Handbook of Fixed-Income Securities

Wiley Handbooks in
FINANCIAL ENGINEERING AND ECONOMETRICS

Advisory Editor
Ruey S. Tsay
The University of Chicago Booth School of Business, USA

A complete list of the titles in this series appears at the end of this volume.

Handbook of Fixed-Income Securities

Edited by

Pietro Veronesi
University of Chicago Booth School of Business

WILEY

Published by John Wiley & Sons, Inc., Hoboken, New Jersey
Published simultaneously in Canada

Library of Congress Cataloging-in-Publication Data

Names: Veronesi, Pietro.
Title: Handbook of fixed-income securities / edited by Pietro Veronesi.
Other titles: Handbook of fixed-income securities (Wiley)
Description: Hoboken, New Jersey : John Wiley & Sons, Inc., [2016] | Includes bibliographical references and index.
Identifiers: LCCN 2015035755 (print) | LCCN 2016000496 (ebook) | ISBN 9781118709191 (cloth) | ISBN 9781118709184 (Adobe PDF) | ISBN 9781118709269 (ePub)
Subjects: LCSH: Fixed-income securities.
Classification: LCC HG4650 .H366 2016 (print) | LCC HG4650 (ebook) | DDC 332.63/2–dc23
LC record available at http://lccn.loc.gov/2015035755

Typeset in 10/12pt TimesLTStd by SPi Global, Chennai, India

10 9 8 7 6 5 4 3 2 1

To Tommaso, Gabriele, Sofia, and Micaela.

Contents

Notes on Contributors

Yacine Aït-Sahalia is the Otto A. Hack '03 Professor of Finance and Economics at Princeton University. He served as the inaugural Director of the Bendheim Center for Finance from 1998 to 2014. He was previously an Assistant Professor (1993–1996), Associate Professor (1996–1998), and Professor of Finance (1998) at the University of Chicago's Graduate School of Business. He is a Fellow of the Econometric Society, a Fellow of the Institute of Mathematical Statistics, a Fellow of the American Statistical Association, an Alfred P. Sloan Foundation Research Fellow, a Fellow of the Guggenheim Foundation, and a Research Associate for the National Bureau of Economic Research (NBER). His research has been widely published in the leading academic journals in finance, econometrics, and statistics. He co-wrote the book *High Frequency Financial Econometrics*, published in 2014, with Jean Jacod. He is the recipient of the 1997 Michael Brennan Award, the 1998 Cornerstone Research Award, the 2001 FAME Research Award, and the 2003 Dennis J. Aigner Award. He recently served as the editor of the Review of Financial Studies and currently serves as the editor of the *Journal of Econometrics*. He received his PhD in Economics from the Massachusetts Institute of Technology in 1993 and is a graduate of France's Ecole Polytechnique.

Pierluigi Balduzzi is Professor of Finance at the Carroll School of Management at Boston College, where he teaches Masters and PhD-level courses in Finance. His main area of research is empirical asset pricing, with a focus on the fixed-income markets. His research has appeared in leading finance and economic journals, such as the *Journal of Finance*, the *Journal of Financial Economics*, and the *American Economic Review*. He currently serves as an Associate Editor of the *Journal of Business and Economic Statistics* and the *Journal of Financial Econometrics*.

Jules van Binsbergen is an Associate Professor at the Wharton School of the University of Pennsylvania and conducts theoretical and empirical research in finance. His current work focuses on asset pricing, in particular the relationship between financial markets and the macroeconomy, and the organization, skill and performance of financial intermediaries. Some of his recent research focuses on measuring the skill of mutual fund managers, the term structure of cash flow growth and stock return predictability, and the implications of good-specific habit formation for asset prices. His research has appeared in leading academic journals, such as the *American Economic Review*, the *Journal of Finance*, the *Journal of Financial Economics*, and the *Journal of Monetary Economics*. He received his PhD from the Fuqua School of Business at Duke University. He previously taught at the Stanford Graduate School of Business and the Kellogg School of Management.

Michael W. Brandt is the Kalman J. Cohen Professor of Business Administration at the Fuqua School of Business of Duke University. He conducts empirical and theoretical research in finance. His current work focuses on quantitative portfolio management, risk management, currency and fixed-income markets, and financial econometrics. Professor Brandt's research has appeared in leading academic journals, including the *American Economic Review*, *Journal of Business*, *Journal of Finance*, *Journal of Financial Economics*, *Journal of Monetary Economics*, and *Review of Financial Studies*. He has served as co-editor of the *Review of Finance*, the official journal of the European Finance Association, and as associate editor of the *Journal of Finance*, the official journal of the American Finance Association. He is also a Faculty Research Associate of the NBER. Before joining Fuqua in 2003, Professor Brandt was at the Wharton School of the University of Pennsylvania for 6 years.

Professor Damiano Brigo is Chair in Mathematical Finance and Stochastic Analysis at the Department of Mathematics at Imperial College London. Former roles include Gilbart Professor at King's College London, Managing Director at Fitch Ratings, Director of the Capco Institute, and Head of Credit Models in Banca IMI. Dr Brigo published 80+ works in *Quantitative Finance*, *Probability and Statistics*, and field reference books in interest rate and credit modeling, and he is in the editorial board of several journals including *Mathematics of Control, Signals and Systems* and the *International Journal of Theoretical and*

Applied Finance. Dr Brigo has been the most cited author in *Risk Magazine* in 2006, 2010, and 2012. His interests include valuation, funding, risk, credit, and stochastic differential geometry. Dr Brigo holds a PhD in Mathematics.

Andrea Buraschi is the Chair in Finance at Imperial College London and a research fellow at the Center for Economic and Policy Research. He has been a visiting professor at the University of Chicago Booth and Columbia University. He earned his PhD from the University of Chicago specializing in Financial Economics. His area of research is empirical asset pricing and general equilibrium models of bond and derivative markets. His work has appeared in several publications, including the *Journal of Finance*, the *Journal of Financial Economics*, *Review of Financial Studies*, *Journal of Derivatives*, *European Financial Management*, and the *Journal of Banking and Finance*. Prof. Buraschi is a recipient of several best paper and teaching awards and serves as Associate Editor for the *Review of Finance*.

Christopher Culp is a Senior Advisor with Compass Lexecon, Adjunct Professor at the Swiss Finance Institute, Research Fellow at the Johns Hopkins Institute for Applied Economics, and Honorarprofessor at Universität Bern in the Institut für Finanzmanagement. His research and teaching specializations include derivatives, structured finance, insurance, risk management, credit markets, and clearing/settlement, and he also provides advisory consulting services and testimonial expertise in these areas. He has written four books, co-edited two books (one with Merton Miller and the other with William Niskanen), and has authored numerous articles on the same topics. Dr Culp is on the editorial advisory boards of the *Journal of Applied Corporate Finance*, the *Journal of Structured Finance*, and *Futures Industry* magazine, and was previously on the editorial advisory boards of *Derivatives Quarterly* (where he was also co-editor), *FMA Online*, and the *Journal of Risk Finance*. He holds a PhD in finance from the University of Chicago's Booth School of Business, where he was also an Adjunct Professor of Finance from 1998 to 2013.

Magnus Dahlquist is the Peter Wallenberg Professor of Finance at the Stockholm School of Economics (SSE). He is also a Research Fellow with the Centre for Economic Policy Research (CEPR), London, and with the Network for Studies on Pensions, Aging and Retirement (NETSPAR) in the Netherlands. Dahlquist's research interests lie in asset management, asset pricing, and international finance. His current research focuses on (i) individuals' and institutions' investment behavior and the design of pension plans, (ii) trading strategies in the bond and currency markets and their relation to fundamentals, and (iii) performance evaluation and practical problems related to portfolio selection. Dahlquist has been an advisor to several financial institutions as well as government authorities.

Alexander David, PhD, is the Haskayne Research Professor of Finance at the Haskayne School of Business at the University of Calgary. Before joining Haskayne, he worked at the Federal Reserve Board in Washington DC as a staff economist and the Olin School of Business at Washington University in St Louis. He has taught classes in financial risk management, advanced corporate finance, options and futures, energy finance, investments, and asset pricing in the undergraduate, MBA, Executive MBA, and PhD programs. His main research interest is the modeling of changing investors' uncertainty about the state of economic fundamentals and their impact on asset prices. His research has been published in leading academic journals such as the *Journal of Political Economy*, *Journal of Finance*, *Review of Financial Studies*, and *Journal of Financial Economics*.

Jens Dick-Nielsen is Associate Professor of Finance at the Center for Financial Frictions (FRIC), Department of Finance, Copenhagen Business School where he teaches Masters and Executive-level courses in finance and credit risk modeling. His research on credit risk and liquidity risk has impacted European Banking regulation and has been published among others in the *Journal of Financial Economics* and the *Journal of Fixed Income*.

Jefferson Duarte is the Gerald D. Hines Professor of Real Estate Finance at the Jesse H. Jones Graduate School of Business at Rice University. He is an expert on fixed-income and mortgage-backed securities. His research has received many awards including the prestigious Fama-DFA prize for the best asset pricing paper published in the *Journal of Financial Economics*. Dr. Duarte's research has also been covered in United States and international media, including the following papers and magazines: *The Wall Street Journal*, *Financial Times*, and *The Economist*. Prior to joining academia, Dr. Duarte worked at the proprietary trading desk of JP Morgan Chase in New York as part of the group managing a multibillion dollar commercial mortgage-backed security (CMBS) portfolio.

Matthias Fleckenstein joined Cornerstone Research, a leading economic and financial consulting firm, after obtaining his PhD at UCLA in 2013. Matthias also has Masters' degrees in Quantitative Finance, Business Administration, and Industrial Engineering and Management. Matthias has consulted on complex financial issues arising in litigation, including securities class actions and antitrust matters in derivatives markets. For joint work with Francis Longstaff and Hanno Lusting on TIPS markets, he received a Distinguished Paper award as part of the Amundi Smith Breeden Prize for the best paper in the *Journal of Finance* on capital markets.

Jean-Sébastien Fontaine is a principal researcher in the Financial Markets Department at the Bank of Canada. In this role, he studies the interaction between monetary policy and fixed-income markets. His research focuses on the effect of funding liquidity on asset prices; macrofinance models of the term structure of interest rates; and the information content of option prices. He holds a PhD from the Université de Montréal, and his research has been published in the *Review of Financial Studies* and the *Review of Finance*.

René Garcia holds a PhD in Economics from Princeton University. He is Chair Professor of Finance at EDHEC Business School in Nice (France). Formerly, he was a professor at University of Montreal, held the Hydro-Québec Chair in Risk Management, and was a Research Fellow of the Bank of Canada. He was also the scientific director of the Centre for Interuniversity Research and Analysis on Organizations (CIRANO). He is a co-founding editor of the *Journal of Financial Econometrics*, published by Oxford University Press and was Editor-in-Chief until June 2012. His recent research focuses on the evaluation of asset pricing models accounting for higher moments, long-run risk asset pricing models, and the funding liquidity premium in bonds and equities. His work has appeared in numerous publications, including the *Journal of Finance*, *Review of Financial Studies*, *Econometrica*, and *Journal of Econometrics*.

Henrik Hasseltoft is an Assistant Professor of Finance at the University of Zurich. He holds a PhD in Finance from the Stockholm School of Economics. Hasseltoft's research on asset pricing lies in the intersection between finance and macroeconomics. His empirical research focuses on predictability of asset returns in equity, bond, and currency markets while his theoretical research focuses on understanding the time-series and cross-sectional aspects of asset prices using consumption-based models. Hasseltoft is affiliated with the Swiss Finance Institute.

Robert L Kimmel is an Associate Professor at the NUS Business School, and the Deputy Director of Research at the Risk Management Institute, at the National University of Singapore. He received his PhD in finance from the University of Chicago Graduate School of Business. Before joining NUS, Prof. Kimmel was at Princeton University, Ohio State University, and EDHEC Business School. His research focuses on the econometrics of continuous-time models for asset prices, and on methods for estimation and testing of linear factor models of asset returns.

David Lando is Professor of Finance at Copenhagen Business School and Director of the Center for Financial Frictions (FRIC) funded by the Danish National Research Foundation. He holds a Master's degree from the joint Mathematics–Economics program at the University of Copenhagen and a PhD in Statistics from Cornell University. His main area of research in finance is credit risk modeling and risk management, and some of his work has appeared in *Econometrica*, *Journal of Financial Economics*, and *Review of Financial Studies*. He has been a visiting scholar at among other places Princeton University, the Federal Reserve Board in Washington, The Federal Reserve Bank of New York. Before joining the Copenhagen Business School, he was a professor at the Department of Applied Mathematics and Statistics at the University of Copenhagen.

Qing (Daphne) Liu is currently a PhD student in Mathematical Finance at Imperial College London under the supervision of Prof. Damiano Brigo. Her main research focus is on developing and studying a consistent derivative valuation framework incorporating counterparty credit risk, collateralization, and funding risk.

Hanno Lustig joined Stanford GSB in 2015. Prior to that, he taught at the University of Chicago, the UCLA Economics department, and UCLA's Anderson School of Management. He graduated in 2002 from Stanford University with a PhD in economics. He has been awarded the JP Morgan Award for the Best Paper on Financial Institutions and Markets in 2012 as well as the NASDAQ OMX Award for the Best Paper on Asset Pricing in 2010. Lustig is a Faculty Research Fellow at the NBER and an associate editor at the *Journal of Finance* and *Econometrica*. Francis Longstaff and Lustig were also awarded a Distinguished Paper distinction as part of the Amundi Smith Breeden Prize for the best paper in the *Journal of Finance* on capital markets for their work on TIPS markets with Matthias Fleckenstein.

Professor Francis Longstaff, PhD, CPA, CFA, is the Allstate Professor of Insurance and Finance at the UCLA Anderson School. His research focuses primarily on fixed-income and derivatives markets, asset pricing, and the valuation of illiquid assets. He has published over 60 articles in top finance, economics, and science journals. He is a research associate of the NBER.

Gerardo Manzo is the Fama-Miller Center Postdoctoral Researcher at the University of Chicago Booth School of Business. He earned his PhD in Money and Finance at the University of Rome "Tor Vergata" in 2013 after an 18-month visiting scholar position at the Booth School of Business. Gerardo conducts research on asset pricing, credit risk, systemic risk, and macrofinance. He is the recipient of several academic awards, including the 2014 UniCredit & Universities Best PhD Thesis Award, the 2014 John A. Doukas Best PhD Paper Award, and the 2011 Orazio Ruggeri Best Master Thesis Award.

Doug McManus is the Director of Financial Research in the Office of the Chief Economist at Freddie Mac where he has worked on issues related to financial markets, credit scoring, credit loss forecasting, fair lending testing, and house price modeling. While at Freddie Mac, he has also served as an advisor to the US Treasury on housing and mortgage modification issues. Prior to joining Freddie Mac, he was at the Board of Governors of the Federal Reserve System where he conducted research on commercial bank risk management, capital requirements, and general econometric methodology. He has published articles in the *Journal of Fixed Income*, *Journal of Banking and Finance*, *Real Estate Economics*, and the *Journal of Econometrics* and has been issued many US patents in the area of house price forecasting and credit scoring. He received his PhD in Economics at the University of Pennsylvania in 1985.

Antonio Mele is a Senior Chair at the Swiss Finance Institute and a Professor of Finance at University of Lugano, after a decade spent as a tenured faculty at the London School of Economics. He is also a research fellow of the CEPR. He holds a PhD in Economics from the University of Paris. His work focuses on capital market volatility, interest rates and credit markets, macrofinance, and information in securities markets, and has appeared in journals such as the *Journal of Financial Economics*, the *Review of Economic Studies*, the *Review of Financial Studies*, and the *Journal of Monetary Economics*. His work outside academia includes developing fixed-income volatility indexes for Chicago Board Options Exchange. He is currently a member of the Securities and Markets Stakeholder Group of the European Securities Markets Authority (ESMA). At ESMA, he is also a member of the Group of Economic Advisers.

Fabio Moneta is an Assistant Professor of Finance at the Stephen J.R. Smith School of Business, Queen's University, Canada. He received his PhD in Finance from the Carroll School of Management, Boston College. He also holds an MSc in Finance from CORIPE Piemonte (Turin, Italy) and a BA in Economics from the University of Pisa in Italy. His research interests concentrate on investments, institutional investors, mutual fund performance, and empirical asset pricing. He has presented his research at the American Finance Association and the European Finance Association meetings, as well as other conferences and universities in Europe and North America. He has published articles on mutual fund performance, forecasting, and international business cycle synchronization in a variety of journals.

Yoshiki Obayashi is a managing director at Applied Academics LLC in New York. The company specializes in developing and commercializing ideas emanating from a growing think tank of academic researchers selected on the basis of their work's relevance to practice in the finance industry. His most recent projects range from running systematic trading strategies for funds to developing fixed-income volatility indexes for Chicago Board Options Exchange. Yoshiki Obayashi previously managed US and Asian credit portfolios for a proprietary fixed-income trading group at an investment bank. He holds a PhD in Finance and Economics from Columbia Business School.

Andrea Pallavicini is the head of equity, FX, and commodity models at Banca IMI, Milan, and visiting professor at the Department of Mathematics of Imperial College, London. He holds a PhD in Theoretical and Mathematical Physics from the University of Pavia for his research activity at CERN. Over the years, he published several papers in financial modeling, theoretical physics, and astrophysics. He is the author of the books "Credit Models and the Crisis: a journey into CDOs, copulas, correlations and dynamic models," Wiley (2010), and "Counterparty Credit Risk, Collateral and Funding with pricing cases for all asset classes," Wiley (2013).

Carolin Pflueger is an Assistant Professor of Finance in the Sauder School of Business at the University of British Columbia. She received her PhD in Business Economics from Harvard University in 2012. Her research focuses on asset pricing and macroeconomics, bond risks and returns, and monetary policy. Her work has appeared in the *Journal of Finance*, *Journal of Monetary Economics*, and *Journal of Business and Economic Statistics*.

Riccardo Rebonato is Professor of Finance at EDHEC Risk Institute and a Professorial fellow at the Edinburgh University. He was previously Global Head of Interest Rates and FX Analytics at PIMCO, a Visiting Lecturer at Oxford University (Mathematical Finance). He sits on the board of Trustees for GARP and was on the Board of ISDA for 11 years. He holds doctorates in Nuclear Engineering and in Condensed Matter Physics (Stony Brook University), and was a postdoctoral Research Fellow in physics at Oxford University (Corpus Christi) and Research Fellow at Brookhaven National Laboratory and Institut Laue Langevin (Grenoble). He is the author of several books in finance and of many papers in academic journals in the same area.

David Sloth is a quantitative strategist/structure in Rate Options and Inflation Trading at Danske Bank Markets, Copenhagen. He holds a PhD in Mathematical Finance from Aarhus University. His research focuses on derivatives pricing, trading strategies, counterparty credit and funding risk, and numerical methods. Dr. Sloth's work has appeared in several publications, including *Quantitative Finance*.

Josephine M. Smith, PhD, is a Vice President in the Model Portfolios Solutions team at BlackRock, where she is responsible for the research, development, and management of strategic and tactical asset-allocation models. Before joining BlackRock, Dr. Smith was an assistant professor of finance at the New York University Stern School of Business, where she taught an advanced fixed income course to undergraduates and MBAs. Before this, she worked on various research projects at the Bureau of Labor Statistics, Federal Reserve Bank of San Francisco, and the Division of Monetary Affairs at the Federal Reserve Board in Washington, DC.

Oleg Sydyak is the Director of the Asset and Liability Strategy group at a major financial services company. Oleg has designed and implemented the firm's strategic positioning and product offering for liability-driven investing (LDI) strategies and asset and liability management (ALM) studies. He is responsible for the ongoing development of LDI strategies and ALM studies, including analysis of the capital markets, modeling of asset and liability cash flows, and making asset allocation recommendations. Oleg regularly contributes to the firm's thought leadership related to LDI strategies and ALM studies through writing white papers and developing and enhancing analytic capabilities.

Claudio Tebaldi is Associate Professor in quantitative methods for economics, finance, and insurance at the Department of Finance of "L. Bocconi" University, Milano. In March 2015, he received the national habilitation for full professorship. In 2004, he visited the Faculty of Finance, Anderson School of Management, UCLA. He owns a PhD in Statistical Mechanics, an MPhil in Complex Systems, Institute for Advanced Studies (SISSA) and a Master in Economics and Finance (Venice International University). His research has appeared in numerous publications, including the *Review of Financial Studies* and *Mathematical Finance*, among others.

Pietro Veronesi is the Roman Family Professor of Finance at the University of Chicago Booth School of Business, where he teaches Masters and PhD-level courses in fixed income, risk management, and asset pricing. His research focuses on asset pricing, and especially on stock and bond valuation, bubbles and crashes, return predictability, stochastic volatility, and recently, on the interaction between government interventions and asset prices. His work has appeared in leading academic journals, such as the *Journal of Finance*, *Journal of Financial Economics*, *Review of Financial Studies*, the *Journal of Political Economy*, the *American Economic Review*, and the *Quarterly Journal of Economics*. He is the recipient of several awards, including the 2015 AQR Insight award, the 2012 and 2003 Smith Breeden prizes from the *Journal of Finance*, the 2006 Fama/DFA prize from the *Journal of Financial Economics*, and the 1999 Barclays Global Investors/Michael Brennan prize from the *Review of Financial Studies*. In 2010, he wrote the popular textbook *Fixed Income Securities*, published by John Wiley and Sons. Veronesi is also a research associate of the NBER, a research fellow of the Center for Economic and Policy Research, and a former co-editor of the *Review of Financial Studies*. He received his PhD in Economics from Harvard University in 1997, his Master in Econometrics and Mathematical Economics from the London School of Economics in 1993, and is a graduate of Bocconi University.

Luis M. Viceira is the George E. Bates Professor at the Harvard Business School, where he has been in the faculty since 1998. He received his MA and PhD in Economics from Harvard University. He is a Research Associate in the NBER's Program on Asset Pricing, a Research Fellow and member of the Scientific Council of Netspar, the Network for Studies on Pensions, Aging, and Retirement, a Fellow of the TIAA-CREF Institute, and a Public Governor of the Financial Industry Regulatory Authority. Viceira is a financial economist interested in the study of asset allocation models, with an emphasis on models that explore the asset allocation implications of empirical regularities in asset pricing and on life-cycle investing, asset pricing, with an emphasis on models of the term structure of interest rates, household finance, and international finance. His research has been published in the *Journal of Finance*, the *Journal of Financial Economics*, the *Review of Financial Studies*, the *American Economic Review*, the *Quarterly Journal of Economics*, and the *Review of Finance*, among others. He is also the author of the book *Strategic Asset Allocation* with John Y. Campbell. Viceira is also interested in the design of pension fund systems, the design of investment strategies for long-term investors, the management and organization of large institutional investors, and product innovation in the money management industry.

Paul Whelan is an Assistant Professor of Finance at Copenhagen Business School where he teaches asset pricing to MSc and PhD students. His research interests are in the areas of asset pricing and financial econometrics with a focus on fixed-income markets. Dr. Whelan has won several awards for his work, including the GARP Risk Management Research Award (2013), Carefin-Bocconi Research in Finance Grant Award (2012), and Q-Group Grant Award (2011).

Preface

Fixed income markets have been changing dramatically over the past few years, especially after the financial crisis. New regulation, aggressive monetary policy that led to zero nominal rates, large expansions of government debt, new empirical behavior of Treasury securities, appearance of new securities, and so on have been changing the way fixed income markets work. Old theories have been challenged and new ones have been proposed. Much new research has been poured into uncovering new empirical properties of fixed income securities. Many of us who teach fixed income courses have had to change substantial portions of class material as many old methodologies and formulas have become obsolete and to make space for new material. All these recent changes make the market for fixed income securities all the more exciting.

I accepted to be the editor of this handbook because I thought it was important to collect the new research and new methodologies all in one place. I tried to balance basic material with more advanced material so that even readers new to fixed income will be able to read and understand most of the chapters. Still, readers that are already well versed in the intricacies of fixed income markets will also find most of the handbook material interesting, both because most of the chapters contain novel research and because some of the chapters deal with very advanced new topics. Finally, I also tried to balance empirical evidence with methodology. Both types of chapters are very informative, and in fact, given the novelty of much of the material, they are complementary to each other and illuminating. Kudos to the contributors who took great effort and did a marvelous job in writing intriguing and engaging chapters.

THE HANDBOOK

I now describe the handbook and the topics in more detail.

The handbook is divided into eight parts that cover different topics. The first part is an overview of current fixed income markets, namely, U.S. Treasuries, money markets, and mortgage-related securities. More specifically, in Chapter 1, I provide an overview of fixed income markets by discussing some recent developments, such as their growth, the recent aggressive monetary policy, and the puzzling behavior of "bond betas" in recent times. I also cover some of the terminologies, concepts, and methodologies that lay the foundations for many of the following chapters. In Chapter 2, Smith teaches us about money market instruments, an important market that played a special role during the financial crisis. In Chapter 3, Fleckenstein, Longstaff, and Lustig cover the U.S. Treasury inflation-protected securities and discuss the ways these securities can be combined with regular Treasury securities to learn about expected future inflation and the inflation risk premium. Finally, in Chapter 4, Duarte and McManus discuss the mortgage-backed securities (MBS) market. The MBS market has been especially affected by the crisis, as the two giant government-sponsored enterprises (GSEs) Fannie Mae and Freddie Mac needed to be placed under government conservatorship in 2008. Duarte and McManus walk us through the changes in the MBS market and the new pricing methodologies that make use of large datasets that are now available from the GSEs.

Part 2 of this handbook is about monetary policy and bond markets, a critical topic especially given the aggressive expansionary policy measures pursued by the Federal Reserve in the United States, the Bank of England in the United Kingdom, and the European Central Bank in Europe in the wake of the financial crisis. Treasury securities played the role of safe havens for investors during the crisis as risk-averse investors sold their holdings of risky securities and searched for safe investments. Numerous questions arise on the size (if any) of the impact of monetary policy on bond prices and the transmission channel through which monetary policy affects short- and long-term yields. In Chapter 5, Buraschi and Whelan discuss the channels through which *conventional* monetary policy affects interest rates and the evidence in favor of the effects. The empirical methodology exploits high-frequency data to identify the impact of monetary policy shocks on the term structure of interest rates. In Chapter 6, Buraschi and Whelan organize the recent evidence about *unconventional* monetary policy, that is, the exceptional measures taken by the Federal Reserve, Bank of England, and European Central Bank to cope with the 2008–2009 crisis, as well as the subsequent slow recovery and the (still ongoing) European debt crisis.

Part 3 covers interest rate risk management, with applications to asset–liability management (ALM). As the number of institutions issuing debt instruments and investing in fixed income securities around the world increases, the issue of interest rate risk management takes center stage. Indeed, as shown in Chapter 1, the size of the interest rate derivatives market increased 10-fold over the last 20 years, as the risk-management needs of institutions increased. Chapter 7, by Sydyak, covers the traditional tools of interest rate risk management, from the concept of duration and convexity to key-rate duration and factor analysis, and illustrates their use in ALM problems. In Chapter 8, Brandt and Van Binsbergen show how modern techniques of dynamic portfolio allocation with constraints can be profitably used to solve ALM problems for numerous types of constrained institutions, such as pension funds and insurance companies. Such modern techniques use advanced numerical methodologies, such as Monte Carlo simulations to identify the optimal strategies, and are becoming widely used in the industry to carry out interest rate risk management.

Part 4 of this handbook deals with the predictability of bond returns, a hot topic that interests both practitioners who look for the best investment strategies and financial economists who try to understand what drives the variation of U.S. Treasury bond prices. In Chapter 9, Dahlquist and Hasseltoft review the empirical methodologies and the empirical evidence supporting the view that bond risk premia are time varying. The chapter does not limit itself to just a review of U.S. Treasuries but also considers other countries, such as the United Kingdom, Switzerland, and Germany. Interestingly, bond risk premia across countries display a strong comovement, which the authors identify with a global predicting factor. In Chapter 10, Pflueger and Viceira survey and provide novel evidence about the predictability of bond returns and especially focus the analysis on the returns of inflation-protected securities. This chapter contains a discussion of the liquidity premium that is apparent in inflation-protected bonds. Finally, in Chapter 11, Balduzzi and Moneta survey the literature that identifies bond risk premia using high-frequency data. This chapter contains an intriguing discussion of the evidence about time variation in risk premia at high frequencies and the impact of market microstructure effects, and it even touches upon the recent literature on high-frequency trading and its impact on bond returns.

Part 5 covers a number of advanced topics on fixed income models and their estimation. In Chapter 12, Rebonato discusses the popular class of affine term structure models. This chapter also covers the concept of market price of risk and the recent evidence about time-varying risk premia, now casted in fully fledged no-arbitrage term structure models. In Chapter 13, Aït-Sahalia and Kimmel review several empirical methodologies used to estimate term structure models, with a detailed discussion of their pros and cons. In Chapter 14, Fontaine and Garcia focus on several recent models and evidence on "old" fixed income topics, including some new evidence about the expectations hypothesis, the importance of liquidity and liquidity premia, and, interestingly, the impact of the zero lower bound of nominal rates – that is, the fact that nominal interest rates cannot become negative – on term structure modeling. The latter issue is especially important in current markets with extremely low interest rates. Finally, in Chapter 15, David and Veronesi discuss the recent theories and evidence about the time-varying correlation of Treasury bond returns with stock market returns, a correlation that was very positive in the 1980s but became very negative in the 2000s. During this time span, U.S. Treasuries moved from being a "risky investment" (their prices drop together with the stock market) to being a "hedging vehicle" (their prices rise when the stock market drops). The question is why.

Part 6 focuses on derivative securities. The financial crisis spurred a large amount of new regulation on interest rate derivatives. In Chapter 16, Culp walks us through the new regulation that shapes the derivatives markets, both in the United States and in Europe. This chapter provides numerous statistics about the current state of derivatives markets and reviews the new infrastructure, such as the introduction of central counterparties ("CCPs") to clear OTC derivatives and the electronic execution platforms ("EEPs"). In Chapter 17, Tebaldi and Veronesi introduce the pricing of derivatives in the familiar – and relatively simple – context of binomial trees. This chapter also provides several real-world examples by applying the binomial – and trinomial – tree methodology to real-world securities. In Chapter 18, I discuss the impact of the crisis and new regulation on the pricing of plain vanilla derivatives and especially the use of double-curve pricing of London Interbank Offered Rate (LIBOR)-based derivatives. This chapter is introductory and mostly highlights the main changes that occurred after the crisis.

Part 7 of this handbook is about advanced topics in derivative pricing. The chapters included in this part of the handbook use rather advanced techniques, such as continuous time models, Monte Carlo simulations, and the like. More specifically, in Chapter 19, Tebaldi and Veronesi develop the pricing formulas for derivatives in continuous time, derive the risk-neutral pricing formulas, and show their implementation using Monte Carlo simulations. In Chapter 20, Mele and Obayashi provide a detailed review of modern derivative pricing techniques. They also focus on modeling and trading volatility, which is an important topic in current fixed income markets. Finally, in Chapter 21, Brigo, Liu, Pallavicing, and Sloth discuss recent modifications to derivative pricing formulas as security dealers and financial institutions were forced to rethink their pricing methodologies in the wake of the 2008–2009 financial crisis. Such adjustments – such as credit value adjustments, funding value adjustments, and so on – make the pricing of OTC derivatives very complex and the chapter covers the new methodologies in detail.

Finally, Part 8 of this handbook looks at another class of fixed income instruments, that is, corporate and sovereign bonds. The focus of this part of the handbook is on the impact of credit risk on the pricing of fixed income securities. In particular, in Chapter 22, Dick-Nielsen and Lando review and discuss the existing pricing methodologies for corporate bonds. The chapter covers both the Merton model and the intensity-based model and provides an overview of their performance when confronted with the data. In Chapter 23, Manzo and Veronesi cover sovereign default risk. After a discussion of the pricing methodology for sovereign bonds, most of the chapter is devoted to the empirical analysis of sovereign credit risk and the credit risk premium, with a special attention to emerging economies and the recent European debt crisis.

The handbook is finally complete. I have to very much thank all of the contributors to this handbook, who have generously contributed their time to write a chapter and make this handbook a reality. I hope – and I am sure – that readers will learn a good deal from these contributions about the new reality of fixed income markets.

PIETRO VERONESI

Chicago
3 June, 2015

PART I

Fixed Income Markets

1

Fixed Income Markets: An Introduction

Pietro Veronesi
Booth School of Business, University of Chicago, Chicago, IL, United States

1.1 INTRODUCTION

The last decade witnessed a profound transformation of fixed-income markets, in no small part due to the 2008–2009 financial crisis. The transformation took different forms: first, in the aftermath of the crisis, a number of countries – and the United States, in particular – had to expand their borrowing capacity in order to "stimulate" the economy. Lower tax revenues due to the economic downturn and higher government spending resulted in a large increase in government debt. As an example, Panel A of Figure 1.1 plots the outstanding U.S. debt from 1985 to 2014, compared to the mortgage-backed securities market, the corporate debt market, and the money market, which include commercial paper, bankers' acceptance, and large time deposits. The first obvious observation is that all debt markets have been trending upward. The second observation is that while the U.S. Treasury debt market was the largest market between 1985 and the late 1990s, by year 2000, it was surpassed in sheer size by two forms of private debt, namely, the mortgage-backed securities market (the mortgage-related debt of individual households) and the corporate debt market (the debt market of private corporations). The United States has steadily becoming more in debt, but until the mid-2000s, this new debt was mainly private debt. With the advent of the financial crisis, the U.S. debt started a quick ascent to then take over both the mortgage-backed securities market and the corporate debt market, both of which instead show no growth after the crisis.

Clearly, the trends in Panel A are partly misleading, as it is true that the United States increased its nominal debt levels considerably since 1985, but the U.S. economy itself also grew substantially over the past 30 years. To take this into account, Panel B plots the same quantities as in Panel A but as a percentage of the U.S. Gross Domestic Product (GDP). The normalized U.S. debt shows a much more stable path over the sample period, as it had been indeed decreasing as a percentage of GDP between 1995 and 2008. The last 4 years, however, have seen the debt-to-GDP ratio rise from 30% to 70%, a clear concern that even led the rating agency Standard & Poor to downgrade the U.S. debt to AA+ from AAA in August 2011. In contrast to the U.S. Treasury debt, both the mortgage-backed securities market and the corporate debt market have been declining in the last few years as percentage of U.S. GDP. Finally, the size of the money markets also reached its peak in 2007, at around 20% of GDP and has been declining ever since. Smith (2015, Chapter 2 in this handbook) covers in detail the recent trends in money markets.

Besides declining in size (relative to the GDP), the mortgage-backed securities market also underwent several transformations on its own during the crisis, starting with U.S. government placing the two mortgage giants Freddie Mac and Fannie Mae under conservatorship. Duarte and McManus (2015, Chapter 4 in this handbook) discuss the evolution of the mortgage-backed

Handbook of Fixed-Income Securities, First Edition. Edited by Pietro Veronesi.

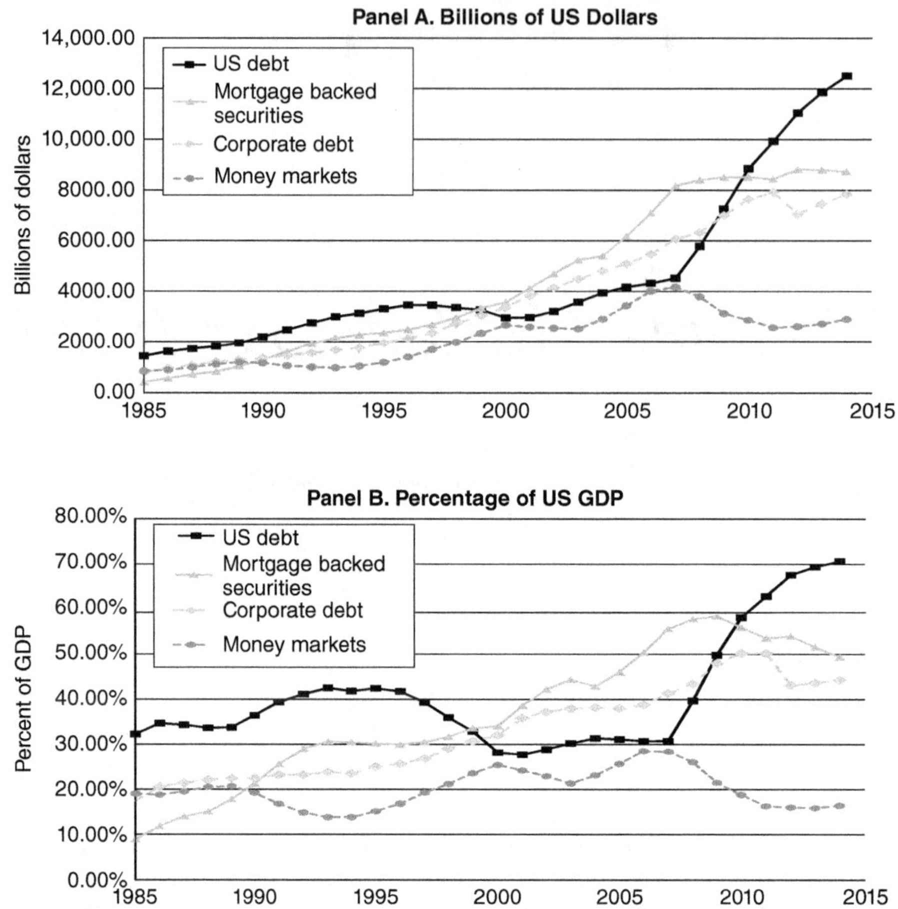

Figure 1.1 The outstanding amount of U.S. debt. Panel A shows the outstanding marketable U.S. debt, mortgage-backed securities, and corporate debt from 1985 to 2014. Panel B reports the same quantities rescaled by U.S. GDP for the same period. Source: SIFMA and FRED at Federal Reserve Bank of St Louis.

securities market after the crisis. In particular, after the crisis, large amounts of new data have become available, and Duarte and McManus discuss new methodologies to price mortgage-backed securities.

A second important change in the U.S. debt market is the unprecedented aggressive monetary policies adopted by the Federal Reserve. In 2008, the Federal Reserve slashed its main reference interest rates – the Federal funds rate – to essentially zero and then moved to the so-called "unconventional" monetary policies, which essentially entailed large purchases of U.S. government debt as well as mortgage-backed securities. Panel A of Figure 1.2 plots the Federal funds rate over time, which highlights its precipitous drop from 5.27% in July 2007, to 2% in June 2008, to 0.25% in November 2008. Panel B shows the entire term structure of interest rates over the same time period, with maturities ranging from 3 months to 30 years.[1] The short-term 3-month Treasury bill rate hit (almost) zero at about the same time as the Federal funds rate, while the long-term yields steadily decreased over time, with some ups and downs in the last few years. Several questions arise on the impact that the Federal Reserve actually has on the term structure of interest rates. Buraschi and Whelan (2015a, 2015b, Chapters 5 and 6 in this handbook) discuss the existing evidence as well as provide new evidence about the impact of monetary policy on the term structure of interest rates.

Third, in the aftermath of the 2008–2009 financial crisis, governments around the world introduced substantial regulatory changes with the aim of regulating trading in derivatives markets and curbing the risk-taking behavior of a number of financial institutions (see Culp (2015, Chapter 16 in this handbook) for a detailed discussion of the new regulatory environment). Indeed, Figure 1.3 shows that the size of the global fixed-income derivatives market has been increasing steadily over the two decades preceding the financial crisis. Panel A shows the increase in the notional amount of Over-the-Counter (OTC) derivatives from June 1998 to June 2013, starting from about \$50 trillion and increasing to over \$560 trillion over the 15-year period.[2]

[1]Note that in Panel B of Figure 1.2, only yields up to 5 years of maturity are available until August 1971, when also the 10-year yield becomes available. The 20-year yield is available from July 1981 and the 30-year yield from November 1985.

[2]Data are from the Bank for International Settlements and are available at *www.bis.org*. The biannual survey result of June 2013 is available at *http://www.bis.org/publ/otc_hy1311.pdf*, accessed on January 17, 2014.

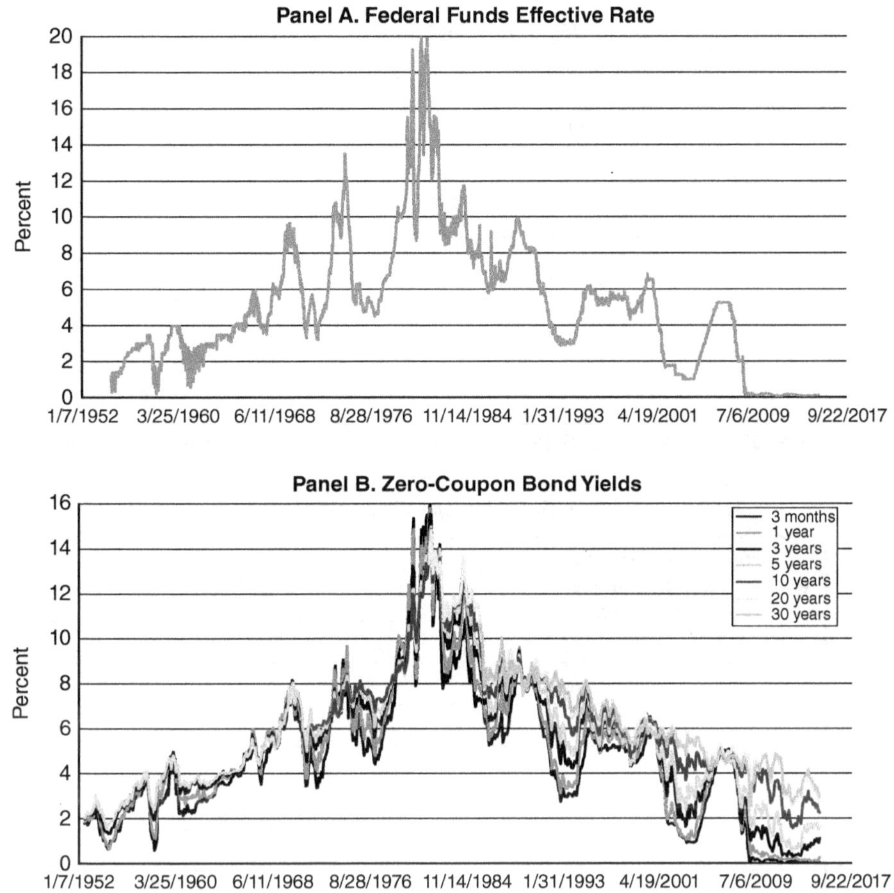

Figure 1.2 Federal funds and U.S. Treasury yields. Panel A shows the Federal funds effective rate from 1954–2014 (Source: Federal Reserve Bank of New York website). Panel B plots the zero-coupon bond yields from 1952–2014. Source: Yields up to 5 years are from the Center for Research in Security Prices (CRSP). Yields from 10 to 30 are from Gürkaynak, Sack, and Wright (2007), updated series.

The figure also shows that interest rate swaps comprise the lion's share of the OTC fixed-income derivatives market. While the tenfold increase in the OTC market is impressive, the global economy also expanded considerably over the same period. Panel B of Figure 1.3 renormalizes the notional amount of OTC derivatives by world GDP. Even after normalization, the total notional of OTC fixed-income derivatives increased from about 1.5 times the global GDP in 1998 to 8 times the global GDP at the end of 2007 and then mildly declined to 7 times the global GDP level by the end of 2012, possibly due to the effects of the financial crisis and the new regulation on derivatives.

One additional important change that came with the new regulation, however, is that the pricing of derivative securities has became even more complex than ever before. Even relatively "simple" plain vanilla securities became challenging to price, as market participants now require (or are required to require) full collateralization of derivative positions, which entail additional costs from holding the positions open. Veronesi (2015, Chapter 18 in this handbook) and Brigo et al. (2015, Chapter 21 in this handbook) discuss a number of pricing issues that arise from the new regulation.

Finally, besides the level of interest rates and additional regulation, the last decade also witnessed substantial changes in the behavior of bond returns themselves. For instance, the left panel of Figure 1.4 shows the quarterly series of the covariance of 5-year U.S. bond returns with the returns of the S&P 500 index. The covariance is computed from daily returns in each quarter. Quite dramatically, the covariance turned from being mostly positive until about the year 2000 to being mostly negative since then. The right panel shows that the realized "beta" of bonds with respect to the S&P 500 index (i.e., the covariance divided by the variance of the S&P 500 index) also experienced a rather dramatic fall over the same period. That is, since 2000, bonds have become an important hedge against stock market fluctuations. But why were not bonds a hedge historically? What has changed recently? The answers to these questions have obvious first-order consequences for asset allocation between two of the largest financial asset classes. David and Veronesi (2015, Chapter 15 in this handbook) review the recent literature on the movement of stock-bond covariance over time.

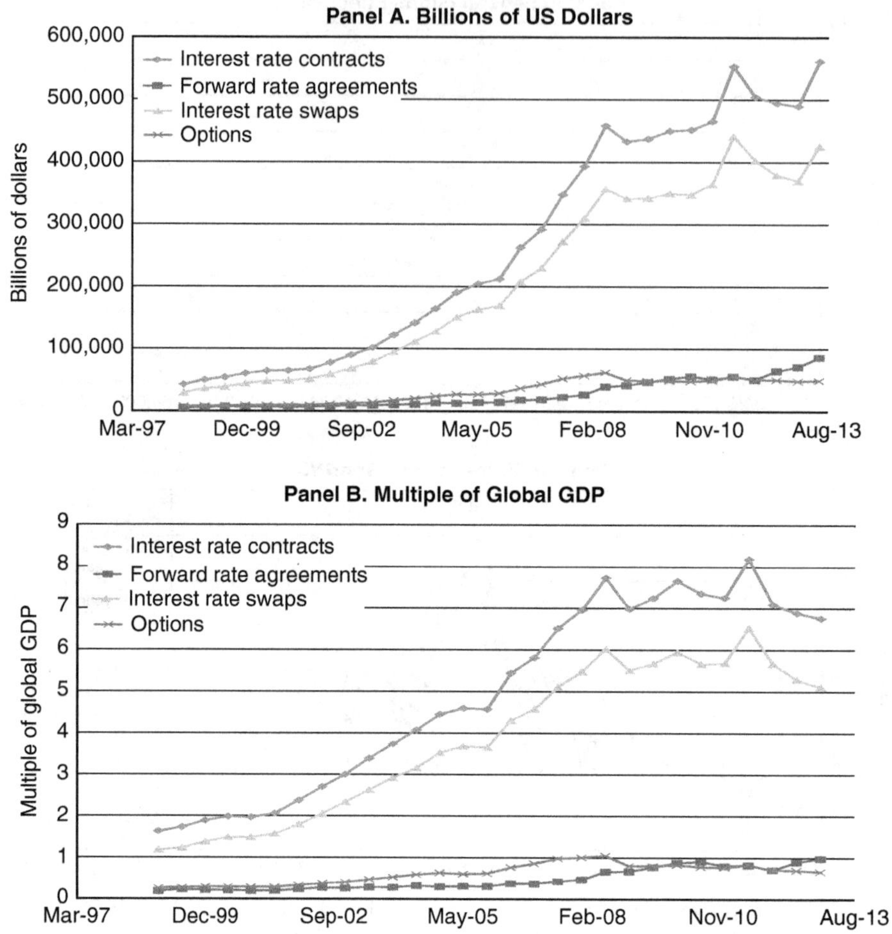

Figure 1.3 The notional amount of over-the-counter derivatives. Panel A shows the notional amount of OTC fixed-income derivatives from June 1998 to June 2013. Panel B reports the notional amount of OTC derivatives rescaled by the world global GDP from 1998 to 2012. OTC derivatives data are from the Bank for International Settlements, while global GDP data are from the World Bank.

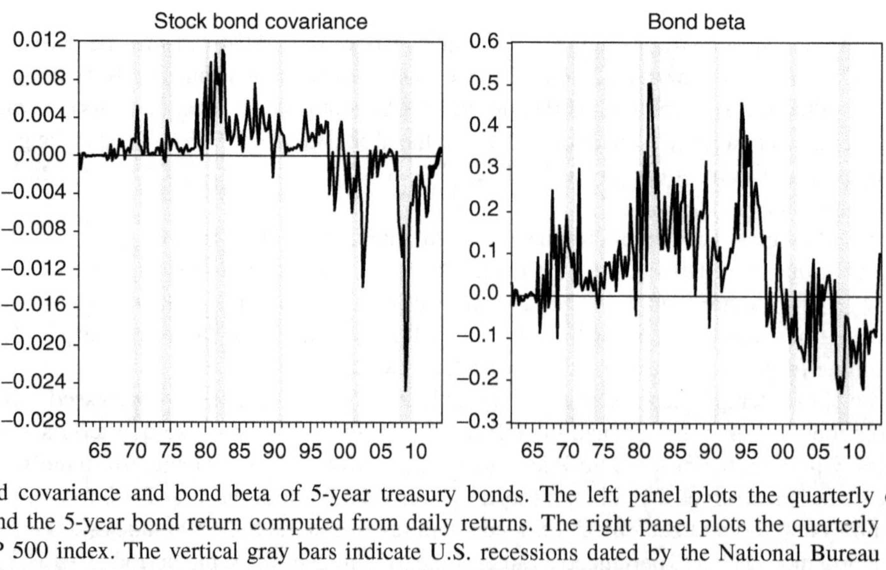

Figure 1.4 Stock-bond covariance and bond beta of 5-year treasury bonds. The left panel plots the quarterly covariance between the S&P 500 daily return and the 5-year bond return computed from daily returns. The right panel plots the quarterly beta of the 5-year bond with respect to the S&P 500 index. The vertical gray bars indicate U.S. recessions dated by the National Bureau of Economic Research. Source: Stock data are from the Center for Research in Security Prices (CRSP) while 5-year zero-coupon bond data are from Gürkaynak, Sack, and Wright (2007, updated series).

This introduction only touched upon a few of the major changes that took place in the last 10–15 years. This handbook collects recent research on these and many more topics. Indeed, in addition to sheer changes to the markets, novel methodologies and new fixed-income instruments have been introduced to fixed-income markets, and the handbook covers such recent topics as well.

In this introductory chapter, I cover some basic notions of fixed-income securities and markets. In the next section, I briefly discuss the U.S. Treasury market. Section 1.3 introduces the notions of interest rate and risk-free discounting. Section 1.4 focuses on the term structure of interest rates and on the economic forces that affect its shape. A brief discussion of the expectations hypothesis as well as forward rates as predictor of future interest rates is included in this section. Section 1.5 discusses U.S. Treasury coupon bonds and notes, as well as the methodologies to estimate the zero-coupon bond curve from coupon bonds. Section 1.6 discusses the real term structure of interest rates, as extracted from the U.S. Treasury Inflation-Protected Securities (TIPS), while Section 1.7 contains a discussion of the pricing of Floating Rate Notes (FRNs), which the U.S. Treasury started issuing in January 2014. Section 1.8 concludes.

1.2 U.S. TREASURY BILLS, NOTES, AND BONDS

A cursory look at the U.S. Treasury website immediately shows the large number of different securities that are available to investors. These securities comprise Treasury bills, Treasury notes, Treasury bonds, TIPS, and FRNs.[3]

The U.S. Treasury conducts regular auctions according to a well-defined calendar in order to place such securities with the public, individual investors or institutional investors. Two types of bids are available: in a competitive bid, the investor quotes the (minimum) rate that he/she will be willing to accept. In a noncompetitive bid, the investor agrees to purchase some amount of securities at the rate that is set at the auction. The Treasury allocates the amount available at the auction to noncompetitive bids and then to competitive bids (from the lowest rate to the highest rate bid) up to the amount available for sale. All investors receive the highest rate bid. Each type of security auctioned off by the U.S. Treasury is normally available with different maturities. For instance, Treasury bills are regularly auctioned off with maturities of 4, 13, 26, and 52 weeks. Treasury notes, by contrast, are regularly auctioned off with maturities of 2, 3, 5, 7, and 10 years. Treasury bonds are now only sold with a maturity of 30 years.

Table 1.1 reports the breakdown of marketable U.S. Treasury securities on March 31, 2015.[4] As can be seen, the majority of U.S. Treasury securities held by the public (65%) are in the form of Treasury notes and thus with maturity ranging between 1 and 10 years. Short-term Treasury bills and long-term Treasury bonds are of about equal size, at 12% and 13% of the total. Securities with floating rate coupons, either tied to inflation (TIPS) or tied to interest rates (FRNs) comprise together about 10% of the total U.S. marketable debt.

TABLE 1.1 Marketable U.S. Treasury Securities (Million of Dollars)

	Debt held by the public		Intragovernmental holdings		
	$	%	$	%	Total
Bills	1,476,540	11.68	1,359	0.01	1,477,900
Notes	8,256,666	65.30	7,767	0.06	8,264,433
Bonds	1,607,585	12.71	62	0.00	1,607,647
Treasury Inflation-Protected Securities	1,075,141	8.50	83	0.00	1,075,224
Floating rate notes	204,991	1.62	0	0.00	204,991
Federal financing bank	0	0.00	13,612	0.11	13,612
Total	12,620,923		22,883		12,643,807

Source: U.S. Treasury website. *https://www.treasurydirect.gov/govt/reports/pd/mspd/2005/2005_mar.htm.*

[3]As of the writing of this chapter, the main web address where to find information about U.S. Treasury debt is *http://www.treasurydirect.gov/*. The products available to individual investors are listed at *http://www.treasurydirect.gov/indiv/products/products.htm.*

[4]Data are from the U.S. Treasury website *https://www.treasurydirect.gov/govt/reports/pd/mspd/2015/2015_mar.htm*. accessed on April 5, 2015. Data in Table 1.1 only reports the total marketable securities, that is, those available to the public. In March 2015, the U.S. government also had $5.508 trillion in nonmarketable securities.

1.3 INTEREST RATES, YIELDS, AND DISCOUNTING

The concept of interest rates is ubiquitous to fixed-income securities. The problem is that the notion of an interest rate is not well defined without explicitly defining a compounding frequency, that is, the number of times within the year in which the interest accrues to the initial investment. For instance, 100,000 dollars invested at 10% annual rate for 10 years yields a final amount in 10 years that crucially depends on how many times per year the interest on the investment is calculated and accrued. If the interest accrues annually (*annual compounding*), then in 10 years we obtain (in thousands of dollar)

$$\$100 \times (1.1)^{10} = \$259.37$$

If instead the interest accrues twice per year (*semiannual compounding*), then we receive 5%(= 10%/2) every 6 months but 20 times (the number of 6 months in 10 years), obtaining

$$\$100 \times (1.05)^{20} = \$265.33$$

If the interest accrues quarterly, then we will receive 2.5%(= 10%/4) every 3 months 40 times, obtaining in 10 years

$$\$100 \times (1.025)^{40} = \$268.51$$

In the limit, if the interest accrues daily, we receive a rate $r = 10\%/365$ every day, 3650 times (approximately, because of leap years), obtaining in 10 years

$$\$100 \times \left(1 + \frac{0.1}{365}\right)^{10 \times 365} = \$271.79$$

In all these cases, the "quoted" interest rate on the $100,000 investment is the same (10%), but the accrual convention makes a difference of over $12,000 between annual compounding and daily compounding.

The general formula for compounding frequency is the following: given a quoted (annualized) interest rate r accrued n times per year for T years, the total amount at maturity from a $1 investment is equal to

$$V = \left(1 + \frac{r}{n}\right)^{n \times T} \tag{1.1}$$

It is often convenient to work with an extremely high compounding frequency, namely, *continuous compounding*, which is the limit of Equation 1.1 as n becomes very large. Indeed, as n goes to infinity, the right-hand side of Equation 1.1 converges to

$$V = \left(1 + \frac{r}{n}\right)^{n \times T} \to e^{r \times T} \tag{1.2}$$

where $e = 2.718281828$ is the "Euler number." The function $f(x) = e^x$ is called the "exponential function," and it is widely used in finance and fixed-income because of its convenient mathematical properties. One can safely think of continuous compounding to be the same as daily compounding frequency and thus that the continuous compounding formula (the exponential) is nothing more than a convenient tool to approximate daily compounding. Indeed, in the previous example, if we compute the total value V using directly the number e (available on any calculator), we obtain

$$\$100 \times e^{0.1 \times 10} = \$271.82$$

which is indeed very similar to the case with daily compounding in the preceding text.

Given an interest rate (and a compounding frequency), we can invert the relations in the preceding text and obtain the discount factors $Z(T)$ to discount dollars paid at time T to dollars today. That is, how much are we willing to pay today to have $1 at time T? Given an interest rate r that is compounded n times per year, by inverting Equation 1.1, we obtain

$$Z(T) = \frac{1}{\left(1 + \frac{r}{n}\right)^{n \times T}}$$

That is, $Z(T)$ is the amount that we have to invest today in order to receive \$1 at T, as $Z(T) \times \left(1 + \frac{r}{n}\right)^{n \times T} = 1$. In the limit as n diverges to infinity, we obtain the discount function

$$Z(T) = \frac{1}{\left(1 + \frac{r}{n}\right)^{n \times T}} \rightarrow e^{-rT}$$

I will mostly use continuous compounding in this chapter, except when other forms of compounding are required for clarity.

1.4 THE TERM STRUCTURE OF INTEREST RATES

In general, when we discount future cash flows to the present, different discount rates apply for different maturities. It is customary to denote such discount rates by $y(T)$, where "y" stands for "yield." Therefore, we denote the discount factor today for a dollar to be received at time T by

$$Z(T) = e^{-y(T)\,T}$$

The function $Z(T)$ (as a function of maturity T) is called zero-coupon discount function. Panel A of Figure 1.5 plots six discount functions at the end of January in 2007–2009, 2011, 2013, and 2015. The discount functions $Z(T)$ have been increasing during these years, meaning that the value of \$1 to be received in the future has been increasing over the period.

Panel B of Figure 1.5 plots the term structures of interest rate. In January 2007, the yields $y(T)$ are essentially constant across maturities. The interest rate on a 1-year risk-free investment is the same as the (annualized) interest rate of a 15-year risk-free investment or a 30-year risk-free investment. However, things are very different in the other years. In 2008, short-term yields were already much lower than long-term yields, and long-term yields themselves also decreased compared to their values in 2007. From 2009 on, short-term rates were at very low levels, while long-term rates went down and up to finally drop dramatically by January 2015.[5]

1.4.1 The Economics of the Nominal Yield Curve

What economics forces affect the term structure of interest rates? While short-term rates may be believed to be greatly affected by monetary policy (but see, e.g., Fama (2013) and the related discussion in Buraschi and Whelan (2015b, Chapter 6 in this handbook)), a number of questions arise as to what factors affect long-term yields.

A standard decomposition of long-term nominal yields is revealing:

$$\text{Nominal yield} = \text{real yield} + \text{expected inflation} + \text{risk premium} \tag{1.3}$$

Thus, a low nominal yield may be due to a low real yield, a low expected inflation, or a low risk premium (or any combination of those). We return to real yields in Section 1.6. What are the other two terms?

"Expected inflation" refers to the market expectation of average inflation over the life of the bond. Such expectations are time varying, depending on market conditions. Panel A of Figure 1.6 plots the realized inflation from 1952 to 2015 and the expected inflation from 1980 to 2015. Expected inflation is computed as the consensus inflation forecast from the Survey of Professional Forecasters available at the Federal Reserve Bank of Philadelphia. As can be seen, inflation expectations dropped substantially in the last 10 years, as inflation itself has decreased over time.

Why does expected inflation affect long-term yields? Intuitively, with the exception of TIPS (see Section 1.6), U.S. Treasury securities' promised payments are expressed in dollars. If investors expect a high rate of inflation over the life of the bond, they are not willing to pay much money today for a security that will pay "deflated" dollars in the future. That is, the price of the U.S. Treasury security will be low today, implying a high yield. Thus, the higher the expected inflation, the higher is the (nominal) yield that investors require to buy the U.S. Treasury securities.

The last term in Equation 1.3 is a risk premium that investors require for holding nominal bonds. What types of risks does an investor in long-term bonds actually bear? While U.S. Treasuries are often referred to as "risk-free," what is really meant is "default risk-free," in the sense that the investor who holds the U.S. Treasury bond to maturity will receive its promised payments with an extremely high probability. However, holding long-term bonds can be quite risky for other reasons. There are two important sources of risk in particular. First, there is an inflation risk: because nominal bonds promise coupons and

[5] The yields in Figure 1.5 use data from Gürkaynak, Sack, and Wright (2007), who fit a six-parameter Nelson–Siegel model to bond data. See Section 1.5.1.

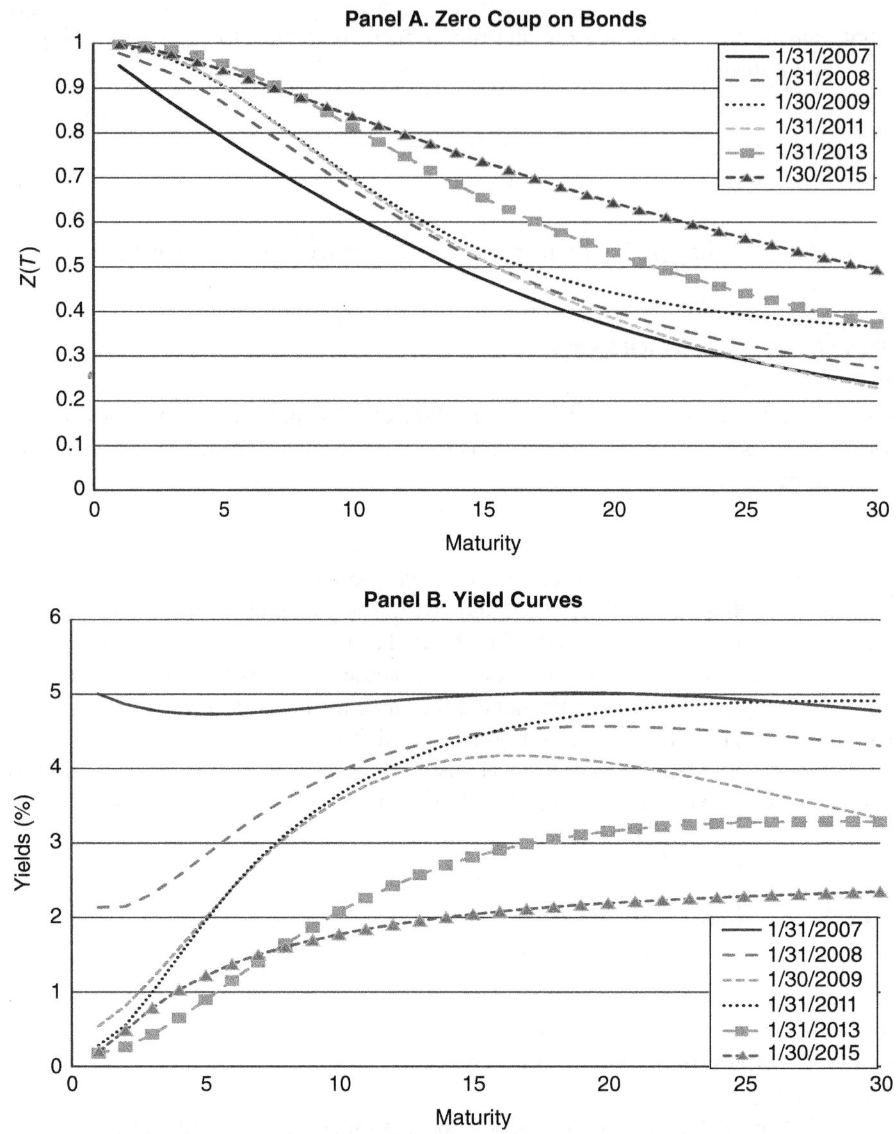

Figure 1.5 Zero-coupon bonds and yield curves. Panel A shows the zero-coupon bonds at the end of January in 2007–2009, 2011, 2013, and 2015. Panel B reports the corresponding yield curves against maturity. Yields are continuously compounded. Source: Data are from Gürkaynak, Sack, and Wright (2007), updated series.

final payoffs in dollars, if inflation unexpectedly increases over the life of the bond, the real value of these promised payments declines, and investors require a premium to hold a security with an uncertain real payoff.

The second source of risk in a long-term bond stems from interest rate risk: if the investor needs to sell the bond before maturity, he/she may suffer potentially severe capital losses if nominal interest rates increased in the meantime. To illustrate, Panel A of Figure 1.7 plots the "life cycle" of a 30-year coupon bond, issued on February 15, 1985, and maturing on February 15, 2015. The coupon rate of the bond is 11.25%. More specifically, Panel A plots the end-of-month price of the coupon bond (solid black line) together with the 1-month Treasury bill rate (dashed gray line). The price of the coupon bond shot up from its issue price of \$100 in February 1985 to \$140 by March 1986 and then dropped to \$113 by September 1987.[6] If an investor bought the bond at \$140 in March 1986 but found it necessary to sell it in September 1987, he/she would have suffered a capital loss of 20%, which would have only partly be compensated from receiving the 11.25% coupon.

Panel B of Figure 1.7 plots the total monthly return (capital gain plus accrued interest) in excess of the 1-month T-bill rate from investing in the 30-year bond (dashed gray line). Monthly excess returns of plus/minus 5% are not uncommon for the first half of the sample. Indeed, the solid black line in the figure reports the monthly standard deviation of excess bond returns

[6]Panel A actually shows the first price in February 1985 as \$94.718 rather than \$100 as the figure reports end-of-month prices. That is, the bond dropped 5.3% in the first 2 weeks after issuance.

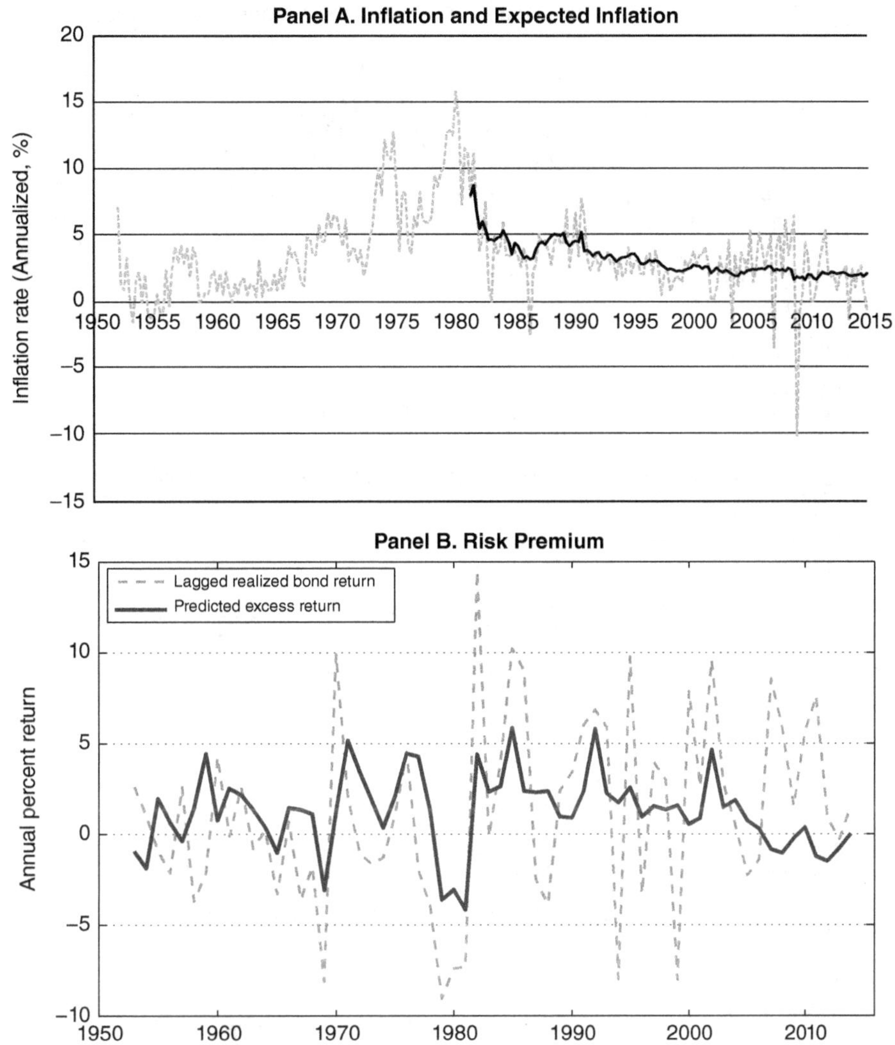

Figure 1.6 Expected inflation and risk premium. Panel A shows the quarterly realized inflation rate (Consumer Price Index (CPI), dashed gray line) and the professional forecasters' consensus forecast of future inflation with 2 years horizon (solid black line). CPI data are from the FRED database at the Federal Reserve Bank of St Louis, while consensus forecasts are from the Survey of Professional Forecasters from the Federal Reserve Bank of Philadelphia. CPI forecasts are only available from 1981 onward. Panel B reports the estimated expected excess return of a 5-year zero-coupon bond computed from the Cochrane and Piazzesi factor. Source: Data for Panel B are from Fama–Bliss zero-coupon bond yields available at the Center for Research in Security Prices (CRSP).

estimated over the previous 3 years, and we find that such bond return volatility was as high as 4% at the beginning of the sample (equivalent to about 13.8% annualized), a sizable variation. Panel B shows that the volatility of bond returns also declines over time as we approach maturity: indeed, long-term bonds are far more volatile than short-term bonds, due to their higher duration (see, e.g., Sydyak (2015, Chapter 7 in this handbook)). In fact, in the very last part of the sample, the price declines almost deterministically (close to zero volatility) toward \$100, which is the promised principal at maturity. The reason why the price declines so steeply is that these bonds carry a coupon of 11.25%. Because short-term interest rates were essentially zero in this period, the steep decline in the coupon bond price must compensate for the high 11.25% coupon for the total bond return to be approximately zero, that is, the same as the return on an alternative investment in Treasury securities with similar short maturity.[7]

For comparison, Panel C plots the returns of the S&P 500 index over the same sample (1985–2014). This sample includes two major drops in the stock market: October 1987 (with a negative excess return of −25%) and October 2008 (with a negative excess return of −19%). Both events are clearly visible in the figure. The S&P 500 index is more volatile than the 30-year bond

[7]For instance, the price dropped from \$112.3594 on December 31, 2013, to \$101.3008 on December 31, 2014. Thus, the total return over the year including the coupon is (\$101.308 + \$11.25 − \$112.3594)/\$112.3594 = 0.1703%, which is very similar to the 1-year T-bill rate on December 31, 2013, given by 0.1691%.

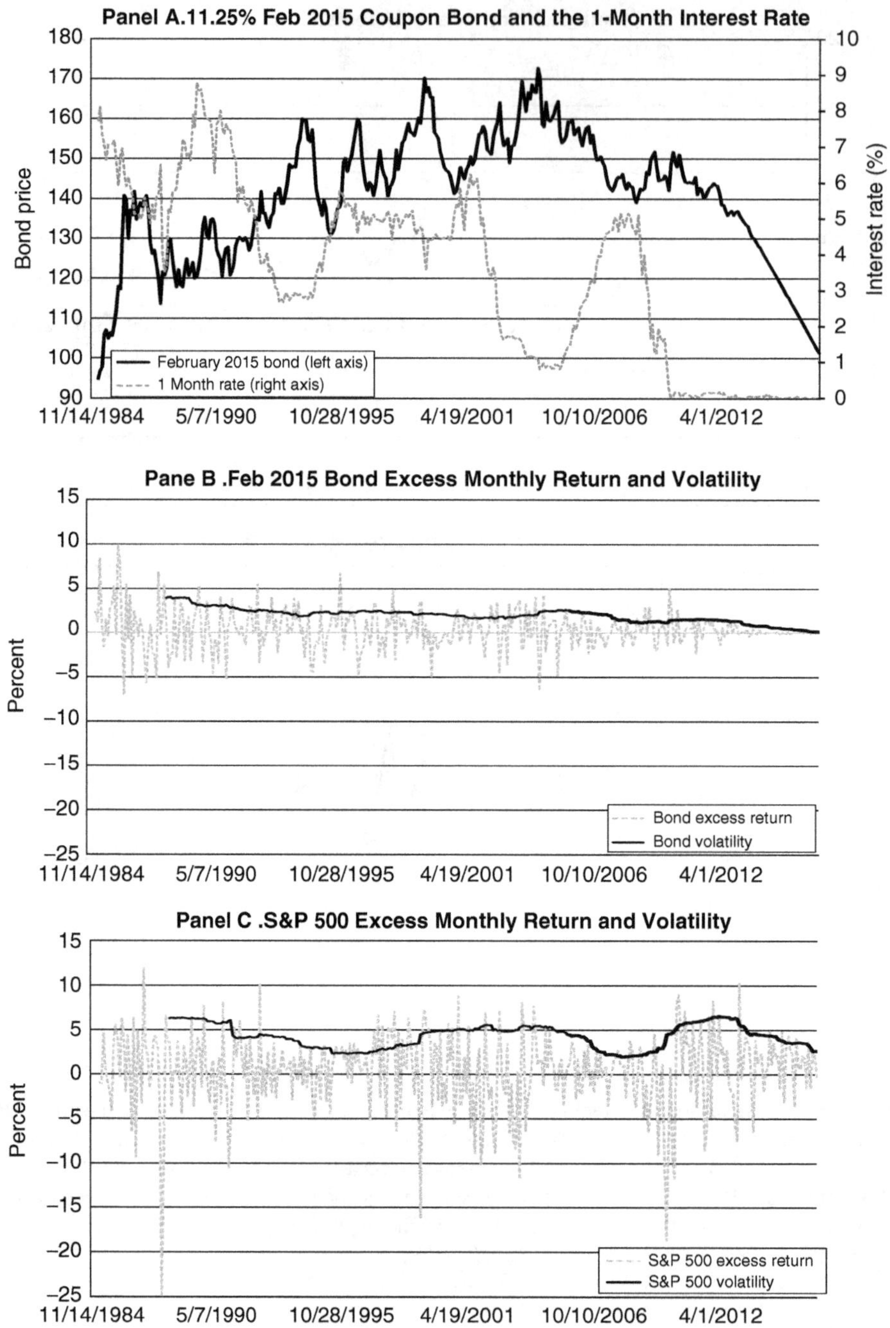

Figure 1.7 The life cycle of a 30-year coupon bond. Panel A shows the monthly (clean) price of 11.25%, 30-year U.S. Treasury coupon bond issued on February 15, 1985, and expiring on February 15, 2015, alongside the 1-month Treasury bill rate. Panel B shows the monthly excess return of the coupon bond and its monthly volatility computed as the 3-year trailing standard deviation of excess returns. Panel C shows the monthly excess return of the S&P 500 index and its monthly volatility computed as the 3-year trailing standard deviation of excess returns. Source: All data are from the Center for Research in Security Prices (CRPS).

on average, as the monthly standard deviation (the black solid line) hovers around 5% (17% annualized). However, the volatility of the S&P 500 index has been as low as 2% (7% annualized) and as high as 6.5% (23% annualized). The 4% volatility of the 30-year bond is sizable even compared to the variation of the stock market. In this sense, U.S. Treasuries represent risky investments for investors who may not hold them to maturity.

The risk premium in the last term of Equation 1.3 is therefore a compensation that investors require to hold risky long-term bonds, which could pay off little when the investors need them the most. Indeed, Panel B of Figure 1.6 plots the expected excess annual return on a 5-year zero-coupon bond computed using the Cochrane–Piazzesi factor as predictor (solid black line).[8] The figure also plots the lagged realized excess return from holding a 5-year zero-coupon bond. When the lines "move together," it means that the predictor is predicting well. Assuming that the Cochrane–Piazzesi factor captures the variation of the bond risk premium well, Panel B shows quite a bit of time variation in the bond risk premium. Interestingly, the bond risk premium computed from the Cochrane–Piazzesi factor turned negative around 2005. From an economic standpoint, a negative risk premium for long-term bonds is realistic in recent years as U.S. Treasury bonds may be considered "hedging instruments" against especially negative economic scenarios (see, e.g., Campbell, Sunderam, and Viceira (2013) and David and Veronesi (2015, Chapter 15 in this handbook) for a discussion). Indeed, recall that the right panel of Figure 1.4 shows that the "beta" of the 5-year zero-coupon bond with respect to the S&P 500 index turned negative after 2000, thereby justifying the "hedge" interpretation of long-term Treasury bonds. Intuitively, bad economic news makes investors drop stocks and buy safe U.S. Treasuries, which push up the value of Treasury bonds in bad times. Treasury bonds, therefore, represent a hedge against negative economic outcomes.

To conclude, Equation 1.3 shows that nominal yields are affected by three components, all of which turned lower in the last few years: real yields declined in the aftermath of the crisis (see Section 1.6), expected inflation has been declining steadily since early 1980s (Panel A of Figure 1.6), and the risk premium has been declining too in the last 10 years, because of the hedging properties of U.S. Treasury securities (Panel B of Figure 1.6). Not surprisingly, nominal yields have been especially low in the last few years (Panel B of Figure 1.5).

1.4.2 The Expectations Hypothesis

The previous section provided a discussion of the economic forces behind the shape of the term structure of nominal interest rates that was grounded on "fundamentals," such as real yield rates, expected inflation, and risk premium. However, there is also a more "finance-related" explanation of the yield curve which is related to investors' expectations about future interest rates and again a risk premium:

$$\text{Long-term yield} = \text{expected future short-term rates} + \text{risk premium}$$

To illustrate, it is useful to consider the case of *perfect foresight* first. Assume investors have perfect foresight about the next 1-year interest rates. That is, they know not only the current 1-year yield $y_t(1)$ but also next year's 1-year yield $y_{t+1}(1)$, where $y_t(\tau)$ denotes the continuously compounded yield at time t of a zero-coupon bond with time to maturity τ (and hence maturity *date* $t+\tau$). Given this knowledge, what is the value of a zero-coupon bond with maturity in 2 years?

Because investors *know* that next year's 1-year yield will be $y_{t+1}(1)$, they also know that the zero-coupon bond price next year will be

$$Z_{t+1}(1) = e^{-y_{t+1}(1)\times 1}$$

Because under these assumptions, $Z_{t+1}(1)$ is known today, its value today is simply the discounted value using the current 1-year yield. That is, the 2-year zero-coupon bond price is

$$Z_t(2) = Z_t(1) \times Z_{t+1}(1) = e^{-(y_t(1)+y_{t+1}(1))}$$

Because the 2-year yield also satisfies $Z_t(2) = e^{-y_t(2)\times 2}$, we obtain that under perfect foresight, the 2-year yield is the average of the two 1 year yields:

$$y_t(2) = \frac{1}{2}(y_t(1) + y_{t+1}(1))$$

Indeed, a similar argument implies that if we have perfect foresight of n future 1-year yields, then the yield of a zero-coupon bond with $n+1$ years to maturity is

$$y_t(n+1) = \text{Average}[y_t(1), y_{t+1}(1), \cdots, y_{t+n}(1)] = \frac{1}{n+1}\sum_{i=0}^{n} y_{t+i}(1)$$

The **expectations hypothesis** substitutes the perfect foresight with an expectation, thereby giving the long-term yield as being equal to the market expectation of future short-term rates. Using the notation above, we have

$$y_t(n+1) = E_t\left[\frac{1}{n+1}\sum_{i=0}^{n} y_{t+i}(1)\right] \tag{1.4}$$

[8]Cochrane and Piazzesi (2005) propose a special combination of forward rates as a predictor of future excess bond returns and find that it does predict returns very well. See also Dahlquist and Hasseltoft (2015, Chapter 9 in this handbook).

Subtracting the current 1-year yield, we can also write

$$y_t(n+1) - y_t(1) = E_t\left[\frac{1}{n+1}\sum_{i=0}^{n} y_{t+i}(1)\right] - y_t(1) \tag{1.5}$$

The left-hand side is the term spread, the difference between the $n + 1$-year yield and the 1-year yield, while the right-hand side is the "expectation spread," the difference between the expected future average interest rate and the current 1-year yield.

Does this relation holds in the data? Heuristically, Panel A of Figure 1.8 plots the expected future 3-month rates from the Survey of Professional Forecasters from 1981 to 2015. The forecasts are for the 3-month T-bill rate for the current quarter, denoted in the figure by $r(t)$, and for the next three quarters, denoted by $r(t + 3m)$, $r(t + 6m)$, and $r(t + 9m)$, respectively. According to the expectations hypothesis, and assuming that the consensus forecasts from the surveys reflect market expectations, the 1-year yield $y_t(1)$ should be equal to the average forecast of future rates. Panel B shows the 1-year term spread, defined as $y_t(1y) - r(t)$,[9] together with the 1-year "expectation spread," which equals the expected average interest rates $\sum_{i=0}^{3} E_t[r(t + i \times 3m)]/4$ minus the 3-month rate $r(t)$. The figure shows that the two series are correlated with each other (correlation of 26%), but they are quite different from each other. Though the term spread is often larger than the expectation spread, we also have cases in which the term spread is actually smaller than the expectation spread. That is, there are occasions when the expected future average rate over the next year is in fact higher than the 1-year yield.

Panels A and B of Figure 1.8 provide simple heuristic evidence to show that the expectations hypothesis is not supported in the data. More formally, using predictive regression techniques, Fama and Bliss (1987), Campbell and Shiller (1991), Cochrane and Piazzesi (2005), and many others (see discussion in Dahlquist and Hasseltoft (2015, Chapter 9 in this handbook) and Fontaine and Garcia (2015, Chapter 14 in this handbook)) show that there is little or no support for the expectations hypothesis in the data.

The violation of the expectations hypothesis suggests the existence of an additional term in Equation 1.4, that is, we have

$$y_t(n+1) = E_t\left[\frac{1}{n+1}\sum_{i=0}^{n} y_{t+i}(1)\right] + RP_t \tag{1.6}$$

where RP_t reflects a risk premium from holding the bond from t. The time variation in RP_t invalidates the expectations hypothesis. Indeed, even if expected future interest rates (the first term in Equation 1.6) does not change, the yield curve changes because RP_t changes. Therefore, movements in the yield curve do not only correspond to variations in expected future short-term yields.

To understand the source of this risk premium in this context, consider again the previous example. Let us now assume that investors do not know at t the 1-year yield at $t + 1$, but they believe it has a normal distribution (for simplicity):

$$y_{t+1}(1) \sim N(\bar{y}, \sigma_y^2)$$

where $\bar{y} = E[y_{t+1}(1)]$ is the expected future 1-year yield and σ_y is the standard deviation. From the eyes of a time t investor, the 1-year zero-coupon bond at $t + 1$ is risky, as $Z_{t+1}(1) = e^{-y_{t+1}(1)}$ and $y_{t+1}(1)$ is random. Therefore, it is possible that the investor at time t would like to discount the next year bond at a higher rate than the risk-free rate. That is, an intuitive formula is

$$Z_t(2) = e^{-(y_t(1)+RP)\times 1} E_t[Z_{t+1}(1)]$$

where RP is a risk premium the investor requires to hold the 2-year bond, and $E_t[Z_{t+1}(1)]$ is the current expected value of the future zero-coupon bond 1 year from now. Using the properties of the normal distribution, we then obtain

$$Z_t(2) = e^{-(y_t(1)+RP)\times 1} e^{-\bar{y}+\frac{1}{2}\sigma_y^2}$$

where $\frac{1}{2}\sigma_y^2$ is a convexity term.[10] Because the 2-year yield is $Z_t(2) = e^{-y_t(2)\times 2}$ and we defined $\bar{y} = E[y_{t+1}(1)]$, we obtain

$$y_t(2) = \frac{1}{2}\{y_t(1) + E[y_{t+2}(1)]\} + \frac{1}{2}\left(RP + \frac{1}{2}\sigma_y^2\right)$$

That is, the yield of the 2-year bond is given by the expected average 1-year yields over the 2 years, plus a term that includes a risk premium and a convexity term. If the risk premium RP (or the volatility σ_y) are time varying, then the expected future average rate may differ from the current 2-year yield in a random manner, generating patterns such as those illustrated in Panel B of Figure 1.8.

[9] Because the time step is less than 1 year, the notation here emphasizes the units used, so that 1y is 1 year, $3m$ is 3 months, and so on.

[10] The convexity term is also called a "Jensen's" term, due to Jensen's inequality that states that if $f(x)$ is convex, then $E[f(x)] > f(E[x])$. In the special case of a normal distribution and exponential function, we have that if $x \sim N(\mu_x, \sigma_x^2)$, then $E[e^x] = e^{\mu_x+\frac{1}{2}\sigma_x^2} > e^{\mu_x}$. Hence, $\frac{1}{2}\sigma_x^2$ quantifies the Jensen's effect.

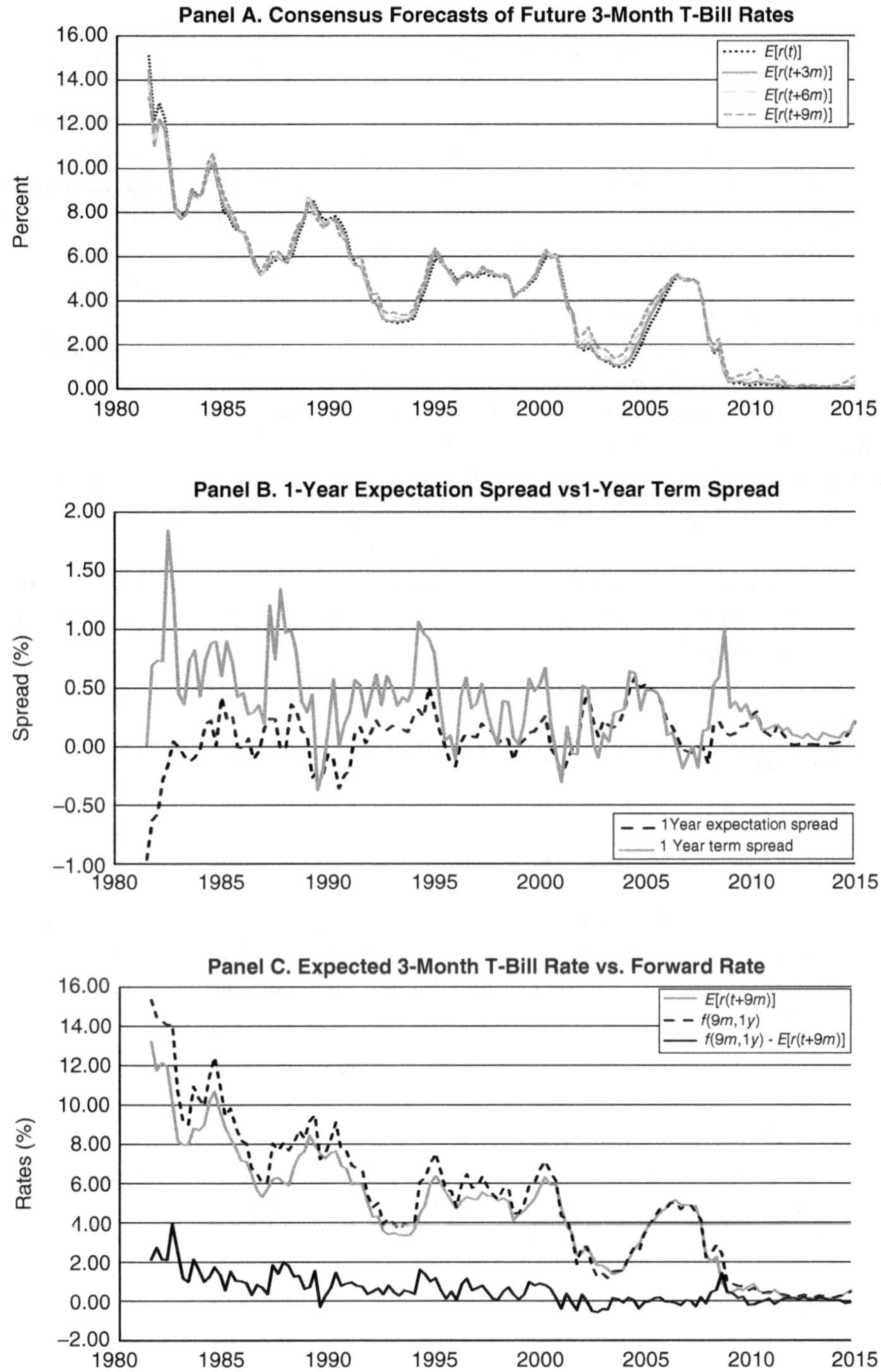

Figure 1.8 Expected future interest rates and the yield curve. Panel A plots the consensus (average) forecasts of the 3-month Treasury bill rate of the current quarter (t) and one, two, and three quarters ahead ($t + 3m$, $t + 6m$, $t + 9m$). Panel B plots the 1-year term spread, defined as the 1-year yield minus the 3-month yield, along with the 1-year "expectation spread," defined as the average expected 1-year rate $\sum_{i=0}^{3} E[r(t + i \times 3m)]/4$ minus the current 3-month yield. Panel C plots the predicted 3-month rate with 9-month horizon (gray solid line) and the corresponding 3-month forward rate $f(9m, 1y)$ (black dashed line). The bottom black line plots the difference between forward rates and expected future rates. Survey data are from the Survey of Professional Forecasters at the Federal Reserve Bank of Philadelphia. Source: Yield data from the Center for Research in Security Prices (CRPS).

1.4.3 Forward Rates as Expectation of Future Interest Rates?

A subject that is closely related to the expectations hypothesis is the relation between forward rates and expected future interest rates.

First, what is a forward rate? Consider an investor who has a receivable of \$1 million in 9 months from now and wants to invest it for 3 months (i.e., from $9m$ to $1y$ from now) by investing in U.S. Treasury securities. One strategy is to wait until the receivable arrives and then invest it in the 3-month T-bill at that time. However, this strategy subjects the investor to interest rate risk: if the interest rate declines, the investor will receive a lower payment in 1 year. An alternative is to design a trading strategy to *lock in* today the future 3-month interest rate. The investor can do the following:

- **Today (time 0):** Set up a zero-cost, long/short strategy:
  1. Short 9-month U.S. Treasury bills with face value of \$1 million. The short sale will yield proceeds of $\$1 \times Z(9m)$ million, where $Z(9m)$ is the unit price of the T-bill with 9 months to maturity.
  2. Use the proceeds from the short sale to purchase M, 1-year T-bills. Given the current price $Z(1y)$ of a 1-year T-bill, the investor can purchase $M = Z(9m)/Z(1y)$ million 1-year T-bills.
- **In 9 months:** Use the receivable of \$1 million to pay off the short position in 9-month T-bills, which has become due.
- **In 1 year:** Redeem the 1-year T-bills purchased at time zero, thereby receiving $\$M = Z(9m)/Z(1y)$ million.

In frictionless markets, this strategy implies no outlays of money today, and from the perspective of the investor, it is *as if* he invests \$1 million in 9 months (the receivable) and receives $\$M = Z(9m)/Z(1y)$ million in 1 year. Thus, the implicit annualized interest rate f in this investment strategy is

$$e^{f\times 0.25} = \frac{Z(9m)/Z(1y)\ \text{million}}{1\text{million}}$$

where 0.25 represents the investment horizon (3 months = 0.25). We thus find that the implicit interest rate f satisfies

$$f(9m, 1y) = \frac{1}{0.25}\ln\left(\frac{Z(9m)}{Z(1y)}\right)$$

where we emphasize that the interest rate f is for an investment from 9 months ($9m$) from now to 1 year ($1y$) from now. $f(9m, 1y)$ is called a **forward rate** and it is an interest rate for a future investment that is implicit in the current zero-coupon bond curve.[11]

In general, the same argument as above but for other investment times and horizons gives the following general formula for the continuously compounded forward rate:

$$f_t(\tau_1, \tau_2) = \frac{1}{\tau_2 - \tau_1}\ln\left(\frac{Z_t(\tau_1)}{Z_t(\tau_2)}\right) \tag{1.7}$$

where t is the time when the forward rate is determined (time 0 in previous example) and τ_1 and τ_2 are the times (from t) at which the investment takes place ($\tau_1 = 9m$ and $\tau_2 = 1y$ in the previous example). Of course, $\tau_2 > \tau_1$.

Substituting $Z_t(\tau_i) = e^{-y_t(\tau_i)\tau_i}$ in Equation 1.7, we find two useful formulas:

(i) The forward rate is related to the slope of the yield curve:

$$f_t(\tau_1, \tau_2) = y_t(\tau_1) + \tau_2\left(\frac{y_t(\tau_2) - y_t(\tau_1)}{\tau_2 - \tau_1}\right) \tag{1.8}$$

(ii) The long-term yield is the average forward rates

$$y_t(\tau_2) = w \quad y_t(\tau_1) + (1 - w) \quad f_t(\tau_1, \tau_2) \tag{1.9}$$

where

$$w = \frac{\tau_1}{\tau_2}$$

[11] I emphasize the "investment" interpretation of the forward rate, but by reversing the trade, the same can be thought as "borrowing" in the future at the locked-in borrowing rate f.

The first expression in Equation 1.8 provides a convenient formula for forward rates: it essentially shows that the forward rate is equal to the corresponding yield $y_t(\tau_1)$ plus a term proportional to the slope of the yield curve between τ_1 and τ_2 $\left(\text{the term } \left(\frac{y_t(\tau_2)-y_t(\tau_1)}{\tau_2-\tau_1}\right)\right)$. That is, if the yield curve is increasing between τ_1 and τ_2, then the forward rate is above the yield curve, while if the yield curve is decreasing between τ_1 and τ_2, then the forward rate is below the yield curve. Hence, the forward rate represents the marginal increase or decrease to the yield curve, and the yield curve is an average of forward rates.

Indeed, Equation 1.9 shows that the long-term yield is an average of the short-term yield and the forward rate. Equation 1.9 can be easily generalized to a sequence of forwards. For instance, consider 1-year forward rates $f_t(1,2), f_t(2,3), \cdots$. Then, we have that the $n+1$-year yield can be written as

$$y_t(n+1) = \frac{1}{n+1}\sum_{i=0}^{n-1} f_t(i, i+1) \tag{1.10}$$

with the notation $y_t(1) = f_t(0,1)$ (the first forward equals the 1-year yield to maturity).

Under the expectations hypothesis in Equation 1.4, we then have that the forward rate is equal to the expected future interest rate[12]:

$$f_t(i, i+1) = E_t[y_{t+i}(1)]$$

A positive risk premium instead generates $f_t(i, i+1) > E_t[y_{t+i}(1)]$. To see this, as shown in Equation 1.6, the existence of a positive risk premium implies $y_t(n+1) > E_t\left[\frac{1}{n+1}\sum_{i=0}^{n} y_{t+i}(1)\right]$ which in turn implies (if $RP > 0$ for every maturity n) that $f_t(i, i+1) > E[y_{t+i}(1)]$.

To check whether the forward rate is in fact equal to the expected future rate in the data, Panel C of Figure 1.8 plots the 9-month forward rate for a 3-month investment horizon ($f_t(9m, 1y)$) along with the predicted 3-month rate at the 9-month horizon ($E_t[r(t+9m)]$). As can be seen, for most of the sample, the forward rate was above the expected future 3-month rate $f_t(9m, 1y) > E_t[r(t+9m)]$, which is consistent with the existence of a risk premium.

1.4.4 Interpreting a Steepening of the Yield Curve

According to the expectations hypothesis, a steepening of the yield curve must be interpreted as an expected increase in future yields. However, one of the main messages of the evidence surrounding the failure of the expectations hypothesis is that essentially the opposite may be true. A steepening of the yield curve may as well signal (under some conditions) an expected *decline* in future yields. To understand the logic, intuitively, if the steepening of the yield curve is due to an increase in the risk premium RP_t in Equation 1.6, then zero-coupon bonds must have a positive expected excess return going forward. The only way a long-term zero-coupon bond may have a high return is for its price to increase, as a zero-coupon bond does not pay any coupons or dividends. For the price of a zero-coupon bond to increase, it ought to be the case that the corresponding yield has to decline. Thus, we have the paradoxical result that if a steepening of the yield curve is due to an increase in risk premium, then future rates should decline, instead of increase. Indeed, the researches carried out by Fama and Bliss (1987), Campbell and Shiller (1991), Cochrane and Piazzesi (2005), and many others (see Dahlquist and Hasseltoft (2015, Chapter 9 in this handbook) for a review and discussion) show that indeed the risk premium appears to be a main driver of the variation in long-term yields, providing the counterintuitive result about the slope of the yield curve and the expected future yields.

1.5 PRICING COUPON NOTES AND BONDS

As shown in Table 1.1, the vast majority of U.S. Treasury debt is made of coupon-bearing notes and bonds. From the table, about 78% of U.S. Treasuries are in fixed-coupon-bearing securities (notes and bonds), while about 12% are in (zero-coupon) Treasury bills and about 10% in securities with floating coupons, either indexed to inflation or to short-term interest rates

How do we value coupon bonds? What is their relation with discount factors introduced in the previous sections? Consider a coupon bond with maturity T_n, with semiannual coupon payments at times $T_1, T_2, \cdots, T_n$, where $T_i = T_{i-1} + 0.5$, and coupon rate c_n. Given a set of discount factors $Z(T_1), Z(T_2), \cdots, Z(T_n)$, the value of a coupon bond is provided by the no-arbitrage relation

$$P(T_n, c_n) = \sum_{i=1}^{n} \frac{c_n}{2} Z(T_i) + Z(T_n) \tag{1.11}$$

[12]The implication stems from observing that both Equations 1.4 and 1.10 must hold for all $n = 1, 2, \cdots$.

If the price of the bond was, say, lower than the right-hand side, then an arbitrageur could buy the bond and sell a portfolio of zero-coupon bonds with principals $c_n/2$ for $i = 1, \cdots, n-1$ and $(1 + c_n/2)$ for $i = n$, making a positive cash inflow today. Because at every future date the trade is perfectly hedged (as on every T_i, the arbitrageur collects the coupon – and principal at T_n – and use it to pay the corresponding zero-coupon sold), this trade represents an arbitrage opportunity.

1.5.1 Estimating the Zero-Coupon Discount Function

While in Equation 1.11 we assumed that we can price coupon bonds from a set of discounts $Z(T_i)$, in reality, we normally go in the opposite direction. In fact, computing the fair value of discount factors $Z(T_i)$ is very useful in practice, as they provide the value today of dollars in the future and thus provide an important benchmark for computing the time value of money. It is therefore common practice to use liquid U.S. Treasury notes and bonds to *extract* the discount factors $Z(T)$ from them.

There are several ways of extracting $Z(T)$ from coupon notes and notes. One possibility, called **bootstrapping**, is to invert Equation 1.11 and directly extract $Z(T)$ in a recursive manner. For instance, if we have coupon notes and bonds prices available with maturities at semiannual frequency, then inverting Equation 1.11 for $n = 1, 2, \cdots$ we obtain

$$Z(T_1) = \frac{P(T_1, c_1)}{1 + \frac{c_1}{2}}$$

$$Z(T_2) = \frac{P(T_2, c_2) - \frac{c_2}{2} Z(T_1)}{1 + \frac{c_2}{2}}$$

$$Z(T_3) = \frac{P(T_3, c_3) - \frac{c_3}{2}(Z(T_1) + Z(T_2))}{1 + \frac{c_3}{2}}$$

$$\vdots \quad \vdots$$

$$Z(T_n) = \frac{P(T_n, c_n) - \frac{c_n}{2} \sum_{i=1}^{n-1} Z(T_i)}{1 + \frac{c_n}{2}}$$

This bootstrapping procedure is widely used in practice, normally after a large filtering of the data to take into account data errors and other noises. For instance, the Fama–Bliss yields that are plotted in Figure 1.2 (those with maturities from 1 to 5 years) are indeed obtained through a bootstrapping procedure, although the methodology is more refined and elaborate than the one just illustrated.[13] An important feature of the bootstrapping methodology is that it does not impose any parametric restriction on the structure of zero-coupon bonds $Z(T_n)$, but they are extracted in a fully nonparametric manner from traded coupon bonds. Several chapters in this handbook use the Fama–Bliss zero-coupon data.

A second possibility is to postulate a parametric functional form for $Z(T_i)$ and then *estimate* the parameters by minimizing the squared difference between the observed bonds and the model bonds. For instance, a popular methodology, called the **extended Nelson–Siegel model**, is to assume that the continuously compounded yield with maturity T_i is given by

$$y(T_i) = \beta_0 + (\beta_1 + \beta_2)\frac{1 - e^{-\frac{T_i}{\lambda_1}}}{\frac{T_i}{\lambda_1}} - \beta_2 e^{-\frac{T_i}{\lambda_1}} + \beta_3 \left(\frac{1 - e^{-\frac{T_i}{\lambda_2}}}{\frac{T_i}{\lambda_2}} - e^{-\frac{T_i}{\lambda_2}} \right) \tag{1.12}$$

For given parameters $(\beta_0, \beta_1, \beta_2, \beta_3, \lambda_1, \lambda_2)$, we can compute

$$Z(T_i) = e^{-y(T_i) T_i} \tag{1.13}$$

[13]The Fama–Bliss methodology extracts forward rates from Treasury bills and notes by iteratively extending the maturity of the zero-coupon curve. The methodology essentially uses Equation 1.10, once it is generalized to any intermediate maturity.

where $y(T_i)$ is given by Equation 1.12. Thus, for given parameters, we can compute a "model price" for each available bond $P^{\text{model}}(T_n, c_n)$ by using Equation 1.11, with $Z(T_i)$ given by 1.13. We can finally estimate the parameters of the model by minimizing

$$\min_{(\beta_0,\beta_1,\beta_2,\beta_3,\lambda_1,\lambda_2)} \sum_{n=1}^{N} (P^{\text{model}}(T_n, c_n) - P^{\text{data}}(T_n, c_n))^2$$

where $P^{\text{data}}(T_n, c_n)$ denotes the observable data. Indeed, the zero-coupon bonds $Z(T_n)$ and the yield curves $y(T_n)$ in Panels A and B, respectively, of Figure 1.5 are estimates of the extended Nelson–Siegel model in Equation 1.12 (see updated series of Gürkaynak, Sack, and Wright (2007)). Several chapters in this handbook use these data.

1.5.2 Data and Bond Illiquidity

Clearly, the type of data used in the computation of discount factors $Z(T_i)$ affects the coupon bond curves. For instance, to illustrate, Table 1.2 contains some U.S. Treasury note and bond data on November 15, 2007, and November 15, 2008. I selected only the notes and bonds that have maturity on consecutive February 15 or August 15, so that we can easily extract the zero-coupon bond curve using the bootstrap methodology.[14] It is evident from Table 1.2 that there are multiple bonds maturing exactly on the same date. Hence, which bonds we use may affect the zero-coupon bonds $Z(T)$ and thus the yields $y(T)$.

To illustrate, Figure 1.9 shows the discount functions (top panels) and the yield curves (bottom panels) on November 15, 2007 (left panels), and on November 15, 2008 (right panels), the last date chosen as the financial crisis was in its full swing. Each panel reports two lines: the line with squares uses the oldest notes or bonds available at each maturity. So, for instance, for the first maturity (2/15/2008) on November 15, 2007, it uses the note issued on 2/15/1998 (see Table 1.2). The line with circles, instead, uses the most recently issued bonds or notes available at each maturity. So, for instance, again for the first maturity on November 15, 2007, it uses the note issued on 2/15/2005, which is the latest issued with that maturity, and so on.

Looking at the top-left panel of Figure 1.9, we see that there is little difference in the two zero-coupon bond curves on November 15, 2007, independently on whether the oldest or the most recent notes and bonds were used in the computation. The bottom-left panel shows that some little difference is visible in yields between the two curves, but the difference is small.

Different is the situation displayed in the top-right panel of Figure 1.9, when on November 15, 2008, the two zero-coupon discount curves show some significant price differences at maturities around 6 through 8 years. In fact, the bottom-right panel shows that on this date, the yield curves displayed a difference as high as 1% at these maturities. What is the source of the discrepancy between old bonds and new bonds? By examining the data in Table 1.2, we see that at these maturities the oldest Treasuries were bonds issued back in the 1980s. Such bonds tend to be less liquid on average compared to other U.S. Treasury notes with the same maturities but issued more recently (some differences in yield curves are in fact visible also on November 2007 on the left-bottom panel). During the financial crisis, the illiquidity of such bonds turned out to be very significant, generating a large spread in the zero-coupon bond curves issued at this time. Fontaine and Garcia (2015, Chapter 14 in this handbook) contains a discussion of the literature that highlights these and other similar events.

1.6 INFLATION-PROTECTED SECURITIES

The U.S. Treasury, as well as the treasury departments of many other countries such as the United Kingdom and Italy, issues inflation-protected bonds, that is, bonds that do not pay a fixed amount but a quantity proportional to the cumulative inflation during the life of the bond (see Fleckenstein, Longstaff, and Lustig (2015, Chapter 3 in this handbook) and Pflueger and Viceira (2015, Chapter 10 in this handbook) for details and discussions about inflation-protected bonds). Figure 1.10 plots the real yields obtained from U.S. TIPS on the same six dates as in Figure 1.5. The variation is quite interesting, as the real yields were all positive in 2007 and then moved to negative for short-term maturities, while they remained mostly positive for long-term maturities. Indeed, negative real rates persisted since the beginning of the 2008–2009 financial crisis up until today. In January 2013, moreover, the short-term real rate was extremely negative, at −2%.

What economic forces determine the real yields, such as the ones plotted in Figure 1.10? A standard decomposition of the real yield is as follows:

$$\begin{aligned} \text{real yield} = a \times {} & \text{expected real economic growth} \\ & -b \times \text{macroeconomic risk} + \text{impatience} \end{aligned} \tag{1.14}$$

where a and b are two positive proportionality factors.

[14] Note that the price data reported are "clean" prices, that is, without accrued interest. In order to extract the zero-coupon bond curve, we need to use "invoice prices" which equal "clean prices" plus "accrued interests." Accrued interest equals the semiannual coupon payment times the fraction of time since the last coupon payment. For instance, on November 15, 2007, the accrued interest of the 3% coupon note expiring on 2/15/2008 is $\frac{3}{2} \times 0.5 = 3 \times 0.25 = \$0.75$.

TABLE 1.2 U.S. Treasury Note and Bond Data on Two Dates with Maturity at Semiannual Frequency

November 15, 2007						November 15, 2008					
Issue Date	Maturity date	Type	Coupon rate	Price		Issue date	Maturity date	Type	Coupon rate	Price	
				Bid	Ask					Bid	Ask
2/18/03	2/15/08	Note	3	99.92188	99.95313	2/17/04	2/15/09	Note	3	100.6172	100.6484
2/15/05	2/15/08	Note	3.375	100.0078	100.0391	2/15/06	2/15/09	Note	4.5	100.9922	101.0234
2/15/98	2/15/08	Note	5.5	100.5313	100.5625	8/16/04	8/15/09	Note	3.5	101.7656	101.7969
8/15/03	8/15/08	Note	3.25	99.85156	99.88281	8/15/06	8/15/09	Note	4.875	102.75	102.7813
8/15/05	8/15/08	Note	4.125	100.4531	100.4844	8/16/99	8/15/09	Note	6	103.5938	103.625
2/17/04	2/15/09	Note	3	99.52344	99.55469	2/15/05	2/15/10	Note	3.5	103.0078	103.0391
2/15/06	2/15/09	Note	4.5	101.3359	101.3672	2/15/07	2/15/10	Note	4.75	104.4297	104.4609
8/16/04	8/15/09	Note	3.5	100.2734	100.3047	2/15/00	2/15/10	Note	6.5	106.5	106.5313
8/15/06	8/15/09	Note	4.875	102.5469	102.5781	8/15/05	8/15/10	Note	4.125	105.2344	105.2656
8/16/99	8/15/09	Note	6	104.4766	104.5078	8/15/00	8/15/10	Note	5.75	108.1484	108.1797
2/15/05	2/15/10	Note	3.5	100.4219	100.4531	2/15/01	2/15/11	Note	5	108.6094	108.6406
2/15/07	2/15/10	Note	4.75	103.0781	103.1094	8/15/01	8/15/11	Note	5	110.4844	110.5156
2/15/00	2/15/10	Note	6.5	106.8828	106.9141	2/15/02	2/15/12	Note	4.875	110.8438	110.875
8/15/05	8/15/10	Note	4.125	102.0781	102.1094	8/15/02	8/15/12	Note	4.375	110.5313	110.5625
8/15/00	8/15/10	Note	5.75	106.2656	106.2969	2/18/03	2/15/13	Note	3.875	108.0781	108.1094
2/15/01	2/15/11	Note	5	104.9219	104.9531	8/15/03	8/15/13	Note	4.25	109.3281	109.3594
8/15/01	8/15/11	Note	5	105.2969	105.3281	2/17/04	2/15/14	Note	4	108.2656	108.2969
2/15/02	2/15/12	Note	4.875	105.0156	105.0469	8/16/04	8/15/14	Note	4.25	109.9063	109.9375
8/15/02	8/15/12	Note	4.375	103.3125	103.3438	2/15/85	2/15/15	Bond	11.25	145.0625	145.0938
2/18/03	2/15/13	Note	3.875	100.9219	100.9531	2/15/05	2/15/15	Note	4	107.2813	107.3125
8/15/03	8/15/13	Note	4.25	102.625	102.6563	8/15/85	8/15/15	Bond	10.625	143.2344	143.2656
2/17/04	2/15/14	Note	4	100.9688	101	8/15/05	8/15/15	Note	4.25	107.5156	107.5469
8/16/04	8/15/14	Note	4.25	102.1094	102.1406	2/18/86	2/15/16	Bond	9.25	135.7813	135.8125
2/15/85	2/15/15	Bond	11.25	145.3594	145.3906	2/15/06	2/15/16	Note	4.5	108.7656	108.7969
2/15/05	2/15/15	Note	4	100.2969	100.3281	8/15/06	8/15/16	Note	4.875	109.9063	109.9375
8/15/85	8/15/15	Bond	10.625	143.7188	143.75	2/15/07	2/15/17	Note	4.625	107.6719	107.7031
8/15/05	8/15/15	Note	4.25	101.5625	101.5938	8/17/87	8/15/17	Bond	8.875	136.4844	136.5156
2/18/86	2/15/16	Bond	9.25	136.0469	136.0781	8/15/07	8/15/17	Note	4.75	108.2344	108.2656
2/15/06	2/15/16	Note	4.5	103.125	103.1563	2/15/08	2/15/18	Note	3.5	99.64063	99.67188
8/15/06	8/15/16	Note	4.875	105.5938	105.625	8/15/08	8/15/18	Note	4	102.8594	102.8906
2/15/07	2/15/17	Note	4.625	103.7813	103.8125						
8/17/87	8/15/17	Bond	8.875	137	137.0313						

Source: CRSP

This table reports data on U.S. Treasury notes and bonds on two dates, November 15, 2007, and November 15, 2008. The data were selected to have maturities at a semiannual frequency (February and August of each year) for as many years as possible without gaps. All bonds and notes available on that maturity calendar are reported.

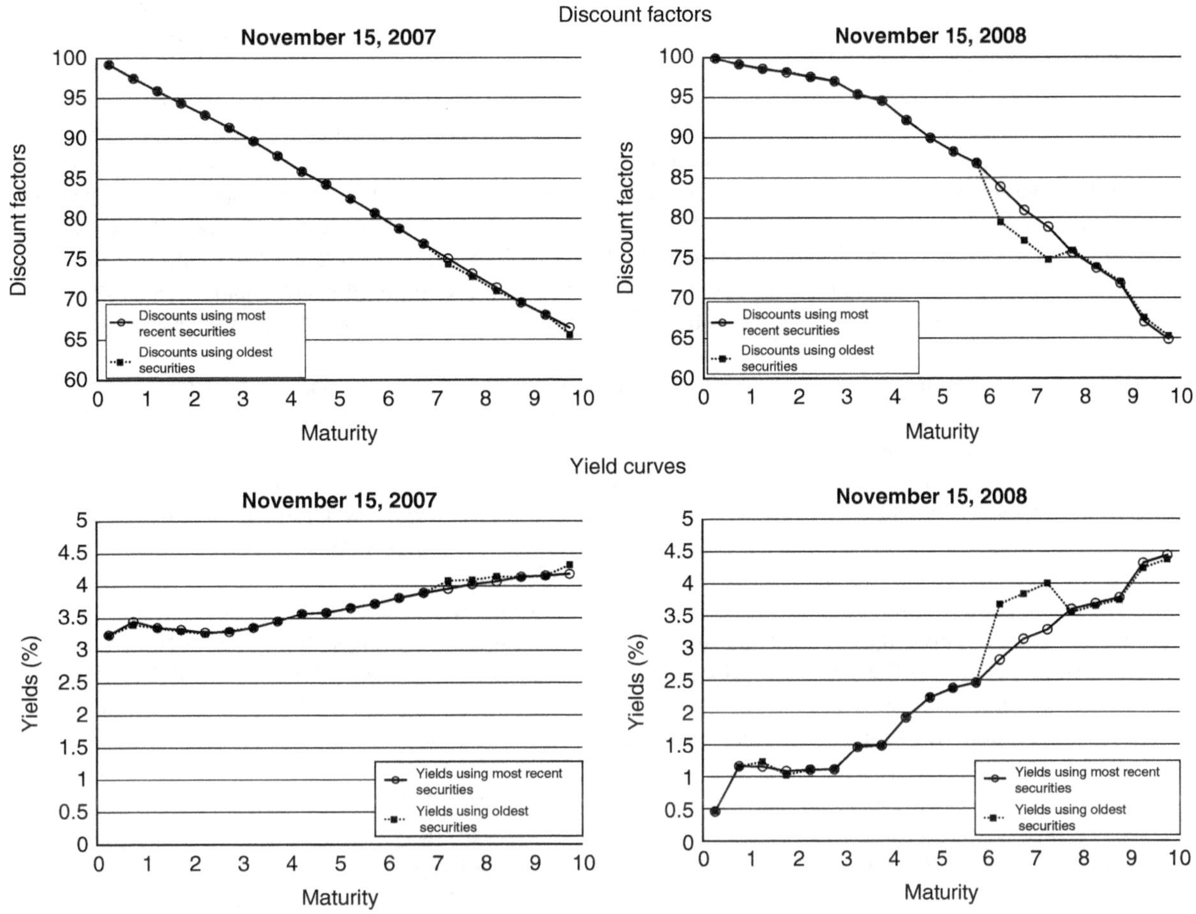

Figure 1.9 Discounts and yields on two dates. The top two panels plot the discount functions $Z(T)$ obtained from bootstrapping on November 15, 2007, and November 17, 2008, while the bottom two panels plot the corresponding yield curves. For each panel, the lines with squares are computed using the oldest securities available, while the lines with circles use the most recent securities available. Source: Data are from the Center for Research on Security Prices (CRSP).

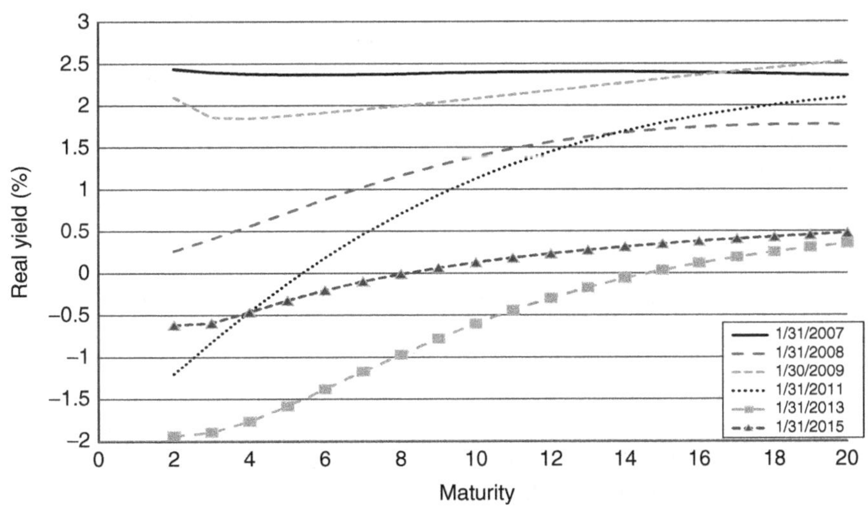

Figure 1.10 TIPS-implied real yield curves. This figure reports the real yield curves extracted from TIPS at the end of January in 2007–2009, 2011, 2013, and 2015. Yields are continuously compounded. Source: Data are from Gürkaynak, Sack, and Wright (2010), updated series.

Intuitively, let us consider an investor who is thinking about how much to borrow or save today. Let the investment or borrowing horizon be denoted by T. Assume there is no inflation, so that the only reason to save or borrow is to transfer "real consumption" from today to time T (if he saves) or vice versa (if he borrows). The logic is as follows: If the investor expects to be very rich at time T, then he knows he will be able to buy a lot of goods in the future, such as a home or a better car, and so on. Thus, it is likely that this investor would like to borrow today to consume more today in expectation of being able to pay back the loan in the future (time T). For instance, many households borrow money to purchase their homes or their cars in the expectation that their income will increase (or at least persist) over time and thus will be able to repay the mortgage or the auto loans. That is, they do not wait to save enough to buy their homes or cars, but rather they buy them today through borrowing. If many households want to borrow today, the strong demand for funds push up the (real) interest rate today, as the higher demand for scarce financial resources induces banks to charge more for borrowing. Extending this argument to the whole economy, we can expect that the higher the expected real growth rate of the economy, the more firms and individuals would like to borrow today and thus the higher the real rate of interest should be.

On the other hand, even if an investor expects to be rich at time T but there is a lot of risk – for instance, he could be fired in the meantime – then he would like to save some money today to cover against the rainy days, so to speak. If a lot of investors want to save because of too much economic uncertainty, they will buy a lot of (inflation-protected) Treasury securities. Such high demand for U.S. Treasuries in turn decreases the real interest rate. Thus, higher macroeconomic risk reduces the risk-free real interest rate. Finally, investors' natural impatience has also an impact on real rates. That is, the more people prefer to consume today versus the future (i.e., the more they are impatient to consume, such as buy new cars or bigger homes), the more they need to borrow today, which in turn pushes up the real rate of interest, as discussed.

These arguments imply that observing low or negative real rates may indicate that investors expect a low or negative real growth of the economy or perceive high macroeconomic risk. Figure 1.10 is consistent with this interpretation: in 2007, before the crisis, macroeconomic risk was low and expectation of economic growth was strong. However, the 2008 financial crisis has slashed agents' expectations of real economic growth and dramatically increased macroeconomic risk. Both channels moved to reduced dramatically the real rate of interest, as agents stop borrowing for the future. Of course, other forces are at play as well, such as an aggressive monetary policy that slashed nominal interest rates in 2008 and kept them close to zero ever since. With low expected inflation, real rates are mechanically negative from Equation 1.3. Still, why was the monetary policy so aggressive that led to a massive decrease in the reference short-term rate to start with? Likely, because the Federal Reserve's own expectations were that real economic growth was predicted to be low and that macroeconomic risk was large. That is, the decomposition 1.14 is a useful reference to interpret the data and the market (or Federal Reserve) expectations about the future of the real economy.

1.7 FLOATING RATE NOTES

The U.S. Treasury started issuing FRNs in January 2014. As of March 2015, 1.6% of U.S. marketable securities are in FRN. FRNs are securities whose coupon is not fixed, but it depends on realized short-term rates. That is, if the short-term interest rate increases, the periodic coupon of the FRN increases, and vice versa. For instance, the new U.S. Treasury FRNs pay coupons at the quarterly frequency using the 13-week U.S. Treasury bill rate as a reference rate, plus a spread determined at the auction of the FRN.

Let $T_1, T_2, \cdots, T_n$ denote the coupon payment dates of the FRN, and let $T_{i+1} = T_i + 0.25$. The standard coupon-adjustment formula is that the (annualized) coupon rate at time T_i is given by

$$c(T_i) = r(T_{i-1}) + \text{ spread} \tag{1.15}$$

where $r(T_{i-1})$ is the quarterly compounded, (annualized) 3-month rate. While the price of FRNs seems very hard to obtain, because its cash flows (coupons) depend on the realization of future interest rates, which are unknown today, it turns out the FRN pricing is relatively simple although conceptually a little complicated.

Indeed, we can obtain the price from a recursive argument. We consider first the case in which the "spread" in Equation 1.15 is zero. Suppose the FRN has maturity date T_n, where n is the total number of coupon payments. Suppose that today is actually T_{n-1} and thus the FRN has only 3 months to maturity. Today we know the reference 3-month rate $r(T_{n-1})$ and therefore we know the full cash flow at time T_n. This is given by the principal \$1 plus the 1/4 of the coupon rate $c(T_n) = r(T_{n-1})$,

$$\text{Cash flow at } T_n = 1 + \frac{1}{4}c(T_n) = 1 + \frac{1}{4}r(T_{n-1})$$

Therefore, denoting by $P^{FRN}(t)$ the value of the FRN at t, the FRN value at time T_{n-1} ought to be equal to the discounted value of its cash flow at T_n, that is

$$P^{FRN}(T_{n-1}) = \frac{\text{Cash flow at } T_n}{1 + \frac{1}{4}r(T_{n-1})} \tag{1.16}$$

$$= \frac{1 + \frac{1}{4}c(T_n)}{1 + \frac{1}{4}r(T_{n-1})} \tag{1.17}$$

$$= \frac{1 + \frac{1}{4}r(T_{n-1})}{1 + \frac{1}{4}r(T_{n-1})} \tag{1.18}$$

$$= 1 \tag{1.19}$$

That is, no matter what the interest rate is at T_{n-1}, the value of the FRN 3 months before maturity is always 1. The intuition is that the interest rate at T_{n-1} affects both the future cash flow *and* the discount rate used for discounting the cash flow next period back to T_{n-1}. A high interest rate implies not only a higher future cash flow but also a higher discount rate, and vice versa. The two effects offset each other, and the value of the security 3 months before maturity is always 1.

Consider now the value of the security 6 months before maturity, that is, at T_{n-2}. At this time, the investor knows that by purchasing an FRN he gets a security that pays the (annualized) coupon $c(T_{n-1}) = r(T_{n-2})$ next period (i.e., T_{n-1}), when the price of the security will revert back to unity $P^{FRN}(T_{n-1}) = 1$. Thus, the FRN value at T_{n-2} ought to be

$$P^{FRN}(T_{n-2}) = \frac{P^{FRN}(T_{n-1}) + \frac{1}{4}c(T_{n-1})}{1 + \frac{1}{4}r(T_{n-2})} \tag{1.20}$$

$$= \frac{1 + \frac{1}{4}r(T_{n-2})}{1 + \frac{1}{4}r(T_{n-2})} \tag{1.21}$$

$$= 1 \tag{1.22}$$

where we used Equations 1.15 and 1.19 to move from the first to the second line. Once again, the FRN is equal to one also at time T_{n-2}.

Using the same logic and using backward induction, we obtain the rule that an FRN is always equal to unity at every reset time T_i:

$$P^{FRN}(T_i) = 1$$

The FRN is going to be slightly different from one outside reset times, however. Consider a time t such that $T_{i-1} < t < T_i$. At this time, the next cash flow at T_i has already been set according to Equation 1.15. However, at t the new interest rate $r_t(T_i)$ with maturity T_i may have changed. Thus, the value at t is the discounted value of $(1 + c(T_i)/4) = (1 + r(T_{i-1})/4)$ using the discount at t with time to maturity $T_i - t$, $Z_t(T_i - t)$:

$$P^{FRN}(t) = Z_t(T_i - t)(1 + r(T_{i-1})/4) \tag{1.23}$$

The discussion so far assumed that the spread in Equation 1.15 is zero. Adding a spread to the coupon payments is simple because the spread is constant over time, and therefore its present value can be computed using the existing zero-coupon discount curve as $\frac{\text{spread}}{4} \times \sum_{i=1}^{n} Z(T_i)$, a quantity that needs to be added to $P^{FRN}(0) = 1$. The spread in U.S. Treasury FRN has been extremely small since their first issuance in January 2014, ranging between 0.045% and 0.84%.[15] Because the default risk of U.S. Treasury FRN is the same as the one of short-term Treasury bills and notes, the additional spread over T-bills is likely due to a compensation for the likely less liquidity of FRN compared to the other short-term U.S. Treasury securities.

[15] Data from treasurydirect.gov accessed on May 4, 2015.

1.8 CONCLUSION

This chapter contains an introductory overview of fixed-income markets. I highlighted a number of recent changes in fixed-income markets as well as some basic methodologies for their analysis, such as zero-coupon discount functions, forward rates, and the various market forces affecting the term structure of interest rates. This handbook covers many of these subjects, and many more, in far more detail.

REFERENCES

Brigo D, Liu Q, Pallavicini A, Sloth D. Nonlinear valuation under margining and funding costs with residual credit risk: a unified approach. In: Veronesi P, editor. *Handbook of Fixed Income*. John Wiley & Sons; 2015.

Buraschi A, Whelan P. Bond markets and monetary policy. In: Veronesi P, editor. *Handbook of Fixed Income*. John Wiley & Sons; 2015a.

Buraschi A, Whelan P. Bond markets and unconventional monetary policy. In: Veronesi P, editor. *Handbook of Fixed Income*. John Wiley & Sons; 2015b.

Campbell JY, Shiller RJ. Yield spreads and interest rate movements: a bird's eye view. Rev Econ Stud 1991;58(3):495–514.

Campbell JY, Sunderam A, Viceira LM. Inflation Bets or Deflation Hedges? The Changing Risks of Nominal Bonds. Working Paper, Harvard University; 2013.

Cochrane JH, Piazzesi M. Bond risk premia. Am Econ Rev 2005;94(1):138–160.

Culp CL. Interest rate derivatives products and recent market activity in the new regulatory framework. In: Veronesi P, editor. *Handbook of Fixed Income*. John Wiley & Sons; 2015.

Dahlquist M, Hasseltoft H. International bond risk premia. In: Veronesi P, editor. *Handbook of Fixed Income*. John Wiley & Sons; 2015.

David A, Veronesi P. The economics of the comovement of stocks and bonds. In: Veronesi P, editor. *Handbook of Fixed Income*. John Wiley & Sons; 2015.

Duarte J, McManus DA. Mortgage related securities (MRS). In: Veronesi P, editor. *Handbook of Fixed Income*. John Wiley & Sons; 2015.

Fama E. Does the fed control interest rates? Rev Asset Pric Stud 2013;3:180–199.

Fama E, Bliss RR. The information in long-maturity forward rates. Am Econ Rev 1987;77(4):680–92.

Fleckenstein M, Longstaff F, Lustig H. Inflation-adjusted bonds and the inflation risk premium. In: Veronesi P, editor. *Handbook of Fixed Income*. John Wiley & Sons; 2015.

Fontaine JS, Garcia R. Recent advances in old fixed-income topics: liquidity, learning, and the lower bound. In: Veronesi P, editor. *Handbook of Fixed Income*. John Wiley & Sons; 2015.

Gürkaynak RS, Sack B, Wright J. The U.S. treasury yield curve: 1961 to the present. J Monet Econ 2007;54:2291–2304.

Gürkaynak RS, Sack B, Wright J. The TIPS yield curve and inflation compensation. Am Econ J Macroecon 2010;2:70–92.

Pflueger CE, Viceira LM. Return predictability in the treasury market: real rates, inflation, and liquidity. In: Veronesi P, editor. *Handbook of Fixed Income*. John Wiley & Sons; 2015.

Smith JM. Money market instruments. In: Veronesi P, editor. *Handbook of Fixed Income*. John Wiley & Sons; 2015.

Sydyak O. Interest rate risk management and asset liability management. In: Veronesi P, editor. *Handbook of Fixed Income*. John Wiley & Sons; 2015.

Veronesi P. Discounting and derivative pricing before and after the crisis: an introduction. In: Veronesi P, editor. *Handbook of Fixed Income*. John Wiley & Sons; 2015.

2

Money Market Instruments

Josephine M. Smith
Model Portfolios & Solutions, BlackRock, San Francisco, CA, United States

2.1 OVERVIEW OF THE MONEY MARKET

The term money market refers to the market for borrowing and lending with maturities ranging from overnight to 1 year. There are a wide range of securities traded in this market, and this chapter will cover a large subset of that range, with an emphasis on securities whose behavior has been potentially highlighted since the recent financial crisis. Figure 2.1 charts the percentage of the U.S. bond market issues outstanding attributable to money market instruments.

There has been a secular decline in issuance since the early 1980s, though more recently the percentage fell by half from 2007 till today (14% to 7%). While this may seem like a small fraction of the overall bond market today, the total value of outstanding money market instruments is currently approaching $3 trillion (or nearly 20% of U.S. real GDP). As a reference to the current state of the U.S. bond market in terms of its components, Figure 2.2 breaks down the current U.S. bond market into its large categories.

Investors use money market instruments in a variety of ways. The market developed as a result of an out-of-equilibrium pool for short-term funds (or paper).[1] There were some investors who had an oversupply of funds that they were willing to lend over a short-term horizon, while there were other investors that needed to borrow funds for the short-term to shore up capital requirements. Some common examples include the following:

- *Corporations:* Short-term funding needs for payroll or other capital requirements through the issuance of commercial paper.
- *Banks:* Excess reserves can be invested short-term in very liquid money market instruments as a means of profit without sacrificing liquidity.
- *Central Banks:* The Federal Reserve performs its open market operations through the buying and selling of U.S. Treasuries in the repurchase agreement market.

This chapter aims to highlight some of the main constituents of money markets. To begin, we will discuss U.S. Treasury bills. We then move to the private money market instruments including commercial paper, discount window loans, Eurodollars, repurchase agreements, and interbank loans.[2]

[1]This is in contrast to longer-term funding in capital markets, which is supplied predominantly through debt and equity issuance.
[2]A more in-depth discussion of the history of money market instruments can be found in Cook and Laroche (1993) and Fabozzi and Mann (2012). The author fully admits that this is a small subset of money market instruments, but this set of instruments was most affected during the recent financial crisis.

Handbook of Fixed-Income Securities, First Edition. Edited by Pietro Veronesi.

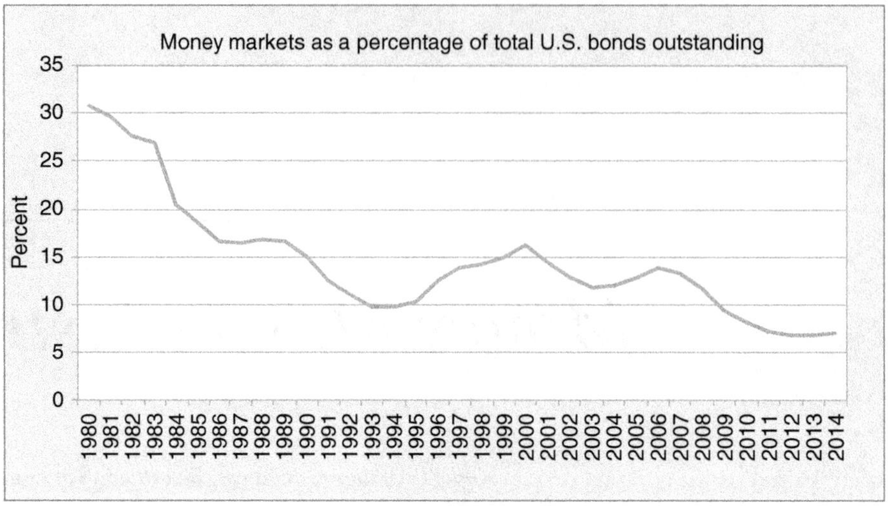

Figure 2.1 Percentage of total U.S. bond market outstanding attributable to the money markets. Source: Securities Industry and Financial Markets Association (SIFMA).

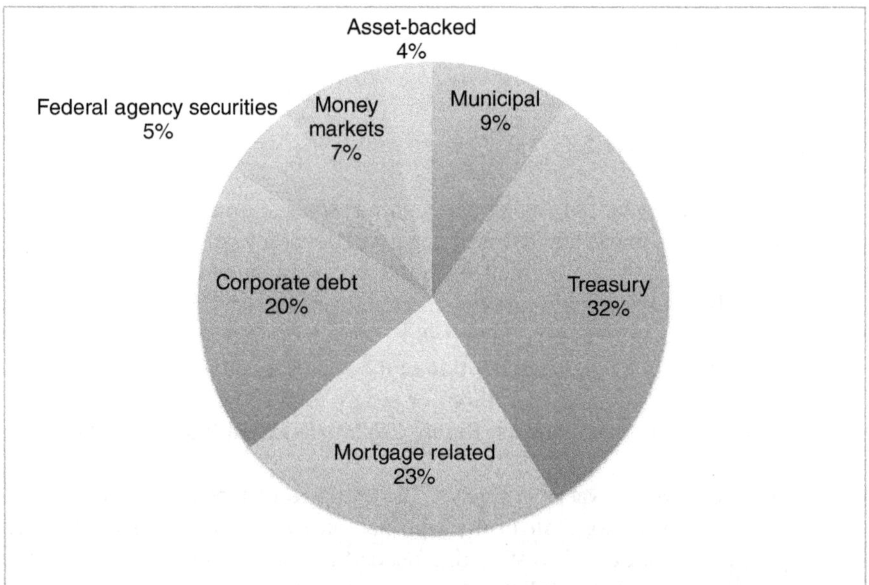

Figure 2.2 Current breakdown of the U.S. bond market. Source: SIFMA.

2.2 U.S. TREASURY BILLS

The U.S government issues a wide set of maturities of nominal, fixed coupon rate debt. Treasury bills are short-term instruments with a maturity of up to 1 year. These issues pay no coupon and principal plus interest on the final maturity date. Treasury bills are auctioned by the U.S. Treasury frequently: every week for bills up to 6 months in maturity and every 4 weeks for bills with 1 year to maturity. Given the implied safety of debt issued by the U.S. government, Treasury bills often provide a benchmark for risk-free rates globally.

Owing to the fact that no cash flows for these issues occur until maturity, Treasury bills are priced at a discount to par, with the discount rate determined at the initial auction of the security. On auction date t, a Treasury bill with maturity $T - t$ will have a price per \$1 par denoted by $Z(t, T)$, a price commonly referred to as the discount factor of the bill. We can derive the implied semiannually compounded discount rate $r_2(t, T)$ using the following conversion:

$$r_2(t, T) = 2 \times \left(\left(\frac{1}{Z(t, T)} \right)^{\frac{1}{2(T-t)}} - 1 \right) \tag{2.1}$$

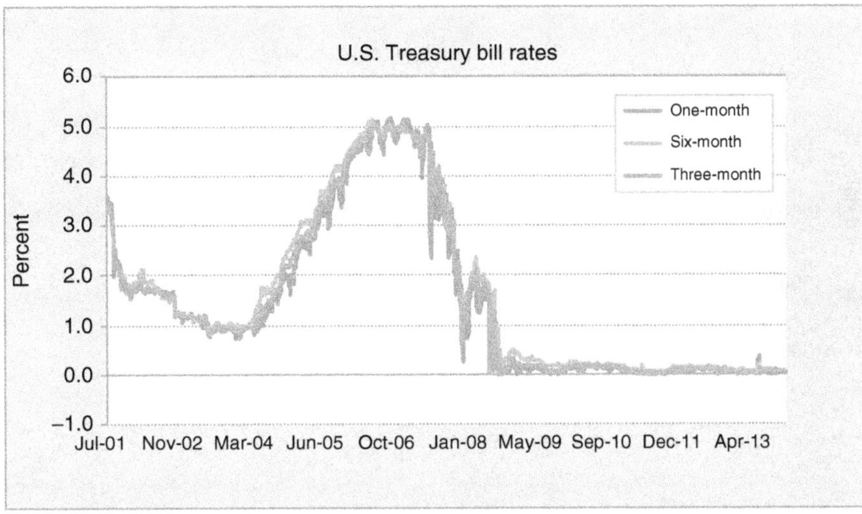

Figure 2.3 Secondary market rates on 1-, 3-, and 6-month Treasury bills. Source: Federal Reserve Bank of St Louis FRED Database.

Figure 2.3 displays the historical behavior of 1-, 3-, and 6-month Treasury bill rates.[3] Later in this chapter, we will compare these short-term rates to securities with comparable maturities yet varied credit risks, such as term federal funds rates and London Interbank Offered Rate (LIBOR) rates.

2.3 COMMERCIAL PAPER

Commercial paper is a debt instrument that provides large corporations with a means of short-term, unsecured funding. For corporations with high credit ratings, commercial paper provides a lower cost alternative to bank borrowing. More recently, lower credit entities have been able to use the commercial paper market for funding via Asset-Backed Commercial Paper (ABCP), notes backed by varying forms of collateral. Before the recent financial crisis, it was the largest U.S. short-term money market instrument and regarded as safe due to its short maturity, high credit rating, and/or safe collateral. Various events in the commercial paper market during the crisis highlighted the fragility of this market, with the end result being major nonconventional interventions by the Federal Reserve to support the issuers and investors in the market. Kacperczyk and Schnabl (2010) provide an in-depth overview of the commercial paper market and detail the major events during the financial crisis that dried up issuance in the market and increased the overall credit risk of the instruments.

2.3.1 General Facts about Commercial Paper

As with Treasury bills, commercial paper is issued as a discount instrument and sold at a price less than the value at maturity, thus implying a discount yield on the issue. Owing to SEC registration restrictions, the maturity of most commercial paper is less than 270 days, with the majority of issues having maturities less than 45 days.[4] To pay off maturing issues, corporations often issue new paper. The main risk that investors face in the commercial paper market stems from the inability of a corporation to issue new paper to pay off existing holders of paper.

Figure 2.4 displays the outstanding amounts of commercial paper in billions of USD. This figure clearly highlights the sharp decrease in commercial paper issuance, both nonasset-backed and asset-backed, since the financial crisis.

2.3.2 Nonasset-Backed Commercial Paper

The majority of commercial paper is issued by financial corporations. Figure 2.5 plots the spread between the 3-month nonasset-backed AA financial commercial paper rate and the 3-month Treasury bill rate. Commercial paper rates lie above comparable Treasury bill rates for three main reasons. First, investors in commercial paper face credit risk. Second, commercial paper does not have the tax exemptions of Treasuries. Finally, the liquidity of the commercial paper market is far lower than that of the Treasury bill market. While the average spread hovers between 0 and 50 basis points, the financial crisis from 2007 to

[3]One-year Treasuries were discontinued after August 2001; thus, we do not include these in Figure 2.3.
[4]To be eligible as collateral for Fed discount window lending, commercial paper must have a maturity of 90 days or less.

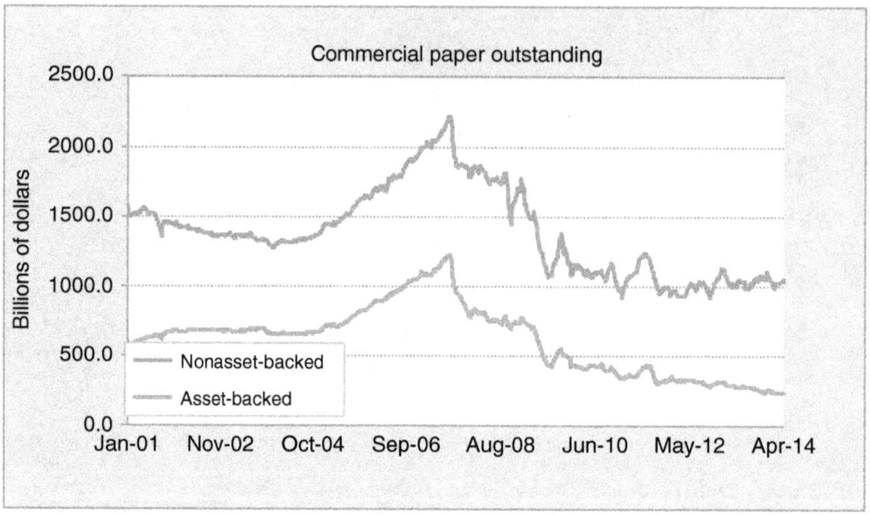

Figure 2.4 Commercial paper oustanding, billions of USD. Source: Federal Reserve Bank of St Louis FRED Database.

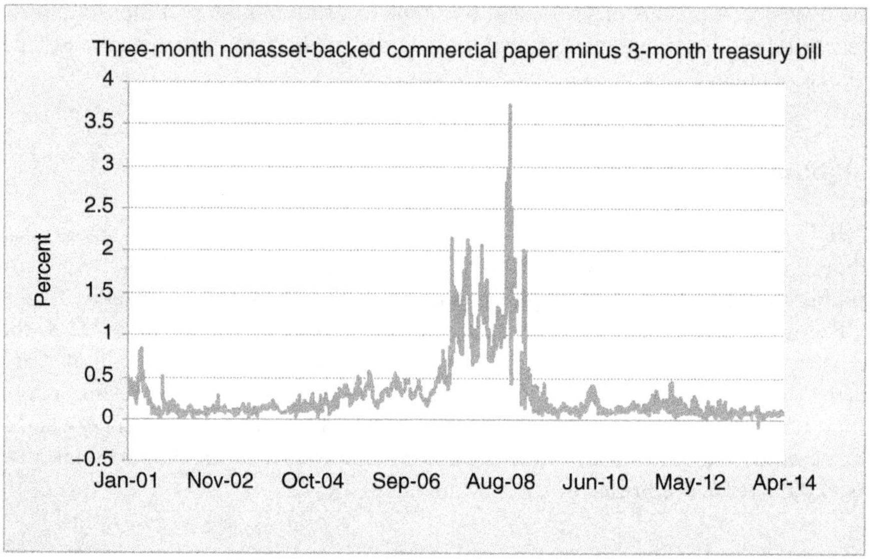

Figure 2.5 Spread between 3-month nonasset-backed AA financial commercial paper rate and 3-month Treasury bill rate. Source: Federal Reserve Bank of St Louis FRED Database.

2009 exhibited spreads upward of 2% for commercial paper of the highest quality relative to the comparable 3-month Treasury bill. Normally, both of these rates track the federal funds rate quite closely, but the commercial paper rate broke from this structural relationship, and the size of this spread reflects the high level of financial risk in the commercial paper market.

2.3.3 Asset-Backed Commercial Paper

Although the typical issuer of commercial paper is a high-credit-quality financial entity, lower credit-quality companies have been able to issue commercial paper more recently by collateralizing the issue with high-credit-quality assets. These issues are known as ABCP and are issued through special-purpose vehicles that pool all of the collateral and issue the securities based on that pool.

The mix of assets used to collateralize this commercial paper spanned from asset-backed securities, mortgages, commercial loans, mortgage-backed securities, and more. While the assets were meant to be of the highest (i.e., AAA or AA) quality, the financial crisis saw a large drop in the value of these assets, thus decreasing the value of the collateral. This caused almost a complete collapse of the ABCP market. Figure 2.6 plots the spread between the 3-month asset-backed financial commercial paper rate and the 3-month Treasury bill rate. Compared with Figure 2.5 for non-ABCP, these spreads are higher due to the

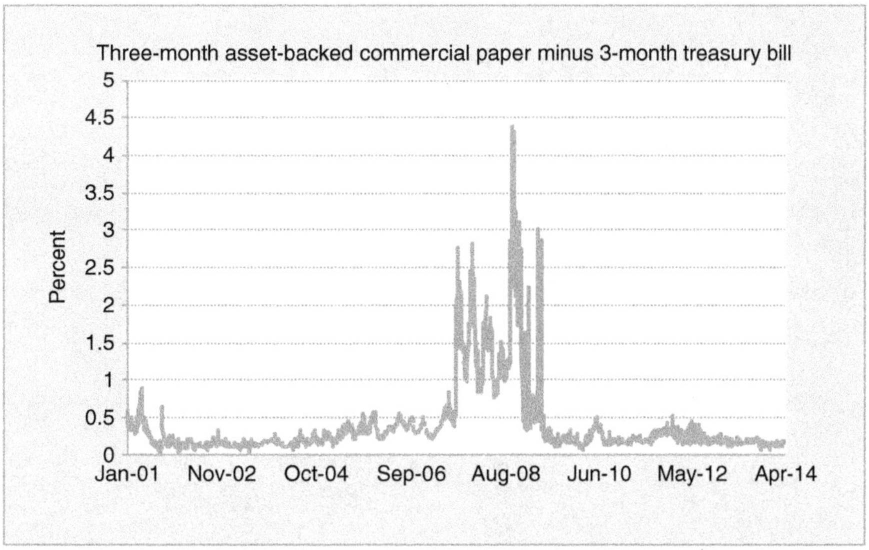

Figure 2.6 Spread between 3-month asset-backed financial commercial paper rate and 3-month Treasury bill rate. Source: Federal Reserve Bank of St Louis FRED Database.

excess credit risk imposed by the quality of the issuing entity (even with the collateralization requirement). During the height of the financial crisis, these issues exhibited spreads over 3-month Treasury bills of over 4%. The predominant force behind these exorbitant spreads was the extreme drop in the value of the collateral assets, and the market completely seized up for some forms of riskier collateral, such as securitized subprime mortgages.[5]

A lesson to be learned from the crisis is that while commercial paper is often issued either by a very high-credit-quality institution or backed by (seemingly) high-credit-quality securities, the fragility of the market was tested during the recent financial crisis, and overall outstanding issuance of commercial paper has dropped by more than half from its precrisis peak. The combination of default risk in both forms of paper and credit risk in asset-backed paper highlights the need for market participants to fully price in these risks. The correct pricing of these assets will require new modeling techniques for the pricing of underlying collateral and will ultimately result in higher spreads (higher interest payments) for these securities.

2.4 DISCOUNT WINDOW

The discount window is an instrument of monetary policy that allows Federal Reserve System banks to borrow directly from the Federal Reserve on a short-term basis to meet temporary liquidity demands. When markets refer to the Federal Reserve as the "lender of last resort," they are referring to borrowing through the discount window. There are a variety of rates used for discount window lending, and Figure 2.7 plots the primary credit rate used by the Federal Reserve. Markets often view borrowing from the discount window as a sign of weakness of a particular bank.

During the recent financial crisis, as liquidity dried up in financial markets, banks were searching for as many funds as they could to protect from the uncertainty and financial shocks they were continuing to face. As a means of lessening the reputation effects of discount window borrowing, the Federal Reserve dropped the discount window borrowing rates to incentivize banks to borrow. Figure 2.8 charts discount window borrowings of depository institutions. During the height of the financial crisis in the fall of 2008, banks were borrowing upward of $400 billion from the discount window, and levels of borrowing remained elevated until the beginning of 2013. While always referred to as a tool of monetary policy, the discount window was particularly effective during this time of high liquidity stress.

2.5 EURODOLLARS

Eurodollars are U.S. dollar-denominated deposits ranging from 1-month to 12-month terms held in a European-based bank.[6] Figure 2.9 displays the historical behavior of 1-, 3-, and 6-month Eurodollar rates. Because these time deposits are held outside

[5]These spreads provided market participants with a gauge of overall financial stress in money markets. For example, Taylor and Williams (2009) control for credit risk in LIBOR–OIS spreads using these commercial paper stress measures.

[6]Even though these deposits are prefixed with "Euro," the prefix is used to refer to U.S. dollar-denominated deposits in any non-U.S. bank.

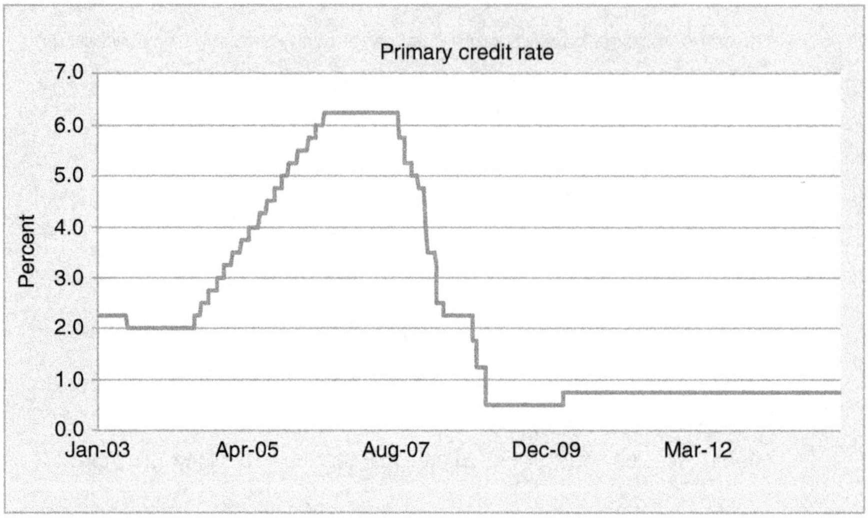

Figure 2.7 Primary credit rate for discount window borrowing. Source: Federal Reserve Bank of St Louis FRED Database.

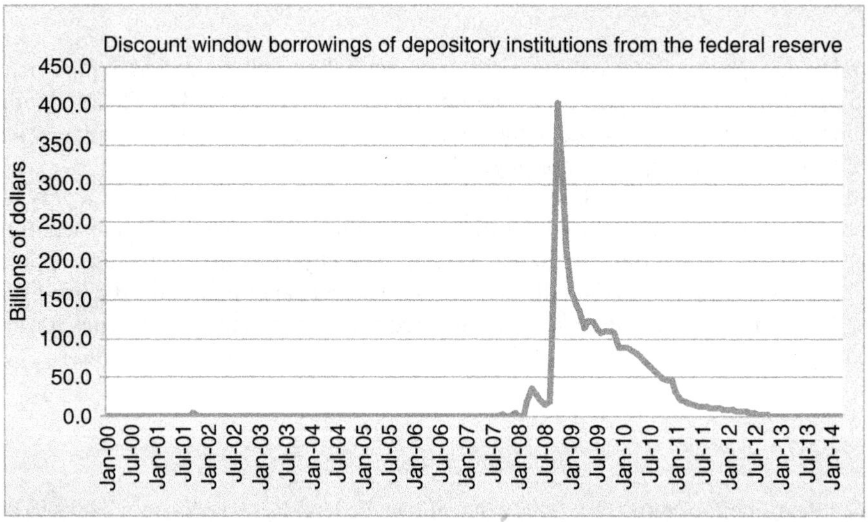

Figure 2.8 Total discount window borrowing. Source: Federal Reserve Bank of St Louis FRED Database.

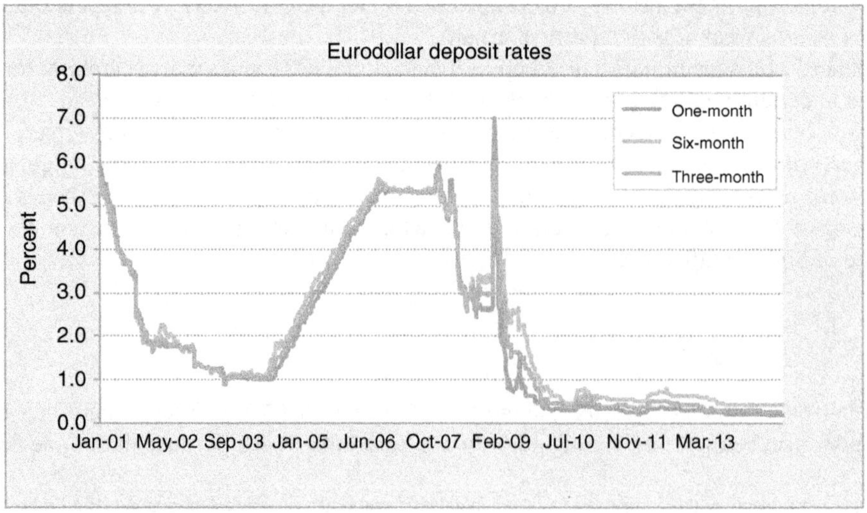

Figure 2.9 One-, three-, and six-month Eurodollar deposit rates. Source: Federal Reserve Bank of St Louis FRED Database.

Figure 2.10 One-month LIBOR rate and one-month Eurodollar deposit rate. Source: Federal Reserve Bank of St Louis FRED Database.

of the United States, they are not under the oversight of the Federal Reserve. This decrease in regulation allows large institutions to operate at lower margins, and the Eurodollar market has expanded rapidly due to this advantage. The majority of Eurdollar time deposits are interbank liabilities.

Although Eurodollar deposits have advantages in terms of regulation, the rates on Eurodollar deposits and comparable deposits at banks inside of the jurisdiction of the Federal Reserve tend to move hand in hand. In addition, Eurodollar deposit rates and comparable LIBOR rates have also exhibited spreads near zero since inception.[7] Figure 2.10 plots the spread between the 1-month Eurodollar rate and the 1-month LIBOR rate.[8] Effectively, these are the same contract, only quoted from different perspectives of the interbank loan. The Eurodollar deposit rate is the rate at which banks want to borrow funds (bid side), while the LIBOR rate is the rate at which banks believe they are capable of borrowing funds (offer side). During the recent financial crisis, the spread between these two rates widened, reflecting that the actual cost of 1-month interbank loans (Eurodollar rate) was well above the surveyed cost of 1-month interbank loans (LIBOR rate).

2.5.1 Eurodollar Futures

While this chapter is meant to focus on basic money market instruments, Eurodollar futures contracts are one of the largest derivative markets. Traded on the Chicago Mercantile Exchange, Eurodollar futures contracts are cash-settled derivates that form a basis for the market's expectations of future LIBOR rates. They allow institutions to lock in an interest rate today for money it intends to borrow or lend at a future settlement date. There are contracts with settlement or expiration dates every month for the nearest 6 months, and then every quarter March, June, September, December out 10 years. The Eurodollar futures contract at time t for settlement on date T has a price $G(t, T)$. On the settlement date, a final futures price is equal to

$$G(T, T) = 100 \times (1 - L(T)) \tag{2.2}$$

where $L(T)$ is the 3-month LIBOR rate at the settlement date T.

Profits and losses in the Eurodollar futures market are realized via daily marking to market. Contracts are written per \$1,000,000 par, and each fluctuation of one basis point in the Eurodollar futures price maps into a \$25 gain or loss for each side of the contract. Many market participants use Eurodollar futures rates to hedge positions in interest rate swaps (which are a portfolio of forward rate agreements). The high liquidity of these futures contracts allows for reliable calibration of LIBOR forward rate curves for market participants and ultimately the short end of the LIBOR term structure for derivative pricing.

[7] See Lee (2003).

[8] LIBOR and term federal funds are term interbank loans for banks in the LIBOR survey and Federal Reserve System, respectively. We will discuss these in more detail in Section 2.7.

2.6 REPURCHASE AGREEMENTS

Repurchase agreements, or repos, are collateralized loans. In particular, a repo is the spot sale of a security combined with a forward contract to buy back that security at some future date. The borrower sells the specified collateral to the lender at a price below its market value. The difference between the market value of the collateral and the loan principal captures the haircut or margin of the repo. At the end of the repo, the lender returns the collateral to the borrower, and the borrower pays the lender back the principal plus any interest that accrues according to the specified repo rate.

2.6.1 Types of Repos and Haircuts

Repos have maturities ranging from overnight (50% of market) out to 12 months. Similar to repos, reverse repos are just a repo contract as viewed from the opposite perspective. If a dealer is a borrower in a repo transaction, then he is a lender in a reverse repo transaction. Figure 2.11 displays the average daily outstanding repo and reverse repo financing by U.S. primary dealers from 1996 through 2013. The overall size of the market exploded in the early 2000s, and there was a contraction of the size of the market during the financial crisis.

Regardless of the type of collateral underlying a repo, both parties in the agreement face credit risk. If the borrower in the contract cannot purchase the security back with the agreed-upon interest (either related or unrelated to the repo itself), the lender is forced to sell the collateral to the open market. If the value of this collateral has dropped significantly since the start of the repo or the liquidity of the collateral has dried up, the lender will suffer a loss.[9] The haircut, or overcollateralization of the repo, provides the main dimension by which the overall exposure to credit risk is reduced. In general, haircuts range between 1% and 3%. But for noncreditworthy borrowers or risky forms of collateral, haircuts can rise well above 10%.

Repos were intially only traded bilaterally. One counterparty would lend the other a prespecified amount of principal in exchange for a form of collateral (i.e., U.S. Treasury bond) that was worth the prespecified amount of principal plus a haircut. The bilateral repo was settled when the borrower paid the previously agreed-upon principal plus interest back to the lender and the lender returned the underlying collateral to the borrower. As always, the repo market is understood from the perspective of the dealer, and therefore the bilateral repo market is segmented into the part where dealers are borrowing and the part where dealers are lending. Main participants in this market include dealer banks and/or hedge funds.

Even withstanding the underlying credit risks of repurchase agreements, the bilateral repo market comes with its challenges, both informationally costly and financially costly. These include marking the underlying collateral of the repo to market every single day and simply maintaining possession of the physical collateral itself. The triparty repo market has provided one way to circumvent some of these issues. The third party (hence the "tri") of the agreement is the repo clearing bank. They are in charge

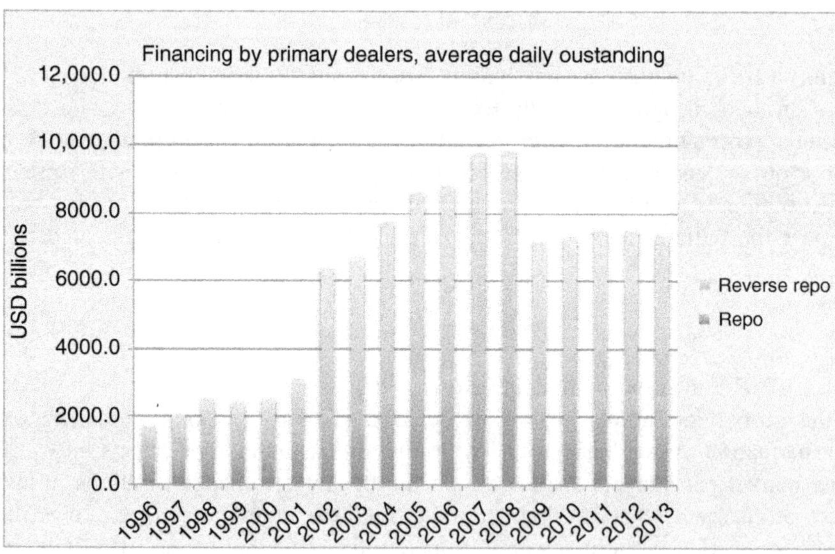

Figure 2.11 Primary dealer financing values include both triparty and bilateral agreements. Covers financing involving U.S. government, federal agency, corporate, and federal agency MBS securities. Beginning in April 2013, figures also include equity and other securities. Source: Federal Reserve Bank of New York and SIFMA.

[9]There is an additional effect of unwinding coming through the triparty repo market. We refer to Krishnamurthy, Nagel, and Orlov (2014) for more details.

of all settlement processes of the repurchase agreement, custodial services, and collateral pricing services (which were the job of the borrowers and lenders themselves in the bilateral agreement).[10] In addition, they can provide a backstop for the collateral given default by the borrower in the repo agreement.

2.6.2 Basic Forms of Repo Collateral

Typical market participants for repurchase agreements vary. Borrowers, or net sellers of collateral, include security dealers, thrifts, and bank portfolios. Lenders, or net buyers of collateral, include bank trust departments, money market funds, municipalities, and corporations.[11] The market participants can also vary based on the type of collateral used in the repurchase agreement. The types of collateral accepted for repos now include Treasuries, agencies, mortgage-backed securities, corporate bonds, equity, or customized collateral. Figure 2.12 displays a more recent breakdown of the types of collateral used in repo contracts. This chapter will focus on the most common forms of collateral: U.S. Treasuries, agencies, and mortgage-backed securities.

U.S. Treasury repos are the safest form of repo transaction. The borrower must post collateral in the form of a prespecified U.S. Treasury security. Given the low credit risk of the U.S. government, this type of repo is thought of as safe, and lenders require small haircuts and charge lower interest rates to borrow in this market.[12]

Agency repos are considered a slightly less safe form of major repo transactions. The collateral posted in this transaction takes the form of federal agency and government-sponsored enterprise (e.g., Fannie Mae and Freddie Mac) securities. Given the potential risks underlying these institutions, agency repos are considered slightly less safe compared to U.S. Treasury repos. However, the recent backing of these institutions via the federal government has driven some to the opinion that these repos are now much safer, though this issue remains a hot topic for discussion.

We also consider mortgage-backed security repos. The collateral underlying these repos takes the form of high-grade mortgage-backed securities and related derivatives. Since their inception, these repos have traded at noticeably higher rates than their U.S. Treasury counterparts, which we believe is due to the higher collateral value risk of these repos. Figure 2.13 displays the Depository Trust and Clearing Corporation's (DTCC) general collateral finance (GCF) Repo Indices written on the three most traded and separate forms of collateral: U.S. Treasuries, agency non-MBS securities, and agency MBS.[13]

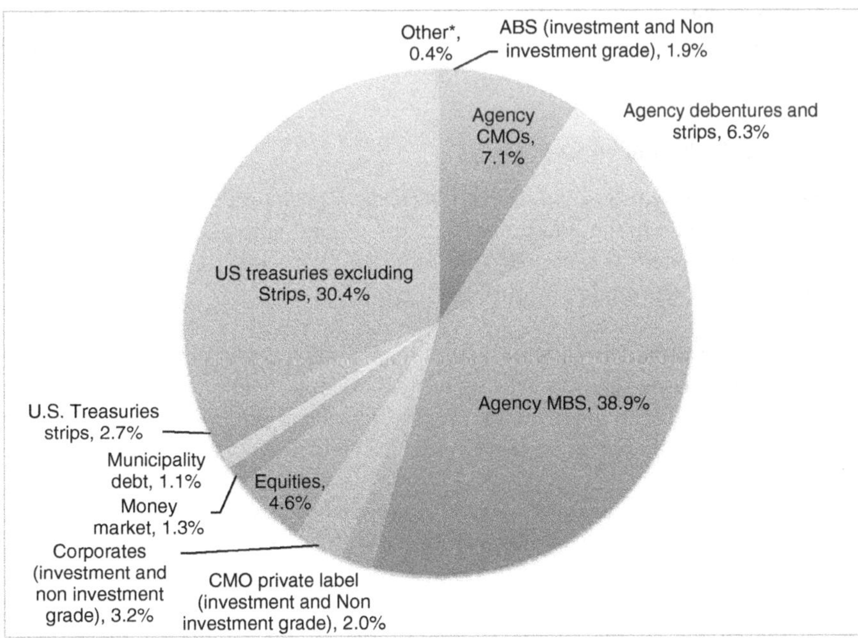

Figure 2.12 Breakdown of repo collateral, July 2013. Source: SIFMA.

[10] In the United States, the two clearing banks are JP Morgan Chase and Bank of New York Mellon.

[11] Hedge funds can act on either side of the market, depending on what type of leverage position they desire in the particular repo market.

[12] Since we do not have U.S. Treasury securities at a maturity of less than 1 month, repo rates have provided practitioners with a measure of short-term, relatively riskless borrowing rates in U.S. fixed-income markets.

[13] Agency refers to the government-sponsored entities Fannie Mae and Freddie Mac.

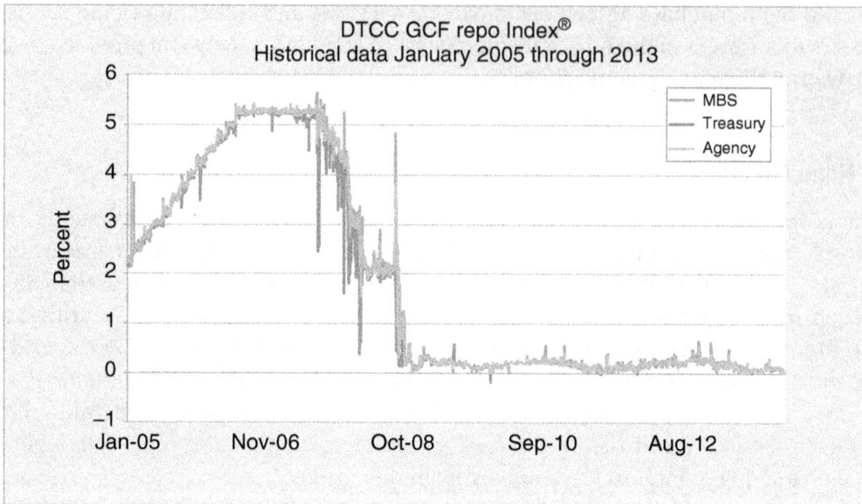

Figure 2.13 DTCC GCF Repo Index rates from 2005 through 2013. Source: DTCC.

2.6.3 Repo Rates and Collateral Value Risks

While haircuts provide a means of controlling for credit risk, Smith (2014) provides a detailed description of the behavior of repo rates for different forms of collateral in the triparty repo market and highlights the relative collateral value risks through a term structure analysis. Using a basic factor analysis, the author hypothesizes that while common factors do exist across repo markets with varying forms of collateral, spreads between repo rates with different forms of collateral provide additional information to market participants regarding risk in the repo market.

In particular, risk premiums embedded in the spread between Treasury-backed repos and MBS-backed repo can be explained by a variety of macroeconomic and financial uncertainty factors, including the uncertainty index created by Baker, Bloom, and Davis (2015), the S&P 500 volatility index (VIX), and the 3-month LIBOR minus 3-month Treasury bill (TED) spread. While this paper just provides a descriptive analysis of the rates, a more detailed term structure analysis can provide an exact breakdown of the risk premiums in short-term money market instruments and assess the exact predictive power of these macro- and financial uncertainty variables for these new measures of risk in the shadow banking sector.

2.6.4 The Run on Repo During the Financial Crisis

Since the financial crisis, there has been an explosion of research on the level of haircuts during the worst of the crisis for particular types of collateral. The (potential) increase in these haircuts highlights a run on repo, or collapse of the shadow banking sector of which repos are a fundamental component. The works of Gorton and Metrick (2012) and Krishnamurthy, Nagel, and Orlov (2014) provide opposing views on the level of haircuts during the crisis.

2.6.4.1 The Shadow Banking Sector The definition of the shadow banking sector is certainly debated among academics and practitioners. At its core, the shadow banking sector is a group of financial intermediaries, unregulated like their traditional bank counterparts, that provide credit and liquidity to financial markets through securitization and maturity transformation (borrowing short-term and lending long-term). To quote former Federal Reserve Chairman Ben Bernanke:

> Shadow banking, as usually defined, comprises a diverse set of institutions and markets that, collectively, carry out traditional banking functions–but do so outside, or in ways only loosely linked to, the traditional system of regulated depository institutions. Examples of important components of the shadow banking system include securitization vehicles, asset-backed commercial paper (ABCP) conduits, money market mutual funds, markets for repurchase agreements (repos), investment banks, and mortgage companies. Bernanke (2012)

The shadow banking sector is a global entity, and its growth has been a main focus of regulators since the financial crisis. As defined by the Financial Stability Board (2014), the Monitoring Universe of Non-Bank Financial Intermediation (MUNFI) is comprised of the financial assets of nontraditional financial intermediaries, or their definition of financial assets of the shadow banking sector. Since the financial crisis, shadow banking has grown to approximately $75 trillion in value and has a consistent share of 25% of the overall market of total financial assets. In GDP terms, this is roughly 120% of the total GDP of the global sample used in the calculations. A total of 80% of all these assets are coming from the United States, United Kingdom, and Euro Area, and there has recently been an uptick in the share of shadow banking coming from emerging markets (particularly China).

2.6.4.2 Repo Markets and the Shadow Banking Sector Repurchase agreement markets have been a main character in the shadow banking sector, and the structure of repurchase agreements and valuation of their underlying collateral has been studied in detail by the academic literature since the financial crisis. The work of Gorton and Metrick (2012) focuses on the bilateral repo market with collateral taking the form of various classes of structured debt. The authors conclude that haircuts on this form of collateral were upward of 45% at the worst of the crisis, essentially confirming the hypothesis of the authors that the shadow banking sector, created to provide liquidity outside of the channels protected by deposit insurance, experienced a dramatic run on repo and (near) insolvency. While the results of this paper are provocative, there are some issues with the implications. First, the collateral used in the bilateral repos analyzed by the authors is only a small fraction of the overall repo market (20–30%), the rest of which is collateralized using high-quality forms of collateral. In addition, the bilateral nature of these agreements exacerbates the effect of the credit risk faced by the borrower and lender.

Krishnamurthy, Nagel, and Orlov (2014) provide another perspective on this run on repo. The authors analyze the triparty repo market with two of the main lenders to the shadow banking system: money market funds and securities lenders. In contrast to the results of Gorton and Metrick (2012), the authors here conclude that the increase in repo lending was not the main force behind the expansion of the shadow banking system before the recent financial crisis, and thus the collapse of the repo market during the crisis was not the main force behind the collapse in the shadow banking sector. In particular, short-term debt did play a very important role, but a much more important channel was through short-term funding via ABCP and the collapse of that market during the crisis discussed in Section 2.3.3. Finally, the authors calculate implied haircuts using the triparty repo data compiled by the authors and find little to no increase in haircuts on the collateral for these repos.

In summary, while these papers deliver different conclusions on the level of haircuts during the financial crisis, they do lead to the same result that there was a run on repo and that it took the form of a credit crunch. However, triparty repos were a much larger share of the total repo market during the financial crisis and remain as such since the financial crisis.[14] Therefore, it is important to understand the distinction between bilateral (interdealer reallocation) repos versus triparty (nonbank to dealer, net source of shadow funding) repos when trying to assess the overall costs associated with a run on the repo market.

2.7 INTERBANK LOANS

The interbank lending market is the market for short-term loans between banks for a specified term. The majority of interbank loans are overnight loans, though the term of these loans can be as long as 12 months. The interest rate charged on these loans is determined in equilibrium from the supply and demand of interbank funds. Banks borrow and lend at the equilibrium interbank rate to manage their liquidity and satisfy reserve regulations. Here, we will be focusing on two interbank markets: the federal funds market and the LIBOR market.

2.7.1 Federal Funds

The federal funds market is the market for interbank lending between banks in the Federal Reserve System. Fed funds are reserves deposited at regional Federal Reserve Banks that provide unsecured loans, predominantly of overnight maturity, between lenders of excess federal funds (smaller banks) and borrowers (larger banks). Loans can be established either bilaterally or through a fed funds broker. The rate charged on overnight federal funds loans is called the federal funds rate, and Figure 2.14 plots the historical path of the market or effective federal funds rate. For terms beyond overnight, the interest rate is called the term federal funds rate.

Depository institutions are required by the Federal Reserve to maintain a specific reserve of federal funds. Until recently, any reserves in excess of required reserves did not collect any interest. At the height of the recent financial crisis, the Federal Reserve started paying interest on excess reserves. Figure 2.15 plots the excess reserves of depository institutions at the Federal Reserve, and Figure 2.16 plots the interest rate paid on excess reserves starting in 2008. Paying interest on reserves was an additional policy tool invoked by the Federal Reserve to maintain liquidity in the market and provide financial stability.

The federal funds rate is the main interest rate tool used by the Federal Reserve to implement monetary policy. Following Taylor (1993), the standard view of monetary policy is that of a policy rule:

$$i_t = \alpha + \beta_1 \pi_t + \beta_2 y_t \tag{2.3}$$

where i_t is the federal funds rate, π_t is the inflation rate,, and y_t is a measure of the output gap. This rule can take a variety of backward-looking and forward-looking forms, but in general it highlights the fact that the Federal Reserve explicitly reacts to

[14]Copeland et al. (2012) estimate the size of the bilateral repo market at approximately \$1 trillion in 2012 versus \$1.8 trillion for the triparty repo market in the same time period.

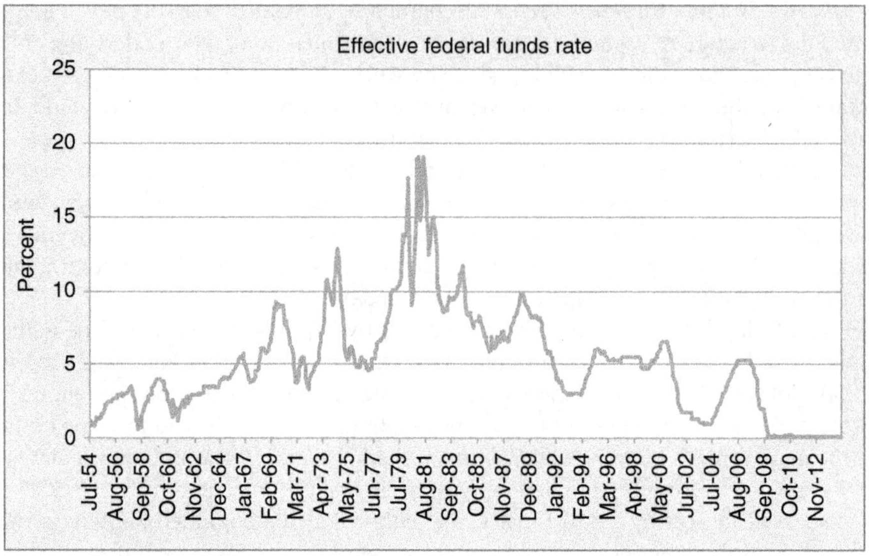

Figure 2.14 The effective federal funds rate. Source: Federal Reserve Bank of St Louis/FRED.

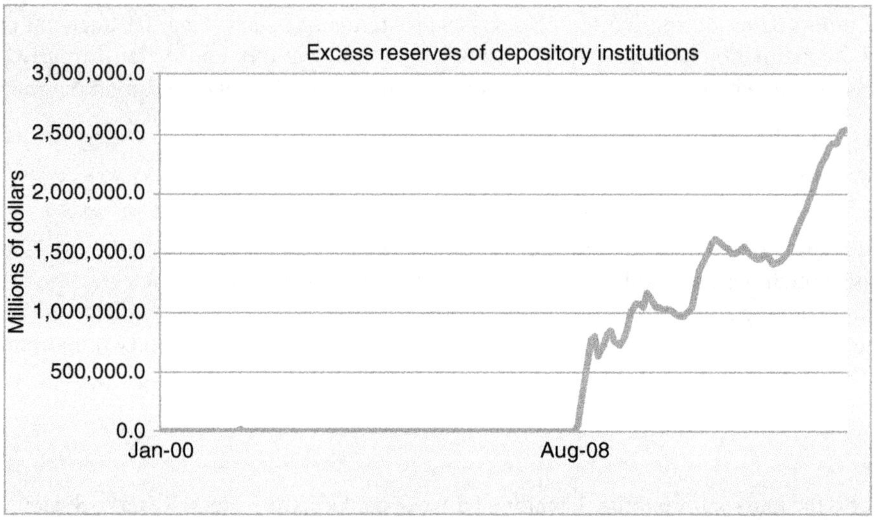

Figure 2.15 Excess reserves of depository institutions. Source: Federal Reserve Bank of St Louis/FRED.

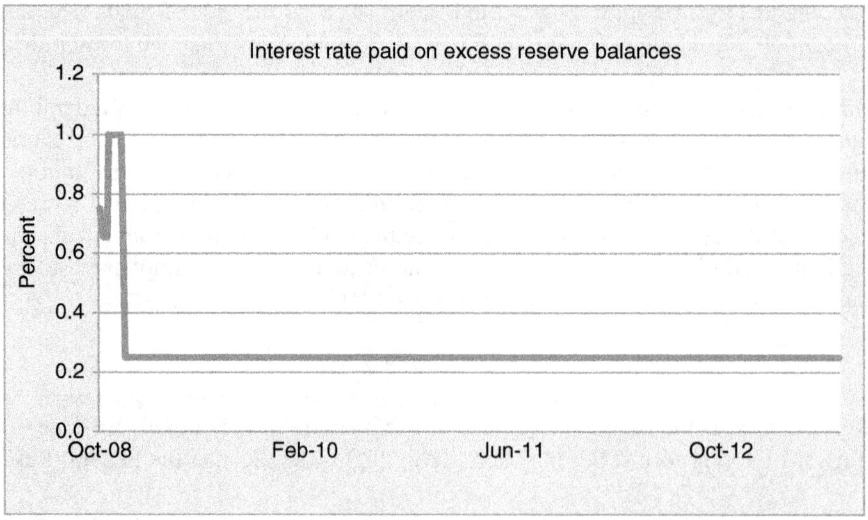

Figure 2.16 Interest rate paid on excess reserve balances. Source: Board of Governors of the Federal Reserve System/FRED.

movements in inflation and growth. While the Federal Reserve cannot explicitly set the fed funds rate, it has a target value or range of the fed funds rate, and it performs large asset purchases and sales (often through the repo market) to alter the supply of fed funds in the market and bring the equilibrium fed funds rate toward the target. Since the financial crisis, the Federal Reserve has also implemented more unconventional monetary policy through more asset purchases and sales in an effort to stabilize the macroeconomy and financial markets. The target fed funds range has been between 0% and 0.25%, and thus conventional policy has essentially hit its lower bound and these unconventional policies provide an additional boost to the markets. Since the extreme policy moved by the Fed and moving into the future of eventual Fed tightening of the federal funds rate, there remains an interesting (and potentially never-ending) debate among academic and practitioners on whether the market is following Fed actions or vice versa.

2.7.2 LIBOR

LIBOR stands for the London Interbank Offered Rate published by the British Banker's Association until February 2014, when it was taken over by the Intercontinental Exchange Benchmark Administration (IBA). Historically, LIBOR indicates the average rate that a participating institution can obtain *unsecured* funding for a given period of time in a given currency in the London money market. The rates are calculated based on the trimmed, arithmetic mean of the middle two quartiles of rate submissions from a panel of the largest, most active banks in each currency. In the case of the U.S. LIBOR, the panel consists of now 16 banks. These rates are a benchmark for a wide range of financial instruments including futures, swaps, variable rate mortgages, and even currencies.

Each participating bank is asked to base its quoted rate on the following question: "At what rate could you borrow funds, were you to do so by asking for and then accepting interbank offers in a reasonable market size just prior to 11 a.m. London time?" An important distinction is that this is an offered rate, not a bid rate, for a loan contract. Actual transactions may not occur at this offered rate, but LIBOR rates do reflect the true cost of borrowing given the sophisticated methods each participating bank has at its disposal to ascertain risks in the underlying financial markets when it chooses to enter financial contracts. Controversy has been raised over the reliability of the offering rates that LIBOR banks were posting during the crisis. Institutions were thought to be quoting lower rates at which they could take on interbank loans in an effort to disguise any default risk they thought was present in their respective institution. Indeed, a number of financial institutions have been under investigation for "rigging" LIBOR rates through the manipulation of their own LIBOR quotes in order to obtain an advantage in markets for LIBOR-based derivatives. Because of these rigging scandals and subsequent settlements, there has been policy worked aimed at changing the way LIBOR is quoted to markets. The IBA recently released what could best be called an instruction manual for LIBOR banks when submitting their daily quotes, and more changes will be formally introduced in 2015.

Before the onset of the financial crisis, LIBOR rates closely tracked the federal funds rate. Yet with the crisis came a decoupling of LIBOR rates from the federal funds rate, with LIBOR rates fluctuating above the federal funds rate. While comparing these two rates is interesting, the federal funds rate is an overnight rate, while LIBOR is a term rate. Figure 2.17 plots the TED spread, or the spread between the 3-month LIBOR rate and the 3-month Treasury bill rate. While the TED spread is measure of risk

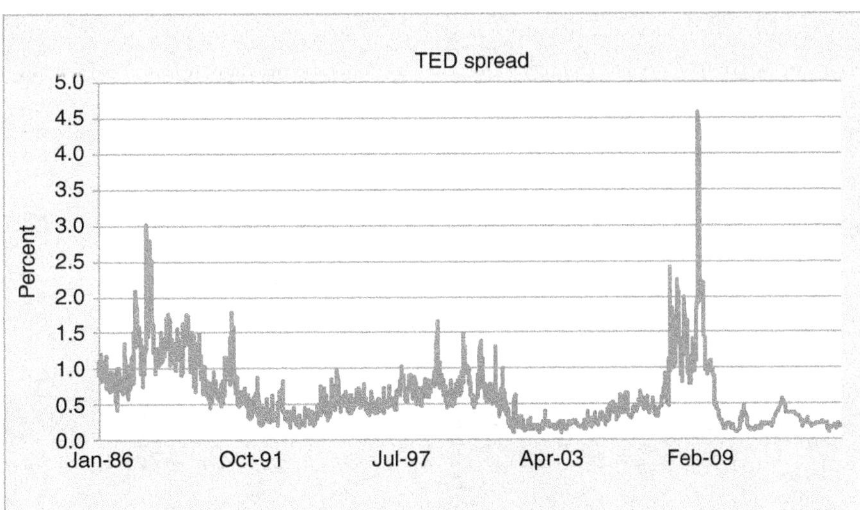

Figure 2.17 The TED spread. Source: Federal Reserve Bank of St Louis/FRED.

embedded in a LIBOR loan, it would be preferred if we could compare interbank loan to interbank loan, and the Treasury bill is not an interbank loan. Therefore, the next section will discuss an interest rate with comparable maturity to the LIBOR rate that captures movements in the federal funds rate.

2.7.3 Overnight Index Swaps and LIBOR–OIS Spreads

An Overnight Indexed Swap (OIS) is a fixed/floating interest rate swap where the floating rate is determined by the geometric average of a published overnight index rate over each time interval of the contract period. The two counterparties of an OIS contract agree to exchange, at maturity, the difference between interest accrued at the agreed fixed rate and the floating rate on the notional amount of the contract. The party paying the fixed OIS rate is, in essence, borrowing cash from the lender that receives the fixed OIS rate. No principal is exchanged at the beginning of the contract. In contrast to a plain vanilla swap, there are no intermediate interest payments on OIS contracts with maturities of less than 1 year.[15] In the case of the United States, the floating rate of the OIS contract is tied to the federal funds rate. The fixed rate of an OIS in the United States is meant the capture the expected federal funds rate over the term of the swap plus any potential risk premiums. Even with the onset of the crisis, OIS rates remained very close to the federal funds rate. Longer-term OIS rates differ from short-term OIS rates due to the longer length of the contract and more uncertainty in movements of the underlying federal funds rate.

A common measure of interbank market stress during the financial crisis was the spread between LIBOR rates and OIS rates of a given maturity, or the LIBOR–OIS spread. Figure 2.18 plots the 3-month LIBOR–OIS spread. Before the crisis, this spread hovered around 10 basis points, reflecting fundamental differences in market characteristics such as market participants and market timing conventions. Starting in the summer of 2007, this spread began to increase, and it reached a peak of nearly 3.5% in the fall of 2008.

2.7.4 A Model of LIBOR–OIS Spreads

In an effort to better understanding the sources of variation in LIBOR–OIS spreads, we could specify a model for the term structure of unsecured, longer-term interbank interest rates. With the yield curve derived from this model, we can price a variety of derivatives, including forward contracts and swaps. Let $i_t^{(1)}$ denote the short-term interbank rate at time t, $i_t^{(n)}$ the longer-term interbank rate at time t that matures at time $t+n$, and $f_t^{(n-1)\to(n)}$ the forward rate at time t for a contract that starts in time $t+n-1$ and ends at time $t+n$. The common way to derive forward rates is by using current, short-term interbank rates using the following formula:

$$f_t^{(n-1)\to(n)} = E_t\left[i_{t+n-1}^{(1)}\right] + c \tag{2.4}$$

Equation 2.4 states that the forward rate is the expected future short rate $E_t[i_{t+n-1}^{(1)}]$ plus a constant term premium c. Therefore, any movements in the short end of the interbank yield curve will directly impact forward rates.

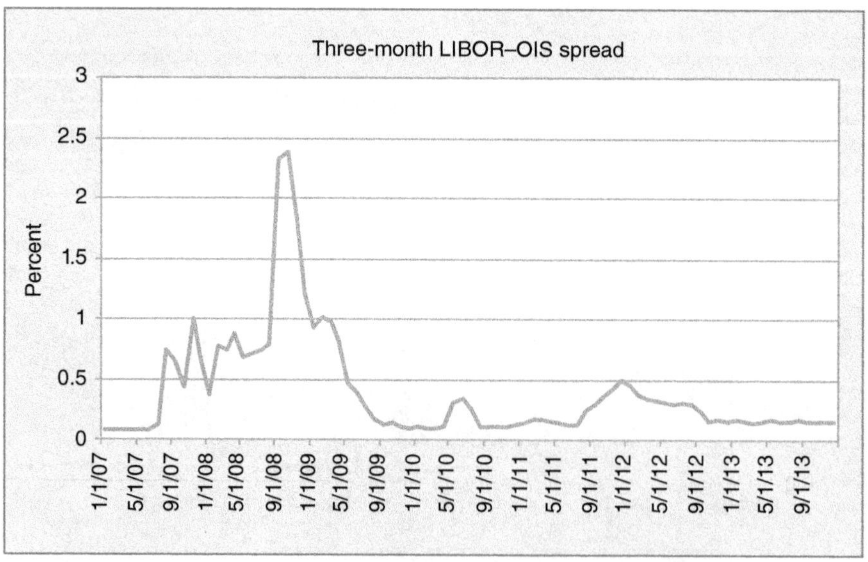

Figure 2.18 Three-month LIBOR–OIS spread. Source: Bloomberg.

[15]Recently, OIS contracts with maturities of longer than 1 year have been established, which do disperse intermediate payments.

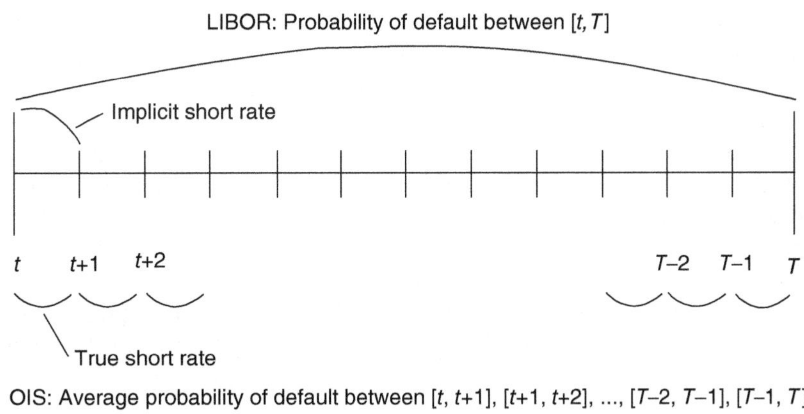

Figure 2.19 Comparison of LIBOR versus OIS.

Interest rate swaps on interbank interest rates are essentially bundles of forward contracts on the underlying short-term interbank interest rate. Therefore, the yield curve for interbank rates will imply a series of forward rates, and bundling these forward rates provides us with swap rates. Figure 2.19 provides a diagram of an unsecured, longer-term interest rate $i_t^{(n)}$ (e.g., the LIBOR rate) and the intervals of short-term interest rates between the start time t and the maturity date $t + T$ from which the swap rate (e.g., the OIS rate) will be calculated. With the entire yield curve for unsecured interbank rates, swap rates can be computed using the short-term interest rate from that yield curve.

Using Figure 2.19, we can back out that the longer-term rate $i_t^{(n)}$ is approximately equal to the probability of default (ignoring liquidity effects) over the time interval $[t, T]$, while the swap rate is the geometric average of the probability of default in the intervals $[t, t + 1], [t + 1, t + 2], \cdots, [T - 1, T]$ generated by rolling over each of the spot rates at each time interval. If it is the case that longer-term rates are high due to the probability of default (i.e., default rates are higher over longer horizons), then forward contracts on the short-term rate must be high as well. This is because any default priced into the unsecured, interbank yield curve will be picked up by the short rate $i_t^{(1)}$, and thus forward rates will reflect it, as well, as seen in Equation 2.4. Therefore, spreads between unsecured, longer-term interbank rates like LIBOR and their swap counterparts like OIS would be low, a prediction rejected by the data during the financial crisis.

Why might LIBOR–OIS spreads be so high? First, the unsecured nature of LIBOR loans implies that the quoted borrowing rates provided by LIBOR-participating institutions must take into account the lack of collateral posted at the start of the contract. A second reason is because the probability of default (and/or liquidity pressures) between, for example, $[T - 1, T]$ is much higher than the probability of default between $[t, t + 1]$, and the geometric averaging performed in computing swap rates creates a large difference between the probability of default between $[t, T]$ and the average of the smaller time intervals. Finally, the parties involved in short- versus longer-term contracts might differ. High-default institutions could show up for longer-term loans, while low-default institutions show up for short-term loans.[16] This implies that the OIS is a derivative that has as the basis a short-term rate for low-default institutions, while the longer-term LIBOR rate is high for high-default institutions. Therefore, taking a geometric average of the short-term rate when computing the forward contracts that make up the OIS rate provides a lower rate than the longer-term LIBOR rate due to the default adjustment.

Smith (2013) develops an affine term structure model for LIBOR–OIS spreads during the financial crisis that incorporates movements in interest rate, credit, and liquidity factors and relies on both the defaultable bond work of Duffie and Singleton (1999) and the no-arbitrage, discrete time affine models of Ang and Piazzesi (2003). LIBOR and OIS are each modeled as zero-coupon bonds, and the assumption of no-arbitrage provides closed-form solutions for both prices and yields of these bonds.[17]

Given the closed-form solutions for LIBOR yields $i_t^{L,(n)}$ and OIS yields $i_t^{O,(n)}$, define the LIBOR–OIS spread for maturity n as

$$\begin{aligned} z_t^{(n)} &= i_t^{L,(n)} - i_t^{O,(n)} \\ &= \left(a_{L,n} + b_{L,n}^T X_t\right) - \left(a_{O,n} + b_{O,n}^T X_t\right) \\ &= a_n + b_n^T X_t \end{aligned} \tag{2.5}$$

[16]Indeed, while only 16 institutions participate in the LIBOR survey, over 30 participate in the OIS market. Therefore, the average probability of default across all of the institutions in the OIS market could be far below that for the LIBOR market.

[17]Admittedly, modeling these two securities as zero-coupon bonds is a highly reduced-form assumption, but it provides a parsimonious analysis of how credit and liquidity factors play a role in the evolution of these spreads during the crisis.

where $a_n \equiv a_{L,n} - a_{O,n}$, $b_n^T \equiv b_{L,n}^T - b_{O,n}^T$, and X_t is the state vector of the economy, which we assume consists of an interest rate factor (the fed funds rate), a credit factor (a credit default swap factor), and a liquidity factor (on-the-run/off-the-run premium). What is of interest in the analysis is the response coefficient vector b_n, since it determines how spreads respond to movements in the underlying factors of the economy.

A critical contribution of the model comes from a partition of the response coefficients b_n that separates LIBOR–OIS spreads into two components. The first is related to time-varying expectations of the future spread between LIBOR and the federal funds rate, while the second is due to time variation in risk premiums caused by changes in risk attitudes of investors. Since the model provides closed-form solutions for the separate components, Smith (2013) can identify how much of the movements in spreads is directly attributable to each. Combining the VAR estimation of the evolution of X_t with estimates of risk premiums, LIBOR–OIS spreads react most sensitively to movements in the credit factor. A substantial proportion of the volatility of spreads can be explained by risk premiums (up to 50% for the 12-month LIBOR–OIS spread), and the response of spreads to shocks to X_t is most sensitive to credit risk premiums.

2.8 CONCLUSION

This chapter has described the money market and its main financial instruments. We discussed these instruments in detail and spent time focusing on the role each of these instruments in the financial sector. In particular, we focused on the role that many of these instruments might have played during the recent financial crisis and how we can better use these instruments going forward in a way that will not shut down the shadow banking sector and provide a solid foundation for credit allocation and maturity transformation for global financial markets.

REFERENCES

Ang A, Piazzesi M. A no-arbitrage vector autoregression of term structure dynamics with macroeconomic and latent variables. J Monet Econ 2003;50:745–787.

Baker S, Bloom N, Davis S. Measuring Economic Policy Uncertainty. NBER Working Paper 21633; 2015.

Bernanke B. Some Reflections on the Crisis and the Policy Response, Russell Sage Foundation and The Century Foundation Conference on "Rethinking Finance."; 2012.

Cook T, Laroche R. Instruments of the Money Market. Federal Reserve Bank of Richmond; 1993.

Copeland A, Duffie D, Martin A, McLaughlin S. Key mechanics of the U.S. tri-party repo market. Econ Policy Rev Fed Reserve Bank N Y 2012;18:17–28.

Duffie D, Singleton K. Modeling term structure of defaultable bonds. Rev Financ Stud 1999;12:687–720.

Fabozzi F, Mann S. *The Handbook of Fixed Income Securities*. 8th ed. New York: McGraw-Hill; 2012.

Financial Stability Board. Global Shadow Banking Monitoring Report 2014; 2014.

Gorton G, Metrick M. Securitized banking and the run on repo. J Financ Econ 2012;104:425–451.

Kacperczyk M, Schnabl P. When safe proved risky: commercial paper during the financial crisis of 2007–2009. J Econ Perspect 2010;24:29–50.

Krishnamurthy A, Nagel S, Orlov D. Sizing up repo. J Finance 2014;69:2381–2417.

Lee YS. The federal funds market and the overnight Eurodollar market. J Bank Finance 2003;27:749–771.

Smith J. The Term Structure of Money Market Spreads During the Financial Crisis, Working Paper; 2013.

Smith J. The Term Structure of Money Market Spreads During the Financial Crisis. 2014. Unpublished manuscript.

Taylor J. Discretion versus policy rules in practice. Carnegie-Rochester Conference Series on Public Policy, Volume 39; Carnegie Mellon; 1993. p 195–214.

Taylor J, Williams J. A black swan in the money market. Am Econ J Macroecon 2009;1:58–83.

3

Inflation-Adjusted Bonds and the Inflation Risk Premium

Matthias Fleckenstein[a], Francis Longstaff[b] and Hanno Lustig[c]

[a]*Cornerstone Research, New York, NY, United States*
[b]*Anderson School of Management, UCLA, Los Angeles, CA, United States*
[c]*Graduate School of Business, Stanford University, Stanford California*

3.1 INFLATION-INDEXED BONDS

Inflation-indexed bonds differ from standard coupon bonds in that the nominal principal of an inflation-indexed bond is indexed to the price level. Since a fixed coupon rate is applied to the principal that varies with the price level, the actual coupon payments vary in response to the realized rate of inflation or deflation.

There is a long history of countries issuing inflation-linked debt. Emerging market countries started to issue inflation-linked bonds in the 1950s. Much later, the United Kingdom's Debt Management Office followed suit with the first inflation-linked gilt issue in 1981, followed by Australia, Canada, and Sweden. The U.S. Treasury only started issuing Treasury Inflation-Protected Securities (TIPS) in 1998. Currently, France, Germany, and Italy are frequent issuers of inflation-linked bonds in the Euro area. Japan recently started issuing inflation-linked bonds again. Australia, Brazil, Canada, Chile, Israel, Mexico, Turkey, and South Africa also issue substantial amounts of inflation-linked bonds.

Governments have several motives for issuing inflation-linked bonds. First, inflation-linked bonds reduce the effect of inflation on the real debt burden. This provides a commitment technology to those countries who want to signal a strong commitment to low inflation. Second, inflation-linked bonds may provide investors with a new asset whose payoffs are not spanned by existing securities and thus help to complete the market. Long-term real bonds are an important asset for long-term investors (Campbell and Viceira, 2001). Third, the Treasury could reduce its funding cost by not paying the inflation risk premium, provided that the inflation risk premium is positive. Fourth, these securities possibly provide policy makers as well as market participants with new tools for gauging the inflation expectations of investors and forecasting inflation. The latter is notoriously hard to do well out of sample using fundamentals (Atkeson and Ohanian, 2001; Stock and Watson, 2007).

In the United States, the Treasury's TIPS program has grown substantially since its inception in January of 1997. By the end of 2013, the total notional of TIPS had grown to $972 billion. That accounts for 8.18% of total marketable Treasury securities.[1]

[1]See Table B-87: U.S. Treasury Securities Outstanding By Kind of Obligation, 1974–2013. Economic Report of the President.

Handbook of Fixed-Income Securities, First Edition. Edited by Pietro Veronesi.

3.1.1 Mechanics of TIPS

The details of how inflation-linked bonds work vary across countries. We will focus on TIPS. The mechanics of the TIPS issued by the U.S. Treasury are straightforward. The principal amount of a TIPS (e.g., \$1000 at issuance) is adjusted daily based on the CPI for All Urban Consumers. The inflation adjustment I_t is computed as the ratio of the reference CPI at the valuation date t divided by the reference CPI at issuance (time 0). The reference CPI for a particular date during a month is linearly interpolated from the CPI reference index for the beginning of that month and the CPI reference index for the beginning of the subsequent month.[2] However, the dollar value of the principal is bounded below at \$1000, its value at issuance. Hence, TIPS offer some deflation protection.

3.1.2 Valuing an Inflation-Indexed Bond

Let s denote the fixed coupon rate on the TIPS. P denotes the principal. The coupon payments and the principal for a 10-year TIPS $s \times P \times I_1, \ldots, s \times P \times I_t, \ldots, s \times P \times I_{20}, P \times I_{20}$ are tied to the reference price level. We abstract from the deflation protection embedded in TIPS, to keep the analysis tractable.

The value of the bond at initiation ($t = 0$) can then be computed as the discounted value of the constant real coupon payments:

$$P_0 = \frac{s \times P}{(1+y)^{6/12}} + \frac{s \times P}{(1+y)^{12/12}} + \cdots + \frac{s \times P}{(1+y)^{240/12}} + \frac{P}{(1+y)^{240/12}}$$

where y denotes the yield to maturity on a 10-year TIPS. This is a real yield.

The appeal of this security is obvious. The stream of cash flows produced by this security $s \times P \times I_1, \cdots, s \times P \times I_t, \cdots, s \times P \times I_{20}, P \times I_{20}$ moves one for one with the CPI and as a result the cash flows are constant in real terms: $s \times P, \cdots, s \times P, \cdots, s \times P, P$. There is no inflation risk in these cash flows, at least not for a tax-exempt investor. Investors who pay taxes are taxed on the principal adjustment $P \times I_t$ in each period t, even though there is no real income that results from this adjustment itself. As a result, tax-paying investors earn lower real after-tax coupon payments when inflation increases.

We have abstracted from the deflation protection embedded in TIPS. In fact, the actual real value of the coupon payments at t is given by

$$\frac{\max(s \times P \times I_t, s \times P)}{I_t}$$

while the actual real value of the principal at maturity t is given by

$$\frac{\max(P \times I_t, P)}{I_t}$$

The real value of the coupons starts to increase when the accrued inflation adjustment I_t dips below 1. To value this stream, we need to price the basket of inflation options. Recently, this embedded deflation option in TIPS has been priced explicitly by Grishchenko, Vanden, and Zhang (2011) as well as Christensen, Lopez, and Rudebusch (2011). During the U.S. financial crisis, this option became highly valuable for some newer TIPS issues.

3.2 INFLATION DERIVATIVES

In addition to the cash inflation market, there is an active derivatives market that consists mainly of inflation swap contracts and inflation options. The inflation swap market in the United States is growing rapidly. Fleming and Sporn (2012) report that the overall market size had approached \$350 million in April 2012, with most of the trading concentrated at the 5- and 10-year tenors.

European inflation derivatives markets are generally described as more developed. In the United Kingdom and Europe, there is an active market in inflation options as well. Recently, volume in the U.S. inflation option market has picked up as well. There is anecdotal evidence of large U.S. asset managers such as PIMCO taking sizable positions in these inflation option markets.

3.2.1 Constructing a Synthetic Nominal Treasury Bond with Inflation Swaps

Let us start with a zero-coupon inflation-linked bond ($P = 1$) with coupon rate s. We can swap the floating coupon payments into fixed payments by taking positions in the zero-coupon inflation swap market. We use F_0^t to denote the zero-coupon inflation

[2]The CPI reference index for the first day of any calendar month is the CPI-U index for the third preceding calendar month. Thus, the reference CPI for April 1 would be the CPI-U index for the month of January, which is reported by the Bureau of Labor Statistics during February. The details of how the principal amount of a TIPS issue is adjusted for inflation is described on the U.S. Treasury's website.

swap rate for delivery at date t. This contract involves the exchange of the inflation index that has accrued at maturity – divided by the inflation index at the start – (I_t) in exchange for a fixed payment ($(1 + F_0^t)^t$). Only cash flows occur at the maturity date of the contract. The fixed swap rate is set such that the value of the contract equals zero at initiation. The party that is paying floating provides the other part with inflation protection or insurance.

Adding the cash flows from an inflation swap position with notional s to the cash flows from the long position in the inflation-linked bond produces $s \times I_t - s \times I_t + s(1 + F_0^t)^t$. Hence, by adding an inflation swap position, we end up with fixed coupon payments – instead of floating ones. We have created a synthetic nominal Treasury bond out of the inflation-linked bond. This synthetic zero-coupon nominal bond only has the following fixed coupon payments at maturity t: $s(1 + F_0^t)^t$. No-arbitrage implies that the value of the TIPS at $t = 0$ has to equal the value of Treasury bond with the same maturity with coupon payment $s(1 + F_0^t)^t$.

The most frequently traded inflation options are caps and floors that pay the difference between the realized annualized inflation π_t between time 0 and t and the strike S on an annual basis. For example, at maturity date $t = 10$, a 10-year zero-coupon cap struck at $S = 1\%$ would pay $\max(0, 1 + \pi_t - (1 + S))$. Kitsul and Wright 2012 and Fleckenstein, Longstaff, and Lustig 2014b provide a detailed discussion of inflation options.

3.3 NO-ARBITRAGE PRICING

3.3.1 Zero-Coupon Bonds

We start by considering a t-period zero-coupon bond. Let $V_0[X_t]$ denote the price of a random payoff at time t. By the same no-arbitrage logic, we know that the price of an indexed t-period zero-coupon bond equals the price of a nominal t-period bond with the inflation swap rate as its payoff t-periods from now:

$$V_0[I_t] = V_0[\exp(tf_0^t)] \tag{3.1}$$

where f_0^t denotes the continuously compounded t-period swap rate. This follows because the inflation swap rate is set such that the contract has zero value at initiation $t = 0$. Alternatively, we can define a risk-neutral measure $\mathbb{Q}$. The same relation in (3.1) can be restated as follows:

$$\exp\left(-ty_0^{t,\$}\right) \mathbb{E}_0^{\mathbb{Q}}[I_t] = \exp\left(t(f_0^t - y_0^{t,\$})\right) E_0^{\mathbb{Q}}[1_t] \tag{3.2}$$

where $y_0^{t,\$} = -(1/t)\log V_0[1_t]$ denotes the log yield on a t-period zero-coupon nominal bond. We use $y_0^t = -(1/t)\log V_0[I_t]$ to denote the log yield on a t-period zero-coupon real bond. This in turn implies that the swap rate can be interpreted as the expected rate of inflation under the risk-neutral measure $\mathbb{Q}$:

$$f_0^t = (1/t)\log \mathbb{E}_0^{\mathbb{Q}}[I_t] \tag{3.3}$$

The spread $y_0^{t,\$} - y^t$ between the nominal yield and the real yield is typically referred to as the break-even rate.

From Equation 3.1, it follows that the log yield on the nominal k-period bond equals the log yield on the real bond plus the inflation swap rate:

$$y_0^{t,\$} = y_0^t + f_0^t$$

Hence, no-arbitrage implies that the break-even rate $y_0^{t,\$} - y^t$ equals the inflation swap rate f_0^t. As a result, both the break-even rate and the inflation swap rate are measures of expected inflation under the risk-neutral measure $\mathbb{Q}$. To extract actual inflation expectations, we need a model that specifies how the pricing kernel covaries with inflation.

3.4 INFLATION RISK PREMIUM

We use π_t to denote the annualized rate of inflation, such that $I_t = \exp(t\pi_t)$. Λ_t denotes the nominal pricing kernel, and Λ_t denotes the real pricing kernel. The multiplicative excess return on a long position in the indexed bond and a short position in the nominal bond is given by

$$Rx_{0\to t} = \frac{[\exp(t\pi_t)]\mathbb{E}_0\left[\frac{\Lambda_t^{\$}}{\Lambda_0}\right]}{\mathbb{E}_0\left[\frac{\Lambda_t^{\$}}{\Lambda_0}\exp(t\pi_t)\right]}$$

This is the return on a long position in inflation, an inflation bet in other words. The annualized log of the multiplicative risk premium on a long position in inflation-linked bonds is given by

$$rp_0 = \left(\frac{1}{t}\right) \log \mathbb{E}[Rx_{0\to t}] = \pi_0^{e,t} + y_0^t - y_0^{\$,t} = \pi_0^{e,t} - f_0^t \tag{3.4}$$

where we define the expected annualized rate of inflation as $\pi_0^{e,t} = (1/t) \log \mathbb{E}_0[\exp(\pi_t)]$. Hence, if the swap rate exceeds the expected rate of inflation, this risk premium is negative.

Similarly, at horizon t, the annualized inflation risk premium is defined as the difference between the nominal yield and the real yield plus expected inflation:

$$\phi_0^t = y_0^{\$,t} - \pi_0^{e,t} - y_0^t = f_0^t - \pi^{e,t} \tag{3.5}$$

Hence, if the swap rate exceeds the expected rate of inflation, the inflation risk premium is positive. Even though it is natural to think investors would be willing to pay an insurance premium in exchange for inflation protection, this inflation risk premium does not have to be positive.

A positive covariance between the nominal pricing kernel and realized inflation $cov(\exp(t\pi_t), \Lambda_t^\$) > 0$ implies a positive log of the multiplicative risk premium on a long position in inflation, because this ratio

$$\mathbb{E}_0[Rx_{0\to t}] = \frac{\mathbb{E}_0[\exp(t\pi_t)]\mathbb{E}_0[\Lambda_t^\$]}{\mathbb{E}_0[\Lambda_t^\$ \exp(t\pi_t)]} = \frac{\mathbb{E}_0[\exp(t\pi_t)]\mathbb{E}_0[\Lambda_t^\$]}{\mathbb{E}_0[\exp(t\pi_t)]\mathbb{E}_0[\Lambda^\$] + cov_0(\Lambda_t^\$, \exp(t\pi_t))}$$

is smaller than 1. Investors are willing to forgo some return and accept a negative risk premium in exchange for the inflation hedge. In that case, the inflation swap rate f_0^t exceeds the expected rate of inflation $\pi^{e,t}$ over that horizon.

In this scenario, investors expect higher inflation under the risk-neutral than under the actual measure; the inflation risk premium is positive. Investors seeking inflation protection pay a swap rate that exceeds expected inflation, in exchange for receiving inflation at maturity. The swap rate includes an insurance premium.

When the covariance $cov(\exp(t\pi_t), \Lambda_t^\$) < 0$, investors demand a positive risk premium for holding inflation-indexed bonds. In that case, the inflation risk premium ϕ_0^t turns negative. This could happen, for example, when investors are mainly concerned about deflation in bad states of the world with high marginal utility growth. Furthermore, it is perfectly feasible that the inflation risk premium switches signs over time.

There is a growing literature that estimates inflation risk premia from Treasury yields and TIPS yields (see, e.g., Buraschi and Jiltsov, 2005; Ang, Bekaert, and Wei, 2008; Christensen, Lopez, and Rudebusch, 2010), as well as from inflation surveys (Chernov and Mueller, 2012) and inflation swap rates (Haubrich, Pennacchi, and Ritchken, 2012; Fleckenstein, Longstaff, and Lustig, 2014). These authors rely on no-arbitrage affine term structure models for real and nominal interest rates, as well as inflation swap rates. Kitsul and Wright (2012) and Fleckenstein, Longstaff, and Lustig (2014) also bring information from inflation option markets to bear.

Recently, we have learned that real and inflation factors have incremental forecasting power for bond excess returns even when controlling for the shape of the yield curve (Ludvigson and Ng, 2009). In standard affine term structure models, all of the relevant information for forecasting is fully summarized in the current yields. This body of emerging evidence flatly contradicts this implication of these models (Duffee, 2011). Joslin, Priebsch, and Singleton (2014) describe a class of arbitrage-free dynamic models of the term structure that allow for inflation and output risk not spanned by yields.

3.4.1 Determinants of the Inflation Risk Premium

Entropy $\mathbb{L}(x) = \log \mathbb{E}_0(x) - \mathbb{E}_0 \log x$ is a generalized risk measure. The concavity of the log function implies that entropy is nonnegative and increases with variability; it is a measure of risk (Backus, Chernov, and Zin, 2014). The risk premium on a long position in indexed bonds and a short position in the nominal bond is given by the entropy of the log nominal pricing kernel minus the entropy of the log real pricing kernel and the entropy of inflation:

$$\begin{aligned} t \times rp_0 = \log \mathbb{E}_0[Rx_{0\to t}] &= \mathbb{L}(\Lambda_t^\$) - \mathbb{L}(\Lambda_t) + \mathbb{L}(I_t) \\ &= \mathbb{L}(\Lambda_t - I_t) - (\mathbb{L}(\Lambda_t) - \mathbb{L}(I_t)) \end{aligned} \tag{3.6}$$

The riskier the real pricing kernel is relative to the nominal pricing kernel, the more valuable the inflation-indexed bond is for the marginal investor, compared to the nominal bond, and the more negative this risk premium becomes (and the higher the inflation risk premium ϕ_0^t is of course).

To develop a better understanding of these expressions, we can use $k(s;x)$ to denote the cumulant generating function $\log \mathbb{E}_0[\exp(sx)]$. Under regularity conditions, this has a power series expansion:

$$k(s) = \sum_{j=0}^{\infty} \kappa_j(x)\frac{s^j}{j}!$$

where the cumulant κ_j denotes the jth derivative of $k()$ at $s = 0$. κ_1 is the mean, κ_2 is the variance, while skewness and kurtosis are related to the higher order cumulants:

$$skewness = \frac{\kappa_3}{\kappa_2^{3/2}}, kurtosis = \frac{\kappa_4}{\kappa_2^2}$$

Lowercase symbols denote logs. The log of the multiplicative risk premium

$$t \times rp_0^t = -\log \mathbb{E}_0[\exp t(\lambda_t^\$ + \pi_t)] + \log \mathbb{E}_0[\exp t(\pi_t)] + \log \mathbb{E}_0[\exp t(\lambda_t^\$)]$$

depends on all of the higher-order moments of the pricing kernel and inflation:

$$t \times rp_0^t = -k(t; \lambda_t^\$ + \pi_t) + k(t; \pi_t) + k(t; \lambda_t^\$)$$

Let us focus on the one-period premium. We can state the risk premium as a function of the cross moments of the real pricing kernel:

$$rp_0^1 = -k(1; \lambda_t) + k(1; \pi_t) + k(1; \lambda_t - \pi_t)$$

We start by considering the simplest case in which the pricing kernel and inflation are jointly log-normal. In that case, the log risk premium on an inflation-indexed bond is given by the covariance of the log pricing kernel and inflation:

$$rp_0^1 = -\sigma_{\lambda_t,\pi_t}$$

To develop some intuition, consider the simplest case of a Breeden–Lucas–Rubinstein economy with a representative agent who has time-separable power utility. α denotes the coefficient of risk aversion. Then the equilibrium risk premium is given by $rp_0^1 = \alpha\sigma_{\Delta c_t,\pi_t}$ if consumption growth and inflation are jointly log-normal. The derivation is in the Appendix.

A negative covariance between aggregate consumption growth and inflation delivers a negative risk premium on the inflation-indexed bond, because the inflation risk exposes the representative investor to more aggregate consumption growth risk when he/she holds the nominal bond. As a result, average inflation is higher under the risk-neutral than under the actual measure. Inflation insurance comes at a cost.

We analyzed the simplest case of time-additive utility. When investors care about the timing of the resolution of uncertainty, the covariance of future inflation and future consumption growth also matters for risk premia. Piazzesi and Schneider (2006) provide evidence that news about future consumption growth is negatively correlated with news about future inflation in the United States. When the stand-in investor has a preference for early resolution of uncertainty, this mechanism will give rise to positive inflation risk premia. The appendix also analyzes the implications of disaster risk for the inflation risk premium. Disaster risk creates a role for higher order moments of consumption growth and inflation in determining the inflation risk premium.

Similarly, in a standard CAPM world in which inflation and the market return are jointly log-normal, the product of the market beta of inflation and the market risk premium rp^m would determine the inflation risk premium: $rp_0^1 = rp^m\sigma_{r_t^m,\pi_t}/\sigma_{r^m}^2 = rp^m\beta_{\pi_t}$.

3.5 A LOOK AT THE DATA

3.5.1 Break-Even Rates

We start by analyzing the behavior of the break-even rates $y^{t,\$} - y^t$ in the U.S. bond markets. Figure 3.1 plots the U.S. break-even rates computed from the constant-maturity yields for nominal Treasuries and TIPS. The U.S. Treasury computes these yields by fitting a spline function for bid yields of on-the-run securities. Between January 2003 and October 2014, the average U.S. break-even rate at the 5-year horizon was 1.94% per annum. This number was 2.18% per annum at the 10-year horizon.

Prior to the financial crisis, the break-even rates remained above 2% almost invariably. After the onset of the U.S. subprime mortgage crisis, the 5-year break-even rate plummeted to −2.10%, while the 10-year break-even rate flirted with the 0% boundary. Under $\mathbb{Q}$, U.S. investors seemed to expect deflation for the next 10 years. We will revisit what these numbers really mean. These rates then gradually recovered after 2009.

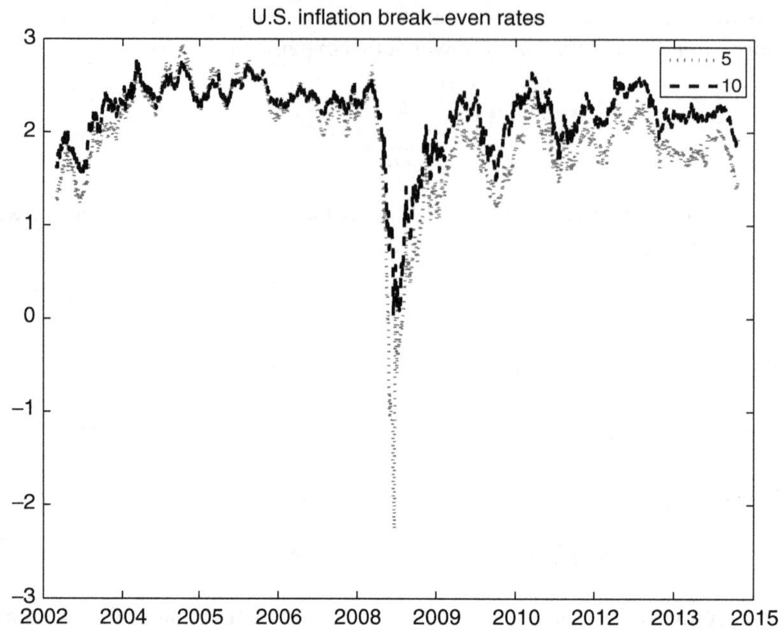

Figure 3.1 U.S. break-even rates. Plot of break-even rates ($y^{t,\$} - y^t$) computed from constant-maturity TIPS and Treasury yields. Source: FRED and U.S. Treasury.

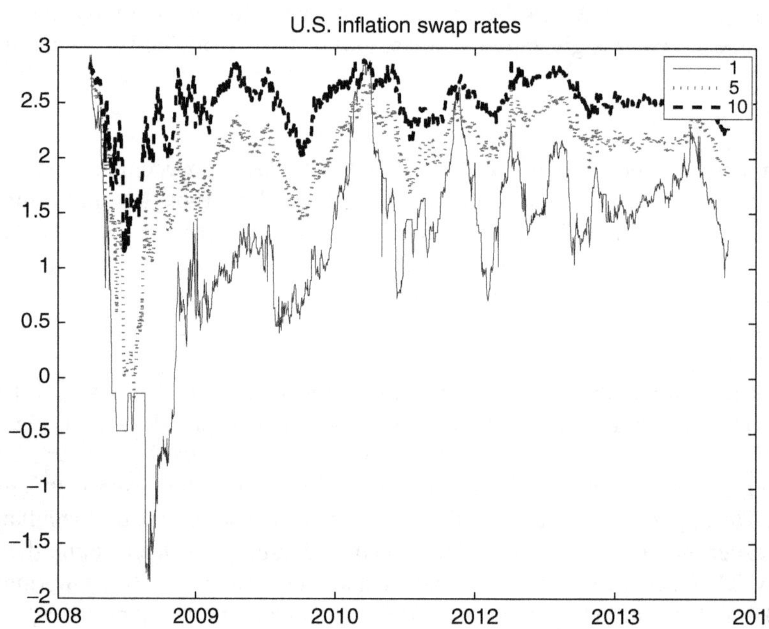

Figure 3.2 U.S. inflation swap rates. Plot of annualized zero-coupon U.S. inflation swap rates F^t of $t = 1, 5$, and 10-year tenors. Source: Thomson Reuters.

3.5.2 Inflation Swap Rates

Next, we confront these measures of expected inflation under the risk-neutral measure from bond markets with another measure from derivatives markets: the inflation swap rates. In Figure 3.2, we plot the time series of annualized U.S. inflation swap rates for 1-year, 5-year, and 10-year maturities. The 10-year inflation swap rate seems firmly anchored around 2.5%, except during the last quarter of 2008 and the first quarter of 2009. The 1-year inflation swap rate drops to 2% in the last quarter of 2008, but the 10-year never falls below 1%. Hence, during the crisis, there is large discrepancy between the break-even rates and the inflation swap rates. U.S. break-even rates suggest a prolonged period of deflation, while inflation swap rates hinted at a much shorter period of deflation.

These U.S. inflation swap rates with maturities ranging from 1 to 30 years (1, 2, 3, …, 10, 15, 20, 25, and 30 years) have a strong low-dimensional factor structure. The first principal component is a level factor that explains 88% of the daily variation in

TABLE 3.1 Inflation Swap Rates

	Maturity	1	5	10	15	20
U.S.	Average	1.268	2.037	2.487	2.622	2.738
	Standard deviation	0.818	0.455	0.265	0.251	0.246
	Correlation	0.117	0.243	0.231	0.176	0.155
Euro	Average	1.403	1.752	2.051	2.249	2.340
	Standard deviation	0.554	0.335	0.251	0.189	0.192
	Correlation	0.078	0.115	0.122	0.105	0.096

Annualized zero-coupon inflation swap rates for U.S. and Euro zone in percentage points. Daily data from 24 July 2008 till October 30, 2014. We report averages and standard deviations of daily data. We also report the correlation of daily changes in inflation rates with the return on the S&P 500.

swap rates across all maturities. At longer maturities, the swap rates do not load as heavily on this level factor because inflation expectations seem firmly anchored, but the level factor does shift inflation swap rates up and down across the maturity spectrum. The second principal component, a slope factor, explains only 8%. Together, these two principal components account for 96% of the variation in the sample. Two factors suffice to characterize the dynamics of inflation swap rates.

Table 3.1 presents the means and volatilities of the inflation swap rates for tenors ranging from 1, 5, 10, 15, to 20 years. The sample only covers July 2008–October 2014. This is the longest sample over which we have data for all of these tenors. On an average, the inflation swap curve slopes upward over this short sample. The average U.S. rates increase from 1.26% at the 1-year horizon to 2.03% at the 5-year, 2.48% at the 10-year, and 2.73% at the 20-year horizon. The spread between the 20-year and the 1-year horizon is 1.47% per annum.

Clearly, the rates are much more volatile at the short end. The standard deviation decreases from 81 bps at the 1-year horizon to 24 bps at the 20-year horizon. Under the risk-neutral measure, there is a lot of mean-reversion built into the U.S. inflation dynamics.

It is interesting to compare the break-even rates to the inflation swap rates. No-arbitrage implies that they are identical. Over the same sample, the 5-year U.S. break-even rate was 1.64% per annum. The 10-year (20-year) break-even rate was only 2.04% (2.28%) per annum. Hence, the break-even rates are between 39 and 44 basis points lower than the inflation swap rates at the same maturity. This confirms the findings of Fleckenstein, Longstaff, and Lustig (2014) who analyze this arbitrage relation on a sample of 29 maturity-matched TIPS and nominal U.S. Treasury (coupon) bonds. They document that the synthetic Treasuries constructed from TIPS and inflation swaps are invariably underpriced relative to the actual, nominal Treasuries. These pricing gaps in the United States between the break-even rates and the inflation swap rates are consistently positive, and they have not dissipated in years since the financial crisis. Figure 3.3 plots the break-even rates against the inflation swap rates. In October 30, the 5-year break-even rate was 1.47%, while the 10-year inflation swap rate was 1.93%. Similarly, the 10-year break-even rate was 1.92%, while the 10-year inflation swap rate was 2.27%.

This pricing discrepancy could arise because TIPS yields are too high, Treasury yields are too low, inflation swap rates are too low, or a combination thereof. Certainly, it is possible that investors seeking protection in the inflation swap market are overpaying systematically, perhaps because of a limited pool of investors willing to supply inflation protection. However, there is independent evidence that TIPS are less liquid than Treasuries (see, e.g., Gürkaynak, Sack, and Wright, 2010). Pflueger and Viceira 2015 estimate that TIPS would have yields that are 64 bps per annum lower if they were as liquid as Treasuries. Especially during crises, investors seem to value the liquidity and safety yielded by nominal Treasuries (Krishnamurthy and Vissing-Jorgensen, 2012), but not by TIPS. It is hard to provide a sound economic rationale for this safety distinction between different securities issued by the Treasury that investors seem to make. Apparently, the flight-to-safety applies only to the nominal securities issued by the Treasury, not the real ones.

The anomalous behavior of TIPS yields in the last quarter of 2008 definitely suggests that the pricing of TIPS may be partly to blame. Figure 3.4 plots the constant-maturity yields on TIPS. TIPS yields declined gradually since the onset of the subprime mortgage crisis in the United States, except during the months following the fall of Lehman in September of 2008. During that brief interval, real TIPS yields, computed by the Treasury using on-the-run TIPS, actually rose dramatically, a radical departure from what standard economic and financial theory would predict for the behavior of the risk-free real interest rate in a high volatility episode. The Barclays 1–5-year TIPS index lost more than 13% from peak to trough in 2 months.

There is anecdotal evidence that Lehman's repo trades were largely backed by TIPS collateral. The wholesale selling of its inventory of TIPS after the Lehman failure may have contributed to the large price declines in the TIPS market at the start of Q4 in 2008.[3]

[3]"Lehman Brothers owned TIPS as part of repo trades or posted TIPS as counterparty collateral. Because of Lehman's bankruptcy, the court and its counterparty needed to sell these TIPS, which created a flood of TIPS on the market. There appeared to be few buyers and distressed market makers were unwilling to take positions in these TIPS. As a result, the TIPS yields rose sharply." Source: GAO Report to the Secretary of the Treasury, September 2009.

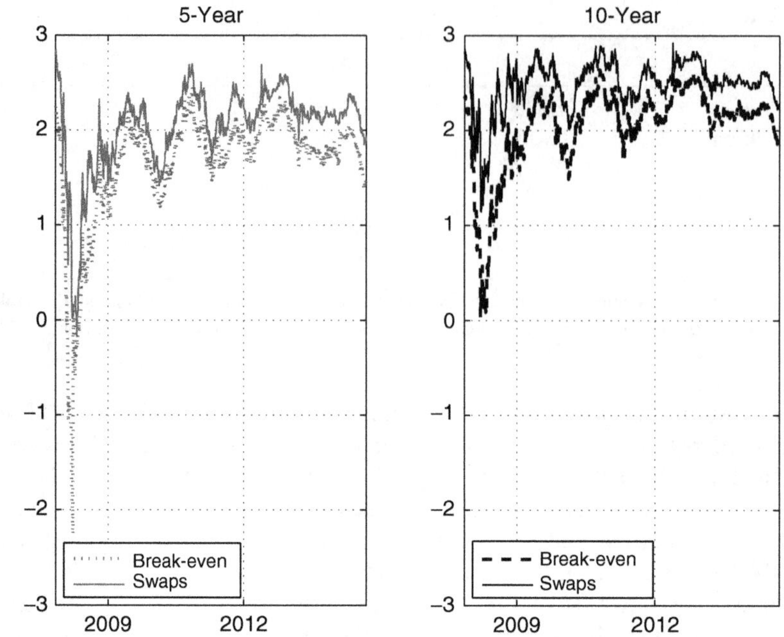

Figure 3.3 U.S. break-even and inflation swap rates. Plot of break-even rates ($y^{t,\$} - y^t$) computed from constant-maturity TIPS and Treasury yields and inflation swap rates for $t = 5$ and $t = 10$ years. Source: FRED and U.S. Treasury for break-even rates, Thomson Reuters for inflation swap rates.

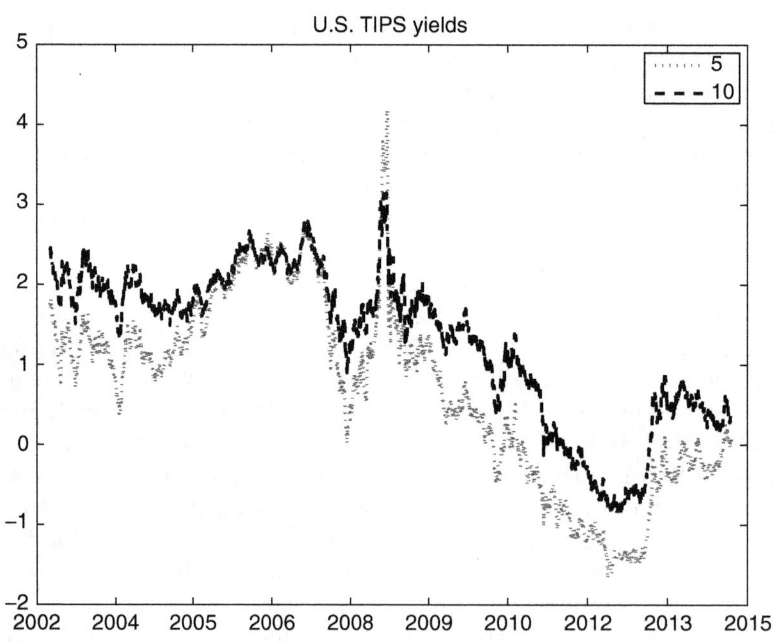

Figure 3.4 U.S. TIPS yields. Plot of constant-maturity TIPS yields. Source: FRED and U.S. Treasury.

Capital was slow to move into TIPS markets to take advantage of this mispricing, possibly because investors with the expertise to put on these trades were leverage constrained in the face of substantial losses in TIPS and other markets. Fleckenstein (2013) relates the size of the TIPS–Treasury mispricing in the United States and other countries to the availability of arbitrage capital. Certainly, this evidence is in line with what we have learned about other arbitrage relations in bond markets. For example, Treasuries were also rich during the crisis relative to corporate bonds after accounting for Credit Default Swap (CDS) spreads (see, e.g., Duffie, 2010). What is more surprising is that there is still a 30 bps spread between break-even rates and inflation swap rates today, as shown in Figure 3.3.

There was another sell-off in TIPS in 2013; this one attributed to rumors that Fed's quantitative easing experiment was about to come to an end. The 10-year real yield jumped from negative 70 basis points to plus 60 basis points between May and June of 2013.

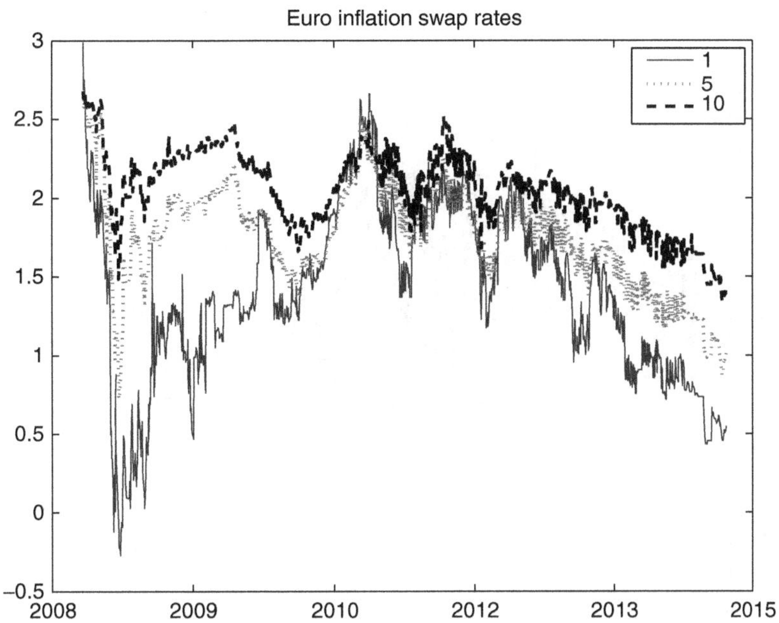

Figure 3.5 Euro inflation swap rates. Plot of annualized zero-coupon Euro inflation swap rates F^t at 1-, 5-, and 10-year tenors. Source: Thomson Reuters.

The Euro swap rate displayed in Figure 3.5 curve looks similar. The swap rates increase from 1.43% at the 1-year horizon to 2.34% at the 20-year horizon. The spread is only 93 bps per annum in the Euro zone. Hence, the Euro curve is not quite as steep as the U.S. curve over this sample. On the other hand, the Euro 10-year inflation swap rate is not as strongly anchored. In fact, the 10-year rate has been drifting down from 250 to 150 basis points over the last 2 years, while the 1-year swap rate declined from 1.5% to 0.5%. We cannot rule out the possibility that much of this decline reflects a decrease in the inflation risk premium.

3.5.3 Inflation Risk Premium

To gauge inflation expectations from inflation swap rates or break-even rates, we need to take a stand on the size and sign of the inflation risk premium. Historical estimates of the U.S. inflation risk premium in the literature at the 10-year horizon vary between 50 and 120 basis points. These estimates require a completely specified model for the joint dynamics of inflation and the pricing kernel. We will try to summarize some of the recent evidence that has emerged about the inflation risk premium.

To develop some intuition for inflation risk premia over the last decade, we compute the correlation of daily changes in the inflation swap rates with daily stock returns, both in the United States and in the Euro area. These numbers are also reported in Table 3.1. In the United States, this correlation is strong and positive at the 5-year maturity at 25%, and it tapers off for higher maturities. These averages hide a substantial amount of time variation. Figure 3.6 plots the correlation over 100-day windows. For the 5- and 10-year tenors, the correlation between changes inflation swap rates and returns on the S&P 500 peaks around 0.8 in early 2009. Based on the simple CAPM logic, investors should require a positive risk premium on TIPS relative to nominal Treasuries, $t \times rp_0^t = rp^m \beta_{\pi_t}$, and hence a negative inflation risk premium. Investors are mostly concerned about deflation in high marginal utility states of the world. Consistent with this, Fleckenstein, Longstaff, and Lustig (2014) estimate a negative inflation risk premium from inflation option and swap data during the U.S. financial crisis. The probability of deflation under the risk-neutral measure is considerably larger than the actual probability.

In the Euro area, we see a similar but weaker correlation pattern. Over the 2008–2014 sample, higher 5-year inflation expectations are good news for stocks, in the form of either lower discount rates or higher cash flow growth rates. Higher inflation over the next 5–10 years on average is interpreted as good news by the average U.S. investor.

Certainly, this is a new development. Before the late 1990s, U.S. stock and nominal bond returns were positively correlated, consistent with the notion that higher inflation is bad news for stocks, as pointed in recent work by Campbell, Sunderam, and Vicera (2013) and Baele, Bekaert, and Inghelbrecht (2009). Between August 1998 and October 2014, the average correlation between daily stock and bond returns on all outstanding U.S. Treasuries, measured using the Barclays U.S. Treasury Index, is −0.18. Borrowing a phrase from Campbell, Sunderam, and Vicera (2013), we could say that nominal bonds have changed from "inflation bets to deflation hedges." Higher expected inflation signals good news for the U.S. stock market. These bond return correlations are consistent with the evidence from the inflation swap market. This same correlation is −0.22 for the Eurozone.

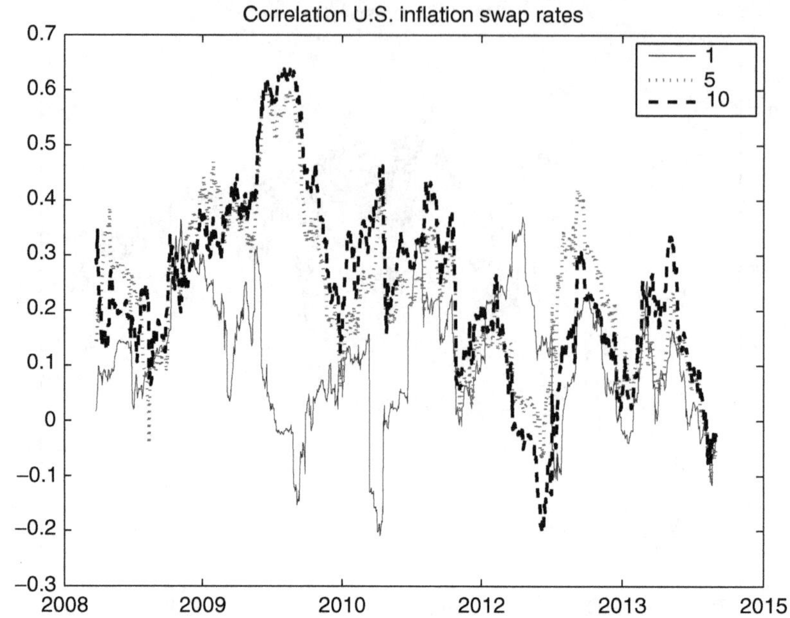

Figure 3.6 Correlation of U.S. inflation swap rates with S&P 500 returns. Plot of correlation between daily changes in swap rates and S&P 500 returns computed over 100-day windows centered around t. Source: FRED and U.S. Treasury and Datastream.

While the variation in stock–bond correlations may seem puzzling, David and Veronesi (2013) manage to explain the time variation in this comovement in an equilibrium in which agents are learning about the economic regime they find themselves in. Depending on the regime, higher inflation can be good or bad news. The chapter by David and Veronesi in this handbook reviews this evidence.

3.6 CONCLUSION

Certainly, the evidence from stock, bond, and inflation swap markets suggests that the inflation risk premium varies quite a bit over time and even switches signs. Over the last decade or more in the United States, this inflation risk premium has probably been negative. U.S. investors were willing to pay a premium to provide inflation protection, presumably in order to hedge against the looming risk of deflation. We detected a similar pattern in the Eurozone. It is challenging to infer the investor's expected inflation from swap rates and break-even rates given that the inflation risk premium switches over time. This always requires a complete model for the joint dynamics of the pricing kernel and inflation.

In today's regime of negative inflation risk premia, actual expected inflation exceeds the inflation swap rate and the break-even rate. Of course, negative inflation risk premia take one of the main motivations behind the Treasury's TIPS program off the table. When the inflation risk premium is negative, it is cheaper to issue nominal bonds than inflation-linked bonds, even if there is no mispricing.

Furthermore, the evidence from the inflation swap markets suggests that even 16 years into the TIPS program, these securities are still underpriced relative to Treasuries, possibly because TIPS are less liquid, even now. In bond markets, Treasuries are special, but TIPS are not. As a result, the expected inflation measures backed out from break-even rates will probably be too low, even when we abstract from the risk adjustment. Inflation swap rates may offer a more reliable gauge of the market's inflation expectations.

3.7 APPENDIX

3.7.1 Breeden–Lucas–Rubinstein Example

We can state the risk premium as a function of the cross moments of the real pricing kernel:

$$rp_0^1 = -k(1;\lambda_t) + k(1;\pi_t) + k(1;\lambda_t - \pi_t)$$

To develop some intuition, consider the simplest case of a Breeden–Lucas–Rubinstein economy with a representative agent who has time-separable power utility. α denotes the coefficient of risk aversion. In the Breeden–Lucas–Rubinstein example, we set $\lambda_t = \beta - \alpha\Delta c_t$. Then the equilibrium risk premium is given by

$$rp_0^1 = -k(1; \beta - \alpha\Delta c_t) + k(1; \pi_t) + k(1; \beta - \alpha\Delta c_t - \pi_t)$$

In the case of joint log normality, the covariance between consumption growth and inflation determines the risk premium; all of the higher order moments drop out. Then $rp_0^1 = \alpha\sigma_{\Delta c_t, \pi_t}$. A negative covariance between aggregate consumption growth and inflation delivers a negative risk premium on the inflation-indexed bond, because the inflation risk exposes the representative investor to more aggregate consumption growth risk when he/she holds the nominal bond. As a result, average inflation is higher under the risk-neutral than under the actual measure. Inflation insurance comes at a cost.

Then the equilibrium risk premium is given by

$$rp_0^1 = -k(1; \beta - \alpha\Delta c_t) + k(1; \pi_t) + k(1; \beta - \alpha\Delta c_t - \pi_t)$$

In the case of joint log normality, the covariance between consumption growth and inflation determines the risk premium; all of the higher order moments drop out. Then $rp_0^1 = \alpha\sigma_{\Delta c_t, \pi_t}$.

3.7.2 Disaster Risk

However, deviations from joint log normality create an interesting role for higher order moments of inflation and aggregate consumption growth. If there is more positive skewness or kurtosis in the real pricing kernel than in the nominal pricing kernel and inflation,

$$\kappa_3(\lambda) > \kappa_3(\lambda^\$) + \kappa_3(\pi) \text{ or}$$
$$\kappa_4(\lambda) > \kappa_4(\lambda^\$) + \kappa_4(\pi)$$

that delivers a negative risk premium on inflation-indexed bonds relative to the nominal risk-free bond and hence a positive inflation risk premium.

This arises naturally in a disaster-style model in which large consumption drops go hand in hand with higher rates of inflation:

$$\kappa_3(\beta - \alpha\Delta c_t) > \kappa_3(\beta - \alpha\Delta c_t - \pi_t) + \kappa_3(\pi_t) \text{ or}$$
$$\kappa_4(\beta - \alpha\Delta c_t) > \kappa_4(\beta - \alpha\Delta c_t - \pi_t) + \kappa_3(\pi_t)$$

In this case, the effect of large drops in consumption (and high growth rates for marginal utility) on the nominal pricing kernel would be mitigated by higher rates of inflation in those rare disaster states. Hence, the nominal pricing kernel and inflation are less risky than the real pricing kernel. That makes a long position in inflation-indexed bonds and a short position in nominal bonds safer, and it produces a more negative risk premium on this strategy rp_t, because the real bond offers insurance against the worst states of the world, while nominal bonds do not.

Gabaix (2008) relies on this mechanism to generate positive inflation risk premia in an equilibrium asset pricing model with time-varying disasters. Nakamura et al. (2013) document that large consumption disasters go together with substantial inflation spikes in a large panel of countries. Frequently, governments effectively default on the outstanding nominal debt by creating inflation.

The recent financial crisis represented a departure from this stylized fact. Several countries around the world including the United States experienced brief deflationary episodes, along with large consumption drops. In this environment, the inflation risk premium would be negative:

$$\kappa_3(\beta - \alpha\Delta c_t) < \kappa_3(\beta - \alpha\Delta c_t - \pi_t) + \kappa_3(\pi_t) \text{ or}$$
$$\kappa_4(\beta - \alpha\Delta c_t) < \kappa_4(\beta - \alpha\Delta c_t - \pi_t) + \kappa_3(\pi_t)$$

3.8 DATA APPENDIX

The U.S. inflation swap rates are U.S. dollar inflation-linked swap n year downloaded from Datastream with mnemonics *USDIS1Y, USDIS2Y, …, USDIS10Y, USDIS20Y, USDIS25Y*, and *USDIS30Y*. The source is Thomson Reuters.

The Euro inflation swap rates are Euro inflation-linked swap *n* year downloaded from Datastream with mnemonics *EURIS1Y, EURIS2Y, ..., EURIS10Y, EURIS20Y, EURIS25Y*, and *EURIS30Y*. The source is Thomson Reuters.

The 5-year break-even inflation rate (*T5YIE*) from FRED is the difference between the 5-year treasury constant-maturity securities (http://research.stlouisfed.org/fred2/series/DGS5) and the 5-year treasury inflation-indexed constant-maturity securities (http://research.stlouisfed.org/fred2/series/DFII5). The 10-year break-even inflation rate (*T10YIE*) is the difference between the 10-year treasury constant-maturity securities (http://research.stlouisfed.org/fred2/series/DGS10) and 10-year treasury inflation-indexed constant-maturity securities (http://research.stlouisfed.org/fred2/series/DFII10).

The Treasury's yield curve is derived using a quasicubic hermite spline function. Our inputs are the Close of Business (COB) bid yields for the on-the-run securities. Because the on-the-run securities typically trade close to par, those securities are designated as the knot points in the quasicubic hermite spline algorithm and the resulting yield curve is considered a par curve. However, Treasury reserves the option to input additional bid yields if there is no on-the-run security available for a given maturity range that we deem necessary for deriving a good fit for the quasicubic hermite spline curve.

The U.S. Bond Return Index is the Barclays U.S. Treasury Index. The Datastream mnemonic is *LHUSTRY*. The U.S. TIPS Return Index is the Barclays U.S. 1–5-Year TIPS Index. The Datastream mnemonic is *LHTP15Y*. The Euro Bond Return Index is Barclays Euro Aggregate Index. The Datastream mnemonic is *LHAGOVE*.

REFERENCES

Ang A, Bekaert G, Wei M. The term structure of real rates and expected inflation. J Finance 2008;63(2):797–849.

Atkeson A, Ohanian L. Are Phillips curves useful for forecasting inflation? Fed Reserve Bank Minneap Q Rev 2001;25(1):2–10.

Backus D, Chernov M, Zin S. Sources of entropy in representative agent models. J Finance 2014;69(1):51–99.

Baele L, Bekaert G, Inghelbrecht K. The determinants of stock and bond return comovements. NBER Working Paper, 15260; 2009.

Buraschi A, Jiltsov A. Inflation risk premia and the expectations hypothesis. J Financ Econ 2005;75(2):429–490.

Campbell JY, Sunderam A, Viceira LM. Inflation bets or deflation hedges? The changing risks of nominal bonds. Working Paper Harvard Business School; Jan 2013.

Campbell JY, Viceira LM. Who should buy long-term bonds? Am Econ Rev 2001;91(1):99–127.

Chernov M, Mueller P. The term structure of inflation expectations. J Financ Econ 2012;106(2):367–394.

Christensen JHE, Lopez JA, Rudebusch GD. Inflation expectations and risk premiums in an arbitrage-free model of nominal and real bond yields. J Money Credit Bank 2010;42(S1):143–178.

Christensen JHE, Lopez JA, Rudebusch GD. Pricing deflation risk with us treasury yields. Unpublished working paper. Federal Reserve Bank of San Francisco (CA); 2011.

David A, Veronesi P. What ties return volatilities to price valuations and fundamentals? J Pol Econ 2013;121(4):682–746.

Duffee GR. Information in (and not in) the term structure. Rev Financ Stud 2011;24(9):2895–2934.

Duffie D. Presidential address: asset price dynamics with slow-moving capital. J Finance 2010;65(4):1237–1267.

Fleckenstein M. The Inflation-Indexed Bond Puzzle (April 1, 2013); 2013. Available at SSRN: http://ssrn.com/abstract=2180251 or http://dx.doi.org/10.2139/ssrn.2180251.

Fleckenstein M, Longstaff FA, Lustig H. The tips-treasury bond puzzle. J Finance 2014a;69(5):2151–2197.

Fleckenstein M, Longstaff FA, Lustig H. Deflation. Working paper; Aug 2014b.

Fleming M, Sporn J. An analysis of OTC interest rate derivatives transactions: implications for public reporting appendix: trading activity and price transparency in the inflation swap market. Federal Reserve Bank of New York Staff Reports No. 557; New York: Federal Reserve Bank of New York; 2012.

Gabaix X. Variable rare disasters: a tractable theory of ten puzzles in macrofinance. Am Econ Rev 2008;98(2):64–67.

Grishchenko OV, Vanden JM, Zhang J. The informational content of the embedded deflation option in tips. Finance and Economics Discussion Series Divisions of Research Statistics and Monetary Affairs; Dec 2011.

Gürkaynak RS, Sack B, Wright JH. The tips yield curve and inflation compensation. Am Econ J Macroecon 2010;2(1):70–92.

Haubrich J, Pennacchi G, Ritchken P. Inflation expectations, real rates, and risk premia: evidence from inflation swaps. Rev Financ Stud 2012;25(5):1588–1629.

Joslin S, Priebsch M, Singleton KJ. Risk premiums in dynamic term structure models with unspanned macro risks. J Finance 2014;69(3):1197–1233.

Kitsul Y, Wright JH. The economics of options-implied inflation probability density functions. Working paper; Jan 2012.

Krishnamurthy A, Vissing-Jorgensen A. The aggregate demand for treasury debt. J Pol Econ 2012;120(2):233–267.

Ludvigson SC, Ng S. Macro factors in bond risk premia. Rev Financ Stud 2009;22(12):5027–5067.

Nakamura E, Steinsson J, Barro R, Ursua J. Crises and recoveries in an empirical model of consumption disasters. Am Econ J Macroecon 2013;5(3):35–74.

Pflueger CE, Viceira LM. Return predictability in the treasury market: real rates, inflation, and liquidity. In: Veronesi P, editor. *Handbook of Fixed Income*. John Wiley & Sons; 2015.

Piazzesi M, Schneider M. Equilibrium yield curves. National Bureau of Economic Analysis Macroeconomics Annual; 2006.

Stock JH, Watson MW. Why has U.S. inflation become harder to forecast? J Money Credit Bank 2007;39:3–33.

4

Mortgage-Related Securities (MRSs)

Jefferson Duarte[a] and Douglas A. McManus[b*]

[a]*Rice University, Jones Graduate School of Business, Houston, TX, United States*

[b]*Freddie Mac, Office of the Chief Economist, McLean, VA, United States*

4.1 PURPOSE OF THE CHAPTER

Mortgage-related securities (MRSs) comprise one of the largest segments of the American fixed income market. Figure 4.1 shows the amount of debt outstanding for three different sectors of the U.S. bond market. This figure reveals that between 1999 and 2010, MRS comprised the largest sector of the American bond market. As of December 2013, there are around \$8.7 trillion of outstanding MRSs, making the MRS sector the third largest segment of the American fixed income market, following only the Treasury sector (\$11.9 trillion outstanding) and the corporate sector (at around \$9.5 trillion outstanding). Of the \$8.7 trillion of MRS outstanding, around \$7 trillion are agency MRSs; that is, they are created through government-sponsored enterprises (GSEs) such as Fannie Mae and Freddie Mac or government backed such as FHA/VA loans securitized through Ginnie Mae. The remainder, \$1.7 trillion, is non-agency MRSs, such as private-label residential mortgage-backed securities (RMBSs) and securities backed by mortgages on commercial properties (commercial mortgage-backed securities, or CMBSs).

It is of course impossible to describe all the issues related to a market of the size of the MRS market in a book, let alone in a chapter. We therefore focus on three objectives: first, we provide a very brief description of the MRS market. Second, we describe an important new class of MRS introduced in 2013. The GSEs, responding to supervisory requests, created instruments to achieve risk sharing with private capital through Freddie Mac's STACR deals and Fannie Mae's C-deals. We provide a textbook description of this type of MRS.[1] Third, we give an example of the evaluation of MRSs with emphasis on the modeling of prepayment and default and their resulting impact on mortgage cash flows. This example would be a good starting place for the more technical reader wishing to better understand a competing risk model of default and prepayment. Throughout the chapter, we focus on the agency MRSs and provide citations for the reader interested in delving further into the MRS literature.[2]

The remainder of this chapter is organized as follows: Section 4.2 describes basic concepts having to do with MRSs. Section 4.3 describes the valuation framework commonly used to price and hedge MRSs. Section 4.4 gives an example of a competing risk model of default and prepayment and an application for the analysis of Freddie Mac's STACR deals. Section 4.5 concludes.

*Any views expressed are solely those of the authors and do not necessarily represent the opinions of Freddie Mac or its board of directors. While the authors attempt to provide reliable, useful information, it does not guarantee that the information is accurate, current, or suitable for any particular purpose.

[1]We focus on the STACR Series 2013-DN1 which is the first Freddie Mac MRS of this type. The other securities of this type share similar characteristics to those of STACR Series 2013-DN1.

[2]We therefore do not discuss CMBS or securities backed by subprime or home equity loans.

Handbook of Fixed-Income Securities, First Edition. Edited by Pietro Veronesi.

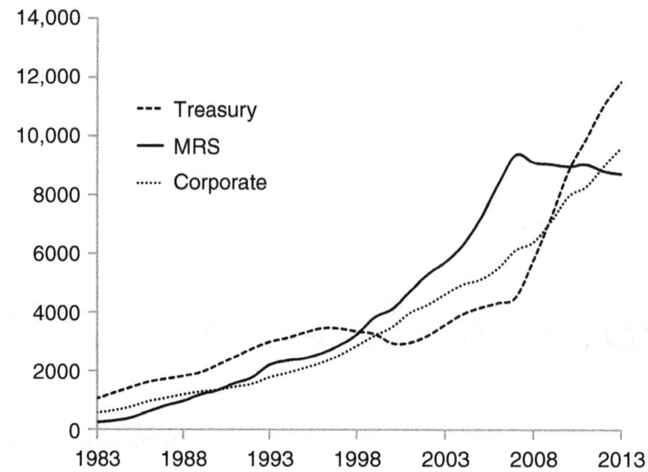

Figure 4.1 The amount outstanding for three different sectors of the U.S. bond market. The amounts are in billions of dollars. Source: Securities Industry and Financial Markets Association (SIFMA).

4.2 INTRODUCTION TO MRSs

4.2.1 Mortgage and Securitization

A mortgage is a debt instrument formed by a promissory note in which the borrower promises to pay certain amounts by specific dates and by a lien that gives the lender the right to possess a specific property (usually a real estate property) in the event that the borrower does not fulfill the obligations related to the promissory note.

Lenders in the United States primarily used to keep mortgages on their balance sheet, but this practice changed in the 1980s due to the S&L crisis. As a result of this crisis, the process of mortgage securitization became common. Mortgage securitization involves packaging mortgages into securities that are relatively liquid and traded in the capital markets. These securities usually receive a credit rating and are a common part of bond investor portfolios. These securities are called mortgage-backed securities (MBSs).[3]

The process of securitization separates the many tasks that traditional lenders once performed themselves across different agents. In the traditional financing model, a lender would find the borrower, perform the due diligence of the mortgage loan origination, receive the loan payments, negotiate with the borrower in case of credit issues, and bear the credit and interest rate risks of the loans. In the securitization process, on the other hand, these tasks are divided across many agents: an originator finds a borrower and performs the necessary origination due diligence, a servicer deals with the borrowers' payments, while investors in the securities provide capital and bear all or some of the risks of the loans.

Because all of these tasks can be separated in different ways, there are different securitization models. The first is the one used by GSEs. We call this model "the credit guarantee" or CG model. The second is the model used by investment firms in private-label securitization. We call this model "the credit tranche" or (CT) model.

In the CT model, the cash flows of all the underlying mortgages are pooled together in a single entity that distributes the cash flows according to some priority rule. The result of this cash flow distribution scheme is that some of the bonds created in the securitization have a very low likelihood of principal losses and a high credit rating, while other bonds have a very high likelihood of write-downs and a low credit rating.

In the CG model, on the other hand, an institution (i.e., Fannie Mae or Freddie Mac along with the U.S. government) promises to pay the full amount that is owed to the investors in the mortgage securities in the event of borrower default. In this model, the provider of credit guarantee commonly receives a guarantee fee in exchange for assuming the credit risk of the mortgages, while the investors in the MBS provide capital and assume the interest rate as well as the prepayment risks. The credit guarantee fee is commonly paid from the mortgage-payment cash flows.

As we pointed out before, our focus in this chapter is on the mortgage securities related to the agency segment of the RMBS market. Theoretically, the techniques described herein can be applied to mortgages that are not securitized by the GSEs, but in practice, market participants usually choose modeling frameworks that emphasize the main risks of the modeled securities. For instance, commercial mortgages usually have a prepayment penalty, while residential mortgages securitized by the GSEs generally do not. As a result, a great deal of attention is devoted to prepayment modeling by investors in RMBSs, while investors

[3]The distinction between an MBS and an MRS is that the cash flows of an MBS are secured by an underlying pool of mortgages, while the cash flows of an MRS are function of the cash flows of a reference pool but they are not necessarily secured by the underlying mortgages.

in CMBSs do not focus on prepayment risk. In addition, we focus our discussion on MRSs that have their cash flows derived from fixed-rate, fully amortizing mortgages instead of mortgages that have floating rates, such as adjustable-rate mortgages (ARMs). This is because the great majority of the mortgages securitized by the GSEs are fully amortizing, 30-year fixed-rate loans.

4.2.2 The Cash Flows of Mortgage Pools

We now describe some basic characteristics of the cash flows of agency MRSs. The explanation provided herein intends to be general. For a detailed explanation of the cash flows of a specific MRS instead, it is necessary to review its respective prospectus.

The most common agency MBS is the participation certificate or PC. PCs are pass-through MBSs, that is, they pass all the cash flows of the underlying pool of mortgages (after servicing and guarantee fees) to the PC investors. An example of a PC is the Gold fixed-rate PC from Freddie Mac. This security pays on the payment date of every month[4] an interest amount equal to

$$UPB_{t-1} \times \frac{Rate}{12} \tag{4.1}$$

where UPB_{t-1} is the unpaid principal balance (UPB) of the mortgage pool on the first day of the previous month and *Rate* is the coupon rate of the Gold PC. The difference between the interest paid by each mortgage in the pool and the coupon paid by the PC is the servicer fee plus Freddie's guarantee fee. The servicer fee compensates the servicer for handling and collecting mortgage payments, while in exchange for the guarantee fee, Freddie Mac buys at the current unpaid loan balance any mortgage loan in the underlying pool once the loan is delinquent by 120 days or more.

The principal amount paid on the payment date of every month to Gold PC investors is equal to the principal paid by the pool of mortgages during the previous month. This principal amount includes the scheduled principal payment and any prepayments. The principal prepayments include the outstanding principal of the mortgages removed by Freddie from the pool because of delinquency, the payments of principal due to refinancing or home sales, and all the curtailment of principal paid by homeowners.

A traditional way to measure prepayments is with the single monthly mortality (SMM) rate. The SMM of a mortgage pool in a given month is

$$SMM_t^P = \frac{PR_t}{(UPB_{t-1} - Scheduled\_Principal_t)} \tag{4.2}$$

where PR_t is the amount of principal prepayment at month t. That is, SMM_t^P is the fraction of the UPB after the scheduled payment that prepays. Although the SMM^P is a monthly measure of prepayment, practitioners typically report this measure as annualized. The annualized SMM^P is called the constant prepayment rate, or CPR, and is equal to

$$CPR_t = 1 - (1 - SMM_t^P)^{12} \tag{4.3}$$

Prepayments have a significant effect on the cash flows of PCs. To demonstrate this, Figure 4.2 shows the cash flows paid by a hypothetical PC under three different CPR scenarios. In this example, we assume a PC that pays a 4% coupon and is composed of a pool of identical, 30-year, fully amortizing fixed-rate mortgages with 4.5% note rate. The scheduled cash flows of the mortgages are computed as are the ones of a level annuity. As this figure shows, the cash flows of the hypothetical pool of mortgages are fairly close to a constant in the case of no prepayments; at a moderate prepayment speed (6%), the pool is completely prepaid in about 20 years and completely prepaid in about 8 years if the prepayment speed is fairly high (40%).

Naturally, this picture does not consider the fact that the CPR of a pool of mortgages is time-varying. In fact, the prepayment speed of a pool of mortgages varies with the age of the loans in the pool. Mortgages that have been recently originated are less likely to prepay than are seasoned mortgages. This seasoning effect on prepayments is well known and is the motivation for one of the main benchmarks on prepayment speed – the PSA standard. This standard assumes that the CPR of a pool of mortgages is equal to 0.2% in the first month, increases by 0.2% every month until it reaches 6% at 30 months, and remains constant at 6% until the mortgages are paid in full. Figure 4.3 plots the PSA standard. The left axis of this figure shows the SMM, while the right axis shows the equivalent CPR. Essentially, the PSA standard sets the CPR of a pool of mortgages as min(0.2% × *WALA*, 6%), where WALA is the average loan age weighted by the loan principals and age is measured in months since origination.

In addition to varying with age, the CPR of a pool of mortgages also varies due to changes in the economic variables that drive prepayment decisions. For instance, a drop in mortgage interest rates results in an increase of refinancing activity, which in turn drives, the CPR of mortgage pools. To illustrate this, Figure 4.4 plots the CPR of the pool of mortgages originated in the year 2000 that are in the sample described in Section 4.4.1.1. Note that even 1 year after origination, the CPR of the pool of mortgages was already very high at about 50%. This prepayment speed started decreasing in 2004 and has been essentially flat around 15% since 2007. The fairly high prepayment speeds for this pool of mortgages in 2001 resulted from low mortgage rates during this

[4]The "payment date" is the 15th day of each month or, if the 15th day is not a business day, the next business day.

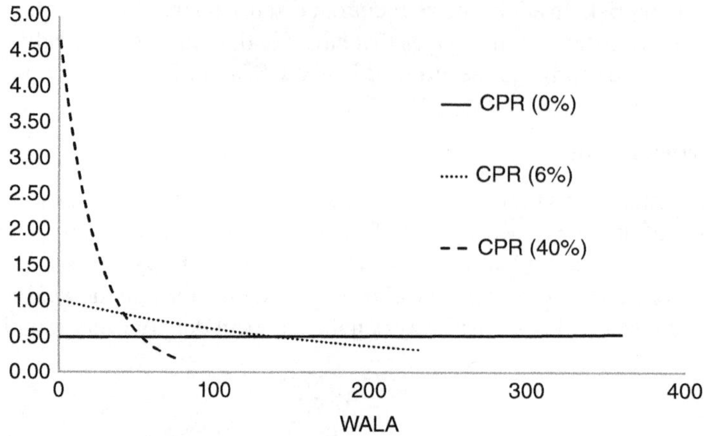

Figure 4.2 The cash flows of a PC with coupon rate 4.0% under different CPR scenarios. Principal amount at time zero is $100. WALA is the weighted average loan age (months) of the loans in the PC.

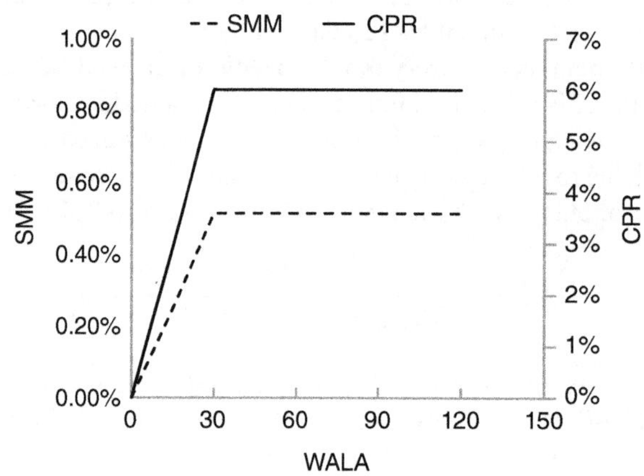

Figure 4.3 The PSA standard. The left axis shows the standard in SMM, while the right axis shows the standard in CPR. WALA is the weighted average loan age of the mortgage pool. WALA is measured in months.

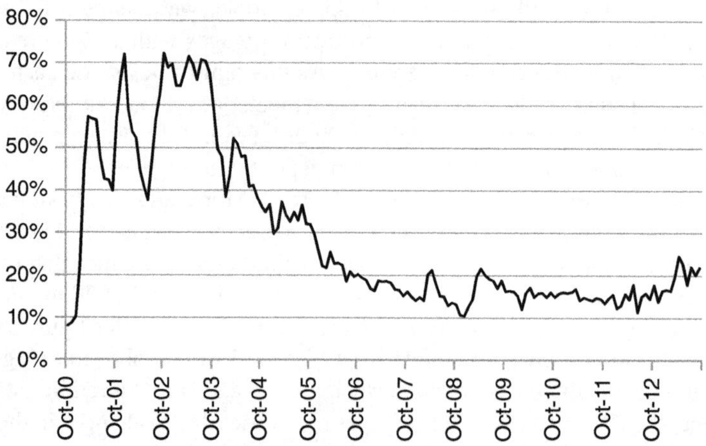

Figure 4.4 The CPR of mortgages originated in the year 2000. Source: Freddie Mac's Single-Family Loan-Level Dataset.

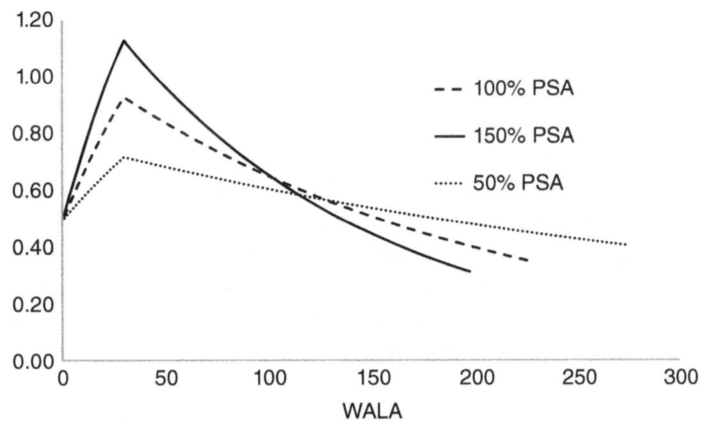

Figure 4.5 The cash flows of a PC with coupon rate 4.0% under different PSA scenarios. Principal amount at time zero is \$100. WALA is the weighted average life (months) of the loans underlying the PC.

period. Indeed, the average rate of the loans originated in 2000 was 8.13%, and 30-year fixed mortgage rate was around 7.03% in January 2001. The difference in these rates provided substantial incentives for homeowners to refinance. On the other hand, the essentially constant prepayment speed since 2007 may result from constraints that some of these homeowners may face to refinance. For instance, due to credit issues, some homeowners may not have been able to refinance even when mortgage rates are much smaller than their loan rates.

The PSA standard is commonly used as a simple metric to build different prepayment speed scenarios. Figure 4.5 shows the cash flows of a PC under three different PSA scenarios. The scenario called 100% PSA assumes that the PC has the same prepayment speed as the one given in the PSA standard. The scenario called 150% PSA assumes that the prepayment speed is given by 1.5 times the one in the PSA standard and the 50% by 0.5.

Both Figures 4.2 and 4.5 clearly show that prepayment speed has a significant effect on the cash flows of PCs. Note that some investors are not willing to take the variation in cash flows of PCs that result from prepayments, while others are willing to take even more. To cater to different investor needs, GSEs and investment banks created securities that go one step beyond just equally distributing all the cash flows of a pool of mortgages to all the investors. These securities are called collateralized mortgage obligations (CMOs).[5] CMOs attend to the needs of investors that want cash flows with different characteristics to those of simple PCs. The idea is to distribute the cash flows of a pool of mortgages or of a pass-through, according to certain rules, thereby creating securities that have different sensitivities to changes in risk factors such as interest rates and prepayment speeds. There are a fairly large number of types of CMOs. For a review of these structures, see Mortgage Research Group, Lehman Brothers (2001).

In the same way that we defined CPR and SMM^P in Equations 4.2 and 4.3, we can define CER credit event rate (CER) and SMM^D due to credit events such as defaults. Indeed, define SMM^D as

$$SMM_t^D = \frac{D_t}{(UPB_{t-1} - Scheduled\_Principal_t)} \tag{4.4}$$

where D_t is the amount of UPB that suffers a credit event at time t. Also define CER_t as

$$CER_t = 1 - (1 - SMM_t^D)^{12} \tag{4.5}$$

The CER_t and the SMM_t^D summarize default scenarios in an analogous way to how the CPR_t and the SMM_t^P summarize prepayment scenarios. See the prospectus of the STACR Series 2013 DN-1 for an example of how these metrics summarize default and prepayment scenarios.

4.3 VALUATION OVERVIEW

The basic framework for evaluating MRSs is the risk-neutral valuation procedure. (See Chapter 17 of Veronesi (2010) for a review of risk-neutral evaluation.) No-arbitrage implies that the price of an MRS can be written as the expected discounted

[5] Real estate mortgage investment conduits (REMICs) and CMOs have different tax treatments for the issuers. They are essentially the same for investors.

payoff using the risk-free rate. The expectation is taken under the risk-neutral measure. That is, the price of an MRS is given by

$$E_t^Q\left[\sum_{i=1}^{J} e^{-\int_t^{T_i} r_\tau d\tau} \times CF_{T_i}(X_{T_i})\right] \tag{4.6}$$

where E_t^Q is the risk-neutral expectation taken at time t, r_τ is the short-term interest at time τ, and $CF_{T_i}(X_{T_i})$ is the cash flow of the MRS paid at time T_i as function of the state variables in the vector X_{T_i}.

There is some flexibility in choosing the "risk-free" rate. The short-term interest rate used in the expression above can be either based on a T-bill rate or LIBOR. Before 1998, a Treasury-based, short-term rate (typically the T-bill rate) was the benchmark in most of the applications. With the LTCM debacle and the decrease in the supply of Treasury notes in the late 1990s, however, many practitioners switched to a LIBOR–swap-based benchmark (e.g., Duarte, 2006). After the 2008 crisis, many practitioners are switching back to Treasury rates as the benchmark, risk-free rates.

In addition to specifying the appropriate discount rates, we also need to specify MRS payoffs (see Eq. 4.6). These payoffs are stochastic, because they are affected by both prepayments and credit events. For instance, Figure 4.4 shows the stochastic nature of the prepayment speed of a pool of mortgages. Although homeowner decisions to prepay their mortgage or to default can be modeled as a result of an optimization problem, because there is a great deal of heterogeneity in homeowner behavior, practitioners normally rely on a statistical model that is estimated with the prepayment and default behavior that has been observed in historic data. The variables in these models (the vector X_{T_i} in Eq. 4.6) are motivated by optimality arguments. For instance, a drop in interest rates would make it optimal for many homeowners to refinance; similarly, a drop in housing prices would trigger a greater percentage of default. Hence, both interest rates and housing prices are commonly used as state variables that affect the cash flows of MRSs.

As we pointed out, the expectation in Equation 4.6 is under the risk-neutral measure. That is, the processes of the state variables X (including housing prices) and the risk-free rate (r) used for pricing are those under the risk-neutral measure. There is a long literature (some of which is discussed in this volume) on how to specify the risk-neutral process of r. The literature on the specification of the risk-neutral process for housing prices is much shorter. One possible way to specify this process is

$$dH_t = (r_t - q_h)dt + \sigma\, dZ_t \tag{4.7}$$

where q_h is the flow of rents accruing to homeowners (see Downing, Stanton, and Wallace (2005)). This specification for the risk-neutral process of house price relies on the assumption that housing is a traded asset and hence its drift under the risk-neutral process should be equal to the risk-free rate minus the housing "dividend rate." Housing is, however, an asset that is not as easily traded as financial assets such as stocks, and there are no liquid instruments that allow investors to short sell housing assets. Hence, the risk-neutral process in Equation 4.7 may work poorly empirically.

The evaluation of the expectation in Equation 4.6 is normally done with Monte Carlo simulations. Armed with the risk-neutral process of the state variables, as well as with the prepayment-default model, a series of paths for the cash flows of the MRS can be simulated, and the price of the MRS is the average of these discounted cash flows across all the simulated paths. This evaluation procedure is the basis of many practical applications. For instance, an MRS investor may wish to evaluate the relative value of different CMOs to detect investment opportunities, or an investor may wish to hedge the interest rate risk of an MRS portfolio. We now describe how the evaluation procedure is used in each of these tasks.

4.3.1 OAS, OAD, and Negative Convexity

One commonly used measure of the relative value of MRSs is the option-adjusted spread or OAS. The idea is that MRSs have embedded options related to prepayment and default. These options have different effects on different types of MRS. For instance, the value of a PC with very high coupon (option to refinance is deep in the money) is not as sensitive to interest rate movements as the value of a PC with low coupon (option to refinance is deep out of money). So to assess whether a given PC is cheap or expensive, one needs to adjust its valuation to account for the optionality embedded in MRSs. One way to accomplish this is with the OAS.

The OAS of a given MRS solves the equation:

$$P_t^{Market} = E_t^Q\left[\sum_{i=1}^{J} e^{-\int_t^{T_i}(r_\tau + OAS)d\tau} \times CF_{T_i}(X_{T_i})\right] \tag{4.8}$$

That is, the OAS is the spread that needs to be added to the risk-free rate to reconcile the pricing model with the market price. The OAS is normally calculated by solving Equation 4.8 with an iterative process in which the expected value in Equation 4.8 is calculated with Monte Carlo simulations.

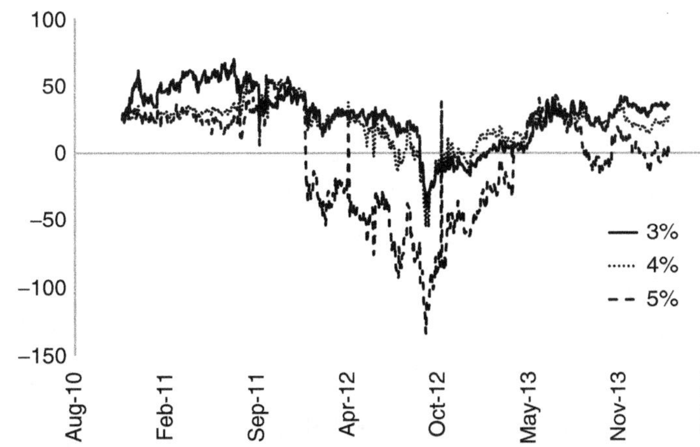

Figure 4.6 Time series of LIBOR-OASs of 30-year fixed-rate Freddie PC with coupons 3%, 4%, and 5%. Source: the Yield Book.

The reader familiar with option pricing will recognize the similarity between the OAS and the implied volatility used in the options literature. Indeed, these concepts are similar in the sense that they are both used to evaluate the relative value of different financial contracts. In fact, a comparison of Equations 4.6 and 4.8 would imply that the OAS of any MRS should be zero if the model fits the market prices perfectly. In reality, however, the OASs of MRSs are not zero, and different MRSs have different OASs. The usual explanation for the fact that OASs are different from zero is that investors require compensation for holding securities that are subject to prepayment risk. Moreover, other factors such as liquidity and compensation for holding interest rate volatility risk also play a role in the prices of MRSs and, hence, affect their OASs.

Investors commonly use the OAS as a measure of the relative prices of different MRSs as well as a measure of the time series variation of the prices of MRSs. Figure 4.6 displays a graph of the LIBOR-OAS[6] of the 30-year fixed-rate Freddie PC with different coupons. This figure shows that at any point in time, different MRSs have different OASs. Moreover, there is a substantial variation in the OAS of any given MRS.

Equation 4.8 is also commonly used to evaluate hedge ratios. Specifically, the option-adjusted duration (OAD) of an MRS is defined as the return in the MRS given a parallel shift in the term structure of interest rates. There is no closed-form solution for this effective duration, and it is calculated numerically. This numerical procedure starts by calculating the OAS of an MRS. Keeping the OAS constant, the procedure calculates the MRS prices after a shift in the entire term structure by Δy (e.g., 1 basis point) and by $-\Delta y$. Let these prices be represented by $P_{\Delta y}$ and $P_{-\Delta y}$. The OAD is given by

$$OAD = \frac{-(P_{\Delta y} - P_{-\Delta y})}{P \times 2\Delta y} \tag{4.9}$$

The OAD is broadly used to hedge the interest rate risk of MRSs; however, it is not without its limitations. For instance, embedded in the OAD is the assumption that the OAS does not change with interest rate movements. The empirical support for this assumption is somewhat limited, as the OAS frequently changes with interest rates.

An important implication of the prepayment feature on the prices of MRSs is that the prices of MRSs in general exhibit negative convexity. That is, the OAD of an MRS decreases as interest rates drop and increases as interest rates increase. It is convenient to think about the cash flows of a mortgage pass-through to understand the origin of the negative convexity. As interest rates drop, homeowners tend to refinance their mortgages. As a result, the principal cash flow of a pass-through tends to be paid sooner when interest rates drop, and the sensitivity of the price of a pass-through to subsequent interest rate movements decreases. The opposite happens when interest rates increase. Figure 4.7 exemplifies the negative convexity of a PC. This figure plots the price of a 30-year fixed-rate PC as function of the 10-year constant maturity Treasury (CMT) rate. The prices are from Bloomberg and the CMT rates are from Federal Reserve Economic Data (FRED). The data are monthly from February 2001 to March 2014. Each dot in this graph is an observation and the line is obtained from fitting a quadratic function by least squares. Note that the fitted curve is concave that shows the negative convexity of this MBS.

The negative convexity of MRSs may lead to significant variations in the P&L of a portfolio of MRSs. Assume, for instance, that a trader buys an MRS and hedges the interest rate movements with interest rate swaps or Treasury securities – that is, the

[6]The OAS with respect to the LIBOR–swap yield curve.

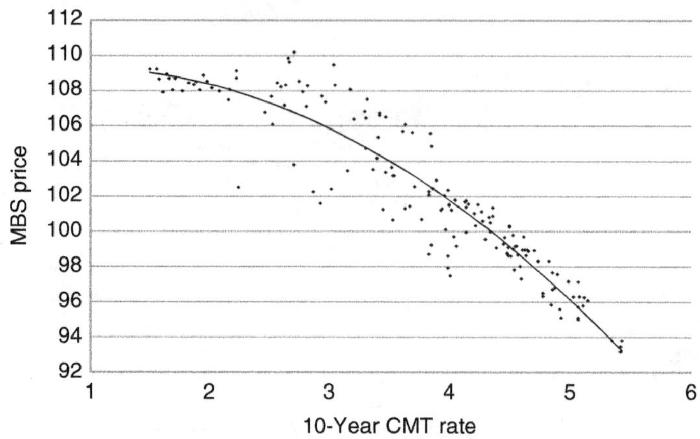

Figure 4.7 The price of 5.5% 30-year Freddie Mac Gold PC as a function of the 10-year CMT rate. Source: Bloomberg.

trader creates a portfolio with zero duration. To be more specific, let us approximate the return of this portfolio with a Taylor expansion:

$$\frac{\Delta\Pi}{\Pi_t} \sim \frac{1}{\Pi_t}\frac{\partial\Pi}{\partial y}(y_t) \times \Delta y + \frac{1}{2\Pi_t}\frac{\partial^2\Pi}{\partial y^2}(y_t) \times (\Delta y)^2 \tag{4.10}$$

where Π_t is the price of the portfolio at time t and y_t is the benchmark interest rate (e.g., the 10-year CMT rate). The assumption that the portfolio has zero duration implies that the first term on the right-hand side of the equation above is zero. Assume that the convexity of the hedging instrument (swap or Treasury) is very close to zero. In this case, the second derivative on the second term of Equation 4.10 is negative. As a result, independently of the sign of Δy, the return of the portfolio is negative as long as interest rates move. In fact, the larger the variation on the rates, the larger is the drop on the value of this portfolio.[7]

4.3.2 Modeling Prepayment and Default

We now present a model of mortgage default and prepayment. The general idea of this type of model is to understand the likelihood that a mortgage is terminated at time $t + dt$ given that it has not been terminated until t. Also, because default and prepayment have different effects on the cash flows of MRSs, it is important to understand not only the likelihood that a mortgage is terminated but also the likelihood that a mortgage is terminated for a given reason (default or prepay). As a result, we model the competing reasons for mortgage termination. In Section 4.3.2.1, we describe the main reasons for prepayment, Section 4.3.2.2 describes the reasons for default, and Section 4.3.2.3 describes a framework to model these competing risks of mortgage termination.

4.3.2.1 The Causes of Prepayment Homeowners prepay their mortgages for a number of reasons: first, and mostly important, most of the residential mortgages in the United States do not have a prepayment penalty. The great majority of the residential mortgages in the agency universe allow homeowners to prepay their mortgages without incurring any fees, other than standard closing costs. This implies that homeowners usually refinance their mortgages when they can get a new mortgage at a lower interest rate. Refinancing is the main factor that drives the prepayment speed of MRSs. In periods of high refinancing activity, it is not uncommon to see PC pools reaching a CPR of more than 60%. The second most common reason for prepayment is house turnover. In fact, house turnover is a particularly important reason for prepayment in periods during which interest rates are high and refinancing activity is low. (See Hayre and Young (2001) for a review of turnover effects on mortgage prepayments.) Third, defaults generate prepayments in agency PCs and CMOs. In fact, as part of the credit enhancement provided by Fannie Mae and Freddie Mac in their MBSs, the GSEs buy any mortgage that is more than 120 days delinquent from the underlying MBS pool for the unpaid principal amount. As a result, agency MBSs receive a prepayment cash flow in the event of deep delinquency or mortgage default. Fourth, some homeowners pay more than the scheduled mortgage payments every month. This is referred to as "curtailment" in the mortgage literature. Fifth, some homeowners pay their mortgages in full when the principal balance is low.

[7]Note, however, that the option to prepay a mortgage is not a "free lunch" for homeowners. Indeed, the coupon of MRS is higher than those of Treasuries to compensate for the fact that MRSs have negative convexity.

4.3.2.2 *The Causes of Credit Events* We define a credit event as any event related to the default of a homeowner in his/her mortgage that leads to a cash flow in the MRS. As mentioned before, a particularly important credit event for investors in agency MBSs is the 120-day delinquency, but there are other credit events that are also relevant in the valuation of MRSs, especially in private-label securities. For instance, a homeowner may sell his/her property for an amount smaller than the current UPB in a process called short sale. In this kind of scenario, the lender will not recover the entire principal amount and will incur a loss. A short sale may nonetheless be a better deal for a lender than actually taking possession of the property in a foreclosure process because the foreclosure process is costly and has an uncertain outcome and timeline. Indeed typically a lender fails to sell a foreclosed property for the UPB, and the property becomes real estate owned (REO).

An investor in an agency MBSs is effectively protected against principal losses due to these credit events since the agency assumes the credit risk of the mortgages underlying an MBS, but an investor in a non-agency MBS may have losses due to credit events. The expected value of such losses is the probability of credit event multiplied by the loss in case of a credit event. An investor in an agency MBS must be concerned about credit events because these may result in prepayments. Such an investor is therefore concerned about modeling the probability of a credit event but is not particularly interested in modeling any associated credit loss, since these are assumed by the GSEs. On the other hand, an investor in a private MRS is usually concerned about both components of the expected losses.

Since our focus is on agency MRSs, we also focus on the variables that drive the probability of a credit event. We can broadly classify these variables in two categories: one category is related to the borrower, such as borrower credit score, and the other is related to the property, such as the ratio of the loan balance to the market value of the property Loan-To-Value (LTV). Such classifications broadly map the two main reasons for borrower defaults on mortgages: first, when the borrower is unable to fulfill his/her credit obligation or, second, when the property value falls below the loan amount.

4.3.2.3 *Competing Risk Model* The probability of prepayment and of a credit event can be jointly modeled in a competing risk Cox model.[8] In this model, the probability that a mortgage loan will either prepay or default between t and time $t + dt$, given that the mortgage loan has not been prepaid or defaulted at t, is

$$h(t) = [h_0^D(t) \times \exp\ (\beta^D \times X_t)] + [h_0^P(t) \times \exp\ (\beta^P \times Y_t)] \tag{4.11}$$

The term $[h_0^D(t) \times \exp\ (\beta^D \times X_t)]$ in Equation 4.11 captures the probability that a loan defaults between t and $t + dt$ given that it has not been prepaid or defaulted at t, while $[h_0^P(t) \times \exp\ (\beta^P \times Y_t)]$ captures the likelihood of prepayment given that the loan has survived until t. The functions $h_0^D(t)$ and $h_0^P(t)$ are the baseline prepay and default hazard functions. They capture the effect of loan age on the probability that a given loan will either prepay or default (i.e., seasoning effects). And X_t and Y_t are (possibly time-varying) vectors of covariates.

The hazard functions $[h_0^D(t) \times \exp\ (\beta^D \times X_t)]$ and $[h_0^P(t) \times \exp\ (\beta^P \times Y_t)]$ are somewhat similar to SMM^D and SMM^P. To see that note that the expected amount of UPB that prepays between t and $t + dt$ given the UPB_t is $E[PR_t] = [h_0^P(t) \times \exp\ (\beta^P \times Y_t)] \times (UPB_{t-1} - Scheduled\_Principal_t)$. This implies that

$$h_0^P(t) \exp\ (\beta^P \times Y_t) = \frac{E[PR_t]}{(UPB_{t-1} - Scheduled\_Principal_t)} \tag{4.12}$$

Equation 4.12 is analogous to the SMM^P definition in Equation 4.2.

In many applications of this type of model, the investigator is interested in understanding the effect that a covariate X has on the probability of an event. In this case there is no need to estimate the baseline hazard functions ($h_0^D(t)$ and $h_0^P(t)$). On the other hand, it is necessary to estimate the baseline hazard functions for the type of applications that mortgage practitioners are normally interested in (e.g., pricing). For instance, an investigator may be interested in understanding whether mortgage loans with one single borrower default more often than mortgage loans with multiple borrowers. To do this, we can estimate a model like the one in Equation 4.11 in which one of the covariates X is a variable that takes value one when the mortgage has more than one borrower and zero otherwise (call this covariate X_1). The coefficient β_1^D on this covariate reveals the effect of multiple borrowers on the likelihood of default. Indeed, the model above implies that mortgages with multiple borrowers have a likelihood of default between t and $t + dt$ that is $\exp\ (\beta_1^D)$ times higher than otherwise identical mortgages with only one borrower. In this case, the investigator may only estimate the parameters β_1^D and not estimate the baseline hazard functions. The estimation of the coefficients β_1^D and β_1^P can be done with maximum likelihood. On the other hand, it is necessary to understand the expected time of the cash flows of an MRS to price it. Consequently, it is necessary to estimate the baseline hazard functions in pricing applications.[9]

[8] See Lam, Dunsky, and Kelly (2013) for an example of a prepayment model that is not within the Cox model framework; see Kalbfleisch and Prentice (2002) as well as Lunn and McNeill (1995) for a detailed description of Cox model.

[9] The model above is semiparametric in the sense that the baseline hazard function is commonly estimated nonparametrically, while the coefficients β^D and β^P are commonly estimated by maximum likelihood.

Economic models of default and prepayment behavior provide a good guideline for the choice of covariates in the vectors X_t and Y_t. For instance, in a model without frictions or transaction costs, homeowners refinance as soon as the current mortgage rate is lower than the loan rate.[10] This motivates the use of the difference between the rate in the mortgage loan and the current mortgage rate as a covariate (which is in fact a common measure of refinancing incentive used in practice). In a structural model of default (e.g., Merton, 1974), the likelihood of default changes nonlinearly with LTV ratios, which motivates the use of splined covariates as $\max(0, LTV - 100\%)$. This covariate helps the model match a nonlinear relationship between LTV and the probability of default that is empirically observed.

4.4 ANALYZING AN MRS

We now estimate a competing risk model of prepayment and default and apply this model to analyze an MRS. Section 4.4.1 describes the model, Section 4.4.2 describes the MRS that we analyze – the STACR Series 2013-DN1, and Section 4.4.3 uses the estimated model to analyze the STACR.

4.4.1 Modeling Prepayment and Default

In this section, we estimate a competing risk model of default and prepayment. Section 4.4.1.1 describes the data used in this model estimation. Section 4.4.1.2 displays the estimation results.

4.4.1.1 Data Used Freddie Mac has made available loan-level credit performance data on approximately 16 million fully amortizing "full documentation" (i.e., verified or waived documentation) 30-year fixed-rate mortgages that the company purchased or guaranteed from 1999 to 2012.[11]

Monthly loan performance data including loan balance and termination events such as prepayments, short sales, deeds in lieu of foreclosure, third-party sales, and real estate owned (REO) properties are available through June 30, 2013. In addition, mortgages repurchased after a termination event but prior to March 31, 2013, are identified, as are mortgages that were modified from the original loan terms. Only approved and closed workouts (e.g., short sales, modifications, and deeds in lieu of foreclosure) prior to the March 31, 2013, are included.[12]

Because of the size of this dataset (there are 706 million unique performance records), Freddie Mac has created a sample dataset composed of a simple random sample of 50,000 loans selected from each origination year and a corresponding file with monthly performance data on this subset of loans. The estimates provided in this chapter are based on a merge of these sample datasets, which results in about 27 million individual performance records. These records cover the period between 7 months from origination to maturity of the loans. The database does not include the performance of loans that are less than 7 months from origination.

Table 4.1 describes the static variables (the ones that remain constant throughout the life of the mortgage loan) in this dataset that are used in our competing risk model. These variables are borrower FICO score, number of units in the property, occupancy status, the origination UPB, the origination LTV, the combined loan-to-value (CLTV), the original debt-to-income (DTI) ratio, property type, loan purpose, and the number of borrowers.[13]

Table 4.2 describes the dynamic variables in the Freddie Mac's loan-level database. These variables are current actual UPB, loan age, zero balance code, zero balance effective date, and current mortgage note interest rate. Recall that in addition to data related to mortgage loans, a competing risk model of prepayment and default also uses time-varying covariates, such as refinancing incentive and marked-to-market total loan to value (MTMTLTV). These variables are related to the current mortgage

[10]Homeowners have an American option to buy their own debt. By refinancing immediately after mortgage rate drops below their loan rate, homeowners save on their interest expense. At the same time, if mortgage rate drops even further after homeowners refinance, they can refinance again at no cost if there are no frictions. Therefore, in a model without refinancing frictions, homeowners should refinance as soon as the current mortgage rate is lower than their loan rate.

[11]Specifically excluded from this dataset are (i) ARMs; (ii) initial interest, balloons, and any mortgages with step rates; (iii) relief refinance mortgages (including Home Affordable Refinance Program or HARP); (iv) Government-insured mortgages, including Federal Housing Administration (FHA) and Veterans Affairs (VA), Guaranteed Rural Housing (GRH), and HUD-Guaranteed Section 184 Native American mortgages; (v) home possible and home possible neighborhood solution mortgages and other affordable mortgages (including lender-branded affordable loan products); (vi) mortgages delivered to Freddie Mac under alternate agreements; (vii) mortgages for which the documentation is not verified or not waived; (viii) mortgages associated with mortgage revenue bonds purchased by Freddie Mac; (ix) mortgages delivered to Freddie Mac with credit enhancements other than primary mortgage insurance, with the exception of certain lender-negotiated credit enhancements; (x) mortgages with original loan terms of 420 months or more and with 300 months or less.

[12]To protect borrower privacy, certain data elements are masked: (i) dates only include month and year, first payment date, maturity date, and zero balance effective date; (ii) origination loan amount is rounded to the nearest $1000; (iii) current unpaid loan balance is missing for first 6 months after loan origination; (iv) small servicers or originators (representing less than 1% of the total origination UPB) are identified as "other sellers" or "other servicers"; (v) The last two digits of the zip code for each loan are replaced with zeroes.

[13]See http://www.freddiemac.com/news/finance/pdf/summary_statistics.pdf for detailed information about Freddie Mac's loan-level data.

TABLE 4.1 Static Variables in Freddie Mac's Loan-Level Database

Name	Description
FICO	The credit score used to originate the mortgage
Number of units	Denotes whether the mortgage is a one-, two-, three-, or four-unit property
Occupancy status	Denotes whether the mortgage type is owner-occupied, second home, or investment property
CLTV	This is the combined loan to value at origination. In the case of a purchase mortgage loan, the ratio is obtained by dividing the original mortgage loan amount plus any disclosed secondary mortgage amount by the lesser of the property's appraised value or its purchase price. For a refinance, the original loan amount plus any disclosed secondary mortgage loan amount is divided by the property's appraised value. The CLTV is in percent
DTI	The debt-to-income ratio at time of origination is based on (i) the sum of the borrower's monthly debt payments, including the mortgage payment divided by (ii) the total monthly income used to underwrite the mortgage
Original UPB	The unpaid principal balance (UPB) of the mortgage on the note date, rounded to the nearest $1000
LTV	This is the origination loan-to-value ratio. For a purchase mortgage loan, the ratio is obtained by dividing the original mortgage loan amount by the lesser of the property's appraised value or its purchase price. For a refinance, the original loan amount is divided by the property's appraised value. For some acquired seasoned mortgages, the property value used in the LTV calculation is based on a new appraisal value. The LTV is in percent
Property type	Denotes whether the property type secured by the mortgage is a condominium, leasehold, Planned Unit Development (PUD), cooperative share, manufactured home, or single-family home. If unknown, this field is set to a missing value code
Loan purpose	Indicates whether the mortgage loan is a cash-out refinance mortgage, no cash-out refinance mortgage, or a purchase mortgage
Number of borrowers	The number of borrowers who are obligated to repay the mortgage note secured by the mortgaged property

TABLE 4.2 Used Time-Varying Variables in Freddie Mac's Databases

Name	Description
Current UPB	The current actual UPB reflects the mortgage ending balance as reported by the servicer for the corresponding monthly reporting period and includes any scheduled and unscheduled principal reductions applied to the mortgage. For mortgages with loan modifications (as indicated by "Y" in the modification flag field) the current actual UPB may include partial principal forbearance. The current actual UPB is missing for the first 6 months after the origination date
Loan age	The number of months since the note origination month of the mortgage
Zero balance codes	Loans may become inactive in the dataset for a variety of reasons, including voluntary payoffs or credit events, known as "termination events." The termination events along their zero balance codes are prepayment (voluntary payoff) or maturity (01), 180-day delinquency or D180 (97), third-party sale prior to D180 (02), short sales prior to D180 (03), deed in lieu of foreclosure prior to D180 (04), repurchased prior to D180 (06), and REO acquisition prior to D180 (08)
Zero balance effective date	Date on which the loan's balance was reduced to zero, due to a termination event
Current interest rate	Reflects the current interest rate on the mortgage note, taking into account any loan modifications. The current mortgage rate is in percent
PMMS rate	This is the average mortgage rate from the "Freddie Mac's" Primary Mortgage Market Survey (PMMS). Each week Freddie Mac surveys lenders on the rates and points for their most popular 30-year fixed-rate mortgage for first-lien prime conventional conforming mortgages with a loan to value of 80%. Currently, about 125 lenders are surveyed each week and the mix of lender types – thrifts, credit unions, commercial banks, and mortgage lending companies – is roughly proportional to the level of mortgage business that each type commands nationwide. The PMMS rate is in percent (Source: http://www.freddiemac.com/pmms/)
HPI	This is the state-level house price appreciation from the Freddie Mac House Price Index (FMHPI). The FMHPI is based on an ever-expanding database of loans purchased by either Freddie Mac or Fannie Mae. (Source: http://www.freddiemac.com/finance/fmhpi/)

rates and to house price appreciation. The refinance incentive is based on rate data from Freddie Mac's Primary Mortgage Market Survey (PMMS) for 30-year fixed-rate mortgages. The House Price Index (HPI) used to calculate MTMTLTV is the Freddie Mac House Price Index (FMHPI^{SM}), which provides monthly values for each of the 50 states and the District of Columbia. These variables are described in Table 4.2.

This dataset is clean relative to most mortgage data, and most of the data fields do not appear to have outlier observations. We note, however, that in some cases, the values of some observations are not consistent with current practices in the market and are treated as data errors. LTV ratios below 6% or greater than 105% are set to missing. Some CLTV are too extreme to be consistent with current market practices and are corrected. Specifically, if the calculated CLTV is less than zero or greater than 200, but the LTV is greater than 80 and less than or equal to 200, then the CLTV is set equal to the LTV. If instead the LTV is less than 80 or greater than 200 or unknown, the CLTV is set to "unknown." If the CLTV is smaller than LTV, the CLTV is also set to "unknown." Also the DTI is set to missing if it is greater than 65% in the raw data.

Both the prepayment event and the credit event in the competing risk model are based on the data field "zero balance code." If this data field is equal to "01," then the loan's balance was reduced to zero because it is either prepaid or matured, indicating a voluntary payoff. A credit event occurred with the mortgage loan if this data field is equal to "97" (180-day delinquency or D180), "02" (third-party sale prior to D180), "03" (short sale or short payoff prior to D180), "04" (deed in lieu of foreclosure prior to D180), and "08" (REO acquisition prior to D180).

4.4.1.2 Model and Estimation Results We estimate a competing risk Cox model as described in Section 4.3.2.[14] Table 4.3 describes all of the variables in the competing risk model. The first column of this table indicates whether the covariate is present in the prepayment or in the default hazard function. The majority of the covariates are in both the prepayment and in the default hazards, with the exception of house price appreciation in the last 12 months (HPA12), the refinance incentive (REFI_INC), and the two variables that accommodate nonlinear relationships between the probability of refinance and the incentive to refinance (REFI_INC_SP0 and REFI_INC_SP1).

In addition to these variables, the MTMTLTV also varies through time. This variable is an estimation of the total LTV at time *t*. To build this variable, we use the origination CLTV, the change in the house price appreciation index between the origination and

TABLE 4.3 Description of Covariates in the Competing Risk Model

Default (D) or prepay (P)	Covariate	Description
D and P	CNT_BORR	1 in case of one borrower. The baseline is 2
D and P	CNT_UNITS	Assume values from 1 to 4 units. The baseline case is 1 – single-family detached home
D and P	FICO	FICO score reported in the mortgage
P only	HPA12	HPI appreciation in the last 12 months
D and P	LOAN_PURPOSE	C (cash-out refinance), N (non-cash-out refinance). The base case is P (purchase)
D and P	MTMTLTV	This is the total loan to value of a given mortgage loan based on the estimate of the property value at time *t* and the total unpaid principal balance of mortgages on the property at *t*. Specifically, the MTMTLTV is $(HPI_0/HPI_t) \times (UPB_t/UPB_0) \times CLTV_0$ where time 0 refers to time of origination and UPB is the unpaid principal balance of the first mortgage lien
D and P	MTMTLTV100	$\text{MAX}(MTMTLTV - 100, 0)$
D and P	MTMTLTV120	$\text{MAX}(MTMTLTV - 120, 0)$
D and P	OCCPY_STS	Occupancy status is I (investment property) and S (second home). The base case is (O) owner-occupied
D and P	PROP_TYPE	Property type is C (condominium), CP (cooperative share), LH (leasehold), MH (manufacture home), and PU (planned unit development). The base case is single-family home (S)
P only	REFI_INC	Difference between rate on the mortgage note and the current PMMS rate
P only	REFI_INC_SP0	$\text{MAX}(REFI\_INC, 0)$
P only	REFI_INC_SP1	$\text{MAX}(REFI\_INC - 1, 0)$
D and P	VDTI	VDTI is equal to debt-to-income (DTI) ratio of the borrower when DTI is not missing from the database and zero otherwise
D and P	ZDTI	ZTI is equal to one when DTI is missing and zero otherwise

[14]The model that we estimate does not deal with curtailments. See Janowiak (2013) for an example of how to model curtailments in a competing risk framework.

time t, and the outstanding balance in the mortgage loan. Specifically, the denominator of the total LTV at time t – the property value at t – is obtained from the property value at origination appreciated by the change in the HPI between the origination and time t. The numerator of the total LTV at time t is the sum of the outstanding principal balance at time t and an estimate of the outstanding principal balance of any additional mortgage(s) on the property. The principal balance of the additional mortgage(s) at time t is assumed to amortize in the proportion to the amortization on the first lien.

We also add two variables that are functions of the MTMTLTV. These variables are MTMTLTV100 and MTMTLTV120, and they vary over the life of a mortgage. They are added to the model to accommodate a nonlinear relationship between MTMTLTV and the probability of default or prepayment.

In addition to these time-varying covariates, we also add a series of covariates to the model that aim to capture heterogeneity on borrowers' behavior with respect to the probability of default or prepayment. Borrowers' behavior can be inferred from a series of variables that are collected at the origination of the mortgage. For instance, borrowers are more likely to default on investment properties than they are on their primary residences. As a result, we include occupancy status at time of origination in the model.[15]

The results of the prepayment model estimation are in Table 4.4.[16] Overall, the signs of the estimated parameters in this table conform to our intuition regarding when homeowners are more likely to refinance. For instance, the point estimate of 0.00186 for the parameter on FICO score implies that a one point increase in FICO score results in an increase in the prepay hazard by a factor of approximately 0.00186. To see this, note that in the Cox model, the prepayment hazard is given by $[h_0^P(t) \times \exp\ (\beta^P \times Y_t)]$, hence an increase in Y of one unit results in a new hazard which is approximately $[h_0^P(t) \times \exp\ (\beta^P \times Y_t)] \times (1 + \beta^P)$. In addition, the nonlinear relationship between the prepayment hazard and the refinancing incentive also conforms to the S-shape relationship between refinancing incentive and prepayment speed. Indeed, for negative refinancing speed, the prepayment hazard is slightly increasing with refinancing incentive (the coefficient on *REFI_INC* is 0.5773); for refinancing incentive above zero and below one, the coefficient on *REFI_INC* is effectively (0.5773 + 0.75307); and for refinancing incentive above one, the coefficient on *REFI_INC* is effectively (0.5773 + 0.75307 − 1.22008).

Figure 4.8 shows the estimated prepayment baseline hazard function. This function is plotted from 0 to 130 months for two reasons: first, the STACR deal has only 120 months to maturity; hence we do not need to go up to the maturity of the loans to

TABLE 4.4 Prepayment Model Estimation Results

Covariate (Y)	β^P	Standard error	Chisquare	p-Value
MTMTLTV	−0.00424	0.0001017	1739.6395	<0.0001
MTMTLTV100	−0.02184	0.0007284	899.0944	<0.0001
MTMTLTV120	0.01788	0.00122	213.139	<0.0001
HPA12	3.13049	0.0209	22435.3635	<0.0001
CNT_BORR 1	−0.27512	0.00351	6148.8248	<0.0001
CNT_UNITS 2	−0.2231	0.01603	193.819	<0.0001
CNT_UNITS 3	−0.18873	0.0388	23.6535	<0.0001
CNT_UNITS 4	−0.10633	0.03994	7.0881	0.0078
VDTI	0.0005545	0.0001484	13.9721	0.0002
ZDTI	0.0355	0.01307	7.3736	0.0066
FICO	0.00186	0.000032	3376.266	<0.0001
REFI_INC	0.5773	0.01144	2545.5273	<0.0001
REFI_INC_SP0	0.75307	0.01613	2181.0845	<0.0001
REFI_INC_SP1	−1.22008	0.00884	19052.3496	<0.0001
LOAN_PURPOSE C	−0.18074	0.00436	1714.9616	<0.0001
LOAN_PURPOSE N	−0.05351	0.00413	167.6853	<0.0001
OCCPY_STS I	−0.6808	0.00894	5793.4589	<0.0001
OCCPY_STS S	−0.33721	0.0101	1115.1773	<0.0001
PROP_TYPE CO	−0.03612	0.00668	29.205	<0.0001
PROP_TYPE CP	−0.43894	0.03381	168.5361	<0.0001
PROP_TYPE LH	−0.3372	0.09368	12.9554	0.0003
PROP_TYPE MH	−0.9847	0.0343	824.1923	<0.0001
PROP_TYPE PU	0.02573	0.00465	30.5652	<0.0001

[15]Practitioners typically include additional variables in their prepayment models such as loan age interactions with certain variables (e.g., refinance incentive). They also normally include additional variables in their default model such as the mortgage spread over the market rate at origination, measures of recent local house price changes, and interactions of LTV with other variables (e.g., FICO score).

[16]We estimate this model with SAS, but statistical packages such as Stata also have functions to estimate this type of model.

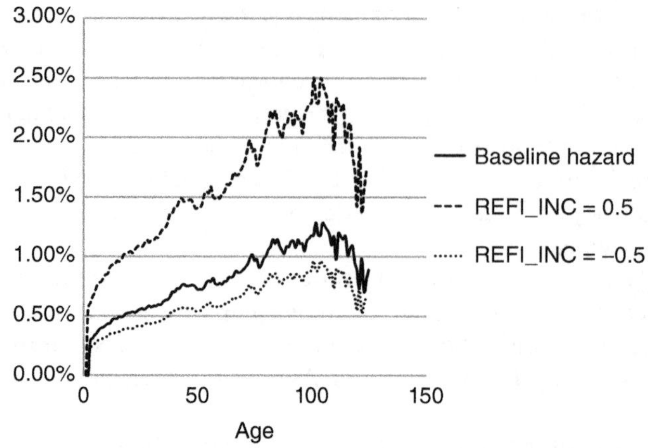

Figure 4.8 The estimated prepayment baseline hazard function. It also shows how the prepayment baseline hazard function is shifted with a movement of 50 basis points on refinancing incentive.

TABLE 4.5 Default Model Estimation Results

Covariate (X)	β^D	Standard error	Chisquare	p-Value
MTMTLTV	0.04573	0.0004823	8990.6348	<0.0001
MTMTLTV100	−0.01975	0.00136	211.1051	<0.0001
MTMTLTV120	−0.00922	0.00141	42.7017	<0.0001
CNT_BORR 1	0.53282	0.01195	1988.8454	<0.0001
CNT_UNITS 2	0.26727	0.04017	44.2605	<0.0001
CNT_UNITS 3	0.25757	0.11124	5.3613	0.0206
CNT_UNITS 4	0.23804	0.1185	4.0349	0.0446
VDTI	0.0191	0.0005284	1307.0499	<0.0001
ZDTI	0.97979	0.04309	517.0546	<0.0001
FICO	−0.01016	0.0001037	9596.0728	<0.0001
LOAN_PURPOSE C	0.54927	0.01389	1564.7973	<0.0001
LOAN_PURPOSE N	0.35309	0.01552	517.5914	<0.0001
OCCPY_STS I	0.42587	0.0245	302.1772	<.0001
OCCPY_STS S	−0.05626	0.03249	2.9974	0.0834
PROP_TYPE CO	−0.2999	0.02272	174.1777	<0.0001
PROP_TYPE CP	−0.60803	0.19265	9.9614	0.0016
PROP_TYPE LH	−0.19652	0.25839	0.5784	0.4469
PROP_TYPE MH	0.24536	0.04816	25.9539	<0.0001
PROP_TYPE PU	−0.05294	0.01804	8.6118	0.0033

analyze this deal. Second, the baseline hazard is very noisy after the loans become seasoned. In fact, some practitioners estimate the baseline hazard as a smooth version of the function plotted in Figure 4.8. Figure 4.8 shows the effect of seasoning on the likelihood of prepayment. The baseline hazard function steadily increases between the origination and about 100 months from the origination, at which point the baseline seems to move around a constant. A comparison between Figure 4.8 and the SMM scale in Figure 4.3 reveals that the seasoning effect that we observe in our data is of about the same magnitude as the one in the PSA standard.

Figure 4.8 also shows the effect that changes on the refinance incentive have on the likelihood of prepayment. To do so, this figure plots the baseline hazard prepay function shifted by the effect of an increase or of a decrease in REFI_INC equal to 50 basis points. Specifically, our model estimation implies that if REFI_INC increases by 50 basis points, the hazard function increases by a factor of exp $((0.5773 + 0.75307) \times 0.5)$, which is equal to 1.94. On the other hand, if REFI_INC decreases by 50 basis points, the hazard function is shifted by a factor of exp (0.5773×-0.5), which is equal to 0.75. Figure 4.8 also plots the baseline hazard prepay function shifted by these factors.

The results of the default model estimation are in Table 4.5. As in the prepayment model, the signs of the estimated parameters in this table also conform to our intuition. Figure 4.9 shows the default baseline hazard function. This figure shows a seasoning pattern on the likelihood of default. Indeed, the likelihood of default increases steadily up to about 40 months from origination

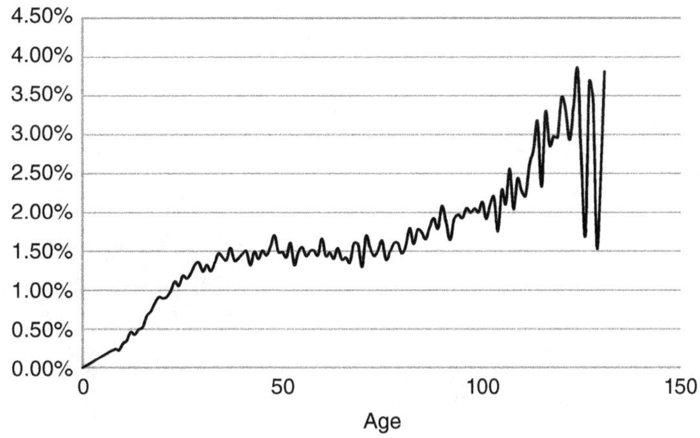

Figure 4.9 The estimated default baseline hazard function.

and then remains constant until about 80 months of origination, and at this point, it starts increasing steadily again. As in the case of prepayment, the baseline hazard function becomes very noisy after 120 months of origination.[17] In the analysis that we perform in Section 4.4.3, we use the baseline hazard function displayed in Figures 4.8 and 4.9 without applying any smoothing technique to it.

4.4.2 Freddie Mac's STACR

An important new class of an MRS was introduced in 2013. The GSEs, responding to supervisory requests, created instruments that would achieve credit risk sharing with private capital through Freddie Mac's STACR and Fannie Mae's C-deals. These bond issuances provide private investors the opportunity to take on a mezzanine slice of the credit risk of a diverse reference pool of GSE mortgages. This section will describe the general structure as well as specific aspects of these securities by providing detail on the first of these deals, the STACR Series 2013-DN1.

The STACR and C-deal mezzanine tranches are structured as a direct senior unsecured debt issuance but with repayments of principal subject to the credit and the prepayment performance of a reference pool of mortgages. This structure preserves the current role of the GSEs in providing credit enhancements in MBSs and the functioning of the to-be-announced (TBA) market,[18] but, at the same time, allows investors to take some of the credit risk of a diversified pool of mortgages securitized by the GSEs.

Figure 4.10 represents each of the tranches in the STACR Series 2013-DN1. The structure of these securities includes mezzanine (M) bonds sold to investors, as well as "reference" tranches (A-H, M1-H, M2-H, and B-H classes) that are utilized to define cash flows for the mezzanine securities. The reference tranches are not issued as debt and do not receive any actual cash flows; their only purpose is to determine cash flows to the issued mezzanine tranches. One way to conceptualize the reference tranches is to imagine that they are retained in Freddie Mac's portfolio. The reference tranches are represented in gray in Figure 4.10, while the traded tranches are represented in black. The reference securities M1-H and M2-H have notional principal cash flows and write-downs identical to those of the mezzanine bonds M1 and M2. As Figure 4.10 shows, the B-H reference tranche absorbs the first losses due to credit events in the reference pool. That is, Freddie Mac retains a first-loss position up to this specified limit. The mezzanine tranches (M1, M1-H, M2, and M2-H) absorb the losses due to credit events in the reference pool beyond the first-loss position up to some ceiling. Finally, in this design, the reference senior CT A-H absorbs all the remaining losses.

Figure 4.11 presents the pricing of the STACR Series 2013-DN1 (the first STACR deal). Interest payments on the mezzanine tranches are tied to the 1-month LIBOR rate. Pricing for the M-1 class was 1 month LIBOR plus a spread of 340 basis points. Pricing for the M-2 class was the 1 month LIBOR plus a spread of 715 basis points. The origination principal amounts of the M-1 and M-2 classes were 250 million. In the case of STACR Series 2013-DN1, the B-H tranche absorbs the first 0.30% of credit losses. This is the initial subordination of the M2 tranche. The mezzanine tranches (M1, M1-H, M2, and M2-H) absorb the losses due to credit events in the reference pool beyond the first-loss position up to 2.70%, resulting in an initial subordination for the A-H tranche of 3% (0.3% + 2.7%). Finally, the reference senior credit tranche A-H absorbs all the remaining losses.

[17]Some of the patterns of the baseline functions in Figures 4.8 and 4.9 do not conform with typical baseline functions. For instance, the baseline prepayment function in Figure 4.8 is not as flat after 3 years as a typical prepayment hazard baseline function. This may be a result of the studied sample, which contains loans that are eligible for the HARP refinance program. This program allows loans originated before May 2009 to refinance even though their current LTV ratios would typically have been a barrier to their refinancing. For the evaluation of loans originated after 2009, HARP-eligible loans would likely be excluded from the model calibration.

[18]The TBA market is the main market in which agency MBSs are traded. See Biby, Modukuri, and Hargrave (2001) for a review of this market.

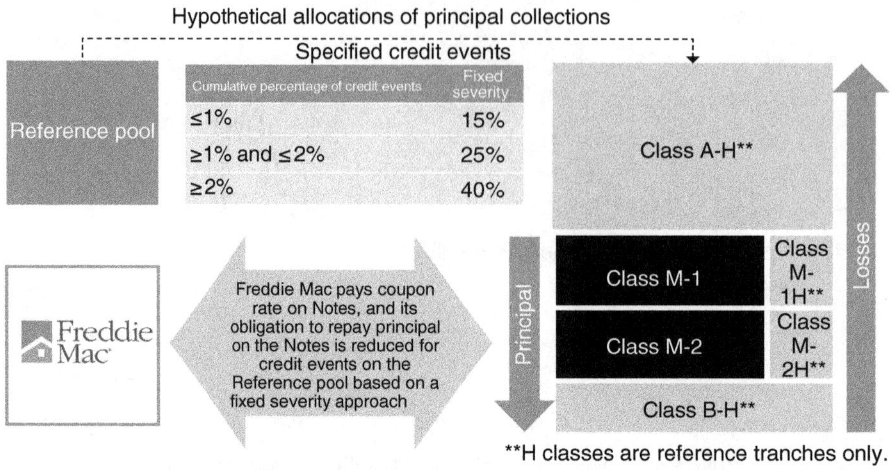

Figure 4.10 The structure of the STACR Series 2013-DN1. Part of this picture is from STACR Series 2013-DN1 prospectus. Source: Reproduced with permission of Freddie Mac.

The reference pool of mortgages in the STACR Series 2013-DN1 had an aggregate, UPB of $22,584,361,520 as of June 15, 2013, and represents a broad diversified pool of 30-year fixed-rate loans. Freddie Mac acquired the mortgages in the reference pool between July 1, 2012, and September 30, 2012, and securitized them into PCs by January 31, 2013, where they remained until July 2, 2013. All the 96,389 mortgages in the reference pool meet an eligibility criterion that includes the requirements (among many other requirements) that the mortgage must be a fully amortizing, fixed-rate mortgage with an original term of 30 years and that the mortgage has an original LTV greater than 60% and smaller than 80%. Table 4.6 summarizes some of the characteristics of the mortgages in the reference pool.

A mortgage in the reference pool suffers a "credit event" if any of the following occurs: (i) the mortgage is 180 days delinquent or greater[19]; (ii) a short sale is settled; (iii) the related mortgage note is sold to a third party during the foreclosure process; (iv) a deed-in-lieu of foreclosure is executed; or (v) there is an REO acquisition. For the purpose of calculating credit losses, only one credit event for each mortgage in the credit pool can occur.

As we pointed out above, the expected credit loss in mortgages is a function of the probability of a credit event (e.g., 180-day delinquency) and of the actual credit loss given the credit event. It is relatively straightforward to gauge whether a credit event occurred, since it is normally just a matter of understanding whether a homeowner is sufficiently delinquent on his/her mortgage. On the other hand, it takes some time to quantify the actual loss given a credit event. This is because the actual loss due to a credit event can only be assessed after the creditor takes the necessary steps to recover the credit losses. The legal process for such steps may take years, since (in case of mortgages) it may involve foreclosing and attempting to sell the property. Moreover, a fraction of the loans that reach 180-day delinquency subsequently recover and become current.

As a result of the lengthy process needed to assess the actual credit losses of a mortgage portfolio, the STACR Series 2013-DN1 uses a proxy of the loss severity given a credit event to calculate the credit losses of the reference pool of mortgages. Specifically, the applicable loss severity (ALS) is assumed to be a step function:

$$ALS = \begin{array}{l} 15\% \text{ if } CNCEP < 1\% \\ 25\% \text{ if } 1\% < CNCEP < 2\% \\ 40\% \text{ if } CNCEP > 2\% \end{array} \tag{4.13}$$

where *CNCEP* is the cumulative net credit event percentage. The *CNCEP* at a given date is the sum of the UPB that suffered a credit event after the cutoff date (here, June 25,2013) divided by the total balance of the reference pool at the cutoff date (here, approximately $22 billion).[20]

For the purpose of defining cash flows for the STACR securities, the write-down amount in the reference pool in a given month is assumed to be equal to the product:

$$write\_down_t = ALS_t \times UPB\_suffered\_credit\_event_t \tag{4.14}$$

[19]Note that the STACR specifies 180 delinquency as a credit event, while Fannie and Freddie remove a mortgage from an MBS pool after 120 delinquency.

[20]The actual calculation of the ALS is slightly more complicated than the one in the step function above. The actual calculation is a weighted average of 15%, 25%, and 40%, where the weights are a function of the CNCEP in the previous month and in the current month. See the STACR Series 2013-DN1 prospectus for further detail.

Classes of Reference Tranches	Initial Class Notional Amount	Initial Subordination (1)
Class A-H	$ 21,906,830,673	3.00%
Class M-1 and Class M-1H(2)	$ 304,888,881(2)	1.65%(3)
Class M-2 and Class M-2H(4)	$ 304,888,881(4)	0.30%(5)
Class B-H	$ 67,753,085	0.00%

(1) Represents the initial subordination and initial credit enhancement of such Class or Classes of Reference Tranches, which is equal to the percentage of the Cut-off Date Balance of the Reference Pool represented by the aggregate initial Class Notional Amount of the Class or Classes of Reference Tranches subordinate to the subject Class or Classes of Reference Tranches.

(2) Pursuant to the hypothetical structure, the Class M-1 and Class M-1H Reference Tranches are *pro rata* with each other. The initial Class Notional Amount shown is the aggregate amount for the Class M-1 and Class M-1H Reference Tranches combined. The initial Class Notional Amount of the Class M-1 Reference Tranche is $250,000,000 (which corresponds to the initial Class Principal Balance of the Class M-1 Notes) and the initial Class Notional Amount for the Class M-1H Reference Tranche is $54,888,881.

(3) Represents the initial subordination and credit enhancement available to the Class M-1 and Class M-1H Reference Tranches in the aggregate.

(4) Pursuant to the hypothetical structure, the Class M-2 and Class M-2H Reference Tranches are *pro rata* with each other. The initial Class Notional Amount shown is the aggregate amount for the Class M-2and Class M-2H Reference Tranches combined. The initial Class Notional Amount of the Class M-2 Reference Tranche is $250,000,000 (which corresponds to the initial Class Principal Balance of the Class M-2 Notes) and the initial Class Notional Amount for the Class M-2H Reference Tranche is $54,888,881.

(5) Represents the initial subordination and credit enhancement available to the Class M-2 and Class M-2H Reference Tranches in the aggregate.

Class of Notes	Initial Class Coupon	Class Coupon Formula
M-1	3.59003%	One-Month LIBOR + 3.40%
M-2	7.34003%	One-Month LIBOR + 7.15%

Figure 4.11 The pricing of the STACR Series 2013-DN1. This picture is from STACR Series 2013-DN1 prospectus. Source: Reproduced with permission of Freddie Mac.

TABLE 4.6 Characteristics of the STACR Series 2013-DN1 Reference Pool

Number of reference obligations	96,389
Aggregate principal balance ($)	22,584,361,520.38
Average principal balance ($)	234,304
Weighted average mortgage rate (%)	3.838
Nonzero weighted average original credit score	766
Weighted average original LTV ratio (%)	75
Nonzero weighted average original CLTV (%)	76
Weighted average loan age as of the cutoff date (months)	10
Nonzero weighted average DTI	32%
Occupancy-type aggregate principal balance (%)	
Owner-occupied	89.24
Second home	5.46
Investment property	5.3
Loan purpose aggregate principal balance (%)	
No cash-out refinance	42.69
Purchase	39.98
Cash-out refinance	17.34
Type of property aggregate principal balance (%)	
1–4-Family dwelling unit	71.06
PUD	23.78
Condo	4.88
Manufactured housing	0.14
Coop	0.08
Leasehold	0.06

The write-down amount (which serves as a proxy for credit losses) is applied to reduce the notional value of the bonds sequentially. Write-downs are applied in a waterfall structure starting with the most subordinate class (the B-H class), then, after this class is extinguished, reducing the notional value of the mezzanine classes, and, after these are extinguished, finally reducing the notional value of most senior class (A-H). There is also a sequential allocation of write-down amounts within the mezzanine classes, with the write-downs applying first to the M-2 class, followed by the M-1 class. This tiered severity allows for a timely and predictable payment of expected losses (in contrast to waiting for the actual credit losses to be realized).

The amount recovered during a credit event is assumed to be equal to

$$Recovery_t = (1 - ALS_t) \times UPB\_suffered\_credit\_event_t \tag{4.15}$$

The recovery amount is applied to decrease the notional amount of the A-H class first. After the A-H class is completely paid off, the recovered amount is applied sequentially to the M1 (and M-1 H) class, to the M2 (and M-2H) class, and to the B-H class.

Principal payments on the underlying reference pool determine reductions in the notional amount. Both scheduled and unscheduled principal payments are paid to tranche holders, and the tranche notional amount is reduced accordingly.

The total scheduled principal payment of the reference pool is divided into components on a pro rata basis. The component that reduces the notional principal amount of the A-H class is equal to

$$Pool\_scheduled\_principal\_payment_t \times AHP_t \tag{4.16}$$

where AHP_t is the notional amount outstanding of the A-H class prior to the principal payment divided by the UPB of the reference pool. The component of the schedule principal that reduces the principal amount of the subordinated tranches (M1, M1-H, M2, M2-H, and B-H) is equal to

$$Pool\_scheduled\_principal\_payment_t \times (1 - AHP_t) \tag{4.17}$$

This component is applied first to the M1 (and M1-H) class until it is completely paid off, then to the M2 (and M2-H) class, and lastly to the B-H class.

As with the scheduled principal payments, the unscheduled principal payment of the reference pool, that is, the prepayment of the reference pool, is also divided among the A-H and the subordinated classes. However, the rules of distribution of these

TABLE 4.7 Time-Varying Threshold for the CNCEP

Payment date occurring in the period	Percentage
August 2013 to July 2014	0.25
August 2014 to July 2015	0.50
August 2015 to July 2016	0.75
August 2016 to July 2017	1.00
August 2017 to July 2018	1.25
August 2018 to July 2019	1.50
August 2019 to July 2020	1.75
August 2020 to July 2021	2.00
August 2021 to July 2022	2.25
August 2022 and thereafter	2.50

cash flows are different from those used to distribute the scheduled principal payments. The distribution of this principal to the tranches depends on a multipart test: if there are few credit events relative to thresholds, that is, if the current cumulative credit experience is relatively benign, then the prepayment cash flows are distributed exactly as the scheduled principal payment distribution described in the previous paragraph. Instead, if the default experience is not benign, then all of the principal payments flow sequentially, starting with the most senior class (A-H), then to the mezzanine classes (M), and finally to the most junior tranche, B-H. In the first STACR transaction (STACR 2013 DN1), the test specifications consisted of requirements that (i) the subordinate percentage remained greater than or equal to 3% and (ii) that the CNCEP does not exceed a time-varying threshold, as presented in Table 4.7.

4.4.3 Analyzing the STACR Series 2013-DN1

We are now in position to use our competing risk model to analyze different securities in the STACR Series. Specifically, we use our model to understand the effect that shocks to house prices and to interest rates have on the cash flows of different STACR securities.

We assume three different interest rate scenarios and five different house price appreciation scenarios. Armed with possible values for interest rates and for house price appreciation, we generate expected principal cash flows and defaults for each of the 96,389 mortgage loans in the STACR reference pool using the competing risk model in Tables 4.4 and 4.5 and in Figures 4.8 and 4.9. These expected cash flows are calculated for each month between the issuance and the maturity of the STACR Series 2013 DN-1 using Equation 4.12.

Once we have ascertained the expected prepayment, schedule principal, and defaulted UPB, we calculate the cash flows of each security in the STACR Series using the cash flow distribution rules explained in Section 4.4.2. Table 4.8 displays the percentage of each tranche principal that is written down as a result of credit losses under different scenarios. Each row shows a different interest rate scenario. The first row shows the scenarios in which the mortgage rate drops 100 basis point below the weighted average mortgage rate of the reference pool (2.838%), the second row shows scenarios in which the mortgage rate remains at 3.838%, and the third row shows scenarios in which the mortgage interest rate increases to 4.838%. Each column displays scenarios with different house price appreciation. The columns display scenarios in which house price appreciation varies from −10% to +10% per year.

The results in the first panel of Table 4.8 reveal that the reference tranche B-H suffers severe write-downs in most of the scenarios. This is natural given the small size of this first-loss tranche. The second panel shows the write-downs of the M2 tranche. The M2 losses are most severe in scenarios of deep housing depreciation. These losses are somewhat sensitive to interest rates. Indeed, for a given drop in house prices, the M2 write-downs are smaller in scenarios with low interest rates. This is expected given that the M2 tranche receives prepayment cash flows after M1 tranche is paid down. As in the case of the M2 tranche, the M1 losses are most severe in scenarios in which house prices drop and interest rates increase. The losses of the M1 tranche are much less severe than those of the M2 in low rate scenarios. The intuition for this result is clear since the M1 tranche receives principal cash flows before M2, and, as a result, the credit losses of M1 are less severe in scenarios with high refinancing activity. Finally, the last panel shows the write-downs of the reference tranche A-H. These write-downs are much smaller than those of the other tranches and are concentrated in scenarios of large house depreciation without interest rate drops.

Table 4.9 calculates the present values of the cash flows of the M1 and M2 tranches in different scenarios. Recall from Figure 4.11 that M1 tranche pays monthly coupons of 340 basis points above LIBOR, while M2 tranche pays 715 basis points above LIBOR. With this information and the principal amounts of M1 and M2, we calculate the interest cash flows for each of these bonds. For such calculation, we assume that LIBOR becomes zero in the case when the mortgage rate drops to 2.838%,

TABLE 4.8 Write-Downs under Different Rate and Housing Appreciation Scenarios (in Percentage of Principal)

		House price appreciation scenarios				
		−10%	−5%	0%	5%	10%
B-H						
	2.838	100	93	34	19	12
Mortgage rate scenarios	3.838	100	100	100	45	28
	4.838	100	100	100	74	39
M2						
	2.838	99	0	0	0	0
Mortgage rate scenarios	3.838	100	100	3	0	0
	4.838	100	100	28	0	0
M1						
	2.838	0	0	0	0	0
Mortgage rate scenarios	3.838	65	9	0	0	0
	4.838	75	58	0	0	0
AH						
	2.838	0	0	0	0	0
Mortgage rate scenarios	3.838	4	0	0	0	0
	4.838	8	1	0	0	0

TABLE 4.9 PV of M2 and M1 Cash Flows under Different Scenarios

		House price appreciation scenarios				
		−10%	−5%	0%	5%	10%
M2						
	2.838	0.47	1.27	1.17	1.14	1.12
Mortgage rate scenarios	3.838	0.27	0.49	1.44	1.34	1.29
	4.838	0.28	0.44	1.38	1.50	1.43
M1						
	2.838	1.11	1.03	1.02	1.02	1.02
Mortgage rate scenarios	3.838	0.49	1.09	1.06	1.05	1.04
	4.838	0.43	0.66	1.17	1.07	1.06

remains at 0.19% when mortgage rates are assumed to remain at the 3.838%, and becomes 1.19% when mortgage rates increase by 100 basis points to 4.838%. The present values are calculated for $1 of principal.

We discount all cash flows (interest plus principal) for the M1 and M2 tranches at the LIBOR rate to calculate the present values in Table 4.9. Naturally, the choice of discount rates should reflect the fact that these cash flows are risky. Recall however that risk-neutral evaluation implies that for pricing purposes, we can either adjust the discount rates or we can adjust the probabilities of each of the scenarios used for pricing. In fact, in Monte Carlo simulations used for pricing, risky cash flows are normally discounted at the risk-free rate, and the probabilities of each of the Monte Carlo scenarios are adjusted to account for risk. That is, Monte Carlo simulations rely on interest rate and house price paths generated under the risk-neutral measure. To get from the present values in Table 4.9 to a price for the M1 and M2 tranches, we would have to associate a probability for each of these scenarios. These probabilities would reflect a risk adjustment.

The results suggest that only in the most extreme scenarios are the present values of the cash flows smaller than 1. The intuition is clear; the interest cash flows of both M1 and M2 bonds compensate for the write-downs in these bonds, ameliorating the losses due to credit events.

4.5 SUMMARY

In this chapter, we explain some basic concepts related to MRSs. We also analyze a new type of agency MRS. Specifically, we estimate a competing risk model of prepayment and default to analyze the Freddie Mac's STACR Series 2013 DN-1.

Although we focus in only one security, the STACR Series 2013-DN1, our analysis can potentially be applied to other securities such as the Fannie Mae's C-deals. Both the Freddie Mac's STACR deals and Fannie Mae's C-deals are new types of instruments in which the GSEs, responding to supervisory requests, achieve risk sharing with private capital. Because of this, understanding the effects of prepayment and credit risk on these securities is important.

Moreover, the competing risk methodology we describe can be used in other contexts in which prepayment and default risk are present. For instance, it is possible to use this methodology to analyze private-label MRS and agency MRSs such as PCs and CMOs. Naturally, the choice of pricing methodology depends on many practical issues such as data availability and importance of different types of risk. The competing risk methodology however is quite general, and it takes into account the competing risk nature of default and prepayment on the determination of cash flows. Therefore, this methodology is a natural candidate as a pricing methodology in a large number of contexts.

REFERENCES

Biby J-D, Modukuri S, Hargrave B. Trading, settlement, and clearing procedures for agency MBS. In: Fabozzi FJ, editor. *The Handbook of Mortgage-Backed Securities*. New York: McGraw-Hill; 2001.

Downing C, Stanton R, Wallace N. An empirical test of a two-factor mortgage valuation model: how much do house prices matter? Real Estate Econ 2005;33:681–710.

Duarte J. The causal effect of mortgage refinancing on interest-rate volatility: empirical evidence and theoretical implications. Rev Financ Stud 2006;21:1689–1731.

Hayre L, Young R. Anatomy of prepayments: the Salomon smith barney prepayment model. In: Hayre L, editor. *Salomon Smith Barney Guide to Mortgage-Backed and Asset-Backed Securities*. New York: John Wiley & Sons; 2001.

Janowiak J. Curtailment in Interest-Only Mortgages. Freddie-Mac working paper; 2013.

Kalbfleisch JD, Prentice RL. *The Statistical Analysis of Failure Time Data*. 2nd ed. Hoboken (NJ): John Wiley & Sons; 2002.

Lam K, Dunsky R-M, Kelly A. Impacts of Down Payment Underwriting Standards on Loan Performance – Evidence from the GSEs and FHA portfolios. FHFA Working Papers, Working Paper 13-3; 2013.

Lunn M, McNeill D. Applying Cox regression to competing risks. Biometrics 1995;51:524–532.

Merton RC. On the pricing of corporate debt: the risk structure of interest rates. J Finance 1974;29:449–470.

Mortgage Research Group, Lehman Brothers. Collateralized mortgage obligations. In: Fabozzi FJ, editor. *The Handbook of Mortgage-Backed Securities*. New York: McGraw-Hill; 2001.

Veronesi P. *Fixed Income Securities: Valuation, Risk, and Risk Management*. New York: John Wiley & Sons; 2010.

PART II

Monetary Policy and Fixed Income Markets

5

Bond Markets and Monetary Policy

Andrea Buraschi[a] **and Paul Whelan**[b]

[a]*Department of Finance, Imperial College, London, United Kingdom*

[b]*Department of Finance, Copenhagen Business School, Copenhagen, Denmark*

5.1 INTRODUCTION

In the 1980s, under the chairmanship of Paul Volcker (1979–1987), the Federal Reserve dropped the federal funds rate as its operating target and introduced a commitment to control the growth rate of money (narrow M1 and M2 aggregates) by adopting a nonborrowed reserves operating target. The economic context of Volcker's appointment was one of high inflation and financial instability as a consequence of the first (1973) and second (1979) oil shocks. To tackle inflation, Volcker adopted procedures that were inspired by the quantity theory of money. This theory argues that inflation is fundamentally determined by the growth rate of money supply and that the demand for money, as reflected by its velocity, is a stable function of nominal income and interest rates. Volcker is largely accredited with quashing inflation, which dropped 8.5% between 1981 and 1987; however, the administration was criticized for inducing a prolonged recession. The general concern was that a policy targeting monetary aggregates created too much interest rate volatility and uncertainty for business borrowers.[1] In 1987, the Federal Open Market Committee (FOMC) abandoned a target for M1 growth and in 1993 the Federal Reserve publicly acknowledged the "downgrading" of its M2 target. Since the early 1990s, and until the 2008 financial crisis, the main policy tool of the FOMC has been a nominal interest rate target.

The FOMC consists of 12 members and holds 8 regularly scheduled meetings per year.[2] At these meetings, the FOMC committee reviews economic and financial conditions in order to determine the appropriate monetary policy stance, which is then (conventionally) implemented by setting the federal funds target rate. The federal funds rate is the interest rate at which depository institutions trade balances held at the Federal Reserve (the Fed) with each other, usually overnight, on an uncollateralized basis. U.S. banks and thrift institutions are obligated by law to maintain a certain level of reserves either as deposits with the Fed or as vault cash. The level of these reserves is determined by the outstanding assets and liabilities of each depository institution, as well as by the Fed itself, but is typically 10% of the total value of the bank's demand accounts (depending on bank size). Institutions with surplus balances in their accounts lend those balances to institutions in need of larger balances. The effective federal funds rate is a weighted average of all federal funds transactions for a group of federal funds brokers who report to the

[1] Milton Friedman, once a supporter of this policy framework, eventually stated that "The use of quantity of money as a target has not been a success." He added: "I'm not sure I would as of today push it as hard as I once did" (Financial Times, June 7, 2003).

[2] The 12 members consist of 7 members of the Board of Governors, the President of the Federal Reserve Bank of New York, and 4 rotating members from 1 of the 11 Reserve Bank presidents.

Handbook of Fixed-Income Securities, First Edition. Edited by Pietro Veronesi.

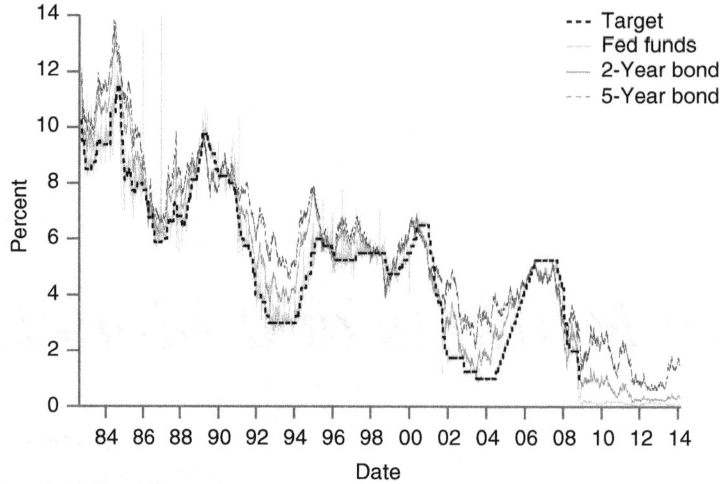

Figure 5.1 Treasury yields. This figure plots the time series of the Federal funds target rate, the Fed funds effect rate, and Treasury yields for 2-year and 5-year maturities. The sample period is from 1982 to 2014. Source: Federal Reserve Economic Data (FRED) at St. Louis Fed.

Federal Reserve Bank of New York each day. It is the outcome of negotiation between banks and should be distinguished from the target rate, which is set by the FOMC and enforced by open market operations.

The effective federal funds rate generally lies within a range of the target rate, as the Fed cannot set an exact value through open market operations. Figure 5.1 shows the evolution over time of the target rate, the federal funds rate, and Treasury yields at 2-year and 5-year maturities.

Three results emerge. First, the target is persistent, which the literature often refers to as interest rate smoothing. Moreover, target changes are often followed by additional changes in the same direction, which the literature often refers to as policy inertia.[3] Second, cycles of monetary policy easing are associated with large spreads between long-term and short-term interest rates. As the target rate is lowered during recessions, the short-term treasury rate tracks its path (the short end is procyclical) while the spread between long and short maturity bond yields often moves in the opposite direction (the term premium is countercyclical). Third, there exists a large high-frequency volatility component in short-term interest rates spreads over the target rate. Indeed, Fama (2013) reports that in the period 1982–2012, the volatility of the spread between the federal funds rate and the target rate was 0.21 bp, which should be compared to a volatility of federal funds rate changes equal to 0.28 bp and an average spread over this period equal to 0.04 bp. Fama (2013) estimates an error correction specification and argues that "the day-to-day variation in rates for maturities of a month or more has little or nothing to do with the Fed target rate." He interprets the result as evidence either of a passive Fed that largely moves the target rate as a consequence of the dynamics of existing market rates or of an active Fed that can control interest rates but whose actions are predictable in advance by the market. Indeed, Fama (2013) reports that if one considers FOMC announcements in which the Fed changed the target rate, the lagged commercial paper rate can explain 83% of the variance of changes in the target rate. When the Fed changes the target rate, it moves strongly toward existing (market) short rates. Moreover, while market rates do react to unexpected changes in the target rate, the effect on long-term bonds is rather limited. While all rates display a significant amount of correlation with the federal funds rate, a closer inspection raises the question of whether it is the federal funds rate that causes long-term yields or the other way around.

This evidence summarizes the challenges that an extensive literature has tried to address in investigating the link between the dynamics of bond yields and monetary policy. A stream in this literature uses high-frequency information in event time to help identifying monetary policy shocks. This literature uses FOMC announcements to identify shocks to market participant's expectations about the current and future monetary policy stance.[4] In this chapter, we investigate this literature and review the empirical evidence on the link between monetary policy shocks and bond markets.

5.2 HIGH-FREQUENCY IDENTIFICATION OF MONETARY POLICY SHOCKS

Empirically, measuring the actions of monetary policy is a challenging task. An important source of difficulty is related to the fact that a significant component of policy actions reflects the systematic response of the policy instrument to the

[3] See for a discussion Goodfriend (2001).

[4] A second stream in this literature studies the low-frequency impact of monetary policy shocks. This literature investigates extensions of real business cycle models that explicitly include reaction functions of the central bank to the real economy and inflation.

macroeconomic environment, rather than exogenous policy shocks. In practice, researchers make identifying assumptions to be able to disentangle the systematic component from the monetary policy shock. Since expectations of Fed policy actions are not directly observable, several scholars have suggested alternative identification methods. For a long time, the common approach was to specify reduced-form vector autoregressive models and impose ad-hoc identification assumptions, as in Christiano, Eichenbaum, and Evans (1996) and Ang, Dong, and Piazzesi (2007), or to specify a structural model with a monetary sector, as in Bakshi and Chen (1996), Buraschi and Jiltsov (2005), and Buraschi and Jiltsov (2007). With both these approaches, however the dynamic properties of the resulting decomposition are highly dependent on the assumptions imposed to achieve identification.

A more recent literature emerged that took advantage of high-frequency information to identify the policy shocks in a model-free framework. Rudebusch (1998) uses federal funds futures data to decompose the federal funds rate into an expected target change and a shock. This approach assumes that the expectations hypothesis holds so that the futures rate is equal to the expected future spot rate. Cochrane and Piazzesi (2002) avoid the expectations hypothesis assumption and the orthogonalization problems of monthly vector autoregressions (VARs) by using daily data around FOMC announcements. They define a monetary shock as the change in the 1-month Eurodollar rate from just before to just after the target change. They find large and persistent responses of bond yields to these shocks: the 10-year yield rises by as much as 52 basis points to a 1% unexpected target change. A third approach is proposed by Kuttner (2001a), who uses daily data on federal funds futures prices to identify target rate surprises from the change in the current month futures rate scaled by a factor related to the number of days in the month affected by the change. He finds that bond yields' response to anticipated changes is essentially zero, while their response to unanticipated movements is large and highly significant. Fleming and Piazzesi (2005) uses the same approach of Kuttner (2001a) but take advantage of tick-by-tick data to more precisely characterize the response of yields to monetary policy shocks. They calculate surprises for 30-minute, 60-minute, and daily intervals around announcement and find that on average the impact of surprise components on yield changes is fairly modest. Interestingly, they document that the response depends on the slope of the term structure.

Gurkaynak, Sack, and Swanson (2005) compare different approaches in identifying monetary policy shocks. They argue that federal funds futures rates dominate all other market interest rates for predicting changes in the federal funds rate over horizons of several months. For horizons longer than a few months, they find that Eurodollar futures provide the most accurate proxy of monetary policy expectations. Hamilton (2009) reviews the time-series properties of daily changes in fed funds futures prices at 1- to 3-month horizons. He concludes that they provide an excellent measure of market's expectation of near-term changes in Fed policy. Bernanke and Kuttner (2005) use the estimation of monetary policy shocks obtained from high-frequency data to study the implications for equity returns. They find that an unanticipated cut to the Fed funds rate results in large positive shocks to the stock market. More recently, Basistha and Kurov (2013) document a large intraday response of energy futures prices to the surprise component of announcements.

In the following section, we adopt the approach proposed by Kuttner (2001a) to investigate and summarize the empirical evidence of monetary surprises and their links with the Treasury yield curve.

5.2.1 Learning About Monetary Policy Surprises

The Chicago Board of Trade (CBOT) began offering federal funds futures contracts in October 1988. Unlike T-bill futures contracts, where the contract is for the T-bill rate on a specific day, the federal funds futures contract is for the simple average of the daily effective federal funds rate during the month of the contract. The CBOT offers future contracts ranging from the current month to 24 months out. Contracts have a nominal value of \$5 million, and their settlement price is equal to 100 minus the average of the effective federal funds rate for the month of the contract. Hence, a market price of 96.5 for a 1-month contract on September 15 means that the current futures rate for October is 3.5 percent (100–96.5).

Kuttner (2001b) and Gurkaynak (2005) suggest a simple way to identify monetary policy surprises. Suppose that at time t the Fed has a planned FOMC meeting. The day before, at time $t-1$, the prevailing effective Fed funds rate is r_{t-1}^0 and the price of the front-month federal funds futures contract is f_{t-1}^0. Then, the equilibrium federal funds futures price is equal to the weighted average of the current effective rate and the expected Fed funds rate over the remaining life of the contract plus a risk premium η_{t-1}^0:

$$f_{t-1}^0 = \frac{d}{m} r_{t-1}^0 + \frac{m-d}{m} E_{t-1}\left[r_t^0\right] + \eta_{t-1}^0$$

where r_t^0 is the target rate announced after the FOMC meeting, d is the day of the month, and m is the number of days in the month. Since immediately after the FOMC announcement the price of the front-month contract is

$$f_t^0 = \frac{d}{m} r_{t-1}^0 + \frac{m-d}{m} r_t^0 + \eta_t^0$$

we can compute the surprise component $e_t^0 \equiv r_t^0 - E_{t-1} r_t^0$ as

$$e_t^0 = \frac{m}{m-d}\left[f_t^0 - f_{t-1}^0\right] - \frac{m}{m-d}\left[\eta_t^0 - \eta_{t-1}^0\right]$$

Assuming that over an interval of 1 day the risk premium variation $\frac{m}{m-d}\left[\eta_t^0 - \eta_{t-1}^0\right]$ is negligible, we can use the dynamics of Fed funds futures to identify the expected and unexpected components of target rate changes ($e_t^0 \simeq \frac{m}{m-d}\left[f_t^0 - f_{t-1}^0\right]$):

$$r_t^0 - r_{t-1}^0 = \underbrace{E_{t-1}(r_t^0 - r_{t-1}^0)}_{\text{Expected}} + \underbrace{e_t^0}_{\text{Unexpected}} \tag{5.1}$$

The first three columns of Table 5.1 report summary statistics for the change in the Fed funds rate, and the above decomposition of expected and unexpected components, for the sample period 1990.1 to 2008.6. We find that a large component of federal funds rate changes is anticipated by the market. Indeed, the variance of the expected component is 0.0457, while the variance of the unexpected component is 0.0353. We also find that during this period the mean unexpected change in federal funds rate has been negative, which implies that, on average, the Fed has surprised markets by reducing rates more aggressively than the market expected. This feature can be visualized by plotting the cumulative unexpected shocks over time. Indeed, since 1990 the overall cumulative unexpected shock in federal funds rates has been −5% (figure 5.3).

Our sample includes 164 FOMC meetings. The futures market predicted no change in the effective rate (or less than 10 bp) in 72 occasions. In 67 out of these 72 occasions, the Fed indeed did not change the target rate. The left panel of Figure 5.4 plots these events; the bold bars indicate those occasions in which future markets predicted no change while a change occurred. The futures market predicted a change in the effective rate (by at least 10 bp) in 92 occasions. In 66 out of these 92 cases, indeed the target rate was changed. However, in 26 of these meetings the FOMC decided to leave the rate unchanged. The right panel of Figure 5.4 shows these events; the bold bars indicate those occasions in which the future market predicted a change while a change did not occur. In 3 of these 66 occasions the future market forecasted the change with the wrong sign. The dates of these meetings are (i) 20-Dec-1991, (ii) 18-Apr-2001, and (iii) 17-Sep-2001. Interestingly, in all these events the type of forecasting error committed by the market was the same: future contracts were forecasting an increase in the rate while the FOMC decided to reduce the rate. All these events occurred during recessions. The evidence from the second event is quite revealing due to the magnitude of the forecasting error and its timing. March 2001 marks the end of an economic expansion period that, according to NBER, started in March 1991 and lasted exactly 10 years, the longest in the NBER's chronology. Nonetheless, on April 18,

TABLE 5.1 Summary Statistics

	Δr	$E[\Delta r]$	e^0	$\Delta FF3$	$\Delta E6$	$\Delta E9$	$\Delta E12$
Mean	−0.0259	0.0060	−0.0319	−0.0226	−0.0138	−0.0155	−0.0140
Var	0.0503	0.0457	0.0353	0.0079	0.0255	0.0202	0.0178

This table reports summary statistics for expected ($E[\Delta r]$) versus unexpected changes (e^0) in the front-month Federal funds futures rate, the change in the third-month contract, and the change in 6-, 9-, and 12-month Eurodollar rates. Our sample includes 164 FOMC meetings between 1990.1 and 2008.6. Source: Datastream (Fed funds and Eurodollar futures) and Federal Reserve Board (FOMC dates).

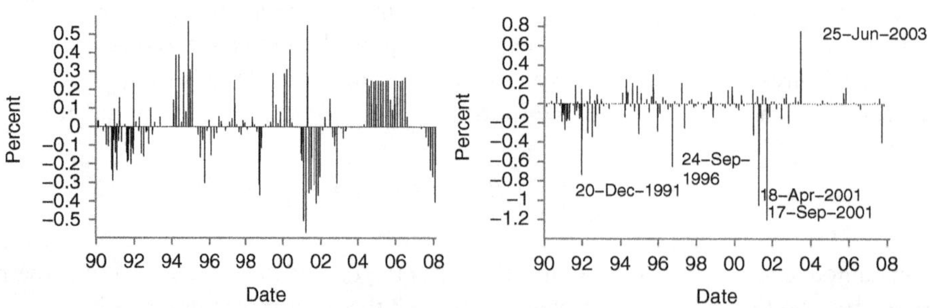

Figure 5.2 Expected versus unexpected changes. This figure plots expected (left panel) versus unexpected (right panel) changes in the front-month Federal funds futures around all FOMC meetings. The sample includes 164 FOMC meetings between 1990.1 and 2008.6. Source: Datastream (Fed funds and Eurodollar futures) and Federal Reserve Board (FOMC dates).

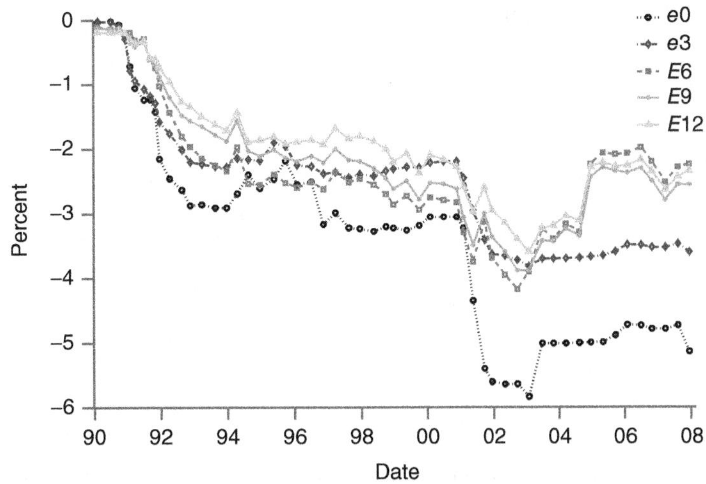

Figure 5.3 Cumulative shocks. This figure plots the cumulative sum of shocks to front- and third-month contract Federal funds futures ($e0$, $e3$) and 6-, 9-, and 12-month Eurodollar rates ($E6$, $E9$, $E12$).

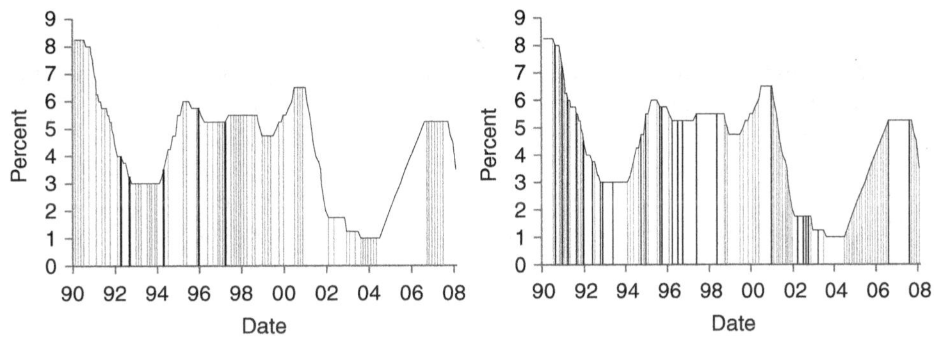

Figure 5.4 Futures predictions. This figure plots predicted changes by the future market. The left panel plots those events when the future markets predicted no change in the effective rate; the bold black bars indicate those occasions when a change *did* occurred. The right panel shows the occasions when future markets predicted a change; the bold black bars highlight those occasions when a change did actually *not* occur. Source: Datastream (Fed funds and Eurodollar futures) and Federal Reserve Board (FOMC dates).

2001, future markets were forecasting an increase of at least 50 basis points. Instead, the FOMC decided to drop the rate by 50 basis points to address the start of an economic recession. The forecast error committed around the September 17, 2001 FOMC event is more idiosyncratic in nature since it is related to an emergency meeting held by the Fed following the September 11 events when markets were closed.

In summary, the implied expected change in the target rate by the future market is remarkably accurate. However, we find that the average absolute magnitude of the unexpected component is significant and similar in size to the expected component.

5.2.2 The Impact on Treasury Bond Yields

The distinction between expected and unexpected components in the dynamics of federal funds rates becomes apparent when we investigate the link between Fed decisions and changes in Treasury bond yields. We use data on (implied) zero-coupon bond yields from January 1990 to June 2008 and regress the 1-day change in bond yields around FOMC announcements on the target changes. We use nominal and TIPS zero-coupon bonds estimated by Gurkaynak, Sack, and Wright (2006, 2010) (GSW) and short-term nominal interest rates with 3- and 6-month maturities from the Fama–Bliss T-bill files available from CRSP.[5] The results are summarized in Table 5.2. The top panel shows that most of the impact of the total change in Fed funds rates on Treasury yields is limited to maturities up to 1 year. After this maturity, the effect is somewhat muted and the slope coefficient is not statistically significant. However, when we decompose the total change in two components (bottom panel), one finds

[5]GSW construct zero-coupon yields by fitting the Nelson–Siegel–Svensson functional form to market quoted coupon bonds and is publicly available from the Federal Reserve Board site.

TABLE 5.2 FOMC Announcements: Expected versus Unexpected Changes

	Bill 3 m	Bill 6 m	1 yr	3 yr	5 yr	10 yr
			Panel A			
Δ target	0.20	0.16	0.11	0.05	0.02	−0.01
	(8.33)	(5.97)	(2.96)	(1.34)	(0.62)	(−0.38)
R^2	0.37	0.28	0.11	0.02	−0.00	−0.00
			Panel B			
$E[\Delta r]$	0.15	0.10	0.05	0.00	−0.02	−0.04
	(5.84)	(5.75)	(1.56)	(0.02)	(−0.73)	(−1.44)
e^0	0.30	0.29	0.22	0.15	0.11	0.04
	(6.15)	(5.50)	(3.70)	(2.52)	(2.23)	(1.12)
R^2	0.50	0.50	0.30	0.13	0.10	0.04

This table reports regressions of the daily change in {3, 6}-month bills rates, and {1, 3, 5, 10}-year zero-coupon rates on target changes (Panel A), and expected ($E[\Delta r]$) versus unexpected (e^0) components of the target change (Panel B). OLS t-stats are reported in parenthesis.
Source: Datastream (Fed funds and Eurodollar futures); Federal Reserve Board (FOMC dates); GSW dataset, Federal Reserve Board (Zero-coupon Treasury yields).

that unexpected changes are strongly significant in explaining changes in Treasury bond yields at maturities between 1 and 5 years. On the other hand, for these maturities the effect of the expected component is indistinguishable from noise. Thus, the reason raw target changes are not significant for longer maturities is due to the polluting effect of the expected component. This is confirmed by the substantially larger R^2 obtained when we run the regression on the two terms separately. In addition to statistical significance, the results show that at short maturities most of the magnitude of yield changes is due to unexpected variations in the target Fed funds rate. The marginal impact of the unexpected component on the 3-month T-bill rate is twice as large as the expected component.

5.2.3 The Timing of Expected Fed Interventions

The previous results show that on five occasions the futures market predicted no change in the target rate when in fact there was a change. Moreover, on three occasions the future markets predicted changes in target rates with the wrong sign. One possible interpretation is that markets may have forecasted incorrectly the timing of decisions that were relatively inevitable. Both Gurkaynak (2005) and Bernanke and Kuttner (2005) discuss this channel as a particularly important component to explain changes in medium and long-term bond yields as these are sensitive, not only to the target rate decided at the next FOMC meeting, but also to future policy decisions. To investigate this conjecture, Figure 5.5 plots unexpected changes in the front-month futures

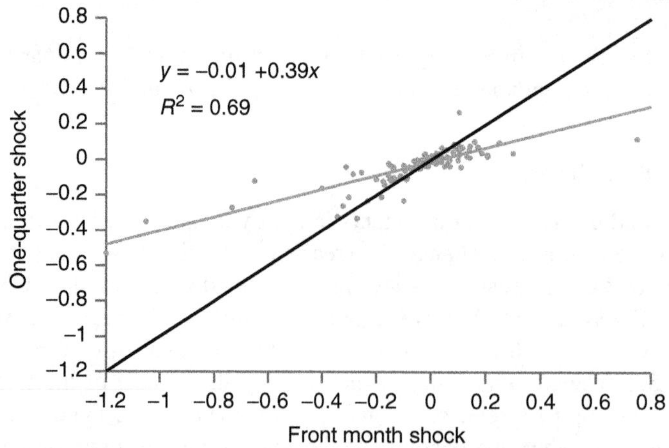

Figure 5.5 Futures predictions. This figure plots unexpected changes in the front-month futures contract (y-axis) with respect to changes in the one-quarter (third-month) contract (x-axis). The back line in the plot is the 45° lines; the gray line is the least squares fit. Source: Datastream (Fed funds futures) and Federal Reserve Board (FOMC dates).

contract (y-axis) with respect to changes in the one-quarter (third-month) contract (x-axis). The bold black line in the plot is the 45° lines; the gray line is the least squares fit. We find that the slope coefficient is far from unity. Moreover, for large positive front-month changes the least square fit is below the 45° line suggesting that the 3-month contract responds less than the front-month contract. Similarly, for large negative front-month changes, innovations in the 3-month contract plots above the 45° line. The R^2 of a linear regression is 70% suggesting that unexpected changes in the target rate obtained from the dynamics of the front-month future contract are not perfectly correlated with changes at longer horizons. A possible reason is that the market interprets the information content of FOMC decisions in the context of the timing of future policy decisions. While these decisions are useful signals, their information content to infer future target rate decisions likely depends in the state of the business cycle and the market surely looks at other signals, such as statements by policy makers.

Thus, in what follows we distinguish between two components of the change in the one-quarter contract. The first component is the unexpected change in the front-month contract as defined by Equation 5.1 (e^0); the second component, the "timing shock," is defined as the vertical distance of the data points from the 45° line in Figure 5.5 (e^{time}). Figure 5.6 summarizes some stylized features of "target" and "timing" shocks. We find that the economic magnitude of "timing" shocks is large and comparable to "target" shocks. Moreover, on several occasions, target and timing shocks are negatively correlated, moving in opposite directions.

This is a potentially important channel to explain the dynamics of long-term yields. To investigate this channel, we run a regression using the same data and sample period as in Table 5.2. Indeed, we find that the timing factor is as important as the target factor to explain variations in the Treasury bond market (see Table 5.3). Moreover, when we compare the R^2 of Table 5.2, Panel B, to those in Table 5.3, we find that the timing factor substantially increases the explanatory power for long-term bonds, with the R^2 for the 5-year note increasing from 10% to 17%.

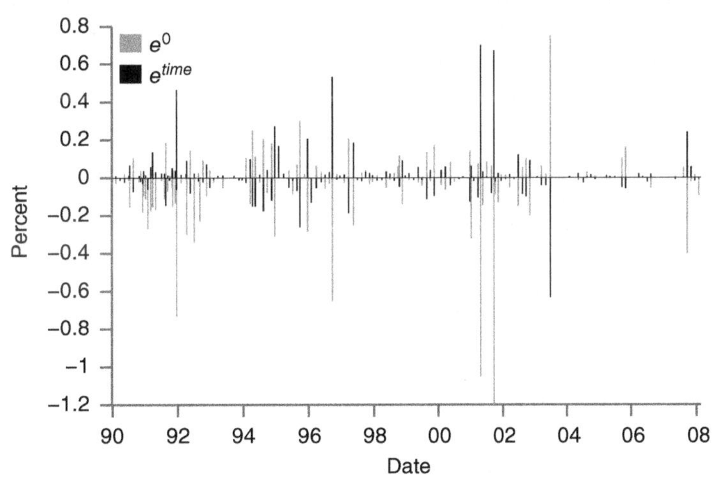

Figure 5.6 Level versus timing. This figure plots the time-series behavior of two components of the change in the one-quarter contract: (i) the "target" shock (e^0); (ii) the timing shocks are defined as the difference between the shock to the one-quarter contract and the target shock (e^{time}). Source: Datastream (Fed funds and Eurodollar futures); Federal Reserve Board (FOMC dates).

TABLE 5.3 FOMC Announcements: Timing versus Target

	Bill 3 m	Bill 6 m	1 yr	3 yr	5 yr	10 yr
e^0	0.55	0.60	0.50	0.44	0.36	0.22
	(5.70)	(6.34)	(4.38)	(3.62)	(3.16)	(2.44)
e^{time}	0.54	0.60	0.49	0.48	0.39	0.27
	(5.52)	(6.41)	(4.13)	(3.38)	(2.70)	(2.12)
R^2	0.46	0.59	0.40	0.23	0.17	0.07

This table reports regressions of the daily change in $\{3,6\}$-month bills rates, and $\{1,3,5,10\}$-year zero-coupon rates on target shocks (e^0) and timing shocks (e^{time}). OLS t-stats are reported in parentheses.

Source: Datastream (Fed funds and Eurodollar futures); Federal Reserve Board (FOMC dates); GSW dataset, Federal Reserve Board (Zero-coupon Treasury yields).

5.3 TARGET VERSUS PATH SHOCKS

Gurkaynak, Sack, and Swanson (2005) conjecture that the surprise component of target rate changes conveys only part of the news about monetary policy on announcement days: market participants update their beliefs by interpreting statements about monetary policy that give information about the path of future monetary decisions. Following this intuition the authors construct a "path factor" from high-frequency data that is, by construction, orthogonal to target shocks. Indeed, the important role played by the timing shocks suggests that monetary policy shocks may be characterized by different frequency components. To review this evidence more formally, we combine two datasets that include data containing information about policy expectations over the coming year. The first two time series provide information on futures on the front-month and 3-month-ahead Federal funds contracts. The remaining three time series include data on longer maturity Eurodollar futures contracts with maturities of two-, three-, and four-quarter ahead. At these maturities, Eurodollar futures are significantly more liquid than Federal fund futures contracts. Over a period of 12 months, there are eight scheduled FOMC meetings. Thus, these data include price information that is sensitive to the decisions in the following eight FOMC meetings. Figure 5.7 shows the magnitude of the five original shocks over time. It is apparent that in several occasions small shocks to the front-month future were contemporaneously associated to large shocks to longer dated futures (and vice versa).

We stack the shocks to these five contracts around each FOMC announcements in a $T \times 5$ matrix and perform a principal component decomposition. The decomposition of the variance explained by the first three principal components (PCs) F_t is summarized in Table 5.4. Indeed, we find that a single factor can only explain 62% of the total variance of the shocks to the term structure of futures rates around FOMC meeting. A second factor is needed to explain about 33% of the remaining variation across maturity. This is strongly suggestive of a multifrequency factor structure underlying the evolution of future monetary policy.

Since the identification of the principal components is only linked to their relative explanatory power for the overall variance, we do not have an interpretation of what the factors might be. To help economic understanding, following Gurkaynak, Sack, and Swanson (2005), we perform a rotation of the first two PCs. Let the original PCs $F_t = [PC_1, PC_2]$. We define the new rotated factors $Z_t = F_t U$, where the matrix U is such that Z_t^2 is orthogonal to the shocks to the front-month future, $E(Z_t^2 e_t^0) = 0$. Because this rotation generates a component that is orthogonal to e_t^0, we label the second factor ($e_t^{path} = Z_t^2$) as the "path" factor.

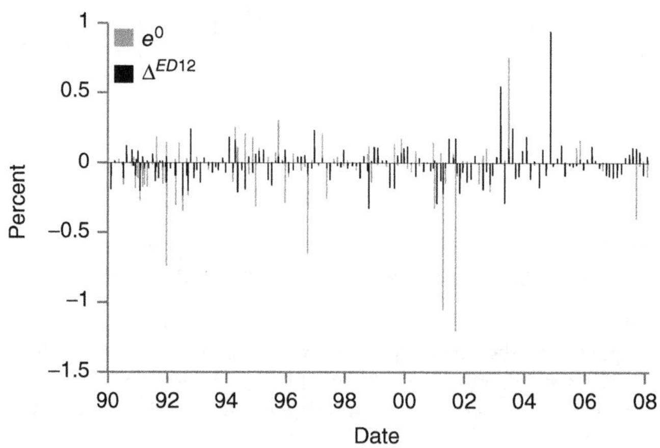

Figure 5.7 All shocks. This figure plots target shocks (e^0) around FOMC announcements in light gray; shocks to the 12-month Eurodollar futures rate ($\Delta ED12$) are reported in black. Source: Datastream (Fed funds and Eurodollar futures); Federal Reserve Board (FOMC dates).

TABLE 5.4 Factor Decomposition

	PC_1	PC_2	PC_3
%	61.98	32.97	3.26

We stack the shocks to five contracts (2 Fed funds and 3 Eurodollar) around each FOMC announcement in a $T \times 5$ matrix and perform a principal component decomposition. This table reports a decomposition of the variance explained by the first three principal components of the covariance matrix of the shocks.

By construction, this factor includes information that affects the expected path for monetary policy but that is orthogonal to decisions about the current target rate. This also implies that the dynamics of e_t^0 can only be explained by Z_t^1. Thus, we interpret the first rotated principal component as a scaled target shock ($e_t^0 = cZ_t^1$). Moreover, to identify the factors uniquely, we impose that Z_t^i have unit variance and $E(Z_t^1 Z_t^2) = 0$.

Figure 5.8 summarizes the difference between the target and path shocks. We find that target and path shocks move in the same direction in 93 of the 164 FOMC meetings. On the other hand, in 71 occasions, they moved in opposite directions.

The result confirms the conjecture about the existence of two distinct monetary policy shocks. The first associated to movements in the front-end of the future curve and a second one linked to future policy decisions. Similar to the importance of distinguishing between expected and unexpected components in Fed funds decisions, it is likely that long-dated Treasury bonds are more sensitive to path shocks than to target shocks.

To investigate this conjecture further, we run a contemporaneous regression of changes in Treasury yields on both types of shocks. Table 5.5 summarizes the results. Indeed, we find that while the yield on the 3-month T-bill is more sensitive to target shocks, both economically and statistically, the opposite is true for long-dated Treasury bonds. For the 5-year bond, the slope coefficient on the path shock is 2.5 times larger than the slope coefficient on the target shock. For the 10-year bond, only path shocks are statistically significant, with a t-statistics of 3.31. This confirms that target rate changes in themselves are not the most important component driving long-term bond changes.

Figures 5.8 shows that the largest unexpected shocks occur at the beginning of recessions when the Fed enters an easing cycle. This motivates the question of the extent to which the significance of shocks is state dependent. To investigate this conjecture, we use the Chicago Fed National Activity Indicator (CFNAI) as a monthly business cycle variable. The CFNAI is the first principal component of 85 economic monthly indicators drawn from four broad categories of data: (i) production and income (23 series), (ii) employment, unemployment, and hours (24 series), (iii) personal consumption and housing (15 series), and (iv) sales, orders, and inventories (23 series). All of the data are adjusted for inflation. A positive value of the *CFNAI* variable signals that the economy is expanding. Thus, we define a dummy variable that takes the value of 1 or 0 depending on whether *CFNAI*

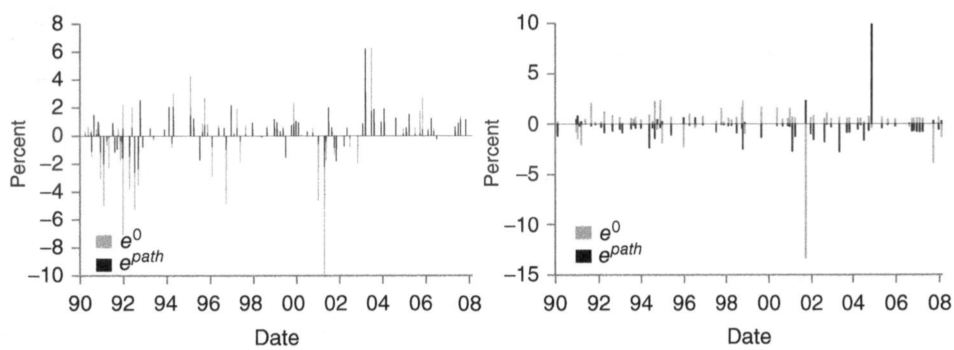

Figure 5.8 Target versus path shocks (in standardized units for comparison purposes). This figure plots target (e_t^0) versus path shocks (e_t^{path}). The left panel plots those occasion when these moved in the same direction, while the right panel plots those occasions when the shocks moved in opposite directions. Source: Datastream (Fed funds and Eurodollar futures); Federal Reserve Board (FOMC dates).

TABLE 5.5 FOMC Announcements: Target versus Path Shocks

	Bill 3 m	Bill 6 m	1 yr	3 yr	5 yr	10 yr
e_t^0	0.68	0.67	0.47	0.28	0.22	0.09
	(4.00)	(4.27)	(3.28)	(2.50)	(2.41)	(1.15)
e_t^{path}	0.17	0.32	0.49	0.57	0.57	0.56
	(1.87)	(2.86)	(3.11)	(3.16)	(3.20)	(3.31)
R^2	0.52	0.63	0.55	0.45	0.41	0.33

This table reports regressions of the daily change in $\{3, 6\}$-month Treasury Bill rates, and $\{1, 3, 5, 10\}$-year Treasury rates on target (e_t^0) and path shocks (e_t^{path}). OLS t-stats are reported in parentheses.

Source: Datastream (Fed funds and Eurodollar futures); Federal Reserve Board (FOMC dates); GSW dataset, Federal Reserve Board (Zero-coupon Treasury yields); Fred St. Louis (T-bill rates).

TABLE 5.6 State Dependence: Target versus Path Shocks

	Bill 3 m	Bill 6 m	1 yr	3 yr	5 yr	10 yr
e_t^0(GOOD)	0.49	0.49	0.42	0.30	0.25	0.14
	(6.40)	(8.71)	(6.29)	(4.32)	(3.72)	(1.91)
e_t^0(BAD)	0.48	0.47	0.29	0.14	0.10	0.02
	(3.34)	(3.61)	(2.63)	(1.74)	(1.44)	(0.29)
e_t^{path}(GOOD)	0.03	0.14	0.27	0.33	0.34	0.36
	(0.64)	(2.65)	(2.27)	(2.03)	(1.97)	(1.00)
e_t^{path}(BAD)	0.21	0.31	0.42	0.47	0.46	0.42
	(2.12)	(3.35)	(3.68)	(4.93)	(5.41)	(5.62)
R^2	0.56	0.67	0.60	0.49	0.44	0.34

Table reports regressions of the daily change in $\{3,6\}$-month bills rates, and $\{1,3,5,10\}$-year zero-coupon rates on target and path shocks conditional on the state of the economy: $\Delta y_t^i = const + \beta_1 e_t^0\, \mathbf{1}_{cfnai>0} + \beta_2 e_t^0\, \mathbf{1}_{cfnai<0} + \beta_3 e_t^{path}\, \mathbf{1}_{cfnai>0} + \beta_4 e_t^{path}\, \mathbf{1}_{cfnai<0} + \epsilon_t^i$ where $\mathbf{1}_{cfnai>0}$ is a good state and $\mathbf{1}_{cfnai<0}$ is a bad state, and cfnai is the Chicago Fed National Activity Index. OLS t-stats are reported in parenthesis. Data source: Datastream (Fed funds and Eurodollar futures); Federal Reserve Board (FOMC dates); GSW dataset, Federal Reserve Board (Zero-coupon Treasury yields); Fred St. Louis (T-bill rates, CFNAI index).

is positive or negative. Then, we repeat the previous regression after interacting this dummy variable with both target and path shocks:

$$\Delta y_t^i = const + \beta_1 e_t^0\, \mathbf{1}_{cfnai>0} + \beta_2 e_t^0\, \mathbf{1}_{cfnai<0} + \beta_3 e_t^{path}\, \mathbf{1}_{cfnai>0} + \beta_4 e_t^{path}\, \mathbf{1}_{cfnai<0} + \epsilon_t^i$$

where $\mathbf{1}_{cfnai>0}$ is a good state and $\mathbf{1}_{cfnai<0}$ is a bad state. Table 5.6 summarizes the results. We find that path shocks are particularly significant in bad states of the world. Indeed, in good states of the world for the 3-year bond the magnitude of the slope coefficients on target and path shocks are broadly similar and both of them are statistically significant. However, in bad states of the world the slope coefficient on path shocks is about three times larger and strongly statistically significant. On the other hand, the target shock is not statistically significant. This may be interpreted as evidence that at the beginning and end of recessions the Treasury market is particularly sensitive to information about changes in the stance of monetary policy. Changes in the target rate are an important, but not exclusive, signal used by the market to learn about future interest rates.

5.3.1 The Economics of FOMC Meetings and Bond Yields

What is the channel responsible for the reaction of Treasury bonds to monetary policy shocks? A first possible channel discussed in the literature is that a positive shock to the Fed funds target rate reduces expected inflation. This should reduce nominal yields on long-term bonds and, if inflation is neutral, it should have no impact on real yields. If inflation have distortive (Mundell–Tobin) effects on the real economy, changes in target rates would also affect both nominal and real yields.[6] A second possible channel could arise if agents have preferences for early resolution of uncertainty. To the extent that monetary policy affects economic uncertainty, FOMC decisions may affect bond markets by affecting the real risk premium in equilibrium. In this case, both real and nominal bonds could be affected by FOMC decisions.

5.3.1.1 FOMC Decisions: Real versus Nominal Yields To investigate the first channel, we collect data on TIPS and run contemporaneous regressions on changes of real yields, break-even rates, and nominal yields around FOMC decisions on target and path shocks. Since the TIPS market is more recent, this constrains us to analyze the effect using data starting in January 2000. Table 5.7 summarizes the results. We find that positive shocks to the target rate reduce the break-even rate. This is consistent with the conjecture that an increase in the Fed funds rate reduces expected inflation. However, slope coefficients are not statistically significant and the R^2 of this regression are very small, suggesting that the link is statistically weak. On the other hand, the slope coefficients on path shocks are highly significant both in the case of the nominal and real yield regressions. Moreover, the slope coefficients on e_t^{path} are very similar in size, implying that changes in TIPS and nominal Treasury yields are strongly correlated following unexpected FOMC shocks. This result is robust across maturities.

[6] See Mundell (1963) and Tobin (1965).

TABLE 5.7 Nominal versus Real Yields: Target versus Path Shocks

	Nominal yield change			Real yield change			Break-even change		
	3 yr	5 yr	10 yr	3 yr	5 yr	10 yr	3 yr	5 yr	10 yr
e_t^0	0.17	0.12	0.00	0.31	0.28	0.19	−0.15	−0.18	−0.23
	(1.09)	(0.85)	(−0.04)	(2.56)	(2.23)	(2.24)	(−1.41)	(−1.10)	(−1.30)
e_t^{path}	0.44	0.43	0.43	0.41	0.45	0.46	0.10	0.08	0.08
	(2.31)	(2.37)	(2.71)	(2.54)	(2.48)	(2.53)	(0.89)	(0.84)	(1.47)
$\bar{R}^2$	0.21	0.18	0.16	0.26	0.28	0.24	0.00	0.01	0.03

This table reports regressions of the daily change in $\{3, 5, 10\}$-year nominal rates, real rates, and break-even inflation rate on target and path shocks. OLS t-stats are reported in parentheses. Sample period 2000.1–2008.6.
Source: Datastream (Fed funds and Eurodollar futures); Federal Reserve Board (FOMC dates); GSW dataset, Federal Reserve Board (Zero-coupon Treasury yields); Fred St. Louis (T-bill rates, CFNAI index).

TABLE 5.8 Nominal versus Real Yields Changes

	3 yr	5 yr	10 yr
Real yield	0.79	0.90	0.94
	(6.98)	(9.65)	(12.81)
R^2	0.51	0.56	0.57

This table reports the regression results for the daily change in $\{3, 5, 10\}$-year nominal rates on the daily change in $\{3, 5, 10\}$-year real rates. OLS t-stats are reported in parenthesis. The sample period is 2000.1–2008.6.
Source: GSW dataset, Federal Reserve Board.

To further investigate the joint behavior of nominal and real bonds around FOMC announcements, we regress the change in nominal yields on the change in TIPS yield in the day surrounding the FOMC announcement. Table 5.8 shows that the slope coefficient for the 5-year bond is 0.90 with a t-statistics of 9.65 and a R-square of 0.56. These results clearly suggest that the channel driving changes in yields is common across nominal and real bonds.

It is possible that the previous results are dominated by state of the world in which the economy is close to recession, when a decision by the Fed to reduce the fed funds rate may signal that indeed the economy is entering a recession. To investigate this possibility, we run a regression by interacting both surprise and path factors with the *cfnai* business cycle dummy variable, $\mathbf{1}_{cfnai>0}$, which takes the value of one if $cfnai > 0$:

$$\Delta y_t^{\$,r(\tau)} = const + \beta_1 e_t^0 \, \mathbf{1}_{cfnai>0} + \beta_2 e_t^0 \, \mathbf{1}_{cfnai<0} + \beta_3 e_t^{path} \, \mathbf{1}_{cfnai>0} + \beta_4 e_t^{path} \, \mathbf{1}_{cfnai<0} + \epsilon_t^{\tau}$$

Table 5.9 summarizes the results. Even in this case, we find that nominal and real bonds have almost identical sensitivities to path shocks after controlling for the business cycle. Similar results are discussed also by Hanson and Stein (2014) who show that distant nominal forward rates respond significantly to changes in the yield of the 2-year nominal Treasury rate on FOMC days. Moreover, the response is driven almost exclusively by movements in real forward rate measured from TIPS data. They report that "a 100 bp shock to the 2-year nominal rate on an FOMC announcement date is associated with a 45 bp increase in 10-year nominal forward rate. And this 45 bp increase can be decomposed into a 42 bp rise in real forwards and a 3 bp rise in forward break-even inflation."

This evidence is difficult to reconcile with New Keynesian models with sticky nominal prices, which imply that monetary policy cannot move real rates over a horizon longer than the time it takes for prices to adjust. Two alternative explanations are consistent with the results. A first explanation is based on the notion that agents believe the Fed to have superior information about the future level of real economic activity. If the Fed unexpectedly reduces short-term nominal rates, it signals lower future real interest rates. In this context, it would be incorrect to say that the monetary policy causes changes in real rates: the explanation is based on an information channel. The second explanation is based on the notion that Fed's unexpected decisions affect real (term) risk premia. Consistent with this hypothesis, Hanson and Stein (2014) find that when long-term forward rates rise on an FOMC announcement day, this predicts a reversal of forward rates over the next 12 months. They argue that this effect may

TABLE 5.9 Nominal versus Real Yields: State Dependence

	Nominal yield change			Real yield change		
	3 yr	5 yr	10 yr	3 yr	5 yr	10 yr
e_t^0(GOOD)	0.14	0.11	0.08	0.26	0.21	0.18
	(1.42)	(1.20)	(0.81)	(2.51)	(2.31)	(1.59)
e_t^0(BAD)	0.14	0.09	−0.02	0.26	0.24	0.15
	(0.97)	(0.69)	(−0.19)	(2.70)	(2.50)	(2.29)
e_t^{path}(GOOD)	0.19	0.19	0.22	0.14	0.16	0.18
	1.29	1.32	1.60	1.61	1.50	1.44
e_t^{path}(BAD)	0.43	0.41	0.38	0.42	0.47	0.46
	4.44	5.57	6.30	6.31	7.01	8.61
$\bar{R}^2$	(0.24)	(0.20)	(0.16)	(0.33)	(0.34)	(0.28)

[a]This table reports regressions of the daily change in $\{3, 5, 10\}$-year nominal note rates and real note rates on target and path shocks conditional of the state of the economy:

$$\Delta y_t^{\$,r(i)} = const + \beta_1 e_t^0 \ \mathbf{1}_{cfnai>0} + \beta_2 e_t^0 \ \mathbf{1}_{cfnai<0} + \beta_3 e_t^{path} \ \mathbf{1}_{cfnai>0} + \beta_4 e_t^{path} \ \mathbf{1}_{cfnai<0} + \epsilon_t^i$$

We define the indicator function $\mathbf{1}_{cfnai>0}$ is a good state and $\mathbf{1}_{cfnai<0}$ is a bad state, and cfnai is the Chicago Fed National Activity Index. OLS t-stats are reported in parentheses. Sample period 2000.1–2008.6.
Source: GSW dataset, Federal Reserve Board; Fred St. Louis (CFNAI index).

occur in economies populated by agents with a preference for yield. In this case, as the Fed reduces short-term nominal rates, agents rebalance their portfolios toward longer-term bonds in an effort to keep their overall portfolio yield from declining too much. The implied price pressure on long-term bonds reduces long-term forward rates.[7]

5.3.1.2 FOMC Decisions: Risk Premia To investigate the extent to which monetary policy surprises may affect distant bond yields because of changes in the (term) risk premium, we adopt the approach proposed by Cochrane and Piazzesi (2005). A common property of several term structure models is that the cross section of bond yields follows a Markov structure and spans expected bond excess returns.[8] In the specific case of affine models, linear combinations of date t bond yields suffice to characterize date t risk factors through so-called yield curve inversion. The Cochrane–Piazzesi return forecasting factor, CP_t, is a tent-shaped linear combination of forward rates that predicts realized excess returns with R^2 statistics as high as 43% (in the authors original sample period) and has been shown to capture a large component of the time variation in expected returns.[9] We estimate the *daily* changes in CP_t and study the extent to which its dynamics around FOMC announcements carries important information for bond excess returns. Specifically, we estimate the CP_t factor using daily bond data with 1-year excess holding period returns.[10]

The single factor construction begins with projecting the average excess return (across maturity) on a constant plus available forward rates:[11]

$$\frac{1}{9}\sum_{n=2}^{10} rx_{t,t+12}^{(n)} = \gamma_0 + \gamma_1 y_t^{(1)} + \gamma_3 f_t^{(3)} + \gamma_5 f_t^{(5)} + \gamma_7 f_t^{(7)} + \gamma_9 f_t^{(9)} + \bar{\epsilon}_{t+12}$$

$$= \underbrace{\gamma' \bar{f}_t}_{CP_t} + \bar{\epsilon}_{t+12}$$

[7]Other important papers that highlight the potential role played by agents searching for yield include Vayanos and Vila (2009), Gagnon et al. (2010), Krishnamurthy and Vissing-Jorgensen (2011, 2012), Greenwood and Vayanos (2010, 2014).
[8]Affine term structure models are no-arbitrage specifications where interest rates and bond risk premia are modeled as an affine (linear) function of some state vector. The seminal works of Vasicek (1977) and Cox, Ingersoll, and Ross (1985) are early examples of equilibrium structural affine models.
[9]For a detailed discussion of CP_t, we refer the reader to Cochrane and Piazzesi (2005).
[10]For robustness, we also estimate the factor loadings at a monthly frequency and apply the loadings to daily forward rates. The quantitative implications are unchanged.
[11]We only include alternate forward rates to avoid well-known multicollinearity associated with the span of GSW forward rates.

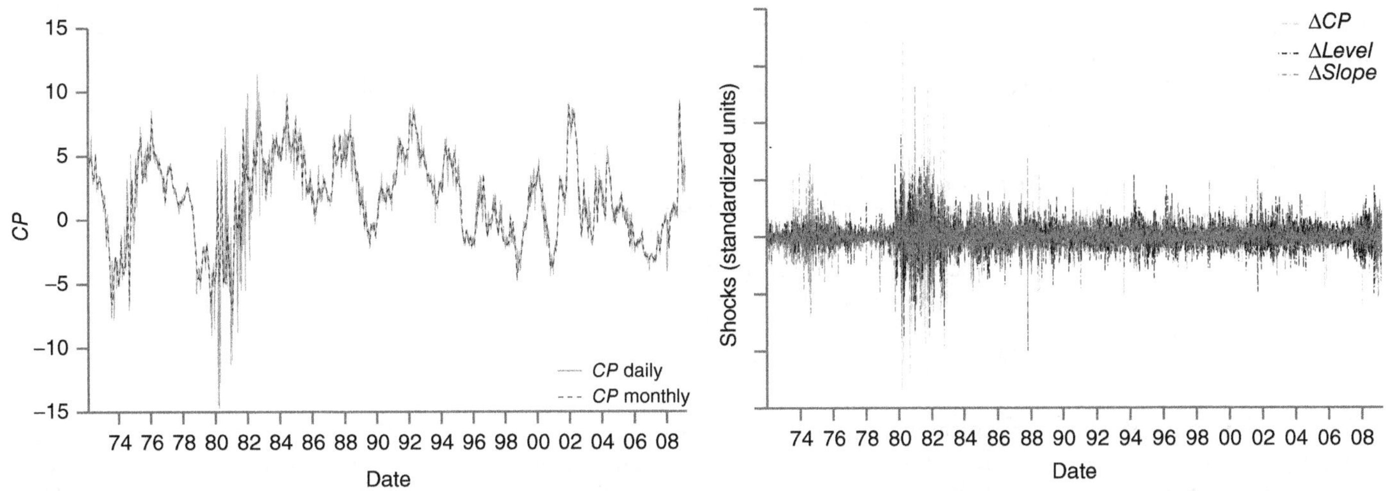

Figure 5.9 Yield curve factors and shocks. The left panel displays the behavior of the Cochrane and Piazzesi (2005) return forecasting factor constructed at monthly and daily frequency. The right panel displays daily changes in the CP_t factor compared to daily changes in the level (PC1) and slope (PC2) of the term structure. Variances in the right panel are standardized for comparison purposes. Source: GSW dataset, Federal Reserve Board.

In traditional predictability regression, the forecasting ability of CP_t is then evaluated in second stage predictability regressions in which the first-stage linear combination of forward rates serves as a single state variable:

$$rx_{t,t+12}^{(n)} = \beta \times CP_t + \epsilon_{t+12}^{(n)}$$

The left panel of Figure 5.9 compares the behavior of the CP-factor at monthly and daily frequency over the sample period 1972–2012. It can be noticed that CP_t estimated at daily and monthly frequencies are almost identical. Both series are countercyclical, peaking in recessions (1973–1975, 1987–1988, 1990–1991, 2000–2001, and 2008–2010), and their volatility is higher during the Volcker's monetary policy experiment.

Then, we study the extent to which target (e^0) and path (e^{path}) shocks explain the dynamics of CP_t around FOMC announcements. Table 5.10 reports the results. Both target and path monetary policy shocks are statistically significant (column 1). The t-statistics are −3.39 and 2.87 for the target and path shocks, respectively, and the $\bar{R}^2$ of the regression is 10%. Positive innovations in the path shocks, which is particularly significant to explain changes in long-term yields (Table 5.5), raise risk premia, proxied by the CP_t factor, consistent with the previous predictability regressions. Target shocks are mostly important at the short end and we find that an unexpected drop in the target increases the risk premium.

Cochrane and Piazzesi (2005) highlight that higher-order principal components of the yield curve are important to explain the dynamics of (term) risk premia. For instance, they argue that "the fourth factor, which is essentially unimportant for explaining the variation of yields, turns out to be very important for explaining expected returns." Thus, we explore whether innovations in these components are significantly different during FOMC announcement days. First, we compute principal components at the

TABLE 5.10 Risk Premia and Yield Curve Shocks on Monetary Policy Shocks

	ΔCP	$\Delta Level$	$\Delta Slope$	$\Delta Curve$	$\Delta PC4$	$\Delta PC5$
e^0	−0.23	0.20	−0.37	0.02	0.28	−0.13
	(−3.39)	(2.73)	(−2.47)	(0.30)	(1.58)	(−0.97)
e^{path}	0.27	0.58	0.09	0.32	−0.06	−0.11
	(2.87)	(3.20)	(1.09)	(2.59)	(−0.76)	(−1.38)
$\bar{R}^2$	0.10	0.42	0.12	0.13	0.06	0.02

This table reports regressions of the daily change in CP_t and yield curve factors PCs on target (e^0) and path factors (e^{path}) shocks around FOMC meetings. OLS t-stats are reported in parentheses.

daily frequency via an eigenvalue decomposition of the covariance matrix of yields.[12] Second, we project changes in ΔCP_t on changes in yield curve factors ΔPCs around the announcement. The right panel of Figure 5.9 displays daily changes to CP_t, level, and slope factors. All series display volatility clustering around recessionary periods. Noticeable periods of inflated variances occur during the monetary policy experiment and the recent 2008 financial crisis:

$$\Delta CP_t = \alpha + \underbrace{0.02}_{(0.35)} \Delta Level_t + \underbrace{0.56}_{(14.35)} \Delta Slope_t + \underbrace{0.51}_{(7.34)} \Delta Curve_t - \underbrace{0.47}_{(-6.51)} \Delta PC_t^4 - \underbrace{0.68}_{(-8.65)} \Delta PC_t^5 + \epsilon_t^i$$

$$\bar{R}^2 = 78\%$$

When we focus on FOMC announcement days, changes in CP_t are unrelated to changes in the level of yields but are strongly explained by shocks to the slope of the term structure. An extensive literature finds the slope to contains information about future expected excess returns (see Fama (1984) and Fama (2006)). Thus, this finding is consistent with the interpretation that FOMC announcements are indeed linked to changes in (term) risk premia. Moreover, consistent with the statement by Cochrane and Piazzesi (2005), we find that shocks to the fourth and fifth principal components are highly correlated with shocks to CP_t. For instance, when we run a separate regression on the fourth and fifth principal components we find

$$\Delta CP_t = \alpha - \underbrace{0.27}_{(-2.16)} \Delta PC_t^4 - \underbrace{0.57}_{(-5.37)} \Delta PC_t^5 + \epsilon_t^i$$

$$\bar{R}^2 = 38\%$$

These factors are indeed highly significant and explain 38% of the variance of shocks to CP_t on announcement days. This is an interesting result and consistent with the interpretation that during FOMC announcement days changes in the term structure contain information about future expected returns. Columns 2–6 summarize the evidence on these links more directly. Target shocks are negatively correlated with slope shocks with a t-statistic of −2.47. This is consistent with the negative loading of ΔCP_t on e^0 and a positive loading of ΔCP_t on $\Delta Slope$. At the same time, path shocks explain 13% of the variance of *Curve* shocks and with a factor loading significant at the 1% level. This finding is interesting as Piazzesi (2005) finds that an increase in the probability of a rate hike at future FOMC meetings generate a hump-shaped (curvature) factor.

Finally, as above, we examine the extent to which these results are state dependent by projection of changes in CP_t on target and path shocks conditional on the CFNAI indicator dummy

$$\Delta CP_t = \alpha - \underbrace{0.09}_{(-1.29)} e_t^0 \, \mathbf{1}_{cfnai>0} - \underbrace{0.22}_{(-3.54)} e_t^0 \, \mathbf{1}_{cfnai<0} + \underbrace{0.17}_{(1.70)} e_t^{path} \, \mathbf{1}_{cfnai>0} + \underbrace{0.22}_{(3.86)} e_t^{path} \, \mathbf{1}_{cfnai<0} + \epsilon_t$$

The magnitude of this effect is larger in bad states of the world: good state loadings are insignificant while bad state loadings jump to highly significant levels. This result is both consistent with the state dependence regressions documented above and suggests that monetary policy indeed affects bond risk premia especially in bad states of the world.

5.4 CONCLUSIONS

An important literature studies the impact of conventional monetary policy decisions on bond yields using "high-frequency data." Indeed, an early challenge of the empirical monetary economics literature was the fact that a significant component of policy

[12]The eigenvector loadings for principal components 1, 2, and 3 have the usual level, slope, and curvature interpretation, while principal components 4 and 5 have display "snake"-like patterns across maturity. We rotate the second principal component so positive shocks to this factor raise long-term yields with respect to short-term yields and rotate the curvature factor so that positive shocks raise maturities 3, 4, 5 with respect to the short and long ends.

actions reflects the systematic response of the policy instrument to the macroeconomic environment, rather than exogenous policy shocks. This literature highlights the importance of using the dynamics of the Federal fund futures around FOMC announcements as a key instrument in identifying policy shocks.

The evidence from this literature shows that after controlling for expected changes in interest rates, surprises to the target Fed funds rate do indeed have a significant effect on long-term bond prices. FOMC decisions affect bonds of all maturity because they are exposed to two types of shock: (i) shocks to the target rate and, perhaps more importantly (ii) shocks to the future *path* of the monetary policy. Interestingly, we present evidence suggesting this effect is unrelated to changes in expected inflation, which would be difficult to reconcile with New Keynesian models with sticky nominal prices. The empirical evidence points to one of the following two explanations. The first explanation assumes the existence of an information channel. When the Fed unexpectedly reduces short-term nominal rates, the market assumes that the Fed has an informational advantage and infers that real rates will be lower in the future. The second explanation is based on a (real) risk premium channel. When the Fed lowers short-term rates, the change in risk compensation induces agents to rebalance their bond portfolios. This channel is observationally equivalent to one in which agents appear to increase their demand of longer-term bonds in search for yield as short-term rates drop. We present empirical evidence in support of both channels.

ACKNOWLEDGMENTS

For providing useful comments we would like to thank Stefania D'Amico and Pietro Veronesi.

REFERENCES

Ang A, Dong S, Piazzesi M. No-arbitrage Taylor rules. NBER Working Paper; 2007.

Bakshi GS, Chen Z. Inflation, asset prices, and the term structure of interest rates in monetary economies. Rev Financ Stud 1996;9(1):241–275.

Basistha A, Kurov A. The impact of monetary policy surprises on energy prices. J Futures Mark 2013;35(1):87–103.

Bernanke BS, Kuttner KN. What explains the stock market's reaction to Federal Reserve policy? J Finance 2005;60:1221–11257.

Buraschi A, Jiltsov A. Inflation risk premia and the expectations hypothesis. J Financ Econ 2005;75:429–4490.

Buraschi A, Jiltsov A. Habit formation and macroeconomic models of the term structure of interest rates. J Finance 2007;62:3009–3063.

Christiano L, Eichenbaum M, Evans C. The effects of monetary policy shocks: some evidence from the flow of funds. Rev Econ Stat 1996;78:16–134.

Cochrane JH, Piazzesi M. The Fed and interest rates - a high-frequency identification. Am Econ Rev 2002;92:90–995.

Cochrane JH, Piazzesi M. Bond risk premia. Am Econ Rev 2005;95:138–1160.

Cox JC, Ingersoll JE Jr., Ross SA. A theory of the term structure of interest rates. Econometrica 1985;53:385–3407.

Fama EF. The information in the term structure. J Financ Econ 1984;13:509–5528.

Fama EF. The behavior of interest rates. Rev Financ Stud 2006;19:359–3379.

Fama EF. Does the Fed control interest rates? Rev Asset Pric Stud 2013;3:180–199.

Fleming M, and Piazzesi M. Monetary policy tick by tick. Stanford University working paper; 2005.

Gagnon J, Raskin M, Remache J, Sack BP. Large-scale asset purchases by the Federal Reserve: did they work? Federal Reserve Bank of New York Staff Reports, no. 441; 2010.

Goodfriend M. *Carnegie-Rochester Conference Series on Public Policy*. Volume 55(1). Elsevier; 2001. p IFC.

Greenwood R, Vayanos D. Price pressure in the government bond market. Am Econ Rev Pap Proc 2010;100:585–5590.

Greenwood R, Vayanos D. Bond supply and excess bond returns. Rev Financ Stud 2014;27:663–6713.

Gurkaynak RS. *Using Federal Funds Futures Contracts for Monetary Policy Analysis*. Volume 5: The Federal Reserve Board Finance and Economics Discussion Series 2005. Divisions of Research & Statistics and Monetary Affairs, Federal Reserve Board; 2005.

Gurkaynak RS, Sack B, Swanson E. Do actions speak louder than words? The response of asset prices to monetary policy actions and statements. Int J Cent Bank 2005;1:55–593.

Gurkaynak RS, Sack B, Wright JH. *The U.S. Treasury Yield Curve: 1961 to the Present*, Federal Reserve Board Working Paper Series. The Federal Reserve Board; 2006.

Gurkaynak RS, Sack B, Wright JH. The tips yield curve and inflation compensation. Am Econ J Macroecon 2010;2(1):70–792.

Hamilton JD. Daily changes in fed funds futures prices. J Money Credit Bank 2009;41:567–582.

Hanson SG, Stein JC. Monetary policy and long-term real rates. J Financ Econ 2014;115(3):429–448.

Krishnamurthy A, Vissing-Jorgensen A. The effects of quantitative easing on interest rates: channels and implications for policy, Discussion paper. National Bureau of Economic Research; 2011.

Krishnamurthy A, Vissing-Jorgensen A. The aggregate demand for treasury debt. J Pol Econ 2012;120:233–267.

Kuttner KN. Monetary policy surprises and interest rates: evidence from the fed funds futures market. J Monet Econ 2001a;47:523–5544.

Kuttner KN. Monetary policy surprises and interest rates: evidence from the fed funds futures market. J Monet Econ 2001b;47:523–5544.

Mundell R. Inflation and real interest. J Pol Econ 1963;71:280.
Piazzesi M. Bond yields and the federal reserve. J Pol Econ 2005;113:311–3344.
Rudebusch GD. Do measures of monetary policy in a VAR make sense? Int Econ Rev 1998;39:907–9031.
Tobin J. Money and economic growth. Econometrica 1965;33(4):671–6684.
Vasicek O. An equilibrium characterization of the term structure. J Financ Econ 1977;5:177–188.
Vayanos D, Vila J-L. A preferred-habitat model of the term structure of interest rates, Discussion paper. National Bureau of Economic Research; 2009.

6

Bond Markets and Unconventional Monetary Policy

Andrea Buraschi[a] **and Paul Whelan**[b]

[a]*Department of Finance, Imperial College, London, United Kingdom*
[b]*Department of Finance, Copenhagen Business School, Copenhagen, Denmark*

6.1 INTRODUCTION

The 2007/2008 financial crisis and its subsequent impact on the global macroeconomy led to a fundamental change in the conduct of monetary policy. Before this crisis, a common goal of monetary policy was to achieve low and stable inflation, implemented through a nominal interest rate target. In deciding the target rate, several empirical studies argue that central bank decisions can be explained by a Taylor rule, whereby policy rates respond linearly to deviations of inflation from a target and fluctuations in the output gap. The left panel of Figure 6.1 displays the evolution of policy rates set by the Federal Reserve, the European Central Bank (ECB), and the Bank of England (BOE) in the run-up to the financial crisis. The extent of the slowdown in economic activity during the crisis was so significant that a normative use of Taylor rules implied setting a negative Federal funds rate. On December 16, 2008, the Federal Open Market Committee (FOMC) decided to reduce the target federal fund rate to a range between 0% and 0.25%. Thereafter, the Federal Reserve abandoned the traditional use of the target rate to control lending channels and began to implement "unconventional" monetary policy.

In the aftermath of the crisis, unconventional monetary policy was initially designed to alleviate distress in the financial sector but was subsequently broadened to stimulate the real economy, promote inflation, support sovereign debt markets, and guide monetary expectations. The Federal Reserve and the BOE chose to implement large-scale asset purchase (LSAP) programs known as quantitative easing (QE). The respective size of these programs was very large, equivalent to ~20% of GDP for both countries, and involved purchase of both government and private sector securities. The ECB, on the other hand, focused on the provision of liquidity and repairing the bank lending channel. The right panel of Figure 6.1 plots the resulting expansion of the balance sheets of the three central banks. Expansion of the Fed balance sheet has been carried out by purchasing Treasuries, agency debt, and agency Mortgage-Backed Securities (MBS). The BOE balance sheet expansion focused more on the purchase of U.K. government bonds in the secondary market. ECB operations were quite different as most of its balance sheet expansion was due to large-scale repurchase agreements. Indeed, while at the end of 2014 the asset side of balance sheets of the Fed and BOE is about $\sim$ 5 times larger than in 2007, the ECB asset value was only $\sim$ 1.5 larger than in 2007.

This chapter surveys unconventional monetary policies adopted by the Federal Reserve (Fed), the ECB, and the BOE (BOE). We begin by discussing the details of the respective programs implemented by each central bank. Next, we discuss the theoretical

Handbook of Fixed-Income Securities, First Edition. Edited by Pietro Veronesi.

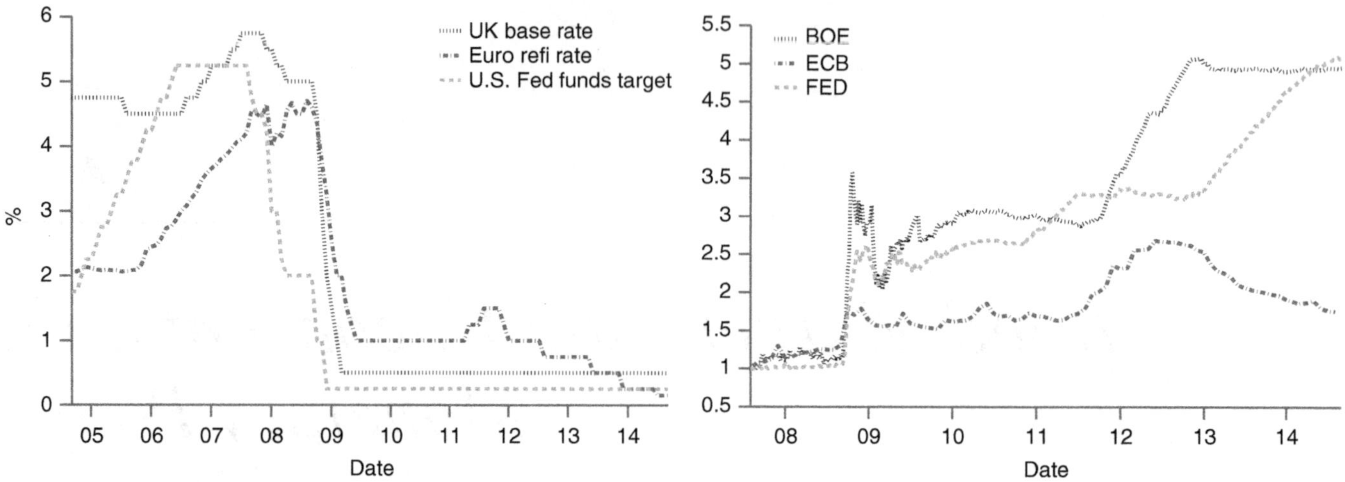

Figure 6.1 Policy rates versus asset growth. The left panel plots the main policy rates for the Fed, ECB, and BOE, which are the Federal funds rate, the main refinancing operations fixed bid rate, and the official Bank rate, respectively. The right panel plots the growth rate of the asset side of the balance sheets of the Fed, the ECB, and the BOE. Each series is indexed to the level of assets held at the start of the sample. Source: FRED, ECB, BOE, Datastream.

channels via which the unconventional policy might operate. Finally, given this framework, we survey the empirical evidence on the effectiveness of unconventional policy operations from the perspective of financial markets.

6.2 UNCONVENTIONAL POLICIES: THE Fed, ECB, AND BOE

6.2.1 Federal Reserve Operations

In 2007, well before the collapse of Lehman Brothers, the U.S. level of economic activity had declined significantly. In the summer of 2007, the Fed responded by using traditional policy tools. Between August and December, it reduced the Fed fund target rate from 5.75% to 4.75%. However, due to increasing evidence of corporate bond illiquidity, a freeze in funding markets, and concerns about the condition of financial institutions, the Federal Reserve began to consider alternative monetary policy tools. Indeed, an important difference emerged between the policy measures taken before and after the collapse of Lehman Brothers. Before Lehman Brothers' bankruptcy, Fed interventions mainly aimed to address market illiquidity. After the bankruptcy of Lehman, the Fed shifted the nature of interventions to directly address credit concerns. We will refer to these two periods as the "Liquidity Crisis" and "Credit Crisis" periods.

Monetary Policy in the "Liquidity Crisis" period (January 2007–September 15, 2008).

In the first part of the crisis, the Federal Reserve became increasingly concerned about market illiquidity. Indeed, on December 12, 2007, the Fed introduced a Term Auction Facility (TAF) designed to lend funds directly to depository institutions (thus including U.S. branches of foreign banks maintaining reserves at the Fed) for a fixed term (28 or 84 days) and to relieve frictions related to interbank borrowing. The important restriction characterizing these measures was that funds were in fixed terms and in limited supply.

On January 9, 2008, the Fed held an emergency conference call during which Ben Bernanke stated, "I think there are a lot of indications that we may soon be in a recession. I think a garden-variety recession is an acceptable risk, but I am also concerned that such a slowdown might morph into something more serious."[1] In fact, the United States had already entered a recession and in an emergency meeting on January 21, 2008, the FOMC committee voted on the biggest rate reduction in two decades, cutting the target rate 75 basis points to 4.0%, and then again on January 30, 2008, cutting the target rate a further 50 basis points to 3.50%.

During the spring of 2008, the secondary market for mortgage-backed securities began to collapse, affecting several financial intermediaries. Locked out from funding markets Bear Stearns was extended an emergency loan by the Federal Reserve Bank of New York. However, the company could not be saved and was sold to JP Morgan Chase for $10 per share, a price less than 1/10th of its preceding 52-week high. In an emergency meeting on March 10, 2008, the Fed announced an expansion of the set of counterparts eligible for liquidity operations as well as provisions for $400 billion. Funding markets continued to be extremely tight, which induced the Fed to lower the target rate to 2.25% in three further meetings between March 16 and April 30.

[1] http://www.federalreserve.gov/monetarypolicy/files/FOMC20080109confcall.pdf.

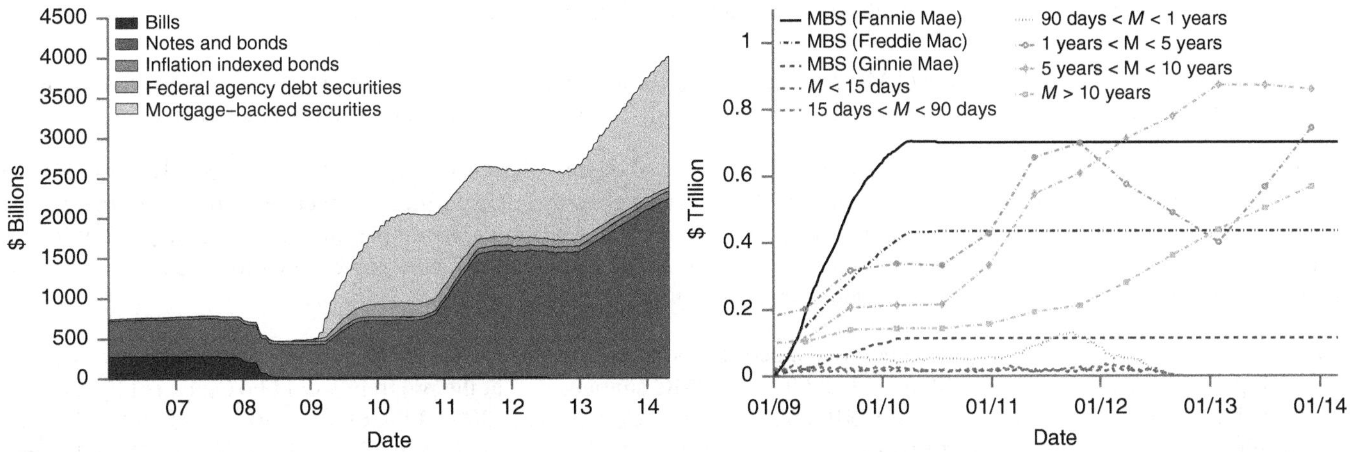

Figure 6.2 Balance sheet and asset purchases: the Fed. The left panel plots the evolution of the asset side of the balance sheet (in \$ billion) of the Fed between 2006.1 and 2014.1. The right panel plots asset purchases of mortgage-backed securities (MBS) from Fannie Mae, Freddie Mac, Ginnie Mae, and purchase of Treasury bills, notes, and bonds (in \$ trillions). Source: Federal Reserve Bank of New York, Federal Reserve Economic Data (FRED) at St Louis Fed.

In addition, it announced the introduction of the Term Securities Lending Facility (TSLF) and the Primary Dealer Credit Facility (PDCF) to address pressures faced by primary dealers. Eligible borrowers included all financial institutions listed as primary dealers. Thus, nonbank institutions such as investment banks, which would have normally fallen outside the Fed's regulatory structure, had access to this facility. Initially the creation of the PDCF generated substantial criticism as it was the first time in history that the Fed had lent directly to investment banks. The nature of the loan was a repurchase agreement, or "repo" loan, whereby the broker dealer sells a security in exchange for funds through the Fed's discount window. In total, \$8.95 trillion in loans were made through the PDCF, which was eventually terminated in February 2010.

In the second half of 2007 and in 2008, evidence emerged that most European financial institutions were finding it difficult to secure USD funding to support conduits for which they had committed backup (dollar) liquidity (see Buraschi, Menguturk, and Sener (2015) and Kacperczyk and Schnabl (2013)).[2] A contributing factor was the general increase in counterpart risk and the capital repatriation by U.S. financial institutions that reduced the supply of USD in the interbank market. To address this friction and facilitate the international provision of USD liquidity, on December 12, 2007, the FOMC authorized bilateral currency swap lines with the ECB and the Swiss National Bank (SNB). On September 29, 2008, the FOMC expanded its swap line program with the BOE, the ECB, the Bank of Japan, and most G8 countries; the total amount involved was about \$330 billion. One month later, on October 29, 2008, the FOMC established new swap lines to the central banks of those emerging market countries that were major U.S. commercial partners. The left panel of Figure 6.2 displays the evolution of the asset side of the Fed's balance sheet during 2005–2014.

Monetary Policy in the "Credit Crisis" period (September 15, 2008–December 2014).

In September 2008, the newly enacted Federal Housing Finance Agency placed Fannie Mae and Freddie Mac in government conservatorship, and then on September 15, Lehman Brothers filed for Chapter 11 bankruptcy protection, the largest filing in U.S. history. Global equity markets reacted dramatically: the S&P 500 dropped 25% by November 15 and the FTSE 100 dropped 35% over the same period. The Fed reported that new issuance of Asset-Backed Securities (ABS) declined precipitously in September and came to a halt in October. At the same time, interest rate spreads on AAA-rated tranches of ABS soared to levels not seen before, reflecting unusually high risk premiums. Because of the importance of the ABS market to fund consumer credit and small business loans, the Federal Reserve and the U.S. Treasury changed the nature of their interventions to directly address these credit concerns. It was decided to intervene by taking three unconventional policies:

- *The Term Asset-Backed Securities Loan Facility (TALF)* allowed the Fed to increase credit availability and supported economic activity by facilitating renewed issuance of consumer and business ABS at normal interest rate spreads.[3]
- *The Commercial Paper Funding Facility (CPFF)* allowed the Fed to fund a Special Purpose Vehicle (SPV) that purchased highly rated unsecured and asset-backed commercial Paper (CP) from eligible issuers. The SPV would buy and

[2]See "Central Bank Action Calms Investor Nerves," *Financial Times*, August 13, 2007; "Fed–ECB Currency Swap Politically Tricky," Reuters, August 13, 2007.

[3]The program was announced on November 25, 2008, and involved the lending of up to \$1 trillion to holders of AAA-rated ABS.

hold the commercial paper for 3 months and on maturity the proceeds would be used to pay back the loan from the NY Fed.[4]

- *The Troubled Asset Relief Program (*TARP*)* aimed at compensating for the lost capital of U.S. banks via purchasing bank preferred stocks.[5] With these measures, the Fed took on credit risk exposure. The final purchase matured on April 26, 2010.

The previous three programs marked the beginning of a policy of quantitative easing (QE). QE can be broadly defined as an unconventional monetary policy in which a central bank purchases government securities or other securities from the market with the final effect of increasing money supply. QE in the United States began in November 2008 and was carried out in five distinct phases. In total, the Fed expanded its balance sheet from \$860 billion at the beginning of 2007 to \$4.2 trillion in 2014. Figure 6.2 displays the evolution of the Fed balance sheet across these phases.

- *QE1*. On November 25, 2008, the Fed announced the purchase of 500 billion in MBS and of 100 billion in agency mortgage-backed securities. On March 18, 2009, the FOMC announced that the program would be expanded by an additional \$750 billion in purchases of MBS, \$100 billion of agency debt, and \$300 billion of long-term Treasury bonds. This would bring its total purchases of MBS up to \$1.25 trillion and of agency debt up to \$200 million. By mid-2009 the Fed held \$1.75 trillion of bank debt, MBS, and Treasury notes.
- *QE2*. On November 10, 2010, the Fed announced a second round of quantitative easing (QE2) with the intention to buy \$600 billion of Treasury securities over a 7-month period (\$85 billion per month). The majority of securities purchased were Treasury bonds with maturities between 1 and 10 years (see right panel of Figure 6.2). During this program the Fed did not purchase MBS. This feature differentiates the design of QE2 from both QE1 and QE3. This program was terminated in June 2011.
- *Maturity Extension Program (Operation Twist)*. On September 21, 2011, the FOMC announced the implementation of "Operation Twist." According to this plan, the Fed intended to purchase \$400 billion of bonds with maturities of 6–30 years and to sell an equal amount of bonds with maturities of 3 years or less, thereby extending the average maturity of the Fed's own portfolio. The objective was to inject more liquidity into the system and hold long-term rates low without expanding the Fed balance sheet.
- *Maturity Extension Program and Reinvestment Policy II*. On June 20, 2012, at the natural expiration of the MEP program, the Fed decided to extend the previous MEP program by an additional \$267 billion in Treasury securities, until the end of 2012. The Committee decided also to maintain its existing policy of reinvesting principal payments from its holdings of agency debt and agency MBSs in agency MBS.
- *QE3*. On September 13, 2012, the Fed announces a third round of quantitative easing with an open-ended commitment to purchase \$40 billion agency MBS per month "until the labor market improves substantially." On December 12, 2012, the FOMC decided to expand the program to \$85 a month by adding \$45 billion worth of longer-term Treasury securities. QE3 was supposed to work alongside Operation Twist, allowing the Fed to "neutralize" longer-term securities purchases by selling shorter-term Treasuries. Eventually, however, the Federal Reserve could no longer sell short-dated Treasury securities to buy longer dated ones due to the lack of sufficient holdings in short-dated Treasuries. On December 18, 2013, the Federal Reserve Open Market Committee announced it would taper QE3 at a rate of \$10 billion at each meeting. The Federal Reserve ended its monthly asset purchase program (QE3) in October 2014.

6.2.2 Bank of England Operations

The monetary policy approach followed by the BOE was similar in spirit to the Fed's. Following the collapse of Lehman Brothers, the BOE's Monetary Policy Committee (MPC) began lowering the U.K. bank rate aggressively, from 4.5% in October 2008 to 0.5% in March 2009 (see Figure 6.1) reaching an effective zero lower bound. Moreover, in response to the developing liquidity crisis in the banking system, the BOE introduced the special liquidity scheme (SLS) in April 2008, allowing banks to swap high-quality MBS for U.K. Treasury bills for up to 3 years. The intention of the SLS was to address the overhang of illiquid assets on banks' balance sheets by exchanging them temporarily for more easily tradable assets. The scheme was initially supposed to operate until January 30, 2009. However, it remained in place until January 30, 2012.[6]

The SLS was not a quantitative easing policy since it did not affect monetary supply. However, in January 2009, the Chancellor of the Exchequer (Secretary of the Treasury) approved a series of QE policies. In particular, the Asset Purchase Facility (APF)

[4] The program was created on October 27, 2008, and lent out a total \$738 billion before it was closed.

[5] The program was signed into law on October 3, 2008, and involved the purchase of troubled assets, such as MBS, from U.S. banks and other financial institutions (initially up to \$700 billion). The Capital Purchase Program (CPP) was a part of TARP that involved the purchase of preferred stocks of U.S. banks.

[6] The BOE reports that all drawings under the scheme were repaid before the scheme closed.

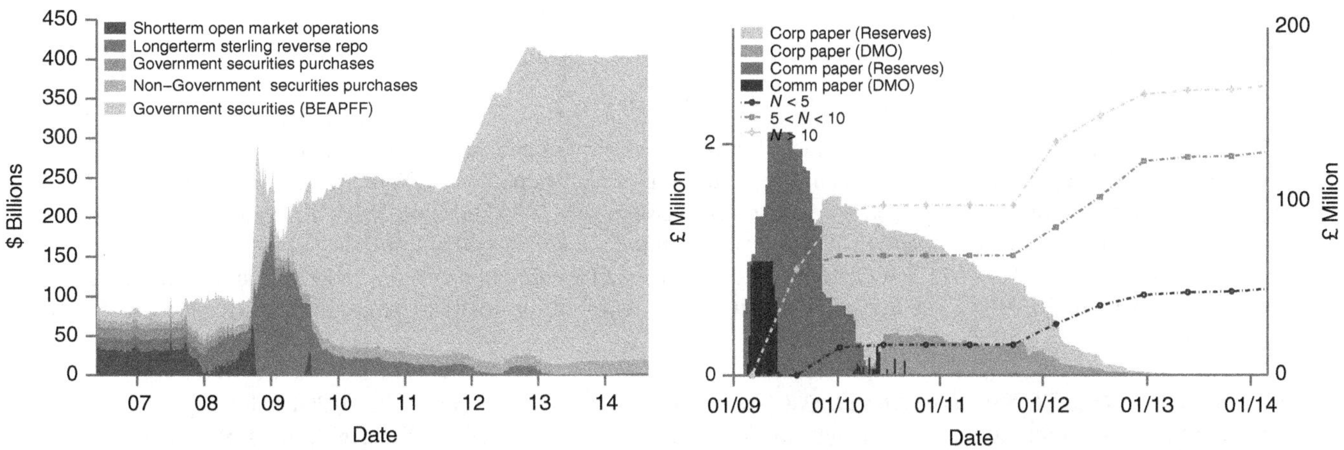

Figure 6.3 Balance sheet and asset purchases: the BOE. The left panel plots the evolution of the asset side of the balance sheet (in $ billion) of the BOE between 2006.1 and 2014.1. The right panel plots asset purchases of corporate paper, commercial paper, and government securities (in $ millions). Purchases of government securities are undertaken by a subsidiary company of the BOE, the Bank of England Asset Purchase Facility Fund Limited (BEAPFF). In turn the BOE finances its lending to BEAPFF by the creation of central bank reserves. Purchases of corporate and commercial paper are financed either by creation of reserves or by the Debt Management Office (right panel). Source: Bank of England.

was created and authorized to buy high-quality assets financed by the creation of central bank reserves and the Debt Management Office's (DMO) cash management operations. The program was designed to purchase medium- to long-term government bonds (Gilts), mostly from nonbank financial institutions (pension funds and insurance companies), to address the significant slowdown of the U.K. economy and reduce deflation risks. Running alongside APF the Commercial Paper Facility (CPF) enabled the purchase of investment grade sterling commercial paper, purchased in large quantities (see right panel of Figure 6.3), and aimed to direct funds to the corporate sector while supporting secondary market activity.

Between March and November 2009, the BOE purchased £200 billion of assets. The MPC voted to extend purchases by £75 billion in October 2011 and, again, at its February 2012 meeting voted to purchase additional £50 billion. In July 2012, citing weak domestic demand the MPC announced a final round of QE, purchasing a further £50 billion bringing total gilt purchases to £375 billion.

6.2.3 European Central Bank Operations

The monetary policy of the ECB differs from both the Fed and the BOE in several respects. Instead of monetizing the debt via outright QE interventions, for several years the ECB focused on providing immediate liquidity to the interbank market. The ECB used as its policy channel the refinancing operations, whereby banks borrow directly against high-quality collateral at one of two maturities: (i) the main refinancing operations (MROs) for a maturity of 2 weeks and (ii) the longer-term refinancing operations (LTROs) for a maturity of 3 months. Until October 2008, normal ECB refinancing was conducted by fixing a quantity of funding and allowing prices to adjust via an auction process.

6.2.3.1 The ECB and the Credit Crisis (2008–2009) Initially, between October 2008 and May 2009, the policy rate was lowered from 4.25% to 1% (Figure 6.1). Then, on October 15, 2008, the ECB changed conventional refinancing operations by announcing a new "unconventional" policy to lend at fixed-rate tender on a full-allotment basis.[7]

While initially the ECB was unwilling (or unable) to conduct outright QE, this decision implied that banks had unlimited access to central bank (short-term) liquidity should they post adequate collateral. The average refinancing rate was 0.75%. This should be compared to Spanish and Italian 2-year (10-year) Treasury yields that averaged 2.00–5.00% (5.00–7.00%) during the early part of this period. In late 2010, collateral requirements on LTROs were expanded to include a larger set of eligible assets and the tenors of the refinancing operations for eligible securities were extended to 6- and 12-month maturities.

[7]The announcement of unlimited funding was in response to a huge spike in the 3-month OIS spread which reached an all-time high of 198 basis points on October 10, 2008, reflecting a dramatic increase in perceived counterparty risk.

In 2009, as the economic conditions deteriorated, the eurozone covered bond market was seriously impaired.[8] In response, on May 7, 2009, the ECB announced its first Covered Bond Purchase Program (CBPP).[9]

- *The CBPP.* Under this program the ECB purchased euro-denominated covered bonds issued in the euro area, for an amount of EUR 60 billion. The purchases were conducted in both the primary and secondary markets and involved holding until maturity securities eligible for use as collateral for Eurosystem credit operations. Three programs were eventually introduced. The first set of interventions (CBPP1) took place between July 2009 and June 2010, it targeted covered bond with a minimum rating of "AA" or equivalent, and it reached a nominal amount of €60 billion. The second interventions (CBPP2) operated between November 2011 and October 2012 and reached a nominal amount of €40 billion. A third program was approved on October 20, 2014. The minimum credit quality required for bonds to be eligible was lowered to "BBB-" or equivalent.

6.2.3.2 The ECB and the EU Sovereign Bond Crisis (2010–2013) During the course of 2010–2012, due to persistent negative economic growth and accelerating government debt stocks, 4 out of 18 eurozone states (Greece, Ireland, Portugal, and Cyprus) were unable to repay or refinance their government debt without some form of explicit economic assistance. The unfolding EU Sovereign Bond Crisis induced the ECB to take several significant measures. The first was the *Securities Markets Program (SMP)*.

- *SMP.* In May 2010, under the SMP, the ECB started purchasing government bonds in secondary markets to alleviate pressures from sovereign debt risk on the balance sheet of financial institutions. However, to limit the risk of inflationary pressures, SMP purchases were "sterilized" by auctioning fixed-term liquidity absorbing deposits. The SMP was active during two periods. The first lasted between May and July 2010, and the second between August 2011 and January 2012. The program purchased a total of €212 billon of sovereign debt issued by Portugal, Ireland, Greece, Spain, and Italy. CBPP and SMP purchases are included in the category "Securities Held for Monetary Policy Purposes" in the left panel of Figure 6.4.

At the same time, the ECB expanded the scope and tenors of the initial LTRO program. In December 2011 and February 2012, the ECB conducted two large refinancing operations (LTRO1 and LTRO2) for tenors with a maturity up to 3 years. The total allotment of LTRO1 and LTRO2 was close to €1 trillion, in part financed by selling shorter maturities, resulting in a net increase in duration of the ECB's balance sheet: as of January 2012 almost all liquidity provided to eurozone banks had a maturity

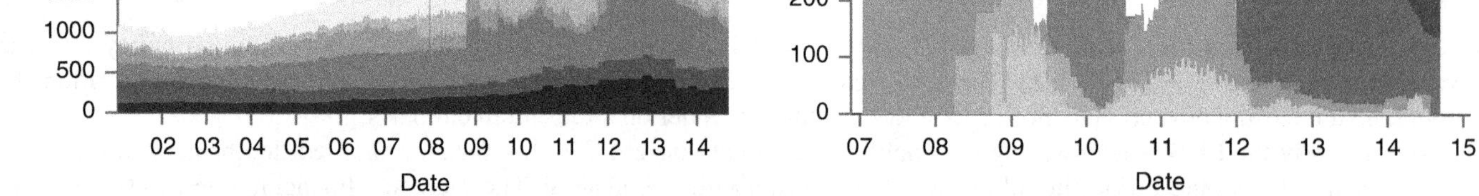

Figure 6.4 Balance sheet and asset purchases: ECB. The left panel plots the evolution of the asset side of the balance sheet (in €billion) of the ECB between 2002.1 and 2014.1. The right panel plots (in €billion) regular refinancing operations (LTROs) for maturities between 30 and 360 days and large refinancing operations LTRO1 and LTRO2. Source: ECB and Eurostat.

[8] Covered bonds are debt securities issued by financial institutions that collateralize the issue with "safe" assets. In the event of a bond default, covered bondholders have recourse to the issuer of the bond and its collateral pool.

[9] The CBPP was designed to "(i) easing funding conditions for credit institutions and enterprises; and (ii) encouraging credit institutions to maintain and expand lending to their clients."

of ∼ 3 years (right panel of Figure 6.4). Unsurprisingly, the LTRO facility was mainly demanded by banks in Portugal, Italy, Greece, Spain, and Ireland who accounted for in excess of 70% of uptake.[10]

The European sovereign debt crisis continued into the summer of 2012, with the solvency of Spain and Italy at risk, and intense debate of the viability of the euro in the financial press. On August 2, 2012, ECB President Mario Draghi announced that the ECB would expand its sovereign debt purchases and stated that "The euro is irreversible." In September 2012, the ECB announced details of Outright Monetary Transactions (OMTs) that would replace the SMP.

- The *OMTs* Program. Under OMT the ECB could buy government-issued bonds with maturities between 1 and 3 years, on the condition that sovereign states agree to certain domestic economic measures, thus enforcing a mechanism for support. As with the SMP, the OMT was intended to be sterilized so as not to affect the monetary base and therefore was not considered outright QE. After the announcement of OMT Spanish bond yields fell from 5.15% on August 2 to 2.80% in January 1, 2013, with a similar drop in yields observed in Italy. One interpretation of this drop is that the sheer existence of OMT was effective in its own right. However, closer inspection reveals that Spanish and Italian yields had already peaked in the weeks preceding the announcement.

6.2.3.3 ECB Starts QE (2014–2016) The year 2014 marks an important change in the conduct of monetary policy by the ECB. In order to reduce liquidity hoarding by banks and encourage lending to the private sector, in June 2014 the ECB introduced a negative deposit facility interest rate of −0.10% to reserve holdings in excess of the minimum requirement. This implied that banks were charged to deposit excess cash. In addition, the ECB approved a program of purchases of ABS and Treasury bonds.

- The *Asset-Backed Securities Purchase Program (ABSPP)*. Alongside the third covered bond purchase program CBPP3, on September 4, 2014, the ECB approved the outright purchase of eligible ABS for at least 2 years. The goal was to provide banks with the necessary funds to offer new lending to the real economy.

Then, on January 22, 2015, the ECB announces the formal start of significant quantitative easing policies, in a context where key ECB interest rates were already at their lower bound.

- The *Expanded Asset Purchase Program (EAPP)* authorizes the purchase of bonds issued by euro area central governments, agencies, and European institutions. The combined intended asset purchases amount to €60 billion monthly between March 2015 and until at least September 2016 (for a total balance sheet expansion of €1.140 trillion). The ECB motivated the decision stating that "asset purchases provide monetary stimulus to the economy in a context where key ECB interest rates are at their lower bound. They further ease monetary and financial conditions, making access to finance cheaper for firms and households. This tends to support investment and consumption, and ultimately contributes to a return of inflation rates towards 2%." The program will encompass the ABSPP and the covered bond purchase program (CBPP3), which were both launched in late 2014. The maturity of the securities covered by the new program is between 2 and 30 years. The purchases will be allocated across issuers from the various euro area countries on the basis of the ECB's capital key. Different than in the past, this program is designed to ensure that national central banks take most of the losses from any default or restructuring of their country's debt. Indeed, 20% of the asset purchases will be subject to a regime of risk sharing. In case of default, the Eurosystem accepts the same (pari passu) treatment as private investors.

6.2.3.4 A Comparison of the Three QE Programs A distinguishing feature of the Fed's and BOE policies after Lehman's bankruptcy is their explicit monetization of Treasury debt with respect to the policy implemented by the ECB. Indeed, unconventional measures implemented by the Fed had a substantially larger impact on the monetary base than the ECB. Figure 6.5 compares the evolution of money supply in Europe, the United Kingdom, and the United States. Indexing M1 to one on January 1, 2007, we see that by January 2015 the level of M1 in the United Kingdom (the United States) is about 2.2 (1.7) times larger. In Europe, on the other hand, the level of M1 in January 2015 is almost the same as in January 2007.

The institutional objectives of the three central banks are very different. The primary goal of the ECB is price and financial stability. The evolution of the crisis in Europe, especially after the Spring of 2010, was a significant outflow of deposits from credit institutions of peripheral countries to banks in core countries. This form of bank run made funding conditions particularly difficult and the ECB long-term refinancing operations were designed to be effective in addressing this liquidity event.

Among the Fed's objectives, on the other hand, there is the level of economic activity and unemployment. Consistent with this objective, the Fed actively tried to reduce the cost of capital of a wide range of assets, especially those used to finance directly economic activity.

[10]The intracountry breakdown of LTRO uptake is available from the consolidated balance sheet of the ECB.

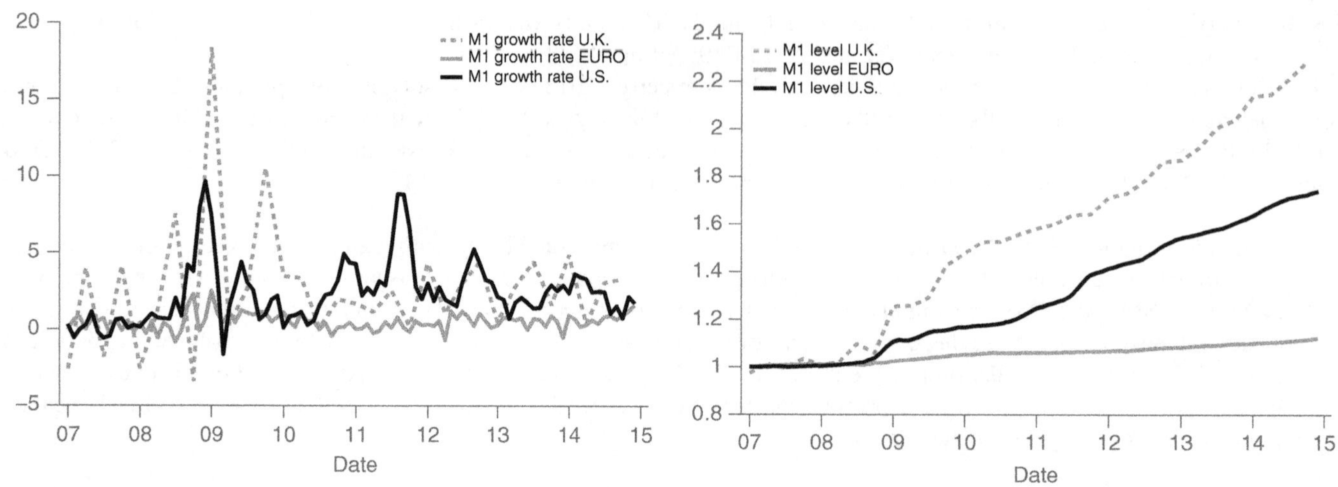

Figure 6.5 Money supply. The left pane plots the growth rate in money supply for the United States, the United Kingdom, and the eurozone. For the United States, this is M1 = Federal Reserve Notes + US Notes + Coins plus the amount of demand deposits, travelers checks, and other checkable deposits. For the United Kingdom, this is M1 (estimated) = cash outside BOE + operational deposits held at the BOE. For the eurozone, this is M1 = currency in circulation + overnight deposits. The right panel plots the level of money supply indexed to 1 on 1.1.2007. Source: McLeay, Radia, and Thomas (2014), FRED, ECB, and BOE.

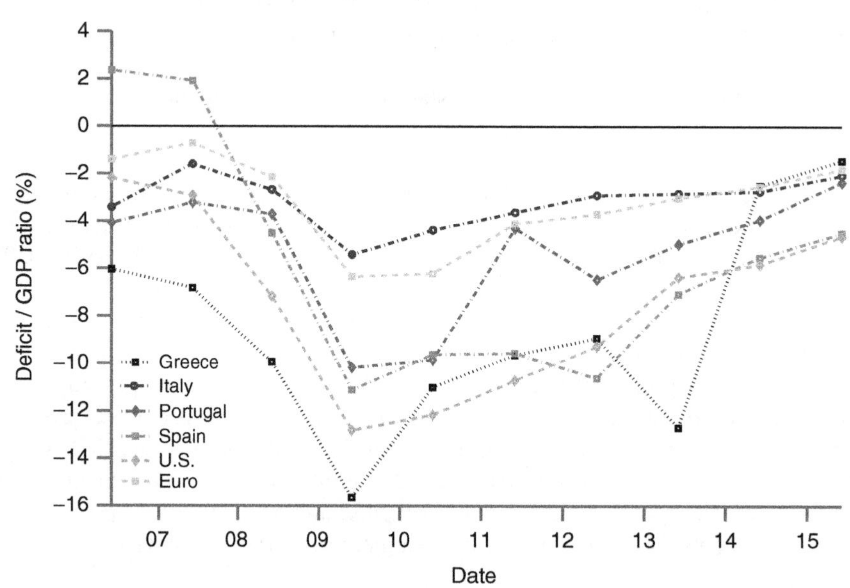

Figure 6.6 Deficit/GDP ratios. This figure displays government deficits as a percentage of GDP for Greece, Italy, Portugal, Spain, the United States, the 15 most recent members of the eurozone common currency block (Euro). Source: IMF and Eurostat.

The QE program introduced by the ECB on January 22, 2015 is very significant as it represents the first time the ECB conducts QE in the traditional sense. Under this program, the ECB buys bonds issued by euro area central governments, agencies, and European institutions in the secondary market against central bank money. The goal is to create incentives for these institutions to use the money to buy other assets and extend credit to the real economy. The implementation of the program relies on the role played by each national central bank in the secondary market, where they retain some level of flexibility in choosing the securities to purchase.

The ECB QE program introduced in January 2015 differs from the Fed QE1–QE3 of 2008–2012 in several respects. First, the relative size of the ECB purchases with respect to the overall budget deficit of EU area countries is larger. In 2009–2010, the United States was running a budget deficit in excess of 12%. In 2015, the average budget deficit in the European Union is about 2% (see Figure 6.6). This implies that while the Fed limited the net increase in duration held by the private sector, the ECB program is designed to remove duration. Figure 6.7 compares the difference between the expected impact of the ECB and Fed QE programs and shows the difference in the potential impact of the two types of quantitative easing programs. Assuming that

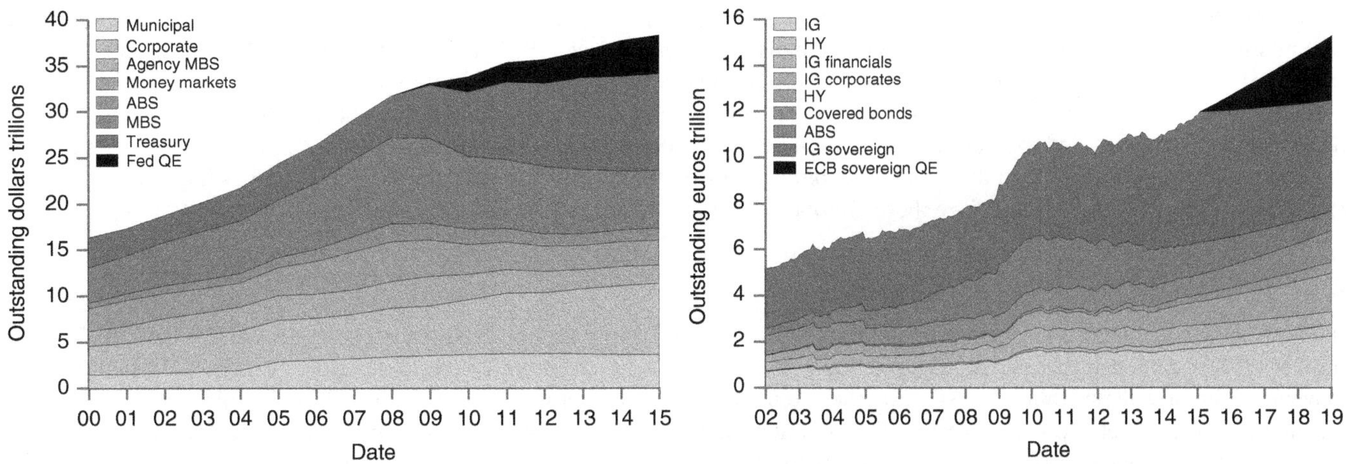

Figure 6.7 QE comparison. This figure displays the difference between the *expected* impact of the ECB QE program and the *realized* impact of the Fed QE program. The left panel plots the Fed impact while the right panel plots the ECB impact. The forecasted ECB impact is computed under the assumption that the budget deficit of EU member countries in 2016–2018 remains the same as in 2015. Source: RBS, SIFMA, and FRED.

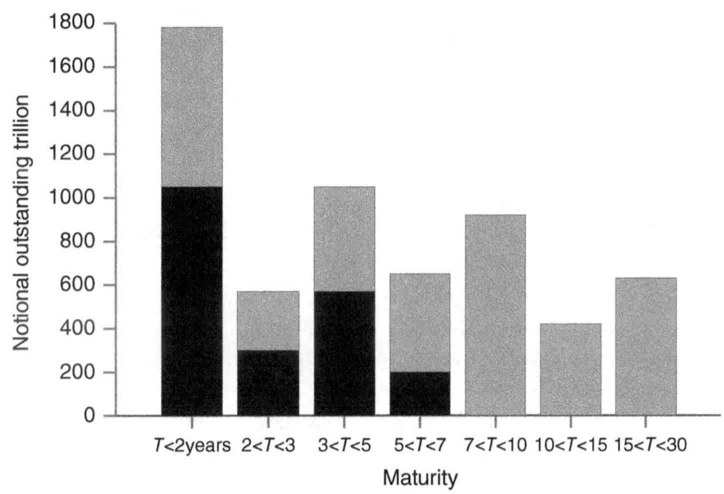

Figure 6.8 Outstanding amounts of sovereign with negative YTM. This figure displays the notional values of euro-denominated government debt securities with positive (gray) and negative (black) YTM. Each bar represents a maturity bucket, so that $2 < T < 3$ represents maturities between 2 and 3 years. The data includes major euro area countries - Germany, France, Italy, Spain, the Netherlands, Belgium, Austria, Finland, Portugal, and Ireland - and excludes inflation-linked securities. Source: Bloomberg, Goldman Sachs Global Investment Research.

the budget deficit of EU member countries in 2016–2018 will remain the same as in 2015, the total amount of bonds outstanding at the net of ECB purchases will compress (gray area in Figure 6.7). Second, the yield to maturity of sovereign bonds of several EU core countries is close to zero or negative. The total amount of sovereign debt trading at a negative yield on March 12, 2015 is shown in Figure 6.8. As a matter of comparison, on November 24, 2008, the day before the announcement of QE1, the yield to maturity on the 5-year U.S. Treasury bond was equal to 2.24%. It should be noticed that ECB's rules preclude buying of securities yielding less than its deposit rate of minus 0.20%. Thus, countries with near-zero yields have limited amount of eligible debt outstanding, implying that assets of countries such as Italy and Spain may become more scarce on a relative basis.

6.3 UNCONVENTIONAL POLICIES: A THEORETICAL FRAMEWORK

LSAPs were decisions about quantities of assets, instead of decisions about the short-term interest rate. LSAPs increased both the liabilities and assets of the central bank by increasing the private sector claims to the central bank (money and reserves) in exchange for assets sold to the central bank.

In a frictionless world, Ricardian irrelevance implies that a simple expansion of the balance sheet of the central bank should have no effect on the real economy. The argument is discussed in Wallace (1981) and Eggertsson and Woodford (2003). In the absence of credit constraints, imperfect or asymmetric information, and market segmentation, any rational agent would interpret the LSAPs by the central bank as a simple asset swap with no aggregate implications. Recent literature has investigated how the presence of frictions and market segmentation may induce deviations from the Ricardian irrelevance. For LSAPs to have an impact, these asset swaps need to make the marginal investor nonindifferent. This literature investigates four main economic channels.[11] First, we briefly summarize these alternative channels; then, we review the empirical evidence.

6.3.1 Portfolio Balance (Duration) Channel

The basic portfolio balance mechanism was initially discussed by Tobin (1961, 1963, 1969), Brunner and Meltzer (1973), and Frankel (1985). Suppose that the supply function of the asset purchased in the LSAP is inelastic. By removing duration and convexity from private portfolios, LSAPs have the potential to reduce the return required for holding a diminished amount of total risk on the balance sheet of private investors. The argument can be easily understood in the context of a mean–variance framework in which the representative private investor needs to clear markets conditional on the portfolio of the U.S. Federal Reserve and Treasury. The investor chooses a vector of portfolio weights ω to maximize $E_t(\omega' R - R_f) - \frac{1}{2}\gamma\omega'\Sigma_t\omega$, where $E_t(R) - R_f$ and $\Sigma_t = Var_t(R)$ are the conditional mean and covariance matrix of excess returns. The first-order conditions imply that $\omega = \frac{1}{\gamma}\Sigma_t^{-1}E_t(R - R_f)$. Suppose that the investor needs to choose between two risky assets, a short-term and long-term Treasury bond, ω_i with $i = s, l$. Let the total supply of Treasury bonds be S_i and let the amount purchased by the Fed via LSAPs be D_i, so that the net supply is $\hat{S}_i = S_i - D_i$. Since in equilibrium the Treasury market must clear, $E_t(R) - R_f = \gamma\Sigma_t[S - D]$. LSAPs swap long-dated assets D_l (Treasury bonds and MBS) for short-dated asset D_s (reserves/bank deposits/short-term Treasury bonds), thus reducing the residual quantity of long-term interest rate risk that agents need to hold in their portfolios. Thus, assuming Σ_t does not change, the model predicts that LSAPs induce a "broad" decline in long-term bond yields due to a reduction in the equilibrium risk (term) premium. This outcome is sometimes referred to as the "duration" channel.

King (2014) notices that the previous result, in which asset quantities can affect asset prices in equilibrium, holds more generally in any economy in which the pricing kernel depends on the return on wealth, the supply of bonds is fixed, and bondholders are isolated from taxpayers. The intuition is simple. Let $B(t, T)$ be the price of a zero-coupon bond with unit face value and maturity $T > t$. In the absence of arbitrage, there exists a stochastic discount factor m such that $B(t, T) = E_t[m \times B(t + s, T)]$ for $\forall s > t$ and $B(T, T) = 1$. Bond risk premia are proportional to $Cov_t[m; B(t + s, T)]$. Let the total supply of face value issued be equal to S_T. Quantities matter for bond risk premia if they affect $Cov_t(m, B(t + s, T))$. An example is given by economies in which the stochastic discount factor $m(t, t + s)$ depends on the return on wealth R^w. Let $S_{t,T}$ be the total face value supply of Treasury bond with maturity T and let $D_{t,T}$ be the purchases of these bonds by the Fed. If the total wealth W_t of the private sector is equal to the total financial value of these assets, then $W_t = (S_{t,T} - D_{t,T})' B(t, T)$ and the total return on wealth is given by $R^w(t, t + s) = [(S_{t,T} - D_{t,T})' B(t, T)]^{-1}(S_{t+s,T} - D_{t+s,T})' B(t + s, T)$. If the stochastic discount factor m depends on the return on financial wealth $R^w(t, t + s)$, then Fed's purchases D can affect risk premia by influencing the distribution of returns of claims with different maturity on the balance sheet of individual agents. For instance, in mean–variance economies the stochastic discount factor is linear in R^w; thus, bond risk premia depends on the LSAP variable D.[12] More generally, in economies with agents endowed with Epstein–Zin recursive preferences, the stochastic discount factor can be written as $m(t, t + s) = \left(\beta \frac{c_{t+s}}{c_t}^{-1/\psi}\right)^{\theta} R^w(t, t + s)^{\theta - 1}$, where θ and ψ are preference parameters.[13] It follows that $\log m(t, t + s) = \theta \log \beta - \frac{\theta}{\psi}\frac{c_{t+s}}{c_t} - (1 - \theta)\log R^w(t, t + s)$. In this case, if bond returns are a considerable component of the return of the wealth portfolio, LSAP can affect bond risk premia:

$$
\begin{aligned}
Cov(\log m_{t,t+s}, \log R^i_{t,t+s}) = {} & \frac{\theta}{\psi} Cov\left(\frac{c_{t+s}}{c_t}, R^i_{t,t+s}\right) \\
& + (1 - \theta) Cov(R^w_{t,t+s}, R^i_{t,t+s})
\end{aligned}
$$

[11] See also Joyce et al. (2012) for a review of the literature.

[12] Greenwood and Vayanos (2014) is an example of a mean–variance economy with this property. Their economy is formed by overlapping generations of short-lived arbitrageurs with mean–variance preferences over instantaneous final wealth. Arbitrageurs absorb a supply factor that is assumed to follow a Gaussian process, so that bond prices are exponentially affine. As common in this family of models, excess returns are proportional to factor variance. However, the factor loading depends on arbitrageurs' total exposure to factor risk.

[13] Epstein and Zin (1991) preferences U_t are defined recursively over current (known) consumption c_t and a certainty equivalent $R_t(U_{t+1})$ of tomorrow utility: $U_t = F(c_t, R_t(U_{t+1}))$. A common specification used in the literature is $U_t = \left((1 - \beta)c_t^{1-\rho} + \beta(E_t U_{t+1}^{1-\alpha})^{\frac{1-\rho}{1-\alpha}}\right)^{1/(1-\rho)}$. Risk aversion is parameterized by ρ, while the intertemporal elasticity of substitution is given by $1/\rho$. The reduced-form parameters θ and ψ of $m(t, t + s)$ are defined as $\theta = (1 - \alpha)/(1 - \rho)$ and $\psi = 1/\rho$. Notice that when $\rho = \alpha$, one recovers the standard time-separable expected utility case. When $\alpha > \rho$, that is, when $RRA > 1/IES$, agents have a preference for early resolution of uncertainty.

In the special case in which $\theta = 1$, preferences are time separable over consumption growth (as with power utility), with $\log m(t, t+s) = \theta \log \beta - \frac{1}{\psi}\frac{c_{t+s}}{c_t}$, one obtains

$$Cov(\log m_{t,t+s}, \log R^i_{t,t+s}) = \frac{1}{\psi} Cov\left(\frac{c_{t+s}}{c_t}, R^i_{t,t+s}\right)$$

Thus, when $\theta = 1$ and assets are enjoyed only for their pecuniary returns, the economy does not generate a portfolio channel effect (see King (2014) for the implications of different parametric assumptions).

6.3.2 Signaling Channel

An additional and distinct reason why LSAP can have broad effects on the economy is that they signal a change of the stance of the future monetary policy. This channel operates mainly thorough the impact on agents' expectations about the future path of interest rates. LSAP may potentially be quite effective in this sense as they increase the credibility of the Fed's commitment to keep interest rates lower than what is implied by the Taylor rule, even after a signal of economic recovery. The reason is that an increase in interest rate would precipitate large capital losses on the portfolio of long-term bonds accumulated during the LSAP (see Clouse et al. (2003); Eggertsson and Woodford, (2003); Woodford, (2012)).

Buraschi, Carnelli, and Whelan (2012) use a novel approach to distinguish between target shocks and innovation in the future path of the monetary policy. Their measure of path shocks is obtained from the residuals of a Taylor rule estimated directly on survey expectations. They find that during the period in which interest rates were close to the zero lower bound, path shocks were highly time varying even though short-term interest rates displayed little volatility. Moreover, they show that path shocks represent a source of priced risk and are important in explaining time variation in bond risk premia.

Similar to the portfolio balance channel, the signaling channel is *broad* in the sense that it affects all long-term interest rates at the same time. In the case of the signaling channel, changes in market prices should take place even before the actual execution of LSAP and as soon as agents revise their expectations.

6.3.3 Credit and Capital Constraint Channel

In general, LSAP may have an impact when the assets being swapped by the central bank are not perfectly substitutable. In this case, agents may not be indifferent to a LSAP decision and the Ricardian equivalence fails. A potential source of limited substitutability is the different liquidity value of short- and long-term assets. An example is discussed in the monetary economy of Kiyotaki and Moore (2012) in which firms can always use money to finance new investment opportunities but have limited ability to issue shares (or other corporate liabilities). In this economy, economic shocks may affect the amount of positive net present value projects undertaken by the firm because the firm may face a credit constraint. The imperfect substitutability between money and long-term financial instruments (such as Treasury bonds) makes LSAPs conducted by the central bank nonneutral since they relax this credit constraint.

A separate channel may arise when certain asset markets are dominated by a small number of specialist investors operating in segmented markets. This may be the case of asset markets requiring specific knowledge and modeling skills that only a small set of specialists may have. MBS and complex securitized products (e.g., cash and synthetic Collateralized Debt Obligations (CDOs)) may be examples of markets with a natural barrier to entry (at least in the short run). If these investors have limited access to funding markets, limits to arbitrage in these products may arise. When credit frictions are elevated, yields and expected rates of returns of these assets need to increase in equilibrium, with respect to an economy with no frictions, to compensate investors for the use of their scarce capital. In such an environment, the central bank decision to engage in LSAP for these assets reduces the relative scarcity of the capital available, thus reducing the impact of the friction on asset prices. Suppose, for instance, that a fraction of these specialists were affected by a negative wealth shock that would force them to unwind their positions in these assets. In the absence of a central bank intervention, remaining specialists would be the only other potential buyers. As a result, yield and expected returns would change. In this context, LSAPs make the central bank a residual provider of scarce capital for these assets so that yields and expected returns on these assets could fall. Examples of models investigating this channel include Curdia and Woodford (2010), Gertler and Karadi (2011), He and Krishnamurthy (2008), and Del Negro et al. (2011).

This channel has *narrow* implications with respect to both the portfolio balance and signaling channels. LSAP can have an impact exactly because these assets are traded in segmented markets. The existence of an externality (yield spillover) to other, seemingly unrelated, assets depends strictly on the extent to which these other assets are on the balance sheet of a specialist. An example would be the case of investors holding both agency and non-agency MBS. In that case, purchases of agency MBS may have a price impact also on non-agency MBS. It should be noticed that while this channel may be significant in segmented market, it might be less significant in international asset markets with small barriers to entry.

6.3.4 Preferred Habitat and Asset Scarcity Channel

The portfolio balance (duration) channel predicts that LSAPs affect equilibrium prices of *all* long-term assets, not just those being purchased. Thus, LSAP effects may be muted by the fact that the market with near-substitute assets is potentially very large (including Aaa corporate bonds, supranational bonds, and sovereign bonds of foreign countries issued in dollars). For this reason, a stream of the literature investigates the effect of segmented markets featuring imperfect asset substitution. Vayanos and Vila (2009) consider an economy with a set of preferred-habitat investors who specialize in securities of certain maturities. Their demand shocks are absorbed by risk-averse universal arbitrageurs who trade across maturities. However, risk aversion prevents these arbitrageurs from taking complete advantage of profit opportunities. If the total supply of bonds is inelastic, LSAPs of securities that are in positive net demand by preferred-habitat agents create a shortage that cannot be filled, at existing asset prices, by arbitrageurs. These assets may become scarce and prices have to adjust. In this model, the effect on yields is more or less narrow, depending on how wide the "habitat" is assumed to be.

In the Treasury bond market, scarcity is an important phenomenon. Indeed, both short-term and long-term bonds may trade at different convenience yields when they become scarce in the market. For instance, when on-the-run Treasury bonds are in excess demand, their owners can borrow at a *special* rate in the overnight repo market, which can be much lower than the general collateral rate. Buraschi and Menini (2002) document a series of empirical regularities of specialness in Treasury repo markets and show that it often affects also off-the-run bonds. Duffie (1996) proposes a search model to explain the dynamics of specialness in the repo markets.

One may argue, however, that the preferred-habitat theory is exposed to a similar criticism of the portfolio balance theory. Investors whose preferred habitat is defined in terms of a specific maturity range can always tap into close substitute assets with similar maturities. In this case, LSAP should generate yield spillovers also to Aaa corporate bonds, supranational bonds, and dollar-denominated foreign sovereign bonds. Thus, preferred habitats need to be narrowly defined in order to generate a significant narrow effect. Krishnamurthy and Vissing-Jorgensen (2012) argue that Treasury bonds are different because they provide a special service in terms of both liquidity and safety. For this reason, their collateral value is high, which is reflected in lower average borrowing rates in repo transactions.

Even within a narrow definition of a habit, the effect depends on the speed at which universal arbitrageurs can transmit shocks across maturities. If their risk aversion is low and capital plentiful, localized shocks are quickly transmitted across maturities. The existence of a set of well-funded universal arbitrageurs blurs the distinction between narrow and broad effects.

Krishnamurthy and Vissing-Jorgensen (2013) apply the scarcity argument to the MBS market. They assume the existence of a demand heterogeneity for old (vintage) and current-production (new) MBS. If current-production MBS provide a convenience yield to investors, the purchase of current-coupon agency MBS may reduce the net supply of these instruments and induce the private sector to create more of the scarce asset. In both cases, the prediction is that the effect of this channel on yields is narrow. It should be noticed that, exactly because this channel assumes heterogeneity in the convenience yields of different bonds, the effect of any LSAP is specific to the bond that is purchased.

6.4 UNCONVENTIONAL POLICIES: THE EMPIRICAL EVIDENCE

6.4.1 The Treasury Bond Market

The first paper to investigate the empirical implications of large-scale open market operations was Modigliani and Sutch (1966) in the context of the first "Operation Twist". The term "Operation Twist" was first used in 1961 – in a reference to the Chubby Checker song "The Twist" that was popular at the time – when the Fed employed a similar policy. Modigliani and Sutch (1966) found no evidence that the maturity structure of the federal debt, or changes in this structure, exert lasting or transient effects on the long–short spread. The authors compute real-time forecasts of interest rate spreads based on a mixed model of extrapolative and mean-reverting expectations and show that ex ante yield forecasts coincide with ex post realizations that were subject to open market operations.

The Operation Twist of the 1960s was, however, more limited in both scale and time than the one started in 2011. Several scholars argued that most recent LSAPs, by removing duration and convexity risk from private portfolios, reduced the return required for holding a diminished amount of this risk. In turn, this reduced the risk premium and the cost of capital of long-term debt. What is the exact amount of Treasury duration risk removed by the Fed? If the Fed made significant purchases of Treasury bonds, two other effects might have limited their impact. First, during the same period the Treasury increased quite significantly the total issuance of Treasury bonds to finance a large budget deficit. Second, the drop in interest rates to near-zero levels mechanically increased the duration of the stock of outstanding bonds. Thus, the net effect is unclear. Figure 6.9 shows the total dollar amount of Treasury bonds outstanding. This amount increased from about 3.9 trillion \$ in 2007 to 11 trillion \$ in 2015. Part of the new issuance of Treasury bonds has been purchased by the Fed.

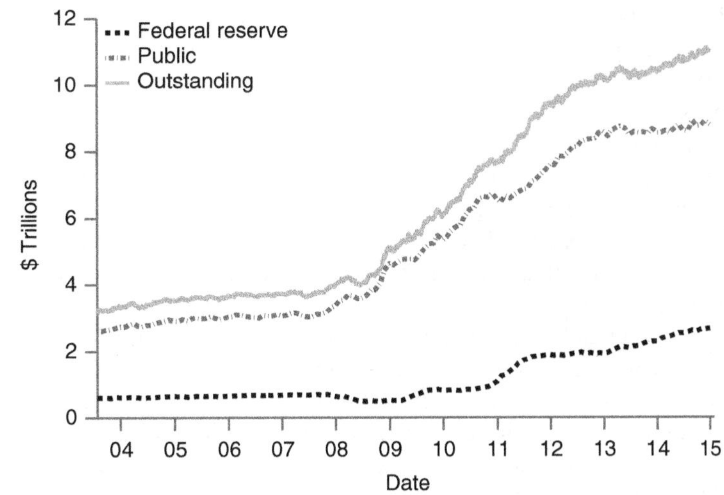

Figure 6.9 Outstanding treasury debt value. This figure shows a time series for the value (in trillions of dollars) of the total outstanding stock of Treasury bonds, the value of Treasury bonds owned by the Federal Reserve, and the residual component owned by the public. Source: CRSP and the New York Fed.

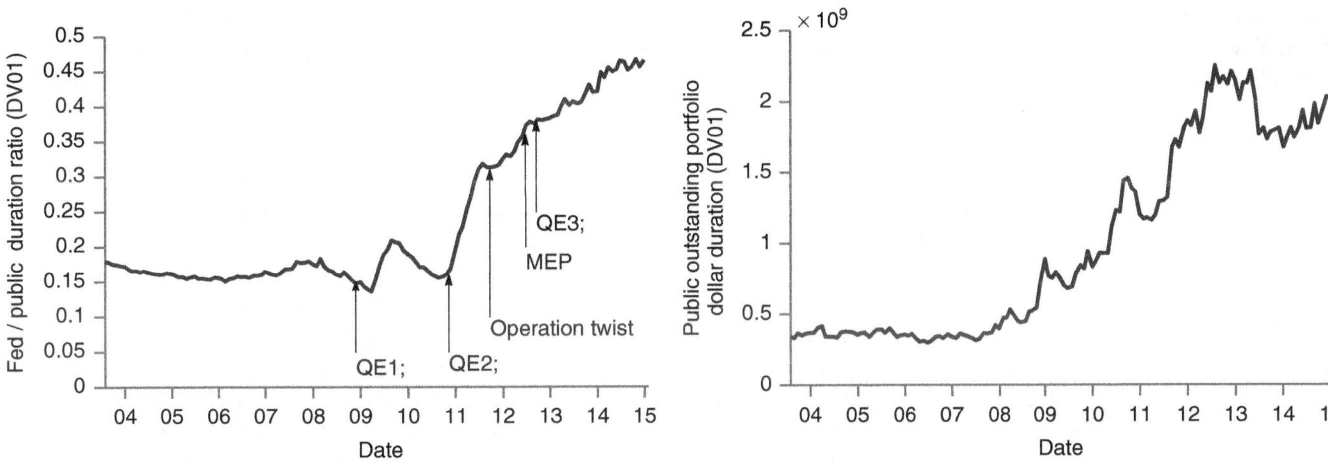

Figure 6.10 Dollar durations. The left panel plots the ratio of the Fed DV01 over the total residual private sector DV01. The right panel plots the absolute level of the total residual private sector DV01. Source: CRSP, the New York Fed, and the Monthly Statement of the Public Debt.

A rigorous quantification of the impact of these programs on the duration requires bond-specific data for both the entire stock of Treasury bond outstanding and the portfolio of Treasury bonds accumulated by the Fed over time. First, we use CUSIP-specific data from CRSP to compute the total outstanding dollar duration (DV01) of U.S. debt.[14] This requires aggregating the whole universe of real and nominal Treasury bills, notes, and bonds.[15]

Then, we use data from the Federal Reserve reporting outright Treasury holdings for the System Open Market Account.[16] Finally, we subtract the DV01 removed by the Fed to calculate the residual DV01 left in the market. Figure 6.10 displays the results.

We find that the DV01 of the Fed portfolio of Treasury bonds increased from about 0.8×10^8 dollars to about 9.3×10^8 in 2013. However, we also find that the total dollar duration of the stock of Treasury bonds increased almost by the same proportion. At the beginning of 2007, the DV01 of the total stock of Treasury bonds (including TIPS) was about 0.35×10^9 dollars. This increased 10-fold to a level slightly above 3×10^9 dollars in 2013. We compute the ratio of the dollar duration of the Fed balance sheet over the total dollar duration of the stock of Treasury bonds in the portfolio of the private sector. In 2007, this ratio is 0.17

[14]The DV01 (i.e., "the dollar value of a basis point") is the dollar change in value of the assets for a 1 basis point change in the yield. It is related to the modified duration *ModD* as $DV01 = [V \times ModD]/10,000$.

[15]The CRSP dataset contains errors. After applying a series of filters to search for these, we manually cross-reference entries with the Monthly Statement of the Public Debt (MSPD) and Downloadable Files http://treasurydirect.gov/govt/reports/pd/mspd/mspd.htm.

[16]http://www.newyorkfed.org/markets/.

and it increases to 0.40 in 2013. We notice that while this ratio increased somewhat slightly during the QE1 period, the greatest accumulation of DV01 on the balance sheet of the Fed starts occurring in 2011 with QE2 and Operation Twist.

The right panel of Figure 6.10 shows the residual DV01 that is on the balance sheet of the private sector. Between November 2010 and February 2011, QE2 was effective in removing dollar duration from the private sector. Notwithstanding these LSAPs, the residual amount of dollar duration in the portfolios of the private sector in 2013 is larger by a factor of 4 than in 2007. This is due both to the net increase in the total amount of Treasuries issued and the drop in interest rates that increased the average DV01 of each bond. It is also important to notice that the previous analysis does not include other assets that are near substitutes to Treasury bonds, such as Aaa corporate bonds and sovereign bonds from high-credit-quality issuers. If one were to account also for these near-substitute assets, the percentage impact of the LSAP in removing dollar duration off the balance sheet of the private sector would be even weaker.

Even if the Fed had managed to remove duration from the portfolio of agents, according to the Ricardian irrelevance argument, this would not necessarily lead to a reduction of equilibrium risk premia. Eventually, interest payments on the larger amount of Treasury debt needs to be financed by the taxpayers. If changes in the maturity structure of the payments made to the government's creditors are paid with nondistortionary changes in taxes, then any increase in the private wealth of bondholders should be matched by an equal increase in the liabilities of taxpayers, as argued by Ricardo (1820) and Wallace (1981), and more recently by Eggertsson and Woodford (2003) in the context of economies at the zero lower bound. Risk premia are affected only if bondholders and taxpayers are segmented, each having different discount rates and required compensation for risk. We conclude that the key argument in support for the portfolio balance effect rests on tenuous grounds. If LSAPs had an effect on the term premium, this occurred notwithstanding the increase in dollar duration in the private sector portfolio, not because of it. Those supporting the transmission mechanism of the portfolio balance channel would argue that in the absence of LSAPs the increase in interest rate risk on the balance sheet on the public would have been substantially higher and long-term yield would have been higher. Tests of this counterfactual argument are not model-free and require the specification and estimation of a model.[17]

Another element that needs to be considered is that the effect of the portfolio balance channel depends on interest rate risk. For instance, in the portfolio balance section we highlighted that in a simple mean–variance framework, expected returns need to satisfy $E_t(R) - R_f = \gamma\Sigma_t[S - D]$. This implies that low-interest-rate volatility reduces the effect of asset purchases D. This is important since the Fed started LSAPs in conjunction with a forward guidance policy that was intended to reduce Σ_t. This may have reduced the potential impact of LSAPs on risk (term) premia. Going forward, on the other hand, the abandonment of forward guidance and the return to a more data-driven monetary policy may increase (within the context of a portfolio balance model) the impact of a reduction of the balance sheet of the Fed on risk (term) premia in an undesirable way.

To investigate further the effect of LSAPs on bond risk premia, we study the CAPM beta of long-term bonds by computing the in-sample covariance of the 10-year Treasury bond return with the S&P 500 return and the variance of the stock market return. The beta is the ratio of the two. In order to highlight the potential dynamics during different QE policies, Figure 6.11 shows the time variation in the long-term bond beta using daily data and a rolling 1-year window. Two results emerge. First, in the 1980s and 1990s long-term bonds had a positive beta on the stock market. In the later part of the sample, the beta declined and has become negative. Bonds have become natural hedges for the stock market. This is consistent with many recent financial commentaries. Second, we find that the bond beta declined during all five QE programs. While these results should be interpreted with caution given the suggestive nature of the exercise, it provides some supporting evidence that LSAPs did indeed reduce bond risk (term) premia.

To gain additional insight on the effect of LSAPs on asset prices, several important studies use alternative methodologies, test assets, and observation frequencies to distinguish and quantify the relative importance of different transmission channels.

6.4.1.1 High-Frequency Studies A first stream of the literature uses event study methods and high-frequency data to address the issue of the identification of the causal relation between Fed interventions and interest rate movement. One of the first examples of this approach is Swanson (2011) who focuses on the reaction of Treasury yields in a narrow window of time surrounding six announcements during the Operation Twist of 1961. The results suggest that in four cases the effect was statistically significant but small in magnitude. For example, the cumulative effect of point estimates suggests long-term Treasury yields were lowered by about 15 basis points. Moreover, the author finds mixed evidence in support of a broad channel. On the one hand, the effect on long-term yields on government agency securities is similar to those on long-term Treasuries; on the other hand, long-term corporate bond yields declined by substantially less (2–4 bp). Gagnon et al. (2010) expand on the previous study by considering the period from December 2008 to March 2010 and including eight official announcements. In addition, they use information concerning the potential or actual expansion of the size, composition, and/or timing of LSAPs. They use 1-day windows around the announcements and consider a broad set of assets with different maturities to investigate the predictions of the portfolio balance channel. The assets used include the 2-year and 10-year Treasury yields, the 10-year agency debt yield, the

[17] See, for instance, King (2014) and Hamilton and Wu (2012).

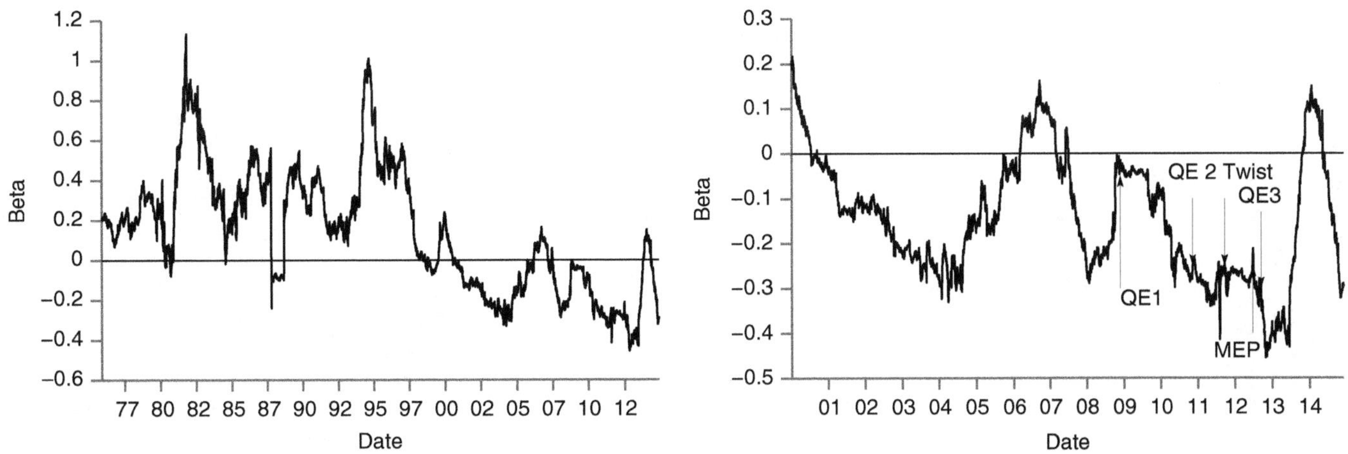

Figure 6.11 CAPM beta on a 10-year zero-coupon bond. The left and right panels display the realized CAPM beta on a 10-year zero- coupon bond. The beta is computed using a 1-year rolling window of daily returns by computing variances and covariances separately. The market index is taken to be the S&P 500.

current-coupon 30-year agency MBS yield, the 10-year Treasury term premium, the 10-year swap rate, and the Baa corporate bond index yield. These authors find that both the level of interest rates and term premium (measured as the spread between the 10-year and 2-year Treasury yields) dropped in seven out of the eight announcement days. On average, across these events, the 10-year Treasury yield, 10-year agency debt yield, and current-coupon agency MBS yield declined 91, 156, and 113 basis points, respectively. Since LSAPs affected also yields of assets that were not directly targeted in these purchases, the authors interpret the results as supporting evidence for a "broad" portfolio balance channel.

D'Amico et al. (2014) is a comprehensive analysis using event study techniques at even higher sampling frequencies. The authors use intraday CUSIP-level data to examine the price reaction to the different information content of separate FOMC and Desk announcements. This is important in order to gain additional insights to distinguish the potential existence of a narrow versus broad channel. The identification strategy is based on the observation that the Fed has often made two announcements. In the first, the Fed has announced the decision to start a new purchasing program; in the second, the Fed has provided specific details about the quantity and duration/maturity of the securities that was intending to target. The sequence of announcements made in March 18, 2009, is a useful example. At 14:15, the Fed communicated the decision to purchase a large amount of long-term Treasury bonds and agency MBS. Later, at 14:44 the Desk announced that the Fed would target Treasury bonds with duration between 2 and 10 years. On the basis of the first announcement, both channels predict that at 14:15 yields of all long-term Treasury bonds (above 2 years) would drop. However, the second announcement, by excluding maturities above 10 years, reduced the average duration of Fed's purchases. This identifies two separate predictions. The duration risk channel predicts that after 14:45 *all* bonds, across the whole maturity spectrum, should reverse the initial effect because the amount of duration risk removed by the Fed is smaller than expected. The narrow channel, on the other hand, predicts that after 14:45 *only bonds with maturities above 10 years* should give up part of the initial yield drop. The authors use high-frequency data on all outstanding bonds (purchased, not purchased, and across different maturities) to identify these two channels. The empirical evidence reported by the authors (see Figure 6.12) shows that maturities above 7.8-year Treasury bonds gave up at least half of the initial change in yields. This rejects that the duration risk channel is the only channel and is consistent with the existence of a narrow channel.

The authors also calculate separate proxies for local-supply shocks (ls_i) and for the duration risk channel (idr_i) defined as the product of security i 's sensitivity to duration risk times the unexpected variation in total Macaulay duration risk due to the program. Then, they extend the analysis to consider five Fed's programs (with the exclusion of QE3) and run a cross-sectional regression on the changes in bond yields around the announcements

$$\Delta y_i = \beta_0 + \beta_1 \times ls_i + \beta_2 \times idr_i + u_i$$

where Δy_i is the bond-specific yield change. They investigate all five program announcements both separately and jointly in a pooled regression. They find that both $\hat{\beta}_1$ and $\hat{\beta}_2$ are statistically significant. On average, the implied effect on the 10-year yield from an unexpected \$100 billion program is a reduction in yield of 5.6 basis points, due to the duration risk channel, and of 3.5 basis points, due to the local scarcity channel. They also argue that there is no evidence that the announcement impact of these two channels has declined since the first LSAP.

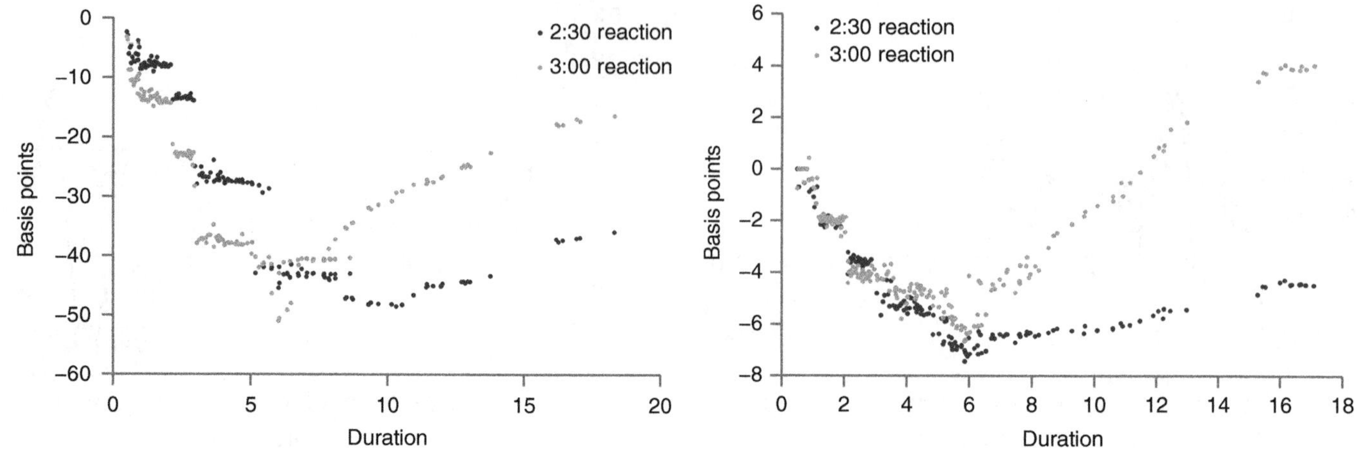

Figure 6.12 LSAP announcement effects (D'Amico et al., 2014). The left figure shows the Treasury market reaction to the "LSAP1" Announcement at 2:30 and 3:00 (March 18, 2009). The right figure shows the evidence for the "Reinvestment" Announcement (August 10, 2010). Source: D'Amico et al. (2014).

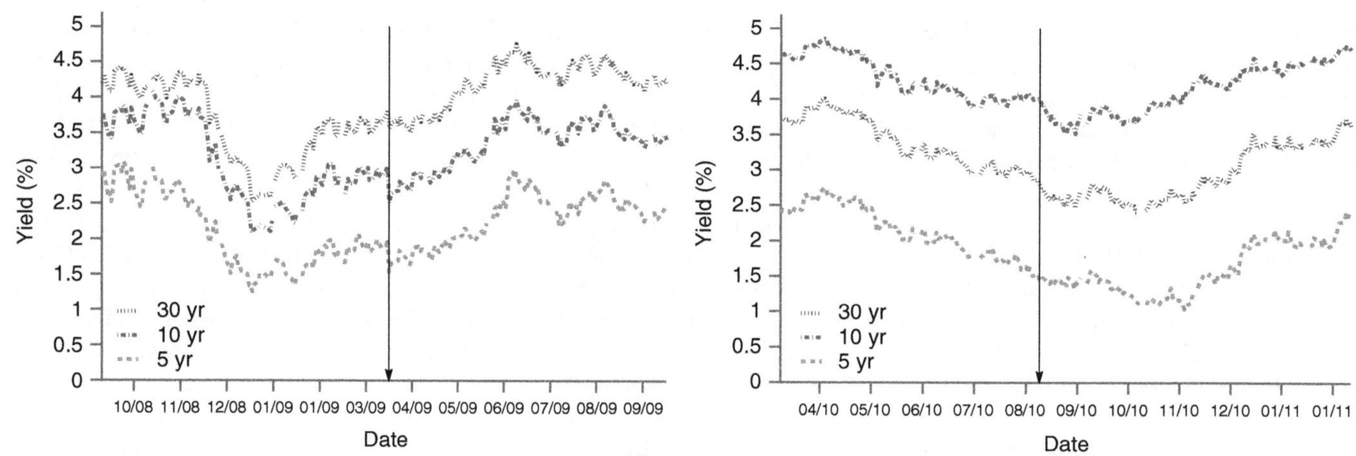

Figure 6.13 LSAP1 and Reinvestment Announcements. The two panels show the dynamics of interest rates 6 months before and after two of the announcements discussed in the high-frequency literature. The first is LSAP1 (March 18, 2009) while the second is the Reinvestment Announcement (August 10, 2010). Both events are discussed in detail in D'Amico et al. (2014). From top to bottom, the two panels plot the 30-year, 10-year, and 5-year U.S. Treasury constant maturity yields. The vertical bar indicates the announcement date. Source: FRED at St Louis Fed.

6.4.1.2 How Persistent is the Effect? The advantage of event studies based on high-frequency data is their ability to address the fundamental identification issue of distinguishing the exogenous effect of LSAPs from other contemporaneous effects, which plagues time-series studies using low-frequency data. During such short intervals of time, economic conditions do not change, and if one detects changes in yields, this can indeed be attributed to the policy announcement.[18] However, whether the effect being documented over such a short window of time is persistent is another question. Figure 6.13 shows the dynamics of interest rates 6 months before and after the two announcements made by the Fed on March 18, 2009 (the "LSAP1 Announcement") and August 10, 2010 (the "Reinvestment Announcement"). These two events are part of the study in D'Amico et al. (2014) in event time and the results are summarized in Figure 6.12. In the 20 minutes following the announcement, the short-term effect is significant. However, if one zoom out from the event window, after a week one can no longer easily conclude that yields are lower than the day before the announcement. The transitory nature of these effects is quite striking if one consider the LSAP1 Announcement. In event time, this is the announcement with the largest intraday impact. However, the effect is completely transitory: long-term Treasury yields start to drift higher shortly after the announcement. A month later long-term yields are higher than immediately before the LSAP1 Announcement. The 10-year Treasury bond yield increased from 2.97 (February 16, 2009) to values ranging between 2.98% (April 17, 2009) and 3.29% (May 7, 2009). Yields of maturities between 2 and 3 years were mainly unchanged.

[18] D'Amico et al. (2014) consider time intervals as short as 20 minutes.

One could be tempted to conclude that LSAP1 had the effect of increasing interest rates, instead of reducing them. It all depends on whether one wants to focus on the temporary or long-term effect. The Reinvestment Announcement looks somewhat more promising. However, even in this case 3, 5, and 10 years U.S. Treasury yields move to 0.88%, 1.59%, and 2.81%, respectively, on September 10, 2010, from 0.81%, 1.54%, and 2.86%, as of August 9, 2010. The difference is hardly significant and in some cases they, again, drift higher. This highlights the risk of drawing strong policy implications using exclusively short-term effects from high-frequency event studies. In summary, the evidence suggests that even if frictions may indeed be responsible of short-term deviations from the Wallace irrelevance proposition, a significant component of these deviations may indeed be transitory. If this were the case, then the documented short-term impact should simply be interpreted as a wealth transfer from the Fed to bond traders. Smart hedge funds would sell to the Fed as soon as it announces its intention to buy. In the case of LSAP1, the profit would have been significant: according to the estimates of D'Amico et al. (2014) the short-term price impact has been about −50 basis points for bonds with 6-year duration. A hedge fund trading with the Fed would have pocketed about $30 million for each $1 billion trade (during LSAP1, the Fed purchased a total of $300 billion).

6.4.1.3 Low-Frequency Studies A second stream of this literature uses time-series and low-frequency information. The duration risk channel argues that the U.S. Treasury pays a premium to arbitrageurs for the ability to lock in a long-term borrowing cost. The Treasury's preferred habit for long-term bonds is motivated by its desire to limit fiscal risks. However, market needs to clear and somebody needs to hold these bonds. If arbitrageurs are risk averse, their net holdings of long-term bonds give rise to a risk premium. In the no-arbitrage heterogeneous agent model by Vayanos and Vila (2009), equilibrium risk premia are proportional to the product of the volatility and the price of risk $\Sigma\lambda_t$. However, the price of risk depends on the arbitrageur total exposure to factor risk, so that the risk premium can be specified as

$$\underbrace{[\gamma\Sigma\Sigma']}_{\Lambda}d_t = \Lambda\sum_{n=2}^{N} z_{t,n}b_{n-1}$$

where b_n are factor loadings of fundamentals on yields and $z_{t,n}$ is the period t portfolio fraction of bond maturity n in the arbitrageurs portfolio. The greater the demand of preferred-habit agents for issuing bonds with maturity n, the greater the fraction of these bonds held by the arbitrageur. Thus, portfolio holdings of arbitrageurs interact with the factors loadings on fundamentals in driving risk compensation and the term premium.

Greenwood and Vayanos (2014) is a rigorous test of the predictions of this model using data on the U.S. Treasury bond market between June 1952 and December 2007. They use bond-specific data from CRSP to compute the maturity structure of aggregate payments on government debt and calculate the average dollar duration of the total stock of Treasury bonds outstanding. They scale this quantity by GDP to obtain the time series of the maturity-weighted debt-to-GDP ratio (MWD/GDP). This is approximately equal to the product of debt to GDP times the average maturity of debt. Figure 6.14, left panel, shows the scatter plot of the excess returns on a 5-year Treasury bond at holding periods of 3 years (Y-axis) against MWD/GDP ratio (X-axis). The figure shows a positive relationship between excess returns and MWD/GDP in the 1952–2007 period. Since the model predicts that an increase in MWD/GDP leads to an increase in yield spreads, in the right panel we also (sample period 1952–2007) show a scatter plot for this relation "in differences" to account for the persistence of both left- and right-hand side variables. Each year we compute the average quarterly change in MWD/GDP and the corresponding change in the 5-year minus 1-year term spread. The variables are labeled as $\Delta(MWD/GDP)$ on the Y-axis and $\Delta(y^{(5)} - y^{(1)})$ on the X-axis. Considering this relationship in differences reveals a weak relationship between bond supply and yield spreads and highlights the dangers of making inference between highly autocorrelated variables.

The authors also run monthly time-series regressions for the yield $y_t^{(\tau)}$ spread over the 1-year yield $y_t^{(1)}$

$$y_t^{(\tau)} - y_t^{(1)} = \alpha + \beta\left(\frac{MWD_t}{GDP_t}\right) + \varepsilon_t, \quad \varepsilon_t = \rho\varepsilon_{t-1} + u_t, u_t \sim N(0,\sigma)$$

The slope coefficient β of the yield regression of the 5- and 20-year yield spread is equal to 0.0030 and 0.0050 with t-statistics equal to 1.729 and 1.936, respectively. The authors are careful in accounting for the presence of overlapping data due both to the use of data sampled at monthly frequency and to the significant persistence of $\frac{MWD_t}{GDP_t}$. Thus, they compute t-statistics assuming an AR(1) process for the residuals (Table C.2 in the original article). This implies that a one-standard-deviation increase in MWD/GDP raises the yield spread on the 5- and 20-year bond by an amount equal to 30 and 50 basis points and its expected return over a 1-year horizon by 110 and 250 basis points. The authors highlight that these results predict that the LSAP carried out by the Fed during QE1 would have a much smaller impact on yields than suggested by previous event studies. The total amount of purchases of Treasury bonds during both the QE1 and QE2 programs was $0.9 trillion. The average maturity of Treasury securities purchased by the Fed was approximately 6.5 years (average duration 5 years). Thus, given that the U.S.

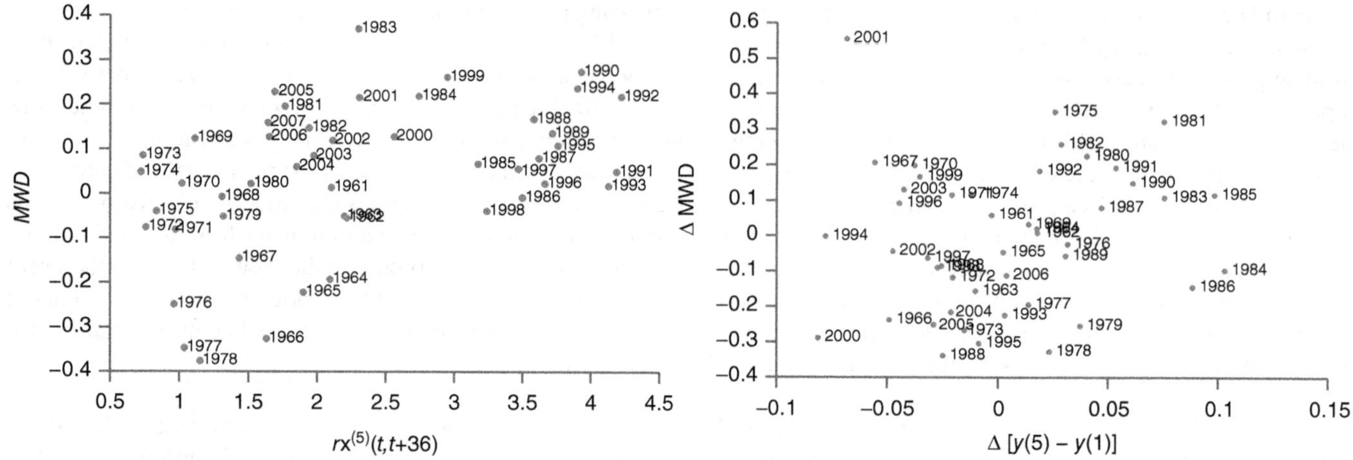

Figure 6.14 Excess bond returns and differences in yield spreads. The left panel of this figure shows a scatter plot of the excess bond returns on a 5-year Treasury bond at holding periods of 3 years (Y-axis) against MWD/GDP ratio (X-axis) for the 1952–2007 period. The right panel shows a scatter plot of the difference in the yield spread of the 2-, 3-, 4-, 5-year Treasury bond minus the 1-year yield at quarterly frequency (Y-axis) against the differences in the MWD/GDP ratio (X-axis). Source: Greenwood and Vayanos (2014), the New York Fed, and the Monthly Statement of the Public Debt.

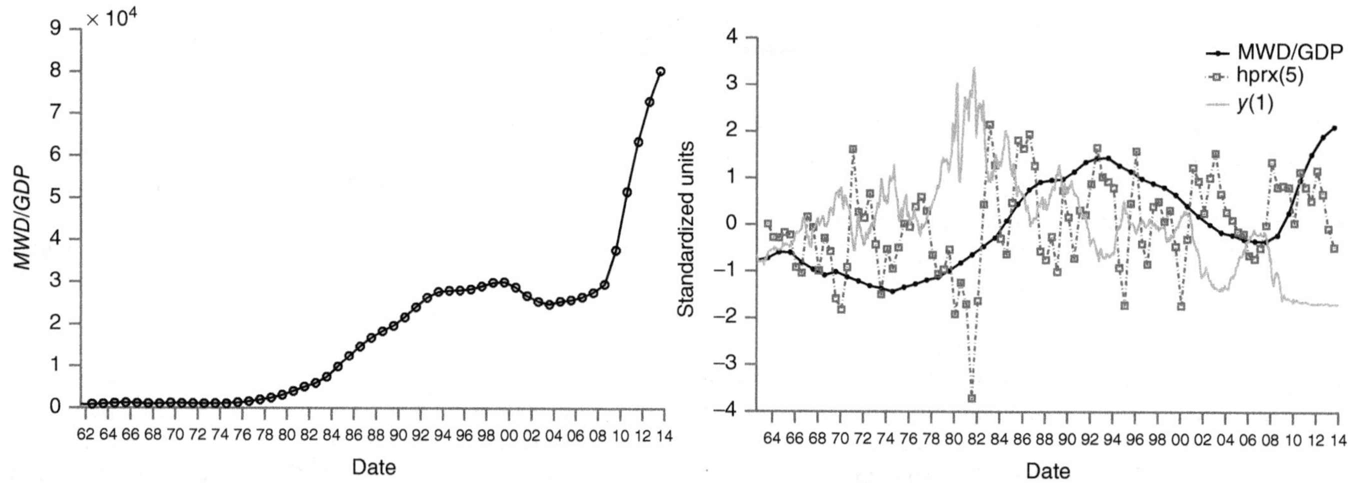

Figure 6.15 Excess returns and MWD/GDP. This figure plots the bond supply factor MWD/GDP computed following Greenwood and Vayanos (2014), whereby for each month outstanding debt payments are sorted by maturity, weighted by maturity, summed across maturities, and then scaled by the GDP index prevailing in the previous quarter. The figure also plots 1-year excess bond returns on a 5-year zero-coupon bond and the 1-year zero-coupon yield. Sample Period: 1961.7–2014.12. Source: the New York Fed and the Monthly Statement of the Public Debt.

GDP was about \$14 trillion, the reduction in $\frac{MWD_t}{GDP_t}$ has been about $\frac{0.9}{14} \times 5 = 0.32$. The model therefore predicts a reduction in the long-term yield by $0.0030 \times 0.32 = 9.6$ basis points. Gagnon et al. (2011) and D'Amico et al. (2012) estimate that the two QE programs together lowered the 10-year Treasury yield by 90–100 basis points. Even if one were to consider *all* purchases (thus including Treasury bonds, MBS, agency and bank debt) during the entire period November 25, 2008, to June 1, 2011, the reduction in $\frac{MWD_t}{GDP_t}$ has been about $\frac{2.35}{14} \times 5 = 0.84$. Thus, the estimates of Greenwood and Vayanos (2014) predict a reduction in long-term yield of only $0.0030 \times 0.84 = 25.2$ basis points.

Figure 6.15, left panel, shows the evolution of the level of MWD_t. During the 2007–2014 period, the level of MWD_t increases by a factor almost equal to 3. This provides a very interesting out-of-sample testing ground for the model. First, we compute and update $\frac{MWD_t}{GDP_t}$ following Greenwood and Vayanos (2014) for the sample period 2007–2014. Second, we compare the realization of $y_t^{(\tau)} - y_t^{(1)}$ to the time series implied by the model $\left[\bar{\alpha} + \bar{\beta}\frac{MWD_t}{GDP_t}\right]$ where the parameter estimates are computed using data up until 2007. The right panel of Figure 6.16 displays out-of-sample predicted term spread. The result shows that the model correctly

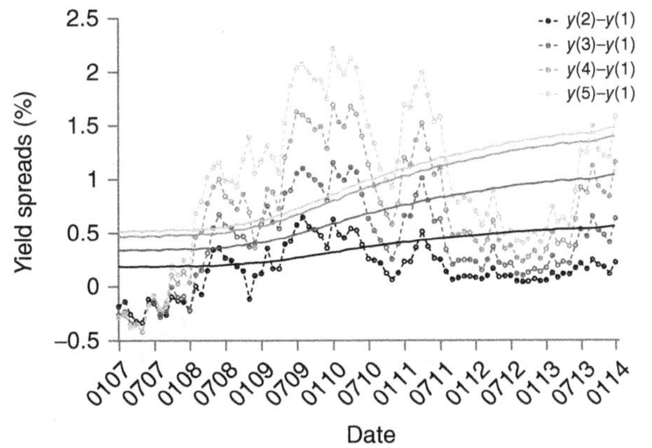

Figure 6.16 Yield spread prediction. This figure plots the out-of-sample forecast (now-cast) implied by the linear regression

$$ys(n) = \alpha + \beta\left(\frac{MWD}{GDP}\right)_t + \varepsilon_t^{(n)}$$

where $ys(n) = [y_t(n) - y_t(1)]$. The in-sample parameter estimates $(\bar{\alpha}, \bar{\beta})$ are computed using the sample period 1961.7–2006.7. Using these estimates, implied yield spreads are computed using the time series for the bond supply factor for the period 2007.1–2014.12

$$\overline{ys}(n) = \overline{\alpha} + \overline{\beta}\left(\frac{MWD}{GDP}\right)_t$$

Source: The New York Fed and the Monthly Statement of the Public Debt.

predicts that the yield spread will increases, due to the increase in $\frac{MWD_t}{GDP_t}$ during the financial crisis. However, the size of the error is quite large: in January 2010, the actual 5-year term spread is 200 basis points while the model implies a spread of 90 basis points. Moreover, it is noticeable that in January 2013, the yield spread compresses to a value equal to a quarter of the term spread in January 2010, while $\frac{MWD_t}{GDP_t}$ does not decrease between 2010 and 2013.

To test more formally the link between yield spreads and bond supply, we revisit the Greenwood and Vayanos (2014) regression specification but run a regression in differences

$$\Delta[y(n) - y(1)] = \alpha + \beta\Delta\left(\frac{MWD}{GDP}\right)_t + \varepsilon_{t,t+4}^{(n)}$$

where quarterly changes are sampled to coincide with reversion to the GDP index for the sample period 1961:Q2 and 2006:Q4. Table 6.1 reports the results. The t-statistics and low R^2 show that once the variables are differenced there is very little empirical evidence of a link between bond supply and interest rates. This is consistent with the scatter plot in Figure 6.14, right panel.

A second prediction of the model is in terms of expected returns. The higher the duration risk that agents need to absorb, the higher the risk premium. The right panel of Figure 6.15 shows the time series of MWD/GDP and the 1-year excess return on a 5-year zero-coupon bond, from July 1961 including the financial crisis period up to December 2014. While one can identify periods in which the two series are positively correlated, one can also identify periods where excess returns on bond supply are negatively correlated.

Some important learning points emerge. First, on average it seems indeed that the higher is the duration risk in the market, the higher is the yield spread. The latest QE period is a good example. However, the statistical link is not compelling. The U.S. bond market has become progressively more international and a substantial component of the demand is by foreign and well-diversified investors. It is possible that a measure of duration risk that accounts for the financial wealth of these foreign countries/investors might provide more precise estimates. Another important challenge that time-series studies face is that changes in average dollar duration are not exogenous and occur contemporaneously with several other economic factors that might affect bond markets. High-frequency event studies have the theoretical advantage that they can better identify policy shocks from other contemporaneous effects. However, they also have the general shortcoming of focusing on relationships that may be transitory.

An alternative estimation of the portfolio balance channel is proposed by Hamilton and Wu (2012). They estimate a linear dynamic specification of the three traditional term structure factors $X_t = [level, slope, curvature]$

$$X_{t+1} = c + \rho X_t + \phi q_t + \varepsilon_{t+1}.$$

TABLE 6.1 Yield Changes on Changes in Supply

	const	$\Delta\left(\frac{MWD}{GDP}\right)_t$	R^2
$\Delta[y(2) - y(1)]$	−0.00	−0.07	0.00
	(−0.21)	(−0.24)	
$\Delta[y(3) - y(1)]$	−0.01	0.02	0.00
	(−0.20)	(0.06)	
$\Delta[y(4) - y(1)]$	−0.01	0.11	0.00
	(−0.22)	(0.21)	
$\Delta[y(5) - y(1)]$	−0.01	0.20	0.00
	(−0.21)	(0.40)	

Source: Greenwood and Vayanos (2014), the New York Fed, and the Monthly Statement of the Public Debt.

This table reports regression of quarterly changes in zero-coupon yield spreads for $n = 2:5$ year bonds on quarterly changes in the maturity-weighted debt-to-GDP ratio

$$\Delta[y(n) - y(1)] = \alpha + \beta\Delta\left(\frac{MWD}{GDP}\right)_t + \varepsilon^{(n)}_{t,t+4}$$

where quarterly changes are sampled to coincide with reversion to the GDP index. t-Statistics are reported in parentheses below the parameter estimated. Sample Period: 1961.7–2006.12. Quarterly frequency.

with q_t being factors based on the effect of QE operation on the bond supply. Then they simulate forward a linear model for bond yields $Y_t^{(n)} = b_n X_t$ to compute the implied impact of changes in q_t onto the future trajectory of $Y_{t+s}^{(n)}$. The process q_t is three-dimensional, with ϕ being a (3×3) matrix, and it is linked to the observable supply factors as $q_t = \Lambda \sum_n z_{t,n} b_{n-1}$, as given above. Thus, the ith component of the vector q_t is given by adding up the product of the fraction of the bonds with maturity n held by the private sector times the factor loadings of a bond with maturity n with respect to the $X_{i,t}$. This allows to interpret $q_{i,t}$ as the amount of the ith factor risk that the private sector is exposed by holding the Treasury bonds. When the Fed intervenes by purchasing (or swapping) specific maturities, it changes the market exposure to the level, slope, and curvature factors depending on the factor loading b_{n-1} of these bonds. The authors find that a single factor z_t^A computed as the average maturity of outstanding debt is not statistically significant and one cannot reject the null hypothesis $H_0 : \phi = 0$. However, a multiple regression using unrestricted ordinary least squares (OLS) estimates of a combination of three supply factors produces "R^2 as high as 0.71 in the case of predicting the 2-over-1 excess return." In his discussion at the NBER Monetary Economics Meeting (March 4, 2011), Cochrane (2011) highlights, however, that the three variables that are part of the vector q_t are highly correlated and he raises concerns about overfitting. Hamilton and Wu (2012) simulate the reduced-form linear model forward and find strong evidence in support for a duration risk channel. On the basis of the estimated value of the (3×3) matrix ϕ, they conclude that if in December 2006, the Fed had sold off all its Treasury holdings of less than 1-year maturity (about \$400 billion) and used the proceeds to retire long-term Treasury debt, the 10-year and 6-month rates would have changed by −14 and +11 basis points, respectively. They notice that when interest rates are at the zero lower bound, the same effect of such maturity swap could have been achieved by swapping new reserves for 10-year Treasury bonds. They calculate, however, that in this case the effect would be a reduction of the 10-year yield by 13 basis points with no change in the short rate.

In the context of a portfolio balance model with capital mobility, LSAP should have broad effects also on international bonds issued by countries with similar credit and liquidity characteristics of the United States. Neely (2010) explores this broad channel implication in the context of international sovereign bond markets. They find that LSAP programs significantly reduced the 10-year yields of Australia, Canada, Germany, Japan, and the United Kingdom. Their yields fell cumulatively by 78, 54, 50, 19, and 65 basis points during the five LSAP event windows. At the same time, they document that (international) short-term rates did not change during these interventions. These two results are consistent with the argument of a broad channel that operates by reducing bond risk premia at the long end of the term structure. Neely (2010) investigates also the effect of LSAP on exchange rates. The Uncovered Interest Rate Parity (UIP) implies that the expected change in the exchange rate over a horizon of N years should be a function of interest differentials at that horizon. This should be true both before and after the announcement. If U.S. yields decline more than foreign yields, UIP would predict that the USD exchange rate should be expected to appreciate over the same horizon, compared to its previous sample path. This implies that the USD exchange rate needs to depreciate instantaneously at the announcement to support a higher than expected return thereafter. The evidence from the five LSAP events suggests that these purchases had strong effects on the USD exchange rate that declined cumulatively between 3.6% and 10.8%, depending on the currency.

Wright (2012) estimates a structural VAR with daily data. To identify the monetary policy shocks, he assumes that monetary policy shocks are heteroskedastic and have higher variance on days of FOMC meetings and specific announcements/speeches. Wright argues that monetary policy shocks had a significant effect on 10-year yields and long-maturity corporate bond yields but that these effects were transitory and died off over the next few months. Effects on shorter rates are much smaller. Initial effects on corporate bond yields are around half the size as the effect on 10-year Treasury yields. Finally, he finds some evidence on real rates with short-term break-even rates rising and long-term forward break-even rates falling. The author suggests that a possible interpretation is that the economic stimulus provided by the LSAPs caused the economy to pick up. Another interpretation is that markets initially overreacted to the news of these quantitative easing actions.

6.4.2 The MBS Market

An important component of the Fed's quantitative easing programs involved the purchase of large amounts of MBS. Hancock and Passmore (2011) analyze the price impact of these purchases on MBS yield spreads and try to empirically distinguish between the potential role played by a signaling effect and the portfolio rebalancing channel. They argue that if asset prices adjust slowly to quantitative easing programs, then a time-series approach may have advantages over event studies. The authors compute the Federal Reserve's share of MBS relative to the total amount of agency MBS assets outstanding, backed by 30-year fixed-rate mortgages. Similarly, they compute the Fed's market share of Treasury bonds for comparison reasons. The authors report that "the cumulative stock of Treasury bond holdings and Federal Reserve agency MBS holdings eventually amounted to about one-fifth of all outstanding Treasury securities and fixed-rate agency MBS." The total share started declining at the end of 2012. They run regressions of the MBS yield on both the Fed's market share of MBS and Treasury bonds and control for the potential effect of changes in expected future interest rates by using the long-term swap rate. They find that an increase in either the Federal Reserve market share of MBS or its market share of U.S. Treasury securities significantly lowered MBS yields during their sample period, which is based on weekly data between July 7, 2000, and June 28, 2013. The average level of MBS yields is 73 basis points lower when the Fed holds 24% of the available MBS securities (on June 30, 2013, this was equivalent to about a $1.21 trillion portfolio). This is equivalent to a decline in MBS rates of 3 basis points for every $50 billion increase in the Federal Reserve's MBS holdings. A regression using dummy variable techniques suggests that MBS yields were more sensitive to additional MBS purchases during QE1 and QE3 than during QE2. The authors interpret the result as evidence that LSAP had a "broad" impact, which is consistent with a portfolio balance or liquidity channel. They also note, however, that the long-term swap rate is a significant explanatory variable for MBS yields. This suggests that the signaling channel plays a statistically important role, in addition to the portfolio balance channel.

This joint result also highlights a common challenge of time-series studies in addressing these types of questions. This is related to the difficulty of being able to separately identify the effect due to the policy decision from contemporaneous effects due to other sources of time variation in expected interest rates and economic conditions. In a series of articles, Krishnamurthy and Vissing-Jorgensen (KVJ) address the identification problem by using an event study methodology for each of the Fed Programs. Indeed, each QE episode had different characteristics. During the QE1 and MEP programs, the Fed purchased both MBS, agency debt and Treasury securities. During QE2, on the other hand, the Fed targeted only Treasury bonds; moreover, during QE3 the Fed focused exclusively on MBS. This is an important source of variation to estimate the impact of Fed purchases. Vissing-Jorgensen and Krishnamurthy (2011) and Krishnamurthy and Vissing-Jorgensen (2012) study the effect of the first two purchases; Krishnamurthy and Vissing-Jorgensen (2013) extend the analysis to include also the evidence from QE3 and summarize the effects in table 6.2 of their paper.

KVJ argue that the results support a narrow channel explanation. The QE3 event is quite informative in this respect since it involves the exclusive purchase of MBS bonds. Indeed, during this event, 15- and 30-year MBS yields decline by 16 and 15 basis points, respectively. The effect on Treasury bonds, on the other hand, is very limited. QE2 offers an interesting counterfactual since during this program the Fed purchases only Treasury bonds. The 10-year Treasury bond rate drops by 18 bps, more than what would be predicted by the variation in Fed fund future rates. Consistent with the narrow channel explanation, the drop in MBS rates is fully accounted by the change in Fed fund futures.

In order to isolate the impact on the risk premium implied in MBS, KVJ provide evidence of the time variation of option-adjusted spreads (OASs) of MBS across the coupon stack. Owing to the decline in interest rates, high-coupon MBS have been issued in earlier years while low-coupon MBS are more closely substitutable to current-production MBS. KVJ argue that the existence of a scarcity channel would predict that assets substitutable with production-coupon MBS would trade relatively rich with respect to old MBS immediately after LSAPs targeting MBS assets (as in QE1 and QE3).

On November 25, 2008, the Fed announced its first round of purchases of up to $500 billion in agency MBS. While the actual start of the program was delayed to early January 2009, a substantial component of the price impact was immediate.

Two results emerge. First, during the QE2 event, OAS are not affected. On the other hand, during both QE1 and QE3, OAS compress quite significantly. Second, OAS of lower coupon MBS have compressed more significantly than higher coupon MBS. Before the announcement of QE1, current-coupon OAS was trading around 75–100 basis points. Immediately after the

TABLE 6.2 Changes in Asset Prices around QE1, QE2, MEP, QE3, and Exit Event Dates

	QE1	QE2	MEP	QE3	Exit
Asset purchase news	MBS and Treasury	Treasury only	MBS and Treasury	MBS only	MBS and Treasury
Treasury yields (CMT)					
5-Year	−74	−17	3	−6	24
10-Year	−107	−18	−7	−3	21
30-Year	−73	−9	−17	1	15
Inflation swaps					
10-Year	96	5	−4	4	−9
Corporate bonds					
Aaa	−77	−9	−16	4	23
Baa	−81	−7	−15	0	28
Aaa CDS	−7	2			
Baa CDS	−40	2			
Agency MBS					
15-Year	−88	−9	−7	−16	26
30-Year	−107	−12	−23	−15	30

Source: Krishnamurthy and Vissing-Jorgensen (2013).
Two-day changes for QE1 and Exit, and 1-day changes for QE2, MEP, and QE3. For QE3 and Exit, corporate yields are Barclays long-term bond index and CDS is from MARKIT. For MBS, yield changes are averaged across the FNMA, Freddie Mac, and GNMA production coupon MBS. For the 30-year MBS, this is GNMA 3%, FNMA 3.5%, and Freddie Mac 3.5% (for QE3 and Exit). For the 15-year MBS, this is the 2.5% coupon for all three securities.

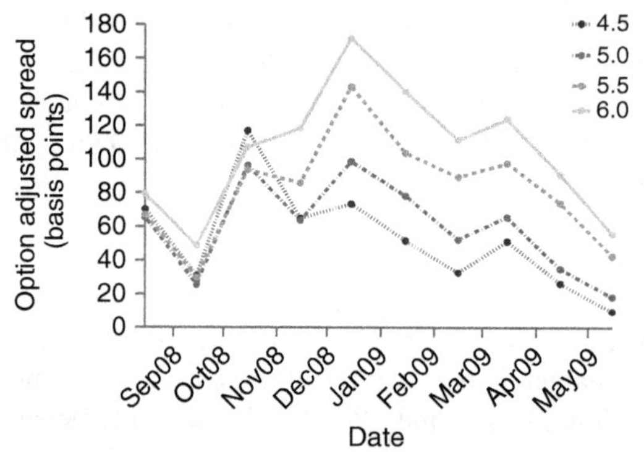

Figure 6.17 OAS during QE1. This figure shows the behavior of the OAS of MBS with coupon rates ranging between 4.5% and 6.0% around the date of the announcement of QE (November 8, 2008). Source: Boyarchenko, Fuster, and Lucca (2014).

announcement, it fell by 30–40 basis points. In the period between the announcement and January 2009, the headline 30-year fixed-rate mortgage rates dropped about one percentage point. The authors conclude that this is supporting evidence of the existence of a scarcity channel.

Boyarchenko, Fuster, and Lucca (2014) argue that a significant component in the cross-sectional behavior of the OAS in MBS is due to the role of interest rate prepayment risk. This is defined as the risk of over- or underpredicting future prepayments due to interest rates. They investigate a simple model in which OAS tend to be lower for ATM coupons MBS than for others and discuss spreads movements around the day of the QE1 announcement. Similar to KVJ, Boyarchenko, Fuster, and Lucca (2014) report significant cross-sectional differences across the coupon stack. Indeed "Between October and November 2008, OAS on low coupons (4.5 and 5) fell, while those on higher coupons were little changed and then even widened through the end of December." The evidence is summarized in Figure 6.17. Different than KVJ, Boyarchenko, Fuster, and Lucca (2014) argue that an important reason for the different impact of LSAPs is due to change in the repayment option value. Changes in mortgage rates, due to these purchases, affect securities' moneyness and shift the OAS along the smile because of changes in the prepayment risk premium. The effect depends on the coupon level. Before the announcement, the OAS of the 4.5 coupon MBS was OTM. Then, after the LSAPs it moves closer to ATM as mortgage rates drop; the 5.5 and 6, which are around ATM in October, move quite deeply ITM. Thus, the prepayment risk premia on the 5.5 and 6 coupons are high from December onward as they move deeply ITM and are more sensitive to prepayment model risk. Consistent with this hypothesis, their OAS widens

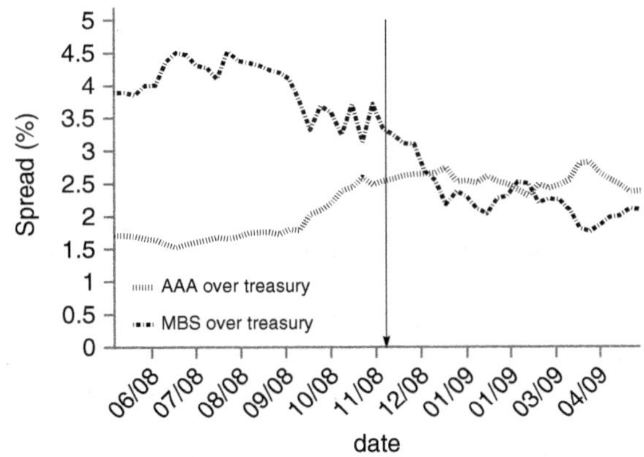

Figure 6.18 MBS–Treasury spreads after QE1. This figure shows the behavior of the 10-year MBS minus 10-year Treasury bond spread and of the 10-year Aaa corporate minus 10-year Treasury bond spread in the period 6 months before and after the announcement of QE (November 8, 2008). Source: Fred.

relative to low-coupon MBS. This suggests an alternative explanation for the cross-sectional differences in OAS changes during LSAP, which does not require assuming cross-coupon segmentation or the existence of a narrow "scarcity" channel, as discussed in Vissing-Jorgensen and Krishnamurthy (2011).

6.4.3 How Persistent is the Effect?

Similar to the case of Treasury bond yields, it is interesting to investigate the extent to which the impact on MBS spread was persistent. To this end, Figure 6.18 compares the MBS and Aaa corporate bond spreads over the 10-year U.S. Treasury bond rate. Different than in the case of the impact on Treasury bonds, which we found to be mainly temporary, the effect on the MBS spreads was significantly more persistent. During the month before the QE1 announcement, the MBS spread was around 350 basis points; 2 months after the start of the program, the MBS spread compressed to about 200 basis points. It interesting to observe that during the same period the Aaa corporate bond spread stayed roughly constant. Although it is difficult to extrapolate strong conclusions from a handful of events, the evidence suggests that the impact of QE programs on MBS spreads was indeed different than on Treasury bond yields.

6.5 CONCLUSIONS

In the past 10 years, a vast literature engaged in studies of the impact of unconventional monetary policies on bond prices. This period is of great importance since it provides a unique laboratory to test theories of unconventional monetary policy. To understand the empirical evidence it is important to distinguish the results related to the U.S. Treasury and MBS bond markets.

In the case of the Treasury bond market, there is clear evidence that LSAPs have a short-term impact on bond yields. The effect on the day of the announcement is quite significant. The largest impact affects the actual bonds that are purchased by the central bank and clearly show the presence of a "narrow" channel. Part of the impact, however, affects also the term premium and it suggests the presence of a "broad" channel. However, the effect is only temporary. Time-series studies do not offer compelling evidence that the effect is persistent. Moreover, the size of the price impact of LSAPs that is predicted by time-series studies is substantially smaller than the one predicted by event studies.

In the case of the MBS market, there is clear evidence that LSAP significantly lowered MBS yields and OAS. There is no consensus, however, about whether the price impact is due to a narrow "scarcity" channel or to a "broad" channel. It is quite possible that both channels are at play. Different than the case of the Treasury bond market, the effect is persistent.

The results of this large body of the literature are very valuable to policy makers as they focus on the design of an optimal exit strategy from the LSAP made during the 2008–2013 period. These results, for instance, show that a reduction of mortgage-backed assets currently on the balance sheet of the Fed may have a significant impact on MBS yield spread unless this exit strategy were to be implemented gradually.

ACKNOWLEDGMENTS

For providing comments and/or supplying data we would like to thank Nina Boyarchenko, Stefania D'Amico, Alberto Gallo, Robin Greenwood, Thomas King, Arvind Krishnamurthy, Dimitri Vayanos, and Pietro Veronesi.

REFERENCES

Boyarchenko N, Fuster A, Lucca DO. Understanding mortgage spreads. FRB of New York Staff Report; 2014.

Brunner K, Meltzer AH. Mr. Hicks and the "Monetarists," Economica 1973;40:44–59.

Buraschi A, Carnelli A, Whelan P. Monetary policy and treasury risk premia. Imperial College Business School Working Paper; 2012.

Buraschi A, Menguturk M, Sener E. The geography of funding markets and limits to arbitrage. Rev Financ Stud 2015;28:1103–1153.

Buraschi A, Menini D. Liquidity risk and specialness. J Financ Econ 2002;64:243–284.

Clouse J, Henderson D, Orphanides A, Small DH, Tinsley PA. Monetary policy when the nominal short-term interest rate is zero. Top Macroecon 2003;3(1):1534–5998.

Cochrane J. Inside the black box: Hamilton. Wu, and QE2, NBER Monetary Economics Program Meeting; Mar 4 2011.

Curdia V, Woodford M. Credit spreads and monetary policy. J Money, Credit Bank 2010;42:3–35.

D'Amico S, English W, Lopez-Salido D, Nelson E. The Federal Reserves large-scale asset purchase programs: rationale and effects. Econ J 2012;122:415–446.

D'Amico S, Li C, Sears JS, Cahill ME. The term premium effect and the Federal Reserve's asset purchase announcements. Federal Reserve Board, Working paper; 2014.

Del Negro M, Eggertsson GB, Ferrero A, Kiyotaki N. The great escape? A quantitative evaluation of the Fed's liquidity facilities. A Quantitative Evaluation of the Fed's Liquidity Facilities; October 1, 2011; FRB of New York Staff Report; 2011.

Duffie D. Special repo rates. J Finance 1996;51:493–526.

Eggertsson G, Woodford M. Zero bound on interest rates and optimal monetary policy. Brookings Pap Econ Act 2003;1:139–233.

Epstein LG, Zin SE. Substitution, risk aversion, and the temporal behaviour of consumption and asset returns: an empirical analysis. J Polit Econ 1991;99(2):263–286.

Frankel JA. Portfolio crowding-out, empirically estimated. Q J Econ 1985;100:1041–1065.

Gagnon J, Raskin M, Remache J, Sack BP. Large-scale asset purchases by the Federal Reserve: did they work? FRB of New York Staff Report; 2010.

Gagnon J, Raskin M, Remache J, Sack BP. Large-scale asset purchases by the Federal Reserve: did they work? Int J Cent Bank 2011;7:3–43.

Gertler M, Karadi P. A model of unconventional monetary policy. J Monet Econ 2011;58:17–34.

Greenwood R, Vayanos D. Bond supply and excess bond returns. Rev Financ Stud 2014;27:663–713.

Hamilton JD, Wu JC. The effectiveness of alternative monetary policy tools in a zero lower bound environment. J Money Credit Bank 2012;44:3–46.

Hancock D, Passmore W. Did the Federal Reserve's MBS purchase program lower mortgage rates? J Monet Econ 2011;58:498–514.

He Z, Krishnamurthy A. Intermediary asset pricing, Discussion paper. National Bureau of Economic Research; 2008.

Joyce M, Miles D, Scott A, Vayanos D. Quantitative easing and unconventional monetary policy an introduction. Econ J 2012;122:271–288.

Kacperczyk M, Schnabl P. How safe are money market funds? Q J Econ 2013;128:1073–1122.

King TB. A portfolio-balance approach to the nominal term structure, Working paper. Federal Reserve Bank of Chicago; 2014.

Kiyotaki N, Moore John. Liquidity, business cycles, and monetary policy, Discussion paper. National Bureau of Economic Research; 2012.

Krishnamurthy A, Vissing-Jorgensen A. The aggregate demand for treasury debt. J Polit Econ 2012;120:233–267.

Krishnamurthy A, Vissing-Jorgensen A. The Ins and Outs of LSAPs. Proceedings - Economic Policy Symposium - Jackson Hole. Kansas City Federal Reserve Symposium on Global Dimensions of Unconventional Monetary Policy: Federal Reserve Bank of Kansas City; 2013.

McLeay M, Radia A, Thomas R. Money creation in the modern economy. Bank Engl Q Bull 2014;Q1:14–27.

Modigliani F, Sutch R. Innovations in interest rate policy. Am Econ Rev 1966;56:178–197.

Neely CJ. *Unconventional Monetary Policy had large international effects*, Federal Reserve Bank of St. Louis Working Paper Series. St. Louis (MO): Federal Reserve Bank of St. Louis; 2010.

Ricardo D. Essay on the funding system. The Works of David Ricardo (McCulloch ed. 1846); 1820.

Swanson E. Let's twist again: A high-frequency event-study analysis of operation twist and its implications for QE2 [with comments and discussion]. Brookings Papers on Economic Activity, Spring 2011. p 151–207.

Tobin J. Money, capital, and other stores of value. Am Econ Rev 1961;51(2):26–37.

Tobin J. *An Essay on the Principles of Debt Management*. New Haven (CT): Cowles Foundation for Research in Economics at Yale University; 1963.

Tobin J. A general equilibrium approach to monetary theory. J Money Credit Banking 1969;1:15–29.

Vayanos D, Vila J-L. A preferred-habitat model of the term structure of interest rates, Discussion paper. National Bureau of Economic Research; 2009.

Vissing-Jorgensen A, Krishnamurthy Arvind. The effects of quantitative easing on long-term interest rates. 2011 Meeting Papers No. 1447. Society for Economic Dynamics; 2011.

Wallace N. A modigliani-miller theorem for open-market operations. Am Econ Rev 1981;71:267–274.

Woodford M. Methods of policy accommodation at the interest-rate lower bound. The Changing Policy Landscape: 2012 Jackson Hole Symposium. Federal Reserve Bank of Kansas City; 2012.

Wright JH. What does monetary policy do to long-term interest rates at the zero lower bound? Econ J 2012;122:F447–F466.

PART III

Interest Rate Risk Management

7

Interest Rate Risk Management and Asset Liability Management

Oleg Sydyak*

7.1 INTRODUCTION

Numerous institutions, such as pension funds and insurance companies, have long-term commitments to their customers and other stake holders. For instance, a defined benefit pension plan promises a given stream of payments to future retirees or an insurance company may be promising annuities or life insurance to its customers. In order to ensure that their long-term liabilities are met, such institutions engage in interest rate risk management and, more specifically, in asset–liability management ("ALM"), that is, the activity of managing and benchmarking an asset portfolio in relation to its liabilities or obligations to pay. In other words, the main investment objective of the so-called "liability centric" portfolio is to provide enough assets over time in order to meet liability payouts when they become due. The purpose of this chapter is to discuss interest rate risk management and to analyze certain ALM strategies in more details based on the research available to date.

There are numerous types of asset pools that exist with the purpose of supporting some form of liabilities for the sponsoring organizations. Such liabilities can be dictated by laws, by contractual agreements, by personal objectives, or in some other way. For example:

- Pension plans have very clearly defined legal obligations as specified by such laws as Employee Retirement Income Security Act ("ERISA") and Pension Protection Act of 2006 ("PPA") and as specified by the accounting standards promulgated by the U.S. GAAP and IFRS.
- Insurance companies also have very clearly defined obligations as outlined by the state and Federal laws.
- Endowments and foundations face other types of requirements according to which they have to finance certain payouts or spending levels over time, such as an annual spending level of 5% of their asset balances, in order to finance their activities.
- Individual investors often define their liabilities in terms of the retirement goals and fund such retirement liabilities over their entire life spans.

*Oleg Sydyak is the Director, Head of Asset and Liability Strategy group, Chief Actuarial Officer at a major financial services institution.

Handbook of Fixed-Income Securities, First Edition. Edited by Pietro Veronesi.

Therefore, in many (if not most) cases, asset pools do not exist in isolation but rather have attached to them very specific financing objectives. In this chapter, we will focus on more clearly defined legal obligations, as in the case of pension plans and insurance companies. But this "liability centric" approach for asset management can be easily applied to numerous other cases where liabilities are not as clearly defined by laws, contracts, or regulations.

7.2 LITERATURE REVIEW

Over the years, many papers and books have been published in order to explore various ALM strategies. One of the most comprehensive reference guides on ALM is Luckner (2003), *Professional Actuarial Specialty Guide: Asset-Liability Management*, published by the Society of Actuaries in 2003. This guide contains outlines of the main building blocks for ALM strategies as well as includes hundreds of references to many books and papers related to each specific functional area of ALM. Furthermore, the ALM references are grouped by (i) the type of institutional investors, that is, defined benefit pension plans, life insurance companies, property and casualty insurance companies, and others, and by (ii) the level of sophistication, that is, basic, intermediate, and advanced. This guide by itself can serve as a very comprehensive source of ALM material.

The purpose of this chapter is to discuss interest rate risk management and to analyze certain ALM strategies in more details based on the research available to date. In particular, the following ALM strategies are illustrated in this chapter, and the recommended literature for further in-depth analysis is the following:

- Immunization Strategy, a.k.a. Duration Matching Strategy:
  The term "immunization" was introduced by Frank M. Redington in his 1952 paper (see Redington (1952) for more details), where he suggested that in order to immunize the Surplus, the "mean term" of assets and liabilities should be the same (among other conditions). The concept of "mean term" was already introduced at that time by Frederick R. Macaulay in his 1938 paper (see Macaulay (1938) for more details), whose term "Duration" became a standard terminology in the modern fixed-income area. Additionally, two Nobel laureates in economics independently came up with "Duration" concepts (see Hicks (1939) and Samuelson (1945) for more details).
  Since then, Immunization Strategies have been researched and analyzed in many papers. Hawawini (1982) and Bierwag (1987) are among the books that deal solely with immunization theory and Duration analysis. Panjer (1998), Fabozzi (2012), and Veronesi (2010) are among the books that cover immunization theory and Duration analysis extensively among other topics discussed.
- Cash Flow Matching Strategy, a.k.a. dedication strategy:
  Asset–liability Cash Flow Matching or "dedication" was introduced by Tjalling C. Koopmans in 1942 (see Koopmans (1942) for more details). The idea was to find the cheapest bond portfolio, such that liability payments in all periods are always met. Mathematical algorithms for solving this problem have been developed and implemented over time as illustrated in Iyengar and Ma (2009), Kocherlakota, Rosenbloom, and Shiu (1988), and Shang and Uryasev (2011).
- Key Rate Duration Matching Strategy:
  Key Rate Duration Matching Strategy is a natural extension of Duration Matching Strategy as outlined in this chapter in the following sections. Ho (1992) contains more information regarding how this strategy is created and implemented.
- Factor Duration Matching Strategy.
  More advanced ALM strategies have been implemented in recent years that involve immunization of assets and liabilities with respect to nonparallel movements of the entire term structure. As a result, Principal Component Analysis has been applied to determine factors inherent in the term structure of interest rates, identified as "level," "slope," and "curvature," and such factors are used as part of Factor Duration Matching Strategy. Additional research in this area can be found in Barber and Cooper (1996), Willner (1996), and Veronesi (2010).
- ALM strategies and total portfolio construction:
  There is an emerging literature regarding how the ALM strategies can be incorporated in the total portfolio construction problem. In particular, Brandt et al. (2005), Bogentoft, Romeijn, and Uryasev (2001), and van Binsbergen and Brandt (2014, Chapter 8 in this handbook) provided algorithms to solve a multiperiod portfolio construction problem for pension plans based on the ALM framework.

7.3 INTEREST RATE RISK MEASURES

The following notation is helpful for the analysis.

We will define $r_t(\tau)$ as a continuously compounded spot rate from the U.S. Treasury yield curve at time t with maturity τ and $Z_t(\tau)$ as the respective zero-coupon bond, that is,

$$Z_t(\tau) = e^{-r_t(\tau)\,\tau} \tag{7.1}$$

We will further define $\mathbf{r_t} = (r_t(\tau))$ and $\mathbf{Z_t} = (Z_t(\tau))$, $\tau = \tau_1, \tau_2, \ldots, \tau_M$, as the respective column vectors of such spot rates and zero-coupon bonds at time t for all maturities τ, that is, $\mathbf{r_t}$ vector represents the entire term structure of interest rates at time t and $\mathbf{Z_t}$ is the corresponding vector of zero-coupon bond prices.

7.3.1 Duration

Similar to the notations introduced in Veronesi (2010), the Duration at time t of a zero-coupon bond $Z_t(\tau)$ with maturity τ and face value $F = 1$ is defined as the sensitivity of such bond to a change in a spot rate $r_t(\tau)$:

$$D_t(\tau) = -\frac{1}{Z_t(\tau)} \frac{\partial Z_t(\tau)}{\partial r_t(\tau)} \tag{7.2}$$

The first derivative of a zero-coupon bond with respect to a spot rate, using $Z_t(\tau)$ functional form as specified in (7.1), is the following:

$$\frac{\partial Z_t(\tau)}{\partial r_t(\tau)} = \frac{\partial}{\partial r_t(\tau)} e^{-r_t(\tau)\,\tau} = -\,\tau\, e^{-r_t(\tau)\,\tau} = -\,\tau\, Z_t(\tau) \tag{7.3}$$

After substituting this result into (7.2), we can see that the Duration of a zero-coupon bond is equal to its maturity:

$$D_t(\tau) = \tau \tag{7.4}$$

As another example, consider a 30-year bond paying semiannual coupons c and face value F. Let $CF(\tau)$ denote the cash flow of the bond at time τ. That is, $CF(\tau) = \frac{c}{2}F$ before maturity and $CF(\tau) = \left(\frac{c}{2} + 1\right) F$ at maturity. The value of such bond at t is

$$P_t = \sum_{\tau} CF(\tau) Z_t(\tau)$$

Because

$$\frac{\partial P_t}{\partial r_t} = \sum_{\tau} CF(\tau) \frac{\partial Z_t(\tau)}{\partial r_t(\tau)}$$

the Duration of a coupon-paying bond is then

$$D_t = \sum_{\tau} D_t(\tau) = \sum_{\tau} \tau\, w_t(\tau) \tag{7.5}$$

where $w_t(\tau) = \frac{1}{P_t} CF_t(\tau) Z_t(\tau)$. Substituting $CF_t(\tau)$, we obtain the explicit formulas for the weights w_τ as

$$w_t(\tau) = \frac{1}{P_t} \frac{c}{2} Z_t(\tau), \text{for } \tau = \frac{1}{2}, 1, \frac{3}{2}, \ldots, 29\frac{1}{2}$$

$$w_t(30) = \frac{1}{P_t} \left(\frac{c}{2} + F\right) Z_t(30)$$

where, explicitly, $P_t = \sum_{\tau} \frac{c}{2} Z_t(\tau) + F\, Z_t(30)$, $\tau = \frac{1}{2}, 1, \frac{3}{2}, \ldots, 30$

The key assumption behind the portfolio Duration calculation, which is implicit in (7.5), is that *the entire yield curve shifts in a parallel manner*. In other words, each spot rate $r_t(\tau)$, $\tau = \tau_1, \tau_2, \ldots, \tau_M$, from the Treasury yield curve is assumed to change by the same amount. Moreover, the parallel shift is assumed small.

Duration allows for the approximation of a change in the bond value through a first-order Taylor approximation as follows:

$$\frac{dP_t}{P_t} \approx -D_t\, dr_t \tag{7.6}$$

Therefore, once we have the Duration estimate, D_t, we can compute the bond value at time $t + dt$, based on the Duration approximation of the bond value at time t, resulting from a small and parallel movement in the term structure

$$P_{t+dt} \approx P_t + (-D_t)\, P_t\, dr_t \tag{7.7}$$

Equation (7.7) is applicable to any fixed-income security, that is, zero-coupon bonds, coupon-paying bonds, floating-rate bonds, and so on. Once the Duration or the sensitivity of such a security to interest rates is estimated, Equation (7.7) can be used in order to estimate the instantaneous bond price change resulting from the parallel shift of the entire term structure.

7.3.2 Convexity

The Duration of a security measures the risk of a security against small, parallel shifts in the term structure of interest rates. This measure may be quite imprecise, however, when there are large interest rate changes.

As shown in Figure 7.1, a zero-coupon bond price is plotted as a solid line based on different interest rate levels. Since the Duration (multiplied by the bond price) is the negative of the first derivative of the bond price with respect to interest rate as shown in (7.2), it is the slope of the bond price. Assuming that today's interest rate is 4%, the slope of the bond price, or its Duration, corresponding to the 4% interest rate level is depicted by the dashed line.

It can be seen from Figure 7.1 that when the interest rate changes are small, as shown by the darker shaded area, the linear approximation of the bond price based on the Duration alone, as shown by the dashed line, is quite close to the actual bond price depicted by the solid line. However, when the interest rate changes are large, as shown by the lighter shaded area, the linear approximation of the bond price based on the Duration alone is not close to the actual bond price any longer, and the distance between the dashed line (Duration approximation) and the solid line (bond price) will increase with larger interest rate changes.

Therefore, we can obtain a more precise measure of a security's interest rate risk by adding its Convexity with respect to interest rates.

The Convexity at time t of a zero-coupon bond $Z_t(\tau)$ with maturity τ and face value $F = 1$ is defined as the "curvature" of such bond with respect to a spot rate $r_t(\tau)$:

$$C_t(\tau) = \frac{1}{Z_t(\tau)} \frac{\partial^2 Z_t(\tau)}{\partial r_t(\tau)^2} \tag{7.8}$$

The second derivative of a zero-coupon bond with respect to a spot rate, using $Z_t(\tau)$ functional form as specified in (7.1), is the following:

$$\frac{\partial^2 Z_t(\tau)}{\partial r_t(\tau)^2} = \frac{\partial^2}{\partial r_t(\tau)^2} e^{-r_t(\tau)\,\tau} = \tau^2 e^{-r_t(\tau)\,\tau} = \tau^2 Z_t(\tau) \tag{7.9}$$

After substituting this result into (7.8), we can see that the Convexity of a zero-coupon bond is equal to its maturity squared:

$$C_t(\tau) = \tau^2 \tag{7.10}$$

As another example, consider again a 30-year bond paying semiannual coupons c and face value F. Because

$$\frac{\partial^2 P_t}{\partial r_t^2} = \sum_\tau CF(\tau) \frac{\partial^2 Z_t(\tau)}{\partial r_t(\tau)^2}$$

the Convexity of a coupon bond is then

$$C_t = \sum_\tau C_t(\tau) = \sum_\tau \tau^2\, w_t(\tau) \tag{7.11}$$

where $w_t(\tau) = \frac{1}{P_t} CF_t(\tau)\, Z_t(\tau)$ are the same as those used in the Duration computation.

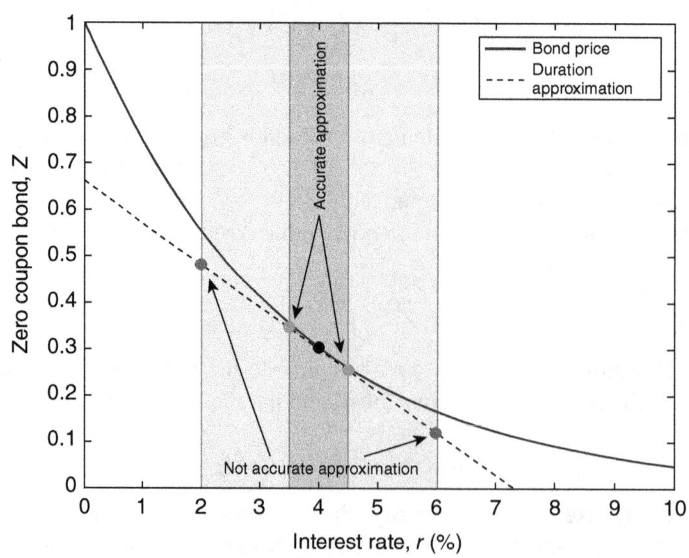

Figure 7.1 Bond price approximation with Duration.

Combining Duration and Convexity allows for the approximation of a change in the bond value through a second-order Taylor approximation as follows:

$$\frac{dP_t}{P_t} \approx -D_t \, dr_t + \frac{1}{2} \, C_t \, dr_t^2 \tag{7.12}$$

which, according to Figure 7.1, will improve the linear approximation of the bond price based on the Duration alone.

Therefore, once we have the estimates of the Duration and Convexity (D and C), it is easy to compute the impact on a bond from a potentially large movement in interest rates

$$P_{t+dt} \approx P_t + (-D_t) \, P_t \, dr_t + \frac{1}{2} \, C_t \, P_t \, dr_t^2 \tag{7.13}$$

Note that while adding Convexity to Duration can help us deal with the potentially large changes in interest rates, the underlying assumption is still unchanged, that is, that the entire term structure will only change in a parallel fashion. The next two measures of risks – the Key Rate Durations and the Factor Durations – move away from this restrictive assumption.

7.3.3 Key Rate Duration

As outlined in Ho (1992), the purpose of Key Rate Durations is to overcome the limitations imposed by the Duration to hedge bond portfolios against nonparallel yield curve shifts. By matching Key Rate Durations at certain maturities, the bond portfolio is designed to be hedged against yield curve movements at those maturities. And since there are comovements, to a certain extent, of spot rates at the closely adjacent maturities, it is possible to hedge a portfolio against nonparallel yield curve shifts with only a few Key Rate Durations.

Key Rate Duration at time t for spot rate $r_t(\tau)$, or $KRD_t(\tau)$, also called spot rate Duration, is defined as the sensitivity of a bond to changes in the respective spot rate $r_t(\tau)$ while keeping all the remaining spot rates unchanged:

$$KRD_t(\tau) = \frac{P_t\left(r_t(\tau) - \Delta\right) - P_t\left(r_t(\tau) + \Delta\right)}{2\,P_t} \tag{7.14}$$

where $P_t(r_t(\tau) \pm \Delta)$ is the bond price at time t when only the spot rate $r_t(\tau)$ increases/decreases by Δ, while all other spot rates in the yield curve remain unchanged and P_t is the current bond price at time t, that is, the price when no spot rates change. Note that P_t can be either a zero-coupon bond with maturity τ or a coupon-paying bond with maturity greater than or equal to τ.

Similar to the Duration-based bond approximation, a change in the bond value can be approximated through a first-order Taylor approximation as follows:

$$\frac{dP_t}{P_t} \approx \sum_{\tau} -KRD_t(\tau) \, dr_t(\tau) \tag{7.15}$$

where $dr_t(\tau)$, $\tau = \tau_1, \ldots, \tau_M$, can all be different amounts and so model nonparallel changes in the term structure.

Therefore, once we have the estimates of the Key Rate Durations, $KRD_t(\tau)$, we can compute the impact on a bond price from nonparallel changes in the interest rates

$$P_{t+dt} \approx P_t + \sum_{\tau} -KRD_t(\tau) \, P_t \, dr_t(\tau) \tag{7.16}$$

Given the definition of Key Rate Durations, zero-coupon bonds are the most logical instrument, since each zero-coupon bond will have only one Key Rate Duration. In other words, Key Rate Duration in (7.14) and Duration in (7.2) are the same for zero-coupon bonds. However, coupon-paying bonds can also be used to approximate Key Rate Duration Matching using a nonlinear optimization technique as shown in the later examples.

Section 7.4.4 illustrates the application of Key Rate Duration to ALM and contains further discussion.

7.3.4 Principal Component Analysis and Factor Duration

Factor analysis is a statistical method used to describe variability among observed, correlated variables in terms of a potentially lower number of unobserved variables called factors. For example, the capital asset pricing model is a factor model where the variability of the observed individual stock returns is described by a single factor, the market return, which represents a linear combination of the returns of the underlying stocks (weighed by their market capitalization).

A similar idea can be applied to the term structure of interest rates where we hypothesize that one or more factors may exist that explain the variability of interest rate term structure over time. For example:

- The average spot rate from a yield curve can be thought of as a factor representing the average level of a yield curve, commonly referred to as a level factor.

- Alternatively, the term spread calculated as the difference between a long-term spot rate and a short-term spot rate can be thought of as a factor representing the slope of a yield curve, commonly referred to as a slope factor.
- Or, the butterfly spread calculated as the sum of a long-term spot rate and a short-term spot rate reduced by twice a midterm spot rate can be thought of as a factor representing the curvature of a yield curve, commonly referred to as a curvature factor.

However, the major challenge is to identify what are the factors that explain well the variability over time of the term structure. Also, ensuring independence among such factors is a very important property because factor independence would make it possible to apply factor neutrality/hedging models in order to better immunize portfolios against movements of such underlying factors. However, if these factors are not independent from each other, then hedging of their correlations will also be required, which would significantly complicate the application of the factor neutrality models.

Principal Component Analysis is a statistical technique that can help us achieve the following:

- Identify the factors by maximizing their ability to explain variations in the spot rates over time.
- Make sure that such factors are independent from each other by construction.

7.3.4.1 *Principal Component Analysis* According to Principal Component Analysis (see Litterman and Scheinkman (1991)), it is assumed that there are a number of independent factors that affect changes in the term structure of interest rates. For simplicity we will assume that there are only three such factors f_t^1, f_t^2, and f_t^3. In other words, the changes of spot rates along yield curves have the following functional forms:

$$\begin{aligned}
\Delta r_t(\tau_1) &= \alpha_1 + \beta_1^1 \Delta f_t^1 + \beta_1^2 \Delta f_t^2 + \beta_1^3 \Delta f_t^3 \\
\Delta r_t(\tau_2) &= \alpha_2 + \beta_2^1 \Delta f_t^1 + \beta_2^2 \Delta f_t^2 + \beta_2^3 \Delta f_t^3 \\
&\ldots\ldots\ldots\ldots\ldots\ldots\ldots\ldots \\
\Delta r_t(\tau_M) &= \alpha_M + \beta_M^1 \Delta f_t^1 + \beta_M^2 \Delta f_t^2 + \beta_M^3 \Delta f_t^3
\end{aligned} \tag{7.17}$$

where $r_t(\tau)$, $\tau = \tau_1, \tau_2, \ldots, \tau_M$, is the term structure of interest rates at time t, Δ denotes the changes in spot rates and factors, and β are the corresponding factor sensitivities.

Initially these factors are not known since they are not observable in the market, but it is assumed that they are linear combinations of the underlying spot rates. As a result, the factors are defined as follows:

$$\begin{aligned}
\Delta f_t^1 &= \gamma_{11} \Delta r_t(\tau_1) + \gamma_{12} \Delta r_t(\tau_2) + \ldots + \gamma_{1M} \Delta r_t(\tau_M) \\
\Delta f_t^2 &= \gamma_{21} \Delta r_t(\tau_1) + \gamma_{22} \Delta r_t(\tau_2) + \ldots + \gamma_{2M} \Delta r_t(\tau_M) \\
\Delta f_t^3 &= \gamma_{31} \Delta r_t(\tau_1) + \gamma_{32} \Delta r_t(\tau_2) + \ldots + \gamma_{3M} \Delta r_t(\tau_M)
\end{aligned} \tag{7.18}$$

Principal Component Analysis is a statistical technique that is used to identify such factors based on the following steps:

1. The covariance matrix of the spot rates, denoted as $\Omega = Cov(\Delta r_t(\tau))$, $\tau = \tau_1, \tau_2, \ldots, \tau_M$, is estimated based on the historical term structures, with the covariance between individual $r_t(\tau_i)$ and $r_t(\tau_j)$ spot rates denoted as

$$\sigma_{ij} = Cov(\Delta r_t(\tau_i), \Delta r_t(\tau_j)) \tag{7.19}$$

Then, principal component factors are determined one at a time in the sequential manner.

2. The first factor, f_t^1, is determined as a result of maximizing its variance as part of the following optimization program:

$$\begin{aligned}
&\underset{\gamma_{11},\gamma_{12},\ldots,\gamma_{1M}}{\text{maximize}} \quad Var\left(\Delta f_t^1\right) = \sum_{i=1}^{M} \sum_{j=1}^{M} \gamma_{1i}\gamma_{1j}\sigma_{ij} \\
&\text{subject to} \quad \sum_{i=1}^{M} \left(\gamma_{1i}\right)^2 = 1
\end{aligned} \tag{7.20}$$

By maximizing the variability of this factor, which is a linear combination of the spot rates, we are maximizing its covariability with the underlying spot rates and therefore maximizing the factor's explanatory power of the spot rate changes. The constraint is a boundary condition that would ensure that the decision variables will not be simply maximized to infinity.

3. Once the maximization problem is solved, we can determine the first factor f_t^1 based on the historical term structures and the estimated parameters $\gamma_{11}, \gamma_{12}, \ldots, \gamma_{1M}$:

$$\Delta f_t^1 = \gamma_{11}\Delta r_t(\tau_1) + \gamma_{12}\Delta r_t(\tau_2) + \ldots + \gamma_{1M}\Delta r_t(\tau_M)$$

4. Subsequently, using this factor as an explanatory variable, we can estimate the following multiple regressions:

$$\begin{aligned} \Delta r_t(\tau_1) &= \alpha_1 + \beta_1^1 \ \Delta f_t^1 + \epsilon_t^1 \\ \Delta r_t(\tau_2) &= \alpha_2 + \beta_2^1 \ \Delta f_t^1 + \epsilon_t^2 \\ &\cdots\cdots \\ \Delta r_t(\tau_M) &= \alpha_M + \beta_M^1 \ \Delta f_t^1 + \epsilon_t^M \end{aligned} \tag{7.21}$$

As a result, the residuals of these regressions will be the following for $i = 1, 2, \ldots, M$:

$$\hat{\epsilon}_t^i = \Delta r_t(\tau_i) - \hat{\alpha}_i - \hat{\beta}_i^1 \ \Delta f_t^1 \tag{7.22}$$

5. The residuals constructed based on the first factor are by definition the elements of the term structure not explained by the first factor. Therefore, the second factor can be defined based on the following:

$$\Delta f_t^2 = \gamma_{21} \ \hat{\epsilon}_t^1 + \gamma_{22} \ \hat{\epsilon}_t^2 + \ldots + \gamma_{2M} \ \hat{\epsilon}_t^M \tag{7.23}$$

where coefficients $\gamma_{21}, \gamma_{22}, \ldots, \gamma_{2M}$ are the solutions of the following maximization problem:

$$\begin{aligned} &\underset{\gamma_{21},\gamma_{22},\ldots,\gamma_{2M}}{\text{maximize}} \quad Var\left(\Delta f_t^2\right) = \sum_{i=1}^{M}\sum_{j=1}^{M} \gamma_{2i}\gamma_{2j}\sigma_{ij} \\ &\text{subject to} \quad \sum_{i=1}^{M} \left(\gamma_{2i}\right)^2 = 1 \end{aligned} \tag{7.24}$$

where σ_{ij} is the covariance between individual residuals $\hat{\epsilon}_t^i$ and $\hat{\epsilon}_t^j$.

6. The additional factors are determined in a similar manner.

The appendix shows how this procedure can be easily implemented.

Using the historical Treasury spot yield curves published by the Federal Reserve, where the spot yield curves are taken from November 1985 through June 2014 in the semiannual intervals, the factor sensitivities $\beta_\tau^1, \beta_\tau^2, \beta_\tau^3, \tau = \tau_1, \tau_2, \ldots, \tau_M$, are estimated and summarized in Figure 7.2. Given the resulting shapes of the factor sensitivities, factors can have the following economic interpretations:

- The first factor, f_t^1, is interpreted as "Level Factor," since sensitivities of changes in spot rates to changes in this factor are relatively uniform across all maturities as shown by the flat line in Figure 7.2. As a result, shifts in this factor will change the general level of the yield curve by about the same amount across all maturities, since this factor influences all spot rates to about the same extent.
- The second factor, f_t^2, is interpreted as "Slope Factor," since sensitivities of changes in spot rates to changes in this factor are negative at the short-term maturities and positive at the long-term maturities as shown by the line with diamonds in Figure 7.2. As a result, shifts in this factor will change the general slope of the yield curve, since this factor influences the short-term maturities differently than the long-term maturities.
- The third factor, f_t^3, is interpreted as "Curvature Factor," since sensitivities of changes in spot rates to changes in this factor are positive at the short-term and long-term maturities and negative at the midterm maturities as shown by the line with triangles in Figure 7.2. As a result, shifts in this factor will change the general curvature of the yield curve, since this factor influences the short-term and the long-term maturities differently than the midterm maturities.

Additionally, it can also be shown that the first three factors explain most of the variability of the interest rate term structures, and therefore the benefit of estimating additional factors is limited. As a result, for practical purposes it is common to limit the application of Principal Component Analysis to the first three factors only.

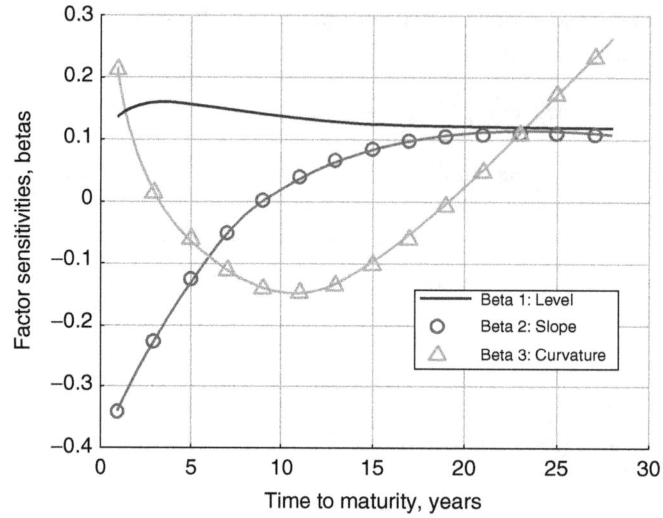

Figure 7.2 Factor sensitivities, $\beta_\tau^1, \beta_\tau^2, \beta_\tau^3$.

7.3.4.2 Factor Durations Factor Duration of a zero-coupon bond $Z_t(\tau)$ is defined as the sensitivity of this bond's price to changes in the underlying factor $f_t^j, j = 1, 2, 3, \ldots$

$$FD_t^j(\tau) = -\frac{1}{Z_t(\tau)} \frac{\partial Z_t(\tau)}{\partial f_t^j} \tag{7.25}$$

which is conceptually similar to the definition of the conventional Duration in (7.2), except now we implement a parallel shift of the factor instead of a parallel shift of the term structure. Also, Factor Duration based on the level factor would be equivalent to the conventional Duration in (7.2).

The intuition for determining Factor Durations can be described as follows. According to the multiple regressions (7.21), factor sensitivities β_τ^j represent sensitivities of the spot rates to changes in the factors, and therefore spot rates depend on such factors by construction

$$\frac{\partial r_t(\tau)}{\partial f_t^j} = \beta_\tau^j \tag{7.26}$$

which is just an interpretation of the multiple regressions (7.21).

Therefore, applying the chain rule to the functional form of the Factor Duration in (7.25), we have the following:

$$FD_t^j(\tau) = -\frac{1}{Z_t(\tau)} \frac{\partial Z_t(\tau)}{\partial f_t^j} = -\frac{1}{Z_t(\tau)} \frac{\partial Z_t(\tau)}{\partial r_t(\tau)} \frac{\partial r_t(\tau)}{\partial f_t^j}$$

Since we know that the Duration of a zero-coupon bond is defined as the sensitivity of such bond to the interest rate changes as shown in (7.2) and (7.4), or equivalently Duration is the time to maturity of a zero-coupon bond

$$D_t(\tau) = -\frac{1}{Z_t(\tau)} \frac{\partial Z_t(\tau)}{\partial r_t(\tau)} = \tau$$

and that sensitivity of a spot rate to a factor is given by (7.26), we can rewrite Factor Duration for a zero-coupon bond as follows:

$$FD_t^j(\tau) = \tau\, \beta_\tau^j \tag{7.27}$$

Similarly, the Factor Duration of an asset portfolio or a liability will be a weighted average of the Factor Durations for each asset and liability cash flow, respectively:

$$FD_t^j = \sum_\tau \tau\, \beta_\tau^j\, w_t(\tau) \tag{7.28}$$

where $\omega_t(\tau) = \frac{CF_t(\tau)\ Z_t(\tau)}{\sum_s CF_t(s)\ Z_t(s)}$, $s = \tau_1, \tau_2, \ldots, \tau_M$, is the weight of each asset or liability cash flow at time t for each future maturity $\tau = \tau_1, \tau_2, \ldots, \tau_M$.

7.4 APPLICATION TO ASSET LIABILITY MANAGEMENT

7.4.1 Nature of Liabilities

Liabilities of insurance companies and pension plans are typically determined as present values of future cash flows or cash payouts associated with such liabilities. Throughout this chapter, we will define $ACF_t(\tau)$ and $LCF_t(\tau)$ as asset and liability cash flows, respectively, measured at time t and payable τ years later, where $\tau = \tau_1, \tau_2, \ldots, \tau_M$. Accordingly, A_t and L_t would denote the present values of such asset and liability cash flows at time t.

Liability cash flows of insurance companies and pension plans are typically determined as part of the actuarial analysis and therefore only represent "expected" future payouts since their calculations are based on future estimates of such contingencies as mortality, disability, termination, retirement, policy lapses, policy surrenders, and others. These contingencies affect the liability levels determined as present value of the liability cash flows. However, ALM in its traditional form is designed to minimize the asset–liability mismatch associated mainly with the liability's interest rate risk. Nevertheless, the ALM approach can be further extended to take into account these other sources of risks faced by insurance companies and pension plans. Also, in order to illustrate the basic ALM strategies, we will assume that liability cash flows themselves are not sensitive to changes in interest rates and are fixed instead. This assumption can be further relaxed, and the ALM strategies discussed in this chapter can be equally applicable to interest rate-sensitive liability cash flows as well.

Additionally, we will focus our analysis on the U.S.-based insurance companies and pension plans, but this approach can easily be generalized to other institutional investors from different countries in the world.

Figure 7.3 illustrates some common shapes of liability cash flows that exist at insurance companies (top row) and pension plans (bottom row). In each panel of Figure 7.3, the x-axis represents time horizon in years, while the y-axis represents the amount of liability cash flows in \$ millions. The key observations are the following:

- Liability cash flows tend to have maturities longer than 30 years.
- The shape of liability cash flows is not flat, and cash flows can be decreasing over time as in the case of the annuity book of business or mature frozen pension plan shown in Panels A and C, or can be increasing/decreasing over time as in the case of insurance book of business and ongoing pension plan shown in Panels B and D.

The actual liability of an insurance company or a pension plan is the present value of the liability cash flows. Since a liability is not a traded security, appropriate interest rates should be used for its determination. This is a highly regulated area, and the type of interest rates is usually either prescribed by the respective federal/state laws and regulations or required by the accounting

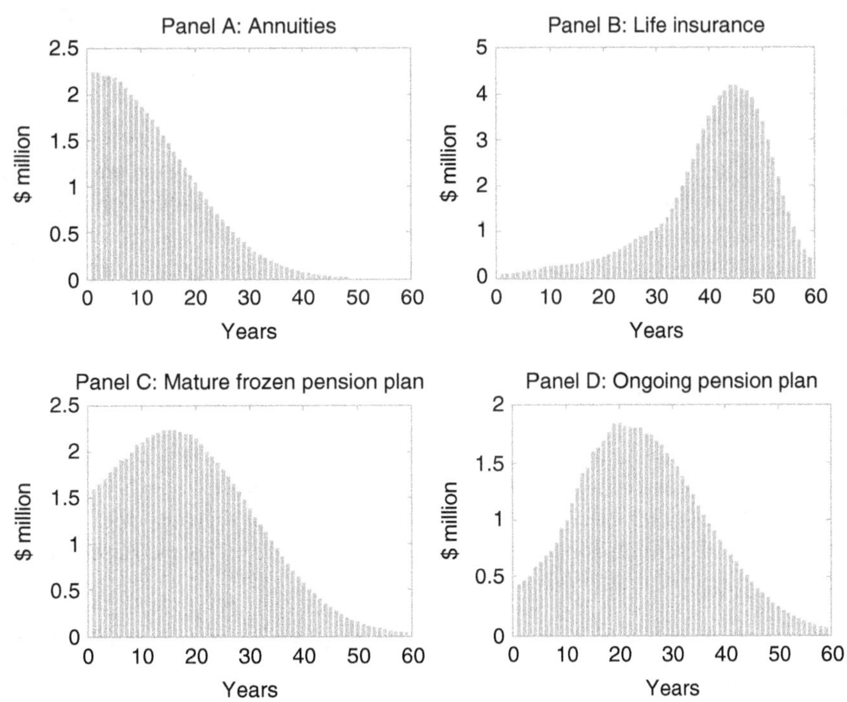

Figure 7.3 Liability cash flows.

standards. In most cases, such interest rates are derived from the U.S. Treasury securities and from the "high-quality" U.S. corporate bonds. In particular, insurance and pension liabilities are either calculated by discounting liability cash flows with the appropriate full yield curves or valued with the use of hypothetical bond portfolios whose cash flows from coupons and principals approximate the liability cash flows.

For example, according to the U.S. GAAP statement ASC 715, paragraph 35–44, "discount rates," the present value of the pension liability cash flows, that is, the pension liability, is determined as follows:

> *...an employer to look to rates of return on high-quality fixed-income investments in determining assumed discount rates. The objective of selecting assumed discount rates using that method is to measure the single amount that, if invested at the measurement date in a portfolio of high-quality debt instruments, would provide the necessary future cash flows to pay the pension benefits when due. Notionally, that single amount, the projected benefit obligation, would equal the fair value of a portfolio of high-quality zero-coupon bonds whose maturity dates and amounts would be the same as the timing and amount of the expected future benefit payments... However, in other than a zero-coupon portfolio, such as a portfolio of long-term debt instruments that pay semiannual interest payments or whose maturities do not extend far enough into the future to meet expected benefit payments, the assumed discount rates (the yield to maturity) need to incorporate expected reinvestment rates available in the future...*

In order to introduce the ALM strategies, we will use the U.S. Treasury securities only, but this analysis can be easily extended to high-quality corporate bonds by including modeling of corporate credit spreads. Given the notation introduced in Section 7.3, an asset portfolio at time t, defined as the present value of future asset cash flows discounted at the Treasury spot yield curve, is denoted as follows:

$$A_t = \sum_{\tau} A_t(\tau) = \sum_{\tau} ACF_t(\tau)\, Z_t(\tau) = \mathbf{ACF_t^T\, Z_t} \tag{7.29}$$

and a liability, defined as the present value of future liability cash flows discounted at the Treasury spot yield curve, is denoted as follows:

$$L_t = \sum_{\tau} L_t(\tau) = \sum_{\tau} LCF_t(\tau)\, Z_t(\tau) = \mathbf{LCF_t^T\, Z_t} \tag{7.30}$$

where $\mathbf{ACF_t} = (ACF_t(\tau))$ and $\mathbf{LCF_t} = (LCF_t(\tau))$, $\tau = \tau_1, \tau_2, \dots, \tau_M$, are the column vectors of asset and liability cash flows at time t, respectively.

Subsequently, a Surplus at time t, defined as the difference between assets and liabilities at time t, is denoted as follows:

$$S_t = A_t - L_t \tag{7.31}$$

For purposes of analyzing different ALM strategies and constructing portfolios in relation to liabilities, we will use insurance company's liability for an annuity book of business, where the annuity buyers exchange single payments upfront for a stream of annuity payments over future periods of time. Such future payouts from the insurance company to the annuity holders as a group are shown in Figure 7.3, Panel A.

For every following example of "liability-centric" strategies, it is assumed that liability cash flows will continue for 50 years and are payable semiannually (for simplicity). Also, it is assumed that liability cash flows are fixed for the purposes of these strategies, and any future changes in liability cash flows resulted from the actuarial or other demographic gains or losses will be funded immediately at that time and therefore will not affect the results of these strategies. However, the proposed strategies can also be implemented for liabilities with the so-called "interest-sensitive" cash flows, and the approach will be the same.

7.4.2 Cash Flow Matching

According to the Cash Flow Matching Strategy and as originally shown in Koopmans (1942), a portfolio of fixed-income securities is created in such a way that asset cash flows from bond coupons and principal maturities are equal to the liability cash flows at each future payment date. In this case, the liability cash flow stream will be fully covered, even though, the present value of the corresponding asset and liability cash flows may not be the same at each future date.

Iyengar and Ma (2009), Kocherlakota, Rosenbloom, and Shiu (1988), and Shang and Uryasev (2011) contain more information regarding mathematical algorithms for creating Cash Flow Matching Strategy. Based on these algorithms, the steps to construct a cash flow matched portfolio are the following:

1. At the inception of the strategy time $t = 0$, the first bond is chosen such that it is the highest yielding bond that matures on the same date as the last liability cash flow, that is, maturity τ_M, and its face value plus coupon is the same as the amount of the last liability cash flow:

$$k_0(\tau_M)(F_0(\tau_M) + c_0(\tau_M)) = LCF_0(\tau_M)$$

Solving for $k_0(\tau_M)$, we get

$$k_0(\tau_M) = \frac{LCF_0(\tau_M)}{F_0(\tau_M) + c_0(\tau_M)} \tag{7.32}$$

where $c_0(\tau_M)$, $F_0(\tau_M)$, and $k_0(\tau_M)$ are the respective coupon amount, the face value, and the number of contracts of a Treasury bond with τ_M years to maturity and $LCF_0(\tau_M)$ is the liability cash flow due τ_M years from now.

2. The second bond is chosen such that it is the highest yielding bond that matures on the same date as the second to last liability cash flow, that is, at time τ_{M-1}, and its face value plus coupon is the same as the amount of the second to last liability cash flow reduced by the coupon payment from the first bond:

$$k_0(\tau_{M-1})(F_0(\tau_{M-1}) + c_0(\tau_{M-1})) = LCF_0(\tau_{M-1}) - c_0(\tau_M)$$

Solving for $k_0(\tau_{M-1})$, we get

$$k_0(\tau_{M-1}) = \frac{LCF_0(\tau_{M-1}) - c_0(\tau_M)}{F_0(\tau_{M-1}) + c_0(\tau_{M-1})} \tag{7.33}$$

3. Continuing in this manner by going backward from later maturities to more recent maturities, the position in Treasury bonds with τ_j years to maturity, $j = M-2, M-3, \ldots, 2, 1$, will be the highest yielding bond that satisfies the following requirements:

$$k_0(\tau_j)(F_0(\tau_j) + c_0(\tau_j)) = LCF_0(\tau_j) - \sum_l c_0(l)$$

where $l = \tau_{j+1}, \tau_{j+2}, \ldots, \tau_M$. Solving for $k_0(\tau_j)$, we get

$$k_0(\tau_j) = \frac{LCF_0(\tau_j) - \sum_l c_0(l)}{F_0(\tau_j) + c_0(\tau_j)} \tag{7.34}$$

4. Once the bond weights are determined in this fashion, there will be no need to change the original bond portfolio at any future time t as long as the original liability cash flows $LCF_0(\tau)$, $\tau = \tau_1, \tau_2, \ldots, \tau_M$, determined at the inception of the strategy time $t = 0$, are unchanged and the bonds do not default.

Advantages of the Cash Flow Matching strategy are as follows:

- If implemented properly, this strategy will result in the complete match of the asset and liability cash flows and therefore will provide zero tracking error by construction.
- Since cash flows from coupons and principals of maturing bonds match liability cash flows exactly, there is no interest rate risk and there is no reinvestment risk.
- Once it is implemented at the inception of the strategy, there is no need for any further rebalancing and no additional transaction costs are incurred.
- If some corporate bonds are included in the matching portfolio, then bond downgrades would have no impact as long as coupon and principal amounts continue to be paid.
- Volatility of the bond portfolio's market value is not important since bonds are held to maturity, as long as there are no defaults.

Disadvantages of the Cash Flow Matching Strategy are as follows:

- As shown in Figure 7.3, the liability cash flows often extend beyond 30 years, and therefore Cash Flow Matching is difficult to implement, since the bond market is very illiquid for such longer maturities. As an approximation, the liability cash flows beyond 30 years can be aggregated at a 30-year maturity, usually on a present value basis, and the Cash Flow Matching Strategy would be implemented then.
- All asset maturities have to match exactly all liability maturities without any gaps, which is a very restrictive requirement.
- Backward induction-based matching works well when liability cash flows gradually decrease over time as shown in Panel A of Figure 7.3. However, when liability cash flows increase and subsequently decrease over time, then backward induction-based matching may be difficult to implement using coupon-paying bonds, and application of zero-coupon bonds may be required, the supply of which is usually limited.

- Cash Flow Matching tends to be quite a restrictive strategy due to its matching nature, and many high yielding bonds may be eliminated as a result. Therefore, portfolio managers may be prevented from taking advantage of potentially mispriced securities, making this strategy more costly.
- If some corporate bonds are included in the matching portfolio, then bond defaults will have a drastic effect on the portfolio, since the portfolio would have to be rematched, and potentially low yielding bonds will be included.
- Additionally, if downgraded corporate bonds violate the sponsor's minimum credit quality requirements and therefore need to be replaced, then the portfolio would have to be rematched as well, and potentially low yielding bonds would need to be included.

Given the restrictive nature of the Cash Flow Matching Strategy and all of its disadvantages, other strategies are often preferred and implemented as a result. Duration Matching is one of the simpler strategies that can be implemented to remedy some of these issues.

7.4.3 Classic Immunization and Duration Matching

Different forms of Classic Immunization and Duration Matching Strategy have been introduced independently by Macaulay (1938), Hicks (1939), Samuelson (1945), and Redington (1952), and over the years, the terms "Duration" and "immunization" became the standard terminology in the modern fixed-income area.

In general, Classic Immunization and Duration Matching Strategy can overcome some of the limitations with Cash Flow Matching, even though additional problems may exist with Duration Matching.

Assets and liabilities at each future time t are portfolios of zero-coupon bonds with maturities τ and face values equal to the respective cash flow amounts or $ACF_t(\tau)$ and $LCF_t(\tau)$, respectively, where maturities are $\tau = \tau_1, \tau_2, \ldots, \tau_M$. Therefore, asset Duration at time t, or AD_t, is a weighted average of Durations, or maturities as shown in (7.4), of individual asset cash flows, where weights are proportional to their present values:

$$AD_t = -\frac{1}{A_t}\frac{\partial A_t}{\partial r_t} = -\frac{1}{A_t}\sum_{\tau}\frac{\partial A_t(\tau)}{\partial r_t(\tau)} = \frac{1}{A_t}\sum_{\tau}\tau\, ACF_t(\tau)\, Z_t(\tau)$$

where $A_t = \sum_{\tau} A_t(\tau) = \sum_{\tau} ACF_t(\tau)\, Z_t(\tau) = \mathbf{ACF}_t^{\top}\, \mathbf{Z}_t$

or, alternatively,

$$AD_t = \sum_{\tau} AD_t(\tau) = \sum_{\tau} \tau\, w_t^A(\tau) \tag{7.35}$$

where $w_t^A(\tau) = \frac{1}{A_t} ACF_t(\tau)\ Z_t(\tau)$.

Similarly, liability duration at time t, or LD_t, is a weighted average of Durations, or maturities as shown in (7.4), of individual liability cash flows, where weights are proportional to their present values:

$$LD_t = -\frac{1}{L_t}\frac{\partial L_t}{\partial r_t} = -\frac{1}{L_t}\sum_{\tau}\frac{\partial L_t(\tau)}{\partial r_t(\tau)} = \frac{1}{L_t}\sum_{\tau}\tau\, LCF_t(\tau)\, Z_t(\tau)$$

where $L_t = \sum_{\tau} L_t(\tau) = \sum_{\tau} LCF_t(\tau) Z_t(\tau) = \mathbf{LCF}_t^{\top}\ \mathbf{Z}_t$

or, alternatively,

$$LD_t = \sum_{\tau} LD_t(\tau) = \sum_{\tau} \tau\, w_t^L(\tau) \tag{7.36}$$

where $w_t^L(\tau) = \frac{1}{L_t} LCF_t(\tau)\, Z_t(\tau)$, $\tau = \tau_1, \tau_2, \ldots, \tau_M$.[2]

The key assumption behind the portfolio duration calculation as shown in (7.35) and (7.36) is that *the entire yield curve shifts in a parallel manner*. In other words, each spot rate $r_t(\tau)$, $\tau = \tau_1, \tau_2, \ldots, \tau_M$, from the Treasury yield curve is assumed to change by the same amount.

As illustrated in Panjer (1998), the Classic Immunization Strategy is designed to balance two sources of risks, interest rate risk and reinvestment risk, because of the following offsetting effects of interest rate changes on a bond portfolio:

[2]As mentioned before, throughout the chapter it is assumed that both asset and liability cash flows are not sensitive to interest rates. Therefore, both (7.35) and (7.36) are only valid for asset and liability cash flows that are not sensitive to interest rates. However, the concept of asset and liability duration can be generalized for the situations when asset and liability cash flows are sensitive to interest rates.

- When interest rates *increase*, the bond portfolio will experience capital losses, while coupons received can be reinvested at higher interest rates, resulting in reinvestment gains.
- When interest rates *decrease*, the bond portfolio will experience capital gains, while coupons received can be reinvested at lower interest rates, resulting in reinvestment losses.

As a result, by structuring a portfolio of bonds such that it has the same Duration as that of the liability, interest rate and reinvestment risks will be balanced and the Surplus amount will be relatively stable, regardless of the direction of the interest rate change.

In order to illustrate how the Classic Immunization Strategy works, we use a 30-year Treasury bond with 4% semiannual coupons in order to hedge insurance company's liability for an annuity book of business as previously described.

The key steps for the strategy implementation are the following:

1. At the inception of the strategy time $t = 0$, the values of the assets and liabilities are assumed to be the same by construction, $A_0 = L_0$. In other words, the annuity book of business is fully funded at that time.
2. As a result, at time $t = 0$ the bond portfolio position $k_0(\tau)$ is created such that the dollar sensitivities of total assets and liabilities to changes in interest rates are the same:

$$L_0\, LD_0 = P_0(\tau)\, AD_0(\tau)\, k_0(\tau)$$

where $\tau = 30$ since we are using a 30-year bond, $AD_0(\tau)$ and LD_0 are the asset and liability Durations determined based on (7.35) and (7.36), respectively, and L_0 and $P_0(\tau)$ are the values of the liability and 30-year bond price at time $t = 0$, respectively. Solving for the bond position, we get the following number of contracts:

$$k_0(\tau) = \frac{L_0\, LD_0}{P_0(\tau)\, AD_0(\tau)} \tag{7.37}$$

The total amount invested in the bond is therefore

$$Bond_0 = k_0(\tau)\, P_0(\tau) \tag{7.38}$$

with the balance invested in cash that earns a short-term interest rate:

$$Cash_0 = L_0 - Bond_0 \tag{7.39}$$

3. At each future coupon payment time $t = t_1, t_2, \ldots, t_T$, the market value of then $29\frac{1}{2}$-year Treasury bond position changes based on the new interest rates at that time, resulting in capital gains or losses. Assuming for simplicity that portfolio rebalancing happens during the coupon payment times only, we have the following bond position:

$$Bond_t = k_{t-\Delta}(\tau)\, P_t(\tau) \tag{7.40}$$

where $\Delta = \frac{1}{2}$ for semiannual rebalancing, $P_t(\tau)$ is the bond price at times t, $k_{t-\Delta}$ is the bond position established at the previous rebalancing time $t - \Delta$, and $\tau = 29\frac{1}{2}$[3]. Cash position increases with interest earned I_t based on the prior period's short-term interest rate $r_{t-\Delta}(\tau)$, $\tau = \frac{1}{2}$, and with the semiannual coupon received, while the tth liability cash flow is paid out from the cash position:

$$Cash_t = Cash_{t-\Delta} + I_t + \Delta\, k_{t-\Delta}(\tau)\, c - LCF_t \tag{7.41}$$

resulting in the following total asset balance at time t:

$$Asset_t = Bond_t + Cash_t \tag{7.42}$$

Total assets $Asset_t$ are then rebalanced between a new 4% 30-year Treasury bond available in the market at time t and cash in order to match Durations of assets and liabilities at that time. The resulting number of bond contracts is the following:

$$k_t(\tau) = \frac{L_t\, LD_t}{P_t(\tau)\, AD_t(\tau)} \tag{7.43}$$

[3] At every time t, we use a new 30-year bond to immunize the current portfolio so that at time $t + \Delta$, $\Delta = \frac{1}{2}$, the bond has $29\frac{1}{2}$ years to maturity.

and the total amount invested in the bond is therefore

$$Bond_t = k_t(\tau)\, P_t(\tau) \tag{7.44}$$

with the cash position being the balancing item:

$$Cash_t = Asset_t - Bond_t \tag{7.45}$$

where now $\tau = 30$, $P_t(\tau)$ is the price of a 30-year Treasury bond with 4% semiannual coupons available in the market at time t.

4. Each following 6-month period, the portfolio is rebalanced in the same manner between cash and a 4% 30-year Treasury bond available in the market at that time in order to match Durations of assets and liabilities.

Figure 7.4 shows the performance of the Classic Immunization Strategy based on two yield curve simulations. The term structure is simulated based on the methodology outlined in Diebold and Li (2006), and model parameters are estimated based on the historical term structure data reported by the U.S. Federal Reserve for the period from 1987 to 2014.

Panel A presents the first random simulation of the term structure over the following 30-year period, and Panel B summarizes the respective levels of assets, liabilities, and Surplus. In this simulation, the strategy performs well resulting in positive Surplus at the end of the horizon. We can see that assets follow liabilities pretty closely and then gradually exceed liabilities over time. Bond position steadily declines to match the Duration of the liability, while the cash position is relatively stable, declining over time as well.

Panel C presents another random simulation of the term structure, which results in Surplus losses as shown in Panel D. Initially, assets follow liabilities closely but then gradually decline below liabilities over time due to large adverse nonparallel movements of the term structure. As before, bond position steadily declines to match the Duration of the liability, while the cash position is more volatile, declining over time as well.

In order to assess the performance of the Classic Immunization Strategy, Treasury spot yield curves were simulated semiannually for 30 years, liabilities were calculated as present values of the liability cash flows at each future date based on the simulated yield curves at that time, and the Duration Matching Strategy was applied at each future semiannual payment date. The results are presented in Figure 7.5, according to which this strategy performs satisfactory when levels of interest rates change randomly, but the entire yield curves shift in a parallel fashion, as shown in Panels A and C. However, as shown in Panels B and D, once we introduced nonparallel yield curve shifts, this strategy produced losses more frequently than gains.

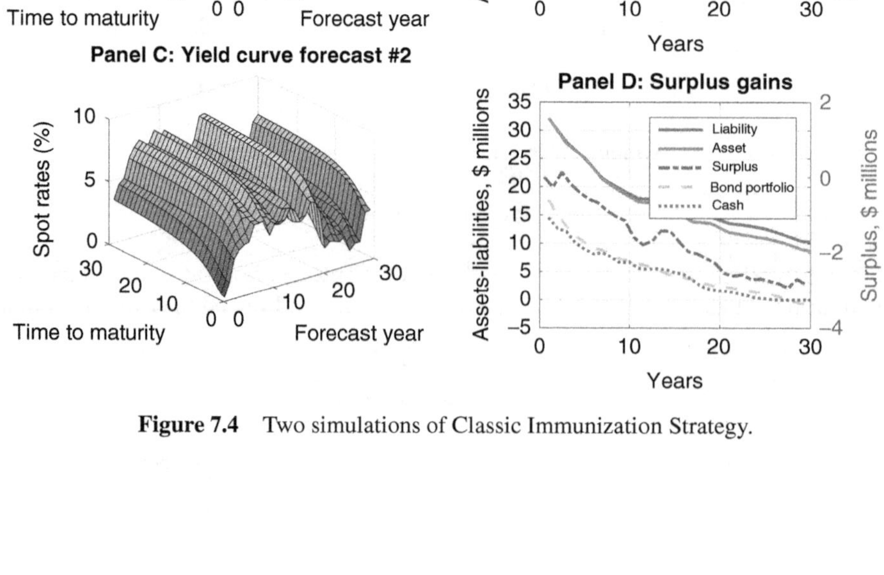

Figure 7.4 Two simulations of Classic Immunization Strategy.

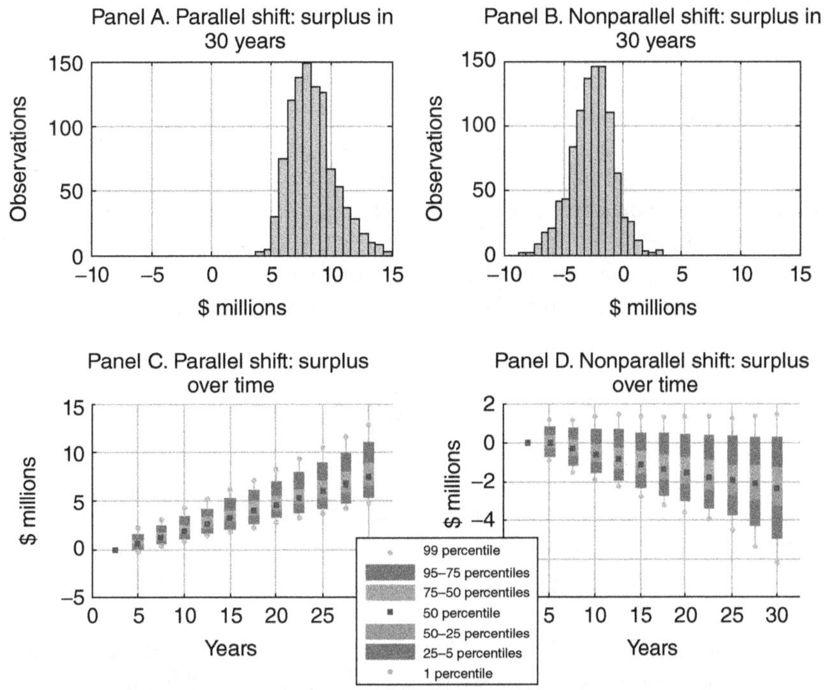

Figure 7.5 Performance of Classic Immunization Strategy.

Advantages of the Classic Immunization Strategy are as follows:

- Simple strategy and easy to implement.
- Duration concept has intuitive interpretation as the sensitivity of a bond to yield curve shift and Duration can be used to compare different fixed-income products.
- In many applications, the Classic Immunization Strategy can provide satisfactory results where high precision is not required.
- It can serve as a good first approximation for the hedging portfolios and as a result be a benchmark for more sophisticated strategies.

Disadvantages of the Classic Immunization Strategy are as follows:

- The main issue is that it only works when yield curves shift in a parallel fashion, which happens quite rarely.
- It requires frequent rebalancing in order to account for nonparallel yield curve shifts, generating large transaction costs.
- It tends to generate more losses than gains if yield curves shift in a nonparallel manner and rebalancing is done infrequently.

In order to hedge or immunize liabilities against nonparallel yield curve shifts, a variation of the Classic Immunization Strategy is used, which requires matching Key Rate Durations of assets and liabilities, as described in the following section.

7.4.4 Key Rate Duration Matching

As discussed earlier and outlined in Ho (1992), the purpose of matching Key Rate Durations is to overcome limitations imposed by the Classic Immunization Strategy and as a result to hedge bond portfolios against nonparallel yield curve shifts. In order to illustrate how the Key Rate Duration Matching Strategy works, we implement liability hedging with a portfolio of zero-coupon bonds, and the liability being hedged is the same as that in the previous example of the Classic Immunization Strategy, that is, the insurance company's liability for an annuity book of business.

In order to hedge this liability against nonparallel movements in the term structure, we selected 10-year, 20-year, and 30-year Key Rates, which means that three zero-coupon Treasury bonds of the corresponding maturities will be used, and therefore $\tau_B = 10, 20, 30$.

The key steps for the strategy implementation are the following:

1. At the inception of the strategy time $t = 0$, the values of the assets and liabilities are assumed to be the same by construction, $A_0 = L_0$. In other words, the annuity book of business is fully funded at that time.
2. As a result, at time $t = 0$ the bond portfolio is created such that Key Rate Durations of three chosen bonds are the same as those of the liability. Recall that $KRD(\tau)$ denotes the Key Rate Duration, defined in Equation (7.14). Since the liability has Key Rate Duration at each spot rate maturity, $KRD_0^L(\tau)$, $\tau = \tau_1, \tau_2, \ldots, \tau_M$, and we only use three zero-coupon bonds and therefore only three-bond Key Rate Durations, $KRD_0^B(\tau_B)$, $\tau_B = 10, 20, 30$; we need to aggregate liability KRDs around each bond's maturity when choosing the number of contracts for each bond.
As a result, a number of contracts needed for 10-year, 20-year, and 30-year zero-coupon bonds, respectively, are the following:
$$k_0(\tau_B) = \frac{\sum_{\tau \subset I_B} KRD_0^L(\tau)\, LCF_0(\tau)\, Z_0(\tau)}{KRD_0^B(\tau_B)\, Z_0(\tau_B)} \tag{7.46}$$
where:
   - $k_0(\tau_B)$, $Z_0(\tau_B)$, and $KRD_0^B(\tau_B)$ are the respective number of contracts, prices, and Key Rate Durations of 10-year, 20-year, and 30-year zero-coupon bonds, $\tau_B = 10, 20, 30$.
   - $LCF_0(\tau)$, $Z_0(\tau)$, and $KRD_0^L(\tau)$ are the respective liability cash flows, zero-coupon bonds, and liability Key Rate Durations with maturities $\tau = \tau_1, \tau_2, \ldots, \tau_M$.
   - $\sum_{\tau \subset I_B}$ is the summation of the liability Key Rate Durations over three maturity sets, where the first maturity set is $I_{10} = \{1, \ldots, 15\}$, the second maturity set is $I_{20} = \{16, \ldots, 25\}$, and the third maturity set is $I_{30} = \{26, \ldots, 50\}$.

   Therefore, the total amount invested in bonds that match liability KRDs at time $t = 0$ is the following:
$$Bond_0 = \mathbf{k}_0^\top\ \mathbf{Z}_0 \tag{7.47}$$
where $\mathbf{Z}_0 = (Z_0(\tau_B))$ and $\mathbf{k}_0 = (k_0(\tau_B))$, $\tau_B = 10, 20, 30$, are the column vectors of prices and positions of 10-year, 20-year, and 30-year zero-coupon bonds at the inception of the strategy time $t = 0$, while the balance is invested in cash earning a short-term interest rate:
$$Cash_0 = L_0 - Bond_0 \tag{7.48}$$
where L_0 is the liability value at the inception of the strategy.
3. At each future rebalancing time $t = t_1, t_2, \ldots, t_T$, the market values of then $9\frac{1}{2}$-year, $19\frac{1}{2}$-year, and $29\frac{1}{2}$-year zero-coupon bond positions change based on the new interest rates at that time, resulting in capital gains or losses. Assuming for simplicity that portfolio rebalancing happens during the coupon payment times only, we have the following bond position:
$$Bond_t = \mathbf{k}_{\mathbf{t}-\Delta}^\top \mathbf{Z}_\mathbf{t} \tag{7.49}$$
where $\Delta = \frac{1}{2}$ for semiannual rebalancing, $\mathbf{Z}_\mathbf{t} = (Z_t(\tau_B))$ is the column vector of bond prices at times t, $\mathbf{k}_{\mathbf{t}-\Delta} = (k_{t-\Delta}(\tau_B))$ is the column vector of bond positions established at the previous rebalancing time $t - \Delta$, and $\tau_B = 9\frac{1}{2}, 19\frac{1}{2}, 29\frac{1}{2}$ [4].
Cash position increases with interest earned, I_t, based on the prior period's short-term interest rate $r_{t-\Delta}(\tau)$, $\tau = \frac{1}{2}$, while the tth liability cash flow is paid out from the cash position:
$$Cash_t = Cash_{t-\Delta} + I_t - LCF_t \tag{7.50}$$
resulting in the following total asset balance at time t:
$$Asset_t = Bond_t + Cash_t \tag{7.51}$$
Key Rate Durations for assets and liabilities at time t are then recalculated based on the interest rate term structure at that time, resulting in the updated values for $KRD_t^B(\tau_B)$, $\tau_B = 10, 20, 30$, and $KRD_t^L(\tau)$, $\tau = \tau_1, \tau_2, \ldots, \tau_M$. Total assets $Asset_t$ are then rebalanced among the new 10-year, 20-year, and 30-year zero-coupon bonds available in the market at time

[4] At every time t, we use new 10-year, 20-year, and 30-year zero-coupon bonds to immunize the current portfolio so that at time $t + \Delta$, $\Delta = \frac{1}{2}$, the bonds have $9\frac{1}{2}$, $19\frac{1}{2}$, and $29\frac{1}{2}$ years to maturity, respectively.

t and cash in order to match these Key Rate Durations of assets and liabilities at that time, resulting in the following bond positions:

$$k_t(\tau_B) = \frac{\sum_{\tau \subset I_B} KRD_t^L(\tau)\, LCF_t(\tau)\, Z_t(\tau)}{KRD_t^B(\tau_B)\, Z_t(\tau_B)} \tag{7.52}$$

and the total amount invested in bonds is therefore

$$Bond_t = \mathbf{k}_t^\top \mathbf{Z}_t \tag{7.53}$$

where $\mathbf{Z}_t = (Z_t(\tau_B))$ and $\mathbf{k}_t = (k_t(\tau_B))$, $\tau_B = 10, 20, 30$, are the column vectors of prices and positions of 10-year, 20-year, and 30-year zero-coupon bonds at time t, while the balance is invested in cash earning a short-term interest rate:

$$Cash_t = Asset_t - Bond_t \tag{7.54}$$

4. Each following 6-month period, the portfolio is rebalanced in the same manner among the new 10-year, 20-year, and 30-year zero-coupon bonds available in the market at that time and cash in order to match Key Rate Durations of assets and liabilities.

Even though zero-coupon bonds are a natural choice for Key Rate Duration Matching, it is also possible to use regular coupon-paying bonds by applying nonlinear optimization in order to approximately match Key Rate Durations of assets and liabilities. In this case, each coupon-paying bond will have a number of smaller Key Rate Durations corresponding to each of its coupon payments and one large Key Rate Duration corresponding to its final payment of coupon plus face value. Therefore, the following nonlinear optimization program has to be solved at each future time t in order to find three bond positions $\mathbf{k}_t = (k_t(\tau_B))$, $\tau_B = 10, 20, 30$, as follows:

$$\begin{aligned} \underset{\mathbf{k}_t}{\text{Minimize}} \quad & \sum_{\tau} \left(KRD_t^L(\tau) LCF_t(\tau) Z_t(\tau) - \sum_{\tau_B} k_t(\tau_B) KRD_t^B(\tau_B) Z_t(\tau_B) \right)^2 \\ \text{subject to} \quad & \left(Asset_t - \mathbf{k}_t^\top \mathbf{Z}_t \right) \geq 0 \end{aligned}$$

where the constraint is introduced in order to prevent leverage, $LCF_t(\tau)$, $\tau = \tau_1, \tau_2, \ldots, \tau_M$, are the liability cash flows, $KRD_t^B(\tau)$ and $KRD_t^L(\tau)$ are the respective bond and liability Key Rate Durations, $\mathbf{Z}_t = (Z_t(\tau))$ is the column vector of the zero-coupon bond prices, and $\mathbf{k}_t = (k_t(\tau_B))$ is the column vector of positions of the coupon-paying bonds with respective maturities $\tau_B = 10, 20, 30$.

Figure 7.6 summarizes the performance of the Key Rate Duration Matching strategy based on the simulated term structure of interest rates as shown in Panels A and C. The term structure is simulated based on the methodology outlined in Diebold and Li (2006), and model parameters are estimated based on the historical term structure data reported by the U.S. Federal Reserve for the period from 1987 to 2014.

Bond portfolios based on zero-coupon bonds and coupon-paying bonds are summarized in Panels B and D, respectively. Even though both bond portfolios resulted in slightly negative and volatile Surplus during some of the projection time, assets tracked liability quite closely over the entire time horizon, which is a much better performance than that of the Classic Immunization Strategy. Bond positions gradually declined over time in order to match Key Rate Durations of liabilities, with the largest bond allocation to the 10-year bond, followed by the 20-year bond, and then followed by the 30-year bond in both portfolios. Cash positions are stable but also declining.

Similar to the previous section, in order to assess the performance of the Key Rate Duration Matching Strategy, Treasury spot yield curves were simulated semiannually for 30 years, liabilities were calculated as present values of the liability cash flows at each future date based on the simulated yield curves at that time, and the Key Rate Duration Matching Strategy was applied at each future semiannual payment date. The results are presented in Figure 7.7, according to which this strategy resulted in some losses over time, as shown in Panels B and E for the zero-coupon bonds and in Panels C and F for the coupon-paying bonds, but such losses were much smaller than those produced by the Classic Immunization Strategy as shown in Panels A and D. Even though liability matching with coupon-paying bonds is less precise than that with zero-coupon bonds, liability hedging happened to be better with coupon bonds as shown in Figure 7.7, since coupon payments produce more Key Rate Durations, which can improve hedging precision in some cases.

Advantages of the Key Rate Duration Matching Strategy are as follows:

- It provides protection against nonparallel yield curve shifts, which is a substantial improvement over the Classic Immunization Strategy.

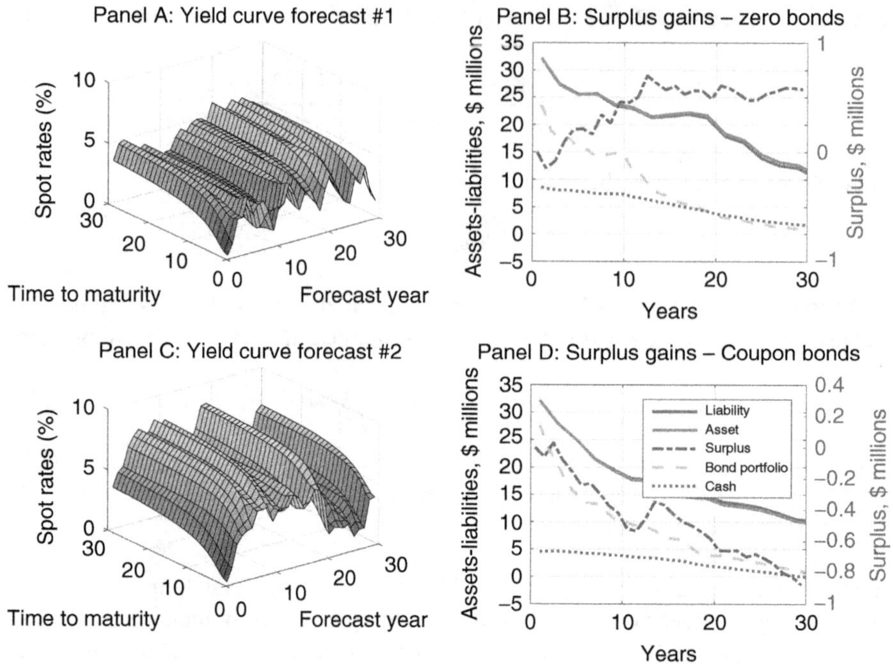

Figure 7.6 Two simulations of Key Rate Duration Matching strategies.

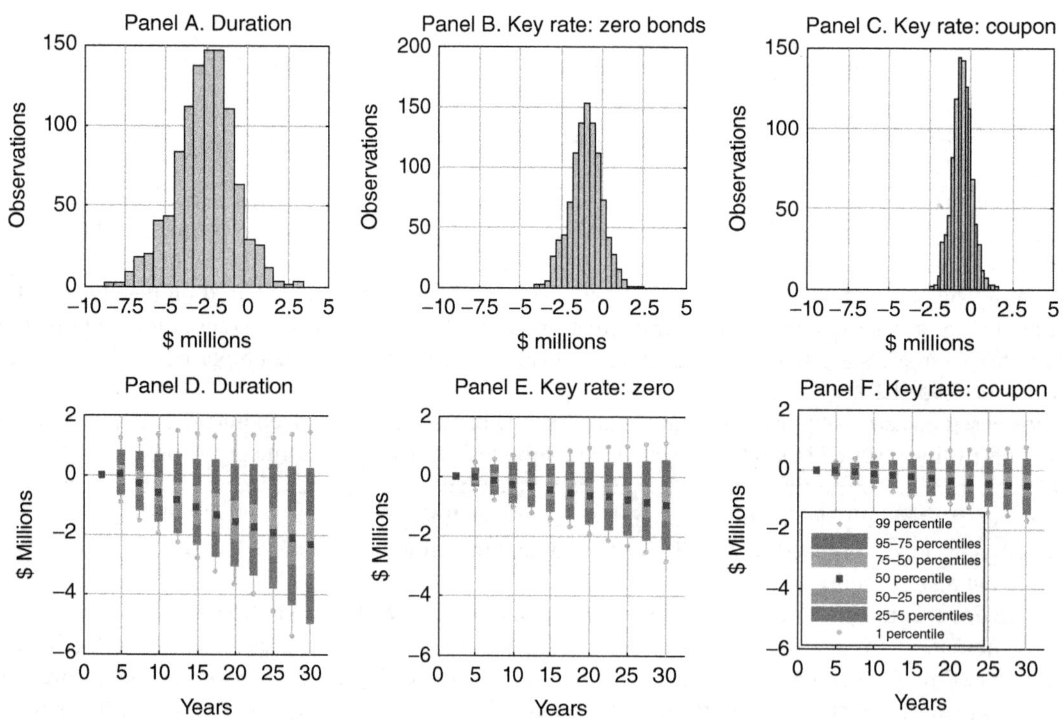

Figure 7.7 Performance of Key Rate Duration Matching strategies.

- If carefully created, this strategy can produce adequate results and relatively low asset–liability tracking error.
- It does not require hedging all or many Key Rates in order to hedge liabilities, since using only a few Key Rates can produce a stable hedge.
- A wide variety of bonds can be used, even though zero-coupon bonds are the most logical choice, while coupon bonds can only provide an approximate Key Rate Matching.

Disadvantages of the Key Rate Duration Matching Strategy are as follows:

- Key Rate Duration may be difficult to interpret and understand since it has no real world equivalent as it is only a "theoretical" sensitivity to a single spot rate change, while in real world many spot rates usually change at the same time.
- Since grouping of some liability Key Rate Durations is required in order to determine the position in bonds, this strategy is only an approximation and can result in large asset–liability tracking errors.
- Determining which Key Rates to hedge may be quite subjective when the liability does not have clearly defined areas of large and highly concentrated cash flows.
- Zero-coupon bonds are the most logical securities for implementing this strategy since they only have one Key Rate Duration per security. But the use of zeros can create a lot of restrictions for the portfolio construction.
- Coupon-paying bonds can also be used in order to match Key Rate Durations, but the solution can only be an approximation achieved with optimization programs.
- It may be challenging to match Key Rate Durations beyond 30-year maturity for liabilities with especially long tails since such long-term bonds are generally not available in the markets.
- As the number of Key Rates hedged increases, the cost of the strategy increases as well, even though tracking errors decline. This strategy converges to Cash Flow Matching as more Key Rates are hedged.

Even though the Key Rate Duration Matching Strategy is a significant improvement over Classic Immunization, many limitations still remain. As a result, factor analysis, which allows for the so-called Factor Duration Matching Strategy, is an alternative that can overcome some of the issues with the Key Rate Duration Matching Strategy while keeping asset–liability tracking errors at acceptable levels.

7.4.5 Factor Duration Matching

In recent years, more advanced ALM strategies have been implemented to further immunize assets and liabilities with respect to nonparallel movements of the entire term structure. As shown in Litterman and Scheinkman (1991), Barber and Cooper (1996), Willner (1996), and Veronesi (2010), Principal Component Analysis has been applied to determine factors inherent in the term structure of interest rates. As a result, the main idea behind factor analysis is that yield curve movements are analyzed and modeled in terms of the movements of yield curves' underlying factors. As discussed in Section 7.3.4, Principal Component Analysis is one of the statistical techniques that can be used in order to determine what those underlying factors can be.

Recall that according to Principal Component Analysis, it is assumed that there are independent factors $f_t^1, f_t^2, f_t^3, \ldots$, that affect changes in the term structure of interest rates as

$$\begin{aligned}
\Delta r_t(\tau_1) &= \alpha_1 + \beta_1^1 \Delta f_t^1 + \beta_1^2 \Delta f_t^2 + \beta_1^3 \Delta f_t^3 \\
\Delta r_t(\tau_2) &= \alpha_2 + \beta_2^1 \Delta f_t^1 + \beta_2^2 \Delta f_t^2 + \beta_2^3 \Delta f_t^3 \\
&\cdots\cdots\cdots\cdots\cdots\cdots\cdots\cdots \\
\Delta r_t(\tau_M) &= \alpha_M + \beta_M^1 \Delta f_t^1 + \beta_M^2 \Delta f_t^2 + \beta_M^3 \Delta f_t^3
\end{aligned} \tag{7.55}$$

where only three factors f_t^1, f_t^2, f_t^3 are considered here, $r_t(\tau)$, $\tau = \tau_1, \tau_2, \ldots, \tau_M$, is the term structure of interest rates at time t, Δ denotes the changes in spot rates and factors, and β are the corresponding factor sensitivities. Principal Component Analysis assumes that these three factors are defined by a linear combination of the underlying spot rates:

$$\Delta f_t^j = \gamma_{j1} \Delta r_t(\tau_1) + \gamma_{j2} \Delta r_t(\tau_2) + \ldots + \gamma_{jM} \Delta r_t(\tau_M) \tag{7.56}$$

As shown in Section 7.3.4, such factors f_t^1, f_t^2, and f_t^3 and the corresponding factor sensitivities β_τ^1, β_τ^2, β_τ^3, $\tau = \tau_1, \tau_2, \ldots, \tau_M$, are estimated from the historical spot rate yield curves. In particular, the factor sensitivities β_τ^1, β_τ^2, and β_τ^3, $\tau = \tau_1, \tau_2, \ldots, \tau_M$, which are plotted in Figure 7.2, have the economic interpretations as "level factor," "slope factor," and "curvature factor."

Once we identified and interpreted three factors that determine the term structure of interest rates, we can also introduce a way of hedging portfolios of assets and liabilities against changes in these factors through the use of the so-called Factor Durations discussed in Section 7.3.4.2.

As shown in Section 7.3.4.2, Factor Duration of a zero-coupon bond $Z_t(\tau)$, $\tau = \tau_1, \tau_2, \ldots, \tau_M$, is defined as the sensitivity of this bond's price to changes in the underlying factor f_t^j, $j = 1, 2, 3$:

$$FD_t^j(\tau) = -\frac{1}{Z_t(\tau)} \frac{\partial Z_t(\tau)}{\partial f_t^j} \tag{7.57}$$

and Factor Duration of a liability or a portfolio of assets is the following:

$$FD_t^j = \sum_\tau \tau\, \beta_\tau^j\, \omega_t(\tau) \tag{7.58}$$

where $\omega_t(\tau)$ are the weights of asset or liability cash flows at time t for each future maturity $\tau = \tau_1, \tau_2, \dots, \tau_M$ as shown in Section 7.3.4.2 and β_τ^j are the respective factor sensitivities from Principal Component Analysis described in Section 7.3.4.1.

In order to illustrate how the Factor Duration Matching Strategy works, we implement liability hedging with a portfolio of coupon-paying bonds, and the liability being hedged is the same as that in the previous example of the Classic Immunization Strategy, that is, the insurance company's liability for an annuity book of business. To hedge this liability against nonparallel movements in the term structure, we use 10-year, 20-year, and 30-year Treasury bonds each paying 4% semiannual coupons, that is, $\tau_B = 10, 20, 30$.

The key steps for the strategy implementation are the following:

1. At the inception of the strategy time $t = 0$, the values of the assets and liabilities are assumed to be the same by construction, $A_0 = L_0$. In other words, the annuity book of business is fully funded at that time.
2. As a result, at time $t = 0$ the bond portfolio is created such that Factor Durations of the bond portfolio are the same as those of the liability. Therefore, the bond positions at time $t = 0$ are the solution to the following system of linear equations:

$$\begin{cases} FD_0^{1,L} = FD_0^{1,B1}\ k_0^1 + FD_0^{1,B2}\ k_0^2 + FD_0^{1,B3}\ k_0^3 \\ FD_0^{2,L} = FD_0^{2,B1}\ k_0^1 + FD_0^{2,B2}\ k_0^2 + FD_0^{2,B3}\ k_0^3 \\ FD_0^{3,L} = FD_0^{3,B1}\ k_0^1 + FD_0^{3,B2}\ k_0^2 + FD_0^{3,B3}\ k_0^3 \end{cases} \tag{7.59}$$

or in matrix notations it will be the following:

$$\mathbf{FD_0^L} = \mathbf{FD_0^B} \cdot \mathbf{k_0} \tag{7.60}$$

where $\mathbf{k_0} = (k_0^1, k_0^2, k_0^3)$ is the column vector of bond positions, $\mathbf{FD_0^L} = (FD_0^{1,L}, FD_0^{2,L}, FD_0^{3,L})$ is the column vector of liability Factor Durations, and $\mathbf{FD_0^B}$ is the matrix of bond Factor Durations:

$$\mathbf{FD_0^B} = \begin{pmatrix} FD_0^{1,B1} & FD_0^{1,B2} & FD_0^{1,B3} \\ FD_0^{2,B1} & FD_0^{2,B2} & FD_0^{2,B3} \\ FD_0^{3,B1} & FD_0^{3,B2} & FD_0^{3,B3} \end{pmatrix} \tag{7.61}$$

As a result, the bond positions will be the solution of the above equation:

$$\mathbf{k_0} = (\mathbf{FD_0^B})^{-1}\ \mathbf{FD_0^L} \tag{7.62}$$

where $(\mathbf{FD_0^B})^{-1}$ is the inverse matrix of the bond Factor Duration matrix (7.61), and the resulting total position in bonds that matches the liability Factor Durations at time $t = 0$ is the following:

$$Bond_0 = \mathbf{k_0^\top}\ \mathbf{P_0} \tag{7.63}$$

where $\mathbf{P_0} = (P_0(\tau_B))$ and $\mathbf{k_0} = (k_0(\tau_B))$, $\tau_B = 10, 20, 30$ are the respective column vectors of prices and positions of 10-year, 20-year, and 30-year bonds at the inception of the strategy time $t = 0$, while the balance is invested in cash earning a short-term interest rate:

$$Cash_0 = L_0 - Bond_0 \tag{7.64}$$

where L_0 is the liability value at the inception of the strategy.

3. At each future coupon payment time $t = t_1, t_2, \dots, t_T$, the market values of then $9\frac{1}{2}$-year, $19\frac{1}{2}$-year, and $29\frac{1}{2}$-year bond positions change based on the new interest rates at that time, resulting in capital gains or losses. Assuming for simplicity that portfolio rebalancing happens during the coupon payment times only, we have the following bond position:

$$Bond_t = \mathbf{k_{t-\Delta}^\top}\ \mathbf{P_t} \tag{7.65}$$

where $\Delta = \frac{1}{2}$ for semiannual rebalancing, $\mathbf{P_t} = (P_t(\tau_B))$ is the column vector of bond prices at times t, $\mathbf{k_{t-\Delta}} = (k_{t-\Delta}(\tau_B))$ is the column vector of bond positions established at the previous rebalancing time $t - \Delta$, and $\tau_B = 9\frac{1}{2}, 19\frac{1}{2}, 29\frac{1}{2}$ [5].

Cash position increases with interest earned I_t based on the prior period's short-term interest rate $r_{t-\Delta}(\tau)$, $\tau = \frac{1}{2}$, and with the semiannual coupons received, while the tth liability cash flow is paid out from the cash position:

$$Cash_t = Cash_{t-\Delta} + I_t + \Delta\, \mathbf{k}_{t-\Delta}^{\mathsf{T}}\, \mathbf{c} - LCF_t \tag{7.66}$$

where $\mathbf{c} = (c(\tau_B))$, $\tau_B = 9\frac{1}{2}, 19\frac{1}{2}, 29\frac{1}{2}$, is the column vector of coupons from the three bonds, resulting in the following total asset balance at time t:

$$Asset_t = Bond_t + Cash_t \tag{7.67}$$

Factor Durations of assets and liabilities are then recalculated at time t based on Principal Component Analysis and the term structure of interest rates at that time, resulting in the updated values $\mathbf{FD_t^B}$ and $\mathbf{FD_t^L}$, respectively. Total assets $Asset_t$ are then rebalanced among the new 10-year, 20-year, and 30-year 4% coupon-paying bonds available in the market at time t and cash in order to match these Factor Durations of assets and liabilities at that time, resulting in the following bond positions at time t:

$$\mathbf{k_t} = (\mathbf{FD_t^B})^{-1}\, \mathbf{FD_t^L} \tag{7.68}$$

and the total amount invested in bonds will therefore be

$$Bond_t = \mathbf{k_t^{\mathsf{T}}}\, \mathbf{P_t} \tag{7.69}$$

where now $\mathbf{P_t} = (P_t(\tau_B))$ and $\mathbf{k_t} = (k_t(\tau_B))$, $\tau_B = 10, 20, 30$ are the respective column vectors of prices and positions at time t of 10-year, 20-year, and 30-year bonds, while the balance is invested in cash earning a short-term interest rate:

$$Cash_t = Asset_t - Bond_t \tag{7.70}$$

4. Each following 6-month period, the portfolio is rebalanced in the same manner among the new 10-year, 20-year, and 30-year 4% coupon-paying bonds available in the market at that time and cash in order to match Factor Durations of assets and liabilities at that time.

Figure 7.8 illustrates the performance of the Factor Duration Matching Strategy based on two simulated term structures of interest rates as shown in Panels A and C. The term structure is simulated based on the methodology outlined in Diebold and Li

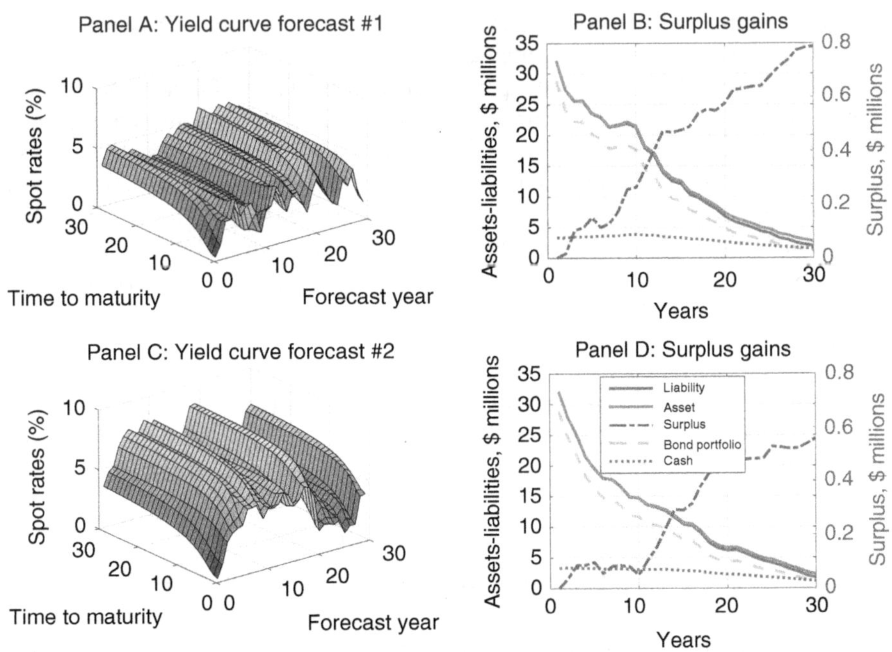

Figure 7.8 Two simulations of Factor Duration Matching Strategy.

[5]At every time t, we use new 10-year, 20-year, and 30-year 4% coupon-paying bonds to immunize the current portfolio so that at time $t + \Delta$, $\Delta = \frac{1}{2}$, the bonds have $9\frac{1}{2}$, $19\frac{1}{2}$, and $29\frac{1}{2}$ years to maturity, respectively.

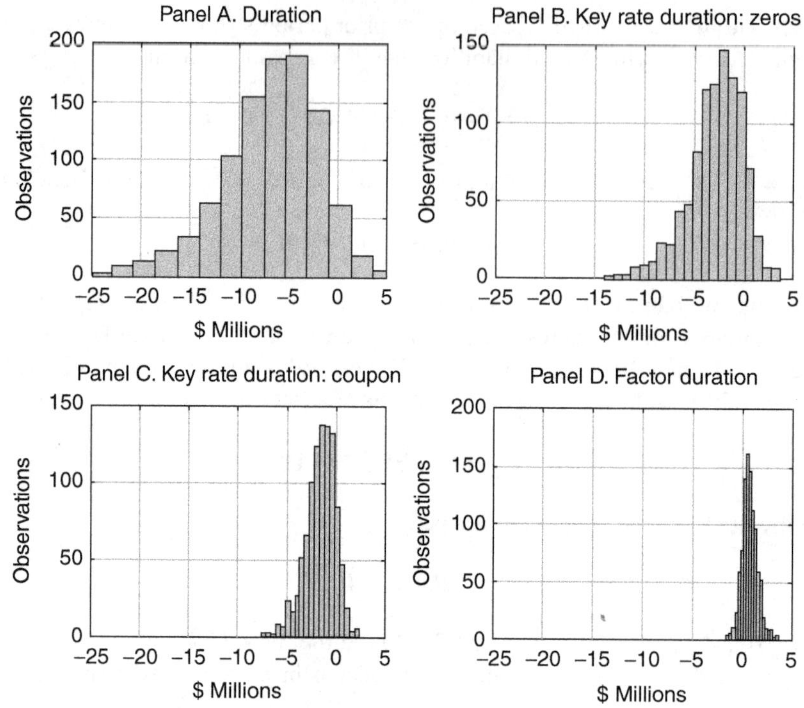

Figure 7.9 Distribution of Surplus at 30-year maturity.

(2006), and model parameters are estimated based on the historical term structure data reported by the U.S. Federal Reserve for the period from 1987 to 2014.

The strategy performed very well in both simulations, resulting in positive and relatively stable Surplus over the entire forecast horizon. Additionally, assets tracked liabilities quite closely over time. The position in bond #2 became negative for some period of time resulting in a minor leverage, which can be eliminated through additional restrictions when the strategy is constructed. Bond #1 has by far the largest position, indicating that "level" is the dominant factor, which is consistent with statistical results. Most of the time, bond positions gradually decline in order to match the liability Factor Durations, which decrease as liability cash flows are paid out. Cash positions are stable while gradually declining as well.

Similar to the previous sections, in order to assess the performance of the Factor Duration Matching Strategy, the Treasury spot yield curves were simulated semiannually for 30 years, liabilities were calculated as present values of liability cash flows at each future date based on the simulated yield curves at that time, and the Factor Duration Matching Strategy was applied at each future semiannual payment date. The results are presented in Figures 7.9 and 7.10, according to which Factor Duration Matching produced some losses over time, as shown in Figure 7.9, but such losses are much smaller than those produced by both Classic Immunization Strategy as shown in Panel A of Figure 7.9 and by Key Rate Duration Matching strategies as shown in Panels B and C of Figure 7.9. Similar results are also shown in Figure 7.10 where the changes of Surplus over time are projected for each strategy.

Advantages of the Factor Duration Matching Strategy are as follows:

- Statistically, three factors f_t^1, f_t^2, and f_t^3 explain more than 99% of the variations in the term structure of interest rates. Therefore, they should possess high hedging and predictive powers.
- The factors have reasonable economic interpretation as level, slope, and curvature, due to the shapes of their respective factor sensitivities.
- Liability cash flows of any maturity can be hedged with bonds based on Factor Durations.
- Asset and liability cash flow maturities do not have to coincide (other than for the near-term liquidity needs) as long as Factor Durations are matched.
- A wide range of bonds can be used for the strategy, including both coupon-paying and zero-coupon bonds.
- Level, slope, and curvature are, in general, among the most important elements of the interest rate term structure. Therefore, having factors with the same interpretation is in line with many modeling approaches used for the term structure forecasts.

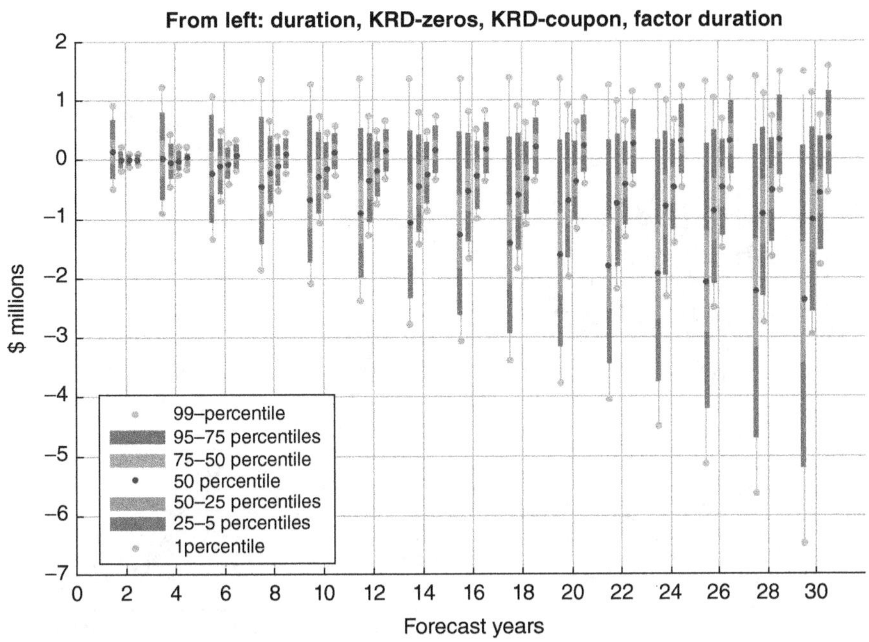

Figure 7.10 Change of Surplus over time.

Disadvantages of the Factor Duration Matching Strategy are as follows:

- Factors are calculated using a statistical technique and are not otherwise observable in the marketplace and therefore not investable.
- Some tracking errors between assets and liabilities still remain since yield curves can move differently than what was predicted and hedged according to Factor Durations.
- Unlike the Cash Flow Matching Strategy, frequent rebalancing is required in order to maintain Factor Duration Matching.

7.5 BACKTESTING ALM STRATEGIES

In the previous sections, we compared the performance of the ALM strategies by considering simulated term structures of interest rates over time. Another way to compare the performance of the ALM strategies is to run them against historical term structures. The historical data is the same as what was used in order to estimate parameters of the models used to simulate the term structures over the future time periods.

In particular, we used a 28-year period that begins in 1987 and ends in 2014 based on the data reported by the U.S. Federal Reserve. Similar to what was done before, to illustrate how the ALM strategies perform, we implemented liability hedging with portfolios of coupon and zero-coupon bonds, while the liability being hedged is the same as in the previous example of the Classic Immunization Strategy, that is, the insurance company's liability for an annuity book of business. To hedge this liability, we use the same bond portfolios as before:

- 30-year Treasury bond with 4% semiannual coupons for the Classic Immunization Strategy
- 10-year, 20-year, and 30-year zero-coupon Treasury bonds for the Key Rate Duration Matching Strategy with zero-coupon bonds
- 10-year, 20-year, and 30-year Treasury bond with 4% semiannual coupons for the Key Rate Duration Matching Strategy with coupon-paying bonds and for the Factor Duration Matching Strategy

Figure 7.11 contains the backtesting results, and the key observations are the following:

- As shown by the line with diamonds, the Duration Matching Strategy exhibited the most volatile pattern of Surplus over time resulting in significant losses by the end of the strategy horizon in 2014.

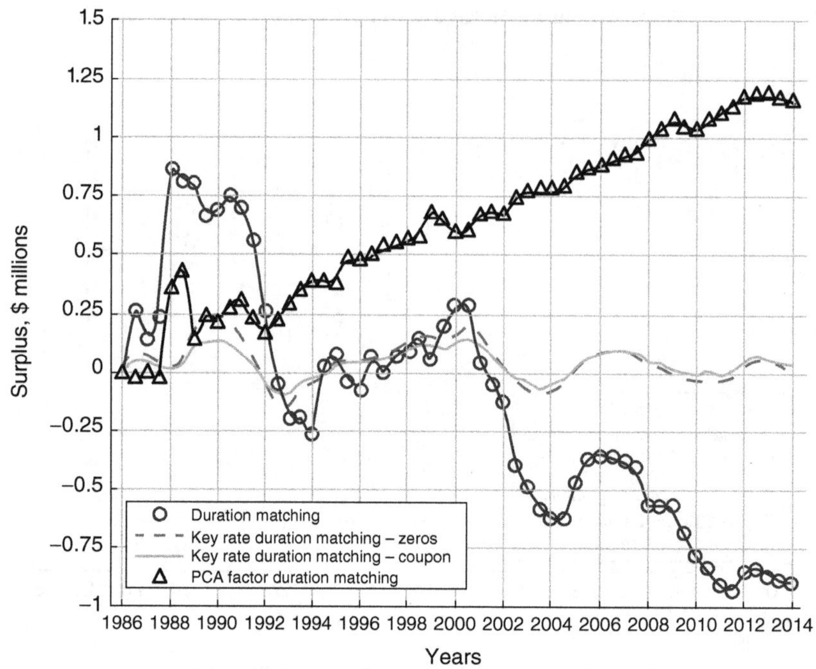

Figure 7.11 Surplus backtesting using historical term structures.

- As shown by the flat and dotted lines, both Key Rate Duration Matching strategies, that is, with zeros and with coupon-paying bonds, exhibited a much more stable pattern than the Duration Matching Strategy, with Surplus fluctuating around zero over time. Both strategies produced results that are comparable to each other, with Surplus exhibiting some swings around zero, while in each instance Surplus would mean revert to zero over time.
- As shown by the line with triangles, the Factor Duration Matching Strategy on the other hand resulted in much smaller fluctuations over time, with Surplus changing almost along a straight line. Even though in this particular example Surplus increased gradually over time, a different bond portfolio would likely produce a slightly different pattern. But the stability of Surplus would still remain when the Factor Duration Matching Strategy is implemented.

7.6 LIABILITY HEDGING AND PORTFOLIO CONSTRUCTION

In recent years, there has been an increase in research of how the ALM strategies can be incorporated in the total portfolio construction problem. In particular, Brandt et al. (2005), Bogentoft, Romeijn, and Uryasev (2001), and van Binsbergen and Brandt (2014) provided algorithms to solve a multiperiod portfolio construction problem for pension plans based on the ALM framework.

So far in this chapter, the main objective of the investment strategies considered was to minimize the asset–liability mismatch and to use the entire asset portfolio in order to match the key liability risk drivers, measured by either Duration, Key Rate Durations, or Factor Durations. In reality, however, a part of portfolio is typically invested in the so-called "return-seeking" asset classes, such as equities, alternatives, high yield bonds, and so on, in order to grow the asset balances.

For example, many frozen pension plans usually still invest part of their portfolios in such "return-seeking" asset classes in order to improve the pension funding levels. Once the pension plan is fully funded, the plan sponsor can either fully immunize their liabilities based on the strategies discussed in the previous sections or transfer liability to an insurance company by buying annuities.

Insurance companies typically have less freedom than pension plans regarding investments in such "return-seeking" asset classes, due to laws, regulations, and accounting standards that insurance companies are subject to. However, there are still some opportunities for insurance companies to invest in such assets.

As a result, Multiperiod Stochastic Portfolio Optimization is usually employed in order to construct asset portfolios with some allocation to "return-seeking" assets, while the balance is allocated to hedging strategies discussed in this chapter. In other words, an asset portfolio is managed in relation to liabilities where allocations can change over time to match liability risk drivers, and the allocations are determined by maximizing the expected "utility" of Surplus subject to the appropriate constraints on asset classes as follows:

$$\begin{aligned}
&\underset{X_0,\ldots X_{T-1}}{\text{maximize}} \quad E\left[U(S_T)\right] \\
&\text{subject to} \quad \sum_{j=1}^{n} X_{t,j} = A_t, t = 0, \ldots, T-1 \\
&S_t = A_t - L_t, t = 0, \ldots, T-1
\end{aligned} \tag{7.71}$$

This is a Multiperiod Stochastic Portfolio Optimization problem, covering periods from $t = 0$ to $t = T - 1$, where the asset allocations $X_t = (X_{t,1}, \ldots, X_{t,n})$ are determined at each future time t, based on assets A_t, liabilities L_t, and Surplus S_t available at that time. $U(S_T)$ is the utility function of Surplus at the end of the horizon time T. In other words, such utility function shows how much value or utility is generated by each level of Surplus.

The utility function is unique for each portfolio allocation problem, but it explicitly reflects liabilities or Surplus of the sponsoring organization. Risk aversion can be either constant over time or changing based on the Surplus levels. For example, frozen pension plans that implement dynamic derisking strategies may need to model increasing risk aversion factors as a function of the funding levels of the plan, because at higher funding levels, they have more incentives to immunize their liabilities and lock in the gains than at the lower funding levels when they still target return-generating objectives.

The Surplus function is also quite unique for each portfolio allocation problem and can reflect future cash inflows to the pension plans according to the requirements of ERISA and PPA, solvency requirements faced by the insurance companies, Surplus volatility limits, and many other requirements.

According to Brandt et al. (2005) and van Binsbergen and Brandt (2014), Chapter 8 in this handbook), one of the ways to solve this complex Multiperiod Stochastic Portfolio Optimization problem (7.71) is through a so-called dynamic programming approach, according to which the problem is solved backward in time as follows:

1. At the beginning of the last period of time $t = T - 1$, the following optimization problem is solved:

$$\begin{aligned}
&\underset{X_{T-1}}{\text{maximize}} \quad E\left[U(S_T)|S_{T-1}\right] \\
&\text{subject to} \quad \sum_{j=1}^{n} X_{T-1,j} = A_{T-1} \\
&S_{T-1} = A_{T-1} - L_{T-1}
\end{aligned} \tag{7.72}$$

   where $E[U(S_T) \mid S_{T-1}]$ is the Expected utility of Surplus at time $t = T$, conditional on the Surplus level at time $t = T - 1$. The resulting optimal asset allocation is $X_{T-1} = [X_{T-1,1}, \ldots, X_{T-1,n}]$.
2. At the beginning of the second to last period of time $t = T - 2$, the following optimization problem is solved:

$$\begin{aligned}
&\underset{X_{T-2}}{\text{maximize}} \quad E\left[U(S_T)|S_{T-2}, X_{T-1}\right] \\
&\text{subject to} \quad \sum_{j=1}^{n} X_{T-2,j} = A_{T-2} \\
&S_{T-2} = A_{T-2} - L_{T-2}
\end{aligned} \tag{7.73}$$

   where $E[U(S_T) \mid S_{T-2}, X_{T-1}]$ is the Expected utility of Surplus at time $t = T$, conditional on the Surplus level at time $t = T - 2$ and conditional on the optimal asset allocation rule at the prior step $t = T - 1$ or X_{T-1} [6]. The resulting optimal asset allocation is $X_{T-2} = [X_{T-2,1}, \ldots, X_{T-2,n}]$.

[6]Optimal asset allocation at time $T - 2$, that is, X_{T-2}, is conditional on the Surplus level available at that time and is also conditional on the asset allocation rule at the future time $T - 1$ determined in the previous step for all possible Surplus levels at time $T - 1$.

3. Going backward in time in a similar manner, the following optimization problem is solved at each time t after the inception of the strategy:

$$\begin{aligned} &\underset{X_t}{\text{maximize}}\ E\left[U(S_T)|S_t, X_{t+1}, \dots, X_{T-1}\right] \\ &\text{subject to}\ \sum_{j=1}^{n} X_{t,j} = A_t \\ &S_t = A_t - L_t \end{aligned} \tag{7.74}$$

where $E[U(S_T) \mid S_t, X_{t+1}, \dots, X_{T-1}]$ is the Expected utility of Surplus at time $t = T$, conditional on the Surplus level at time t and conditional on the optimal asset allocation rules at all prior steps, $X_{t+1}, \dots, X_{T-1}$ [7]. The resulting optimal asset allocation is $X_t = [X_{t,1}, \dots, X_{t,n}]$.

This approach is very flexible by its construction and can accommodate a wide variety of different liability cash flow patterns, utility functions, risk aversion profiles, Surplus functions, funding requirements, Surplus volatility thresholds, and other metrics relevant to each sponsoring organization as well as the specific time horizons over which liability cash flows are paid out.

Additionally, since this approach is based on stochastic optimization, distributions for stochastic processes of asset returns and term structures have to be determined and respective random variables simulated over the projection horizon. Such distributions can be as sophisticated as required for each portfolio construction problem and potentially include stochastic volatility and correlations for returns and yields, asymmetric distributions with fat tails, mean reversion of yields, volatilities and correlations, and other models.

As a result, this approach is fully consistent with the so-called "liability-centric" approach for the portfolio management, according to which portfolios are designed to support certain liability streams over time.

7.7 CONCLUSIONS

Throughout this chapter, different portfolio strategies were considered, all of which have the same common idea: they are designed in relation to the liability streams that sponsoring organizations are responsible for and therefore would like to hedge. As a result, the demand from the sponsoring organizations for the "liability-centric" investment approaches is the cornerstone and the main driving force behind ALM.

Once the sponsoring organizations decide to hedge their liability streams with assets, a few different strategies are available with respective strengths and weaknesses:

- *Cash Flow Matching Strategy* is the most basic approach for managing assets in relation to liabilities. Once the liability cash flows are matched, the portfolio of assets will always be enough to match the stream of future liability cash flows, provided there are no defaults. However, due to its restrictive nature, this strategy may be quite costly to implement, may not work well with the liability payouts beyond 30-year maturities, and may not be well suited for investment policy statements with substantial restrictions on bond credit quality and downgrades.
- As a result, *Duration Matching Strategy* is an alternative that allows for more flexibility in bond selection, resulting in potentially higher yielding portfolios, as it is a much less restrictive strategy. The Duration Matching Strategy is based on the idea that when Durations of assets and liabilities are matched, interest rate risks and reinvestment risks are balanced. However, the Duration Matching Strategy only hedges against small and parallel yield curve shifts, and as soon as the term structure changes in a nonparallel fashion, this strategy would produce losses more frequently than gains.
- The natural alternative for the Duration Matching Strategy that would overcome this problem with hedging against nonparallel yield curve movements is *Key Rate Duration Matching Strategy*. As its name suggests, several Key Rates along the spot yield curve are selected and a bond portfolio is created such that its sensitivity to those Key Rates is the same as that of the liability. As a result, a bond portfolio is created specifically to hedge a liability against nonparallel changes in the interest rate term structure. Potential issues arise when determining which Key Rates to hedge and how many as well as which bonds to use especially for maturities beyond 30 years. As a result, approximations are frequently implemented, resulting in tracking errors between assets and liabilities.

[7] Optimal asset allocation at time t, that is, X_t, is conditional on the Surplus level available at that time and is also conditional on the asset allocation rules at all future times $t+1, t+2, \dots, T-1$ determined in all previous steps for all possible Surplus levels.

- *Factor Duration Matching Strategy* is introduced in order to explicitly manage assets and liabilities with respect to their sensitivities to changes in certain factors embedded in the term structure of interest rates. Principal Component Analysis is used to identify such factors as "level," 'slope,' and "curvature" of the term structure, and Factor Durations are then defined in terms of the respective factor sensitivities. This strategy works well for any liability cash flow maturity and for any type of bonds. Furthermore, it has an intuitive interpretation due to its linkage to the key elements of the term structure of interest rates, such as "level," "slope," and "curvature." However, similar to any other matching strategy, it requires frequent rebalancing and therefore can result in some losses over time, even though such losses are usually smaller than those produced by other considered strategies.
- Finally, both assets and liabilities should be analyzed as part of the larger portfolio construction problem, where the sponsoring organization's expected utility is maximized and portfolio Surplus is explicitly reflected. By constructing portfolio in such a way, the allocation between "return-seeking" and "hedging" parts of the portfolio is done in an optimal fashion over time as part of a very flexible approach called Multiperiod Stochastic Portfolio Optimization, which can be solved through dynamic programming approach.

7.8 APPENDIX: THE IMPLEMENTATION OF PRINCIPAL COMPONENT ANALYSIS

The actual implementation of Principal Component Analysis is relatively straightforward by applying a technique that involves eigenvalues and eigenvectors.

Let us consider maximization problem (7.20) where $\boldsymbol{\gamma}_1 = (\gamma_{11}, \gamma_{12}, \dots, \gamma_{1M})$ is the column vector of the variables that we are trying to solve for and $\boldsymbol{\Omega}$ is the covariance matrix of the interest rate term structure determined in (7.19). Rewriting this problem in a matrix form, we get the following:

$$\begin{aligned} &\underset{\gamma_1}{\text{maximize}}\ \boldsymbol{\gamma}_1^{\mathsf{T}}\ \boldsymbol{\Omega}\,\boldsymbol{\gamma}_1 \\ &\text{subject to}\quad \boldsymbol{\gamma}_1^{\mathsf{T}}\,\boldsymbol{\gamma}_1 = 1 \end{aligned} \tag{7.75}$$

As a result, the following Lagrangian can be formed for this problem:

$$L(\boldsymbol{\gamma}_1) = \boldsymbol{\gamma}_1^{\mathsf{T}}\,\boldsymbol{\Omega}\,\boldsymbol{\gamma}_1 - \lambda\,(\boldsymbol{\gamma}_1^{\mathsf{T}}\,\boldsymbol{\gamma}_1 - 1) \tag{7.76}$$

and the first-order condition is

$$\frac{\partial L(\boldsymbol{\gamma}_1)}{\partial \boldsymbol{\gamma}_1} = \boldsymbol{\Omega}\,\boldsymbol{\gamma}_1 - \lambda\,\boldsymbol{\gamma}_1 = 0 \tag{7.77}$$

or, rewriting it, we get

$$\boldsymbol{\Omega}\,\boldsymbol{\gamma}_1 = \lambda\,\boldsymbol{\gamma}_1 \tag{7.78}$$

which is satisfied when $\boldsymbol{\gamma}_1$ and λ are the respective eigenvectors and eigenvalues of matrix $\boldsymbol{\Omega}$.

Therefore, the typical steps in order to implement Principal Component Analysis are the following:

1. Determine the covariance matrix of the changes in spot rates as specified in (7.19) based on the historical term structures with maturities $\tau = \tau_1, \tau_2, \dots, \tau_M$
$$\boldsymbol{\Omega} = Cov(\Delta r_t(\tau)) \tag{7.79}$$
2. Estimate eigenvalues, $\lambda_1, \lambda_2, \dots, \lambda_M$, and eigenvectors, $\mathbf{v_1}, \mathbf{v_2}, \dots, \mathbf{v_M}$, of matrix $\boldsymbol{\Omega}$ and rank eigenvalues from highest to lowest
$$\lambda_1 > \lambda_2 > \dots > \lambda_M \tag{7.80}$$
3. According to the first-order condition (7.77), eigenvector $\mathbf{v_1}$, corresponding to the *largest* eigenvalue λ_1, is the solutions to the maximization problem (7.20) for the first factor. Therefore, the first factor is determined as
$$\Delta f_t^1 = \mathbf{v}_1^{\mathsf{T}}\,\Delta\mathbf{r_t} \tag{7.81}$$
where $\Delta\mathbf{r_t} = (\Delta r_t(\tau))$, $\tau = \tau_1, \tau_2, \dots, \tau_M$ is the column vector of changes in the term structure of interest rates at time t.

4. Accordingly, eigenvector $\mathbf{v}_2$, corresponding to the **second largest** eigenvalue λ_2, is the solutions to the maximization problem (7.24) for the second factor. Therefore, the second factor is determined as

$$\Delta f_t^2 = \mathbf{v}_2^{\mathrm{T}} \, \Delta \mathbf{r}_t \tag{7.82}$$

where $\Delta \mathbf{r}_t = (\Delta r_t(\tau))$, $\tau = \tau_1, \tau_2, ..., \tau_M$ is the column vector of changes in the term structure of interest rates at time t.
5. The third factor is determined in a similar manner.

REFERENCES

Barber JR, Cooper ML. Immunization using principal component analysis. J Portf Manage 1996;23:1.
Bierwag GO. *Duration Analysis: Managing Interest Rate Risk.* Cambridge (MA): Ballinger; 1987.
van Binsbergen, JH, Brandt, MW. Optimal asset allocation in asset liability management. In: Veronesi P, editor. published in the *Handbook of Fixed Income.* Hoboken (NJ): John Wiley & Sons; 2014.
Bogentoft E, Romeijn HE, Uryasev S. Asset/liability management for pension funds using CVaR constraints. J Risk Finance 2001;3(1):57–71.
Brandt MW, Goyal A, Santa-Clara P, Stroud JR. A simulation approach to dynamic portfolio choice with an application to learning about return predictability. Rev Financ Stud 2005;18:831–873.
Diebold FX, Li C. Forecasting the term structure of government bond yields. J Econometrics 2006;130:337–364.
Fabozzi F, editor. *Handbook of Fixed Income Securities.* 8th ed. Two Penn Plaza, New York, NY 10121-2298: McGraw-Hill; 2012.
Hawawini GA. *Bond Duration and Immunization: Early Developments and Recent Contributions.* New York: Garland; 1982.
Hicks JR. *Value and Capital.* Oxford: Clarendon Press; 1939.
Ho T. Key rate durations: measures of interest rate risks. J Fixed Income 1992;2(2):29–44.
Iyengar G, Ma A. Cash flow matching: a risk management approach. North Am Actuar J 2009;13(3):370–78.
Kocherlakota R, Rosenbloom ES, Shiu ESW. Algorithms for cash flow matching. Trans Soc Actuar 1988;40(Pt 1):477–484.
Koopmans KC. *The Risk of Interest Rate Fluctuations in Life Insurance Companies.* Philadelphia (PA): Penn Mutual Life Insurance Company; 1942.
Litterman R, Scheinkman J. Common factors affecting bond returns. J Fixed Income 1991;1:54–61.
Luckner WR. Society of Actuaries Professional Actuarial Specialty Guide: Asset-Liability Management, BB-1-03; 2003.
Macaulay FR. *Some Theoretical Problems Suggested by the Movements of Interest Rates, Bond Yields and Stock Prices in the United States Since 1856.* New York: Bureau of Economic Research; 1938.
Panjer H, editor. *Financial Economics: With Applications to Investments, Insurance and Pensions.* Schaumburg (IL): Actuarial Foundation; 1998.
Redington FM. Review of the principles of life-office valuations. J Inst Actuar 1952;78:286–315. Discussion, 316–40.
Samuelson PA. The effects of interest rate increases on the banking system. Am Econ Rev 1945;36:16–27.
Shang D, Uryasev S. Cash flow matching problem with CVaR constraints: a case study with portfolio Safegurd. Research Report 2011–1. Gainesville (FL) 32611: ISE Department, University of Florida; 2011.
Veronesi P. *Fixed Income Securities: Valuation, Risk, and Risk Management.* Hoboken (NJ): John Wiley & Sons; 2010.
Willner R. A new tool for portfolio managers level, slope, and curvature durations. J Fixed Income 1996;6(1):48–59.

8

Optimal Asset Allocation in Asset Liability Management

Jules H. van Binsbergen[a] **and Michael W. Brandt**[b]

[a]*The Wharton School, University of Pennsylvania, Philadelphia, PA, United States*
[b]*Fuqua School of Business, Duke University, Durham, NC, United States*

8.1 INTRODUCTION

Asset liability management (ALM) refers to the portfolio choice problem of an investor who uses the principal and investment returns on assets to satisfy future liabilities.[1] One leading example is a defined benefits pension plan that must pay promised benefit payments using pension contributions and the investment returns accumulated on those contributions. Because liabilities are typically modeled as coupon payments of more or less known timing and magnitude, ALM is at the heart a fixed-income problem.

The traditional and most conservative approach to ALM is cash flow matching, where assets are invested in fixed-income securities for which the coupon and principal payments match as closely as possible the liabilities both in terms of timing and magnitude, thereby eliminating most if not all risk. In larger liability portfolios, such as for an insurance company, however, liability cash flow matching is difficult so instead of matching individual payments, traditional ALM matches the risk profile, specifically interest rate risk and liquidity risk, of the liabilities. Cash flow or risk matching is commonly referred to as "immunization."

Both liability cash flow or risk matching rely critically on the liabilities being fully funded. ALM in this case is simply a fixed-income risk management problem. Unfortunately, a growing number of defined benefits pension plans in particular are materially underfunded. For example, in 2013, the largest 100 pension plans in the United States reported US$ 3.77 trillion of liabilities guaranteed with only US$ 2.58 trillion of asset, which represents and underfunding of more than 30%.[2] With such degree of underfunding, the plan sponsor cannot rely simply on interest to make up the shortfall. Instead, the assets must be invested in more sophisticated investment portfolio that earns risk premia in order to generate higher expected returns. A recent study by investment consultant Tower Watson shows the average asset allocation of U.S. pension plans to be 57% equities, 23% bonds, and 20% others (typically real assets and alternatives).[3] Therefore, ALM is no longer just a risk management problem. It has become a portfolio choice problem, and a rather complex and very dynamic one at that.

[1]Investment professionals have in recent years relabeled ALM as liability-driven investing (LDI). For our purposes the two are synonymous.
[2]See Milliman 2013 Public Pension Funding Study, www.milliman.com
[3]See Tower Watson, Global Pension Assets Study 2014, www.towerswatson.com

Handbook of Fixed-Income Securities, First Edition. Edited by Pietro Veronesi.

ALM (or its recent popularized version LDI) has become increasingly the standard for pension management. A 2013 survey by SEI, a pension consultant, found that the use of modern portfolio choice techniques for pension management has increased from 20% in 2007 to almost 60% in 2013 with the primary objective being control of the level and volatility of the funding status of the plan.[4] Although pension plans are the primary focus of ALM in the academic and practitioner literature, because of their vastly underfunded nature, they are not the only financial institutions that face ALM problems. Other users of ALM are insurance companies, banks with liabilities on their balance sheet, and even central banks. Any institution that approaches asset management from a balance sheet perspective, meaning takes both assets and liabilities into account when making decisions, is solving an ALM problem and potentially has a different objective than simply maximizing the Sharpe ratio of return on assets. As a consequence, the total amount of assets that are involved in ALM problems is many times larger than the amounts discussed above.

In this chapter, we use an easy-to-implement dynamic programming algorithm to solve for the optimal asset allocation of a financial intermediary that faces an ALM problem under regulatory constraints. As an application, we focus on the ALM problem of a defined benefits pension plan. The defined plan faces a dynamic investment opportunity set with time-varying expected bond and stock returns, as well as two types of constraints, ex ante and ex post risk constraints, and we study examples of both. For the ex ante constraint, we consider a Value-at-Risk (VaR) constraint. The ex post constraint we study is the legal requirement for plan sponsors to make mandatory additional financial contributions (AFCs) once the plan is underfunded relative to the accounting definition of liabilities. This accounting definition can (and does) deviate from the market value of the liabilities, which we explicitly account for in our method.

Using this framework, we examine the impact of regulations on pension investment decisions. Because many plans invested heavily in stocks and only had limited positions in long-term bonds, the recent decrease in interest rates combined with the poor performance of global stock markets has further lowered the funding status of many plans. This raises the important question why pension funds hedge interest rate risk so poorly by investing in asset classes, such as stocks, that have a low correlation with interest rate changes. We argue in this paper that this investment behavior is (at least partially) due to the regulatory environment. In response to the underfunded status of many plans, the congress has passed a law as part of the Transportation Bill (June 2012) that allows corporate-defined benefit plans to discount their liabilities using a rolling average of yields over the past 25 years. Not only does this interest smoothing rule lead to a large deviation of the reported value of liabilities from their market value (by a factor 2 in 2012), but we show that it further discourages the hedging of interest rate risk. We study in this chapter the optimal asset allocation decisions of a pension manager as a function of the plan's funding ratio (defined as the ratio of its assets to liabilities), interest rates, and the equity risk premium. We compare the optimal investment decisions under several policy alternatives to understand better the real effects of financial reporting and risk management rules.

Arguably the most important aspect of the ALM problem faced by defined benefits retirement plans is the discount rate used for computing the present value of the plan's liabilities.[5] Historically, two methodologies have been implemented, namely, the use of current market yields and the use of a weighted average of yields over a longer horizon (yield smoothing). On the one hand, discounting by current yields guarantees an accurate description of the fund's financial situation. On the other hand, proponents of yield smoothing argue that discounting by smoothed yields gives a more long-term view of the funds financial position, as the liabilities are not subject to "short-term" interest rate fluctuations. The 2012 Transportation Bill, which established a 25-year smoothing period to compute the discount rate for liabilities, is the third time in a decade that discounting rules have been changed. The Pension Protection Act of 2006 introduced a 2-year smoothing period, replacing the 4-year smoothing period of corporate bond rates established under the Pension Funding Equity Act of 2004.

In this context, we make the following three points. First, regardless of whether or not yield smoothing leads to a long-term view of a pension plan's financial position, it can (and arguably has) led to an upward-biased view. This upward bias is induced by a regulator who, in response to political pressure from the private sector and pension sector, changes the length of the smoothing rule depending on the path of interest rates. Figure 8.1 shows that under the 25-year smoothing rule, reported liabilities are twice as small as they would be under market-based discounting in 2012. However, the figure also shows that when interest rates were high, 25-year smoothing would have led to higher reported liabilities than what market-based accounting implied. Not surprisingly, 25-year smoothing was not the rule at the time. Surely, when in the next decades interest rates are high once again, the 25-year smoothing rule will be abandoned, and market-based accounting methods will be applied, lowering reported liabilities.

Second, yield smoothing distorts incentives and leads to poor hedging against interest rate risk. We show that even when the long-term objective of a plan manager is to maximize the ratio of assets and *market-based* liabilities, his/her short-term objective (and/or requirement) of satisfying risk constraints and/or avoiding AFCs from the plan sponsor (which are based on the reported liabilities) can induce poor interest rate hedging and inadvertently increase risk-taking behavior. We investigate portfolio choice under different discounting regimes, taking a given policy as fixed. This provides a lower bound on how distorting yield

[4] See SEIC: 7th Annual Global Liability-Driven Investing (LDI) Poll, 2013.

[5] See also Novy-Marx and Rauh (2010).

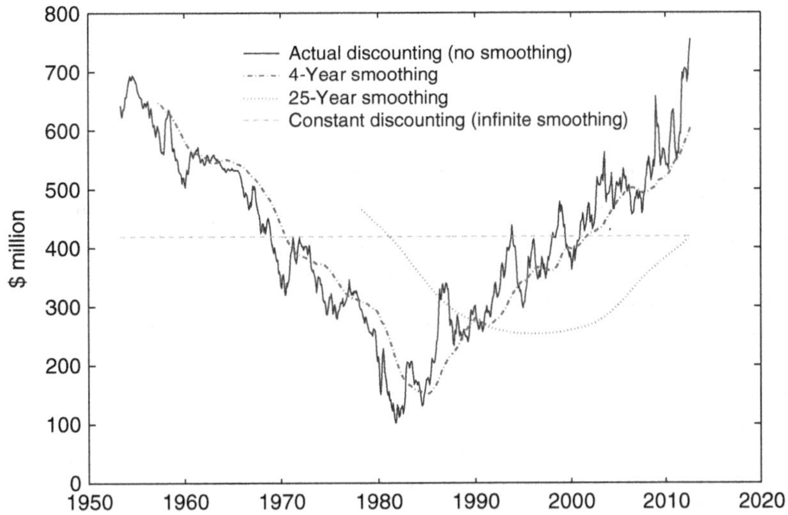

Figure 8.1 Smoothing the 15-year government bond yield and the value of liabilities. We plot the present value of 1 billion in future liabilities with an assumed duration of 15 years under four discounting regimes. Actual discounting (no smoothing), 4-year smoothing, 25-year smoothing, and constant discounting (infinite smoothing) between 1956 and 2012. Source: Federal Reserve Bank.

smoothing can be. If we add to the model the realistic feature that smoothing rules can be adjusted by a regulator to minimize reported liabilities, for example, as a consequence of political pressure, the effects become even stronger. Adjusting the smoothing rule forms a put option on funds' reported financial positions, encouraging risk taking and further lowering incentives to hedge interest rate risk.

Third, we investigate the influence of ex ante versus ex post risk constraints on the investment decisions of pension managers. At first glance, ex ante and ex post risk constraints may seem similar as both aim to decrease the risk-taking behavior of the manager. However, we show that they can have different implications for the gains to dynamic, as opposed to myopic, decision making. We hypothesize that ex ante (preventive) constraints, such as a VaR constraint, can *decrease* the gains to dynamic investment, as these constraints restrict the choice set of the manager and hence do not allow the manager to respond to the time-varying investment opportunity set. Ex post (punitive) constraints, such as ACFs, in contrast, can *increase* the gains from solving the dynamic program. In other words, under ex ante constraints, the myopic solution may provide a good approximation for the optimal solution, whereas under ex post constraints it requires dynamic optimization to make the optimal investment decision. As such, ex post constraints induce the manager to behave strategically.

ALM problems are inherently long-horizon problems with potentially important strategic aspects.[6] They differ from standard portfolio choice problems (Markowitz (1952), Merton (1969, 1971), Samuelson (1969), and Fama (1970)), not only because of the short position in the pension liabilities but also because of the regulatory risk constraints and mandatory AFCs discussed above. We assume that the investment manager dislikes drawing AFCs from the plan sponsor and directly model this dislike as a "utility" cost. We interpret this utility cost as a reduced form for the loss of compensation or reputation of the investment manager. In other words, drawing mandatory AFCs serves as an ex post (punitive) risk constraint. The associated utility cost introduces a kink in the value function of the investment manager's dynamic optimization problem that causes the manager to become first-order risk averse whenever the (reported) funding ratio approaches the critical threshold that triggers AFCs.[7] We show that this kink in the value function leads to substantial hedging demands and large certainty equivalent utility gains from dynamic investment.

The investment behavior of corporate pension plans has been studied by Sundaresan and Zapatero (1997) and by Boulier, Trussant, and Florens (1995). Sundaresan and Zapatero (1997) model the marginal productivity of the workers of a firm and solve the investment problem of its pension plan assuming a constant investment opportunity set consisting of a risky and a riskless asset. We instead allow for a time-varying investment opportunity set including cash, bonds, and stocks. More importantly, we consider the ALM problem from the perspective of the investment manager as a decision maker and investigate how regulatory rules influence the optimal investment decisions. In order to focus attention on the asset allocation side of the ALM problem, we model the liabilities of the pension plan in reduced form by assuming a constant duration of 15 years.

[6]Recent strategic asset allocation studies include Kim and Omberg (1996), Campbell and Viceira (1999), Brandt (1999, 2010), Aït-Sahalia and Brandt (2001), and Sangvinatsos and Wachter (2005).

[7]First-order risk aversion implies that even over very small lotteries investors are very risk averse. This is different for second-order risk aversion where, as the lottery becomes smaller and smaller, the investor essentially becomes risk neutral.

Boulier, Trussant, and Florens (1995) also assume a constant investment opportunity set with a risky and a risk-free asset. In their problem, the investment manager chooses his/her portfolio weights to minimize the expected discounted value of the contributions over a fixed time horizon, with the constraint that the value of the assets cannot fall below that of the liabilities at the terminal date. This problem setup implicitly assumes that the pension plan terminates at some known future date and that the investment manager's horizon is equal to this terminal date. By taking the investment manager's preferences and horizon as the primitive, our perspective is different. The manager has a motive to minimize (the disutility from) the sponsor's contributions, captured by the AFCs in our case. However, the manager also wants to maximize the funding ratio at the end of his/her investment horizon, for example, due to career concerns. The end of the manager's investment horizon may be long before the pension plan terminates, which is why we hold the duration of the liabilities fixed.

Our contributions to the portfolio choice literature are the following. First, we attempt to bridge further the gap between the dynamic portfolio choice literature and the ALM literature.[8] We pose the ALM problem as a standard dynamic portfolio choice problem by defining terminal utility over the ratio of assets and liabilities, as opposed to over assets only. This approach allows a parsimonious representation of the ALM problem under a time-varying investment opportunity set. Solving this dynamic program is relatively straightforward compared to the usual, more complicated, stochastic programming techniques. We then assess the interplay between dynamic hedging demands, risk constraints, and first-order risk aversion. We show that the solution to the ALM problem under ex post (punitive) constraints involves economically significant hedging demands, whereas ex ante (preventive) constraints decrease the gains from dynamic investment. Finally, we explicitly model the trade-off between the long-term objective of maximizing terminal utility and the short-term objective of satisfying VaR constraints and avoiding AFCs from the plan sponsor.[9] We show that if these short-term objectives are based on reported liabilities that are different from actual liabilities, they can lead to large utility losses with respect to the long-term objective.

For ease of exposition, there are at least three important aspects of the ALM problem that we do not address explicitly. First, there is a literature, starting with Sharpe (1976), that explores the value of the so-called "pension put" arising from the fact that U.S. defined benefit pension plans are insured through the Pension Benefit Guaranty Corporation. Sharpe (1976) shows that if insurance premiums are not set correctly, the optimal investment policy of the pension plan may be to maximize the difference between the value of the insurance and its cost. This obviously induces perverse incentives.[10] Second, we do not incorporate inflation. Besides affecting the allocation to real versus nominal assets (Hoevenaars et al. (2004)), inflation drives another wedge between the long-term objective of maximizing the real funding ratio, computed with liabilities that are usually pegged to real wage levels, and the short-term objective of satisfying risk controls and avoiding AFCs based on nominal valuations. Third, we ignore the taxation issues described by Black (1980) and Tepper (1981).

The chapter proceeds as follows. Section 8.2 describes the different smoothing rules that have been proposed to compute the discount factor and then assesses their impact on discount rates and reported liabilities. Section 8.3 describes the return dynamics, the preferences of the investment manager, and the constraints under which the manager operates. Section 8.4 describes our numerical solution method for the dynamic optimization problem. Sections 8.5 and 8.6 present our results, and Section 8.7 concludes.

8.2 YIELD SMOOTHING

As mentioned earlier, the 2012 Transportation Bill, which established a 25-year smoothing period to compute the discount rate for liabilities, is the third time in a decade that discounting rules have been changed. The Pension Protection Act of 2006 introduced a 2-year smoothing period, replacing the 4-year smoothing period of corporate bond rates established under the Pension Funding Equity Act of 2004. To illustrate the impact of yield smoothing, Figure 8.1 plots the net present value of \$1 billion in future 15-year liabilities (nominal) under four different discounting regimes: (i) market-based accounting using the 15-year (nominal) government bond yield, (ii) 4-year smoothing of the 15-year government bond yield, (iii) 25-year smoothing of the 15-year bond yield, and (iv) constant discounting using the average 15-year yield between 1956 and 2012. The graph shows that as of July 2012, the present value of \$1 billion in liabilities using market-based accounting methods is \$760 million, whereas under the

[8]Campbell and Viceira (2002) and Brandt (2010) survey the dynamic portfolio choice literature.

[9]We could easily incorporate other short-term objectives, such as beating a benchmark portfolio over the course of the year (see also Basak, Shapiro, and Teplá (2006) and Basak, Pavlova, and Shapiro (2007)). Whenever this short-term objective is defined with respect to reported liabilities that are different from actual liabilities, this leads to a similar misalignment of incentives as the one we explore in this chapter. It is interesting to note that in practice pension fund managers are often assessed relative to an assets-only benchmark, which is a benchmark that implicitly assumes constant liabilities (see van Binsbergen, Brandt, and Koijen (2008)).

[10]The PBGC pays pension benefits for failed defined benefit plans up to the maximum guaranteed benefit of \$54,000 (2011) to participants who retire at age 65.

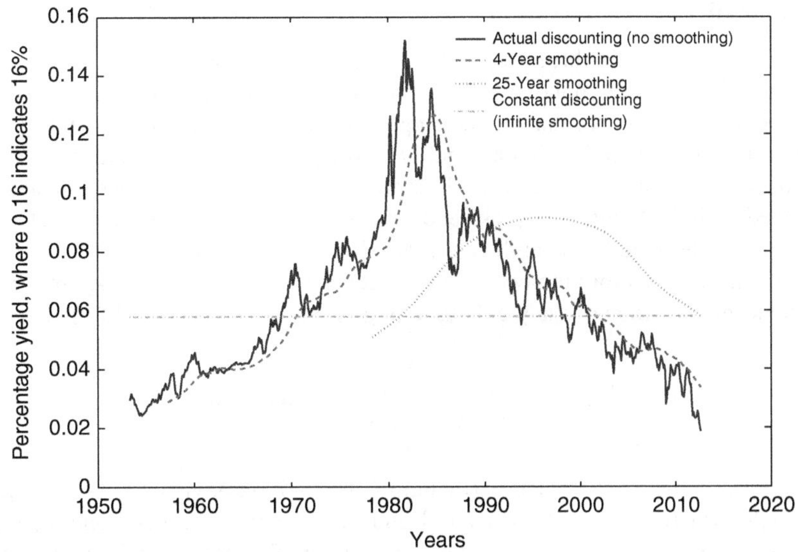

Figure 8.2 Smoothing the 15-year government bond yield. We plot the discount rate under four different discounting regimes. Actual discounting (no smoothing), 4-year smoothing, 25-year smoothing, and constant discounting (infinite smoothing) between 1956 and 2012. Source: Federal Reserve Bank.

newly approved 25-year smoothing rule, this present value is reduced by almost half to \$420 million.[11] The assumption that all liabilities are due at 15 years is obviously a simplification, but using the usual duration arithmetic, this is accurate up to a first-order approximation.

The underlying yields used to compute the liabilities in Figure 8.1 are plotted in Figure 8.2. The graph shows that the unconditional variance of the 15-year bond yield is close to the unconditional variance of the 4-year smoothed 15-year bond yield. In other words, the 15-year yield is so persistent that a 4-year smoothing rule is not long enough to decrease its unconditional variance.[12] To the extent that the purpose of yield smoothing is to create "stability" (as defined by its proponents) in the pension system by decreasing the unconditional variance of the discount factor, we have to conclude that this goal was not reached by previous regulations that allowed for 2-year or 4-year smoothing but is achieved by 25-year smoothing.

There is however another important implication of yield smoothing that can have large (potentially unintended) consequences even with 2-year or 4-year smoothing. Denote by $y_{15,t}$ the yield to maturity of a 15-year government zero-coupon bond at time t. The conditional variance of the N-year smoothed series (conditional on time t information) is given by

$$var_t\left[\frac{1}{N}\sum_{i=0}^{N-1} y_{15,t+1-i}\right] = \frac{1}{N^2}\text{var}_t\left[y_{15,t+1}\right] \tag{8.1}$$

where N is the smoothing period. This conditional variance of the N-year smoothed series is a factor N^2 smaller than the conditional variance of the actual (market based) yield series. For example, for 2-year smoothing, the formula simplifies to

$$\text{var}_t\left[\frac{y_{15,t+1}+y_{15,t}}{2}\right] = \frac{1}{4}\text{var}_t\left[y_{15,t+1}\right] \tag{8.2}$$

which shows that the variance is reduced by a factor 4. For 25-year smoothing, the conditional variance is reduced by a factor 625, essentially eliminating interest rate risk in reported liabilities.

8.3 ALM PROBLEM

The ALM problem requires that we specify the investment opportunity set (or return dynamics), the preferences of the investment manager, and the risk constraints the investment manager faces. The next three subsections describe these three items in turn.

[11] In the rest of this chapter, we use the 15-year government bond yield as the discount rate as for many plans, 15 years is their average duration. As the dynamics of the 15-year and the 30-year yields are very similar, our conclusions do not change when using the 30-year bond yield.

[12] As noted before, similar results hold for the 30-year bond yield.

8.3.1 Return and Yield Dynamics

We consider a pension plan that can invest in three asset classes: stocks, bonds, and the risk-free asset. Stocks are represented by the Standard and Poors (S&P) 500 index, bonds by a 15-year constant maturity Treasury bond, and the risk-free asset by a 1-year Treasury bill. We consider an annual rebalancing frequency. We reduce the investment opportunity set to three asset classes driven by two state variables to keep the dimensionality of the problem low. Considering only three asset classes may seem restrictive, however, these asset classes can also be interpreted as broader categories where long-term bonds represent assets that are highly correlated with the liabilities; stocks and 1-year Treasury bills represent assets that have a low correlation with liabilities and have, respectively, a high risk/high return and low risk/low return profile. We assume that the 1-year and 15-year yield levels follow a first-order vector autoregression (VAR) process. We model stock returns with a time-varying risk premium that depends on the level and slope of the yield curve (e.g., Ang and Bekaert (2007)). We model the return dynamics as follows:

$$\begin{bmatrix} r_{s,t} \\ \ln\left(y_{1,t}\right) \\ \ln\left(y_{15,t}\right) \end{bmatrix} = A + B \begin{bmatrix} \ln\left(y_{1,t-1}\right) \\ \ln\left(y_{15,t-1}\right) \end{bmatrix} + \varepsilon_t \text{with } \varepsilon_t \sim MVN(0, \Sigma)$$

where $r_{s,t}$ is the annual log return on the S&P 500 index (including distributions), $y_{1,t}$ and $y_{15,t}$ are the annualized continuously compounded zero-coupon yields for the 1-year Treasury bill and the 15-year Treasury bond, ε_t is a three-by-one vector of innovations, and Σ is a three-by-three covariance matrix of the innovations. We model the dynamics of the log yields in the spirit of Black and Karasinski (1991) to ensure that nominal yields are positive.[13] The return dynamics we propose allow for both a time-varying risk-free rate, time-varying expected bond returns, and a time-varying equity risk premium, all as a function of two state variables, the short-term and the long-term yields.[14] The estimation results are presented in Appendix A.

We assume that the pension plan has liabilities with a fixed duration of 15 years. We measure the value of these liabilities in three ways. First, we compute the actual present value of the liabilities by discounting by the actual 15-year government bond yield:[15]

$$L_t = \exp\left(-15y_{15,t}\right) \tag{8.3}$$

Our second measure is based on recent regulations prescribing that the appropriate discount factor is the 4-year average bond yield:

$$\hat{L}_t = \exp\left(-15\hat{y}_{15,t}\right) \tag{8.4}$$

where

$$\hat{y}_{15,t} = \frac{y_{15,t} + y_{15,t-1} + y_{15,t-2} + y_{15,t-3}}{4} \tag{8.5}$$

Finally, we compute the value of the liabilities using a constant yield equal to the steady-state value of the long-term bond yield $\bar{y}_{15}$ implied by the VAR (see Appendix A):

$$\bar{L}_t = \exp\left(-15\bar{y}_{15}\right) \tag{8.6}$$

With all the three measures, the liabilities follow a stationary stochastic process. The model could easily be extended to include a deterministic time trend representing demographic factors. However, to maintain a parsimonious representation, we focus on the detrended series. Our specification also abstracts from inflows (premium payments) and outflows (pension payments) to the fund. We assume that in each year the inflows equal the outflows, which allows us to focus purely on the investment management part of the fund. The only inflows we consider are cash injections by the plan sponsor required to meet the regulator's minimal funding level. Note further that the three liability measures mentioned previously are driven by only one risk factor, the 15-year government bond yield. This could suggest that a one-factor model for the term structure would suffice in our model. However, we assume a two-factor model to allow for a time-varying risk-free rate.

We compute the simple gross returns on the three asset classes as follows:

$$\begin{aligned} R_{f,t} &= \exp\left(y_{1,t-1}\right) \\ R_t &= \begin{bmatrix} R_{s,t} \\ R_{b,t} \end{bmatrix} = \begin{bmatrix} \exp(r_{s,t}) \\ \exp(-14y_{15,t}) / \exp(-15y_{15,t-1}) \end{bmatrix} \end{aligned} \tag{8.7}$$

[13]We assume here that asset returns are homoskedastic. Evidence by Chacko and Viceira (2005) suggests that the volatility of stock returns is not variable enough to create sizeable hedging demands.

[14]For recent work on return predictability, see van Binsbergen and Koijen (2010), Ang and Bekaert (2007), Lewellen (2004), Campbell and Yogo (2005), and Torous, Valkanov, and Yan (2005) for stock returns, as well as Dai and Singleton (2002) and Cochrane and Piazzesi (2005) for bond returns.

[15]To maintain a parsimonious representation, we use the 15-year bond yield to determine the discount factor instead of the 30-year bond yield. Since the dynamics of both yields are very similar, this simplification does not alter our results.

where $R_{s,t}$ is the simple gross return on stocks, $R_{f,t}$ is the return on the 1-year T-bill (risk-free), and $R_{b,t}$ is the simple gross return on long-term bonds. Our expression for the bond return assumes that the yield curve is flat between 14 and 15 years to maturity.[16]

The funding ratio of the pension plan is defined as the ratio of its assets to liabilities:

$$S_t = \frac{A_t}{L_t} \tag{8.8}$$

where assets evolve from one period to the next according to

$$A_t = A_{t-1}(R_{f,t} + \alpha_{t-1} \cdot (R_t - R_{f,t})) + c_t \exp\,(-15y_{15,t}) \text{ for } t \geq 1 \tag{8.9}$$

and $\alpha_t \equiv [\alpha_{s,t}, \alpha_{b,t}]'$ denotes the portfolio weights in stocks and bonds. We let $c_t$denote the contributions of the plan sponsor at time t as a percentage of the liabilities which, under actual discounting, are equal to exp $(-15y_{15,t})$. Note that defining the contributions as a percentage of the liabilities is equivalent to expressing contributions in future $(t + 15)$ dollars. When liabilities are determined through constant discounting or 4-year average discounting, we define the contributions as a percentage of those liability measures and the last term in expression 8.9 is adapted accordingly. We use $\hat{S}_t$ and $\bar{S}_t$ to denote the funding ratios computed using the liability measures $\hat{L}_t$ and $\bar{L}_t$, respectively.

Finally, we define A_t^* as the assets in period t before the contributions are received and S_t^* as the ratio of A_t^* and the liabilities

$$A_t^* = A_{t-1}\left(R_{f,t} + \alpha_{t-1} \cdot \left(R_t - R_{f,t}\right)\right) \text{ for } t \geq 1 \tag{8.10}$$

$$S_t^* = \frac{A_t^*}{L_t} \tag{8.11}$$

8.3.2 Preferences

We take the perspective of an investment manager facing a realistic regulatory environment. We assume that the manager's utility is an additively separable function of the funding ratio at the end of the investment horizon, S_T, and the requested extra contributions from its sponsor as a percentage of the liabilities, c_t. We assume that the manager suffers disutility in the form of unmodeled reputation loss or loss in personal compensation for requesting these contributions. The utility function of the manager is given by

$$\begin{aligned} U\left(S_T, \{c_t\}_{t=1}^{T-1}\right) &= E_0\left[u\left(S_T\right) - \sum_{t=1}^{T} v(c_t, t)\right] \\ &= E_0\left[\beta^T \frac{S_T^{1-\gamma}}{1-\gamma} - \lambda \sum_{t=1}^{T} \beta^t c_t\right], \text{ where } \gamma \geq 0 \text{ and } \lambda \geq 0 \end{aligned} \tag{8.12}$$

The first term in the utility function is the standard power utility specification with respect to the funding ratio at the end of the investment horizon. We call this wealth utility. We assume that this wealth utility always depends on the actual funding ratio. That is, we use the actual yields to compute the liabilities in the denominator, regardless of government regulations, as opposed to using a smoothed or constant yield. The motivation for this assumption is that ultimately the manager is interested in maximizing the actual financial position of the fund, which is also the position the pension holders care about.[17] If we assumed that wealth utility was also based on the smoothed liability measure, this would further strengthen our results, as the incentive to hedge interest rate risk would be even further reduced.

The term $\sum_{t=1}^{T} \beta^t v(c_t)$ represents the investment manager's disutility (penalty) for requesting and receiving extra contributions c_t from the plan sponsor. This penalty can be interpreted as loss in reputation or compensation. The linear function just reflects the

[16]To check that this implicit assumption is innocuous, we also considered a specification in which the 14-year yield is included in the VAR. The results from this slightly expanded specification are identical. Recall that short positions are not allowed.

[17]It is interesting to note that even when both wealth utility and the risk constraints/AFCs are determined through 4-year average discounting, there is still a misalignment of incentives for a multiperiod investment problem. The risk constraints (which apply in every period) still induce the use of the risk-free asset. This is a consequence of the large reduction of the *conditional* variance that yield smoothing induces: $\text{var}_t(\hat{y}_{15,t+1}) = \text{var}_t\left[\frac{1}{4}(y_{15,t+1} + y_{15,t} + y_{15,t-1} + y_{15,t-2})\right] = \frac{1}{16}\text{var}_t\left[y_{15,t+1}\right]$. Wealth utility, on the other hand, depends on the funding ratio in year T. The conditional variance of $\hat{y}_{15,T}$ is given by $\text{var}_t(\hat{y}_{15,T}) = \text{var}_t\left[\frac{1}{4}(y_{15,T} + y_{15,T-1} + y_{15,T-2} + y_{15,T-3})\right]$. Note that for a 10-year investment problem, $T = 10$, the yields in year 10, 9, 8, and 7 (which jointly determine the liabilities in year 10) are all unknown before year 7. Therefore, in periods 1–6, long-term bonds are still the preferred instrument to hedge against liability risk when maximizing wealth utility, but in years 7 through 10 they are not.

first-order effect of these penalties and higher order terms could be included in our analysis.[18] Furthermore, when contributions from the sponsor are set equal to the funding ratio shortfall, linearity of the function $v(\cdot)$ implies that the utility penalties are scaled versions of the expected loss, which, next to a VaR constraint, is often used as a risk measure. As noted by Campbell and Viceira (2006), the weakness of a VaR constraint is that it treats all shortfalls greater than the VaR as equivalent, whereas it seems likely that the cost of a shortfall is increasing in the size of the shortfall. They, therefore, propose to incorporate the expected loss directly in the utility function, which in our framework is achieved by the linearity of the function $v(\cdot)$. Finally, the investment manager discounts next period's utility and disutility by the subjective discount factor β.

Another appealing interpretation of our utility specification is the following. In the context of private pension plans, the investment manager acts in the best interest of two stakeholders of the plan, (i) the pension holders who are generally risk averse and (ii) the sponsoring firm, which we assume to be risk neutral. The parameter λ then measures the investment manager's trade-off between these two stakeholders. If one believes that the investment manager merely acts in the best interest of the firm, the value of λ is high. Conversely, if one believes that the investment manager acts mainly in the interest of the beneficiaries, λ is low.

Finally, we can interpret the proposed utility specification in yet two other interesting ways. First we can interpret it as a portfolio choice problem with intermediate consumption and bequest. In the literature on lifetime savings and consumption, it is common to assume that utility from consumption is additively separable from bequest utility. The only difference is that, in our case, consumption is strictly negative and not strictly positive. In other words, the investment manager can increase his wealth by suffering negative consumption, which leads to a trade-off between maximizing (the utility from) the funding ratio at the end of the investment horizon and minimizing (the disutility from) the contributions along the way. The second interpretation is that similar utility specifications have been used in the general equilibrium literature with endogenous default, where agents may choose to default on their promises, even if their endowments are sufficient to meet the required payments (e.g., Geanakoplos, Dubey, Shubik (2005)). Agents incur utility penalties, which are linearly increasing in the amount of real default. The idea of including default penalties in the utility specification was first introduced by Shubik and Wilson (1977).

The trade-off between the disutility from contributions and wealth utility is captured by the coefficient λ. When we impose that in each period the sponsor contributions are equal to the funding ratio shortfall, and this shortfall is determined through actual discounting, a value of $\lambda = 0$ implies that the investment manager owns a put option on the funding ratio with exercise level $S^* = 1$. This gives the manager an incentive to take riskier investment positions. When $\lambda \to \infty$, the disutility from contributions is so high that the investment manager will invest conservatively to avoid a funding ratio shortfall when the current funding level is high. Depending on how liabilities are computed, investing conservatively either implies investing fully in the risk-free asset or investing fully in bonds (to immunize the liabilities) or a mixture of the two.[19]

Increasing the funding ratio at time zero affects the expected utility in three ways. First, it increases current wealth and therefore, keeping the investment strategy constant, also increases expected wealth utility. Second, if there is a period-by-period risk constraint, a higher funding ratio will make the risk constraint less binding in the current period and also decreases its expected impact on future decisions. Third, keeping the investment strategy constant, the probability of incurring contribution penalties in future periods decreases.

8.3.3 Constraints

8.3.3.1 Short-Sale Constraints We assume that the investment manager faces short-sales constraints on all three assets:

$$\alpha_t \geq 0 \text{ and } \alpha_t' \iota \leq 1 \tag{8.13}$$

8.3.3.2 VaR Constraints Pension funds often operate under VaR constraints. A VaR constraint is an ex ante (preventive) risk constraint. It is a risk measure based on the probability of loss over a specific time horizon. For pension plans, regulators typically require that over a specific time horizon the probability of underperforming a benchmark is smaller than some specified probability. The most natural candidate for this benchmark is the fund's reported liabilities. In this case, the VaR constraint requires that in each period the probability of being underfunded (i.e., reported liabilities exceeding assets) in the next period is smaller than probability δ. We set δ equal to 0.025. Depending on prevailing regulations, the relevant benchmark can be the actual liabilities (L_t), constant liabilities ($\bar{L}_t$), or, as under current regulations, $\hat{L}_t$.

We also compute the optimal portfolio weights and certainty equivalents when there are no additional contributions from the sponsor. In that case, there is no external source of funding that guarantees the lower bound equal to 1 on the funding ratio. It may

[18] Nonlinear specifications for the function $v(\cdot)$, for example, a quadratic form, do not change our qualitative results.

[19] When $\lambda \geq 1$, concavity of the utility function is guaranteed under actual discounting. For $\lambda = 1$, the utility is smooth, but for $\lambda > 1$, it is kinked at $S^* = 1$. The right derivative of the function $\frac{1}{1-\gamma}[\max(S^*, 1)]^{1-\gamma} - \lambda \max(1 - S^*, 0)$ is 1, whereas its left derivative equals λ. The risk neutrality over losses combined with the kinked utility function at $S^* = 1$ resembles elements of prospect theory (Kahneman and Tversky (1979)).

therefore be that in some periods the fund is underfunded to begin with. In those cases, the VaR constraint described previously cannot be applied and requires adaptation. When at the beginning of the period the fund has less assets than liabilities, we impose that the probability of a decrease in the funding ratio is less than 0.025. In other words, if the fund is underfunded to begin with, the manager faces a VaR constraint as if the funding ratio equals 1.

8.3.3.3 ***AFCs*** Under current regulations, a pension plan is required to receive AFCs from its sponsor whenever it is underfunded. As the manager dislikes drawing AFCs from the plan sponsor, this requirement serves as an ex post (punitive) risk constraint. The government regulation around these mandatory AFCs is not at all trivial and has changed over time. The Bush era reforms have substantially shortened the amortization period over which shortfalls can be amortized. This amortization period is generally equal to 7 years but extensions can be applied in certain cases. Previous regulation has also allowed for building up so-called credits, in which excess contributions in the past could be used to lower current contributions, regardless of the current financial position of the fund.

In our setup, we set the contributions of the sponsor equal to the funding ratio shortfall in each period. The measurement of this shortfall depends on the way liabilities are computed, which is what we study in this paper. We do not allow for credits nor do we allow for amortization of the shortfall. Since the latter can easily be mimicked by a bond that amortizes over time in combination with a different value for λ, we do not consider this to be a severe restriction in our model.

8.3.4 Data Description and Estimation

To obtain a reasonably representative data generating process, we use the following annual data from June 1954 through June 2008. For stock returns we take the natural logarithm of the return on the S&P 500 composite index including distributions. For bond yields we use the continuously compounded constant maturity yields as published by the Federal Reserve Bank. Whenever data on 15-year government bonds is missing, we take an average of the 10- and 20-year bond yields. We estimate the model by ordinary least squares (OLS) and we include dummy variables for the period 1978–1983 in our estimation to correct for this exceptional period with high inflation.[20] The estimation results are given in Appendix A.

8.4 METHOD

The ALM investment problem, even in stylized form, is a complicated and path-dependent dynamic optimization program. We use the simulation-based method developed by Brandt et al. (2005) to solve this program. The main idea of their method is to parameterize the conditional expectations used in the backward recursion of the dynamic problem by regressing the stochastic variables of interest across simulated sample paths on a polynomial basis of the state variables.[21] More specifically, we generate $N = 25,000$ paths of length T from the estimated return dynamics. We then solve the dynamic problem recursively backward, starting with the optimization problem at time $T-1$:

$$\max_{\alpha_{T-1}} U(S_T) = \max_{\alpha_{T-1}} \mathrm{E}_{T-1}\left[\frac{\beta}{1-\gamma} S_T^{1-\gamma} - \lambda\beta c_T\right] \tag{8.14}$$

subject to Equations 8.7 –8.9 as well as the short-sale constraints and the definition of the required contributions.

The solution of this problem depends on S_{T-1}. To recover this dependence, we solve a range of problems for S_{T-1} varying between 0.4 and 3. For each value of S_{T-1}, we optimize over the portfolio weights α_{T-1} by a grid search over the space $[0,1] \times [0,1]$. This grid search over the portfolio weights avoids a number of numerical problems that can occur when taking first-order conditions and iterating to a solution. We then evaluate the conditional expectation $\mathrm{E}_{T-1}(S_T^{1-\gamma})$ by regressing for each value of S_{T-1} and each grid point of α_{T-1} the realizations of $S_T^{1-\gamma}(N \times 1)$ on a polynomial basis of the two state variables $y_{15,T-1}$ and $y_{1,T-1}$. Define

$$z = \begin{bmatrix} z_1 & z_2 \end{bmatrix} = \begin{bmatrix} y_{1,T-1} & y_{15,T-1} \end{bmatrix} \tag{8.15}$$

then

$$X = \begin{bmatrix} 1 & z_{1,1} & z_{2,1} & (z_{1,1})^2 & (z_{2,1})^2 & (z_{1,1})(z_{2,1}) & \cdots \\ 1 & z_{1,2} & z_{2,2} & (z_{1,2})^2 & (z_{2,2})^2 & (z_{1,2})(z_{2,2}) & \cdots \\ \vdots & \vdots & \vdots & \vdots & \vdots & \vdots & \cdots \\ 1 & z_{1,N} & z_{2,N} & (z_{1,N})^2 & (z_{2,N})^2 & (z_{1,2})(z_{2,N}) & \cdots \end{bmatrix} \tag{8.16}$$

[20] The dummies correct for the average level of interest rates over this period and also lower the persistence estimate of yields. We also run a version of the VAR where we exclude these dummy variables. This does not change any of our conclusions and leads to highly similar quantitative results.

[21] This approach is inspired by Longstaff and Schwartz (2001) who first proposed this method to price American-style options by simulation. See Tebaldi and Veronesi (2015, Chapter 19 in this handbook) for a review of this methodology.

where each row of X corresponds to a different simulation. The conditional expectation can then be computed as

$$\mathrm{E}_{T-1}\left(S_T^{1-\gamma}\right) = X'\hat{\beta} \tag{8.17}$$

where

$$\hat{\beta} = \left(X'X\right)^{-1}X'\left(S_T^{1-\gamma}\right) \tag{8.18}$$

When liabilities are discounted by the rolling 4-year average yield, we have to include polynomial expansions of all four lags of both state variables in our solution method. To evaluate the conditional expectation of the contributions in period T, $\mathrm{E}_{T-1}\left(c_T\right)$, we first regress $1 - S_T^*$ on X:

$$\hat{\xi} = (X'X)^{-1}X'(1 - S_T^*) \tag{8.19}$$

Assuming normality for the error term in the regression and letting $\hat{\sigma}$ denote its standard deviation, we find

$$\mathrm{E}_{T-1}(c_T) = \mathrm{E}_{T-1}[\max(1 - S_T^*, 0)] = \Phi\left(\frac{X'\hat{\xi}}{\hat{\sigma}}\right)X'\hat{\xi} + \hat{\sigma}\phi\left(\frac{X'\hat{\xi}}{\hat{\sigma}}\right) \tag{8.20}$$

where $\Phi(\cdot)$ and $\phi(\cdot)$ denote, respectively, the cumulative and probability density functions of the standard normal distribution. Note that this conditional expectation also represents the expected loss of the fund over the next period. In the exposition previously, contributions are determined by actual discounting. When we use constant or 4-year average discounting, we simply replace S_T by $\bar{S}_T$ or $\hat{S}_T$ and we replace S_T^* by $\bar{S}_T^*$ or $\hat{S}_T^*$.

Given the conditional expectations in (8.17) and (8.20), we can finally solve problem (8.14), obtaining the optimal weights α_{T-1}. These weights depend on S_{T-1}. Given the solution at time $T-1$, meaning the mapping from S_{T-1} to the optimal α_{T-1}, we iterate backwards through time. The iterative steps are as described previously with just a few additions. For ease of exposition we now describe these additions for period $T-2$, but they equally apply for periods $T-3, T-4, \cdots, 1$. At time $T-2$ we determine for each grid point of α_{T-2} the return on the portfolio in path $i \in N$ from $T-2$ to $T-1$. Using this return to compute $S_{T-1,i}$, we can then compute the return in path i from $T-1$ to T by interpolating over the mapping from S_{T-1} to α_{T-1} derived in the previous step. Similarly, we interpolate in each path the expected penalty payments.

In the case of a VaR constraint, we impose the constraint in each period and along each path. For given values of S_t, we determine for each α_t the conditional mean and conditional variance of the funding ratio in period $t+1$ through regressions on the polynomial basis of the state variables. By assuming lognormality, we then evaluate whether the probability of a funding ratio shortfall (i.e., a funding ratio smaller than 1) in period $t+1$ is less than δ. If this requirement is not met, those particular portfolio weights are excluded from the investment manager's choice set. As described above, the VaR can be imposed with respect to S_t^* (discounting at actual yields), $\bar{S}_t^*$ (discounting at constant yields), or $\hat{S}_t^*$ (discounting at the 4-year average yield).

For ease of exposition, we will use first-order approximations throughout our simulations, but higher order terms in the matrix X can easily be accommodated.

8.5 SINGLE-PERIOD PORTFOLIO CHOICE

In this section, we investigate the investment manager's optimal portfolio choice when he/she is faced with risk constraints that are based on the smoothed liability measure. We consider a VaR constraint as the ex ante (preventive) constraint. For the ex post (punitive) constraint, we consider the requirement to draw AFCs whenever the plan becomes underfunded. Note again that both the VaR constraint and the AFCs are short-term considerations based on the *smoothed* liability measure, whereas the long-term objective of wealth utility is defined with respect to the *actual* liability measure. We quantify in this section the losses that result from the wedge that yield smoothing drives between these short- and long-term considerations. We first solve a one-period problem to explain the main intuition in a parsimonious setting. We then explain how the results change in a multiperiod setup.

8.5.1 ALM with a VaR Constraint

First we investigate optimal portfolio decisions and corresponding certainty equivalents in a one-period context ($T = 1$) under a VaR constraint. We set the state variables at time zero equal to their long-run averages. We set the VaR probability δ=0.025 and

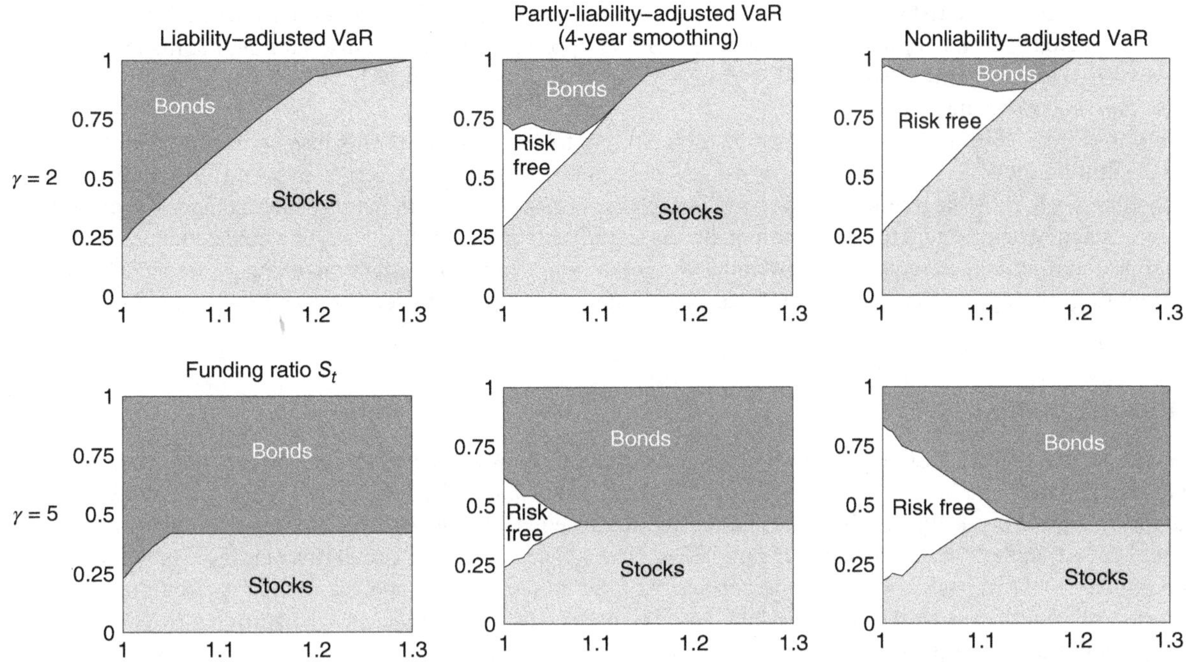

Figure 8.3 Portfolio weights: one-period CRRA ALM problem under a VaR constraint ($\delta = 0.025$). The VaR constraint is determined under actual liability discounting (liability-adjusted VaR), 4-year average discounting (part-liability-adjusted VaR) and constant discounting (nonliability-adjusted VaR). We solve the problem for relative degrees of risk aversion equal to 2 and 5.

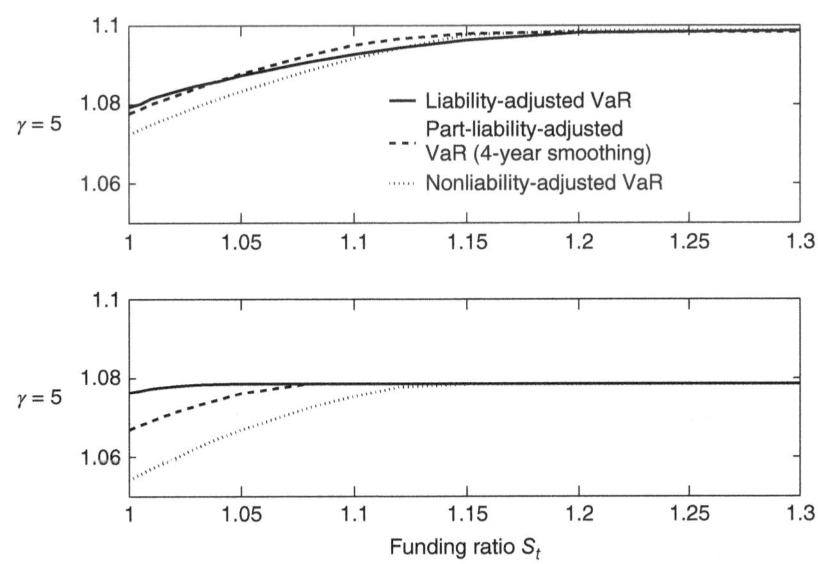

Figure 8.4 Scaled certainty equivalents for a one-period CRRA ALM problem under a value-at-risk constraint ($\delta = 0.025$). The VaR constraint is determined under actual liability discounting (liability-adjusted VaR) 4-year average discounting (part-liability-adjusted VaR) and constant discounting (nonliability-adjusted VaR). We solve the problem for relative degrees of risk aversion equal to 2 and 5. We report certainty equivalents that are scaled by the initial funding ratio S_0, comparable to an annual gross risk-free return (so 1.06 means a 6% return).

we do not include contributions from the sponsor (i.e., $c_T = 0$). We compare a VaR constraint imposed on S_T (discounting at actual yields) with one imposed on $\bar{S}_T$ (discounting at a constant yield) and one on $\hat{S}_T$ (discounting at the 4-year average yield).

Figures 8.3 and 8.4 present the optimal portfolio weights and scaled certainty equivalents for a VaR based on actual (market based) discounting, 4-year average discounting, and constant discounting, for two different levels of risk aversion, $\gamma = 2$ and $\gamma = 5$. Note that the VaR constraint is more binding when the funding ratio at time zero, denoted by S_0, is lower. Therefore, as S_0 decreases, the manager has to substitute away from stocks to satisfy the constraint. The key insight of these results is that under actual discounting the manager substitutes into the long-term bond, whereas under constant discounting he/she moves into the risk-free asset. Because the utility from wealth depends on the actual (market based) funding ratio, which is computed using current yields, investing in the riskless asset leads to large utility losses. The riskless asset does not hedge against liability risk and has a low expected return. In other words, when the VaR is imposed with constant discounting, the manager is torn between the objective of maximizing utility from wealth and satisfying the VaR constraint. When the VaR constraint is based on actual yields, these two objectives are more aligned.

The utility loss from constant discounting can be large and up to 4% of wealth. This loss is increasing in the degree of risk aversion. Substituting away from bonds into the riskless asset and stocks leaves a larger exposure to liability risk, leading to larger utility losses when the degree of risk aversion is higher. As risk aversion increases, the manager's preferred position in stocks decreases and he/she prefers to invest more in bonds to hedge against liability risk. As a consequence, the VaR constraint under actual discounting, which requires a substantial weight in bonds, does not affect the manager much. The VaR constraint under constant discounting, on the other hand, forces the manager into the risk-free asset and stocks leading to large welfare losses.

8.5.2 ALM with AFCs

We now assess the impact of smoothing yields by comparing optimal portfolio decisions and corresponding certainty equivalents when the investment manager has to request AFCs whenever the fund is underfunded. The notion of being underfunded depends on the liability measure used. We set the contributions at time 1 equal to the realized funding ratio shortfall, which implies $c_T = \max(1 - \bar{S}_T^*, 0)$ under constant discounting and $c_T = \max(1 - S_T^*, 0)$ under actual discounting. As before, we consider a one-period setup ($T = 1$). We set $\lambda > 1$ to ensure concavity of the utility function and, for ease of exposition, we do not impose the VaR constraint. Finally, we set the state variables equal to their long-run averages at time zero.

Figures 8.5 and 8.6 present the optimal portfolio weights and certainty equivalents for $\lambda = 2$ for degrees of risk aversion γ equal to 2 and 5 as a function of the funding ratio $S_0 \geq 1$. Figures 8.7 and 8.8 show the results for $\lambda = 5$. The graphs show that when sponsor contributions and their consequent reputation loss are determined under smoothed yield measures, the investment manager does not substitute into bonds but hedges against the utility penalties through a higher weight in the risk-free asset combined with a higher weight in stocks. This goes against the investment manager's desire to maximize wealth utility, leading to large welfare losses.

Again we conclude that yield smoothing leads to perverse investment incentives. Whereas the AFCs should induce the manager to take less risky positions when the funding ratio approaches the critical threshold of one, smoothing induces the manager to take riskier positions. We can therefore conclude once again that smoothing yields can lead to perverse investment behavior accompanied by large welfare losses.

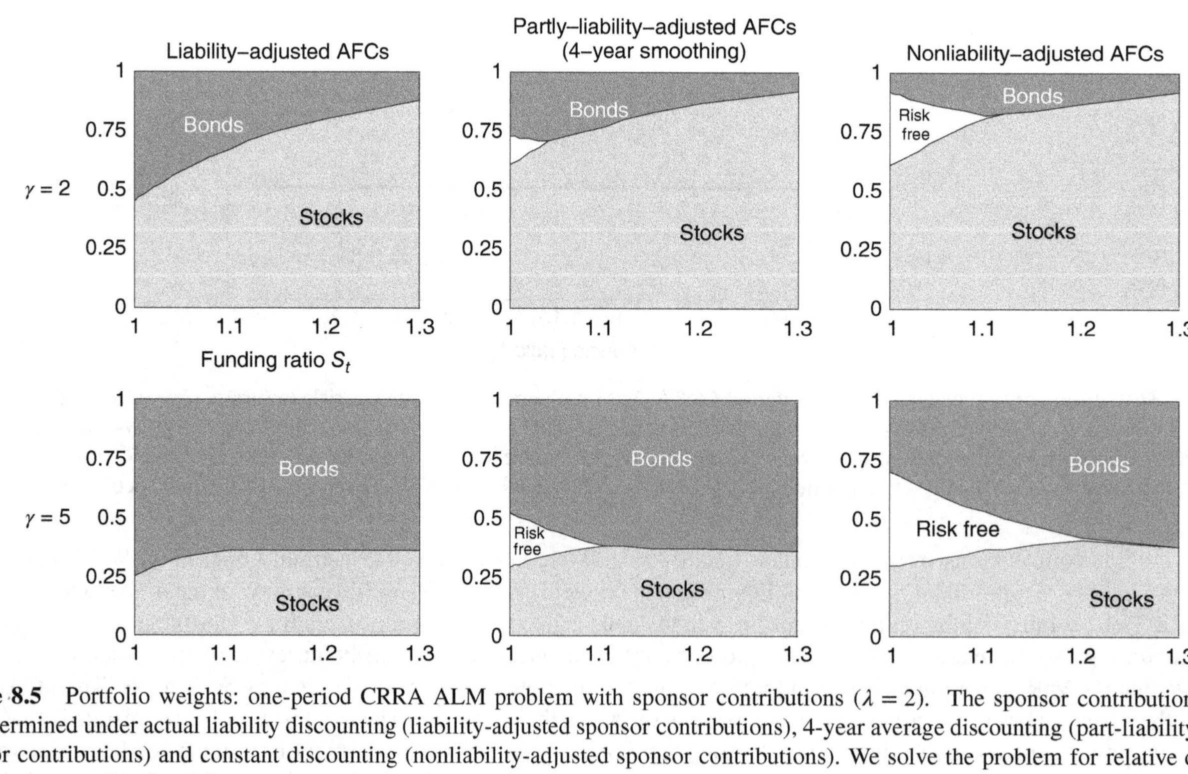

Figure 8.5 Portfolio weights: one-period CRRA ALM problem with sponsor contributions ($\lambda = 2$). The sponsor contributions (AFCs) are determined under actual liability discounting (liability-adjusted sponsor contributions), 4-year average discounting (part-liability-adjusted sponsor contributions) and constant discounting (nonliability-adjusted sponsor contributions). We solve the problem for relative degrees of risk aversion equal to 2 and 5.

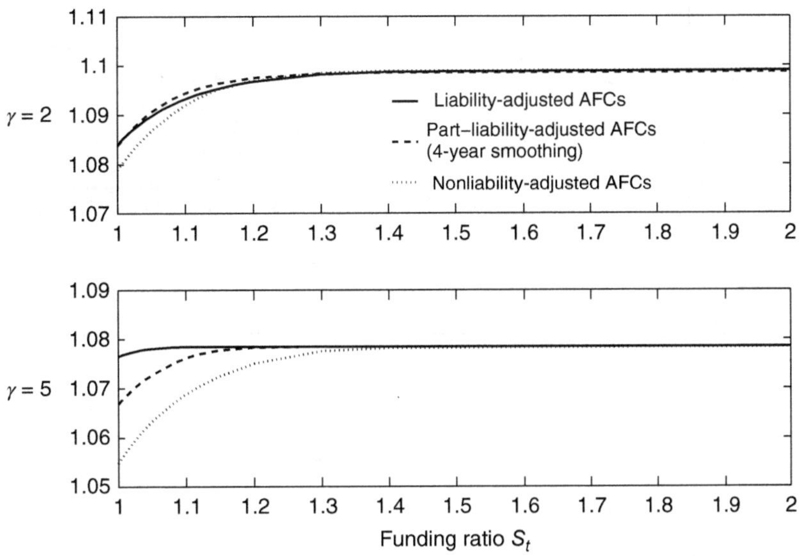

Figure 8.6 Certainty equivalents: one-period CRRA ALM problem with AFCs ($\lambda = 2$). The sponsor contributions (AFCs) are determined under actual liability discounting (liability-adjusted sponsor contributions), 4-year average discounting (part-liability-adjusted sponsor contributions), and constant discounting (nonliability-adjusted sponsor contributions). We solve the problem for relative degrees of risk aversion equal to 2 and 5. We report certainty equivalents that are scaled by the initial funding ratio S_0, comparable to a gross annual risk-free return (so 1.06 means a 6% return).

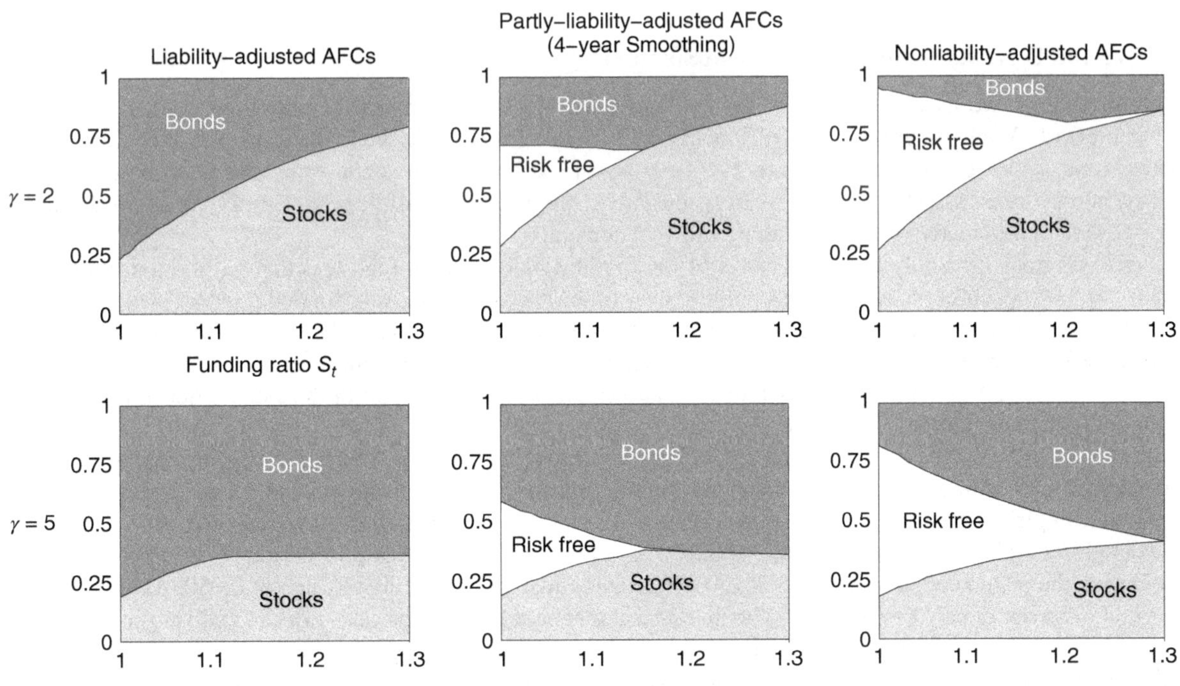

Figure 8.7 Portfolio weights: one-period CRRA ALM problem with AFCs ($\lambda = 5$). The sponsor contributions are determined under actual liability discounting (liability-adjusted sponsor contributions), 4-year average discounting (part-liability-adjusted sponsor contributions), and constant discounting (nonliability-adjusted sponsor contributions). We solve the problem for relative degrees of risk aversion equal to 2 and 5.

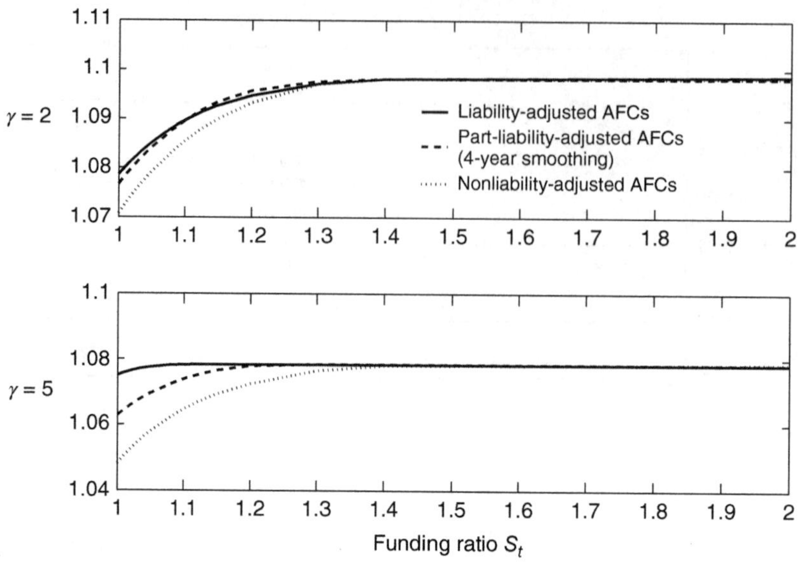

Figure 8.8 Certainty equivalents: one-period CRRA ALM problem with AFCs ($\lambda = 5$). The sponsor contributions (AFCs) are determined under actual liability discounting (liability-adjusted sponsor contributions), 4-year average discounting (part-liability-adjusted sponsor contributions), and constant discounting (nonliability-adjusted sponsor contributions). We solve the problem for relative degrees of risk aversion equal to 2 and 5. We report certainty equivalents that are scaled by the initial funding ratio S_0, comparable to a gross annual risk-free return (so 1.06 means a 6% return).

8.6 DYNAMIC PORTFOLIO CHOICE

8.6.1 Welfare and Portfolio Implications of Yield Smoothing

In the previous section, we have assessed the welfare and portfolio choice impact of smoothing yields in a parsimonious one-period framework. When we extend our analysis to a multiperiod framework, we find results that are highly comparable to the one-period case, with welfare losses of up to 2–4% per year in certainty equivalent terms and portfolio choices that hedge poorly against interest rate risk. That said, there are a few subtle but important differences with the one-period framework that are worth discussing, particularly when considering the VaR constraint.

Because the VaR constraint only binds for levels of the funding ratio close to (and less than) 1 and the funding ratio has a positive drift, the VaR becomes *on average* less binding over time. Therefore, for fully funded pension plans, the impact of the VaR and the difference between constant and actual discounting decreases over time as the plan's funding ratio increases. However, highly underfunded plans without AFCs can be confronted with the VaR constraint over a very long time span. Therefore, the welfare loss of constant discounting for such underfunded plans is very large and in the same order of magnitude as in the one-period model, that is, between 2% and 4% per year.

We would expect that, as in the one-period model, the impact of 4-year average discounting takes an average of the impacts of constant and actual discounting. However, another important implication of smoothing yields now emerges: in around 10–20% of the cases, not a single portfolio weight in the choice space satisfies the VaR constraint. The reason is as follows. Consider the following example of a plan with a funding ratio equal to 1. Suppose that in the last four periods ($t-3$, $t-2$, $t-1$, and t) the 15-year yield took the path 0.060, 0.055, 0.045, and 0.040, leading to a 4-year rolling average of 0.050. Assume further that the short-term yield is currently very low at 0.020. The investment manager knows that next year the yield at time $t-3$ (i.e., 0.060) will be dropped from the average and the yield at $t+1$ will be added. The 15-year bond yield is expected to rise, due to mean reversion, but it is unlikely to rise back to 0.060 in one period. Therefore, the 4-year average yield will most probably decrease, leading to a deterioration of the fund's position. Investing fully in the riskless asset is not allowed because the expected return is too low to compensate for the deterioration of the fund's reported position. As a result, investing fully in the riskless asset leads to an almost certain shortfall, whereas the maximum allowed probability of a shortfall under the VaR constraint is only 0.025. Investing in bonds is not too attractive either, as the long-term yield is expected to rise, leading to low expected returns on long-term bonds. The investment manager needs to offset a *drop* in the 4-year rolling average yield, whereas the long-term yield is expected to increase. Therefore, the probability of a shortfall will be larger than 0.025 for all available portfolio weighs. Surprisingly, it turns out that in cases like this, the portfolio composition that leads to the lowest probability of a shortfall is

TABLE 8.1 Portfolio Weights and Standardized Certainty Equivalents for a 10-Period CRRA ALM Portfolio Optimization Without VaR Constraint or Sponsor Contributions

	Myopic				Dynamic				Gains (bp/a)
γ	Stocks	Risk-free	Bonds	CE scaled	Stocks	Risk-free	Bonds	CE scaled	
2	0.96	0.00	0.04	2.951	1.00	0.00	0.00	2.956	1.5
	(0.028)	(0.000)	(0.028)	(0.009)	(0.032)	(0.000)	(0.000)	(0.012)	(0.1)
5	0.37	0.00	0.63	2.415	0.43	0.00	0.57	2.426	4.1
	(0.008)	(0.000)	(0.008)	(0.010)	(0.028)	(0.000)	(0.028)	(0.009)	(1.0)

Due to the power utility specification over the funding ratio, the weights are independent of the funding ratio at time zero. The portfolio weights are rebalanced annually. We run 50 simulations and report averages and standard deviations (between brackets). In the last column (gain in basis points per year), we take the ratio of the certainty equivalents to the power 1/10, subtract 1 and multiply by 10,000, to get the gains to dynamic (strategic) investment compared to myopic (tactical) investment in basis points per year.

investing 100% in stocks, which is undesirable from a wealth utility perspective. We conclude once again that smoothing yields can lead to excessive risk taking and large welfare losses.[22]

8.6.2 Hedging Demands and Regulatory Constraints

In the previous sections, we have discussed the welfare implications of yield smoothing in a dynamic framework. In this section, we address the impact of regulatory constraints on *hedging demands*. That is, the differences between the dynamic (also called strategic) and myopic portfolio weights. They hedge against future changes in the investment opportunity set. It is well-known that the value function of standard CRRA utility function is relatively flat at the maximum, implying that moderate deviations from the optimal portfolio policy only lead to small utility losses (e.g., Cochrane (1989) and Brandt (2010)). As a consequence, the economic gains to dynamic (strategic) as opposed to myopic (tactical) investment are usually small even when the hedging demands are large in magnitude. Intuitively, ex ante (preventive) risk constraints could enhance these gains as it could be profitable to strategically avoid the constraints in future periods. Specifically when the investment opportunity set is time-varying, the investment manager might want to avoid being constrained in the future when expected returns are high. We show that for the return-generating process that we consider, the exact opposite result seems to hold: ex ante risk constraints further decrease the gains to dynamic investment. However, we also show that under ex post (punitive) constraints, such as the requirement to draw AFCs when the plan becomes underfunded, strategically (dynamically) avoiding these contributions can lead to economically large utility gains.

8.6.2.1 Dynamic ALM Benchmark As a benchmark, we first present the optimal portfolio weights for an ALM problem without sponsor contributions, AFCs, or VaR constraint.[23] Table 8.1 shows the optimal portfolio weights and certainty equivalents for the dynamic and the myopic investor for different values of γ. Given the short position in the liabilities, it is no longer optimal to invest in the riskless asset, so the manager spreads his wealth between stocks and bonds. The dynamic investor now substitutes away from long-term bonds into stocks. When investing myopically, the uncertainty caused by the liabilities induces the manager to invest more in long-term bonds, which are a good hedge against liability risk. However, when investing dynamically, liability risk is not as important due to the mean-reverting nature of yields. In other words, future bond returns are negatively correlated with current bond returns. Suppose that the 15-year yield is at its long-run average and is hit by a negative shock. Current liabilities will increase, which leads to a deterioration of the funds financial position. However, yields are consequently expected to increase, which will ameliorate the fund's position. In other words, in our setup bonds are a good hedge against changes in the investment opportunities for bonds. Apparently, this effect even dominates the use of bonds as a hedge against changes in the investment opportunities for stocks. The gains to dynamic investment are again small, not exceeding 10 basis points per year.

8.6.2.2 Dynamic ALM with a VaR Constraint We now investigate the impact of ex ante (preventive) risk constraints on hedging demands. In particular, we focus on a VaR constraint. We set the VaR probability δ equal to 0.025 and maintain the assumption of no sponsor contributions, so $c_t = 0$ for all times t.

[22]When long-term yields have been rising consistently, and the short-term yield is high, the opposite argument holds, and the investment environment is very favorable to the manager. In this case he/she is less restricted by the VaR constraint under 4-year average discounting than under actual discounting.

[23]An even more basic benchmark is to study an asset-only (no liabilities) problem given the return dynamics, which we do in Appendix B.

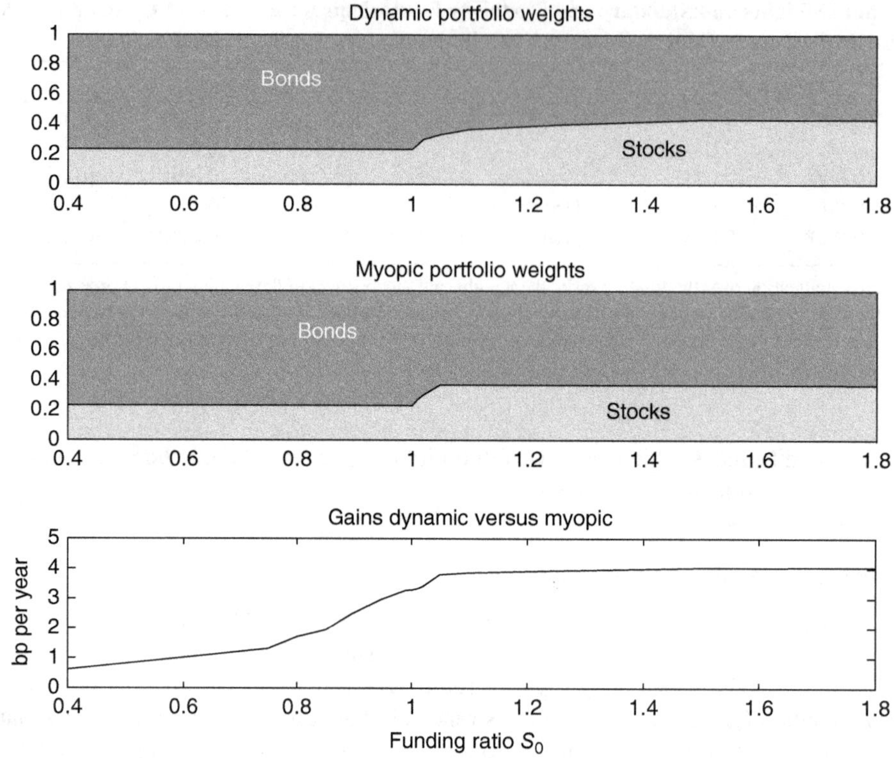

Figure 8.9 Dynamic versus Myopic Portfolio Choice under a VaR. Dynamic and myopic portfolio weights and certainty equivalent gains for a 10-period CRRA ($\gamma = 5$) ALM problem (no sponsor contributions) with a VaR constraint imposed on the actual (actual discounting) funding ratio ($\delta = 0.025$). The top panel summarizes the dynamic (strategic) portfolio weights, and the middle panel summarizes the myopic (tactical) ones. The bottom panel shows the certainty equivalent gains, which are computed in basis points per year by taking the ratio of the certainty equivalents of the 10-year problem, raising this to the power 1/10, subtract 1 and multiply by 10,000.

Intuitively we would expect the VaR constraint to increase the value of solving the dynamic program. Strategically avoiding the VaR constraint should lead to utility increases. Our results indicate exactly the opposite: the VaR constraint further reduces the already small gains to dynamic investing. Figures 8.9 and 8.10 show the optimal portfolio weights for $\gamma = 5$ as a function of the funding ratio at time zero for both the dynamic and myopic investor. The graphs also plot the certainty equivalent gains of dynamic investing relative to the myopic solution. In Figure 8.9, the VaR is imposed with respect to S_t (discounting at current yields), and in Figure 8.10 it is imposed with respect to $\bar{S}_t$ (discounting at a constant yield). Recall that the VaR constraint applies period by period for both the dynamic and the myopic investor. For ease of exposition, let us consider low and intermediate levels of the funding ratio at time zero. In this case the VaR constraint binds and it reduces the weight in stocks. That is, the VaR constraint leads the investor away from the preferred portfolio weight in stocks, leading to a utility loss. The upper bound on the weight in stocks as required by the VaR depends on the funding ratio at time zero and is the same for the dynamic and the myopic investor. From the unconstrained ALM problem presented in the previous section, we know that to hedge against changes in the investment opportunity set, the dynamic investor wants to invest more in stocks than the myopic one. However, the VaR constraint prevents him/her from doing so, thereby eliminating the gains to dynamic investment.

Even though the dynamic investor cannot invest more in stocks than the myopic one, he/she could choose to invest less in stocks in the current period, thereby strategically lowering the probability of being constrained by the VaR in the future. However, the current VaR already decreases his weight in stocks, which already lowers the probability of being constrained by the VaR in the future. The current period's portfolio loss of decreasing the weight in stocks even further outweighs the potential future gains. As a result, both investors make the same portfolio choices, leading to almost equal certainty equivalents. The VaR constraint in the current period is a strong remedy in trying to avoid the VaR constraint in the future. Furthermore, it is interesting to note that the expected returns on stocks are high when the 15-year yield is high. This means that the liabilities are low when stock returns are high. This ameliorates the negative impact of the VaR in future periods and allows the manager to invest in stocks when it is most profitable for him to do so. However, this last argument only holds when the VaR is imposed on the actual funding ratio S_t and may not hold when liabilities are smoothed. This is yet another unattractive feature of yield smoothing.

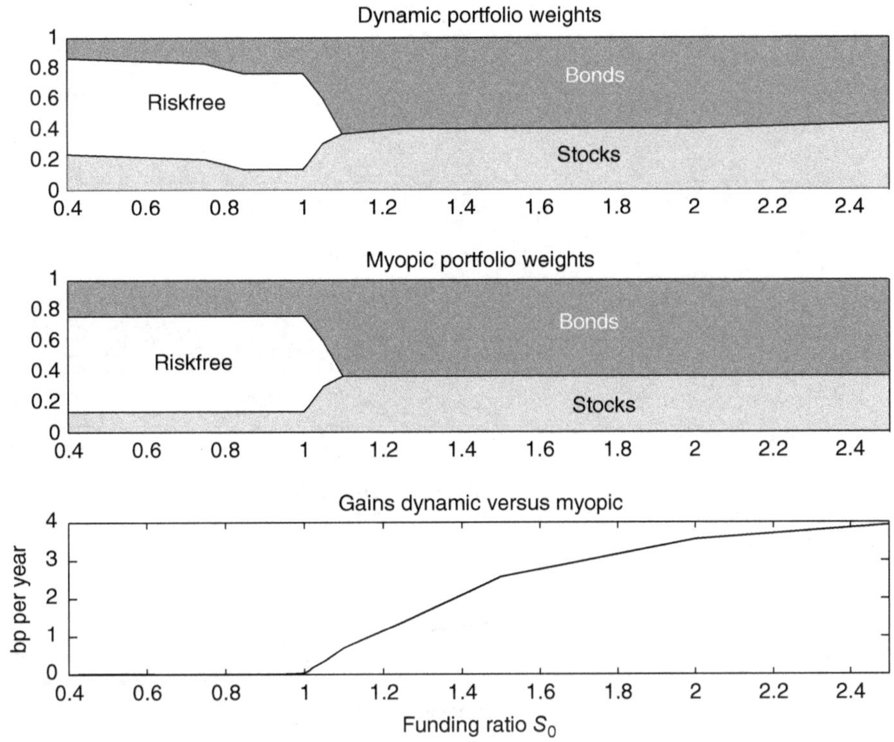

Figure 8.10 Dynamic versus Myopic Portfolio Choice under a VaR. Dynamic and myopic portfolio weights and certainty equivalent gains for a 10-period CRRA ($\gamma = 5$) ALM problem (no sponsor contributions) with a VaR constraint imposed on the smoothed (constant discounting) funding ratio ($\delta = 0.025$). The top panel summarizes the dynamic (strategic) portfolio weights, and the middle panel summarizes the myopic (tactical) ones. The bottom panel shows the certainty equivalent gains, which are computed in basis points per year by taking the ratio of the certainty equivalents of the 10-year problem, raising this to the power 1/10, subtract 1 and multiply by 10,000.

We conclude that the dynamic investor faces a trade-off between forming an optimal portfolio in the current period given the current VaR and lowering the probability and impact of hitting the VaR in the future. Our results suggest that the current loss from decreasing the weight in stocks by more than is prescribed by the current VaR outweighs the gain of a lower probability of hitting the VaR in the future, at least for the return-generating process (VAR) that we consider. When the 15-year yield at time zero is no longer at its unconditional mean but below it, investing in stocks in the current period becomes less appealing compared to investing in stocks in the future. However it also implies that current liabilities are high and are expected to decrease. This downward trend in liabilities decreases the impact of the VaR constraint in the future under actual discounting but not under constant discounting.

8.6.2.3 Dynamic ALM with AFCs Finally, we consider ex post (punitive) risk constraints. In particular, we focus on the investment manager's requirement to request AFCs from the plan sponsor whenever the plan becomes underfunded. In the previous section, we showed that lowering the weight in stocks today to strategically avoid the VaR constraint in the future does not payoff. Now, however, lowering the weight in stocks to lower the probability of being underfunded in the future can lead to very large utility gains. Including sponsor contributions in the utility function leads to a kinked utility function. The induced first-order risk aversion enhances the gains to dynamic investment. Furthermore, contributions have a direct utility impact and apply each period as opposed to utility from wealth, which only depends on the funding ratio in time T. We set the subjective discount factor $\beta = 0.99$ and set $\delta = 1$ (no VaR constraint).[24] Recall that λ is the parameter that describes the trade-off between the sponsor contributions and wealth utility. When λ is set sufficiently high, the gains of lowering the probability of being underfunded in the future will outweigh the portfolio loss of lowering the weight in stocks today. In this case the gains to dynamic investment are very large. Figure 8.11 shows the portfolio weights and certainty equivalent gains for $\lambda = 2$ when in each period the contributions are set equal to the realized funding ratio shortfall under actual discounting ($c_t = \max(1 - S_t^*, 0)$). The certainty equivalent gains are in terms of wealth, which assumes that the utility penalties associated with AFCs can be converted into monetary amounts according to the trade-off in the utility function.

[24]Setting the subjective discount factor β to 0.95 or 0.9 does not influence our results.

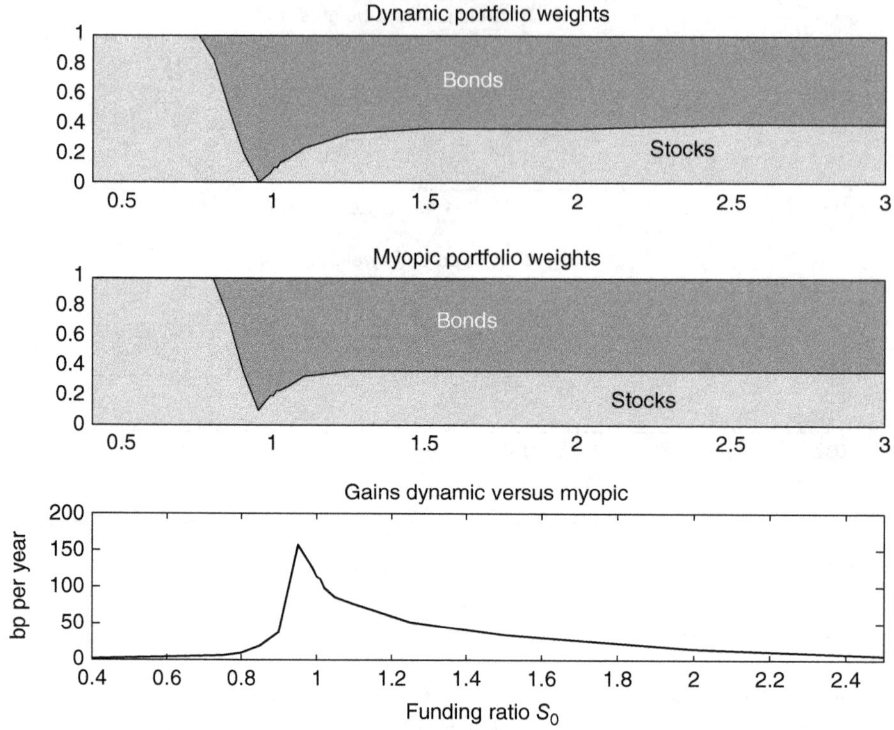

Figure 8.11 Dynamic versus myopic portfolio choice under AFCs. Dynamic and myopic portfolio weights and certainty equivalent gains for a 10-period CRRA ($\gamma = 5$) ALM problem with sponsor contributions (AFCs), where AFCs are computed on the actual funding ratio ($\lambda = 2$). The top panel summarizes the dynamic (strategic) portfolio weights, and the middle panel summarizes the myopic (tactical) ones. The bottom panel shows the certainty equivalent gains, which are computed in basis points per year by taking the ratio of the certainty equivalents of the 10-year problem, raising this to the power 1/10, subtract 1 and multiply by 10,000.

The figure shows that highly underfunded plans invest heavily in stocks, which is a consequence of the linearity of the utility penalties, which effectively make the managers risk neutral for low levels of the funding ratio. This gambling for resurrection in our model also illustrates that including the pension put (i.e., the fact that U.S. defined benefit pension plans are insured through the Pension Benefit Guaranty Corporation) in our framework would not change the portfolio weights very much.[25] The manager already invests 100% in stocks when the plan is highly underfunded. The figure also shows that the gains from dynamic investment are very large. By lowering the weight in stocks today, the investment manager can avoid costly contributions from the sponsor in the future, thereby realizing large utility gains.

8.7 CONCLUSION

We address in this chapter the investment problem of the investment manager of a defined benefits pension plan and show that financial reporting and risk control rules have real effects on investment behavior. The requirement to discount liabilities at a rolling average yield can induce grossly suboptimal investment decisions, both myopically and dynamically. Both a VaR constraint and mandatory AFCs by the plan sponsor should *decrease* the manager's risky holdings as the funding ratio approaches the critical threshold of 1. We show that when these short-term objectives are defined with respect to the smoothed liability measure, they can inadvertently induce the manager to *increase* the riskiness of the portfolio. We therefore conclude that smoothing yields may lead to highly perverse investment behavior and large welfare losses. Furthermore, if the regulator yields to political pressure by allowing additional smoothing when interest rates are low, and less smoothing when interest rates are high, this encourages additional risk-taking behavior, thereby increasing the probability of underfunded pension plans relative to the nonsmoothed (true market value) of liabilities.

We compared the influence of preventive and punitive constraints on the gains to dynamic decision making. We conclude that ex ante (preventive) constraints, such as VaR constraints, short-sale constraints, and an upper bound on the share of stocks in the portfolio, decrease the size of the choice set (i.e., the space of admissible portfolio weights) and thereby substantially decrease

[25]For a similar V-shaped policy function of portfolio weights, see Berkelaar and Kouwenberg (2003).

the gains to dynamic investment. However, ex post (punitive) constraints, such as mandatory AFCs from the plan sponsor, make the investment manager first-order risk averse at the critical threshold that triggers the constraint, leading to large utility gains to dynamic investment. In other words, if the investment manager is concerned about being underfunded and dislikes the resulting AFCs, a dynamic investment strategy leads to large expected utility gains by strategically avoiding to be underfunded in the future.

8.8 APPENDIX: RETURN MODEL PARAMETER ESTIMATES

We estimate the VAR of order 1 that describes the return dynamics by OLS equation by equation. The estimates are given below with their respective standard errors within brackets:

$$A = \begin{bmatrix} 0.252 & (0.1677) \\ -0.518 & (0.4189) \\ -0.309 & (0.1562) \end{bmatrix} \tag{8.21}$$

$$B = \begin{bmatrix} -0.1548 & (0.0821) & 0.2193 & (0.1336) \\ 0.5324 & (0.1916) & 0.3101 & (0.2832) \\ 0.0058 & (0.0714) & 0.8771 & (0.1056) \end{bmatrix} \tag{8.22}$$

$$\Sigma = \begin{bmatrix} 0.0234 & 0.0064 & -0.0048 \\ 0.0064 & 0.1226 & 0.0408 \\ -0.0048 & 0.0408 & 0.0208 \end{bmatrix} \tag{8.23}$$

As the starting values, we take the unconditional average of the yields in the data, which differs slightly from the average yields implied by the VAR.

8.9 APPENDIX: BENCHMARK WITHOUT LIABILITIES

As a second benchmark, we solve a standard dynamic portfolio optimization problem without liabilities, AFCs, utility penalties, or a VaR constraint. We compare the certainty equivalent achieved under the solution of the dynamic 10-year investment problem with that of a myopic setup. The myopic problem involves solving 10 sequential 1-year optimizations. Hence the only difference between the dynamic and the myopic problems is the utility function that the manager maximizes. In the myopic problem, the manager optimizes the one-period utility function 10 times, and in the dynamic problem he/she optimizes the 10-period utility function. We then use the optimal weights for both problems to compute certainty equivalents with respect to the 10-period utility function. In other words, we use the myopic and dynamic policy functions to compute the certainty equivalent when the investment manager has a 10-year utility function. In this case, the myopic policy function is suboptimal. The important question is how suboptimal it is. We define the gains to dynamic investment as the ratio of the dynamic and myopic certainty equivalents.

Table 8.2 shows for different values of γ the optimal portfolio weights and certainty equivalents for the dynamic and the myopic problem. In the myopic case, the manager spreads his funds between stocks and the riskless asset and hardly invests in long-term bonds. In the dynamic case, however, it is optimal to invest part of the funds in long-term bonds as a hedge against

TABLE 8.2 Portfolio Weights and Standardized Per-Period Certainty Equivalents for a 10-Year CRRA Portfolio Optimization Problem Without Liabilities, VaR Constraint, or Sponsor Contributions

	Myopic				Dynamic				Gains (bp/a)
γ	Stocks	Risk-free	Bonds	CE scaled	Stocks	Risk-free	Bonds	CE scaled	
2	1.00	0.00	0.00	2.881	1.00	0.00	0.00	2.888	2.7
	(0.000)	(0.000)	(0.000)	(0.008)	(0.000)	(0.000)	(0.000)	(0.012)	(0.1)
5	0.50	0.50	0.00	2.384	0.57	0.07	0.36	2.439	23.08
	(0.01)	(0.02)	(0.01)	(0.007)	(0.01)	(0.01)	(0.02)	(0.008)	(1.14)

Due to the power utility specification over wealth, the weights are independent of the wealth level at time zero. The portfolio weights are rebalanced annually. We run 50 simulations and report averages and standard deviations (within parentheses). In the last column (gain in basis points per year), we take the ratio of the certainty equivalents to the power 1/10, subtract 1 and multiply by 10,000, to get the gains to dynamic (strategic) investment compared to myopic (tactical) investment in basis points per year.

changes in the investment opportunity set for stocks. When there is a drop in the 15-year yield, the return on bonds in the current period are high, which forms a hedge against the lower future risk premium on stocks. Even though the hedging demands can be large, the utility gains, as expressed by the net ratio of the dynamic and myopic certainty equivalents, are relatively small. They vary between 3 and 23 basis points per year depending on the degree of risk aversion. These low gains to dynamic investment are caused by the relatively flat peak of the 10-period value function.

ACKNOWLEDGMENTS

We thank Jonathan Berk, Tim Bollerslev, Peter DeMarzo, Frank de Jong, Joachim Inkmann, Ralph Koijen, Vinay Nair, Theo Nijman, Anamaría Pieschacón, Josh Rauh, George Tauchen, Bas Werker, Marcus Whitehead, and the seminar participants at the 2005 SAMSI conference on Financial Mathematics, Statistics, and Econometrics, the Asset Allocation in Uncertain Times conference at Cass University, Duke University, Tilburg University, and ABP Investments for helpful discussions and comments. Jules van Binsbergen thanks the Prins Bernhard Cultuurfonds for generous financial support.

REFERENCES

Aït-Sahalia Y, Brandt MW. Variable selection for portfolio choice. J Finance 2001;56(4):1297–1350.
Ang A, Bekaert G. Stock return predictability, is it there? Rev Financ Stud 2007;20(3):651–707.
Basak S, Pavlova A, Shapiro A. Optimal asset allocation and risk shifting in money management. Rev Financ Stud 2007;20(5):1583–1621.
Basak S, Shapiro A, Teplá L. Risk management with benchmarking. Manage Sci 2006;52:542–557.
Berkelaar A, Kouwenberg R. Retirement saving with contribution payments and labor income as a benchmark for investments. J Econ Dyn Control 2003;27/6:1069–1097.
van Binsbergen JH, Brandt MW, Koijen RSJ. Optimal decentralized investment management. J Finance 2008;4:1849–1895.
van Binsbergen JH, Koijen RSJ. Predictive regressions: a present-value approach. J Finance 2010;65:1439–1471.
Black F. The tax consequences of long-run pension policy. Financ Anal J 1980;36(4):21–28.
Black F, Karasinski P. Bond and option pricing when Short rates are Lognormal. Financ Anal J 1991;47:52–59.
Boulier J, Trussant E, Florens D. A dynamic model for pension funds management. Proceedings of the 5th AFIR International Colloquium, Volume 1; 1995. p 361–384.
Brandt MW. Estimating portfolio and consumption choice: a conditional Euler equations approach. J Finance 1999;54(5):1609–1645.
Brandt MW. Portfolio choice problems. In: Ait-Sahalia Y, Hansen LP, editors. *Handbook of Financial Econometrics: Tools and Techniques*. Volume 1. North Holland; 2010. p 269–336.
Brandt MW, Goyal A, Santa-Clara P, Stroud JR. A simulation approach to dynamic portfolio choice with an application to learning about return predictability. Rev Financ Stud 2005;18:831–873.
Campbell JY, Viceira LM. Consumption and portfolio decisions when expected returns are time varying. Q J Econ 1999;114:433–495.
Campbell JY, Viceira LM. *Strategic Asset Allocation: Portfolio Choice for Long-Term Investors*. New York: Oxford University Press; 2002.
Campbell JY, Viceira LM. Strategic asset allocation for pension plans. In: Clark G, Munnell A, Orszag J, editors. *Oxford Handbook of Pensions and Retirement Income*. Oxford University Press; 2006.
Campbell JY, Yogo M. Efficient tests of stock return predictability. J Financ Econ 2005;81(1):27–60.
Chacko G, Viceira L. Dynamic consumption and portfolio choice with stochastic volatility in incomplete markets. Rev Financ Stud 2005;18(4):1369–1402.
Cochrane JH. The sensitivity of tests of the intertemporal allocation of consumption to near-rational alternatives. Am Econ Rev 1989;79:319–337.
Cochrane JH, Piazzesi M. Bond risk premia. Am Econ Rev 2005;95(1):138–160.
Dai Q, Singleton KJ. Expectation puzzles, time-varying risk premia, and affine models of the term structure. J Financ Econ 2002;63(3):415–441.
Fama EF. Multiperiod consumption-investment decisions. Am Econ Rev 1970;60:163–174.
Geanakoplos J, Dubey P, Shubik M. Default and punishment in general equilibrium. Econometrica 2005;73:1–37.
Hoevenaars R, Molenaar R, Schotman P, Steenkamp T. Strategic asset allocation with liabilities: beyond stocks and bonds, working paper. Maastricht University; 2004.
Kahneman D, Tversky A. Prospect theory: an analysis of decision under risk. Econometrica 1979;47:263–292.
Kim TS, Omberg E. Dynamic nonmyopic portfolio behavior. Rev Financ Stud 1996;9(1):141–162.
Lewellen J. Predicting returns with financial ratios. J Financ Econ 2004;74(2):209–235.
Longstaff FA, Schwartz ES. Valuing American options by simulation: a simple least-squares approach. Rev Financ Stud 2001;14:113–147.
Markowitz HM. Portfolio selection. J Finance 1952;7:77–91.
Merton RC. Lifetime portfolio selection under uncertainty: the continuous time case. Rev Econ Stat 1969;51:247–257.
Merton RC. Optimum consumption and portfolio rules in a continuous-time model. J Econ Theory 1971;3:373–413.
Novy-Marx R, Rauh J. Public pension promises: how big are they and what are they worth? J Finance 2010;66(4):1207–1245.
Samuelson PA. Lifetime portfolio selection by dynamic stochastic programming. Rev Econ Stat 1969;51:239–246.

Sangvinatsos A, Wachter J. Does the failure of the expectations hypothesis matter for long-term investors? J Finance 2005;60(1):179–230.
Sharpe WF. Corporate pension funding policy. J Financ Econ 1976;3:183–193.
Shubik M, Wilson C. The optimal bankruptcy rule in a trading economy using fiat money. Z Nationalokon 1977;37:337–354.
Sundaresan SM, Zapatero F. Valuation, asset allocation and incentive retirements of pension plans. Rev Financ Stud 1997;10:631–660.
Tebaldi C, Veronesi P. Risk neutral pricing: Monte Carlo simulations. In: Veronesi P, editor. *Handbook of Fixed Income*. John Wiley & Sons; 2015.
Tepper I. Taxation and corporate pension policy. J Finance 1981;36:1–13.
Torous W, Valkanov R, Yan S. On predicting stock returns with nearly integrated explanantory variables. J Bus 2005;77(4):937–966.

PART IV

The Predictability of Bond Returns

9

International Bond Risk Premia

Magnus Dahlquist[a] **and Henrik Hasseltoft**[b]

[a]*Department of Finance, Stockholm School of Economics, Stockholm, Sweden*
[b]*Department of Banking and Finance, University of Zurich, Zurich, Switzerland*

9.1 INTRODUCTION

The endeavor to understand bond returns and the term structure of interest rates has generated an extensive literature, ranging from papers on return predictability and affine term structure models to theoretical contributions in the form of equilibrium models. While most of the empirical literature focuses on U.S. data, a large body of work applies an international perspective. This chapter reviews the relevant literature while also providing empirical evidence on international bond risk premia and the link to the macroeconomy.

The expectations hypothesis of interest rates is commonly expressed in three forms: long-term interest rates equal average expected future short-term rates plus a risk premium, forward rates equal expected future interest rates plus a risk premium, and the expected one-period return on bonds equals the one-period interest rate plus a risk premium. All formulations of the expectations hypothesis restrict risk premia on government bonds to being zero or at least constant over time.[1] As such, the expectations hypothesis leaves no room for time-varying risk premia or compensation for risk.

An extensive literature has empirically examined whether risk premia on government bonds are indeed constant over time. The standard way of testing the expectations hypothesis is by running predictability regressions in which future realized bond returns in excess of the risk-free rate are regressed on predictive variables such as the spread between yields on long- and short-term bonds or the spread between forward and spot rates. A statistically significant slope coefficient in such a regression implies that future bond excess returns are predictable or, equivalently, that bond risk premia are time varying. Hence, excess return predictability and time-varying risk premia are two sides of the same coin, both violating the expectations hypothesis.

For academic researchers, the interest in predictability lies mainly in understanding why investors' required risk compensation should vary over time. Such time variation may arise through either rational or irrational channels. Asset pricing theory suggests that rational variation in risk premia and therefore predictability may arise from either time-varying economic risks or time-varying risk aversion among investors. This suggests that future excess returns can be predictable even if markets are efficient. For example, academic evidence suggests that investors require higher risk premia on nominal bonds during economic

[1]The pure expectations hypothesis sets risk premia to zero. Cox, Ingersoll, and Ross (1981) demonstrate that various formulations of the pure expectations hypothesis are inconsistent with one another when interest rates are random due to Jensen's inequality. Campbell (1986) demonstrates that this is generally not the case for the less restrictive form of the expectations hypothesis in which risk premia are nonzero but constant, which is what the empirical literature is mostly concerned with. We will consider alternative ways of empirically evaluating the expectations hypothesis.

Handbook of Fixed-Income Securities, First Edition. Edited by Pietro Veronesi.

recessions, when economic uncertainty and investors' risk aversion arguably increase. However, rather than reflecting rational variation in risk premia, predictability may also arise from market inefficiencies and irrational investor behavior. For example, empirical evidence in behavioral finance suggests that predictability of bond returns may reflect expectational errors made by investors whose expectations deviate from rational expectations.

For investors, predictability of returns is naturally attractive from an asset management perspective. Rather than implying that future returns are known with certainty, predictability of returns implies that a statistically significant return-forecasting variable can turn the odds slightly in favor of the investor compared with making a 50:50 bet. Furthermore, diversifying across several predictive variables that are less than perfectly correlated is likely to yield even greater benefits in terms of risk-adjusted returns. In practical implementation, the distinction between in-sample and out-of-sample predictability is particularly important. While evidence suggests that several variables do predict returns in sample, significant out-of-sample predictability is typically harder to come by.

The empirical analysis presented in this chapter builds on Dahlquist and Hasseltoft (2013), who found time-varying risk premia across four international bond markets. Both local and global factors were found to drive international bond risk premia, the global factor being closely linked to U.S. bond risk premia and to international business cycles. In this chapter, we expand the cross section of countries examined and refine the analysis of bond risk premia and economic growth.

We document that the standard Fama and Bliss (1987, Fama–Bliss (FB)) regressions fail to predict excess returns across a broad set of countries; in contrast, Cochrane and Piazzesi (2005, Cochrane–Piazzesi (CP)) regressions seem to capture substantial predictability. Furthermore, we construct a global return-forecasting factor that, jointly with local factors, predicts excess returns across countries. International bond risk premia seem to be driven by both local and global factors, the global factor being closely linked to U.S. bond risk premia. The fact that global and U.S. risk premia are closely related is consistent with the literature on real integration in which, for example, Kose, Otrok, and Whiteman (2003) identify a common factor in world business cycles that is highly correlated with U.S. output growth.

Consistent with asset pricing theory, we find that a rise in global bond risk premia is contemporaneously negatively correlated with global economic growth, a 1% rise in global risk premia being associated with a drop of 0.5–1% in annualized economic growth in three large economic areas, that is, the European Monetary Union (EMU), OECD, and United States. In addition, we find that the global factor positively predicts economic growth, a one-percentage-point increase in global bond risk premia being associated with a 0.5–1.3% annualized increase in future economic growth. Hence, a rise in global bond risk premia is contemporaneously associated with bad economic times but signals improved times ahead.

Though bond risk premia are positive on average, we find that bond risk premia turn negative during some periods. Negative bond risk premia suggest that nominal bonds act as hedging assets rather than risky assets. To further analyze the riskiness of bonds, we calculate rolling betas of nominal bonds with equity and find that bond betas turned negative around year 2000 in all countries, bottoming around the time of the financial crisis. These findings are consistent with what Campbell, Sunderam, and Viceira (2013) document for U.S. data. In addition, we find that movements in bond betas are highly correlated across countries, again suggesting that global and systematic factors may drive changes in the riskiness of nominal bonds.

We also analyze whether global bond risk premia display any state dependency with respect to economic recessions and expansions. Evidence from equity markets suggests that traditional return predictors such as price–dividend ratios mainly predict returns in bad economic times (e.g., Henkel, Martin, and Nardari, 2011). We test this by predicting international bond excess returns using our global factor, conditioning on the state of the economy. We define recessions outside the United States using data from the Economic Cycle Research Institute while using NBER-dated recessions for the United States. Unlike in equity markets, we find no evidence of state dependency in bond markets, meaning that our global factor predicts returns across business cycles.

The chapter proceeds as follows. Section 9.2 reviews the literature on bond return predictability and term structure modeling. Section 9.3 presents our notation and data on international bond markets. Section 9.4 presents and discusses the unconditional properties of international bond risk premia. Section 9.5 examines conditional bond risk premia by running various predictability regressions. Section 9.6 interprets the findings and links international bond risk premia to global economic growth and business cycles. Section 9.7 concludes the chapter.

9.2 LITERATURE REVIEW

As far back as the 1960s, Kessel (1965) studied whether the expectations hypothesis of interest rates could explain the level and cyclical behavior of interest rates, and Van Horne (1965) studied the risk premium component embedded in forward rates. More recently, the expectations hypothesis has typically been tested by running predictability regressions in which excess bond returns are regressed on one or several predictive variables. The seminal contributions of FB (1987) and Campbell and Shiller (1991) use the spread between forward and spot rates and the slope of the spot yield curve, respectively, as forecasting variables. They find significant evidence of time-varying risk premia in U.S. bond markets, soundly rejecting the expectations hypothesis. CP (2005) identify a factor in the form of a linear combination of U.S. forward rates that predicts excess returns with roughly double the explanatory power of traditional regressions. Interestingly, the CP factor is largely unrelated to the traditional level, slope, and curvature factors that drive variation in interest rate levels (e.g., Litterman and Scheinkman, 1991). This raises the question of how an interest rate factor can contain important information about risk premia while having a small effect on the cross section of yields. Duffee (2011) analyzes this question and documents a hidden factor in yields that has offsetting effects on risk premia and expectations of future short-term interest rates, leaving the level of yields largely unaffected. Hence, it seems that certain information about future bond returns is not easily summarized by current interest rates. This possibility is supported by Ludvigson and Ng (2009) and Cooper and Priestley (2009), who identify U.S. macro factors that add incremental predictive power beyond the yield-based factors.

In contrast to the fairly robust U.S. evidence against the expectations hypothesis, the international evidence is mixed. For example, Ilmanen (1995) constructs a proxy for risk aversion in the form of the inverse of the real stock market level and finds that it significantly predicts international bond returns, while Hardouvelis (1994) and Bekaert and Hodrick (2001) both find it difficult to reject the expectations hypothesis based on international data. In addition, Dahlquist and Hasseltoft (2013) find weak international evidence against the expectations hypothesis when running FB regressions. However, they document substantial international predictive power when running local and global CP (GCP) regressions, suggesting that there is significant time variation in international bond risk premia after all.

A different stream of literature centers on affine term structure models. The list of relevant contributions in this stream is too long to cite in full but includes Duffie and Kan (1996), Dai and Singleton (2000, 2002), Duffee (2002), Ang and Piazzesi (2003), CP (2008), and Joslin, Priebsch, and Singleton (2014). The affine models typically use a set of latent variables, such as the level, slope, and curvature factors of interest rates, to price bonds, sometimes complementing them with macroeconomic variables. Focusing on international yields, Diebold, Li, and Yue (2008) build on Nelson and Siegel (1987) and document global yield curve factors that appear to be linked to global macroeconomic factors such as inflation and real activity. Wright (2011) decomposes a cross section of international yields into term premia and expected future short-term rates. He finds that term premia have declined globally, in line with the level of yields, since the 1990s and links this to a drop in inflation uncertainty and changes in monetary policy. Bauer, Rudebusch, and Wu (2014) address Wright's (2011) estimation and demonstrate that correcting for small-sample bias in the estimation of affine term structure models changes the conclusion regarding international term premia. Rather than mirroring the long-term downward trend in interest rates, adjusting for small-sample bias renders international term premia countercyclical and consequently more consistent with asset pricing theory.

The endeavor to understand movements in interest rates and bond risk premia has produced a large number of equilibrium models, with early contributions such as Cox, Ingersoll, and Ross (1985), Dunn and Singleton (1986), and Backus, Gregory, and Zin (1989). Building on Campbell and Cochrane's (1999) consumption-based framework of habit formation in which investors' risk aversion rises in bad economic times but the amount of economic risk is constant, Brandt and Wang (2003), Wachter (2006), and Buraschi and Jiltsov (2007) all find that habit formation can generate time-varying bond risk premia. In contrast, Hasseltoft (2012) and Bansal and Shaliastovich (2013) build on the long-run risk framework of Bansal and Yaron (2004), in which investors' risk aversion is constant but the amount of economic risk varies, and demonstrate that time-varying macroeconomic volatility can generate bond return predictability similar to that observed in the data. Another area of relevant theoretical models is the disaster risk models. Barro (2006) builds on Rietz (1988) and demonstrates that the presence of low-probability but large economic disasters, such as the Great Depression, can account for the equity risk premium and the volatility of stock returns. Gabaix (2012) argues that a disaster risk model in which the severity of disasters varies over time can explain several asset pricing puzzles, including the predictability of bond excess returns. In this model, inflation is assumed to increase in periods of economic disaster, leading to low bond returns in bad times and therefore making nominal bonds risky assets. Time variation in the severity of disaster risk allows for time-varying risk premia and therefore predictable excess returns.

Moreover, work has been done to explain interest rates and bond returns using theories of portfolio rebalancing and preferred habitats (see Culbertson, 1957; Tobin, 1958; and Modigliani and Sutch, 1966, for early contributions). The portfolio rebalancing theory suggests that changes in the supply of government bonds affect interest rates. For example, increasing the supply increases the interest rate risk for investors, who consequently demand higher expected returns, leading to higher interest rates. The preferred-habitat theory moves away from the common assumption of a representative agent and models a segmented market with various investor clienteles along the yield curve, each having its own demand effect on the term structure. Krishnamurthy and Vissing-Jorgensen (2011, 2012) note that changes in the supply of government debt affect the level and slope of the yield curve. Greenwood and Vayanos (2010) provide empirical support for the preferred-habitat view in the forms of the U.S. Treasury buyback program of 2000–2001 and the U.K. pension reform of 2004. Furthermore, Greenwood and Vayanos (2014) find that an increased supply of long-term government debt steepens the yield curve and predicts excess returns on long-term bonds.

Finally, there are several extensive reviews of the term structure of interest rates. Shiller (1990) reviews fundamental concepts and theories of interest rates. Dai and Singleton (2003) and Piazzesi (2010) relate fixed-income pricing to term structure models, while Gürkaynak and Wright (2012) and Duffee (2013) review the link between the term structure of interest rates and the macroeconomy. While the empirical analysis in these reviews centers on U.S. data, less is known about international term structures, which are the focus of this chapter.

9.3 NOTATION AND INTERNATIONAL BOND MARKET DATA

9.3.1 Notation

We use standard notation throughout the chapter. The annual return on an n-period bond is defined as $r^n_{t+1} = p^{n-1}_{t+1} - p^n_t$, where p denotes the log bond price and the maturity, n, and time, t, are defined in terms of years. (We will consider data sampled on annual as well as monthly bases. For convenience, we keep the notation for time in years even when we are sampling data on a monthly basis.) The log yield of a bond is computed as $y^n_t = -p^n_t/n$. The annual return in excess of the 1-year yield is defined as $rx^n_{t+1} = r^n_{t+1} - y^1_t$. We define the 1-year forward rate between periods $n-1$ and n as the differential in log bond prices, $f^n_t = p^{n-1}_t - p^n_t$. We consider returns for several countries but typically suppress the country indexation, c, of variables unless we find it is necessary to avoid confusion.

9.3.2 International Bond Market Data

We consider four datasets when analyzing unconditional and conditional bond risk premia. First, we use the Dimson, Marsh, and Staunton (DMS) dataset, obtained from Morningstar and used by Dimson, Marsh, and Staunton (2002, 2014). This dataset contains annual bond excess returns on long-term bonds, covering 21 countries over the 1900–2013 period.[2] Taking a long-term perspective is interesting because the international bond market data used in academic studies typically start in the 1970s or later. Second, we use an updated version of the dataset used in Dahlquist and Hasseltoft (2013), which allows us to run predictability regressions starting in the 1970s. This dataset covers four countries, that is, Germany, Switzerland, the United Kingdom, and the United States, and covers the period from January 1975 to December 2013. All yields are based on zero-coupon bonds for maturities of 1–5 years: German yields are obtained from the Bundesbank; Swiss yields are obtained from Jorion and Mishkin (1991) until December 1987, after which yields from the Swiss National Bank are used; U.K. yields are obtained from the Bank of England; and U.S. yields are obtained from the Fama–Bliss discount bond file from the Center for Research in Security Prices.

Third, we consider a shorter-term dataset that contains a richer cross section of countries. We obtain yields on derived zero-coupon bonds for ten countries from Datastream covering the period from December 1999 to December 2013.[3] Fourth, we consider a dataset from Datastream consisting of returns on Citigroup bond indexes for 19 countries. For each country, five indexes cover five maturity buckets, that is, 1–3 years, 3–5 years, 5–7 years, 7–10 years, and 10+ years. In addition, we use several complementary data in our analysis. We collect yields on long-term bonds from Global Financial Data starting in the early 1900s and spanning the same set of countries as in DMS. We obtain annual PPP-adjusted gross domestic product (GDP) data from Datastream, which are used to construct a global return-forecasting factor, and we also consider data on industrial production and economic leading indicators from the OECD. Finally, we relate bond and equity returns as described later.

9.4 UNCONDITIONAL RISK PREMIA

We start by describing the unconditional properties of bond excess returns around the world. We do so by first applying a broad long-term approach using the DMS dataset, providing us with an understanding of excess returns on long-term bonds since 1900. We then apply a more refined and detailed approach to how excess returns have evolved across countries and maturities since the 1970s.

9.4.1 A Long-Term Perspective

Before reporting and discussing long-term risk premia, it is helpful first to consider some caveats regarding the data. Some countries in particular have undergone extreme episodes since 1900. The German hyperinflation from 1922 to 1923 caused investors in German bonds and bills to lose their entire investment. Austria also experienced extreme volatility in the 1920s and 1930s. Furthermore, international bond markets have undergone periods of turbulence due to two World Wars, several instances of civil war, and regulatory changes or financial repression over the years. These events all represent periods in which yields were not subject to regular market forces. Two examples of many in terms of regulations include those of the United States, where

[2]The DMS bond indexes are equal-weighted portfolios of long-term bonds with a desired maturity of 20 years. If no such bonds are available, either perpetuals or shorter-maturity bonds are used.

[3]The zero-coupon yields provided by Datastream are derived from interbank instruments such as futures and swaps and therefore contain a credit risk component; however, using these yields provides us with a richer cross section of markets. Furthermore, yields from Bundesbank, the Swiss National Bank, and Datastream use annual compounding, while the remaining yields use continuous compounding. We accordingly convert annually compounded yields to continuously compounded yields.

TABLE 9.1 Means and Standard Deviations of Bond Excess Returns

	Mean	Standard deviation	Mean I	Mean II	Mean III
Australia	0.83	10.16	1.51	−0.34	1.34
Austria	4.35	43.02	11.11	−0.98	2.91
Belgium	0.48	9.18	0.02	−1.19	2.60
Canada	0.59	8.21	−0.93	0.03	2.69
Denmark	0.93	8.51	−0.30	−0.33	3.43
Finland	0.55	5.56	−0.47	0.28	1.85
France	2.81	7.51	−0.43	3.14	5.72
Germany	0.77	10.29	−1.66	0.90	2.94
Ireland	0.73	11.38	−0.21	−1.39	3.78
Italy	2.19	8.10	1.13	1.79	3.64
Japan	0.91	13.55	−0.60	−0.57	3.89
Netherlands	0.89	7.47	0.05	−0.15	2.78
New Zealand	0.37	6.88	0.28	0.42	0.42
Norway	0.62	8.17	−0.59	1.37	1.08
Portugal	1.73	17.47	8.52	−3.85	0.53
South Africa	0.86	7.85	1.56	0.12	0.90
Spain	1.13	9.27	0.34	1.36	1.71
Sweden	0.65	8.73	0.76	−1.14	2.34
Switzerland	1.41	5.94	0.24	1.36	2.62
United Kingdom	0.50	10.25	−0.30	−1.26	3.06
United States	0.98	8.22	−0.51	0.08	3.36

This table presents means and standard deviations of annual log returns on bonds in excess of log returns on bills. The sample period is 1900–2013, yielding 114 annual observations. The right-hand side of the table presents means for three subperiods: I. 1900–1937, II. 1938–1975, and III. 1976–2013. Each subperiod has 38 annual observations. The statistics for Germany exclude the hyperinflationary period 1922–23. Means and standard deviations are expressed in percentage per year. Data sources are given in Section 9.3.2.

long-term rates were capped at 2.5% throughout the 1940s, and of Japan, where bond yields experienced extended periods of tight regulation before the start of financial liberalization in 1975.[4]

Table 9.1 reports the means and volatilities of annual realized bond excess returns for the DMS dataset covering the 1900–2013 period. In addition to the means and standard deviations of the entire sample period, we also report the means for three subsamples: 1900–1937, 1938–1975, and 1976–2013. The table shows that the averages for the entire sample period were positive in all countries, albeit subject to high volatility, making standard errors large (untabulated). Austria experienced the highest annual volatility at 43%, while Finland experienced the lowest at approximately 5%. The last three columns in the table refer to the three subsamples. Historical bond risk premia have increased over time, with most countries exhibiting realized risk premia of 2% or more since 1976. The level of risk premia for a particular subperiod is related to the initial yield of that period, as interest rates tend to exhibit mean reversion over time. This is evident from Figure 9.1, in which the solid line plots the average long-term nominal yield across 21 countries, using data from Global Financial Data. The average nominal yield peaks in 1981, after which there is a continued downward drift with consequently high realized returns. A principal component analysis of the international long-term nominal yields reveals a first factor that explains 76% of the variation, suggesting significant commonality across countries. This commonality has increased over time, with the first factor explaining 50% of the variation in the first half of the sample period and 78% in the second half.

Nominal interest rates can be decomposed into three components: the real interest rate, expected inflation over the maturity of the bond, and an inflation risk premium. The real interest rate is an interesting and useful concept but is difficult to measure accurately for several reasons, particularly on an ex ante basis. Reliable statistical projections of long-term inflation are difficult to compute, and reliable surveys of long-term expected inflation are scarce. In addition, the inflation risk premium is difficult to measure accurately, and the result depends greatly on the methods used. A direct way of measuring the real interest rate is to use yields on real government bonds, that is, inflation-protected bonds or index-linked bonds. A drawback of this approach is that the available time series are short as, for example, real bonds began to be issued in 1981 in the United Kingdom and 1997 in the United States. The principal and coupon payments on a real bond are typically indexed to a measure of consumer price inflation, protecting the investor against inflation risk. Campbell, Shiller, and Viceira (2009) describe the history of real bonds

[4] See Homer and Sylla (2005) for a long-term review of international bond markets.

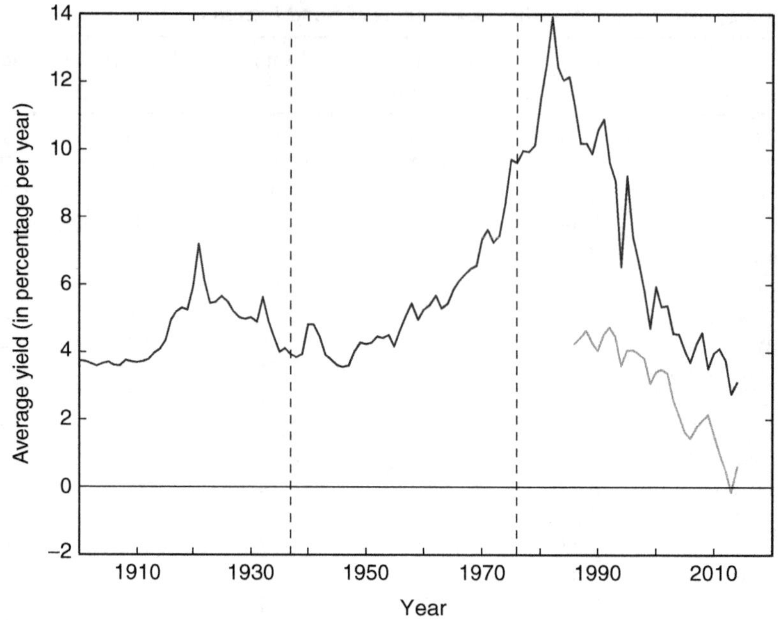

Figure 9.1 Average long-term international yields. This figure shows global nominal and real interest rates. The black line represents the equal-weighted average of nominal 10-year government yields across 21 countries, excluding Germany for the hyperinflationary period 1922–23. The grey line represents the equal-weighted average of 10-year real interest rates across G7 countries, as computed by King and Low (2014). The dashed vertical lines indicate the subperiods considered in Table 9.1. Source: Global Financial Data and King and Low (2014).

in the United States and United Kingdom and highlight various institutional factors, such as market segmentation and liquidity, that affect yields on real bonds. Pflueger and Viceira (2011) also study nominal and real bonds in the United States and United Kingdom and find the expectations hypothesis to be violated in both markets, implying that excess returns on real bonds are also predictable. Related to the international focus of this chapter is King and Low (2014), who describe the market for real bonds across a number of countries and construct a "world" real interest rate comprising 10-year real yields from the G7 countries. Their estimate of the global real rate starts in 1985 and is plotted as the dotted line in Figure 9.1. The figure shows that both real and nominal rates have been in a downward trend since the 1980s, though the difference between the two rates, referred to as the break-even inflation rate, has varied over time. The drop in break-even inflation over time suggests that inflation expectations have declined from elevated levels in the 1980s to lower levels today. However, it is noteworthy that the break-even inflation rate reflects not only the expected inflation but also the inflation risk premium and potentially a liquidity premium.

9.4.2 More Recent Evidence

The sample with yields since 1975 allows us to make a more detailed examination of historical bond risk premia. Table 9.2 reports the first four moments and the Sharpe ratios of annual bond excess returns for Germany, Switzerland, the United Kingdom, and the United States over the 1976–2013 period. Measured risk premia for maturities of 2–5 years are considered. First, average excess returns and volatility tend to be significantly different from zero across countries and increase with maturity. Second, the skewness of excess returns tends to be insignificantly different from zero, except for the German bonds, which exhibited negative skewness throughout the period. Third, excess returns in all countries display kurtosis close to 3, being in the region of the normal distribution. It is noteworthy that the skewness and kurtosis of bond returns differed from those of equity returns during this period, which in each country display large negative skewness and positive kurtosis (untabulated). Fourth, the Sharpe ratios across countries and maturities lie in the 0.30–0.40 region where, for example, the Sharpe ratio of U.S. bonds declines with maturity. The Sharpe ratios tend to be significantly different from zero and larger than the corresponding Sharpe ratios for equities, which are approximately 0.20 in Switzerland and the United States and close to zero in Germany and the United Kingdom.

In line with Litterman and Scheinkman (1991), the variation in yields can be summarized into three principal components, that is, the level, slope, and curvature factors, with the level factor accounting for more than 97% of the variation within each country. Pooling all international yields reveals a level factor that explains 90% of the variation, indicating the existence of a global-level factor in local term structures. A principal component analysis of the pooled excess bond returns results in a common factor that explains 70% of the variation. These observations relate to Driessen, Melenberg, and Nijman (2003), who examine variations in international bond returns and identify a world-level factor that explains approximately 50% of the variation. Furthermore,

TABLE 9.2 Summary Statistics for Bond Excess Returns

	Maturity	Mean	Standard deviation	Skewness	Kurtosis	Sharpe ratio
Germany	2	0.64	1.40	−0.52	3.74	0.45
		(0.20)	(0.13)	(0.30)	(0.82)	(0.17)
	3	1.25	2.61	−0.51	3.30	0.48
		(0.37)	(0.22)	(0.26)	(0.70)	(0.16)
	4	1.77	3.66	−0.56	3.26	0.48
		(0.52)	(0.31)	(0.25)	(0.67)	(0.16)
	5	2.20	4.57	−0.60	3.29	0.48
		(0.64)	(0.39)	(0.24)	(0.65)	(0.17)
Switzerland	2	0.40	1.73	0.22	4.23	0.23
		(0.25)	(0.19)	(0.31)	(0.68)	(0.14)
	3	0.94	2.98	0.22	3.77	0.31
		(0.42)	(0.31)	(0.28)	(0.61)	(0.14)
	4	1.45	4.00	0.10	3.53	0.36
		(0.56)	(0.39)	(0.27)	(0.58)	(0.14)
	5	1.81	4.85	−0.02	3.38	0.37
		(0.67)	(0.46)	(0.28)	(0.54)	(0.15)
United Kingdom	2	0.54	1.76	0.43	4.78	0.31
		(0.23)	(0.19)	(0.37)	(0.95)	(0.13)
	3	1.07	3.21	0.38	4.32	0.33
		(0.40)	(0.30)	(0.30)	(0.66)	(0.12)
	4	1.51	4.54	0.35	4.35	0.33
		(0.55)	(0.42)	(0.32)	(0.59)	(0.12)
	5	1.93	5.72	0.31	4.41	0.34
		(0.69)	(0.54)	(0.33)	(0.58)	(0.12)
United States	2	0.73	1.81	−0.19	3.76	0.40
		(0.26)	(0.17)	(0.29)	(0.49)	(0.15)
	3	1.27	3.40	−0.28	3.64	0.37
		(0.48)	(0.32)	(0.27)	(0.45)	(0.15)
	4	1.78	4.73	−0.25	3.52	0.38
		(0.67)	(0.44)	(0.26)	(0.40)	(0.15)
	5	2.04	5.85	−0.26	3.45	0.35
		(0.82)	(0.54)	(0.26)	(0.40)	(0.15)

The table presents summary statistics (i.e., means, standard deviations, skewness, kurtosis, and Sharpe ratios) for 1-year returns on bonds with maturities of 2, 3, 4, and 5 years in excess of the return on 1-year bonds (i.e., rx^n_{t+1} with $n = 2$, 3, 4, and 5) for Germany, Switzerland, the United Kingdom, and the United States. The sample period is from January 1976 to December 2013, yielding 456 monthly return observations. Central moments are estimated using Hansen's (1982) generalized method of moments, while the standard errors of the reported statistics are derived using the delta method. The standard errors, accounting for serial correlation up to 12 lags as in Newey and West (1987), are reported within parentheses. Means and standard deviations are expressed in percentage per year. Data sources are given in Section 9.3.2.

Perignon, Smith, and Villa (2007) find that U.S. bond returns share one common factor with German and Japanese bond returns and link this to changes in the level of interest rates. Also related are the findings of Jotikasthira, Le, and Lundblad (2015), who study the high correlation of yield changes across countries and argue that a world inflation factor drives risk compensation for long-term bonds. Moreover, the yields in our sample can be well summarized as all exhibiting upward-sloping yield curves, yield levels being highly persistent, short-term rates being more volatile than long-term rates, and yield levels being highly positively correlated both within and across countries. These summary statistics for yields are not tabulated.

9.5 CONDITIONAL RISK PREMIA

Having described unconditional bond risk premia, we next consider conditional bond risk premia. As discussed earlier, an extensive literature has documented time-varying risk premia in international bond markets using a broad set of predictive variables. We focus on regressions that use yield-based predictive variables. Using several datasets, we run FB regressions, CP regressions, and regressions using a global factor constructed as the GDP-weighted average of local CP factors.

Our predictability regressions consider annual excess returns sampled on a monthly basis. Hence, there is a data overlap, inducing serial correlation in error terms. All regression results are therefore reported together with Newey and West (1987) standard errors, which account for conditional heteroskedasticity and serial correlation, with the number of lags set equal to the forecasting horizon in months. We do not consider bootstrapped standard errors in this chapter but instead refer the reader to Dahlquist and Hasseltoft (2013), who ran similar regressions. They computed bootstrapped confidence intervals for the R^2 values stemming from the predictive regressions, using the stationary block bootstrap simulation of Politis and Romano (1994) with the optimal block size of Politis and White (2004) and Politis, White, and Patton (2009). They found that incorporating bootstrapped confidence bounds in the analysis did not change the main findings. We do not address further econometric challenges such as small-sample biases due to persistence in yields and measurement errors (see, e.g., Bekaert, Hodrick, and Marshall, 1997, and Bekaert and Hodrick, 2001).

9.5.1 Local Predictors of Returns

We start by predicting excess returns using FB regressions, doing so using two datasets, one starting in 1975 and the Datastream sample starting in 1999. Annual excess returns are regressed on the differential between forward and spot rates, as follows:

$$rx^n_{t+1} = a^n + b^n FB^n_t + \epsilon^n_{t+1}, \tag{9.1}$$

where a^n and b^n are parameters, FB^n_t equals the forward–spot spread $f^n_t - y^1_t$, and ϵ^n_{t+1} is an error term. The first columns in Table 9.3 present the results for the 1975 sample. Consistent with earlier results in the literature, we find statistically significant coefficients for the United States with R^2 values ranging from 6% to 12%. Switzerland too has highly statistically significant slope coefficients. However, the results for Germany and the United Kingdom are less encouraging, suggesting that the international support for FB regressions is mixed. This is consistent with earlier findings in the literature that it is more difficult to reject the expectations hypothesis for samples outside the United States. We later consider alternative ways of evaluating the expectations hypothesis, namely, by using predictability regressions as in Campbell and Shiller (1991) and Backus et al. (2001).

The first columns in Table 9.4 present the results for the sample starting in 1999. We report the results for bonds with maturities of 2 and 5 years; the results for bonds with 3- and 4-year maturities are similar and typically lie between those for maturities of 2 and 5 years. These results paint a different picture, as only one country, Japan, is subject to statistically significant slope coefficients across maturities. There could be two reasons for the difference in results: either the sample period of 1999–2013 is too short to permit detection of predictability or the forward–spot spread lost its predictive power during this period. To shed further light on this, we next run CP regressions for the two datasets and compare the outcomes to those of the FB regressions.

We follow CP (2005) and construct local CP factors for each country for the two datasets. A CP factor is constructed by regressing average excess returns across maturities at each time, t, on the 1-year yield and four 1-year forward rates, as follows:

$$\overline{rx}_{t+1} = \gamma_0 + \gamma_1 y^1_t + \gamma_2 f^2_t + \gamma_3 f^3_t + \gamma_4 f^4_t + \gamma_5 f^5_t + \bar{\epsilon}_{t+1} \tag{9.2}$$

where $\overline{rx}_{t+1} = \sum_{n=2}^{5} rx^n_{t+1}/4$. Let the right-hand side variables, including the constant term, for each country be collected in vector f_t and let the corresponding estimated coefficients be collected in vector $\hat{\gamma}$. A local CP factor, CP_t, is then given by $\hat{\gamma}' f_t$. The CP factors as of date t are later used to predict future excess returns.[5] By construction, the CP factor at time t contains some forward-looking information, as the entire sample period is used in the construction. Dahlquist and Hasseltoft (2013) report that a recursively constructed CP factor for the United States, using only information up to time t, has a positive correlation of 0.85 with the full-sample factor. This is consistent with results presented in the appendix to CP (2005), which documents that full-sample forecasts of bond returns and real-time forecasts are quite similar.

The average pairwise correlation of CP factors in the 1975 sample is 0.28, suggesting a positive comovement of bond risk premia across countries, a comovement that has increased over time. In the first half of the 1975–2013 period, the average pairwise correlation was 0.13, while it was 0.58 in the second half. Figure 9.2 plots the local CP factors for the four countries starting in 1975. The gray areas in the graphs represent economic contractions as measured by the NBER for the United States and by the Economic Cycle Research Institute for the remaining countries.[6] Overall, the CP factors and therefore bond risk premia tend to increase during bad economic times, while there are large variations outside recessions.

[5]Cochrane and Piazzesi (2005) note that the estimated γ values are tent shaped. We also find a tent-shaped pattern for the United States, using the sample starting in 1975. However, the patterns differ for the remaining countries. Dai, Singleton, and Yang (2004) emphasize that different ways of smoothing yield curves give rise to different patterns, yields that are choppy and less smoothed producing patterns that are more tent shaped. While the U.S. yields we use are unsmoothed yields, yields for the remaining countries are smoothed, so the patterns differ. However, including only the 1-year yield, the 3-year forward rate, and the 5-year forward rate on the right-hand side tends to produce tent shapes for smoothed yields as well, without substantially changing the dynamics of the CP factor.

[6]Recession dates for the United States produced by the Economic Cycle Research Institute line up closely with the ones from NBER.

TABLE 9.3 Fama–Bliss and Cochrane–Piazzesi Regressions, 1975–2013 Sample

	Maturity	FB_t^n	R^2	CP_t	R^2
Germany	2	0.37	0.03	0.40	0.07
		(0.37)		(0.16)	
	3	0.59	0.05	0.83	0.09
		(0.42)		(0.30)	
	4	0.73	0.05	1.22	0.10
		(0.47)		(0.42)	
	5	0.84	0.06	1.55	0.10
		(0.52)		(0.53)	
Switzerland	2	0.83	0.21	0.56	0.30
		(0.22)		(0.11)	
	3	0.91	0.14	0.92	0.27
		(0.29)		(0.17)	
	4	1.00	0.12	1.17	0.24
		(0.38)		(0.21)	
	5	1.15	0.11	1.35	0.22
		(0.49)		(0.25)	
United Kingdom	2	0.34	0.03	0.41	0.08
		(0.25)		(0.15)	
	3	0.49	0.03	0.85	0.10
		(0.31)		(0.27)	
	4	0.54	0.03	1.23	0.10
		(0.36)		(0.41)	
	5	0.53	0.02	1.50	0.10
		(0.40)		(0.53)	
United States	2	0.74	0.08	0.43	0.17
		(0.29)		(0.09)	
	3	1.07	0.11	0.85	0.19
		(0.35)		(0.18)	
	4	1.25	0.12	1.26	0.21
		(0.42)		(0.25)	
	5	1.00	0.06	1.46	0.19
		(0.48)		(0.32)	

This table presents the results of Fama and Bliss (1987) and Cochrane and Piazzesi (2005) regressions, corresponding to regression equations 9.1 and 9.3. Estimates of constant terms are not tabulated. The sample period is from January 1975 to December 2013. Point estimates are reported with Newey and West (1987) standard errors, accounting for conditional heteroskedasticity and serial correlation up to 12 lags, within parentheses. Adjusted R^2 values are also reported. Data sources are given in Section 9.3.2.

We next predict annual excess returns using the local CP factors, as follows:

$$rx_{t+1}^n = a^n + b_{CP}^n CP_t + \epsilon_{t+1}^n \tag{9.3}$$

The last columns in Table 9.3 present results for the 1975 sample and constitute strong evidence of predictability. The slope coefficients are highly significant across all countries, with R^2 values varying between 7% and 30%. For countries in which the FB regressions indicate significance, the explanatory power of the CP regressions is roughly doubled. For countries in which the FB regressions indicate no evidence of predictability, the CP regressions indicate strong evidence in favor of predictability. A potential explanation for this difference in results is that the CP regressions use more information from the yield curve than do the FB regressions.

We consider the time variation in bond risk premia using fitted values from the estimated regression in 9.3. In untabulated results, we find that the bond risk premia occasionally turn negative, particularly during the period after year 2000.[7] Negative bond risk premia imply that nominal bonds in fact are hedges against bad economic times as opposed to being risky assets, such as equity. We analyze this further by computing rolling 60-day betas of nominal bonds with equity for each country. We do so

[7] A fall in term premia on long-term bonds during the 2000s, albeit not to negative levels, has been documented by, for example, Backus and Wright (2007).

TABLE 9.4 Fama–Bliss and Cochrane–Piazzesi Regressions, 1999–2013 Sample

	Maturity	FB_t^n	R^2	CP_t	R^2
Australia	2	−0.15	0.00	0.38	0.21
		(0.52)		(0.19)	
	5	0.00	0.00	1.58	0.35
		(1.30)		(0.54)	
Canada	2	0.41	0.12	0.43	0.26
		(0.18)		(0.10)	
	5	0.72	0.06	1.56	0.34
		(0.48)		(0.21)	
Denmark	2	0.24	0.03	0.39	0.11
		(0.23)		(0.19)	
	5	0.82	0.05	1.57	0.18
		(0.70)		(0.57)	
Germany	2	−0.14	0.00	0.50	0.20
		(0.58)		(0.15)	
	5	0.60	0.02	1.42	0.15
		(0.90)		(0.55)	
Japan	2	0.38	0.12	0.21	0.32
		(0.19)		(0.06)	
	5	1.27	0.19	1.87	0.52
		(0.56)		(0.27)	
Norway	2	−0.35	0.03	0.48	0.03
		(0.41)		(0.45)	
	5	−0.07	0.00	1.48	0.04
		(0.55)		(1.26)	
Sweden	2	−0.22	0.01	0.53	0.28
		(0.47)		(0.14)	
	5	0.02	0.00	1.37	0.19
		(0.88)		(0.42)	
Switzerland	2	0.17	0.00	0.46	0.33
		(0.44)		(0.11)	
	5	0.64	0.03	1.49	0.31
		(0.64)		(0.33)	
United Kingdom	2	0.35	0.01	0.33	0.06
		(0.47)		(0.12)	
	5	0.98	0.09	1.61	0.16
		(0.59)		(0.48)	
United States	2	0.23	0.01	0.50	0.27
		(0.45)		(0.13)	
	5	0.59	0.04	1.41	0.25
		(0.60)		(0.34)	

This table presents the results of Fama and Bliss (1987) and Cochrane and Piazzesi (2005) regressions, corresponding to regression equations 9.1 and 9.3. Estimates of constant terms are not tabulated. The sample period is from December 1999 to December 2013. Point estimates are reported with Newey and West (1987) standard errors, accounting for conditional heteroskedasticity and serial correlation up to 12 lags, within parentheses. Adjusted R^2 values are also reported. Data sources are given in Section 9.3.2.

by collecting daily returns on 10-year bond indexes and daily returns on broad stock market portfolios for each country from Datastream. Consistent with Campbell, Sunderam, and Viceira (2013), who document negative bond betas during the 2000s in U.S. data, we find that bond betas in Germany, Switzerland, and the United Kingdom also turned negative around year 2000 and reached a trough during the financial crisis of 2008 and 2009. Interestingly, the evolution of bond betas is highly positively correlated across countries, suggesting the existence of systematic and global factors driving the riskiness of nominal bonds. A potential explanation for the time-varying nature of bond risk is the time-varying relationship between inflation and economic growth, as pointed out by Burkhardt and Hasseltoft (2012) and David and Veronesi (2013).

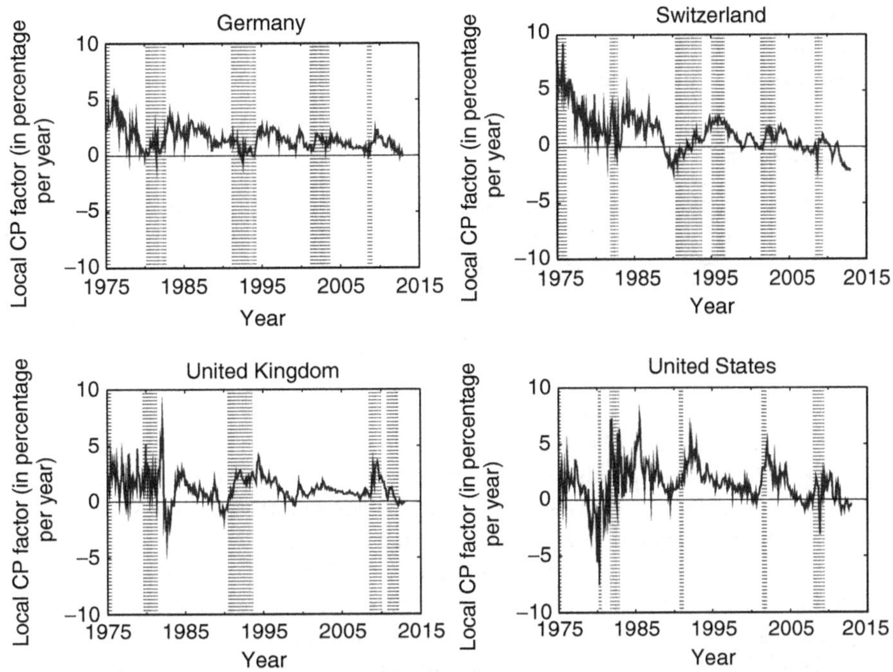

Figure 9.2 Local CP factors. The figure shows the local CP factors (in % per year) for Germany, Switzerland, the United Kingdom, and the United States. The shaded areas indicate contractions (peak to trough) as dated by the NBER for the United States and by the Economic Cycle Research Institute for the other countries. Source: CRSP, NBER, Economic Cycle Research Institute, and central banks.

We also run the regression in 9.3 using the Datastream sample starting in 1999, with the results being reported in the last columns of Table 9.4. In this broader cross section of countries, we also find support for the CP regressions. Slope coefficients are statistically significant for all countries except Norway, with R^2 values as high as 52% in the case of Japan. These results stand in stark contrast to those of the earlier FB regressions, which indicate no predictability for the sample starting in 1999. As the same sample period is used for the FB and CP regressions, the differences in results suggest that the forward–spot spread lost its predictive power over the last 13 years, whereas the CP factors seem to embody predictive information.

In addition to predicting annual excess returns, we also consider the prediction of monthly excess returns (untabulated). For the United States, we collect monthly returns from CRSP for seven portfolios of bonds sorted by maturity. We then construct a monthly CP factor in the same manner as the annual CP factor previously. The results suggest that monthly returns are also predictable but mainly for bonds with maturities greater than 3 years and with R^2 values of approximately 1–2%. Since we do not have corresponding monthly returns for the remaining countries, we construct approximate monthly returns using our existing data.[8] As with the U.S. data, we find evidence of monthly predictability mainly for bonds with maturities in excess of 3 years, except in the case of Germany, for which the predictability is weaker. We also analyze the relationship between monthly and annual CP factors within countries, finding that they have correlations of approximately 0.60–0.80. Hence, monthly and annual bond risk premia are positively but not perfectly correlated, suggesting a time variation in the term structure of risk premia.

Following Campbell and Shiller (1991) and Backus et al. (2001), we consider two alternative ways of evaluating the expectations hypothesis. Campbell and Shiller predict the change in long-term rates using the yield spread between long- and short-term bonds, that is, $y^{n-1}_{t+1} - y^n_t = a^n + b^n(y^n_t - y^1_t)/(n-1) + \epsilon^n_{t+1}$, where the expectations hypothesis implies a slope coefficient equal to one. The results for our 1975 sample are similar to those of the FB regressions, as we find statistically significant violations of the expectations hypothesis for Switzerland and the United States but not for the remaining countries. Backus et al. (2001) consider a different form of the expectations hypothesis, namely, that forward rates equal expected future interest rates, that is, $f^n_t = E_t(y^1_{t+n-1})$, which implies that forward rates are martingales, that is, $f^n_t = E_t(f^{n-1}_{t+1})$. Consequently, they suggest the regression $f^{n-1}_{t+1} - y^1_t = a^n + b^n(f^n_t - y^1_t) + \epsilon^n_{t+1}$, where the expectations hypothesis implies a slope coefficient equal to one. We run this regression for our 1975 sample and obtain results similar to those of the FB and Campbell–Shiller regressions, except for Germany, for which the expectations hypothesis is violated for 4- and 5-year bonds. Overall, the estimated slope coefficients are less than one and increase with maturity.

[8]Since we only have data on bonds with annual maturities, we approximate the monthly returns by assuming one buys an n-year bond and sells it 1 month later at a price computed from the yield of an n-year bond but with a maturity equal to n years minus 1 month. The excess return of a bond is over a 1-month rate for the United States but over a 3-month rate for the remaining countries due to data availability.

To summarize our results, the regressions of FB (1987), Campbell and Shiller (1991), and Backus et al. (2001) provide strong evidence against the expectations hypothesis in U.S. data but considerably weaker evidence in international data. In contrast, CP regressions document statistically significant predictability across all countries.

9.5.2 Global Predictors of Returns

Having established time variation in bond risk premia stemming from country-specific factors, we next analyze whether there also exists a common global factor driving risk premia. We construct a GCP factor as the GDP-weighted average of all local CP factors, now denoted with subscript c for each country, at time t, as follows:

$$GCP_t = \sum_{c=1}^{C} w_{c,t} CP_{c,t} \tag{9.4}$$

where $w_{c,t} = GDP_{c,t} / \sum_{c=1}^{C} GDP_{c,t}$ and where $C = 4$ for the 1975 sample and $C = 10$ for the 1999 sample. The GDP weights used in 1 year are based on the GDP of the previous year. For example, the average weights for the months in the 1975 sample are based on the GDP in 1974 and are 0.19 for Germany, 0.02 for Switzerland, 0.10 for the United Kingdom, and 0.69 for the United States. Hence, the size-weighted global risk factor is dominated by the United States in this sample. Using GDP weights to construct the global factor as opposed to, for example, using the first principal component of the covariance matrix of local CP factors is appealing as it does not introduce an extra layer of forward-looking information. Figure 9.3 plots the global factor together with U.S. recessions and suggests that the level of global bond risk premia tend to increase during U.S. recessions. The figure also shows that global bond risk premia on occasions have turned negative, in particular around 1980 and during the most recent years.

We run the following monthly regression, predicting annual bond excess returns with the global factor, as follows:

$$rx_{t+1}^{n} = a^{n} + b_{GCP}^{n} GCP_t + \epsilon_{t+1}^{n} \tag{9.5}$$

Table 9.5 reports results for the 1975 sample and shows that the global factor predicts local bond returns across all four countries, with the economic magnitude of the regression coefficients and the explanatory power being similar to when using local CP factors, except in the case of Germany, where the global factor doubles the R^2 to 20%. As the local U.S. CP factor receives approximately 70% of the weight of the global factor, our results suggest that U.S. bond risk premia carry economically great predictive power for bond returns outside the United States.

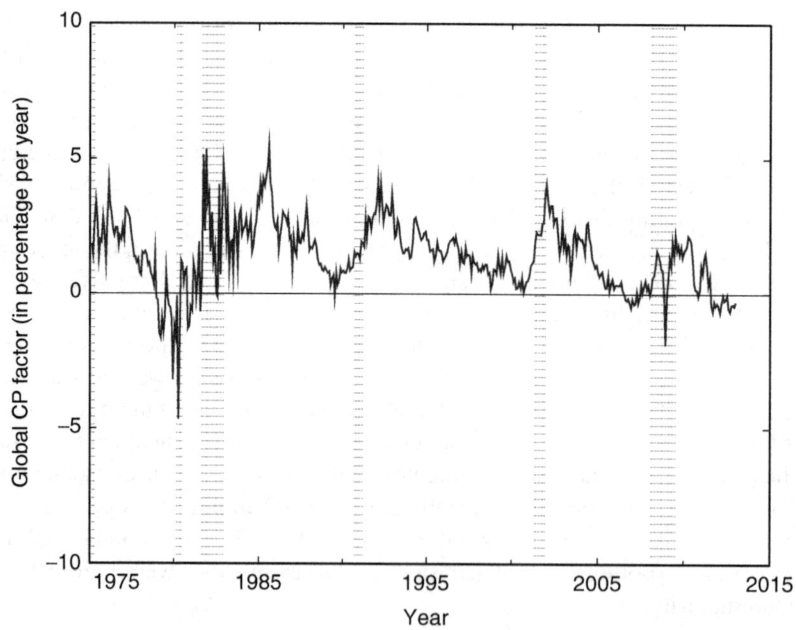

Figure 9.3 Global CP factor. The figure shows the global CP factor (in % per year). It is a GDP-weighted average of the local CP factors for Germany, Switzerland, the United Kingdom, and the United States. The shaded areas indicate U.S. contractions (peak to trough) as dated by the NBER. Source: CRSP, NBER, and central banks.

TABLE 9.5 Local and Global Cochrane–Piazzesi Regressions, 1975–2013 Sample

	Maturity	GCP_t	R^2	CP_t	GCP_t	R^2	Wald
Germany	2	0.50	0.21	0.15	0.50	0.22	[0.00]
		(0.08)		(0.14)	(0.08)		
	3	0.93	0.20	0.40	0.93	0.22	[0.00]
		(0.15)		(0.27)	(0.15)		
	4	1.26	0.19	0.65	1.26	0.22	[0.00]
		(0.21)		(0.40)	(0.22)		
	5	1.55	0.19	0.87	1.55	0.21	[0.00]
		(0.28)		(0.50)	(0.29)		
Switzerland	2	0.60	0.19	0.46	0.60	0.36	[0.00]
		(0.11)		(0.13)	(0.13)		
	3	1.05	0.20	0.72	1.15	0.34	[0.00]
		(0.21)		(0.20)	(0.24)		
	4	1.41	0.20	0.90	1.41	0.33	[0.00]
		(0.29)		(0.26)	(0.33)		
	5	1.70	0.20	1.01	1.70	0.30	[0.00]
		(0.35)		(0.30)	(0.40)		
United Kingdom	2	0.40	0.08	0.34	0.40	0.13	[0.00]
		(0.14)		(0.14)	(0.13)		
	3	0.72	0.08	0.72	0.72	0.15	[0.00]
		(0.26)		(0.26)	(0.23)		
	4	1.04	0.08	1.04	1.04	0.15	[0.00]
		(0.36)		(0.38)	(0.32)		
	5	1.35	0.09	1.24	1.35	0.15	[0.00]
		(0.43)		(0.49)	(0.40)		
United States	2	0.57	0.16	0.42	0.57	0.17	[0.00]
		(0.13)		(0.46)	(0.12)		
	3	1.11	0.17	1.12	1.11	0.19	[0.00]
		(0.27)		(0.82)	(0.25)		
	4	1.65	0.20	1.67	1.65	0.21	[0.00]
		(0.38)		(1.03)	(0.35)		
	5	1.91	0.17	1.67	1.91	0.18	[0.00]
		(0.48)		(1.25)	(0.45)		

The table presents the results of local and global Cochrane and Piazzesi (2005) regressions, corresponding to regression equations 9.5 and 9.6 for maturities $n = 2, 3, 4$, and 5. Estimates of constant terms are not tabulated. When both local and global CP factors are included, the local factor is orthogonalized relative to the global factor. The sample period is from January 1975 to December 2013. Point estimates are reported with Newey and West (1987) standard errors, accounting for conditional heteroskedasticity and serial correlation up to twelve lags, within parentheses. Adjusted R^2 values are also reported. P-Values from Wald tests of joint significance are presented in square brackets. Data sources are given in Section 9.3.2.

Table 9.6 presents results for the shorter sample period. Again, we only report results for maturities of 2 and 5 years. Results are consistent with those for the longer sample period in that the global factor predicts local bond returns in all but two countries. In general, the magnitude of the slope coefficients and the explanatory power are somewhat less than when using local CP factors, except in the case of the United States, where in fact the global factor seems to have a somewhat larger effect on bond risk premia.[9]

We also run regressions in which we predict annual excess returns on Citigroup bond indexes using the global factor across 19 countries. For each country, we predict excess returns on five different maturity buckets. In untabulated results, we find estimated slope coefficients to be positive across all countries except Ireland, suggesting that the global factor raises risk premia across countries and maturities. However, the statistical significance is lower in this sample, with only about half the countries having statistically significant regression coefficients.

Finally, we consider predictive regressions with both local and global factors as independent variables, as follows:

$$rx^n_{t+1} = a^n + b^n_{CP}CP_t + b^n_{GCP}GCP_t + \epsilon^n_{t+1} \tag{9.6}$$

[9]We have also predicted returns for the sample starting in 1999 using the global factor computed from the 1975 sample; the slope coefficients are statistically significant, but the explanatory power is somewhat lower.

TABLE 9.6 Local and Global Cochrane–Piazzesi Regressions, 1999–2013 Sample

	Maturity	GCP_t	R^2	CP_t	GCP_t	R^2	Wald
Australia	2	0.27	0.04	0.38	0.27	0.21	[0.03]
		(0.19)		(0.18)	(0.25)		
	5	0.70	0.02	1.77	0.70	0.37	[0.00]
		(0.62)		(0.41)	(0.76)		
Canada	2	0.47	0.20	0.31	0.47	0.28	[0.00]
		(0.13)		(0.14)	(0.13)		
	5	1.75	0.28	1.11	1.75	0.37	[0.00]
		(0.31)		(0.28)	(0.31)		
Denmark	2	0.28	0.06	0.39	0.28	0.11	[0.03]
		(0.17)		(0.37)	(0.15)		
	5	1.11	0.10	1.57	1.11	0.17	[0.00]
		(0.53)		(1.14)	(0.45)		
Germany	2	0.37	0.12	0.54	0.37	0.20	[0.00]
		(0.15)		(0.26)	(0.13)		
	5	1.04	0.09	1.56	1.04	0.15	[0.01]
		(0.53)		(0.99)	(0.47)		
Japan	2	0.10	0.19	0.17	0.10	0.35	[0.00]
		(0.04)		(0.06)	(0.03)		
	5	0.70	0.21	1.69	0.70	0.54	[0.00]
		(0.26)		(0.24)	(0.20)		
Norway	2	0.12	0.00	0.52	0.12	0.02	[0.24]
		(0.19)		(0.44)	(0.19)		
	5	0.52	0.02	1.35	0.52	0.04	[0.24]
		(0.54)		(1.33)	(0.52)		
Sweden	2	0.42	0.13	0.59	0.42	0.28	[0.00]
		(0.14)		(0.20)	(0.12)		
	5	1.41	0.15	1.05	1.41	0.20	[0.00]
		(0.44)		(0.60)	(0.41)		
Switzerland	2	0.49	0.33	0.26	0.49	0.36	[0.00]
		(0.13)		(0.16)	(0.13)		
	5	1.37	0.23	1.38	1.37	0.31	[0.00]
		(0.36)		(0.48)	(0.35)		
United Kingdom	2	0.44	0.12	0.00	0.44	0.12	[0.00]
		(0.14)		(0.26)	(0.14)		
	5	1.18	0.09	1.47	1.18	0.15	[0.00]
		(0.47)		(0.82)	(0.51)		
United States	2	0.77	0.32	−0.89	0.77	0.34	[0.00]
		(0.22)		(0.51)	(0.24)		
	5	2.30	0.32	−4.98	2.30	0.43	[0.00]
		(0.55)		(1.49)	(0.67)		

The table presents the results of local and global Cochrane and Piazzesi (2005) regressions, corresponding to regression equations 9.5 and 9.6 for maturities $n =$ 2 and 5. Estimates of constant terms are not tabulated. When both local and global CP factors are included, the local factor is orthogonalized relative to the global factor. The sample period is from December 1999 to December 2013. Point estimates are reported with Newey and West (1987) standard errors, accounting for conditional heteroskedasticity and serial correlation up to twelve lags, within parentheses. Adjusted R^2 values are also reported. *P*-Values from Wald tests of joint significance are presented in square brackets. Data sources are given in Section 9.3.2.

To simplify interpretation of the results, we first orthogonalize the local factors relative to the global factor. More specifically, we regress the local factors on the global factor and treat the residuals as the truly local factors. The last columns in Table 9.5 present the results for the 1975 sample. First, the local and global factors are jointly significant in all countries. Second, for all countries except the United States, the explanatory power of these joint regressions is greater than when using only local factors. A similar picture emerges when we run the regressions for the broader sample of ten countries, as reported in the last columns of Table 9.6. The local and global factors are jointly significant in all countries except Norway. Overall, our regression results suggest that the expectations hypothesis is violated in international data, local bond risk premia being driven by both local and global factors, and that U.S. bond risk premia matter for international risk premia.

We find that the global factor had significant predictive power across all countries leading up to the financial crisis in 2007 but experienced a marked decrease in predictive power over the 2008–2013 period. The deterioration in the predictive power of the CP factor during the financial crisis has also been noted by Sekkel (2011) and Buraschi and Whelan (2012). The underlying reason for this is unclear but may be related to the extraordinary monetary policy measures employed since 2008 and to the large contemporaneous changes in liquidity funding that are not necessarily captured by the CP factor. Analyzing the latter, Fontaine and Garcia (2012) find that tightness of liquidity funding indeed affects risk premia on U.S. bonds. It is also possible that the so-called zero bound on nominal interest rates affected predictability, as the Federal Funds rate and other short-term rates dropped to virtually zero in 2008 and 2009. However, the effect of the zero bound on the predictability of annual excess returns on long-term bonds is less clear and might even be muted, as the dynamics and responsiveness to news of long-term rates remained similar to their previous levels, as documented by Swanson and Williams (2014a,b). However, the fact that the predictive power of the CP factor dropped fairly significantly during and after the Great Recession suggests that there are state dependencies in bond risk premia. We explore one such potential dependency in Section 9.6.2.

In addition, it is noteworthy that all our results pertain to predicting bond excess returns in local currencies. One might wonder whether the predictive power of the global factor carries over to an international bond strategy that takes into account movements in exchange rates. Dahlquist and Hasseltoft (2013) conduct such an analysis by considering the excess return for a U.S. investor who borrows for 1 year in USD, invests in a foreign government bond with maturities of 2–5 years, and then converts the proceeds back into USD after 1 year.

The return on such a strategy can be written as $rx^n_{FX,t+1} = \Delta s_{t+1} + r^n_{t+1} - y^1_{U.S.,t}$ for a foreign currency versus the USD, where $y^1_{U.S.,t}$ is the 1-year yield in the United States. Dahlquist and Hasseltoft (2013) find that the global factor loses most of its predictive power in such a strategy. To understand why, one can decompose the overall return into two parts by adding and subtracting the local short-term rate, y^1_t. The first part equals the 1-year FX excess return, $\Delta s_{t+1} + y^1_t - y^1_{U.S.,t}$, and the second part equals the 1-year local bond excess return, $r^n_{t+1} - y^1_t$. While the global factor predicts the second part, that is, the local bond excess return, it cannot predict exchange rate movements. Including FX returns in the overall strategy therefore introduces noise from the perspective of the global factor, with a corresponding drop in predictive power. However, Dahlquist and Hasseltoft (2013) demonstrate that one can construct a global factor based on dollar returns, called FXGCP, which has predictive power similar to that of GCP for local returns. The FXGCP factor has a correlation of approximately 0.50 with the local return GCP factor.

While our study concerns in-sample regressions, results concerning the out-of-sample performance of the FB and CP regressions are mixed. For example, Kessler and Scherer (2009) note that the CP regressions generate positive out-of-sample performance with information ratios reaching 1.5, the best performance being achieved with a short forecasting horizon of 1 month. On the other hand, Thornton and Valente (2012) find that predictive models using forward rates generate no significant economic value for investors. They also note a deterioration in predictive performance during the Great Recession, as we discussed earlier.

Finally, Dahlquist and Hasseltoft (2013) incorporate the global factor into an affine term structure model and analyze how the factor affects the cross section of yields. They find that the yield level is only slightly affected by variations in the global factor. While a rise in the global factor increases yields through higher risk premia, it also decreases yields as it is associated with lower expectations of future short-term rates. Movements in the global factor give rise to two offsetting effects, leaving the effect on yield levels muted. The global factor therefore seems to act as a hidden factor in the term structure, as discussed in the introduction to this chapter.

9.6 UNDERSTANDING BOND RISK PREMIA

The fact that bond excess returns contain a strongly predictable component raises the natural question of "Why?" Can we explain the strong evidence on predictability using rational risk-based explanations? The classical risk-based argument suggests that assets whose returns covary positively with investor well-being should be subject to positive risk premia on average. Furthermore, investors' required compensation for risk seems to move countercyclically, being high in bad times and low in good times as documented by, for example, Fama (1986), Stambaugh (1988), and Fama and French (1989).

9.6.1 Links to Economic Growth

We study whether the evidence of predictability provided previously can be explained by business cycles and economic growth. Our empirical evidence suggests that a global factor of risk premia exists, and if it is linked to global economic growth, the classical risk-based explanation may be true.

We evaluate this by relating the estimated global factor to global economic growth. More specifically, we consider growth in industrial production in three large economic areas, that is, the EMU, OECD, and United States. We start by regressing annualized economic growth over 1, 2, and 3 years on the change in the global factor across the same time horizons, measuring

TABLE 9.7 The Global CP Factor and Industrial Production Growth

	Horizon	ΔGCP_t	R^2	GCP_t	R^2
EMU	1	–0.57	0.02	0.37	0.01
		(0.27)		(0.39)	
	2	–0.59	0.11	0.67	0.07
		(0.19)		(0.33)	
	3	–0.48	0.18	0.83	0.22
		(0.12)		(0.24)	
OECD	1	–0.72	0.05	0.56	0.03
		(0.23)		(0.30)	
	2	–0.70	0.20	0.87	0.17
		(0.18)		(0.27)	
	3	–0.58	0.30	0.96	0.35
		(0.11)		(0.21)	
United States	1	–1.02	0.09	0.96	0.08
		(0.25)		(0.33)	
	2	–0.90	0.22	1.26	0.24
		(0.21)		(0.31)	
	3	–0.75	0.30	1.30	0.38
		(0.14)		(0.27)	

The table presents the results of regressions of industrial production growth on the global CP factor. The left-hand side of the table presents contemporaneous regressions run for annualized growth in industrial production on the change in the global CP factor across horizons of 1, 2, and 3 years for the EMU, OECD, and United States. Estimates of constant terms are not tabulated. The right-hand side of the table presents a predictability regression run for annualized growth in industrial production on the global CP factor across horizons of 1, 2, and 3 years for the EMU, OECD, and United States. The sample period is from January 1975 to December 2013. Point estimates are reported with Newey and West (1987) standard errors, accounting for conditional heteroskedasticity and serial correlation up to and including the forecasting horizon, within parentheses. Adjusted R^2 values are also reported. Data sources are given in Section 9.3.2.

the contemporaneous relationship between economic growth and changes in risk premia. If the notion of countercyclical risk premia holds true, we would expect negative and significant slope coefficients. Indeed, we find that to be the case, as reported in the first columns of Table 9.7. A one-percentage-point increase in global bond risk premia is associated with a contemporaneous drop of 0.5–1% in annualized economic growth, all regression coefficients being statistically significant.

Having established a contemporaneous negative link between growth and bond risk premia, we turn to predictive regressions. We study whether the global factor has predictive power for growth by regressing future 1-, 2-, and 3-year annualized economic growth on the global factor as of time t. As reported in the last columns of Table 9.7, we find significant evidence of predictive power. For the OECD and United States, the global factor is a statistically significant predictor across all horizons, whereas for the EMU it is significant only across the 2- and 3-year horizons. A one-percentage-point increase in global bond risk premia is associated with a 0.5–1.3% annualized increase in future economic growth. Our results are consistent with those of Plosser and Rouwenhorst (1994), who document that term structures in Germany, the United Kingdom, and the United States can forecast future economic activity and with those of the NBER working paper version of CP (2005), which demonstrates that the CP factor can predict GDP growth across horizons longer than 1 year.

In addition, we consider the relationship between global bond risk premia and the OECD composite leading indicator. The OECD economic leading indicator is a time series formed by aggregating various economic indicators (e.g., consumer sentiment indicators, business climate indicators, and the purchasing managers' index) for each country to form a composite indicator that anticipates economic movements and turning points. Figure 9.4 plots the lead–lag correlation between the global factor at time t and the OECD indicator at time $t + l$, where l extends from −36 months to 36 months. The figure shows a negative contemporaneous correlation between risk premia and the economic leading indicator. Furthermore, a drop in the leading indicator leads a rise in risk premia by 1 year with a correlation of approximately −0.40. Moreover, a rise in risk premia signals improved economic conditions starting 1 year hence. Overall, the figure supports our earlier regression findings.

To summarize, our results suggest that a rise in global bond risk premia is associated with a contemporaneous drop in economic growth but signals improved future growth. These results are supportive of the classical risk-based explanations, suggesting a tight link between bond risk premia and business cycles.

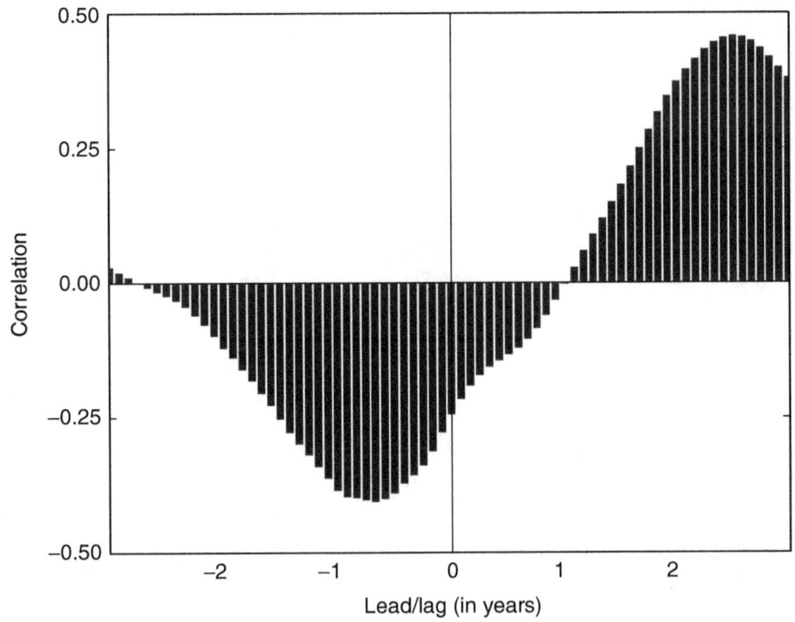

Figure 9.4 Relationship between global CP factor and OECD leading indicator. The figure shows the lead–lag correlations between the global CP factor and an economic leading indicator covering all 30 OECD member countries. The global CP factor is as of date t and the OECD leading indicator is as of date $t + l$, where l refers to the lead (if negative) or lag (if positive). The OECD economic leading indicator is a time series formed by aggregating various economic indicators (e.g., consumer sentiment indicators, business climate indicators, and the purchasing managers' index) for each country to anticipate economic movements and turning points. Source: CRSP, NBER, and central banks.

9.6.2 State Dependency

While an extensive literature has analyzed whether asset returns are predictable, fewer papers have conditioned the predictive regressions on the state of the business cycle. Theory suggests that risk premia on risky assets should be higher in bad economic times than in good times. Focusing on G7 equity markets, Henkel, Martin, and Nardari (2011) combine predictive return regressions with a regime-switching model and indeed find that risk premia in equity markets are higher during recessions. In fact, they find that traditional return predictors, such as dividend yields and term structure variables, are statistically significant only during recessions and are insignificant during business cycle expansions. This suggests a state dependency in risk premia on risky assets.

We build on this notion and analyze whether a similar dependency exists for global bond risk premia. We consider only our sample starting in 1975, as a longer time period is necessary for capturing business cycle variations. We predict local bond returns using our global factor, introducing a dummy variable, D_t, that takes the value of one in recessions. We use data from the Economic Cycle Research Institute to define recessions for Germany, Switzerland, and the United Kingdom but use NBER-dated recessions for the United States. Using our dummy variables, we run the following regression:

$$rx^n_{t+1} = a^n D_t + b^n(1 - D_t) + c^n GCP_t D_t + d^n GCP_t(1 - D_t) + \epsilon^n_{t+1} \tag{9.7}$$

We report the results in Table 9.8, which shows statistically significant coefficients for both regimes with similar economic magnitudes. Testing the null hypothesis of equal slope coefficients fails to reject, as shown by the p-values. Hence, the global factor seems to drive risk premia during both economic expansions and contractions. Interestingly, this stands in contrast to earlier findings regarding equity markets. The explanation for this may lie either in differences between the dynamics of equity and bond returns or in the dynamics of the typical predictors used in stock and bond markets. We leave this matter for further research.

9.7 CONCLUSION AND OUTLOOK

This chapter provides empirical evidence regarding the predictability of international bond risk premia. Our results suggest that the expectations hypothesis is violated in international data, as we document considerable time variation in bond risk premia. While the classical FB (1987) regressions fail to consistently predict excess returns internationally, the well-known CP (2005) regressions do predict excess returns across countries. We also consider a global forecasting factor that we find predicts local bond excess returns significantly, suggesting a commonality in risk premia across international bond markets. The global factor is

TABLE 9.8 State-Dependent Global Cochrane–Piazzesi Regressions

	Maturity	GCP_tD_t	$GCP_t(1-D_t)$	R^2	Wald
Germany	2	0.46	0.52	0.21	[0.71]
		(0.18)	(0.10)		
	3	0.84	0.99	0.20	[0.58]
		(0.27)	(0.19)		
	4	1.17	1.36	0.19	[0.58]
		(0.36)	(0.29)		
	5	1.47	1.68	0.19	[0.62]
		(0.43)	(0.38)		
Switzerland	2	0.45	0.50	0.23	[0.79]
		(0.20)	(0.10)		
	3	0.83	0.85	0.25	[0.95]
		(0.37)	(0.18)		
	4	1.15	1.16	0.25	[0.98]
		(0.48)	(0.26)		
	5	1.35	1.41	0.24	[0.90]
		(0.56)	(0.33)		
United Kingdom	2	0.30	0.52	0.13	[0.16]
		(0.17)	(0.16)		
	3	0.56	0.95	0.13	[0.20]
		(0.32)	(0.28)		
	4	0.79	1.36	0.13	[0.19]
		(0.46)	(0.39)		
	5	0.98	1.77	0.14	[0.15]
		(0.57)	(0.46)		
United States	2	0.58	0.58	0.22	[0.95]
		(0.11)	(0.16)		
	3	1.22	1.12	0.23	[0.57]
		(0.23)	(0.32)		
	4	1.78	1.65	0.23	[0.61]
		(0.33)	(0.45)		
	5	1.96	1.95	0.20	[0.98]
		(0.51)	(0.56)		

This table presents the results of global Cochrane and Piazzesi (2005) regressions with state-dependent coefficients, corresponding to regression equation 9.7. The recession dummy corresponds to economic contractions according to the Economic Cycle Research Institute for Germany, Switzerland, and the United Kingdom and to NBER-dated recessions for the United States. Estimates of state-dependent constant terms are not tabulated. The sample period is from January 1975 to December 2013. Point estimates are reported with Newey and West (1987) standard errors, accounting for conditional heteroskedasticity and serial correlation up to 12 lags, within parentheses. Adjusted R^2 values are also reported. p-Values from Wald tests of equal coefficients are presented in square brackets. Data sources are given in Section 9.3.2.

closely related to U.S. bond risk premia, which indicates that U.S. risk premia matter for international bond returns. Furthermore, the dynamics of the global factor are consistent with classical asset pricing theory, as they are countercyclical and predict future economic growth. However, the predictive performance of the CP regressions across countries deteriorated starting in the Great Recession. The exact reason for this is unclear, but potential explanations are the extraordinary measures taken by the central banks worldwide, the rise in fiscal policy uncertainty, and the great time variation in funding and liquidity conditions – none of which are likely to be fully captured by typical yield-based predictors. Furthermore, the high levels of government debt around the world are likely to reinforce the roles of fiscal policy, credit risk, and liquidity risk in determining bond risk premia around the world. The good news is that this leaves plenty of opportunities for researchers.

ACKNOWLEDGMENTS

We are grateful to David Backus, Mikhail Chernov, Michael Halling, Rafael De Rezende, Lars E.O. Svensson, Pietro Veronesi, and Irina Zviadadze for their helpful comments and to Vasilis Dedes for his excellent research assistance.

REFERENCES

Ang A, Piazzesi M. A no-arbitrage vector autoregression of term structure dynamics with macroeconomic and latent variables. J Monet Econ 2003;2003:745–787.

Backus DK, Foresi S, Mozumdar A, Wu L. Predictable changes in yields and forward rates. J Financ Econ 2001;59:281–311.

Backus DK, Gregory AW, Zin SE. Risk premiums in the term structure: evidence from artificial economies. J Monet Econ 1989;24:371–399.

Backus D, Wright J. Cracking the conundrum. Brookings Pap Econ Act 2007;1:293–329.

Bansal R, Shaliastovich I. A long-run risks explanation of predictability puzzles in bond and currency markets. Rev Financ Stud 2013;26:1–33.

Bansal R, Yaron A. Risks for the long run: a potential resolution of asset pricing puzzles. J Finance 2004;59:1481–1509.

Barro R. Rare disasters and asset markets in the twentieth century. Q J Econ 2006;121:823–866.

Bauer MD, Rudebusch GD, Wu JC. Term premia and inflation uncertainty: empirical evidence from an international panel dataset: comment. Am Econ Rev 2014;104:323–337.

Bekaert G, Hodrick RJ. Expectations hypotheses tests. J Finance 2001;56:1357–1394.

Bekaert G, Hodrick RJ, Marshall DA. On biases in tests of the expectations hypothesis of the term structure of interest rates. J Financ Econ 1997;44:309–348.

Brandt MW, Wang KQ. Time-varying risk aversion and unexpected inflation. J Monet Econ 2003;50:1457–1498.

Buraschi A, Jiltsov A. Habit formation and macroeconomic models of the term structure of interest rates. J Finance 2007;62:3009–3063.

Buraschi A, Whelan P. Term structure models with differences in beliefs. Working Paper; 2012.

Burkhardt D, Hasseltoft H. Understanding asset correlations. Working Paper; 2012.

Campbell JY. A defense of traditional hypotheses about the term structure of interest rates. J Finance 1986;41:183–193.

Campbell JY, Cochrane JH. By force of habit: a consumption-based explanation of aggregate stock market behavior. J Polit Econ 1999; 107:205–251.

Campbell JY, Shiller RJ. Yield spreads and interest rate movements: a bird's eye view. Rev Econ Stud 1991;58:495–514.

Campbell JY, Shiller RJ, Viceira LM. Understanding inflation-indexed bond markets. Brookings Pap Econ Act 2009;1:79–120.

Campbell J, Sunderam A, Viceira L. Inflation bets or deflation hedges? The changing risks of nominal bonds. Working Paper; 2013.

Cochrane JH, Piazzesi M. Bond risk premia. Am Econ Rev 2005;95:138–160.

Cochrane JH, Piazzesi M. Decomposing the yield curve. Working Paper; 2008.

Cooper I, Priestley R. Time-varying risk premiums and the output gap. Rev Financ Stud 2009;22:2801–2833.

Cox JC, Ingersoll JE, Ross SA. A re-examination of traditional hypotheses about the term structure of interest rates. J Finance 1981;36:769–799.

Cox JC, Ingersoll JE, Ross SA. A theory of the term structure of interest rates. Econometrica 1985;53:385–408.

Culbertson JM. The term structure of interest rates. Q J Econ 1957;71:485–517.

Dahlquist M, Hasseltoft H. International bond risk premia. J Int Econ 2013;90:17–32.

Dai Q, Singleton KJ. Specification analysis of affine term structure models. J Finance 2000;50:1943–1978.

Dai Q, Singleton KJ. Expectation puzzles, time-varying risk premia, and affine models of the term structure. J Financ Econ 2002;63:415–441.

Dai Q, Singleton KJ. Fixed-income pricing. In: Constantinides GM, Harris M, Stulz RM, editors. *Handbook of the Economics of Finance*. Volume 1. Amsterdam: North-Holland; 2003.

Dai Q, Singleton KJ, Yang W. Predictability of bond risk premia and affine term structure models. Working Paper; 2004.

David A, Veronesi P. What ties return volatilities to price valuations and fundamentals? J Polit Econ 2013;121:682–746.

Diebold FX, Li C, Yue VZ. Global yield curve dynamics and interactions: a dynamic Nelson-Siegel approach. J Econom 2008;146:351–363.

Dimson E, Marsh P, Staunton M. *Triumph of the Optimists: 101 Years of Global Investment Returns*. Princeton (NJ): Princeton University Press; 2002.

Dimson E, Marsh P, Staunton M. *Credit Suisse Global Investment Returns Yearbook and Sourcebook 2014*. Zurich: Credit Suisse Research Institute; 2014.

Driessen J, Melenberg B, Nijman T. Common factors in international bond returns. J Int Money Finance 2003;22:629–656.

Duffee GR. Term premia and interest rate forecasts in affine models. J Finance 2002;57:405–443.

Duffee GR. Information in (and not in) the term structure. Rev Financ Stud 2011;24:2895–2934.

Duffee GR. Bond pricing and the macroeconomy. In: Constantinides GM, Harris M, Stulz RM, editors. *Handbook of the Economics of Finance*. Volume 2. Amsterdam: North-Holland; 2013.

Duffie D, Kan R. A yield-factor model of interest rates. Math Finance 1996;6:379–406.

Dunn K, Singleton K. Modeling the term structure of interest rates under non-separable utility and durability of goods. J Financ Econ 1986; 17:27–55.

Fama EF. Term premiums and default premiums in money markets. J Financ Econ 1986;17:175–196.

Fama EF, Bliss RR. The information in long-maturity forward rates. Am Econ Rev 1987;77:680–692.

Fama EF, French KR. Business conditions and expected returns on stocks and bonds. J Financ Econ 1989;25:23–49.

Fontaine J-S, Garcia R. Bond liquidity premia. Rev Financ Stud 2012;25:1207–1254.

Gabaix X. Variable rare disasters: an exactly solved framework for ten puzzles in macro-finance. Q J Econ 2012;127:645–700.

Greenwood R, Vayanos D. Price pressure in the government bond market. Am Econ Rev Pap Proc 2010;100:585–590.

Greenwood R, Vayanos D. Bond supply and excess bond returns. Rev Financ Stud 2014;27:663–713.

Gürkaynak RS, Wright JH. Macroeconomics and the term structure. J Econ Lit 2012;50:331–367.

Hansen LP. Large sample properties of generalized method of moments estimators. Econometrica 1982;50:1029–1054.

Hardouvelis GA. The term structure spread and future changes in long and short rates in the G7 countries. J Monet Econ 1994;33:255–283.

Hasseltoft H. Stocks, bonds, and long-run consumption risks. J Financ Quant Anal 2012;47:309–332.
Henkel SJ, Martin JS, Nardari F. Time-varying short-horizon predictability. J Financ Econ 2011;99:560–580.
Homer S, Sylla R. *A History of Interest Rates*. 4th ed. Hoboken (NJ): Wiley Finance; 2005.
Ilmanen A. Time-varying expected returns in international bond markets. J Finance 1995;50:481–506.
Jorion P, Mishkin F. A multicountry comparison of term-structure forecasts at long horizons. J Financ Econ 1991;29:59–80.
Joslin S, Priebsch M, Singleton KJ. Risk premiums in dynamic term structure models with unspanned macro risks. J Finance 2014;69: 1197–1233.
Jotikasthira C, Le A, Lundblad C. Why do term structures in different currencies co-move? J Financ Econ 2015;115:58–83.
Kessel RA. *The Cyclical Behavior of the Term Structure of Interest Rates*, Occasional paper No. 91. New York: NBER; 1965.
Kessler S, Scherer B. Varying risk premia in international markets. J Bank Finance 2009;33:1361–1375.
King M, Low D. Measuring the "World" real interest rate. NBER Working Paper; 2014.
Kose A, Otrok C, Whiteman CH. International business cycles: world, region, and country-specific factors. Am Econ Rev 2003;93:1216–1239.
Krishnamurthy A, Vissing-Jorgensen A. The effects of quantitative easing on interest rates: channels and implications for policy. Brookings Pap Econ Act 2011;43:215–287.
Krishnamurthy A, Vissing-Jorgensen A. The aggregate demand for treasury debt. J Polit Econ 2012;120:233–267.
Litterman R, Scheinkman J. Common factors affecting bond returns. J Fixed Income 1991;1:54–61.
Ludvigson SC, Ng S. Macro factors in bond risk premia. Rev Financ Stud 2009;22:5027–5067.
Modigliani F, Sutch R. Innovations in interest rate policy. Am Econ Rev 1966;56:178–197.
Nelson CR, Siegel AF. Parsimonious modeling of yield curves. J Bus 1987;60:473–489.
Newey WK, West KD. A simple, positive semi-definite, heteroskedasticity and autocorrelation consistent covariance matrix. Econometrica 1987;55:703–708.
Perignon C, Smith DR, Villa C. Why common factors in international bond returns are not so common. J Int Money Finance 2007;26:284–304.
Pflueger CE, Viceira LM. Inflation-indexed bonds and the expectations hypothesis. Annu Rev Financ Econ 2011;3:139–158.
Piazzesi M. Affine term structure models. In: Aït-Sahalia Y, Hansen LP, editors. *Handbook of Financial Econometrics: Tools and Techniques*. Amsterdam: North-Holland; 2010.
Plosser CI, Rouwenhorst KG. International term structures and real economic growth. J Monet Econ 1994;33:133–155.
Politis DN, Romano JP. The stationary bootstrap. J Am Stat Assoc 1994;89:1303–1313.
Politis DN, White H. Automatic block-length selection for the dependent bootstrap. Econom Rev 2004;23:53–70.
Politis DN, White H, Patton A. Correction to "Automatic block-length selection for the dependent bootstrap" by D. Politis and H. White. Econom Rev 2009;28:372–375.
Rietz T. The equity risk premium: a solution. J Monet Econ 1988;22:117–131.
Sekkel R. International evidence on bond risk premia. J Bank Finance 2011;35:174–181.
Shiller RJ. The term structure of interest rates. In: Friedman BM, Hahn FH, editors. *Handbook of Monetary Economics*. Volume 1. Amsterdam: North-Holland; 1990.
Stambaugh RF. The information in forward rates: implications for models of the term structure. J Financ Econ 1988;22:613–652.
Swanson ET, Williams JC. Measuring the effect of the zero lower bound on yields and exchange rates in the U.K. and Germany. J Int Econ 2014a;92:2–21.
Swanson ET, Williams JC. Measuring the effect of the zero lower bound on medium- and longer-term interest rates. Am Econ Rev 2014b; 104:3154–3185.
Thornton DL, Valente G. Out-of-sample predictions of bond excess returns and forward rates: an asset allocation perspective. Rev Financ Stud 2012;25:3141–3168.
Tobin J. Liquidity preference as behavior towards risk. Rev Econ Stud 1958;25:65–86.
Van Horne JC. Interest-rate risk and the term structure of interest rates. J Polit Econ 1965;73:344–351.
Wachter JA. A consumption-based model of the term structure of interest rates. J Financ Econ 2006;79:365–399.
Wright J. Term premia and inflation uncertainty: empirical evidence from an international panel dataset. Am Econ Rev 2011;101:1514–1534.

10

Return Predictability in the Treasury Market: Real Rates, Inflation, and Liquidity

Carolin E. Pflueger[a] and Luis M. Viceira[b]

[a]*Sauder School of Business, University of British Columbia, Vancouver, Canada*
[b]*Harvard Business School, Boston, MA, United States*

10.1 INTRODUCTION

There is wide consensus among financial economists that returns on nominal U.S. Treasury bonds in excess of Treasury bills are predictable at different investment horizons or, equivalently, that the expected excess return on nominal government bonds is time varying. Predictor variables include forward rates (Fama and Bliss, 1987), the slope of the yield curve (Campbell and Shiller, 1991), and a linear combination of forward rates (Cochrane and Piazzesi, 2005).

However, the question of whether the expected excess returns on inflation-indexed bonds is time varying remains relatively unexplored. This is partly due to the short history of inflation-indexed bonds in the United States and in other countries (Campbell, Shiller, and Viceira, 2009). Answering this question is important on its own, since inflation-indexed bonds are widely used by institutional and retail investors and are a significant source of government funding.

It is also important because it can help understand the economic determinants of predictability in nominal bond excess returns (Campbell, Pflueger, and Viceira, 2013). Research in financial economics has proposed several theories to explain predictability in excess nominal bond returns. One hypothesis is that excess return predictability results from time variation in the aggregate price of risk. Building on the habit preferences model of Campbell and Cochrane (1999), Wachter (2006) shows that a model with time-varying real interest rates can generate nominal bond excess return predictability.

Another hypothesis is that excess return predictability could result from time variation in expected aggregate consumption growth or its volatility. The long-run consumption risk model of Bansal and Yaron (2004) and Bansal, Kiku, and Yaron (2010) emphasizes this possibility. Bansal and Shaliastovich (2013) show that this, combined with time-varying inflation volatility, can explain nominal bond predictability.

If excess bond return predictability is entirely due to time-varying habit or long-run consumption risk, then excess returns on real bonds should be predictable, since prices of both real and nominal government bonds change with the economy-wide real interest rate. Prices of nominal, but not real, government bonds also vary with expected inflation, so excess returns on nominal bonds over real bonds should not be predictable.

Handbook of Fixed-Income Securities, First Edition. Edited by Pietro Veronesi.

A third hypothesis is that the nominal nature of bonds is an important source of time-varying risk premia. In this case, the wedge between nominal and real bond returns should be predictable. Time-varying inflation risk premia are an important source of bond risks in Buraschi and Jiltsov (2005); Piazzesi and Schneider (2007); Gabaix (2012); Bansal and Shaliastovich (2013); Campbell, Sunderam, and Viceira (2013); and Campbell, Pflueger, and Viceira (2013).

We present in this chapter a joint empirical analysis of the sources of excess bond return predictability in nominal and inflation-indexed bonds in the United States and the United Kingdom. This analysis establishes four main stylized facts or empirical findings. The first fact is that the yields of inflation-indexed bonds incorporate an economically significant time-varying liquidity premium with respect to the yields of nominal bonds of similar maturity. The second fact is that, adjusting yields and returns for this liquidity premium, inflation-indexed bonds exhibit excess return predictability, which we can attribute to a time-varying real interest rate risk premium. The third fact is that both a time-varying real interest rate risk premium and a time-varying inflation risk premium are quantitatively important in explaining time variation in excess returns on nominal bonds.

The fourth fact is that the liquidity component in the yield differential between nominal and inflation-indexed bonds of similar maturity – also known as breakeven inflation – also predicts the return differential between nominal and inflation-indexed bonds. The estimated U.S. return differential due to liquidity exhibits a significantly positive stock market capital asset pricing model (CAPM) beta, suggesting that investors in U.S. inflation-indexed bonds (Treasury Inflation-Protected Securities or TIPS) bear systematic liquidity risk and should be compensated in terms of a positive return premium. While the return differential due to liquidity is not directly tradable, this result is relevant to investors who may differ in terms of their exposure to liquidity crises.

We start our analysis by proposing an empirically flexible approach to estimate the liquidity differential between inflation-indexed and nominal bond yields. This approach consists in regressing breakeven inflation onto bond market liquidity proxies while controlling for inflation expectation proxies. Liquidity proxies explain almost as much variation in U.S. breakeven as do inflation expectation proxies. We estimate that the sample average 10-year U.S. TIPS yield would have been 64 basis points (bps) lower if TIPS had been as liquid as nominal Treasury bonds. Liquidity variables have smaller, but still significant, explanatory power for U.K. breakeven. We find no evidence that residuals from liquidity regressions are nonstationary, alleviating concerns that results might be spurious.

Conditional on estimates of liquidity-adjusted returns, we find strong evidence that returns on nominal bonds in excess of return on real bonds are predictable from the breakeven term spread. We find that excess real bond returns are predictable from the real term spread. Time-varying liquidity risk contributes statistically and economically significantly to predictability in inflation-indexed bond excess returns. Our results suggest that a well-specified model of bond return predictability should match substantial predictability in liquidity-adjusted real bond excess returns and in the liquidity-adjusted differential between nominal and real bond excess returns.

Interpreting expected real bond excess returns as real rate risk premia and expected returns on nominal bonds in excess of real bonds as inflation risk premia, we find that both are similarly variable and strongly correlated with the nominal term spread. Therefore, both inflation and real rate risk appear quantitatively important in explaining the predictability of nominal bond excess returns documented by Campbell and Shiller (1991). Moreover, we find that real rate risk premia and inflation risk premia can contribute either positively or negatively to expected nominal bond excess returns. These empirical findings are consistent across the United States and the United Kingdom.

10.2 BRIEF LITERATURE REVIEW

There is a limited body of academic research investigating excess return predictability in inflation-indexed bonds. Early work includes the studies of Barr and Campbell (1997) and Evans (1998) for the United Kingdom, one of the first countries to issue inflation-indexed bonds in modern times (Campbell, Shiller, and Viceira, 2009). The study of Barr and Campbell (1997) tests for the expectations hypothesis of the term structure of interest rates in inflation-indexed bonds, or equivalently the hypothesis that the expected excess return on inflation-indexed bonds is constant, and it does not reject the hypothesis at short horizons. By contrast, Evans (1998) finds evidence of predictability at long horizons.

Recent work by Pflueger and Viceira (2011) shows that the slope of the real term structure forecasts positively excess returns on inflation-indexed bonds in both the United Kingdom and the United States, consistent with the existing evidence of excess return predictability for nominal bonds (Campbell and Shiller, 1991). The study also shows evidence that breakeven inflation forecasts positively the return differential between nominal and inflation-indexed bonds in both markets. Huang and Shi (2012) show that macroeconomic indicators also forecast inflation-indexed bond excess returns.

None of these studies controls for the impact of liquidity on the pricing of inflation-indexed bonds. Yet Campbell, Shiller, and Viceira (2009) and Gurkaynak, Sack, and Wright (2010) suggest that historically the market for TIPS has not been as liquid as the market for nominal Treasury bonds.[1] Liquidity could potentially explain part or all of the estimated predictability of

[1] For additional evidence of relatively lower liquidity in U.S. TIPS, see Fleming and Krishnan (2009); Dudley, Roush, and Steinberg Ezer (2009); or Christensen and Gillan (2011).

excess returns on inflation-indexed bonds or the return differential between nominal and inflation-indexed bonds,[2] complicating interpretations of this predictability in terms of time-varying risk premia related to fundamentals such as real interest rate risk or inflation risk.

The question of what explains bond excess return predictability also arises in the context of the literature in fixed income that investigates the determinants of interest rates. This literature specifies no-arbitrage models of the term structure of interest rates to decompose nominal bond yields into components due to expected inflation, expected real rates, and risk premia related to fundamentals. Before pricing data on inflation-indexed bonds was rich enough to be of use in empirical research, studies estimated the models using nominal bond yield data combined with macroeconomic data on variables such as realized inflation or survey measures of expected inflation (Campbell and Shiller, 1996; Campbell and Viceira, 2001; Ang, Bekaert, and Wei, 2008). Model estimates were then used to back out the unobserved term structure of real interest rates conditional on the specific parameterization of the model.

As data on U.S. TIPS have become richer in both the time series dimension and in the cross-sectional dimension (Gurkaynak, Sack, and Wright, 2010), studies of the term structure of interest rates have started to make use of such data for model estimation and testing. Some examples include Chen, Liu, and Cheng (2010); Christensen, Lopez, and Rudebusch (2010); D'Amico, Kim, and Wei (2008); and Campbell, Sunderam, and Viceira (2013). With the exception of Campbell, Sunderam, and Viceira (2013), these studies do not focus explicitly on bond return predictability, but they produce estimates of the time series of real interest and inflation risk premia implied by their models.

A potential issue with these studies is that model-implied estimates of expected inflation, real interest rates, and risk premia can be distorted if liquidity is an important determinant of bond yields, and the model does not account for that possibility. D'Amico, Kim, and Wei (2008) is the only study that allows for the potential existence of a liquidity premium in inflation-indexed bond yields and shows that indeed model-implied estimates of the inflation risk premium and inflation expectations change significantly after accounting for such premium. Along these lines, Haubrich, Pennacchi, and Ritchken (2012) use nominal bond yields and inflation swap rates instead of TIPS yields to estimate a model of the nominal and real term structure of interest rates arguing that the inflation swap market is more liquid than the TIPS market. Fleckenstein, Longstaff, and Lustig (2014) show evidence of price discrepancies between U.S. inflation swap and TIPS markets, which they attribute to mispricing of TIPS. We are not aware of any prior estimates of liquidity differentials between U.K. inflation-indexed and nominal bond markets.

This handbook chapter proposes a decomposition of nominal bond risk premia that does not rely on a specific parameterization of the stochastic discount factor. Thus it can provide guidance for a much wider range of asset pricing models. This chapter also uses a well-developed array of tools to address identification concerns in the presence of persistent variables, which can plague both ordinary least squares and affine term structure models (Bauer, Rudebusch, and Wu, 2012).

10.3 BOND DATA AND DEFINITIONS

10.3.1 Bond Notation and Definitions

Let $y^{\$}_{n,t}$ and $y^{TIPS}_{n,t}$ denote nominal and inflation-indexed log (or continuously compounded) yields with maturity n. We use the superscript *TIPS* for both U.S. and U.K. inflation-indexed bonds. Breakeven inflation is the difference between nominal and inflation-indexed bond yields:

$$b_{n,t} = y^{\$}_{n,t} - y^{TIPS}_{n,t} \tag{10.1}$$

Log excess returns on nominal and inflation-indexed zero-coupon n-period bonds held for one period before maturity are given by[3]

$$xr^{\$}_{n,t+1} = ny^{\$}_{n,t} - (n-1)y^{\$}_{n-1,t+1} - y^{\$}_{1,t} \tag{10.2}$$

$$xr^{TIPS}_{n,t+1} = ny^{TIPS}_{n,t} - (n-1)y^{TIPS}_{n-1,t+1} - y^{TIPS}_{1,t} \tag{10.3}$$

Inflation-indexed bonds are commonly quoted in terms of *real* yields, but since $xr^{TIPS}_{n,t+1}$ is an excess return over the *real* short rate, it can be interpreted as a real or nominal excess return.

[2]For example, the study of Fontaine and Garcia (2012) shows that liquidity predicts excess returns on nominal bonds, although it does not provide evidence on inflation-indexed bonds.

[3]These expressions follow directly from the fact that the log return on a one-period bill is given by its log yield, $y_{1,t}$, and that the one-period log return on an n-period zeron coupon bond is given by the change in its log price, $p_{n-1,t+1} - p_{n,t}$, where $p_{n,t} = -ny_{n,t}$ by definition. See Campbell, Lo, and Mackinlay (1997), Chapter 10, p. 298.

We define the log excess one-period breakeven return as the log return on a portfolio long one nominal bond and short one inflation-indexed bond with maturity n. This portfolio will have positive returns when breakeven inflation declines:

$$xr^{b}_{n,t+1} = xr^{\$}_{n,t+1} - xr^{TIPS}_{n,t+1} \tag{10.4}$$

The yield spread is the difference between a long-term yield and a short-term yield:

$$s^{\$}_{n,t} = y^{\$}_{n,t} - y^{\$}_{1,t} \tag{10.5}$$

$$s^{TIPS}_{n,t} = y^{TIPS}_{n,t} - y^{TIPS}_{1,t} \tag{10.6}$$

$$s^{b}_{n,t} = b_{n,t} - b_{1,t} \tag{10.7}$$

10.3.2 Yield Data

We obtain zero-coupon off-the-run U.S. yields from the smoothed yield curves by Gurkaynak, Sack, and Wright (2007) and Gurkaynak, Sack, and Wright (2010, GSW henceforth). Using yields derived from a smoothed yield curve is likely to reduce nonfundamental fluctuations in yields and therefore to bias downward the volatility of the estimated liquidity premium. We focus on 10-year nominal and real yields, because this maturity has the longest sample period. We compute quarterly log returns by substituting 10-year and 9.75-year zero-coupon log yields into 10.2 and 10.3. Our sample period is 1999.3–2014.12 for yields and 1999.6–2014.12 for quarterly excess returns. We measure U.S. inflation with the all-urban seasonally adjusted Consumer Price Index (CPI), computed by the Bureau of Labor Statistics. The U.S. 3-month nominal interest rate is from the Fama – Bliss riskless interest rate file available on CRSP and Bloomberg.[4]

We use U.K. constant-maturity zero-coupon yield curves from the Bank of England, which are estimated with spline-based techniques (Anderson and Sleath, 2001). We use 20-year yields because those have the longest history. We compute quarterly log returns on 20-year nominal and real bonds using 20-year and 19.75-year zero-coupon log yields.[5] Our sample covers 1999.11–2014.12 for U.K. yields and 2000.2–2014.12 for U.K. quarterly excess returns because liquidity variables only become available at the end of 1999. We use the nonseasonally adjusted Retail Price Index, which is also used to calculate inflation-indexed bond payouts. U.K. 3-month Treasury bill rates are from the Bank of England (IUMAJNB).

The nominal principal value of U.S. TIPS adjusts with the CPI, but it can never fall below its original nominal face value. Consequently, a recently issued TIPS whose nominal face value is close to its original nominal face value contains a potentially valuable deflation option (Wright, 2009; Grishchenko, Vanden, and Zhang, 2011). The 10-year TIPS yield used for our empirical analysis is based on off-the-run TIPS issuances, which typically have high nominal face values relative to the deflation floor. Our empirical measure of the 10-year TIPS yield therefore likely does not contain a significant deflation option. U.K. inflation-indexed bonds do not contain a deflation option.[6]

Since neither the U.S. nor the U.K. governments issue inflation-indexed bills, we build a hypothetical short-term real interest rate following Campbell and Shiller (1996) as the predicted real return on the nominal 3-month T-bill.[7] We use this real rate to construct excess returns on inflation-indexed bonds. Finally, although our yield data is available monthly, we focus on quarterly overlapping bond returns to reduce the influence of high-frequency noise in observed inflation and short-term nominal interest rate volatility in our tests.

10.4 ESTIMATING THE LIQUIDITY DIFFERENTIAL BETWEEN INFLATION-INDEXED AND NOMINAL BOND YIELDS

Breakeven inflation should reflect investors' inflation expectations plus any compensation for bearing inflation risk. However, if the inflation-indexed bond market is not as liquid as the nominal bond market, inflation-indexed bond prices might reflect a liquidity discount relative to nominal bonds or equivalently a liquidity premium in yields. This liquidity differential will impact breakeven inflation negatively.

[4]We use the CRSP 3-month T-bill for 1999.3–2013.12. We extend the data using month-end T-bill rates from Bloomberg (USGG3M) for 2014.1–2014.12. Monthly 3-month T-bill rates from CRSP and Bloomberg are 99.99% correlated for the period 1999.3–2013.12.

[5]The Bank of England only publishes 19.5 – and 20-year zero-coupon yields. We approximate the 19.75-year zero-coupon log yield with the arithmetic average of 19.5 – and 20-year log yields.

[6]There are further details such as in inflation lags in principal updating and tax treatment of the coupons that slightly complicate the pricing of these bonds. More details on TIPS can be found in Viceira (2001); Roll (2004); Campbell, Shiller, and Viceira (2009); and Gurkaynak, Sack, and Wright (2010). Campbell and Shiller (1996) offer a discussion of the taxation of inflation-indexed bonds.

[7]We predict the real return on a nominal T-bill using the lagged real return on the nominal 3-month T-bill, the lagged nominal T-bill, and lagged four-quarter inflation over the sample 1982.1–2014.12. For simplicity we assume a zero liquidity premium on one-quarter real bonds.

We pursue an empirical approach to identify the liquidity differential between inflation-indexed and nominal bond markets in the United States and the United Kingdom. We estimate the liquidity differential by regressing breakeven inflation on measures of liquidity as in D'Amico, Kim, and Wei (2008) and Gurkaynak, Sack, and Wright (2010), while controlling for inflation expectation proxies. We capture different notions of liquidity through three different liquidity proxies: the nominal off-the-run spread, relative transaction volume of inflation-indexed bonds and nominal bonds, and proxies for the cost of funding a levered investment in inflation-indexed bonds.

Time-varying market-wide desire to hold only the most liquid securities, such as "flight-to-liquidity" episodes, might drive part of the liquidity differential between nominal and inflation-indexed bonds. We capture this notion of liquidity by the nominal U.S. off-the-run spread. The Treasury regularly issues new 10-year nominal notes, and the newest "on-the-run" note is considered the most liquidly traded security in the Treasury bond market. The older "off-the-run" bond typically trades at a discount – that is, at a higher yield – despite offering almost identical cash flows (Krishnamurthy, 2002).[8] The U.K. Treasury market does not have on-the-run and off-the-run bonds in a strict sense, since the Treasury typically reopens existing bonds to issue additional debt. We capture liquidity in the U.K. nominal government bond market with the difference between a fitted par yield and the yield on the most recently issued 10-year nominal bond, similarly to Hu, Pan, and Wang (2013). Hu, Pan, and Wang (2013) argue that such a measure captures market-wide liquidity and the availability of arbitrage capital. We refer to this U.K. measure as the "off-the-run spread" for simplicity.

Liquidity developments specific to inflation-indexed bond markets might also generate liquidity premia. When U.S. TIPS were first issued in 1997, investors might have had to learn about them and the TIPS market might have taken time to get established. More generally, following Duffie, Garleanu, and Pedersen (2005, 2007) and Weill (2008), one can think of the transaction volume of inflation-indexed bonds as a measure of illiquidity due to search frictions.[9] We proxy for this idea with the transaction volume of inflation-indexed bonds relative to nominal bonds for the United States and the United Kingdom, a measure previously used by Gurkaynak, Sack, and Wright (2010) for U.S. TIPS. Fleming and Krishnan (2009) also provide evidence that trading activity is a good measure of cross-sectional TIPS liquidity.

Finally, we want to capture the cost of arbitraging between inflation-indexed and nominal bond markets for levered investors, and more generally the availability of arbitrage capital and the shadow cost of capital (Garleanu and Pedersen, 2011). In the United States and the United Kingdom, a nonlevered investor who perceives inflation-indexed bonds to be underpriced relative to nominal bonds can enter a zero-price portfolio long \$1 of inflation-indexed bonds and short \$1 of nominal bonds. If held to maturity, this position will effectively pay the investor cumulative inflation over the remaining life of the bonds, in exchange for paying breakeven inflation – or the yield differential between the nominal and inflation-indexed bonds – plus any funding costs of the position. The investor can effectively fund the long position in inflation-indexed bonds by borrowing against his/her nominal bond in the repo market.

A levered investor with no nominal bonds to borrow against in the repo market can replicate this position by entering into an inflation swap. A zero-coupon inflation swap is a contract where at maturity one party pays cumulative CPI inflation in exchange for a predetermined fixed rate. The fixed rate is often referred to as synthetic breakeven inflation. A zero-coupon inflation swap does not require any initial capital. An inflation swap position paying fixed and receiving floating is functionally equivalent to being long inflation-indexed bonds and short nominal bonds.

In practice, synthetic breakeven inflation and cash breakeven inflation are not equal, and the difference between the two varies over time reflecting variation in funding costs or the cost of arbitraging between the cash market and the inflation swap market (Viceira, 2011). The synthetic-cash breakeven inflation spread and the off-the-run spread in the United States are likely related to specialness of nominal Treasuries in the repo market and the lack of specialness of TIPS, which can vary over time.[10] Differences in specialness might be the result of variation in the relative liquidity of securities, which make some securities easier to liquidate and hence more attractive to hold than others.

The spread between synthetic and cash breakeven inflation could potentially reflect mispricing or arbitrage opportunities between the two markets (Fleckenstein, Longstaff, and Lustig, 2014). When inflation-indexed bonds and inflation derivatives are not traded by the same marginal investor and investors face borrowing constraints, derivatives may not reflect all nonfundamental

[8]In the search model with partially segmented markets of Vayanos and Wang (2007), short-horizon traders endogenously concentrate in one asset, making it more liquid. Vayanos (2004) presents a model of financial intermediaries and exogenous transaction costs, where preference for liquidity is time varying and increasing with volatility.

[9]See Duffie, Garleanu, and Pedersen (2005, 2007) and Weill (2008) for models of over-the-counter markets, in which traders need to search for counter parties and incur opportunity or other costs while doing so.

[10]A Treasury instrument is considered "on special" when its holders can use it as collateral to borrow at rates significantly below prevailing market rates in the market for repurchase (or "repo") agreements. The prices of Treasury bonds "on special" tend to be larger than the prices of comparable bonds, reflecting their ability to produce interest rate savings when used in collateralized repo loans (Duffie, 1996; Buraschi and Menini, 2002). The repo "specialness"is the difference between the repo rate quoted for Treasury bonds that are not "on special" and the repo rate quoted for bonds that are "on special." In private email Conversations, Michael Fleming and Neel Krishnan report that for the period February 4, 2004, to the end of 2010 average repo specialness was as follows. On-the-run coupon securities: 35 bps; off-the-run coupon securities: 6 bps; T-Bills: 13 bps; TIPS: 0 bps.

related fluctuations in inflation-indexed bond prices. However, the spread has historically tracked very closely the funding differentials between Treasury bonds and TIPS. We therefore control for investors' ability to finance a levered bond position, as reflected by mispricing between derivatives and bond markets, as an important but not the only potential source of nonpayoff-related fluctuations. We use the cash-synthetic breakeven inflation spread as our benchmark variable in the United States, since it most closely captures the relative financing cost and specialness of TIPS over nominal Treasuries.

U.K. inflation swap data is not available. We use the London Interbank Offered Rate – General Collateral (LIBOR – GC) repo interest rate spread, as suggested by Garleanu and Pedersen (2011), to proxy for arbitrageurs' shadow cost of capital. In contrast to the cash-synthetic breakeven inflation spread, this measure cannot capture time-varying margin requirements of inflation-indexed bonds relative to nominal bonds.[11]

The estimated liquidity premium likely represents a combination of current ease of trading and the risk that liquidity might deteriorate: if the liquidity of inflation-indexed bonds deteriorates during periods when investors would like to sell, as in "flight-to-liquidity" episodes, risk averse investors will demand a liquidity risk premium (Amihud, Mendelson, and Pedersen, 2005; Acharya and Pedersen, 2005). While the relative transaction volume of inflation-indexed bonds likely only captures the current ease of trading, the off-the-run spread, the smoothness of the nominal yield curve, the asset-swap spread, and the LIBOR – GC spread likely represent both current liquidity and liquidity risk.

10.4.1 Estimation Strategy

Let $b_{n,t}$ be breakeven inflation, X_t a vector of liquidity proxies, and π_t^e a vector of inflation expectation proxies. We estimate

$$b_{n,t} = a_1 + a_2 X_t + a_3 \pi_t^e + \epsilon_t \tag{10.8}$$

Let $\hat{a}_2$ denote the vector of slope estimates in (10.8). The estimated liquidity premium in inflation-indexed yields over nominal yields is the negative of the variation in $b_{n,t}$ explained by the liquidity variables:

$$\hat{L}_{n,t} = -\hat{a}_2 X_t \tag{10.9}$$

Variables indicating less liquidity in the inflation-indexed bond market, such as the off-the-run spread, the smoothness of the nominal yield curve, the asset-swap spread, and the LIBOR – GC spread, should enter negatively in 10.8. The relative transaction volume of the inflation-indexed bonds should enter positively.

We normalize liquidity variables to equal zero in a world of perfect liquidity. With perfect liquidity, the off-the-run spread, the smoothness of the nominal yield curve, the asset-swap spread, and the LIBOR – GC spread should be zero. U.S. and U.K. relative transaction volumes are normalized to a maximum of zero. This assumption might bias the estimated liquidity differential downward and does not affect the liquidity differential's estimated variability.

In order to obtain consistent liquidity estimates, the regression residual ϵ_t needs to be uncorrelated with liquidity proxies, controlling for inflation expectations. We do not include inflation risk proxies in the liquidity estimation 10.8 so as not to not preclude the outcome of our analysis. Not controlling for inflation risk premia is conservative in the following sense: if the estimated liquidity premium also happens to pick up on inflation risk premia in nominal bonds, then this should bias us against finding predictability in liquidity-adjusted breakeven returns.

If our liquidity proxies contain information on inflation expectations not already captured by included inflation variables, our estimate of the liquidity premium may be biased. We think that this is unlikely given that we control comprehensively for inflation expectations. In any case, changes in inflation expectations are not predictable if agents are rational. In that case, even if our estimate of the liquidity premium is correlated with inflation expectations, this type of potential misestimation will not introduce return predictability in either liquidity or liquidity-adjusted bond returns.

While our liquidity estimate most likely reflects liquidity fluctuations in both nominal bonds and in inflation-indexed bonds, we have to make an assumption in computing liquidity-adjusted inflation-indexed bond yields. We could assume that all of the liquidity premium is in nominal bonds, in which case we would not need to correct inflation-indexed bond yields. Here, we make the alternative assumption and adjust inflation-indexed assuming that the relative liquidity premium is entirely attributable to inflation-indexed bond illiquidity.[12] We refer to the following variables as liquidity-adjusted inflation-indexed bond yields and liquidity-adjusted breakeven:

$$y_{n,t}^{TIPS,adj} = y_{n,t}^{TIPS} - \hat{L}_{n,t} \tag{10.10}$$

$$b_{n,t}^{adj} = b_{n,t} + \hat{L}_{n,t} \tag{10.11}$$

[11]We obtain the 3-month London Interbank Offered Rate (LIBOR), based on British Pound from the St Louis Fed Fred database http://research.stlouisfed.org/fred2/series/GBP3MTD156N. The GC 3-month repo rate is from the Bank of England (IUDGR3M).

[12]See Pflueger and Viceira (2011) for evidence on predictability of TIPS excess returns with no liquidity adjustment.

10.4.2 Data on Liquidity and Inflation Expectation Proxies

The U.S. off-the-run spread is the difference between the 10-year GSW off-the-run par yield and the 10-year on-the-run nominal bond yield from Bloomberg (USGG10YR). For the United Kingdom, we use the difference between the fitted 10-year nominal par yield available from the Bank of England (IUMMNPY) and the 10-year nominal on-the-run yield from Bloomberg.

We calculate U.S. and U.K. relative transaction volume as log ($Trans_t^{TIPS}/Trans_t^{\$}$) smoothed over the past 3 months. Here, $Trans_t^{TIPS}$ and $Trans_t^{\$}$ denote average monthly transaction volume for inflation-indexed and long-term nominal bonds. We use transaction volume for long-term nominal coupon bonds to capture the liquidity differential between inflation-indexed and equivalent maturity nominal bonds.[13]

Data on 10-year zero-coupon inflation swaps are available from Bloomberg (USDSW10Y) from July 2004 onward. The U.K. LIBOR – GC spread is the difference between 3-month British Pound LIBOR and 3-month British Pound GC rates.

Panels A and B of Figure 10.1 plot the time series of the U.S. and U.K. liquidity variables. The U.S. off-the-run spread was high during the late 1990s, declined during 2005–2007, jumped to over 50 bps during the financial crisis, and continued its decline afterward. U.S. relative transaction volume rises linearly through 2004 and then stabilizes.[14] The differential between synthetic and cash breakeven inflation varies within a relatively narrow range of 15–45 bps during our sample period excluding the financial crisis period. Therefore, during our sample period it has always been more expensive to finance a long position in TIPS than in nominal Treasury bonds. This cost differential rose sharply during the financial crisis, reaching 113 bps in December 2008. Campbell, Shiller, and Viceira (2009) argue that the Lehman bankruptcy significantly affected TIPS liquidity because Lehman Brothers had been very active in the TIPS market. The unwinding of its large TIPS inventory, combined with a sudden increase in the cost of financing long positions in TIPS, appears to have induced unexpected downward price pressure in the TIPS market.

Panel B of Figure 10.1 shows a steady increase in the U.K. relative transaction volume. Greenwood and Vayanos (2010) argue that the U.K. pension reform of 2004, which required pension funds to discount future liabilities at long-term real rates, increased demand for inflation-indexed gilts and it seems plausible that the same reform also increased trading volume. Panel B of Figure 10.1 shows that the LIBOR – GC spread peaked during the financial crisis, consistent with the notion that arbitrageurs' capital was scarce during this period. The smoother U.K. off-the-run spread might indicate that during flight-to-liquidity episodes investors have a preference for U.S. on-the-run nominal Treasuries.

We proxy for U.S. inflation expectations with the median 10-year CPI inflation forecast from the Survey of Professional Forecasters (SPF), consistent with bond maturities. We also include the Chicago Fed National Activity Index (CFNAI) to account for the possibility that shorter-term inflation expectations enter into breakeven (Stock and Watson, 1999).[15] We proxy for U.K. inflation expectations using the median response to the question "How much would you expect prices in the shops generally to change over the next 12 months?" from the Bank of England Public Attitudes survey. Unfortunately, no longer forecasting horizon is available for our sample.

Summary statistics in Table 10.1 suggest that there was a substantial liquidity premium in U.S. TIPS yields relative to nominal yields or a substantial negative inflation risk premium in nominal yields. Over our sample, U.S. average breakeven was 2.25% per annum (p.a.), average TIPS yields were 1.87% p.a., and average U.S. survey inflation was 2.43% p.a. If breakeven exclusively reflected investors' inflation expectations, the negative gap between U.S. breakeven and survey inflation would be surprising, especially given that the SPF tends to underpredict inflation in low inflation environments (Ang, Bekaert, and Wei, 2007). In contrast, average U.K. breakeven exceeded survey inflation over the similar period 1999.11–2014.12.

Table 10.1 shows that realized log excess returns on U.S. Treasury bonds averaged 5.57% p.a. and exceeded average log excess returns on U.S. TIPS by 71 bps over our sample. This differential reverses in the United Kingdom At 4.14% p.a., average log excess returns on U.K. inflation-indexed bonds exceeded U.K. nominal log excess returns by 82 bps p.a.

10.4.3 Estimating Differential Liquidity

Panels A and B of Table 10.2 estimate the relation 10.8 for the United States and the United Kingdom, respectively. We add liquidity proxies one at a time. For both panels, column (4) presents our benchmark estimate with all liquidity proxies and inflation expectation controls. The last two columns verify that results are robust to excluding the financial crisis.

[13]For the United States, we use Primary Dealers' transaction volumes from the New York Federal Reserve FR-2004 survey. We are grateful to the U.K. Debt Management Office for providing us with U.K. turnover data. In 2001, the Federal Reserve changed the maturity cutoffs. Before June 28, 2001, we use the transaction volume of Treasuries with 6 or more years to maturity, while starting June 28, 2001, we use the transaction volume of Treasuries with 7 or more years to maturity. The series after the break is scaled so that the growth in $Trans^{\$}$ from June 21, 2001 to June 28, 2001 is equal to the growth in transaction volume of all government coupon securities.

[14]Interestingly, the U.S. Treasury's renewed commitment to the TIPS issuance program (Bitsberger, 2003) and the development of synthetic markets occurred at a similar time.

[15]SPF survey expectations are available at a quarterly frequency and are released toward the end of the middle month of the quarter. We create a monthly series by using the most recently released inflation forecast.

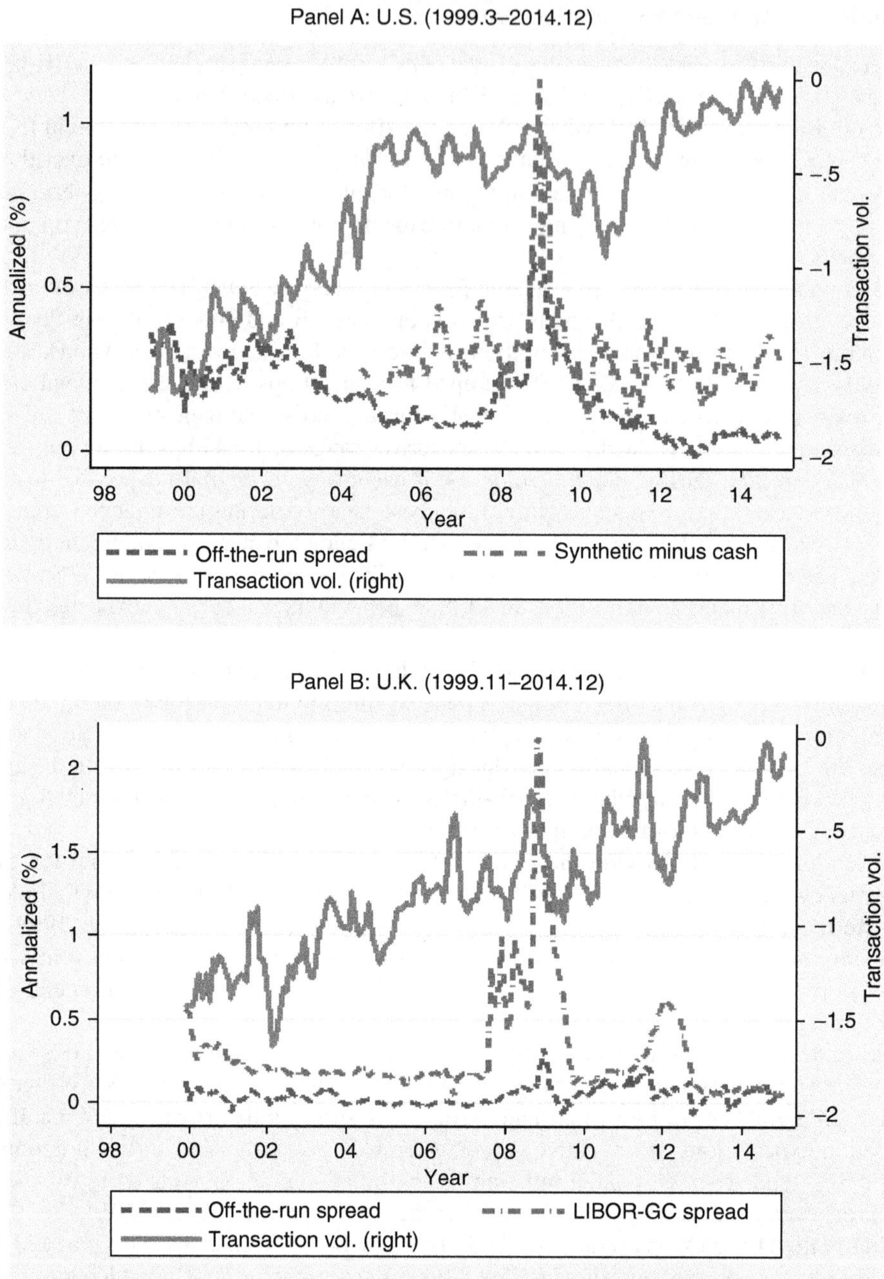

Figure 10.1 U.S. and U.K. liquidity proxies. We use liquidity proxies to estimate differential liquidity between inflation-indexed and nominal government bonds. For the United States, we use the spread between off-the-run and on-the-run 10-year nominal bond yields, the relative inflation-indexed bond log transaction volume, and the difference between synthetic and cash breakeven. For the United Kingdom, we use the difference between a 10-year nominal fitted par yield and the 10-year nominal generic Bloomberg yield, denoted "off the run." We normalize the maxima of relative transaction volumes to zero. The asset-swap spread differential, synthetic minus cash breakeven, and the GBP 3-month LIBOR – GC spread proxy for the cost of funding a levered investment in inflation-indexed bonds. Source: New York Federal Reserve FR-2004 Survey; Bloomberg; St Louis Federal Reserve Fred Database; U.K. Debt Management Office; Bank of England; Gurkaynak, Sack, and Wright (2010); Anderson and Sleath (2001).

Panel A of Table 10.2 column (1) shows that inflation expectation proxies jointly explain 31% of the variability in U.S. breakeven. CFNAI enters positively and significantly, suggesting that short-run inflation expectations influence investors' long-run inflation expectations. Table 10.2 shows that SPF inflation expectations exhibit very little time variation. Table 10.2 suggests that this variation is unrelated to breakeven after controlling for liquidity proxies and CFNAI.

Panel A shows that liquidity measures explain significant variation in U.S. breakeven inflation. The regression R^2 increases with the inclusion of every additional liquidity variable and reaches 59% in column (4). Column (2) shows that the off-the-run

TABLE 10.1 Summary Statistics

Panel A: United States (1999.3–2014.12)		Mean	Std	Min	Max
Nominal yields	$y^{\$}_{n,t}$	4.12	1.26	1.55	6.70
Inflation-indexed yields	$y^{TIPS}_{n,t}$	1.87	1.30	−0.79	4.29
Breakeven	$b_{n,t}$	2.25	0.36	0.39	2.87
Nominal excess ret.	$xr^{\$}_{n,t+1}$	5.57	8.74	−40.11	58.56
Infl.-indexed excess ret.	$xr^{TIPS}_{n,t+1}$	4.86	7.64	−64.78	58.58
Breakeven excess ret.	$xr^{b}_{n,t+1}$	0.71	6.79	−41.26	76.74
Survey inflation	π^E	2.43	0.10	2.20	2.55
Chicago Fed nat. activity	CFNAI	−0.27	0.89	−4.57	1.16
Off-the-run spr.		0.17	0.12	−0.01	0.63
Log transaction vol.		−0.66	0.47	−1.68	0.00
Synthetic-cash		0.29	0.15	0.10	1.13
Panel B: United Kingdom (1999.11–2014.12)		**Mean**	**Std**	**Min**	**Max**
Nominal yields	$y^{\$}_{n,t}$	4.14	0.57	2.45	5.01
Inflation-indexed yields	$y^{TIPS}_{n,t}$	1.14	0.82	−0.79	2.44
Breakeven	$b_{n,t}$	3.00	0.45	2.14	3.95
Nominal excess ret.	$xr^{\$}_{n,t+1}$	3.31	11.32	−49.72	77.67
Infl.-indexed excess ret.	$xr^{TIPS}_{n,t+1}$	4.14	8.93	−67.51	45.25
Breakeven excess ret.	$xr^{b}_{n,t+1}$	−0.82	8.48	−49.34	68.35
Survey inflation	π^E	2.77	0.68	1.50	4.40
Off-the-run spr.		0.05	0.06	−0.06	0.32
Log transaction vol.		−0.79	0.37	−1.64	0.00
LIBOR-GC spr.		0.30	0.32	0.04	2.19

Nominal and inflation-indexed bond yields, excess returns, inflation expectation proxies, and liquidity proxies. U.S. 10-year nominal and TIPS yields from Gurkaynak, Sack, and Wright (2010). U.K. 20-year nominal and inflation-indexed yields from Anderson and Sleath (2001). U.S. 3-month log excess returns (1999.6–2014.12) and U.K. 3-month log excess returns (2000.2–2014.12) are computed using zero-coupon log yields. U.S. survey inflation is the median 10-year CPI inflation forecast from the Survey of Professional Forecasters. The Chicago Fed National Activity Index (CFNAI) is as in Stock and Watson (1999). U.K. survey inflation reflects Bank of England Public Attitudes Survey 12-month inflation expectations. U.S. difference between synthetic and cash breakeven (2004.7–2014.12), and U.K. 3-month GBP LIBOR minus general collateral (GC) spread capture cost of arbitraging between nominal and inflation-indexed bonds. We normalize the maxima of relative transaction volumes to zero. Both GBP LIBOR and GC rates are from Bloomberg. The U.K. off-the-run spread reflects the spread between a fitted 10-year nominal par yield and the generic 10-year nominal U.K. bond yield from Bloomberg. Spreads and zero-coupon yields continuously compounded in annualized percent.

spread alone increases the regression R^2 by 17 percentage points. Column (5) adds a time trend to the regression, which enters significantly but does not impact the magnitude and statistical significance of the other variables, suggesting that our estimates of liquidity are not driven by a time trend, particularly in relative TIPS trading volume.

The coefficients in Panel A of Table 10.2 are consistent with intuition, and they are statistically significant. Breakeven inflation decreases in the off-the-run spread, suggesting that TIPS yields reflect a strong market-wide liquidity component. A one standard deviation move in the off-the-run spread of 12 bps tends to go along with a decrease in breakeven of 11.2 bps in our benchmark estimation (0.93×12 bps). These magnitudes are substantial relative to average breakeven of 225 bps. This empirical finding indicates that during flight-to-liquidity episodes, investors prefer nominal on-the-run U.S. Treasuries over U.S. TIPS, even though both types of bonds are fully backed by the U.S. Treasury.

Relative TIPS trading volume enters positively and significantly, indicating that search frictions impacted inflation-indexed bond prices during the early period of inflation-indexed bond issuance. As TIPS trading volume relative to nominal Treasury trading volume increased, TIPS yields fell relative to nominal bond yields. Our empirical estimates suggest that an increase in relative trading volume from its minimum in 1999 to its maximum in 2014 was associated with a decrease in the TIPS liquidity premium of 29 bps.

TABLE 10.2 Estimating Differential Liquidity

Panel A: United States (1999.3–2014.12)

$y^{\$}_{n,t} - y^{TIPS}_{n,t}$	(1)	(2)	(3)	(4)	(5)	(6)	(7)
Off-the-run spr.		−1.69**	−1.44**	−0.93**	−0.98**		−1.56**
		(0.29)	(0.28)	(0.32)	(0.30)		(0.44)
Synthetic-cash			−1.13**	−1.32**	−1.31**		−0.68
			(0.29)	(0.30)	(0.29)		(0.61)
Transaction vol.				0.17*	0.35**		0.10
				(0.07)	(0.09)		(0.08)
Month × 10^{-2}					−0.25*		
					(0.11)		
Survey inflation	0.25	1.10**	0.92**	1.06**	0.47	0.77	0.55
	(0.32)	(0.36)	(0.32)	(0.33)	(0.46)	(1.65)	(0.63)
CFNAI	0.23**	0.12**	0.04	0.07*	0.06	0.27**	0.18**
	(0.05)	(0.04)	(0.03)	(0.03)	(0.03)	(0.05)	(0.04)
Adjusted R-squared	0.31	0.48	0.57	0.59	0.60	0.28	0.58
ADF of residuals	−4.43 **	−4.75 **	−4.29 **	−4.84 **	−4.91 **	−4.54 **	−3.22 *
Period	Full	Full	Full	Full	Full	1999.3–2006.12	

Panel B: United Kingdom (1999.11–2014.12)

$y^{\$}_{n,t} - y^{TIPS}_{n,t}$	(1)	(2)	(3)	(4)	(5)	(6)	(7)
Off-the-run spr.		0.19	0.10	−0.52	0.02		−3.11 **
		(0.65)	(0.76)	(0.72)	(0.61)		(0.60)
LIBOR-GC spr.			0.05	0.19	0.20 *		0.32
			(0.15)	(0.14)	(0.10)		(0.31)
Transaction vol.				0.68 **	−0.07		0.47 **
				(0.12)	(0.21)		(0.13)
Month × 10^{-2}					0.64 **		
					(0.16)		
Survey inflation	0.45 **	0.45 **	0.44 **	0.20 **	0.11	0.54 **	0.22 **
	(0.06)	(0.07)	(0.07)	(0.06)	(0.09)	(0.12)	(0.08)
Adjusted R-squared	0.46	0.46	0.46	0.61	0.71	0.28	0.64
ADF of residuals	−2.62	−2.64	−2.66	−3.67 **	−3.45 *	−2.79 *	−3.03 *
Period	Full	Full	Full	Full	Full	1999.11–2006.12	

We regress the difference between nominal and inflation-indexed bond yields (breakeven inflation) onto liquidity proxies. The variables are as described in Table 10.1. Newey – West standard errors with three lags in parentheses. * and ** denote significance at the 5% and 1% levels, respectively. Authors' calculations are based on the following data sources: Gurkaynak, Sack, and Wright (2010); Anderson and Sleath (2001); Survey of Professional Forecasters; Chicago Federal Reserve; Bank of England Public Attitudes Survey; Bloomberg; St Louis Federal Reserve Fred Database; U.K. Debt Management Office.

When the marginal investor in TIPS is levered, we would expect breakeven to fall one for one with the synthetic minus cash breakeven inflation spread. The estimated slope on the synthetic-cash breakeven inflation spread is at −1.32 just one standard deviation away of the theoretical value of −1. This slope estimate suggests that disruptions to securities markets and constraints on levered investors were important in explaining the sharp fall in breakeven during the financial crisis when the synthetic-cash breakeven inflation differential spikes up.

We also find a strong relation between breakeven and liquidity proxies during the precrisis period. Column (6) in Panel A shows that before 2007, proxies for inflation expectations explain 28% of the variability of breakeven inflation. Column (7) shows that adding liquidity proxies more than doubles the regression R^2 to 58% and that the off-the-run spread enters with a strongly negative and significant coefficient.

Since some liquidity variables are persistent, one might be concerned about spuriousness. If there is no slope vector so that the regression residuals are stationary, ordinary least squares is quite likely to produce artificially large R^2s and t-statistics (Granger and Newbold, 1974; Phillips, 1986; Hamilton, 1994). Table 10.2 shows that the augmented Dickey – Fuller test rejects the presence of a unit root in regression residuals for all regression specifications at conventional significance levels, including those specifications that include a time trend.

Panel B of Table 10.2 shows that U.K. survey inflation explains a significant 46% of the variability in U.K. breakeven inflation. Liquidity proxies enter with the predicted signs and increase the regression R^2 substantially to 61%. However, column (5) shows that introducing a time trend in the regression reduces both the magnitude and statistical significance of the coefficients survey inflation expectations and relative transaction volume, while it has the opposite effect on the LIBOR – GC spread, suggesting that market-wide liquidity conditions are an important determinant of high-frequency variation in the yield differential between nominal and inflation-indexed bonds in the United Kingdom.

Columns (6) and (7) show that prior to the financial crisis, liquidity variables have somewhat greater explanatory power of the variability in U.K. breakeven inflation. In the pre-2007 sample, including the liquidity variables increases the regression R^2 to 67%. Interestingly, while in the full sample only relative transaction volume is individually statistically significant, in the pre-2007 sample the smoothness of the nominal yield curve also becomes statistically significant. Again, the augmented Dickey – Fuller tests reject the presence of a unit root for all regression specifications in the panel. Overall these results suggest that liquidity factors are important for understanding the time series variability of breakeven inflation both in the United States and the United Kingdom.

Panels A and B of Figure 10.2 and 10.2 plot estimated U.S. and U.K. liquidity premia from (4) of Panels A and B of Table 10.2. The estimated U.S. liquidity premium averages 64 bps with a standard deviation of 26 bps over our sample. This high average reflects periods of very low liquidity in this market. Panel A of Figure 10.2 shows a high liquidity premium in the early 2000s (about 70–100 bps) but a much lower liquidity premium between 2004 and 2007 (35–70 bps). The premium shoots up again beyond 200 bps during the crisis and finally comes down to 40 bps at the end of our sample.

The estimated U.S. liquidity time series is consistent with previous estimates (D'Amico, Kim, and Wei, 2008; Dudley, Roush, and Steinberg Ezer, 2009; Gurkaynak, Sack, and Wright, 2010; Christensen and Gillan, 2011; Haubrich, Pennacchi, and Ritchken, 2012; Fleckenstein, Longstaff, and Lustig, 2014). However, we consider a more comprehensive set of liquidity proxies and estimate U.S. liquidity over a longer time period. We are not aware of any previous estimates of the liquidity differential between U.K. inflation-indexed and nominal bond yields.

The large liquidity premium in TIPS is puzzling given narrow TIPS bid – ask spreads. Haubrich, Pennacchi, and Ritchken (2012) report TIPS bid – ask spreads of at most 10 bps during the financial crisis. It seems implausible that the liquidity premium in TIPS yields simply serves to amortize transaction costs of a long-term investor.[16] If TIPS are held by buy-and-hold investors, as previously argued, then transaction costs of 10 bps can only justify a 1 bp liquidity premium for 10-year TIPS (Amihud, Mendelson, and Pedersen, 2005).

A simple calculation shows that the estimated liquidity premium in U.S. TIPS, though puzzlingly large when compared to bid – ask spreads, gives rise to liquidity returns in line with those on off-the-run nominal Treasuries. The on-the-run/off-the-run liquidity differential converges in 6 months when the new on-the-run nominal 10-year bond is issued. Thus, an average U.S. off-the-run spread of 17 bps yields an annualized return on the liquidity differential of 340 bps (annualized yield differential, 17×2 bps, times the maturity of the bonds, 10 years). In contrast, the 10-year U.S. TIPS liquidity premium might take as long as 10 years to converge, yielding an average annualized return on U.S. TIPS liquidity of only 64 bps.

The estimated U.K. liquidity premium has a lower average (50 bps) but a similar standard deviation (25 bps) compared to U.S. liquidity. Panel B of Figure 10.2 shows that the estimated U.K. liquidity premium was initially similar to the U.S. liquidity premium (around 100 bps) but declined to 10 bps toward the end of our sample. It even became briefly negative during the financial crisis, reflecting extremely high relative transaction volume in U.K. inflation-indexed bonds.

Panel A of Figure 10.3 shows that liquidity-adjusted U.S. breakeven was substantially more stable than raw U.S. breakeven. Estimated liquidity-adjusted U.S. breakeven averaged 2.90% with a standard deviation of 25 bps over our sample. Adjusting breakeven for liquidity suggests that while investors' U.S. long-term inflation expectations fell during the crisis, there was never a period when investors feared substantial long-term deflation in the United States.

Panel B of Figure 10.3 partly attributes the strong upward trend in U.K. breakeven inflation to liquidity. However, even after adjusting for liquidity U.K. breakeven has trended upward from around 3% to 3.5% over our sample. In contrast to the U.S., U.K. breakeven does not exhibit a pronounced drop during the financial crisis. Both raw and liquidity-adjusted U.K. breakeven become highly volatile during 2008–2010, potentially reflecting inflation uncertainty.

10.5 BOND EXCESS RETURN PREDICTABILITY

This section decomposes government bond excess returns into returns due to real interest rates, changing inflation expectations, and liquidity. We test for predictability in each component separately: predictability in liquidity-adjusted real bond excess returns would indicate a time-varying real interest rate risk premium, while predictability in liquidity-adjusted breakeven returns would

[16] See also Wright (2009).

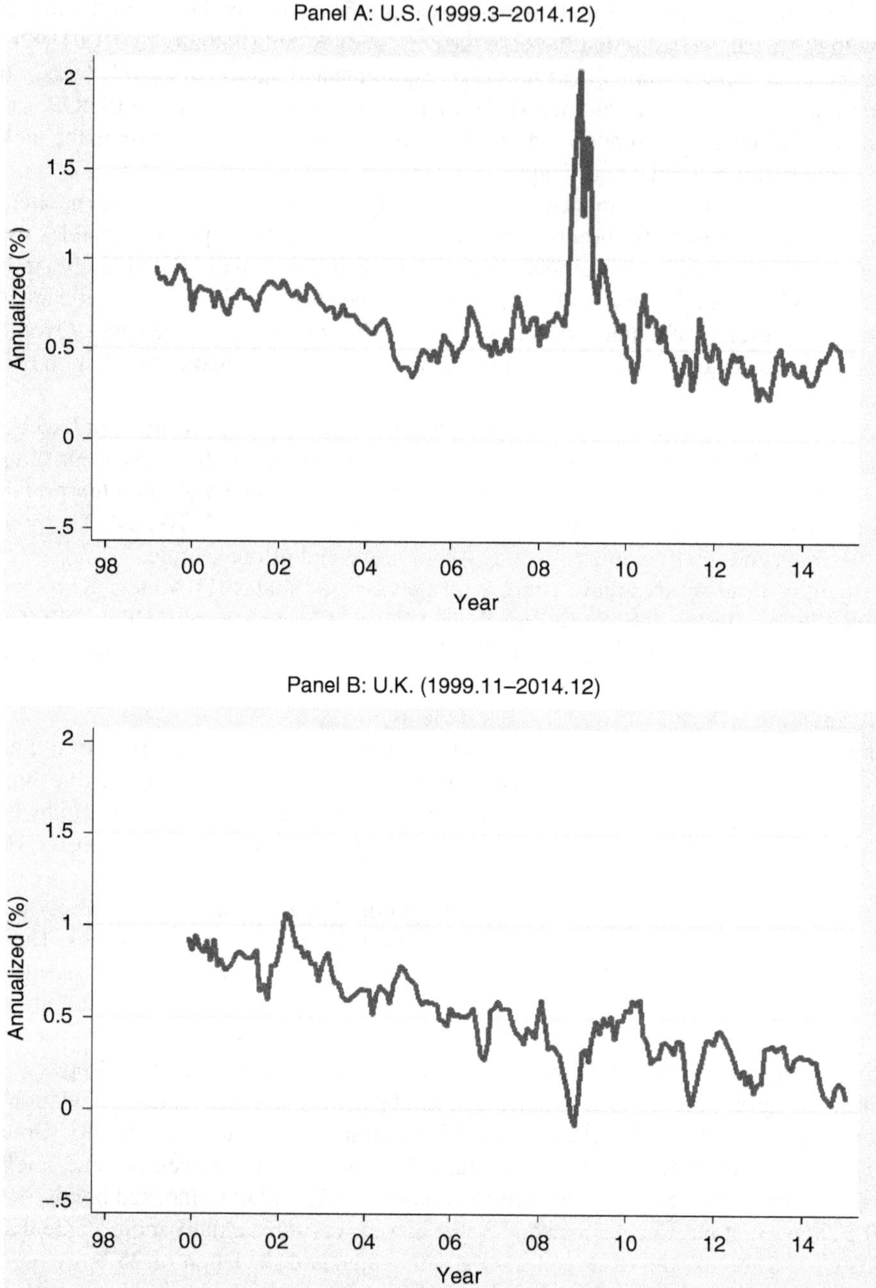

Figure 10.2 Estimated U.S. and U.K. liquidity premia. We estimate liquidity premia as the negative of the variation in breakeven explained by liquidity proxies. Formally, $\hat{L}_{n,t} = -\hat{a}_2 X_t$, where X_t is the vector of liquidity variables and $\hat{a}_2$ is the vector of corresponding estimated coefficients in Table 10.2, column (4), Panels A and B. Authors' calculations are based on the following data sources: Gurkaynak, Sack, and Wright (2010); Anderson and Sleath (2001); Survey of Professional Forecasters; Chicago Federal Reserve; Bank of England Public Attitudes Survey; Bloomberg; St Louis Federal Reserve Fred Database; U.K. Debt Management Office.

indicate a time-varying inflation risk premium. Predictability in the liquidity component of inflation-indexed returns would indicate a time-varying liquidity risk premium.[17]

[17]Relative supply shocks and market segmentation of the type implied by the preferred habitat hypothesis of Modigliani and Sutch (1966) as formalized by Vayanos and Vila (2009) can also generate bond excess return predictability from the relative supply of inflation-indexed bonds (Greenwood and Vayanos, 2008; Hamilton and Wu, 2012). However, in unreported results we find that relative bond supply measures neither do not explain variation in breakeven inflation nor predict bond excess returns. Thus we rule out this potential channel of excess return predictability for the remaining analysis.

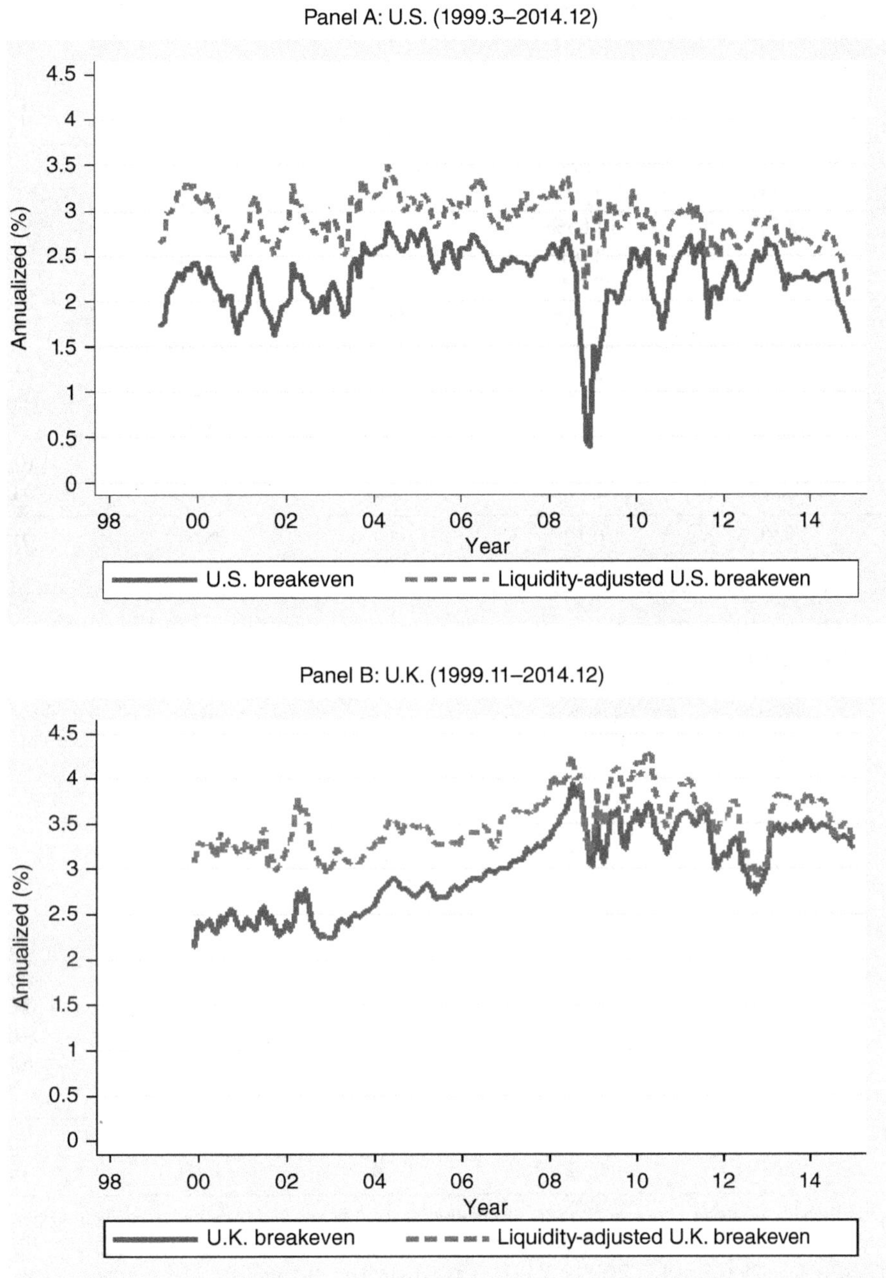

Figure 10.3 Liquidity-adjusted U.S. 10-year breakeven and U.K. 20-year breakeven. Liquidity-adjusted breakeven equals breakeven plus the liquidity premium shown in Figure 10.2. Authors' calculations are based on the following data sources: Gurkaynak, Sack, and Wright (2010); Anderson and Sleath (2001); Survey of Professional Forecasters; Chicago Federal Reserve; Bank of England Public Attitudes Survey; Bloomberg; St Louis Federal Reserve Fred Database; U.K. Debt Management Office.

We adjust inflation-indexed and breakeven excess returns for liquidity and compute inflation-indexed bond returns due to illiquidity:

$$xr_{n,t+1}^{TIPS-L} = ny_{n,t}^{TIPS,adj} - (n-1)y_{n-1,t+1}^{TIPS,adj} - y_{1,t}^{TIPS} \tag{10.12}$$

$$xr_{n,t+1}^{b+L} = xr_{n,t+1}^{\$} - xr_{n,t+1}^{TIPS-L} \tag{10.13}$$

$$r_{n,t+1}^{L} = -(n-1)L_{n-1,t+1} + nL_{n,t} \tag{10.14}$$

TABLE 10.3 Liquidity-Adjusted Bond Return Predictability

Panel A: United States (1999.6–2014.12)

	(1) $xr^{TIPS-L}_{n,t+1}$	(2) $xr^{TIPS-L}_{n,t+1}$	(3) $xr^{b+L}_{n,t+1}$	(4) $xr^{b+L}_{n,t+1}$	(5) $r^{L}_{n,t+1}$	(6) $r^{L}_{n,t+1}$
$(y^{TIPS}_{n,t} - L_{n,t}) - y^{TIPS}_{1,t}$	3.00	2.60		−0.41		0.45
	(1.24)	(1.31)		(1.11)		(0.65)
	7.45%	14.85%		30.40%		42.00%
$(b_{n,t} + L_{n,t}) - b_{1,t}$		1.76	4.14	4.02		−0.49
		(2.80)	(1.69)	(1.91)		(1.82)
		38.75%	0.00%	0.00%		40.00%
$L_{n,t}$		2.59		−3.65	12.60	11.91
		(8.79)		(5.91)	(3.51)	(4.26)
		22.05%		30.75%	0.00%	0.00%
Const.	−0.00	−0.01	−0.00	0.00	−0.02	−0.02
	(0.01)	(0.02)	(0.00)	(0.01)	(0.01)	(0.01)
	74.00%	15.75%	7.30%	46.20%	0.00%	0.25%
p-Value	0.02	0.12	0.02	0.04	0.00	0.00
Adjusted R-squared	0.04	0.04	0.06	0.07	0.17	0.16

Panel B: United Kingdom (2000.2–2014.12)

	(1) $xr^{TIPS-L}_{n,t+1}$	(2) $xr^{TIPS-L}_{n,t+1}$	(3) $xr^{b+L}_{n,t+1}$	(4) $xr^{b+L}_{n,t+1}$	(5) $r^{L}_{n,t+1}$	(6) $r^{L}_{n,t+1}$
$(y^{TIPS}_{n,t} - L_{n,t}) - y^{TIPS}_{1,t}$	4.80	3.32		−0.82		−0.49
	(1.72)	(2.43)		(2.62)		(1.23)
	14.60%	14.70%		28.80%		40.90%
$(b_{n,t} + L_{n,t}) - b_{1,t}$		−3.62	5.46	6.48		3.17
		(2.93)	(3.02)	(3.38)		(1.86)
		6.35%	0.10%	0.05%		11.50%
$L_{n,t}$		−21.04		7.42	13.08	13.64
		(13.43)		(15.71)	(4.73)	(6.40)
		36.40%		35.75%	0.00%	0.00%
Const.	0.00	0.04	−0.01	−0.02	−0.01	−0.02
	(0.01)	(0.02)	(0.01)	(0.03)	(0.01)	(0.01)
	67.50	33.65	2.30%	19.50%	6.70%	6.75%
p-Value	0.01	0.00	0.07	0.27	0.00	0.01
Adjusted R-squared	0.08	0.12	0.04	0.04	0.09	0.12

We predict 3-month overlapping liquidity-adjusted excess log returns of inflation-indexed bonds and of nominal bonds in excess of inflation-indexed bonds using the liquidity-adjusted inflation-indexed term spread, the liquidity-adjusted breakeven term spread, and the liquidity differential $L_{n,t}$. $L_{n,t}$ is estimated as the negative of the variation explained by liquidity variables in Table 10.2(4). $r^{L}_{n,t+1}$ is the return on inflation-indexed bonds due to illiquidity. Newey – West standard errors with three lags within parentheses. The p-value of the F-test for no predictability is shown. We show one-sided bootstrap p-values from 2000 replications to account for the fact that liquidity is estimated. We use block bootstrap with block length 24 months. Authors' calculations are based on the following data sources: Gurkaynak, Sack, and Wright (2010); Anderson and Sleath (2001); Survey of Professional Forecasters; Chicago Federal Reserve; Bank of England Public Attitudes Survey; Bloomberg; St Louis Federal Reserve Fred Database; U.K. Debt Management Office.

Table 10.3 regresses quarterly excess returns 10.12–10.14 onto the lagged liquidity-adjusted real term spread $(y^{TIPS}_{n,t} - L_{n,t}) - y^{TIPS}_{1,t}$, the lagged liquidity-adjusted breakeven term spread $(b_{n,t} + L_{n,t}) - b_{1,t}$, and the lagged estimated liquidity differential between inflation-indexed and nominal yields $L_{n,t}$. Intuitively, the three right-hand side variables decompose the nominal term spread, used by Campbell and Shiller (1991) to predict nominal bond excess returns, into real term structure, inflation, and liquidity components. The table reports Newey – West standard errors with three lags and one-sided bootstrap p-values accounting for generated regressors.[18]

[18]We use a nonparametric block bootstrap with block length 24 months and 2000 replications. We resample the data on inflation-indexed and nominal yields, liquidity variables, and inflation expectation proxies from nonoverlapping blocks of length 24 with replacement. See Horowitz (2001) for a survey of bootstrap methods with serially dependent data.

TABLE 10.4 Decomposing Bond Risk Premia

Panel A: United States (1999.6–2014.12)	$\hat{E}(xr_{n,t})$	$\hat{\beta}(xr_{n,t})$	$\hat{\sigma}(E_t xr_{n,t+1})$	$\widehat{corr}(E_t xr_{n,t+1}, y^{\$}_{n,t} - y^{\$}_{1,t})$
Liquidity-adjusted breakeven	1.63	−0.07	1.33	0.65
Liquidity-adjusted inflation-indexed	3.94	−0.16*	1.52	0.88
Log return liquidity	0.92	0.12**	1.62	0.13
Panel B: United Kingdom (2000.2–2014.12)	$\hat{E}(xr_{n,t})$	$\hat{\beta}(xr_{n,t})$	$\hat{\sigma}(E_t xr_{n,t+1})$	$\widehat{corr}(E_t xr_{n,t+1}, y^{\$}_{n,t} - y^{\$}_{1,t})$
Liquidity-adjusted breakeven	0.74	−0.27 **	2.15	0.71
Liquidity-adjusted inflation-indexed	2.58	0.15	3.32	0.92
Log return liquidity	1.56	−0.04	1.60	−0.54

We show statistics for realized and predicted 3-month overlapping log excess returns on real bonds and breakeven and average log liquidity returns. Realized log excess returns are denoted $xr_{n,t}$, while predicted log excess returns are denoted $E_t(xr_{n,t+1})$. We report the average log excess return $\hat{E}(xr_{n,t})$, stock market beta $\hat{\beta}(xr_{n,t})$, standard deviation of predicted log excess returns $\hat{\sigma}(E_t xr_{n,t+1})$, and the correlation between predicted log excess return and the nominal term spread $\widehat{corr}(E_t xr_{n,t+1}, y^{\$}_{n,t} - y^{\$}_{1,t})$. Betas are with respect to excess log stock returns on the S&P 500 (United States) and the FTSE (United Kingdom). We obtain predicted excess returns as fitted values from the regressions shown in (1), (3), and (5) of Table 10.3(1). Numbers shown are annualized (%). Newey – West standard errors for $\hat{\beta}$ are computed with three lags. * and ** denote the significance at the 5% and 1% levels for $\hat{\beta}$, respectively. Authors' calculations are based on the following data sources: Gurkaynak, Sack, and Wright (2010); Anderson and Sleath (2001); Survey of Professional Forecasters; Chicago Federal Reserve; Bank of England Public Attitudes Survey; Bloomberg; St Louis Federal Reserve Fred Database; U.K. Debt Management Office.

Ordinary least squares can overstate return predictability in small samples, when the regressor is persistent and innovations are negatively correlated with returns (Stambaugh, 1999). In contrast, this correlation is typically negative for bond return predictability regressions (Bekaert, Hodrick, and Marshall, 1997). Therefore, the same small sample bias should bias us toward finding no predictability in real bond excess returns and breakeven returns.

Columns (1) and (2) in Table 10.3 show that the real term spread forecasts real bond excess returns positively, even controlling for liquidity, in the United States and the United Kingdom. Bootstrap p-values in Columns (1) and (2) in Table 10.3 indicate that these positive coefficients are not statistically significant at conventional significance levels, even though Newey – West standard errors would indicate statistical significance. Of course, the relatively short sample may make it hard to detect predictability and bias our results toward finding no predictability. The liquidity-adjusted breakeven term spread and lagged liquidity do not enter significantly in Columns (1) or (2) either in the United States or the United Kingdom, as one might expect if those variables are unrelated to real interest rate risk.

Columns (3) and (4) in Panels A and B of Table 10.3 and show that liquidity-adjusted breakeven term spreads predict breakeven excess returns with coefficients that are large, statistically significant, and similar across both countries. This empirical finding indicates that that time-varying inflation risk premia are a source of predictability in nominal bond excess returns and that the nominal term spread partly reflects time-varying inflation risk premia.

Remarkably, liquidity does not predict liquidity-adjusted real bond or breakeven excess returns in the United States or the United Kingdom. The estimated liquidity differential does not appear related to fundamental bond cash flow risk, alleviating concerns that estimated liquidity might capture time-varying inflation risk premia as a result of our estimation strategy.

The last two columns in Panels A and B of Table 10.3 show that liquidity $L_{n,t}$ predicts liquidity returns $r^L_{n,t+1}$ with large positive and highly significant coefficients. Time-varying and predictable liquidity premia are a source of inflation-indexed bond excess return predictability both in the United States and the United Kingdom. Equivalently, the liquidity component in breakeven exhibits mean reversion. When liquidity in the inflation-indexed bond market is scarce, inflation-indexed bonds enjoy a higher expected return relatively to nominal bonds, rewarding investors who are willing to invest into a temporarily less liquid market.

10.5.1 Economic Significance of Bond Risk Premia

Table 10.4 evaluates the economic significance of time-varying real rate risk premia, inflation risk premia, and liquidity risk premia. For simplicity, we refer to the expected liquidity excess return as a liquidity risk premium, the expected liquidity-adjusted breakeven return as an inflation risk premium, and expected liquidity-adjusted TIPS returns as a real rate risk premium. We note that our average return calculations are based on log returns with no variance adjustments for Jensen's inequality.

By construction, the average excess return on inflation-indexed bonds equals the sum of the liquidity risk premium plus the real rate risk premium. Column (1) of Panel A shows that, at 92 bps, the liquidity risk premium accounts for one-fifth of the average realized U.S. TIPS excess return over this period. Although the average estimated inflation risk premium is economically significant at 163 bps, it is substantially smaller than the average real interest rate risk premium of 394 bps over the same time period. Panel B shows that at 156 bps, the average estimated U.K. liquidity risk premium is even more substantial. The estimated inflation risk premium in U.K. nominal bonds is much lower at 74 bps, helping to explain low average log excess returns on nominal U.K. bonds.

Column (2) of Panel A of Table 10.4 shows that the CAPM beta on U.S. liquidity-adjusted breakeven excess returns is negative, small, and not significant. By contrast, the CAPM beta on liquidity-adjusted TIPS excess returns is negative, large in absolute value, and significant, and the CAPM beta on U.S. liquidity returns is positive and significant. The positive liquidity beta implies that TIPS tend to become illiquid relative to nominal Treasury bonds – or conversely, nominal bonds become liquid relative to TIPS – during stock market drops.[19] The strong positive covariation between U.S. estimated liquidity returns and stock returns suggests that investors should earn a premium on TIPS for bearing systematic variation in liquidity.

In contrast, Panel B of Table 10.4 shows that the U.K. liquidity beta is indistinguishable from zero. The CAPM beta of U.K. liquidity-adjusted breakeven returns is large, negative, and statistically significant, indicating procyclical inflation expectations and nominal interest rates during our sample. Both procyclical nominal interest rates and low inflation risk premia are consistent with a view that nominal Treasuries were safe assets and provided investors with sizable diversification benefits over our sample.

The last two columns in Table 10.4 tie our results back to the initial motivation and theory. Column (3) of Table 10.4 reports roughly similar standard deviations for estimated real rate risk premia, inflation risk premia, and liquidity risk premia. The estimated components of bond excess returns therefore contribute quantitatively similarly to the predictability in standard Campbell and Shiller (1991) bond return forecasting regressions.

Column (4) of Table 10.4 shows that the nominal term spread, shown by Campbell and Shiller (1991) to forecast nominal bond excess returns, is highly correlated with estimates of both inflation risk premia and real rate risk premia. The correlations between the nominal term spread and inflation risk premia range from 65% to 71%, while the correlations with real rate risk premia range from 88% to 92%.

Figure 10.4 shows predicted 3-month excess returns or real rate risk premia, inflation risk premia, and liquidity risk premia. While magnitudes may appear large, Figure 10.4 shows predicted 3-month returns in annualized units and not predicted 12-month returns. Panel A of Figure 10.4 shows a negative U.S. inflation risk premium in the early part of the sample, which turns positive in 2003. The inflation risk premium became highly positive during the period of high oil prices in 2008 and fell to almost −10% at the beginning of 2009, just when the U.S. real rate risk premium increased sharply.

A large and positive U.S. real interest rate risk premium during the crisis indicates that real bonds were considered risky, so a deepening of the recession was considered likely to go along with high long-term real interest rates. The liquidity risk premium on real bonds relative to nominal bonds spiked in the United States, but not in the United Kingdom, during the financial crisis. The U.K. liquidity risk premium even declined, suggesting that investors did not consider U.K. real bonds risky due to illiquidity.

U.S. and U.K. inflation risk premia present a contrasting picture during the financial crisis, mirroring contrasting inflation experiences. In contrast to the U.S., the U.K. inflation risk premium shot up during the financial crisis. This high inflation risk premium likely reflected the high level and volatility of U.K. inflation during the financial crisis.

10.6 CONCLUSION

This chapter explores the sources of time variation in bond risk premia in nominal and inflation-indexed bonds in the United States and the United Kingdom. We find strong empirical evidence in both markets that excess nominal bond return predictability is related to time variation in inflation risk premia. Inflation risk premia exhibit significant time variation, are low on average, and take both positive and negative values in our sample. We find strong evidence in U.K. data that predictability in nominal bond excess returns is also related to time-varying real interest rate risk premia.

We find strong empirical evidence for both time-varying real rate and time-varying liquidity risk premia in inflation-indexed bonds in both markets. Liquidity risk premia in U.S. TIPS account for 92 bps of TIPS excess returns over our sample. Our results suggest that bond investors receive a liquidity discount for holding inflation-indexed bonds. However, this time-varying discount exposes them to systematic risk as measured by a positive and statistically significant CAPM beta.

The estimated liquidity premium in U.S. TIPS yields relative to nominal yields is economically significant and strongly time varying. We estimate a large premium early in the life of TIPS, a decline after 2004, and a sharp increase to over 200 bps during the height of the financial crisis in the fall of 2008 and winter of 2009. Since then, the premium has declined to much lower levels of 40–50 bps. The estimated relative liquidity premium might partly reflect a convenience yield on nominal bonds (Krishnamurthy and Vissing-Jorgensen, 2012), rather than a liquidity discount specific to TIPS. In this case, TIPS are not undervalued securities, but instead investors may be willing to pay a liquidity premium on nominal Treasury bonds.

[19] We compute CAPM betas using the stock market as the proxy for the wealth portfolio. The U.S. excess stock return is the log total return on the S&P 500 in excess of the log 3-month interest rate. The U.K. excess stock return is the log quarterly total return on the FTSE in excess of the log 3-month interest rate.

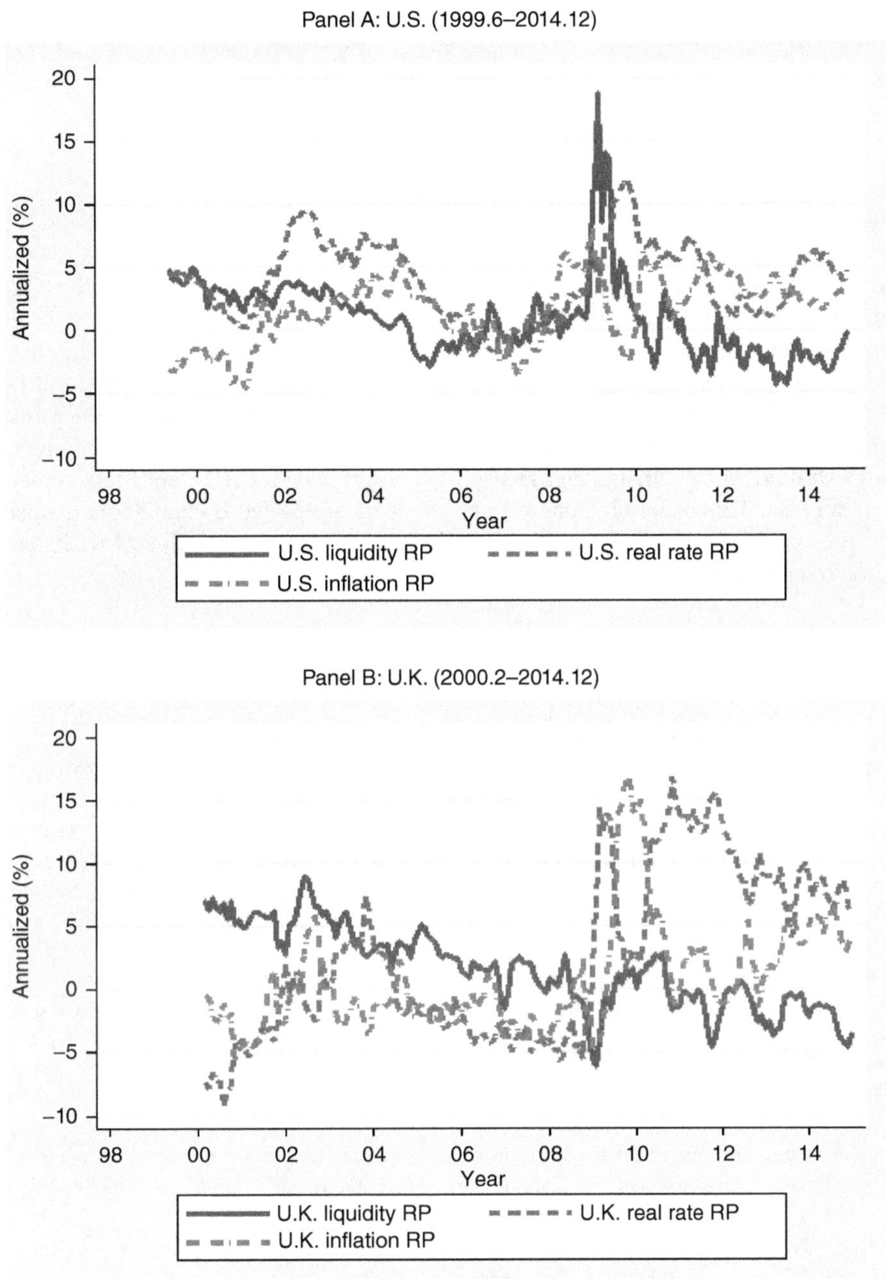

Figure 10.4 U.S. and U.K. estimated risk premia. Predicted 3-month excess returns in annualized units, labeled real rate risk premia, inflation risk premia, and liquidity risk premia. We obtain predicted excess returns as fitted values from the regressions shown in Columns (1), (3), and (5) of Panels A and B of Table 10.3. Authors' calculations are based on the following data sources: Gurkaynak, Sack, and Wright (2010); Anderson and Sleath (2001); Survey of Professional Forecasters; Chicago Federal Reserve; Bank of England Public Attitudes Survey; Bloomberg; St Louis Federal Reserve Fred Database; U.K. Debt Management Office.

Estimated inflation risk premia, real rate risk premia, and liquidity risk premia are roughly equally quantitatively important as sources of bond excess return predictability. Inflation risk premia and real rate risk premia are strongly correlated with the nominal term spread, while liquidity risk premia are not. The empirical results in this chapter have important implications for modeling and understanding predictability in bond excess returns. We find an important role for time-varying real interest rate risk, which can be modeled either in a model of time-varying habit (Wachter, 2006) or in a model of time variation in expected aggregate consumption growth or its volatility (Bansal and Yaron, 2004; Bansal, Kiku, and Yaron, 2010). However, our results indicate that time-varying inflation risk is equally important for understanding the time-varying risks of nominal government bonds. A model that aims to capture predictability in nominal government bond excess returns therefore has to integrate sources of real interest rate risk and inflation risk.

Our results suggest directions for future research. Different classes of investors have different degrees of exposure to time-varying liquidity risk, real interest rate risk, and inflation risk. Exposures may vary with shares of real and nominal liabilities and time horizons. Understanding the sources of bond return predictability can therefore have potentially important implications for investors' portfolio management and pension investing.

ACKNOWLEDGMENTS

We thank Tom Powers, Haibo Jiang, Shuangyi Cao, and Uyseok Lee for the excellent research assistance. We are grateful to John Campbell, Kent Daniel, Graig Fantuzzi, Peter Feldhütter, Michael Fleming, Josh Gottlieb, Robin Greenwood, Arvind Krishnamurthy, George Pennacchi, Michael Pond, Matthew Richardson, Josephine Smith, and Jeremy Stein, to the seminar participants at the NBER Summer Institute 2011, the Econometric Society Winter Meeting 2011, the Federal Reserve Board, the European Central Bank, the New York Federal Reserve, the Foster School of Business at the University of Washington, the HBS-Harvard Economics Finance Lunch, and the HBS Finance Research Day for helpful comments and suggestions. We are also grateful to Martin Duffell, Anna Christie, and Henry Luckhoo from the U.K. Debt Management Office for their help providing us with U.K. bond data. This material is based upon the work supported by the Harvard Business School Research Funding. This paper was previously circulated under the title "An Empirical Decomposition of Risk and Liquidity in Nominal and Inflation-Indexed Government Bonds."

REFERENCES

Acharya VV, Pedersen LH. Asset Pricing with Liquidity Risk. J Financ Econ 2005;77:375–410.

Amihud Y, Mendelson H, Pedersen LH. Liquidity and asset prices. Found Trends Finance 2005;1(4):269–364.

Anderson N, Sleath J. New Estimates of the U.K. Real and Nominal Yield Curves, Bank of England Working Paper; 2001. ISSN: 1368-5562.

Ang A, Bekaert G, Wei M. Do macro variables, asset markets, or surveys forecast inflation better? J Monet Econ 2007;54:1163–1212.

Ang A, Bekaert G, Wei M. The term structure of real rates and expected inflation. J Finance 2008;63(2):797–849.

Bansal R, Kiku D, Yaron A. Long run risks, the macroeconomy, and asset prices. Am Econ Rev 2010;100(2):542–546.

Bansal R, Shaliastovich I. A long-run risks explanation of predictability puzzles in bond and currency markets. Rev Financ Stud 2013;26(1):1–33.

Bansal R, Yaron A. Risks for the long run: a potential resolution of asset pricing puzzles. J Finance 2004;59:1481–1509.

Barr DG, Campbell JY. Inflation, real interest rates, and the bond market: a study of UK nominal and index-linked government bond prices. J Monet Econ 1997;39:361–383.

Bauer MD, Rudebusch GD, Wu JC. Correcting estimation bias in dynamic term structure models. J Bus Econ Stat 2012;30(3):454–467.

Bekaert G, Hodrick RJ, Marshall DA. On biases in tests of the expectations hypothesis of the term structure of interest rates. J Financ Econ 1997;44:309–348.

Bitsberger T. Why the treasury issues TIPS, chart presentation of deputy assistant secretary for federal finance timothy S. Bitsberger to the Bond Market Association's Inflation-Linked Securities Conference; New York; 2003. Available at http://www.treasury.gov/press-center/press-releases/Pages/js505.aspx. Accessed 2015 Sept 26.

Buraschi A, Jiltsov A. Inflation risk premia and the expectations hypothesis. J Financ Econ 2005;75:429–490.

Buraschi A, Menini D. Liquidity risk and specialness. J Financ Econ 2002;64:243–284.

Campbell JY, Cochrane JH. By force of habit: a consumption-based explanation of aggregate stock market behavior. J Polit Econ 1999;107:205–251.

Campbell JY, Lo AW, MacKinlay AC. *The Econometrics of Financial Markets*. Princeton (NJ): Princeton University Press; 1997.

Campbell JY, Pflueger C, Viceira LM. Monetary Policy Drivers of Bond and Equity Risks, Manuscript. Harvard University and University of British Columbia; 2013.

Campbell JY, Shiller RJ. Yield spreads and interest rate movements: a bird's eye view. Rev Econ Stud 1991;58:495–514.

Campbell JY, Shiller RJ. A scorecard for indexed government debt. In: Bernanke BS, Rotemberg J, editors. *National Bureau of Economic Research Macroeconomics Annual 1996*. Cambridge (MA): MIT Press; 1996.

Campbell JY, Shiller RJ, Viceira LM. Understanding inflation-indexed bond markets. In: Romer D, Wolfers J, editors. *Brookings Papers on Economic Activity: Spring 2009*. Washington (DC): Brookings Institution Press; 2009.

Campbell JY, Sunderam A, Viceira LM. Inflation Bets or Deflation Hedges? The Changing Risks of Nominal Bonds, Manuscript. Harvard University; 2013.

Campbell JY, Viceira LM. Who should buy long-term bonds? Am Econ Rev 2001;91:99–127.

Chen R-R, Liu B, Cheng X. Pricing the term structure of inflation risk premia: theory and evidence from TIPS. J Empir Finance 2010;17:702–721.

Christensen, JE, Gillan JM. A Model-Independent Maximum Range for the Liquidity Correction of TIPS Yields, Manuscript. Federal Reserve Bank of San Francisco; 2011.

Christensen JE, Lopez JA, Rudebusch GD. Inflation expectations and risk premiums in an arbitrage-free model of nominal and real bond yields. J Money Credit Bank 2010;42(6):143–178.
Cochrane JH, Piazzesi M. Bond risk premia. Am Econ Rev 2005;95(1):138–160.
D'Amico S, Kim DH, Wei M. Tips from TIPS: The Informational Content of Treasury Inflation-Protected Security Prices, BIS Working Papers, No 248; 2008.
Dudley WC, Roush JE, Steinberg Ezer M. The case for TIPS: an examination of the costs and benefits. Econ Policy Rev 2009;15(1):1–17.
Duffie D. Special repo rates. J Finance 1996;51(2):493–526.
Duffie D, Gârleanu N, Pedersen LH. Over-the-counter markets. Econometrica 2005;73(6):1815–1847.
Duffie D, Gârleanu N, Pedersen LH. Valuation in over-the-counter markets. Rev Financ Stud 2007;20(5):1865–1900.
Evans MD. Real rates, expected inflation and inflation risk premia. J Finance 1998;53(1):187–218.
Fama EF, Bliss RR. The information in long-maturity forward rates. Am Econ Rev 1987;77:680–692.
Fleckenstein M, Longstaff FA, Lustig H. The TIPS-treasury bond puzzle. J Finance 2014;69(5):2151–2197.
Fleming MJ, Krishnan N. The microstructure of the TIPS market. Fed Reserve Bank N Y Econ Policy Rev 2012;18(1):27–45.
Fontaine J-S, Garcia R. Bond liquidity premia. Rev Financ Stud 2012;25(4):1207–1254.
Gabaix X. Variable rare disasters: an exactly solved framework for ten puzzles in macro-finance. Q J Econ 2012;127:645–700.
Gârleanu N, Pedersen LH. Margin-based asset pricing and deviations from the law of one price. Rev Financ Stud 2011;24(6):1980–2022.
Gürkaynak RS, Sack B, Wright JH. The U.S. Treasury yield curve: 1961 to the present. J Monet Econ 2007;54(8):2291–2304.
Gürkaynak RS, Sack B, Wright JH. The TIPS yield curve and inflation compensation. Am Econ J Macroecon 2010;2(1):70–92.
Granger CWJ, Newbold P. Spurious regressions in econometrics. J Econom 1974;2:111–120.
Greenwood R, Vayanos D. Bond Supply and Excess Bond Returns. NBER Working Paper Series, No. 13806; 2008.
Greenwood R, Vayanos D. Price pressure in the government bond market. Am Econ Rev 2010;100(2):585–590.
Grishchenko OV, Vanden JM, Zhang J. *The Informational Content of the Embedded Deflation Option in TIPS*, Finance and Economics Discussion Series. Washington (DC): Federal Reserve Board; 2011.
Hamilton J. *Time Series Analysis*. Princeton (NJ): Princeton University Press; 1994.
Hamilton JD, Wu JC. The effectiveness of alternative monetary policy tools in a zero lower bound environment. J Money Credit Bank 2012;44:3–46.
Haubrich JG, Pennacchi GG, Ritchken PH. Inflation expectations, real rates, and risk premia: evidence from inflation swaps. Rev Financ Stud 2012;25(5):1588–1629.
Horowitz JL. The bootstrap. In: Heckman JJ, Leamer EE, editors. *Handbook of Econometrics*. Volume 5. Amsterdam: North-Holland Publishing Co.; 2001.
Hu GX, Pan J, Wang J. Noise as information for illiquidity. J Finance 2013;68(6):2341–2382.
Huang J-Z, Shi Z. Understanding Term Premia on Real Bonds, Manuscript. Penn State University; 2012.
Krishnamurthy A. The bond/old-bond spread. J Financ Econ 2002;66(2):463–506.
Krishnamurthy A, Vissing-Jorgensen A. The aggregate demand for treasury debt. J Polit Econ 2012;120(2):233–267.
Modigliani F, Sutch R. Innovations in interest-rate policy. Am Econ Rev 1966;56:197–178.
Phillips PCB. Understanding spurious regressions in econometrics. J Econom 1986;33(3):311–340.
Piazzesi M, Schneider M. Equilibrium yield curves. In: Acemoglu D, Rogoff K, Woodford M, editors. *NBER Macroeconomics Annual 2006*. Cambridge (MA): MIT Press; 2007. p 317–363.
Pflueger CE, Viceira LM. Inflation-indexed bonds and the expectations hypothesis. Annu Rev Financ Econ 2011;3:139–158.
Roll R. Empirical TIPS. Financ Anal J 2004;60:31–53.
Stock J, Watson M. Forecasting inflation. J Monet Econ 1999;44:293–335.
Stambaugh R. Predictive regressions. J Financ Econ 1999;54:375–421.
Vayanos D. Flight to Quality, Flight to Liquidity, and the Pricing of Risk, NBER Working Paper Series, No. 10327; 2004.
Vayanos D, Vila J-L. A Preferred-Habitat Model of the Term Structure of Interest Rates, NBER Working Paper Series, No. 15487; 2009.
Vayanos D, Wang T. Search and endogenous concentration of liquidity in asset markets. J Econ Theory 2007;136:66–104.
Viceira LM. The Harvard Management Company and Inflation-Protected Bonds, HBS Case # 201-053; 2001.
Viceira LM. Discussion of 'Why Does The Treasury Issue TIPS? The TIPS-Treasury Bond Puzzle'. slide presentation prepared for the NBER Asset Pricing Group Meeting of April 29, 2011; Chicago; 2011. Available upon request.
Wachter JA. A consumption-based model of the term structure of interest rates. J Financ Econ 2006;79:365–399.
Weill P-O. Liquidity premia in dynamic bargaining markets. J Econ Theory 2008;140:66–96.
Wright JH. Comment on understanding inflation-indexed bond markets. In: Romer D, Wolfers J, editors. *Brookings Papers on Economic Activity: Spring 2009*. Washington (DC): Brookings Institution Press; 2009.

11

U.S. Treasury Market: The High-Frequency Evidence

Pierluigi Balduzzi[a] **and Fabio Moneta**[b]
[a]*Finance Department, Boston College, Chestnut Hill, MA, United States*
[b]*The Stephen J.R. Smith School of Business, Queen's University, Kingston, ON, Canada*

11.1 INTRODUCTION

This chapter reviews the existing empirical evidence on the time-series behavior of the U.S. Treasury markets at *high frequency*: daily and intraday data. We believe that the use of high-frequency data in econometric analyses is a major recent development in the study of the fixed income markets and has important implications for our understanding of how financial markets work. The response of prices to scheduled and unscheduled news, for example, can be examined much more precisely with high-frequency data, by isolating behavior within *narrow* windows surrounding the news releases.[1] The *instantaneous* adjustment to news is what we would expect in a rational, frictionless market. If we were to detect a sluggish response to news, on the other hand, then we would conclude that behavioral effects and/or transaction costs and limits to arbitrage play an important role in these markets.

One can also take advantage of high-frequency data in the study of conditional-volatility dynamics, by relating volatility to macro news and *intraday* seasonal patterns and by constructing realized-volatility measures that approximate the true volatility process as sampling becomes more frequent. In addition, jump and diffusion behavior becomes easier to separate at high frequency.

High-frequency data are also important for the characterization of the trading environment. For example, researchers are able to investigate how liquidity changes during the trading day and around news releases. By using high-frequency data, it is also possible to examine the immediate impact of trading on prices and how this impact is affected by the presence of macro news.

Moreover, bond risk premia can be better estimated using high-frequency data. It is possible to distinguish between days with and without macro news announcements and, within announcement days, between volatile price behavior surrounding announcements and behavior further away from the announcements. This allows us to better understand the way bond risk premia are earned: for example, the possible time variation of conditional risk premia versus the constant risk premia implied by the expectation hypothesis (EH) and the possible compensation for macro risks.

[1] Andersen et al. (2007), for example, show that the response to U.S. macroeconomic news is stronger in the bond market than in the equity and foreign exchange markets.

Handbook of Fixed-Income Securities, First Edition. Edited by Pietro Veronesi.

Finally, the advent of high-frequency trading (HFT) in several markets – including the fixed income markets – has attracted a great deal of attention.[2] By definition, the presence of HFT can only be identified by analyzing high-frequency data. Indeed, several studies using high-frequency data for the U.S. Treasury markets have appeared during the last two decades, and this is an ideal moment to review them.

This is a *selective* review, though, which emphasizes what *we* think are the most important issues when looking at the Treasury markets through a "high-frequency lens." Our upfront apology is offered to any researchers whose papers we have omitted.

The U.S. Treasury market is one of the largest and most important financial markets in the world. Having a better understanding of how this market works is obviously important to practitioners – the main target audience of this review. Specifically, we believe that the studies reviewed in this chapter are relevant for the management, hedging, and pricing of Treasury securities and the many other instruments that are benchmarked against the Treasury yield curve and also for trading and implementation strategies.

In our review, we start with motivating evidence on the behavior of the U.S. Treasury market during the recent financial crisis. We then focus on literature covering the following four topics: (i) the reaction of prices and rates to macroeconomic news, (ii) market-microstructure effects, (iii) bond risk premia, and (iv) the effects of HFT.[3,4] Each section concludes with a brief summary of the main results reviewed.

11.2 THE U.S. TREASURY MARKETS DURING THE FINANCIAL CRISIS

It is well known that the financial crisis brought about disruption throughout the fixed income markets. In addition, the Federal Reserve took some unprecedented actions, some of which directed specifically at the Treasury market. Hence, it is natural to ask if and how the U.S. Treasury market was affected. As a first step in addressing this question, we provide a description of several features of the U.S. Treasury markets (cash and futures), during a sample period inclusive of the financial crisis. Specifically, we focus on yields, price volatility, the on-the-run/off-the-run yield spread, trading volume and price impact, settlement fails, and the intraday price behavior on March 18, 2009.

11.2.1 Yields

Figure 11.1 presents the daily behavior of the Fed funds rate target, the 3-month T-bill rate, and the 10-year note yield.[5] In this, as well as in the remaining figures, the following dates are highlighted:

1. July 31, 2007: Bear Stearns liquidates two mortgage-backed securities funds – the crisis "begins."
2. January 22, 2008: In an intermeeting conference call, the Federal Open Market Committee (FOMC) votes to reduce its target for the Federal funds rate 75 basis points, to 3.5%.
3. March 17, 2008: First trading day after Bear Stearns was sold to JPMorgan Chase.
4. September 15, 2008: Lehman Brothers Holdings Incorporated files for Chapter 11 bankruptcy protection.
5. November 25, 2008: The Federal Reserve Board announces the creation of the Term Asset-Backed Securities Loan Facility, under which the Federal Reserve Bank of New York will lend up to $200 billion on a nonrecourse basis to holders of AAA-rated asset-backed securities and recently originated consumer and small-business loans. The Federal Reserve Board also announces a new program to purchase direct obligations of housing-related government-sponsored enterprises (GSEs) – Fannie Mae, Freddie Mac, and Federal Home Loan Banks – and mortgage-backed securities (MBS) backed by the GSEs.
6. December 16, 2008: The FOMC votes to establish a target range for the effective Federal funds rate of 0–0.25%.

[2]On June 17, 2014, for example, Bradley Katsuyama testified in front of a Senate panel on the impact of HFT on the equity markets. Katsuyama cited market instability (e.g., the 2010 "flash crash"), co-location (high-speed traders gaining trading-time advantage by placing their computer servers as close as possible to trading venues), and conflicts of interest (e.g., fees that trading venues pay brokers to execute transactions on their platforms) as troubling HFT-related developments. Katsuyama had gained notoriety as the main character in Lewis (2014), which chronicles the "discovery" of HFT on the part of Katsuyama and his team at the Royal Bank of Canada. In the wake of the publication of Lewis (2014) in March 2014, several regulatory agencies disclosed that they were taking action against HFT firms.

[3]There are also studies formulating and testing models of the term structure of interest rates at high frequency (weekly and daily data), such as Rudebusch (1995), Balduzzi, Bertola, and Foresi (1997), Farnsworth and Bass (2003), Piazzesi (2005), and Lu and Wu (2009). These studies are beyond the scope of this review.

[4]The review of studies of HFT in the bond markets could have been incorporated in the other three sections. Yet the recent interest in the effects of HFT has prompted us to dedicate a separate section to the topic. We expect that future editions of this chapter will devote even more space to this important trend.

[5]The Fed funds rate target is from the Federal Reserve Bank of New York, whereas the T-bill rate and the 10-year note yield are the constant-maturity series from the U.S. Department of the Treasury.

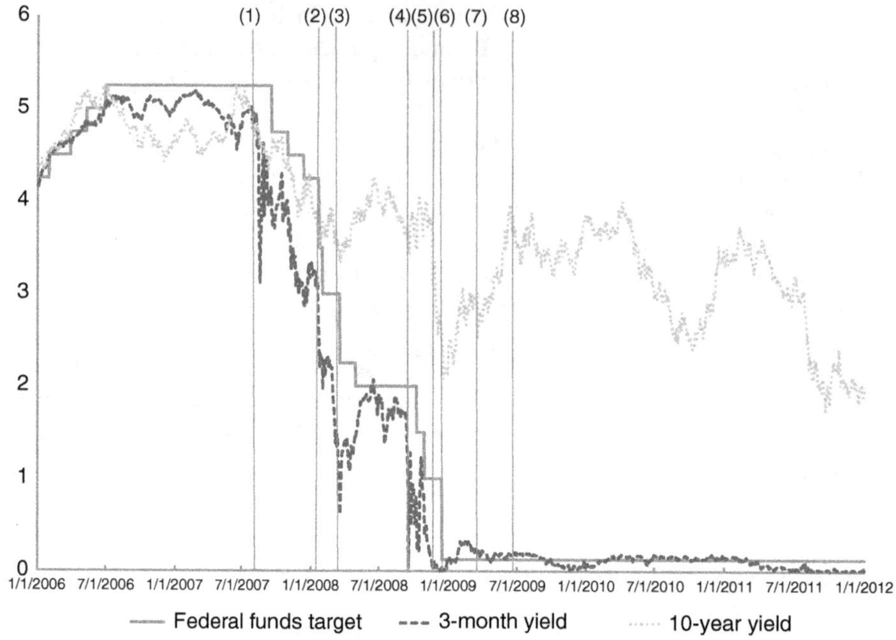

Figure 11.1 Yields and Fed funds rate target.

7. March 18, 2009: The FOMC decides to increase the size of the Federal Reserve's balance sheet by purchasing up to an additional \$750 billion of agency MBSs, bringing its total purchases of these securities to up to \$1.25 trillion this year, and to increase its purchases of agency debt this year by up to \$100 billion to a total of up to \$200 billion. The FOMC also decides to purchase up to \$300 billion of longer-term Treasury securities over the next 6 months to help improve conditions in private credit markets.
8. June 24, 2009: The Fed announces extensions of and modifications to a number of its liquidity programs – the crisis "ends."

The figure highlights the "leading" behavior of the U.S. Treasury markets: as early as July 2006, both the T-bill rate and the T-note yields were trading *below* the overnight Fed funds rate target (5.25%). Indeed, the T-bill rate plots below the Fed funds rate target throughout most of the crisis period, into January 2009. In addition, the 10-year T-note rate was trading below the 3-month T-bill between July 2006 and May 2007, leading to an *inverted* yield curve during that period.

Also noteworthy are the dramatic reductions in the 3-month rate between September 12 and September 17, 2008 (from 1.49 to 0.03%), and in the 10-year yield between October 14 and December 18, 2008 (from 4.08 to 2.08%), and between March 17 and March 18, 2009 (from 3.02 to 2.51%). These reductions are associated with episodes of flight to quality (during September 2008, after Lehman Brothers filed for bankruptcy), cuts in the Fed funds target rate (on December 16, 2008, the target was cut to a historically low level), and the Federal Reserve's large-scale asset purchases (on March 18, 2009, the Fed decided to start to buy long-term Treasury securities), respectively.

11.2.2 Volatility

Figure 11.2 presents the annualized 24-hour realized volatility of the 10-year note futures contract, based on intraday 5-minute returns.[6] The figure highlights an increase in volatility during the financial crisis, with the highest spike on March 18, 2009 (40 basis points, annualized). Interestingly, realized volatility remains somewhat higher and substantially more volatile well *after* the end of the financial crisis, with pronounced spikes on May 6, 2010, and August 9, 2011.[7]

[6]Daily realized volatility is calculated as

$$RV_t = \sqrt{250} \times 100 \times \sqrt{\sum_{n=1}^{N} r_{nt}^2}$$

where r_{nt} denotes 5-minute continuously compounded returns during the 24-hour trading day.

[7]May 6, 2010, is the day of the "flash crash" when the Dow Jones Industrial Average experienced the greatest intraday point decline (almost 1000 points). On August 9, 2011, a Federal Reserve's statement indicated plans to keep "exceptionally low" interest rates in place until at least mid-2013.

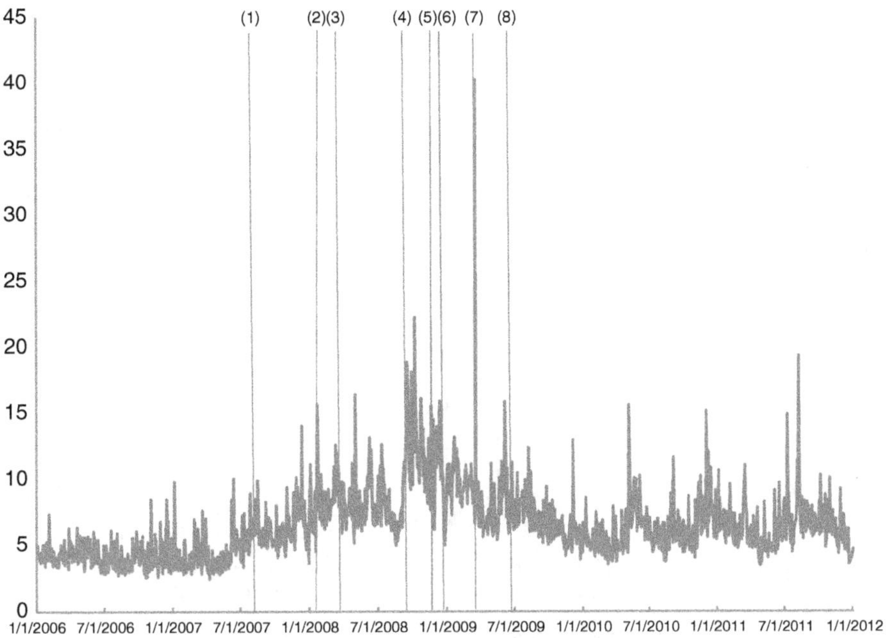

Figure 11.2 10-year T-note futures, daily realized volatility.

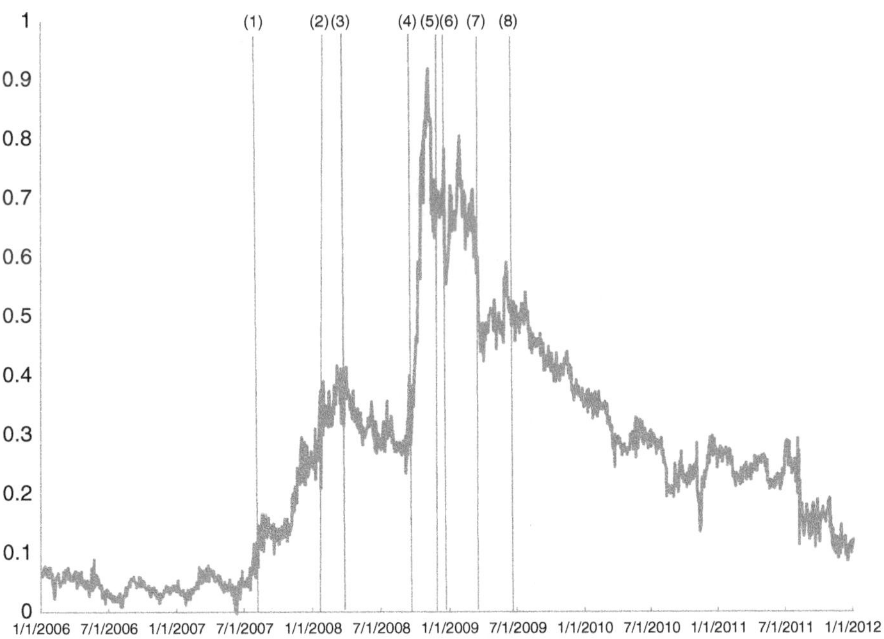

Figure 11.3 Off-the-run/on-the-run spread.

11.2.3 Off-the-Run/On-the-Run Yield Spread

Figure 11.3 highlights the behavior of the off-the-run/on-the-run spread for 10-year securities.[8] This liquidity indicator seems to track very well some of the salient episodes during the financial crisis. The spread quickly increases from 0 to 18 basis points between June 12 and August 20, 2007, and spikes on March 17, 2008, to 41 basis points. In the aftermath of the Lehman default, the spread climbs from 40 basis points (9/15/2008) to an overall peak of 91 basis points (11/3/2008). The spread then follows a downward trend, with a substantial reduction between March 17 (60 basis points) and April 2 (42 basis points).

[8]The 10-year *off-the-run* par-yield series is computed by Gürkaynak, Sack, and Wright (2007) from the CRSP daily U.S. Treasury file and updated by the Board of Governors of the Federal Reserve. The 10-year *on-the-run* yield is calculated by the authors, also based on the CRSP daily U.S. Treasury file.

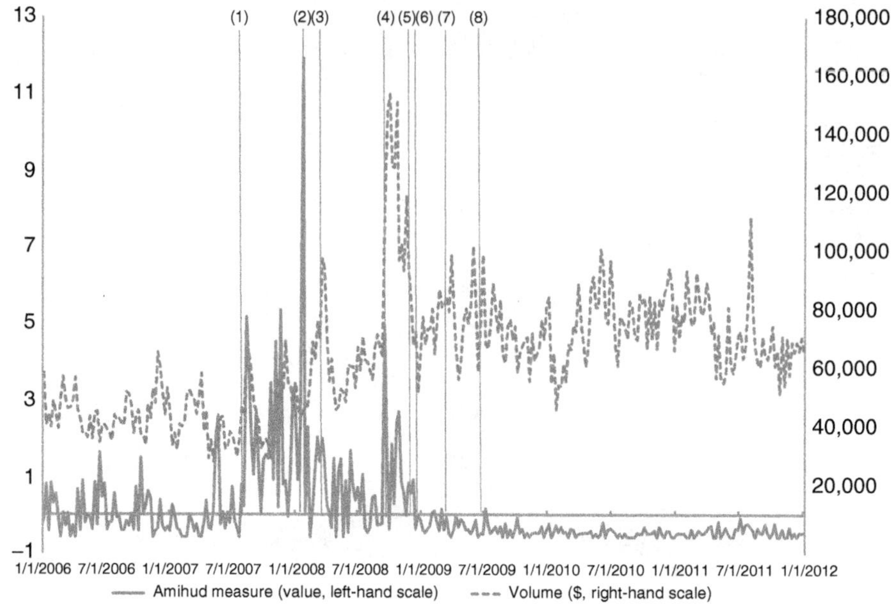

Figure 11.4 T-bills, volume, and Amihud measure.

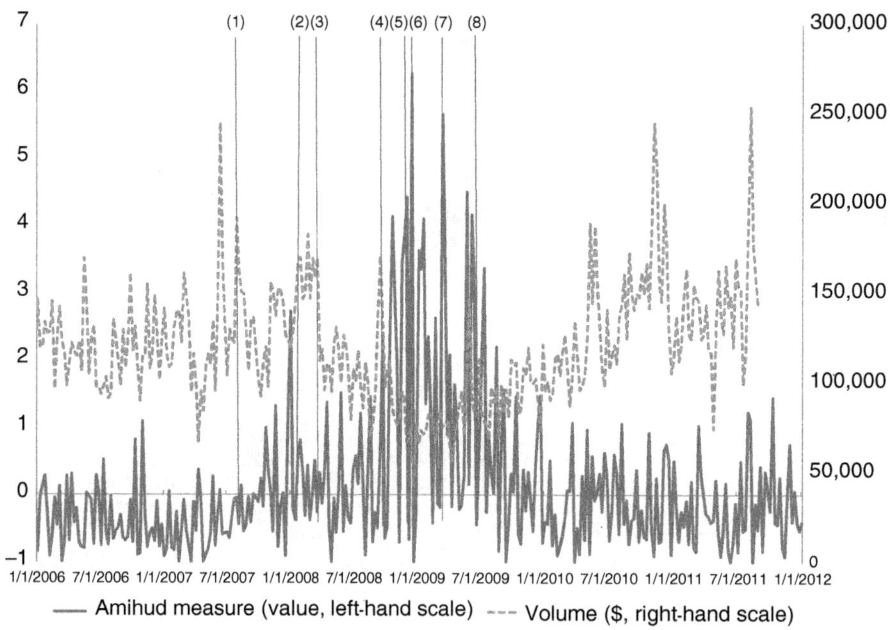

Figure 11.5 Six- to eleven-year notes and bonds, volume, and Amihud measure.

11.2.4 Trading Volume and Price Impact

In Figures 11.4 and 11.5, we present the behavior of weekly trading volume in the interdealer market as well as the (standardized) Amihud illiquidity measure (Amihud, 2002), for the T-bill sector and for the T-note and T-bond sector around the 10-year maturity.[9,10]

[9]The data on interdealer trading volume is from the Federal Reserve Bank of New York. The series presented in the figures are deseasonalized, to eliminate end-of-the-year effects.

[10]The Amihud measure is calculated as the absolute value of the weekly change in yield, divided by weekly trading volume. For the T-bill sector, we use the 6-month T-bill rate; for the T-note and T-bond sector, we use the 10-year yield. For ease of interpretation, the illiquidity measure is demeaned and standardized. Goyenko, Holden, and Trzcinka (2009) demonstrate the usefulness of the Amihud measure as a measure of price impact, in the context of equity trading.

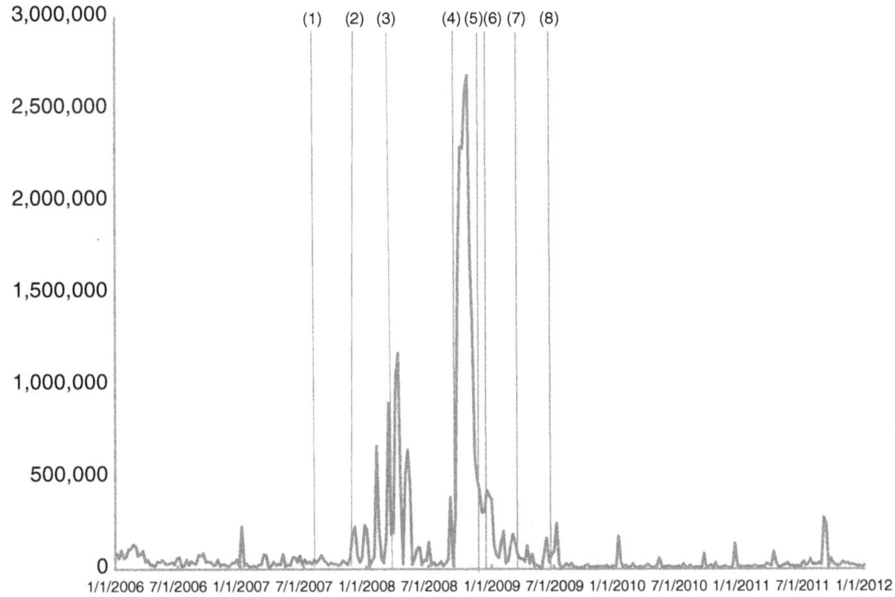

Figure 11.6 Delivery fails.

Trading volume in the T-bill sector is generally upward trending and displays higher volatility during the crisis. In the notes and bonds sector, on the other hand, trading volume trends downward, during the crisis, and upward, after the crisis. The illiquidity measure displays pronounced volatility during the crisis, for both T-bills and notes/bonds. The T-bill illiquidity measure exhibits the most pronounced spikes during the first year of the crisis, with the highest increase during the week that includes January 22, 2008, when the Fed funds rate target was cut by 75 basis points. Especially apparent, in the case of T-bills, is also the reduction of the level and volatility of the illiquidity measure after December 16, 2009. The T-bond/T-note illiquidity measure, on the other hand, exhibits the largest spikes during the second year of the crisis, especially after the Lehman Brothers bankruptcy.

11.2.5 Fails

A "fail" is a transaction that did not settle. Figure 11.6 reports the weekly dollar value (in \$ millions) of transactions in the U.S. Treasury market that failed to settle.[11] Settlement fails had been observed prior to the financial crisis – most notably, after September 11, 2001, as a result of the destruction of market infrastructure. Yet the financial crisis brings about some dramatic spikes in the dollar amount of fails. In particular, during the week ending on October 22, 2008, the dollar volume of fails reaches \$2.683 trillion. For a comparison, during the week ending on September 19, 2001, settlement fails amounted to "only" \$1.330 trillion.

As discussed by Fleming and Garbade (2005), fails are typically caused by the inability/unwillingness of the *seller* to deliver the securities. The main incentive for a seller to avoid a fail is the interest that could have been earned on the transaction proceeds, proxied by the Fed funds or general collateral (GC) repo rate. In turn, the cost of avoiding a fail is the cost of borrowing the securities to be delivered. Note that securities are borrowed by first borrowing cash though a repo, at the GC repo rate, and then by lending cash and borrowing securities through a *reverse* repo, at the special repo rate. Hence, the cost of borrowing securities is the differential between the GC and special repo rates. As special repo rates approached zero, as they did during the financial crisis, the GC/special repo rate differential approaches the GC rate itself, the incentive to borrow securities to avoid failing declines.[12]

11.2.6 Intraday Evidence on March 18, 2009

At 2:20 P.M. (ET) on March 18, 2009, the Fed announced a program of outright purchases of Treasury securities, in addition to other securities. As noted earlier, this announcement brought about a substantial adjustment in rates and prices. In Figure 11.7,

[11] The series is available from the Federal Reserve Bank of New York and covers settlement fails on the part of dealers. The Federal Reserve Bank of New York reports separately "fails to deliver" and "fails to receive." If a transaction between two dealers fails to settle, it is counted as both a fail to deliver and a fail to receive. If a transaction between a dealer and a customer does not settle, it is counted only as a fail to deliver or a fail to receive. We report the series of fails to deliver. The series of fails to receive behaves in an almost identical similar way, as the vast majority of settlement fails are for interdealer transactions. A transaction is counted as a fail for each day that it does not settle, including nontrading days. The fails include both outright and financing transactions (repos).
[12] Note that, in May 2009, the Treasury Market Practices Group introduced a "dynamic fails charge" incentivizing timely settlement; see Garbade et al. (2010).

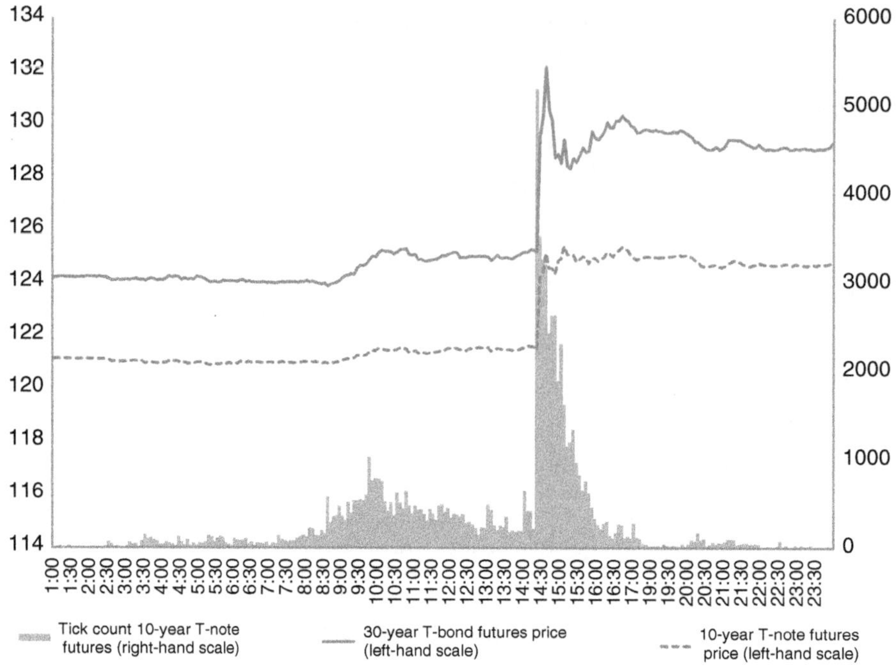

Source: Tick Data.

Figure 11.7 30-year T-bond and 10-year T-note futures prices on March 18, 2009.

we present the intraday price behavior of the 30-year T-bond and 10-year T-note futures prices on that day, together with the 5-minute tick count for the T-note futures contract.

Both futures prices adjust very quickly to the new information, with a surge in tick count for the T-note, and some evidence of overreaction for the T-bond contract. There is also a moderate increase in both prices during the morning, relative to overnight values, together with an increase in the T-note tick count.[13]

11.2.7 Summary

The main findings of our review of market indicators during the crisis highlight the following stylized facts:

- Treasury rates, the 3-month T-bill rate, in particular, seem to anticipate the drastic reductions in the Fed funds target rate implemented during the 2007–2008 period.
- Intraday price volatility increases and becomes more volatile with the crisis, but it remains elevated and volatile well after the end of the crisis.
- The off-the-run/on-the-run spread tracks well the salient episodes of the crisis and also persists at elevated levels after the end of the crisis.
- The price impact of trades increases and becomes more volatile with the crisis for both the T-bill and T-note markets, although following different patterns. For the T-bill sector, the level and volatility of price impact revert to values *below* those of the precrisis period, after the crisis, whereas they remain at a somewhat higher level for longer maturity Treasuries.
- Settlement fails increase and become more volatile during the crisis, likely as a result of the increased cost of borrowing Treasury securities.
- The adjustment to the March 18, 2009, announcement of the Fed's Treasury purchase program is a good example of almost instantaneous reaction to the release of "unexpected" news.[14]

[13]Some of the morning activity could be explained by some traders anticipating the Fed decision. Indeed, on December 1, 2008, Chairman Bernanke had delivered a speech indicating that "the Fed could purchase longer-term Treasury or agency securities on the open market in substantial quantities." (Bernanke, Ben S., "Federal Reserve Policies in the Financial Crisis." Speech at the Greater Austin Chamber of Commerce, Austin, Texas, December 1, 2008.)
[14]The FOMC meeting was a regularly scheduled meeting, but the announcement of Treasury purchases was *unexpected*.

The evidence summarized above naturally prompts several questions on the behavior of the U.S. Treasury markets. For example:

- How efficient are the U.S. Treasury markets in incorporating information on future interest rate behavior and Fed policy?
- What are the factors behind the time-varying volatility of bond returns?
- How important are jumps?
- What affects bond-market liquidity?
- Overall, what is the role of macro news in affecting all the above variables?
- Is HFT partly responsible for the surge in trading activity after important announcements?

It is to these questions that we turn next, starting with the response to the release of scheduled macro news.

11.3 THE REACTION OF BOND PRICES AND INTEREST RATES TO MACROECONOMIC NEWS

This section reviews studies of the impact of macro news (i.e., the surprise component of scheduled macroeconomic announcements such as nonfarm payrolls and CPI). We first discuss *level* effects: the impact of macro announcements on the prices of U.S. Treasury securities. We then turn to *volatility* effects: general volatility patterns associated with macro news, the effect of macro news on implied volatilities, autoregressive conditional heteroskedasticity (ARCH) and generalized autoregressive conditional heteroskedasticity (GARCH) effects, and the presence of jumps. Note that the response of the U.S. Treasury bond markets to macro news is an ideal "laboratory" to test the informational efficiency of financial markets: (i) macro news is public; (ii) the timing of the release of macro news is known in advance and there is no evidence of leakages; (iii) macrovariables are recognized as the main determinants of Fed decisions and the future path of short-term rates; and (iv) if we focus on a small window around the announcements, the price change is likely to reflect exclusively the causal impact of the news.

11.3.1 Level Effects

Balduzzi, Elton, and Green (2001) examine the impact of 26 U.S. macroeconomic announcements on Treasury prices, using intraday data from GovPX for the July 1, 1991–September 29, 1995, sample period.[15] The four securities examined are the *on-the-run* 3-month T-bill, 2-year T-note, 10-year T-note, and 30-year T-bond. Separately for each announcement k, they estimate the model:

$$R_t = \alpha_k + \beta_{1k} S_{kt} + \sum_{j=1}^{J} \beta_{2j} S_{jt} + \epsilon_t \tag{11.1}$$

where R_t is the intraday announcement-window return – from 5 minutes *before* to 30 minutes *after* the announcement – during day t, S_{kt} is the (standardized) surprise component of announcement k, and S_{jt} is the surprise component of concurring announcements. Money market services (MMS) forecasts are used to derive the surprise component of the different macroreleases.[16]

Their main results can be summarized as follows. First, 17 news releases have a significant impact on the price of at least one of the four securities. Second, these effects vary significantly according to maturity. While nine announcements affect the price of the T-bill, 13 announcements affect the price of the 2-year note, 16 announcements affect the price of the 10-year note, and 10 announcements affect the price of the 30-year bond.[17] For the 10-year note, the largest significant effect is for nonfarm payrolls (−16 basis points for a one standard deviation surprise), whereas the smallest significant effect is for the money-supply measure M2 (−1.1 basis points). Third, macrosurprises explain a substantial fraction of price volatility in the aftermath of announcements: the R^2 of the regression model in 11.1 is as high as 56.7% when the authors focus on the response

[15]GovPX is a service collecting and disseminating price information from the brokered *voice* market for Treasury securities. With the only exception of Jiang, Lo, and Verdelhan (2011), all the studies of intraday behavior in the cash market reviewed in this chapter use the GovPX data set. One earlier study using the GovPX data to analyze the effect of macro news on Treasury prices is Fleming and Remolona (1997), who consider the August 23, 1993–August 19, 1994, sample period. They find that each of the 25 sharpest price changes in the price of the on-the-run 5-year T-note during that period can be associated with a just-released announcement.

[16]Since the beginning of the 1980s, MMS surveyed around 40 market participants weekly (every Friday, except on holidays) for their forecasts of major economic indicators. MMS was acquired by Informa in 2003 and no longer exists; Action Economics is now providing the same survey service.

[17]Gürkaynak, Sack, and Swanson (2005b) focus on *forward rates* to better gauge the reaction to macro announcements of yields of different maturity. They use daily data on 1-year forward rates, 1, 5, and 10 years forward, for the sample period from January 1990 to December 2002, to evaluate the response to 13 types of macro news and to monetary policy surprises. They find several significant responses as far out as the 10-year forward date.

to the employment report. Moreover, the adjustment to news generally occurs within 1 minute after the announcement. Indeed, for the 10-year note, out of 16 significant announcements, only six impact prices beyond 1 minute after the release and none after 15 minutes.[18,19] While the level effect of macro news is exhausted quickly, heightened volatility persists for up to 60 minutes.[20] In summary, the two main messages of this study are that macro news matters for bond prices and that the bond markets are remarkably efficient at incorporating new information, as exemplified earlier in Section 11.2.6 with the reaction to the March 18, 2009, Fed announcement. In other words, market participants typically reach very quickly a consensus on what macro news implies for the future trajectory of short-term rates and the future compensation for interest rate risk.[21]

In addition to analyzing jump behavior (reviewed later on in this section), Beber and Brandt (2010) also study the effect of macro announcements on bond returns. They use daily data on T-bill, T-note, and T-bond futures, for the February 1980–December 2003 sample period, where the macro announcements being considered are the CPI, the unemployment rate, the producer price index (PPI), and nonfarm payrolls. The authors employ a regression specification that allows for an *asymmetric* impact of good and bad macro news during different phases of the business cycle:

$$R_t = \alpha_k + \beta_{1k}(1 - X_t)S^+_{kt} + \beta_{2k}(1 - X_t)S^-_{kt} + \beta_{3k}X_tS^+_{kt} + \beta_{4k}X_tS^-_{kt} + \epsilon_t \tag{11.2}$$

where X_t is a business-cycle indicator and S^+_{kt} (S^-_{kt}) equals the surprise component of the kth announcement, when the surprise is positive (negative) and equals zero otherwise.

The authors find that announcements are most important when they contain *bad* news for the bond market in *expansions* and, to a lesser extent, good news for the bond market in contractions. The strongest response to bad news is in the release of nonfarm payrolls during expansionary periods. This effect is significant at all maturities. The documented asymmetry in price responses is important because it is consistent with a perceived *asymmetric* Fed reaction function, by which positive economic news induces a strong increase in the likelihood of higher future target rates, in expansions, but only a marginal increase, in contractions. In such a setting, the response of bond prices to macroeconomic news depends critically on *both* the content of the news *and* on the phase of the business cycle.

11.3.2 The Impact of Monetary Policy

The studies reviewed above have not considered FOMC announcements of changes in the stance of monetary policy, as captured by changes in the Fed funds rate target.[22] In addition, the Fed, through its open market operations (OMO), can directly convey to the markets the stance of monetary policy. The next three articles present evidence on the reaction of the Treasury markets to changes in monetary policy.

Kuttner (2001) uses daily data on yields on bills, notes, and bonds, to estimate the effect of target changes on interest rates. The sample covers the June 6, 1989–February 2, 2000, period, for a total of 42 changes in Fed funds rate target. One key element of the analysis is the use of daily changes in the Fed funds futures rate to measure the unexpected component of the target change:[23]

$$\Delta r^*_{ft} - E_{t-1}(\Delta r^*_{ft}) = \frac{m}{n_t}\Delta f_t \tag{11.3}$$

[18]The speed of adjustment is estimated by regressing returns from τ to 30 minutes after the announcement on the announcement surprises, for different values of τ. The adjustment is complete after τ minutes if the announcement surprise is no longer significant.

[19]This result is in partial contrast with Becker, Finnerty, and Kopecky (1996) who analyze T-bond futures data for the sample period from November 8, 1988, to December 28, 1990, period. They find evidence of *underreaction* to news about the consumer price index (CPI): the T-bond futures price systematically responds in the same direction in two of the ensuing 15-minute intervals, until 9:45 A.M. In addition, there is evidence of a reversal in the direction of movement of T-bond prices between 2 and 3 hours after the CPI news is released. Furthermore, the response to news about the merchandise trade balance is delayed by 15 minutes.

[20]The authors also examine some microstructure effects. They find that trading volume increases immediately after the announcements and persists also for up to 60 minutes, whereas bid-ask spreads widen at the time of the announcements but then revert to normal values after 5–15 minutes. More discussion of high-frequency microstructure effects can be found in Section 11.4.

[21]Note that Ederington and Lee (1995) refine this result; see Section 11.3.3. Also note that the advent of HFT is likely to have further accelerated the price response to news in recent years.

[22]An earlier study of the effect of changes in the Fed funds rate on Treasury rates during the 1974–1979 period is Cook and Hahn (1989). Cook and Hahn (1988), on the other hand, study market reactions to changes in the Fed's *discount* rate. More recently, Gürkaynak, Sack, and Swanson (2005a) examine the intraday effect of monetary policy announcements from January 1990, through December 2004, finding that in addition to changes in the Fed funds rate target, Treasury yields also respond to a "path" factor, which they relate to soft information contained in FOMC statements. van Dijk, Lumsdaine, and van der Wel (2014) find that macro news, central bank officials' speeches, and congressional testimony significantly impact the volatility of *expected* Fed funds rate targets, using daily data for the July 31, 2001–September 30, 2008, sample period. Expected Fed funds rate targets are constructed using Fed funds futures prices, as in Kuttner (2001).

[23]A similar approach to the identification of monetary policy shocks is used by Faust, Swanson, and Wright (2004) in the context of a standard vector autoregression (VAR).

where r^*_{ft} is the target, m is the number of days in the month, n_t is the remaining number of days in the month, and f_t is the spot month's Fed funds futures rate.[24] Note that f_t can be viewed as the market's time-t expectation of the average fed funds rate for the current month. The author then regresses Treasury yield changes on unanticipated target changes, finding significant responses at all maturities, albeit decreasing with maturity and ranging from 0.2 (30-year bond) to 0.8 (3-month bill).[25]

Harvey and Huang (2002) examine intraday volatility patterns in the bond futures markets, as they relate to the Fed's OMO. The analysis uses data for the 1982–1988 sample period.[26]

For both T-bill and T-bond futures contracts, volatility during the 11:30 A.M.–12:00 P.M. Eastern Time (ET) interval ("Fed time") is higher than during the prior and following 1-hour intervals. For example, for the T-bill contract, volatility first increases from 0.99 basis points to 2.06 basis points and then decreases to 1.62 basis points, going from 10:30 A.M.–11:30 A.M. to 11:30 A.M.–12:30 P.M. and 12:30 P.M.–1:30 P.M.. Interestingly, though, Fed time volatility is generally higher when there are no OMO than on days with OMOs, consistent with Fed actions smoothing market expectations. In addition, the average returns often go in the *opposite* direction of the effect of the OMOs: for example, negative returns are observed for every year in the sample for the T-bond contract, for reserve-adding operations. This is consistent with the market being unable to decode Fed policy targets from Fed's actions.

Fama (2013) replicates the analysis of Kuttner (2001), using daily data on bill, note, and bond yields, for the September 27, 1983–December 31, 1993, and January 3, 1994–December 16, 2008, sample periods. During the first sample period, target changes had to be inferred from OMO; during the second sample period, on the other hand, the Fed publicly announced target changes. The unexpected component of a target change is computed here as the difference between the new target and the previous day's commercial paper rate. During the first sample period, both short-term and long-term rates respond significantly to unexpected target changes. During the second sample period, on the other hand, it is only short-term rates to be affected.

The author argues that the evidence above can be interpreted as supportive of the notion that the Fed controls interest rates. This interpretation, though, is tempered by (i) the fact that the responses of rates to unexpected target changes are smaller at longer maturities and (ii) the fact that unexpected target changes are a small part (17%) of the variance of total target changes. Moreover, one can argue that the Fed is an informed agent with private information about how market rates will evolve and uses this information when it changes the target. It is then rational that rates respond to unexpected changes in the target, even when the Fed does not seek to affect rates.

11.3.3 Realized-Volatility Patterns

While the previous two sections have focused on the immediate price response to macro news, this section turns to volatility patterns induced by macro news. Essentially, there are two aspects of volatility dynamics that have caught the attention of researchers. First, there is an obvious "burst" in volatility at announcement times, as a result of the immediate reaction of prices to news. Second, volatility may persist at heightened levels as market participants further adjust their views on the economic implications of the just-released economic quantities. The relative importance of the two effects sheds further light on the informational efficiency of the U.S. Treasury market.

Ederington and Lee (1993) document that macroeconomic announcements are responsible for most of the time-of-day and day-of-the-week volatility patterns in the U.S. Treasury markets. Focusing on the November 7, 1998–November 29, 1991, sample period, the authors first note that prices in the T-bond (futures) markets are much more volatile between 8:30 and 8:35 A.M. ET than during any other 5-minute trading period, including the 5 minutes following the market open (8:20 A.M.) and preceding the market close (3:00 P.M.). Indeed, the standard deviation of 8:30 A.M. to 8:35 A.M. returns is approximately 2.5 times the next highest 5-minute return standard deviation. Since several major macroeconomic statistical releases, including the employment report, the CPI, the PPI, gross national product (GNP), the index of leading indicators, and the merchandise trade deficit, are released at 8:30 A.M., these releases are obvious candidates for explaining the pattern. In addition, when the authors control for these announcements, volatility is basically flat across both the trading day and the trading week.

[24] This is the contract that settles based on the current month's *average* Fed funds rate.

[25] Rigobon and Sack (2004) note that the change in the expected average fed funds rate could, in turn, be affected by the behavior of bond yields. In other words, there may be a simultaneous-equation bias affecting the estimates of the impact of target changes on interest rates. Hence, the authors use an identification-through-heteroskedasticity approach (see Rigobon (2003) for details) to estimate the impact of target-change shocks on interest rates. Studying the sample January 3, 1994–November 26, 2001, they find that the estimated response of rates on far-dated Eurodollar futures contracts is much reduced after correcting for the simultaneous-equation bias. A similar approach to identification has been used recently by Wright (2012) to estimate the effect of monetary policy shocks during a recent sample when the Fed funds rate has been kept essentially at the zero lower bound.

[26] Fleming and Piazzesi (2005) also use intraday data, but they focus on FOMC announcements, during the more recent January 1, 1994–December 31, 2004, sample period. They find that the impact of target-change surprises is conditional on the slope of the yield curve (10-year minus 3-month yield): a steeper yield curve reduces the impact of target-change surprises.

The authors then examine the impact of the announcements using the regression model:

$$|r_{nt} - \bar{r}_n| = \alpha_n + \sum_{k=1}^{K} \beta_{kn} I_{kt} + \epsilon_{nt} \tag{11.4}$$

where r_{nt} is the log return during the nth 5-minute interval on day t, $\bar{r}_n$ is the average return for interval n across all days, and I_{kt} is a dummy variable, which equals one if announcement k is released on day t and equals zero otherwise. The regression model above is estimated separately for each of the 5-minute intervals. The following *seven* announcements (listed in order of decreasing impact) have a significant (0.005 p-level) effect on the T-bond futures prices: employment report, the PPI, the CPI, durable goods orders, industrial production–capacity utilization, construction spending National Association of Purchasing Managers (NAPM) survey, and the federal budget.[27] More importantly, after controlling for these announcements, volatility is basically flat both across the trading day and the trading week.

The authors also explore the speed at which the market adjusts to these news releases, focusing on both market efficiency (serial correlation of returns) and volatility. The major price adjustment occurs within *1 minute* of the release, and the direction of subsequent price adjustments is basically independent of the first minute's price change. Nonetheless, prices continue to be considerably more volatile than normal for roughly 15 minutes and slightly more volatile for several hours.

The analysis of Ederington and Lee (1993) is taken one step further by Ederington and Lee (1995), who focus on the T-bond futures price adjustment *immediately* following the releases, using both 10-second interval returns and tick-by-tick data for the November 7, 1988–October 30, 1992, sample period. The authors find that prices adjust almost immediately following a news release – generally within the first *10 seconds*. The price adjusts in a series of small, but rapid, price changes, and the major adjustment to the initial release is basically complete within 40 seconds after the release. There is weaker evidence that the market tends to overreact in this first 40 seconds and that a small correction occurs in the second or third minute following the release. Volatility remains higher than normal after 3 minutes. However, consistent with the findings of Ederington and Lee (1993), these later price adjustments are independent of the initial price change.

11.3.4 Macro News and Option-Implied Volatilities

The section above focused on the impact of macro news on *realized* bond volatility. The articles reviewed in this section, on the other hand, examine the relations between macro news and *implied* volatilities and other indicators derived from option prices.[28] In this way, we can assess whether macro announcements also have an impact on the volatility *expected* by market participants.

Ederington and Lee (1996) focus on the prices of futures options, where the measure of market uncertainty is the implied standard deviation (ISD). The ISD is the value of σ_t obtained from Black's (1976b) model for futures options:

$$C_t = \exp(-r_{ft}T_t)[F_t N(d_{1t}) - EN(d_{2t})] \tag{11.5}$$

and

$$d_{1t} = [\ln\,(F_t/E) + \sigma_t^2 T_t/2]/(\sigma_t\sqrt{T_t}) \tag{11.6}$$

$$d_{2t} = d_{1t} - \sigma_t\sqrt{T_t} \tag{11.7}$$

where C_t is the call price, r_{ft} is the instantaneous riskless rate, T_t is the time to expiration, F_t is the futures price, $N(.)$ is the cumulative normal distribution, and E is the exercise price. The impact of macro announcements on ISDs is evaluated with the regression model:

$$\ln\,(\sigma_t/\sigma_{t-1}) = \alpha + \sum_{k=1}^{K} \beta_k I_{kt} + \epsilon_t \tag{11.8}$$

The analysis is performed on daily data on T-bond futures options contracts for the sample period from November 11, 1988, to September 30, 1992. The macro announcements being considered are the construction spending–NAPM survey, the CPI, durable

[27] Since 2002 the NAPM survey is called Institute for Supply Management (ISM) survey.

[28] The implied volatility of *equity* index options, on the other hand, has been employed to study the *comovement* of stock and bond returns; see Connolly, Stivers, and Sun (2005).

goods orders, the employment report, federal budget, GNP, industrial production–capacity utilization, merchandise trade deficit, the PPI, and retail sales.

The ISD declines following the release of price-impacting scheduled announcements, where the decline tends to be greater, the shorter the option's time to expiration and the greater the announcement's impact on actual volatility. ISDs also tend to fall on Fridays and rise on Mondays, due to the tendency for scheduled announcements to be bunched on Fridays. Since ISDs tend to decline following major scheduled announcements, the authors also investigate whether it is possible to exploit this predictability to earn abnormal returns, by selling options in anticipation of a fall in σ_t. In particular, a strategy selling options in anticipation of the release of the employment report has the highest potential to be profitable. The authors find that this is not the case. The major reason is that even for delta neutral positions, losses due to the convexity of option prices and the high price volatility on the day of the announcement offset the profits due to the anticipated ISD decline.[29]

The results of Ederington and Lee (1996) are revisited by Beber and Brandt (2006) for a different sample period, using both daily and *tick-by-tick* data, from January 1995 to December 1999. Moreover, the analysis is extended beyond ISDs to the entire state-price density (SPD) of bond futures prices, where the SPDs are obtained as Edgeworth expansions around log-normal densities. Specifically, the price of a call option is approximated as

$$\begin{aligned} C_t \approx{} & \exp\,(-r_{ft}T_t)[F_tN(d_{1t}) - EN(d_{2t})] \\ & + F_t\exp\,(-r_{ft}T_t)\varphi(d_{1t})\sigma_t\sqrt{T_t}\left[\frac{\gamma_{1T_t}}{3!}\left(2\sigma_t\sqrt{T_t} - d_{1t}\right)\right. \\ & \left. - \frac{\gamma_{2T_t}}{4!}\left(1 - d_{1t}^2 + 3d_{1t}\sigma_t\sqrt{T_t} - 3\sigma_t^2T_t\right)\right] \end{aligned} \tag{11.9}$$

where the first term in the RHS is Black's (1976a) formula, $\varphi(.)$ is the standard normal density, and γ_{1T_t} and γ_{2T_t} measure *skewness* and *excess kurtosis*, respectively. The three parameters, $\mu_t = \{\sigma_t, \gamma_{1T_t}, \gamma_{2T_t}\}$, are estimated from the cross section of futures options with the same time to maturity T_t but different strike prices.

Daily changes in these parameters are then used as dependent variables in the model:

$$\Delta\mu_t = \alpha + \sum_{k=1}^{K} \beta_{1k}I_{kt} + \beta_2 T_t + \epsilon_t \tag{11.10}$$

where the announcements being considered are CPI, PPI, unemployment rate, nonfarm payrolls, retail sales, industrial production, consumer confidence, NAPM index, Fed funds rate target, and housing starts. In addition, the authors also estimate a model that includes macrosurprises (instead of announcement dummies),

$$\Delta\mu_t = \alpha_k + \beta_{1k}S_{kt} + \sum_{j=1}^{J} \beta_{2j}S_{jt} + \beta_{3k}T_t + \epsilon_{kt} \tag{11.11}$$

separately for each announcement k but controlling for contemporaneous announcements. The authors also estimate a version of the regression model above, where the β_1 and β_2 coefficients are allowed to vary depending on whether the surprises are good or bad news for the bond markets.

Consistent with the results in Ederington and Lee (1996), the release of macro news (CPI, PPI, and employment report) reduces the uncertainty implicit in the second moment of the SPD, *regardless* of the news content. The direction and magnitude of the changes in the higher-order moments of the SPD, in contrast, depend on the information content. The SPD becomes less (more) negatively skewed and less (more) fat-tailed in response to bad (good) news for the bond market. Furthermore, the results are asymmetric, in that bad news have a greater impact on the higher-order moments of the SPD than do good news.

The changes in the higher-order moments of the SPD cannot be attributed to variation in the physical price process, that is, changes in the higher-order moments of the objective probability density function (PDF). In fact, the effect of the announcements on the higher-order moments of the PDF is often exactly *opposite* to the effect on the higher-order moments of the SPD. Conversely, the changes in the higher-order moments are consistent with countercyclically varying risk aversion. Combining estimates of the SPD with estimates of the PDF obtained from a jump model for the underlying futures price, the authors recover estimates of the implied risk aversion before and after the announcements. They then relate the changes in the implied risk aversion directly to the content of macroeconomic news, finding that *good* news for the economy leads market participants to become *less* risk averse.

[29] The profitability of intraday trading strategies related to macro news is also explored by Faust and Wright (2009).

Beber and Brandt (2009) examine how and to what extent the *ex-post* resolution of uncertainty in financial markets due to the release of macro news is related to the *ex-ante* uncertainty of market participants about the state of the economy. Ex-ante macroeconomic uncertainty is measured using prices of economic derivatives traded in a new auction-based market, launched in 2002 jointly by Goldman Sachs and Deutsche Bank.[30] The underlying is the initial release of a given macroeconomic statistic (nonfarm payrolls, ISM index, retail sales, and initial jobless claims) on the scheduled announcement date. These economic derivatives are bets on macro news, and their option-implied second moments are a direct measure of uncertainty regarding the news release. The data set covers 233 auctions during the sample period from October 2002 to August 2006.

The authors extract a model-free measure of macroeconomic uncertainty from the observed prices of economic derivatives, $\sigma_{\mathrm{ECO}t}$, based on the relationship:

$$\sigma^2_{ECOt} = 2\int_0^\infty \frac{C(T_t, E) - \max(0, F_t - E)}{E^2} dE \tag{11.12}$$

where F_t, the expected outcome of the release, is calculated based on the prices of puts and calls, using put–call parity. The relationship above is also used to extract ISDs from the prices of options on the 10-year T-note futures contract and the 30-year T-bond futures contract. Changes in (squared) ISDs from before to after the macro announcements are then related to the measured macroeconomic uncertainty:

$$\Delta\sigma_t^2 = \alpha + \beta\sigma^2_{ECOt} + \epsilon_t \tag{11.13}$$

Across contracts and option expiration dates, higher ex-ante uncertainty about macrofundamentals is significantly associated with greater reduction in the implied volatility of bond options when the economic data are released and the effect appears to be permanent. Specifically, focusing on the nonfarm payrolls announcement, the degree of uncertainty about the economy explains between 26% and 39% of the variance of the change in the volatility of T-bond futures. This effect is also economically significant. For example, a high degree of uncertainty equal to one standard deviation above the average macroeconomic uncertainty in the sample predicts more than a one-third drop in the implied volatility of bond options, compared to less than a 15% drop when macroeconomic uncertainty is low (one standard deviation below the average).[31] While the authors do not comment on the nature of the reduction in implied volatilities, we can observe that it must be due to a combination of (i) a reduction in the volatility of bond returns and (ii) a reduction of the risk premium associated with the pricing of interest rate option. The disentangling of these two effects seems to be a worthwhile exercise to be pursued in future research.

11.3.5 ARCH and GARCH Effects

Given the evidence reviewed above regarding the impact of macro news on both realized and implied volatilities, it is natural to ask how the arrival of macro news affects the dynamics of the conditional second moments of bond returns.[32] This is important in order to understand if the stylized facts concerning the dynamic behavior of the conditional volatility of returns and yields are driven by macro news. Hence, we next examine the dynamics of volatility. We first review studies implemented at the daily frequency. We then turn to the intraday evidence.

11.3.5.1 Daily Evidence The motivation of Jones, Lamont, and Lumsdaine (1998) is to understand the drivers of the time variation in the volatility of returns. In particular, while it is a well-documented fact that volatility in financial markets is correlated over time, relatively little is known about *why* financial market volatility is autocorrelated. One possibility is that the news-arrival process is serially correlated. However, macro news releases are events where a "lump" of information arrives to the markets, without further information disclosure. Hence, one would expect volatility to display weaker (stronger) persistence after announcement (nonannouncement) days. This is the main test performed by the authors, using daily data on returns on 5-, 10-, and 30-year Treasury securities for the October 9, 1979, to December 31, 1995, period. The announcements that they focus on are the employment report and the PPI.

[30]Gürkaynak and Wolfers (2006) provide an initial analysis of this market, estimating market-based forecasts from the prices of digital options, for the October 2002–July 2005 sample period. They then construct two types of macro news using market-based forecasts and survey forecasts, respectively. They use intraday data to show that Treasury prices react significantly to the first type of news – nonfarm payrolls, in particular – but the reaction to the second type of news is mainly insignificant.

[31]The authors also use macroeconomic uncertainty to explain trading behavior. They find that higher macroeconomic uncertainty is associated with a *greater* increase in transacted volume after the news release. Conversely, there is a negative relation between macroeconomic uncertainty and the change in open interest after the news release; that is, higher ex-ante uncertainty translates into a larger reduction in open interest after the announcement.

[32]Note that some authors have also investigated the role of macro news for the stock-bond *correlation*; see Christiansen and Ranaldo (2007). Brenner, Pasquariello, and Subrahmanyam (2009) also examine the *joint* effect of macroeconomic announcements on the conditional moments of U.S. Treasury bonds, stocks, and corporate bonds.

The authors estimate an extended GARCH(1,1) model modified to account for differential ARCH and GARCH effects on announcement and nonannouncement days:

$$R_t = \mu + \theta I_t^A + \phi R_{t-1} + \sqrt{s_t}\epsilon_t \tag{11.14}$$

$$s_t = \left(1 + \delta_0 I_t^A\right)\left(1 + \delta_1 I_{t-1}^A\right) \tag{11.15}$$

$$h_t = \omega + \left[\alpha_0 + \alpha_A I_{t-1}^A\right]\epsilon_{t-1}^2 + \left[\beta_0 + \beta_A I_{t-1}^A\right]h_{t-1} \tag{11.16}$$

where R_t is the return, I_t^A is an announcement-day dummy, and ϵ_t has conditional variance h_t. Across maturities, the ARCH effect is much weaker for announcement shocks ($\alpha_A < 0$). Indeed, the null hypothesis that the impact of announcement-day shocks is zero ($\alpha_0 = -\alpha_A$) cannot be rejected, consistent with the market quickly incorporating public information. Conversely, the GARCH effect after announcement and nonannouncement days is essentially the same: on the day after announcement days, conditional volatility decays at the same rate as on other days ($\beta_A \approx 0$). Finally, while announcement-day volatility is significantly higher than nonannouncement-day volatility (δ_0 is positive and significant), on days after announcement days, the unconditional volatility is also not statistically greater than on other days (δ_1 is insignificant).[33]

In Christiansen (2000), the focus is shifted from univariate volatility patterns to the *covariance* structure of bond returns. Specifically, the author investigates the effect of macroeconomic announcements (employment report and PPI) in a heteroskedastic *multivariate* model of daily excess returns of six government notes and bonds with different maturities (2-, 3-, 5-, 7-, 10-, and 30-year) for the period from January 1, 1983, to December 31, 1998.

The author estimates an extended GARCH(1,1), with constant conditional correlations. The ARCH effect for bond i is allowed to depend on whether the previous day there was an announcement and whether the previous announcement-day's return innovation was positive or negative:

$$h_{ii,t} = \omega_i + \left[\alpha_{i0} + \alpha_{iA} I_{t-1}^A + \alpha_{i-} I_{t-1}^A I_{i,t-1}^-\right]\epsilon_{i,t-1}^2 + \beta_i h_{ii,t-1} \tag{11.17}$$

where $I_{i,t}^-$ is a dummy for negative return innovations. The conditional correlation between any two bond returns is allowed to differ depending on whether there is an announcement:

$$h_{ij,t} = \rho_{ij}\left(1 + \rho_{ijA} I_t^A\right)\sqrt{h_{ii,t}h_{jj,t}} \tag{11.18}$$

Consistent with Jones, Lamont, and Lumsdaine (1998), the author finds that announcement shocks do not persist at all; that is, there are no announcement-day ARCH effects ($\alpha_{i0} + \alpha_{iA} \approx 0$) nor evidence of asymmetries ($\alpha_{i-} \approx 0$). On the other hand, there are significant ARCH effects on nonannouncement days ($\alpha_{i0} > 0$). The conditional variance is high and similarly persistent across bonds of different maturity: $\beta \approx 0.94$. In general, bond returns are strongly correlated ($\rho_{ij} > 0.78$), and the correlation is stronger, the closer the bonds are with respect to the time to maturity. The maturity dependency is substantially dampened on announcement days, which implies that releases of macroeconomic news induce common movements in the government bond market. The rise on macroeconomic announcement days in the conditional covariance of two government bonds is of economic importance (ρ_{ijA} is as high as 0.11) and is a decreasing function of the time to maturity of either of the bonds.

de Goeij and Marquering (2006) investigate whether there is an *asymmetric* ARCH effect associated with announcement days and with large macro surprises. Specifically, the authors estimate the volatility model:

$$h_t = \omega_0 + \omega_A I_t^A + \left[\alpha_0 + \alpha_A I_{t-1}^A\right]\epsilon_{t-1}^2 + \left[\beta_0 + \beta_A I_{t-1}^A\right]\left(\epsilon_{t-1}^-\right)^2 + \gamma_0 h_{t-1} \tag{11.19}$$

where $\epsilon_{t-1}^- = \min\{0, \epsilon_t\}$. A variation of the model above is also estimated, where the announcement-day dummy is replaced by a dummy capturing large macrosurprises (greater than one standard deviation, in absolute value). The analysis is implemented on daily data from January 1982 to September 2004 for 1-, 3-, 5-, and 10-year Treasury securities. The main results are as follows. First, conditional variances are much higher on macroeconomic announcement days ($\omega_A > 0$ and significant), and FOMC announcements are especially important for short-term bonds, whereas for long-term bonds, PPI and the employment report are the most important announcements. Second, consistent with Jones, Lamont, and Lumsdaine (1998) and Christiansen

[33] Interestingly, Li and Engle (1998) obtain different results by studying the futures market, rather than the cash market. They use daily T-bond futures data for the sample period from November 9, 1988, to December 31, 1997, and focus on the CPI, PPI, and employment announcements. The authors find that GARCH effects are smaller on announcement days, whereas the opposite is true for ARCH effects. Furthermore, they distinguish between the effects of positive and negative return shocks, finding that positive shocks on announcement days depress volatility on successive days, while negative shocks on announcement days increase volatility. They explain the existence of the announcement leverage effect by the fact that investors take highly leveraged positions in the futures market, which is not the case in the cash bond market.

(2000), announcement-day volatility does not persist ($\alpha_0 + \alpha_A \approx 0$). Third, the asymmetric volatility parameters (β_0 and β_A) are mainly insignificant, consistent with Christiansen (2000).

Note that the lack of asymmetric volatility effects in bond returns is in contrast with the widely documented "leverage" effect in equities (see Black 1976a), where bad news has a larger impact on volatility than good news.[34] The absence of leverage effects in the volatility of Treasury bonds is to be expected, though, as financial leverage is not applicable to government bonds.

11.3.5.2 Intraday Evidence While Jones, Lamont, and Lumsdaine (1998) study ARCH and GARCH patterns at the daily frequency, Bollerslev, Cai, and Song (2000) turn their attention to *intraday* T-bond futures returns.[35] The analysis is based on a 4-year sample period of 5-minute returns, from 1994 to 1997, where the key element is a regression model of intraday seasonal patterns:

$$\begin{aligned} 2\ln \frac{|R_{nt} - \bar{R}|}{\sqrt{h_t}/\sqrt{80}} &= \alpha + \sum_{k=1}^{K} \beta_k I_{knt} + \beta_1 n + \beta_2 n^2 \\ &\quad + \sum_{p=1}^{P} \left(\gamma_{cp} \cos \frac{2\pi p}{80} n + \gamma_{sp} \sin \frac{2\pi p}{80} n \right) \\ &\quad + \delta D_{nt} + \epsilon_{nt} \end{aligned} \tag{11.20}$$

where R_{nt} is the nth 5-minute return on day t, $\bar{R}$ is the average 5-minute return, h_t is the estimated daily variance, 80 is the number of 5-minute returns during the trading day, I_{knt} is a dummy variable for announcement and week-day effects, and D_{nt} is an expiration-day dummy. The third and fourth terms on the RHS of 11.20 capture a linear and a quadratic intraday time trend, respectively, whereas the fifth term is a Fourier transform capturing more complex intraday seasonal patterns. The authors consider a comprehensive list of 27 macroeconomic announcements, and the estimation is carried on in two steps, where h_t is estimated in a first step from a fractionally integrated GARCH model, which does not account for announcement effects and seasonal patterns.

Consistent with Ederington and Lee (1993), there are *two* spikes in intraday volatility at 8:30 A.M. and 10:00 A.M. (ET), respectively, corresponding to the regularly scheduled macroeconomic announcements in the United States at these times. There is also an overall U-shaped pattern in the volatility across the day, which gives rise to a strong daily pattern in the autocorrelation of the absolute 5-minute returns. After filtering out this periodic pattern, it is possible to identify rapid initial decay in the autocorrelations, lasting 1 day or so, followed by an extremely slow rate of decay, lasting for up to 10 days.

Moreover, the largest returns in the U.S. T-bond market are linked to the release of macroeconomic announcements. At both the daily and intraday frequencies, the announcement effects have the highest marginal explanatory power for the volatility among the three components (calendar, announcement, and ARCH effects). Most notably, the release of the Humphrey–Hawkins testimony and the employment report generates an average instantaneous jump in volatility of about 2100% and 1400%, respectively, along with a 93% and 75% increase in the cumulative absolute return for trading days that contain these two particular announcements.[36] Moreover, the 15 most important regularly scheduled macroeconomic news reports result in an increase in the daily cumulative absolute returns in excess of 10%.

11.3.6 Jumps

As mentioned earlier, macro news represents lumpy arrivals of information and generates sudden increases in bond return volatility. This evidence motivates the study of the presence of jumps in interest rates and bond prices. Establishing the presence and importance of jumps is important from an asset pricing perspective. Standard continuous-time term structure models, such as Vasicek (1977) and Cox, Ingersoll, and Ross (1985), postulate "smooth" behavior of the short rate – that is, the short rate follows a diffusion process, which is characterized by *continuous* sample paths – and derive implications for yields of different maturities.

[34] The leverage effect is due to equity being a leveraged claim on the assets of the firm: a drop in the value of equity increases financial leverage, which makes equity more risky and increases its volatility.

[35] In the same vein as Bollerslev, Cai, and Cai (2000), Ederington and Lee (2001) explore ARCH–GARCH effects, the impact of macro news, and seasonality patterns for the intraday volatility of T-bond futures contracts. The analysis is performed on 10-minute return data for T-bond futures contracts, from July 3, 1989, to May 28, 1993. Among their main findings is that ARCH effects are *less pronounced* when seasonal patterns and announcement effects are incorporated into the model. Moreover, the GARCH(1,1) model underestimates the impact of the most recent and very distant shocks and overestimates the impacts of shocks with intermediate lags. Finally, volatility persists much longer after unscheduled announcements, as compared to scheduled announcements, and, consistent with Christiansen (2000), there is little difference in volatility persistence after positive and negative price shocks.

[36] The Humphrey–Hawkins testimony, or Monetary Policy Report, is delivered by the Chairman of the Board of Governors twice a year, in February and July, and reports on the basic state of the U.S. economy and its financial welfare.

The presence of jumps invalidates those relations.[37] Moreover, models of bond options also assume diffusion behavior of interest rates and prices. The presence of jumps requires the modification of those pricing models as well.

11.3.6.1 Daily Frequency Johannes (2004) examines the statistical and economic role of jumps in *continuous-time* interest rate models. The analysis is implemented on daily data on 3-month T-bill data, for the sample period from January 1965 to February 1999.

To test for the presence of jumps, this chapter compares the unconditional and conditional nonnormalities in interest rates with analogs generated by candidate diffusion models. The approach is based on a simulation exercise and involves four *steps*:

1. Compute sample measures of kurtosis of interest rate changes.
2. For a given diffusion model (the no-jump null), simulate a large number of sample paths.
3. For each sample path, recompute the measures of kurtosis.
4. Compare the sample test statistics with the percentiles of the simulated distribution under the null.

Two diffusion benchmarks are used to generate the simulated data. The first benchmark is a flexible single-factor model:

$$dr_{ft} = \mu(r_{ft})dt + \sigma(r_{ft})dW_t \tag{11.21}$$

where r_{ft} is the short rate, $\mu(.)$ and $\sigma^2(.)$ are flexible functions of r_{ft}, and dW_t is the increment of a Wiener process. The second benchmark is a stochastic-volatility model:

$$dr_{ft} = \kappa_r(\mu_r - r_{ft})dt + r_{ft}^{\gamma}\sqrt{V_t}dW_{1t} \tag{11.22}$$

$$d\ln\,(V_t) = \kappa_v(\mu_v - \ln\,(V_t))dt + \sigma_v dW_{2t} \tag{11.23}$$

where dW_{1t} and dW_{2t} are increments of Wiener processes.

Neither of the two diffusion models can generate kurtosis measures consistent with those of observed 3-month T-bill rates. For example, at the daily frequency, the 99th percentile of the empirical distribution of the unconditional kurtosis measure is 15.48, whereas the sample unconditional kurtosis is 24.30.

The author then introduces a flexible short-rate model that allows for jumps:

$$d\ln\,(r_{ft}) = \mu(r_{ft})dt + \sigma(r_{ft-})dW_t + d\left(\sum_{n=1}^{N_t} Z_n\right) \tag{11.24}$$

where N_t is a point process with random intensity $\lambda(r_{ft})$ and Z_n is normally distributed, with mean zero and constant variance σ_Z^2. The fourth and sixth moments of (log) interest rate differences allow to identify $\lambda(.)$ and σ_Z^2, whereas the first and second moments allow to identify $\mu(.)$ and $\sigma(.)$, respectively.

Jumps play a *dominant role* in interest rate dynamics. At low rates ($r_{ft} \approx 5\%$), jumps generate more than half of the conditional variance of interest rate changes. At high rates ($r_{ft} \approx 15\%$), jumps generate almost two-thirds of the conditional variance of interest rate changes. The daily probability of a jump is about 6%, at low rates, and more than 20% at high rates, with a three standard deviation jump move corresponding to approximately 50 basis points, at low rates, and as much as 150 basis points at high rates.

The author then estimates jump times and sizes and examines the 1979–1982 and 1991–1993 periods in detail. Each of the large interest rate moves during these two periods can be identified as jumps and coincide with *unexpected* news arrivals, both scheduled and unscheduled.

The author also examines the pricing implications of jumps in interest rates. While jumps have little impact on the yield curve, they are important in the pricing of out-of-the-money options.

Beber and Brandt (2010) focus specifically on the role of *scheduled* macro news in affecting the arrival rate and size of jumps in bond prices. They use daily data on T-bill, T-note, and T-bond futures, for the February 1980–December 2003 sample period. The macro announcements being considered are CPI, unemployment rate, PPI, and nonfarm payrolls.

The authors estimate a model of bond futures returns:

$$r_t = \mu_t + \epsilon_{1t} + \epsilon_{2t} \tag{11.25}$$

[37] See Piazzesi (2005) for an example of a term structure model that incorporates short-rate jump behavior induced by Fed policy.

where ϵ_{1t} is normal with mean zero and variance h_t, whereas ϵ_{2t} follows the jump process:

$$\epsilon_{2t} = \sum_{n=1}^{N_t} Z_{jt} - \theta_t \lambda_t \tag{11.26}$$

where Z_{jt} is normal with mean θ_t and constant variance. The conditional mean return depends on the phase of the business cycle:

$$\mu_t = \mu_{1t}(1 - X_t) + \mu_{2t} X_t \tag{11.27}$$

Similarly, the conditional variance of the normal innovation follows the GARCH(1,1) process:

$$h_t = \omega_0 + \omega_t \epsilon_{t-1}^2 + \gamma_0 h_{t-1} \tag{11.28}$$

where the ARCH effect ω is *time-varying* and depends on X_t and the ex-post time t estimate of the likely number of jumps occurred between time $t - 1$ and time t. The jump arrival rate λ_t is a function of what announcements are taking place on a given day:

$$\lambda_t = \lambda_0 + \sum_{k=1}^{K} \lambda_k I_{kt} \tag{11.29}$$

The mean jump size θ_t depends on four announcement surprises (CPI, PPI, unemployment rate, and nonfarm payrolls) in a way that, in turn, is business-cycle-dependent:[38]

$$\theta_t = (1 - X_t)\left(\theta_{01} + \sum_{k=1}^{K+1} \theta_{1k} S_{kt}\right) + X_t \left(\theta_{02} + \sum_{k=1}^{K+1} \theta_{2k} S_{kt}\right) \tag{11.30}$$

The estimates of the model in 11.25 show that macroeconomic news has a substantial impact on bond volatility, by increasing jump intensities – especially in the case of the employment report – and by affecting the distributions of the jump size. The relation between macroeconomic news and jumps depends on the combination of the announcement type, the maturity of the bond, and the phase of the business cycle. Specifically, the proportion of releases resulting in a jump decreases dramatically for short maturities and is generally lower in recessions. Jumps on announcement days are associated predominantly with nonfarm payrolls releases, but CPI news becomes relatively more associated with jumps in recessions and at medium maturities. As in prior studies, jump volatility is not persistent: the ARCH effect is all but muted after a jump is likely to have taken place.

11.3.6.2 Intraday Frequency The analysis of jumps is taken to the *intraday* frequency by Andersen, Bollerslev, and Diebold (2007), who study tick-by-tick transaction prices for the T-bond futures contract. The sample covers the period from January 1990 through December 2002.

In the presence of jumps, as the sampling frequency increases, the realized bond return volatility,

$$RV_{t+1}(\Delta) \equiv \sum_{n=1}^{1/\Delta} r_{t+n\Delta,\Delta}^2 \tag{11.31}$$

converges to

$$\lim_{\Delta \to 0} RV_{t+1}(\Delta) = \int_t^{t+1} \sigma^2(s) ds + \sum_{t < s \leq t+1} Z^2(s) \tag{11.32}$$

where the second term is the sum of the squared jumps that occurred between t and $t + 1$. Hence, in order to separately identify the two components of the realized quadratic variation, the authors use the concept of *realized bipower variation,*

$$BV_{t+1}(\Delta) \equiv \frac{1}{(2/\pi)} \sum_{n=2}^{1/\Delta} |r_{t+n\Delta,\Delta}||r_{t+(n-1)\Delta,\Delta}| \tag{11.33}$$

[38]Because the unemployment rate is released together with nonfarm payrolls, there are only three announcement dummies I_{kt}.

which converges to

$$\lim_{\Delta \to 0} BV_{t+1}(\Delta) = \int_t^{t+1} \sigma^2(s)\, ds \tag{11.34}$$

The contribution of jumps to the volatility of returns can then be estimated by[39]

$$\lim_{\Delta \to 0} RV_{t+1}(\Delta) - BV_{t+1}(\Delta) = \sum_{t<s\leq t+1} Z^2(s) \tag{11.35}$$

Based on sample counterparts of 11.34 and 11.35, the authors construct estimates of the components of the realized variation attributable to continuous-sample-path variation, $C_{t+1}(\Delta)$, and to jump variation, $J_{t+1}(\Delta)$. They then formulate and estimate a heterogeneous autoregressive realized-volatility model that differentiates between the two components:

$$\begin{aligned} RV_{t,t+h} = {} & \beta_0 + \beta_{CD} C_t + \beta_{CW} C_{t-5,t} + \beta_{CM} C_{t-22,t} \\ & + \beta_{JD} J_t + \beta_{JW} J_{t-5,t} + \beta_{JM} J_{t-22,t} + \epsilon_{t,t+h} \end{aligned} \tag{11.36}$$

where $C_{t-h,t}$ and $J_{t-h,t}$ are h-day trailing averages of C_t and J_t, respectively.

The authors find that jumps dynamics are much less persistent (and predictable) than continuous-sample-path dynamics. In addition, the estimates of 11.36 show that the continuous-variation measures are always significant in predicting realized volatility, whereas, in most cases, the jump-variation measures are not.

Jiang, Lo, and Verdelhan (2011) identify jumps in bond prices based on the "variance-swap" approach: in the absence of jumps, the difference between *simple* returns and *log* returns captures 1/2 of the instantaneous return variance. The variance-swap measure is defined as

$$SWV_{t+1} \equiv 2 \sum_{n=1}^{1/\Delta} \left(R_{t+n\Delta,\Delta} - r_{t+n\Delta,\Delta} \right) \tag{11.37}$$

Under the no-jumps null, $SWV_{t+1}(\Delta)$ is "close" to $RV_{t+1}(\Delta)$.

The analysis is implemented on intraday (5-minute) BrokerTec data for 2-, 3-, 5-, and 10-year T-note and the 30-year bond for the sample period from January 2004 to June 2007.[40] The authors identify a large number of jumps for all maturities. For example, there are 120 jumps in the 2-year note prices during the sample period. Overall, the average jump size is more than ten times the 5-minute return standard deviation.

With identified jumps, the authors search for potentially related economic news or events. They identify an extensive list of pre-scheduled macroeconomic news and events as potential causes of bond price jumps. The list includes major news announcements widely considered in the existing literature, such as initial jobless claims, CPI, nonfarm payrolls, retail sales, PPI, consumer confidence, and the ISM index. The list also includes announcements that have been considered less important and thus largely omitted in previous studies, for example, the NY Empire State Index (a regional economic indicator published by the Federal Reserve Bank of New York). Overall, the authors find that a large number of jumps occur during prescheduled macroeconomic news announcements. For example, about 90% of jumps in the 2-year note prices occur within 10 minutes of prescheduled news announcement times.[41]

11.3.7 Summary

This section has reviewed several articles analyzing the high-frequency, time-series properties of interest rates and bond prices. The organizing theme of this section is the impact of macro news. In summary, the following main patterns arise:

- Among the different macro announcements impacting prices, the nonfarm payrolls announcement, often referred by market participants as the "king" of announcements, dominates both level and volatility effects. Other important announcements across studies are the NAPM/ISM index and the PPI.
- Announcements regarding the Fed funds rate target are also important, with a stronger effect at short maturities. However, it is difficult to determine whether this is a causal or simply an information effect.

[39] Since the difference between realized volatility and realized bipower variation can turn negative, in estimation, the authors use the quantity $\max\{RV_{t+1}(\Delta) - BV_{t+1}(\Delta), 0\}$.

[40] BrokerTec is an electronic trading platform supported by ICAP.

[41] The authors also study the relation between jumps and liquidity shocks; we will review their analysis in Section 11.4.

- Macro news is responsible for most of the time-of-day and day-of-the-week volatility patterns in the Treasury markets. In particular, macro news leads to significant increases in bond price volatility on the day and at the time when the news is released.
- The release of macro news reduces option-implied volatility, more so, the higher is the ex-ante uncertainty on the news release.
- The increase in volatility is not persistent, though: ARCH effects in the aftermath of macro news are not significant.
- Interest rates and bond prices "jump" at the time of news announcements, but also at the time of important unscheduled news.

11.4 MARKET-MICROSTRUCTURE EFFECTS

This section reviews literature studying high-frequency market-microstructure effects in the U.S. Treasury markets.[42] By microstructure effects, we denote a variety of patterns related to trading activity, execution costs, and the informational environment, such as trading volume, bid–ask spreads, and the price impact of trades. The recognition of these patterns is crucial for the effective implementation of trading strategies on the part of market participants. For example, Green (2004) documents that the price impact of trades is higher after macro announcements. This should lead *uninformed* traders to avoid implementing trades in the aftermath of announcements. It is also worth noting that the studies referenced in this section analyze sample periods during which HFT was not yet likely to be prevalent. In Section 11.6, we turn specifically to how HFT has recently affected the trading environment in the U.S. Treasury market.

11.4.1 Microstructure Effects in the Cash Market

Fleming and Remolona (1999) use intraday data to examine not only the volatility effects of macro announcements, as Ederington and Lee (1993) do for bond futures, but also the behavior of trading volume and bid–ask spreads. The authors focus on three 8:30 A.M. ET announcements: the employment report, the CPI, and the PPI.[43] The sample period is from August 23, 1993, to August 19, 1994.

In characterizing the market's response, they uncover *two* distinct stages of adjustment. During a brief first stage (2 minutes), the release of a major macroeconomic announcement induces a sharp and nearly instantaneous price change – the 8:30–8:31 A.M. standard deviation on announcement days is more than 13 times higher than on nonannouncement days – with a *reduction* in trading volume. At the time of the sharp price change, the bid–ask spread widens dramatically – the 8:30–8:31 A.M. spread is more than seven times higher than on nonannouncement days. Since it is public information what drives prices at the time of the announcement, it is likely to be inventory control to drive the spread.[44]

In a prolonged second stage (90 minutes for volume and 60 minutes for volatility), trading volume surges and then persists along with high price volatility and moderately wide bid–ask spreads. During the 9:30–9:35 A.M. interval, for example, volatility and trading volume are 1.4 and 1.7 times higher than on nonannouncement days, respectively. This extension of the adjustment process is consistent with residual disagreement among investors about the information content of the just-released announcement.

Green (2004) studies the informational role of trading on macro announcement days, using trade-by-trade data for the July 1, 1991, to September 29, 1995, sample period. Specifically, the author focuses on trading taking place between 8:00 and 9:00 A.M. ET, since many important announcements are made at 8:30 A.M. The model used by the author explains *transaction* price changes, ΔP_t, as a function of signed order flow and macrosurprises,

$$\Delta P_t = \beta_1 \Delta V_t + \beta_2 (V_t - \rho V_{t-1}) + \sum_{k=1}^{K} \beta_{3k} S_{kt} + \epsilon_t \tag{11.38}$$

where $V_t = 1$ if the trade is buyer-initiated and $V_t = -1$ if the trade is seller-initiated, ρ is the serial correlation coefficient for V_t, and t measures time in transactions. The parameter β_1 quantifies the effect of two trades of *different* sign (a purchase followed by a

[42] A few studies provide a descriptive analysis of liquidity patterns in the voice and electronic markets. Fleming (1997) studies liquidity during both day and overnight trading, using intraday data for the April 4, 1994–September 19, 1994, sample period. Fleming (2003) estimates and evaluates a set of different liquidity measures using intraday data for on-the-run bills and notes during the December 30,1996–March 31, 2000, sample period. Mizrach and Neely (2006) document the transition of trading from the voice market to an electronic market, the eSpeed electronic communication network (ECN), founded by Cantor Fitzgerald and Co. Fleming and Mizrach (2009) use data from January 2001 to February 2006 to characterize trading activity and liquidity on the BrokerTec ECN for the on-the-run 2-, 3-, 5-, 10-, and 30-year Treasury securities.

[43] Nonannouncement days, though, are identified based on the absence of any announcement from a broader set of 18 announcements.

[44] By "inventory control," we denote the compensation required by market makers for the price risk faced on their inventory.

sale or a sale followed by a purchase) and captures compensation for *liquidity provision*: the cost of order processing and holding inventory. The parameter β_2, on the other hand, isolates the *informational* effect of innovations in the trading flow $(V_t - \rho V_{t-1})$: the compensation for trading with informed traders (adverse-selection costs). The two price-impact parameters, as well as ρ, are allowed to take on different values depending on whether the observation takes place before or after an announcement or on a day when there are no announcements.[45]

Estimates of β_1 are *negative* and significant and more so after economic announcements; that is, a buyer-initiated trade followed by a seller-initiated (a seller-initiated trade followed by a buyer-initiated) trade leads to a price increase (decrease), which is larger after announcements. This suggests that, on average, dealers *consume* liquidity in the U.S. Treasury interdealer market. Estimates of β_2, on the other hand, are positive and significant, and larger after economic announcements; that is, an unexpected buyer-initiated (seller-initiated) trade impacts positively (negatively) prices and more so after economic announcements. In other words, the informational impact of trades is stronger after announcements. This is consistent with the explanation suggested by Fleming and Remolona (1999) of a disagreement among investors about the information content of the announcements.

The analysis is further refined by allowing the announcement-day parameter estimates to differ across the four time intervals: 8:00–8:15 A.M., 8:15–8:30 A.M., 8:30–8:45 A.M., and 8:45–9:00 A.M.. Both β_1 and β_2 increase, in absolute value, until the 8:30–8:45 A.M. time interval and then decrease. This suggests that both the (negative) compensation for providing liquidity and the informational role of trading increase up to and immediately after the announcements but then tend to revert to normal levels.

Huang, Cai, and Wang (2002) examine the trading behavior of primary dealers in the 5-year Treasury note interdealer broker market using intraday (10-minute intervals) data for 1998. First, the authors focus on the impact of macro news on liquidity variables. The authors estimate the regression model,

$$Y_{nt} = \sum_{n=1}^{N} \alpha_n D_{nt} + \sum_{k=1}^{K} \beta_k I_{knt} + \beta \tau_{nt} + \epsilon_{nt} \tag{11.39}$$

where Y_{nt} is a liquidity variable, D_{nt} is a time-of-the-day dummy, I_{knt} is a nonlinear function of the time since the release of announcement k on day t, and τ_{nt} is a time trend. I_{knt} captures the gradual dissipation of the announcement effect as time elapses.

The liquidity variables are (i) trading volume, (ii) trade frequency, (iii) average trade size, and (iv) average bid–ask spread. The authors find that 17 macroindicators have a significant positive impact on trade frequency, whereas no announcement has a significant positive impact on trade size. Of the 17 announcements significantly impacting trade frequency, the most important are the employment report, employment costs, and the Beige book. Twelve announcements also have a significant positive impact on the bid–ask spread: employment report, employment costs, and the PPI.

The authors then investigate further the nature of the widening of bid–ask spreads. In a similar spirit as Green (2004), they separate liquidity and informational effects, by computing the *effective* spread and the *adverse-selection* component of the spread.[46] The effective half-spread is defined as $|P_t Q_t|$, where P_t is the transaction price and Q_t is the midpoint of the prevailing quotes at the time of the trade. The adverse information component is calculated as the difference between the effective and realized half-spreads, where the realized half-spread is defined as the (negative of the) price change for initial trades at the (ask) bid. They find that the adverse-selection component of the spread significantly increases 30 minutes after all the most significant announcements, suggesting trading based on private knowledge of inventory and/or order flow.

Finally, the authors investigate the volume-volatility relationship. They estimate the regression model:[47]

$$|r_t| = \alpha + \beta E_{t-1}(V_t) + \epsilon_t \tag{11.40}$$

where r_t is here the 10-minute return, V_t is a measure of trading volume, and t measures time in 10-minute intervals. The conditional expectation $E_{t-1}(V_t)$ is assumed to be a linear function of lagged volume and volatility. In one specification, trade volume is replaced by trade frequency and trade size. Interestingly, the authors find that while trade frequency impacts volatility positively, the impact of trade size is *negative*. The authors conclude that trade frequency reflects the presence of information-based trading, but trade size does not.

[45]More recently, Menkveld, Sarkar, and van der Wei (2012) estimate a similar regression model using data from the futures market, allowing them to isolate *customer* order flow out of total flow (both dealer and customer). They consider two samples: a sample covering the open-outcry market from 1994 to 1997 and a sample covering the electronic market from February 3, 2009, until February 11, 2010. They find that customer flow is more informative on macro announcement days than on nonannouncement days and that the announcement-day informativeness of flow is strongest when analyst forecasts are most dispersed.

[46]This approach follows Huang and Stoll (1996).

[47]While the articles reviewed here focus on the impact of order flow on bond prices, Cohen and Shin (2003) also study how trading activity is affected by lagged returns, finding evidence of *positive-feedback* trading at high frequency.

While Green (2004) focuses on the informativeness of trades on days of macro announcements, Brandt and Kavajecz (2004) measure the response of yields to order-flow imbalances on days *without* major macroeconomic announcements, using intraday data from January 1992 to December 1999. The main result is that yields respond significantly and negatively to contemporaneous net order flow. Interestingly, most yields react to net order flow for *all* maturities, as opposed to each bond reacting only to its own order flow. In particular, each maturity range has a strong reaction to its own order-flow imbalance, but an even stronger reaction to the order-flow imbalance at the *2- to 5-year* maturity range. The explanatory power of order flow is substantial, as high as 25% (adjusted R^2) for the on-the-run securities in the 2- to 5-year maturity range and as high as 28% for the first principal component of on-the-run yields.

The evidence that yields react to net order flow for other maturities is consistent with the impact of order flow capturing a *price-discovery* effect – the aggregation of heterogeneous private information (or heterogeneous interpretation of public information) through trading – rather than an inventory effect. Further evidence of this interpretation is that off-the-run yields only respond to on-the-run order flow and that lagged order flow does not impact yields. Indeed, if the price impact of trades was driven by an inventory effect, we would expect yields to react to order flow for the same maturity range. Moreover, we would expect off-the-run yields to respond to off-the-run flow. Finally, given that the effect of inventory buildup would not last, we would expect a positive correlation between yield changes and lagged order-flow imbalances.

Finally, the authors examine the differential impact of order flow when liquidity is high and when liquidity is low. Consistently across maturities, the incremental impact of flow when liquidity is low is negative and significant in most instances. This finding is consistent with market participants paying more attention to order flow when the subjective valuations are relatively uncertain and liquidity is therefore low.

The goal of Pasquariello and Vega (2007) is to measure the effect of two complementary mechanisms responsible for daily price changes: (i) the aggregation of public news and (ii) the aggregation of order flow. These mechanisms were also considered by Green (2004) and Brandt and Kavajecz (2004), but Pasquariello and Vega (2007) extend both studies by assessing the relevance of each mechanism conditional on the dispersion of beliefs among traders and the public signals' noise. The analysis is performed using intraday data for the January 1992–December 2000 period.

Following Hasbrouck (1991), the authors first specify an empirical model for intraday net order flow, where half-hour net order flow is regressed on lagged half-hour returns and order flow. The residuals, aggregated at the daily frequency, are used as the innovations $\Omega_t^\star$ in net order flow. In turn, order-flow innovations, together with macro news on announcement days, explain daily bond returns:[48]

$$R_t = \beta_1 \Omega_t^\star + \sum_{k=1}^{K} \beta_{2k} S_{kt} + \epsilon_t \tag{11.41}$$

The price-impact parameter β_1 is allowed to differ for days with and without announcements. In particular, on non-announcement days, β_1 varies with the dispersion of analyst forecasts concerning upcoming macro-announcements. On announcement days, β_1 varies with both the dispersion of analyst forecasts and the public signals' noise, measured by the absolute difference between the actual announcement and its last revision.

During nonannouncement days, adverse-selection costs of unanticipated order flow are higher when the dispersion of beliefs is high. For instance, one standard deviation innovations in order flow decrease the 2-year, 5-year, and 10-year bond yields by 7.19, 10.04, and 6.84 basis points, respectively, on high-dispersion days, compared to 4.08, 4.07, and 2.86 basis points on low-dispersion days. These differences are economically and statistically significant.

These higher adverse-selection costs translate into a higher contemporaneous correlation between order-flow changes and bond yield changes. For example, the adjusted R^2 of regressing daily 5-year T-bond yield changes on unanticipated order flow is 41.38% on high-dispersion days, compared to 9.65% on low-dispersion days. When information heterogeneity is high, informed traders' behavior leads to a "cautious" equilibrium where changes in unanticipated order flow have a greater impact on bond yields.

The release of macro news induces informed traders to trade more aggressively on their private information. Accordingly, the correlation between unanticipated order flow and bond yield changes is lower during announcement days. For example, comparing nonannouncement days with announcement days when the employment report is released, the explanatory power of order flow decreases from 15.31% to 6.47%, 21.03% to 19.61%, and 6.74% to 3.59% for the 2-year, 5-year, and 10-year bonds, respectively. Yet when both the dispersion of beliefs and the noise of the public signal are high, the importance of order flow in setting bond prices increases.

[48] The authors actually use yield changes in the analysis, rather than returns.

He et al. (2009) contrast the informational role of trades in the U.S. Treasury market during and outside the regular domestic trading hours, using intraday data on the 5-year on-the-run Treasury note for the January 1, 1992–December 31, 1999, sample period. The model is the same as the one estimated in Green (2004), which allows to identify the degree of information asymmetry and the compensation for liquidity provision.

The main results are as follows. First, the informational impact of trades varies considerably over the 24-hour day. Informational impact is greatest during the preopen period (7:30–8:30 A.M. ET) than during any other trading period. Notably, the informational impact during the overnight period (5:30 P.M.–7:30 A.M.) is comparable to that during the regular daytime trading period (8:30 A.M.–3:00 P.M.).

Second, consistent with the intraday price-impact pattern, the informed-trading component of the bid–ask spread is highest in the pre-open period, whereas the liquidity component is highest in the post-close period (3:00–5:30 P.M.). The magnitude of the informed-trading component during the overnight period is comparable to that during the regular daytime trading period.

Third, distinguishing between nonannouncement and announcement days, the informational impact of trades peaks during the preopen period, on days with no macro announcements, whereas it peaks after the news release at 8:30 A.M., on days with macro announcements. On average, information asymmetry is higher in the preopen period on Mondays than on other weekdays. In addition, information asymmetry is higher immediately before than after the opening of the futures market (8:20 A.M.), suggesting that private information of client order flow is another important source of information asymmetry in the preopen period.

In their analysis of the role of jumps, Jiang, Lo, and Verdelhan (2011) find that while a majority of jumps occur at prescheduled news announcement times, the announcement surprises have limited power in explaining jumps in bond prices. They find that *pre-announcement* liquidity shocks also play an important role in bond price jumps. They use several liquidity measures constructed from the BrokerTec data to capture liquidity shocks, including the bid–ask spread, trading volume, and various measures of market depth. Consistent with Fleming and Remolona (1999), they find that there is generally a widening of the bid–ask spread and a sharp drop in market depth prior to a news announcement. Interestingly, the widening of the spread and the drop in market depth during the preannouncement period are more significant on days with jumps than on those without jumps.

To examine the explanatory power of information shocks versus liquidity shocks for jumps in bond prices, they specify and estimate a probit model for the occurrence of jumps. First, preannouncement liquidity shocks, in particular shocks to the bid–ask spread and market depth, have significant predictive power regarding jump frequency in bond prices. Second, there is a significantly positive relation between announcement surprises and jumps. Third, liquidity shocks remain significant in predicting jumps even after controlling for the effect of announcement surprises.

On the other hand, when it comes to the price impact of net order flow, net order flow has significantly less effect on bond prices *after* jumps occurred at announcement times. This suggests that when uncertainty at announcement times is resolved in the form of jumps, the dispersion of investor belief is reduced, and thus, order flow becomes less informative.

11.4.2 Joint Microstructure Effects in the Cash Market and Futures Markets

The previous articles characterize microstructure effects in the cash market. The futures market for contracts on U.S. Treasury securities, though, is an important ancillary market. The next article studies the interaction between the two markets.[49,50]

Mizrach and Neely (2008) model the interaction between the spot voice markets and the futures market, using data on the on-the-run 2-, 5-, and 10-year notes, over the October 1, 1995–March 30, 2001, sample period. The authors base their analysis on two related measures of *information share*: (i) the contribution of shocks to a market to the total variance of the permanent component of prices (ii) the limits of the changes in the price with respect to the elements of the vector of shocks, as the time horizon goes to infinity. The information shares are based on a vector error correction model estimated daily, using 1-minute returns.[51]

This chapter highlights the role of the futures markets in U.S. Treasury price discovery. Specifically, the estimates of 5- and 10-year spot market information shares typically fail to reach 50% from 1999 on. The spot market information shares for the 2-year note are higher than those of the 5- and 10-year maturities, but also decline after 1998. Relative bid–ask spreads, number of trades, and realized volatility are statistically significant in explaining daily information shares and capture up to 21% of the variability. The authors also regress information shares on daily dummies for 11 macro and FOMC-related announcements. In roughly 1/4 of cases, the release of public information increases the futures market's information share, but macroeconomic announcements rarely explain information shares independently of liquidity.

[49] See also Brandt, Kavajecz, and Underwood (2007), who use daily data for the 1995–2000 sample period, to study the interaction between the cash and futures markets. The authors identify the differential impact of different categories of trading in the futures markets on the cash and futures markets.

[50] While our focus is on the bond markets, some authors have also investigated the joint dynamics of liquidity measures in the bond and *stock* markets; see Chordia, Sarkar, and Subrahmanyam (2005).

[51] A similar analysis of information shares is performed by Man, Wang, and Wu (2013) for the electronic and voice-based spot markets. They find that the electronic market has a much higher information share than the voice market.

11.4.3 Summary

This section has reviewed several articles analyzing high-frequency market-microstructure effects in the cash and futures markets for U.S. Treasury securities. In summary, the following main features emerge:

- Prices adjust almost instantaneously to the releases of macroeconomic announcements, whereas volatility and trading volume remain at an abnormal higher level for more than 1 hour. This could be consistent with disagreement among investors about the information content of the just-released announcement.
- Trading impact prices, although with considerable variations throughout the day and across days. In particular, on announcement days, trading is more informative in the aftermath of macro announcements and depending on the degree of information heterogeneity about macroeconomic fundamentals among market participants.
- Bond futures markets contribute substantially to price discovery, especially for long-maturity Treasury securities.

Hence, despite the fact that most (if not all) "fundamental" information relevant for U.S. Treasury securities is public, liquidity in this market is not perfect. In particular, there seem to be important price-discovery effects related to the way public information is processed. This feature should be incorporated into bond valuation models.

11.5 BOND RISK PREMIA

In this section, we review the evidence on bond risk premia at high frequency. We start with articles documenting the evidence in daily bond returns, and we then turn to the intraday evidence. High-frequency data allow researchers to study the way risk premia are earned in relation to the release of economic announcements. In addition, the benchmark EH postulates constant expected log returns, in excess of the log risk-free rate. By examining bond returns at high frequency, researchers may be better able to detect time variation in risk premia and, hence, assess the validity of this important benchmark.

11.5.1 Daily Evidence

Jones, Lamont, and Lumsdaine (1998) find that average excess returns are significant on the days when employment and PPI data are announced.[52] Specifically, announcement-day average bond excess returns on announcement days exceed nonannouncement-day returns between 6.3 (5-year note) and 10.8 (30-year bond) basis points, after controlling for day-of-the week effects.

Li et al. (2009) provide a connection between microstructure effects and bond risk premia. Specifically, the authors study the effect of liquidity *risk* and liquidity on the pricing of U.S. Treasury securities. The authors employ intraday, daily, and monthly data for the January 1992–December 2002 sample period.

To estimate a bond's exposure to liquidity risk, the authors use *daily* data to estimate the regression model:

$$R^e_{i,n+1t} = \alpha_{i,t} + \alpha_{i,1t} R_{nt} + \alpha_{i,2t}\,\text{sign}\left(R^e_{i,n+1t}\right) V_{i,nt} + \epsilon_{i,n+1t} \tag{11.42}$$

where $R^e_{i,nt}$ is the ith bond return, in excess of the return on an equally weighted Treasury portfolio, on day n, in month t; R_{nt} is the bond return; sign($R^e_{i,nt}$) is an indicator function that equals 1 if $R^e_{i,nt} > 0$, and minus 1, otherwise; and $V_{i,nt}$ is the trading volume measured in par value. The model is estimated each month for each bond, and the average of $\hat{\alpha}_{i,2t}$ across bonds, $\hat{\alpha}_{2t}$, is used as the liquidity measure for the Treasury market.

Innovations in the liquidity measure are computed as the residuals of the *monthly* regression model:

$$\Delta\hat{\alpha}_{2t} = \beta_0 + \beta_1 \Delta\hat{\alpha}_{2t-1} + \beta_2 \hat{\alpha}_{2t-1} + e_t \tag{11.43}$$

In turn, $L_t \equiv 1000 \times \hat{e}_t$ is used as a regressor in the augmented Fama and French (1993) factor model for monthly excess returns:

$$\begin{aligned} R_{it} - R_{ft-1} = \gamma_{0i} &+ \gamma_{iMKT}(R_{mt} - R_{ft-1}) \\ &+ \gamma_{iSMB} R_{SMBt} + \gamma_{iHML} R_{HMLt} \\ &+ \gamma_{iTERM} R_{TERMt} + \gamma_{iL} L_t + \upsilon_t \end{aligned} \tag{11.44}$$

[52]Note that Li and Engle (1998) test for a GARCH-in-mean effect, where the conditional bond volatility is allowed to impact expected excess returns on announcement days, but not on nonannouncement days; that is, they allow for a risk-return trade-off but only on announcement days. They find the effect to be insignificant. Christiansen (2000) also fails to identify a significant differential risk premium on announcement days.

where R_{ft-1} is the monthly risk-free rate, R_{mt} is the stock market return, R_{SMBt} is the size factor, R_{HMLt} is the value factor, and R_{TERMt} is the excess return on a long-term government bond. The parameter γ_{iL} captures the liquidity risk associated with bond i. In addition to liquidity risk, the authors estimate a monthly measure of the probability of information-based trading (PIN_{it}), which is derived from a sequential trade model (Easley, Hvidkjaer, and O'Hara, 2002). The authors then perform a sequence of *cross-sectional* regressions for monthly excess returns,

$$R_{it} - R_{ft-1} = \phi_{0t} + \phi_{MKTt}\hat{\gamma}_{iMKT} + \phi_{SMBt}\hat{\gamma}_{iSMB} + \phi_{HMLt}\hat{\gamma}_{iHML} + \phi_{TERMt}\hat{\gamma}_{iTERM} + \phi_{Lt}\hat{\gamma}_{iL} + \phi_{PINt}\widehat{PIN}_{it} + \text{controls} + u_{it} \tag{11.45}$$

where $\widehat{PIN}_{it}$ is the average PIN_{it} over the previous 6 months. The average values of $\hat{\phi}_{Lt}$ and $\hat{\phi}_{PINt}$ provide an indication of whether liquidity level and liquidity risk are priced.

Results of the asset pricing test described above show that liquidity risk is important over and beyond the effect of the level of liquidity. Moreover, there is a *positive* relation between expected Treasury returns and information risk in the cross-sectional regressions. Finally, the compensation for exposure to liquidity risk is economically important. A difference of 10 percentage points in liquidity risk leads to a difference in Treasury excess return of 9 basis points per annum, which accounts for 6% of the mean excess return. By contrast, the same amount of change in information risk leads to a difference in Treasury excess return of six basis points per year or 4% of the mean excess return. Hence, while both liquidity and information matter, the economic effect of liquidity risk appears to be greater than that of information risk.

Savor and Wilson (2013) examine announcement-day and non announcement-day bond returns for 30-day T-bills and notes and bonds with maturities 1, 2, 10, 20, and 30 years, for the 1958–2009 sample period (1961–2009, for T-bills), focusing on inflation, unemployment, and FOMC announcements.

They find that average T-bill daily returns are significantly lower on announcement days: 0.7 basis points lower, relative to a sample mean of 2.3 basis points for nonannouncement days. On the other hand, similar to Jones, Lamont, and Lumsdaine (1998), average note and bond excess returns (maturity above 1 year) are significantly higher on announcement days, and they increase with the maturity of the instrument. The average excess return differential ranges between 2.6 (5-year note) and 4.5 (30-year bond) basis points.[53]

11.5.2 Intraday Evidence

Balduzzi and Moneta (2012) focus on the *cross section* of risk premia at announcement and non-announcement times.[54] In addition, within announcement days, the authors distinguish between return behavior in the immediate vicinity of macro announcements ("announcement-window" returns) and behavior further away from the announcements ("non- announcement-window" returns). They examine intraday futures contracts on 2-, 5-, 10-, and 30-year notes and bonds, for the March 2, 1993-March 31, 2008, sample period, finding that the distinction between announcement- and nonannouncement-window returns affords an interesting novel insight: announcement-day bond risk premia are significant but only for the portion earned outside the announcement windows.

The authors then perform *three* main exercises. First, they estimate the sensitivity of futures returns to 22 announcement surprises and use the estimated sensitivities to construct portfolios mimicking the surprises: "unit-beta" mimicking portfolios. They then estimate the Sharpe ratios earned by the mimicking portfolios. They find that the Sharpe ratios (in absolute value) are remarkably similar across announcements being tracked, which is consistent with a single-factor structure in the response of returns to surprises, and that the Sharpe ratios are mainly earned on announcement days but outside the announcement windows. They also find significant evidence of predictability in mimicking-portfolio (excess) returns: portfolios mimicking procyclical (countercyclical) macro news earn negative (positive) risk premia, more negative (positive) as interest rates increase and the economy slows down.

The second exercise is to impose and test a single-factor structure in the response of returns to macro news, that is, they assume that the day-t announcement-window return on the ith contract, r_{it}^{aw}, follows:[55]

$$r_{it}^{aw} = \alpha_i + \beta_{iy}y_t + \epsilon_{it} \tag{11.46}$$

[53]Savor and Wilson (2014) also examine announcement-day and nonannouncement-day bond returns, for the 1964–2011 sample period, focusing on the same three macro announcements. They find that on announcement days, average bond excess returns are positively related to their equity market beta.

[54]Faust and Wright (2009) study *conditional* bond risk premia at the intraday frequency. They examine intraday futures returns on 5- and 30-year notes and bonds for the November 1988 to December 2007 period. They show that bond return predictability is mainly driven by price behavior *within* a 15-minute window surrounding the employment, CPI, PPI, trade balance, retail sales, personal income, durable goods, initial unemployment claims, industrial production, and scheduled FOMC announcements.

[55]The authors allow for *multiple* announcement windows within the day.

where

$$y_t = \sum_{k=1}^{K} \delta_k S_{kt} \tag{11.47}$$

is a "latent" economic-news factor through which all macro surprises affect bond futures prices. The authors find that the single-factor structure cannot be rejected, where the latent factor mainly loads on the nonfarm payrolls, FOMC, and the ISM index announcements.

Third, the authors test the *asset pricing* implications of the single-factor model, that is, they test the implication that

$$E_{t-1}(r_{it}) = \beta_{iy}\lambda_{yt-1} \tag{11.48}$$

where λ_{yt-1} is the conditional risk premium associated with the exposure to the latent factor. The restrictions of the asset pricing model are not rejected.

11.5.3 Summary

This section has reviewed articles characterizing risk premia in the U.S. Treasury markets. In summary, these are the main results:

- Bond risk premia are mainly earned on announcement days.
- Both the level of liquidity and the exposure to liquidity shocks explain the cross section of (monthly) bond risk premia.
- Announcement-day unconditional risk premia are only significant for the portion earned *outside* of the announcement windows. There is also significant time variation in the intraday risk premia, with different predictability patterns across different trading periods.
- The cross section of bond risk premia is explained by the exposure to a single factor capturing macro news.

Overall, the main message is that bond risk premia are earned *unevenly* over time and also display uneven time variation. The fact that both the average risk premia and the time variation of risk premia are especially significant in the proximity of macro announcement releases supports the notion that macro risk is indeed priced.

11.6 THE IMPACT OF HIGH-FREQUENCY TRADING

A recent development in the fixed income markets is the increasing role played by HFT.[56,57] The literature on the topic is still evolving and there are no published articles yet. Hence, in this section, we review two studies still at the working paper stage.

11.6.1 The Effects of HFT on Liquidity, Volatility, and Risk Premia

Jiang, Lo, and Valente (2013) study the price data from BrokerTec on the 2-, 5-, and 10-year note. They examine the January 2, 2004–June 30, 2007, sample. Crucial to their analysis is the identification of high-frequency (HF) trades and limit orders. The authors use information on the time of order submission in reaction to changes in market conditions and its subsequent

[56]Note that there are subtle differences between algorithmic trading (AT), automated trading, and HFT. AT is typically understood as the implementation of automated trade execution strategies on the part of fund managers to buy or sell large amounts of assets. Automated trading is the complete automation of the investment *and* trading process. HFT is understood as a subset of automated trading where trading opportunities arise and are taken advantage of on very small timescales.

[57]While the interest in HFT in the fixed income markets is *very* recent, a few studies have analyzed the effects of AT and HFT on the stock markets; see, for example, Hendershott, Jones, and Menkveld (2011), Hendershott and Riordan (2013), and Brogaard, Hendershott, and Riordan (2014). The overall conclusion of these studies is that AT and HFT improve liquidity and informational efficiency.

alteration, such as cancellation or execution, to classify HF trades and orders as those that are placed at a speed deemed beyond manual capacity.[58]

The authors characterize HF and non-HF trading and orders before and after macro announcements, finding that both HF and non-HF activities greatly intensify after macro announcements. They then examine two main issues. First, they explore whether HF trades and orders improve or reduce liquidity and whether they increase or decrease bond volatility. In order to address this issue, they regress the abnormal component of the bid–ask spread and market depth – the deviations from a 5-day trailing moving average for the same time of day – on HF trades and orders. They find that HF trades and orders impact positively (negatively) the bid–ask spread before (after) macro announcements. On the other hand, HF trades and orders impact negatively market depth at the best quote, both before and after macro announcements. They also regress abnormal return volatility on HF trades and orders, finding that HF trades increase volatility, more so before than after announcements, and that HF orders only increase volatility before announcements. The authors conclude that HF trading has a negative (mixed) effect on preannouncement (postannouncement) liquidity.

Second, the authors investigate how informative HF trades and orders are relative to non-HF trades and orders and what their role is in affecting price efficiency. Specifically, they implement the test of Kaniel and Liu (2006), which quantifies the probability that a trade or order anticipates price changes in the right direction. They find that non-HF limit orders are *more* informative than their non-HF counterparts, especially during the postannouncement periods. The authors also regress the 5-minute serial correlation in tick-by-tick returns on HF trades and orders. They find that HF trades reduce serial correlation and, thus, improve price efficiency, during the postannouncement period.

In summary, while HF trades and orders generate higher (subsequent) bond return volatility, their effect on market liquidity depends on the information environment. HF activities generally have a negative impact on liquidity before announcements, but they are associated with lower bid–ask spreads, especially during postannouncement periods, when information uncertainty is resolved. Moreover, during the postannouncement period, HF trades (limit orders) are more (less) informative than their non-HF counterparts. Finally, their results show that only HF trades have a significant effect in enhancing price efficiency during the postannouncement period.

Liu et al. (2014) investigate whether the *intensity* of HF trading has an impact on average returns. They construct a daily HFT intensity factor defined as the average ratio between the number of HF trades and orders and the total number of overall trades and orders across bonds:

$$HFTI_t = \frac{1}{N}\sum_{n=1}^{N}\left(\frac{HFTO_{nt}}{ALLTO_{nt}}\right) \tag{11.49}$$

where $HFTO_{nt}$ is the number of HF trades and orders for bond n during day t and $ALLTO_{nt}$ is the total number of trades and orders. The authors conjecture that exposure to $HFTI_t$ commands a premium. The rationale behind this conjecture is that HFT can entail both benefits and risks. Among the possible risks are that HFT may overload exchanges, make it more difficult to trade at posted prices, and reduce liquidity at volatile times or when market making is difficult. Combined together, these effects mean that shocks to HFT intensity may generate systematic market disruptions and increase risk.

To test the conjecture above, the authors construct a portfolio of long (short) low (high) HFT-beta bonds, where HFT betas are estimated using daily data for the previous 12 months. They then test whether such a long-short HFT mimicking portfolio earns positive excess returns, after controlling for the exposure to several other risk factors.

The analysis is based on the data from BrokerTec covering the January 2, 2004–December 30, 2011, sample. The main finding is that the HFT mimicking portfolio does earn a significant risk premium and that this premium does not disappear when the excess returns are regressed on the returns of several other factor mimicking portfolios. In summary, exposure to HFT intensity is priced in the bond markets.

[58] Specifically, HF trades are identified as those market orders that are placed within a second of a change in the best quote on either side of the market. HF orders are identified as those orders that belong to one of the three different categories: (i) orders that are canceled or modified within 1 second of their placement, (ii) orders at the best quote that are modified within 1 second of a change in the best quote on either side of the market, and (iii) orders at the second best quote that are modified within 1 second of a change in the best quote on either side of the market.

11.6.2 Summary

This section has reviewed two recent working papers studying the effects of HFT on the U.S. Treasury markets. In summary, these are the main results:

- HFT is substantially higher after scheduled macro news announcements.
- HFT worsens (improves) liquidity before (after) macro news announcements.
- Exposure to HFT is priced.

11.7 CONCLUSIONS

This chapter has reviewed studies of the high-frequency behavior of the U.S. Treasury markets. We believe that the recent focus in the literature on high-frequency data has dramatically improved our understanding of bond-market dynamics, but, in some sense, our scientific journey has just began. For example, while macro news is important, it still explains a relatively small portion of return behavior at announcement times. Moreover, even after controlling for macro news, there are still pronounced residual volatility dynamics that one would like to relate to fundamentals. Order flow moves prices in the Treasury markets, and more so in the aftermath of macro news announcements, precisely when public information should dominate. Moreover, recent years have witnessed a severe financial crisis, unprecedented responses by the Federal Reserve, and the increasing role of HFT. More research is warranted to better understand if any of these changes have caused a structural break in any of the key variables of the U.S. Treasury market. These are only some of the issues that are worth of further exploration within this exciting area of research.

REFERENCES

Amihud Y. Illiquidity and stock returns: cross-section and time-series effects. J Financ Mark 2002;5:31–56.

Andersen T, Bollerslev T, Diebold FX. Roughing it up: including jump components in the measurement, modeling, and forecasting of return volatility. Rev Econ Stat 2007;89:701–720.

Andersen T, Bollerslev T, Diebold FX, Vega C. Real-time price discovery in global stock, bond and foreign exchange markets. J Int Econ 2007;73:251–277.

Balduzzi P, Bertola G, Foresi S. A model of target changes and the term structure of interest rates. J Monet Econ 1997;39:223–249.

Balduzzi P, Elton EJ, Green TC. Economic news and bond prices: evidence from the U.S. Treasury market. J Financ Quant Anal 2001;36:523–543.

Balduzzi P, Moneta F. Economic risk premia in the fixed income markets: The Intra-day Evidence, Working Paper; 2012.

Beber A, Brandt MW. The effect of macroeconomic news on beliefs and preferences: evidence from the options market. J Monet Econ 2006;53:1997–2039.

Beber A, Brandt MW. Resolving macroeconomic uncertainty in stock and bond markets. Rev Finance 2009;13:119–155.

Beber A, Brandt MW. When it cannot get better or worse: the asymmetric impact of good and bad news on bond returns in expansions and recessions. Rev Finance 2010;14:1–45.

Becker K, Finnerty JE, Kopecky K. Macroeconomic news and the efficiency of international bond futures markets. J Financ Mark 1996;16:131–145.

Black F. Studies in stock price volatility changes. Proceedings of the 1976 Business Meeting of the Business and Economics Statistics Section; American Statistical Association; 1976a. p 177–181.

Black F. The pricing of commodity contracts. J Financ Econ 1976b;3:167–179.

Bollerslev T, Cai J, Song FM. Intraday periodicity, long memory volatility, and macroeconomic announcement effects in the US Treasury bond market. J Empir Finance 2000;7:37–55.

Brandt MW, Kavajecz KA. The impact of order flow and liquidity on the yield curve. J Finance 2004;59:2623–2654.

Brandt MW, Kavajecz KA, Underwood SE. Price discovery in the treasury futures market. J Futures Mark 2007;27:1021–1051.

Brenner M, Pasquariello P, Subrahmanyam M. On the volatility and comovement of U.S. financial markets around macroeconomic news announcements. J Financ Quant Anal 2009;44:1265–1289.

Brogaard J, Hendershott T, Riordan R. High-frequency trading and price discovery. Rev Financ Stud 2014;27:2267–2306.

Chordia T, Sarkar A, Subrahmanyam A. An empirical analysis of stock and bond market liquidity. Rev Financ Stud 2005;18:85–129.

Christiansen C. Macroeconomic announcement effects on the covariance structure of government bond returns. J Empir Finance 2000;7:479–507.

Christiansen C, Ranaldo A. Realized bond-stock correlation: macroeconomic announcement effects. J Futures Mark 2007;27:439–469.

Cohen BH, Shin HS. Positive Feedback Trading Under Stress: Evidence From the US Treasury Securities Market, Working Paper; 2003.

Connolly R, Stivers C, Sun L. Stock market uncertainty and the stock-bond return relation. J Financ Quant Anal 2005;40:161–193.

Cook T, Hahn T. The information content of discount rate announcements and their effect on market interest rates. J Money Credit Bank 1988;20:167–180.
Cook T, Hahn T. The effect of changes in the federal funds rate target on market interest rates in the 1970s. J Monet Econ 1989;24:331–351.
Cox JC, Ingersoll JE Jr., Ross SA. A theory of the term structure of interest rates. Econometrica 1985;53:385–407.
van Dijk D, Lumsdaine RL, van der Wel M. Market Set-Up in Advance of Federal Reserve Policy Rate Decisions, Working Paper; 2014.
Easley D, Hvidkjaer S, O'Hara M. Is information risk a determinant of asset returns? J Finance 2002;57:2185–2221.
Ederington LH, Lee JH. How markets process information: news releases and volatility. J Finance 1993;48:1161–1191.
Ederington LH, Lee JH. The creation and resolution of market uncertainty: the impact of information releases on implied volatility. J Financ Quant Anal 1995;31:513–539.
Ederington LH, Lee JH. The short-run dynamics of the price adjustment to new information. J Financ Quant Anal 1996;30:117–134.
Ederington LH, Lee JH. Intraday volatility in interest-rate and foreign-exchange markets: ARCH, announcement, and seasonality effects. J Financ Mark 2001;21:517–552.
Fama EF. Does the Fed control interest rates? Rev Asset Pricing Stud 2013;3:180–199.
Fama EF, French KR. Common risk factors in the returns on stocks and bonds. J Financ Econ 1993;33:3–56.
Farnsworth H, Bass R. The term structure with semi-credible targeting. J Finance 2003;58:839–865.
Faust J, Swanson ET, Wright JH. Identifying VARS based on high frequency futures data. J Monet Econ 2004;51:1107–1131.
Faust J, Wright JH. Risk Premia in the 8:30 Economy, Working Paper; 2009.
Fleming MJ. The round-the-clock market for U.S. treasury securities. Fed Reserve Bank N Y Econ Policy Rev 1997;3:9–32.
Fleming MJ. Measuring Treasury market liquidity. Fed Reserve Bank N Y Econ Policy Rev 2003;9:83–108.
Fleming MJ, Garbade KD. Explaining settlement fails. Fed Reserve Bank N Y Curr Issues Econ Finance 2005;11:1–7.
Fleming MJ, Mizrach B. The Microstructure of a U.S. Treasury ECN: The BrokerTec Platform. Federal Reserve Bank of New York Staff Reports, No. 381. New York: Federal Reserve Bank of New York; 2009.
Fleming MJ, Piazzesi M. Monetary Policy Tick-by-Tick, Working Paper; 2005.
Fleming MJ, Remolona EM. What moves the bond market? FRBNY Econ Policy Rev 1997;3(4):31–50.
Fleming MJ, Remolona EM. Price formation and liquidity in the U.S. Treasury market: the response to public information. J Finance 1999;54:1901–1915.
Garbade KD, Keane FM, Logan L, Stokes A, Wolgemuth J. The introduction of the TMPG fails charge for U.S. treasury securities. FRBNY Econ Policy Rev Oct 2010:45–71.
de Goeij P, Marquering W. Macroeconomic announcements and asymmetric volatility in bond returns. J Bank Finance 2006;7:2659–2680.
Goyenko RY, Holden CW, Trzcinka CA. Do liquidity measures measure liquidity? J Financ Econ 2009;92:153–181.
Green TC. Economic news and the impact of trading on bond prices. J Finance 2004;59:1201–1233.
Gürkaynak RS, Sack B, Swanson E. Do actions speak louder than words? The response of asset prices to monetary policy actions and statements. Int J Cent Bank 2005a;1:55–93.
Gürkaynak RS, Sack B, Swanson E. The sensitivity of long-term interest rates to economic news: evidence and implications for macroeconomic models. Am Econ Rev 2005b;95:425–436.
Gürkaynak RS, Sack B, Wright JH. The U.S. treasury yield curve: 1961 to the present. J Monet Econ 2007;54:2291–2304.
Gürkaynak RS, Wolfers J. Macroeconomic Derivatives: An Initial Analysis of Market-based Macro Forecasts, Uncertainty, and Risk, NBER Working Paper 11929; 2006.
Harvey CR, Huang RD. The impact of the federal reserve bank's open market operations. J Financ Mark 2002;5:223–257.
Hasbrouck J. Measuring the information content of stock trades. J Finance 1991;46:179–207.
He Y, Lin H, Wang J, Wu C. Price discovery in the round-the-clock U.S. Treasury market. J Financ Intermed 2009;18:464–490.
Hendershott T, Jones CM, Menkveld AJ. Does algorithmic trading improve liquidity? J Finance 2011;66:1–33.
Hendershott T, Riordan R. Algorithmic trading and the market for liquidity. J Financ Quant Anal 2013;48(4):1001–1024.
Huang RD, Cai J, Wang X. Information-based trading in the treasury note interdealer broker market. J Financ Intermed 2002;11:269–296.
Huang RD, Stoll HR. Dealer versus auction markets: a paired comparison of execution costs on NASDAQ and the NYSE. J Financ Econ 1996;41:313–357.
Jiang GJ, Lo I, Valente G. High Frequency Trading around Macroeconomic News Announcements: Evidence from the US Treasury Market, Working Paper; 2013.
Jiang GJ, Lo I, Verdelhan A. Information shocks, liquidity shocks, jumps, and price discovery – evidence from the U.S. Treasury market. J Financ Quant Anal 2011;49:527–551.
Johannes M. The statistical and economic role of jumps in continuous-time interest rate models. J Finance 2004;49:227–260.
Jones CM, Lamont O, Lumsdaine RL. Macroeconomic news and bond market volatility. J Financ Econ 1998;47:315–337.
Kaniel R, Liu H. So what orders do informed traders use? J Bus 2006;79:1867–1913.
Kuttner KN. Monetary policy surprises and interest rates: evidence from the fed funds futures market. J Monet Econ 2001;47:523–544.
Lewis M. *Flash Boys (A Wall Street Revolt)*. New York: W. W. Norton; 2014.
Li L, Engle RF. Macroeconomic Announcements and Volatility of Treasury Futures, Working Paper; 1998.
Li H, Wang J, Wu C, He Y. Are liquidity and information risks priced in the treasury bond market? J Finance 2009;64:467–503.
Liu X, Lo I, Nguyen M, Valente G. High-Frequency Trading and Treasury Bond Returns, Working Paper; 2014.
Lu B, Wu L. Macroeconomic releases and the interest rate term structure. J Monet Econ 2009;56:872–884.
Man K, Wang J, Wu C. Price discovery in the U.S. Treasury market: automation vs. intermediation. Manage Sci 2013;59:695–714.

Menkveld AJ, Sarkar A, van der Wei M. Customer order flow, intermediaries, and discovery of the equilibrium risk-free rate. J Financ Quant Anal 2012;47:821–849.

Mizrach B, Neely C. The transition to electronic communications networks in the secondary Treasury market. Fed Reserve Bank St Louis Rev 2006;88:527–541.

Mizrach B, Neely C. Information shares in the U.S. Treasury market. J Bank Finance 2008;32:1221–1233.

Pasquariello P, Vega C. Informed and strategic order flow in the bond markets. Rev Financ Stud 2007;20:1976–2019.

Piazzesi M. Bond yields and the federal reserve. J Polit Econ 2005;113:311–344.

Rigobon R. Identification through heteroskedasticity. Rev Econ Stat 2003;85:777–792.

Rigobon R, Sack B. The impact of monetary policy on asset prices. J Monet Econ 2004;51:1553–1575.

Rudebusch GD. Federal reserve interest rate targeting, rational expectations, and the term structure. J Monet Econ 1995;35:245–274.

Savor P, Wilson M. How much do investors care about macroeconomic risk? Evidence from scheduled economic announcements. J Financ Quant Anal 2013;48:343–375.

Savor P, Wilson M. Asset pricing: a tale of two days. J Financ Econ 2014;113:171–201.

Vasicek O. An equilibrium characterization of the term structure. J Financ Econ 1977;5:177–188.

Wright J. What does monetary policy do to long-term interest rates at the zero lower bound? Econ J 2012;122:447–466.

PART V

Advanced Topics on Term Structure Models and Their Estimation

12

Structural Affine Models for Yield Curve Modeling

Riccardo Rebonato

Professor of Finance, EDHEC Risk Institute, London, United Kingdom

12.1 PURPOSE AND STRUCTURE OF THIS CHAPTER

In this chapter, I intend to look at term structure modeling from a "structural" perspective. By this I mean that I will look at models created with the goal to *explain* (as opposed to *describe*) the yield curve. For reasons that will become apparent in what follows, these models almost invariably straddle the real-world and the risk-neutral measures.

I intend to show how three "building blocks" (expectations, risk premia, and convexity) can be linked together by the conditions of no-arbitrage to produce a rich description of the evolution of the yield curve.

Because of their intuitional appeal and tractability, I deal with a popular class of models (the affine class).[1] By starting my discussion from the simplest incarnation of affine models, I try to give a transparent understanding of how these models weave together these three building blocks to determine the shape of the yield curve.

The simple affine version I present first is unparalleled for the intuitive understanding it affords. However, recent empirical evidence suggests that its explanation of risk premia is *qualitatively* wrong.

Luckily, the same empirical evidence also suggests how first generation affine models can be modified and enriched. I therefore explain in the middle part of this chapter what we now know about term premia and how this can be incorporated in the affine framework. Indeed, we shall see that much of the "modern" affine term structure modeling revolves around the combination of the econometric (statistical) research strand with the traditional no-arbitrage approach.

I then conclude the chapter by analyzing and comparing the predictive outputs of these new-generation models. When it comes to the risk premia, I will find a remarkable, and surprising, congruence of predictions. I will offer an explanation of why this might be the case and of whether this should be seen as an encouraging or a worrying feature.

[1]See, for instance, Dai and Singleton (2000) for a systematic classification of affine models and Duffee (2002) for a discussion of *essentially* affine models – loosely speaking, models that remain affine both in the real-world and in the pricing measures.

Handbook of Fixed-Income Securities, First Edition. Edited by Pietro Veronesi.

12.2 STRUCTURAL MODELS

All structural models (affine or otherwise) provide answers to a handful of fundamental questions:

1. What drives the yield curve? On which state variables does the evolution of the term structure depend? Should we choose these variables *a priori* (perhaps on the basis of a macroeconomic picture of what drives the economy)? Or should we use unspecified ("latent") variables and allow the data to speak for themselves?
2. Are there conditions of the economy when investors require a greater or a smaller compensation for risk? Or is the market price of risk instead a constant? If it isn't, how does it depend on the chosen state variables?
3. What risk do investors require compensation for?[2]
4. How do different portions of the yield curve respond to movements in the state variables? This, of course, will determine both the value of convexity and how much compensation investors demand for investing in a particular segment of the yield curve. The point here is that we *assign* how much the nontradable state variables move (their "volatility") and we *derive*, using the model, how much the traded instruments respond.
5. How does the model account for expectations?
6. What, according to the model, is the value of convexity?

If, indeed, the shape of the yield curve is just a function of expectations, risk premia, and convexity, there is precious little else to term structure modeling than providing answers to these questions. All models, no matter how complex, can therefore be seen as tools to provide simplified, but self-consistent, answers to these questions.

The last three questions are important but, in a sense, more "technical": they refer to how expectations, convexity, and risk premia are *transmitted* along the yield curve. They are silent about where the risk premia come from.

It is the first three questions that are truly "fundamental": they tell us which variables "drive" the yield curve and how and when uncertainty about these variables affect the risk premia – if at all.

At first blush, the standard (affine) modeling framework, which has been built since the 1970s to answer these questions, looks self-evidently convincing and deceptively simple - so much so that a visiting Martian may well surmise that, after decades of working in this conceptual framework, practitioners and academics must by now be arguing about the fourth decimal figure. This is, alas, not the case. Most surprisingly, we are still learning new facts about how the yield curve behaves – for instance, what drives excess returns. This, in turn, is telling us in which direction existing models should be tinkered with and where they are in need of fundamental replumbing. Affine term structure modeling is still very much in a work-in-progress, and exciting, phase.

12.3 A SIMPLE TAXONOMY

There are many types of term structure model. In part they are different because they have been created with different purposes in mind, in part because they look at the same problem from different angles. A reasonable taxonomy may look as follows:

1. *Statistical models* aim to *describe* how the yield curve moves. There are (at least) two main workhorses in this class of models, often harnessed together: principal component analysis, which points to a handful of factors (say, "level," "slope," and "curvature") to describe parsimoniously and efficiently the dynamics of the yield curve, and vector autoregression (VAR) models, which are often employed to forecast interest rates and to estimate the risk premium as the difference between the forward rates and the forecasted rates. This task sounds easy, but as I discuss immediately below, the quasi-unit-root nature of the level of rates (and many more statistical pitfalls) makes estimations purely based on time-series analysis arduous and the "error bars" embarrassingly large (see, e.g., the discussion in Cochrane and Piazzesi (2008)).[3] In the attempt to improve on this state of affairs, no-arbitrage structural models, which add *cross-sectional* information to the time-series data, come to the fore.
2. *Structural no-arbitrage models* (of which the Vasicek (1977) and CIR (1985a,b) are the earliest and best-known examples) make assumptions about how a handful of important driving factors behave; they ensure that no-arbitrage is satisfied; and they derive how of the three components that drive the yield curve (expectations, risk premia, and convexity) should affect the shape of the yield curve. The no-arbitrage conditions ensure that the derived prices of bonds do not offer free lunches. I speak of "structural" models when they straddle the physical ($\mathbb{P}$) and risk-neutral ($\mathbb{Q}$) measures – as opposed to "restricted"

[2]It is important to note the subtle difference between questions 2 and 3. The first asks: "*When* do investors most require compensation for risk?"; the second asks: "*What* do investors require compensation for?"

[3]See, in particular, the discussion of their Panel 1 on page 2 of their paper.

no-arbitrage models that are only formulated in the $\mathbb{Q}$ measure. The distinction is important at least for two reasons. First, if we want to understand how bond prices are formed from expectations and risk aversion, we cannot just look at one measure: market prices are compatible with an infinity of different combinations of expectations and market prices of risk. The second reason is subtler. If we only look at the risk-neutral ($\mathbb{Q}$) measure, it is well known that three factors (the first three principal components (PCs)) explain the movements in prices extremely well. However, if we also want to explain excess returns (risk premia), we may have to use more variables (up to five, according to Cochrane and Piazzesi (2005) and Hellerstein (2011)).[4] The message here is that variables virtually irrelevant in one measure may become important when the two measures are linked (more about this later).

3. *"Snapshot" models* (e.g., Nelson–Siegel, splines, etc.) are cross-sectional devices to *interpolate* prices or yields of bonds that we cannot observe, once given prices or yields that we can observe. They also produce as a by-product the model yields of the bonds we *do* observe. If supplemented with the ubiquitous but somewhat *ad hoc* assumption that the residuals (the differences between the model and the market prices) are mean reverting, these models give practitioners suggestions about whether a given observed bond yield (hence, price) is "out of line" with a reasonable smooth interpolation of where it should lie.[5] In general, there is no deep "meaning" to the parameters of a fitted snapshot models. However, some recent developments have given a time series, dynamic interpretation to their parameters and married them with principal component analysis (see, e.g., Diebold and Rudebush, 2013). So, these latest developments combine features of structural, statistical, and snapshot models. We shall revisit this approach later in the chapter.
4. *Derivatives models* (e.g., HJM, BGM, Hull and White, BDT, etc.) are based on *relative* pricing and on the enforcement of no-arbitrage. Because of this, they strongly rely on first-order cancellation of errors (between the derivative they are designed to price and the hedging instruments used to build the riskless or minimum variance portfolio – see the discussion in Nawalkha and Rebonato (2011)). Therefore, they do not strive to provide a particularly realistic description of the underlying economic reality. After the first generation (Vasicek, CIR), they have squarely set up camp in the risk-neutral $\mathbb{Q}$ measure and affect a disdainful lack of interest for risk premia. I will not deal with this class of models in this chapter.

12.4 WHY DO WE NEED NO-ARBITRAGE MODELS AFTER ALL?

Suppose that one were interested in estimating the time-varying risk premium. More specifically, suppose that we want to find an answer to the following question. Consider the strategy of investing in an n-year maturity bond, funding it with a 1-year-maturity bond, and that we unwind this package after 1 year. In what configurations of the yield curve (level, slope, curvature), or in what states of the economy, do we expect this strategy to be profitable? After the quick sketch provided by the taxonomy above, one may well ask why statistical models are not enough to answer this question. Granted, by themselves they may lack a deep explanatory dimension, but as far as detecting empirical regularities, surely they should be unsurpassed. Or are they?

One way of explaining why relying only on statistical information is unsatisfactory goes back to the quasi-unit-root nature of rates and to the overliberal parameterization of unconstrained statistical models. The two issues are closely linked. Suppose that one embraces a Newtonian "*hypotheses non fingo*" approach and shies away from assigning *a priori* an economic interpretation to the state variables. This is indeed the approach chosen by latent variable models, of which we discuss a popular incarnation in the following. If this agnostic modeler wants the statistical model to be sufficiently rich to capture the complexity of the yield curve, she is quickly faced with a very large number of parameters eager to be estimated[6]. Lots of parameters need lots of data. But if rates are very weakly mean reverting (if at all), almost every reasonable sample becomes a "small sample"[7], and unguided estimation very difficult. And, as luck would have it, those quantities that are relatively easy to estimate (say, the reversion speed of the second and third principal component) matter little, and those that matter a lot (say, the reversion speed and the reversion level of rates) come with unhelpfully large uncertainty bars.

A structural no-arbitrage model that straddles the $\mathbb{P}$ and $\mathbb{Q}$ measures can help. It does so by adding cross-sectional information, by significantly reducing the parameters that need estimation, and by constraining the signs and relative magnitudes of those that are left. For instance, structural no-arbitrage models can guide the statistical estimation task by stating which variables the market price of risk should depend on and by specifying the nature of the dependence.[8] We will give a concrete example of what we mean in Section 12.11.

[4]See in this respect the discussion on page 140 of Cochrane and Piazzesi (2005) and on page 3 of Hellerstein (2011).

[5]Snapshot models are also important because all structural models use as their building blocks discount bonds, which are not traded in the market, but which make mathematical analysis (immensely) easier. The output of snapshot models (the discount curve) is therefore the input to structural models.

[6]See below for an estimate of the number of parameters that an unconstrained latent variable model requires.

[7]For a discussion, see, for example, Kim (2007).

[8]In the approach by Cochrane and Piazzesi (2005, 2008), for instance, the market price of risk is made to depend on one single (carefully chosen) combination of forward rates. In other approaches (see, e.g., Duffee (2002)), it is linked to the slope of the yield curve. In the Vasicek model, it is simply a constant. In general, every structural model makes some simplifying assumptions about the market price of risk, implies some testable model properties (e.g., when excess returns should be large or small), and lays itself open to empirical testing.

Of course, to be plausible, a well-specified no-arbitrage models, once calibrated (i.e., once its parameters have been estimated), should be able to recover reasonably well the cross-sectional snapshots of the market yield curve for *some* values of the state variables.[9] But this is just a necessary condition for a satisfactory model specification. A more stringent test looks at the time series of the state variables historically fitted to the observed yield curves and checks that the fitted values indeed behave (in the $\mathbb{P}$ measure) as the model assumes they do.

This extra cross-sectional information is very precious, but does not come "for free," and the modeler is faced with difficult modeling choices: the need (or the desire) for tractability, for intuitional appeal (as humans, we like to *understand* models), and for estimation stability often forces such drastic simplifications on the structure of no-arbitrage models (e.g., term premia that are constants or affine functions of the state variables) that the predictive power of the models is very seriously deteriorated. When the process of simplification and structural "constrainment" is pushed too far, the model *can* be solved, but unfortunately, it ends up being *qualitatively* wrong. Flexible and rich models, on the other hand, can explain *in sample* the observed empirical regularities but leave the user with difficult-to-interpret results, hard-to-estimate parameters, and little confidence that out-of-sample the models would still perform as well.

My plan is therefore to progressively build from the simplest (and most constrained) models in the affine class (the Vasicek) all the way to relatively complex ones (the Kim–Wright and the affine principal component-based models), adding along the way those model features required to explain a wider range of observed empirical phenomena.

12.5 AFFINE MODELS AND THE DRIVERS OF THE YIELD CURVE

As briefly mentioned above, the perspective embraced in this chapter points to three components – expectations, term (risk) premia, and convexity – as the drivers of the evolution of the yield curve. The overarching constraint linking these three drivers is the principle of no-arbitrage. In this section I show how these three building blocks enter the construction of term structure models in general and of affine models in particular.

12.5.1 Expectations

The impact of expectations on the shape of the yield curve is intuitively obvious – perhaps too much so. Admittedly, it is well known that the expectations hypothesis has been robustly rejected.[10] However, the rejection of the expectations hypothesis does not mean that expectations play *no* role in determining the shape of the yield curve. It only means that *expectations alone cannot explain all of the shape of the yield curve* – other factors must be at play: namely, term premia and convexity.

Which part of the yield curve do we expect to be most affected by views? It is reasonable to assume that market participants have well-formed expectations about the path of rates in the next few months, or perhaps a year or two. Beyond this horizon, "views" are unlikely to display much more structure than bland statements, say, "long-term rates are currently uncharacteristically high/low," or "the yield curve is unusually steep/flat." Definitely, expectation-motivated kinks and "sharp bends" in the yield curve (such as the V-shaped recovery yield curve of early 2001) should be localized at the short end. *So, we expect views to influence most short-dated bonds.*

This can create a modeling problem for affine mean-reverting models. These models "know about" expectations through a mean-reverting component (see Equation 12.17). Simplifying somewhat, this term accounts for how the state variables are attracted to a *long-term* (fixed or stochastic) reversion level (assuming that they do). It is ill-suited to describing highly structured, *short-term* expectations – such as the short rate will remain close to zero for 2 years, and then it will quickly rise. The danger is that later-generation affine models come equipped with enough variables and parameters to allow, if one really wanted, a very close, and "optically good," cross-sectional fit to all portions of the yield curve, even when they display very complex shapes. However, this is a blessing in disguise, because an undisciplined use of the degrees of freedom of a model is a certain recipe for modeling nonsense.

12.5.2 Term (Risk) Premia

Term (risk) premia are the compensation above the riskless rate an investor expects to receive for bearing some risk (say, "level," or, perhaps, "slope" and "curvature" risk, or volatility risk, or, etc.).

What can we say about these risk premia? Which yields are they most likely to affect?

[9]See Diebold and Rudebush (2013), page 38 in the context of the EM algorithm and Cochrane and Piazzesi (2008) (Panel 1 on page 2) for a discussion of the estimation of parameters and state variables.
[10]See, for example, Fisher (2004) and references therein.

A first important observation is that each source of uncertainty can have its own market price of risk. Risk factors, however, are not (directly) traded. What is traded are bonds. To go from market prices of risk for a factor to expected return for a bond, we start by thinking of the yield curve as driven by some (perhaps principal component-like) factors, x_i. The expected return from holding a T-maturity bond will then embed different compensations for unit risk, $a_i^{t,T}$, each of the form

$$a_i^{t,T} = \frac{\partial P_t^T}{\partial x_i}\sigma_i^t \lambda_i^t \tag{12.1}$$

where σ_i^t is the time-t volatility of the ith factor (always positive), λ_i^t is the time-t compensation (positive or negative) for unit risk associated with that risk factor, and the term $\frac{\partial P_t^T}{\partial x_i}$ describes how the price of the $(T-t)$-maturity bond changes when the ith factor changes. (If one of the factors were "the level of the yield curve," then we can roughly think of this term as the "duration" of the bond.) This means that at time t the expected return for a bond of maturity T is given by

$$\frac{E\left[dP_t^T\right]}{P_t^T}/dt = r_t + \sum_i \frac{1}{P_t^T}\frac{\partial P_t^T}{\partial x_i}\sigma_i^t \lambda_i^t \tag{12.2}$$

where r_t is the short rate at time t, to which we add "compensation components" from each risk factor, $\sigma_i^t \lambda_i^t$. Each risk contribution is transmitted down the curve by the responsiveness of a given bond to the risk factor, $\frac{\partial P_t^T}{\partial x_i}$.

To build our intuition, suppose that we have a single factor, that this is the short rate, and that the market price of risk is a constant, λ. With Vasicek (1977), let us assume that the process for the short rate in the real-world measure, $\mathbb{P}$, is a simple mean reversion, with the short rate reverting to a fixed reversion level, θ, with a reversion speed, κ:

$$dr_t = \kappa(\theta - r_t)dt + \sigma_r dz_t^{\mathbb{P}} \tag{12.3}$$

Then it is easy to show that we have

$$\frac{E\left[dP_t^T\right]}{P_t^T}/dt = r_t - \frac{1}{P_t^T}\frac{\partial P_t^T}{\partial r}\sigma_r \lambda_r = r_t + B_t^T \sigma_r \lambda_r \tag{12.4}$$

with

$$B_t^T = \frac{1 - \exp\left[-\kappa(T-t)\right]}{\kappa} \tag{12.5}$$

where κ is the speed of mean reversion, and the behavior of the "duration" term B_t^T as a function of maturity is displayed in Figure 12.1.

Figure 12.1 shows clearly the key message of mean-reverting models: for zero reversion speed, the "duration" of a discount bond (its responsiveness, $-\frac{1}{P_t^T}\frac{\partial P_t^T}{\partial x_i}$, to a change in the state variable) is a linear function of its maturity. As we increase the reversion speed, the state variables become more and more strongly attracted to some fixed level, and the uncertainty about their location (their variance) does not grow indefinitely with time, but remains finite. As a consequence, the stronger the "spring" (the speed of mean reversion, κ) that pulls the state variables toward their reversion levels, the less pronounced the growth of the duration with maturity.

Why does this matter? If the market price of risk is a compensation for the risk (read, the "volatility") of bonds, then the importance of the strength of mean reversion is obvious: the model-specific "duration" functions B_t^T (or, more generally, the model-specific "durations" $-\frac{1}{P_t^T}\frac{\partial P_t^T}{\partial x_i}$) determine, for each risk factor, how the risk premium "per unit risk" is assigned to bonds of different maturity. Even if we did a splendid job at estimating the *risk factor* risk premia, that is, the term λ_r, but our model described poorly how the various maturity bonds move when the risk factors move, the terms $-\frac{1}{P_t^T}\frac{\partial P_t^T}{\partial x_i}$, that is, our apportionment of risk premia across the yield curve, could be very wrong.

Similarly, if convexity arises because of a nonlinear dependence between the state variables and the traded instruments, what matters (quadratically so!) is not the volatility of the state variables, but the duration-mediated volatility of the nonlinear prices.

The sublinearity of the responsiveness term B_t^T is a consequence of a *statistical* property of our model: the variance of the driving factor does not increase indefinitely with time, but is "tucked in" by the speed of mean reversion to reach an asymptotic value. This part of the story is therefore about how much, according to our model, the "risk" increases with maturity. The other part of the story is how the investor responds to this risk – that is, the market price of risk. We will look at this later.

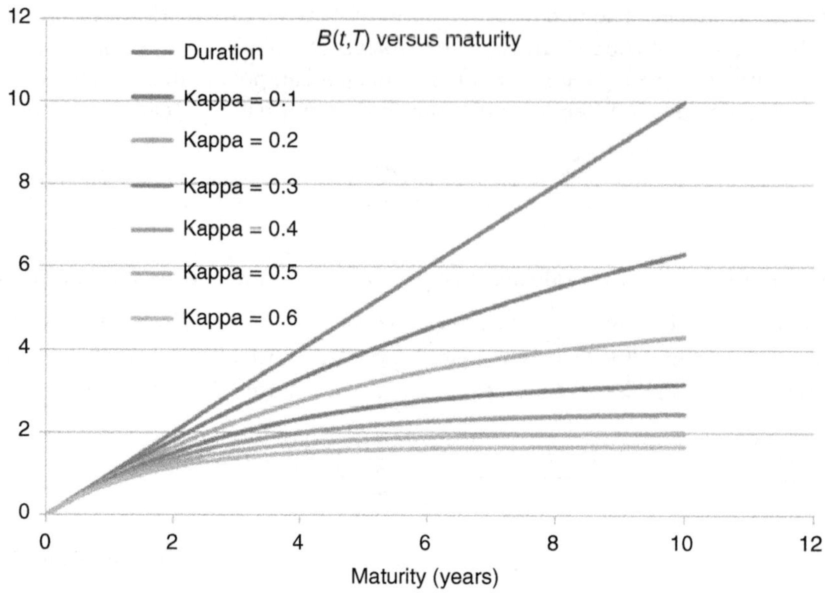

Figure 12.1 The term B_t^T as a function of maturity (x axis, in years) for different values of the reversion speed, from $\kappa = 0.1$ to $\kappa = 0.6$. The line labeled "Duration" shows the term B_t^T when the reversion speed is zero – in which case for a discount bond it corresponds to its maturity and hence its duration.

An observation is in order: if we introduce the seemingly "innocuous" assumption of requiring the market price of risk to be a constant, we cannot have at different times or for different yield curves positive and negative risk premia (because the duration is always positive). In reality, as we discuss at length in Section 12.10, one tends to find that excess returns are positive when the yield curve is steep, and zero or negative when it is flat or inverted. We shall see ways to enrich the simple Vasicek-like models to account for this feature, but the important message at this stage is that an apparently minor and reasonable assumption ("let's set the market price of risk to a constant") is far from being innocuous when it comes to a model's ability to recover essential empirical features about term premia.

For a positive market price of risk, term premia provide a possibly declining but never negative contribution to the shape of the yield curve. Yield curves, however, are not always to be monotonically increasing at the very long end. For very long maturities, convexity kicks in, and its effect can provide a significant contribution to yields of very long maturities.

12.5.3 Convexity

Where does convexity come from?

Take a yield of a given maturity, y_t^T. Let's assume that an upward yield move by x basis points is just as likely as a downward move by the same amount. For a yield move of a given size, the bond price will move up in price (in correspondence with the down move in yield) by more than it declines (for the up move in the yield). This is because the relationship between yields and prices is not linear – more precisely, because of Jensen's inequality.

The market "knows about" this nice feature of bonds, and, *everything else being equal*, long-dated bonds will command a higher price (a lower yield) than short-dated ones.

We can see how this works from the expansion for the bond price as a function of the yield. Starting from

$$P_t^T = \exp\left[-y_t^T (T-t)\right] \tag{12.6}$$

one obtains

$$\frac{E\left[dP_t^T\right]}{P_t^T} = \frac{1}{P_t^T}\left[\frac{\partial P_t^T}{\partial t}dt + \frac{\partial P_t^T}{\partial y_t^T}E\left[dy_t^T\right] + \frac{1}{2}\frac{\partial^2 P_t^T}{\partial \left(y_t^T\right)^2}\left(dy_t^T\right)^2 + \cdots\right] \tag{12.7}$$

$$= \left[y_t^T + \frac{1}{2}(T-t)^2\left(\sigma_{y_t^T}\right)^2 + \cdots\right]dt \tag{12.8}$$

wherein the last line $\sigma_{y_t^T}$ is the absolute volatility (i.e., the basis point volatility) of the $(T-t)$ maturity yield, and we have neglected the term in $E[dy_t^T]$, which is all important when it comes to no-arbitrage, but a nuisance in the discussion of convexity.

Equation 12.8 shows that the expected return gets an extra boost by the term, $\frac{1}{2}(T-t)^2(\sigma_{y_t^T})^2$, which is always positive and grows quadratically with maturity and with the yield volatility. But we know from the previous section that in a Vasicek-like model the volatility of the $(T-t)$-maturity yield, $\sigma_{y_t^T}$, does not grow linearly with maturity, but is "tucked in" by the reversion speed, κ, and is given by

$$\sigma_{y_t^T} = \frac{B_t^T}{T-t}\sigma_r \tag{12.9}$$

Therefore, we see that the magnitude of this yield boost depends *quadratically* on the volatility of the state variable and on the "duration" term, B_t^T. For low reversion speed, the term B_t^T behaves almost like the maturity but grows less and less with T as the reversion speed increases. In any case, the convexity effect should dominate at the long end. Yield curves, sooner or later, should become downward sloping. However, the stronger the mean-reversion "spring" (κ), the less the change in the duration B_t^T for long maturities, and the smaller the convexity contribution: which means that, for very long maturities, the convexity contribution begins to "saturate."

In practice, for reasonable values of volatility and of reversion speeds, convexity contributes a handful of basis points for maturities up to 5 years and used to be regarded as an annoying technical distraction. However, as issuers take advantage of the investors' hunger for yields and of historically low rates[11], convexity is being progressively pushed to center stage.

12.6 INTRODUCING NO-ARBITRAGE

Pasting together as one pleases expectations, risk premia, and convexity contributions does not produce a viable description of the evolution of the yield curve. What is missing is the glue (or constraint) of no-arbitrage.

The derivation of the no-arbitrage conditions is found in many good references. For our purposes, we simply have to recall one fundamental result: to prevent arbitrage, in the presence of risk arising from a vector $\vec{x}$ of factors, the expected return from holding a T-maturity bond must be given by

$$\frac{E_t^{\mathbb{P}}\left[P_{t+dt}^{T-dt}\right] - P_t^T}{P_t^T} = r_t dt + \frac{1}{P_t^T}\left(\sum_i \frac{\partial P_{t+dt}^{T-dt}}{\partial x_i}\lambda_t^i(\vec{x})\,\sigma_{x_i}\right)dt \tag{12.10}$$

In words, the risk adjustment over and above the riskless rate, r_t, is given the sum of three contributions coming from each risk factor: for each risk factor, the term $\frac{\partial P_{t+dt}^{T-dt}}{\partial x_i}$ tells us how the price of the $(T-t)$-maturity bond depends on the ith risk factor, $\lambda_t^i(\vec{x})$ is the compensation for the risk introduced by the ith risk factor, and σ_{x_i} is the volatility of the ith risk factor.

Note that the market price of risk can depend on calendar time and, in principle, on all the risk factors – indeed specifying realistically and parsimoniously on *which* state variables the market price of risk should depend is at the heart of a large portion of the current econometric work in term structure modeling. However, the market price of risk, which describes a *behavioral* response of investors to risk, cannot depend on the specific security and hence on the maturity T of a bond.

This way of looking at term premia affords a very elegant decomposition: the "duration" terms, $\frac{\partial P_{t+dt}^{T-dt}}{\partial x_i}$,[12] tell us how *specific securities* respond to the risk factors; the market price of risk tells us how *investors* respond to these sources of risk; and the model we have chosen tells us where the risk comes from (the short rate? The principal components? Some macroeconomic variables? Some latent quantities?) and how it behaves.

As long as we ensure that the conditions in Equation 12.10 are satisfied, we can rest assured that no free lunches will be allowed by our model.

12.7 WHICH VARIABLES SHOULD ONE USE?

We move in this section to the question of how the state variables of the model should be chosen.

In very general terms, the state variables used in no-arbitrage models provide a "basis" onto which to project information in yield and other data (Kim, 2007).[13] These variables can be exogenously (*a priori*) specified, perhaps on the basis of one's macroeconomic understanding of what drives the yield curve (say, expected inflation or real economic activity), or of a statistical

[11] At the time of this writing, Mexico is preparing a 100-year \$-denominated issue.

[12] As we have seen, in Vasicek-like model these are the B_t^T-like terms.

[13] See the discussion on page 2.

description of the yield curve (say, its "level," "slope," and "curvature"). Alternatively, they can be interpretation-free latent variables, to be estimated using econometric techniques such as Kalman filters (see, e.g., D'Amico, Kim, and Wei, 2010).

If the chosen state variables are endowed with an economic meaning or link, the modeler is faced with two problems. The first is obvious: she must hope that the empirical or theoretical mappings she is using (say, the Taylor rule or the Phillips curve) are robust and well founded. More subtly, the modeler must also be confident that the chosen variables can capture effectively and parsimoniously the yield curve dynamics. As Kim (2007) points out, "no-arbitrage guarantees the existence of *some* pricing kernel, but it does not mean that the pricing kernel can be described well by*a priori* selected variable."[14]

The seemingly obvious alternative is to use latent factors and let statistical analysis suggest their behavior. Life, however, is not without problems also in this case.

The first, and most obvious, problem lies in the opaqueness of the factors (i.e., in the difficulty to interpret them). Absent an understanding of what these factors are, it is very difficult to set up "sanity tests" to check whether they behave plausibly – and, hence, whether the model has been adequately specified. More fundamentally, it is difficult to "understand" the model.

The second well-known problem is that of overparameterization: once p observable variables and their q lags are added to m latent variables, one has to deal with $(p+m)(pq+m)$ parameters, which can quickly add up to $O(10^1)$ if not $O(10^2)$ "degrees of freedom."[15] As John von Neumann pointed out, " [w]ith four parameters I can fit an elephant, and with five I can make it wiggle his trunk". As Mayer, Khairy, and Howard (2009) prove in their Figure 1, this is no empty boast, and they show how they indeed manage to achieve the feat with four (complex) parameters.

The problem is compounded by the fact that the "level" of rates (for which the first principal component can be taken as a reasonable proxy) is close to unit root. As the principal component that "matters" most is the first, this in turn means that, whatever the latent variables of the model, the parameters that "matter" are likely to be estimated with great imprecision, and the confidence levels for market observables are too wide to be of much use.[16,17]

Because of this, working with clearly identifiable quantities rather than latent variables seems to have a strong appeal. However, there are subtle problems associated with specifying variables. A good place to understand the nature of this problem is to start with the work by Dai and Singleton (2000).

In an important paper published at the beginning of the new millennium, they produced a very general classification of affine models, and they obtained the following result. Start from N state variables (factors), $\vec{x}_t$, and impose that they should follow a diffusive process of the form

$$d\vec{x}_t = \vec{a}(\vec{x}_t)dt + \underline{b}(\vec{x}_t)d\vec{z}_t \tag{12.11}$$

As for the "drift" and "volatility" coefficients' $\vec{a}(\vec{x}_t)$ and $\underline{b}(\vec{x}_t)$, they can depend on the state variables, $\vec{x}_t$, but only in an affine fashion:

$$\begin{aligned} \vec{a}(\vec{x}_t) &= \vec{a}_0 + \underline{a}_1\vec{x}_t,\ a_0 \in R^N, a_1 \in R^{N\times N} \\ \underline{b}(\vec{x}_t)\underline{b}(\vec{x}_t)^T &= \underline{b}_0 + \underline{b}_1\vec{x}_t,\ b_0 \in R^{N\times N}, b_1 \in R^{N\times N\times N} \end{aligned} \tag{12.12}$$

Now, if the short rate, r_t, can be written as a linear combination of these N factors plus a constant,

$$r_t = c_0 + c_1^T\vec{x}_t \tag{12.13}$$

then Dai and Singleton (2000) show that the bond prices, P_t^T, can always be written as exponentially affine functions of the factors, that is, as a function of the form

$$P_t^T = e^{A_t^T + (\vec{B}_t^T)'\vec{x}_t} \tag{12.14}$$

Note that, apart from the short-rate requirement that $r_t = c_0 + c_1^T\vec{x}_t$, the factors can be totally general. However, we know that the time-t yield for maturity T is defined as

$$y_t^T = -\frac{1}{T-t}\log P_t^T \tag{12.15}$$

[14]Page 3, emphasis in the original. To make an extreme example, suppose that a macroeconomic variable (say, the real activity) were linked to the slope of the yield curve. Then it is intuitively clear that this variable would not constitute a good basis onto which to project a one-factor model of the yield curve – because we know that most of the yield curve moves can be explained by a quasi-parallel shift in the rates.

[15]The Ang and Piazzesi (2003) model, with its 2 observable variables, their associated 12 lags, and the 3 latent factors, requires 135 parameters for the pricing kernel to be defined. Similarly, the Gaussian QMLE affine model discussed in Diebold and Rudebush (2013) comes equipped with 139 parameters eager to be estimated: in their words " a challenging if not absurd situation" (page 37–38).

[16]Kim (2007), page 27.

[17]When a time series displays close-to-unit-root behavior, even extremely large datasets suffer from "small-sample" limitations; these limitations are made more acute by the occurrence of structural breaks, of which the post- 2008 year could be one example.

By taking the logarithm of the exponentially affine expression for the bond price (Eq. 12.14), it is always the case that for exponentially affine models yields should have this very simple form:

$$\vec{y}_t^T = \vec{u}_t + \underline{U}_t \vec{x}_t \tag{12.16}$$

Now, in specified variable approaches, the modeler assigns *a priori* the link between the state variables and the yields. For instance, Duffie and Kan (1996) simply identify the factors with the yields themselves ($\vec{u}_t = 0$ and $\underline{U}_t = I$). More interestingly, macrofinancial models link the observable yields (or linear functions thereof) to macroeconomic observables via some structural models. Or, again, we may use as state variables some special combinations of yields, such as their principal components. In general, modifying the terminology in Saroka (2014), let us call *specified variable models*[18] all models where the loadings $\vec{u}_t$ and $\underline{U}_t$ are assigned *a priori* by the modeler on the basis of her domain knowledge of how the world works.

Equation 12.16 immediately suggests that working with prespecified factors must bring about strong issues of internal consistency, and, once absence of arbitrage is imposed, any exogenous, *a priori* specification of the loadings $\vec{u}_t$ and $\underline{U}_t$ places severe restrictions on the admissible stochastic behavior of the state variables.[19]

For instance, suppose that we choose to work with principal components as state variables. As principal components are a linear combination of yields, our PC-based model would certainly fall in the specified variable model category. In an affine framework, we may then *like* to require that each principal component should display a nice and simple mean-reverting behavior, whereby, as it strays away from its own reversion level, it is attracted back toward it by a "spring" of appropriate strength. We may well *like* to impose this simple behavior, but the internal consistency constraints mentioned above and discussed in Rebonato, Saroka, and Putiatyn (2014) and Saroka (2014)) tell us that it is not in our gift to do so: the reversion-speed matrix becomes strongly constrained once the state variables are identified to be principal components.

The problem is general: by specifying the variables we gain in intuition, but we lose the ability to assign *a priori* a simple and intuitively understandable dynamics. No-arbitrage restrictions and the constraints imposed by Equation 12.16 will dictate a significant part of their dynamics. So, we *can* choose principal components as state variables, *or* we can choose (latent) state variables and assign a nice and simple mean reversion to their behavior. What we *cannot* do is choose principal components as state variable *and* impose that they should follow a "nice and simple" mean-reverting behavior.

As mentioned above, there is nothing special about principal components in this impossibility result. Once we have made *a priori* the modeling choice of Equation 12.16, that is, once, on the basis of our domain knowledge, we choose to assign the link between the yields and the state variables, we lose part of our ability to assign the precise nature of their dynamics.

All of this may sound rather abstract at this stage, but it will become clearer when we deal with the various models.

12.8 RISK PREMIA IMPLIED BY AFFINE MODELS WITH CONSTANT MARKET PRICE OF RISK

Irrespective of whether we choose to work with specified or latent variables, let us generalize Equation 12.3 as follows:

$$d\vec{x} = \underline{\mathcal{K}}(\vec{\theta} - \vec{x})dt + \underline{\Sigma} d\vec{w}^{\mathbb{P}} \tag{12.17}$$

where $\vec{x}$, $\vec{\theta}$, and $d\vec{w}$ are now $[n \times 1]$-vectors, $\underline{\mathcal{K}}$ and $\underline{\Sigma}$ are $[n \times n]$-matrices, and the superscript $\mathbb{P}$ indicates that we are working in the objective (real-world) measure. If we require that the market price of risk, $\vec{\lambda}$, should also depend on the state variables in an affine manner, we have

$$\vec{\lambda} = \vec{\lambda}_0 + \underline{\Lambda}\vec{x} \tag{12.18}$$

where $\underline{\Lambda}$ is an $[n \times n]$-matrix that expresses the dependence of the market price of risk on the state variables.

Moving to the risk-neutral measure, $\mathbb{Q}$, Equation 12.17 becomes

$$d\vec{x} = [\underline{\mathcal{K}}(\vec{\theta} - \vec{x}) + \underline{\Sigma}\vec{\lambda}]dt + \underline{\Sigma} d\vec{w}^{\mathbb{Q}} \tag{12.19}$$

To gain intuition, we can think of the factors as principal components. Then we know that the eigenvalue associated with the level (its "variance") is much larger than the eigenvalue associated with the slope and the latter in turn much larger than the curvature eigenvalue. Looking at expression 12.10, we therefore expect that, when explaining excess returns, uncertainty in the level of the yield curve should be the variable that "matters" most.

[18] Saroka (2014) calls them *observable affine-factor models*.

[19] This topic is discussed in detail in Joslin, Singleton, and Zhu (2011).

At this point, absent specific information to the contrary, it is tempting to posit that a time- and state variable-independent (i.e., Vasicek-like) market price of risk[20] should be a useful starting point. Then we can rewrite Equation 12.19 as

$$d\vec{x} = \left[\underline{\mathcal{K}}\left(\vec{\theta}' - \vec{x}\right)\right] dt + \underline{\Sigma} d\vec{w}^{\mathbb{Q}} \tag{12.20}$$

with

$$\vec{\theta}' = \underline{\mathcal{K}}^{-1}\underline{\Sigma}\vec{\lambda}_0 \tag{12.21}$$

To see with clarity what the measure change entails in the constant-λ-case, consider the one-factor Vasicek-like model. Then we have

$$dr_t = \kappa(\theta - r_t)dt + \sigma_r dz_t^{\mathbb{P}} =$$

$$dr_t = \kappa(\theta - r_t + \lambda_0\sigma_r)dt + \sigma_r dz_t^{\mathbb{Q}} = \tag{12.22}$$

$$dr_t = \kappa(\theta' - r_t)dt + \sigma_r dz_t^{\mathbb{Q}} \tag{12.23}$$

So, if the market price of risk is a constant ($\lambda(r_t, t) = \lambda_0$), moving from the objective to the risk-neutral measure therefore simply entails shifting (upward if λ_0 is positive) the reversion level by the amount $\Delta\theta$:

$$\Delta\theta = \theta' - \theta = \lambda_0\sigma_r \tag{12.24}$$

This makes sense: if we are risk averse, we need an extra compensation for bearing risk, which lowers the price of a bond with respect to the risk-neutral case and raises the level of rates (by raising the reversion level to which they are attracted).

In this entry-level approach, how much extra compensation should we get when we buy a particular bond? It depends, via λ_0, on how risk averse we are; according to our provisional modeling framework, our degree of risk aversion does *not* depend on the state variables – say, the state of the economy, or the slope of the yield curve; it depends, via σ_r, on how volatile the risk factor is; and, finally, it depends, via the term $\frac{1}{P_t^T}\frac{\partial P_{t+dt}^{T-dt}}{\partial x_i}$, on how much the particular bond we have bought is affected by the risk factor.

Note that, in the simple constant-market-price-of-risk case, the reversion speed has not changed. This would be extremely convenient, because the statistical estimation of all quantities related to the reversion speeds (the degree of persistence of principal components, for instance, or the volatility of long-dated yields) would remain invariant across measures. This would make the calibration of the model much simpler.

This state of prelapsarian simplicity no longer applies if we allow instead the market price of risk to have the functional form $\lambda(r_t, t) = \lambda_0 + \lambda_r r_t$. In this case we would have

$$dr_t = \kappa'(\theta'' - r_t)dt + \sigma_r dz_t^{\mathbb{Q}} \tag{12.25}$$

with

$$\theta'' = \theta'\frac{\kappa}{\kappa'} \tag{12.26}$$

$$\kappa' = \kappa - \lambda_r\sigma_r \tag{12.27}$$

This also makes sense: if λ_r is positive, the reversion level is lifted even further (because $\kappa' < \kappa$), bond prices are depressed, and the yield demanded increased. Furthermore, a smaller "effective" reversion speed means that the variance of the risk factor is "tucked in" less, and therefore that bond prices are more uncertain, and that the "duration" (see expression 12.5) becomes longer: investors' risk aversion makes them price bonds as if they were more volatile than they are in the real-world measure.

However, the price to pay for this richer description of the market price of risk is that we can no longer estimate reversion speeds statistically in the real-world measure and use them in the risk-neutral measure.

For the sake of simplicity and parsimony, we would very much like to work with a constant market price of risk. But how far can this working hypothesis take us?

[20]Historically, some early affine models (e.g., CIR) have posited a functional dependence of the market price of risk on the state variable(s). However, they have done so on the basis of analytical tractability, not because of the desire to account for some empirical features.

12.9 TESTABLE PREDICTIONS: CONSTANT MARKET PRICE OF RISK

The answer, unfortunately, is "not very far."

If the simple picture we have painted up to this point were substantially correct, excess returns produced by Vasicek-like single- or multifactor models should at least be positively correlated with the variance of the yields. Empirical evidence fails to detect this feature[21]. After fitting models of this type to four decades' worth of data, Duffee (2002) finds yield forecasts produced by a constant-λ affine model even a bit worse than those predicted by assuming that yields follow a random walk.[22]

What is more, the residuals are not just large: they also display an easily identifiable "structure," because they are strongly negatively correlated with the slope of the yield curve.

The second finding points to a misspecified model, but the first (the absence of any detectable dependence of excess returns on volatility) throws into questions the validity of the whole conceptual approach: if investors do not require excess return for bearing volatility risk, what are they compensated for? Whatever it is, constant market price of risk[23] seems to offer no obvious answer.

The simple Vasicek-like modeling framework sketched with a broad brush above has another very obvious consequence: how much compensation per unit risk investors demand should not depend on the state variables. However, copious empirical evidence (see Section 12.10 below) suggests that it does. As we shall see, the two shortcomings are linked: they stem from the need to distinguish between what the compensation per unit risk should depend on (the Vasicek-like models answer "nothing") and which risk investors are sensitive to.

The picture, fortunately, is not as bleak as it seems, and the modeling approach presented so far needs enrichment, not a waste basket. In order to understand what is missing, it is useful to review briefly what we *do* know about expected excess returns and yield predictions.

12.10 WHAT DO WE KNOW ABOUT EXCESS RETURNS?

Recall that we have

$$\frac{E_t^{\mathbb{P}}[P_{t+dt}^{T-dt}] - P_t^T}{P_t^T} = r_t dt + \frac{1}{P_t^T}\left(\sum \frac{\partial P_{t+dt}^{T-dt}}{\partial x_i} \lambda_t^i(\vec{x})\,\sigma_{x_i}\right) dt \tag{12.28}$$

The n model factors, $\vec{x}$, could be latent variables, macroeconomic quantities, or identifiable statistical quantities. To fix ideas, let these factors be principal components, and let the first factor be associated with the level of rates. Each market price of risk could in principle be of the form

$$\lambda_t^i = \lambda_t^i\left(x_1, x_2, \cdots, x_n, t\right) \tag{12.29}$$

If we want to remain in a tractable affine setting, this general dependence can be written as

$$\vec{\lambda} = \vec{\lambda}_0 + \underline{\Lambda}\vec{x} \tag{12.30}$$

The empirical evidence collected in the last decade tells us the following about the structure of the matrix $\underline{\Lambda}$ and of the vector $\vec{\lambda}_0$:

1. "Expected future interest rates are quite different from forward rates"[24] and therefore "[r]isk premia are large. […] A pure forecasting approach leaves them as simple undigested residuals."
2. The forecasting "errors" (residuals) are strongly negatively correlated with the slope of the yield curve.[25]
3. Average expected excess returns to Treasury bonds are *on average* small.
4. These small average excess returns can be reconciled with the statement that "risk premia are large," if the market price of risk depends on a quantity of time-varying sign, giving at times a (large) positive contribution and at times a (large) negative contribution.
5. The correlation of the residuals with the slope of the yield curve suggests that this latter quantity could be the sign-changing quantity that can account for the large risk premia – or, at least, that it might contain part of the explanation.

[21] See, for example, Tab I on page 410 in Duffee (2002). Work by Chan et al. (1992) and Andersen and Lund (1997) suggests that volatility *is* linked to the slope of the yield curve, but when it comes to excess returns, slope does not seem to proxy for volatility.

[22] Duffee (2002), page 406.

[23] The same applies to market prices of risk that vary as a function of time, $\lambda = \lambda(t)$, but retain the same sign.

[24] Cochrane and Piazzesi (2008), page 3.

[25] Duffee (2002) page 406. See also Chan et al. (1992) and Andersen and Lund (1997) for links between the volatility and the slope of the yield curve.

6. Compensation for shocks other than level shocks is essentially zero.[26]
7. The degree of compensation for bearing level risk is proportional to a " return-forecasting factor". As mentioned above, earlier studies indicated that this factor should be the slope of the yield curve[27]; using US Treasury data over the last 40 years, we replicate these results, we elaborate on this finding below. More recent work by Cochrane and Piazzesi (2005, 2008), Hellerstein (2011), and others suggests that this factor may be described by a special (tent-shaped) function, $f(\cdot)$, of five forward rates (and hence of five principal components)[28]:

$$\lambda_t^1 = f(x_1, x_2, \cdots, x_5) \tag{12.31}$$

8. This more recent ("tent") return-forecasting factor is imperfectly spanned by level, slope, and curvature.

Taken together, this relatively recent empirical evidence suggests what needs fixing in the Vasicek + model: the assumption that the market price of risk is independent of the shape of the yield curve (i.e., its slope, its curvature, or the factor-predicting factor).

The last of the empirical findings reported above is somewhat subtle and is worth analyzing in some detail. From Finding 5, we know that what investors want from compensation for is *level* risk. However, from Findings 4 and 7, we also know that *how much* they want to be compensated does not depend on the level of rates, but on the return-forecasting factor –either the slope, or the curvature, or the "tent." To the extent that the return-forecasting factor can be proxied by the slope of the yield curve, this can be rephrased by saying that investors seek a compensation for bearing *level* risk whose *sign and magnitude* depends on the slope of the yield curve: when the curve is upward sloping, the amount of compensation *per unit risk* is large and positive; when the slope is zero or negative, the amount of compensation is small or negative. And *the* single market price of risk does depend on time, but this dependence only comes about because the return-forecasting factor depends on time.

12.11 UNDERSTANDING THE EMPIRICAL RESULTS ON TERM PREMIA

The "distilled" results presented above are terse and concise. It pays, however, to look a bit more carefully under the bonnet.

To do so, we used over 40 years of yield curve data provided by Gürkaynak, Sack, and Wright (2007). Mimicking the procedure by Cochrane and Piazzesi (2005), every month we entered the 1-year strategy of buying the T -year maturity bond, funding it with the 1-year bond, selling after 1 year the then-$T - 1$-year maturity bond, and repaying the loan. We call the profit or loss from these (overlapping) strategies the T-maturity excess return. The name is apposite: if forward rates were noisy but unbiased expectations of future rates, the excess return would be zero. We display the time series of the excess returns for the 10-year bond (together with various regressions discussed later) in Figure 12.2.

We found that the "slope" regressor is strongly significant, and its beta very stable, irrespective of the number of regressors used. The R^2 obtained using the slope regressor only is 19.39%, and it is barely changed when the first and third principal components are added.

Interestingly, when the volatility of the yield curve is used as regressors to predict the excess returns, the intercept and slope coefficients are not significant, and the R^2 is statistically indistinguishable from zero. However, when the absolute value of the excess returns is regressed against the volatility of the first principal component, the R^2 becomes a respectable 11.8%, and both intercept and slope are highly significant.

Figure 12.3 explains what is happening: in the presence of a state-dependent term premium, by itself volatility fails to have any explanatory power, as Duffee (2002) observed. However, once the slope of the yield curve determines whether the excess return is expected to be positive or negative, the volatility contributes to the explanation of the *magnitude* of the return. This ties in well with the empirical findings reported in Section 12.10: the slope determines the compensation (positive or negative) per unit risk; what investors are compensated for is then the volatility of the yield curve level.

Understanding excess return data requires careful analysis, which we cannot report here for reasons of space (see, however, Rebonato (2014a and 2014b)). As mentioned above, it may be possible to identify more powerful return-predictive factors. However, the overall message remains clear: the slope of the yield curve is an important, robust, and parsimonious predictor of

[26]Cochrane and Piazzesi (2008), page 4.
[27]Fama and Bliss (1987) and Fama and French (1989, 1993) report early work in this area. See also the discussion in Duffee (2002), pages 407 and 409.
[28]Hellerstein (2011) extends the study to several other countries and finds qualitatively similar results.

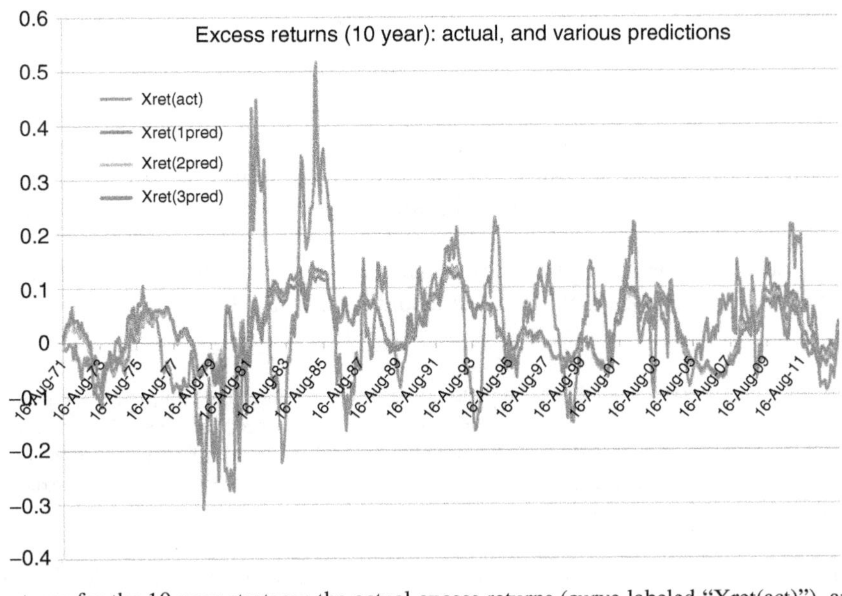

Figure 12.2 The excess returns for the 10-year strategy: the actual excess returns (curve labeled "Xret(act)"), and the predictions obtained using as regressors the second principal component only (curve labeled "Xret(1pred)"), the first two principal components (curve labeled "Xret(2pred)"), and the first three principal components (curve labeled "Xret(3pred)"). Source: Gürkaynak, Sack, and Wright (2007, updated series).

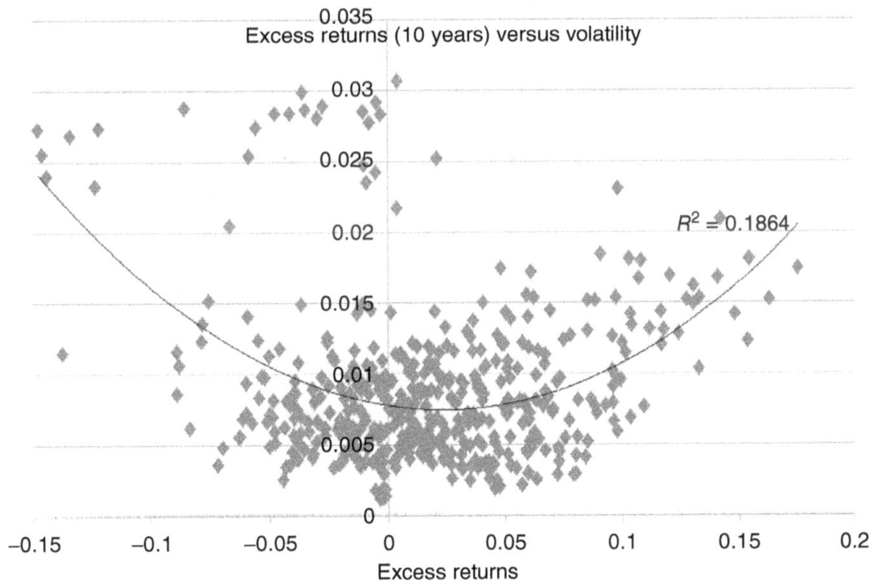

Figure 12.3 The 10-year excess returns (x axis) against the rolling (25-day) volatility of the yield curve (y axis). Source: Gürkaynak, Sack, and Wright (2007, updated series).

excess returns; excess returns are, on average, large and positive when the curve is steep, and zero or negative when the yield curve is flat or inverted; and the *absolute* excess returns are positively correlated with the volatility of the yield curve (but the signed excess returns are uncorrelated with the volatility).

This clearly shows the way to improve the first-generation affine models: if we want to use them for predictive purposes in a structural manner (i.e., straddling the $\mathbb{P}$ and $\mathbb{Q}$ measures), it is the constant-market-risk assumption that needs fixing, as expected excess returns must become state dependent. Once this is done, we will also recover the dependence of excess returns on volatility, which, intuitively, we always expected to be there.

12.12 ENRICHING THE FIRST-GENERATION AFFINE MODELS

We now have a modeling blueprint ahead.

Our goal is to look for models that enrich the specification of the market price of risk so as to reflect the empirical information above. These models will do so by making the market price of risk depend either on the slope (or, if we prefer, on the Cochrane–Piazzesi) return-forecasting factor. By using a theoretically sound model (rather than just relying on statistical estimation), we will add the condition of no-arbitrage to our description. And, for tractability, we will want the no-arbitrage model at hand to be of the affine family.

This "marriage" of the traditional statistical estimation approach to yield curve modeling with the arbitrage-free modeling framework is a recurrent feature of modern research. As Diebold and Rudebush (2013) say speaking of their recently introduced model,

> "[it] blends two important and successful approaches to yield curve modeling: the [...] empirically based and the no-arbitrage theoretically based one. Yield curve models in both traditions are impressive successes, albeit for different reasons. Ironically, both approaches are equally impressive failures, and for the same reasons, swapped. That is, models in the [statistical] tradition fit and forecast well, but they [...] may admit arbitrage possibilities, while the models in the arbitrage-free tradition are theoretically rigorous [...], but they may fit and forecast poorly."[29]

Their approach, the authors continue, "bridges the divide with a [statistically]-inspired model that enforces absence of arbitrage."[30]

Diebold and Rudebush (2013) are not alone in attempting this marriage. Indeed, their contribution can be seen as one strand in the recent body of work by D'Amico, Kim, and Wei (2010), Cochrane and Piazzesi (2008), Adrian, Crump, and Moench (2013), and Rebonato, Saroka, and Putyatin (2014).

What mainly differentiates these modeling approaches is the choice of state variables. Historically, "traditional" affine modeling approaches tended to start from a "financial story," which had well-specified variables (such as the target rate, or the long-term reversion level of the short rate) as its characters, specified a "model" to link the state variables in a way compatible with the "story," and tried to ensure that the optimized model parameters were consistent with their interpretation.

More modern approaches tend to employ a less prescriptive approach: either they directly employ latent variables (see, e.g., D'Amico, Kim, and Wei (2010) or Kim and Wright (2005)) or are rather casual about their choice of variables, as long as their properties can be estimated statistically. Adrian, Crump, and Moench (2013), for instance, say that they use "linear combinations of yields" that "could be principal components." The title of their paper, *Pricing the Term Structure with Linear Regressions*, clearly suggests that the no-arbitrage "glue" will be applied to the results of the statistical analysis. The recent work by Diebold and Rudebush (2013) and Rebonato, Saroka, and Putyatin (2014) can also be seen in this light, as the variables they use (principal components or their proxies) are chosen, at least in part, because of the wealth of statistical information that has accumulated about them.

In the next sections, we briefly sketch the modeling approach employed in these strands of research, and we focus on the predictions they make about rate expectations and risk premia – which is what structural models should after all provide.

12.13 LATENT VARIABLES: THE D'AMICO, KIM, AND WEI MODEL

In the Kim and Wright (2005) and in the D'Amico, Kim, and Wei (2010) models, real yields, nominal yields, and inflation are modeled by using three latent factors.[31] The three latent factors follow a familiar affine process:

$$d\vec{x}_t = \underline{\mathcal{K}}\left(\vec{\theta} - \vec{x}_t\right) + \underline{\Sigma} d\vec{z}_t^{\,\mathbb{Q}} \tag{12.32}$$

As long as the eigenvalues of the $\mathcal{K}$ matrix are positive, a "rotation of axes" can always be carried out such as either the matrix $\mathcal{K}$ or the matrix $\underline{\Sigma}$ is diagonal and the system is stable (see Ahn, Dittmar, and Gallant (2002)).

D'Amico, Kim, and Wei (2010) then link the nominal rates, $r^N(x_t)$, the real rates, $r^R(x_t)$, the instantaneous expected inflation, $\pi(x_t)$, the nominal market prices of risk, $\lambda^N(x_t)$, and the real market prices of risk, $\lambda^R(x_t)$, to their latent factors by requiring that

$$r^{R,N}(x_t) = \rho_0^{R,N} + \rho_1^{R,N} x_t \tag{12.33}$$

[29] Diebold and Rudebush (2013), page 76.

[30] *ibid*, page 76.

[31] Four in later versions, to include liquidity. For simplicity, we deal here with the three-factor version, for which all the considerations we want to make already apply.

$$\lambda^{R,N}(x_t) = \lambda_0^{R,N} + \Lambda_1^{R,N} x_t \tag{12.34}$$

$$\pi(x_t) = \rho_0^{\pi} + \rho_1^{\pi} x_t \tag{12.35}$$

and the superscripts N and R signify "nominal" and "real," respectively.

Assume now that the chosen state variables follow in the real world a process of the type[32]

$$dx_t = \mathcal{K}(\theta - x_t)dt + S dz_t \tag{12.36}$$

Given the discussion of the Vasicek problem, it will come to no surprise that if we make the affine assumption, we can write

$$P^i_{t,T} = e^{A_{t,T}+(B_{t,T})' x_t} \tag{12.37}$$

where the A_t^T and B_t^T coefficients have the usual Vasicek-like structure.

Without loss of generality, D'Amico, Kim, and Wei (2010) then impose that[33]

$$\theta = \begin{bmatrix} 0 \\ 0 \\ 0 \end{bmatrix} \tag{12.38}$$

$$\mathcal{K} = \begin{bmatrix} k_{11} & 0 & 0 \\ 0 & k_{22} & 0 \\ 0 & 0 & k_{33} \end{bmatrix} \tag{12.39}$$

Then they require that

$$S = \begin{bmatrix} 0.01 & 0 & 0 \\ \Sigma_{21} & 0.01 & 0 \\ \Sigma_{31} & \Sigma_{32} & 0.01 \end{bmatrix} \tag{12.40}$$

The equations obtained above specify and formally "solve" the model. The parameters and the state variables must now be estimated. D'Amico, Kim, and Wei (2010) obtain the parameters using a Kalman filter technique in order to estimate the real-world model parameters using data up to 2008. They supplement this information with survey data. Given the economic meaning of these quantities, one can show that the 5 ("intercepts") $+3 \times 5$ ("slope") loading coefficients cannot be independent, but must be related by four equations. This somewhat reduces the number of degrees of freedom, but one is still left with about 10 parameters to estimate. This is a tall order. Not only are the parameters overplentiful; they are also difficult to estimate, because of the close-to-unit-root nature of rates and because, given the latent nature of the state variables, we have no intuition about their plausible values.

We discuss the results of this model (i.e., its predictions for risk premia and rate expectations) in what follows.

12.14 FROM LINEAR REGRESSORS TO AFFINE MODELS: THE ACM APPROACH

Latent variables offer flexibility at the cost of opaqueness. Adrian, Crump, and Moench (2013) follow a different, and, in a sense, complementary, strategy: they do choose identifiable state variables (either linear combinations of yields or macroeconomic variables), but their choice is dictated by their ability to estimate econometrically their regression loadings on excess returns. Their estimation procedure is rather involved, but, in essence, they:

1. choose some linear combination of yields (for instance, principal components) as state variables;
2. impose that bonds should be priced as expectations of the state-price deflator (doing so ensures absence of arbitrage);
3. enforce the affine assumption for the market price of risk;

[32] To remain consistent with the notation used in this chapter, we have slightly changed the notation in Kim and Wright (2005) and D'Amico, Kim, and Wei (2010): their reversion-level vector, μ, is our θ, and their matrix Σ is our matrix S. Also, for consistency their quantities $a^i_{t,T}$ and $b^i_{t,T}$ (Eq. 22 and 23 in Kim and Wright (2005)) have been changed to $\alpha^i_{t,T}$ and $\beta^i_{t,T}$. When no ambiguity can arise, in what follows we no longer use an arrow for a vector and an underscore for a matrix.

[33] Why "without loss of generality?" Because it is always possible to orthogonalize either $\mathcal{K}$ or S. What is not possible, under $\mathbb{Q}$, is to have both $\mathcal{K}$ and S diagonal. Here D'Amico, Kim, and Wei (2010) choose to diagonalize the reversion-speed matrix, rather than the "volatility" matrix, under $\mathbb{P}$.

4. express the excess returns in terms of the affinely constrained state-price deflator;
5. recast the resulting equations in such a form that they lend themselves to an econometric estimation of the parameters of the process for these state variables;
6. establish a connection between the parameters of the statistical models and the "yield coefficients" of the underlying exponentially affine model.

The "heart" of this procedure is point 5 (the econometric estimation). By carrying out this estimation, the authors are able to estimate the state-dependent market price of risk, which constitutes the key "structural" bridge in their explanatory view of yield curve dynamics.

A striking feature of the approach is that a "traditional" affine model has almost receded in the background. By "traditional" I mean a model that starts from a financial "story," adds a clear identification of the "meaning " of the state variables (by stipulating that they should be, say, the principal components or the target rate), and provides a specification of their dynamics motivated by the identification of the variables.

The approach by Adrian, Crump, and Moench (2013), which is typical of much modern work in affine models, is rather different, in that it mixes some features of the latent and specified variable methods. Admittedly, it starts from identifiable state variables, but the authors are rather casual about what these variables should be, as they simply gesture to some linear combinations of yields, which, they say, could, but need not, be principal components. The salient feature of the variables they choose is not the interpretability, but their statistical estimability. A good model, in their approach, is a linear model that can be easily estimated (in their case, by linear regressions but, in general, by any statistical technique, such as Kalman or particle filters).[34]

They enrich the statistical estimation that constitutes the backbone of their empirical work with the no-arbitrage conditions and the affine assumption, and from these they directly derive recursive relationships on the quantities A_t^T and B_t^T in $P_t^N = e^{A_t^T + (B_t^T)^T X_t}$, without ever going through the explicit solution of the continuous-time differential equations.

The "model," of course, is still present but has been pushed to the background. The (constrained) estimation takes center stage – and, indeed, the title of their paper is not, say, "*A New Model of the Term Structure*," but "*Pricing the Term Structure with Linear Regressions*."

The difference with more traditional approaches is not fundamental, but the shift of emphasis is significant, and representative of modern affine modeling.

I examine the output (i.e., the estimates of risk premia and of the rate expectations) in Section 12.16, alongside a discussion of the results from the other models briefly surveyed. The questions of greatest interest, of course is: " Does the difference in the approach translate in a difference in predictions? And, if so, which model should we trust?"

12.15 AFFINE MODELS USING PRINCIPAL COMPONENTS AS FACTORS

The idea of using principal components or their proxies as state variables for affine models has recently been embraced by Christensen, Diebold and Rudebush (2013), Ungari and Turc (2012), and Rebonato, Saroka, and Putyatin (2014).[35]

We can look at this popular choice of state variables as a variation on the Adrian, Crump, and Moench (2013) criterion to choose the state variables: they set estimability of the regression coefficients that link the state variables with the excess returns as the hallmark of a good choice of state variables. The estimability criterion is certainly satisfied by principal components (after all, the slope has been known since the 1970s to be one of the strongest return-predicting factors). In addition, PCs are probably the best studied descriptive statistics of the yield curve, and they have been the subject of dozens of studies – which means that we know *a lot* about them, and we can readily ensure that the model reproduces these empirical facts.

But there is another very important advantage. For a model to be well specified, the time series of the calibrated state variables (obtained by fitting them day after day for fixed parameters to the yield curve) should display the same statistical features that the model imposes: they should have, for instance, the same covariance matrix, they should be (in the correct measure) as mean reverting as model assumes, and so on. But if one calibrates a principal component model to their well-known and stable statistical features, and one accurately recovers every day (to within a small pricing error) the realization of the principal components themselves, *then we are automatically assured of the consistency between the stochastic component of the dynamics for the state variables the model posits and the diffusive behavior displayed by the fitted state variables.*

In practice, Diebold and Rudebush (2013) start from an unabashedly snapshot model (the ever-popular Nelson and Siegel (1987) parameterization), carry out a clever transformation of three of its four parameters, endow them with a state variable

[34] To be precise, Adrian, Crump, and Moench (2013) (page 12) say that "our approach does not require pricing factors to be linear combinations of yields but can also be readily applied to models that use observable (and economically interpretable) pricing factors such as macroeconomic variables."

[35] See Joslin, Singleton, and Zhu (2011), Joslin, Le, and Singleton (2013), Joslin, Priebsch, and Singleton (2014) for a discussion.

interpretation, and then impose that these new variables should display a mean-reverting behavior, with a reversion-speed matrix, $\mathcal{K}$, a reversion-level vector, $\vec{\theta}$, and a volatility matrix, Σ:

$$d\vec{x} = \mathcal{K}\left(\vec{\theta} - \vec{x}\right) dt + \Sigma d\vec{z} \tag{12.41}$$

The three parameters in the Nelson–Siegel model, which have been "promoted" to variables, are denoted by β_1, β_2, and β_3. Shocks to the short rate (which is the limit of the yield of vanishingly short maturity) are then just given by the sum of shocks to the first and second variables:

$$dr_t = d\beta_1^t + d\beta_2^t \tag{12.42}$$

The rather artificial decomposition of the Nelson–Siegel snapshot model is unexpectedly interesting because shocks to the first variable move yields in a parallel fashion (and therefore changes the *level* of the yield curve), changes to the second affect the *slope* of the yield curve, and changes to the third create a hump in the yield curve (and therefore changes its *curvature*). The suggestive choice of words ("level," "slope," and "curvature") points to an obvious similarity between shocks to the variables, $\{\beta_1^t, \beta_2^t, \beta_3^t\}$, and shocks to the three first principal components.[36]

As Diebold and Rudebush show, this decomposition lends itself well to statistical estimation. They also show that it can be turned into an affine arbitrage-free model.[37] Indeed, Diebold and Rudebush look at the family of arbitrage-free affine models in the taxonomy provided by Duffie and Kan (1996) and pick the family member that most closely resembles the dynamic factors described above. More precisely, if the reversion-speed matrix, $\mathcal{K}$, is chosen to be

$$\mathcal{K} = \begin{bmatrix} 0 & 0 & 0 \\ 0 & \lambda & -\lambda \\ 0 & 0 & \lambda \end{bmatrix} \tag{12.43}$$

and if, inspired by Equation 12.42, the mapping from the state variables to the short rate is given by

$$r_t = x_1^t + x_2^t \tag{12.44}$$

then we know that the bond price, P_t^T, is given by

$$P_t^T = e^{A_t^T + (\vec{B}_t^T)' \vec{x}_t} \tag{12.45}$$

Rebonato, Saroka, and Putyatin (2014) follow a similar approach, but choose exact principal components as state variables, and require that they should evolve following a set of stochastic differential equations (SDEs) as in Equation 12.41, with the matrix Σ diagonal, and with elements on the main diagonal equal to the square root of the respective eigenvalues. This ensures exact recovery of the covariance matrix and of the yield curve for the reference yields. They also show, however, that absence of arbitrage imposes strong constraints on the reversion-speed matrix in the $\mathbb{Q}$ measure. In particular, they show that, for true principal components, this matrix cannot be diagonal and must contain "large" negative entries – where "large" means of the same order of magnitude as the diagonal elements. This gives rise to complex $\mathbb{Q}$ measure dynamics.

Rebonato, Saroka, and Putyatin (2014) then make use of the results of excess return studies on the dependence of the market price of risk on the second principal component in order to link the reversion-speed matrix and the reversion-level vectors in the $\mathbb{P}$ and $\mathbb{Q}$ measures.

The results from these two similar approaches suggest some interesting considerations. In both cases, the reversion-speed matrix, $\mathcal{K}$, is chosen in the $\mathbb{Q}$ measure. Now, if we want to interpret the variables $\{x\}$ as exact or quasi-principal components, their $\mathbb{P}$ measure dynamics should be statistically determinable. In particular, for the interpretation to hold, their Σ volatility matrix should be (close to) diagonal, and the $\mathbb{P}$ measure reversion-speed matrix, $\mathcal{K}^{\mathbb{P}}$, should be whatever comes out from the econometric analysis. (As Diebold and Rudebush make clear in the opening chapters, we do know a lot about the $\mathbb{P}$ measure behavior of the principal components – such as their degree of persistence – and this is precisely one of the features that makes their approach more appealing than latent variable models).

Now, once the reversion-speed matrix under $\mathbb{Q}$ (Eq. 12.43) is chosen, and once the $\mathcal{K}^{\mathbb{P}}$ matrix turns out to be whatever we estimate it to be, the affine market price of risk, $\vec{\Lambda} = \vec{\Lambda}_0 + \underline{\Lambda}_1 \vec{x}$, is fully specified. However, it would be an incredible fluke if the "implied" market price of risk turned out to bear more than a passing resemblance with the market price of risk that can be estimated from excess return studies.

[36]Note however (i) that the "slope factor" has the same sign for all yields, while the second principal component moves yields on opposite sides of the "pivot point" in opposite directions; (ii) that the first true principal component is not a constant as a function of yield maturity (it actually resembles a combination of the first and the third factors, β_1^t and β_3^t); and (iii) that the Nelson–Siegel loadings are not orthogonal, as true principal components should be (they cannot be, as they are all positive).

[37]See Sections 3.2 and 3.3, pages 62–78.

As we discussed in Section 12.10, from Fama and Bliss onward we know that the slope of the yield curve "contains," if not all, certainly a lot of the return-predicting factor (see also Adrian, Crump, and Moench (2013), Cochrane and Piazzesi (2005)). But if this is the case, and if the second state variable of the Diebold and Rudebush approach is to be interpreted as a "yield curve slope," then the matrix Λ_1 should have the form

$$\underline{\Lambda}_1 = \begin{bmatrix} 0 & \lambda_{21}^1 & 0 \\ 0 & \lambda_{22}^1 & 0 \\ 0 & \lambda_{23}^1 & 0 \end{bmatrix} \tag{12.46}$$

It is easy to see that there is a potential incompatibility between (i) the $\mathbb{Q}$ measure reversion-speed matrix, $\mathcal{K}$, Diebold and Rudebush choose, (ii) a market price of risk matrix, $\underline{\Lambda}_1$, that reflects some well-established facts about excess returns, (iii) a statistically determined reversion-speed matrix, $\mathcal{K}^{\mathbb{P}}$, and iv) the interpretation of the state variables as (quasi) principal components. Once the market price of risk is made to depend in a *specified* (affine) manner on the state variables, the modeler loses her ability to assign the nature of the variables *and* their $\mathbb{Q}$ measure reversion-speed matrix, $\mathcal{K}$.

With this proviso in mind, we present in the next section the predictions for risk premia and rate expectations produced by all the models discussed in the last three sections.

12.16 THE PREDICTIONS FROM THE "MODERN" MODELS

Since the modeling approaches presented above use very different estimation techniques and a variety of state variables (latent variables for Kim–Wright and D'Amico–Kim–Wei, "flexible" linear combinations of yields for the Adrian, Crump, and Moench model, and principal components for the Rebonato, Saroka, and Putyatin approach), one would *a priori* expect very different predictions for the risk premia and rate expectations. Figure 12.4 shows whether this is indeed the case.

More precisely, Figure 12.4 plots the 10-year risk premium for the models by Kim and Wright, and D'Amico, Kim and Wei (curve labeled "10yRPKW"), by Adrian, Crump, and Moench (curve labeled "10yRPACM"), and by Rebonato, Saroka, and Putyatin (curve labeled "10yPCAff") for the period from August 1999 to June 2014. The same figure also displays the slope of the yield curve (proxied for simplicity as the difference between the 10- and the 1-year yields) over the same period (curve labeled "slope").

It is obvious that there is a striking similarity in the predicted risk premia – if not between their levels, certainly between their changes. The similarity is even more striking when we compare the risk premia with the slope of the yield curve. What is happening?

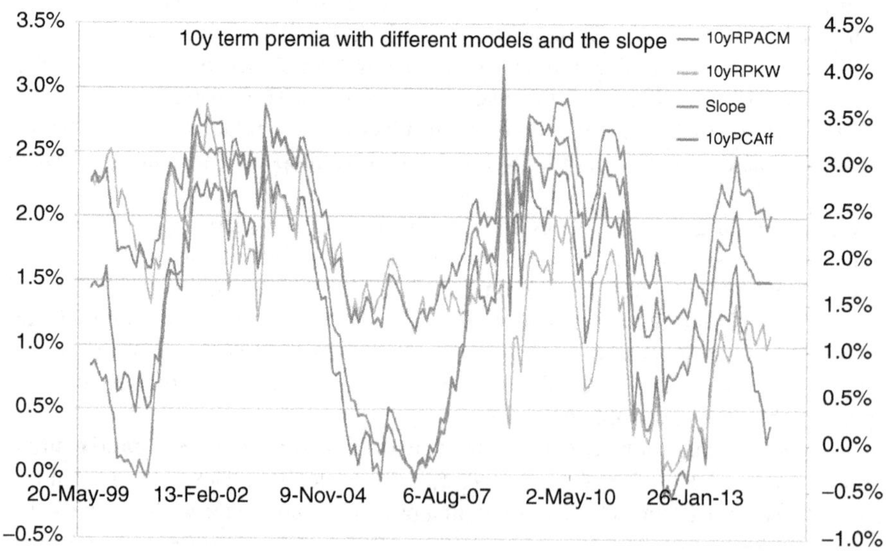

Figure 12.4 The 10-year risk premium for the models by Kim and Wright, and D'Amico, Kim, and Wei (curve labeled "10yRPKW"), by Adrian, Crump, and Moench (curve labeled "10yRPACM"), and by Rebonato, Saroka, and Putyatin ((curve labeled "10yPCAff")). The curve labeled "Slope" shows the slope of the yield curve (August 1999 to June 2104). For ease of visual comparison of the similarities in changes in term premia, a fixed positive shift of 0.01 has been added to the Kim–Wright term premium. Source: Gürkaynak, Sack, and Wright (2007, updated series).

Recall that all these models, directly or indirectly, "impound" information about the statistical links between excess returns and the shape of the yield curve when the strategy was put in place. Recall also that, whatever the potential additional information contained in return-predicting factors such as Cochrane and Piazzesi's "tent," the slope certainly explains a lot of the observed excess returns. What we observe, therefore, is simply the "regurgitation" by the apparently very different models of the same statistical information about excess returns fed into them during the calibration phase.

For all the sound and fury of the no-arbitrage conditions and of the various modeling assumptions, the predictions of the risk premia produced by these models are very similar to what is achieved by a purely statistical approach. Rather crudely, one may be tempted to say that, once we know the slope, we know almost everything there is to know about risk premia (and hence expectations). The marriage between statistical and no-arbitrage models that Diebold and Rudebush advocate in the quote in Section 12.15 has indeed been consummated, but the offsprings have turned out to bear a striking resemblance to only one of the parents.

Why are the *levels* of the risk premia rather different? When Rebonato, Saroka, and Putyatin (2014) examine the statistical estimates of the regression coefficients from the excess return studies, they find much larger standard errors associated with the intercepts than with the regression "betas." So, even the differences in levels of risk premia could be a reflection of little more than statistical uncertainty.

In reality the similarities run even deeper. Figures 12.5, 12.6 and 12.7 show the 10-year yield and its decomposition in term premium and rate expectations for the PCA-based model by Rebonato, Saroka, and Putyatin (2014), the Kim and Wright (2005) model, and the Adrian, Crump, and Moench (2013) model, respectively.

As one can readily see, all the affine models we have looked at imply that, from the late 1990s to early 2009, the observed market 5-year yields were overwhelmingly driven by expectations (with correlation in levels between $\mathbb{P}$ and $\mathbb{Q}$ measure yields as high as 88% for the KW model); after the Lehman crisis and the zero-bound regimes for U.S.-$ rates, changes in market yields are predominantly attributed by *all* the models to changes in risk premia.

Whether the model predictions for the post-2008 years are to be trusted or not is a different and lengthy discussion (see Rebonato ((2015)) in this respect). However, the relevant observation for the present discussion is that, despite their apparent differences, all these affine models produce deeply similar results.

What is one to make of this unsettling congruence? Do all these models uncover, after following very different routes, the same deep "truth" about risk premia? Or are the same answers somehow "backed into" the apparently different models in the calibration phase?

In order to answer these questions, recall that all essentially affine models specify the market price of risk as a deterministic (affine) function of the state variables. This means, conditional on a future realization of these variables, the market price of risk (and hence the risk premia and the expectations) can have one and only one value. Statistical regressions of excess returns come equipped with the residuals (and the smallness of the R^2 statistics associated even with the most optimistic regressions indicate that the residuals are large indeed). Once the affine mapping is made, however, this residual flexibility (e.g., the ability for the

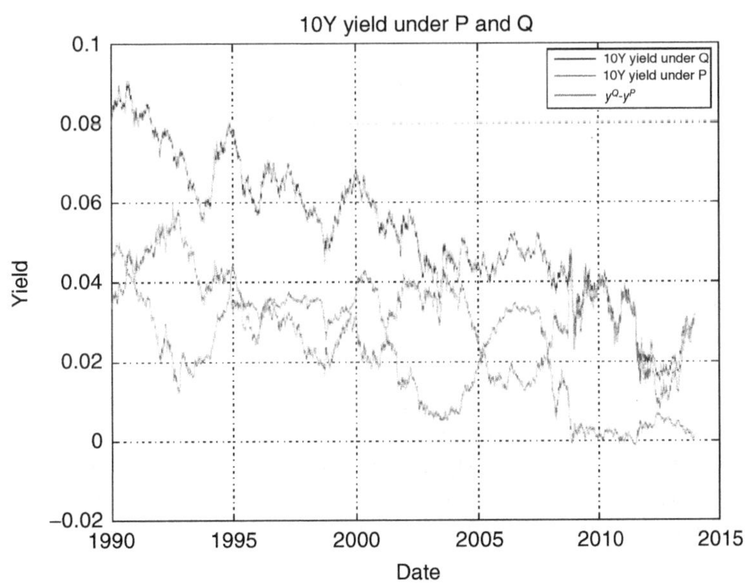

Figure 12.5 The 10-year yield under $\mathbb{P}$ (the market yield), under $\mathbb{Q}$ (pure expectation component), and the difference between the two (the risk premium) for the Rebonato, Saroka, and Putyatin (2014) model. Source: Gürkaynak, Sack, and Wright (2007, updated series).

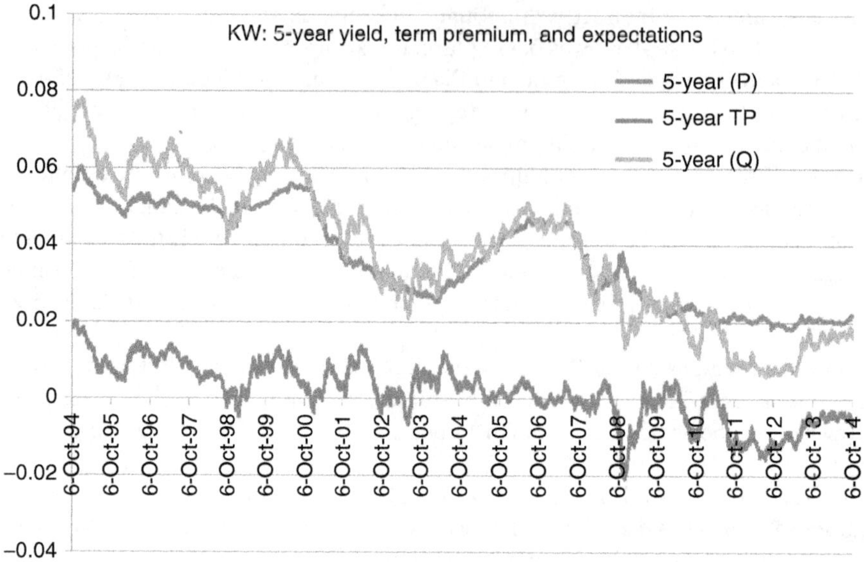

Figure 12.6 The 5-year yield under $\mathbb{P}$ (the market yield), under $\mathbb{Q}$ (pure expectation component), and the difference between the two (the risk premium) for the Kim and Wright (2005) model. Source: Gürkaynak, Sack, and Wright (2007, updated series).

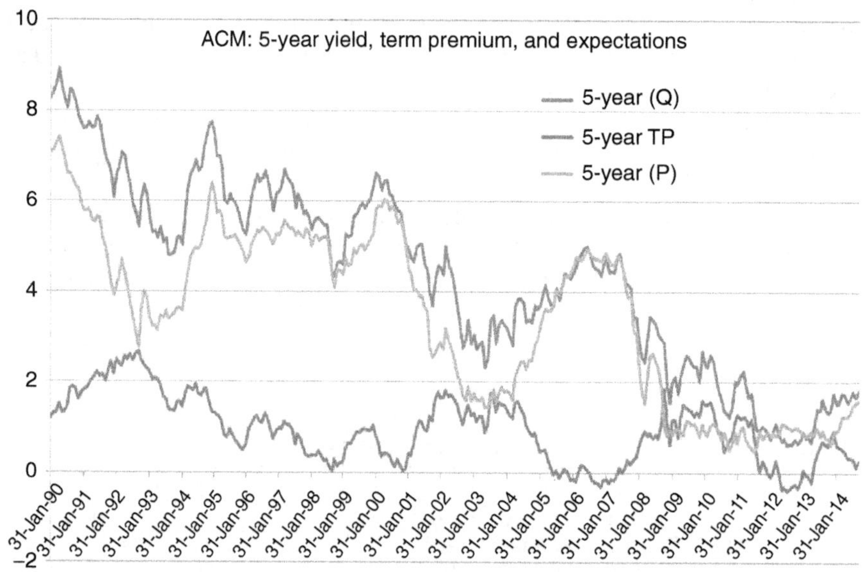

Figure 12.7 The 5-year yield under $\mathbb{P}$ (the market yield), under $\mathbb{Q}$ (pure expectation component), and the difference between the two (the risk premium) for the Adrian, Crump, and Moench (2013) model. Source: Gürkaynak, Sack, and Wright (2007, updated series).

market price of risk to be at one point in time small or negative even if the slope of the yield curve is high) is lost.[38] So, all essentially affine models require that for a given configuration of the state variables the market price of risk should be uniquely determined.

Next, all these models are "trained" on the same excess return data. The precise estimation techniques are different (ranging from Kalman filter, to traditional regressions, to more complex multistage techniques). However, ultimately, all these approaches discover that the slope of the yield curve explains a significant part of the excess returns. And, to the extent that the chosen state variables recover accurately day after day the market yield curves (a feat that all of these modern approaches easily achieve), they also recover accurately the principal components, and, in particular, the slope of the yield curve – that is, the main

[38]Recently, there have been some modeling attempts (see, e.g., Rebonato (2014)) to break this deterministic link while retaining both the affine framework and the long-term correlation between the market price of risk and the slope of the term structure. It is probably too early to tell how successful these developments will prove.

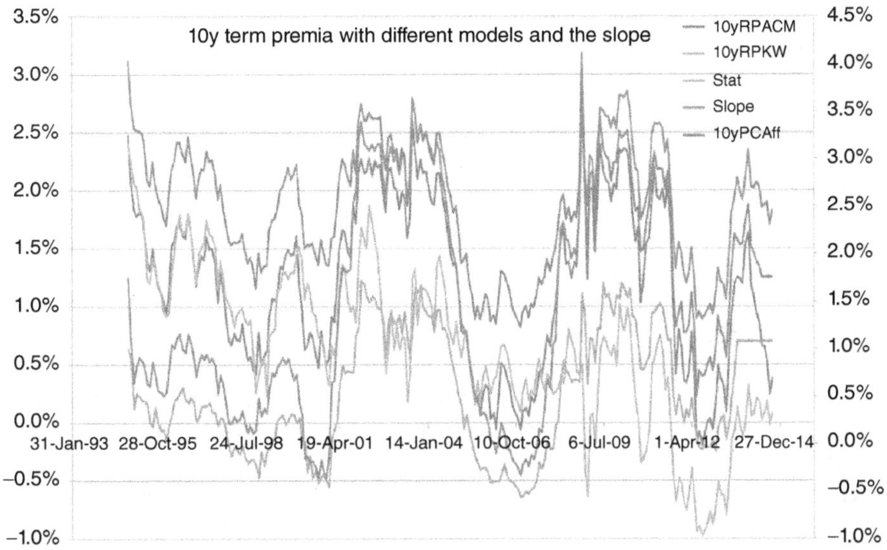

Figure 12.8 The same information conveyed in Figure 12.5, but with the addition of the prediction of the excess return coming from the regression study (the curve labeled "Stat"). Source: Gürkaynak, Sack, and Wright (2007, updated series).

return-predicting factor. So, from a bird's-eye view, all these models to first order seem simply to "regurgitate" the statistical information available from the statistical regressions of excess returns on slope (and other return-predicting factors). And, indeed, Figure 12.8 shows how little they add to the predictions of excess return over what is afforded by a pure statistical estimate (the curve labeled "Stat").

Admittedly, the levels are different, but as discussed above, the intercepts in the regressions (which determine the levels of the market price of risk) are much more uncertain than the "betas." So, a cynic may say, what the models predict well is already largely known from regression studies; and what they add, it cannot be trusted. Is such a jaded conclusion justified? In the quote above, Diebold and Rudebush spoke of a marriage of the statistical and modeling traditions. But what are the affine models bringing to the wedding party?

12.17 CONCLUSIONS

It would be wrong to draw the conclusion that no-arbitrage models are a wasteful encumbrance that adds little to what has been statistically estimated beforehand – the "stuttering regurgitator" picture of models.

12.17.1 Models as Enforcers of Parsimony and Builders of Confidence

The first reason why relying *only* on statistical information is unsatisfactory even if we are just interested in predictions goes back to the overliberal parameterization of unconstrained statistical models. Models are useful not just because they tell us what the phenomenon at hand depends on but also which variables it does *not* depend on. Absent a model, the econometrician is faced with a bewildering number of state variables, and their lags, as potentially "significant regressors." So, the first virtue of a model is to enforce some drastic pruning.

But there is more. Most of the interesting features of yield curve dynamics (say, the reversion level in the real world or the deviations from the local expectations hypothesis) are very hard to estimate statistically. Take again excess returns. With the long investment horizons needed to obtain meaningful returns,[39] either we have to use overlapping data or we are left with very few data points. After running a number of fancy statistical tests, we may then well find statistical significance for some of our regressors. But if we do not understand *why* these combinations of yields or forward rates should be able to predict excess returns, it is difficult to "trust" the results of our regression analysis even if they have passed the standard battery of statistical tests.

[39]Cochrane and Piazzesi (2005, p. 139), for instance, justify their use of monthly overlapping yearly returns by arguing that estimating 1-month (nonoverlapping) returns because "to see the effect [they discover] you must look directly at the 1-year horizon" and 1-month returns "completely miss the single factor representation" that they uncover is necessary because the noise (that roughly scales as the square root of time step) overwhelms the signal (that grows roughly lineally in the time step).

Of course, one thing is to make investment decisions on the basis of the statistical result that, somewhat mysteriously, excess returns are linked to, say, the slope of the yield curve; another is to make the same investment decision, after linking the slope of the yield curve to, say, some business cycle properties that help us understand *why* the slope dependence of excess returns might occur.

12.17.2 Models as Enforcers of Cross-Sectional Restrictions

Let me move to the second reason why structural models can be useful.

Suppose that we have full faith in the statistical significance of the regressors we have chosen to account for, say, excess returns. Even so, the regression parameters we have estimated will in reality still have very significant uncertainty bars – which means that they are informationally meaningful, but very noisy.

Suppose that, on the basis of these statistically significant but imperfect estimates, we want to predict the risk premia for the 3-, 5-, and 10-year maturity bonds. (Perhaps we have our own real-world expectations about the future path of rates[40], and we want to see what today's yields "should be," given the risk premia we have estimated.)

Now, our statistical estimates have been obtained from time series of market yield data that (presumably) impounded the no-arbitrage conditions. However, our noisy statistical estimates do not *directly* "know about" no-arbitrage. In the presence of unavoidable *and large* measurement error, the projections of term premia for different-maturity yields may not be compatible with absence of arbitrage. If we embed the statistical information into a model that knows about no-arbitrage, we may be able to improve our predictions, by making sure that they reflect not only the imperfectly estimated statistical regularities but also the additional information about differences in yields brought about by enforcing absence of arbitrage.

This is (in part) what is meant in the literature when people speak about "imposing cross-sectional restrictions": no-arbitrage condition link yields of different maturities at the same point in time (and in this sense they are cross-sectional) and complement this with time-series information about excess returns, yields, and so on.

This way of looking at models – the models-as-statistical-regularizers view –can be seen as a special case of statistical shrinkage in a direction reflecting prior views.[41] For readers familiar with Bayesian thinking, the prior views toward which the "raw" estimate is shrunk can either be diffuse or informative. In the case at hand, absence of arbitrage can be seen as the highly informative prior view toward which the solution should be "encouraged" to converge. The analogy is not perfect, but, I think, suggestive and helpful enough.

12.17.3 Models as Revealers of Forward-Looking Informations

Models are also useful because, by virtue of being fitted to today's yield curve, they know about the *forward-looking* information embedded in the prices. Using our historical record, we may well estimate, say, the volatilities of yields of different maturities. But this does not mean that these historically based estimates of volatilities are used by the forward-looking market participants to arrive at prices, especially when structural breaks occur – that is, when, arguably, we need most the help from models. The days after Lehman's default provide a vivid case in point.

The output from models calibrated to market prices can therefore differ from the output from statistical analyses for two reasons, one bad and one good.

The bad recovery failure stems from the model inability to account for some established empirical features: a state-independent market price of risk is an example of one such inability.

The "good" failure to produce the same predictions for market observables (say, yield volatilities) as suggested by a backward-looking statistical analysis is that the market-calibrated model knows something that the econometric analysis does not. This "something" is the market (measure-adjusted) forward-looking estimates of the same quantities.

12.17.4 Models as Enhancers of Understanding

Important as they are, these three reasons why models are not redundant but complement statistical information are only a (small) part of the story of why models matter. There is, I believe, far more to model building than the regularization of noisy inputs, the enforcement of parsimony, and the revelation of forward-looking information. And there is more to models, I claim, than enforcement of no-arbitrage.

[40] Of course, we also have to throw convexity into the pot.

[41] For an early discussion of shrinking techniques in statistical estimation, see Stein (1956).

Structural models afford an *understanding* of what drives the yield curve that is very difficult for a purely statistical analysis to provide. Statistical information is essentially associative and does not lend itself to a ready causal interpretation. Yet the human mind readily works in a causal mode but often falters when presented with association-based information. Faced with empirical findings, we naturally like to build explanations ("financial stories"). These causal accounts – these "models" –allow us to make sense of reality, to sieve the noise from the signal, and to understand the inadequacies of our current thinking. These causal accounts are dynamic, because they naturally point to the direction in which the model should be enriched.

This is more true than ever when our models suggest answers that are difficult to understand or to reconcile with our expectations, or with empirical evidence. Nothing stimulates thought and fosters progress more keenly than a recalcitrant piece of statistical evidence or a "paradox." After all, it was after observing the predictive deficiencies of the early constant market price of risk that researchers began thinking about what was missing – namely, the slope information.

In general, the main virtue of models is the power they confer on their thoughtful users to engage in a critical analysis of what the model may be lacking and of how it should be improved. When we look at modeling from this perspective, one can fairly say that we are in the midst of one of the more vibrant phases in the many-decades-old history of affine term structure modeling.

REFERENCES

Adrian T, Crump RK, Moench E. Pricing the term structure with linear regressions. J Financ Econ 2013;110(1):110–138.

Ahn D, Dittmar RF, Gallant AR. Quadratic term structure models: theory and evidence. Rev Financ Stud 2002;15:243–288.

Andersen TG, Lund J. Estimating continuous-time stochastic volatility models of the short-term interest rate. J Econom 1997;77:343–377.

Ang A, Piazzesi M. A no-arbitrage vector autoregression of term structure dynamics with macroeconomic and latent variables. J Monet Econ 2003;50:745–787.

Chan KC, Karoly A, Logstaff FA, Sanders AB. An empirical comparison of alternative models of the short-term interest rate. J Finance 1992;47:1209–1227.

Cochrane JH, Piazzesi M. Bond risk premia. Am Econ Rev 2005;95(1):138–160.

Cochrane JH, Piazzesi M. Decomposing the Yield Curve, University of Chicago and NBER working paper; March 2008.

Cox J, Ingersoll J, Ross S. An intertemporal general equilibrium model of asset prices. Econometrica 1985a;53:363–384.

D'Amico S, Kim DH, Wei M. Tips from TIPS: The Informational Content of Treasury Inflation Protected Security Prices, working paper, Finance and Economics Discussion Series. Washington (DC): Federal Reserve Board; 2010.

Dai Q, Singleton KJ. Specification analysis of affine term structure models. J Finance 2000;LV(4):1943–1978.

Diebold FX, Rudebush GD *Yield Curve Modelling and Forecasting – The Dynamic Nelson-Siegel Approach.* Princeton (NJ); Oxford: Princeton University Press; 2013.

Duffee GR. Term premia and interest rate forecasts in affine models. J Finance 2002;LVII(1):405–443.

Duffie D, Kan R, (1996), *A Yield-Factor Model of Interest Rates*, Mathematical Finance, Vol 6, No 4, (October), 379–406.

Fama E, Bliss R. The information in long-maturity forward rates. Am Econ Rev 1987;77:680–692.

Fama E, French K. Business conditions and expected returns on stocks and bonds. J Financ Econ 1989;25:23–49.

Fama E, French K. Common risk factors in the returns on stocks and bonds. J Financ Econ 1993;33:3–56.

Fisher M. Modeling the term structure of interest rates: an introduction. Fed Reserve Bank Atlanta Econ Rev 2004:41–62. Available at https://www.frbatlanta.org/research/publications/economic-review/2004/q3/vol89no3_modeling-term-structure-of-interest-rates.aspx Last Accessed 2015 August 6.

Gürkaynak RS, Sack B, Wright JH. The US Treasury yield curve: 1961 to the present. J Monet Econ 2007;54:2291–2304.

Hellerstein R. Global Bond Risk Premiums. Federal Reserve Bank of New York Staff Report No. 499, June 2011. Available at http://www.nyfedeconomists.org/research/staff&uscore;reports/sr499.pdf Last Accessed 2015 June 4.

Joslin S, Le A, Singleton KJ. Why Gaussian macro-finance models are (Nealry) unconstrained factor-VARs. J Financ Econ 2013;109(3):604–622.

Joslin S, Priebsch M, Singleton KJ. Risk premiums in dynamic term structure models with unspanned macro risks. J Finance 2014;LXIX(3):1197–1233.

Joslin S, Singleton KJ, Zhu H. A new perspective on Gaussian dynamic term structure models. Rev Financ Stud 2011;24:926–970.

Kim DH. Challenges in Macro-Finance Modelling, BIS working paper No. 240; Dec 2007.

Kim DH, Wright JH. An Arbitrage-Free Three-Factor Term Structure Model and the Recent Behavior of Long- Term Yields and Distant-Horizon Forward Rates, Federal Reserve Board, Working Paper; 2005.

Mayer J, Khairy K, Howard J. Drawing an elephant with four complex parameters. Am J Phys 2010;78(6):648–649.

Nelson CR, Siegel AF. Parsimonious modeling of yield curves. J Bus 1987;60:473–489.

Rebonato R. Why does the market price of risk depend on the slope of the yield curve? J Fixed Income SSRN Work Pap 2014a. Submitted to. Available at http://papers.ssrn.com/sol3/papers.cfm?abstract&uscore;id=2518985.

Rebonato R. An extension of the double vasicek model to account for stochastic risk premia. J Fixed Income SSRN Work Pap 2014b. Submitted to. Available at http://papers.ssrn.com/sol3/papers.cfm?abstract&uscore;id=2516775.

Rebonato R, (2015), RETURN-PREDICTING FACTORS FOR US TREASURIES: ON THE SIMILARITY OF "TENTS" AND "BATS". International Journal of Theoretical and Applied Finance, Volume 18, Issue 04, pages 1550028-1-1550028-14.

Rebonato R, Saroka I, Putyatin V. A principal-component-based affine term structure model. Appl Math Finance 2014. Submitted to. Available at http://papers.ssrn.com/sol3/papers.cfm?abstract&uscore;id=2451130.

Saroka I. Arbitrage-free modelling of affine principal components of the yield curve [unpublished thesis for MSc in Mathematical Finance]. Oxford: Oxford University; 2014.

Ungari S, Turc J. Macro-Financial Model, working paper SocGen Cross, Asset Quantitative Research, 19 October 2012.

Vasicek O. An equilibrium characterization of the term structure. J Financ Econ 1977;5:177–188.

13

The Econometrics of Fixed-Income Markets

Yacine Aït-Sahalia[a] **and Robert L. Kimmel**[b]

[a]*Department of Economics and Bendheim Centre for Finance, Princeton University, Princeton, NJ, United States*
[b]*NUS Business School and NUS Risk Management Institute, Singapore*

13.1 INTRODUCTION

This chapter deals with the estimation of a fairly broad class of term structure models, which can be used for both forecasting and derivatives pricing. Ideally, estimation methods should have the following properties: they should be applicable to continuous-time models with diffusions and/or jumps yet account for the discrete time interval between observations; be applicable to factor models with many different specifications, including nonlinear drifts and/or diffusions, that is, not be restricted to affine diffusions; have desirable statistical properties (at a minimum, consistency, and, if possible, efficiency); be computationally feasible and tractable, meaning that estimation results including standard errors are generated in a reasonable amount of time; and be, to the extent possible, robust to at least some forms of potential misspecification.

These goals may sometimes be in conflict, requiring some trade-off. However, the range of available estimation techniques has improved considerably over the last few years, making estimation of sophisticated continuous-time models feasible with discretely sampled data. Even estimation methods that are usually thought of as very straightforward can present serious challenges in a continuous-time setting. For example, a simple method of moments estimation strategy based on conditional means and variances quickly encounters the difficulty that, for most diffusions, neither of these quantities is known explicitly without a discrete approximation error. For latent variable models, the extraction of the state variables of the underlying model from observed quantities (such as bond yields) is typically difficult and may require numeric methods. This relation also typically depends on the model parameters being estimation and must therefore be repeated for each parameter vector considered during the estimation procedure.

Furthermore, model identification is often problematic (see Aït-Sahalia and Kimmel (2010) and Hamilton and Wu (2012)), at a minimum complicating numeric optimization. In a typical term structure model, the yield corresponding to any particular maturity can be expressed as a function of a set of benchmark yields, without any error at all. In practice, this model prediction is never observed exactly, so an estimation with " extra" yields is overidentified, and the observed data are generally inconsistent with any value of the parameter vector at all. However, performing an estimation with only the benchmark yields often leads to underidentification. In this case, there are many different values of the parameter vector that have identical implications for the behavior of the benchmark yields but different implications for other yields.

Handbook of Fixed-Income Securities, First Edition. Edited by Pietro Veronesi.

Consider the following example where the interest rate process is specified by the model of Cox, Ingersoll, and Ross (CIR) (1985):

$$dr_t = \kappa(\theta - r_t)dt + \sigma\sqrt{r_t}dW_t$$

under the true probabilities, but

$$dr_t = \kappa'(\theta' - r_t)dt + \sigma\sqrt{r_t}dW_t^Q$$

under the risk-neutral probabilities. If a series of observations of the short rate, r_t, is used to perform the estimation, then the κ, θ, and σ parameters are identified, but the κ' and θ' parameters are not; the time series of r_t observations contains no information about the investors' attitude toward interest rate risk and therefore no information that would allow estimation of the risk-neutral parameters. However, if we introduce, in addition to the r_t, a series of observations of a bond yield for a particular maturity, the result is overidentification. There are two additional parameters that can be used to try to fit the newly observed data, but these two parameters must fit the entire time series of yield observations, without any error at all. This will almost certainly not happen in any real-world dataset. So, for this model, observations of only a single yield (or the short rate) are not enough for identification, but observations of two yields are too much.

We focus in this chapter on maximum likelihood estimation. For maximum likelihood estimation, there are very few diffusions that have transition likelihoods that are actually known in closed form. However, the recent development of closed-form approximation methods that are extremely accurate, well beyond the accuracy required in applications, has made the estimation of these models feasible, computationally efficient due to their closed-form nature, and statistically efficient due to their reliance on maximum likelihood.

This chapter is organized as follows. We start by describing briefly in Section 13.2 the different types of term structure models, primarily to establish a typology that is useful when considering different estimation methods. We then turn our attention in Section 13.3 to the different types of estimation methods available, before focusing in Section 13.4 on maximum likelihood. Section 13.5 explains how to construct the likelihood function. Section 13.6 concludes.

13.2 DIFFERENT TYPES OF TERM STRUCTURE MODELS

Term structure modeling has a long history, but methods for constructing models have changed considerably over time. Some early modeling approaches specified the behavior of bond prices or yields of all maturities explicitly; for example, the approach of Macaulay (1938), which gave birth to the well-known duration and convexity concepts, assumed that the yield curve made parallel shifts. However, a more modern understanding of term structure evolution tells us that there are strong consistency conditions needed for absence of arbitrage; the parallel yield curve shift model does not satisfy these conditions. Most modern term structure models take a different approach of modeling the short interest rate and deriving bond prices as a consequence.

13.2.1 Factor Models

A typical modern yield curve model (see Vasicek (1977) for an early example) is based on a set of factors, which follow a continuous-time or discrete-time Markov process. For example, a continuous-time diffusion model might be specified as

$$dX_t = \mu(X_t)dt + \sigma(X_t)dW_t$$

where X_t and μ are vectors, σ is a square matrix, and W_t is a vector of independent Brownian motions; this general model includes one-dimensional models as a special case.[1]

The short (or instantaneous) interest rate is some function

$$r_t = f(X_t)$$

of the state vector X_t; note that this includes the special case in which r_t is simply one of the elements of X_t. This is typically the case for so-called " arbitrage-free" models, often used for derivatives pricing; in such models, the interest rate may be the only element of X_t, but the μ and σ functions are usually explicitly time dependent.

This model specification is incomplete, because it is inadequate to determine the prices or yields of any bonds. Except for the degenerate case where the interest rate r_t is a deterministic process, bonds have interest rate risk, since they depend on the

[1] We assume throughout that the coefficients of the diffusion (and also the interest rate function) are not time dependent. However, the estimation method can be extended to incorporate explicit time dependence in any or all of these coefficients; see Egorov, Li, and Xu (2003).

evolution of the Brownian motions W_t. Unless we know what risk premium investors demand for facing this risk, we cannot find bond prices. A fully specified term structure model therefore also includes a market price of risk (in effect, the instantaneous Sharpe ratio for each element of W_t) or, equivalently, an alternative set of probabilities that are risk neutral, under which the $\mu(X_t)$ function is different, that is,

$$dX_t = \mu^Q(X_t)dt + \sigma(X_t)dW_t^Q$$

where W_t^Q is a set of independent Brownian motions under the risk-neutral probabilities.

A complete specification of $\mu(X_t)$, $\mu^Q(X_t)$, $\sigma(X_t)$, and $f(X_t)$ therefore defines fully a term structure model under which we can, in principle at least, price bonds and interest rate derivatives, and also forecast yields, for portfolio management or risk management purposes. To perform these tasks, we need to estimate the parameters governing these four functions; how this task is performed depends on the nature of the factors underlying a particular model.

13.2.2 Observable Factors

The elements of X_t could correspond to quantities that are readily observed. For example, these elements could be the short interest rate, the yields of bonds of varying maturities, macroeconomic variables, or other observed quantities. Alternatively, the elements of X_t could be abstract latent variables that do not map in a simple way to any easily observed or easily interpreted economic quantities. Both of these approaches have been used in term structure modeling, and both present their own unique challenges.

The advantage of observable factors is, unsurprisingly, that they are observed. No difficult procedure is required to extract the value of the state vector X_t indirectly from other observed quantities, such as prices/yields of bonds, or perhaps interest rate derivatives. Since X_t is observed, any technique for estimation of the parameters of a model of a diffusion process may be used.

13.2.3 Latent Factors: Filtering versus Indirect Observation

By contrast, when the state variables are latent, filtering or some other creative approach is required for estimation, introducing an extra level of complexity to the process. Two distinct approaches are possible.

First, a traditional filtering method may be used. For example, if the function $\mu(X_t)$ is linear in X_t and the function $\sigma(X_t)$ is constant, then the distribution of X_t, conditional on $X_{t-\Delta}$, is multivariate Gaussian, and the Kalman filter may be used. For more complicated diffusion processes, the filtering process is still possible in principle but is considerably more difficult in practice. Different filtering approaches applied to term structure models include Duan and Simonato (1999) for affine term structure models, Geyer and Pichler (1999), Bates (2006) for a filtration-based maximum likelihood approach, and Christoffersen et al. (2014). But, regardless of the particular diffusion, the filtering procedure requires that at least some of the elements of X_t are observed.

Second, latent variables may be considered indirectly observed, through bond yields or the prices of interest rate derivative securities. For example, assuming indirect observability with yields, the value of X_t can be inferred by the shape of the yield curve at time t. This simple idea is fraught with practical difficulties:

- The relation between bond yields and the state X_t may be complicated, requiring numeric methods to derive if it is not known in closed form.
- This relation may not be easily invertible.
- This relation may be parameter dependent and therefore have to be recalculated for every set of parameters considered during a search.
- If a model is not constructed carefully, with suitable restrictions imposed, some of the parameters may be unidentified; that is, there may be multiple processes for the evolution of X_t, which have identical implications for the evolution of the entire yield curve.
- There may be inconsistency, if too many parameter restrictions are imposed.

Despite these difficulties, many term structure models are written in terms of latent variables and estimated using information extracted from the yield curve.

13.2.4 Macroeconomic Models

One particular special case of a model with observable factors is one in which those factors correspond to macroeconomic variables. Such models are not commonly used for applications involving term structure derivatives pricing, but are often used when yield curve forecasting is considered in the context of a more general macroeconomic model. Examples of models in this class include Ang and Piazzesi (2003); Gallmeyer, Hollifield, and Zin (2005); Ang, Piazzesi, and Wei (2006); Diebold, Rudebusch, and Aruoba (2006); Rudebusch and Wu (2008); Bikbov and Chernov (2010); Ludvigson and Ng (2010); Gürkaynak and Wright (2012); and Joslin, Priebsch, and Singleton (2014).

For estimation purposes, it might seem that macroeconomic models should not be any different than any other model with observed factors, although for many applications, it is not so important to ensure that these models are free from arbitrage. However, the mismatch between the frequencies of observation of different variables can give rise to significant challenges. Many macroeconomic variables are available on a quarterly basis, or even less frequently, whereas the yield curve is observed on a daily or even transactional basis.

The principal benefit of such models is the relation between the yield curve and other macroeconomic variables. Observed macroeconomic quantities may add predictive power when forecasting the yield curve, relative to forecasts based on the shape of the yield curve alone. Furthermore, it might be possible to use information from the yield curve to produce better forecasts of the macroeconomic variables.

13.2.5 Affine Models

One extremely popular family of term structure models is the so-called "affine yield" family. These models are of the latent factor type, and the μ function, $\sigma\sigma^T$, and the f function all have elements that are affine functions of X_t.

The reason for the popularity of affine models is that the affine structure simplifies many of the computational tasks that must be performed. For example, bond prices are known in closed form for only a very few highly restricted diffusion models and must be found using numeric methods; specifically, prices are solutions to a second-order parabolic partial differential equation. This remains the case for most affine yield models; however, in this case, the partial differential equation (PDE) can be decomposed into a system of ordinary differential equations, which can be solved numerically much faster than a general PDE. This analytic tractability is not confined to finding bond prices; although likelihoods are not known for most affine yield models, conditional moments of bond yields are relatively easy to derive.

Early examples of affine yield models are Vasicek (1977) and Cox, Ingersoll, and Ross (1985), who develop simple models in which the short interest rate is a Markov process. In these models, returns of bonds of all maturities are instantaneously perfectly correlated, which implies somewhat unrealistic yield curve behavior; for example, the risk of a 30-year bond could be hedged with a 1-month bond, if these models were the literal truth. The subsequent years saw development of more complicated multiple-factor models, such as Chen (1996) and Balduzzi et al. (1996), which allowed for independent sources of variation for bonds of different maturities. Duffie and Kan (1996) did not focus on specific models, but rather derived a number of results for a broad family of affine models, which included nearly all previously developed models as special cases. Many subsequent studies such as Dai and Singleton (2000); Duffee (2002); Mosburger and Schneider (2005); Gouriéroux and Sufana (2006); Cheridito, Filipović, and Kimmel (2007); Thompson (2008); Aït-Sahalia and Kimmel (2010); Duffee (2011); Joslin, Le, and Singleton (2013); and Egorov, Hong, and Li (2006) studied the broad classes of affine models, in contrast to the earlier practice of focusing on particular special cases.

Examples of term structure models based on an explicitly specified process for the short rate that are *not* affine are relatively uncommon in the literature; however, for an example, see Longstaff (1989), Constantinides (1992), Beaglehole and Tenney (1992), Aït-Sahalia (1996b), Ahn and Gao (1999), and Ahn, Dittmar, and Gallant (2002). Cai and Swanson (2011) examine the performance of several affine and nonaffine models over various time periods and also examine some discrete-time models.

13.2.6 Yield-Based Models

Given many of the challenges involved with estimation of factor models, it might seem tempting to bypass these problems by using term structure models based directly on yields, that is, in which the elements of X_t are yields of bonds with different maturities. This approach is suitable for some applications, but when no-arbitrage restrictions are important, it is very difficult to incorporate these into yield-factor models.

For risk management purposes, it may not be important to impose the no-arbitrage conditions. The concepts of duration and convexity, based on a model of parallel yield curve shifts, are taught widely in investment management courses and used extensively in industry, despite the fact that parallel yield curve shifts offer exploitable arbitrage opportunities. Similarly, yield curve evolution is sometimes described in terms of level, slope, and curvature (see, e.g., Litterman and Scheinkman (1991)); however, a yield curve that evolves in this way offers arbitrage opportunities. Unless one believes such arbitrage opportunities really exist, such a model is clearly misspecified; however, for risk management purposes, the model may still be useful. However, models inconsistent with the absence of arbitrage are unsuitable for applications such as derivatives pricing.

The crux of the issue is that there are strong consistency conditions between the evolutions of yields of different maturities. For example, consider a two-factor model, and write the evolution of X_t under risk-neutral probabilities

$$d\begin{bmatrix} X_{1,t} \\ X_{2,t} \end{bmatrix} = \begin{bmatrix} \mu_1^Q(X_t) \\ \mu_2^Q(X_t) \end{bmatrix} dt + \begin{bmatrix} \sigma_{11}(X_t) & \sigma_{12}(X_t) \\ \sigma_{21}(X_t) & \sigma_{22}(X_t) \end{bmatrix} d\begin{bmatrix} W_{1,t}^Q \\ W_{2,t}^Q \end{bmatrix}$$

The prices of bonds are fully specified through the relation

$$P_{t,\tau} = E_t^Q\left[e^{-\int_t^\tau r_u du}\right] \tag{13.1}$$

where $P_{t,\tau}$ is the time t price of a zero-coupon bond with a face value of 1 and a time of maturity τ and the Q superscript indicates that the expectation is taken under the risk-neutral probabilities. If the short rate is given by $r_t = X_{1,t}$ and $X_{2,t}$ is a latent variable, then estimation of the model must be by filtering or some similar technique, as previously discussed. But, given the parameters of the model and the current values of $X_{1,t}$ and $X_{2,t}$, the current values of all yields are fully specified, as are their drifts and diffusions.

But suppose that, instead of being latent, $X_{2,t}$ is identified with the yield of a particular maturity of bond. The model is then based entirely on observed quantities, with all the advantages thereof. However, the parameters μ_2^Q, σ_{12}, and σ_{22} must be consistent with the evolution of this bond yield as implied by 13.1. This is unlikely to happen by coincidence, and it is in general quite difficult to construct any nontrivial models that satisfy this property.

With some exceptions, the state vector X_t in an affine yield models can be replaced with an alternate state vector whose elements are yields of zero-coupon bonds; see Duffie and Kan (1996). The model, expressed in terms of the alternate state vector, remains affine. However, the elements of the μ and σ functions (in the alternate model) are, in general, known only as a solutions to differential equations. Similar problems will exist with nonaffine models; even when a model can theoretically be expressed in a form with X_t containing only observed yields, in practice, it is quite difficult to impose the no-arbitrage constraint explicitly. For a method for expressing Gaussian models in terms of observed quantities, see Joslin, Singleton, and Zhu (2011).

13.2.7 Forward-Based Models

A completely different approach to term structure modeling has been developed over the last two decades, in which the short interest rate does not play such a prominent role. Rather, in the approach of Heath, Jarrow, and Morton (HJM) (1992), as further developed by Brace, Gątarek, and Musiela (BGM) (1997), all yields (or, more typically, all forward rates) are modeled simultaneously, as in the parallel yield curve shift model of Macaulay (1938). However, restrictions necessary to ensure absence of arbitrage are imposed. Specifically, under risk-neutral probabilities, once the diffusion coefficient is specified for forward rates of all maturities, their drifts must have a specific form.

HJM and BGM models are very widely used in industry but less often in academic studies. They offer tremendous flexibility, being able to match any arbitrarily shaped yield curve, with further degrees of freedom to match yield volatility and correlation. Being used mostly for derivatives pricing, such models are typically calibrated from current market data, rather than estimated from historic data.

In general, the short rate process implied by a particular HJM or BGM model (which is typically not derived explicitly) is non-Markovian. When strong restrictions are imposed on the parameters of an HJM or BGM model, the short interest rate process can be made to be Markov, although, in this case, the particular model can be viewed as a factor model instead.

We do not discuss HJM models in general, although every factor model can be viewed as a special case of the general HJM model.

13.3 PARAMETRIC ESTIMATION METHODS

We consider only methods that are designed to estimate the parameters of a prespecified model, that is, parametric methods. In particular, we do not discuss semi- or nonparametric methods (see Aït-Sahalia (1996a)) or methods that are designed to assess the fit of a particular parametric model by comparing it to its nonparametric counterpart (see Aït-Sahalia (1996b)).

There are many other parametric approaches, besides maximum likelihood, for estimation of continuous-time term structure models. Most are some variation of method of moments, and each has its own advantages/disadvantages and may be appropriate for particular situations. Duffee and Stanton (2012) provide a comparison of different estimation techniques.

13.3.1 GMM

The generalized method of moments (GMM) is a very powerful and flexible method for estimation of model parameters, allowing estimation under very general distributional assumptions. The logic of the method of moments is quite simple and intuitive – model parameters are chosen so that population moments match their sample counterparts. When applied to continuous-time problems and latent variable settings, however, the method encounters certain challenges.

The first challenge is the derivation of moment conditions when data are observed at discrete time intervals. For some very simple diffusion processes (such as arithmetic or geometric Brownian motions or Ornstein–Uhlenbeck processes), first-, second-, and possibly higher-order moments are known explicitly. However, for most other diffusion processes, not even first moments can be found in closed form; some numeric or other approximation method is needed.

The second challenge is that even a relatively rich set of moment conditions may fail to capture all the information in the full distribution of the state variables of a model. Some term structure models will impose positivity or other range restrictions on the values its state variables may assume, and estimation by method of moments will not necessarily respect these restrictions. In latent variable models (discussed in detail in Section 13.4.2), the underlying state variables of the model are not observed directly; rather, we observe functions, possibly complicated, of the state variables. (In a typical term structure setting, the observed quantities would be yields.) The relation between the observed quantities and the latent state variables can depend on the parameters being estimated. To take an example, in the model of Cox, Ingersoll, and Ross (1985), the interest rate process follows

$$dr_t = \kappa(\theta - r_t)dt + \sigma\sqrt{r_t}dW_t \tag{13.2}$$

In this model, the interest rate cannot become negative, and the parameter restriction $\kappa\theta \geq 0$ is necessary to enforce this nonnegativity. The first and second conditional moments of the interest rate r_t are linear and quadratic, respectively, functions of r_t itself. These functions extend quite readily to negative values of r_t, even though such values make no sense in terms of the stochastic process specified by 13.2. But, notwithstanding recent policy decisions of the European Central Bank, negative interest rates do not occur in most real-world datasets, so estimation of the parameters of 13.2 from direct observation of the interest rate process r_t is possible.

However, a particular estimation may be based on yields of zero-coupon bonds, which, in this model, are linear functions of the interest rate r_t, that is,

$$y_{t,\tau} = a(\tau - t;\theta) + b(\tau - t;\theta)r_t \tag{13.3}$$

where $a(\tau - t;\theta)$ and $b(\tau - t;\theta)$ are known functions and $y_{\tau,t}$ is a continuously compounded yield to maturity. (The parameter vector θ also includes risk preference parameters, as discussed in Section 13.2.1.) The moments of $y_{t,\tau}$ can be expressed in terms of the moments of r_t, and it is possible to perform method of moments estimation without ever determining the implied process of r_t.

However, the nonnegativity restriction on r_t also translates directly into a restriction on the allowable values of $y_{t,\tau}$, but the allowable yields depend on the model parameters θ. A method of moments estimation based directly on observations of $y_{t,\tau}$ may well produce an estimated parameter vector $\hat{\theta}$ for which some of the values of r_t implied by 13.3 are actually negative. The method of moments estimate of θ, based on observations of $y_{t,\tau}$, may therefore be a value for which the observed data sample could not have occurred. This problem becomes substantially worse in more complicated models; the relation between latent variables and observed quantities can be complicated and dependent on the model parameters in ways that defy simple characterization. Expressing a restriction, given a particular data sample, on the allowable values of θ, is no simple task.

The issues that occur with a traditional method of moments estimation also arise when GMM is used. The first issue of calculating moment conditions in a continuous-time environment is no worse than similar issues with other methods; for example, in maximum likelihood estimation, calculation of the likelihood function (as discussed in Section 13.3.2) also requires numeric or other approximation. However, enforcement of range restrictions on model parameters is almost impossible in a method of moments (or GMM) estimation, unless the implied values of latent variables in the model are calculated explicitly, thereby negating one of the principal advantages of method of moments estimation.

Although not an estimation method per se, Song (2011) discusses specification testing of continuous-time models based on the infinitesimal generator. Hamilton and Wu (2012) propose an estimation method based on minimum chi-square as an alternative to maximum likelihood estimation (MLE).

13.3.2 Maximum Likelihood

Although typically thought of as an alternative to method of moments estimation, maximum likelihood can also be thought of as a special case; it is method of moments with a particular set of moment conditions. Those conditions are the scores of the likelihood, or conditional probability density, function. The advantages of maximum likelihood estimation are well known; it is efficient, producing estimates that have lower asymptotic standard errors than any other consistent estimation method. For this reason, maximum likelihood is the estimation method we focus on in Sections 13.4 and 13.5.

The principal challenge to be overcome for maximum likelihood estimation is the evaluation of the likelihood function of a continuous-time process, observed only at discrete time intervals. This is essentially the analogous issue to the evaluation of moment conditions in a method of moments or GMM estimation; like the conditional moments, conditional likelihoods are known explicitly for only a few very simple diffusion processes. Cases where it is known include the Vasicek and CIR models, and MLE was successfully employed by Chen and Scott (1993) and Pearson and Sun (1994). For more general models, some form of numeric or other approximation is needed if maximum likelihood estimation is to be used; how to do it is discussed in Sections 13.4 and 13.5.

Unlike method of moments (or GMM), maximum likelihood enforces range restrictions on latent variable models. As discussed in detail in Section 13.4, the values of the latent variables are identified explicitly during the estimation, and the particular parameter vector being evaluated can be assigned a likelihood of zero if any of the state variables are out of range. Implemented in this way, maximum likelihood avoids estimating impossible models.

Although we use closed-form approximations to the likelihood function, it is also possible to use simulations to approximate it, at the cost of losing a closed-form expression. See Beskos, Papaspiliopoulos, and Roberts (2009) and Beskos et al. (2006) for details on this approach.

13.3.3 QML

Quasi-maximum likelihood (QML) is similar to our maximum likelihood method, except that a simple approximation to the likelihood function is used, based on an Euler discretization of the diffusion process. In general, QML will be neither consistent nor efficient, although, if the time between observations is small, the approximation might not be bad.

Within the context of affine models, QML has in recent years taken on a somewhat different meaning, which is discussed separately later.

13.3.3.1 Traditional QML The QML approximation, which can be applied to any diffusion, simply takes the drift and diffusion coefficients at a particular point of time to be fixed until the next observation of the data. That is,

$$l_X \sim \mathcal{N}(\Delta\mu(t,X_t;\theta), \Delta\sigma(t,X_t;\theta)\sigma^T(t,X_t;\theta))$$

where Δ is the time between observations.

The procedure for estimation by QML is similar, whether the state vector is observed or latent, to our MLE procedure; the only difference is that a different likelihood approximation is used. The most obvious differences in the properties of the estimators are that QML is neither consistent nor efficient and the extent of the loss of accuracy depends on the time between observations, the nonlinearity of the drift function, and the nonconstancy of the diffusion function. For some applications, the use of QML may be perfectly acceptable; in particular, when a data series is very volatile, and also very short, the loss of accuracy due to use of an inaccurate likelihood function may well be negligible compared to the uncertainty inherent in maximum likelihood estimation in a finite data sample.

For an example of this approach, see Nowman (1997).

13.3.3.2 Affine Models For affine yield models, it is possible to use an estimation procedure that is sometimes referred to as QML, even though it differs from traditional QML. Specifically, these studies exploit the fact that the first and second moments for affine diffusions can be derived much more easily than likelihood functions. Conditional means, conditional variances, and conditional covariances of affine diffusions are all linear functions of the state X_t and are known in closed form.[2] This form of QML still uses a Gaussian approximation to the transition likelihood function, but uses the true first and second moments. The likelihood approximation of traditional QML is (potentially) inaccurate for two reasons. First, it is assumed to be Gaussian, even though it is generally not, and second, Euler approximations to the first and second moments are used. The modified version of QML retains the first source of inaccuracy, but not the second, and therefore might potentially be more accurate than traditional QML. One example of QML estimation of affine yield models is Duffee (2002).

13.3.4 Efficient Method of Moments

The efficient method of moments (EMM) of Gallant and Tauchen (1996) is a simulation-based method. It can be viewed as a special case of the GMM of Hansen (1982), in which the moments to be matched are generated by an auxiliary model.

[2] The definition of " closed form" here in a multidimensional setting includes certain linear algebra operations, such as calculation of the spectral or Jordan decomposition of a matrix.

The efficiency of estimates using this method depends on how close the auxiliary model is to the true model. If the auxiliary model includes the true model as a special case, then EMM is as efficient as maximum likelihood. By contrast, if the auxiliary model is misspecified, then the EMM estimates will not be efficient, but if the degree of misspecification is small, then the amount of inefficiency is also likely to be small. So by using a very general seminonparametric model, it is possible to approach, if not quite achieve, the efficiency of maximum likelihood. However, the more general the auxiliary model is, the more computationally intensive EMM tends to be. Examples of EMM estimations in a term structure setting include Andersen and Lund (1997), Dai and Singleton (2000), and Ahn, Dittmar, and Gallant (2002).

Some potential problems beyond efficiency, in the case where the auxiliary model does not include the true model as a special case, is the possibility that the estimated model may violate existence or other constraints on the parameters. In a model with observed factors, existence, no-arbitrage, and other constraints can generally be imposed in the estimation process without too much difficulty. However, in latent variable models, existence and other constraints are joint restrictions on both the parameters and the data; that is, the estimated model may satisfy all applicable constraints but may imply that it is impossible for the observed data series to have occurred. For some applications, this may not be critical, but for others, it might be important. Duffee and Stanton (2012) report rather negative results regarding the finite sample properties of EMM in the context of estimating term structure models; other authors have reached more positive conclusions.

13.3.5 Estimation Bias in Mean-Reversion Parameters

Aït-Sahalia (1996b) and Ball and Torous (1996) discuss the near unit root behavior of interest rates. As happens in the classical estimation problem of an AR(1) coefficient near a unit root, estimates of the speed of mean reversion (the corresponding continuous-time parameter) can be biased when the speed of mean reversion is close to zero (corresponding to an autoregressive parameter close to one in discrete time). This effect can be large and should not be ignored in empirical applications.

Phillips and Yu (2005) propose a general method of bias reduction for pricing bond options based on the jackknife; see also Tang and Chen (2009). Zhou (2001) reports Monte Carlo results on various methods under the scenario of near unit root behavior. He finds that MLE is overall the most efficient method. Bauer, Rudebusch, and Wu (2012) discuss the issue of bias in estimating affine term structure models, document the impact of the bias on estimates of expected future short-term interest rates and of long-maturity term premia, and provide bias-correction methods.

13.4 MAXIMUM LIKELIHOOD ESTIMATION

We now describe a technique for maximum likelihood estimation based on the methods developed in Aït-Sahalia (1999, 2002, 2008). We begin under the assumption that the state vector X_t is observed and then modify the technique to cover the case in which X_t is latent. Assuming that the complete state vector is observable simplifies maximum likelihood estimation, and the remaining challenge is then the calculation of the likelihood function, which we discuss in Section 13.5. From the term structure modeling perspective, assuming full observability of the factors (or state variables) has the drawback that the absence of arbitrage restrictions is difficult or impossible to impose explicitly, which can result in inconsistent term structure models.

13.4.1 Observed State Variables

In this situation, the specification of the functions μ and σ is known, but they depend upon a vector of unknown parameters θ, which is to be estimated:

$$dX_t = \mu(X_t;\ \theta)dt + \sigma(X_t;\ \theta)dW_t \tag{13.4}$$

In the simplest case, the data consist of direct observations on the process X_t sampled at dates $0, \Delta, 2\Delta, \ldots, n\Delta$, on a time interval $[0, T]$ with $T = n\Delta$.

Maximum likelihood estimation of θ is the efficient choice of estimation technique. Let $p_X(x|x_0, \Delta; \theta)$ denote the transition density of the process X, that is, the probability that X will go from x_0 to x in the amount of time Δ, when the parameter vector is θ and the model is 13.4. In what follows, we will work with the logarithm $l_X = \ln p_X$. Using Bayes' rule and the Markov property, the joint probability of observing $\{X_0, X_\Delta, \ldots, X_{n\Delta}\}$ is

$$\begin{aligned}
&\mathbb{P}(X_{n\Delta}, X_{(n-1)\Delta}, \ldots, X_0; \theta)\\
&= \mathbb{P}(X_{n\Delta}|X_{(n-1)\Delta}, \ldots, X_0; \theta)\mathbb{P}(X_{(n-1)\Delta}, \ldots, X_0; \theta)\\
&= \mathbb{P}(X_{n\Delta}|X_{(n-1)\Delta}; \theta)\mathbb{P}(X_{(n-1)\Delta}, \ldots, X_0; \theta)\\
&= \mathbb{P}(X_{n\Delta}|X_{(n-1)\Delta}; \theta) \times \cdots \times \mathbb{P}(X_\Delta|X_0; \theta) \times \mathbb{P}(X_0; \theta)
\end{aligned} \tag{13.5}$$

Ignoring the likelihood of the initial observation, the objective is therefore to maximize over values of θ the log-likelihood function

$$\ell_n(\theta) \equiv \sum_{i=1}^{n} l_X(X_{i\Delta}|X_{(i-1)\Delta}, \Delta; \theta) \tag{13.6}$$

With X fully observable, the problem therefore reduces to replacing the unknown function l_X with some form of numeric approximation. Explicit, closed-form expansions for l_X are described in Section 13.5. This method has been shown to be substantially more accurate and much faster to implement in practice than simulation-based, tree-based, or PDE-based alternatives; see, for example, Jensen and Poulsen (2002); Hurn, Jeisman, and Lindsay (2007); and Stramer and Yan (2007) for comparisons.

13.4.2 Latent State Variables

We now revise the estimation method to allow for the case where the state vector X_t is latent and observed indirectly through bond yields. This approach solves the consistency problem, as bond yields are assumed to satisfy the no-arbitrage conditions. However, it introduces additional complexity to the estimation process. The state vector X_t must be extracted from a panel of observed yields; since the relation between the state X_t and the observed bond yields depends on the model parameters, this relation must be recalculated for every value of the parameter vector searched. However, in addition to resolving the consistency problem, this procedure provides estimates of the model parameters governing the evolution of X_t (and implicitly of bond yields) under both true and risk-neutral probabilities and can therefore be used for both derivatives pricing purposes (for which it is the risk-neutral probabilities that matter) and forecasting/risk management purposes (for which it is the true probabilities that matter). One issue that can arise with this approach, however, is that additional information is sometimes needed to identify fully all the parameters under both probability measures, as discussed in Section 13.2.1; this issue is addressed later.

Under risk-neutral probabilities, X_t evolves according to

$$dX_t = \mu^Q(X_t;\theta)dt + \sigma(X_t;\theta)dW_t^Q$$

The price of a zero-coupon bond, with maturity at time τ and face value of 1, is given (subject to some regularity restrictions) by the probabilistic relation

$$P_{t,\tau} = P(t,\tau,X_t;\theta) = \mathbb{E}_t^Q\left[e^{-\int_t^\tau r_u du}\right]$$

where $r_t = f(t,\ X_t;\ \theta)$, with yields then given by

$$y_{t,\tau} = -\frac{1}{\tau - t}\ln P_{t,\tau}$$

There exist probabilistic techniques (such as Monte Carlo simulation) to find the bond prices (or, equivalently, yields), but it is more common in practice to exploit the relation between the probabilistic problem and a corresponding PDE problem. Specifically, bond prices satisfy

$$\begin{aligned}
&\frac{\partial P}{\partial t}(t,\tau,X_t;\theta) + \sum_{i=1}^{m} \mu_i^Q(t,X_t;\theta)\frac{\partial P}{\partial X_{i,t}}(t,\tau,X_t;\theta) \\
&+\frac{1}{2}\sum_{i=1}^{m}\sum_{j=1}^{m}\left[\sigma\left(t,X_t;\theta\right)\sigma^T(t,X_t;\theta)\right]_{ij}\frac{\partial^2 P}{\partial X_{i,t}\partial X_{j,t}}(t,\tau,X_t;\theta) \\
&= f(t,X_t;\theta)P(t,\tau,X_t;\theta)
\end{aligned} \tag{13.7}$$

with the final condition $P(\tau,\tau,X_t;\theta) = 1$, where m is the number of elements in X_t and the instantaneous interest rate is $r_t = f(t,X_t;\theta)$. The appropriate technique for finding the solution depends on the particular coefficients of the model. For affine models, in which μ_t^Q, $\sigma\sigma^T$, and f are all affine functions of X_t, the solution is of the form

$$P(t,\tau,X_t;\theta) = e^{-\left[\phi_0(\tau-t;\theta)+\sum_{i=1}^{m}\phi_i(\tau-t;\theta)X_t\right](\tau-t)} \tag{13.8}$$

or, expressed in terms of yields instead of prices,

$$y_{t,\tau} = y(t,\tau,X_t;\ \theta) = \phi_0(\tau - t;\ \theta) + \sum_{i=1}^{m}\phi_i(\tau - t;\ \theta)X_t$$

If 13.8 is substituted into 13.7, all terms are proportional to either $P(t,\tau,X_t;\theta)$ or $X_{i,t}P(t,\tau,X_t;\theta)$ for some value of i; by gathering like terms, the PDE can be rewritten as a system of ordinary differential equations:

$$\begin{bmatrix} \phi_0(t,\tau;\theta), \\ \text{with} \\ \phi_m(t,\tau;\theta) \end{bmatrix} = \begin{bmatrix} g_0\left(\phi_0(\tau - t;\theta), \ldots, \phi_m(\tau - t;\theta)\right), \\ \text{with} \\ g_m(\phi_0(\tau - t;\theta), \ldots, \phi_m(\tau - t;\theta)) \end{bmatrix}$$

$$\phi_i(0;\theta) = 0 \qquad \text{for } 0 \le i \le m,$$

where the $g_0, \ldots, g_m$ are linear or quadratic functions. For a few specific affine yield models, the $g_0, \ldots, g_m$ functions can be found explicitly. In general, they must be found numerically, but there exist very fast quadrature techniques for this type of system of ordinary differential equations. Furthermore, the relation between yields and state can be inverted; given a set of m bond yields, then

$$\begin{bmatrix} X_{1,t} \\ \vdots \\ X_{m,t} \end{bmatrix} = \begin{bmatrix} \phi_1(\tau_1 - t;\theta) & \cdots & \phi_m(\tau_1 - t;\theta) \\ \vdots & \cdots & \vdots \\ \phi_1(\tau_m - t;\theta) & \cdots & \phi_m(\tau_m - t;\theta) \end{bmatrix}^{-1} \begin{bmatrix} y_{t,\tau_1} - \phi_0(\tau_1 - t;\theta) \\ \vdots \\ y_{t,\tau_m} - \phi_0(\tau_m - t;\theta) \end{bmatrix} \tag{13.9}$$

Although this method allows us to extract X_t from the observed yields, it is not appropriate simply to apply maximum likelihood to the derived X_t, that is, to find

$$\hat{\theta} = \underset{\theta \in \Theta}{\operatorname{argmax}}\, \ell_n(\theta) = \underset{\theta \in \Theta}{\operatorname{argmax}} \sum_{i=1}^{n} l_X(X_{i\Delta} | X_{(i-1)\Delta}, \Delta;\theta)$$

where $l_X(\bullet)$ is the log-likelihood transition function of the process X_t.[3] The problem is that the X_t are implicitly functions of the parameters θ and therefore are not fixed during a search through the space of admissible θ; it is the yields $y_{t,\tau_1}, \ldots, y_{t,\tau_m}$ that are fixed.

It is instead necessary to find the log-likelihood of the yields, which is

$$l_y\left(y_{i\Delta} | y_{(i-1)\Delta}, \Delta;\theta\right) = l_X(X_{i\Delta} | X_{(i-1)\Delta}, \Delta;\theta) - \ln \left| \det \begin{bmatrix} \phi_1(\tau_1 - t;\theta) & \cdots & \phi_m(\tau_1 - t;\theta) \\ \vdots & \cdots & \vdots \\ \phi_1(\tau_m - t;\theta) & \cdots & \phi_m(\tau_m - t;\theta) \end{bmatrix} \right|$$

where

$$y_t = \begin{bmatrix} y_{t,\tau_1} \\ \vdots \\ y_{t,\tau_m} \end{bmatrix}$$

is the vector of the yields with maturities $\tau_1, \ldots, \tau_m$, observed at time t. More generally, for potentially nonaffine models, the relation between the log-likelihood of the state vector X_t and the log-likelihood of the yields is

$$l_y\left(y_{i\Delta} | y_{(i-1)\Delta}, \Delta;\theta\right) = l_X(X_{i\Delta} | X_{(i-1)\Delta}, \Delta;\theta) - \ln \left| \det \begin{bmatrix} \frac{\partial y(t,\tau_1,X_t;\theta)}{\partial X_{1,t}} & \cdots & \frac{\partial y(t,\tau_1,X_t;\theta)}{\partial X_{m,t}} \\ \vdots & \cdots & \vdots \\ \frac{\partial y(t,\tau_m,X_t;\theta)}{\partial X_{1,t}} & \cdots & \frac{\partial y(t,\tau_m,X_t;\theta)}{\partial X_{m,t}} \end{bmatrix} \right|$$

Note that it is typical practice (although not required) to use rolling maturity yields in the estimation, that is, at each point in time, the yields used have the same time remaining until maturity (rather than the same time of maturity). In other words, it is not the times of maturity, $\tau_1, \ldots, \tau_m$, that are held fixed, but the times until maturity, $\tau_1 - t, \ldots, \tau_m - t$.

One final issue that needs to be addressed for latent variable models is that of identification. The parameters of some models may be fully identified in the estimation procedure described here, in which the number of yields used is equal to the number

[3]The unconditional likelihood of the initial observation is generally omitted. Apart from the difficulty in calculating it (since it is based on the unconditional, rather than conditional, probability density of the diffusion process), it may not even exist, if the underlying process is not stationary. Asymptotically, this should not matter, since the estimation will be dominated by the transition densities.

of state variables in the model. However, for affine models, this is typically not the case, as in the example of the model of Cox, Ingersoll, and Ross (1985), as discussed in the Introduction. However, introduction of additional yields results in overidentification. The model predicts the price of the extra bonds *exactly*, without any error at all, and no real-world dataset ever conforms to such a model's predictions that closely. Because the model is underidentified with the original set of yields, there are still degrees of freedom remaining that can be used to fit the information in the additional yields. However, the number of degrees of freedom is typically small and must be used to fit the entire time series of the additional yields. Inevitably, the likelihood of the entire panel (the original yields and these additional yields) is zero for any parameter vector. Although the problem of maximum likelihood estimation is simplified (since any parameter vector achieves the maximum of zero), a less trivial model and estimation technique would be strongly preferred.

The typical resolution to this problem is to assume that the additional yields are contaminated by "observation error." A set of m benchmark yields, so one for each latent variable in the model, are assumed to be observed without any error. An additional set of m_2 yields are also observed with error, that is,

$$y_{t,\tau} = y(t,\tau,X_t;\theta) = \phi_0(\tau - t;\theta) + \sum_{i=1}^{m} \phi_i(\tau - t;\theta)X_t + \psi_{t,\tau} \tag{13.10}$$

If τ is one of the benchmark maturities, then $\psi_{t,\tau} = 0$. However, for other maturities, some statistical model for the observation errors is assumed; for example, the $\psi_{t,\tau}$ for the extra yield(s) might be assumed to be an i.i.d. series of multivariate normal random variables with mean zero, with an unspecified covariance matrix, independent of the Brownian motions driving the evolution of the latent state variables. Evaluation of the likelihood of the full set of yields then proceeds as follows: for a given parameter vector θ, the value of the latent variables X_t can be found from 13.9. Then for each of the "extra" yields, the theoretical value can be found by calculating the first two terms on the right-hand side of 13.10. The observation error is then just the difference between the observed and theoretical values of the extra yields.

Since the observation errors are assumed independent of the latent variable processes, the joint likelihood of the entire panel of yields is the product of the likelihood of the benchmark yields and the likelihood of the observation errors (or, alternately, the sum of the log-likelihoods). Addition of sufficiently many extra yields to the observed panel then allows full identification of all model parameters, including those in the covariance matrix of the observation errors.

Although this method of observing extra yields with observation error certainly solves the identification problem, it does so in a very ad hoc and rather inelegant way. No stochastic evolution of the observation errors is specified; rather, they are specified only on the specific dates on which data observations are available. The implications of the presence of observation errors on the absence of arbitrage and other desirable modeling features are generally left unexplored. Whether a better method for resolving the identification problem is possible remains a topic for future exploration.

Numeric maximization of the likelihood (or in fact any other objective function such as a GMM criterion or one derived from simulations) can be difficult in practice when the model involves a large number of parameters; in our experience with affine models, this tends to happen with models in dimension 3 and above. Creal and Wu (2015) propose an approach based on linear regression to reduce the dimension of the numeric optimization problem in maximum likelihood by eliminating parameters from the objective function.

13.5 CONSTRUCTING THE LIKELIHOOD FUNCTION: EXPANSION OF THE TRANSITION DENSITY

In this section, we describe the construction of the function l_X in 13.6, following Aït-Sahalia (1999) (examples and application to interest rate data), Aït-Sahalia (2002) (univariate theory), and Aït-Sahalia (2008) (multivariate theory). The output of this section will be an explicit expression for l_X : that theoretical derivation needs to be done only once for a given model. Once we have derived the closed-form expansion corresponding to that model, it can be reused and reevaluated at different parameter values (θ), different transition variables (x and x_0), or different time intervals (Δ). This is of course a major advantage over alternative approaches that require a new numeric evaluation of $l_X(x|x_0, \Delta; \theta)$ every time the parameter vector θ changes, since, in the course of maximizing the log-likelihood function 13.6 over θ, changing θ is exactly what needs to be done. Other methods for constructing approximate likelihoods have also been developed; see, for example, Corielli, Foschi, and Pascucci (2010) or Jacod (2006).

The method is applicable also to other estimation strategies that require an expression for p_X, such as Bayesian methods where one needs a distribution for θ, to generate simulated paths at the desired discrete frequency from the continuous-time model or to serve as the instrumental or auxiliary model in indirect inference and simulated/efficient methods of moments.

Computations using a closed-form p_X are straightforward and fast because everything is in closed form, compared to other methods, such as solving numerically the PDE satisfied by p_X(Lo (1988)), simulating the process to determine p_X by Monte Carlo integration (Pedersen, 1995 and Brandt and Santa-Clara, 2002), or using binomial or other trees (Jensen and Poulsen, 2002).

In particular, the computation of the closed-form expression for p_X corresponding to a given model is only done once and for all[4] and is not repeated at different data points or parameter values. This is unlike simulation-based methods where each new set of parameter values and pair of successive observations (x, x_0) call for a new evaluation of the transition density, itself to be followed by the optimization step to find the parameter estimates.

13.5.1 Reducibility

Whenever possible, it is advisable to start with a change of variable. A diffusion X is defined in Aït-Sahalia (2008) as *reducible* if and only if there exists a one-to-one transformation of the diffusion X into a diffusion Y whose diffusion matrix σ_Y is the identity matrix. That is, there exists an invertible function $\gamma(x;\theta)$ such that

$$Y_t \equiv \gamma(X_t;\theta) \tag{13.11}$$

satisfies the stochastic differential equation

$$dY_t = \mu_Y(Y_t;\theta)dt + dW_t$$

Every univariate diffusion is reducible, through the simple transformation

$$Y_t = \int^{X_t} du/\sigma(u;\theta)$$

However, not every multivariate diffusion is reducible. The diffusion X is reducible if and only if the inverse diffusion matrix $\sigma^{-1} = \left[\sigma^{-1}_{i,j}\right]_{i,j=1,..,m}$ satisfies the condition that

$$\frac{\partial\sigma^{-1}_{ij}(x;\theta)}{\partial x_k} = \frac{\partial\sigma^{-1}_{ik}(x;\theta)}{\partial x_j}$$

for each triplet $(i,j,k) = 1,\dots,m$ such that $k > j$. Each model corresponds to a particular $\sigma(x;\theta)$, and so this can be checked for the model of interest.

Whenever a diffusion is reducible, an expansion can be computed for the transition density p_X of X by first computing it for the density (resp. log density) p_Y (resp. l_Y) of the reduced variable Y. An additional transformation is needed from Y to Z such that Z that is sufficiently close to a normal random variable, expanding the transition density p_Z of Z around a normal density and then reverting the transformations $Z \mapsto Y \mapsto X$ to obtain an expansion for p_X and l_X.

The expansion for l_Y is of the form

$$l_Y^{(K)}\left(y|y_0,\Delta;\theta\right) = -\frac{m}{2}\ln(2\pi\Delta) + \frac{C_Y^{(-1)}(y|y_0;\theta)}{\Delta} + \sum_{k=0}^{K} C_Y^{(k)}(y|y_0;\theta)\frac{\Delta^k}{k!} \tag{13.12}$$

The coefficients of the expansion are given explicitly by

$$C_Y^{(-1)}(y|y_0;\theta) = -\frac{1}{2}\sum_{i=1}^{m}(y_i - y_{0i})^2 \tag{13.13}$$

$$C_Y^{(0)}(y|y_0;\theta) = \sum_{i=1}^{m}(y_i - y_{0i})\int_0^1 \mu_{Yi}(y_0 + u(y-y_0);\theta)du \tag{13.14}$$

and, for $k \geq 1$,

$$C_Y^{(k)}(y|y_0;\theta) = k\int_0^1 G_Y^{(k)}(y_0 + u(y-y_0)|y_0;\theta)u^{k-1}du \tag{13.15}$$

where $G_Y^{(k)}(y|y_0;\theta)$ is given explicitly as a function of μ_{Yi} and $C_Y^{(j-1)}, j = 1,\dots,k$.

[4] A Matlab library for existing models is now available at http://www.princeton.edu/~yacine.

Given an expansion for the density p_Y of Y, an expansion for the density p_X of X can be obtained by a direct application of the Jacobian formula reverting the effect of the transformation 13.11:

$$l_X^{(K)}(x|x_0,\Delta;\theta) = -\frac{m}{2}\ln(2\pi\Delta) - D_v(x;\theta) + \frac{C_Y^{(-1)}(\gamma(x;\theta)|\gamma(x_0;\theta);\theta)}{\Delta} + \sum_{k=0}^{K} C_Y^{(k)}(\gamma(x;\theta)|\gamma(x_0;\theta);\theta)\frac{\Delta^k}{k!} \tag{13.16}$$

from $l_Y^{(K)}$ given in 13.12, using the coefficients $C_Y^{(k)}$, $k=-1,0,\ldots,K$ given above, and where

$$D_v(x;\theta) \equiv \frac{1}{2}\ln(\det[v(x;\theta)]) \tag{13.17}$$

with

$$v(x;\theta) \equiv \sigma(x;\theta)\sigma^T(x;\theta) \tag{13.18}$$

13.5.2 The Irreducible Case

When the diffusion is not reducible, the expansion of the log-likelihood l_X is obtained directly in the form

$$l_X^{(K)}(x|x_0,\Delta;\theta) = -\frac{m}{2}\ln(2\pi\Delta) - D_v(x;\theta) + \frac{C_X^{(-1)}(x|x_0;\theta)}{\Delta} + \sum_{k=0}^{K} C_X^{(k)}(x|x_0;\theta)\frac{\Delta^k}{k!} \tag{13.19}$$

Without the intermediary Y process, it is not possible in general to obtain the closed-form expressions of the coefficients $C_X^{(k)}$. Instead, the approach is to calculate a Taylor series in $(x-x_0)$ of each coefficient $C_X^{(k)}$, at order j_k in $(x-x_0)$. Such an expansion will be denoted by $C_X^{(j_k,k)}$ at order $j_k = 2(K-k)$, for $k=-1,0,\ldots,K$.

The resulting expansion will then be

$$\tilde{l}_X^{(K)}(x|x_0,\Delta;\theta) = -\frac{m}{2}\ln(2\pi\Delta) - D_v(x;\theta) + \frac{C_X^{(j_{-1},-1)}(x|x_0;\theta)}{\Delta} + \sum_{k=0}^{K} C_X^{(j_k,k)}(x|x_0;\theta)\frac{\Delta^k}{k!}$$

Such a Taylor expansion was unnecessary in the reducible case: the expressions given above provide the explicit expressions of the coefficients $C_Y^{(k)}$, and then in 13.16 we have the corresponding ones for $C_X^{(k)}$. However, for an irreducible diffusion, what is possible is to compute the coefficients $C_X^{(j_k,k)}$ explicitly.

For each $k=-1,0,\ldots,K$, the coefficient $C_X^{(k)}(x|x_0;\theta)$ in 13.19 solves an equation of the form

$$f_X^{(k-1)}(x|x_0;\theta) = C_X^{(k)}(x|x_0;\theta) - G_X^{(k)}(x|x_0;\theta) - \sum_{i=1}^{m}\sum_{j=1}^{m} v_{ij}(x;\theta)\frac{\partial C_X^{(-1)}(x|x_0;\theta)}{\partial x_i}\frac{\partial C_X^{(k)}(x|x_0;\theta)}{\partial x_j} = 0 \tag{13.20}$$

Each function $G_X^{(k)}$, $k=0,1,\ldots,K$ involves only the coefficients $C_X^{(h)}$ for $h=-1,\ldots,k-1$, so this system of equation can be utilized to solve recursively for each coefficient at a time. Specifically, the equation $f_X^{(-2)}=0$ determines $C_X^{(-1)}$; given $C_X^{(-1)}$, $G_X^{(0)}$ becomes known and the equation $f_X^{(-1)}=0$ determines $C_X^{(0)}$; given $C_X^{(-1)}$ and $C_X^{(0)}$, $G_X^{(1)}$ becomes known and the equation $f_X^{(0)}=0$ then determines $C_X^{(1)}$; and so on. It turns out that this results in a system of linear equations in the coefficients of the polynomials

$C_X^{(j_k,k)}$, so each one of these equations can be solved explicitly in the form of the Taylor expansion $C_X^{(j_k,k)}$ of the coefficient $C_X^{(k)}$, at order j_k in $(x - x_0)$.

In practice, even in the case where a diffusion is theoretically reducible, it is sometimes simpler to compute its irreducible expansion. Also, every univariate diffusion is reducible, but a closed-form formula requires that the integral of the function $1/\sigma$ be available in closed form. If that is not the case, then the corresponding irreducible expansion will still be available in closed form. An alternative method to circumvent the integrability of $1/\sigma$ is provided by Bakshi and Ju (2005).

For example, the model for the short-term interest rate in Aït-Sahalia (1996b)

$$dX_t = (\alpha_{-1}X_t^{-1} + \alpha_0 + \alpha_1 X_t + \alpha_2 X_t^2)dt + (\beta_0 + \beta_1 X_t + \beta_2 X_t^{\beta_3})dW_t$$

is such that $1/\sigma$ cannot be integrated in closed form in the general case. Using the irreducible method in that case bypasses the need for the $X \mapsto Y$ transformation. At order $K = 1$ in Δ, the irreducible expansion for the generic model $dX_t = \mu(X_t)dt + \sigma(X_t)dW_t$ is

$$\begin{aligned} \tilde{l}_X^{(1)}(\Delta, x|x_0;\theta) = &-\frac{1}{2}\ln(2\pi\Delta) - \ln(\sigma(x;\theta)) + \frac{C_X^{(4,-1)}(x|x_0;\theta)}{\Delta} \\ &+ C_X^{(2,0)}(x|x_0;\theta) + C_X^{(0,1)}(x|x_0;\theta)\Delta \end{aligned}$$

and the coefficients $C_X^{(j_k,k)}$, $k = -1, 0, 1$ are given by

$$\begin{aligned} C_X^{(4,-1)}(x|x_0;\theta) = &\frac{(4\sigma(x_0;\theta)\sigma''(x_0;\theta) - 11\sigma'(x_0;\theta)^2)}{24\sigma(x_0;\theta)^4}(x - x_0)^4 \\ &+ \frac{\sigma'(x_0;\theta)}{2\sigma(x_0;\theta)^3}(x - x_0)^3 - \frac{1}{2\sigma(x_0;\theta)^2}(x - x_0)^2 \\ C_X^{(2,0)}(x|x_0;\theta) = &\frac{\left(\left(\sigma'(x_0;\theta)^2 + 2\mu'(x_0;\theta)\right)\sigma(x_0;\theta) - 4\mu(x_0;\theta)\sigma'(x_0;\theta) - \sigma''(x_0;\theta)\sigma(x_0;\theta)^2\right)}{4\sigma(x_0;\theta)^3}(x - x_0)^2 \\ &+ \frac{(2\mu(x_0;\theta) - \sigma(x_0;\theta)\sigma'(x_0;\theta))}{2\sigma(x_0;\theta)^2}(x - x_0) \\ C_X^{(0,1)}(x|x_0;\theta) = &\frac{1}{8}\left(\begin{aligned} &2\sigma(x_0;\theta)\sigma''(x_0;\theta) - \frac{4\mu(x_0;\theta)^2}{\sigma(x_0;\theta)^2} \\ &+ \frac{8\sigma'(x_0;\theta)\mu(x_0;\theta)}{\sigma(x_0;\theta)} - \sigma'(x_0;\theta)^2 - 4\mu'(x_0;\theta) \end{aligned}\right) \end{aligned}$$

An extension to processes with jumps is provided by Yu (2007) and Schaumburg (2001). DiPietro (2001) has extended the methodology to make it applicable in a Bayesian setting. Li (2013) considers the case of damped diffusion processes.

The method has been employed by Aït-Sahalia and Kimmel (2007); Aït-Sahalia and Kimmel (2010); Bakshi, Ju, and Ou-Yang (2006); Cheridito, Filipović, and Kimmel (2007); Mosburger and Schneider (2005); Thompson (2008); and Egorov, Li, and Ng (2011).

Instead of expanding the transition function in orthogonal polynomials around a leading term, an alternative strategy for constructing closed-form approximations consists in using the saddle point method (see Aït-Sahalia and Yu (2006)): they replace the characteristic function by an expansion in Δ, with the expansion being then computed from the infinitesimal generator of the diffusion process.

Series expansion approaches in the same spirit have also been applied to the problem of finding asset prices directly, without going through the intermediate step of finding a density: see Kristensen and Mele (2011) for the case of options and Kimmel (2013b) and Kimmel (2013a) for the case of bond prices.

Comparison studies that have compared this method to others include Jensen and Poulsen (2002); Hurn, Jeisman, and Lindsay (2007); and Stramer and Yan (2007).

13.6 CONCLUDING REMARKS

In this chapter, we have described a method for estimation of arbitrage-free continuous-time term structure models using approximate maximum likelihood estimation. Although other estimation methods are possible, maximum likelihood has the advantage of statistical efficiency and avoids some problems that can occur with some other techniques, such as the estimation of models that imply that the observed data could not have occurred.

Although recent years have seen considerable advances in this area, it seems unlikely that the final word has been written on continuous-time term structure model estimation. The technique we have described applies to nonlinear diffusions under true probabilities; however, nonlinearity under risk-neutral probabilities complicates pricing and therefore identification of the state in latent variable models. Future research may result in improved techniques for solving this problem. Better techniques for dealing with the identification problem, without the use of observation errors that are outside the scope of the arbitrage-free model, may also be found in the future.

ACKNOWLEDGMENTS

Aït-Sahalia's research was supported by the Bendheim Center for Finance at Princeton University. Kimmel's research was supported by the Risk Management Institute at NUS. Professor Kimmel thanks the Singapore Ministry of Education for its support through the Academic Research Fund, Grant #R-315-000-106-133.

REFERENCES

Ahn D-H, Dittmar RF, Gallant AR. Quadratic term structure models: theory and evidence. Rev Financ Stud 2002;16:459–485.

Ahn D-H, Gao B. A parametric nonlinear model of term structure dynamics. Rev Financ Stud 1999;12:721–762.

Aït-Sahalia Y. Nonparametric pricing of interest rate derivative securities. Econometrica 1996a;64:527–560.

Aït-Sahalia Y. Testing continuous-time models of the spot interest rate. Rev Financ Stud 1996b;9:385–426.

Aït-Sahalia Y. Transition densities for interest rate and other nonlinear diffusions. J Finance 1999;54:1361–1395.

Aït-Sahalia Y. Maximum-likelihood estimation of discretely-sampled diffusions: a closed-form approximation approach. Econometrica 2002;70:223–262.

Aït-Sahalia Y. Closed-form likelihood expansions for multivariate diffusions. Ann Stat 2008;36:906–937.

Aït-Sahalia Y, Kimmel R. Maximum likelihood estimation of stochastic volatility models. J Financ Econ 2007;83:413–452.

Aït-Sahalia Y, Kimmel R. Estimating affine multifactor term structure models using closed-form likelihood expansions. J Financ Econ 2010;98:113–144.

Aït-Sahalia Y, Yu J. Saddlepoint approximations for continuous-time Markov processes. J Econom 2006;134:507–551.

Andersen TG, Lund J. Estimating continuous time stochastic volatility models of the short term interest rate. J Econom 1997;77:343–378.

Ang A, Piazzesi M. A no-arbitrage vector autoregression of term structure dynamics with macroeconomic and latent variables. J Monet Econ 2003;50:745–787.

Ang A, Piazzesi M, Wei M. What does the yield curve tell us about GDP growth? J Econom 2006;131:359–403.

Bakshi GS, Ju N. A refinement to Aït-Sahalia's (2002) "Maximum likelihood estimation of discretely sampled diffusions: a closed-form approximation approach". J Bus 2005;78:2037–2052.

Bakshi G, Ju N, Ou-Yang H. Estimation of continuous-time models with an application to equity volatility dynamics. J Financ Econ 2006;82:227–249.

Balduzzi P, Das S, Foresi S, Sundaram R. A simple approach to three factor affine term structure models. J Fixed Income 1996;6:43–53.

Ball CA, Torous WN. Unit roots and the estimation of interest rate dynamics. J Empir Finance 1996;3:215–238.

Bates DS. Maximum likelihood estimation of latent affine processes. Rev Financ Stud 2006;19:909–965.

Bauer M, Rudebusch G, Wu J. Correcting estimation bias in dynamic term structure models. J Bus Econ Stat 2012;30:454–467.

Beaglehole D, Tenney M. Corrections and additions to 'a nonlinear equilibrium model of the term structure of interest rates'. J Financ Econ 1992;32:345–353.

Beskos A, Papaspiliopoulos O, Roberts G. Monte Carlo maximum likelihood estimation for discretely observed diffusion processes. Ann Stat 2009;37:223–245.

Beskos A, Papaspiliopoulos O, Roberts G, Fearnhead P. Exact and computationally efficient likelihood-based estimation for discretely observed diffusion processes. J R Stat Soc B 2006;68:333–382.

Bikbov R, Chernov M. No-arbitrage macroeconomic determinants of the yield curve. J Econom 2010;159:166–182.

Brace A, Gątarek D, Musiela M. The market model of interest rate dynamics. Math Finance 1997;7:127–154.

Brandt M, Santa-Clara P. Simulated likelihood estimation of diffusions with an application to exchange rate dynamics in incomplete markets. J Financ Econ 2002;63:161–210.

Cai L, Swanson NR. In- and out-of-sample specification analysis of spot rate models: further evidence for the period 1982–2008. J Empir Finance 2011;18:743–764.

Chen L. Stochastic mean and stochastic volatility - a three-factor model of the term structure of interest rates and its application to the pricing of interest rate derivatives. Financ Mark Inst Instrum 1996;5:1–88.

Chen R-R, Scott L. Maximum likelihood estimation of a multi-factor equilibrium model of the term structure of interest rates. J Fixed Income 1993;3:14–31.

Cheridito P, Filipović D, Kimmel RL. Market price of risk specifications for affine models: theory and evidence. J Financ Econ 2007;83:123–170.

Christoffersen P, Dorion C, Jacobs K, Karoui L. Nonlinear Kalman filtering in affine term structure models. Manage Sci 2014;60:2248–2268.

Constantinides GM. A theory of the nominal term structure of interest rates. Rev Financ Stud 1992;5:531–552.

Corielli F, Foschi P, Pascucci A. Parametrix approximation of diffusion transition densities. SIAM J Financ Math 2010;1:833–867.

Cox JC, Ingersoll JE, Ross SA. A theory of the term structure of interest rates. Econometrica 1985;53:385–408.

Creal DD, Wu JC. Estimation of affine term structure models with spanned or unspanned stochastic volatility. J Econom 2015;185:60–81.

Dai Q, Singleton KJ. Specification analysis of affine term structure models. J Finance 2000;55:1943–1978.

Diebold FX, Rudebusch G, Aruoba SB. The macroeconomy and the yield curve: a dynamic latent factor approach. J Econom 2006;31:309–338.

DiPietro M. Bayesian inference for discretely sampled diffusion processes with financial applications [PhD thesis]. Department of Statistics, Carnegie-Mellon University; 2001.

Duan J, Simonato J-G. Estimating and testing exponential-affine term structure models by Kalman filter. Rev Quant Finance Account 1999;13:111–135.

Duffee GR. Term premia and interest rate forecasts in affine models. J Finance 2002;57:405–443.

Duffee GR. Information in (and not in) the term structure. Rev Financ Stud 2011;24:2895–2934.

Duffee GR, Stanton RH. Estimation of dynamic term structure models. Q J Finance 2012;2:Article ID: 125008–.

Duffie D, Kan R. A yield-factor model of interest rates. Math Finance 1996;6:379–406.

Egorov AV, Hong Y, Li H. Validating forecasts of the joint probability density of bond yields: can affine models beat random walk? J Econom 2006;135:225–284.

Egorov AV, Li H, Ng D. A tale of two yield curves: modeling the joint term structure of dollar and euro interest rates. J Econom 2011;162:55–70.

Egorov AV, Li H, Xu Y. Maximum likelihood estimation of time inhomogeneous diffusions. J Econom 2003;114:107–139.

Gallant AR, Tauchen GT. Which moments to match? Economet Theory 1996;12:657–681.

Gallmeyer M, Hollifield B, Zin S. Taylor rules, McCallum rules and the term structure of interest rates. J Monet Econ 2005;52:921–950.

Geyer A, Pichler S. A state-space approach to estimate and test multifactor Cox-Ingersoll-Ross models of the term structure. J Financ Res 1999;22:107–130.

Gouriéroux C, Sufana R. A classification of two-factor affine diffusion term structure models. J Financ Econom 2006;4:31–52.

Gürkaynak RS, Wright JH. Macroeconomics and the term structure. J Econ Lit 2012;50:331–367.

Hamilton JD, Wu JC. Identification and estimation of Gaussian affine term structure models. J Econom 2012;168:315–331.

Hansen LP. Large sample properties of generalized method of moments estimators. Econometrica 1982;50:1029–1054.

Heath D, Jarrow R, Morton A. Bond pricing and the term structure of interest rates: a new methodology for contingent claims evaluation. Econometrica 1992;60:77–105.

Hurn S, Jeisman JI, Lindsay KA. Seeing the wood for the trees: a critical evaluation of methods to estimate the parameters of stochastic differential equations. J Financ Econom 2007;5:390–455.

Jacod J. Parametric inference for discretely observed non-ergodic diffusions. Bernoulli 2006;12:383–401.

Jensen B, Poulsen R. Transition densities of diffusion processes: numerical comparison of approximation techniques. J Derivatives 2002;9:1–15.

Joslin S, Le A, Singleton KJ. Why Gaussian macro-finance term structure models are (nearly) unconstrained factor-VARs. J Financ Econ 2013;109:604–622.

Joslin S, Priebsch M, Singleton KJ. Risk premiums in dynamic term structure models with unspanned macro risks. J Finance 2014;69:1197–1233.

Joslin S, Singleton KJ, Zhu H. A new perspective on Gaussian dynamic term structure models. Rev Financ Stud 2011;24:926–970.

Kimmel R. Asset pricing and conditional moments under non-affine diffusions. Technical report. National University of Singapore; 2013a.

Kimmel R. The pricing problem in non-linear models. Technical report. National University of Singapore; 2013b.

Kristensen D, Mele A. Adding and subtracting Black-Scholes: a new approach to approximating derivative prices in continuous-time models. J Financ Econ 2011;102:390–415.

Li M. An examination of the continuous-time dynamics of international volatility indices amid the recent market turmoil. J Empir Finance 2013;22:128–139.

Litterman R, Scheinkman J. Common factors affecting bond returns. J Fixed Income 1991; 1 (1):54–61.

Lo AW. Maximum likelihood estimation of generalized Itô processes with discretely sampled data. Economet Theory 1988;4:231–247.

Longstaff FA. A nonlinear general equilibrium model of the term structure. J Financ Econ 1989;23:195–224.

Ludvigson S, Ng S. Macro factors in bond risk premia. Rev Financ Stud 2010;22:5027–5067.

Macaulay FR. *Some Theoretical Problems Suggested by the Movements of Interest Rates, Bond Yields and Stock Prices in the United States Since 1856*. New York: National Bureau of Economic Research; 1938.

Mosburger G, Schneider P. Modelling international bond markets with affine term structure models. Technical report. Vienna University of Economics and Business Administration; 2005.

Nowman KB. Gaussian estimation of single-factor continuous time models of the term structure of interest rates. J Finance 1997;52:1695–1706.

Pearson ND, Sun T-S. Exploiting the conditional density in estimating the term structure: an application to the Cox, Ingersoll, and Ross model. J Finance 1994;49:1279–1304.

Pedersen AR. A new approach to maximum-likelihood estimation for stochastic differential equations based on discrete observations. Scand J Stat 1995;22:55–71.

Phillips PCB, Yu J. Jackknifing bond option prices. Rev Financ Stud 2005;18:707–742.

Rudebusch GD, Wu T. A macro-finance model of the term structure, monetary policy, and the economy. Econ J 2008;118:906–926.
Schaumburg E. Maximum likelihood estimation of jump processes with applications to finance [PhD thesis]. Princeton University; 2001.
Song Z. A martingale approach for testing diffusion models based on infinitesimal operator. J Econom 2011;162:189–212.
Stramer O, Yan J. On simulated likelihood of discretely observed diffusion processes and comparison to closed-form approximation. J Comput Graph Stat 2007;16:672–691.
Tang CY, Chen SX. Parameter estimation and bias correction for diffusion processes. J Econom 2009;149:65–81.
Thompson S. Identifying term structure volatility from the LIBOR-swap curve. Rev Financ Stud 2008;21:819–854.
Vasicek O. An equilibrium characterization of the term structure. J Financ Econ 1977;5:177–188.
Yu J. Closed-form likelihood approximation and estimation of jump-diffusions with an application to the realignment risk of the Chinese yuan. J Econom 2007;141:1245–1280.
Zhou H. Finite sample properties of EMM, GMM, QMLE, and MLE for a square-root interest rate diffusion model. J Comput Finance 2001;5:89–122.

14

Recent Advances in Old Fixed-Income Topics: Liquidity, Learning, and the Lower Bound

Jean-Sébastien Fontaine[a] **and René Garcia**[b]
[a]*Financial Markets Department, Bank of Canada, Ottawa, Canada*
[b]*EDHEC Business School, Accounting, Law, Finance and Economics Department Nice (France)*

14.1 INTRODUCTION

The expectations hypothesis (EH) paradigm dominates the world of term structure modeling. Formal tests of the hypothesis go back at least to Meiselman (1962), but the possibility that long-term rates provide biased forecasts of future short rates has long preoccupied economic discourse (see, e.g., the discussion in Culbertson, 1957). True, bond yields are the sum of the expected interest rate and a risk premium, but this blurs different types of deviations from the EH. What distinguishes modern literature is the emphasis on interest rate risk as the leading (or sole) determinant of the risk premium. This is apparent in, for instance, the reviews by Dai and Singleton (2003), Piazzesi (2005), Gürkaynak and Wright (2012), and Duffee (2013). The older literature emphasized several mechanisms that could cause deviations from the expectations hypothesis.

Sources of risk premium other than interest rate risk found a refuge in undergraduate textbooks, while the academic agenda leapt forward, developing an array of sophisticated yet tractable no-arbitrage models. Tractability may lead to progress, nudging aside some old themes for a time, but the empirical evidence eventually catches up as theory matures. In this chapter, we selected old topics that have returned to the forefront in fixed-income research: liquidity, learning, and the bound underlying nominal yields. Progress has been rapid in these fields in recent years.

First, the importance of liquidity and of intermediation frictions has reemerged in the face of large deviations from no-arbitrage relationships during and around the 2008 financial crisis. The prices of neighboring Treasury bonds became widely misaligned to an extent unjustified by the small differences in their cash flows. But the fact that similar bonds often bear dissimilar prices had not escaped those estimating smooth zero-coupon curves from observed coupon bond prices (e.g., Bliss, 1997). This dispersion of prices has been attributed to bid–ask spreads, search frictions, short-selling costs, and clientele effects but was generally felt to be unimportant in broader contexts. We discuss recent advances, showing how these apparent deviations from arbitrage reveal important state variables and possibly generate their own risk premium.

Handbook of Fixed-Income Securities, First Edition. Edited by Pietro Veronesi.

Second, several recent works have revisited an old conundrum: testing whether yields conform to the EH relies on the auxiliary assumptions that investors' expectations are rational and based on a complete information set. Combining observed yields with data from surveys of yield forecasts can break this conundrum, and early results confirm that expectational "errors" could explain part of the evidence against the EH. Modern term structure models use a flexible reduced-form specification of the pricing kernel and should capture shifts in investors' forecasts within an encompassing risk premium. Nonetheless, the required variability of the pricing kernel appears hard to square with macro risk implicit in the evolution of the consumption growth or the inflation rate. Incorporating the subjective expectations embodied in survey data as well as the effect of learning within term structure models, whether structural or based on a no-arbitrage argument, has produced a stimulating research agenda.

Our final topic builds on the observation that nominal rates are bounded from below. As the Federal Reserve target rate hovers near zero for yet another year – since the end of 2008 – and as Japan, Europe, and other countries reach the lower bound, the challenge to benchmark models continues to grow. In the previous era of relatively high rates, the literature had escaped from the limitations of the square-root model and taken refuge in Gaussian high grounds. The lower bound underlying yields change most stylized facts about yield, requiring different but yet tractable models.

Section 14.2 first reviews how differences in prices between apparently similar bonds can persist, defying arbitrage activities. Notions of segmented markets or preferred habitats are discussed, as well as empirical evidence on liquidity premia in the fixed-income markets. Section 14.3 starts with the older literature on tests of the expectations hypothesis, describes the new models distinguishing subjective expectations extracted from surveys and expectations based on statistical models, and concludes with adaptive learning, in particular the ability of learning models to fit professional forecasts, including in the context of structural models. Section 14.4 reviews term structure models recently introduced to face an ever-growing sample where the target rate is close to its lower bound in the United States and Japan as well as in and around the eurozone.

14.2 LIQUIDITY

14.2.1 Bills, Notes, and Bonds

Nowadays, investors can trade more than three hundred U.S. Treasury securities with maturities between only a few days and up to 30 years (excluding inflation-indexed securities). Their prices tend to move together, since the underlying rates used to discount each security's cash flows are highly correlated. Figure 14.1 reports estimates of the yield curve for par coupon bonds at the end of April, May, and June 2013, respectively. The yield curve steepened significantly over this period, coinciding with intense speculation as to the pace at which the FOMC would "taper" its asset purchases.

Most importantly, Figure 14.1 illustrates the tight correlations between yields of different maturities. In fact, the entire curve of yields necessary to discount any U.S. Treasury security can be closely approximated with a small number of risk factors – generally 3 – and the fit of term structure models is assessed with respect to smoothed yield curves. Nonetheless, some significant information is lost as we move between the observed yields to maturity (*ytm*) and the unobserved smoothed yields depicted in

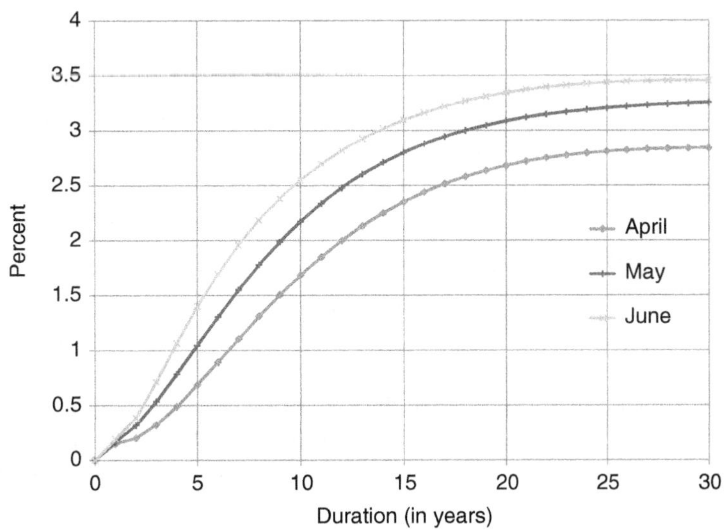

Figure 14.1 Yield-to-maturity curves. Yields to maturity for par Treasury securities at the end of April, May, and June of 2013 from the Gürkaynak, Sack, and Wright (2006) dataset and available from the Federal Reserve Board website.

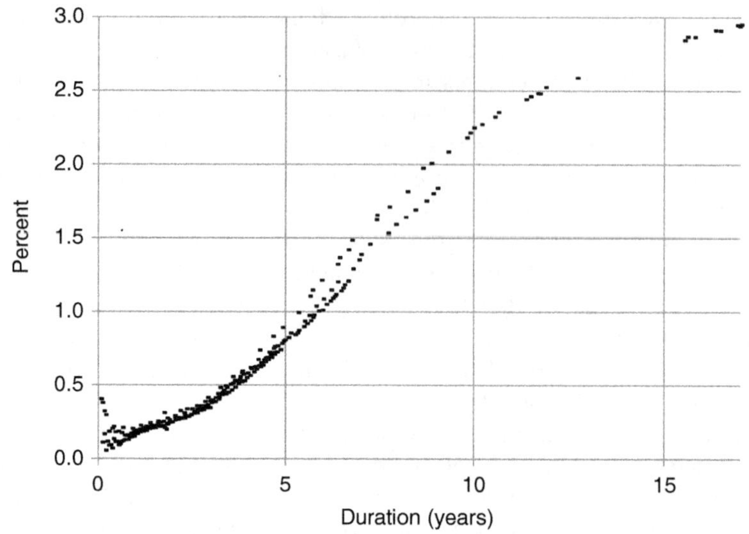

Figure 14.2 U.S. Treasury yield-to-maturity curve on March 28, 2013. Source: CRSP.

Figure 14.1. To illustrate, Figure 14.2 reports the *ytm* against duration on the x-axis, for every security in the Center for Research in Security Prices (CRSP) dataset and for 1 day at the end of March 2013.[1]

Figure 14.2 shows a bird's eye view of what is depicted in Figure 14.1: bonds of a similar duration have a similar *ytm*. One could draw a curve connecting maturities, with yields ranging from 0% to 3%. But Figure 14.2 also reveals large departures from a smooth curve. There is a clear separation – a difference of around 20 basis points (bps) – between the (lower) yields of recently issued 10-year notes and the (higher) yields of bonds originally issued with 30 years to maturity – located between years 5 and 10 on the duration axis. The separation cannot be attributed to a transitory on-the-run effect due to the recent issue being "special" in the repo (funding) market (Duffie, 1996): the difference between the recent 10-year issue and the just-off-the-run issue is only 4 bps on that day. This is also not due to differences in market liquidity: the bid–ask spreads are similar across all recent and old issues.

We observe a similar separation at the short end of the maturity spectrum between the yields on bills, which were originally issued with less than 1 year to maturity, and the yields on older notes and bonds. Again, the separation arises in the age dimension. The largest deviations correspond to old 30-year bonds maturing soon. For a small intermediate range of maturities – around 2 years to maturity – the *ytm* dispersion seems more compressed, probably within twice the bid–ask spreads for off-the-run issues, and appears consistent with a smooth yield curve. We can also find episodes where the yield curve appears dislocated. Figure 14.3 shows the observed *ytm* at the end of October 2008, revealing what were perhaps the worst conditions in financial markets. Again, we observe a clear separation between old bonds and recent notes, but the yield difference between nearly identical securities has more than doubled to around 50 bps. We also observe a similar separation for short maturities where, again, the deviations are much larger than in Figure 14.2.

Figure 14.3 reveals an additional pattern. There are significant troughs at regular intervals along the duration axis: the yield curve appears flat or even downward sloping at some points. These humps are typically close to maturity points with regular issuances. The most recent issue typically lies near the lowest point, but the yields of older issues located nearby are also pulled downward by arbitrage forces.

14.2.2 Market Liquidity and Short-Selling Costs

The market for bills appears partially segmented from the markets for old notes and bonds (Garbade, 1984; Kamara, 1994; Duffee, 1996). Similarly, the market for old bonds appears partially segmented from the market for more recently issued bonds (Cornell and Shapiro, 1989). Figures 14.2 and 14.3 suggest that this segmentation offers arbitrage strategies. Traders should buy the older bonds and short the recent issues. For instance, Warga (1992) compares excess returns from holding recent issues or from holding older bonds while matching durations. In practice, the older bonds are less liquid and more costly to trade. Nonetheless, this effect is larger than bid–ask spreads and larger than the dispersion of prices quoted by different dealers for a

[1] We plot *ytm* against duration since, for our purpose, we want to emphasize yield differences that are not accounted for by differences in cash flows. Controlling for duration provides a first-order adjustment for coupon differences. In addition, the volatility of yields implicit in bond options was close to a multiyear low at the end of March 2013. This minimizes the effect due to differences in bond convexity.

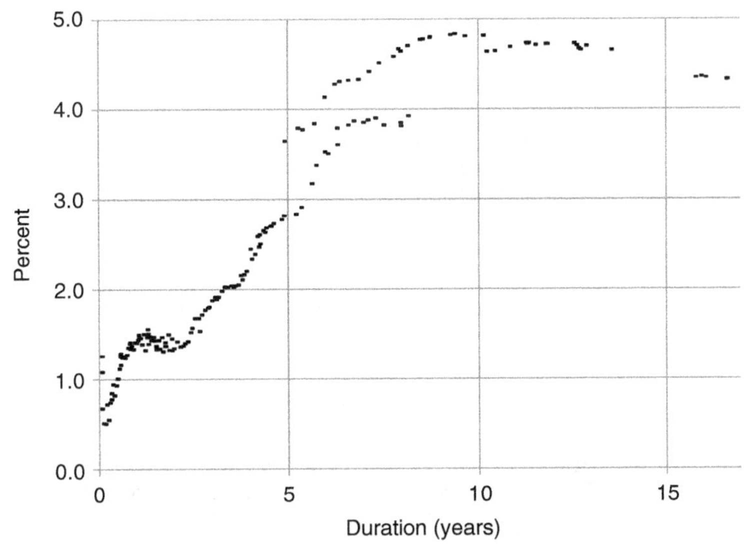

Figure 14.3 U.S. Treasury yield-to-maturity curve on October 31, 2008. Source: CRSP.

given bond (Garbade and Silber, 1976). Amihud and Mendelson (1991) also find that the difference in market liquidity is not sufficient to explain the note–bills yield differential.

Amihud and Mendelson (1991) conjecture that sufficiently high costs for borrowing a security in order to sell it short could rationalize the observed yield differential. In practice, short-sellers can obtain the security from a bond holder, via a reverse repo transaction, or from the holder's custodian, via a securities lending agreement. In the case of the repo transaction, the cost of borrowing the security is given by the spread S between the "special" repo rate offered by short-sellers to borrow specific securities and the repo rate for general collateral. Duffie (1996) examines this link formally in an equilibrium where the general collateral rate, the special repo rates (or borrowing fee), and the prices of two bonds are determined jointly.[2] In equilibrium, the borrowing costs s are such that the demand for short-selling the bond $D(s)$ equals the supply by lenders of securities. In his notation,

$$D(s) = \frac{q_L S}{\overline{\lambda}} \tag{14.1}$$

where q_L is the quantity of bonds held by potential lenders and $\frac{S}{\overline{\lambda}}$ is the fraction of lenders with opportunity costs $\lambda \leq S$. Duffie shows that the spread increases with the demand for short-selling this bond and the opportunity costs of lenders. He also shows that specialness increases with the market liquidity of the bond. Krishnamurthy (2002) provides an extension where bond holders' liquidity preference identifies a unique equilibrium.

Empirically, Jordan and Jordan (1997), for Treasury notes, and Krishnamurthy (2002), for 30-year bonds, show that borrowing costs contribute to a large extent to observed price differences between recent issues. Expanding on these results, Fontaine and Garcia (2012) extract a funding liquidity factor FL from the observed mispricings between pairs of Treasury securities across a range of 11 maturities (see also the discussion in Section 14.2.6). Expanding the range of maturities helps filter the persistent and systematic price dispersions. Following Duffie (1996), this funding factor should reflect expectations of future special repo rates across a range of maturities. To check this, Figure 14.4 reports the funding factor FL against the first principal component of *future* repo spreads to borrow on-the-run bonds with 2, 5, 10, and 30 years to maturity. For each maturity, we average the spreads over the next 3 months. We then extract the first principal component PC across maturities. The relationship is clearly positive (a regression of PC on FL produces an R^2 of 28%). The relationship is statistically and economically significant. A one-standard deviation change in FL yields one-half of a standard deviation increase common across future repo spreads.

Duffee (1996) and Krishnamurthy (2002) take the relative liquidity of different bonds as given. But why are older bonds less liquid? Garbade and Silber (1976) argue that "seasoning […] measures whether the issue is trading actively because it has not yet been 'locked away' in investor portfolios." See also Sarig and Warga (1989), Amihud and Mendelson (1991), and Vayanos and Weill (2006). Warga (1992) confirms that excess returns of the arbitrage strategy increase when the age of the seasoned bonds increases. Can this clientele effect rationalize at once the observations that recent issues have higher market liquidity, higher prices, and higher borrowing costs?

[2]The active literature on Treasury auctions is related to the discussion in this section. Several papers emphasize predictable price variations and apparent overpricing for Treasury securities following the issuance auction cycle (Jegadeesh, 1993; Cheria, Jacquier, and Jarrow, 2004; Lou, Yan, and Zhang, 2013).

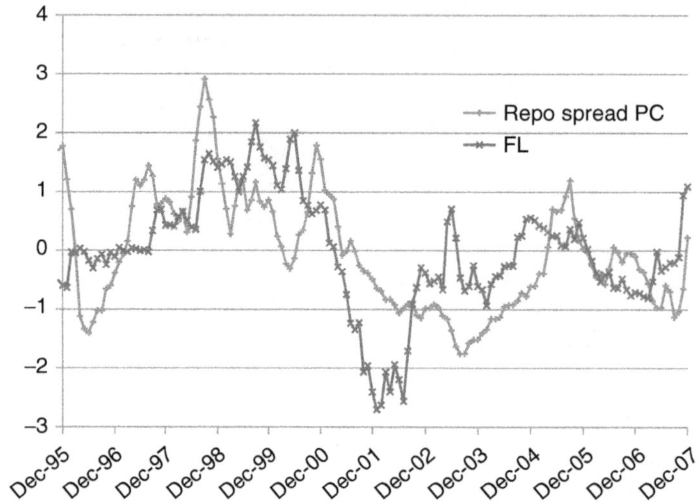

Figure 14.4 Funding risk and future repo spreads. Funding liquidity risk factor *FL* at the end of each month against the first principal component extracted from the special repo spread for bonds with maturities of 2, 5, 10, and 30 years where we use the average spread over the next 3 months for each maturity. Both series are normalized with a mean zero and unit standard deviation. The FL factor is estimated using data from CRSP. The repo spread data are from ICAP.

Vayanos and Weill (2006) provide a positive answer. Liquidity and specialness are not independent explanations. Since a short-seller must eventually buy back the security borrowed, the short-sellers concentrate activity around the security that is easier to locate, which is the same that other short-sellers are borrowing. Today's short-sellers are tomorrow's buyers, increasing the liquidity and the price of the bond. The combination of short-selling and search frictions generates asymmetries between the equilibrium price *and* liquidity of each asset. Adding search in the repo market, Vayanos and Weill (2006) also generate lower special repo rates (higher borrowing costs), adding to the price difference. As in most equilibrium models with search frictions, the value of a trade is shared between a buyer and a seller according to an exogenous "bargaining power" parameter. Empirically, Banerjee and Graveline (2013) decompose the premium between on-the-run and just-off-the-run 5-year and 10-year notes and estimate that, from November 1995 through July 2009, short-sellers bore 22% and 37% of the premium, respectively. Consistent with existing results, they also find that profits from the arbitrage strategies are quite volatile but that they are statistically different than zero.

14.2.3 Hedging Demand

The demand for hedging duration risk is perhaps the most important determinant of the short-selling demand in the Treasury market. Indeed, Graveline and McBrady (2011) find that proxies for hedging demand and proxies for buy-and-hold investors' demand to own liquid securities explain roughly the same share of repo spread variations. Much of the duration risk variation comes from the interest rate convexity of mortgage-backed securities (MBS).[3] Fernald, Keane, and Mosser (1994) detail how higher current or expected interest rates reduce the mortgage prepayment and refinancing rates, increase the duration of MBS portfolios, and increase the hedging demand of dealers and investors with large MBS inventories. As an illustration, Figure 14.5 compares Barclay's index of MBS duration with the notional amount of derivatives held by Fannie Mae for risk management purposes between 2000 and 2012.[4] The two series are clearly correlated and the changes in Fannie Mae's hedging demand are economically large, varying between 400 and 1200 billion U.S. dollars.

As made clear in Vayanos and Weill (2006), the increase in short-selling demand makes the limits to arbitrage more severe in the Treasury market, increasing the spread between new and old bonds. In addition, theoretical results link the price of interest rate risk to changes in aggregate duration (Hanson, 2014; Malkhozov et al., 2014). Again, the spread between new and old bonds then takes a new significance: it contains information about the compensation for interest rate risk. In addition, the same authors show that duration risk predicts bond returns, and this information is not subsumed by factors from the (smoothed) yield curve.[5]

[3]Hedging interest rate futures or options risk is another source of short interest in the Treasury market.

[4]We thank Aytek Malkhozov for sharing these data.

[5]Gabaix, Krishnamurthy, and Vigneron (2007) also show that prepayment risk carries a positive risk premium in the MBS market itself. These results add to the documented effect of MBS duration on option-implied and realized volatility of bond yields (Perli and Sack, 2003; Duarte, 2008).

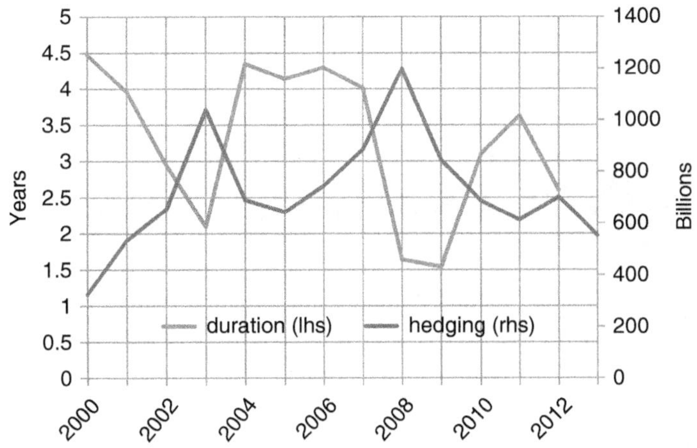

Figure 14.5 MBS duration and Fannie Mae's hedging. Barclay's MBS duration index (in years) and the Fannie Mae notional amount of derivatives used for risk management purposes (billions USD). Annual data, 2000–2012. The duration index data are from Barclay's. The notional derivative balance is from Fannie Mae annual accounts.

14.2.4 Risky Arbitrage

Banerjee and Graveline (2013) find that "variation in the repo premium does not completely account for variation in the price premium" (p. 650). In addition, Figure 14.2 shows that off-the-run notes initially issued with 10 years to maturity have a lower yield than old bonds initially issued with 30 years to maturity. These two securities have different market liquidity, explaining part of the yield difference, but they carry the same borrowing costs on the repo market (excluding the few most recent issues). Similarly, Longstaff (2004) shows that the spread between the yield on RefCorp bonds and seasoned Treasury bonds with identical cash flows is not commensurate with the lower bid–ask spreads and lower repo rate of Treasury issues.

The evidence is inconsistent with the prediction that the price differences between similar bonds should compensate for the expected transaction costs and borrowing costs until bond prices converge (see, e.g., Proposition 1 in Duffie, 1996, or Equation 8 in Krishnamurthy, 2002). But these models do not consider the effect of risk. First, rolling over overnight short positions is risky. For instance, Bartolini et al. (2011) find that the general collateral repo rates of Treasury securities vary significantly, while the (higher) repo rates on agency securities and MBS collateral are not meaningfully different from the unsecured rates. Buraschi and Menini (2002) ask whether *term* special repo rates correctly predict future *overnight* special repo spreads. This is an analog to tests of the expectations hypothesis between long-term rates and the short-term interest rate. They conclude that forward spreads implicit in term repo spreads overestimate changes in future overnight repo spreads. The effect is significant and largely explained by the volatility of the overnight special repo rate. In other words, rolling over a short position generates an exposure to an unexpectedly large aggregate short interest rate in the future.

Figure 14.6 illustrates the large variability of the repo spread in transactions involving the on-the-run 10-year note. The repo spread can be large, often as large as the underlying general collateral repo rate. More importantly, its volatility can be low at times but with rapid and persistent increases. Panel C of Figure 14.6 displays the conditional volatility from an EGARCH(1,1) model fitted to the data. Estimates confirm a strong leverage effect: periods of high volatility are also periods of high repo spreads, increasing the risk associated with short-selling securities. Liu and Longstaff (2004) find that the optimal strategy between new bonds and old bonds rarely fully exploits the arbitrage, since the speculator's final wealth is inversely related to the probability of hitting the speculator's borrowing constraint.

14.2.5 Segmented Markets and Preferred Habitats

The clientele demand for new and old bonds is similar in spirit to the view that investors have "preferred habitats" (Culbertson, 1957; Modigliani and Sutch, 1967). The clientele demand may be scattered across bond maturities, but it can also be scattered across the illiquidity spectrum – as in Krishnamurthy (2002) – across bonds with different ages. The effect of preferred habitats is analyzed formally in Vayanos and Vila (2009), where investors have clienteles' preference for specific maturities. Empirically, Chen et al. (2014) find that the aggregate portfolios of insurance firms exhibit a liability habitat – driven by the need to immunize the interest rate risk of operating liabilities – and a horizon habitat – due to the preference for holding risk-free securities over a specific investment horizon.

In Vayanos and Vila (2009), risk-averse arbitrageurs integrate the maturity-specific markets, eliminating risk-free arbitrage. However, the risk premium required by arbitrageurs propagates local clientele shocks across the term structure of yields. Building on this prediction, Greenwood and Vayanos (2014) show that a maturity-weighted measure of debt to GDP is positively related

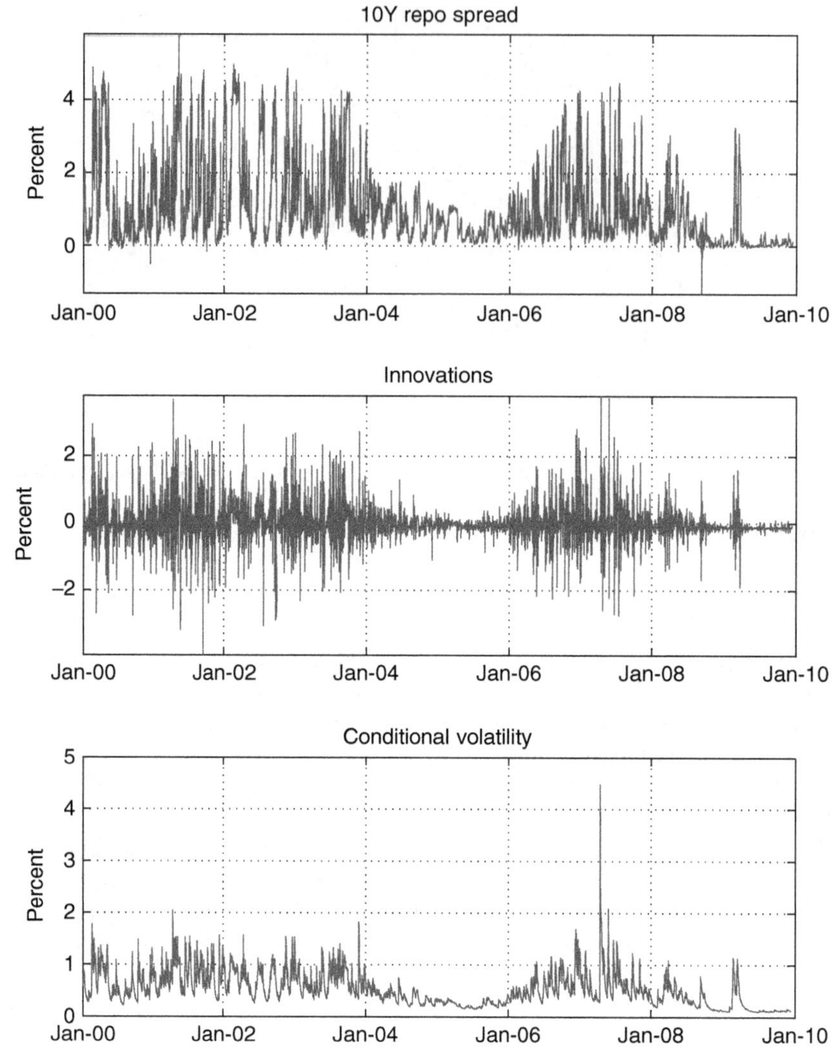

Figure 14.6 10-year repo spreads. Repo spreads for transactions involving the on-the-run 10-year note (Panel A). Innovations from fitting an ARMA(1,1) model to the repo spreads (Panel B). Estimated conditional volatility from fitting an EGARCH(1,1) model to the innovations (Panel C). All series in percentage points. Daily data from ICAP, November 1995 to July 2010.

to bond returns and argue that the effect is stronger when intermediaries' wealth has declined. More generally, interest rate risk increases when intermediaries wealth' decreases (or if their risk aversion increases). Guibaud, Nosbusch, and Vayanos (2013) study the optimal maturity structure of government debt within a clientele-based equilibrium model of the yield curve. Consistent with their model, they find that the median age of the population is correlated with the slope between 10- and 30-year bonds in the cross section of Organization for Economic Cooperation and Development (OECD) countries. Countries with older populations have relatively more investors with shorter investment horizons.

14.2.6 Funding Risk

Funding risk provides a channel between conditions in the repo markets, limits to arbitrage, and the bond risk premiums. Krishnamurthy (2002) shows that the expected repo spreads and bond spreads increase when the clientele's preference for the more-liquid assets increases. Adrian and Shin (2008) show that broker-dealers' leverage is procyclical and that the repo market is the marginal source of broker-dealers' funds. The reduction of leverage also implies that dealers are less willing to lend bonds or funds for the purpose of the arbitrage strategy. The evidence suggests that shocks to intermediaries' or to bondholders' liquidity preferences lead to wider *apparent* arbitrage opportunities across Treasury securities. Summing up, the spread between new and old bonds then takes on an important significance: it contains information about intermediaries' funding risk.[6]

[6]This is also analogous to results in Vayanos and Vila (2009) where the limited arbitrageur's ability to integrate segmented markets generates a risk premium.

Fontaine and Garcia (2012) provide direct evidence that measures of limits to arbitrage from the Treasury market can predict bond excess returns. They estimate a standard affine term structure model using observed coupon bond prices instead of the smoothed zero-coupon yields. They add a funding risk factor discounting the price of older bonds,

$$P(F_t, L_t, Z_{n,t}) = \sum_{m=1}^{M_n} D_t(m) \times C_{n,t}(m) + \zeta(L_t, Z_{n,t}) \tag{14.2}$$

where $Z_{n,t}$ summarizes any security-specific characteristics. The specification of $\zeta(L_t, Z_{n,t})$ in Fontaine and Garcia (2012) relies on the observation that older bonds become less liquid and less expensive. The price premium is given by

$$\zeta(L_t, Z_{n,t}) = L_t \times \beta_{M_n} \exp\left(-\frac{1}{\kappa} age_{n,t}\right) \tag{14.3}$$

where $age_{n,t}$ is the age, in years, of the bond at time t and β_M controls the average premium at each fixed maturity M. The filtered estimates of funding risk capture the price differences observed in Figure 14.2 that are (i) persistent, (ii) common across maturities, and (iii) correlated with age. As predicted by theory, the funding risk factor is correlated with measures of liquidity: it is correlated with current bid–ask spreads, and it predicts future bid–ask spreads. Funding risk predicts future repo spreads. However, the funding risk factor is also correlated with broader liquidity indicators, including the shape of the yield curve, investment flows into money market mutual funds, banks' nonborrowed reserves at the Fed, the growth of the shadow banking sector, and changes in monetary aggregates. Consistent with Krishnamurthy (2002), the dispersion of prices in Figures 14.2 and 14.3 is associated with investors' liquidity preference.

Fontaine and Garcia (2012) then check whether the funding risk factor predicts the risk premium across fixed-income markets. Figure 14.7 reproduce their factor but updated to a more recent sample. Conditions in the U.S. funding market exhibit a spike during the October 1987 crash, the Mexican peso crisis, toward the end of the millennium, and in 2005 when Ford and GM were downgraded to junk status. More recently, conditions spiked in 2008, in the summer of 2010, and throughout most of the sovereign crisis in Europe.

Table 14.1 reproduces some of the predictability results in Fontaine and Garcia (2012) (see their Table 8B) and reports the R^2 and coefficients on the funding risk factor in the following regressions of annual Treasury bond returns on funding risk:

$$xr^{(m)}_{t+12} = \alpha^{(m)} + \delta^{(m)} L_t + \beta^{(m)T} f_t + \varepsilon^{(m)}_{(t+12)} \tag{14.4}$$

where $xr^{(m)}_{t+h}$ are the annual excess returns on a zero-coupon bond with m years to maturity (from CRSP data), L_t is the liquidity factor, and f_t is a vector of annual forward rates $f_t^{(h)}$ from 1 to 5 years. We include f_t to control for the information content of forward rates.

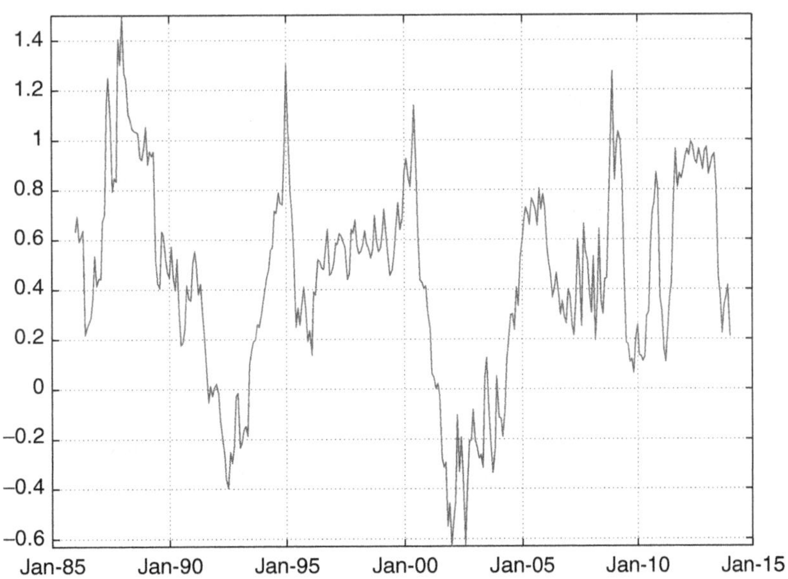

Figure 14.7 Funding liquidity risk. Filtered estimates of the funding risk factor L, as in Fontaine and Garcia (2012), but normalized to a mean of zero and a variance of 1 and updated in a monthly sample from January 1986 to December 2013.

TABLE 14.1 Treasury Excess Returns and Funding Risk

Maturity	α	$f_t^{(1)}$	$f_t^{(2)}$	$f_t^{(3)}$	$f_t^{(4)}$	$f_t^{(5)}$	L_t	R^2
2y	0.72	0.29	−1.31	1.88	0.93	−0.95	−0.78	41.65
	(3.49)	(0.49)	(−1.18)	(1.50)	(1.04)	(−1.60)	(−5.97)	
3y	1.31	0.15	−2.26	4.32	0.76	−1.49	−1.55	41.66
	(3.41)	(0.14)	(−1.13)	(1.89)	(0.48)	(−1.27)	(−5.93)	
4y	1.79	−0.51	−1.74	4.58	1.53	−1.85	−2.18	42.82
	(3.53)	(−0.35)	(−0.66)	(1.51)	(0.75)	(−1.13)	(−6.07)	
5y	1.98	−1.51	−0.24	4.57	0.36	−0.81	−2.66	40.87
	(3.23)	(−0.84)	(−0.07)	(1.24)	(0.15)	(−0.39)	(−5.83)	

Results from the regressions of annual excess returns $xr_{t+h}^{(m)}$ on a zero-coupon bond with m years to maturity,

$$xr_{t+12}^{(m)} = \alpha^{(m)} + \delta^{(m)} L_t + \beta^{(m)T} f_t + \epsilon_{(t+12)}^{(m)}$$

where f_t is a vector of annual forward rates $f_t^{(h)}$ from 1 to 5 years and L_t is the liquidity factor. Regressors are demeaned and divided by their standard deviations. Newey–West t-statistics (within parentheses) with 15 lags. End-of-month CRSP data (1985:12–2007:12).

The expected return on Treasury bonds is lower when the funding risk factor increases. This is consistent with an increase of lenders' or bondholders' liquidity preference driving up prices. The effect is economically significant: a one-standard deviation increase of the funding risk factor lowers expected returns by 0.8% and 2.7% for a bond with 2 and 5 years to maturity, respectively. The R^2s are doubled compared with the ones obtained when excluding the funding risk factor (unreported). The results cannot be attributed to the 2008–2009 crisis: the regressions are estimated using data between 1986 and 2007. Adding data from the crisis period only strengthens the results.

Fontaine and Garcia (2012) also find that an increase in the funding risk factor predicts higher returns across the LIBOR, swap, agency, and corporate bond markets. Importantly, the estimated predictability coefficients follow a flight-to-liquidity pattern. Limits to arbitrage in the Treasury market reflect liquidity preferences and funding risk, transmitting shocks to the risk premium across markets. Minimally, the results show that shocks to intermediaries' willingness or ability to facilitate arbitrage activities are correlated to shocks driving the risk premium across markets. In addition, these shocks potentially cause some of the risk premium variations.

Because repo markets play an essential role in the provision of liquidity across the fixed-income market, the evidence strongly suggests that intermediaries amplify and propagate those shocks when managing their funding risk. Fontaine, Garcia, and Gungor (2015) show that funding risk is transmitted to other markets. They find that funding shocks generate cross-sectional variations in liquidity and volatility, that funding shocks are correlated with contemporaneous returns in the cross section of stock returns, and that this risk is priced across a broad set of test portfolios.

14.2.7 Implication for Term Structure Models

The predictive power of the funding risk factor is robust to the inclusion of forward rates. In fact, the information content of these two factors appears largely independent. In other words, observed bond prices contain information about the future risk premium that is not spanned in the smoothed zero-coupon yield curve.[7]

Funding shocks are correlated with contemporaneous bond returns. We estimate a VAR(1) for the three term structure factors and the funding factor, jointly, and we compute the residuals based on the estimated dynamics. Table 14.2 reports the results from contemporaneous regressions of monthly bond returns on funding and term structure shocks:

$$r_{t+1}^{(m)} = \alpha + \beta_u^{\top} u_{t+1} + \beta_X^{\top} X_t + \epsilon_{t+1} \tag{14.5}$$

where $r_{t+1}^{(m)}$ is the monthly log-returns from an off-the-run zero-coupon bond with maturity m, $X_t = [L_t\ F_t]$ stacks the funding liquidity and term structure factors from the no-arbitrage model with liquidity and u_{t+1} is the Cholesky decomposition of X_{t+1} −

[7] The principal components (PCs) computed from the Fama–Bliss CRSP files (T-bill rates at maturities of 1, 2, 3, 4, 5, and 6 months; zero-coupon yields at maturities of 1, 2, 3, 4, and 5 years) span only 47% of funding liquidity variations. PCs from the dataset of Gürkaynak, Sack, and Wright (2006), computed using maturities of 3, 6, 9, and 12 months as well as 1, 2, 3, 4, 5, 7, and 10 years, span 54% of the funding liquidity variations. See Joslin, Priebsch, and Singleton (2014) for a discussion of unspanned risk within dynamic no-arbitrage term structure models.

TABLE 14.2 Funding Liquidity and Contemporaneous Treasury Bond Returns

	3m	6m	9m	1y	2y	3y	4y	5y	7y	10y
α	0.41	0.43	0.45	0.46	0.52	0.57	0.61	0.65	0.71	0.78
					Funding liquidity innovations					
$u_{liq,t+1}$	0.011	0.013	0.008	0.004	0.017	0.057	0.103	0.145	0.216	0.299
	(5.746)	(7.319)	(3.932)	(1.749)	(4.647)	(10.530)	(11.317)	(12.525)	(15.569)	(6.688)
					Nelson–Siegel factor innovations					
$u_{lvl,t+1}$	−0.006	−0.031	−0.070	−0.119	−0.370	−0.658	−0.953	−1.246	−1.806	−2.571
$u_{slp,t+1}$	−0.028	−0.076	−0.123	−0.164	−0.278	−0.337	−0.368	−0.384	−0.395	−0.395
$u_{crv,t+1}$	−0.003	−0.031	−0.073	−0.123	−0.336	−0.520	−0.653	−0.736	−0.785	−0.680
					Funding liquidity					
L_t	−0.018	−0.025	−0.038	−0.054	−0.131	−0.204	−0.266	−0.316	−0.392	−0.467
	(−10.091)	(−14.852)	(−21.013)	(−25.969)	(−45.261)	(−44.930)	(−37.740)	(−34.771)	(−30.051)	(−13.147)
					Nelson–Siegel factors					
$F_{1,t}$	0.143	0.160	0.175	0.190	0.250	0.306	0.355	0.398	0.476	0.584
$F_{2,t}$	0.146	0.148	0.147	0.146	0.143	0.137	0.127	0.116	0.094	0.074
$F_{3,t}$	0.003	0.004	0.006	0.010	0.033	0.060	0.087	0.111	0.149	0.184
R^2	97.7	98.3	98.4	98.6	99.3	99.4	99.4	99.4	99.2	97.6

[a]Results from the contemporaneous regressions

$$r_{t+1}^{(m)} = \alpha + \beta_u^\top u_{t+1} + \beta_X^\top X_t + \varepsilon_{t+1}$$

$r_{t+1}^{(m)}$ is the monthly log-returns from an off-the-run zero-coupon bond with maturity m, $X_t = [L_t \quad F_t]$ stacks the funding liquidity and term structure factors from the AFENS model with liquidity and where u_{t+1} is the Cholesky decomposition of $X_{t+1} - E_t[X_{t+1}]$. Regressors are demeaned and divided by their standard deviations. Newey–West standard errors (3 lags) in parentheses. End-of-month CRSP data (1985:12–2007:12).

$E_t[X_{t+1}]$ computed from a VAR(1). We include lagged funding and term structure factors as conditioning information to increase precision.

The evidence is unambiguous. Funding shocks are associated with positive bond returns contemporaneously. For a 10-year bond, a funding shock is associated with 0.3% monthly returns. Consistent with predictability regressions, this higher current value of funding liquidity is associated with lower expected returns in the future. This holds for every maturity. Coefficients of lagged term structure factors and of their innovations have the expected sign.

We identify the shocks via a Cholesky decomposition of the estimated covariance matrix where funding risk is ordered first. A structural interpretation suggests that an economically significant share of the term structure factor innovations is attributable to funding shocks. For instance, this will be the case if Treasury bonds provide a hedge against funding liquidity shocks. Overall, the evidence points to the important role of intermediation frictions in the level and variability of yields.

14.3 LEARNING

The expectations hypothesis is certainly a good point of departure to study the term structure of yields and the predictability of bond returns. Indeed, testing the EH was a major concern for researchers in the eighties. To set the problem clearly, one can start with a fundamental asset pricing equation for bond excess returns:

$$E_t^*\left[xR_{t+1}^{(n)} M_{t+1}\right] = 0 \tag{14.6}$$

where $xR_{t+1}^{(n)}$ is the returns from an n-period bond between t and $t+1$, M_{t+1} denotes the marginal utility of an investor, and the expectation $E_t^*[\cdot]$ is taken under the subjective beliefs of the investor (denoted by *). Applying the covariance formula and introducing an expected excess return under the true probability measure, $E_t\left[xR_{t+1}^{(n)}\right]$, one obtains

$$E_t\left[xR_{t+1}^{(n)}\right] = \left(E_t\left[xR_{t+1}^{(n)}\right] - E_t^*\left[xR_{t+1}^{(n)}\right]\right) - \frac{cov_t^*\left[M_{t+1}, xR_{t+1}^{(n)}\right]}{E_t^* M_{t+1}} \tag{14.7}$$

The first term on the right-hand side captures the difference between the expected excess returns computed using the investor's beliefs or using the true measure. The second term captures the risk premium. The larger part of the literature assumes that the first term is zero, since investors are typically endowed with full-information rational expectations (FIRE). The expectations hypothesis implies that the risk premium is either zero or constant through time. Therefore, predictability regressions of bond returns – the workhorse in this literature – provide only a test of the joint hypothesis that investors' expectations conformed with the expectations hypothesis and with FIRE. The literature provides quite different interpretations of the evidence that bond returns were predictable. Most authors argue that time-varying term premia are responsible for the predictability, but others argue for the importance of expectation errors, invoking the underreaction of long rates (or expected future short rates).[8]

14.3.1 Yield Survey Forecasts

Some authors avoid the conundrum by relying on survey data on interest rate expectations. From the EH, investors' forecasts should be unbiased, efficient, and consistent, and forecast errors should be orthogonal with respect to freely available information. Strikingly, the use of survey data as a means to test the EH makes an appearance as early as Meiselman (1962). Friedman (1980) uses the survey conducted in the *Goldsmith and Nagan Bond and Money Market Letter* among a selected panel of market professionals. The data provide the median response for one-quarter-ahead and two-quarter-ahead predictions of several interest rates. Friedman (1980) concludes that survey forecasts were biased, that they failed to be consistent, and that they did not efficiently exploit the information in past interest rate movements. Moreover, he finds that common current macroeconomic and macropolicy variables forecast ex post prediction errors for long-term rates (but not for short rates).

Froot (1989) also uses the survey conducted in the *Goldsmith and Nagan Bond and Money Market Letter*. He runs two sets of tests with survey data. First, he constructs a direct test of the EH by regressing survey forecasts of yields on short- and long-term instruments on forward premia:

$$s_{t+j}^{(k-j)} = \alpha + \beta fp_t^{(j,k)} + \varepsilon_{t,j} \tag{14.8}$$

where

- $s_{t+j}^{(k-j)}$ is the survey expected yield on a $k-j$-period bill, purchased at time $(t+j)$ less the yield at time t on a j-period bill, purchased at time t
- $fp_t^{(j,k)} = f_t^{(j,k)} - i_t^{(j)}$ is the forward premium at time t on a $k-j$-period bill, j periods into the future, less the yield on a j-period bill.

The forecast $s_{t+j}^{(k-j)}$ is a median survey measure, and it measures the spread with error. The test verifies whether the biased prediction is attributable to a time-varying term premium. Froot (1989) concludes that the expectations theory on short-term instruments is rejected, since the regression coefficient β is statistically less than one. However, the survey data tend to show that expected long-rate changes conform to the expectations theory: changes in the spread are reflected one for one in changes in expected future long rates (β is statistically not different from one). So it appears that term premia are more important in short-duration instruments.

A second test involves expectational errors – that is, the survey prediction error of the spread $i_{t+j}^{(k-j)} - i_t^{(j)}$. Froot (1989) runs the regressions of these errors on the forward premium defined in 14.8. For short maturities, expectational errors appear to be unsystematic. For longer-maturity instruments, results show that expectational errors are systematic, which explains the poor predictive power of the spread for future long-rate changes.

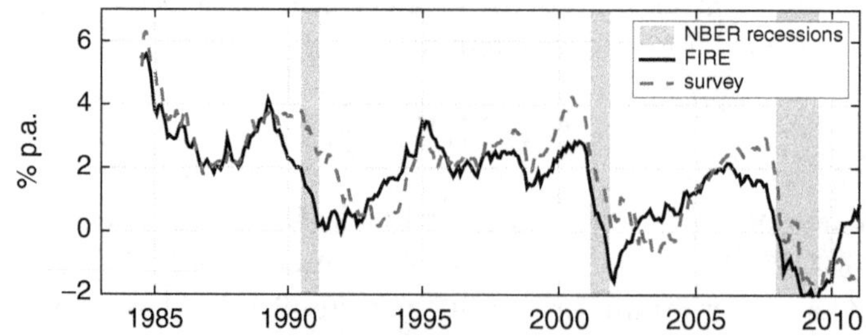

Figure 14.8 Ex-ante real fed funds rates based on FIRE and based on survey-expectations forecasts from Cieslak and Povala (2013).

[8] See Shiller and McCulloch (1987) for a survey of this literature.

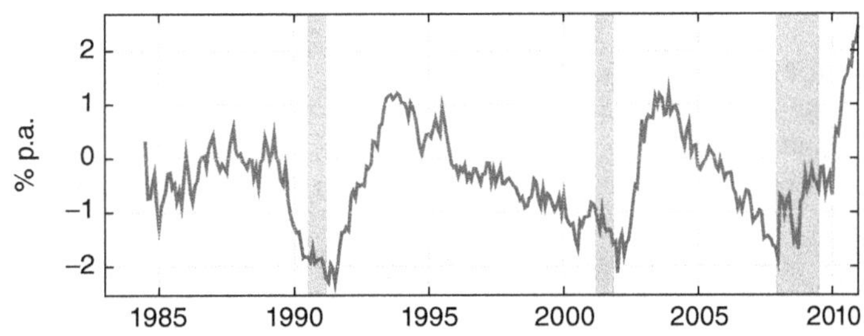

Figure 14.9 Difference $MP^{\perp}$ between survey expectation $r_t^{e,surv}$ and rational expectation $\hat{r}_t^{e,FIRE}$ forecasts of real fed funds rate from Cieslak and Povala (2013).

Recently, Cieslak and Povala (2013) have shown that the expected real federal funds rate implied by surveys differs from its statistical counterpart obtained under the assumption of FIRE. Figure 14.8 compares the forecasts of the federal funds rate based on survey data – labeled $r_t^{e,surv}$ – and based on a projection of realized $t+1$ federal funds rates on lagged instruments – labeled $\hat{r}_t^{e,FIRE}$.[9] The results show that survey forecasts miss both downturns and upturns. In particular, forecasts of future rates are systematically above statistical forecasts throughout all recessions but one. Figure 14.9 reports the difference between the forecasts $r_t^{e,FIRE}$ and $\hat{r}_t^{e,surv}$, which Cieslak and Povala (2013) label $MP^{\perp}$. They show that $MP^{\perp}$ is persistent at the business cycle frequency, it becomes notably large at the beginning of recessions, and it is closely correlated with errors in unemployment forecast errors from surveys. Important to our discussion, they find that several conditioning variables used in predictive regressions of bond returns, especially variables related to the real activity, predict the unexpected returns associated with $MP^{\perp}$ and that these are essentially uncorrelated with the survey-implied risk premia.

Recent work provides additional evidence against the rationality of survey forecasts. Gourinchas and Tornell (2004) use forecasts of 3-month euro rates, 3, 6, and 12 months ahead, for the G7 countries.[10] Jongen, Verschoor, and Wolff (2005) use survey data on 3-month maturity euro, interbank, and T-bill rates.[11] As in Froot (1989), they find that survey forecast errors are linked to the forward premium. Bacchetta, Mertens, and van Wincoop (2009) find systematic evidence that survey forecasts are predictable across markets, across sample periods, and across countries.[12] Coibion and Gorodnichenko (2012) document that mean forecasts in surveys of consumers, firms, central bankers, and professional forecasters do not adjust fully after shocks. These deviations are significant, both statistically and economically, and they are consistent with the predictions of models in which agents face information constraints.

14.3.2 Affine Term Structure Models

The modern term structure literature has mostly proceeded on the assumption that predictable variations in bond returns come from risk premia. This section briefly reviews the risk premium channel in the context of benchmark dynamic term structure models (DTSMs), while subsequent sections will discuss (i) recent attempts to use the information in survey data and (ii) attempts to address the limitations of survey forecasts.

14.3.2.1 Bond Prices As usual, we start from a set of latent risk factors $\mathcal{Z}_t \in \mathbf{R}^{\mathcal{N}_{\mathcal{Z}}}$. Following Feunou and Fontaine (2014), we will construct a conditional mean DTSM (CM-DTSM) based on the conditional mean of $\mathcal{Z}_t$ under the (true) historical measure $\mathbb{P}$:

$$\mathcal{E}_t \equiv E_t[\mathcal{Z}_{t+1}] \tag{14.9}$$

where we adopt a forward-looking specification of the one-period nominal interest rate i_t:

$$i_t = \rho_0 + \rho_1' \mathcal{E}_t \tag{14.10}$$

[9]*FIRE* stands for full-information rational expectations. As instruments, Cieslak and Povala (2013) use time t year-on-year CPI inflation, federal funds rate, annual change in the rate of unemployment, 1-year nominal yield, and the term spread. They also include the $t-1$ term spread. We thank Anna Cieslak for sharing these results.

[10]The data are based on the Financial Times Currency Forecaster, with 48 respondents from both large banks and multinational companies active in the foreign exchange market.

[11]Jongen, Verschoor, and Wolff (2005) use data from the Consensus Economics of London on 3-month-ahead expectations of interest rates in 20 industrialized countries by 250 professional forecasters worldwide.

[12]Bacchetta, Mertens, and van Wincoop (2009) use the survey of exchange rate and interest rate expectations by Forecasts Unlimited Inc. For interest rates, the survey provides the expectations of 3-month LIBOR, 12-month LIBOR, and 10-year government bond yields 3, 6, and 12 months ahead.

Using a specification based on $\mathcal{E}_t$ will make the connection with survey forecasts more transparent. A standard formulation would use $\mathcal{Z}_t$ instead of $\mathcal{E}_t$ in the short rate i. This is innocuous at this point: simply neglect $\mathcal{Z}_t$, take $\mathcal{E}_t$ as the latent risk factor, and follow (say) Joslin, Singleton, and Zhu (2011) to derive the pricing equation.

We leave the dynamics of $\mathcal{E}_t$ (and $\mathcal{Z}_t$) under $\mathbb{P}$ unspecified for now. At this point, we need the dynamics of $\mathcal{E}_t$ under the risk-neutral measure $\mathbb{Q}$ to derive the pricing equation for yields. For tractability, we use a Markovian specification of order 1:

$$\Delta\mathcal{E}_{t+1} = K_0^{\mathbb{Q}} + K_1^{\mathbb{Q}}\mathcal{E}_t + \Sigma_{\mathcal{E}}\varepsilon_{t+1}^{\mathbb{Q}} \tag{14.11}$$

where $\varepsilon_{t+1}^{\mathbb{Q}}$ is a Gaussian white noise. Proposition 1 in Feunou and Fontaine (2014) translates the identification assumptions from Joslin, Singleton, and Zhu (2011) to the dynamics for $\mathcal{E}_t$. The n-period nominal bond price is defined by

$$P_t^{(n)} \equiv E_t^Q\left[\exp\left\{-\sum_{j=0}^{n-1} r_{t+j}\right\}\right] = E_t^Q\left[\exp\ \{-r_t\}\,P_{t+1}^{(n-1)}\right]$$

Guess that $P_t^{(n)} = \exp\ (A_n + B_n'\mathcal{E}_t)$ – using the fact that the model is affine – and substitute for $P_{t+1}^{(n-1)}$ to solve for the coefficients A_n and B_n:

$$\begin{aligned} B_{n+1} =& (I_{\mathcal{N}_Z} + K_1^{\mathbb{Q}\prime})B_n - \rho_1 \\ A_{n+1} =& A_n + K_0^{\mathbb{Q}\prime}B_n + \frac{1}{2}B_n'\Sigma_{\mathcal{E}}\Sigma_{\mathcal{E}}'B_n - \rho_0 \end{aligned} \tag{14.12}$$

It follows that yields are given by $y_t^{(n)} = -\frac{1}{n}\log\ (P_t^{(n)}) = a_n + b_n'\mathcal{E}_t$. One important implication is that yields span time t forecasts of the future risk factors $\mathcal{Z}_{t+1}$ but that they do not span Z_t unless $\mathcal{E}_t$ and $\mathcal{Z}_t$ are linearly dependent.

14.3.2.2 Historical Dynamics The change of measure ξ_t is assumed to be exponential affine:

$$\xi_{t+1} \equiv \frac{\exp\ \left(\lambda_t'\varepsilon_{t+1}^{\mathbb{Q}}\right)}{E_t^{\mathbb{P}}\left[\exp\ (\lambda_t'\varepsilon_{t+1}^{\mathbb{Q}})\right]} \tag{14.13}$$

which guarantees that $\xi_{t+1} > 0$ and $E_t^{\mathbb{P}}[\xi_{t+1}] = 1$, as required by the absence of arbitrage. This change of measure also implies that the (log-) stochastic discount factor is given by

$$m_t = \log\ M_t = \exp\ (-i_t)\xi_{t+1} = -i_t - \frac{1}{2}\lambda_t'\lambda_t + \lambda_t'\varepsilon_{t+1}^{\mathbb{Q}} \tag{14.14}$$

We derive the historical dynamics from the conditional Laplace transform of the innovations:

$$\begin{aligned} E_t^{\mathbb{P}}\left[\exp\ (u'\varepsilon_{t+1}^{\mathbb{Q}})\right] =& E_t^{\mathbb{Q}}\left[\frac{\exp\ (u'\varepsilon_{t+1}^{\mathbb{Q}})}{\xi_{t+1}}\right] \\ =& E_t^{\mathbb{P}}\left[\exp\ (\lambda_t'\varepsilon_{t+1}^{\mathbb{Q}})\right]\exp\ \left(-\frac{1}{2}(u-\lambda_t)'(u-\lambda_t)\right) \\ =& \exp\ \left(-\frac{1}{2}u'u + u'\lambda_t\right) \end{aligned} \tag{14.15}$$

where the first line in 14.15 follows, since ξ_{t+1} is the change of measure between $\mathbb{Q}$ and $\mathbb{P}$, while the second line uses the definition in 14.13.[13] This conditional Laplace transform of $\varepsilon_{t+1}^{\mathbb{Q}}$ under $\mathbb{P}$ defines a Gaussian distribution with unit variance but with a conditional mean given by

$$E_t^{\mathbb{P}}\left[\varepsilon_{t+1}^{\mathbb{Q}}\right] = \lambda_t \tag{14.16}$$

[13]The last line in 14.15 follows from evaluating the left-hand side at $u = 0$, which requires that

$$1 = E_t^{\mathbb{P}}\left[\exp\ (\lambda_t'\varepsilon_{t+1}^{\mathbb{Q}})\right]\exp\ (-\frac{1}{2}\lambda_t'\lambda_t)$$

Assuming that the $\mathcal{N}_Z \times 1$ vector of prices of risk λ_t is also affine,

$$\lambda_t \equiv \tilde{\lambda}_0 + \tilde{\lambda}_1 \mathcal{E}_t \tag{14.17}$$

and using Equations 14.11 and 14.16 to compute $E_t^{\mathbb{P}}[\Delta\mathcal{E}_{t+1}]$, it follows that the dynamics of $\mathcal{E}_{t+1}$ under the historical measure $\mathbb{P}$ is given by

$$\Delta\mathcal{E}_{t+1} = K_0^{\mathbb{P}} + K_1^{\mathbb{P}}\mathcal{E}_t + \Sigma_{\mathcal{E}}\varepsilon_{t+1}^{\mathbb{P}} \tag{14.18}$$

with parameters given by

$$K_0^{\mathbb{P}} = K_0^{\mathbb{Q}} - \Sigma_{\mathcal{E}}\tilde{\lambda}_0 \tag{14.19}$$

$$K_1^{\mathbb{P}} = K_1^{\mathbb{Q}} - \Sigma_{\mathcal{E}}\tilde{\lambda}_1 \tag{14.20}$$

Dai and Singleton (2002) and Duffee (2002) show that essentially affine Gaussian term structure models are able to explain stylized facts of the bond risk premium reported by Fama and Bliss (1987) and Campbell and Shiller (1991), whereby projections of bond returns on the slope of the yield curve produce coefficients that contradict the implications of the traditional expectations theory. DTSMs neglect frictions in the formation of expectations as a possible channel. The interpretation of the pricing kernel in Equation 14.13 is that investors demand compensation for bearing the $\mathcal{N}_Z$ risks captured by $\varepsilon_{t+1}^{\mathbb{P}}$. The vector λ_t corresponds to the market prices of risk. Essentially affine models generalize the completely affine models of Duffie and Kan (1996) and Dai and Singleton (2000), where the market prices of risk are simply proportional to the yield volatility. The additional reduced-form parameters introduce the potential for overfitting. In addition, DTSMs are typically estimated using yield data only, neglecting the restrictions that prices of risk should reflect investors' preferences and economic fundamentals. The interpretation of λ_t estimates may attribute too much of the risk premium to interest rate risk.

14.3.2.3 Unspanned Macroeconomic Variables Consider the links between economic variables such as inflation and consumption growth to the observed yields.[14] Duffee (2013) explores the spanning properties of various measures of inflation and consumption growth for yields, and vice versa, and concludes that a large fraction of nominal yield variations is not related to current and past inflation and economic growth. Smoothing the inflation or the consumption data only slightly reduces the cross-sectional deviations relative to unsmoothed data. On the other hand, this reduces the accuracy of inflation and consumption forecasts. Moreover, the risk premia inferred from these affine no-arbitrage models with macroeconomic data are not well estimated and they are inconsistent with evidence from bond returns. Duffee (2013) concludes that one cannot use nominal term structure to obtain reasonable risk compensation for inflation and consumption growth.

14.3.2.4 Closing the Model Feunou and Fontaine (2014) propose one mechanism that directly introduces a wedge between the dynamics for $\mathcal{Z}_t$ and the evolution of the expectations $\mathcal{E}_t$ driving yields. The key feature of the model is that the yield curve must produce efficient forecasts of the state variables, potentially spanning forecasts forecasts of macro variables but not their current values. In the example of inflation, bond yields would span inflation expectations but not inflation itself. The mechanism driving this wedge is distinct from that in Joslin, Priebsch, and Singleton (2014), who introduce a class of DTSMs where macro variables are not spanned by the yield curve (i.e., with unspanned macro variables) due to restrictions on the prices of risk.

From Equation 14.9, the yield factors $\mathcal{E}_t$ span the conditional expectations of $\mathcal{Z}_{t+1}$ by construction: $\mathcal{Z}_{t+1} = \mathcal{E}_t + u_{t+1}$ for some zero-mean unpredictable innovation u_{t+1}. The key assumption to complete the CM-DTSM specifies the dynamics of $\mathcal{Z}_{t+1}$. We assume that the innovation u_{t+1} corresponds to a rotation of the innovations in $\mathcal{E}_{t+1}$,

$$\mathcal{Z}_{t+1} = \mathcal{E}_t + \Sigma\varepsilon_{t+1}^{\mathbb{P}} \tag{14.21}$$

where Σ is the lower diagonal and positive definite. In other words, we have that $u_{t+1} \equiv \Sigma\varepsilon_{t+1}^{\mathbb{P}}$. Combining Equations 14.10 and 14.21 yields

$$\mathcal{E}_{t+1} = K_0^{\mathbb{P}} + (I_{\mathcal{N}_Z} + K_1^{\mathbb{P}})\mathcal{E}_t + \Sigma_{\mathcal{E}}\Sigma^{-1}u_{t+1} \tag{14.22}$$

from which we can easily see that $\mathcal{Z}_t$ a VAR(1) if $\mathcal{E}_{t+1} = K_0^{\mathbb{P}} + (I_{\mathcal{N}_Z} + K_1^{\mathbb{P}})\mathcal{Z}_t$. This arises only if

$$\Sigma_{\mathcal{E}}\Sigma^{-1} = I_{\mathcal{N}_Z} + K_1^{\mathbb{P}} \tag{14.23}$$

with cross-equation restrictions given in Feunou and Fontaine (2014).

[14] Alternatively, one can impose statistical restrictions more than economic ones, replicating the effects of investors' preferences and constraints.

14.3.2.5 Introducing Macro Variables If condition 14.23 holds, then we have that yields must span the forecasts $\mathcal{E}_t$ *and* the state variables $\mathcal{Z}_t$:

$$y_t = a_n + b_n'\mathcal{E}_t = (a_n + b_n' K_0^{\mathbb{P}}) + b_n'(I_{\mathcal{N}_Z} + K_1^{\mathbb{P}})Z_t$$

Otherwise, yields only span $\mathcal{E}_t$ in the unrestricted case, leaving a separate role for $\mathcal{Z}_t$ to span the information contained in the macro variables. Take a number $0 \leq \mathcal{N}_M < \mathcal{N}_Z$ of macro variables $\mathcal{M}_t$ that are spanned by the state $\mathcal{Z}_t$,

$$\mathcal{M}_t = \gamma_0 + \gamma_1 \mathcal{Z}_t \tag{14.24}$$

where γ_0 is a $\mathcal{N}_M \times 1$ vector and γ_1 is a $\mathcal{N}_M \times \mathcal{N}_Z$ rectangular matrix. In addition, take $\mathcal{N}_L = \mathcal{N}_Z - \mathcal{N}_M$ observed portfolios of yields $\mathcal{P}_t$ that are measured without errors,

$$\mathcal{P}_t = W y_t = a_W + b_W \mathcal{E}_t$$

where y_t stacks the cross section of $\mathcal{N} \geq \mathcal{N}_Z$ individual yields, W is a $\mathcal{N}_L \times \mathcal{N}$ matrix of weights, $a_W \equiv W[a_{n_1} \cdots a_{n_{\mathcal{N}}}]'$, and $b_W = W[b_{n_1} \cdots b_{n_{\mathcal{N}}}]'$. This framework can accommodate different numbers of observable macro variables $\mathcal{M}_t$ and yield portfolios $\mathcal{P}_t$. Feunou and Fontaine (2014) show that any canonical conditional mean macrofinance term structure model (CM-MTSM) based on $\mathcal{Z}_t$ is equivalent to a unique canonical CM-MTSM whose $\mathcal{N}_Z \times 1$ state variables are the observable macro variables and yield factors $\mathcal{X}_t' = [\mathcal{M}_t\ \mathcal{P}_t']$ with

$$\begin{aligned}\mathcal{X}_{t+1} &= \mathcal{E}_{\mathcal{X},t}^{\mathbb{Q}} + \Sigma_X \varepsilon_{\mathcal{X},t+1}^{\mathbb{Q}} \\ \mathcal{X}_{t+1} &= \mathcal{E}_{\mathcal{X},t}^{\mathbb{P}} + \Sigma_X \varepsilon_{\mathcal{X},t+1}^{\mathbb{P}}\end{aligned} \tag{14.25}$$

and where the dynamics of $\mathcal{E}_{\mathcal{X},t}^{\mathbb{P}} \equiv E_t[\mathcal{X}_{t+1}]$ under $\mathbb{Q}$ and $\mathbb{P}$ are given by

$$\begin{aligned}\Delta\mathcal{E}_{\mathcal{X},t+1}^{\mathbb{P}} &= K_{0X}^{\mathbb{Q}} + K_{1X}^{\mathbb{Q}}\mathcal{E}_{\mathcal{X},t}^{\mathbb{P}} + \Sigma_{\mathcal{E}_{\mathcal{X}}}\varepsilon_{\mathcal{X},t+1}^{\mathbb{Q}} \\ \Delta\mathcal{E}_{\mathcal{X},t+1}^{\mathbb{P}} &= K_{0X}^{\mathbb{P}} + K_{1X}^{\mathbb{P}}\mathcal{E}_{\mathcal{X},t}^{\mathbb{P}} + \Sigma_{\mathcal{E}_{\mathcal{X}}}\varepsilon_{\mathcal{X},t+1}^{\mathbb{P}}\end{aligned} \tag{14.26}$$

14.3.2.6 Bond Risk Premium Importantly, $\mathcal{E}_t$ is not the conditional mean of $\mathcal{Z}_{t+1}$ under the risk-neutral measure $\mathbb{Q}$. This is given by

$$\begin{aligned}\mathcal{E}_t^{\mathbb{Q}} &\equiv E_t^{\mathbb{Q}}\left[\mathcal{Z}_{t+1}\right] \\ &= \mathcal{E}_t + \Sigma E_t^{\mathbb{Q}}\left[\varepsilon_{t+1}^{\mathbb{P}}\right] \\ &= \mathcal{E}_t + \Sigma\Sigma_{\mathcal{E}}^{-1}E_t^{\mathbb{Q}}\left[\Delta\mathcal{E}_{t+1} - K_0^{\mathbb{P}} - K_1^{\mathbb{P}}\mathcal{E}_t\right] \\ &= \mathcal{E}_t + \Sigma\Sigma_{\mathcal{E}}^{-1}(K_0^{\mathbb{Q}} - K_1^{\mathbb{Q}}\mathcal{E}_t - K_0^{\mathbb{P}} - K_1^{\mathbb{P}}\mathcal{E}_t) \\ &= \mathcal{E}_t + \Sigma\Sigma_{\mathcal{E}}^{-1}(K_0^{\mathbb{Q}} - K_0^{\mathbb{P}}) + \Sigma\Sigma_{\mathcal{E}}^{-1}(K_1^{\mathbb{Q}} - K_1^{\mathbb{P}})\mathcal{E}_t\end{aligned} \tag{14.27}$$

Therefore, the risk premium $\mathcal{E}_t^{\mathbb{Q}} - \mathcal{E}_t$ is given by a rotation of the volatilities $\Sigma\Sigma_{\mathcal{E}}^{-1}$. However, the risk factors driving the variation of the risk premium satisfy the additional restrictions that they must forecast both the yields and the macro variables $\mathcal{M}_t$.

14.3.2.7 Results Empirically, Feunou and Fontaine (2014) fit a different version of a CM-MTSM to yields, inflation swaps, surveys of inflation forecasts and unemployment data. The estimates imply that yields span macro expectations in the CM-MTSM. Figure 14.10 reports the loadings on expected inflation and expected unemployment from the unrestricted CM-MTSM and the nested VAR-MTSM. Estimates from the CM-MTSM imply that yield loadings on expected inflation range from 1.16 to 0.61 between the short rate and the 10-year bond, and loadings on expected unemployment range between 0.36 and 0.20. In contrast, these loadings are essentially zero in the VAR. In addition, the CM model produces the best inflation forecasts, supporting the assumptions that yields span $\mathcal{E}_t$. Forecasts from the CM model and forecasts from surveys produce similar out-of-sample root-mean-squared errors (RMSEs) for both Canada and the United States. Relative to the VAR, the CM model reduces the RMSE by as much as 20% when forecasting 2-year cumulative inflation.

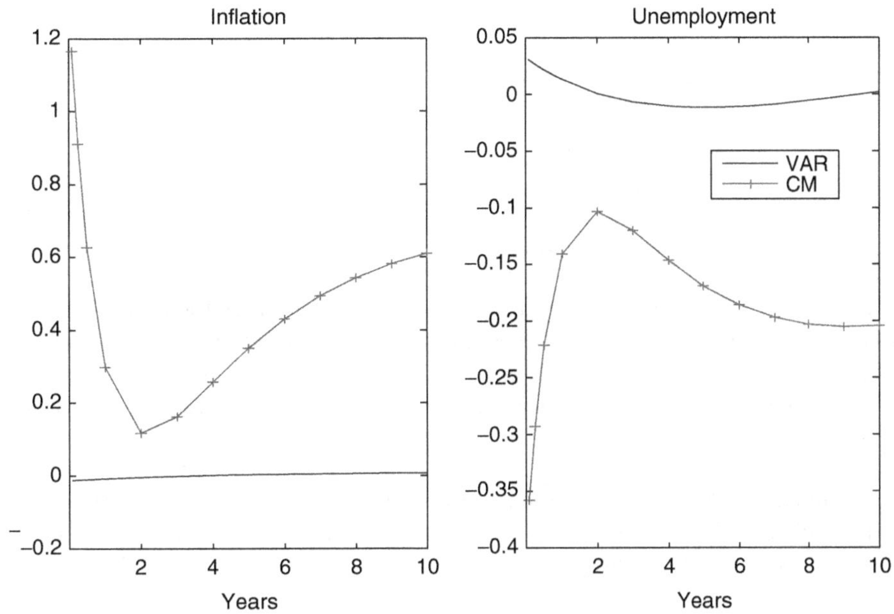

Figure 14.10 Nominal yield loadings. Loadings of nominal yields on the conditional mean of inflation and on the conditional mean of unemployment from the benchmark CM model.

14.3.3 Spanning Survey Forecasts

CM-MTSMs reconcile two strands of the literature. The first uses observed macro variables as risk factors driving yields (inflation, say). The second uses (inflation) survey forecasts (Chun, 2011). However, in the latter case, shocks to macro variables are left outside the model and the corresponding risk premium (the inflation-risk premium) is unidentified. In contrast, CM-MTSMs can include *both* macro variables and their survey forecasts among the state variables *and* guarantee that statistical forecasts correspond to the survey forecast up to a measurement error.

To see how this works, consider a simple case where inflation π_t and its survey forecast $\overline{\pi}_t^s$ are included in the vector of observables $\mathcal{M}_t$, potentially with other macro variables. By assumption, we have that

$$\pi_t = \gamma_{\pi 0} + \gamma_\pi' \mathcal{Z}_t \tag{14.28}$$

but also that

$$\mathcal{E}_{\pi,t} = E_t[\pi_{t+1}] = \gamma_{\pi 0} + \gamma_\pi' E_t[\mathcal{Z}_{t+1}] = \gamma_{\pi 0} + \gamma_\pi' \mathcal{E}_t \tag{14.29}$$

Suppose that $\overline{\pi}_t^s$ and $\mathcal{E}_{\pi,t}$ differ by some measurement errors $\eta_{\pi,t}^s$

$$\overline{\pi}_t^s = \gamma_{\pi 0} + \gamma_\pi' \mathcal{E}_t + \eta_{\pi,t}^s \tag{14.30}$$

With no loss of generality, consider the case where π_t and $\overline{\pi}_t^s$ are ordered first and second in the vector $\mathcal{X}_t$, respectively.[15] Then, the following conditions

$$e_1' K_{0X}^{\mathbb{P}} = 0 \quad \text{and} \quad \delta \equiv e_2 - (I + K_{1X}^{\mathbb{P}})' e_1 = 0$$

guarantee that (i) $E^{\mathbb{P}}[\eta_{\pi,t}^s] = 0$ and (ii) $\text{cov}(\eta_{\pi,t}^s, \eta_{\pi,t+h}^s) = 0 \quad h > 0$ so that $\eta_{\pi,t}^s$ is a measurement error (e_i has its ith element equal to 1 and equal to 0 otherwise). In other words, $e_1' K_{0X}^{\mathbb{P}} = 0$ requires that the first element of the constant be zero and $\delta = 0$ requires that the second line of the autoregressive matrix be equal to e_2'. Clearly, these conditions can be implemented easily. They also

[15] Feunou and Fontaine (2014) discuss the general case with several macro variables included, along with their corresponding survey forecasts.

have an intuitive economic interpretation:

$$\begin{aligned}\mathcal{E}_{\pi,t} = e_1'\mathcal{E}_{\mathcal{X},t} &= e_1'\left(K_{0X}^{\mathbb{P}} + \left(I + K_{1X}^{\mathbb{P}}\right)\mathcal{E}_{\mathcal{X},t-1} + \Sigma_{\mathcal{E}_{\mathcal{X}}}\varepsilon_t^{\mathbb{P}}\right)\\ &= e_2'\mathcal{E}_{\mathcal{X},t-1} + e_1'\Sigma_{\mathcal{E}_{\mathcal{X}}}\varepsilon_t^{\mathbb{P}}\\ &= e_2'\mathcal{X}_t + (e_1'\Sigma_{\mathcal{E}_{\mathcal{X}}} - e_2'\Sigma_X)\varepsilon_t^{\mathbb{P}}\\ &= \overline{\pi}_t^s - e_1'\theta_X^{\mathbb{P}}\Sigma_X\varepsilon_t^{\mathbb{P}}\end{aligned} \tag{14.31}$$

where $\theta_X^{\mathbb{P}} \equiv I + K_{1X}^{\mathbb{P}} - \Sigma_{\mathcal{E}_{\mathcal{X}}}\Sigma_X^{-1}$. The model-implied forecast corresponds to the survey forecasts plus a rotation of innovations in $\mathcal{X}_t$ (including the innovations in survey forecasts). This guarantees that Equation 14.30 holds.[16] Equation 14.31 also shows that Markovian VAR(1) models (i.e., if $\theta_X^{\mathbb{P}} = 0$) can accommodate Equation 14.30 but only at the added cost that $var(\eta_t^s) = 0$. In other words, the inflation forecasts from the model must correspond *exactly* to the survey forecasts, again leading to the counterfactual prediction that yields span the survey forecasts exactly.

14.3.3.1 Subjective Expectations So far, we assumed that investors' historical predictions were identical to predictions produced by statistical models estimated in-sample today up to a measurement error. However, the evidence discussed in Section 14.3.1 forces the question as to whether the assumption of rational expectations is an appropriate assumption in the context of term structure models.

As in Cieslak and Povala (2013), Piazzesi, Salomao, and Schneider (2013) conclude that subjective interest rate expectations deviate from the expectations computed from statistical models and these deviations seem to explain most of the statistical bond premia. They then proceed to study the relative contribution of beliefs and risk assessment for bond return predictability within a no-arbitrage model. They introduce a subjective change of measure causing a wedge between forecasts from the statistical model and from surveys (see also Chernov and Mueller, 2011). Introducing a subjective probability measure allows a more general approach to model the dynamics of survey forecasts relative to including the survey forecasts among the state variables.

We can use the notation introduced above while staying close to the approach in Piazzesi, Salomao, and Schneider (2013). Suppose the following subjective change of measure:

$$\xi_{t+1}^* \equiv \frac{\exp\,(\lambda_t^{*\prime}\varepsilon_{t+1}^{\mathbb{Q}})}{E_t^*[\exp\,(\lambda_t^{*\prime}\varepsilon_{t+1}^{\mathbb{Q}})]} \tag{14.32}$$

and the following subjective prices of risk:

$$\lambda_t^* \equiv \lambda_0^* + \lambda_1^{*\prime}\mathcal{E}_t \tag{14.33}$$

Then, following the same argument as in Equation 14.15, it follows that the dynamics of $\mathcal{E}_t$ under the subjective measure are given by

$$\Delta\mathcal{E}_{t+1} = K_0^* + K_1^*\mathcal{E}_t + \Sigma_{\mathcal{E}}\varepsilon_{t+1}^* \tag{14.34}$$

with parameters given by

$$K_0^* = K_0^{\mathbb{Q}} - \Sigma_{\mathcal{E}}\lambda_0^* \tag{14.35}$$

$$K_1^* = K_1^{\mathbb{Q}} - \Sigma_{\mathcal{E}}\lambda_1^* \tag{14.36}$$

Equation 14.34 provides the dynamics of the state variables under the subjective measure and yields a set of measurement equations corresponding to observable survey forecasts. We can write

$$\overline{X}_t^s = E_t^*[X_{t+1}] + \eta_t^s = K_0^* + (I + K_1^*)\mathcal{E}_t + \eta_t^s \tag{14.37}$$

where $\overline{X}_t^s$ is the observed survey forecast and η_t^s is a measurement error.

Piazzesi, Salomao, and Schneider (2013) implement a three-factor model that includes a change of measure due to risk, as in Equation 14.13, as well as a change of measure due to subjective beliefs, as in Equation 14.32. As observable state variables,

[16]The necessary and sufficient conditions for $\text{cov}(\eta_t^s, \eta_{t+h}^s) = 0 \quad h > 0$ are given in Appendix A6 of Feunou and Fontaine (2014). The sufficient conditions introduced above impose no restrictions on the covariance matrix (which are not free in the canonical form).

Piazzesi, Salomao, and Schneider (2013) use the level of yields, the slope of the yield curve and expected inflation. They estimate each set of parameters sequentially. First, they estimate the historical dynamics of the state vector by maximum likelihood. Second, they estimate parameters of the risk-neutral measure using observed yields. Together with the historical dynamics, Piazzesi, Salomao, and Schneider (2013) can then compute estimates of the "statistical" risk premium. Finally, they estimate parameters of the subjective measure using survey forecasts. Together with the risk-neutral dynamics, they can then compute estimates of the subjective risk premium.

Piazzesi, Salomao, and Schneider (2013) find that the level and slope of the yield curve are less persistent under the subjective measure – estimated from surveys – than under the statistical model. Hence, the subjective risk premium is much less cyclical than the statistical premium. In the statistical models, a high level of yields and a high slope in the yield curve predict higher excess bond returns. Survey forecasters, who view the level and the slope as more persistent, predict lower excess bond returns. Overall, this reduces the volatility of subjective risk premia and lengthens the frequency of its variations.

Garcia and Luger (2012) also explore investors' perceived factor dynamics but in a framework with recursive utility and a time-varying subjective discount parameter.[17] They use VAR(1) dynamics for the state variables $Z_t = (y_t^{(1)}, y_t^{(20)} - y_t^{(1)}, r_t, \pi_t, c_t)'$), where the first two variables are the one-quarter and the 5-year spread, r_t is the log-return on the wealth portfolio, π_t the inflation rate and c_t the log-consumption growth. The Euler equation defines the logarithm of the nominal stochastic discount factor:

$$\log m_{t+1}^{\$} = -y_t^{(1)} + J' \mathcal{Z}_{t+1} \tag{14.38}$$

where $J = (0, 0, \gamma - 1, -1, \alpha - \gamma)'$. The parameters γ and α determine the coefficients of intertemporal substitution and risk aversion, respectively. Bond prices are parameterized as exponential linear functions of the state vector so that

$$P(t, n) = \exp\ (A(n) + B(n)' \mathcal{Z}_t) \tag{14.39}$$

with coefficients $A(n)$ and $B(n)$ determined by the backward recursions

$$\begin{aligned} A(n+1) &= A(n) + [J + B(n)]' \mu + \frac{1}{2} [J + B(n)]' \Sigma \Sigma' [J + B(n)] \\ B(n+1) &= \Phi' [J + B(n)] - e_1 \end{aligned} \tag{14.40}$$

and these also depend on the parameters of the VAR(1) dynamics (with $e_1' = (1, 0, 0, 0, 0)$).

Since the compensation for risk is driven by only two parameters, Garcia and Luger (2012) note that the observation equation for yields identifies all the parameters of the historical dynamics. Hence, they proceed to estimate all the parameters directly from market yields. The recovered dynamics must be consistent with the expectations of a representative investor with recursive utility who is pricing observed market yields.

Estimates of the preference parameters are economically plausible: the coefficient of relative risk aversion is around 6 and the elasticity of intertemporal substitution is around 0.36. The estimates for μ, Φ, and Σ correspond to the *historical* dynamics of Z_t. These produce bond yields and returns that match empirical stylized facts. In regressions of future excess returns on forward rates, as in Cochrane and Piazzesi (2005), the recursive utility model produces slope coefficients with the correct pattern across maturities, and the confidence intervals cover most of the coefficients estimated via direct OLS in market data. Furthermore, the hump-shaped pattern in the term structure of unconditional volatilities of yields and yield changes is apparent.

The perceived dynamics implicit in bond yields differ from the estimates obtained by an econometrician using the available data for Z_t. To illustrate this wedge, they transpose the autoregressive (AR) coefficients estimated directly from the bond yields but using the equilibrium model into a standard reduced-form no-arbitrage version of the model. This modified reduced-form model then becomes competitive with the recursive utility model in reproducing empirical stylized facts for bond returns, but it does not provide any improvement over the equilibrium approach, despite the fact that 30 prices of risk are estimated to fit bond yields.

14.3.4 Adaptive Learning and Survey Forecasts

One reading of the evidence – following Kim and Orphinides (2012), say – is that survey data should be used as additional information to estimate the dynamics of yield factors (as perceived by bond investors). An alternative reading, however, is that surveys do not offer a reliable basis to estimate the historical dynamics. But is it plausible that bond prices carry the same expectation "errors" as surveys? In a sense, this brings us back to our original conundrum.

[17] Following Obstfeld (1990), the subjective discount parameter is linked to the short-term rate and becomes a state variable in their framework.

One approach to this question is to consider that agents observe the relevant state variables, but that they are learning about unknown parameters. A first question to ask is whether the adaptive learning approach is able to replicate the expectations of professional forecasters in survey data. A recent paper by Markiewicz and Pick (2014) argues that learning models provide a good fit of survey forecasts for a range of macroeconomic and financial variables. They consider simple time-series autoregressive models to make predictions of the survey forecasts and update the parameters – generically $y_t = \theta_t' x_t + \varepsilon_t)$ – using recursive least squares, as follows:

$$\begin{aligned} \theta_t &= \theta_{t-1} + \gamma_t \mathbf{R}_t^{-1} x_t (y_t - \theta_{t-1}' x_t), t = 1, 2, \cdots, T, T+1 \\ \mathbf{R}_t &= \mathbf{R}_{t-1} + \gamma_t (x_t x_t' - \mathbf{R}_{t-1}) \end{aligned} \tag{14.41}$$

where θ_t is a $k \times 1$ vector of parameters and x_t is the $k \times 1$ vector of regressors, possibly including lags, and γ_t is the gain parameter. Decreasing gain learning uses $1/t$ and corresponds to standard OLS with a widening window. Constant-gain learning set γ to a constant that is estimated in a second step by minimizing the distance with survey forecasts. Markiewicz and Pick (2014) find that constant-gain learning provides a much closer fit to the survey forecasts of inflation, the 3-month bill rate and the 10-year bond yield.

A second question to ask is whether allowing for learning can rationalize the evidence against the expectations hypothesis based on predictability regressions of bond returns. Bulkley and Giordani (2011) provide one positive answer. They assume that the short-rate process is subject to repeated stochastic structural breaks, in which the break points are not observed but have to be inferred in real time from short-rate data. Agents must judge whether an interest rate surprise denotes a break and they must estimate new parameter values conditional on that inference. In this context, Bayesian learning induces changes in rational expectations – hence changes in long yields – that are consistent with the evidence recovered in Campbell–Shiller regressions. Their calibration is based on estimates from fitting a model of stochastic breaks to U.S. short rate data.

14.3.5 Equilibrium Models of the Term Structure

Duffee (2013) reviews several dynamic stochastic general equilibrium (DSGE) models that have been proposed to model the term structure of interest rates. He notes that expected bond returns appear countercyclical: the correlations between bond returns with consumption or industrial growth are negative. Therefore, the workhorse representative agent model with power utility cannot generate a positive average slope, since nominal bonds appear to be a hedge. Allowing for recursive preferences, and considering the case where the elasticity of intertemporal substitution is one, the real stochastic discount factor is given (in log) by

$$m_{t+1} = \log\ \beta - \Delta c_{t+1} - (\gamma - 1)\zeta_{t+1} - \frac{\gamma - 1^2}{2}\ Var_t(\zeta_{t+1}) \tag{14.42}$$

where β is the discount rate, Δc_{t+1} is the consumption growth, γ is the coefficient of risk aversion and ζ_{t+1} is the innovation to expectations of discounted consumption growth:

$$\zeta_{t+1} = (E_{t+1} - E_t) \sum_{i=1}^{\infty} \beta^i \Delta c_{t+1} \tag{14.43}$$

Nominal bond returns have negative covariance with consumption growth. Therefore, nominal bonds carry a negative risk premium in the benchmark case with power utility ($\gamma = 1$). With recursive utility, the covariance with innovation to future consumption growth also plays a role. For instance, if inflation shocks are positively correlated with lower expected consumption in the future (stagflation), bond returns may be risky if the positive covariance with future consumption growth is high enough. Based on a variety of statistical models estimated in different sample periods, Duffee (2013) concludes that there is not enough information in the estimated joint dynamics of consumption growth and inflation to support the stagflation interpretation of risk premia.

A recent line of research introduced extensions to existing equilibrium models with recursive utility. However, equilibrium models that include elements of learning also appear promising. It turns out that the dynamics of the pricing kernel can differ considerably from the dynamics of realized consumption, because of subjective beliefs. Collin-Dufresne, Johannes, and Lochstoer (2013) study a long-risk economy with recursive utility similar to Bansal and Yaron (2004).[18] They show that parameter learning strongly amplifies the impact of macro shocks on marginal utility when the representative agent has a preference for early resolution of uncertainty. This occurs as rational belief updating generates subjective long-run consumption risks. For instance, even

[18]Early examples where asset pricing implication are driven by learning in a general equilibrium model include Detemple (2011), Dothan and Feldman (1986).

a small update to the mean of consumption growth can have a large effect on the continuation utility, since the shock will affect the expected consumption growth far into the future. The authors derive the term structure in a setting with an intertemporal elasticity of substitution equal to 1. With similar parameter settings as in Bansal and Yaron (2004), they obtain a flat yield curve, which is quite different from the strongly downward-sloping curve obtained by Bansal and Yaron (2004). The difference derives from the fact that updates in beliefs are permanent, as opposed to the mean-reverting process assumed by Bansal and Yaron (2004) for mean consumption growth.

Looking beyond asset pricing, Del Negro and Eusepi (2011) investigate whether DSGE models estimated under rational expectations or models with learning about target inflation are a better fit with inflation forecasts from surveys. Ormeno (2009) also estimates learning models with data on inflation expectations extracted from surveys. Milani (2007) estimates a small-scale DSGE model with learning using only historical data on macroeconomic variables and not survey forecast data. He shows that adaptive learning enhances the propagation mechanism and reduces the scale of rational frictions and the persistence that they cause. Slobodyan and Wouters (2012) extend their work in a medium-scale DSGE model. Their results illustrate that learning models fit the data as well as, or better than, the rational-expectations model.[19]

14.4 LOWER BOUND

Currency yields no interest but coexists with interest-bearing bonds. The risk-free bond may be preferable as a store of value (it yields a higher return), but holding currency may nonetheless be desirable for its use as a medium of exchange. With no frictions, currency becomes a better store of value if the interest rate on the risk-free bond becomes negative, $r_t < 0$. In this case, investors should issue, sell or short the bond; hold currency; and expect a sure profit. This arbitrage keeps the interest rate above zero.

With transaction costs or short-selling frictions, bond yields remain bounded but not necessarily at zero, which explains the choice of title for this section. If holding currency is costly – banks charge a fee to store currency – then the bond could carry a negative yield. On the other hand, if holding the safe bond is costly – the money market mutual funds charge a fee – then the bond yield may be bounded above zero. The Federal Reserve banks and several other central banks refrained from pinning down their target rates to zero. More recently, the European Central Bank, the Swiss National Bank and others lowered their target rate below zero. In any case, the short rate can be written as

$$r_t = lb_t + r_t^* \tag{14.44}$$

where lb_t is the lower bound for the nominal short rate and r_t^* is a positive process. If lb_t is stochastic, it becomes one of the factors driving the observed short rate. In the following, we take $lb_t = 0$ for simplicity.

14.4.1 Square-Root and Autoregressive Gamma Models

Consider the standard affine specification of the short rate:

$$r_t = \delta_0 + \delta_1' x_t \tag{14.45}$$

where x_t includes K risk factors. For $\delta_0 \geq 0$ and $\delta_1 \geq 0$, the short rate remains positive whenever each risk factor remains positive. Cox, Ingersoll, and Ross (1985) introduced the continuous-time square-root process to the term structure literature. In this case, each $x_{i,t}$ for $i = 1, \cdots, K$ follows an independent square-root process:

$$dx_{i,t} = \kappa_i(\theta_i - x_{i,t}) + \sigma_i \sqrt{x_{i,t}} dW_{i,t} \tag{14.46}$$

with parameters κ_i, θ_i, and σ_i. This process is strictly positive when Feller's condition is satisfied: $\frac{2\kappa\theta}{\sigma^2} \geq 1$. Otherwise, zero is an absorbing state: the process may reach zero, but if it does it cannot leave zero.

The square-root process has a discrete-time counterpart: the autoregressive gamma (ARG) process. Let us detail how the ARG process is constructed. Its basic ingredients are the Poisson distribution $\mathcal{P}(\lambda)$ with intensity $\lambda > 0$ and the standard gamma distribution $\gamma(\nu)$ with shape $\nu > 0$. In the univariate case, following Gourieroux and Jasiak (2006) and Le, Singleton, and Dai (2010), the conditional distribution of $x_{i,t}$ is defined as a Poisson mixture of standard gamma distributions:

$$x_{i,t}|x_{i,t-1} \sim \gamma(\nu_i + W_i) \quad \text{where} \quad W_i \sim \mathcal{P}(\rho_i x_{i,t-1}/c_i) \tag{14.47}$$

[19]However, their findings are crucially dependent on the assumptions made about initial beliefs. The best models correspond to the case where initial beliefs are optimized to explain the in-sample data. In this case, the updating of beliefs through constant gain learning brings only a low estimated gain.

with parameter $c_i > 0$, $v_i > 0$ and $0 \leq \rho_i < 1$. The conditional mean of $x_{i,t}$ is autoregressive:

$$x_{i,t} = c_i v_i + \rho_i x_{i,t-1} + \sigma_{i,t} \varepsilon_{i,t} \tag{14.48}$$

where $\varepsilon_{i,t}$ has mean zero, $E_t[\varepsilon_{i,t}] = 0$ and with conditional variance given by

$$\sigma_{i,t}^2 = c_i^2 v_i + 2c_i \rho_i \quad x_{i,t-1} \tag{14.49}$$

The conditional Laplace transform of $x_{i,t}$ is exponential affine (see Gourieroux and Jasiak, 2006):

$$E_{t-1}[e^{ux_{i,t}} | x_{i,t-1}] = \exp\left(-v_i \ln\,(1 - c_i u) + \frac{u \rho_i x_{i,t-1}}{1 - c_i u} \right), u < 1/c_i \tag{14.50}$$

If $v > 1$, then the limit of 14.48 as the time interval Δt shrinks to zero is a square-root process. Conversely, when the continuous-time process satisfies Feller's condition, $\frac{2\kappa\theta}{\sigma^2} \geq 1$, then the distribution given by 14.46 when sampling at frequency Δt corresponds exactly to the distribution given by 14.50. The exact mapping between parameters is given by

$$\rho = e^{-\kappa \Delta t} \quad c = (1 - \rho)\frac{\sigma^2}{2\kappa} \quad v = \frac{2\kappa\theta}{\sigma^2} = (1 - \rho)\frac{\theta}{c} \tag{14.51}$$

which also makes clear the connection between the Feller condition and the discrete-time parameter v.

14.4.1.1 Reaching the Lower Bound If $v < 1$, then zero is an absorbing state for the continuous-time process. However, it should be clear from 14.47 that zero is not an absorbing state for the ARG process even if $v < 1$. In fact, as long as $v > 0$, this process never reaches zero. However, there is no equivalence with the continuous-time case when $v < 1$.

Monfort et al. (2014) build the ARG_0 process, allowing $x_{i,t}$ to reach zero, stay at zero for extended periods of time, and eventually leave zero. This is achieved by setting $v_i = 0$ but introducing a constant α_i in the intensity of the Poisson distribution (compare with Equation 14.47):

$$x_{i,t} | x_{i,t-1} \sim \gamma(W_i) \quad \text{where} \quad W_i \sim \mathcal{P}(\alpha_i + \rho_i' x_{i,t-1}/c_i) \tag{14.52}$$

for the multivariate case ($\rho_i > 0$ is a vector), recognizing that $\gamma(v)$ converges to the Dirac distribution when v reaches zero. Heuristically, the mixing variable W_i is zero with strictly positive probability, in which case the realization of $x_{i,t}$ is also zero (almost surely). The conditional Laplace transform of the ARG_0 process differs substantially from 14.50:

$$E_{t-1}[e^{ux_{i,t}} | x_{i,t-1}] = \exp\left(\frac{u(\alpha_i c + \rho_i' x_{i,t-1})}{1 - c_i u} \right), u < 1/c_i \tag{14.53}$$

The parameter α_i quantifies the average persistence of zero lower-bound regimes. First, the probability that $x_{i,t}$ reaches zero h periods from now is

$$P(x_{i,t} = 0 | x_{i,t-1}) = \exp\,(-h\alpha_i - \rho_i' x_{i,t-1}/c_i) \tag{14.54}$$

Second, denote $p = P(x_{i,t} = 0 | x_{i,t-1} = 0)$, the probability of staying at zero. Fixing $h = 1$ and $x_{i,t-1} = 0$, it follows that $p = e^{-\alpha_i}$. Of course, the probability of leaving zero is $P(x_{i,t} > 0 | x_{i,t-1} = 0) = 1 - p$. Third, the probability of leaving zero after $h - 1$ periods at zero is

$$P(x_{i,t} = 0, \cdots, x_{i,t+h-1} = 0, x_{i,t+h} > 0 | x_{i,t-1} = 0) = (1 - p)p^{h-1} \tag{14.55}$$

and, finally, the average sojourn time at zero if $x_{i,t} = 0$ is given by

$$\frac{1}{1 - p} = (1 - e^{-\alpha_i})^{-1} \tag{14.56}$$

14.4.1.2 Term Structure Models Monfort et al. (2014) mix ARG and ARG_0 processes to construct a new family of term structure models with positive interest rates where the short rate can stay at its lower bound for long periods of time. This is a significant step forward relative to the standard square-root or ARG cases. On the other hand, models based on ARG_0 processes retain some notable weaknesses: (i) it is hard to imagine using (possibly) negative macro variables extensively in this context; (ii) the correlation structure between risk factors is severely limited, since every correlation must be nonnegative; and (iii) the admissibility constraint gives rise to a tension in simultaneously fitting of the physical and risk-neutral yield forecasts (Joslin and Le, 2011).

The short-rate process is given by

$$r_t = \delta_1' x_t^{(1)} + \delta_2' x_t^{(2)} = \delta' x_t \tag{14.57}$$

where $x^{(1)}$ includes n_1 components and $x_t^{(2)}$ includes n_2 components (with $n = n_1 + n_2$) and with $x_t' = [x^{(1)'} \quad x^{(2)'}]$. The dynamics of each component $x_{i,t}$ under the historical probability measure $\mathbb{P}$ is characterized by its Laplace transform $\varphi_{i,t}(u) \equiv E_{t-1}[e^{ux_{i,t}} | x_{i,t-1}]$:

$$\varphi_{i,t}(u) = \exp\left(-v_i \ln\,(1 - c_i u) + \frac{u(\alpha_i c_i + \rho_i' x_{t-1})}{1 - c_i u}\right) \quad u < 1/c_i \tag{14.58}$$

while the asset pricing implications follow from the corresponding transform $\varphi_{i,t}^{\mathbb{Q}}(u)$ under the risk-neutral measure $\mathbb{Q}$:

$$\varphi_{i,t}^{\mathbb{Q}}(u) = \exp\left(-v_i \ln\,(1 - c_i^{\mathbb{Q}} u) + \frac{u(\alpha_i^{\mathbb{Q}} c_i^{\mathbb{Q}} + \rho_i^{\mathbb{Q}'} x_{t-1})}{1 - c_i^{\mathbb{Q}} u}\right) \quad u < 1/c_i \tag{14.59}$$

which is similar to the multivariate extension of the ARG process in Le, Singleton, and Dai (2010). The novel feature is the parameter α_i and the allowance for $v_i \geq 0$. In addition to $c_i > 0$ and $\rho > 0$ (element by element), their family of models has that

1. $0 <, \rho_{ii}^{\mathbb{P}}, \rho_{ii}^{\mathbb{Q}} < 1, i = 1, \cdots, n$
2. $c_i^{\mathbb{Q}} = 1, i = 1, \cdots, n$
3. $v_i^{\mathbb{P}} = v_i^{\mathbb{Q}} = 0, i = 1, \cdots, n_1$
4. $\delta_i^{(2)} = 0, i = 1, \cdots, n_2$

Assumption 1 implies that x_t is stationary. Assumption 2 is required for identification. More importantly, Assumptions 3 imply that the first n_1 factors are ARG_0 processes. Note that the absence of arbitrage requires that v_i cannot be zero under the historical measure and different from zero under the risk-neutral measure.[20] Assumption 4 implies that the short rate is driven by the $n_1 ARG_0$ factors. Together, these two assumptions imply that the short rate has a probability mass at zero.

Under Assumptions 1–4, the solution for bond prices $P_t^{(n)}$ is exponential affine $P_t^{(n)} = \exp\,(A_n + B_n' \mathcal{E}_t)$, as in the previous section, but with coefficients given by

$$\begin{aligned} B_{n+1} &= -\delta + \rho^{\mathbb{Q}'}\left(\frac{B_n \odot \iota}{1 - A_n \odot \iota}\right) \\ A_{n+1} &= A_n + \alpha^{\mathbb{Q}'}\left(\frac{B_n \odot \iota}{1 - A_n \odot \iota}\right) - v' \log\,(1 - A_n \odot \iota) \end{aligned} \tag{14.60}$$

where, following Monfort et al. (2014), $\odot$ denotes the Hadamard product, while the division and log operators apply to the vector element by element (see Proposition 3.2 in Monfort et al. (2014) for closed-form expressions for bond prices).

14.4.2 Black (1995) – Tobin (1958)

Black (1995) builds on the observation that money provides an option to the bondholder: the bondholder can choose to hold money if the bond yield becomes negative. From a pure time-series perspective, this problem corresponds to an environment with censored observations: a "shadow" short-rate process may become negative, but the corresponding observations are censored

[20] The probability measures must be equivalent.

(Tobin, 1958). Economically, the short rate corresponds to the combination of a (possibly negative) shadow rate s_t and the currency option:

$$r_t = \max(0, \delta_0 + \delta' x_t) \tag{14.61}$$

where the shadow rate is linear $s_t = \delta_0 + \delta' x_t$. An important perceived advantage is that x_t can have Gaussian dynamics. As Dai and Singleton (2002) show, Gaussian models provide a better fit for the risk premium than models with square-root (i.e., ARG) dynamics when interest rates are far from zero. Arguably, the gains in fitting bond excess returns were considered worth the small probability that yields became negative when the short rate was far from zero. This trade-off is no longer palatable: a Gaussian short rate near zero has nearly 50% of its probability mass below zero.

It was long thought that asset pricing implications could be hard to derive with a max function for the short-rate process. Specifically, even if the risk factor dynamics are tractable,

$$\Delta x_t = K_0^{\mathbb{Q}} + K_1^{\mathbb{Q}} x_{t-1} + \Sigma \varepsilon_t^{\mathbb{Q}} \quad \varepsilon_t^{\mathbb{Q}} \sim N(0, I) \tag{14.62}$$

the computation of bond yields via the Laplace transform,

$$B_t^{(n)} = E_t^{\mathbb{Q}} \left[\exp \left(-\sum_{i=0}^{n} \max(0, s_{t+i}) \right) \right] \tag{14.63}$$

is no longer available. Ichiue and Ueno (2007) and Kim and Singleton (2012) compute the integral (the expectation) via a discretization scheme. Alternatively, Bauer and Rudebusch (2013) proceed via Monte Carlo simulations. Krippner (2013) provides a broader survey of these numerical approaches.

In the following, we detail a second-order approximation based on the series expansion of 14.63 :

$$B_t^{(n)} \approx 1 - E_t^{\mathbb{Q}} \left[\sum_{i=0}^{n} r_{t+i} \right] + \frac{1}{2} E_t^{\mathbb{Q}} \left[(\sum_{i=0}^{n} r_{t+i})^2 \right] \tag{14.64}$$

Priebsch (2013), in continuous time, and Wu and Xia (2013), in discrete time, follow a similar route based on the series expansion of log $B_t^{(n)}$. We follow a different route to exploit the recursive structure of a discrete-time model. Krippner (2012) introduces an alternative to the representation of 14.63 using the price of a call option. This approximation appears to be slightly less accurate in practice.

Rearranging, we obtain the following recursion for bond prices:

$$\begin{aligned} B_t^{(n+1)} = B_t^{(n)} - E_t^{\mathbb{Q}} \left[\max(0, s_{t+n}) \right] + E_t^{\mathbb{Q}} [\max(0, s_{t+n})^2] \\ + \sum_{i=0}^{n-1} E_t^{\mathbb{Q}} [\max(0, s_{t+i}) \max(0, s_{t+n})] \end{aligned} \tag{14.65}$$

for $n = 1, 2, \cdots,$, with $B_t^{(0)} = 0$. To compute bond prices, each term in 14.65 can be computed explicitly using moments of a truncated bivariate normal distribution (Priebsch, 2013; Rosenbaum, 1961). Note that

$$\begin{pmatrix} s_{t+i} \\ s_{t+n} \end{pmatrix} | x_t \sim N^{\mathbb{Q}} \left[\begin{pmatrix} \mu_{i|t} \\ \mu_{n|t} \end{pmatrix}, \begin{pmatrix} \sigma_{i|t}^2 & \sigma_{i,n|t} \\ \sigma_{i,n|t} & \sigma_{n|t}^2 \end{pmatrix} \right] \quad 0 \leq i < n \tag{14.66}$$

where the mean and covariance terms are once again given by straightforward recursions:

$$\begin{aligned} \mu_{i+1|t} &= \mu_{i|t} + \delta'(I + K_1^{\mathbb{Q}})^i (K_0^{\mathbb{Q}} + K_1^{\mathbb{Q}} X_t) \\ \sigma_{i+1|t}^2 &= \sigma_{i|t}^2 + \delta'(I + K_1^{\mathbb{Q}})^i \Sigma\Sigma' (I + K_1^{\mathbb{Q}})^{i'} \delta \\ \sigma_{i+1,n|t} &= \sigma_{i,n|t} + \delta'(I + K_1^{\mathbb{Q}}) \Sigma\Sigma' (I + K_1^{\mathbb{Q}})^{n-1-i'} \delta \end{aligned} \tag{14.67}$$

for $n = 1, 2, \cdots$. The initial conditions are $\mu_{0|t} = \delta_0 + \delta' x_t$, $\sigma^2_{0|t} = 0$ and $\sigma_{0,n|t} = 0$. Then, the bond prices in 14.65 are given explicitly in terms $\mu_{i+1|t}$, $\sigma^2_{i+1|t}$, and $\sigma_{i+1,n|t}$ and in terms of the Gaussian cumulative and probability distribution functions (see Appendix at the end of the chapter).

This approximation is exact if r_{t+i} is Gaussian (i.e., if $r_{t+i} = \delta_0 + \delta' x_{t+i}$), but higher-order terms come into play once we introduce the max function. Nonetheless, simulation evidence suggests that these terms are small when x_{t+i} is Gaussian (Priebsch, 2013; Wu and Xia, 2013). On the other hand, if x_{t+i} is not Gaussian, the computation of the truncated moments becomes intractable *and* the higher-order terms may not be negligible.

14.4.3 No-Dominance Term Structure Models

The limitations and challenges of no-arbitrage models arise because of the desire for tractability and the difficulty of computing expectations, for example, in 14.63. Exploiting the first fundamental theorem of asset pricing is a powerful tool to guarantee the absence of arbitrage among a set of model prices. Nonetheless, the requirement that yields remains positive limits the choice of dynamic specifications for which we can obtain analytical solutions. Of course, simulation is an acceptable way to compute 14.63, but the benefits of closed forms are unambiguous.

Feunou, Fontaine, and Le (2014) circumvent the computation of expectations and the need to specify the risk-neutral measure $\mathbb{Q}$ for bond pricing. Instead, they directly specify bond prices in terms of primitive functionals:

$$B_t^{(n)} \equiv 1 \tag{14.68}$$

$$B_t^{(n)} = B_t^{(n)}(g(X_t)) \times \exp\,(-m(X_t)) \tag{14.69}$$

for arbitrary functions $m(\cdot)$ and $g(\cdot)$ such that $g(x_t) \in X$ for every $x_t \in X$ the support of the risk factors. They show that bond prices given by Equations 14.68 and 14.69 are free of dominant trading strategies. A dominant trading strategy exists if a zero-cost portfolio has strictly positive payoffs. This portfolio's price,

$$\sum_n w_n B_t^{(n)} = \exp\,(-m(x_t)) \times \sum_n w_n B_t^{(n)}(g(x_t)) \tag{14.70}$$

is strictly positive since its payoff is strictly positive ($g(x_t) \in X$), hence forbidding dominant strategies. No-dominance still allows for zero-cost portfolios that have zero or positive payoffs. These are knife-edge arbitrage opportunities that, arguably, should be disregarded at *some* level of transaction costs. In fact, Feunou, Fontaine, and Le (2014) show that these arbitrage opportunities are precluded in the model as soon as transactions are not zero, either in establishing or selling the portfolio.

14.4.3.1 Example 1: Affine Short-Rate and Nelson–Siegel models From 14.69, we have that $B_t^{(1)} = \exp\,(-m(x_t))$, implying that $r_t = m(x_t)$. For instance, the choice of $m(x_t) = \delta_0 + \delta' x_t$ and $g(x_t) = K x_t$ leads to the following bond yields:

$$y_t^{(n)} = \delta_0 + (b_n/n) x_t \tag{14.71}$$

with b_n given by the recursion:

$$b_n = b_{n-1} K + \delta' \tag{14.72}$$

with $b_0 = 0$. The risk-factor loadings in 14.72 are identical to the results for the canonical term structure models in Joslin, Singleton, and Zhu (2011). However, the constant in the no-arbitrage model,

$$a_n = a_{n-1} + \delta_0 - \frac{1}{2} b_{n-1} \Sigma b'_{n-1} \tag{14.73}$$

differs from the constant in the no-dominance specification, due to the (small) Jensen's term. Indeed, Feunou, Fontaine, and Le (2014) show that three-factor affine no-dominance and no-arbitrage models exhibit no visible pricing differences. Interestingly, restricting the matrix K as in Christensen, Diebold, and Rudebusch (2011) produces the Nelson–Siegel (NS) loadings. In fact, the continuous-time limit corresponds squarely to the adaptation by Diebold and Li (2006) of the static NS model. Therefore, the fact that no-dominance and no-arbitrage models affine models can hardly be distinguished empirically is consistent with a large body of evidence showing the empirical success of NS-based models. Conversely, the results in Feunou, Fontaine, and Le (2014) provide a theoretical justification based on no-dominance of the empirical success of dynamic NS models.

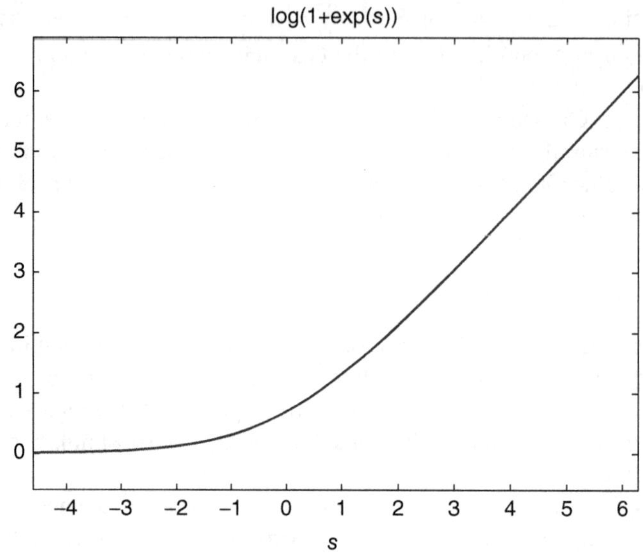

Figure 14.11 Logistic transformation of the short rate.

14.4.3.2 Example 2: Positive Short Rate It is easy to see that any choice of functionals with $m(\cdot) > 0$ guarantees that yields are positive. Feunou, Fontaine, and Le (2014) advocate choosing specifications such that the one-period bond is nondecreasing on the $[0, 1]$ interval to guarantee positive forward rates. The logistic transformation is a natural choice: $B_t^{(1)} = 1/(1 + e^{s_t})$, implying that $r_t = \log\ (1 + e^{s_t})$ is always positive. The logistic function captures the effect that the max function applied to the instantaneous rate in Black (1995) has on longer-maturity yields. Figure 14.11 shows the one-period bond yields as a function of s_t. This is analogous to the difference between an option-like payoff, which exhibits a kink, and its price one-period ahead, which is smooth. Building on this intuition, Feunou, Fontaine, and Le (2014) use a linear specification for $g(x)$ and a minor generalization to the logistic function for $m(x)$:

$$\begin{aligned} g(x) &= Kx \\ m(x) &= \theta_t \log\ (1 + \exp\ ((\delta_0 + \delta_1' x)/\theta_t) \end{aligned} \tag{14.74}$$

where θ_t is given in terms of the macro variables $\mathcal{M}_{t-1}$:

$$\theta_t = \theta_0 + \theta_1' \mathcal{M}_{t-1} \tag{14.75}$$

and controls how quickly the transformation affects the observed short rate r_t as the shadow rate s approaches its lower bound. The short rate in 14.74 can be inverted, and therefore, the shadow rate $s = \delta_0 + \delta_1' x$ can be inverted from a suitable number of forward rate portfolios: estimation can proceed very quickly without the need for a cumbersome filtering step. No-dominance term structure models allow for flexible time-series specifications. There is no restriction either on the choice of functions $m(\cdot)$ or $g(\cdot)$, except for $g(x) \in \mathrm{X}$(and technical conditions for the purpose of estimation).

14.4.4 Recent Empirical Results

Feunou, Fontaine, and Le (2014) perform an early implementation of a truncated, or Black's, version of the benchmark Gaussian DTSM (B-DTSM) to Japanese data in their case. They find that a two-factor B-DTSM provides a good fit of the yield cross section between 1996 and 2006. Kim and Singleton (2012) also study Japanese yield data and compare two-factor DTSMs with the affine and quadratic short rate and Black's version of these models, where the shadow rate is either affine or quadratic. Their results favor B-DTSMs. Empirical work has turned its attention to the United States, where the short rate reached its lower bound at the end of 2008. Most of this work focuses on variants of the B-DTSMs. While some of these results are still preliminary, the results suggest the following empirical regularities.

First, there is ample evidence that $\hat{s}_t$ has different properties – level, persistence, and shocks – depending on the model specification. Hence, estimates of the shadow rate $\hat{s}_t$ may provide a misleading measure of the stance of monetary policy. There seems to be a consensus to use model implications that are more directly tied to observable variables. For instance, Bauer and Rudebusch (2013) advocate computing the *modal path* of the future policy rate and, in particular, calculating the time until the modal path crosses the lower bound as a measure of monetary stance.

Second, incorporating the lower bound is sufficient to capture (i) changes in yield volatilities across the term structure, (ii) changes in correlation between yields, and (iii) dampening of the risk premium when the short rate has reached its lower bound. This can be seen from estimation results for the following specification (see Feunou, Fontaine, and Le (2014) for details). First, bond prices are given by Equations 14.69 and 14.74. Second, the risk factor $\mathcal{P}$ has autoregressive dynamics,

$$\mathcal{P}_{t+1} = K_0^{\mathbb{P}} + K_1^{\mathbb{P}}\mathcal{P}_t + \sqrt{\Sigma_t}\varepsilon_{t+1} \tag{14.76}$$

Third, risk factors' innovations have a dynamic conditional correlation (DCC) specification, as in Engle (2002), to capture the time-varying variances and correlations across yields. Formally, the covariance matrix is given by

$$\Sigma_t = D_t C_t D_t \tag{14.77}$$

where $D_t = \text{diag}(\sigma_{1,t}, \cdots, \sigma_{K,t})$ is a diagonal matrix containing the conditional volatility of each risk factor and C_t is the conditional correlation matrix. Each element of D_t follows an EGARCH(1, 1):

$$\log\,\sigma_{k,t}^2 = \omega_k + \beta_k \log\,\sigma_{k,t-1}^2 + \alpha_k Z_{k,t} + \kappa_k(|Z_{k,t}| - E[|Z_{k,t}|]) \tag{14.78}$$

where $Z_{k,t} = \varepsilon_{k,t}/\sigma_{k,t}$ is the standardized innovation in the kth risk factor. The conditional volatility exhibits a "leverage" effect whenever $\kappa \neq 0$: the conditional volatility is then correlated with the level of the risk factor. The correlation matrix C_t is defined via the autoregressive matrix Q_t:

$$Q_t = (1 - a - b)\overline{Q} + a(Z_t Z_t') + bQ_{t-1} \tag{14.79}$$

which is a symmetric positive definite matrix if $a > 0$, $b > 0$, and $a + b < 1$ and $\overline{Q}$ is symmetric positive definite. The following standardization yields the correlation matrix:

$$C_t = Q_t./\left(\text{diag}\left[Q_t\right]^{-1/2} \otimes \text{diag}[Q_t]^{-1/2}\right) \tag{14.80}$$

where ./ is the element-by-element division of the matrix, $\otimes$ is the Kronecker product, and $\text{diag}[Q_t]$ is the vector whose elements are the main diagonal of Q_t. Needless to say, the EGARCH, leverage, and conditional correlations cannot be integrated within affine no-arbitrage term structure models.

Panel A of Figure 14.12 compares the conditional volatility of the 2-year yield from a range of no-dominance models. Panel A reports the conditional volatility for three models where the covariance is kept constant: one *affine* model, one *nonaffine* constant (C) model where the θ parameter is constant, and one *nonaffine* time-varying (TV) model where the θ_t parameter is time varying. The conditional volatility of the 5-year yield measured from the univariate EGARCH is higher in periods when the short rate is decreasing: toward the end of the easing cycle in 1991, early in 1995, in 2001, and in 2007–2008. The volatility is constant and close to 22% annually in the *affine* model.

The *nonaffine* models can only produce a lower volatility when yields are sufficiently close to the lower bounds. In particular, the model volatilities are very close to the EGARCH volatilities after 2008, when the short rate reaches its lower bound in the United States. By design, these models do not produce time-varying volatilities from the lower bounds and cannot match the EGARCH evidence.

Panel B of Figure 14.12 provides the same comparison for models with DCC. What is key for our discussion is that (i) the affine model with DCC cannot match the conditional volatility of the 2-year yield after 2008 and that (ii) adding more complicated dynamics does not change the volatilities in the nonaffine model after 2008. We conclude that the compression due to the lower bound is the dominant feature of the recent sample, and it is sufficient to capture the compressed volatility since 2009.

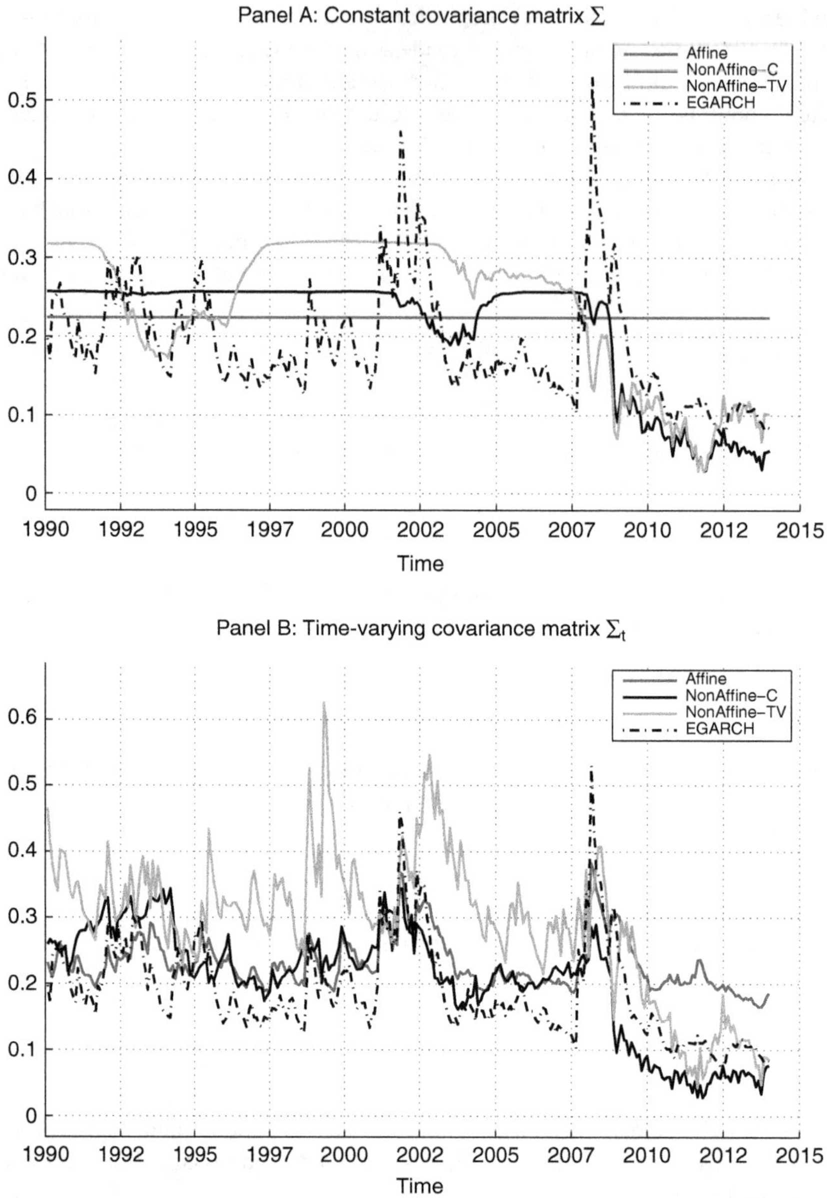

Figure 14.12 Conditional volatility of the 2-year yield. Conditional volatility of the 2-year yield from an unrestricted EGARCH and from no-dominance models without EGARCH or DCC in the risk factor innovations (Panel A) and from no-dominance models with EGARCH and DCC (Panel B). *Affine* is a no-dominance affine specification, *nonaffine*-C is a specification enforcing the lower bound but with constant θ parameters, *nonaffine*-TV is a specification enforcing the lower bound with time-varying θ_t parameters. U.S. monthly data 1990–2014. Source: CRSP and Federal Reserve Board.

This result extends to the correlation between yields. We expect the correlation structure between yields to tighten due to the lower bound. Figure 14.13 compares the share of the conditional variance of all yields explained by the first principal component (where the principal component is computed using the full sample). Panel A reports the results for models where the covariance of innovations is constant. The share of variance explained by the first component is constant in the *affine* model, close to 90%. Again, the nonaffine models can only increase this share when yields are close enough to the lower bound. In particular, the share of variance explained remains close to 95% in the period following 2008.

Panel B reports results for models where the covariance of innovations is time varying. The conclusions reached from Figure 14.12 remain: (i) the share is much lower after 2008 in the *affine* model even allowing for DCC and (ii) allowing for DCC does not change the share of variance explained by the first component in the *nonaffine* model. We conclude that the compression due to the lower bound is the dominant feature of the recent sample, and it is sufficient to capture the increased correlation since 2009.

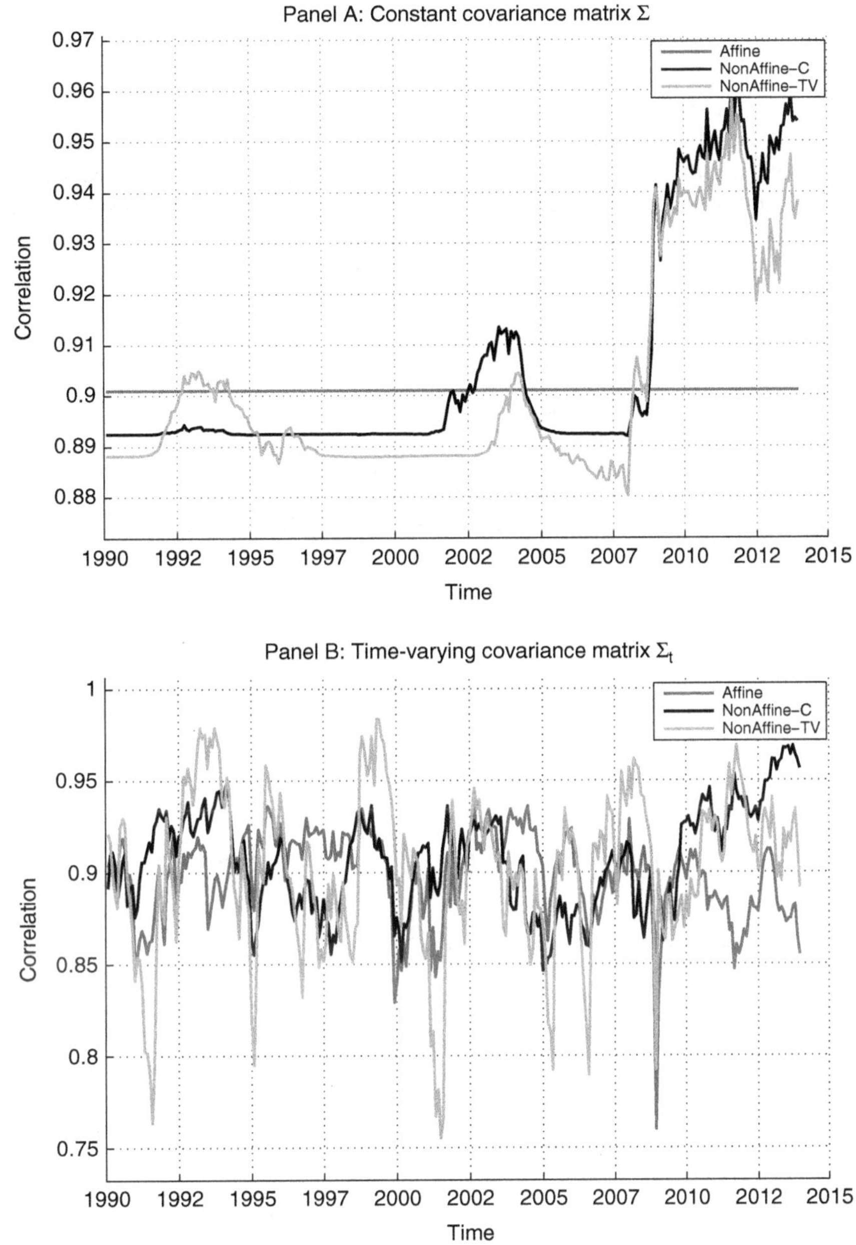

Figure 14.13 Variance share of the first principal component. Share of yield conditional variance explained by the first principal component extracted from the full sample from no-dominance models without EGARCH or DCC in the risk factors' innovations (Panel A) and from no-dominance models with EGARCH and DCC (Panel B). *Affine* is a no-dominance affine specification, *nonaffine*-C is a specification enforcing the lower bound but with constant θ parameters, *nonaffine*-TV is a specification enforcing the lower bound with time-varying θ_t parameters. U.S. monthly data 1990–2014. Source: CRSP and Federal Reserve Board.

14.5 CONCLUSION

We have reviewed three old topics that once were pervasive in macrofinance fixed-income research: liquidity, learning, and the lower bound. The dispersion of bond prices, funding risk, and short-selling pressures predict the risk premia across fixed-income markets such as Treasury, LIBOR, swap, agency, and corporate bond markets. Since most empirical studies of term structure models were conducted with smoothed zero-coupon bond yields, these liquidity premia were obscured. Therefore, going back to coupon bond prices brings important information but entails some loss of model tractability.

Information from surveys on forecasts by economic agents and professionals plays an important role in explaining expected returns. Expectational errors explain part of the statistical bond premia and may be interpreted as waves of optimism or pessimism that make agents depart from their rational expectations. The role played by expectation shocks has not been fully explored and is a promising area for future research. Both the magnitude and the dynamics of bond premia otherwise obtained in no-arbitrage or equilibrium models with rational expectations will likely be affected in a substantial way.

Estimation of term structure models over the past 50 years or so faces with a serious empirical challenge, with very high rates in the beginning of the eighties and rates close to zero in the recent period. The evidence so far suggests that any model imposing a lower bound on yields can capture the compression in volatility and the increased correlations when yields are close to the bound. On the other, matching the bond risk premium and volatility when yields are away from their bound remains a challenge for most implementation. Progress has been made, but the work has just begun. In sum, the return to the forefront of old topics in fixed-income research has produced a stimulating agenda, which holds promise for continued rapid advancement in the future.

ACKNOWLEDGMENTS

We thank Bruno Feunou for several helpful discussions, we thank Pietro Veronesi, Florian Pelgrin, Jean-Paul Rennes, and Francisco Rivadeneyra Sanchez for comments on earlier drafts of this chapter, and we thank Glen Gleeleyside for editorial assistance.

14.6 APPENDIX: MOMENTS OF TRUNCATED BIVARIATE DISTRIBUTION

As in the text, define

$$\begin{aligned} \mu_{i|t} &= E_t^{\mathbb{Q}}[s_{t+i}] \\ \sigma_{i|t}^2 &= Var_t^{\mathbb{Q}}[s_{t+i}] \\ \sigma_{i,n|t} &= Cov_t^{\mathbb{Q}}(s_{t+i}, s_{t+n}) \end{aligned} \tag{14.81}$$

so that

$$\begin{pmatrix} s_{t+i} \\ s_{t+n} \end{pmatrix} |X_t \sim N^{\mathbb{Q}} \left[\begin{pmatrix} \mu_{i|t} \\ \mu_{n|t} \end{pmatrix}, \begin{pmatrix} \sigma_{i|t}^2 & \sigma_{i,n|t} \\ \sigma_{i,n|t} & \sigma_{n|t}^2 \end{pmatrix} \right] \quad 0 \le i \le n \tag{14.82}$$

for $n = 1, 2, \cdots$. The first two moments of the truncated distribution are given by

$$E_t[\max(0, s_{t+i})] = \mu_{i|t}\Phi(\hat{\mu}_{i|t}) + \sigma_{i|t}\phi(\hat{\mu}_{i|t}) \tag{14.83}$$

and

$$\begin{aligned} E_t[\max(0, s_{t+i})\max(0, s_{t+n})] &= \left(\mu_{i|t}\mu_{n|t} + \sigma_{i,n|t}\right)\Phi_2^d\left(\hat{\mu}_{i|t}, \hat{\mu}_{n|t}; \rho_{i,n|t}\right) \\ &+ \sigma_{n|t}\mu_{i|t}\phi(\hat{\mu}_{n|t})\Phi\left(\frac{\hat{\mu}_{n|t} - \hat{\mu}_{t+i|t}\rho_{i,n|t}}{\sqrt{1-\rho_{i,n|t}^2}}\right) \\ &+ \sigma_{i|t}\mu_{n|t}\phi(\hat{\mu}_{i|t})\Phi\left(\frac{\hat{\mu}_{i|t} - \hat{\mu}_{t+n|t}\rho_{i,n|t}}{\sqrt{1-\rho_{i,n|t}^2}}\right) \\ &+ \sigma_{1|t}\sigma_{n|t}\sqrt{\frac{1-\rho_{i,n|t}^2}{2\pi}}\phi\left(\sqrt{\frac{\hat{\mu}_{i|t}^2 - 2\rho_{i,n|t}\hat{\mu}_{i|t}\hat{\mu}_{n|t} + \hat{\mu}_{n|t}^2}{1-\rho_{i,n|t}^2}}\right) \end{aligned} \tag{14.84}$$

where we defined $\hat{\mu}_{i|t} \equiv \mu_{i|t}/\sigma_{i,n|t}$ and $\rho_{i,n|t} \equiv \frac{\sigma_{i,n|t}}{\sigma_{i|t}\sigma_{n|t}}$, where $\Phi(\cdot)$ is the normal cumulative distribution function and $\phi(\cdot)$ is the normal probability distribution function, and where

$$\Phi_2^d(z_1, z_2; \rho) = 1 - \Phi(z_1) - \Phi(z_2) + \Phi_2(z_1, z_2; \rho) \tag{14.85}$$

with $\Phi_2(z_1, z_2; \rho)$ the bivariate normal cumulative distribution function. The proof follows directly from Lemmas A.1 and A.2 in Appendix A.2 of Priebsch (2013).

REFERENCES

Adrian T, Shin H. Liquidity and leverage. Staff Report 361. Federal Reserve Bank of New York; 2008.

Amihud Y, Mendelson H. Liquidity, maturity and the yields on U.S. Treasury securities. J Finance 1991;46(4):1411–1425.

Bacchetta P, Mertens E, van Wincoop E. Predictability in financial markets: what do survey expectations tell us? J Int Money Finance 2009;28(3):406–426.

Banerjee S, Graveline JJ. The cost of short-selling liquid securities. J Finance 2013;68(2):1540–6261.

Bansal R, Yaron A. Risks for the long run: a potential resolution of asset pricing puzzles. J Finance 2004;59(4):1481–1509.

Bartolini L, Hilton S, Sundaresan S, Tonetti C. Collateral values by asset class: evidence from primary security dealers. Rev Financ Stud 2011;24(1):248–278.

Bauer MD, Rudebusch GD. Monetary Policy Expectations at the Zero Lower Bound, Working paper, Federal Reserve Bank of San Francisco; 2013.

Black F. Interest rates as options. J Finance 1995;50(5):1371–1376.

Bliss R. Testing term structure estimation methods. Adv Futures Opt Res 1997;9:197–231.

Bulkley G, Giordani P. Structural breaks, parameter uncertainty, and term structure puzzles. J Financ Econ 2011;102(1):222–232.

Buraschi A, Menini D. Liquidity risk and specialness. J Financ Econ 2002;64(2):243–284.

Campbell J, Shiller R. Yield spreads and interest rate movements: a bird's eye view. Rev Econ Stud 1991;58:495–514.

Chen X, Sun Z, Yao T, Yu T. In Search of Habitat, Working paper; 2014.

Cheria J, Jacquier E, Jarrow R. A model of the convenience yields in on-the-run Treasuries. Rev Deriv Res 2004;7:79–97.

Chernov M, Mueller P. The term structure of inflation expectations. J Financ Econ 2011;106(2):367–394.

Christensen J, Diebold F, Rudebusch G. The affine arbitrage-free class of Nelson-Siegel term structure models. J Econom 2011;164(1):4–20.

Chun AL. Expectations, bond yields, and monetary policy. Rev Financ Stud 2011;24(1):208–247.

Cieslak A, Povala P. Expecting the Fed, Working paper. Northwestern University; 2013.

Cochrane J, Piazzesi M. Bond risk premia. Am Econ Rev 2005;95(1):138–160.

Coibion O, Gorodnichenko Y. What can survey forecasts tell us about information rigidities? J Polit Econ 2012;120(1):116–159.

Collin-Dufresne P, Johannes M, Lochstoer L. Parameter Learning in General Equilibrium: The Asset Pricing Implications, Working paper. Columbia Business School; 2013.

Cornell B, Shapiro AC. The mispricing of US treasury bonds: a case study. Rev Financ Stud 1989;2(3):297–310.

Cox J, Ingersoll J, Ross S. An intertemporal general equilibrium model of asset prices. Econometrica 1985;53(2):363–384.

Culbertson JM. The term structure of interest rates. Q J Econ 1957;71(4):485–517.

Dai Q, Singleton K. Specification analysis of affine term structure models. J Finance 2000;55(5):1943–1978.

Dai Q, Singleton K. Expectation puzzles, time-varying risk premia and affine model of the term structure. J Financ Econ 2002;63(3):415–441.

Dai Q, Singleton K. Fixed income pricing. In: Constantinides C, Harris M, Stulz R, editors. *Handbook of Economics and Finance*. Chapter 20. North Holland; 2003. p 1207–1246.

Del Negro M, Eusepi S. Fitting observed inflation expectations. J Econ Dyn Control 2011;35(12):2105–2131. Detemple JB. Asset pricing in a production economy with incomplete information. J Finance 1986;41(2):383–391.

Diebold F, Li C. Forecasting the term structure of government bond yields. J Econ Dyn Control 2006;130(2):337–364.

Dothan MU, Feldman D. Equilibrium interest rates and multiperiod bonds in a partially observable economy. J Finance 1986;41(2):369–382.

Duarte J. The causal effect of mortgage refinancing on interest rate volatility: empirical evidence and theoretical implications. Rev Financ Stud 2008;21(4):1689–1731.

Duffee G. Idiosyncratic variation of treasury bill yields. J Finance 1996;51(2):527–551.

Duffee G. Term premia and interest rate forecasts in affine model. J Finance 2002;57:405–443.

Duffee G. Bond pricing and the macroeconomy. In: *Handbook of Economics and Finance*. Chapter 13. Elsevier; 2013. p 907–967.

Duffie D. Special repo rates. J Finance 1996;51(2):493–526.

Duffie D, Kan R. A yield-factor model of interest rates. Math Finance 1996;6(4):379–406.

Engle R. Dynamic conditional correlation - a simple class of multivariate GARCH models. J Bus Econ Stat 2002;17(3):339–350.

Fama E, Bliss R. The information in long-maturity forward rates. Am Econ Rev 1987;77(4):680–692.

Fernald JD, Keane F, Mosser PC. Mortgage security hedging and the yield curve. Q Rev Fed Reserve Bank N Y 1994;19:92–100.

Feunou B, Fontaine J-S. Non-Markov Gaussian term structure models: the case of inflation. Rev Finance 2014;18(5):1953–2001.

Feunou B, Fontaine J-S, Le A. Term Structure Modeling when Monetary Policy is Unconventional, Working paper. Bank of Canada; 2014.

Fontaine J-S, Garcia R. Bond liquidity premia. Rev Financ Stud 2012;25(4):1207–1254.

Fontaine J-S, Garcia R, Gungor S. Funding Liquidity, Market Liquidity, and the Cross-section of Stock Returns, Working paper. Bank of Canada; 2015.

Friedman BM. Survey evidence on the rationality of interest rate expectations. J Monet Econ 1980;6(4):453–465.

Froot KA. New hope for the expectations hypothesis of the term structure of interest rates. J Finance 1989;44(2):283–305.

Gabaix X, Krishnamurthy A, Vigneron O. Limits of arbitrage: theory and evidence from the mortgage-backed securities market. J Finance 2007;62(2):557–595.

Garbade K. Analyzing the Structure of Treasury Yields: Duration, Coupon and Liquidity Effects, Topics in Money and Securities Markets. Bankers Trust Co.; 1984.

Garbade K, Silber WL. Price dispersion in the government securities market. J Polit Econ 1976;84(4):721–740.

Garcia R, Luger R. Risk aversion, intertemporal substitution, and the term structure of interest rates. J Appl Econom 2012;27(6):1013–1036.

Gourieroux C, Jasiak J. Autoregressive gamma process. J Forecast 2006;25(2):129–152.

Gourinchas P-O, Tornell A. Exchange rate puzzles and distorted beliefs. J Int Econ 2004;64(2):303–333.

Graveline J, McBrady MR. Who makes on-the-run treasuries special? J Financ Intermed 2011;20(4):620–632.

Greenwood R, Vayanos D. Bond supply and excess bond returns. Rev Financ Stud 2014;27(3):663–713.

Guibaud S, Nosbusch Y, Vayanos D. Bond market clienteles, the yield curve, and the optimal maturity structure of government debt. Rev Financ Stud 2013;26(8):1914–1961.

Gürkaynak R, Sack B, Wright J. The U.S. Treasury Curve: 1961 to the Present, Working paper 2006-28. Federal Reserve Board; 2006.

Gürkaynak R, Wright JH. Macroeconomics and the term structure. J Econ Lit 2012;50(2):331–367.

Hanson S. Mortgage convexity. J Financ Econ 2014;113(2):270–299.

Ichiue H, Ueno Y. Equilibrium Interest Rates and the Yield Curve in a Low Interest Rate Environment, Working Paper 2007-E-18. Bank of Japan; 2007.

Jegadeesh N. Treasury auction bids and the salomon squeeze. J Finance 1993;48(4):1403–1419.

Jongen R, Verschoor W, Wolff C. Time Variation in Term Premia: International Evidence, Discussion paper. CEPR; 2005.

Jordan B, Jordan S. Special repo rates: an empirical analysis. J Finance 1997;52(5):2051–2072.

Joslin S, Le A. Interest Rate Volatility and No-Arbitrage Affine Term Structure Models, Working paper. Kenan-Flagler Business School; 2011.

Joslin S, Priebsch M, Singleton KJ. Risk premiums in dynamic term structure models with unspanned macro risks. J Finance 2014;69(3):1197–1233.

Joslin S, Singleton KJ, Zhu H. A new perspective on gaussian dynamic term structure models. Rev Financ Stud 2011;24(3):926–970.

Kamara A. Liquidity, taxes, and short-term Treasury yields. J Financ Quant Anal 1994;29(3):403–417.

Kim DH, Orphanides A. Term structure estimation with survey data on interest rate forecasts. J Financ Quant Anal 2012;47(1):241–272.

Kim DH, Singleton KJ. Term structure models and the zero bound: an empirical investigation of Japanese yields. J Econom 2012;170(1):32–49.

Krippner L. Modifying Gaussian Term Structure Models when Interest Rates are Near the Zero Lower Bound, Working paper. Reserve Bank of New Zealand; 2012.

Krippner L. A theoretical foundation for the Nelson-Siegel class of yield curve models. J Appl Econom 2013;30(1):97–118.

Krishnamurthy A. The bond/old-bond spread. J Financ Econ 2002;66(2-3):463–506.

Le A, Singleton KJ, Dai Q. Discrete-time affine $\mathbb{Q}$-term structure models with generalized market prices of risk. Rev Financ Stud 2010;23(5):2184–2227.

Liu J, Longstaff FA. Losing money on arbitrage: optimal dynamic portfolio choice in markets with arbitrage opportunities. Rev Financ Stud 2004;17(3):611–641.

Longstaff F. The flight-to-liquidity premium in U.S. Treasury bond prices. J Bus 2004;77(3):511–526.

Lou D, Yan H, Zhang J. Anticipated and repeated shocks in liquid markets. Rev Financ Stud 2013;26(8):1891–1912.

Malkhozov A, Mueller P, Vedolin A, Venter P. Mortgage Risk and the Yield Curve, Working paper. McGill University; 2014.

Markiewicz A, Pick A. Adaptive learning and survey data. J Econ Behav Organ 2014;107(B):685–707.

Meiselman D. *The Term Structure of Interest Rates*, Ford Foundation Dissertation Series. Prentice-Hall; 1962.

Milani F. Expectations, learning and macroeconomic persistence. J Monet Econ 2007;54(7):2065–2082.

Modigliani F, Sutch R. Debt management and the term structure of interest rates: an empirical analysis of recent experience. J Polit Econ 1967;75(4):569–589.

Monfort A, Pegoraro F, Renne J-P, Roussellet G. Staying at Zero with Affine Processes: A New Dynamic Term Structure Model, Working paper. Banque de France; 2014.

Obstfeld M. Intertemporal dependence, impatience, and dynamics. J Monet Econ 1990;26(1):45–75.

Ormeno A. Inflation Expectations, Learning, and DSGE Model Estimation, Working paper. Universitat Pompeu Fabra; 2009.

Perli R, Sack B. Does mortgage hedging amplify movements in long-term interest rates? J Fixed Income 2003;13(3):7–17.

Piazzesi M. Affine term structure models. In: *Handbook of Financial Econometrics*. Chapter 12. Elsevier; 2005; p 691–766.

Piazzesi M, Salomao J, Schneider M. Trend and Cycle in Bond Premia, Working paper. Stanford University; 2013.

Priebsch M. Computing Arbitrage-Free Yields in Multi-Factor Gaussian Shadow-Rate Term Structure Models, Working paper. Federal Reserve Board; 2013.

Rosenbaum S. Moments of a truncated bivariate normal distribution. J R Stat Soc Ser B (Methodological) 1961;23(2):405–408.

Sarig O, Warga A. Some empirical estimates of the risk structure of interest rates. J Finance 1989;44(5):1351–1360.

Shiller R, McCulloch J. The term structure of interest rates. In: *Handbook of Monetary Economics*. Volume 1, Chapter 13. Elsevier; 1987. p 627–722.

Slobodyan S, Wouters R. Learning in a medium-scale DSGE model with expectations based on small forecasting models. Am Econ J Macroecon 2012;4(2):65–101.

Tobin J. Estimation of relationships for limited dependent variables. Econometrica 1958;26(1):24–36.

Vayanos D, Vila J-L. A Preferred-Habitat Model of the Term Structure of Interest Rates, Working paper, W15487. NBER; 2009.

Vayanos D, Weill P-O. A search-based theory of the on-the-run Phenomenon. J Finance 2006;63(3):1361–1398.

Warga A. Bond returns, liquidity and missing data. J Financ Quant Anal 1992;27:605–617.

Wu C, Xia FD. Measuring the Macroeconomic Impact of Monetary Policy at the Zero Lower Bound, Working paper. University of Chicago Booth School of Business; 2013.

15

The Economics of the Comovement of Stocks and Bonds

Alexander David[a] and Pietro Veronesi[b]

[a]*Haskayne School of Business, University of Calgary, Calgary, Canada*
[b]*Booth School of Business, University of Chicago, Chicago, IL, United States*

15.1 INTRODUCTION

The purpose of this chapter is to provide some recently uncovered facts about the dynamics of the covariance of stocks and bonds as well as to provide a brief literature survey that attempts to explain this covariation. Given our taste for explaining stylized facts about asset prices with models of investors' learning about the state of fundamentals, we give more than a fair share of space to this line of research. In particular, we develop a model-based measure of investors' uncertainty about fundamentals and explicitly consider its implications for the stock–bond covariance. We then show that beliefs of professional forecasters extracted from survey data collected by the Federal Reserve Bank of Philadelphia are highly correlated with the model-based beliefs and have almost the same implications for the stock–bond covariance. We also find some supporting evidence for our model's predictions in international data as well.

The left panel of Figure 15.1 shows the quarterly realized series of covariance of returns on the S&P 500 (stocks) and 5-year Treasuries (bonds) constructed from daily returns in each quarter. Quite dramatically, the covariance turned from being mostly positive until about 2000 to being mostly negative since. The right panel shows that the realized beta of bonds also experienced this same sign reversal. That is, since 2000, bonds have become an important hedge against stock market fluctuations. But why were not bonds a hedge historically? What has changed recently? The answers to these questions have obvious first-order consequences for asset allocation between two of the largest financial asset classes.

15.2 A BRIEF LITERATURE SURVEY

We start with the early work on the stock–bond covariance. Important theoretical relations of the stock and real bond covariance are developed in Barksy (1989). In a two-period general equilibrium model, he considers the roles of increased risk and reduced productivity growth in determining the stock–bond covariance. Both disturbances unambiguously lower the real riskless rate but may cause the stock market to respond negatively depending on the elasticity of intertemporal substitution. This model does not have inflation but provides valuable intuition for at least a part of the stock and nominal bond covariance. Campbell and Ammer (1993) decompose the returns on stocks and bonds into cash flow and discount rate components and argue that stock–bond

Handbook of Fixed-Income Securities, First Edition. Edited by Pietro Veronesi.

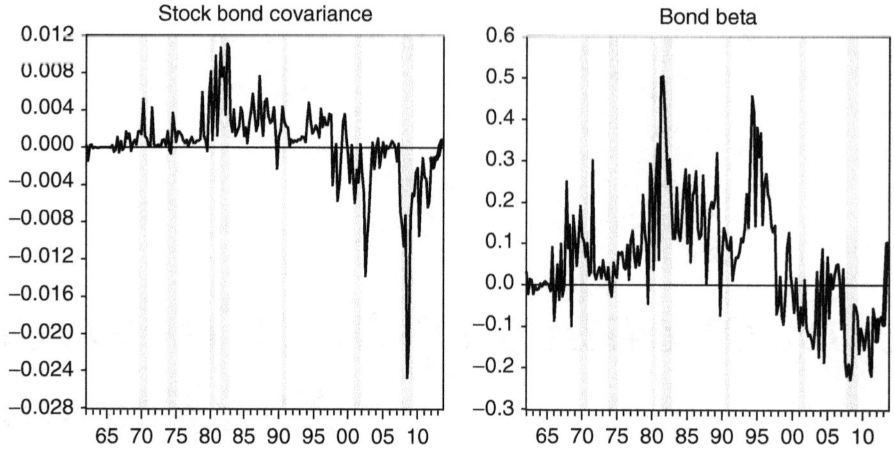

Figure 15.1 Stock–bond covariance and beta of 5-year treasury bonds. Source: Center for Research in Security Prices (CRSP) and Gürkaynak, Sack, and Wright (2007, updated series).

covariance should be low. The only component that is common to both assets is the real interest rate, which has relatively low variability. They do find a common component to news about future excess returns on bonds and stocks but find that it is unable to produce a large stock–bond covariance since news is not a large component of bond returns.

The massive sign flip in the stock–bond covariance in the data has been picked up in more recent work, and efforts have been made to understand this time variation. Baele, Bekaert, and Inghelbrecht (2010) use a linear dynamic factor setting to study the ability of economic factors to explain the dynamics of the stock–bond correlation.[1] The set of factors that they use is large, including interest rates, inflation, the output gap, and cash flow growth, as well as measures of risk aversion and uncertainty proxies for real growth and inflation. These authors conclude that fundamental factors contribute little to the stock–bond correlation, but instead argue that liquidity factors play a larger role in explaining its dynamics. Despite having much of the same macroeconomic information as our model, these authors do not explain the stock–bond correlation mainly due to their linear specification. In contrast, we will see in Section 15.3 that in a learning-based framework, asset volatilities and covariances are nonlinear functions of fundamentals.

Building on the "proxy hypothesis" of Fama (1981), researchers have generally thought of rising inflation as a signal for deteriorating fundamentals. For example, using a state space framework, Piazzesi and Schneider (2006) assume that investors dislike surprise inflation not only because it lowers the payoff on nominal bonds but also because it's bad news for future consumption growth. This effect is large when investors have recursive utility with preference for early resolution of uncertainty, as in the long-run risks channel of Bansal and Yaron (2004). Hasseltoft (2009) extends this framework by including dividend growth in the specification and studies the implications for the "Fed Model" and the stock–bond covariance. A high stock–bond covariance is generated by the common variation in bond and stock risk premia, which is induced by the variation in macroeconomic volatility. The model is able to generate a mild negative stock–bond correlation in the last decade by using the covariance between fundamentals as state variables. Indeed, the author estimates a positive covariance between inflation and real dividend growth in the last decade, which in turn induces a mild negative correlation between stocks and bonds in his model.

Indeed, more recent models are now able to generate both positive and negative stock–bond covariance. Campbell, Sunderam, and Viceira (2013) use a quadratic term structure model with a latent variable, which determines the sign of the relation between real and nominal variables in the economy. After fitting their model to macroeconomic, yield, and stock data from mid-1950s to late 2000, they show that their model implies a stock–bond covariance that endogenously switches sign as a function of the latent state variable. Their fitted model also implies that bond risk premia should have switched sign over time, as bonds turned from being "inflation bets" in the 1980s to "deflation hedges" after 2000. In fact, especially during the 2008–2009 financial crisis , nominal bonds were considered a "safe haven" that provides insurance against particularly severe adverse economic conditions. That is, bad economic news would make the stock market drop but at the same time make nominal bonds gain value, as investors dump stocks for bonds in search of safety. Their status as a hedge against severe economic conditions would induce investors to purchase those bonds even at a premium, that is, purchase them with a yield below expected inflation.

[1]Their model is as follows: Let $r_t = (r_{e,t}, r_{b,t})'$ be the vector of stock and bond returns. Then

$$r_t = E_{t-1}(r_t) + \beta_t' F_t + \epsilon_t,$$

where F_t is the vector of economic factors and $\epsilon_t \sim N(0, \Sigma_t)$. The betas as well as Σ_t are allowed to be regime dependent.

Campbell, Pflueger, and Viceira (2014) use a New Keynesian framework to understand the time variation in the stock–bond covariance. A key intuition of their model is that the response of monetary policy changes over time in reaction to supply versus demand shocks, which leads to a different stock–bond relation. The effects are magnified by changes in risk aversion, particularly in bad times, which make the model's covariance closer to that in the data.

Kozak (2013) proposes a stylized model of production featuring two investment technologies, adjustment costs, and agents with time-varying risk aversion. The model's equilibrium produces a time-varying covariance between returns to the risky technology and long-term claims to safe debt. The main driver of this covariance is the time variation in the level of risk aversion, which induces a negative covariance between stocks and bonds ("flight to safety") especially during periods of high-risk aversion.

An interesting observation made by Connolly, Sun, and Stivers (2005) is that the stock–bond covariance becomes more negative in periods of high stock market volatility. This has certainly been true since 2000. These authors argue that in periods of high stock market volatility, investors seek the safety of bonds, so that bond returns are high precisely when stock returns are low. We discuss this issue in the following section, since the second half of the last century showed the opposite empirical pattern.

15.3 THE STOCK–BOND COVARIANCE AND LEARNING ABOUT FUNDAMENTALS

In David and Veronesi (2013), we study an endowment economy in which the drift rates of real earnings growth and inflation follow an unobserved composite regime switching model. Investors also observe a smoothed version of "true" consumption growth with some noise, although its drift is unknown but constant.[2] Market participants cannot observe the current regime and thus must learn about it by observing fundamentals and other signals.[3] Inflation has a signaling role in predicting real growth as in the "proxy hypothesis" of Fama (1981). In addition, we allow for very low inflation (close to zero) to also be an adverse signal about real fundamentals, an observation that is influenced by the recent evidence in Japan, the United States, and perhaps more recently, in Western Europe. This nonlinear signaling role of inflation is tractably modeled with the specification of the transitions among the composite regimes of real fundamentals and inflation.

We extract investors' beliefs about fundamentals from data on both fundamentals as well as asset prices. We use asset prices since they undoubtedly contain forward-looking information that investors have about fundamentals, while fundamental data by definition are at best current. A key aspect of our methodology is to develop closed-form formulas for stock and Treasury bond prices, as well as their volatilities and covariances as functions of investors' beliefs about fundamentals. We then estimate an overidentified simulated method of moments objective function, which attempts to explain not only the stock–bond covariance but also the complete dynamics of fundamentals, stock and Treasury bond (1-year and 5-year) prices, and volatilities of stocks and bonds.[4] In the following discussion, we leave out the estimates of all the parameters and implications for a range of issues in David and Veronesi (2013) and focus mainly on the narratives of the composite regimes and their implications for the stock–bond covariance.

We start by looking at the closed-form expressions for the volatility of stocks and bonds and discuss their determinants. The volatility of nominal stock returns is[5]

$$\sigma^N(\pi_t) = \sigma_Q + \sigma_E + \frac{\sum_{i=1}^n G_i\, \pi_{it}\, (v^i - \bar{v}(\pi_t))'(\Sigma')^{-1}}{P/E(\pi_t)} \tag{15.1}$$

There are three sources of variation in nominal stock returns: the volatilities of stocks due to inflation Q_t, to real earnings E_t, and to beliefs $\sum_{i=1}^n \pi_{it} G_i$. In the latter, π_{it} denotes investors' belief to be in the composite regime i in period t, G_i is the P/E ratio for stocks in regime i, v^i is a vector of fundamental drifts of inflation and earnings growth, and $\bar{v}(\pi_t)$ is its conditional expectation. In particular, the last term in 15.1 is a learning-based, time-varying endogenous component that depends on beliefs π_{it}. It is important to note that unlike the recent literature on modeling uncertainty (see, e.g., Bansal and Yaron (2004) or Bloom (2009)), we assume homoskedastic fundamentals (σ_Q and σ_E are constant) so that *any* variation in volatility is *endogenous* in our model and arises from learning. Also, importantly, our model implies that stock valuation has an important impact on volatility

[2] The smoothing coefficient of consumption (we estimate that true consumption is about five times more volatile than aggregate consumption) is estimated by our procedure and reflects the government's aggregation procedure across households as well as errors in its sampling and data collection. Having a more volatile true consumption brings our model's equity premium closer to the data.

[3] In our model, investors also suffer from some degree of "money illusion," that is, they partly discount future real cash flows using a nominal stochastic discount factor. The main impact on asset prices is that *ceteris paribus,* it raises the real rate in periods of higher expected inflation. We show that this feature is mainly useful for getting a better fit for the term structure but has only a small impact on the stock–bond covariance.

[4] We must use simulated method of moments (SMM) rather than generalized method of moments (GMM) since we specify a continuous time model, with discrete observations of fundamentals whose likelihood function is not available in closed form.

[5] With some abuse of terminology, we refer to the diffusion of a return process as its volatility. Equations 15.1 and 15.2 show the diffusion vectors of the return processes. Strictly speaking, the "volatility" of stock returns, for instance, is the scalar given by $\sqrt{\sigma^N(\pi)\sigma^N(\pi)'}$.

and that uncertainty about regimes in itself does not fully explain the impact of learning on volatility. In fact, valuations (G_i in Equation 15.1) change the relative weights given to the alternative sources of uncertainty (inflation and earnings) during different periods in our sample.

The volatility of nominal zero-coupon bond returns is

$$\sigma^B(\pi_t, \tau) = \frac{\sum_{i=1}^{n} B_i(\tau)\, \pi_{it}\, (v^i - \bar{v}(\pi_t))'(\Sigma')^{-1}}{B(\tau)} \tag{15.2}$$

The form of the bond's volatility in 15.2 is similar to the stock's volatility in 15.1, except that the conditional P/E ratio G_i in any regime i is replaced by the conditional bond price $B_i(\tau)$ in that regime. In addition, there is no exogenous fundamental component since the bond payoff is fixed at maturity. Intriguingly, bond return volatility is nonlinearly related to the long-term yield, being higher when the long-term yield is both high or low. This result is consistent with agents' uncertainty about entering either a hyperinflation regime or a deflationary regime, each of which has weak real fundamentals. In either case, bond return volatility is high because uncertainty is high, but the level of long-term yields are at their opposite extremes. This insight may also explain the weak evidence in favor of a linear relation between volatility and bond yields (see, e.g., Collin-Dufresne and Goldstein (2002)).

From these two volatilities, the stock–bond covariance at different maturities is simply

$$Cov\left(\frac{dP_t^N(\pi_t)}{P_t^N(\pi_t)}, \frac{dB_t(\pi_t, \tau)}{B_t(\pi_t, \tau)}\right) = \sigma^N(\pi_t)\, \sigma^B(\pi_t, \tau)'. \tag{15.3}$$

15.3.1 Investors' Beliefs About Composite Regimes

Figure 15.2 shows the implied beliefs of investors about each composite growth and inflation regime using our methodology. The beliefs are for the period from 1958 to 2013 based on parameters estimated until 2010 in David and Veronesi (2013). Our estimation procedure revealed that six regimes were required to provide a reasonable fit for the time series of fundamentals, prices, and volatilities (12 series overall) and also to match the unconditional Sharpe ratio on stocks of 0.3 (consistent with the equity premium literature).

The left panels show the conditional probabilities of the three low growth regimes (recessions), while the right panels show those for the medium and high growth regimes (booms). The top-left panel shows that investors believed the recessions in the second half of the 1900s typically had low growth accompanied by medium inflation. The probability of such recessions increased in the recessions in the 1970s, 1980s, and 1990s. The middle-left panel shows that the beliefs about stagflation only spiked once in our sample around 1979–1980, a period that preceded the Volcker regime when interest rates increased dramatically and were consequently followed by two recessions. Finally, the bottom panel shows the beliefs about deflationary (zero inflation) recessions, which spiked in the recessions of the current millennium. Overall, the three panels show the changing nature of recessions in our sample.

The right panels show the beliefs about the three kinds of booms. The top panel shows the most likely regime of low inflation and medium growth. There were long periods in the 1960s, 1990s, and the 2000s in which investors strongly believed that they were in such a regime. The middle panel shows beliefs about the "overheating" boom. We call it that since the estimated transition probability (not shown) shows a higher than typical likelihood of falling into stagflation from this regime than other boom regimes. This instability in real earnings growth not only leads to more volatile beliefs but also lower stock price valuations. Finally, the bottom panel shows the beliefs of the low inflation and high growth regime, which was nontrivial only during the dot com boom and some part of the mid-2000s. These were periods of unusually strong productivity growth in the United States. While it is natural to expect high valuations in such periods, there was also an unusual positive correlation between fundamental news and uncertainty. Why was that? As seen, investors' belief of this regime was at its highest points around 0.2 so that positive earnings during these periods increased the uncertainty on whether this extremely strong regime was really driving the fundamentals.

15.3.2 Valuations and the "Fed Model"

Sometime around the 1990s, practitioners on Wall Street noticed that the correlation between the earnings yield on the S&P 500 index and 5-year Treasuries was positive. This relative valuation commonality was called the "Fed Model," since the Fed's efforts to fight inflation generally raised rates and yields for both stocks and bonds. In the left panel of Figure 15.3, we do see the strong positive correlation in the period until 2000 (correlation coefficient of 0.7). However, quite remarkably, this correlation turned negative after 2000 (correlation coefficient of –0.6) with the two series showing opposite movements especially during and after the two recent recessions.

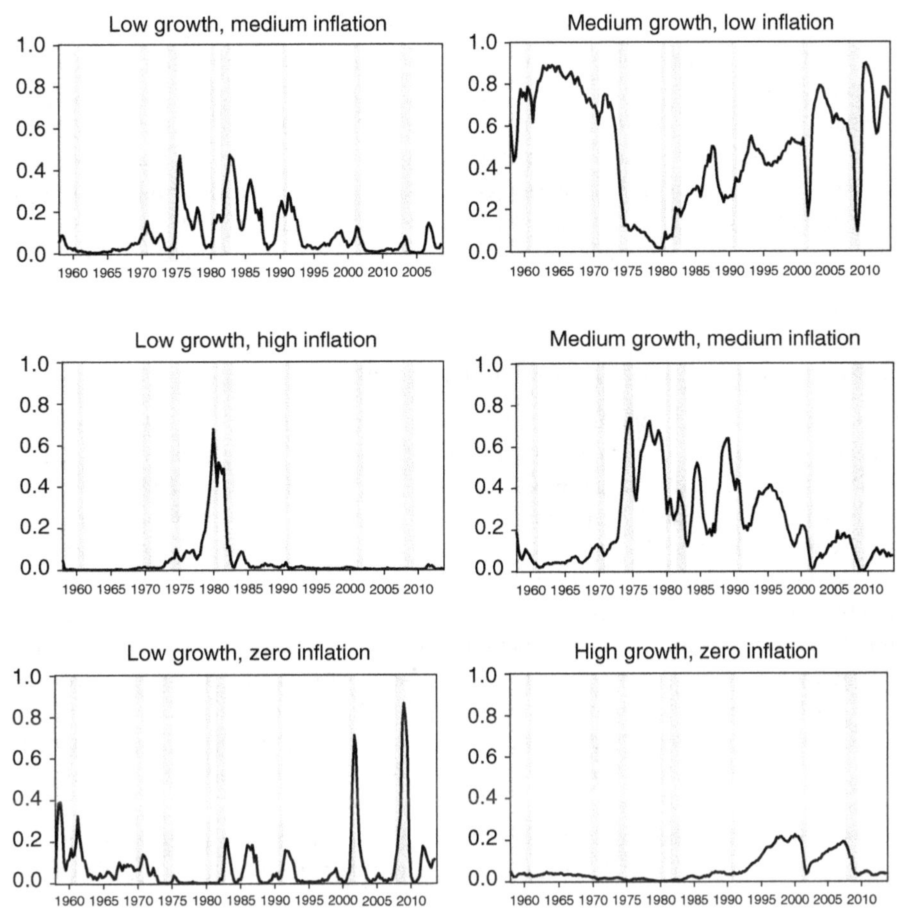

Figure 15.2 Investors' beliefs about fundamentals implied from regime switching model of David and Veronesi (2013). This figure is an updated version of Figure 4 in David and Veronesi (2013).

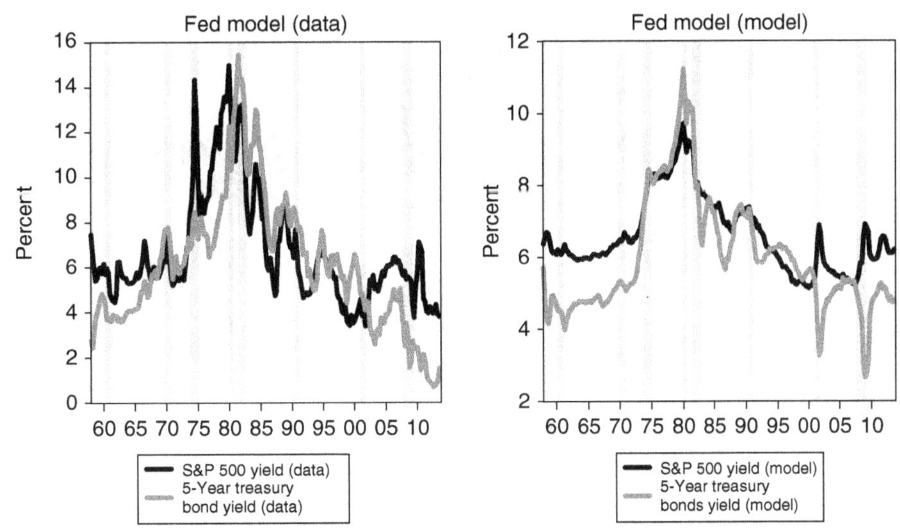

Figure 15.3 Fed model for data and for composite regime switching model of David and Veronesi (2013). Source: Standard and Poor and Gürkaynak, Sack, and Wright (2007, updated series).

What happened? Why did the relative valuation relationship break down at the turn of the millennium? According to our model, the inversion is due to investors' beliefs about the composite regimes that we discussed earlier. Specifically, until 2000, the recessions were generally followed by periods of increased inflation risk (the overheating booms). In such periods, positive inflation news would lead to not only higher bond yields due to higher expected inflation but also higher stock yields due to a drop in stock valuations in anticipation of lower future earnings growth. After 2000, the recessions were of the deflationary type, and thus negative inflation news lead to lower bond yields due to lower expected inflation, but higher dividend yield, again due to the drop in stock valuation in anticipation of lower earnings growth. Therefore, the changing signaling role of inflation, which investors picked up on, implied the reversal of the relative valuation relationship, which is the Fed model. The right panel of Figure 15.3 indeed shows that our fitted model yields such inversion in comovement between the dividend yield and the 5-year bond yield.

15.3.3 Explaining the Time Variation in the Stock–Bond Covariance

Investors' beliefs about composite regimes not only explain the dynamics of the relative valuations between stocks and bonds but also the comovement of their returns, as can be seen in Figure 15.4. The signs of the historical and model-based covariance almost always agree, and the magnitudes are similar as well. Overall, the model covariance explains 42% of the variation in the data covariance. It must be noted that the stock–bond covariance is one of the overidentifying moments used in our estimation. In the following sections, we will provide evidence that the economic logic of our model has additional evidence (from surveys), and the success of our model in not just an artifact of our fitting procedure.

Why does the model covariance explain the time-varying dynamics in the data? Once again, during the overheating boom periods of the 1970s and 1980s, any CPI reading above market expectations was taken as an indication that the economy could shift to stagflation battering the prices on both stocks and bonds. Hence, stock and bond covariance was positive. Since 2000, the opposite has happened. With investors now experiencing fears of a *deflationary* recession regime, positive inflation news is good news for stocks (but bad for bonds) as it signals that the bad deflationary regime could be averted, a channel that leads to a negative covariance between stocks and bonds. Thus, the changing signaling role of inflation explains the change in sign of the covariance between stocks and bonds.

Our model not only provides a unified economic framework explaining the relative valuations of stock and bonds, but it also provides several additional testable relationships between stocks' and bonds' valuations, and their volatilities, which we test in David and Veronesi (2013).

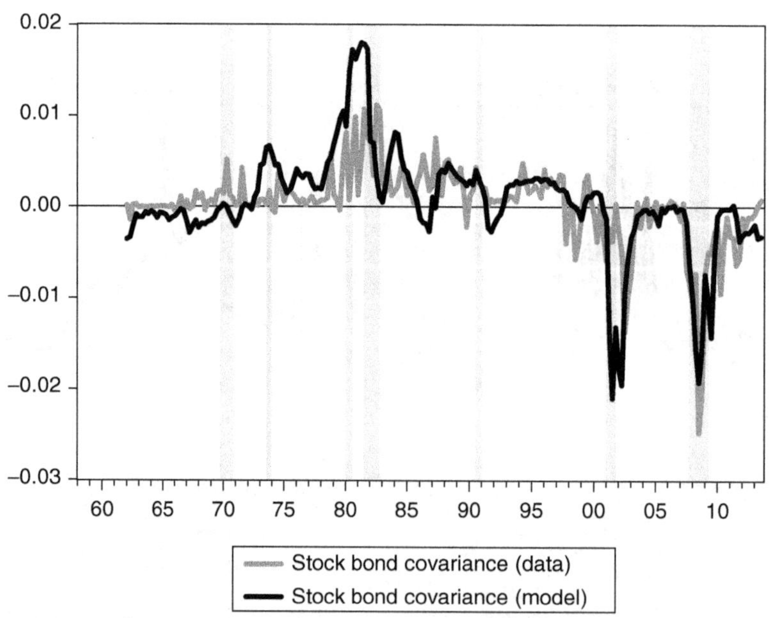

Figure 15.4 Stock–bond covariance in the data and implied by regime switching model of David and Veronesi (2013). This figure is an updated version of Panel D of Figure 7 in David and Veronesi (2013).

15.4 BELIEFS FROM SURVEYS AND FROM THE MODEL

Above we discussed investors' beliefs about fundamentals extracted from the estimation of a structural model. Another way to measure investors' beliefs is from surveys. Here we briefly describe a method for calculating the average beliefs of agents, which we introduced in David and Veronesi (2013), and compare these beliefs with our model-based beliefs.

We use data from the Survey of Professional Forecasters (SPF), which we obtained from the Federal Reserve Bank of Philadelphia. The survey asks respondents to provide probabilities of economic fundamentals falling in specific ranges. We average these probabilities across forecasters. To compare survey-based beliefs with those from our model, we form intervals of fundamentals centered around the means of our estimated regimes. For example, for inflation, we form four intervals and label them as "high," "medium," "low," and "zero," similar to those for our model.

In addition, we use the average beliefs to form first and second moments of expected fundamentals in the following quarter. For example, average inflation uncertainty is measured as

$$UncInf_t = V_t[I] = \sum_{j=1}^{n} p_{j,t}(I^j - E_t[I])^2, \tag{15.4}$$

where I^j are midpoints of inflation unit intervals and $p_{j,t}$ is the average forecasters' probability that inflation will be in the given interval I^j. A similar procedure can be used to compute a proxy for real economic growth uncertainty. The question on the SPF only asks about the probability, p_t, of a decline in real gross domestic product (GDP), without specifying the exact amount of the decline (or the increase in case of growth). Hence, we rely on the following proxy:[6]

$$UncEarn_t = p_t(1 - p_t). \tag{15.5}$$

It is useful to note the distinction between average uncertainty and the dispersion of beliefs across forecasters. The latter is used by a number of researchers as a proxy for uncertainty, which might explain a large part of its variation, but it can also arise from disagreement among forecasters about information or opinions on the structure of fundamentals.

In Figure 15.5, we directly compare the beliefs from the surveys and those from our model fitted to fundamentals, stock, and bonds data. The top and middle panels show the two sets of beliefs about inflation in the following quarter. As can be seen, the two sets of beliefs mostly move together with correlations ranging from 41% for zero inflation to 81% for high inflation. Moreover, the magnitude of the variations is very similar, except in Panel D, in which the model beliefs exceed 70%, while the survey beliefs were only in the 30% range. The bottom left panel shows that the two sets of beliefs about low real growth in the following quarter are each highly countercyclical and strongly move together with a correlation of 50%.

The model's asset prices and volatilities are functions of beliefs, which could also be called "factors," like those in the exponential affine models prevalent in the term structure literature. However, the evidence presented in Figure 15.5 casts some doubts on such a reduced-form interpretation. In fact, by construction our model-based beliefs are fully consistent with Bayes' laws and observations of fundamental data. Moreover, the strong similarity between model-based beliefs and survey-based beliefs is quite reassuring for our modeling methodology and interpretation because the survey beliefs are generated completely independently from any aspect of our model. Instead, the similarity of the two sets of beliefs suggests that our filtering model and professional forecasters are tracking similar historical information and forecasting fundamentals similarly.

15.5 SURVEY AND MODEL BELIEFS AND THE STOCK–BOND COVARIANCE

As discussed in Section 15.3, our model implies that the stock and bond volatilities depend on the two fundamental uncertainties, inflation and earnings, which we have modeled. In periods of higher uncertainty, investors have low confidence in their knowledge about fundamentals and revise their beliefs more in response to news, leading to higher volatility. However, depending on valuations, the two uncertainties are weighted differently over time. In Tables 15.1 and 15.2, we test whether SPF-based and model-based uncertainty measures are able to explain the variation in the stock–bond covariance. We provide results for the covariance of stocks with 1-year and 5-year Treasury bonds.

[6] We note that 15.5 is proportional to the conditional variance of GDP growth in the case of two regimes ("decline" and "no decline"), as $V_t[\theta] = \sum_{i=1}^{2} p_{it}(\theta^i - E_t[\theta])^2 = p_{1t}(1 - p_{1t})(\theta^1 - \theta^2)^2$.

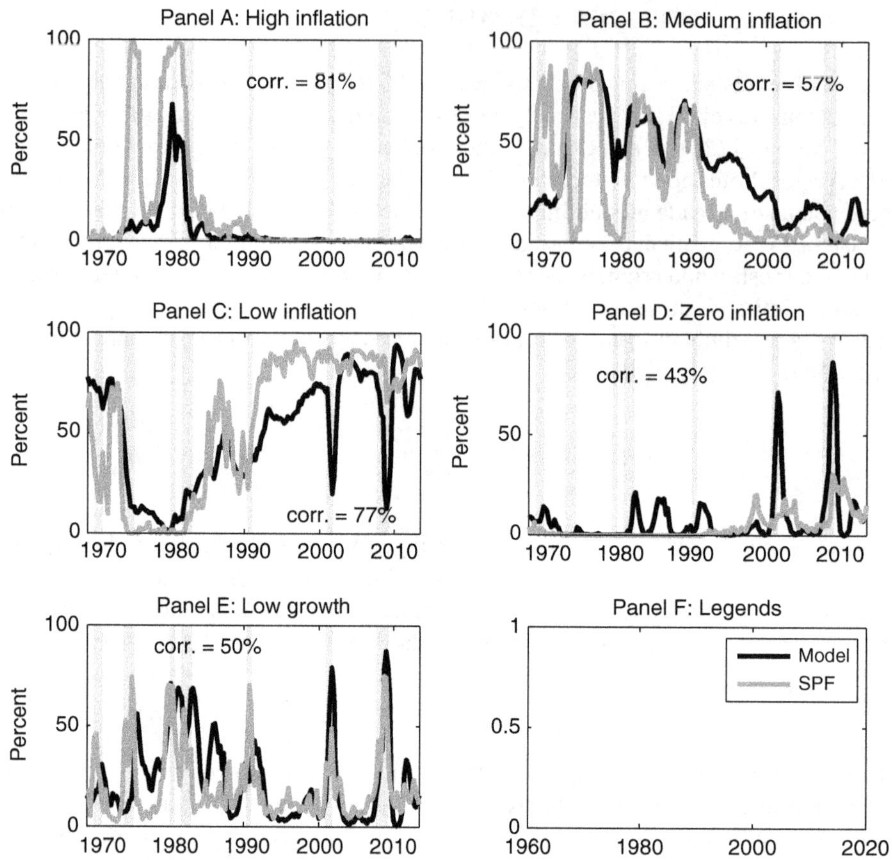

Figure 15.5 Marginal beliefs about fundamentals: survey of professional forecasters and implied by regime switching model of David and Veronesi (2013). This figure is an updated version of Figure 5 in David and Veronesi (2013).

In both tables, regression 1 tests if the stock–bond covariance depends on inflation and earnings uncertainty from the two sets of beliefs. For both sets of beliefs, we find that inflation uncertainty has a positive coefficient and is statistically significant, while earnings uncertainty has a negative but insignificant coefficient. The model-based R^2 is almost twice as high as the SPF-based R^2. The negative coefficient on earnings uncertainty implies that the stock–bond covariance declines on average in recessions when earnings uncertainty has been high.

In regression 2, we use expected inflation and earnings rather than their uncertainties. The results are similar to regression 1, although the R^2 are higher for the SPF-based measures. Why did we use expectations? The mechanism suggested by our model is in fact very much related to expected inflation. A regime of low earnings growth occurs either during periods of very high inflation (stagflation regime) or during periods of very low inflation (deflation regime). When expected inflation is high, positive inflation news (inflation realization above expectation) increase expected inflation and also the probability of stagflation, which is bad for the stock market. Hence, we should expect a positive covariance between stocks and bonds when expected inflation is high. In contrast, when expected inflation is very low, positive inflation news raises expected inflation and lowers the probability of deflation, which is *good* for the stock market. Hence, we should expect a negative relation between stocks and bonds when expected inflation is very low. Overall, we should expect a positive relation between stock–bond covariance and expected inflation, as corroborated by regression 2 in Tables 15.1 and 15.2. No such direct channel exists for expected earnings, as the covariance between stocks and bonds could be positive or negative when expected earnings is low, depending on whether we are in a high inflation regime or low inflation regime. Indeed, the lack of significance on ExpEarn in regression 2 is consistent with this theoretical prediction.

To see if an earnings-based measure enters nonlinearly, in regression 3, we continue to use a measure of inflation expectations but use the belief of a boom for the real measure. The R^2 of both sets of beliefs for both 1-year and 5-year bonds increase, and for 5-year bonds we get statistical significance for the boom probability. The regressions show that stock–bond covariance is higher in booms. In Section 15.3, we discussed that this arises because higher inflation news in booms typically hurts both stock and bond returns as it signals future instability of earnings growth rate.

The key point in our explanation of the changing sign of the stock–bond covariance is the changing signaling role of inflation and the difference in inflation expectations in different recessions. Therefore, in periods of high inflation, stocks and bonds have

TABLE 15.1 Model Beliefs and the Stock Bond Covariance

Variable	α	β_1	β_2	β_3	R^2
Regression 1: Cov = $\alpha + \beta_1$UncInf + β_2UncEarn + ϵ					
Stock 1-year bond cov.	−0.0059	2.5755	−0.3608		0.2678
	[−.7085]	**[4.2433]**	[−1.6079]		
Stock 5-year bond cov.	−0.0317	14.2149	−2.4341		0.2208
	[−0.5311]	**[3.0320]**	[−1.6109]		
Regression 2: Cov = $\alpha + \beta_1$ExpInf + β_2ExpRCP + ϵ					
Stock 1-year bond cov.	−0.0885	0.0305	−0.0013		0.2950
	[−2.7063]	**[4.2317]**	[−0.2558]		
Stock 5-year bond cov.	−0.6412	0.1858	0.0245		0.2713
	[−2.5729]	**[3.5246]**	[0.7350]		
Regression 3: Cov = $\alpha + \beta_1$ExpInf + $\beta_2(1 -$ RECESS$) + \epsilon$					
Stock 1-year bond cov.	−0.0862	0.0308	−0.0067		0.2944
	[−1.5478]	**[4.3144]**	[−0.1506]		
Stock 5-year bond cov.	−0.7916	0.1866	0.2373		0.2735
	[−1.9683]	**[3.5995]**	[0.8051]		
Regression 4: Cov = $\alpha + \beta_1$PrHigh + β_2PrLow + ϵ					
Stock 1-year bond cov.	0.0133	0.2486	−0.1387		0.2552
	[2.0562]	**[6.0368]**	**[−3.1002]**		
Stock 5-year bond cov.	0.0799	0.9778	−1.1860		0.2465
	[1.4556]	**[4.2245]**	**[−3.3843]**		
Regression 5: Cov = $\alpha + \beta_1$UncInf + β_2UncEarn PrHigh + β_3UncEarn PrLow + ϵ					
Stock 1-year bond cov.	−0.0186	2.1844	−0.4288	−1.1287	0.3142
	[−1.7666]	**[2.9008]**	[−0.7478]	**[−3.1257]**	
Stock 5-year bond cov.	−0.1804	17.0241	−9.0707	−8.9414	0.3380
	[−2.3470]	**[3.8225]**	**[−2.3482]**	**[−3.3016]**	
Regression 6: Cov = $\alpha + \beta_1$StockVol PrHigh + β_3StockVol PrLow + $\epsilon(t)$					
Stock 1-year bond cov.	0.0085	10.9658	−1.0425		0.3225
	[1.1137]	**[4.5101]**	**[−12.2772]**		
Stock 5-year bond cov.	0.0212	49.8083	−7.2808		0.3144
	[0.3568]	**[5.5908]**	**[−10.5375]**		

t-Statistics are within square brackets. Bold type indicates significance at 1% level. Standard errors are Newey–West adjusted for heteroskedasticity and autocorrelation.

positive covariance, and in periods of zero inflation, they have negative covariance. In regression 4, we directly use the beliefs of high and low inflation as explanatory variables. For both sets of beliefs, and for both maturities, we now obtain statistical significance and the right signs. The R^2 of the two sets of beliefs are also quite similar.

To resolve the issue about statistical insignificance of earnings uncertainty, in regression 5, we now interact it with low and high inflation probabilities. Our model predicts that during the two subperiods with high and low inflation, we should have positive and negative coefficients, respectively. We indeed find that this is the case in Table 15.2 using SPF measures, with strong significant coefficients for the interaction terms, and R^2 as high as 36.9%.

We finally return to the issue of the "flight-to-safety" phenomenon that was discussed in Connolly, Sun, and Stivers (2005). Using stock options, these authors show that in recent data the stock–bond covariance is more negative during periods of higher implied volatility. Our model is consistent with their findings, but it also implies that bonds do not offer the safe haven comfort in periods of high inflation (which has not really been a concern in recent data). So in regression 6, we use stock volatility as an explanatory variable, and interact it with high and low inflation probabilities from the two sets of beliefs. We find that in both specifications, the stock–bond covariance is high when volatility is high and the probability of high inflation is high, and negative when volatility is high but the probability of low inflation is high. The R^2 for these specifications are the highest among all the specifications considered.

TABLE 15.2 Survey Beliefs and the Stock Bond Covariance

Variable	α	β_1	β_2	β_3	R^2
Regression 1: Cov $= \alpha + \beta_1$UncInf $+ \beta_2$UncEarn $+ \epsilon$					
Stock 1-year bond cov.	−0.0357	3.7294	−0.0431		0.1229
	[−1.6192]	**[3.0856]**	[−0.1829]		
Stock 5-year bond cov.	−0.2068	24.9435	−1.0357		0.1493
	[−1.8577]	**[3.4423]**	[−0.7583]		
Regression 2: Cov $= \alpha + \beta_1$ExpInf $+ \beta_2$ExpRCP $+ \epsilon$					
Stock 1-year bond cov.	−0.0566	0.019	0.0005		0.2559
	[−2.9334]	**[4.0778]**	[0.7469]		
Stock 5-year bond cov.	−0.3755	0.1064	0.0054		0.2227
	[−2.3276]	**[3.4012]**	[1.2307]		
Regression 3: Cov $= \alpha + \beta_1$ExpInf $+ \beta_2(1 -$ RECESS$) + \epsilon$					
Stock 1-year bond cov.	−0.1311	0.021	0.0009		0.2804
	[−1.6368]	**[3.6682]**	[1.1152]		
Stock 5-year bond cov.	−1.0687	0.1241	0.0081		0.2814
	[−1.8714]	**[3.2930]**	[1.5302]		
Regression 4: Cov $= \alpha + \beta_1$PrHigh $+ \beta_2$PrLow $+ \epsilon$					
Stock 1-year bond cov.	0.0129	0.0964	−0.2592		0.2370
	[1.2167]	**[3.4995]**	**[−2.7316]**		
Stock 5-year bond cov.	0.1343	0.2767	−3.1301		0.2984
	[2.0485]	[1.9383]	**[−5.7920]**		
Regression 5: Cov $= \alpha + \beta_1$UncInf $+ \beta_2$UncEarn PrHigh $+ \beta_3$UncEarn PrLow $+ \epsilon$					
Stock 1-year bond cov.	−0.0179	2.0581	0.0042	−0.0165	0.2964
	[−1.1236]	**[2.7608]**	**[4.1114]**	**[−2.5946]**	
Stock 5-year bond cov.	−0.0645	11.9819	0.0117	−0.2004	0.3694
	[−0.6319]	**[3.1091]**	**[2.1207]**	**[−4.8363]**	
Regression 6: Cov$(t) = \alpha + \beta_1$StockVol PrHigh $+ \beta_3$StockVol PrLow $+ \epsilon$					
Stock 1-year bond cov.	0.0153	2.9613	−5.279		0.3072
	[1.9400]	**[2.1170]**	**[−5.0879]**		
Stock 5-year bond cov.	0.0946	9.9221	−47.8387		0.4160
	[1.6078]	[1.4604]	**[−5.2753]**		

t-Statistics are within square brackets. Bold type indicates significance at 1% level. Standard errors are Newey–West adjusted for heteroskedasticity and autocorrelation.
Source: CRSP, Gürkaynak, Sack, Wright (2007, updated series), and Survey of Professional Forecasters from the Federal Reserve of Philadelphia.

15.6 SOME INTERNATIONAL EVIDENCE

Most of the literature discussing the time variation in stock–bond covariance, including David and Veronesi (2013), only use data from the United States. In an early paper, Li (2002) estimates the stock–bond correlation across several countries and documents that it relates both to expected inflation and inflation uncertainty, which is consistent with the predictions of David and Veronesi (2013). The paper, however, proxies for both expected inflation and inflation uncertainty by using the results of predictive regressions of future inflation.

In this section, we consider the evidence across four countries, namely, Germany, Japan, Switzerland, and United Kingdom, for which daily stock and bond data are available on a relatively long sample, and importantly, default risk may be considered small on an *ex ante* basis. Daily bond indexes are from DataStream while daily stock indexes are from Bloomberg. Bond indexes are only available at the 10-year horizon. For these countries, however, we do not have available survey forecasts as we do for the United States. Because we are interested in using *ex ante* forecasts of future inflation and future real GDP growth as explanatory variables, we employ the projections of future inflation (GDP deflator) and future real GDP growth published by the OECD's semiannual economic outlook publications. Unfortunately, this dataset does not allow us to compute measures of uncertainty like for the SPF, but they still allow us to discuss the relation between fears of deflation and stock–bond covariance. Indeed, the model

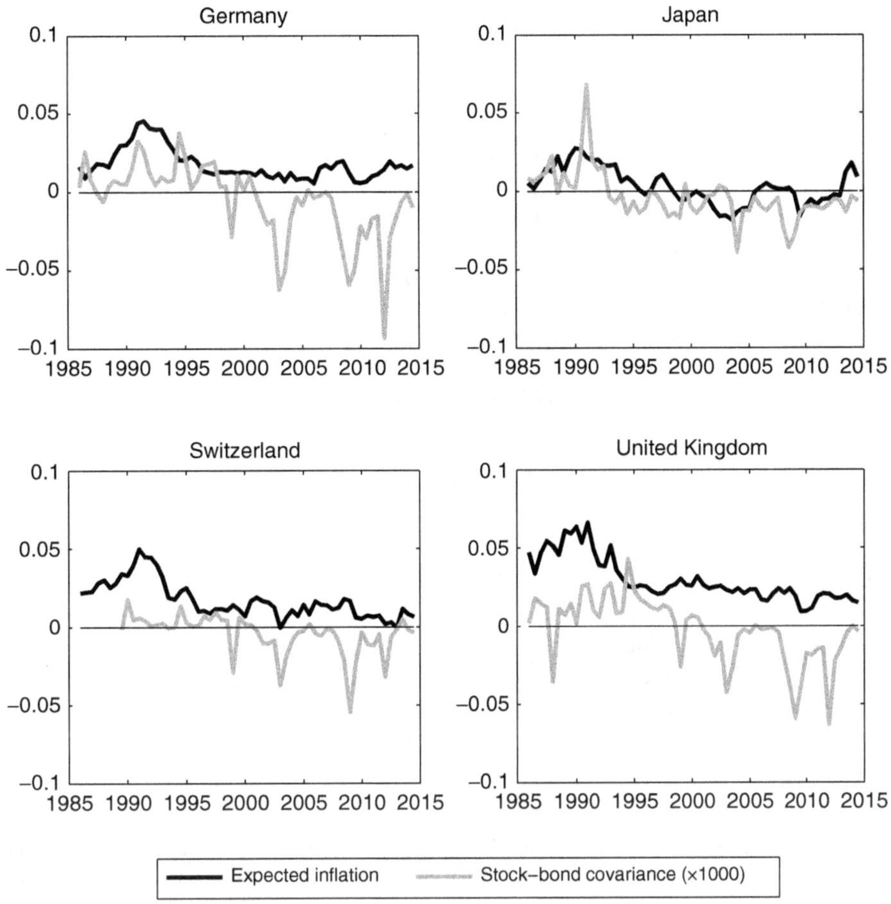

Figure 15.6 Inflation expectation and stock–bond covariances across countries. Source: DataStream, Bloomberg, and OECD economic outlook publications.

by David and Veronesi (2013) predicts that as investors' inflation expectations become too low, agents increase the probability of entering a deflationary regime, which is bad for the stock market. Thus, stock–bond covariance should turn negative in an environment of low expected inflation. The overall sample across these four countries is shorter than the one used for the United States and spans 1985–2014 at the semiannual frequency.

The four panels of Figure 15.6 plot the OECD-based 1-year ahead inflation expectations across the four countries, together with the stock–bond covariance (multiplied by 1000 for a better visual impression). Across the four panels, we see similar dynamics of expected inflation and stock–bond covariance. In particular, Japan's expected inflation is lower than other countries, and in fact Japan experienced negative expected inflation on several occasions starting from the mid-1990s. Indeed, we see also that the stock–bond covariance turned negative in Japan earlier than in other countries, around early 1990s. Moreover, most countries exhibit two negative "spikes" in stock–bond covariances around 2002 and during the financial crisis of 2008–2009, which resemble similar events observed in the United States (see Figure 15.1).

The top panel of Table 15.3 reports the results of individual regressions of stock–bond covariance on expected inflation and expected GDP growth. These regressions correspond to regression 2 reported in previous tables. Across the four countries, the covariance between stocks and bonds is positively related to expected inflation but not expected GDP growth. This result is similar to what we found in regression 2 of Tables 15.1 and 15.2. The R^2 for the cases of Germany, Japan, and United Kingdom are also relatively large, between 23% and 32%, while the R^2 for Switzerland is just 7%. In the last line of the top panel of Table 15.3, we also report the same regression but for the United States, now using the same sample and data sources as for the other four countries. As we can see, the same result as in regression 2 of Table 15.2 holds with the alternative data sources and alternative sample.

We check the robustness of the regression results in Table 15.3 by adding a lag of the dependent variable as an additional explanatory variable in the regression. Such lags are meant to instrument for additional unobservable factors that may be affecting both the explanatory variables and the dependent variable. The bottom panel of Table 15.3 reports the regression results. Expected inflation remains a significant explanatory variable for the covariance between stocks and bonds for three of the five countries,

TABLE 15.3 OECD Expectations and the Stock–Bond Covariance across Countries

	α	β_1	β_2	β_3	R^2
	Regression: Cov = $\alpha + \beta_1$ ExpInf + β_2 ExpGDP + ϵ				
Germany	−0.0035	0.0919	0.0651		0.2311
	[−3.9658]	**[3.8698]**	1.8375		
Japan	−0.001	0.0622	0.0206		0.3202
	−1.9031	**[3.0395]**	0.9916		
Switzerland	−0.001	0.0291	0.0062		0.0732
	−1.7308	**[3.6716]**	0.2603		
United Kingdom	−0.0042	0.0601	0.1016		0.3106
	[−5.8747]	**[4.0401]**	**[3.3277]**		
United States	−0.0055	0.1241	0.0797		0.3215
	[−3.0969]	**[4.7759]**	1.8024		
	Regression: Cov = $\alpha + \beta_1$ ExpInf + β_2 ExpGDP + β_3 Cov(−1) + ϵ				
Germany	−0.0004	0.0445	−0.0274	62.7844	0.4633
	−0.7389	**[2.1854]**	−0.9008	**[5.1954]**	
Japan	−0.0006	0.0362	0.0133	44.1053	0.4642
	−1.702	1.8757	0.9552	**[4.0415]**	
Switzerland	−0.0002	0.0123	−0.0146	43.6717	0.2275
	−0.3218	1.2646	−0.496	**[2.608]**	
United Kingdom	−0.0015	0.0279	0.0255	49.9762	0.4314
	−2.2179	**[2.8772]**	0.8633	**[3.7832]**	
United States	−0.0025	0.0582	0.0328	47.3362	0.4509
	−2.0163	**[2.3468]**	1.1096	**[4.5809]**	

t-Statistics are within square brackets. Bold type indicates significance at 1% level. Standard errors are Newey–West adjusted for heteroskedasticity and autocorrelation. Data source: DataStream, Bloomberg, and OECD economic outlook publications.

namely, Germany, United Kingdom, and United States. Instead, ExpInf is no longer significant for Japan and Switzerland.[7] While it is known that simple measurement error of the explanatory variables may be responsible for their lack of significance once a lag of the dependent variable is inserted in the regression, these weaker results for Japan and Switzerland caution against overinterpreting the causal effect of expected inflation on the covariance between stocks and bonds for those two countries in the top panel of Table 15.3.

A related implication of the model of David and Veronesi (2013) concerns the relation between the stock–bond covariance and the long-term bond yield. Indeed, nominal yields equal real yields plus expected inflation plus a risk premium. The real interest rate itself in David and Veronesi (2013) is also positively related to expected inflation because of money illusion, which makes long-term nominal yields positively related to expected inflation both directly and indirectly through its impact on the long-term real rate.[8] It follows that if the time variation in the covariance between stocks and bonds is related to hyperinflation fears (for positive covariance) and deflation fears (for negative covariance), we should find a positive relation between long-term yields and the covariance between stocks and bonds. David and Veronesi (2013) report empirical evidence to this effect for the United States on the long sample 1960–2010. The top panel of Table 15.4 shows this to be the case also for international data. In particular, in this table we regress the stock–bond covariance for each individual country onto their 10-year bond yield, whose data are obtained from DataStream. Because yields themselves are endogenous quantities, we lag the 10-year yield in these regressions to partly address issues of reverse causality. The sample is still 1985–2014, but the frequency of observation is now quarterly – as in David and Veronesi (2013) – since for this empirical exercise we are not limited by the semiannual frequency of OECD economic projections. The results support the prediction from David and Veronesi (2013) that the level of yields and the covariance between stocks and bonds should be positively related. Indeed, the bottom panel of Table 15.4 shows that adding a lag of the dependent variable to the explanatory variables as an instrument for unobservable factors does not change the significance

[7] We did not report results with lags of the dependent variables as regressors in Tables 15.1 and 15.2 as almost all explanatory variables remain significant once lags are included. The only exception are the regressions involving PrLow in Table 15.2 and in regression 4 in Table 15.1, whose coefficients turn insignificant. Of course, measurement error and the short sample in which PrLow is different from zero may well explain this result.

[8] The empirical literature has documented a positive relation between long-term real rates and expected inflation, although the evidence at the short-horizon is mixed. See, for example, Ang, Baekert, and Wei (2008); Haubrich, Pennacchi, and Ritchen (2013); and David and Veronesi (2014) for recent contributions.

TABLE 15.4 Ten-Year Yields and the Stock–Bond Covariance across Countries

	α	β_1	β_2	$t(\alpha)$	$t(\beta_1)$	$t(\beta_2)$	R^2
	Regression: Cov = $\alpha + \beta_1$ 10-year Yield(-1)) + ϵ						
Germany	−0.0040	0.0675		−4.2522	4.7773		0.2945
Japan	−0.0017	0.0462		−5.6002	4.0770		0.3484
Switzerland	−0.0014	0.0278		−3.3495	3.2440		0.0998
United Kingdom	−0.0030	0.0430		−4.6854	5.4767		0.2790
United States	−0.0039	0.0589		−4.0187	4.3836		0.2997
	Regression: Cov = $\alpha + \beta_1$ 10-year Yield(-1) + β_2 Cov(−1) + ϵ						
Germany	−0.0013	0.0220	0.5976	−2.7382	2.7026	9.6095	0.5181
Japan	−0.0009	0.0226	0.4929	−5.1099	4.0566	8.5982	0.5002
Switzerland	−0.0007	0.0124	0.4430	−2.8559	2.1304	5.7815	0.2658
United Kingdom	−0.0018	0.0259	0.3542	−3.0788	3.7167	1.9041	0.3613
United States	−0.0010	0.0149	0.6662	−2.6119	2.7307	9.6401	0.5769

Notes: Standard errors are Newey–West adjusted for heteroskedasticity and autocorrelation.
Source: DataStream and Bloomberg.

of the long-term yield as an explanatory variable. Therefore, so long as the main variation of the long-term yield over the sample is due to time variation in expected inflation, the prediction of David and Veronesi (2013) is supported in the international data.[9]

15.7 SUMMARY

The covariance of stocks and bonds switched signs from being predominantly positive in the second half of the last century to being predominantly negative in the current century. The main intuition that we offer is that investors' fear of high inflation in the 1980s switched to fear of deflation in recent years, both of which signal weakness in the real growth of fundamentals. Thus, bonds offer a safe haven only in periods of low inflation. During high inflation periods, they are hurt by the same fundamental factors as stocks and have positive conditional betas. Our explanation is line with other recent work on the dynamics of the stock–bond covariance that also feature a time-varying relation between inflation and the real economy.

ACKNOWLEDGMENTS

We thank Ben Charoenwong and Paulo Mateus for excellent research assistance.

REFERENCES

Ang A, Bekaert G, Wei M. The term structure of real rates and expected inflation. J Finance 2008;6:797–849.

Baele L, Bekaert G, Inghelbrecht K. The determinants of stock and bond return comovements. Rev Financ Stud 2010;23:2374–2428.

Bansal R, Yaron A. Risks for the long term: a potential resolution of asset pricing asset pricing puzzles. J Finance 2004;59:1481–1510.

Barksy RB. Why don't the prices of stocks and bonds move together? Am Econ Rev 1989;79:1132–1145.

Bloom N. The impact of uncertainty shocks. Econometrica 2009;77:623–685.

Campbell JY, Ammer J. What moves the stock and bond markets? A variance decomposition for long-term asset returns. J Finance 1993;48:3–37.

Campbell JY, Pflueger C, Viceira L. Monetary Policy Drivers of Bond and Equity Risks, Working Paper 20070. National Bureau of Economic Research; 2014.

Campbell JY, Sunderam A, Viceira L. Inflation Bets or Deflation Hedges? The Changing Risks of Nominal Bonds, Harvard University Working Paper; 2013.

Collin-Dufresne P, Goldstein R. Do bonds span the fixed-income markets: theory and evidence for unspanned stochastic volatility. J Finance 2002;57:1685–1730.

Connolly R, Sun L, Stivers CT. Stock market uncertainty and the stock-bond return relation. J Financ Quant Anal 2005;40:161–194.

[9]The positive relation between the covariance between stocks and bonds and long-term yields may also be due to time-varying risk premia. Indeed, in a CAPM-like world the lower covariance between stocks and bonds may in fact imply lower risk premia and therefore lower long-term yield (see also Campbell, Sunderam, and Viceira (2013)).

David A, Veronesi P. What ties return volatilities to price valuations and fundamentals. J Polit Econ 2013;121:682–746.

David A, Veronesi P. Investor's and central bank's uncertainty embedded in index options. Rev Financ Stud 2014;27(6):1661–1716.

Fama EF. Stock returns, real activity, inflation and money. Am Econ Rev 1981;71:545–565.

Gürkaynak RS, Sack B, Wright J. The U.S. Treasury yield curve: 1961 to the present. J Monet Econ 2007;54:2291–2304.

Hasseltoft H. The "Fed-Model" and the Changing Correlations of Stock and Bond Returns: An Equilibrium Approach, Stockholm School of Economics Working Paper; 2009.

Haubrich J, Pennacchi G, Ritchen P. Inflation expectations, real rates, and risk premia: evidence from inflation swaps. Rev Financ Stud 2012;25(5):1588–1629.

Kozak S. Endogenous risk-taking and risk premia dynamics [PhD thesis]. University of Chicago; 2013.

Li L. Macroeconomic Factors and the Correlation of Stock and Bond Returns, Yale Working Paper; 2002.

Piazzesi M, Schneider M. Equilibrium yield curves. In: Acemoglu D, Rogoff K, Woodford M, editors. *NBER Macroeconomics Annual*. Volume 21. Cambridge (MA): MIT Press; 2006.

PART VI

Derivatives: Markets and Pricing

16

Interest Rate Derivatives Products and Recent Market Activity in the New Regulatory Framework

Christopher L. Culp[a,b,c]

[a]*Johns Hopkins Institute for Applied Economics, Global Health, & Study of Business Enterprise, Baltimore, MD, United States*
[b]*Swiss Finance Institute, Zurich, Switzerland*
[c]*Compass Lexecon*

16.1 INTRODUCTION

Since the first appearance of interest rate derivatives in the early 1980s, the interest rate derivatives market has generally been characterized by explosive growth in trading volumes and notional amounts outstanding, numerous and rapid new product innovations, increased liquidity, and declining transaction costs. Virtually all of those changes were driven primarily by market-based demand and supply considerations. Since 2009, sweeping changes in global financial regulations implemented in the wake of the global credit crisis have already impacted and could further affect volumes, product design, and liquidity in the global interest rate derivatives marketplace.

During the 1980s and much of the 1990s, derivatives were distinguished by two archetypes based on how they were traded and cleared. Over-the-counter ("OTC") derivatives have historically been viewed as dealer-centric and bilateral contracts in which counterparties negotiated all significant terms (and could customize those terms fully) and relied on bilateral credit risk mitigation. Exchange-traded derivatives, by contrast, were (and still are) exchange-centric contracts traded in organized multi-participant markets and are multilaterally cleared by a central counterparty ("CCP"). (Table 16.1 summarizes abbreviations and acronyms for reference purposes.)

Beginning in the late 1990s, innovations in both trading and clearing gave rise to shades of gray between the once-dichotomous categories of OTC and exchange-traded derivatives. In particular, an amorphous new category of derivatives known as "cleared swaps" began to emerge. Cleared swaps are bilaterally negotiated, standardized OTC derivatives that are subsequently cleared by a CCP.[1] Since 2009, regulatory changes have established cleared swaps as a distinct third category of derivatives.

[1]For a review of the historical background and regulation of cleared swaps, see Culp (2010).

Handbook of Fixed-Income Securities, First Edition. Edited by Pietro Veronesi.

TABLE 16.1 Abbreviations and Acronyms

AVA	Additional valuation adjustment
BCBS	Basel Committee on Banking Supervision
BDSR	Bloomberg Swap Data Repository
BIS	Bank for International Settlements
CCP	Central counterparty
CFTC	Commodity Futures Trading Commission (United States)
CLOB	Central limit-order book
CME	Chicago Mercantile Exchange/CME Group
CPO	Commodity pool operator (United States)
CSA	Credit support annex
CVA	Credit valuation adjustment
DCM	Designated contract market (United States)
DSF	Deliverable swap future
DTCC	Depository Trust & Clearing Corporation
DVA	Debit valuation adjustment
ECP	Eligible contract participant
EEP	Electronic execution platform
EMIR	European Market Infrastructure Regulation (E.U.)
ESMA	European Securities and Markets Authority (E.U.)
EONIA	Euro Overnight Indexed Average
EURIBOR	European Interbank Offered Rate
FC	Financial counterparty (E.U.)
FEU	Financial end user (United States)
FRA	Forward rate agreement
FRTB	Fundamental Review of the Trading Book
FVA	Funding valuation adjustment
G20	The Group of 20
ICE	Intercontinental Exchange
IOSCO	International Organization of Securities Commissions
ISDA	International Swaps and Derivatives Association
LIBOR	London Interbank Offered Rate
MAT	Made available to trade
MiFID 2	Markets in Financial Instruments Directive 2 (European Union)
MSP	Major swap participant (United States)
MTF	Multilateral trading facility (European Union)
NFC	Nonfinancial counterparty (European Union)
NFEU	Nonfinancial end user (United States)
OIS	Overnight indexed swap
OTC	Over the counter
OTF	Organized trading facility (European Union)
RFQ	Request for quote
QMTF	Qualifying multilateral trading facility (United States)
SD	Swap dealer (United States)
SDR	Swap Data Repository (United States)
SEC	Securities and Exchange Commission
SEF	Swap execution facility (United States)
SIFMA	Securities Industry and Financial Markets Association
SONIA	Sterling Overnight Indexed Average
TR	Trade repository (European Union)
WGMR	Working Group on Margin Requirements

No longer are cleared swaps simply an alternative available to market participants. Now, the clearing of many OTC derivatives is mandated, and, for those OTC derivatives that must be cleared by a CCP, trading on organized exchanges or electronic execution platforms ("EEPs") is also now a matter of law. Some market participants contend that the costs of the new regulations are so high that many aspects of interest rate derivatives trading and clearing are no longer be economically viable.[2]

[2]See, for example, Devasabai (2014), and Brush (2014).

This chapter reviews the major interest rate derivatives products and recent market activity in the context of the new regulatory framework. Throughout this chapter, the focus is on interest rate derivatives negotiated in and/or executed by market participants domiciled in the United States and the European Union.

Section 16.2 provides a brief introduction to the new regulatory framework governing the global interest rate derivatives marketplace. Sections 16.3–16.5 discuss the most significant products, execution mechanisms, credit risk mitigation and clearing techniques, and recent market activity in exchange-traded interest rate derivatives, noncleared OTC interest rate derivatives, and cleared OTC interest rate derivatives, respectively. Section 16.6 presents a comparative analysis of recent market activity across different interest rate derivatives execution venues – specifically exchange-traded versus OTC interest rate derivatives and OTC interest rate derivatives executed on EEPs versus bilaterally. Section 16.7 analyzes the bifurcation of liquidity that has recently occurred in certain nondollar OTC interest rate derivatives (EUR-denominated swaps, in particular), apparently in response to ongoing disparities and uncertainties regarding the cross-border implementation of U.S. and E.U. regulations. Section 16.8 briefly concludes by considering the potential impact of the recent shift in the derivatives regulation paradigm on interest rate derivatives product and market volumes, new product development, and liquidity. An Appendix appears as Section 16.9 that provides more details on the new regulatory framework and some of the important cross-border and extraterritoriality issues to which disparate new regulations have given rise. The Appendix is provided as background for the rest of the discussion in the chapter but can also be read as a stand-alone introduction to the new regulatory framework for interest rate derivatives in the United States and Europe. All discussions of regulations in this chapter were current through December 2014, but some may have changed since then.

16.2 BACKGROUND ON THE NEW DERIVATIVES REGULATORY FRAMEWORK

In the wake of the financial crisis that began in 2007, lawmakers and financial regulators throughout much of the world began to implement a coordinated redesign of the financial regulatory framework. A significant aspect of the new regulatory environment involves the regulation of derivatives products, markets, and users.

In September 2009, the heads of state of the G20 nations indicated their commitment to help build "a fundamentally stronger financial system than existed prior to the crisis."[3] One significant aspect of the G20 proposal was the following:

> All standardized OTC derivative contracts should be traded on exchanges or electronic trading platforms, where appropriate, and cleared through central counterparties by end-2012 at the latest. OTC derivative contracts should be reported to trade repositories. Noncentrally cleared contracts should be subject to higher capital requirements.[4]

In 2011, the G20 amended its initial recommendations and tasked the Basel Committee on Banking Supervision ("BCBS") of the Bank for International Settlements ("BIS") and the International Organization of Securities Commissions ("IOSCO") to develop a consistent set of minimum margin and capital requirements for noncleared swaps.[5] The expanded "G20 Principles" thus can be summarized as follows:

1. *Clearing:* All standardized OTC derivatives should be cleared by a CCP.
2. *Execution:* All standardized OTC derivatives should be traded on regulated exchanges or recognized EEPs.
3. *Reporting:* All OTC derivatives should be reported to a trade/data repository.
4. *Margin:* Noncleared OTC derivatives should be subject to a consistent set of minimum margin requirements.
5. *Capital:* Noncleared OTC derivatives should be subject to higher capital requirements.

National regulators in North America, member countries of the European Union ("E.U."), several non-E.U. European countries (e.g., Switzerland), and some Asian countries have adopted various new legislation and/or regulations to transform their financial systems and regulatory regimes into markets and infrastructures that conform to the G20 Principles. These changes have redefined the global derivatives marketplace.[6]

Because the new regulatory framework has so significantly impacted the market microstructure of interest rate derivatives, some background discussion of the new regulatory environment is necessary before discussing interest rate derivatives products and market activity in more detail. The following sections provide the relevant background on the first three issues noted earlier (i.e., clearing, execution, and reporting). The Appendix (Section 16.9) provides a more detailed discussion of the new regulatory framework, including clearing, execution, and reporting requirements, as well as margin and capital requirements for noncleared swaps and issues involving cross-border implementation and extraterritoriality.

[3] G-20 (2009) (hereinafter "G-20 Pittsburgh Declaration"), p. 8.
[4] G-20 (2011) (hereinafter "G-20 Cannes Summit Declaration"), p. 5.
[5] G-20 Cannes Summit Declaration, op. cit.
[6] A review of the status of the implementation of these reforms as of April 2014 can be found in Financial Stability Board (2014).

TABLE 16.2 Status as of April 2014 of OTC Derivatives Clearing Mandate Implementation

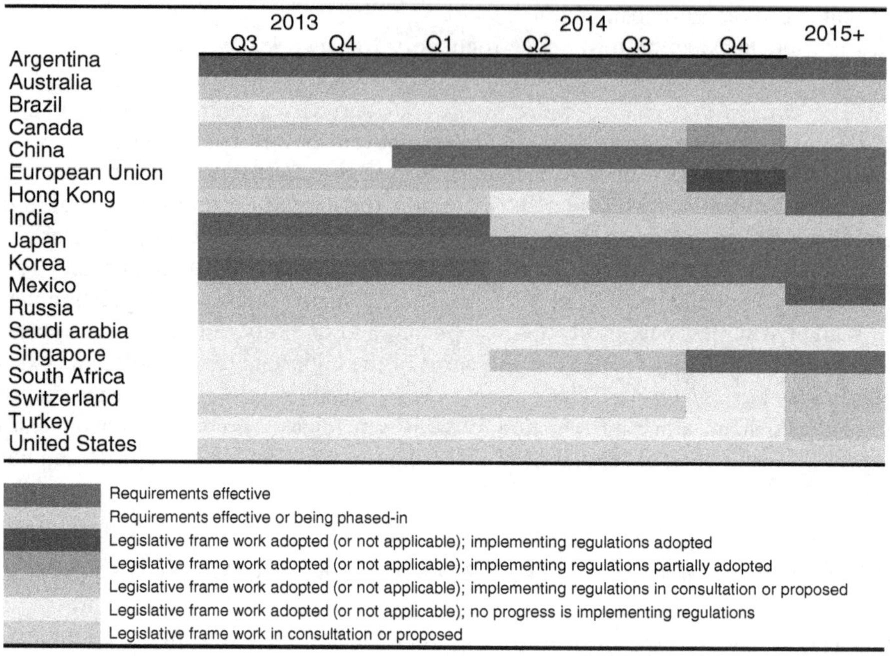

Source: Financial Stability Board, Seventh Progress Report on Implementation (April 8, 2014).

16.2.1 Clearing

All derivatives contracts oblige counterparties to make certain payments. Such payments may occur at the inception of a contract (e.g., the payment of premium on purchased options or the initial exchange of principal in physically settled currency swaps), over the life of the contract (e.g., periodic cash flows on swaps or variation margin cash flows on futures), at the end of the life of a contract (e.g., futures that are not rolled over at expiration, in-the-money options that are exercised, or currency swaps that require an exchange of principal at maturity), or following an early termination event. "Clearing" is the process by which payment obligations between two or more firms are computed (often using an applicable netting scheme), risk-reducing margin and collateral requirements are applied, related risk measures (e.g., value at risk) are calculated, and the like.

Clearing by CCPs has been an integral component of exchange-traded derivatives for more than a century.[7] Derivatives that are cleared through CCPs expose traders only to the credit risk of the CCP itself and not to the credit risk of the original trading counterparty. To protect the integrity of the marketplace, CCPs typically maintain strict safeguards and ample access to capital and liquidity (as discussed in more detail in Section 16.3.3). CCPs, moreover, have withstood the failures of various large market participants over time (e.g., Drexel Burnham Lambert, Barings, Refco, Lehman Brothers) and helped prevent the impact of those failures from spreading to other firms.

In the wake of the global financial crisis that began in 2007, many regulators viewed the nature and role of CCPs and their successful track records as compelling reasons to believe that systemic risk could be reduced by shifting certain types of derivatives transactions out of the traditional bilateral OTC world and into the CCP-cleared environment. As previously noted, OTC-cleared derivatives were already becoming more popular for certain products among some market participants. Regulators around the world took a significant step further and began to *mandate* CCP clearing for certain OTC derivatives.

Table 16.2 shows the status of the implementation of various clearing mandates for OTC derivatives globally as of April 2014. The next subsections discuss the U.S. and E.U. clearing mandates in more detail.

16.2.1.1 United States The United States was the first country to adopt sweeping new reforms of financial regulation with the passage of the "Dodd–Frank Wall Street Reform and Consumer Protection Act" ("Dodd-Frank Act") by the U.S. Congress on July 15, 2010, signed into law by President Obama on July 21, 2010. Title VII of the Dodd–Frank Act requires that all swaps not otherwise excluded by the Commodity Futures Trading Commission ("CFTC") be submitted for clearing to a CFTC-regulated CCP (or a CCP that is recognized by the CFTC but exempt from CFTC regulation).[8] CCPs must submit swaps they wish to

[7]For general discussions on the evolution and function of CCP clearing, see, for example, Edwards (1984), Moser (1998), Kroszner (1999), Norman (2011), and Pirrong (2011).
[8]Dodd–Frank Act §723(a)(3).

clear for review and approval by the CFTC. In addition, the Dodd–Frank Act requires the CFTC to perform its own independent assessment of specific swaps and classes of swaps that should be subject to the clearing mandate.

The U.S. clearing mandate was implemented in 2013 on a phased-in basis and was fully in effect as of September 9, 2013. Certain "end users" of swaps (i.e., firms that engage in swaps for commercial or risk management purposes and not as an intermediary) are exempt from the mandated clearing requirement. Additional details of the Dodd–Frank clearing mandate (and the end-user exception) are discussed in Section 16.9.2.1 of the Appendix.

16.2.1.2 European Union The European Market Infrastructure Regulation ("EMIR") went into force on August 16, 2012,[9] and included a swap clearing mandate for E.U. member nations. The EMIR clearing mandate is generally comparable to the Dodd–Frank clearing mandate in the United States, and the operational and technical details of the mandate are (as of this writing) now being discussed and reviewed by market participants and European regulators. The mandate is expected to be implemented beginning in 2015 with a 3-year compliance phase-in period.

The responsibility for implementing the EMIR clearing mandate on an ongoing basis lies with the European Securities and Markets Authority ("ESMA"), the independent E.U. authority charged with "ensuring the integrity, transparency, efficiency and orderly functioning of securities markets, as well as enhancing investor protection."[10] As of October 2014, five European CCPs have been authorized by ESMA to clear interest rate derivatives: CME Clearing Europe, Eurex Clearing, LCH.Clearnet, Nasdaq OMX, and Poland's KDPW.

Additional details of the EMIR clearing mandate are provided in the Appendix in Section 16.9.2.2.

16.2.2 Execution

Derivatives can generally be "traded" or executed along a spectrum of market microstructures ranging from direct bilateral negotiation to full exchange trading. In between those two extremes are a variety of alternatives including voice brokerage, EEPs, and prime brokers – all of which are discussed in more detail in Section 16.4.2.

As Table 16.3 indicates, a number of countries either have already implemented or are in the process of putting in place execution mandates for certain OTC derivatives. In contrast to the clearing and reporting principles articulated by the G20, however, most countries are much further behind in implementing these regulations, and a few countries have rejected this requirement outright.

16.2.2.1 United States Following the adoption of the Dodd–Frank Act and related CFTC regulations, all OTC derivatives for which clearing has been mandated and that are traded by U.S. market participants must now be traded on an exchange or through a type of EEP known as a "swap execution facility" ("SEF"). (SEFs are discussed in more detail in Sections 16.4.2.3 and 16.9.3.1, and the applicability of SEF requirements on an international basis is discussed further in Section 16.9.7.2)

As discussed in more detail in Section 16.9.3.1, end users executing certain swap transactions are granted an exception from the Dodd–Frank execution mandate.

16.2.2.2 European Union The revised Markets in Financial Instruments Directive (known as "MiFID 2") delegates authority to ESMA for determining which types of derivatives are subject to mandatory execution requirements. Transactions subject to execution mandates include swaps subject to the EMIR clearing mandate that are made available to trade (MAT) on a regulated exchange, multilateral trading facility ("MTF"), organized trading facility ("OTF"), or an equivalent platform outside the European Union.[11]

As discussed in more detail in Section 16.5.1, the OTC derivatives that now must be traded on a recognized exchange or trading facility are generally the same in the United States and Europe and include most standardized interest rate swaps, forward rate agreements ("FRAs"), and several other types of popular swaps based on interest rates.

16.2.3 Reporting

In the postcrisis regulatory paradigm, most countries have adopted new regulations that require explicit disclosures and reporting for OTC derivative transactions. Reporting requirements generally include most or all OTC derivatives and are not limited to OTC derivatives that are subject to a clearing and/or execution mandate. Table 16.4 summarizes the status of those regulations as of April 2014, and the next two subsections outline the new reporting requirements for the United States and Europe in more detail.

[9]Regulation (E.U.) No. 648/2012 (2012) (in force as of August 16, 2012) (hereinafter "EMIR").

[10]http://www.esma.europa.eu/page/esma-short (last visited April 19, 2014).

[11]Cleared swaps also must be sufficiently liquid to be subject to mandatory execution requirements.

TABLE 16.3 Status as of April 2014 of OTC Derivatives Execution Mandate Implementation

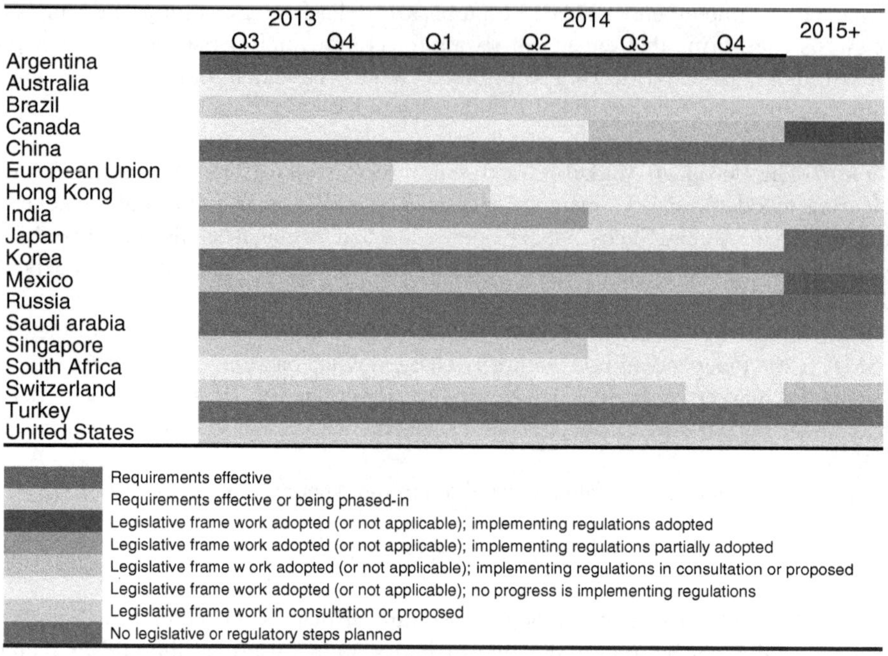

Source: Financial Stability Board, Seventh Progress Report on Implementation (April 8, 2014).

TABLE 16.4 Status as of April 2014 of OTC Derivatives Reporting Implementation

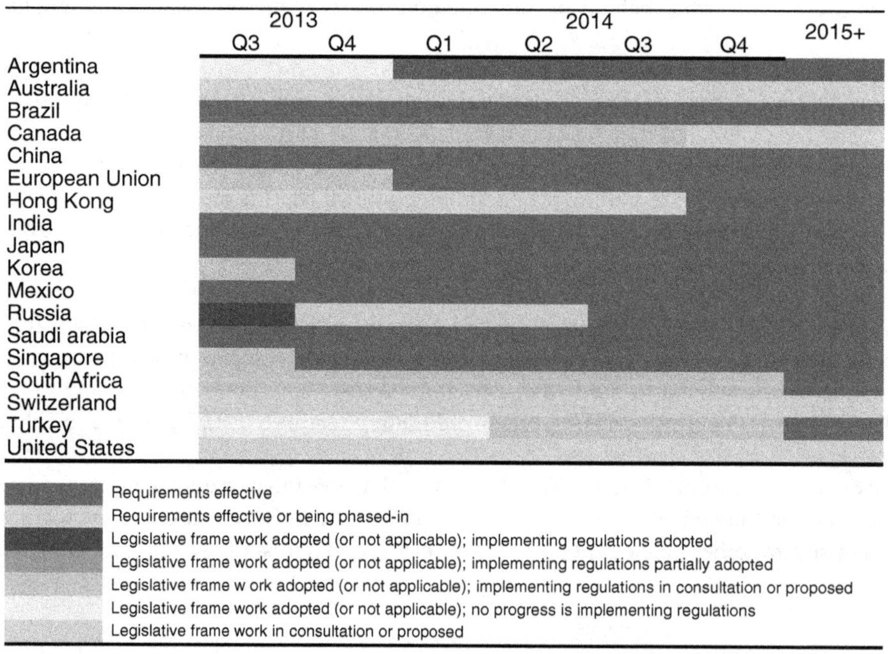

Source: Financial Stability Board, Seventh Progress Report on Implementation (April 8, 2014).

16.2.3.1 United States The Dodd–Frank Act and CFTC regulations establish various mandatory reporting requirements for certain OTC derivatives (including most interest rate derivatives). The specific requirements and the dates on which compliance was required vary depending on the type of OTC derivatives contract, the type of market participant, and the specific reporting requirement (of which there are three).[12] Section 16.9.4.1 in the Appendix reviews the reporting requirements for transactions

[12]For a summary of the reporting requirements for different market participants, see Davis & Wardwell LLP (2012a), and Nazareth and Rosenberg (2013).

involving at least one U.S. market participant in more detail. Transactions involving two counterparties that are not classified as U.S. market participants are not subject to these reporting requirements. (*See* Section 16.9.7.1 for a discussion of the exceptions.)

The first reporting requirement generally obligates U.S. market participants to report certain details of all new OTC interest rate derivatives transactions to a recognized swap data repository ("SDR") as of January 2013. As of this writing, U.S. SDRs that are registered with the CFTC include SDRs operated by the Depository Trust & Clearing Corporation ("DTCC") (as of September 19, 2012), the Intercontinental Exchange ("ICE") (as of June 27, 2012), Chicago Mercantile Exchange (CME) (as of November 20, 2012), and Bloomberg (as of January 17, 2014).

The second reporting requirement is a real-time reporting mandate that requires certain key information about new swap trades (i.e., time and date of execution, effective start and end dates, whether the swap is cleared, and pricing information) to be provided to an SDR and to be publicly distributed by the SDR in a manner that keeps counterparty identities anonymous. Most trades must be reported as soon as operationally possible after their execution, although large block trades are publicly disseminated by SDRs subject to a reporting delay.

The third requirement is a historical requirement for the "back loading" of basic economic data for swaps that were executed before the enactment of the Dodd–Frank Act ("preenactment swaps"), as well as swaps entered into on or after the date on which the Dodd–Frank Act was signed into law (i.e., July 21, 2010) ("transition swaps"). These two categories are collectively referred to as "historical swaps."[13] Mandatory reporting for historical swaps began on January 30, 2013.

Much of the data analyzed later in this chapter is based on trades registered with DTCC or the Bloomberg Swap Data Repository ("BSDR") as collected and filtered by the International Swaps and Derivatives Association ("ISDA"). Specifically, ISDA excludes all registered transactions that represent terminations, novations, or back loads of previously executed trades so that only new trades are represented in its data, which is reported each day on its Swapsinfo.org platform.[14]

16.2.3.2 European Union EMIR requires all counterparties and CCPs in the European Union to report the details of any swap transaction to a trade repository ("TR") recognized by ESMA within one business day of its execution or any major event in the life of an existing swap transaction.[15] New swaps were required to be reported beginning on February 12, 2014. As of this writing, six TRs have been registered with ESMA: CME Trade Repository Ltd., DTCC Trade Repository Ltd. ("DDRL"), ICE Trade Vault Europe Ltd., Krajowy Depozyt Papierw Wartosciowych S.A., Regis-TR S.A., and UnaVista Ltd. As of September 2014, the largest of these six TRs – DTCC's DDRL – reported receiving an average of 12.35 million trade reports per week.[16]

The data that must be transmitted is broadly similar to the data U.S. swap participants must report to an SDR. Unlike the U.S. regulations, however, the EMIR reporting requirement applies to *both* counterparties and includes nonfinancial corporate end users of interest rate derivatives. Like the Dodd–Frank Act, EMIR also mandates the reporting of both historical and new swaps to an SDR. Historical transactions that must be reported include any swaps executed from August 16, 2012 (i.e., the date EMIR was in force), up to the compliance date for new swap transaction reporting.

Since the February 2014 mandated compliance date of the EMIR reporting mandate, numerous problems with compliance and reconciliation have been reported. In particular, many counterparties submit information to different TRs, and market participants report that the details of the transactions often cannot be reconciled across TRs. DTCC indicated that about 60% of all trades registered in its E.U. TR could not be matched.[17] Reports also indicate that many market participants still may not be reporting trades as required under the EMIR mandate.[18]

16.3 EXCHANGE-TRADED DERIVATIVES

16.3.1 Major Products

As their name suggests, exchange-traded derivatives are listed for trading by organized financial exchanges and are cleared by CCPs. Exchange-traded derivatives include futures, options on futures, and certain other options – all of which have the common denominator that they are negotiated within the confines of an exchange's contract specifications and rules. Contract terms typically include the size/quantity of the underlying deliverable or reference asset, the minimum quote/price increment for the contract, the dates on which trading ceases (i.e., the expiration or maturity date) and delivery/settlement occur, and the like. The primary contractual term that is determined by negotiations between trading participants and that is *not* predefined by the exchange is the price at which an exchange-traded derivatives contract is traded.

[13]Dodd–Frank Act §723(h)(5).

[14]Data reported by ISDA's SwapsInfo from January 2013 through May 9, 2014, reflects only data reported to DTCC, whereas data from May 12, 2014, onward reflects aggregate data reported to DTCC's SDR and BSDR. All subsequent references to trades reported to DTCC and/or BSDR adhere to this dating convention.

[15]For additional information, see Gibson, Dunn, & Crutcher LLP (2014).

[16]Maxwell (2014b).

[17]Maxwell (2014a).

[18]See, for example, Maxwell (2014b).

Popular exchange-traded interest rate derivatives may be cash-settled or physically settled. In a cash-settled futures contract, the final settlement of the contract at maturity involves a cash payment by the long to the short for the cash equivalent of the underlying reference product or rate. The most popular and actively traded cash-settled exchange-traded interest rate derivatives are futures contracts based on Eurodeposit index rates. For example, one of the earliest exchange-traded interest rate derivatives is the 3-month Eurodollar futures contract that was first listed for trading by CME in December 1981. The CME Eurodollar futures contract has a value that is based on an index of the 3-month London Interbank Offered Rate ("LIBOR") – i.e., the rate on a "hypothetical" 3-month noncallable certificate of deposit ("CD") negotiated in the London Eurodollar market and averaged across multiple banks that contribute to the index. Similar contracts based on different underlying currencies and maturities are listed for trading by several global futures exchanges.

Unlike a cash-settled contract that involves only transfers of cash between the long and the short at maturity, a physically settled exchange-traded interest rate derivatives contract requires the short to deliver physically (e.g., through electronic transfer of book ownership) a security that is eligible for delivery to the long upon expiration of the contract. The most popular physically settled exchange-traded interest rate derivatives are futures based on government bonds. For example, the 10-year T-Note futures contract listed by the Chicago Board of Trade ("CBOT") is based on one U.S. Treasury Note with a face value at maturity of $100,000 that has at least 6.5 years to maturity but no greater than 10 years to maturity. The contract stops trading on the seventh business day preceding the last business day of the delivery month. During the delivery month, a short that opts to deliver (instead of offsetting the position with a long) must deliver any eligible T-Note to the long via the Federal Reserve's book-entry wire transfer settlement system.[19]

16.3.2 Execution

Exchange-traded derivatives are, by definition, traded on organized derivatives exchanges. An "exchange" is an organization that provides an integrated "all-to-all" trading venue for trading participants. Furthermore, a derivatives exchange is always functionally and legally integrated with a designated CCP to enable access and anonymous liquidity formation in this all-to-all trading setup.

Most exchange trading of interest rate derivatives today is accomplished electronically through central limit-order books ("CLOBs"). On some exchanges (notably the CME Group), open outcry is also used for negotiating interest rate derivatives prices and executing interest rate derivatives transactions. In open outcry trading, market participants gather in physical trading pits and literally shout bids, offers, and order sizes until a transaction is consummated, at which point it is then reported and confirmed.

Panel A of Figure 16.1 illustrates the simplified mechanics of an exchange-traded interest rate derivatives transaction (e.g., a Eurodollar futures contract in which Firm ABC is the long and Firm XYZ is the short). Step 1 requires that Firm ABC, Firm XYZ, and all other trading participants on the exchange deposit initial margin, as discussed in Section 16.3.3.2. (Steps or stages of transaction negotiation and execution are shown in Panel A of Figure 16.1 and in later figures as the number of the step inside a circle.) In this example, trading counterparties ABC and XYZ are presumed to be "clearing members" of the CCP – that is, they have a direct relationship to the CCP, which includes the requirement to deposit initial margin with the CCP or the CCP's designated clearing bank. Clearing members and their distinction from nonclearing members are discussed in Section 16.3.3.1.

Step 2 of the example involves the submission of bids or offers by Firm ABC and any other trading participants on the exchange for a given interest rate derivatives product. In Step 3, the bids and offers submitted by Firm ABC and the other trading participants active in that product market are matched either in the exchange's CLOB or through the open outcry process. If and when those bids and offers are matched, the trade is executed and registered with the exchange (and the parties are notified accordingly once the trade is confirmed). At that point, the exchange-designated CCP becomes the counterparty to both Firms ABC and XYZ on the newly executed trade, as shown in Step 3 of Panel A of Figure 16.1.

As of Step 4 in the trading process, the two trades between Firms ABC and XYZ and the CCP are now open contracts and thus subject to ongoing margin requirements. The solid arrows between Firms ABC and XYZ and the CCP reflect the at-least-daily (usually twice-daily) variation margin flows that continue as long as the trade remains open.

16.3.3 Clearing

All exchange-traded derivatives are centrally cleared by a CCP affiliated with or designated by the exchange. As noted in Section 16.2.1 and illustrated in Panel A of Figure 16.1, the original counterparties that execute an exchange-traded derivatives trade are not exposed to each other's credit risk and are instead both exposed to the credit risk of the CCP. Because trading participants whose transactions are cleared and settled by a CCP are essentially exchanging the credit risk of their original counterparties for the credit risk of the CCP, the CCP must maintain financial resources and risk management policies and procedures

[19] For further contract specifications, see CME Group (2014).

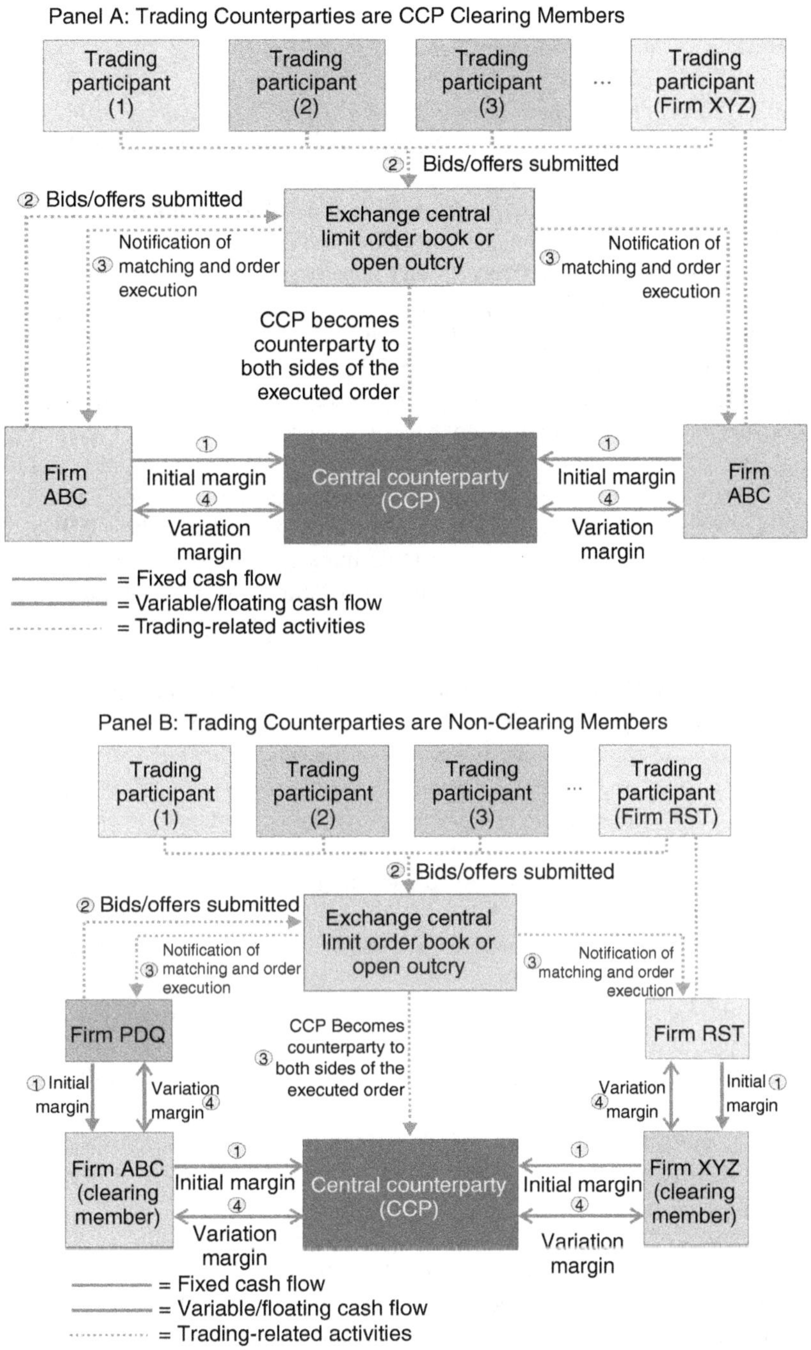

Figure 16.1 Eurodollar futures contract executed on-exchange and cleared by CCP.

sufficient to preserve the confidence of their members as well as market stability and the integrity of the global payment system. In addition, shareholder-owned CCPs have equity investors that seek to avoid catastrophic losses.[20] For all of these reasons, CCPs have historically maintained relatively conservative risk management practices based on a multitiered system of risk controls, policies, and procedures designed to manage the credit exposure of the CCP and its participating clearing members.

16.3.3.1 Clearing Member-Centric Structure The first tier is the clearing member-centric structure of CCPs. More specifically, all CCPs have certain clearing members that are subject to various membership, risk management, and minimum capital

[20]CCPs that are not shareholder owned also have an incentive to avoid catastrophic losses, although the incentive for managers of such CCPs is more in the form of reputation than explicit financial claims on the CCP's earnings.

requirements. In the event that a clearing member of a CCP cannot honor all of its open obligations to the CCP, the CCP steps in and guarantees all amounts owed to other clearing members of the CCP.

All transactions cleared through a CCP must be guaranteed by a clearing member of that CCP. In Panel A of Figure 16.1, we assumed that Firms ABC and XYZ were clearing members of the CCP. Panel B of Figure 16.1 illustrates how this process works when two *non*clearing members are the original trading counterparties whose orders are matched in the exchange's CLOB or other trading mechanisms.

In Panel B of Figure 16.1, continue to assume that Firms ABC and XYZ are clearing members, but now assume that non-clearing member Firms PDQ and RST are the original trading firms. Firm PDQ has its trades cleared and guaranteed by Firm ABC, and Firm RST clears through Firm XYZ. In the event that nonclearing Firms PDQ or RST cannot honor their payment obligations to clearing member Firms ABC or XYZ, respectively, the clearing firms are still obliged to make any corresponding payments due to the CCP arising from PDQ and RST's trading activity.

In Step 1 in Panel B of Figure 16.1, the trading counterparties Firms PDQ and RST now deposit initial margin not with the CCP but rather their designated clearing members ABC and XYZ, respectively (or the clearing banks nominated by the clearing members). Clearing members then deposit initial margin to the CCP on a gross basis – that is, the total initial margin requirement of each clearing member to the CCP for its customer positions is the sum of all the minimum initial margin requirements for all customers. The Step 1 initial margin cash flows (or deposits of eligible securities) thus now show up in four places in Panel B of Figure 16.1 – that is, between Firms PDQ and RST and their respective clearing members ABC and XYZ and again between clearing members ABC and XYZ and the CCP. Similarly, variation margin in Step 4 now flows between the CCP and clearing members ABC and XYZ, and the clearing members collect and distribute corresponding variation margin to their customers Firms PDQ and RST.

16.3.3.2 Initial Margin Requirements CCPs require clearing members to collateralize their risk by posting initial margin as a performance bond for all newly opened positions. Initial margin is posted for any newly established positions, and all open positions must satisfy minimum margin requirements on an ongoing basis. CCPs have strict policies regarding the types of collateral that can be used to satisfy these margin requirements. These margin requirements are intended to ensure that, in the event of a clearing member failure following significant adverse price movements, sufficient liquid funds will be available to cover the losses on its open positions.

As noted in the previous section, clearing members also collect margin from their customers. In practice, clearing members of CCPs generally require more margin from nonclearing customers than the exchange-affiliated CCP demands as minimum initial margin from clearing members. Initial margin deposits are shown as Step 1 in Figure 16.1.

16.3.3.3 Marking to Market and Variation Margin CCPs mark all open positions of clearing members to current market prices and calculate the resulting profits and losses at least once each day (and twice at most large CCPs). Losses on any accounts must be settled with a CCP, usually in cash or cash-equivalent securities such as Treasury bills, or, in some cases, with excess margin on deposit.[21,22] In this manner, the CCP ensures that its exposure to the risk of a clearing member failure is limited by the time between mark-to-market intervals and the time it takes to close out the positions of a failing clearing member. The payments and collections that result from marking open positions to market are known as variation margin and are shown as Step 4 in Figure 16.1.

16.3.3.4 Financial Safeguards and Default Resolution Plans In addition to the three risk management tiers discussed earlier, if the financial resources of a clearing member are inadequate to cover any unsettled obligations to the CCP, the clearing member may be declared in default by the CCP. Following a clearing member default, the CCP assumes any net unsettled obligations and open positions from the defaulting clearing member. Most CCPs then attempt to hedge or liquidate those positions in a timely and nondestabilizing manner based on a default resolution plan maintained by CCPs. All CCPs maintain default resolution plans that govern their hedging or liquidation of open positions at defaulting clearing members.

If the failure of a clearing member occurs as a result of losses unrelated to its futures trading activities or losses in the firm's house trading account, the accounts of the customers of that firm (e.g., Firms PDQ and RST in Panel B of Figure 16.1) are transferred to a nondefaulting firm. Customers may suffer a brief inconvenience but generally do not experience any losses or limited access to their funds.

If the failure of a clearing member occurs as a result of losses in its customer accounts, however, customers of the defaulting clearing member can experience losses. Known as "fellow customer risk," these losses can occur if one or more customers of

[21] Clearing members generally maintain excess funds in their margin accounts to avoid the risk of becoming undermargined.

[22] Some CCPs allow certain members to cover only losses that cause an account to fall below a specified maintenance margin level, where the maintenance margin is below the initial margin requirement. If the value of the account falls below the maintenance margin level, sufficient funds must be paid to the CCP to cover the losses and restore the value of the account back to the initial margin requirement.

the clearing member fail to make a required variation margin payment *and* the clearing member lacks the financial resources to cover any resulting open payment obligation to the CCP. In that situation, the CCP is entitled to liquidate the open *customer* positions of the defaulting clearing member and apply the proceeds from those liquidations to the defaulting member's unmet obligations to the clearinghouse.[23]

In the event that any losses realized by a CCP are not fully covered by the margin, position liquidations, and other available assets of the defaulting clearing member, CCPs rely on their "risk capital structures" to absorb those losses. In particular, CCPs maintain mutualized clearing default guarantee funds to which all clearing members must contribute. In general, the total size of a CCP's clearing default guarantee fund must be large enough to cover losses arising from the default of the two largest clearing members in the CCP during extreme but plausible market conditions.[24] Each individual clearing member's required contribution to the clearing default guarantee fund is determined by a CCP based on the amount of risk to which the CCP is exposed as a result of the clearing member's trading activities.

If a defaulting clearing member's losses exceed its margin and other assets held by the CCP, the defaulting clearing member's contribution to the CCP's clearing default guarantee fund is applied next. Any remaining CCP losses are then covered by some combination of the CCP's retained earnings (or a portion thereof), the remainder of the guarantee fund (which consists of the contributions of the *non*defaulting clearing members), and (at some CCPs) postloss assessments on nondefaulting clearing members. These layers of protection are referred to as the clearinghouse's waterfall, and the types and order of these protections may differ from CCP to CCP.

16.3.4 Market Activity

Figure 16.2 shows the total notional amounts of exchange-traded interest rate derivatives outstanding on a quarterly basis from March 1993 through June 2014, where the dotted and striped bars indicate futures and options, respectively. The incredible growth of the market in the period from 2000 through its peak in June 2007 is immediately apparent. Over that period, notional amounts outstanding rose by 614%. Following the onset of the global financial crisis in 2007, however, market activity has ebbed and flowed. In the most recent quarter as of this writing (i.e., the quarter ending in June 2014), the notional amounts of exchange-traded interest rate derivatives traded had returned to levels in excess of volumes in 2005 and earlier but had not recovered to 2007 precrisis levels.

Also noteworthy in Figure 16.2 is the relative increase in the popularity of option-based exchange-traded interest rate derivatives vis-à-vis futures products. For the quarter ending in March 1993, options represented only 34% of total notional open interest, whereas options accounted for 58% of open interest in the quarter ending June 2014.

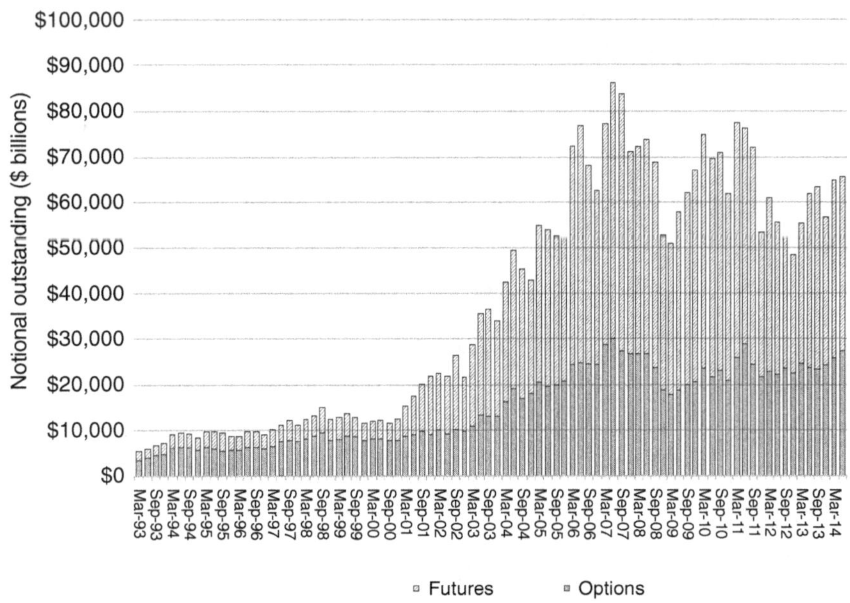

Figure 16.2 Notional amounts of exchange-traded interest rate derivatives outstanding. Source: Bank for International Settlements.

[23]In practice, this has only occurred once in the history of U.S. futures markets – in 1998 with the failure of Griffin Trading. "Fellow customer risk" thus is a real risk, but a relatively remote one as history has shown. For a more detailed discussion, see Compass Lexecon (2013).

[24]Committee on Payment and Settlement Systems and Technical Committee of the International Organization of Securities Commissions (2012).

In 2013, about 200 distinct interest rate futures and options contracts were listed for trading on more than 20 exchanges. Roughly \$3.3 billion of these contracts were traded in 2013. Figure 16.3 shows the most popular types of exchange-traded interest rate derivatives based on total 2013 trading volume. About 85% of all volume involved futures contracts based on government bonds, 3-month interest rates on depository or banking instruments, and overnight interest rates (including interbank rates like the U.S. Fed Funds rate and overnight repo rates). The types of products that accounted for the remaining roughly 15% of total contracts traded in 2013 include futures on 1-month deposit rates, futures on interest rates swaps, options on 3-month deposit rate futures, options on government bond futures, and options on overnight rate futures.

To get a more specific look at the particular contracts that accounted for the largest amounts of 2013 volume (as shown in Figure 16.3), Figure 16.4 shows the total 2013 trading volume for the 15 most actively traded exchange-traded interest rate

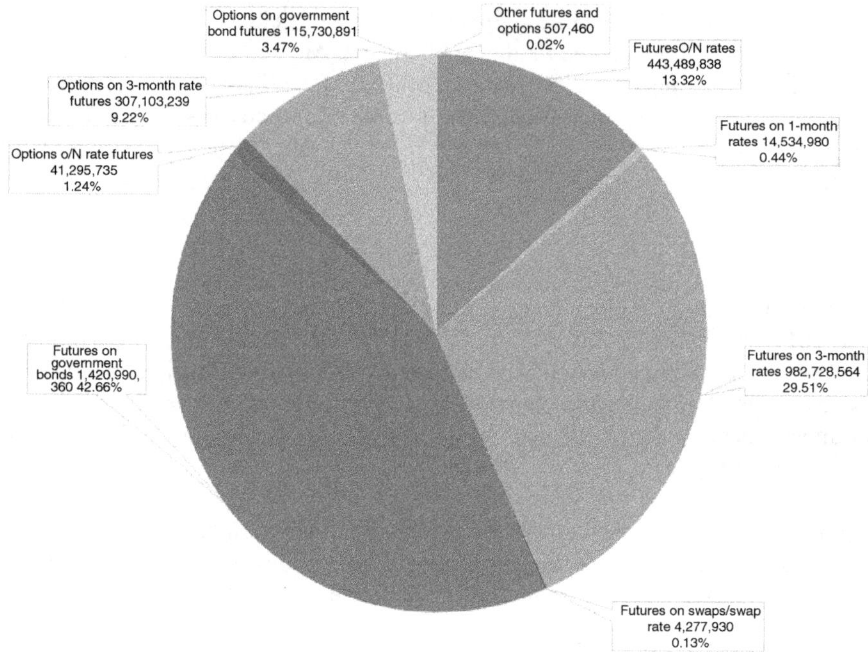

Figure 16.3 Total 2013 volume (number of contracts traded) of top 150 exchange-traded interest rate derivative contracts by type. "O/N" denotes an overnight rate and includes O/N interbank and repo rates. Source: FIA & author's calculations.

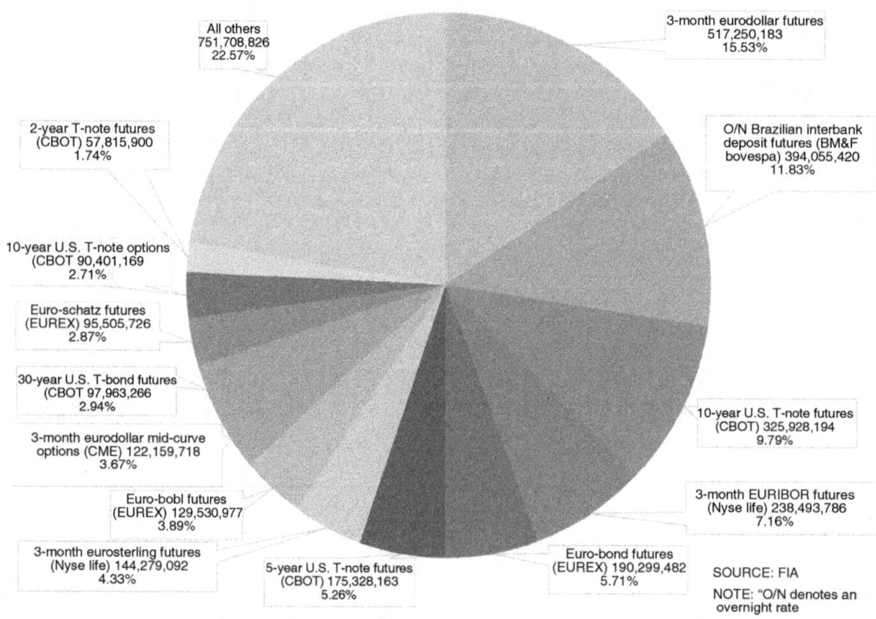

Figure 16.4 Total 2013 volume (number of contracts traded) of top 15 interest rate futures and options contracts. "O/N" denotes an overnight rate. Source: FIA.

derivatives. The data labels in Figure 16.4 indicate the names of the contracts and the exchanges on which they are traded (within parentheses), followed by the total numbers of contracts traded in 2013 and the percentage of total 2013 exchange-traded interest rate derivatives volume. By far the most actively traded contracts were the Eurodollar futures contract based on 3-month LIBOR listed by CME, the overnight interbank deposit futures contract traded on Brazil's BM&FBOVESPA, and the futures contract listed by the CBOT – a division of CME Group – on 10-year U.S. Treasury Notes, which accounted for 15.53%, 11.83%, and 9.79% of total 2013 exchange-traded interest rate derivatives volume, respectively. As Figure 16.4 also shows, the 13 most actively traded contracts represented 77% of all trading activity in 2013.

16.4 NONCLEARED SWAPS

16.4.1 Major Products

OTC derivatives (a.k.a. "swaps") have historically referred to bilateral derivatives contracts that are not negotiated on an organized financial exchange. The primary distinguishing feature of swaps is that the counterparties can customize the contract across virtually any terms. The key terms of the most common swaps include the following:

- Underlying reference rate(s) (e.g., Eurodeposit rates like LIBOR or the Euro Interbank Offered Rate ("EURIBOR"), 30-day commercial paper rate, Prime, Fed Funds) or fixed-income security prices or rates (e.g., 30-year constant maturity Treasury, 3-month T-Bill, long-term Japanese government bond)
- Additional pricing information, such as spreads to be added to the underlying reference rate(s) or amounts to be paid up front
- Dates relevant to the transaction, including trade date, maturity date, value and calculation date(s), and settlement date(s)
- Events that would lead to the early termination of the contract (e.g., changes in tax policy or regulation, corporate actions, events of default)
- Definition of events of default
- Credit enhancements required by one or both counterparties (as discussed in Section 16.4.3)
- Representations and warranties by both counterparties

Virtually all swaps today are negotiated pursuant to pro forma documents known as master agreements that specify the standard terms for a typical swap transaction along the lines above. Although those terms can be customized by the counterparties through the use of schedules and amendments, master agreements serve as foundational legal agreements on which all covered transactions between two counterparties with an executed master agreement are based.

The most prevalent OTC interest rate derivatives include the following:

- *Fixed-for-floating swaps:* Fixed-for-floating interest rate swaps are contracts in which counterparties periodically exchange a fixed payment for a payment based on an underlying reference rate (calculated with respect to a notional principal amount) at specified intervals over a fixed life of the contract. A "plain vanilla" fixed-for-floating swap is an interest rate swap in which the floating reference rate is usually a 3-month Eurodeposit rate (e.g., 3-month LIBOR or 3-month EURIBOR). The floating leg involves quarterly payments (usually calculated on a settled-in-arrears basis), the fixed leg generally involves semiannual payments, and the settlement dates often correspond to the maturity dates of the corresponding March, June, September, and December 3-month Eurodeposit futures contracts. Quarterly reset or settlement dates that correspond to futures contract expirations are called International Monetary Market ("IMM") reset or settlement dates.
- *FRAs*: FRAs are forward contracts on interest rates based on the difference at maturity between the underlying reference rate prevailing on the FRA maturity date and a fixed rate specified on the trade date. Payments are calculated with respect to a notional principal amount. For example, a 2x5 USD FRA is a 2-month forward contract in which the long receives (pays) the difference between 3-month LIBOR observed when the FRA matures 2 months after the trade date and the agreed fixed rate (adjusted for day counting) where payments are calculated with respect to a specified notional amount.
- *Overnight index swaps ("OISs")*: OISs are fixed-for-floating interest rate swaps in which the floating reference rate is generally a geometric average of an overnight lending rate (e.g., the U.S. Fed Funds rate or the Euro Overnight Index Average ("EONIA") rate) over each periodic settlement period.
- *Cross-currency swaps:* Cross-currency swaps are swaps in which the principal amounts of the fixed and floating legs are denominated in different currencies and exchanged at both the inception and the maturity of the swap. Fixed-for-floating cross-currency swaps involve a fixed leg and a floating leg in which periodic payments are based on an underlying reference rate corresponding to the currency denomination for that leg of the swap. Cross-currency swaps can also be basis swaps in

which both legs are floating. In general, cross-currency swaps can be viewed as combinations of fixed-for-floating interest rate swaps with "forex swaps" where the latter involve exchanges of the face value of the swap at the spot rate (on the trade date of the swap) and at the forward rate prevailing on the trade date (with the exchange of currency occurring at the end of the life of the swap).

- *Inflation swaps:* An inflation swap is a fixed-for-floating interest rate swap in which the floating leg is based on the actual change in some reference price level measure (e.g., the U.S. consumer price index). Most inflation swaps are zero-coupon swaps in which a single payment is exchanged at maturity based on the difference between actual inflation over the life of the swap and a fixed swap rate based on the difference between yields on government securities and inflation-protected securities (e.g., Treasury Inflation Protected Securities) on the trade date.
- *Caps and collars:* Caps and collars are portfolios of options on interest rates bundled and sold as single financial products. In a typical cap, the long receives periodic payments (on "caplets" corresponding to each reset period) if the underlying reference rate exceeds a fixed strike rate. Conversely, a floor involves payments by the short to the long when rates are below the fixed strike rate in any given reset period (i.e., on any given "floorlet"). Payments are calculated with respect to notional principal amounts, and underlying reference rates are usually 3-month Eurodeposit rates. Combinations of caps and floors are used to create collars, which are also separately negotiated as bundled financial products.
- *Swaptions:* A swaption is an option to enter into an interest rate swap at or before the swaption's maturity date at a predefined rate on the fixed leg of the underlying interest rate swap. In a receiver swaption, the purchaser has the right but not the obligation to enter into an interest rate swap as the floating leg payer and fixed leg receiver. Conversely, a payer swaption enables its purchaser to enter into the underlying interest rate swap as the fixed-rate payer.
- *Exotics:* The "exotics" category essentially includes "all other" OTC interest rate derivatives. Some exotics are not that complicated, but are classified as exotic because of their relatively limited demand and low liquidity – for example, cross-currency swaptions for exotic currency pairs. Other exotics are highly customized, bilateral transactions between a counterparty with very specific investment or risk management objectives and a swap dealer that is willing to take the other side of the trade. Exotic OTC interest rate derivatives include constant maturity swaps, yield curve flattener/steepener swaps, callable capped floaters, callable inverse floaters, callable "snowballs," and so on.[25]

16.4.2 Execution

The trading and execution of noncleared swaps can be accomplished in a variety of specific ways. For pedagogical simplicity, we can classify noncleared swap execution into two categories: bilateral execution or execution through EEPs.

16.4.2.1 Bilateral Execution Literally for centuries, OTC derivatives have been negotiated bilaterally between two "end users" (i.e., nonintermediary firms with comparable but offsetting risk exposures and risk management objectives).[26] OTC derivatives began to emerge as popular tools of corporate treasury risk management and finance in the early 1980s. In the beginning, most swaps were one-off interest rate or currency transactions arranged by banks and negotiated between two corporate end users. In those days, banks acted as brokers for and advisors to their corporate customers by helping them identify other end users with which a swap might be done, but the swap was executed between the two corporations. Banks were not typically principals or counterparties in those transactions.

For each transaction, the advising bank had to identify two different end users with essentially equal but opposite risk management objectives – for example, one end user that wanted to pay a fixed rate and another that wanted to pay a floating rate over the same time period and on the same notional principal amount. The first such modern transaction between two end users of OTC derivatives occurred in 1981 when the World Bank and IBM executed a swap agreement arranged by Salomon Brothers.[27]

Figure 16.5 illustrates a hypothetical transaction involving a plain vanilla interest rate swap in which Firm ABC agrees to make periodic (e.g., semiannual) fixed-rate payments to Firm XYZ in exchange for receiving periodic (e.g., quarterly) floating-rate payments based on 3-month EURIBOR ("3mEURIBOR"). Both the fixed and floating payment amounts are calculated with respect to a notional principal of €100 million, and the hypothetical swap has a tenor of 2 years. In this transaction, counterparties ABC and XYZ negotiate all the terms of the swap either bilaterally or through a voice broker.

As Figure 16.5 also indicates, either or both of Firms ABC and XYZ may be required to post initial collateral to mitigate the ongoing bilateral credit exposure to which the swap may expose them. As interest rates change over the life of the transaction, the credit exposure of the swap will change. Most credit support annexes ("CSAs") to the master agreements under which swaps are negotiated call for periodic cash resettlements or variation margin.

[25] See, for example, Belomestny, Kolodko, and Schoenmakers (2009).
[26] See, for example, De Roover (1948, 1999), Swan (2000), and Culp (2004).
[27] Park (1984), and Flavell (2010).

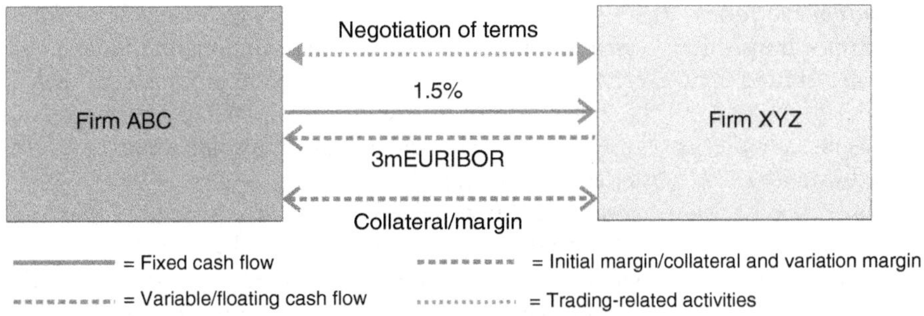

Figure 16.5 Bilateral noncleared plain vanilla 2-Year EURIBOR swap.

As corporate end users began increasingly to use swaps for financing and risk management purposes, the practice of banks directly matching two end users became inefficient and impractical. In response, banks began to function as financial intermediaries in which they were principals to the transactions. These "swap dealers" began to negotiate interest rate swaps with corporate end users *before* identifying an offsetting counterparty. Dealers treated the transactions negotiated with end users as if they were put into a warehouse, and relied on exchange-traded derivatives and interdealer OTC derivatives transactions to hedge the residual risks of their warehouse of customer transactions.

Because swaps exposed both counterparties to bilateral credit risk on often long-dated transactions, customers gravitated toward dealers with relatively greater capital and higher credit ratings (primarily highly rated and well-capitalized European and U.S. banks). A few large nonbank firms also emerged as dealers in certain markets. For example, then-AAA-rated insurance company AIG was a major dealer in OTC currency and interest rate derivative markets.

Many OTC derivatives today are still negotiated between a dealer and an end user or between two dealers. As noted earlier in discussing Figure 16.5, voice brokers also play important roles in OTC derivatives by helping dealers (and sometimes end users) identify willing counterparties and compare different transaction quotes and prices. The involvement of a broker does not, however, change the fundamentally bilateral nature of the OTC derivatives they help arrange; the execution of the ultimate contract is still private and bilateral. In other words, the broker is generally not a principal in the transaction, but is rather a facilitator in matching principals in order to help reduce search costs.[28]

As of June 2010 (prior to the imposition of any clearing or execution mandates), IOSCO estimated that 87.7% of interest rate swaps were negotiated through voice brokers.[29] The primary arena in which brokers operate is the interdealer market – that is, the marketplace in which OTC derivatives are negotiated between dealers. Interdealer brokers have historically been primarily voice brokers. In the past decade, interdealer brokers have also begun to offer a variety of electronic communication services to participants of the OTC derivatives market segment, as discussed in the next section.

Interdealer voice brokerage services have also played an important role historically in the execution of "noncontinuously liquid" transactions that occur on a more ad hoc basis. Indeed, the perception that the primary function of interdealer brokerage dealers is to operate "flow desks" to facilitate transactions in benchmark and exchange look-alike OTC derivatives is somewhat misplaced. In fact, perhaps the most significant source of value that interdealer brokers bring to OTC derivatives participants is their role in facilitating the execution of complex and multilegged trades by dealers.[30] For example, if a dealer wishes to execute a complex transaction and simultaneously wishes to enter into one or more "dynamic" hedges of that transaction, interdealer brokers can help dealers identify contemporaneous transaction opportunities across multiple asset classes and product types. Or if a dealer wishes to transact simultaneously in two related products, interdealer brokers can help the dealer ascertain the price impacts of the trades in both markets. In this manner, interdealer brokers help OTC derivatives dealers manage their own risks and act as risk transfer intermediaries for certain end users of derivatives.

Interdealer brokers may also provide a bridge to exchange-traded derivatives by offering "exchange give-up" services. Specifically, interdealer brokers can engage in exchange-traded derivatives trading on behalf of their clients as executing brokers on organized exchanges. After the trade occurs, the interdealer broker gives up the position to the client's regular clearing broker, which then manages the open position as a traditional exchange-traded derivative between the client and the CCP affiliated with the exchange on which the exchange-traded derivative was executed.[31]

[28] There are exceptions. Some interdealer brokers are willing to act as principals to OTC derivatives in certain circumstances. See Wholesale Markets Brokers' Association/London Energy Brokers' Association (2010), p. 44 (hereinafter "WMBA/LEBA 2010").

[29] Technical Committee of the International Organization of Securities Commissions (2011).

[30] See, for example, WMBA/LEBA 2010, op. cit., pp. 37 & 46.

[31] See, for example, WMBA/LEBA 2010, op. cit., p. 44.

16.4.2.2 Electronic Execution Platforms EEPs generally encompass a broad range of execution forums that facilitate transactions in an organized electronic transactional venue governed by a set of nondiscretionary rules and objective criteria for trade execution. In some cases, the resulting trade executed on the EEP is then novated to or registered with a CCP, which becomes the counterparty to both sides of the trade. If the transaction is not cleared, then, after the execution of the transaction on the EEP, the resulting contract is just a traditional bilateral agreement between the two counterparties for the life of the transaction and is generally documented with an ISDA master agreement and CSA.

EEPs typically have a core group of one or more "liquidity providers," which are generally swap dealers that are willing to make markets in some or all of the EEPs' supported product types. One-to-many EEPs involve a single sponsoring entity that establishes an EEP as a mechanism for trading with multiple counterparties, whereas many-to-many EEPs involve multiple liquidity providers trading with multiple swap participants. Users of EEPs include other dealers, as well as major swap participants ("MSPs") and eligible contract participants ("ECPs"). (*See* Section 16.9.1.2 of the Appendix for definitions of these terms.)

Some EEPs provide request-for-quote ("RFQ") facilities in which participants can request firm price quotes from a specific subset of one or more liquidity providers, which enables swap participants to negotiate with one or more market participants without negotiating with the entire universe of sell-side participants on the EEP.[32] Other EEPs provide request-for-stream ("RFS") services in which firm prices are published in real time by one or more liquidity providers in response to a request from another market participant. Execution facilities that offer the economic equivalent of a CLOB have also emerged in recent years.

Figure 16.6 illustrates the mechanics of the same swap shown in Figure 16.5 that is now executed by Firm ABC through an EEP. The EEP in this example is a one-to-many platform with multiple liquidity providers and customers (of which Firm ABC is one). In this example, Firm ABC submits an RFQ for the swap through the EEP in Step 1.[33] The EEP then notifies the liquidity providers (or the subset of liquidity providers specified by Firm ABC) of Firm ABC's RFQ on a 2-year €100 million plain vanilla swap in which the liquidity providers would receive 3mEURIBOR quarterly. The liquidity providers then respond in Step 2 with their offered fixed rates to pay in the swap. In the example, Firm ABC selects the 1.5% fixed rate offered by Firm XYZ in Step 3. At that point, Firms ABC and XYZ enter into a bilateral agreement that formally executes the swap (and any required documentation, such as a master agreement and CSA).

Once the counterparties have been matched and the transactions has been executed, the EEP in Step 4 reports the transaction to a registered SDR (United States) or TR (European Union) as discussed in Section 16.2.2. The life of the swap begins in Step 5, at which point any initial margin or collateral is exchanged. After that, the frequency and nature of variation margin cash flows and periodic net interest settlements are dictated by the terms of the underlying master agreement and CSA.

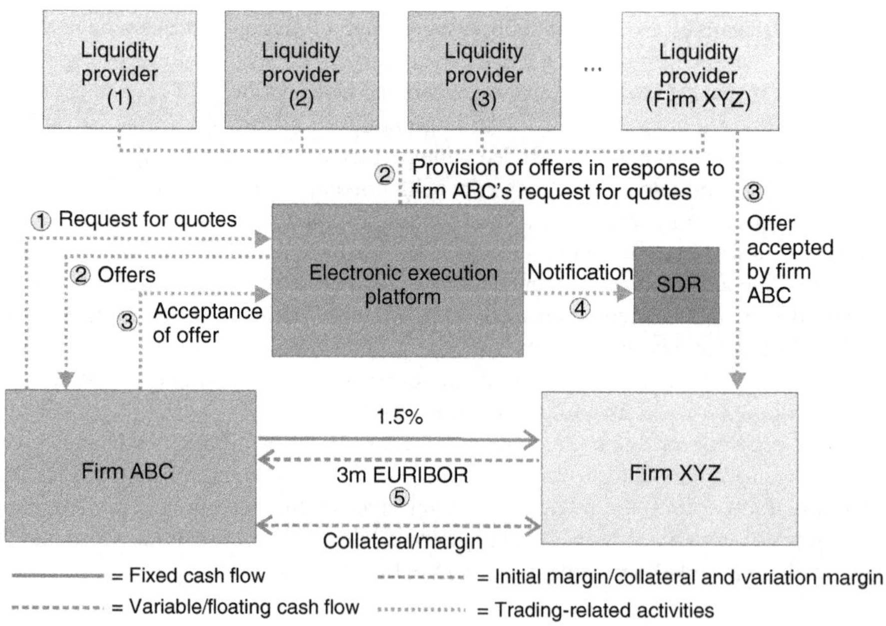

Figure 16.6 Noncleared plain vanilla 2-year EURIBOR swap executed on an EEP.

[32]Transactions on EEPs that offer multilateral negotiation opportunities with multiple dealers are still executed as bilateral transactions.

[33]In this example, Firm ABC may submit its RFQ by contacting a voice broker at the EEP. If Firm ABC preferred to trade through the EEP's electronic platform, then the submission of the original order by Firm ABC would be electronic.

16.4.2.3 Swap Execution Facilities As noted in Section 16.2.2, the Dodd–Frank Act requires that certain OTC derivatives be executed on particular types of EEPs known as SEFs, which are discussed in more detail in Section 16.9.3.1 of the Appendix. Compliance with SEF registration requirements was required as of October 2, 2013.

SEFs are permitted to execute two types of transactions. First, "Required Transactions" are transactions involving swaps that must be executed on SEFs. Required transactions that must be executed on a SEF as of this writing include all swaps subject to the Dodd–Frank clearing mandate, as long as such swaps are designated as MAT by at least one SEF. If one SEF designates a swap as MAT, then all SEFs must make the product available for trading. On this basis, the implementation date for the mandatory trading on SEFs for OTC interest rate derivatives designated as MAT transactions was February 15, 2014.[34]

Second, "Permitted Transactions" are transactions involving swaps that regulations do not require to be executed on a SEF but that a SEF may choose to accept if swap participants are interested in trading the product in that manner. As discussed in Section 16.6.2, about 10% of all trades executed on SEFs involved derivatives that are not subject to the clearing mandate (i.e., noncleared swaps).

16.4.3 Credit Risk Mitigation

The credit risks of noncleared swaps are managed bilaterally by the swap counterparties using credit risk mitigation methods that have been common features of swaps for more than two decades. More specifically, in the 1980s and early 1990s, swap participants managed and controlled their bilateral counterparty exposures primarily through the use of credit enhancements that reduced losses in the event of a counterparty default. Popular credit enhancements included collateral, periodic marking to market and cash resettlement of open positions, and third-party performance guarantees.[35] Attention to such credit risk mitigation techniques intensified significantly between 1989 and 1992 after five companies with then-substantial amounts of outstanding swaps failed (i.e., Development Finance Corporation of New Zealand in 1989, Drexel Burnham Lambert in 1990, British & Commonwealth Merchant Bank in 1990, Bank of New England in 1991, and Olympia and York in 1992).[36,37]

In the current noncleared swaps marketplace, three significant mechanisms for managing bilateral counterparty exposures on noncleared swaps are the use of master agreements and their bilateral netting provisions, the use of collateral, and the use of prime brokers by some swap end users, all of which are discussed in Sections 16.4.3.1–16.4.3.3, respectively. In addition, recent and important advances in clearing-related posttrade services (discussed in Section 16.4.3.4) also help facilitate ongoing credit risk management for noncleared swaps.

16.4.3.1 Bilateral Payment and Closeout Netting As explained in Section 16.4.2, swaps are almost always negotiated under *pro forma* master agreements that specify a set of commonly used definitions and contractual terms and provisions. Any particular transaction can be customized, but the use of master agreements provides contract language that is generally accepted among swap participants, thereby greatly reducing the marginal transaction costs of each individual deal and reducing the legal risk of contractual ambiguities and inconsistencies. The most popular such master agreements for interest rate derivatives are the ISDA master agreements.

Among the standard terms of the ISDA master agreements is the bilateral netting of periodic cash flows and closeout netting in the event of a counterparty default or early termination event. Bilateral netting (primarily closeout netting) significantly reduces counterparty credit exposures by distilling gross payments into smaller net payments, both over the life of a transaction and following a termination.[38]

Bilateral netting, moreover, is not limited to single types of contracts or products. The ISDA master agreements also facilitate cross-product bilateral netting. Two counterparties with significant bilateral credit exposures across several products (e.g., interest rate swaps and CDSs) thus can bilaterally net their same-currency payment obligations across all their asset classes and transactions, provided they are covered by a single master netting agreement.

The exposure-reducing benefits of bilateral netting for swaps have increased steadily over time. Figure 16.7 shows the percentages of credit exposure reduction realized as a result of netting from 1998 through 2013 based on call report data for U.S. commercial banks and savings associations reported to the U.S. Office of the Comptroller of the Currency ("OCC"). In the first quarter of 1998, netting reduced gross credit exposures by only 50.6%. By the fourth quarter of 2002, the netting benefit (i.e., ratio of net current credit exposure to gross positive fair value) exceeded 80% and has not dropped below 80% since then. By the

[34]Javelin SEF LLC submitted a MAT determination for certain interest rate swaps on October 18, 2013. Similar MAT determinations were submitted by trueEX LLC and TW SEF LLC on October 21 and 28, respectively. For more details on the compliance schedule, see Sidley Austin LLP (2013).

[35]See, for example, The Group of Thirty, Global Derivatives Study Group (1994a), and The Group of Thirty, Global Derivatives Study Group (1994b).

[36]See Culp and Kavanagh (1994).

[37]In addition to heightened concerns about credit risk among swap market participants following these five firms' failures, regulators were also paying significant attention to swap credit risk management around the same time. See, for example, Bank for International Settlements (1989) (a.k.a. the Angell Report); Bank for International Settlements (1990) (a.k.a. the Lamfalussy Report); and Bank for International Settlements (1992) (a.k.a. the Promisel Report).

[38]See, for example, Mengle (2010).

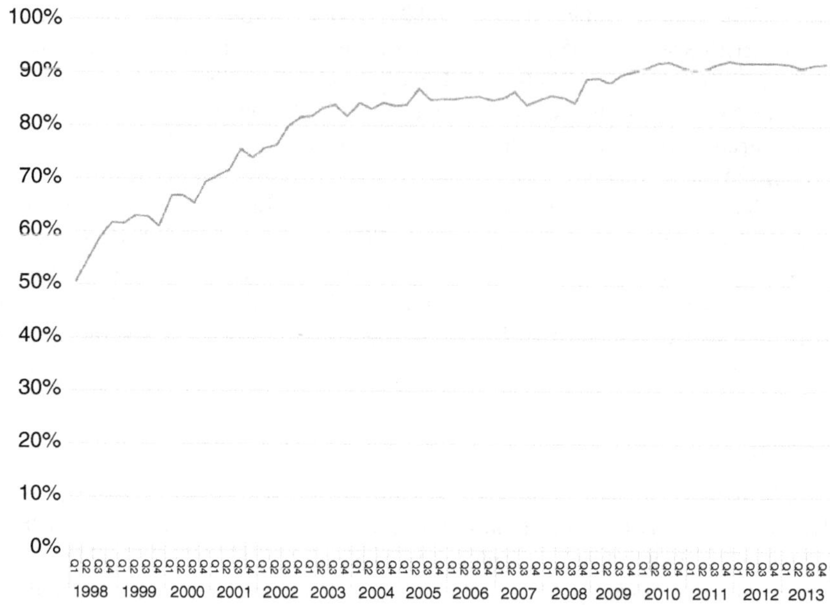

Figure 16.7 Exposure reduction from bilateral closeout netting. Data is based on the call reports of U.S. commercial banks and savings associations. Exposure reduction (i.e., the netting benefit) is defined as the ratio of total reported net current credit exposure to gross positive fair value of swaps. Source: Data from OCC Quarterly Reports on Bank Trading and Derivatives Activities (2010–2013).

first quarter of 2014, netting reduced the $3.169 trillion reported total gross positive fair value of swaps to a $279 billion net current credit exposure (i.e., a 91.2% netting benefit).[39]

16.4.3.2 Collateral/Margin Swaps documented under popular master agreements typically include collateral and/or other credit support provisions. At the end of 2013, 61 ISDA members indicated that 86% of all noncleared bilateral interest rate swaps were performed under a CSA to a master agreement or some other collateral agreement.[40]

Figure 16.8 shows the total collateral reported to and estimated by ISDA backing all noncleared swaps from year-end 1999 through year-end 2013. Total collateral grew steadily from 1999 through 2006 and then surged as the financial crisis erupted and spread in 2007 and 2008. After experiencing declines in 2009 and 2010, total collateral backing noncleared swaps grew again in 2011 and 2012. By year-end 2013, collateral backing noncleared swaps declined again, primarily as a result of the implementation of clearing mandates and the resulting migration of volume from noncleared swaps to cleared swaps. At year-end 2013, total collateral backing noncleared swaps was estimated by ISDA to be $3.171 trillion.

Figure 16.9 shows collateral received and delivered by respondents to the annual ISDA margin survey by asset type from 2005 through 2013. During this period, cash was overwhelmingly the primary asset used as collateral. On average, 78.5% of collateral received (ranging from a low of 72.9% to a high of 83.5% over the 9 years) and 79.8% of collateral delivered (ranging from a low of 75.6% to a high of 83.3%) was in the form of cash. Government securities issued by various countries accounted for 10.9% and 17.1% of collateral received and delivered (respectively) over the period. From 2005 through 2007, other securities (including agency securities, corporate bonds, and equities) accounted for an average of 14% of collateral received and 2.8% of collateral delivered. In the crisis and postcrisis years from 2008 through 2013, however, other securities accounted for 9% of collateral received on average and 3.2% of collateral delivered on average. Although the composition of collateral types has changed a little from 2005 through 2013, cash and government securities – that is, relatively low-risk and liquid assets – have generally represented about 89% of collateral received and 97% of collateral delivered in the past 9 years.

Unlike exchange-traded derivatives margin requirements that are based solely on potential market movements (*see* Sections 16.3.3.2 and 16.3.3.3), margin requirements for noncleared swaps often take into account the potential default risk of the bilateral swap counterparty. Collateral or margin posted pursuant to a CSA or equivalent agreement generally comes in two forms. The first is the initial amount of collateral required to be posted at the inception of the transaction. The initial amount is often a function of economic variables like the credit rating of the posting firm vis-à-vis its counterparty, the estimated market risk and potential credit exposure of the transaction, and the size of the transaction. For noncleared swaps, this initial collateral requirement is often referred to as the "independent amount" because it does not depend on market movements. The second

[39]The fourth quarter of 2014 is not shown in Figure 16.3 to preserve the scale of the x-axis.
[40]ISDA (2014e).

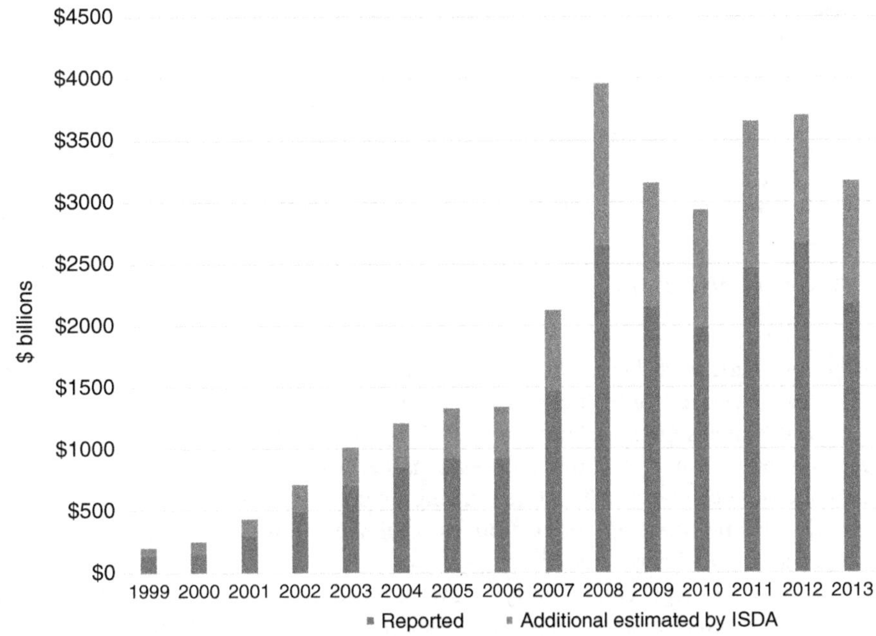

Figure 16.8 Total collateral outstanding on noncleared swaps. Collateral reflects gross amounts of collateral delivered and received and does not adjust for double counting, include rehypothecation. Actual amounts reported to ISDA in the margin survey ("Reported") are adjusted by ISDA to estimate the additional collateral held at nonrespondents ("Additional Estimated"). Source: Data from ISDA, Margin Survey 2014 (April 2014).

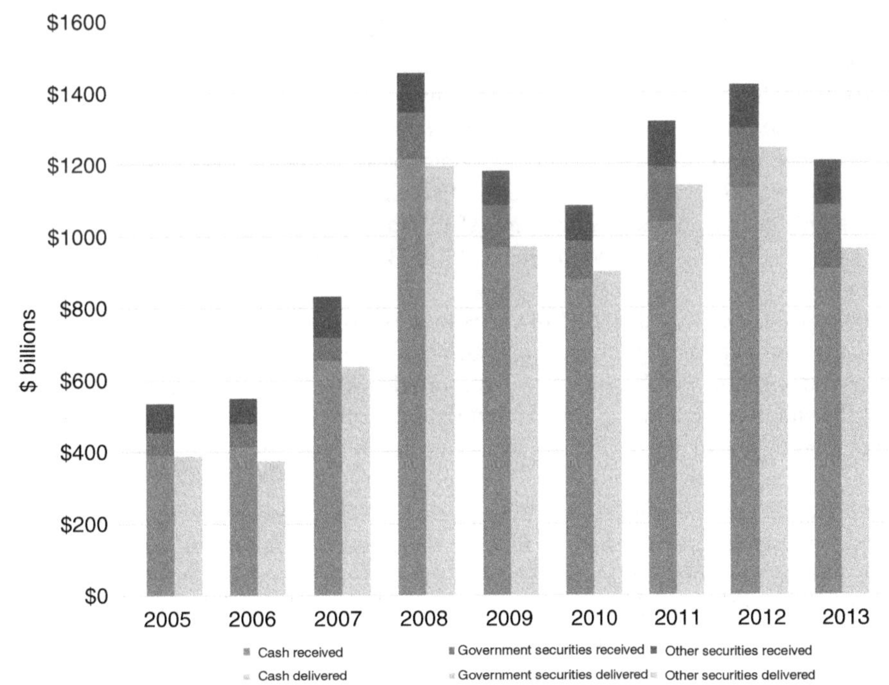

Figure 16.9 Collateral received/delivered on noncleared swaps by collateral type. Collateral values represent values reported by respondents to the ISDA Survey. Source: Data from ISDA Margin Surveys (2006–2014).

collateral flow is variation margin, which primarily involves collateral flows based on market movements that change the value and credit exposure of the swap.

Table 16.5 shows the composition of assets received and delivered to satisfy initial and variation margin requirements as of December 31, 2013. Some firms do not separately track collateral flows for initial and variation margin, and, as such, the table also includes a row that reports commingled initial amounts and variation margin by asset type. For both collateral received and delivered, cash is being used more frequently vis-à-vis government and other securities for variation margin calls.

TABLE 16.5 Initial and variation margin received and delivered on noncleared swaps by asset type as of 12/31/2013.

	Collateral received			Collateral delivered		
	Cash	Government bonds	Other	Cash	Government bonds	Other
Initial	63.5%	13.7%	22.8%	61.9%	14.1%	24.0%
Variation	76.0%	14.8%	9.2%	80.7%	16.9%	2.4%
Commingled	72.5%	6.6%	20.9%	87.0%	10.6%	2.5%

Source: ISDA, *ISDA (2014e), Table 7.*

16.4.3.3 Prime Brokerage and Customer-Level Clearing Although noncleared swaps are not cleared by a CCP, dealers sometimes offer CCP-like clearing services for their customers. In the noncleared swaps arena, such arrangements often involve prime brokerage agreements between customer end users and dealers acting as prime brokers.

Prime brokerage is an institutional arrangement that enables a market participant (e.g., a hedge fund) to conduct transactions with multiple (sometimes numerous) counterparties while keeping its credit risk, collateral, and settlements concentrated at a small number of intermediaries. Prime brokerage in derivatives originated in the foreign exchange market and subsequently expanded across the full spectrum of OTC derivatives.[41]

A prime broker interposes itself as the legal counterparty for swaps originally negotiated with multiple other swap counterparties that the prime broker has authorized as eligible for such give-up trades. From a credit risk management standpoint, a prime broker guarantees the trades of its customers against losses arising from *both* settlement *and* replacement cost risk following a default by any of the customer's original trading counterparties.

To illustrate how swap prime brokerage works, suppose a hedge fund executes a €100 million notional 2-year interest rate swap with Dealer ABC in which the hedge fund pays a fixed par swap rate of 1.5% per annum and receives 3mEURIBOR. At the same time, suppose the hedge fund executes a 2-year €100 million notional basis swap with Dealer XYZ in which the hedge fund pays 3mEURIBOR and receives EONIA plus 50 basis points ("bps"). Panel A of Figure 16.10 illustrates the two swaps if the hedge fund executes each trade bilaterally with Dealers ABC and XYZ.

Panel B of Figure 16.10 shows how the transactions would look if instead the hedge fund had a prime brokerage agreement with Prime Broker PDQ and executed the two swaps with Dealers ABC and XYZ pursuant to give-up agreements with Prime Broker PDQ. In that situation, the hedge fund would still negotiate the terms of the two swaps and execute them with Dealers ABC and XYZ. But unlike the two bilateral trades depicted in Panel A, in Panel B Prime Broker PDQ becomes the principal counterparty to (i) two bilaterally netted swaps with Dealers ABC and XYZ (identical to the swaps shown in Panel A) and (ii) a single bilaterally netted swap with the hedge fund in which Prime Broker PDQ pays EONIA plus 50bps and the hedge fund pays 1.5% fixed.

From an end user's perspective (like the hedge fund in the example), prime brokerage relationships have several advantages. Although the end user usually transacts through more than one prime broker, the number of prime brokers is generally much smaller than the number of counterparties with which the end user wishes to trade. One immediate benefit of prime brokerage thus is the replacement of the end user's credit exposure to multiple execution counterparties with the credit exposures of only its prime brokers. In the example shown in Figure 16.10, two swaps with two dealers are replaced with a single swap with the prime broker.

Not only does a prime brokerage relationship reduce the end user's total gross credit exposure, but it also consolidates that exposure with a single counterparty (i.e., Prime Broker PDQ in the example). In the original case of two separate trades, by contrast, the hedge fund would have two ongoing credit relationships with Dealers ABC and XYZ, two credit lines and limits to monitor, two counterparties exposing the hedge fund to default risk, two master agreements to negotiate (with possibly different terms), two collateral requirements to administer, and so on.

Apart from credit and settlement risk reduction, the prime brokerage relationship also helps end users realize greater efficiencies arising from economies of scale and scope, lower expenses, and less operational risk. All of those benefits trace to the fact that a prime broker allows an end user to reduce the number of counterparties with which it has ongoing principal/legal relationships by replacing those with the prime broker.

16.4.3.4 Clearing-Related Posttrade Services In recent years, several types of posttrade services have arisen that are related to clearing. These services either enhance the ability of noncleared swap users to manage their collateral efficiently, further reduce their bilateral credit exposures, or both. Three such services are discussed below.

[41] See, for example, the Foreign Exchange Committee (2005), Holt (2008), and Risk (2011).

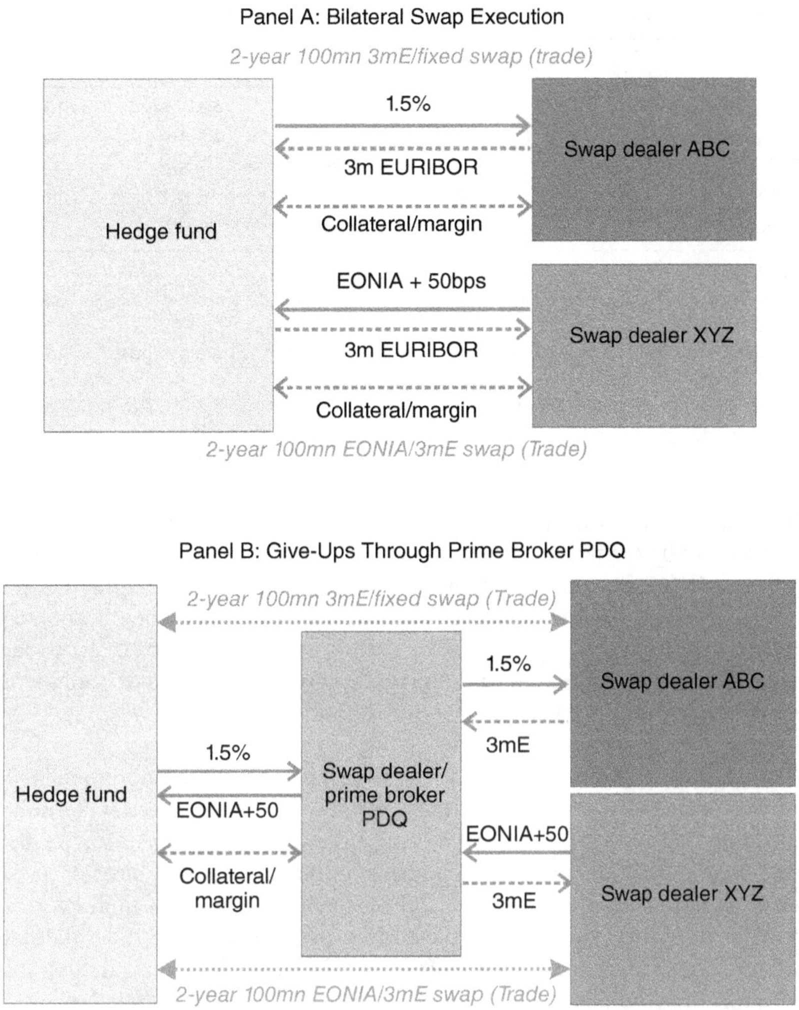

Figure 16.10 Bilateral versus prime brokerage swap execution. All rates are expressed per annum. Differences in settlement dates and frequencies of cash flows are not shown. Interest rates and spreads are for illustrative purposes and not intended to be realistic.

Collateral Reconciliation. A challenge facing noncleared swap market participants is the calculation of mark-to-market values of open positions for the purpose of variation margin calls. Counterparties must reconcile their exposure estimates with one another and agree on a pricing source for collateral valuations and how to calculate variation margin. Although perhaps a straightforward process during normal market conditions, the events of the credit crisis demonstrated that this reconciliation process is far from trivial during periods of market instability.

Through the use of various posttrade service providers, swap participants have been able to streamline the collateral reconciliation process. Such services not only enhance the efficiency of the collateral administration process but also help market participants avoid potentially contentious and costly valuation disputes that might arise during periods of market instability.

At year-end 2013, 84% of all large firms responding to the ISDA margin survey reported that they reconciled their collateral for all portfolios on a daily basis. In contrast, only 16% and 0.3% of medium- and small-sized firms (respectively) reported reconciling collateral on a daily basis. Between 31% and 61% of medium-sized firms, however, reconciled collateral on a weekly, monthly, quarterly, or annual basis. Small-sized firms, however, rarely engage in collateral reconciliation – that is, collateral is reconciled less than 11% of the time.[42]

Collateral Optimization. Swap market participants have increasingly sought to optimize their management of delivered, received, and rehypothecated collateral by carefully considering factors such as costs of funding, transaction costs, liquidity in the underlying collateral markets, haircuts on collateral types specified by CSAs and other collateral agreements, opportunity

[42] ISDA (2014a,b).

TABLE 16.6 Collateral Optimization by Firm Size as of 12/31/13

	All	Large [a]	Medium [b]	Small [c]
Collateral optimization	62.7%	35.1%	54.1%	10.8%
Systematic	75.7%	39.3%	46.4%	14.3%
Daily	62.2%	47.8%	43.5%	8.7%
When needed	48.6%	33.3%	55.6%	11.1%
Other	2.7%	0.0%	100.0%	0.0%

ISDA (2014e), Table 15.

[a]Large firms had more than 3000 active noncleared swaps and comprised 22% of the ISDA survey respondents.

[b]Medium firms had between 100 and 3000 active noncleared swaps and comprised 51% of the ISDA survey respondents.

[c]Small firms had less than 100 active noncleared swaps and comprised 27% of the ISDA survey respondents.

costs of reinvestment, and other economic variables relevant to their collateral management decisions.[43] Such concerns among market participants are driven largely by the potential for certain types of collateral to become illiquid or scarce.

As Table 16.6 indicates, about 63% of all firms responding to the annual ISDA margin survey engaged in some form of collateral optimization at year-end 2013. About 76% of respondents indicated that they optimized collateral systematically, and 62% optimized their collateral receipts and deliveries on a daily basis. Medium-sized respondents were the most frequent users of collateral optimization methods and services. End users of swaps, moreover, have been increasingly utilizing collateral optimization services since mid-2013.[44]

Portfolio Compression. Although the proliferation of master agreements and the netting provisions they contain have significantly reduced bilateral credit exposures in swaps over the last several decades (*see* Figure 16.7), noncleared swaps do not easily lend themselves to *multilateral* netting. Whereas bilateral netting involves the netting of payments or positions between two counterparties, multilateral netting involves the netting of payments or positions across three or more counterparties.

Through the use of posttrade clearing services, however, a close economic cousin of multilateral netting certain swap exposures has become more prevalent in recent years. One of the earliest providers of posttrade multilateral netting and clearance services was the clearinghouse of the CBOT, founded in 1883.[45] At the time, the clearinghouse was not a CCP and provided no direct default protection to trading participants. Nevertheless, the clearinghouse facilitated offsets of positions and calculated trading members' net margin and payment obligations on a multilateral basis. According to the *Chicago Tribune*, the CBOT clearinghouse processed 29,986 checks in its first 14 weeks of operation, as compared to the approximately 260,000 checks that would have been exchanged prior to the advent of the clearinghouse netting system.[46]

More recently, portfolio compression and "tear-up" services have become prevalent as a means of providing the economic equivalent of multilateral netting for swaps.[47] In a typical portfolio compression service, participants submit trades that are then evaluated and compared by the compression service provider. All redundant matching trades are identified and then terminated legally and voluntarily (assuming all involved counterparties agree) and replaced with economically equivalent bilateral trades. The net cash flows and risk exposures on the compressed bilateral trades are identical to the original portfolio, but the *gross* notional amounts and numbers of trades can be reduced significantly in this process.[48]

Portfolio compression services were first offered in 2003 by TriOptima through its triReduce facility for Euro-denominated interest rate swaps. Working as a stand-alone portfolio compression service provider and also together with LCH.Clearnet's SwapClear, TriOptima had reduced notional principal outstanding of swaps denominated in 27 currencies by more than $500 trillion through August 2014.[49]

[43]ISDA (2014), p. 21.

[44]Kentz (2014a).

[45]The CBOT was formed in 1848 as a voluntary membership organization to promote agricultural commerce in Chicago. When the CBOT imposed formal trading rules and standardized trading contracts in 1865, the first true U.S. futures market was born. By the late 1870s, the CBOT was calculating and enforcing margin requirements on behalf of CBOT members. See Kroszner (1999), p. 599.

[46]Moser (1998), p. 29.

[47]Lewandowska and Mack (2010).

[48]See generally ISDA (2014c).

[49]In addition to the compression of interest rate derivatives, this number also includes compression of credit default swaps. In the last several years, however, the total notional compression volume for credit default swaps has represented a negligible fraction of triReduce's total compression volume. See http://www.trioptima.com/resource-center/statistics/triReduce.html (last visited on August 23, 2014).

TABLE 16.7 Estimated Amounts of Notional Amounts Outstanding of Noncleared versus Cleared OTC Interest Rate Derivatives as of 8/31/12

	Total notional Outstanding ($ billions)	Notional Outstanding on a CCP [a] ($ billions)	Noncleared (%)
Fixed/floating swaps	$196,661	$98,399	50.0%
OISs	$33,856	$17,457	48.4%
Basis swaps	$22,089	$6,512	70.5%
Inflation swaps	$2,430	$0	100.0%
Cross-currency swaps	$15,779	$0	100.0%
FRAs	$52,205	$23,801	54.4%
Options	$39,536	$0	100.0%
Exotics	$4,877	$0	100.0%
Other	$959	$88	90.8%
Total	*$368,392*	*$146,257*	*60.3%*

Source: Financial Stability Board, *OTC Derivatives Market Reforms: Fourth Progress Report on Implementation* (October 31, 2012), Appendix IV.
[a]Adjusted for double counting.

Note that portfolio compression is not uniquely beneficial to noncleared swaps. On the contrary, compression also provides significant benefits for users of *cleared* swaps, as will be discussed again in Section 16.5.2.

16.4.4 Market Activity

As discussed in Section 16.2.1, the voluntary clearing of certain OTC interest rate derivatives was occurring on platforms like LCH.Clearnet's SwapClear for at least a decade before the various postcrisis clearing mandates went into effect. Nevertheless, the bulk of OTC interest rate derivatives were still executed bilaterally and noncleared. Table 16.7 summarizes the estimated total notional amounts of OTC interest rate derivatives outstanding and the amounts and proportions of those interest rate derivatives cleared by a CCP as of August 31, 2012. Even for the product that was most amenable to and popular among market participants for clearing (i.e., fixed/floating interest rate swaps), only half of the total estimated notional amount outstanding was cleared as of this date. For all other product types except OISs, more than half of total notional open interest was in noncleared swaps in August 2012.

As explained in Section 16.2.1.1, the U.S. clearing mandate under the Dodd–Frank Act was phased in during 2013. By the end of February 2014, the gross notional total of all OTC interest rate derivatives reported by a group of large swap dealers had grown to $191 trillion, which accounted for about 59% of all OTC interest rate derivatives that were available for CCP clearing at the time and about 46% of total notional outstanding across all OTC interest rate derivatives.[50] Even with the U.S. clearing mandate in effect, however, 54% of all outstanding OTC interest rate derivatives in February 2014 were noncleared, including *all* cross-currency swaps, swaptions, caps, and floors.

Figure 16.11 shows the monthly notional trading volumes of all noncleared interest rate derivatives trades (for all currencies) reported to DTCC or BSDR from January 2013 through August 2014 along with the percentage of noncleared interest rate derivatives trades. The amounts of noncleared interest rate derivatives traded in 2013 were generally lower than in 2014. Average monthly notional volume in 2013 was $1.545 trillion, as compared to average monthly notional volume in 2014 (through August) of $2.708 trillion. As Figure 16.11 further indicates, the proportion of noncleared swaps declined sharply in 2013 from 47% in January to just 19% in December 2013, and, in 2014, noncleared swaps represented only 22% of all reported new OTC interest rate derivatives trades on average. This pattern is not surprising given that the data underlying Figure 16.11 only reflects trades involving at least one U.S. market participant and the gradual phase-in of the U.S. clearing mandate during 2013.

16.4.4.1 By Product Figure 16.12 shows the total notional amounts by product type of all noncleared OTC interest rate derivatives denominated in all currencies that were traded and reported to DTCC or BSDR from January 2013 through August 2014. As Figure 16.12 indicates, fixed/floating swaps were the specific product type that accounted for the largest amount (i.e., 29%) of newly reported trades (in notional terms) in the January 2013 to August 2014 period. (The "other" category is clearly the largest, representing 33% of total notional amounts traded. This category does not indicate a single specific product type, however, and includes customized products not already reflected in Figure 16.12 as well as trades that may not have been properly classified when reported.) Caps, floors, and other options were the second most actively traded noncleared interest rate derivatives

[50]Financial Stability Board (2014), p. 15.

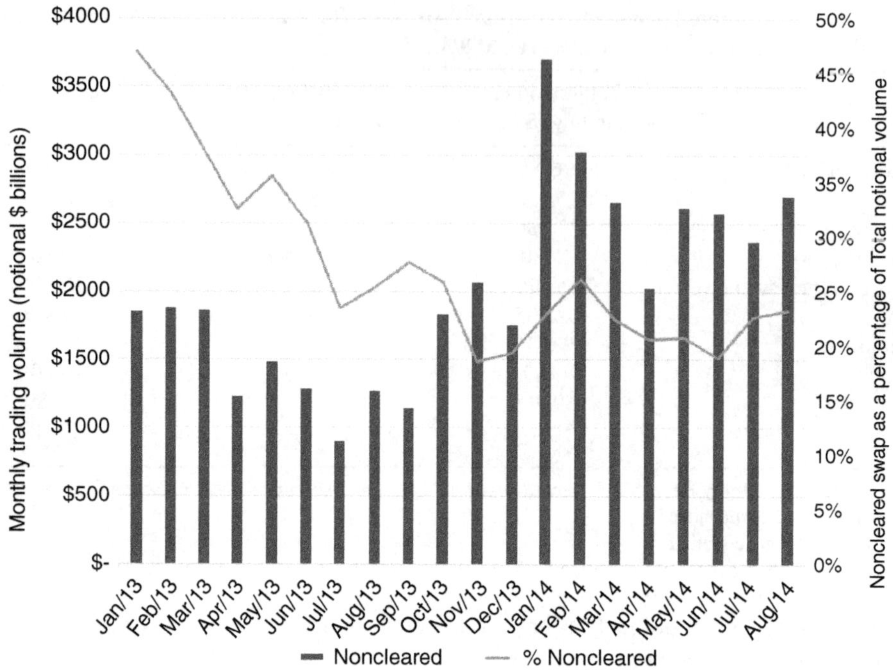

Figure 16.11 Noncleared OTC interest rate derivatives trading volume reported to DTCC/BSDR. Source: Data from ISDA.

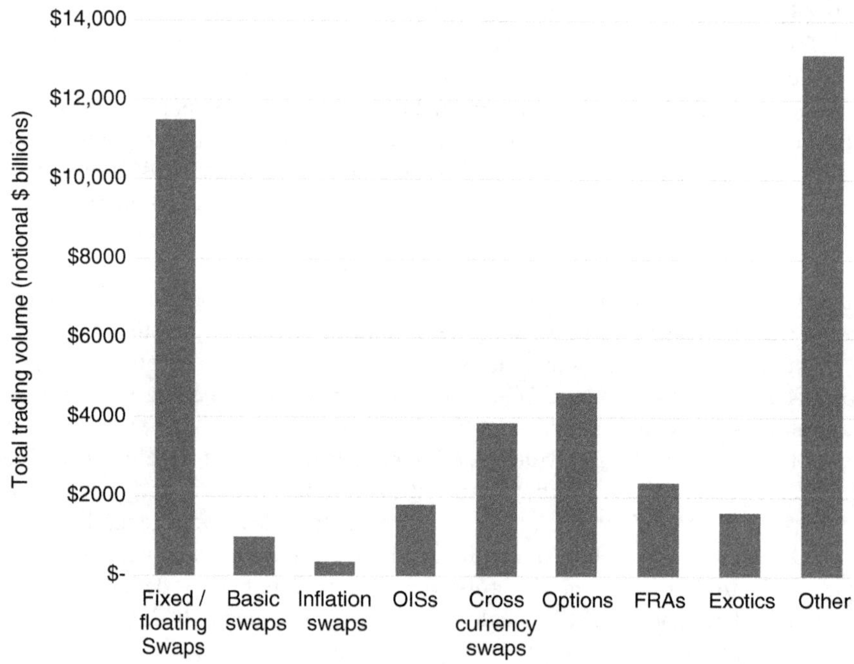

Figure 16.12 Total notional trading volume of noncleared interest rate derivatives reported to DTCC/BSDR by product. January 2013–August 2014. Notional amounts are USD equivalents across all reportable currencies. Source: Data from ISDA.

during this period, accounting for 12% of total gross notional volume. Cross-currency swaps are a close third, reflecting 10% of the total notional trading volume reported to DTCC or BSDR over this period.

16.4.4.2 ***By Currency*** Figure 16.13 shows the total notional amounts of new noncleared OTC interest rate derivatives trades denominated in the G3 currencies and the British pound ("GBP") that were reported to DTCC or BSDR from January 2013 through August 2014. (The G3 currencies are the U.S. dollar ("USD"), Euro ("EUR"), and Japanese yen ("JPY").) Most transactions were USD-denominated, although the trend has been toward relatively more nondollar interest rate derivatives over time.

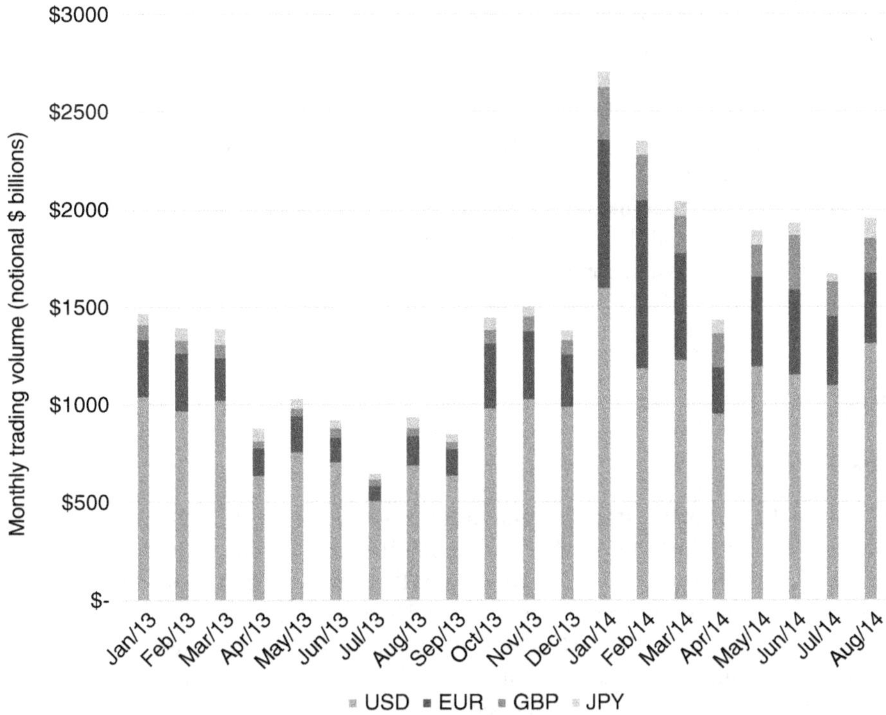

Figure 16.13 Notional amount of noncleared interest rate derivatives trades reported to DTCC/BSDR by currency. Notional amounts are USD equivalents. Source: Data from ISDA.

TABLE 16.8 Noncleared OTC Interest Rate Derivatives Trading Volume[a] 1/1/13–8/29/14

	Panel A: All Currencies			Panel B: USD		
Product Type	Avg size ($billions)[b]	Total trades	Avg trades per day	Avg size ($billions)[b]	Total trades	Avg trades per day
Fixed/floating swaps	$45,100,441	254,644	510	$53,214,587	84,403	194
OISs	$177,954,253	10,160	22	$226,375,075	1,541	4
Basis swaps	$107,538,363	9,044	14	$105,483,730	7,744	12
Inflation swaps	$42,557,267	8,106	14	$38,698,390	3,579	5
Cross-currency swaps	$93,136,909	41,392	74	$86,260,455	40,002	71
FRAs	$230,307,004	10,214	23	$209,971,169	5,678	13
Options	$91,499,216	50,613	101	$88,725,631	36,160	73
Exotics	$85,109,159	18,833	41	$73,654,213	16,958	37
Other	$140,930,371	93,240	178	$134,472,434	35,264	70

Source: ISDA.
[a]Trading volume reflects trades registered with DTCC and BSDR.
[b]Average trade size is calculated as total notional volume over the period divided by total number of trades for the period.

In 2013, 72.5% of total notional reported trading volume was USD-denominated, whereas that percentage fell to 61.4% in 2014. The dollar dominance reflected in Figure 16.13, however, must be kept in context. As noted in Section 16.2.3.1, only trades involving at least one U.S. market participant are required to be reported to DTCC or BSDR. Trades between two non-U.S. entities (which presumably might include a higher proportion of nondollar interest rate derivatives) and trades reported to other registered U.S. SDRs are not reflected in this data.

As Figure 16.13 further indicates, Euro-denominated transactions also accounted for a significant proportion (i.e., 20.5%) of volume in the January 2013–August 2014 period. GBP- and JPY-denominated interest rate derivatives accounted for 7% and 4.4% (respectively) of notional trading volume reported to DTCC or BSDR during the period.

Table 16.8 shows the trading activity in noncleared swaps by product type based on the number of trades reported daily to the DTCC SDR from January 2013 through August 2014. Specifically, columns two through four (Panel A) show the average notional daily trade size, total number of trades in the sample, and average trades per day for all currencies. Columns five through seven (Panel B) report the same summary statistics for noncleared USD interest rate derivatives in the sample period.

For all currencies, the number of trades summarized in Panel A of Table 16.8 echo the notional totals shown in Figure 16.13 and indicate that fixed/floating swaps, options, and cross-currency swaps are the most actively traded noncleared interest rate swaps. Based on the total number of trades and average trades per day, fixed/floating swaps are by far the most actively traded product. The average trade size for fixed/floating swaps, however, is a relatively small $45.1 billion. By comparison, FRAs exhibit an average trade size of about $230.3 billion, despite a relatively low average of 23 trades per day (as compared to 510 fixed/floating swap trades per day on average).

The results in Panel B of Table 16.8 show that noncleared USD swap activity is broadly consistent with the trading activity across all currencies shown in Panel A. Fixed/floating swaps are again the most actively traded product by far but also once more have a relatively small average trade size when compared to other less actively traded noncleared OTC interest rate derivatives products like FRAs.

16.5 CLEARED SWAPS

16.5.1 Major Products

In December 2012, the CFTC indicated that certain OTC interest rate derivatives were subject to the Dodd–Frank clearing mandate.[51] Those interest rate derivatives subject to mandatory clearing include certain single-currency fixed/floating swaps, basis swaps, OISs, and FRAs denominated in any of the G3 currencies or the GBP.[52] The interest rate derivatives subject to the CFTC clearing mandate that were designated as MAT and subject to the Dodd–Frank/SEF execution mandate (*see* Section 16.4.2.3) as of February 15, 2014, are summarized in Table 16.9. In October 2014, ESMA designated essentially the same interest rate derivatives as subject to the EMIR clearing mandate which begins phase-in during 2015.

Section 16.9.2 in the Appendix provides further discussion of the products currently subject to a clearing mandate in the United States and European Union and the exclusions of certain transactions from the clearing mandates.

TABLE 16.9 OTC Interest Rate Derivatives Subject to CFTC Clearing Mandate as of April 2014

Currency:	USD	EUR	GBP	JPY
Panel A: Fixed-for-Floating and Basis Swaps				
Floating reference rate:	LIBOR	EURIBOR	LIBOR	LIBOR
Stated termination date range:	28 days to 50 yrs	28 days to 50 yrs	28 days to 50 yrs	28 days to 30 yrs
Optionality?	No	No	No	No
Dual currencies?	No	No	No	No
Conditional notional amounts?	No	No	No	No
Panel B: OIS				
Floating reference rate:	Fed Funds	EONIA	SONIA	–
Stated termination date range:	7 days to 2 yrs	7 days to 2 yrs	7 days to 2 yrs	–
Optionality?	No	No	No	–
Dual currencies?	No	No	No	–
Conditional notional amounts?	No	No	No	–
Panel C: FRAs				
Floating reference rate:	LIBOR	EURIBOR	LIBOR	LIBOR
Stated termination date range:	3 days to 3 yrs	3 days to 3 yrs	3 days to 3 yrs	3 days to 3 yrs
Optionality?	No	No	No	No
Dual currencies?	No	No	No	No
Conditional notional amounts?	No	No	No	No

Source: 17 CFR §50.4.

LIBOR, London Interbank Offered Rate; EURIBOR, Euro Interbank Offered Rate; EONIA, Euro Overnight Index Average; SONIA, Sterling Overnight Index Average. LIBOR, London Interbank Offered Rate;

[51] CFTC (2012c) (hereinafter "CFTC Clearing Determination").

[52] 17 CFR §50.4.

16.5.2 Market Activity

As of June 30, 2013, ISDA estimates that about 90% of the global interest rate derivatives market that is clearable and/or subject to a clearing mandate has in fact been cleared. ISDA further estimates that less than 10% of the total notional amount outstanding of interest rate derivatives as of June 2013 consists of trades that were clearable but were not actually cleared. At the end of June 2013, moreover, about $73 trillion notional (13%) of the global interest rate derivatives market consisted of nonclearable trades, which included about $65 trillion in nonclearable products and $8 trillion in clearable products denominated in nonclearable currencies. In addition, the end-June 2013 data includes about $29 trillion of interest rate derivatives involving an end user as a counterparty and thus not subject to a clearing mandate.[53]

Figure 16.14 shows the total notional amounts of all new cleared OTC interest rate derivatives trades (for all currencies) reported to DTCC or BSDR from January 2013 through August 2014 along with the percentage of all trades (noncleared and cleared) occurring in all OTC interest rate derivatives products. Figure 16.14, including cleared products, thus is comparable to Figure 16.11 which includes noncleared swaps.

Like noncleared interest rate derivatives, the total trading volumes of cleared swaps were higher in 2014 than in 2013. Average monthly notional volume in 2013 was $3.910 trillion, as compared to average monthly notional volume in 2014 (through August) of $9.476 trillion. Note that these average monthly volumes for cleared swaps significantly exceeded average volume for noncleared swaps (which, by comparison, were $1.545 and $2.708 trillion in 2013 and 2014, respectively). As we also saw in Figure 16.11, the relative proportion of all swaps occurring in the cleared market segment increased fairly steadily in 2013 from 53% in January to 81% in December 2013, which is consistent with the phase-in of the Dodd–Frank clearing mandate during 2013.

As discussed in Section 16.2.3.1, OTC interest rate derivatives trades are required to be reported to U.S. SDRs only for transactions involving at least one U.S. market participant. As a result, the trade volume shown in Figure 16.14 is biased toward the United States. For a more global picture of cleared swap activity, we can look instead to cleared volumes at SwapClear, a European CCP operated by LCH.Clearnet that has provided clearing services for OTC interest rate derivatives since 1999. Interest rate derivatives cleared by SwapClear involving at least one U.S. market participant should be reflected in the data shown in Figure 16.14, whereas transactions involving two non-U.S. participants are not. Although SwapClear is not the only CCP that provides clearing services for interest rate derivatives, an estimated 95% of all cleared interest rate derivatives are cleared through SwapClear – that is, SwapClear market activity is a good indicator of the *global* cleared interest rate derivatives market generally.

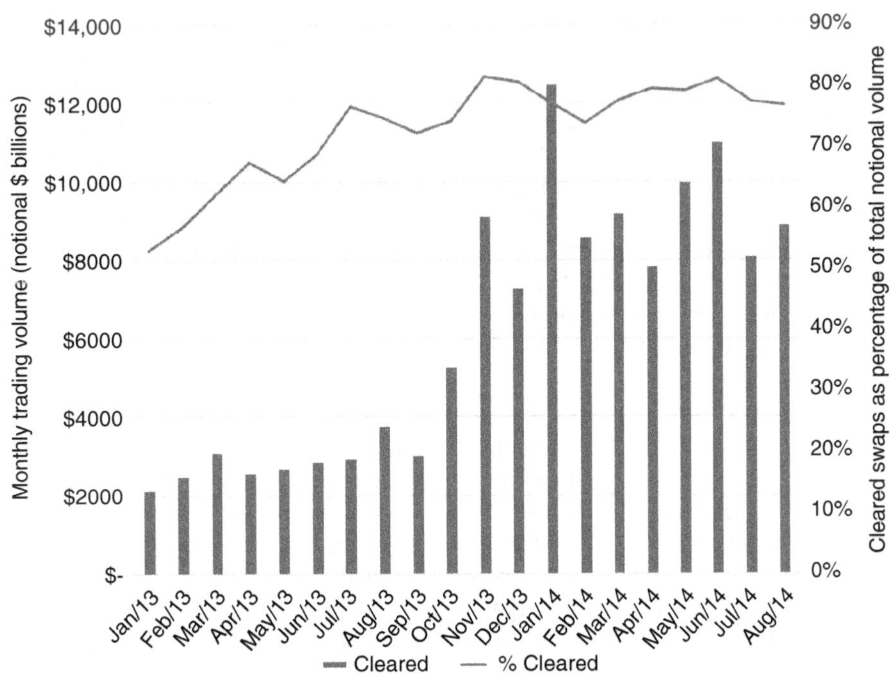

Figure 16.14 Cleared OTC interest rate derivatives trading volume reported to DTCC/BSDR.

[53] ISDA (2014).

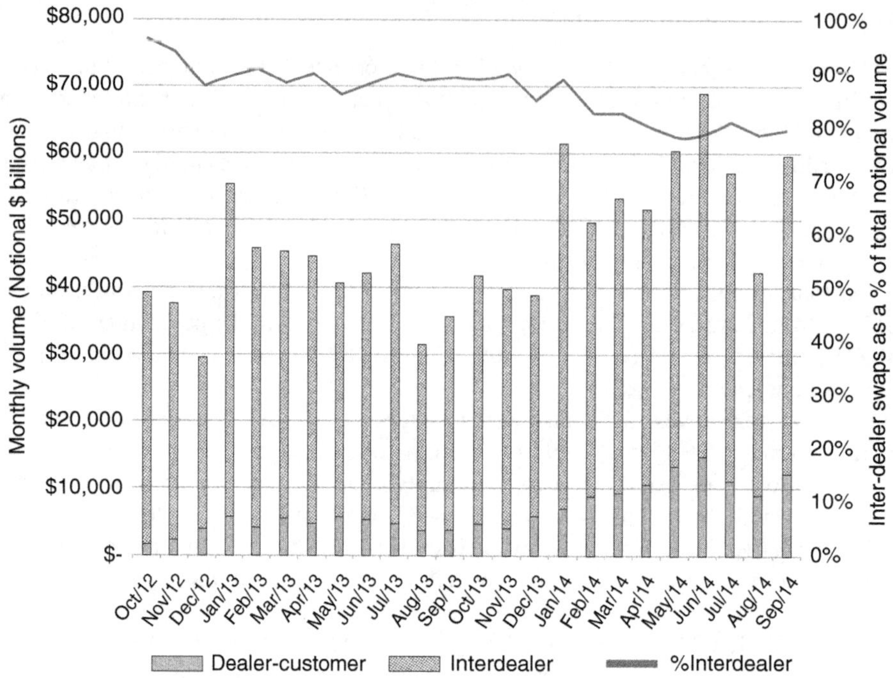

Figure 16.15 Cleared OTC interest rate derivatives volume at SwapClear. Source: Data from LCH.Clearnet.

Figure 16.15 shows the notional amounts of interest rate derivatives cleared through SwapClear from October 2012 through September 2014. The circle-filled columns represent interdealer transactions negotiated between two swap dealers, whereas the triangle-filled columns indicate the volume of "client" transactions negotiated between a swap dealer and an end user customer. The proportion of total notional volume attributable to interdealer transactions is also shown in Figure 16.15.

Although perhaps less obvious than in Figure 16.14, Figure 16.15 also shows the same pattern of increased clearing volume in 2014 vis-à-vis 2013. Average monthly cleared interest rate derivatives volume in 2014 (through September) on SwapClear was $56.1 trillion as compared to average monthly trading volume for interest rate derivatives cleared through SwapClear in 2013 of $42.3 trillion. The total volume on SwapClear, moreover, significantly exceeds the total volume of cleared interest rate derivatives reported to DTCC or BSDR (which were $3.910 trillion in 2013 and $9.476 trillion in 2014 on average).

Figure 16.15 also illustrates that SwapClear remains a predominantly interdealer clearing facility. In January 2013, dealer–customer swaps accounted for only 4% of total cleared volume. Nevertheless, the percentage of SwapClear's volume attributable to dealer–customer swaps has been increasing and reached 21% of the total cleared volume by September 2014.

Figure 16.16 shows the total notional amounts outstanding at SwapClear from October 2012 through September 2014. The amount of notional open interest reduced through SwapClear's collaboration with TriOptima's triReduce compression facility (as discussed in Section 16.4.3.4) is also shown in Figure 16.16. At year-end 2013, compression had reduced total notional amounts outstanding at SwapClear by about 31%, and by September 2014 that number had risen to 45.5% (i.e., a cumulative reduction of $334 trillion as compared to the $733 trillion that would otherwise have been outstanding at end-September 2014 without compression).

16.5.2.1 By Product Figure 16.17 shows the total notional amounts of cleared interest rate derivatives outstanding at SwapClear on October 30, 2014, by product type. The black portion of each column indicates dealer-to-dealer trades, and the relatively small white parts of each column reflect dealer-to-customer client trades. Of the total $411.2 trillion in notional amounts outstanding on that date, about 52% was comprised of fixed/floating swaps. The next two most popular cleared interest rate derivatives are FRAs and OISs, accounting for 22.7% and 21.2% (respectively) of the total outstanding notional amount on October 30, 2014. The remaining two reported product types reflect significantly smaller shares of the market.

Fixed/floating swaps represent a relatively larger proportion of the cleared global market than the noncleared U.S. OTC interest rate derivatives market (*see* Figure 16.12) but are significant in both. By contrast, OISs and FRAs are a much larger relative portion of the cleared global OTC interest rate derivatives market than the noncleared U.S. market.

For a more apples-to-apples comparison with Figure 16.12, Figure 16.18 shows the relative proportions of the total notional trade activity reported to DTCC/BSDR for U.S. interest rate derivatives across all currencies from January 2013 through August 2014. As in Figure 16.12, OISs are significantly more prevalent as a cleared product than a noncleared product (relative to the

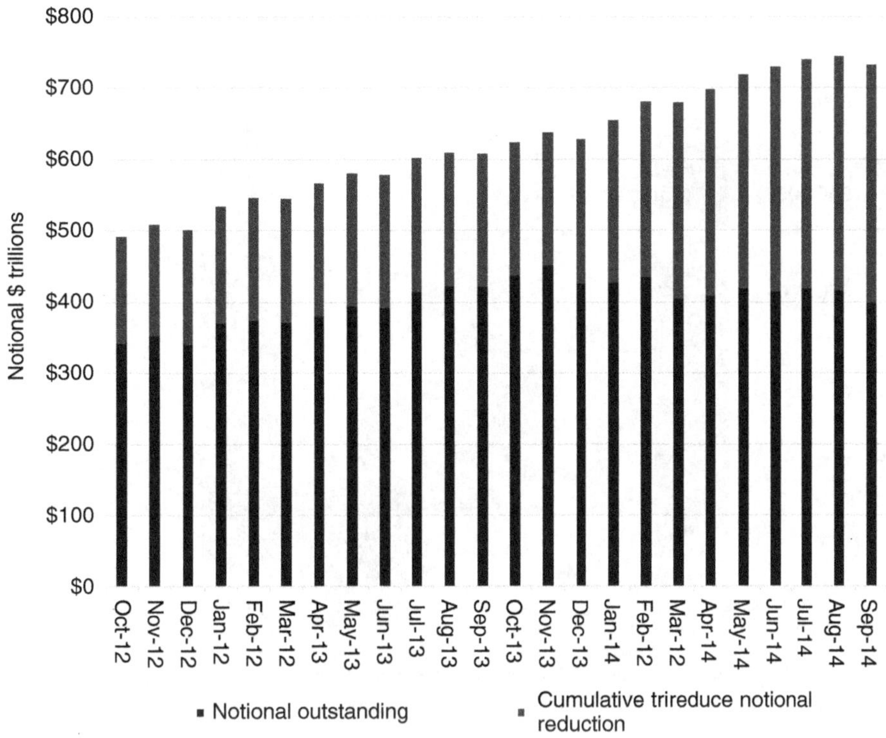

Figure 16.16 Cleared OTC interest rate derivatives notional amount outstanding and impact of trade compression at SwapClear. Source: Data from LCH.Clearnet.

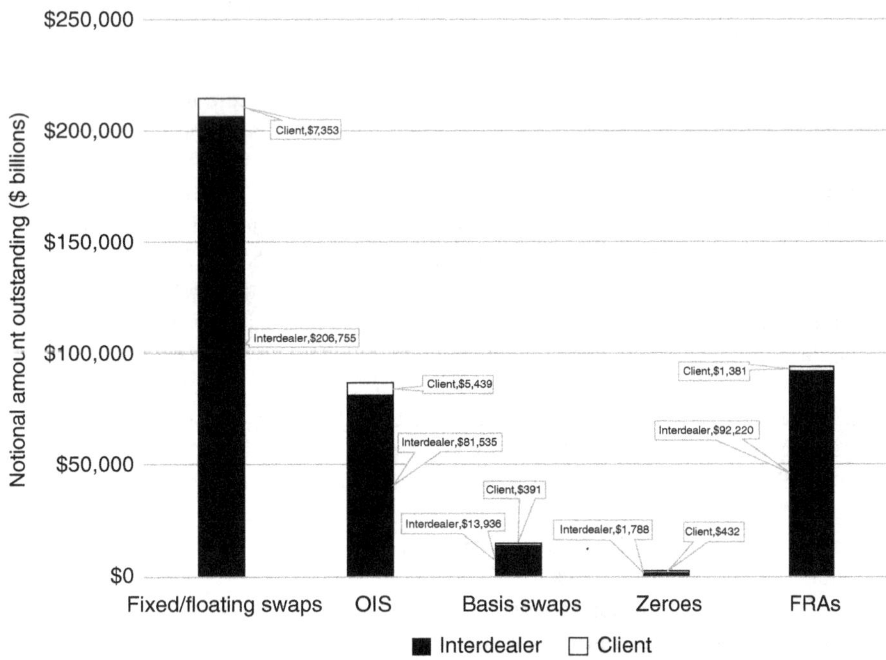

Figure 16.17 Notional amount outstanding at SwapClear of cleared OTC interest rate derivatives on 10/30/2014 by product and counterparty type. All nondollar notional amounts are converted to USD at the prevailing 10/30/14 spot exchange rates. Source: Data from LCH.Clearnet.

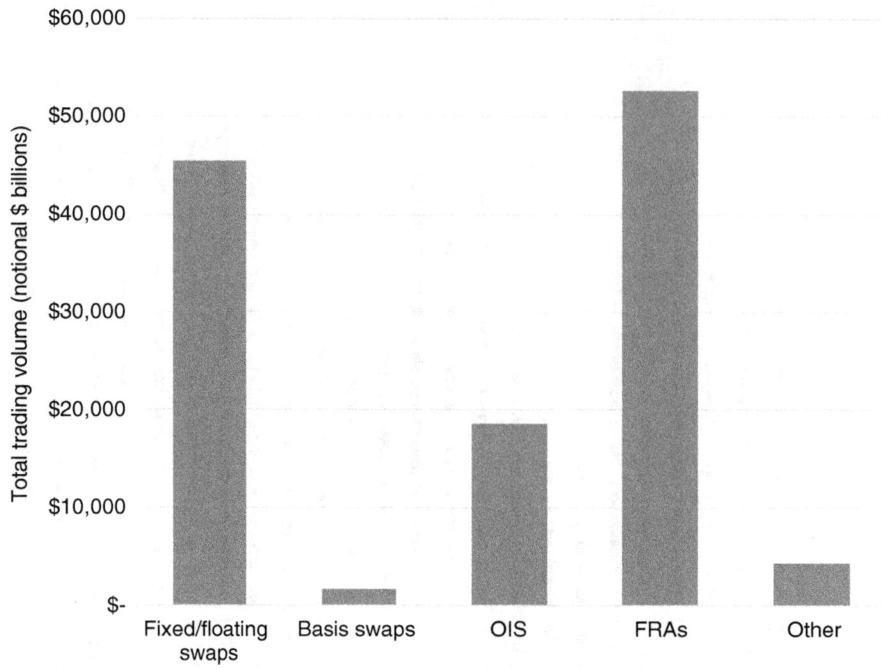

Figure 16.18 Total notional trading volume of cleared OTC interest rate derivatives reported to DTCC/BSDR by product. January 2013–August 2014. Notional amounts are USD equivalents across all reportable currencies. Source: Data from ISDA.

total trade activity in each market). Figure 16.18 suggests, however, that FRAs are the most popular overall cleared interest rate derivatives for U.S. market participants reporting to DTCC or BSDR. This observation must be interpreted with caution. In particular, although ISDA attempts to restrict trades reported in Swapinfo to new transactions, a number of FRAs are done for operational reasons (e.g., booking individual legs of non-settled-in-arrears swaps) and do not actually represent new transactions. Although not evident from Figure 16.18, fixed/floating swaps are again likely to be the dominant product type.

16.5.2.2 By Currency Figure 16.19 shows another snapshot of the total notional amounts outstanding in the global SwapClear facility as of October 30, 2014. Whereas Figure 16.17 showed notional amounts by product, Figure 16.19 displays notional amounts outstanding by currency denomination. The dominant currency denomination for LCH-cleared interest rate derivatives is the Euro, which accounted for 39.7% of the total notional outstanding on October 30, 2014. USD transactions represent another 29.5% of open interest, and 17.3% of LCH-cleared interest rate derivatives are denominated in GBP. Lesser but nevertheless active currencies include the JPY, CAD, AUD, and CHF, which reflected 4.6%, 3.5%, 2.2%, 2.0%, and 1.1% of open interest on October 30, 2014, respectively. The remaining 10 currencies in which SwapClear transactions were denominated accounted for the remaining 3.5% of total notional interest rate derivatives outstanding on the selected date.

Figure 16.20 shows the notional amounts of new cleared interest rate derivatives trades by currency reported to DTCC or BSDR from January 2013 through August 2014. Unlike the October 2014 amounts shown for SwapClear in Figure 16.19, the USD is now by far the dominant currency denomination. Over the whole period, an average of 59% of all new registered trades were USD-denominated, and 64% of August 2014 volume was denominated in dollars. This is not surprising because, as discussed in Section 16.2.3.1, only trades involving at least one U.S. market participant are required to be reported to a registered U.S. SDR.

As Figure 16.20 also indicates, Euro-denominated transactions (which, as shown in Figure 16.19, are the dominant transactions on SwapClear) accounted for an average of 29% of all new trades (on a notional basis) over the full period and only for 20% in August 2014. As in Europe, GBP transactions are in third place, reflecting 9% of average volume over the period and 14% in August 2014. JPY-denominated cleared interest rate derivatives accounted for only 3% of notional monthly volume over the 20-month period shown in Figure 16.20.

Table 16.10 (comparable to Table 16.8 for noncleared swaps) shows the trading activity in cleared swaps by product type based on the number of trades reported daily to the DTCC SDR from January 2013 through August 2014. As in Table 16.8, Panel A shows the average notional daily trade size, total number of trades, and average trades per day for all currencies, and Panel B reports similar statistics for USD-denominated cleared swaps.

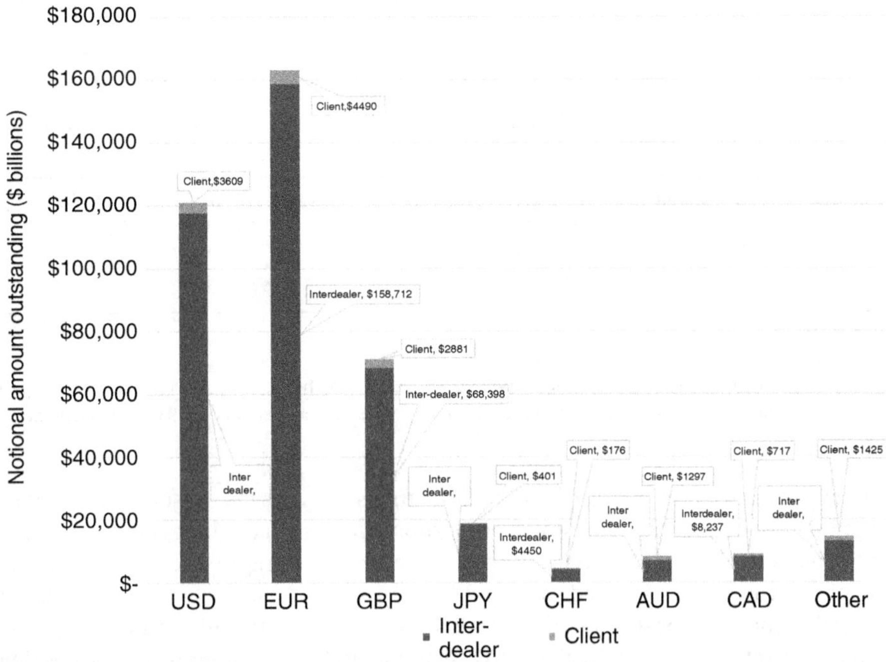

Figure 16.19 Notional amount outstanding at SwapClear of cleared OTC interest rate derivatives on 10/30/2014 by currency and counterparty type. All nondollar notional amounts are converted to USD at the prevailing 10/30/14 spot exchange rates. "Other" currencies include CZK, DKK, HKD, HUF, NOK, NZD, PLN, SEK, SGD, and ZAR. Source: Data from LCH.Clearnet.

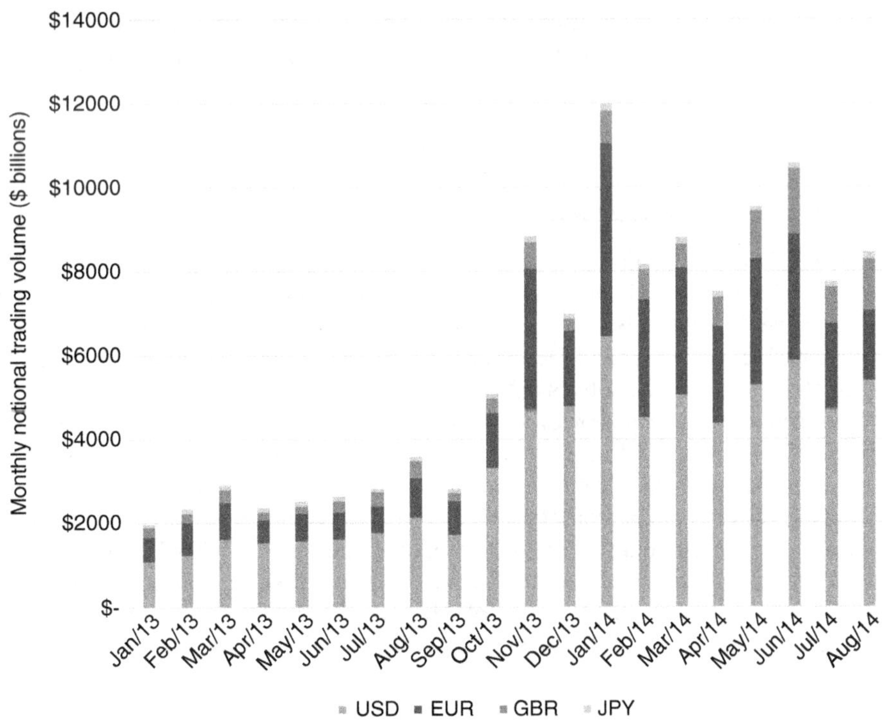

Figure 16.20 Cleared OTC interest rate derivatives trading volume reported to DTCC/BSDR by currency. Source: Data from ISDA.

TABLE 16.10 Cleared OTC Interest Rate Derivatives Trading Volume Reported to DTCC/BSDR, 1/1/13–8/29/14[a]

	Panel A: All Currencies			Panel B: USD		
Product type	Avg size ($bns)[b]	Total trades	Avg trades per day[c]	Avg size ($billions)[b]	Total trades	Avg trades per day[c]
Fixed/floating swaps	$81,709,090	556,478	828	$81,709,077	346,307	515
Basis swaps	$186,406,217	8,982	13	$210,214,315	6,602	10
OIS	$960,830,045	19,359	29	$642,506,263	6,538	10
FRAs	$299,758,160	175,834	262	$335,689,539	96,727	144

Source: Data from ISDA.
[a]Trading volume reflects trades reported to DTCC and BSDR.
[b]Average trade size is calculated as total notional volume over the period divided by total number of trades for the period.
[c]Average trades per day is calculated for the full sample for bilateral swaps and from October 2, 2013, for swaps executed on SEFs.

The total number of trades in Table 16.10 indicate that fixed/floating swaps are the most actively traded product. By contrast, Figure 16.18 indicates that FRAs accounted for the largest proportional notional amount of cleared swaps during the period (for all currencies and for USD transactions). As Table 16.10 shows, however, the average trade size of FRAs was significantly larger than the average fixed/floating swap transaction. Indeed, fixed/floating swaps have the smallest average transaction size across all products, despite accounting for the largest proportion of total trades (in both the all-currency and USD categories).

Comparing Panels A and B of Table 16.10 reveals that USD-denominated cleared interest rate swaps dominate trading activity in several segments of the cleared interest rate swap market. In particular, the total number of USD fixed/floating cleared swap trades over the period represents 62% of the total number of fixed/floating cleared swap trades in all currencies as compared to the 33% of USD fixed/floating noncleared swaps relative to fixed/floating noncleared swaps in all currencies. Similarly, the total number of trades in cleared USD OIS accounts for 34% of all cleared OIS trades, whereas noncleared USD OISs represent only 15% of noncleared OIS trades in all currencies. By contrast, the proportion of the FRA market accounted for by USD transactions is about the same relative to all currencies for both cleared and noncleared FRAs. And for basis swaps, the USD portion of the market is relatively smaller for cleared transactions than for noncleared basis swaps denominated in all currencies.

16.6 COMPARATIVE MARKET ACTIVITY ACROSS EXECUTION VENUES

16.6.1 OTC versus Exchange-Traded Interest Rate Derivatives

16.6.1.1 Volume versus Open Interest Figure 16.21 shows the total notional amounts outstanding from June 1998 through December 2013 for OTC and exchange-traded interest rate derivatives. As Figure 16.21 indicates, the notional amount outstanding in OTC interest rate derivatives significantly exceeded the corresponding notional amount of outstanding exchange-traded interest rate derivatives in all periods. At the end of December 2013, OTC interest rate derivatives accounted for over 90% of the total notional amount of all interest rate derivatives outstanding.

Trading volume and transaction frequency, however, tell a different story, as we can see by comparing plain vanilla USD-denominated interest rate swaps and CME Eurodollar futures, the latter of which are the building blocks for the exchange-traded economic equivalents of plain vanilla interest rate swaps and are known as “Eurodollar strips” or “synthetic swaps.”[54] On October 31, 2014, for example, a total of 1190 USD fixed/floating interest rate swap trades were registered with DTCC and BSDR, as compared to a total volume in CME Eurodollar futures of 1,970,632 contracts traded on that day. The total notional amount of OTC interest rate swaps that day was $73,976,703,000, as compared to the total notional volume of CME Eurodollar futures (equal to $1 million per contract) of $1,970,632,000,000. The trading volume of Eurodollar futures thus significantly exceeds the trading volume of OTC interest rate swaps both in terms of the number of trades and total notional amounts.

Yet, the average trade size is significantly larger for interest rate swaps as compared to Eurodollar futures. On October 31, 2014, the average size of a single USD interest rate swap registered with DTCC or BSDR was $62,165,297, as compared to the average size of a CME Eurodollar futures trade of $1,000,000.

Structural differences in the product terms and transaction mechanisms that differ across interest rate swaps and economically equivalent Eurodollar futures strips naturally lead to higher turnovers in futures. Specifically, a typical plain vanilla interest rate

[54]See, for example, Burghardt (2003).

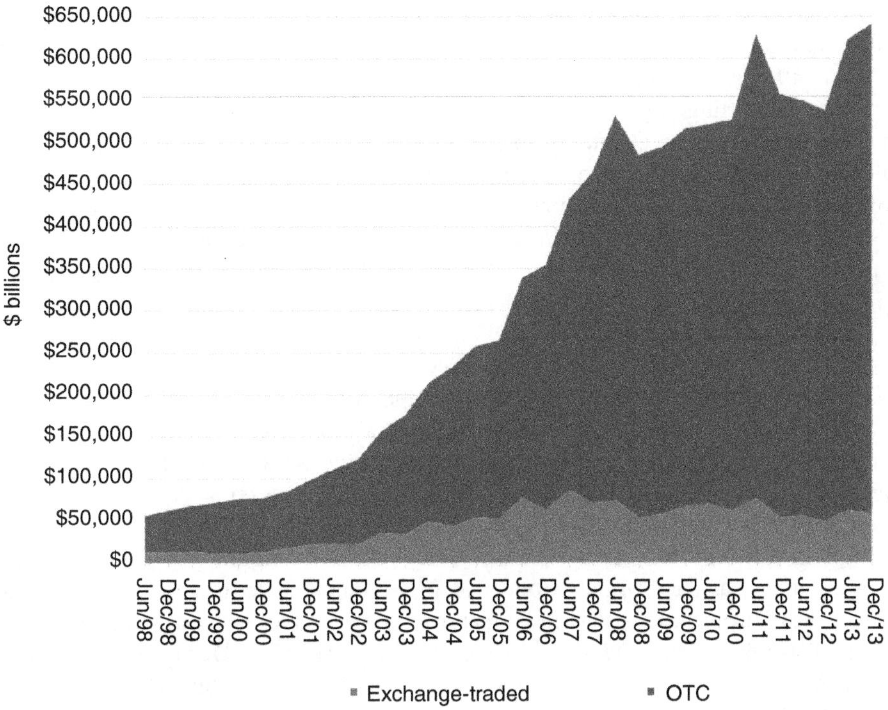

Figure 16.21 Notional amount of exchange-traded and OTC interest rate derivatives outstanding. Source: Bank for International Settlements.

swap is a single contract that involves a sequence of cash flows.[55] A Eurodollar futures strip, by contrast, is actually a portfolio of individual Eurodollar futures contracts, each of which can be viewed as a cash-settled futures contract on a hypothetical 90-day LIBOR CD with a $1 million face value that is issued on the date the futures contract matures. Replicating an interest rate swap with futures thus requires multiple futures trades as compared to a single interest rate swap trade.

Consider, for example, a 2-year plain vanilla USD interest rate swap with a notional principal of $10 million and quarterly IMM settlement dates. The interest rate swap involves eight quarterly settlement dates but is executed as a single transaction and shows up as a single transaction for purposes of turnover calculations. The economically equivalent Eurodollar futures strip, however, requires establishing positions in one cash instrument (corresponding to the first reset date) and seven different futures contracts.[56] With a $10 million total notional amount, that means the Eurodollar strip involves about 70 Eurodollar futures contracts. In this simple example, the $10 million notional turnover in interest rate swaps thus equates to about $68 million (given hedge ratios based on reasonable discount rates) in notional turnover in Eurodollar futures despite the fact that the transactions are essentially economically equivalent.

16.6.1.2 The "Futurization" of Swaps? As a result of the panoply of new regulations that went into effect in 2011 and afterward, some users of swaps have chosen to eschew the new mandated execution requirement for swaps and have instead turned to futures listed on regulated exchanges. Exchanges have capitalized on this demand from swap participants by heavily promoting exchange-traded swap futures as an alternative to interest rate swaps. The result has been a significant surge in the use of deliverable swap futures.

The value proposition for swap futures vis-à-vis swaps traded on SEFs and then submitted to CCPs for clearing is the ostensible cost savings arising from greater efficiencies in capital and margin for all-futures trades as compared to cleared swaps. Specifically, futures in general enjoy several potential benefits vis-à-vis cleared swaps in the new regulatory regime. For example, margin requirements for swap futures are typically based on potential 1- or 2-day price movements, whereas margins on cleared swaps are generally based on price movements over 5–7 days.[57] Interest rate swap futures are also eligible for cross-product

[55] An interest rate swap can be viewed as a portfolio of settled-in-arrears FRAs with a common fixed rate, equal to the par swap rate. See, for example, Smithson (1998).

[56] The actual number of contracts held is based on the hedge ratio that equates the present value of a one basis point change in rates on the Eurodollar futures strip to the present value of a one basis point change in the rates on the interest rate swap. In addition, a convexity adjustment is generally also made to determine the appropriate number of futures contracts to hold. See, for example, Burghardt (2003).

[57] See, for example, Madigan (2013).

margin and netting with related products like Eurodeposit rate futures, whereas cross-margining is not always available for cleared swaps and related futures. Providers of interest rate swap futures currently claim that market participants can realize margin costs that are as low as 40–80% of collateral costs on corresponding cleared swaps.[58] Deliverable swap futures, moreover, are not subject to the new trade reporting requirements.

Futures on interest rate swaps or interest rate swap-like exposures are not a recent invention. NYSE Liffe first listed Swapnote® futures in March 2001.[59] Swapnote futures are cash-settled contracts whose value essentially mimics the value of the fixed leg in a forward-starting plain vanilla interest rate swap with a €100,000 notional principal amount. NYSE Liffe listed Swapnote futures on USD interest rate swaps in July 2002, which were also based on a plain vanilla interest rate swap with a notional principal of $200,000 and IMM settlement dates for the floating leg. Swapnote futures are available on both USD and EUR interest rate swaps with tenors of 2, 5, and 10 years to maturity, and options are listed for trading on 2-, 5-, and 10-year Swapnote futures for Euros only. Variation margin and settlements of Swapnote futures are based on revaluations of the synthetic bond by NYSE Liffe using the interbank/swap discount curve.

In 2009, CME listed a product similar to NYSE Liffe's USD Swapnote futures.[60] The CME interest rate swap futures contract was cash-settled to the ISDA Benchmark Rate.[61] The underlying nondeliverable swap was a plain vanilla USD interest rate swap with IMM floating reset dates and a notional principal of $100,000 (the same as the size of the interest rate swap futures contract). CME listed interest rate swap futures based on swaps with 5-, 7-, 10-, and 30-year tenors, as well as options on interest rate swap futures based on all four interest rate swap maturities.[62]

CME interest rate swap futures were delisted by CME in June 2013.[63] A significant reason for the delisting of the CME interest rate swap futures contract was the CME's introduction of a competing set of swap futures contracts in late 2012. For these new contracts, CME opted for physical settlement at maturity into an actual interest rate swap that would subsequently be cleared by CME. CME first listed these USD *deliverable* swap futures ("DSFs") in December 2012 and later listed EUR DSFs in April 2014. The USD DSFs are available on interest rate swaps with 2-, 5-, 10-, and 30-year tenors. The underlying swaps have notional amounts of $100,000 and are plain vanilla interest rate swaps with semiannual fixed payments and IMM floating reset dates.

In addition to CME and NYSE Liffe, several other exchanges also list interest rate swap futures. For example, the Brazilian futures exchange BM&FBOVESPA lists several actively traded futures contracts based on interest rate swaps. The most popular such contract also includes an embedded exchange rate adjustment to the USD.

New exchanges have also begun offering USD interest rate swap futures contracts.[64] Eris Exchange was established in 2010 by five Chicago-based trading firms and was approved by the CFTC in October 2011 as a new U.S. exchange. Eris exclusively offers interest rate swap futures for trading.[65] Initially, Eris operated as an EEP that offered "flexible" interest rate swap futures that could be traded either through a CLOB or an RFQ process.[66] The flexible interest rate swap futures were cleared by CME and revalued based on the CME swap curve using OIS discounting. The Eris contract consolidates all cash flows on the underlying reference swap (i.e., net fixed and floating payments, any up-front or termination payments, and interest paid on collateral) into a single settlement price while still ensuring that all cash flows occur through traditional variation margin payments administered by CME Clearing.

In December 2012, Eris introduced its "Standards" futures based on plain vanilla USD interest rate swaps with maturities of 2, 5, 10, and 30 years, a $100,000 notional principal, IMM floating reset dates, and a final cash settlement at maturity. Eris Standards futures are also cleared through CME.[67]

Figure 16.22 shows annual volumes of the various futures contracts based on interest rate swaps discussed earlier (except for BM&FBOVESPA swaps, which are excluded because they also include a currency exposure element) from 2009 through October 2014. The surge in volume in 2013 and 2014 leading up to and following the final adoption of the U.S. SEF rules is apparent.

[58] See, for example, Eris Exchange (2012). See also Sapient Global Markets (2013).

[59] Swapnote® is a registered trademark of ICAP plc. Subsequent uses of the symbol ® are dropped for simplicity, but all references to Swapnote herein are intended to respect the reserved rights of ICAP.

[60] USD Swapnote futures have not experienced the same brisk volumes as EUR Swapnote futures.

[61] The ISDA Benchmark Rate is the ISDAFIX midmarket par swap rate collected by Reuters and ICAP daily at 11am Eastern Time and published by Reuters and Bloomberg.

[62] For more details on the original CME interest rate swap futures contract, see CME Group (2009).

[63] CME Group (2013).

[64] Although I only discuss Eris Exchange here as an example, there are other platforms which have obtained CFTC approval as full designated contract markets ("DCMs") specifically to offer interest rate swap futures such as trueEX (https://www.trueex.com/about-us (last visited April 14, 2014)).

[65] See Grant et al. (2010), and Eris Exchange (2011b). Prior to its approval as a DCM, Eris operated as an "exempt board of trade" under CFTC regulations. See, for example, Eris Exchange (2010).

[66] See, for example, Eris Exchange (2011a).

[67] Eris Exchange (2012).

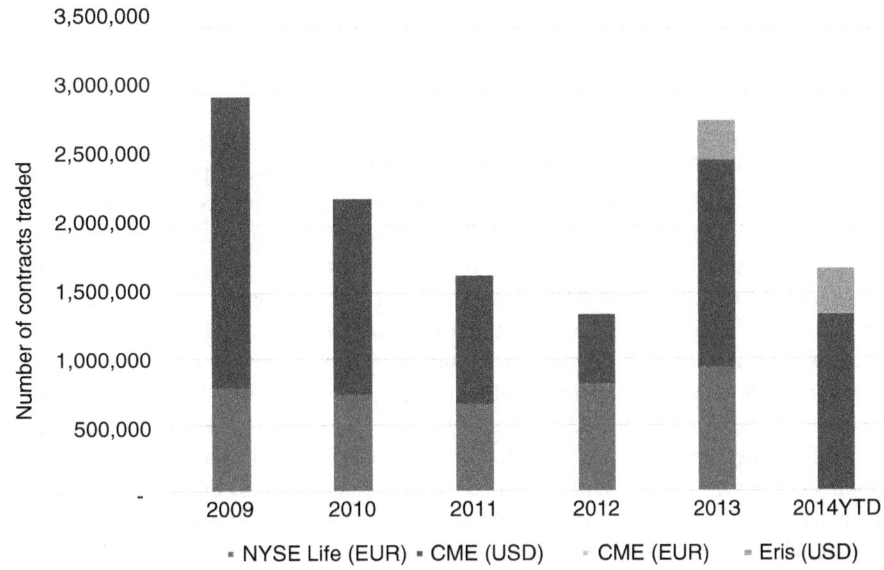

Figure 16.22 Annual volumes of major interest rate swap futures contracts. CME (USD) futures include both deliverable swap futures and IRS futures. Source: Data from CME Group.

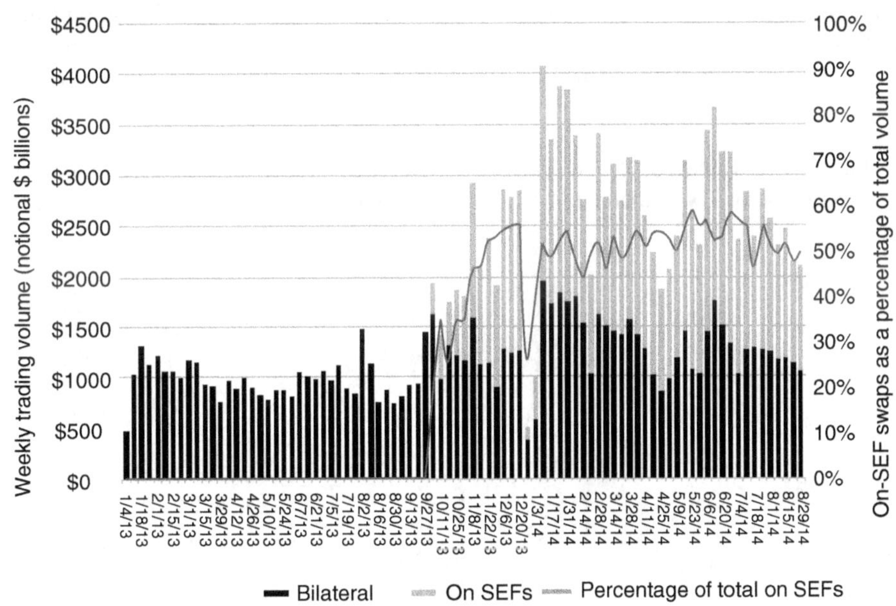

Figure 16.23 Notional trading volume of OTC interest rate derivatives reported to DTCC/BSDR by execution mechanism. Source: Data from ISDA.

16.6.2 Bilateral versus SEF Execution of OTC Interest Rate Derivatives

In the swap world, a significant current issue involves the Dodd–Frank execution mandate (and the analogous pending European mandate under MiFID 2) that requires certain swaps to be executed on EEPs registered with the CFTC as SEFs. Recall that the first SEF registrations occurred in 2013 and that October 2, 2013, was the first day that all trades covered by the execution mandate had to be executed on SEFs.

Figure 16.23 shows the weekly total notional amounts of OTC interest rate derivatives trades (across all products and currencies) registered with DTCC or BSDR based on the execution venue. From October 2013 through August 2014, the black bars represent bilateral swaps, and the gray bars reflect trades executed on SEFs. Bilateral weekly volume from January 2013 through September 2013 is also shown for comparison purposes, along with the percentage of total weekly notional volume executed on SEFs.

As Figure 16.23 shows, the proportion of OTC interest rate derivatives executed on SEFs rose steadily from 25% for the week ending October 18, 2013, to 56% the week ending December 20, 2013. SEF volumes stabilized around the percentage thereafter, accounting for just over 50% of all trade volume on average for 2014 (through August).

16.6.2.1 By Clearing Status As noted in Section 16.4.2.3, not all transactions executed on SEFs involve products that are subject to the clearing and execution mandates of the Dodd–Frank Act. Indeed, market participants were already utilizing EEPs (some of which have registered as SEFs) prior to the advent of the new regulations. Not surprisingly, some activity on SEFs continues to reflect trading volume in noncleared products that are not subject to the execution mandate.

Figure 16.24 shows weekly total notional trading volumes (for all OTC interest rate derivatives products across all currencies) and weekly total numbers of trades for interest rate derivatives executed on SEFs based on the clearing status of those trades. In the months of October 2013 when the Dodd–Frank execution mandate first went into effect, just over 10% (by notional amount) of all products traded on SEFs were noncleared. Since then, noncleared products have accounted for less than 10% of weekly notional trading volume. In other words, the vast majority of products traded on SEFs – but not all – are CCP cleared.

Figure 16.24 also indicates that the amount of trading activity on SEFs in noncleared OTC interest rate derivatives has been relatively stable in 2014 (despite representing a small proportion of the SEF marketplace). In 2014, the number of noncleared trades per week and the total weekly notional amounts of those trades remained fairly close to the annual averages of about 700 and $87.45 billion, respectively (indicating an average trade size of $123.8 million notional).

From Figure 16.24, the weekly volumes of cleared SEF trades appear to have been more volatile than for noncleared SEF trades both in terms of notional amounts and numbers of trades. In 2014, the average weekly notional volume of cleared SEF trades was $1.28 trillion, and the average number of trades per week was 5,962 (indicating an average cleared SEF trade size of $215.4 million – i.e., about $90 million larger than the average size of a noncleared SEF trade). Looking at the total number of trades per week, however, the ratio of the standard deviation to the average number of trades per week is about the same for cleared and noncleared swaps. In terms of weekly notional trading volumes, however, the ratio of the standard deviation to the average for 2014 is about 0.28 for cleared SEF trades as compared to a ratio of 0.21 for noncleared SEF trades. Notional volumes of cleared trades thus did vary more (relative to the average) in 2014 for cleared trades vis-á-vis noncleared trades executed on SEFs.

16.6.2.2 By Product Panel A of Table 16.11 summarizes the trading volume of swaps executed on SEFs (as reported to DTCC and BSDR) since SEF trading was mandated in early October 2013 through August 2014. The table shows daily

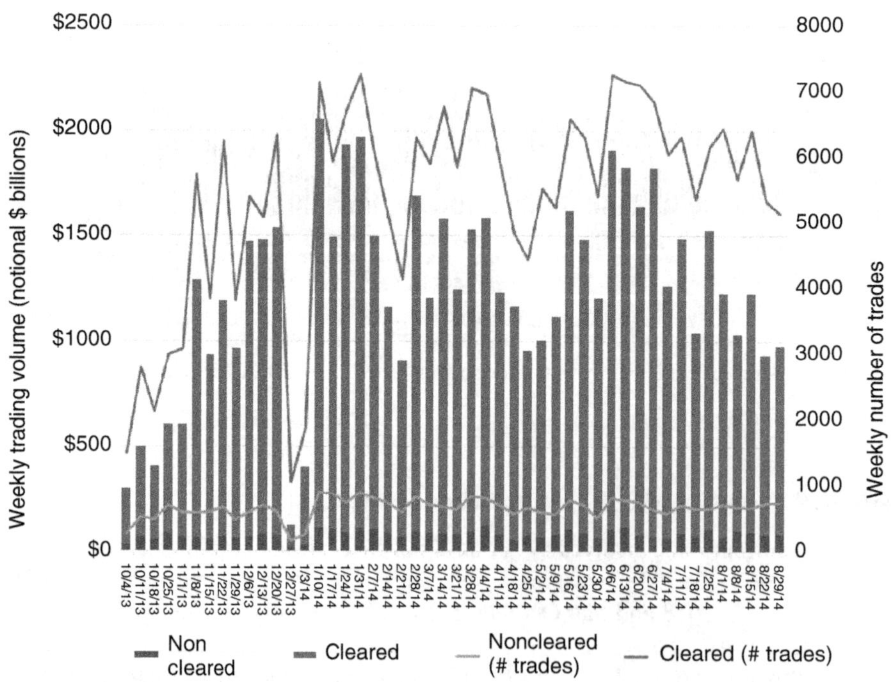

Figure 16.24 Notional trading volume of OTC interest rate derivatives executed on SEFs reported to DTCC/BSDR by clearing status. Source: Data from ISDA.

TABLE 16.11 OTC Interest Rate Derivatives Executed on SEFs as Reported to DTCC and BDSR Notional $ Billions (# Trades)

	Average	Median	Standard deviation	Maximum
	Panel A: October 2013–August 2014			
Fixed/floating swaps	$59.64 (842)	$62.27 (860)	$21.24 (311)	$107.16 (1,504)
OIS	$25.74 (22)	$20.83 (21)	$19.31 (11)	$118.8 (54)
Basis swaps	$4.77 (30)	$4.34 (29)	$3.15 (15)	$18.85 (100)
Inflation swaps	$0.33 (8)	$0.28 (7)	$0.23 (6)	$1.15 (29)
Cross-currency swaps	$4.24 (40)	$3.89 (40)	$2.63 (19)	$17.9 (85)
FRAs	$148.35 (413)	$25.74 (51)	$241.34 (690)	$1,346.66 (3,164)
Options	$3.35 (28)	$3.19 (27)	$1.6 (12)	$9.63 (64)
Exotics	$0.62 (4)	$0.06 (3)	$2.18 (4)	$21.27 (23)
Other	$16.04 (80)	$14.73 (78)	$9.17 (43)	$57.65 (279)
All products	*$263.07 (1,466)*	*$162.38 (1,312)*	*$257.08 (844)*	*$1,461.11 (4,119)*
	Panel B: June 2014–August 2014			
Fixed/floating swaps	$68.44 (1,048)	$66.85 (1,044)	$17.86 (247)	$104.63 (1,504)
OIS	$34.77 (25)	$31.64 (23)	$22.71 (12)	$118.8 (54)
Basis swaps	$3.95 (27)	$3.54 (27)	$2.26 (12)	$14.23 (57)
Inflation swaps	$0.36 (9)	$0.32 (8)	$0.23 (6)	$1.15 (24)
Cross-currency swaps	$4.6 (45)	$3.66 (41)	$2.67 (18)	$11.19 (85)
FRAs	$156.26 (417)	$27.67 (97)	$234.65 (620)	$993.33 (2,340)
Options	$3.39 (27)	$3.16 (27)	$1.68 (11)	$9.63 (59)
Exotics	$1.13 (6)	$0.17 (4)	$3.32 (6)	$21.27 (23)
Other	$17.16 (84)	$15.22 (80)	$9.44 (37)	$49.55 (218)
All products	*$290.06 (1,688)*	*$199.21 (1,566)*	*$250.45 (728)*	*$1,115.9 (3,447)*

Source: Data from ISDA.

averages, medians, standard deviations, and maximums for each major OTC interest rate derivatives product type. Notional amounts are shown along with the number of trades within parentheses. Table 16.11 reports results aggregated across all reported currencies.

As Panel A of Table 16.11 indicates, fixed/floating interest rate swaps were the most actively traded product in terms of average number of daily trades, whereas FRAs exhibited the largest average daily gross notional trading amount. Comparing the average to the median and looking at the standard deviations, however, indicate that the FRA statistics are skewed by several very active trading days. For the most part, the most actively traded product thus is (not surprisingly) fixed/floating interest rate swaps. OISs and other products also experienced relatively robust trading activity during the period.

Panel B of Table 16.11 shows the same summary statistics for the 3-month period from June 2014 through August 2014. The same general patterns of activity can be observed across products as in the full sample shown in Panel A. Notably, Panel B indicates that volumes have generally increased and are noticeably higher in the recent 3-month period than over the full sample.

Table 16.11 includes all trades executed through SEFs regardless of whether the products are cleared or subject to a clearing mandate. For example, cross-currency swaps and exotics are not subject to any clearing mandate and are not available for central clearing. Nevertheless, Table 16.11 indicates (as did Figure 16.24) that at least some market participants have chosen to execute such contracts through SEFs instead of bilaterally.

16.6.2.3 By Currency Figure 16.25 shows weekly notional volumes of OTC interest rate derivatives trades executed on SEFs from October 2, 2013, through August 29, 2014, by the currency in which the swaps were denominated (for the G3 currencies and the GBP). Figure 16.25 also shows the percentage of weekly notional volume attributable to USD-denominated OTC interest rate derivatives.

Given that the SEF trading mandate under the Dodd–Frank Act applies only to U.S. market participants, it is not surprising that USD-denominated interest rate derivatives dominate SEF trading activity. For the entire period, the average notional volume of USD interest rate derivatives executed on SEFs represented 68% of all SEF trades in the G3 currencies plus the GBP. From May through August 2014, moreover, the proportion of USD trading activity increased from about 65% to 78% of trades in these four currencies.

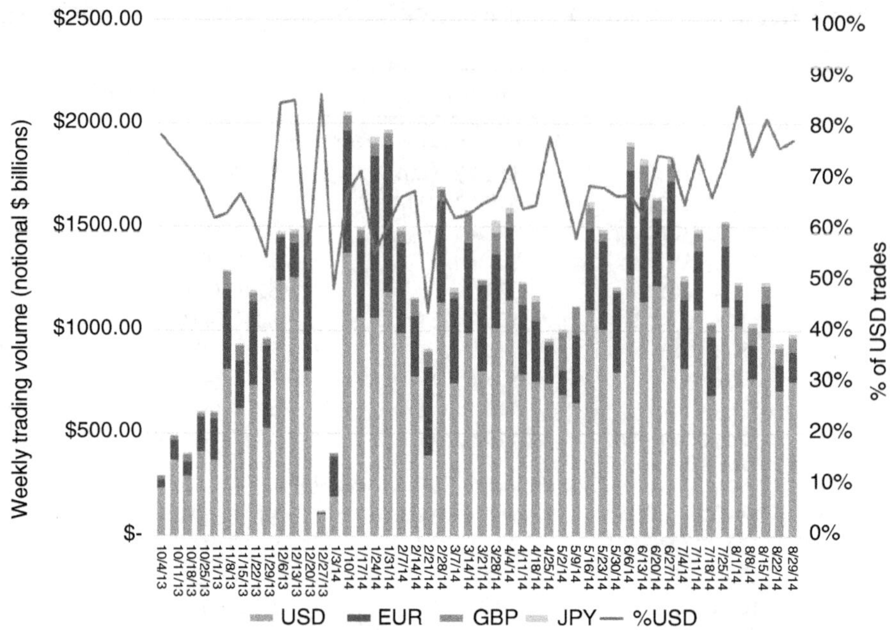

Figure 16.25 Notional trading volume of OTC interest rate derivatives executed on SEFs reported to DTCC/BSDR by currency. Source: Data from ISDA.

16.7 LIQUIDITY FRAGMENTATION IN NONDOLLAR SWAPS

Since the introduction of the Dodd–Frank execution requirements and the SEF regime in the United States (and its cross-border implementation, as discussed further in Appendix Section 16.9.7), market participants and regulators have expressed concerns that the new regulatory framework has caused a fragmentation in what was previously a global liquidity pool for the execution of certain OTC interest rate derivatives. As discussed further in the Appendix (Section 16.9.7), the cross-border implementation of new regulations – and the uncertainties to which it has given rise – has been largely responsible for the bifurcation of liquidity across U.S. and E.U. markets.[68]

More specifically, market participants contend that the new U.S. regulatory framework has driven certain OTC interest rate derivatives trading volume overseas and has led non-U.S. market participants to eschew U.S. counterparties on certain transactions in order to avoid the Dodd–Frank execution mandate and other U.S.-specific regulations (including reporting requirements and other new regulations, as reviewed in the Appendix).[69] The problem has not significantly affected USD-denominated OTC interest rate derivatives (which was already primarily a U.S. marketplace), but EUR-denominated OTC interest rate derivatives have experienced a significant and pronounced bifurcation of liquidity across U.S. and E.U. regulatory regimes since the adoption of the new regulations that characterize the current revamped regulatory framework.[70]

The data supports these concerns.[71] Figure 16.26 shows weekly notional trading volumes of MAT interest rate swaps denominated in USD, EUR, and GBP reported to DTCC and BSDR from October 2013 through October 2014 as a percentage of total SEF trading volumes for interest rate swaps (MAT and non-MAT) denominated in all currencies over the same time period. Trades are not explicitly reported to SDRs as MAT or non-MAT, so the data underlying this figure is based on ISDA's identification of trades that meet the MAT transaction criteria. The period following the introduction of the U.S. SEF regime in October 2013 is shown as the dark gray-shaded area in Figure 16.26, and the period following the imposition of the mandated execution of MAT transactions on February 15, 2014, is shown as the light gray-shaded area in Figure 16.26.

As Figure 16.26 illustrates, the October 2, 2013, introduction of the SEF framework in the United States does not itself seem to have had a significant impact on the relative trading volume of MAT interest rate swaps in any of the three currencies vis-à-vis total SEF interest rate swaps trading volume across all currencies. Following the implementation of the Dodd–Frank execution mandate in February 2014, however, a clear and significant impact can be seen in Figure 16.26. USD-denominated MAT interest rate swaps experienced an increase in relative market share for several months but then declined and then seem to have stabilized around an average of roughly 51% of the total SEF interest rate swap volume from June through October 2014. The stabilized

[68] See, for example, Burne (2014).

[69] See, for example, ISDA (2013a, 2014b,f,g), Madigan (2014b,d), and Burne (2014).

[70] See, for example, Madigan (2014g).

[71] See the references in supra note 69.

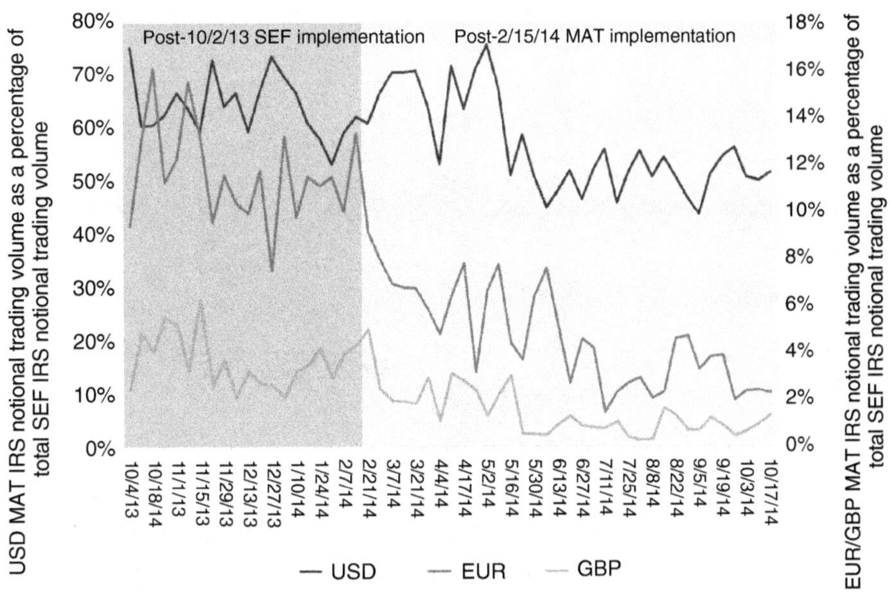

Figure 16.26 Trading volume of MAT interest rate swaps traded on SEFs as a percentage of total self interest rate swap trading volume reported to DTCC/BSDR. Percentages for USD-,EUR-, and GBP-denominated MAT swaps are calculated as weekly total notional amounts of MAT swaps traded in each currently divided by the total reported notional amounts traded of swaps (MAT and non-MAT) denominated in all reported currencies (USD, EUR, GBP, JPY, AUD, BRL, CAD, CLP, CNY, HUF, KRW, MXN, NZD, PLN, TRY, ZAR, and Other). Source: Data from ISDA.

market share of USD-denominated MAT interest rate swaps executed on SEFs since June 2014, however, is appreciably lower in the post-February 2014 period after the Dodd–Frank execution mandate went into effect than in the previous period. This suggests that market participants have indeed sought non-U.S. execution mechanisms and markets and that the volume has migrated from regulated U.S. markets abroad.

Trading volumes of EUR- and GBP-denominated MAT interest rate swaps on SEFs are even more revealing. As Figure 16.26 indicates, such trading has declined on average following the February 2014 imposition of the Dodd–Frank execution mandate. For the week ending February 14, 2014, the notional volume traded of EUR- and GBP-denominated interest rate swaps designated as MAT products accounted for 13% and 4% of total SEF trading volume, respectively. By the week ending October 17, 2014, however, those market shares had declined to 2% and 1%, respectively. The data thus also validates concerns expressed by market participants that the implementation of the new regulatory regimes in the United States and Europe have caused a fragmentation in liquidity that has resulted in a decline in nondollar swap trades on U.S. SEFs.

Figure 16.27 paints a similar picture using total monthly notional cleared interdealer interest rate swap transaction volume at SwapClear, shown in Figure 16.27 based on the different domiciles of swap dealers (i.e., European-to-European, European-to-U.S., and U.S.-to-U.S.). Panels A and B present these clearing volumes for USD- and EUR-denominated interest rate swaps, respectively. Both panels of Figure 16.27 also indicate the time periods in which the two significant U.S. SEF-related regulations were implemented – that is, the period following October 2, 2013, when SEFs first began to execute OTC interest rate derivatives, and the period beginning February 15, 2014, when the trading of OTC interest rate derivatives classified as MAT was mandated.

Panel A of Figure 16.27 for USD-denominated interest rate swaps does not reveal any particular structural pattern following the formal introduction of SEFs in October 2013 or the mandatory execution of MAT swaps in February 2014. For the first few months after the formal introduction of the SEF regime in the United States in October 2013, USD interest rate swap clearing volumes between two European dealers did rise noticeably, which could indicate a desire by European swap dealers to avoid U.S. regulations. The overall time series of trading activity, however, does not suggest any significant fragmentation of the geographical liquidity pool for USD-denominated swaps.

For EUR-denominated swaps, however, the same noticeable shift in liquidity shown in Figure 16.26 is also apparent in Panel B of Figure 16.27, which shows notional volumes of EUR-denominated interest rate swaps cleared by SwapClear from January 2013 through May 2014.[72] Following the introduction of the U.S. SEF regulatory regime in October 2013, the notional volume of EUR-denominated interest rate swaps executed by two European swap dealers rose appreciably, while, at the same

[72]Panel B of Figure 16.27 looks essentially the same if shown using percentages of total interdealer volume instead of total notional amounts.

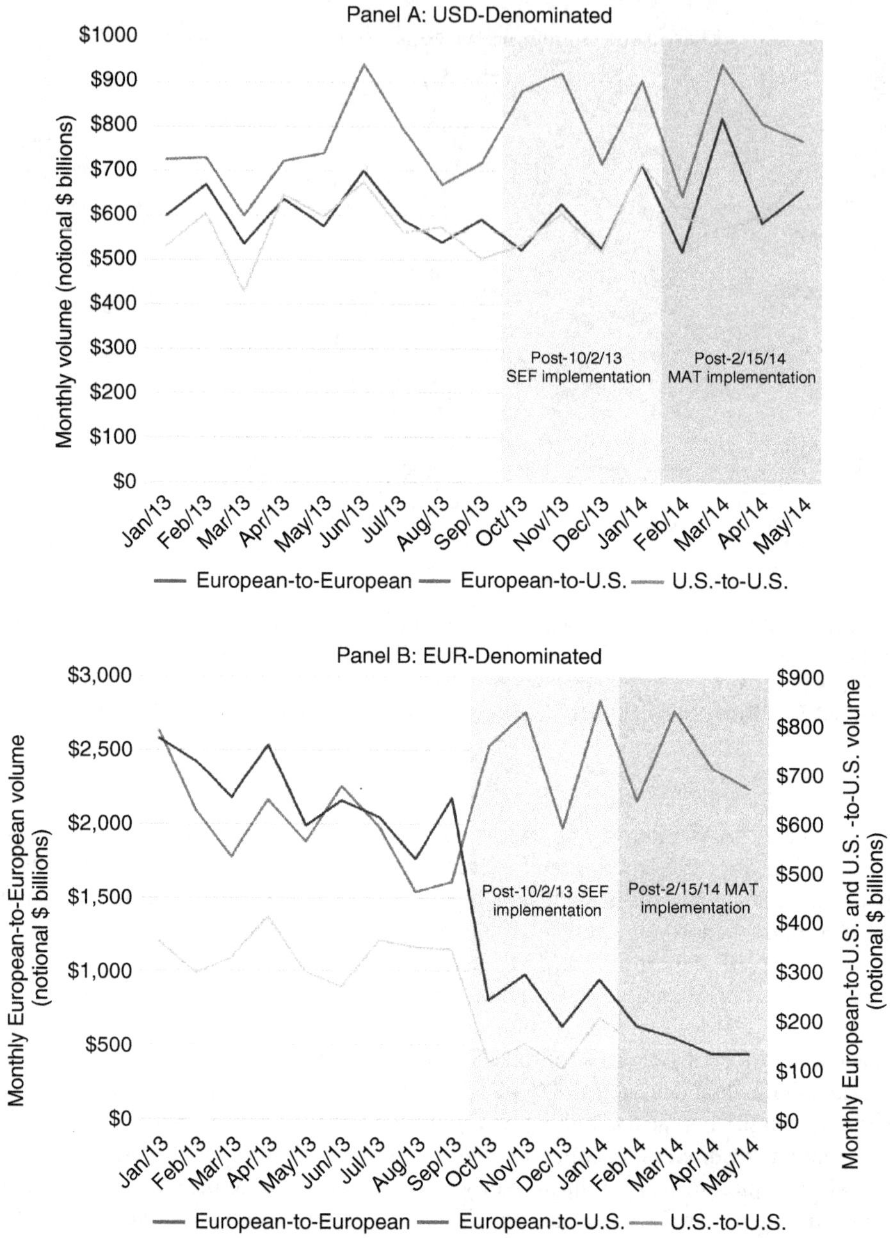

Figure 16.27 Total amounts of interdealer interest rate swaps cleared on SwapClear by counterparty domicile. Source: Data from ISDA & LCH.Clearnet.

time, EUR-denominated interest rate swaps transactions between European and U.S. swap dealers declined precipitously (as did EUR-denominated interest rate swaps executed by two U.S. dealers). Notional volumes of EUR-denominated interest rate swaps executed between European and U.S. dealers or two U.S. dealers continued to decline following the introduction of the Dodd–Frank execution mandate in February 2014.

Figures 16.26 and 16.27 both confirm the concerns that market participants and regulators have expressed regarding the impact of various new regulations on the global liquidity pools for trading EUR- and GBP-denominated interest rate swaps. The empirical evidence indicates a decline in the execution of nondollar swaps by transactions involving at least one non-U.S. counterparty and also suggests a migration of at least some dollar swap volume to non-U.S. regulatory regimes.

16.8 PROSPECTS FOR THE FUTURE

As new regulations continue to be implemented and evolve, market participants respond to those new regulations, which often triggers further refinements and changes to the regulations. In particular, market participants often respond to changes in new regulations by engaging in regulatory avoidance (i.e., identifying and exploiting loopholes) and regulatory arbitrage (i.e., structuring transactions and activities in a manner that reduces exposure to costly regulations by substituting those activities into lower-cost regulatory regimes).[73]

Regulators typically respond to regulatory avoidance and arbitrage by refining the regulations that engendered those activities or by promulgating new regulations. Market participants then respond to those changes, as well, and the cycle continues. Kane refers to this "regulatory dialectic" as

> [the] cyclical interaction between political and economic pressures in regulated markets. It treats political processes of *regulation* and economic processes of *regulatory avoidance* as opposing forces that, like riders on a see saw, adapt continually to each other. This alternating adaptation evolves as a series of lagged responses, with regulators and regulatees seeking to maximize their own objectives, conditional on how they perceive the opposing party to behave. [emphasis in original][74]

Financial markets in general and derivatives in particular are well acquainted with this regulatory dialectic.[75] In some historical cases, relatively minor changes in regulations have precipitated significant changes in financial product design.[76] Given the significant nature of the recent changes in the interest rate derivatives regulatory framework, it stands to reason that at least some market participants will design (or redesign) interest rate derivatives, interest rate derivatives-related activities, and organizational forms (e.g., legal entity status by jurisdiction) either to avoid costly or undesirable new regulations or to accommodate the new regulations in the least disruptive manner possible.

To take a specific example, when the benefits of customization and private negotiation are sufficiently high relative to the costs of EEP or exchange execution, market participants might devote potentially considerable resources to "design-arounds" in which interest rate derivatives are constructed specifically to avoid execution mandates. Numerous ad hoc examples of such responses to new regulations have already been frequently observed in the United States. Some market participants have reportedly avoided U.S. execution mandates by making small changes to interest rate derivatives, apparently for the purpose of ensuring that their transactions are technically distinct from MAT transactions. For instance, some swaps that would otherwise be MAT products have settlement dates and/or day-count conventions that differ just slightly from the MAT definitions but that are sufficient to make the products non-MAT and hence outside the Dodd–Frank execution mandate.

Given the complex dynamics of the interactions between regulators and market participants, the medium- and long-term impacts of the new regulatory environment on the product design, liquidity, and activity of interest rate derivatives are impossible to predict. Even the short-term outlook, moreover, is hazy given how many regulations underlying the new regime are still being implemented.

The data examined in this chapter do provide some clues as what the future of interest rate derivatives marketplace may look like, but these are at best stylized facts and glimpses of one possible market reality. Only time will tell how the interest rate derivatives marketplace will evolve as the regulatory dialectic between regulators and regulatees plays out. What follows in the next three sections thus are not predictions of the future, but rather are commentaries on certain specific issues that have been identified as relevant for the future of interest rate derivatives activity in cleared OTC interest rate derivatives and exchange-traded interest rate derivatives, interest rate swap futures, and noncleared OTC interest rate derivatives, respectively.

16.8.1 Cleared Swaps and Exchange-Traded Interest Rate Derivatives

An obvious and explicitly stated objective of the new regulations in the United States and Europe (and under the G20 Principles generally) is to try and shift as much volume in standardized interest rate derivatives as possible into CCPs for clearing and toward EEPs and exchanges for execution (*see* Sections 16.2.1 and 16.2.2). Market participants that use interest rate derivatives covered by clearing and/or execution mandates are necessarily forced to adhere to these mandates and must shift any such transactions into regulated clearing and execution environments.

All else equal, the ostensible ramification of the new regulations is to force a redirection of significant volumes of OTC interest rate derivatives onto EEPs and CCPs. The empirical evidence presented in Sections 16.3 through 16.6 indicates that trading volumes and market activity have already begun to adjust to this new regulatory environment. The evidence also indicates that such shifts were occurring voluntarily prior to the implementation of the new regulatory regime.

[73]Given the existence of a regulation, regulatory avoidance and arbitrage (and the resources allocated to those activities) is not necessarily problematic. Those activities (or the threat that they may occur) can provide an important source of discipline on regulators. For a discussion in the context of derivatives, see, for example, Culp (1995a).
[74]Kane (1981). See also Kane (1977, 1983), and Kane (1988).
[75]See, for example, Miller (1986), and Miller (1992). See also Silber (1983), Kane (1988), and Merton (1995). For a review of historical derivatives regulations in this context, see, for example, Culp (1991, 1995b), and Culp (2010).
[76]See, for example, Miller (1986).

Nevertheless, there will inevitably be some "leakage" in this process – that is, some market participants that were previously using noncleared bilateral OTC interest rate derivatives may decide that the marginal costs of the new regulations are too high relative to the underlying benefits of using derivatives. In other words, the regulatory edicts in numerous countries that divert transactions from a bilateral noncleared environment into an EEP/exchange and cleared environment do not guarantee that *all* such volume will be successfully diverted. Some firms may, in fact, decide that the forced changes give rise to costs high enough that they are better off desisting in their use of derivatives than migrating into the new environment. (Section 16.8.3 discusses this issue more explicitly with respect to end users.)

16.8.2 Swap Futures

Although interest rate swap futures have experienced some growth since the implementation of the new regulations (*see* Section 16.6.1.2), swap futures have not displaced cleared swaps in the marketplace. Swap futures have experienced less-than-expected volume increases, which indicates that many market participants still prefer to execute OTC interest rate derivatives in lieu of using similar exchange-traded interest rate derivatives. Nevertheless, many market participants remain optimistic that the new regulatory regime will help usher in an increasing shift toward the "futurization" of interest rate swaps.

As discussed in Section 16.6.1.2, the advantages of DSFs and cash-settled swap futures vis-à-vis cleared swaps depend largely on potential margin and collateral efficiencies. Market participants that can take advantage of cross-margining on CCPs for products like interest rate swaps and Eurodollar or EURIBOR futures could experience relatively significant cost savings, whereas firms using only interest rate swaps may not. Also as previously noted, trade reporting requirements for swap futures are less costly than similar requirements for cleared swaps.

Especially in the European Union where implementation of the clearing and execution mandates has lagged behind the United States, the experience of the United States could provide a blueprint and enable a much more rapid adoption of swap futures, especially by institutional asset managers.[77] On the other hand, the cross-margining efficiencies offered by swap futures might not be significant enough – in Europe or the United States – to facilitate the futurization of swaps, in which case swap futures may survive as another weapon in the interest rate risk management arsenal but are unlikely to be the weapon of choice.[78]

16.8.3 Noncleared Swaps and End Users

Noncleared swaps will by necessity continue to be the risk management solution for nonclearable interest rate derivatives products. As discussed in Section 16.5.2, nonclearable products include products for which CCPs have not (yet) offered a clearing solution for certain products (e.g., cross-currency swaps and swaptions) or for products (both nonclearable and clearable) in nonclearable currencies. Until CCPs make such products available for clearing, noncleared swaps will remain the primary available product available to market participants that wish to execute such products. As discussed in Section 16.4, a significant amount of interest rate swaps are nonclearable products or clearable products in nonclearable currencies.

OTC interest rate derivatives that are clearable but not subject to a clearing or execution mandate and OTC interest rate derivatives executed by market participants that are excluded from those mandates pose a larger question regarding future market activity. For such products and market participants, the relative appeal of OTC interest rate derivatives will depend on the final implemented rules regarding minimum margin and capital requirements for noncleared swaps (as discussed in Appendix Sections 16.9.5 and 16.9.6), as well as the implementation of exclusions from mandated clearing and execution requirements – the end-user exclusion in particular.

As discussed in Sections 16.2.1 and 16.2.2 (and Sections 16.9.2.1 and 16.9.3.1 in the Appendix), the CFTC granted exceptions from the Dodd–Frank clearing and execution mandates for certain transactions executed by end users.[79] Specifically, an OTC interest rate derivatives contract executed by an end user is not subject to the clearing and execution mandates if the end user is not a financial entity, is using the swap to hedge or reduce commercial risks, can meet the financial obligations associated with the swap, and provides certain information to the CFTC (via an SDR or to the CFTC directly if no SDR is available). Public companies registered with the Securities and Exchange Commission ("SEC") must also take certain corporate actions to avail themselves of the end-user exception.[80] According to the CFTC, a swap is a hedging or commercial risk-mitigating transaction if the OTC derivatives transaction is "economically appropriate" to reduce the normal business risks of the enterprise, qualifies as a "bona fide hedge" for purposes of determining position limits under the Commodity Exchange Act, or qualifies as a hedge under an applicable accounting standard.

[77] See, for example, Osborn (2013).
[78] Id.
[79] CFTC (2012a). See also
[80] See, for example, Architzel and Bernstein (2012), Cravath, Swaine & Moore LLP (2012), Cleary Gottlieb (2013), Gibson, Dunn & Crutcher LLP (2013), and Sidley Austin LLP (2014).

As noted in Section 16.2.1.2, the European Union does not have a specific end-user exemption from the EMIR clearing mandate. Nevertheless, as discussed in Section 16.9.2.2, the European Union does exempt nonfinancial companies with total OTC derivatives activities below specified thresholds from the EMIR clearing mandate.

The U.S. and E.U. exemptions from mandatory clearing and execution requirements are fairly restrictive (more so in the United States than the European Union). The applicability of various new regulations to OTC interest rate derivatives end users not exempt from these regulations could have a dramatic impact on the future use of such derivatives by nonfinancial corporate hedgers. In particular, OTC derivatives executed by end users that are not exempt from clearing and execution mandates impose several potentially significant costs on OTC interest rate derivatives end users that ultimately could exceed those firms' perceived benefits of hedging and result in their cessation of derivatives hedging entirely.

First, swaps cleared by CCPs are subject to initial margin and twice-daily mark-to-market variation margin requirements that could impose significant costs on end users. For end users of derivatives with limited debt capacity and high leverage, the cash flow volatility of CCP-cleared products can be disruptive to treasury and cash management operations. At the other extreme, well-capitalized and highly rated corporate end users with easy access to unsecured borrowing may find mandatory margin requirements to be unnecessarily burdensome.[81]

Second, CCP clearing and EEP execution require some degree of standardization in the underlying products. Some OTC transactions, which are typically valued for their ease of customization, may pose too many practical problems for CCPs to clear. Being forced to use cleared swaps with standardized dates could expose end users to what they might perceive as excessive basis risk, thereby mitigating the potential benefits of the hedge.

Popova and Simkins demonstrate that end users subject to clearing and execution mandates could experience potentially significant additional costs associated with their interest rate hedging activities as compared to hedging with OTC interest rate derivatives. Such costs could arise from a loss in hedging effectiveness and efficiency, the potential liquidity strain posed by initial margin and variation margin requirements, and the change in accounting treatment in case of standardized exchange-traded interest rate derivatives not qualifying for hedge accounting treatment by end users.[82] Facing such potentially significant higher marginal costs, some end users may opt to eschew derivatives and let their shareholders retain the interest rate risks of their core businesses in lieu of incurring the costs of transferring that risk to other market participants.

16.9 APPENDIX: THE NEW REGULATORY FRAMEWORK FOR INTEREST RATE DERIVATIVES IN THE UNITED STATES AND EUROPEAN UNION

This Appendix provides additional details for interested readers on some of the specific aspects of the new U.S. and E.U. regulations involving interest rate derivatives. In addition, the Appendix is intended to provide a self-contained overview of the new regulatory framework for readers that may be more interested in the new regulations than the discussion of interest rate derivatives products and market activity presented in the body of this chapter.

Section 16.9.1 provides an overview of the regulatory classifications of different market participants that participate in interest rate derivatives transactions, which is at the core of many of the new U.S. and E.U. regulations. Sections 16.9.2 through 16.9.6 provide an overview of new U.S. and E.U. regulations regarding the five G20 principles regarding interest rate derivatives – that is, clearing, execution, reporting, and margin and capital requirements for noncleared. Section 16.9.7 summarizes some of the most significant issues that have arisen in recent years involving the cross-border implementation of U.S. and E.U. regulations that differ in substance, the timing of implementation, or both.

16.9.1 Classifications of Market Participants

16.9.1.1 Historical Context and Regulatory Classifications of Interest Rate Derivatives Users When OTC derivatives began to emerge as popular tools of corporate treasury risk management and finance in the early 1980s, most swaps were one-off interest rate or currency transactions arranged by banks and negotiated between two corporate end users. In those days, banks acted as brokers for and advisors to their corporate customers by helping them identify other end users with which a swap might be done, but the swap was executed directly between the two corporations. Banks were not typically principals or counterparties in those transactions.

For each transaction, the advising bank had to identify two different end users with essentially equal but opposite risk management objectives – for example, one end user that wanted to pay a fixed rate and another that wanted to pay a floating rate over the same time period and on the same notional principal amount.[83] As corporate end users began to use swaps

[81] See, for example, Murphy (2009).
[82] Popova and Simkins (2014).
[83] See, for example, Smithson (1998), pp. 150-151.

increasingly for financing and risk management purposes, the practice of banks directly matching two end users became inefficient and impractical.

In response, banks began to function as financial intermediaries in which they were principals to the transactions. These "swap dealers" began to negotiate interest rate swaps with corporate end users *before* identifying an offsetting counterparty. Dealers treated the transactions negotiated with end users as if they were put into a warehouse and relied on exchange-traded derivatives and interdealer swap transactions to hedge the residual risks of their warehouse of customer transactions.

Because swaps exposed both counterparties to bilateral credit risk on often long-dated transactions, customers gravitated toward dealers with relatively greater capital and higher credit ratings (primarily highly rated and well-capitalized European and U.S. banks). A few large nonbank firms also emerged as dealers in certain markets. For example, then-AAA-rated insurance company AIG was a major dealer in interest rate swaps markets.

Although the dealer/end user taxonomy has proven historically convenient, it is not without its interpretational problems. In particular, the distinction is generally used to differentiate between *institutions*, but the concepts of dealers and end users relate more to *transactions* than companies.[84] Indeed, swap "dealers" routinely enter into both exchange-traded derivatives and swaps in end-user capacities. A swap dealer may enter into derivatives on its own account (i.e., in an end-user capacity) for purposes of treasury and asset/liability management, proprietary trading, market making, and more.[85]

The term "end user" is equally vague and problematic and encompasses a broad universe of institutions. Even end users that have no intermediation or customer-oriented activities whatsoever can have large, sophisticated, high-volume derivatives trading activity. Large-scale proprietary trading firms, for example, often engage in frequent (and sizable) transactions and have sophisticated infrastructures and systems to support their trading. Such firms are quite different from, say, a nonfinancial corporation (e.g., a consumer electronics firm) that does a handful of swaps per year. Yet, both would be considered "end users."

Although the distinction between "dealers" and "end users" can be problematic for the reasons noted earlier, derivatives regulation has long embraced these distinctions, which make these classifications more than just pedagogical. For example, the 1997 edition of the OCC handbook defines a swap dealer as "[a] bank that markets derivative products to customers ... " and an end user as a bank that "engages in derivative transactions for its own account."[86] But the OCC also defines two categories of end users: "active position takers" and "limited end users." An active position taker is defined by the OCC as a bank that "employs derivatives to dynamically manage risk, either to reduce risk or purposefully increase the risk profile of the institution ... [and] generally have large derivative positions relative to their total asset size ... [and] also tend to use more complex derivative structures than other end-users."[87] Limited end users, by contrast, "are characterized by smaller portfolios and lower transaction volume than active position-takers ... [and] primarily [use] derivatives as an investment alternative or to manage interest rate risk."[88]

In the postcrisis regulatory environment, both U.S. and European regulators have promulgated new regulations that classify (and in some cases reclassify) various participants in swap activities based on the nature of their market activities. The new regulatory taxonomy is relevant for two reasons. First, a number of new regulations have implications that differ depending on the type of market participant involved. Second, some jurisdictions (notably the United States) require certain types of market participants to register with a regulator.

16.9.1.2 United States In the United States, new CFTC regulations went into effect on July 23, 2012, defining three categories of swap participants: swap dealers, MSPs, and ECPs.[89] Swap dealers and MSPs are required to register as such with the CFTC.

According to these new definitions, swap dealers are institutions that make markets in swaps, hold themselves out to be dealers, engage in activities that cause themselves to be known by market participants as a dealer or market maker, or regularly engage in swaps "as an ordinary course of business for one's own account."[90] The latter criterion is subject to a *de minimis* exemption (initially $8 billion notional or less per annum of swaps related to dealing activities) and excludes commercial hedging transactions.[91] Insured depository institutions are also excluded from the swap dealer classification to the extent that they are entering into swaps with customers in conjunction with loans they are originating.[92]

An MSP is defined under the new regulations as any institution that is not a swap dealer and that satisfies any one of three tests: (i) it maintains a "substantial position" in swaps (excluding hedging positions); (ii) its outstanding swaps "create substantial

[84] The exact same definitional problem exists in the classification of "hedgers" and "speculators."

[85] See, for example, Bank for International Settlements (1983), and Bank for International Settlements (1992).

[86] See Comptroller of the Currency (1997), pp. 4–5.

[87] See Comptroller of the Currency (1997), p. 5.

[88] Id.

[89] CFTC and SEC (2012) (hereinafter "Swap Participant Definitions").

[90] Swap Participant Definitions, op. cit., p. 30597.

[91] Swap Participant Definitions, op. cit., p. 30597, pp. 30610–30614, and pp. 30628–30635. See also Mayer Brown (2012), and Davis Polk & Wardwell LLP (2012b).

[92] Swap Participant Definitions, op. cit., pp. 30620–30624. See also Mayer Brown (2012), pp. 3–4.

counterparty exposure that could have serious adverse effects on the financial stability of the U.S. banking system or financial markets"[93]; or (iii) it maintains a "substantial position" in any category of swaps and is "a 'financial entity' that is 'highly leveraged' relative to the amount of capital it holds (and that is not subject to capital requirements established by an appropriate Federal banking agency)...."[94] A "substantial position" in OTC interest rate derivatives is presently defined as a position in which the daily average current uncollateralized exposure in a calendar quarter exceeds $3 billion or if the daily average in a calendar quarter of the sum of the current uncollateralized exposure *plus* potential future exposure exceeds $6 billion.[95]

Although ECPs are not required to register with the CFTC, it is unlawful under the Dodd–Frank Act for any person or institution that is not an ECP to enter into a swap unless the swap is executed on or subject to the rules of a CFTC "DCM" (i.e., an organized financial exchange recognized by the CFTC). ECPs are swap users that are not dealers or MSPs but that satisfy certain other minimum eligibility requirements (e.g., at least $10 million in total assets). ECPs resemble "limited end users" when compared to the 1997 OCC definitions. ECPs, moreover, must satisfy certain minimum requirements for participating in swaps. For example, governmental institutions are only considered ECPs if they own or invest more than $50 million on a discretionary basis. The new definitions also articulate various restrictions on when a commodity pool is considered an ECP.[96]

16.9.1.3 European Union In the European Union, EMIR rejects the dealer/end user paradigm and instead classifies swap participants based on their business purposes – specifically either as financial counterparties ("FCs") or nonfinancial counterparties ("NFCs"). FCs include investment firms, banks and other credit institutions, insurance and reinsurance companies, and certain asset managers. NFCs are any swap participants that are neither FCs nor CCPs. NFCs are subcategorized based on the total amount of their derivatives outstanding for purposes of determining the applicability of the E.U. swaps clearing mandate. An NFC with more than €3 billion (gross notional) in swaps is subject to the clearing mandate and is known as an "NFC+." An "NFC-" is an NFC with less than €3 billion in swaps that is excluded from the clearing mandate. Unlike U.S. regulations, swap participants in Europe are not required to register with ESMA.

16.9.2 Clearing

16.9.2.1 United States The Dodd–Frank Act requires that certain swaps be submitted for clearing to a CFTC-regulated CCP or a CCP that is recognized by the CFTC but exempt from CFTC regulation. Swaps that are required to be cleared include (at present) interest rate derivatives and CDS that are not excluded from the clearing mandate by the CFTC.[97] CCPs must submit swaps they wish to clear for review and approval by the CFTC. In addition, the Dodd–Frank Act requires the CFTC to perform its own independent assessment of specific swaps and classes of swaps that should be subject to the clearing mandate.

Mandated clearing for interest rate derivatives subject to the clearing mandate went into effect on March 11, 2013, for swap dealers and MSPs, as well as active funds. Mandated clearing commenced on June 10, 2013, for banks and other financial institutions that were not swap dealers or MSPs, hedge funds, and commodity pool operators ("CPOs"). All remaining participants not otherwise exempt from the clearing mandate had to comply with the mandated clearing requirement by September 9, 2013.

Certain clearable swaps are exempt from certain provisions of Dodd–Frank Act Title VII, including the clearing mandate. The most important such exclusions fall into three categories.

The first is the so-called end-user exception, which allows a nonfinancial firm to hedge or manage its commercial risks by using noncleared swaps provided that the end user is not a financial entity, is using the swap to hedge or reduce commercial risks, can meet the financial obligations associated with the swap, and provides certain information to an SDR or the CFTC (if no SDR is available). Public companies registered with the SEC, moreover, must take certain corporate actions to avail themselves of the end-user exception.[98]

To qualify as a nonfinancial end user (NFEU) under the CFTC end-user exception, a firm must *not* be an SD, MSP, CPO, private fund (defined in the Investment Advisers Act of 1940), employee benefit plan (defined in the Employee Retirement Income Security Act of 1974), or an entity engaged primarily in banking or financial activities (as defined in the Bank Holding Company Act of 1956). To qualify as a hedging or commercial risk-mitigating transaction, moreover, the swap must be "economically appropriate" for reducing the normal business risks of the firm, qualify as a "bona fide hedge" for purposes of determining position limits under the Commodity Exchange Act, or qualify as a hedge under an applicable accounting standard.

The second exemption is for some intragroup transactions executed between certain affiliated entities.

[93] Swap Participant Definitions, op. cit., p. 30661.
[94] Swap Participant Definitions, op. cit., p. 30661.
[95] Swap Participant Definitions, op. cit., p. 30663. For definitions of current and potential exposure, see, e.g., Culp (2001), Chapter 16.
[96] See, for example, Mayer Brown (2012), pp. 7–8.
[97] Dodd–Frank Act §723(a)(3).
[98] See, for example, Architzel and Bernstein (2012), Cravath, Swaine & Moore LLP (2012), Cleary Gottlieb (2013), Gibson, Dunn & Crutcher LLP (2013), and Sidley Austin LLP (2014).

The third exclusion occurs in the event that no CCP agrees to provide clearing services for a given product. Specifically, nothing in the Dodd–Frank Act "authorizes the Commission to adopt rules requiring a derivatives clearing organization to list for clearing a swap, group, category, type, or class of swaps if the clearing of the swap, group, category, type, or class of swaps would threaten the financial integrity of the derivatives clearing organization . . . ."[99]

Nevertheless, the CFTC has considerable authority to investigate and address such situations. If no CCP agrees to clear a swap that is otherwise subject to the mandated clearing provisions, the CFTC can investigate, issue a public report, and take additional actions to ensure that the noncleared swap does not expose the financial system to unnecessary risks. As a noted expert in derivatives regulation observes, "This protection [for CCPs to refuse to clear a given product], however, appears to be minimal and may only allow derivatives clearing organizations to refuse required clearing in the most dire circumstances and, in any case, will require a derivatives clearing organization to perform a defensive analysis in order to fend off an unwanted swap."[100]

As discussed in Section 16.5.1, the CFTC has designated certain OTC interest rate derivatives and CDS as subject to the Dodd–Frank clearing mandate. Those products were shown in Table 16.9. Note from the last three rows of each panel in Table 16.9 that certain interest rate derivatives are currently excluded from the clearing mandate based on product-specific features – that is, swaps with embedded optionality, multicurrency interest rate derivatives (e.g., cross-currency swaps), and swaps with "conditional notional amounts."

A conditional notional amount is defined as "a specification included in the swap at the time of execution that provides that the notional amount will change during the stated term of the swap in an unscheduled manner upon the occurrence of defined events or conditions."[101] For example, a fixed/floating interest rate swap with a notional amount tied to the amount outstanding on a hedged loan or credit facility with an unpredictable drawdown date is considered nonclearable and excluded from the clearing mandate. Similarly, index amortizing swaps (whose notional amounts amortize based on the evolution of an unpredictable reference rate like LIBOR) are also excluded. Voluntary reductions in notional amounts (e.g., voluntary early terminations), however, are *not* considered conditional notional amounts because a party could achieve the same result by executing an offsetting cleared swap.[102]

16.9.2.2 European Union EMIR went into force on August 16, 2012,[103] and articulated a swap clearing mandate for E.U. member nations that is generally comparable to the Dodd–Frank clearing mandate for the United States. The responsibility for implementing the EMIR clearing mandate on an ongoing basis lies with ESMA, and EMIR provides ESMA with two avenues (analogous to those in the Dodd–Frank Act) for determining which swaps are subject to the clearing mandate.[104] First, ESMA can independently identify classes of swaps subject to the clearing mandate for which no CCP has yet sought or been given approval to clear. ESMA then calls for proposals from CCPs to clear such products.

Second, CCPs may apply with their national regulators to clear a particular class of swaps. ESMA is notified of any such approvals and must then determine whether the clearing mandate should apply to such products (i.e., whether or not all such products in the E.U. should be subject to the clearing mandate for the product that a single CCP has been approved to clear). ESMA and other E.U. regulators may also reject an application for clearing even if the national regulator has approved the request.

For example, the application submitted by Eurex Clearing (owned and operated by Deutsche Börse AG) was initially rejected by the European college of regulators, notwithstanding a full risk review by Eurex's primary regulator of domicile (i.e., Bundesanstalt für Finanzdienstleistungsaufsicht ("BaFin") – Germany's Federal Financial Supervisory Authority). Nevertheless, Eurex Clearing was eventually approved as a recognized CCP by both BaFin and the European regulatory congress on April 10, 2014.[105]

There are two exemptions to the EMIR clearing mandate. The first is an exemption for pension scheme arrangements, which expires on August 15, 2015. The second is an exemption for intragroup transactions provided that the relevant national authority either agrees to the exemption or does not explicitly object to it.

Unlike the Dodd–Frank Act, EMIR does *not* provide a specific exemption or exclusion for end users. Nevertheless, swaps executed with an NFC whose derivatives activities are less than a prespecified threshold are not subject to the clearing mandate. As of this writing, NFCs with more than €3 billion in gross notional outstanding in OTC interest rate derivatives are subject to the EMIR clearing mandate.[106]

[99]Dodd–Frank Act §723(a)(3).
[100]Salzman (2007), p. 59.
[101]CFTC Clearing Determination, op. cit., p. 74306.
[102]Id.
[103]Regulation (E.U.) No. 648/2012 (2012) (in force as of August 16, 2012) (hereinafter "EMIR").
[104]ESMA (2013), p. 8.
[105]Eurex Clearing (2014).
[106]ISDA (2014a), p. 23.

In October 2014, ESMA issued a final draft of its Regulatory Technical Standards ("RTS") for the clearing of OTC interest rate derivatives. As noted in Section 16.5.1, ESMA proposed essentially the same interest rate derivatives product universe as the CFTC for interest rate derivatives subject to the EMIR clearing mandate. The European Commission has up to 3 months to endorse the RTS (subject to approval by the European Parliament and Council), and, if approved, the RTS will come into force 20 days later (likely in late January 2015).

Clearing firms must ensure that all swaps in the RTS are cleared by ESMA-authorized CCPs within 6 months of the RTS effective date. Active FCs and alternative investment funds must comply within a year of the RTS effective date, whereas FCs with *de minimis* derivatives activities are given a further 6-month extension. NFCs must comply with the clearing mandate within 3 years of the RTS effective date.

16.9.3 Execution

16.9.3.1 United States The Dodd–Frank Act requires that all swaps for which clearing has been mandated must be traded on a DCM (i.e., exchange) or through a SEF. End users of swaps that are subject to the CFTC clearing exception (*see* Section 16.9.2.1) are exempt from the mandated execution requirement.

Any person or entity "operating a facility that offers a trading system or platform in which more than one market participant has the ability to execute or trade swaps with more than one other market participant on the system or platform" must register with the CFTC as a SEF unless the facility is already a DCM.[107] The definition necessarily excludes one-to-many EEPs (*see* Section 16.4.2.2) but obligates most many-to-many EEPs to register with the CFTC (and, in turn, to satisfy the various requirements set forth by the CFTC for the required services and obligations of a registered SEF). Compliance with SEF registration requirements was required as of October 2, 2013.

EEPs required to register with the CFTC as SEFs must provide a minimum trading functionality – that is, the SEF "must, at a minimum, offer trading services to facilitate Required Transactions by providing market participants with the ability to post both firm and indicative quotes on a centralized electronic screen accessible to all market participants who have access to the SEF."[108] SEFs are also subject to a wide range of additional regulatory and supervisory requirements.

In addition to providing the minimum trading functionality for Required Transactions, SEFs are permitted to offer RFQ services (*see* Section 16.4.2.2) so that market participants can negotiate with multiple counterparties but not necessarily the entire market. SEFs may also petition the CFTC to include additional execution methods for Required Transactions and may offer any execution method for Permitted Transactions.[109] Indeed, despite efforts by regulators to push cleared swaps trading toward exchange-like CLOBs, most trading on SEFs since the mandatory execution requirement went into effect have been on RFQ-based platforms.[110]

A particularly problematic area in the U.S. implementation of SEF regulations involves the treatment of "package trades" – that is, single trades in which multiple legs of related transactions are simultaneously executed at a single bid–ask spread. Examples of popular package OTC interest rate derivatives trades are curve trades (i.e., trades that package multiple interest rate swaps with different tenors), swap spread trades (i.e., trades that package an interest rate swap with a U.S. Treasury security of the same tenor), and invoice spread trades (i.e., package trades in which Treasury futures contracts are executed simultaneously with an interest rate swap). Package trades comprise a relatively significant portion of the OTC interest rate derivatives market. For example, in August 2014 invoice spread trades alone reportedly accounted for up to 20% of total interest rate swap volume.[111] A relatively significant amount of dealer-to-customer OTC interest rate derivatives trading volume, moreover, involves package trades.[112]

The CFTC initially granted a 90-day reprieve to market participants from the February 2014 imposition of the MAT execution mandate for package trades in which one leg involved a MAT product.[113] Beginning in May 2014 with the expiration of the CFTC's no-action relief, all components of package trades that included a MAT component were required to be executed on SEFs based on a phased-in compliance timeline depending on the complexity of the underlying product legs. The final compliance date of November 15, 2014, has been further delayed by the CFTC with compliance dates that vary based on the specific types of products underlying package trades.[114]

The application of SEF execution rules to package trades involving a MAT trade leg presents a variety of challenges to regulators and market participants. First, as a result of SEFs not being able or willing to execute both legs of package trades,

[107] Commodity Futures Trading Commission (2013b), p. 33583 (hereinafter "Final SEF Rules").
[108] Final SEF Rules, op. cit., p. 33483.
[109] Final SEF Rules, op. cit., p. 33483.
[110] Bartholomew (2014).
[111] Kentz (2014c).
[112] Madigan (2014a), and Meyer and Mackenzie (2014).
[113] Madigan (2014a).
[114] CFTC (2014c).

market participants may be forced to break apart some such transactions for execution on different SEFs. That exposes market participants to "legging risk" (i.e., the risk that two legs of a combined package trade cannot be executed simultaneously in two different execution venues). For example, invoice spread packages involve an interest rate swap and a Treasury futures leg. Whereas the interest rate swap is a MAT that must be executed on a SEF, futures trades cannot be executed by SEFs that are not also recognized futures exchanges. Mandated execution of both legs on SEFs that, for practical reasons, must be executed on different SEFs thus exposes firms to basis risk that would not otherwise exist apart from the regulations implementing the execution mandate.[115]

Second, to the extent that market participants cannot execute both legs of package trades at a single bid–ask spread (which is likely for packages whose legs are split across different SEFs), the CFTC SEF requirements involving package trades could dramatically increase execution costs for market participants. For example, one estimate indicates that swap spread and curve trades were three times more expensive when the two legs of the package trades were broken into two outright trades executed separately.[116]

Third, certain package trades involve a leg that is subject to regulation by the SEC rather than the CFTC. In particular, the SEC regulates transactions involving cash U.S. Treasury securities. Market participants have expressed concerns that the SEC and CFTC could get into a "turf war" in which the SEC might decree that products like U.S. Treasuries cannot be executed on a SEF, which would render the implementation of the CFTC SEF rules involving package trades intractable. Even if such a turf war does not arise, market participants have also expressed concerns that the costs of dual CFTC–SEC oversight for package trades involving legs subject to separate CFTC and SEC regulation could be significant enough to depress market activity in such transactions.[117]

16.9.3.2 European Union MiFID 2 delegates authority to ESMA for determining which classes of cleared swaps are subject to mandatory execution requirements. Transactions subject to such execution requirements in the E.U. include swaps subject to the EMIR clearing mandate that are MAT on a regulated exchange, MTF, OTF, or an equivalent platform outside the E.U.[118] MTFs are EEPs that had certain characteristics under the original Markets in Financial Instruments Directive (adopted in 2004), and OTFs are the European analogs of U.S. SEFs that are EEPs (not already considered MTFs or exchanges) in which multiple third parties can interact to execute a swap. OTFs include broker-crossing networks in which brokers attempt to match their clients' trading orders without using an EEP or regulated exchange. OTFs do not include, however, bilateral OTC execution or order routing systems.

As noted in Section 16.5.1, ESMA designated essentially the same products that the CFTC as MAT as subject to a clearing mandate.

ESMA published two lengthy discussion papers in May 2014 regarding the details of MiFID 2 implementation, and comments from market participants were due on August 1, 2014.[119] As of this writing, ESMA is still reviewing the comments, and a final version of the technical standards has not yet been released.

16.9.4 Reporting

16.9.4.1 United States The Dodd–Frank Act and CFTC regulations establish various mandatory reporting requirements for certain OTC derivatives (including most interest rate derivatives) that vary by the type of transaction, type of market participant, and nature of the reporting requirement.[120] Transactions involving two counterparties that are not classified as U.S. market participants are not subject to these reporting requirements.

U.S. market participants have been required since January 2013 to report certain details of all new OTC interest rate derivatives transactions to a recognized SDR. Only one counterparty to an OTC derivatives trade is required to report the trade to an SDR. For swaps executed on an exchange or SEF, the reporting party is the exchange or SEF. For most bilateral transactions, the reporting party is either a swap dealer or MSP. End users generally must only report new bilateral trades to SDRs if the swap counterparty is another end user.

Information must be reported to SDRs both when a new trade is executed and upon the occurrence of any significant changes in the swap over its lifetime (including novations and terminations). For new trades, most information must be reported as soon after the confirmation as is technologically practicable subject to certain permissible delays ranging from 15 minutes to

[115]The two legs of invoice spread trades could be uniquely executed as a package through the CME's SEF because CME is also the exchange that lists Treasury futures. Under the CME's rules, similar package trades involving other SEFs would be impossible to execute on the same terms. See Madigan (2014f).

[116]Madigan (2014a).

[117]See, for example, Kentz (2014b), and Madigan (2014e).

[118]Cleared swaps also must be sufficiently liquid to trade on an MTF, OTF, or regulated exchange to be subject to mandatory execution requirements.

[119]See ESMA (2014a), and ESMA (2014b).

[120]For a summary of the reporting requirements for different market participants, see Davis Polk & Wardwell LLP (2012b), and Nazareth and Rosenberg (2013).

48 hours after confirmation. The information that must be submitted to SDRs presently includes the notional amount, currency denomination, time and date of the transaction, effective start and end dates, whether or not the swap is cleared, and all terms as agreed to at the confirmation of the trade.

In addition, a real-time reporting mandate requires that certain key information about new swap trades (i.e., time and date of execution, effective start and end dates, whether the swap is cleared, and pricing information) be provided to an SDR and publicly distributed by the SDR in a manner that keeps counterparty identities anonymous. Most trades must be reported as soon as operationally possible after their execution, although large block trades are publicly disseminated by SDRs subject to a reporting delay. The back loading of data on OTC derivatives entered into after July 21, 2010, was also required as of January 30, 2013.

Very few exceptions have been provided to the new swap reporting requirements. The new regulations cover "(i) Any executed swap that is an arm's-length transaction between two parties that results in a corresponding change in the market risk position between the two parties; or (ii) Any termination, assignment, novation, exchange, transfer, amendment, conveyance, or extinguishing of rights or obligations of a swap that changes the pricing of the swap."[121] Examples of swaps exempt from the reporting requirement are swaps between wholly owned subsidiaries of the same parent company and new swaps resulting from portfolio compression services (as discussed in Section 16.4.3.4).

In addition, certain exceptions to the real-time reporting requirements are provided for large swaps or block trades that exceed certain CFTC-specified thresholds. Swaps need not be reported in real time for tenors of up to 2 years if the notional amount exceeds $250 million, for tenors greater than two and up to 10 years with notional amounts of more than $100 million, and for tenors of more than 10 years and notional amounts above $75 million.

16.9.4.2 European Union EMIR requires all counterparties and CCPs to report the details of any swap transaction to a TR within one business day of its execution or any major event in the life of an existing swap transaction. The data to be transmitted is broadly similar to the data U.S. swap participants must report to an SDR. Unlike U.S. regulations, the EMIR reporting requirement applies to both counterparties in any OTC interest rate derivatives transaction. In particular, NFC end users (even with *de minimis* derivatives activity) are not exempt, nor are intragroup transactions between affiliated parties.

Like the Dodd–Frank Act, EMIR also mandates the reporting of both historical and new swaps to a TR. Historical transactions that must be reported include any swaps executed from August 16, 2012 (i.e., the date EMIR was in force), up to the compliance date for new swap transaction reporting. New swaps were required to be reported to a TR beginning no later than February 12, 2014.

16.9.5 Margin Requirements for Noncleared Swaps

The fourth G20 principle that defines the new derivatives regulatory framework requires higher and more conservative margin for noncleared swaps. The international effort to establish a consistent regulatory framework for margining noncleared swaps has been run by the Working Group on Margin Requirements ("WGMR"), a joint task force of the BCBS and IOSCO. The WGMR published a consultative proposal for noncleared swap margin in July 2012, a second consultative proposal in February 2013, and the final rule in September 2013.[122] The main elements of the WGMR final policy on margin requirements include the following:[123]

- Appropriate margining practices should be in effect for all derivatives not cleared by a CCP with the exception of physically settled foreign exchange forwards and swaps.
- All financial firms and "systemically important nonfinancial entities" using noncleared swaps ("covered entities") must exchange both initial margin and variation margin "as appropriate to the counterparty risks posed by such transactions." Initial margin requirements are subject to a maximum threshold of €50 million. Counterparties are not required to collect initial margin under the threshold amount and, for exposures in excess of the threshold, are only required to collect the amount in excess of the threshold.
- Initial and variation margin requirements should be consistent across regulated entities, calculated to reflect both potential future exposure (i.e., initial margin) and current exposure (i.e., variation margin) of the portfolio of noncleared swaps in question, and calculated to "ensure that all counterparty risk exposures are fully covered with a high degree of confidence."
- Assets collected as collateral for initial or variation margin must be "highly liquid" and "should, after accounting for an appropriate haircut, be able to hold their value in times of financial stress."

[121] 17 CFR §43.2.
[122] BCBS and IOSCO (2013).
[123] BCBS and IOSCO (2013), p. 4.

- Initial margin should be exchanged by both parties on a gross basis (i.e., without application of any bilateral netting). Assets posted as collateral to satisfy initial margin requirements should be "immediately available to the collecting party in the event of the counterparty's default" and should be subject to arrangements that protect the posting party (to the extent possible) under insolvency and bankruptcy laws that are applicable if the collecting party goes bankrupt.

The margin rules will be phased in beginning in December 2015 for covered entities with an aggregate month-end average notional principal outstanding of more than €3 trillion in noncleared swaps for June, July, and August 2015. The phase-in period will continue until all covered entities with average notional principal amounts of noncleared swaps of more than €8 billion are subject to the margin requirements by December 2018.

The amount of initial margin required on a given noncleared swap portfolio can be determined either using a standardized table or a regulator-approved internal value-at-risk ("VaR") model. The WGMR also gave market participants the opportunity to develop a common, transparent model. In that connection, ISDA introduced a standard initial margin model ("SIMM") in September 2014 shortly after the WGMR final rules were published. The ISDA SIMM is a sensitivity-based methodology that utilizes a 99% confidence interval over a 10-day risk horizon and that does not give offsets for exposures across different asset classes.[124] ISDA estimates that the SIMM would result in an aggregate market-wide initial margin requirement of about $1 trillion as compared to about $10 trillion under the standardized table-based approach. The latter allows essentially no netting, whereas the SIMM takes some within asset-class netting into account while ostensibly remaining compliant with the WGMR requirements.[125]

16.9.5.1 United States The Dodd–Frank Act did not specifically impose margin requirements for NFEUs of OTC interest rate derivatives. Nevertheless, U.S. banking regulators (i.e., the Board of Governors of the Federal Reserve System, Federal Deposit Insurance Corporation, and Office of the Comptroller of the Currency) together with the Farm Credit Administration and Federal Housing Finance Authority (collectively the "Prudential Regulators" ("PRs'')) have indicated that they may require regulated banking enterprises to collect margin on OTC derivatives even from NFEUs.[126]

Both the U.S. PRs and the CFTC proposed regulations governing the collection of initial and variation margin for noncleared swaps in 2011. In September 2014, the agencies reproposed revised rules that incorporate the guidance from the WGMR's final rules on margin for noncleared swaps.[127] Under the proposed regulations by the PRs, the specific requirements for a noncleared swap user to post initial margin, variation margin, or both depend on the regulatory classification of the two counterparties. There are four such classifications: (i) a "swap entity" (which includes both registered swap dealers and MSPs, as defined in Section 16.9.1), (ii) a financial end user with material swap exposure ("FEU+"), (iii) a financial end user without material swap exposure ("FEU-"), and (iv) an NFEU". In general, the proposed rule requires the following:

- For noncleared swaps between two swap entities or between a swap entity and FEU+, initial margin must be posted/collected by both counterparties at the inception of the transaction and variation margin must be posted/collected at least daily.
- For noncleared swaps between a swap entity and FEU-, the collection of initial margin by the swap entity is at the discretion of the swap entity, and the posting of initial margin by the swap entity is not mandatory. The daily collection and posting of variation margin with an FEU-, however, is required.
- For noncleared swaps between a swap entity and NFEU, the collection and posting of both initial and variation margin is at the discretion of the swap entity. Nevertheless, swap entities are required to perform a counterparty credit analysis of each NFEU counterparty and to impose initial margin and/or variation margin requirements to the extent dictated by that counterparty credit risk assessment.

As in the WGMR final rules, the proposed PR regulation for noncleared swap margin includes a threshold of $65 million. For noncleared swap portfolios with credit exposures below that amount, a swap entity is not required to collect or post initial margin with other swap entities or FEU+ entities. There is no threshold, however, for variation margin, which must be posted/collected daily regardless of the amount.

A variety of assets may be posted as collateral to satisfy initial margin requirements, subject to the imposition of specified risk-based haircuts on certain asset types. For variation margin requirements, however, only cash (denominated in the same currency as the underlying transaction) is eligible collateral.

[124]See ISDA (2013b), and ISDA (2014d).

[125]Whittall (2014).

[126]See, for example, Markets Media (2014).

[127]Department of the Treasury Office of the Comptroller of the Currency, Board of Governors of the Federal Reserve System, Federal Deposit Insurance Corporation, Farm Credit Administration, and Federal Housing Finance Agency (2014), and CFTC (2014b).

The proposed CFTC rules for noncleared swap margin are broadly similar to the rules proposed by the U.S. PRs, albeit not identical. Numerous additional nuances and details apart from the broad discussion earlier, moreover, are contained in both proposals. Interested readers are referred both to the proposed rules themselves and to the references provided for further details.[128]

One study of the proposed CFTC margin requirements for noncleared swaps estimates that the requirements would result in a $411 million annual cost (during normal financial market conditions) to market participants as a result of the requirements regarding assets that would be considered acceptable collateral by the CFTC. The study also emphasizes that the procyclicality of the proposed CFTC regulations could exacerbate rather than ameliorate systemic risk.[129]

16.9.5.2 European Union In April 2014, draft RTS regarding margin requirements for noncleared swaps were published for consultation purposes by the Joint Committee of the European Supervisory Authorities (which includes ESMA, the European Banking Authority, and the European Insurance and Occupational Pensions Authority).[130] The proposed E.U. rules are essentially a reflection of the WGMR rules and are broadly similar to the proposed U.S. rules in applying initial and variation margin requirements to different types of entities.

One particular issue that has led to concerns among some market participants is that the proposed E.U. rules treat E.U. NFEUs differently from non-E.U. NFEUs. Specifically, E.U. NFEUs are not obliged to post margin on noncleared swaps, whereas non-E.U. NFEUs are. As a result, non-E.U. corporate users of OTC derivatives would have a disincentive to transact with E.U. swap dealers in order to avoid potentially costly initial and variation margin funding requirements.[131]

In addition, the proposed E.U. rules impose a 50% maximum concentration limit on any single asset type (apart from cash) posted as collateral to satisfy noncleared swap margin requirements. The WGMR final rules do not include this requirement, and no other jurisdiction has imposed a comparable concentration limit on assets posted as collateral to satisfy margin requirements. Market participants have expressed concern that this requirement could give non-E.U. counterparties a further disincentive to execute noncleared swaps with E.U. counterparties. In particular, Japanese banks have expressed particular concerns because they routinely post more than 50% of collateral in Japanese government bonds largely as a result of the relatively small size of the Japanese corporate bond market and the unavailability of alternative collateral.[132]

16.9.6 Capital Requirements for Noncleared Swaps

The final G20 principle is that larger amounts of capital should be required to support portfolios of noncleared swaps. A comprehensive review of all proposed relevant changes to capital requirements is beyond the scope of this chapter and Appendix. The proposed rules implementing this aspect of the new regulatory framework, moreover, remain in flux as of this writing. Instead of discussing the various proposals in any detail, the basic ideas and some of the important specific aspects of the new regulatory framework are discussed in the following sections.

16.9.6.1 Basel 1 & 2 The BCBS promulgated the Basel Capital Accord in 1988 primarily to strengthen bank safety and soundness and level the international playing field. Together with its five substantive amendments, the original accord (a.k.a. "Basel 1") specified minimum capital requirements for internationally active banks. A bank's compliance with its capital requirements is *aggregate*, so that the bank either *is* or *is not* compliant at any given time. But compliance itself is determined by adding up the "risk weights" assigned to assets and liabilities with different risk characteristics.

Under Basel 1, derivatives were assigned risk weights based on current exposures plus a table-based add-on for potential future exposure (reflecting the maturity and asset class of the OTC derivatives contract). The "market risk amendments" to Basel 1 – adopted in 1996 – further require banks to hold capital against the risk of market price fluctuations in the values of certain assets, such as equities or derivatives. Banks were permitted to choose among several methods to determine these risk weights, including both a standardized approach and banks' use of their own internal models (provided that they complied with broad requirements).

International banking regulators announced in 1999 a plan to revise the Accord. First proposed in 2004 and ultimately implemented in 2006, "Basel 2" required banks to maintain adequate capital to cover losses arising from credit, market, and operational risks. To measure credit risk, banks were permitted to use their own internal portfolio-based credit risk measurement models (or, alternatively, to adopt more simplified standardized credit risk measures). For market risk, Basel 2 advanced a VaR-based risk measurement approach and again permitted banks to use their own internal models for capital adequacy calculations. The Basel 2 market risk capital charge for banks using their own internal models was based on a 99% VaR estimated over a 10-day risk horizon.

[128] See, for example, Sullivan & Cromwell LLP (2014a,b), Skadden, Arps, Slate, Meagher & Flom LLP & Affiliates (2014), Katten Muchin Rosenman LLP (2014), ISDA (2014h), and ISDA (2014i).

[129] Brown-Hruska and Wagener (2014).

[130] Joint Committee of the European Supervisory Authorities (2014).

[131] See, for example, Cameron (2014a), ISDA and the Securities Industry and Financial Markets Association (2014j), and Maxwell and Wood (2014).

[132] Vaghela (2014).

16.9.6.2 Basel 2.5 Following the global financial crisis that erupted in 2007, the BIS announced that it would propose a "Basel 3" framework to address a variety of issues related to liquidity and capital adequacy. Prior to the proposal of Basel 3, the BIS adopted rules in July 2009 (which were revised slightly in June 2010) known as "Basel 2.5." Under the Basel 2.5 rules, banks were required to change the methods they used to calculate minimum capital required to support assets in their trading books, including derivatives.

Specifically, under Basel 2.5, banks that used internal models to compute market risk capital requirements were required to modify their estimation methods in two significant ways: (i) banks that were permitted to model specific market risks had to calculate an incremental capital charge measured at a 99.9% confidence level over a 1-year risk horizon that took into account the liquidity risk of the portfolio, and (ii) banks using internal models to measure market risk for capital adequacy were required to consider a "stressed VaR" scenario that involved measuring 10-day VaR at the 99% confidence level over a 1-year period of assumed ongoing systemic financial stress.

16.9.6.3 Basel 3 The Basel 3 framework was proposed by the BCBS in 2013. Basel 3 includes a wide range of additional risks that banks must consider in calculating the minimum capital required to support their derivatives activities. In particular, Basel 3 proposes new specific requirements for minimum leverage and liquidity ratios.

Following the outbreak of the financial crisis, many active participants in swap markets began to change the way that swaps were valued for internal valuation and risk management purposes, accounting purposes (i.e., estimating the fair values of swaps), and regulatory purposes. Some of these valuation adjustments (e.g., the inclusion of the credit valuation adjustment ("CVA"), the funding valuation adjustment ("FVA"), the additional valuation adjustment ("AVA"), and the exclusion of debit valuation adjustment ("DVA")), directly or indirectly affect capital requirements for financial institutions subject to risk-based capital requirements under Basel 3.

First, the CVA attempts to quantify the mark-to-market impact of changes in counterparty credit risk. A CVA adjustment, in principle, should measure the difference between the value of a swap asset assuming the counterparty is default-risk-free and the value of that same asset as measured using the actual perceived credit risk of the counterparty. Because so many losses during the financial crisis arose from changes in mark-to-market credit spreads rather than realized defaults, the BIS has incorporated an explicit capital charge for CVA into the Basel 3 framework. In essence, the CVA capital requirement is based on the perceived need for banks to allocate capital to potential losses arising purely from mark-to-market losses on the values of assets resulting from perceived increased in counterparty credit risk.

Second, DVA, which is the cousin of CVA, involves an adjustment to the estimated fair value of liabilities for the credit risk of a financial institution. Whereas CVA adjusts a bank's asset values for the perceived mark-to-market credit risk of its counterparties, DVA adjusts a bank's liability values for its own mark-to-market credit risk as perceived by the rest of the market. In principle, DVA thus measures the difference between a bank's swap liabilities valued under the assumption that the bank is default-risk-free and the value of its swap liabilities valued at current credit spreads.

In the past, both accountants and national regulators have generally allowed banks to include DVA in equity capital estimates. For example, both U.S. FAS 157 and the Federal Reserve have historically allowed banks to pass through DVA adjustments into equity capital valuations. Basel 3 together with a DVA-specific proposal by the BIS's BCBS in December 2011 would require the *full* exclusion of DVA from bank calculations of equity.[133] In other words, the impact of changes in DVA on quarterly equity valuations would be excluded in Basel 3, and the impact of DVA on *initial* trade valuations would also be excluded under the December 2011 proposal.

Third, adjustments to swaps for funding benefits and costs have also become increasingly popular with swap dealers, in particular. The logic underlying an "FVA" is the need to address a bank's funding benefit or cost when it hedges an uncollateralized swap with a swap involving two-way collateral posting requirements. If the dealer is in the money on the client trade and, hence, out of the money on the hedge, the dealer would be required to make a net delivery of collateral on the hedge. At virtually all large banks, that necessitates an actual or virtual borrowing from the bank's funding desk and an allocation of the resulting funding costs to the swap desk. Conversely, when a dealer is out of the money on the client swap and in the money on the hedge, the swap desk receives a credit from the funding desk (assuming the collateral received can be rehypothecated).

Finally, an AVA" has been proposed by the European Banking Authority that requires banks to adjust market values of open derivatives positions for capital adequacy purposes to reflect factors such as market price uncertainty, closeout costs, model risks, concentration risks, and more.[134]

16.9.6.4 Fundamental Review of the Trading Book The BCBS published a market risk framework, referred to as the Fundamental Review of the Trading Book ("FRTB"), which is related to Basel 3 and the G20 principle that larger amounts of capital should be required to support noncleared swaps. In May 2012, the BCBS issued a consultative document regarding FRTB that

[133] BIS (2011).
[134] EBA (2014).

would revise the assessments by national regulators of the capital required to support the market risk of derivatives and other capital market exposures. The BCBS issued a revised FRTB consultative document in October 2013.[135]

The proposed FRTB framework would fundamentally change the way that banks calculate minimum capital requirements to support their trading activities. The FRTB framework advocates an extension of the Basel 2.5 requirement that banks consider a stressed financial environment in measuring capital adequacy. The FRTB framework also proposes a move away from VaR-based capital requirements toward the use of an expected shortfall measure of market risk at the 97.5% confidence level.[136] In addition, the FRTB framework proposes to extend Basel 2.5 to incorporate varying liquidity risk horizons and incremental risk charges, as well as introduce capital add-ons that address potential jumps in liquidity risk premia that are not reflected in historical price data.

16.9.6.5 Capital Requirements for CCP Exposures Whereas the BIS previously assigned a zero risk weight to CCP-cleared exchange-traded derivatives, a proposal by the BIS (first advanced in 2010 and included in Basel 3) requires clearing members of CCPs to hold capital to cover potential exposures to those CCPs arising from their risk capital structures and default funds (as discussed in Section 16.3.3.4). BIS proposals regarding capital that banks must hold to cover their potential liabilities to CCP default funds have been offered and revised multiple times since 2010.

The BIS first proposed to impose capital requirements on bank clearing members of CCPs in July 2012.[137] In that proposal, the BCBS proposed that capital requirements for the CCP exposures of bank clearing members should be calculated either using a standardized noninternal model method in which banks' risk exposures to CCPs would be based on a 1250% (sic.) risk weight (subject to a cap of 20% of a bank's trading exposures to the CCP) or a "risk-sensitive" approach based on banks' current exposures to CCPs. Current exposures under that proposed calculation, however, were largely based on gross notional exposures and did not allow banks to include netting in their capital calculations. The BCBS received numerous comment letters from market participants that were highly critical of the proposed approach.[138]

In June 2013, the BCBS proposed two new alternatives for banks to calculate their capital requirements for CCP default fund exposures.[139] The alternatives (known as "ratio" and "tranche" approaches) were both based on a concept known as "Cover*" (or "Cover Star") – that is, the minimum prefunded financial resources required by a CCP to cover a default by its two largest clearing members – and represented a departure from previous BIS guidance that CCP default funds should be sized to cover the expected losses arising from the default of a single clearing member.

Again, market participants balked at the revised BCBS proposals.[140] Specifically, market participants contended that the Cover* requirement was neither risk weighted nor subject to the traditional 8% risk-weighted capital charge, thereby resulting in the Cover* requirement almost always being higher than the current exposure requirement in the 2012 proposal. As a result, the revised proposal would have resulted in capital requirements for bank CCP clearing members that were generally equal to their CCP default fund contributions.

The BCBS apparently agreed with market participants' criticisms and provided a final proposed rule in April 2014 that dropped the Cover*-based ratio and tranche proposals.[141] Instead, the final proposed rule includes a standardized approach and a pro rata approach based on bank clearing members' current exposures to CCP default funds subject to a floor of a risk-weighted 2% of members' contributions to CCP default funds.

16.9.7 Cross-Border and Extraterritoriality Issues

Differences between U.S. and E.U. regulations and disparities in the timing of the implementation of new regulations have led to significant complications and regulatory uncertainty during the phasing in of the new regulatory regime to date. Especially because U.S. regulations have been implemented in advance of many corresponding European regulations, the applicability (or lack thereof) of U.S. regulations to non-U.S. market participants has been a source of ongoing debate and questions about policy interpretations.

The primary objective of international regulators in implementing various regulatory changes to date has been the concept of "substituted compliance" when applicable. The concept of substituted compliance is reflected in the following statement by the G20 leaders in 2013: "[J]urisdictions and regulators should be able to defer to each other when it is justified by the quality of their respective regulatory and enforcement regimes, based on similar outcomes, in a nondiscriminatory way, paying due respect to home country regulation regimes."[142]

[135] BCBS (2013b).
[136] VaR versus expected shortfall risk metrics are discussed in Culp (2012).
[137] BCBS (2012).
[138] See, for example, Cameron (2014b).
[139] BCBS (2013a).
[140] Cameron (2014b).
[141] BCBS (2014).
[142] G-20 (2013) (hereinafter "G-20 St Petersburg Declaration"), p. 17.

A complete review of all the various complex aspects of cross-border issues in the new regulatory environment is beyond the scope of this Appendix. Some of the most significant issues that market participants and regulators face, however, are reviewed in the following subsections.

16.9.7.1 Applicability of U.S. CFTC Regulations Section 2(i) of the Commodity Exchange Act as amended defines the scope of the CFTC's regulation of foreign swaps and related activities as follows:

> The provisions of this chapter relating to swaps that were enacted by the [Dodd-Frank Act] (including any rule prescribed or regulation promulgated under that Act), shall not apply to activities outside the United States unless those activities – (1) have a direct and significant connection with activities in, or effect on, commerce of the United States; or (2) contravene such rules or regulations as the Commission may prescribe or promulgate as are necessary or appropriate to prevent the evasion of any provision of this chapter that was enacted by the [Dodd-Frank Act].[143]

The phrase "direct and significant connection with activities in, or effect on, commerce of the United States" opens the door for a potentially very broad interpretation of the extraterritorial application of the Dodd–Frank Act.

On June 29, 2012, the CFTC issued its first proposed interpretive guidance and policy statement concerning cross-border swap regulation (the "Proposed Guidance"). The Proposed Guidance indicated that all swap dealers and MSPs that are not "U.S. Persons" are required to comply with all relevant CFTC regulations but allowed for "substituted compliance" with U.S. regulations (at least in principle). Specifically, the CFTC's Proposed Guidelines state:

Substituted compliance means that a non-U.S. swap dealer or non-U.S. MSP is permitted to conduct business by complying with its home regulations, without additional requirements under the [Commodity Exchange Act]. Specifically, the Commission proposes to permit non-U.S. swap dealers and non-U.S. MSPs to substitute compliance with the requirements of the relevant home jurisdiction's law and regulations, in lieu of compliance with the [Commodity Exchange Act] and Commission's regulations, if the Commission finds that such requirements are comparable to cognate requirements under the [Commodity Exchange Act] and Commission regulations....The Commission proposes that it would make comparability determinations on an individual requirement basis, rather than the foreign regime as a whole.[144]

The Proposed Guidance articulated specific "Transaction-Level" requirements that included compliance with U.S. clearing and execution mandates, margin requirements for noncleared swaps, swap documentation requirements, and the like. Non-U.S. dealers and MSPs would be required under the Proposed Guidance to comply with Transaction-Level requirements (without substituted compliance) for all swaps executed with U.S. Persons as counterparties (excluding foreign branches of U.S. entities). Swaps with non-U.S. Persons as counterparties that are guaranteed or financially supported by U.S. Persons *are* subject to Transaction-Level regulations, although substituted compliance is a possibility for such transactions.[145]

The compliance date for registration with the CFTC as a swap dealer was October 12, 2012. As the date approached, the CFTC acknowledged that its final cross-border guidance and exemptive order would not be completed by the October 12, 2012, registration requirement date and that it was unfair to require U.S. and non-U.S. dealers to register while the registration criteria remained in flux. So, the CFTC issued a no-action letter (effective on October 12, 2012) in which the CFTC indicated that it would not enforce its swap dealer registration requirements until its final rules were promulgated. The no-action letter further clarified the definition of a U.S. Person and the amounts to be included in calculations by non-U.S. swap dealers and MSPs to determine their registration requirements (or lack thereof).[146]

On December 21, 2012, the CFTC issued an exemptive order and further proposed guidance regarding the cross-border regulation of swaps ("Further Proposed Guidance").[147] The exemptive order essentially extended the October 2012 no-action letter and gave non-U.S. swap dealers and MSPs an extension to meet certain Entity-Level and Transaction-Level requirements under the Dodd–Frank Act until July 12, 2013, provided that such noncompliance arose from technical impediments or interpretational uncertainty about the relevant regulations. The Further Proposed Guidance also revised the proposed definition of a U.S. swap dealer from the version in the June 2012 Proposed Guidance to a version resembling the definition in the October 2012 no-action letter and articulated similar clarifications to the calculation method for determining *de minimis* exemptions.

On July 11, 2013 – the day before the earlier exemptive order expired – the CFTC and European Commission issued a joint statement that articulated a "common path forward" for the harmonization of U.S. and E.U. regulations on swaps and swap participants. In particular, the joint statement indicated that "[w]e will not seek to apply our rules (unreasonably) in the other jurisdiction, but will rely on the application and enforcement of the rules by the other jurisdiction."[148] On July 12, 2013,

[143]7. U.S.C. §2(i).
[144]CFTC Proposed Cross-Border Guidance, op. cit., p. 41229.
[145]For various addition details, see, for example, Mayer Brown (2012).
[146]CFTC (2012b).
[147]CFTC (2013a), p. 909.
[148]CFTC and EC (2013) (hereinafter "Path Forward Statement").

the CFTC issued a time-limited exemptive order that essentially extended the terms of the December 2012 exemptive order for non-U.S. swap dealers and MSPs.[149] Specifically, the order indicated that non-U.S. swap dealers and MSPs domiciled in Australia, Canada, the European Union, Hong Kong, Japan, or Switzerland were exempt from most Entity-Level requirements until the earlier of December 21, 2013, or 30 days following the CFTC's determination of acceptable substituted compliance. The order also provided delayed compliance for certain Transaction-Level regulations.

On the same day, the CFTC approved the issuance of an interpretive guidance and policy statement (the "Guidance") that was intended to revise and "finalize" the Proposed Guidance (June 2012).[150] The definition of a U.S. Person in the July 2013 Guidelines reverted to virtually the same definition in the initial Proposed Guidelines. Although the July 2013 Guidance largely disregarded the intervening refined definition of a U.S. Person in the December 2012 Further Proposed Guidance, swap dealers and MSPs were nevertheless given until October 9, 2013, to rely on those interim definitions for compliance purposes.

The July 2013 Guidance defines Entity-Level regulations into Category A (including capital adequacy, chief compliance offers, risk management, and swap data recordkeeping regulations) and Category B (including SDR reporting, recordkeeping related to marketing and sales or complaints, and large trader reporting regulations). Similarly, Transaction-Level regulations are also split into Category A (including swap clearing, execution, margin and segregation for noncleared swaps, swap trading relationship documentation, portfolio reconciliation, portfolio compression, real-time public reporting, trade confirmation, and daily trading records regulations) and Category B (exclusively consisting of external business conduct standards). The CFTC then provides the equivalent of a matrix that indicates required compliance with Category A and B Entity-Level and Category A and B Transaction-Level regulations based on whether a firm and its counterparty are a U.S. or non-U.S. swap dealer, or MSP.[151]

The CFTC continued to permit substituted compliance in its July 2013 Guidance. Unlike the Proposed Guidance, the July 2013 Guidance also indicates the CFTC's willingness to rely on foreign regulations that are comparable (even if undefined) to U.S. regulations. In defining comparability of foreign regulations to the requirements under the Dodd–Frank Act, the CFTC indicates that it will take into account factors like the comprehensiveness of the foreign requirements, the scope and objectives of those requirements, the comprehensiveness of the foreign regulator's supervisory and compliance management approach, and the ability of an entity's home regulatory to support and enforce its oversight.[152] The July 2013 Guidance states: "In this context, comparable does not necessarily mean identical. Rather, the [CFTC] would evaluate whether the home jurisdiction's regulatory requirement is comparable to and as comprehensive as the corresponding U.S. regulatory requirement(s)."[153] If the CFTC determines that a non-U.S. regulatory regime lacks critical components for some or all participants, the CFTC indicates that it will work with the foreign regulator and the applicable foreign registered swap dealers and MSPs to identify alternatives for achieving substituted compliance, if possible.

In its July 2013 Guidance, the CFTC did not, however, provide comprehensive guidance on the applicability of Transaction-Level requirements to swaps between non-U.S. swap dealers and non-U.S. Persons that are arranged, executed, or negotiated by personnel of the non-U.S. swap dealer located in the United States. In response to questions from market participants in that regard, the CFTC issued Staff Advisory No. 13-69 ("Staff Advisory") on November 14, 2013.[154] In the Staff Advisory, the CFTC indicated its belief that "the Commission intended substituted compliance to be available, or Transaction-Level Requirements to not apply, where the activities of the non-U.S. SD take place outside the United States....[but that] the Commission has a strong supervisory interest in swap dealing activities that occur within the United States, regardless of the status of the counterparties."[155]

More specifically, the Staff Advisory indicated that the CFTC would consider swaps executed by non-U.S. swap dealers with non-U.S. Persons to be subject to Transaction Level requirements if the swap is arranged, executed, or negotiated by personnel located in the United States. The CFTC further noted that its interpretation was applicable whether or not the non-U.S. swap dealer was an affiliate of a U.S. Person and regardless of whether the swap was booked in a non-U.S. branch of a non-U.S. swap dealer.

On December 4, 2013, the Securities Industry and Financial Markets Association ("SIFMA"), ISDA, and the Institute of International Bankers ("IIB") filed a lawsuit against the CFTC in which they claimed that the Cross-Border Guidance and Staff Advisory were improper rulemakings. They requested that the Court vacate the Cross-Border Guidance and bar the CFTC from applying the Dodd–Frank Act on an extraterritorial basis.

Following the filing of the lawsuit, the CFTC took the following three actions: (i) issued a no-action letter that deferred the compliance date for Transaction-Level requirements involving non-U.S. swap dealers until December 31, 2014, (ii) suspended

[149]CFTC (2013c).

[150]CFTC (2013d) (hereinafter "CFTC July 2013 Guidance").

[151]See also Mayer Brown (2012), Appendices A and B.

[152]CFTC July 2013 Guidance, op. cit., p. 45343.

[153]CFTC July 2013 Guidance, op. cit., p. 45343.

[154]CFTC Division of Swap Dealer and Intermediary Oversight (2013e) (hereinafter "Staff Advisory").

[155]Staff Advisory, op. cit., p. 2.

the Staff Advisory and solicited further comments on the underlying issues, and (iii) filed a motion to dismiss and a motion for summary judgment on the lawsuit filed by SIFMA, ISDA, and IIB.

On September 16, 2014, the U.S. District Court for the District of Columbia dismissed the lawsuit filed by SIFMA, ISDA, and IIB. The Court ruled that the Cross-Border Guidance was a nonbinding policy statement and not a formal legislative rule. The Court's ruling thus left intact the CFTC's Cross-Border Guidance, as well as the CFTC's indicated extraterritorial application of the Guidance.[156]

16.9.7.2 Extraterritoriality and U.S. SEF Regulations In February 2014, the CFTC and European Union reached an agreement that essentially gives an extension to European-approved swap trading platforms until the regulations pursuant to MiFID 2 eventually come into full force.[157] Consistent with the CFTC's commitment in the Common Path Forward joint statement, the CFTC issued a no-action letter to provide regulatory relief to EEP trading swaps in the European Union on April 9, 2014.[158] In the no-action letter, the CFTC defines a Qualifying MTF ("QMTF") as an MTF overseen by a competent E.U. regulatory authority. In certain situations, QMTFs are exempt from SEF registration requirements, parties executing swaps on QMTFs are exempt from the U.S. mandatory execution requirement, and swap dealers and MSPs executing trades on QMTFs are exempt from certain business conduct, confirmation, and documentation regulations to which they would otherwise be subject.

In order to receive this regulatory relief from the full range of SEF regulations, a QMTF must demonstrate to the CFTC that all of the following are true: (i) the MTF is compliant with its local regulator with regulatory requirements that are "in accordance with certain SEF regulatory requirements concerning trading methodology"[159] ; (ii) the entity is "subject to and compliant with regulatory requirements established by the appropriate governmental authorities in the home country of the facility that are comparable to, and as comprehensive as, certain SEF regulatory requirements concerning non-discriminatory access by market participants and an appropriate level of oversight"[160] ; and (iii) the MTF satisfies certain clearing and reporting requirements; and (iv) the MTF does not permit "U.S. Persons" that are not ECPs to trade on its platform.

The requirement that a QMTF cannot have U.S. Persons and non-ECP trading on its platform has contributed significantly to ongoing regulatory uncertainties among market participants, notwithstanding the CFTC no-action letter. For that and other reasons (not the least of which is concern by some market participants that the CFTC might change the rules of the game yet again), not a single European MTF had applied to the CFTC for QMTF status as of April 7, 2014.[161]

In addition to ongoing regulatory uncertainties, the CFTC also apparently told interested MTFs not to apply as a QMTF but rather to wait for a later revised set of rules (notwithstanding that the U.K.'s Financial Conduct Authority ("FCA") had been working with MTFs to help ensure cross-border compliance). One interdealer broker commented as follows: "No MTF has taken the CFTC up on this offer because we were effectively told not to by the commission. One of the big five interdealer broker MTFs was willing to make an attempt for QMTF status but that platform was told to hold off by the CFTC because it was planning to issue reworked guidance, clarifying what the commission was looking to achieve."[162]

Indeed, London-based ICAP Plc – the world's largest swaps interdealer broker – launched a SEF called ICAP Global Derivatives Limited ("IGDL") in 2014 to complement its existing U.S.-domiciled ICAP SEF (US) LLC. IGDL will providing a trading platform for interest rate swaps, OIS, FRAs, inflation swaps, and certain interest rate options denominated in USD, EUR, and GBP.[163] ICAP opted to register IGDL as *both* an FCA-regulated MTF *and* as a CFTC-regulated SEF.[164] In other words, notwithstanding the CFTC's no-action letters, ICAP still chose to register IGDL as a SEF and to be subject to CFTC regulation in addition to FCA regulation. ICAP explains its reasoning as follows: "By registering to be a SEF with the CFTC, IGDL will be able to provide direct access to market participants in both the United States and [European Economic Area] in a manner which satisfies SEF transaction-level requirements and EEA regulatory rules via its electronic order books and U.S. and London-based voice brokers."[165] Peter Best, chief operating officer of ICAP's SEF, further explained the decision: "The core of US liquidity is U.S.-based and the popular feedback [from customers] we had is that it ought to be on a Sef....They didn't want two liquidity pools. Given that it was a U.S.-centric market, we decided to go with the Sef."[166]

16.9.7.3 CCP Default Fund Capital Requirements As of this writing, non-U.S. CCPs doing business in the United States are required to be compliant with U.S. regulations. Similarly, U.S. CCPs doing business in Europe must satisfy European regulations.

[156] For a more detailed analysis of the Court's ruling, see, for example, Sullivan & Cromwell LLP (2014c); and Brown et al. (2014).

[157] Stafford and Chon (2014b).

[158] CFTC Division of Market Oversight and Division of Swap Dealer and Intermediary Oversight (2014a) (hereinafter "SEF No-Action Letter").

[159] SEF No-Action Letter, op. cit., p. 2.

[160] Id.

[161] Madigan (2014).

[162] Madigan (2014c).

[163] http://www.icap.com/what-we-do/global-broking/sef.aspx (last visited April 21, 2014).

[164] Id.

[165] Id.

[166] Quoted in Stafford (2014a).

Such CCPs were given until December 15, 2014, to be compliant with E.U. regulations, but the implementation date for enforcement of that compliance requirement for U.S. CCPs doing business in Europe has been delayed to June 15, 2015.[167] With two separate regimes in place, a significant amount of potential "regulatory arbitrage" could result in which market participants shift their derivatives activities into regimes with the lowest relative costs and highest relative legal certainties.[168] One such cost involves capital that clearing members are obliged to hold against potential exposures to CCPs.

Specifically, whereas the BIS previously assigned a zero risk weight to CCP-cleared exchange-traded derivatives, a proposal by the BIS (first advanced in 2010 and included in Basel 3) will require clearing members to hold capital to cover potential exposures to CCPs arising from CCPs' risk capital structures (as discussed in Section 16.3.3.4).

As of this writing, the U.S. and E.U. regulatory regimes differ in how they would implement minimum default fund requirements for CCPs. In the United States, CCPs must currently maintain adequate financial resources to cover the failure of the single largest clearing member of the CCP. European CCPs, however, are required to maintain sufficient financial resources to cover potential losses arising from the contemporaneous default of the largest *two* clearing members.

ACKNOWLEDGMENTS

I am grateful to Audrey Costabile Blater, Peter Clayburgh, John Cochrane, Kevin Foley, Yue Malan, Andrea Neves, Irene Perdomo, Bettina Stärkle, and Pietro Veronesi for their suggestions and comments on earlier drafts. I also thank Charmaine Alcain and Laura Yergesheva for their capable research assistance. The usual disclaimer applies, of course, and I alone am responsible for any remaining errors.

REFERENCES

Ackerman A. Europe presents olive branch to U.S. in derivatives skirmish. Wall St J 2014.

Architzel PM, Bernstein GC. CFTC's final rule on the end-user exception to the mandatory clearing of swaps. Wilmer Hale Advisory; 2012.

Bank for International Settlements. The International Interbank Market: A Descriptive Study. BIS Economic Paper No. 8; Basel; July 1983.

Bank for International Settlements. Report on netting schemes. Prepared by the Group of Experts on Payment Systems of the Central Banks of the Group of Ten Countries; Basel; Feb 1989.

Bank for International Settlements. Report of the Committee on Interbank Netting Schemes of the Central Banks of the Group of Ten Countries; Basel; Nov 1990.

Bank for International Settlements. Recent developments in international interbank relations. Prepared by a Working Group Established by the Central Banks of the Group of Ten Countries; Basel; Oct 1992.

Bartholomew H. ISDA AGM: RFQ dominates SEF execution. Int Financ Rev 2014.

BCBS. Application of Own Credit Risk Adjustments to Derivatives. BIS Consultative Document; Dec 2011.

BCBS. Capital Requirements for Bank Exposures to Central Counterparties. Bank for International Settlements; Basel; July 2012.

BCBS. Capital Treatment of Bank Exposures to Central Counterparties. BIS Consultative Document; Basel; June 2013a.

BCBS. Fundamental Review of the Trading Book: A Revised Market Risk Framework. BIS Consultative Document. Basel; Oct 2013b.

BCBS. Capital Requirements for Bank Exposures to Central Counterparties. Bank for International Settlements; Basel; April 2014.

BCBS and IOSCO. Margin Requirements for Non-Centrally Cleared Derivatives. Bank for International Settlements; Basel; Sept 2013.

Belomestny D, Kolodko A, Schoenmakers J. Pricing of Callable LIBOR Exotics, Working Paper; Feb 23 2009.

Brown R, Howell N, Sackheim M, Schwartz J. What SIFMA v. CFTC Means for U.S. Swaps Regulation. Futures Industry; Nov 2014.

Brown-Hruska S, Wagener T. Cost-Benefit Analysis of the CFTC's Proposed Margin Requirements for Uncleared Swaps. NERA Economic Consulting; Dec 2 2014.

Brush S. State Street Exiting Swaps Clearing Business, Citing New Rules. Bloomberg; Dec 4 2014.

Burghardt G. *The Eurodollar Futures and Options Handbook*. New York: McGraw-Hill; 2003.

Burne K. CFTC's Giancarlo: new rules divide swaps market. Wall St J 2014.

Cameron M. Dealers rail at 'Absurd' EU margin rules. Risk June 2014a.

Cameron M. Default fund capital will halve under final rule, banks say. Risk June 2014b.

CFTC. Final rule: end-user exception to the clearing requirement for swaps. Fed Regist 2012a;77(139).

CFTC. No-Action Letter No. 12-22; Oct 12; 2012b.

CFTC. Final rule: clearing requirement determination under section 2(h) of the CEA. Fed Regist 2012c;77(240).

CFTC. Proposed rules: further proposed guidance regarding compliance with certain swap regulations. Fed Regist 2013a;78(4).

CFTC. Final rule: core principles and other requirements for swap execution facilities. Fed Regist 2013b;78(107).

CFTC. Exemptive order regarding compliance with certain swap regulations. Fed Regist 2013c;78(140).

CFTC. Interpretive guidance and policy statement regarding compliance with certain swap regulations. Fed Regist 2013d;78(144).

[167] Ackerman (2014).

[168] The importance and role of regulatory certainty/uncertainty in derivatives regulations and activities are explored in Culp (1995a,b).

CFTC. Applicability of Transaction-Level Requirements to Activity in the United States. CFTC Staff Advisory No. 13-69; Nov 14 2013e.
CFTC. No-Action Letter No. 14-46; Apr 9 2014a.
CFTC. Proposed Rule; Advance Notice of Proposed Rulemaking: Margin Requirements for Uncleared Swaps for Swap Dealers and Major Swap Participants; Sept 23 2014b.
CFTC. No-Action Letter No. 14-137; Nov 10 2014c.
CFTC and EU. Cross-Border Regulation of Swaps/Derivatives: Discussions between the Commodity Futures Trading Commission and the European Union – A Path Forward. Joint Statement; July 11 2013.
CFTC and SEC. Joint final rule: further definition of 'Swap Dealer,' 'Security-Based Swap Dealer,' 'Major Swap Participant,' 'Major Security-Based Swap Participant,' and 'Eligible Contract Participant."' Fed Regist 2012;77(100).
Cleary Gottlieb. Navigating Key Dodd-Frank Rules Related to the Use of Swaps by End Users. Alert Memo; Apr 9; 2013.
CME Group. Interest Rate Swap Futures Reference Guide; 2009.
CME Group. Market Data Notices; June 17 2013.
CME Group. 10-Year T-Note Futures Contract Specs; 2014. Available at http://www.cmegroup.com/trading/interest-rates/us-treasury/10-year-us-treasury-note_contract_specifications.html. Last visited 2014 March 28.
Committee on Payment and Settlement Systems and Technical Committee of the International Organization of Securities Commissions. Principles for Financial Market Infrastructures. Bank for International Settlements and IOSCO; Apr 2012.
Compass Lexecon. Customer Asset Protection Insurance for U.S. Futures Market Customers. White Paper Sponsored by CME Group, Futures Industry Association, Institute for Financial Markets, and National Futures Association; Nov 15 2013.
Comptroller of the Currency. Comptroller's Handbook: Risk Management of Financial Derivatives; Jan 1997.
Cravath, Swaine & Moore LLP. Derivatives Rules under the Dodd-Frank Act Affecting End-Users – An Update Memorandum; Aug 6 2012.
Culp CL. Stock index futures and financial market reform. George Mason Univ Law Rev 1991;13(3).
Culp CL. Regulation and the growth of derivatives in the global banking system. Deriv Q 1995a;1(4).
Culp CL. Regulatory uncertainty and the economics of derivatives regulation. Financier 1995b;2(5).
Culp CL. *The Risk Management Process*. New York: John Wiley & Sons; 2001.
Culp CL. *Risk Transfer: Derivatives in Theory and Practice*. New York: John Wiley & Sons; 2004.
Culp CL. OTC-cleared derivatives: benefits, costs, and implications of the 'Dodd-Frank Wall Street Reform and Consumer Protection Act.' J Appl Finance 2010 (2).
Culp CL. The 'At-Risk' metrics and measures. In: Lane M, editor. *Alternative (Re)insurance Strategies*. London: Risk Books; 2012.
Culp CL, Kavanagh BT. Methods of resolving over-the-counter derivatives contracts in failed depository institutions: restrictions on regulators from federal banking law. Futures Int Law Lett 1994;14(3-4):1–19.
Davis Polk & Wardwell LLP. CFTC Adopts Rules Establishing Swap Reporting Regime. Client Memorandum; Jan 11 2012a.
Davis Polk & Wardwell LLP. CFTC and SEC Adopt Final Swap Dealer, Major Swap Participant and Eligible Contract Participant Definitions. Client Memorandum; May 2 2012b.
De Roover R. *Money, Banking and Credit in Mediaeval Bruges*. Cambridge (MA): The Mediaeval Academy of America; 1948.
De Roover R. *The Rise and Decline of the Medici Bank*. Washington (DC): Beard Books; 1999 [1963].
Department of the Treasury Office of the Comptroller of the Currency, Board of Governors of The Federal Reserve System, Federal Deposit Insurance Corporation, Farm Credit Administration, and Federal Housing Finance Agency. Proposed rule: margin and capital requirements for covered swap entities Fed Reg 2014;79(185).
Devasabai K. Deutsche bank CRO: derivatives becoming loss leader. Risk 2014.
EBA. Prudent Valuation under Article 105(14) of Regulation (EU) No. 575/2013 (Capital Requirements Regulation – CRR). Final Draft Regulatory Technical Standards EBA/RTS/2014/06; March 31 2014.
Edwards FR. The clearing association in futures markets: guarantor and regulator. In: Anderson RW, editor. *The Industrial Organization of Futures Markets*. New York/London: Lexington Books; 1984.
Eris Exchange. *Newedge Executes and Clears $2 Billion in Interest Rate Swap Futures on Eris Exchange*. Press Release; 2010.
Eris Exchange. *Eris Exchange Successfully Launches Eris SwapBookTM Electronic Trading Platform for Transparent Execution of Flexible, OIS-Discounted Eris Interest Rate Swap Futures*. Press Release; 2011a.
Eris Exchange. *Eris Exchange Receives CFTC Approval to Become a Designated Contract Market and Announces the Launch of Benchmark Forward Starting Interest Rate Swap Futures*. Press Release; 2011b.
Eris Exchange. *Eris Exchange to Launch New, Margin-Efficient Interest Rate Swap Futures*. Press Release; 2012.
ESMA. The Clearing Obligation Under EMIR, Discussion Paper; July 12 2013.
ESMA. Consultation Paper MiFID II/MiFIR; May 22 2014a.
ESMA. Discussion Paper MiFID II/MiFIR; May 22 2014b.
Eurex Clearing. *Eurex Clearing Receives EMIR Authorisation*. Press Release; 2014.
European Parliament and the Council of the European Union. Regulation (EU) No. 648/2012; July 4 2012.
Financial Stability Board. OTC Derivatives Market Reforms: Seventh Progress Report on Implementation; April 8 2014.
Foreign Exchange Committee. Foreign Exchange Prime Brokerage: Product Overview and Best Practice Recommendations in the 2005 Annual Report; Dec 2005.
Flavell R. *Swaps and Other Derivatives*. 2d ed. New York: John Wiley and Sons; 2010.
G-20. Leaders' Statement – The Pittsburgh Summit; Sept 24-25 2009.
G-20. Cannes Summit Final Declaration; Nov 4 2011.
G-20. Leaders' Declaration – The St. Petersburg Summit; Sept 5-6 2013.

Gibson, Dunn & Crutcher LLP. Public Companies and the 'End-User Exception' for Swaps: Governance Action Items. Gibson Dunn Letter to Clients and Friends; June 17 2013.

Gibson, Dunn & Crutcher LLP. Are You Ready to Report? European Market Infrastructure Regulation (EMIR) Derivatives Reporting Obligation Becomes Effective on February 12, 2014. Gibson Dunn Letter to Clients and Friends; March 11 2014.

Grant J, Weitzman H, Mackenzie M. Chicago traders launch new derivatives exchange. Financial Times July 13 2010.

Holt C. Prime Brokerage: Not Just for Equities and Fixed Income Anymore JPMorgan Thought (Q4/2007), Global Custodian, OTC Derivatives Prime Brokerage Survey; 2008.

ISDA. Footnote 88 and Market Fragmentation: An ISDA Survey ISDA Research Note; Dec 2013a.

ISDA. Standard Initial Margin Model for Non-Cleared Derivatives. White Paper; Dec 2013b.

ISDA. Overview of U.S. and EU OTC Derivatives Regulatory Reforms; 2014a.

ISDA. Cross-Border Fragmentation of Global OTC Derivatives: An Empirical Analysis ISDA Research Note. Jan; 2014b.

ISDA. Interest Rate Derivatives: A Progress Report on Clearing and Compression ISDA Research Note. Feb 2014c.

ISDA. Appendix: Risk Factors and Idiosyncratic Risk, White Paper; March 2014d.

ISDA. ISDA Margin Survey 2014; Apr 2014e.

ISDA. Made-Available-to-Trade (MAT): Evidence of Further Market Fragmentation ISDA Research Note. Apr 2014f.

ISDA. Revisiting Cross-Border Fragmentation of Global OTC Derivatives: Mid-year 2014 Update ISDA Research Note. July 2014g.

ISDA. Margin and Capital Requirements for Covered Swap Entities. Comment Letter to the U.S. Prudential Regulators; Nov 24 2014h.

ISDA. RE: Margin Requirements for Uncleared Swaps for Swap Dealers and Major Swap Participants. Comment Letter to the Commodity Futures Trading Commission; Nov 24 2014i.

ISDA and the Securities Industry and Financial Markets Association. RE: Consultation Paper Regarding Draft Regulatory Technical Standards on Risk-Mitigation Techniques for OTC-Derivative Contracts not Cleared by a CCP. Comment Letter to the Joint Committee of the European Supervisory Authorities; July 14 2014j.

Joint Committee of the European Supervisory Authorities. Draft Regulatory Technical Standards on Risk-Mitigation Techniques for OTC-Derivative Contracts Not Cleared by a CCP under Article 11(15) of Regulation (EU) No. 648/2012. Consultation Paper JC/CP/2014/03; April 14 2014.

Kane EJ. Good intentions and unintended evil: the case against selective credit allocation. J Money Credit Bank 1977;9(1):55–69.

Kane EJ. Accelerating inflation, technological innovation, and the decreasing effectiveness of banking regulation. J Finance 1981;36(2):355–367.

Kane EJ. Policy implications of structural changes in financial markets. Am Econ Rev 1983;73(2):96–100.

Kane EJ. Interaction of financial and regulatory innovation. Am Econ Rev 1988;78(2):328–334.

Katten Muchin Rosenman LLP. The Re-Proposed Margin Rules for Non-Cleared Swaps: Some Issues and Suggestions for End Users. Financial Services Advisory; Oct 31 2014.

Kentz M. Collateral Optimisation Strategies Come to the Fore. International Financing Review; Apr 23 2014a.

Kentz M. Swap Packages Raise Dual Oversight Fears. International Financing Review; May 30 2014b.

Kentz M. Swap Market Fears CFTC Deadline. International Financing Review; Oct 27 2014c.

Kroszner RS. Can the financial markets privately regulate risk? The development of derivatives clearinghouses and recent over-the-counter innovations. J Money Credit Bank 1999;31(3, Part 2):596–618.

Lewandowska O, Mack B. Squaring the circle: clearing arrangements in over-the-counter derivatives markets. Paper Presented at 2nd International Conference: The Industrial Organisation of Securities Markets: Competition, Liquidity and Network Externalities; Frankfurt; June 2010.

Madigan P. SEFs: dead on arrival? Risk; Mar 2013.

Madigan P. Packaged swaps get three-month SEF reprieve from CFTC. Risk; Feb 2014a.

Madigan P. Dealers Benefit from OTC Liquidity Split, Buy-Siders Claim. Risk; Apr 2014b.

Madigan P. CFTC Told EU Platforms Not to Seek SEF Equivalence. Risk; Apr 2014c.

Madigan P. U.S. End Users are Losers in Swaps Liquidity Split. Risk; Apr 2014d.

Madigan P. SEC Silence on Swap Spread SEF Trading Frustrates Market. Risk; June 2014e.

Madigan P. CME Plans to Corner Invoice Spread Trading, Dealers Claim. Risk; Oct 2014f.

Madigan P. Fragmentation of Swap Markets 'Tragic', Says FCA. Risk; Nov 2014g.

Markets Media. End Users Face Swap Margin Requirements; Nov 11 2014.

Maxwell F. Repositories Call on ESMA to Help Fix EMIR Reporting Problems. Risk; May 2014a.

Maxwell F. Catch Me if You Can: EMIR Reporting Crackdown Looks Tricky. Risk; Sep 2014b.

Maxwell F, Wood D. EBA: Objections over WGMR Rules Not Our Fault. Risk; Sep 2014.

Mayer Brown. The New CFTC and SEC Swap 'Entity' Definitions – Highlights. Legal Update; Apr 30 2012.

Mengle D. The Importance of Close-Out Netting. ISDA Research Notes No. 1; 2010.

Merton RC. A functional perspective of financial intermediation. Financ Manage 1995;24(2):23–41.

Meyer G, Mackenzie M. Slow Start to Swaps Trading Revolution. Financial Times Apr 22 2014.

Miller MH. Financial innovation: the last twenty years and the next. J Financ Quant Anal 1986;21(4):459–471.

Miller MH. Financial innovation: achievements and prospects. J Appl Corp Finance 1992;4(4):4–11.

Moser JT. Contracting Innovations and the Evolution of Clearing and Settlement Methods at Futures Exchanges. Federal Reserve Bank of Chicago Working Paper WP-98-26; Aug 1998.

Murphy T. Statement for the Record." Before the House Financial Services Subcommittee on Capital Markets, Insurance, and Government-Sponsored Enterprises – Hearing on the Effective Regulation of Over-the-Counter Derivatives Markets; June 9 2009.

Nazareth AL, Rosenberg GD. Swap Reporting: Who and When? Futures Industry; Mar 2013.

Norman P. *The Risk Controllers: Central Counterparty Clearing in Globalised Financial Markets*. John Wiley & Sons; 2011.

Osborn T. Europe Set for Swap Futures Shoot-Out. Risk; Dec 3 2013.

Park YS. Currency swaps as a long-term international financing technique. J Int Bus Stud 1984;15(3):47–54.

Pirrong C. The Economics of Central Clearing: Theory and Practice. ISDA Discussion Paper Series No. 1; May 2011.

Popova I, Simkins B. The Value of OTC Derivatives: Case Study Analyses of Hedges by Publicly Traded Non-Financial Firms. ISDA Discussion Paper; Mar 2014.

Risk H. RBS Hangs Hat on Prime Brokerage to Boost FX Revenues. Euromoney; Dec 2011.

Salzman JE. *Swap Clearinghouses and Markets." The Dodd-Frank Act: Commentary and Insights*. New York: Skadden, Arps, Slate, Meagher & Flom LLP & Affiliates; 2007.

Sapient Global Markets. The Cost of Clearing: A Buy-Side Investigation. June 2013.

Sidley Austin LLP. First Swaps Proposed for Mandatory Trading: Next Phase of Dodd-Frank Implementation Begins. Derivatives Update; Oct 31 2013.

Sidley Austin LLP. End-User Exception from the Clearing Mandate and the Trade Execution Requirement Under Dodd-Frank Act. Derivatives Update; Aug 13 2014.

Silber WL. The process of financial innovation. Am Econ Rev 1983;73(2):8995.

Skadden Arps, Slate, Meagher & Flom LLP & Affiliates. Prudential Regulators and CFTC Re-Propose Margin Requirements for Non-Cleared Swaps. Memorandum; Sept 19 2014.

Smithson C. *Managing Financial Risk: A Guide to Derivative Products, Financial Engineering, and Value Maximization*. 3rd ed. New York: McGraw-Hill; 1998.

Stafford P. US Regulators to Monitor London Over-the-Counter Swaps. Financial Times; April 20 2014a.

Stafford P, Chon G. Regulators Reach Deal on Over-the-Counter Derivatives Rules. Financial Times; Feb 12 2014b.

Sullivan & Cromwell LLP. Proposed Margin Requirements for Uncleared Swaps Under Dodd-Frank. Memorandum; Sept 10 2014a.

Sullivan & Cromwell LLP. Court Dismisses Challenge to CFTC Cross-Border Guidance. Memorandum; Sept 18 2014b.

Sullivan & Cromwell LLP. CFTC Proposed Margin Requirements for Uncleared Swaps Under Dodd-Frank. Memorandum; Sept 30 2014c.

Swan EJ. *Building the Global Market: A 4000 Year History of Derivatives*. London: Kluwer Law; 2000.

Technical Committee of the International Organization of Securities Commissions. Report on Trading of OTC Derivatives; Febr 2011.

The Group of Thirty, Global Derivatives Study Group. Derivatives: Practices and Principles – Appendix III: Survey of Industry Practice. Washington (DC); Mar 1994a.

The Group of Thirty, Global Derivatives Study Group. Derivatives: Practices and Principles – Follow-Up Surveys of Industry Practice. Washington (DC); Dec 1994b.

Vaghela V. Japan Slams European Rules on Bilateral Swaps. Asia Risk; Aug 11 2014.

Whittall C. Trillions Saved as Swaps Margining Standards Agreed. IFRAsia; Sept 25 2014.

Wholesale Markets Brokers' Association/London Energy Brokers' Association. Comments to the Committee of European Securities Regulators (CESR) Consultation Paper: Standardization and Exchange Trading of OTC Derivatives. Committee of European Securities Regulators; 2010.

17

Risk-Neutral Pricing: Trees

Claudio Tebaldi[a] **and Pietro Veronesi**[b]

[a]*Department of Finance and IGIER, Bocconi University, Milano, Italy*
[b]*Booth School of Business, University of Chicago, Chicago, IL, United States*

17.1 INTRODUCTION

Risk-neutral pricing has become the main tool for computing the value of derivative securities in the industry. Unfortunately, it also generates substantial confusion for students and practitioners who are not too familiar with the foundations of no-arbitrage pricing. Part of the confusion may arise from the terminology itself, "risk-neutral pricing," which seems to suggest that we assume agents in the economy are neutral to risk, which is definitely *not* one of the assumptions required.

In this chapter, we review the foundations of risk-neutral pricing using simple binomial trees. The binomial tree structure is especially useful because of its simplicity. Moreover, as the number of steps of the tree increases – a simple task when one uses computers – then the binomial tree methodology actually becomes a rather powerful, yet simple, tool to price even very complicated securities. In this chapter, we thus begin by reviewing small trees in order to provide the intuition behind the concepts of no-arbitrage, risk-neutral pricing, market price of interest rate risk, and risk premium. We then move on to illustrate the methodology to fit bigger trees by introducing a number of interest rate models widely used in the industry to value real-world securities. The final part of the chapter covers yet another generalization of binomial trees, namely, *tri*nomial trees, and again applies the risk-neutral methodology to price real-world securities. We will illustrate the various procedures through a couple of running examples, namely, the pricing of two recent Freddie Mac callable securities.

17.2 BINOMIAL TREES

17.2.1 One-Step Binomial Trees

Consider the generic one-step binomial interest rate tree displayed in Table 17.1. The interest rates r_0, $r_{1,u}$, and $r_{1,d}$ are semi-annually compounded interest rates, and the probability p is the "true" probability, reflecting the real expectation of market participants (or yours) about future interest rates. Denote by $\Delta t = 0.5$ the time step on the binomial tree and the generic (time, node) by (i, j).

In addition to the information contained in this binomial tree, it is known also the value of a zero-coupon bond with maturity $t = 1$ year, that is, in two periods from now $i = 2$. We denote the value today of such zero-coupon bond as $Z_0(2)$, where the "2" in the parentheses denotes the maturity of the bond. Combining this information with the interest rates in the binomial tree in

Handbook of Fixed-Income Securities, First Edition. Edited by Pietro Veronesi.

TABLE 17.1 A One-Period Binomial Interest Rate Tree

period ⇒ time ⇒	$i = 0$ $t = 0$	$i = 1$ $t = 0.5$	prob.
		$r_{1,u} = 0.04$	p
	$r_0 = 0.03$		
		$r_{1,d} = 0.02$	1–p

TABLE 17.2 A One-Period Binomial Zero-Coupon Bond Tree

period ⇒ time ⇒	$i = 0$ $t = 0$	$i = 1$ $t = 0.5$	prob.
		$Z_{1,u}(2) = \frac{1}{1 + r_{1,u}\Delta t} = 0.9804$	p
	$Z_0(2) = 0.97$		
		$Z_{1,d}(2) = \frac{1}{1 + r_{1,d}\Delta t} = 0.9901$	1–p

TABLE 17.3 Zero-Coupon Bond and Derivative Tree

$i = 0$ $t = 0$	$i = 1$ $t = 0.5$	prob.
	$Z_{1,u}(2) = \frac{1}{1 + r_{1,u}\Delta t} = 0.9804$ $V_{1,u} = 100\max(r_{1,u} - k, 0) = 1$	p
$Z_0(2) = .97$ $V_0 = ?$		
	$Z_{1,d}(2) = \frac{1}{1 + r_{1,d}\Delta t} = 0.9901$ $V_{1,d} = 100\max(r_{1,d} - k, 0) = 0$	1–p

Table 17.1, we obtain the binomial tree of a two-period zero-coupon bond in Table 17.2, where recall that $Z_0(2)$ is known today. Note that we do not indicate the value of the zero-coupon bond $Z_{i,j}(2)$ at maturity, because in any node j, $Z_{2,j}(2) = 1$.

Consider now another fixed-income security with value $V_{1,u}$ and $V_{1,d}$ at time $i = 1$. Such security could be a derivative that pays at time $i = 1$ different amounts depending on the realized interest rate. For instance, an interest rate option has payoff at $i = 1$ given by $V_{1,j} = \max(r_{i,j} - k, 0)$, where k is a strike rate ($k = 0.03$ in the example in Table 17.3). Or $V_{1,j}$ could also be another zero-coupon bond with another maturity, for example, $i = 3$. Whatever security we consider with values $V_{1,u}$ and $V_{1,d}$ at time $i = 1$, there must exist a no-arbitrage relation between the zero-coupon bond price in the binomial tree in Table 17.2 and the security $V_{i,j}$.

The question is: What is the value of this security at time 0, V_0? We proceed as follows:

1. **Portfolio**: Set up a portfolio today that is long one unit of the security V_0 and N units of the zero-coupon bond with maturity $i = 2$, $Z_0(2)$. The value of this portfolio today is

$$\Pi_0 = V_0 + NZ_0(2) \tag{17.1}$$

2. **Hedging**: Choose N to make the portfolio riskless, that is, such that its value is independent of the interest rate scenario at time $i = 1$. That is, impose

$$\Pi_{1,u} = \Pi_{1,d} \tag{17.2}$$

By definition, this condition can be rewritten as

$$V_{1,u} + NZ_{1,u}(2) = V_{1,d} + NZ_{1,d}(2) \tag{17.3}$$

We can solve for N to get

$$N = -\frac{V_{1,u} - V_{1,d}}{Z_{1,u} - Z_{1,d}} \tag{17.4}$$

3. **No-Arbitrage**: The portfolio Π is risk-free, because given N its value is independent of the interest rate movement. Therefore, its value at time $i = 0$ must equal the risk-free present value

$$\Pi_0 = Z_0(1)\Pi_{1,u} \quad \text{or, equivalently,} \quad \Pi_0 = Z_0(1)\Pi_{1,d} \tag{17.5}$$

Which of these two formulas we use does not matter because $\Pi_{1,u} = \Pi_{1,d}$ and so we would get the same result. In fact, and this step is critical to understand the pricing formulas, consider *any* probability $\tilde{p}$ and denote by $E^{\tilde{p}}[.]$ the expectation taken using such probability. In particular, we have

$$E^{\tilde{p}}[\Pi_1] = \tilde{p}\ \Pi_{1,u} + (1 - \tilde{p})\ \Pi_{1,d} = \Pi_{1,u} = \Pi_{1,d}$$

This equation is a tautology. Because we know the value of $\Pi_{1,u} = \Pi_{1,d}$, its expected value is also known and independent of the probability $\tilde{p}$ that we use to mix the two outcomes. Therefore, we have the no-arbitrage relation

$$\Pi_0 = Z_0(1)E^{\tilde{p}}[\Pi_1] \tag{17.6}$$
$$= Z_0(1)E^{\tilde{p}}[V_1] + Z_0(1)NE^{\tilde{p}}[Z_1(2)] \tag{17.7}$$

4. **Reshuffle and Solve for V_0**: The no-arbitrage relation 17.7 generates an equation, which is obtained by substituting Π_0 from 17.1 on the left-hand side:

$$V_0 + NZ_0(2) = Z_0(1)E^{\tilde{p}}[V_1] + Z_0(1)NE^{\tilde{p}}[Z_1(2)]$$

Solve for V_0 and obtain

$$V_0 = Z_0(1)E^{\tilde{p}}[V_1] + N\{Z_0(1)E^{\tilde{p}}[Z_1(2)] - Z_0(2)\} \tag{17.8}$$

The key is to realize that this pricing equation holds for *any* $\tilde{p}$, without restrictions. That is, independently of what we choose for $\tilde{p}$, we get always the same price of the security.

5. **Risk-Neutral Probabilities**: If the value of V_0 coming from solving 17.8 is independent of $\tilde{p}$, why not choose a value of $\tilde{p}$ that makes the calculations simple? In particular, we could choose $\tilde{p}$ to get rid of the second term. That is,

$$\text{choose } \tilde{p} \text{ such that} \quad Z_0(1)E^{\tilde{p}}[Z_1(2)] - Z_0(2) = 0 \tag{17.9}$$

Denote by q the probability $\tilde{p}$ that satisfies condition 17.9. Given $Z_0(1) = \frac{1}{1+r_0\Delta t}$ we obtain that under q:

$$E^q\left[\frac{Z_1(2)}{Z_0(2)} - 1\right] = r_0\Delta t \tag{17.10}$$

That is, under the probability q, the expected return from purchasing the zero-coupon bond is just the risk-free rate r_0 (times the time step Δt). Because $r_0\Delta t$ is the return that a hypothetical risk-neutral investor would require as rate of return from purchasing the two-period bond, the probability q is called the **risk-neutral probability**. This probability can be obtained explicitly by solving 17.10. From

$$\underbrace{qZ_{1,u}(2) + (1 - q)Z_{1,d}(2)}_{E^q[Z_1(2)]} = Z_0(2)(1 + r_0\Delta t)$$

we obtain

$$q = \frac{Z_0(2)(1 + r_0\Delta t) - Z_{1,d}(2)}{Z_{1,u}(2) - Z_{1,d}(2)} \tag{17.11}$$

Note that we have all of the information to compute the value of the risk-neutral probability. Given the risk-neutral probability, the **risk-neutral pricing formula** is then

$$V_0 = Z_0(1)E^q[V_1] \tag{17.12}$$

TABLE 17.4 Derivative Value V_0 for Various Probabilities $\tilde{p}$

$\tilde{p}$	$Z_0(1)$	$Z_0(2)$	$E^{\tilde{p}}[V_1]$	N	$E^{\tilde{p}}[Z_1(2)]$	V_0
0.1	0.985222	0.97	0.1	103.02	0.989128	0.563211
0.5	0.985222	0.97	0.5	103.02	0.985246	0.563211
0.571659	0.985222	0.97	0.571659	103.02	0.98455	0.563211
0.9	0.985222	0.97	0.9	103.02	0.981363	0.563211

17.2.1.1 Example: Valuation and Risk-Neutral Probability Consider the tree depicted in Table 17.3, and assume $p = 0.5$. Given the values $Z_{1u}(2)$, $Z_{1d}(2)$, V_{1u}, and V_{1d} in the table, we find from 17.4[1]

$$N = -\frac{V_{1,u} - V_{1,d}}{Z_{1,u} - Z_{1,d}} = 103.02$$

We now notice from Equation 17.8 that the value of V_0 is always the same independently of the choice of probability $\tilde{p}$. The calculations are shown in Table 17.4. The first column reports $\tilde{p}$. The second and third columns just report the two zero-coupon bonds $Z_0(1)$ and $Z_0(2)$ at time 0, whose values are independent of $\tilde{p}$. Next we have a column that reports the expected value of the final payoff of the derivative $E^{\tilde{p}}[V_1]$, which instead does depend on $\tilde{p}$. The hedge ratio N is in column 5, while the expected value of the two-period zero-coupon bond $E^{\tilde{p}}[Z_1(2)]$ is next. The last column finally reports the value of the security according to the valuation formula 17.8.

We note that even if both $E^{\tilde{p}}[V_1]$ and $E^{\tilde{p}}[Z_1(2)]$ change across rows, depending on $\tilde{p}$, the value of the security in the last column is the same across rows. The reason is that as the probability increases, the expected value $E^{\tilde{p}}[V_1]$ increases but $E^{\tilde{p}}[Z_1(2)]$ decreases, exactly in the proper amount to make the value of the derivative independent of $\tilde{p}$.

Given that the value of the derivative is independent of the chosen $\tilde{p}$, we choose one value for which the formula is particularly convenient. This is the risk-neutral probability, given by formula 17.11. We obtain

$$q = 0.571659$$

The value of the security is then

$$V_0 = Z_0(1)E^q\left[V_1\right] = Z_0(1)(q\,1 + (1-q)\,0] = 0.563211$$

17.2.1.2 Multistep Trees All of the computations performed in points 1–5 could be done for any subtree in a longer tree. That is, given the current (time, node) = (i, j) in a long tree, we have the one-step risk-neutral pricing formula

$$V_{i,j} = Z_{i,j}(i+1)\;E^{q_{i,j}}[V_{i+1}] \tag{17.13}$$

where

$$E^{q_{i,j}}[V_{i+1}] = q_{i,j}V_{i+1,j+up} + (1-q_{i,j})V_{i+1,j+down} \tag{17.14}$$

We use the notation $q_{i,j}$, with subscript (i, j), as the risk-neutral probability may depend on the current node (i, j). We return in Section 17.3 to discuss how to operationalize this recursive formula.

[1]Note that Tables 17.3 and 17.4 report approximated numbers. The exact values of all of the quantities, without any rounding, are necessary to obtain the result that V_0 is independent of $\tilde{p}$; otherwise, some small discrepancies can be observed. All of the computations in the table, as well as N in the next equation, use true values and not rounded values.

17.2.2 The Market Price of Risk

Consider again the pricing Equation 17.8 and specialize it for the true probabilities, that is, $\tilde{p} = p$, where p is in the original tree in Table 17.2. Moving the first term on the right-hand side of 17.8 to the left-hand side, substituting for N in 17.4 and reshuffling leads to

$$\frac{Z_0(1)E^p[V_1] - V_0}{V_{1,u} - V_{1,d}} = \frac{Z_0(1)E^p[Z_1(2)] - Z_0(2)}{Z_{1,u}(2) - Z_{1,d}(2)} \tag{17.15}$$

Note that the expression on the left-hand side for V is identical to the expression on the right-hand side for $Z(2)$. To gain intuition, we can rewrite this equivalently as

$$\frac{E^p\left[\frac{V_1}{V_0} - 1\right] - r_0\Delta t}{\frac{V_{1,u}}{V_0} - \frac{V_{1,d}}{V_0}} = \frac{E^p\left[\frac{Z_1(2)}{Z_0(2)} - 1\right] - r_0\Delta t}{\frac{Z_{1,u}(2)}{Z_0(2)} - \frac{Z_{1,d}(2)}{Z_0(2)}} \tag{17.16}$$

These expressions have simple economic intuition. Consider the left-hand side. The numerator is the *expected return* from purchasing the security V_0 at $i = 0$ and selling it at time $i = 1$ (first term) minus the risk-free rate. That is, this is a *risk premium* or *expected excess return*. The denominator is the "risk" from purchasing the security that is due variation in interest rates. The right-hand side of condition 17.16 has an identical interpretation but for the bond $Z_0(2)$. In English, we can write

$$\frac{\text{Risk premium of } V}{\text{Risk of } V} = \frac{\text{Risk premium of } Z(2)}{\text{Risk of } Z(2)} \tag{17.17}$$

This has an important implication, namely, that *all fixed-income securities* must have the same risk/return trade-off. It follows that we can provide a name for this common component and call it λ:

$$\lambda = \frac{\text{Risk premium of } V}{\text{Risk of } V} = \frac{E^p\left[\frac{V_1}{V_0} - 1\right] - r_0\Delta t}{\frac{V_{1,u}}{V_0} - \frac{V_{1,d}}{V_0}} \tag{17.18}$$

This ratio λ is called the **market price of interest rate risk** and as seen it is independent of the security that we are considering. The market price of (interest rate) risk can be estimated from the current price of the two-period zero-coupon bond and the interest rate tree, as shown in the next example.

17.2.2.1 Example: Estimating and Interpreting the Market Price of Interest Rate Risk How can we estimate λ? Because it is independent of the particular security used, we can use the two-period zero-coupon bond in Table 17.2 to find its value. In particular, assuming the true probability is $p = 0.5$ and using the entries in Table 17.2, we find

$$\lambda = \frac{E^p\left[\frac{Z_1(2)}{Z_0(2)} - 1\right] - r_0\Delta t}{\frac{Z_{1,u}(2)}{Z_0(2)} - \frac{Z_{1,d}(2)}{Z_0(2)}} = -0.071659002 \tag{17.19}$$

A negative λ implies a positive risk premium $E^p\left[\frac{Z_1(2)}{Z_0(2)} - 1\right] - r_0\Delta t > 0$, because zero-coupon bonds move *inversely* with the interest rate, which is the risk factor. Specifically, the denominator $\frac{Z_{1,u}(2)}{Z_0(2)} - \frac{Z_{1,d}(2)}{Z_0(2)}$ is negative, as $Z_{1,u}(2) < Z_{1,d}(2)$, as seen in Table 17.2.

17.2.2.2 An Equivalent Pricing Formula Given an estimated value of λ, we can then invert Equation 17.18 to solve for V_0 and obtain another equivalent pricing formula

$$V_0 = Z_0(1)\left\{E^p[V_1] - \lambda(V_{1,u} - V_{1,d})\right\} \tag{17.20}$$

That is, the value of the security is equal to the present value of the expected payoff $Z_0(1)E^p[V_1]$, discounted at the risk-free rate, minus an adjustment equal to the market price of interest rate risk (λ) times the amount of risk ($V_{1,u} - V_{1,d}$). This formula is equivalent to the risk-neutral pricing formula obtained earlier (see 17.12). If we apply it to price the derivative security in Table 17.3, we still obtain $V_0 = 0.563211$. In other words, the risk-neutral pricing formula is a convenient tool to price derivatives, but as shown in expression 17.20 there is no assumption that agents are risk-neutral. In fact, under the true probabilities, there is an adjustment due to risk.

We can also relate the market price of risk to the difference in expectations between risk-neutral and true probabilities. Indeed, equating V_0 from the risk-neutral formula 17.12 and the risk-adjusted formula 17.20, we obtain

$$E^q[V_1] = E^p[V_1] - \lambda(V_{1,u} - V_{1,d}) \tag{17.21}$$

That is, the expected risk-neutral value of a security is equal to its true expected value minus an adjustment due to risk. In particular, we obtain an alternate definition of the market price of risk. In other words, the market price of risk is the quantity that allows us to move from the true probability p to the risk-neutral probability q. Or, in the jargon, "from P to Q":

$$\lambda = \frac{E^p[V_1] - E^q[V_1]}{(V_{1,u} - V_{1,d})} \tag{17.22}$$

How does λ behave over a longer tree? In general, λ need not be a constant but it may vary along the tree. If we have a multistep tree, then in general we would have $\lambda_{i,j}$ for a generic (time, node) = (i, j). The important point is that no-arbitrage requires such $\lambda_{i,j}$ to be *the same* across all fixed-income securities at that time/node (i, j) of the tree. The market price of risk is not security specific; otherwise, there is an arbitrage opportunity.

17.3 RISK-NEUTRAL PRICING ON MULTISTEP TREES

In the previous section, we have seen that under no-arbitrage, there are risk-neutral probabilities $q_{i,j}$ such that the value of the security can be computed simply through the recursive relation

$$V_{i,j} = Z_{i,j}(i+1)\left[q_{i,j}V_{i+1,j+up} + (1-q_{i,j})V_{i+1,j+down}\right] \tag{17.23}$$

where $Z_{i,j}(i+1)$ is the value of a one-period zero-coupon bond in time/node (i, j) and $V_{i+1,j+up}$ and $V_{i+1,j+down}$ denote the values of the security if the underlying interest rates go up ($j + up$) or down ($j + down$) at time $i + 1$ from its current position (time/node (i, j)). We can now proceed with the calibration of interest rate models so as to value securities through this recursive relation. In fact, we do not even need the original interest rate model under the "true" probabilities. If we just want to price a derivative, we just need the risk-neutral probabilities $q_{i,j}$ and the interest rate tree nodes $r_{i,j}$. The idea is to use the current value of liquid, traded interest rate securities, such as zero-coupon bonds or liquid interest rate options, in order to estimate the current values of $q_{i,j}$ and $r_{i,j}$ from the tree.

Because of the large number of degrees of freedom, many models simply assume $q_{i,j} = 0.5$ and proceed to obtain the nodes $r_{i,j}$ that best fit a number of derivative securities. Of course, this restriction is arbitrary, but it does provide some simple formulas, as shown below.

We need though one more "notational convention" in order to make the methodology operative, namely, what "$j + up$" and "$j + down$" are in the expression 17.23. A simple way to deal with this is to think about a tree as being a "triangle" on a spreadsheet. Columns correspond to time (index i) while rows correspond to nodes (index j). As we move across columns on the same row, we are moving "up" the tree as time goes by. Moving instead along the diagonal, we are moving "down" the tree. Table 17.5 provides a simple illustration with four rows and four columns. As we move "up" the tree, the node index j is constant, while when we move "down" the tree, the node index increases. We can represent the movements on the tree as follows:

$$r_{i,j} \rightarrow \begin{cases} r_{i+1,j} & \text{an upward movement in interest rate} \\ r_{i+1,j+1} & \text{a downward movement in interest rate} \end{cases} \tag{17.24}$$

Given this convention in denoting up-and-down movement, we can rewrite the recursive formula 17.23 as

$$V_{i,j} = Z_{i,j}(i+1)[q_{i,j}V_{i+1,j} + (1-q_{i,j})V_{i+1,j+1}] \tag{17.25}$$

where recall $Z_{i,j}(i+1)$ is a one-period zero-coupon bond in time/node (i, j). Given a tree (i.e., nodes $r_{i,j}$ and risk-neutral probabilities $q_{i,j}$), we can compute the value of any derivative security by moving backward on the tree by utilizing 17.25. In particular, given that we know the final value of the derivative $V_{n,j}$, where n is the number of steps to maturity, we can initiate the valuation procedure at maturity n and then simply loop back for every i from $n - 1$ to 0.

TABLE 17.5 Interest Rate Tree

$i \Rightarrow$	0	1	2	3	4
j					
0	$r_{0,0}$	→ $r_{1,0}$	→ $r_{2,0}$	→ $r_{3,0}$	→ $r_{4,0}$
	↘	↘	↘	↘	
1		$r_{1,1}$	→ $r_{2,1}$	→ $r_{3,1}$	→ $r_{4,1}$
		↘	↘	↘	
2			$r_{2,2}$	→ $r_{3,2}$	→ $r_{4,2}$
			↘	↘	
3				$r_{3,3}$	→ $r_{4,3}$
				↘	
4		$q = 1/2$			$r_{4,4}$

17.3.1 Calibration of Risk-Neutral Trees to the Yield Curve

We assume we have zero-coupon bond data available. A first requirement to build a tree should be to have a "recombining" tree, namely, an up-and-down movement should lead to the same node as a down-and-up movement. While theoretically there is no problem in working with nonrecombining trees, there are issues with computational speed and feasibility. For instance, imagine we want to value a 30-year mortgage-backed security with monthly payments. Even assuming monthly steps in building the tree, we have 360 steps between now and maturity. If for each node we generate two more nodes at each step, by maturity time $i = 360$ we have $2^{360} = 2.3485 \times 10^{108}$ possible nodes, a pretty large number! If instead the tree is recombining, we have just 361 nodes at maturity.

The calibration methodology is relatively simple: once one has designed an algorithm to generate a recombining tree, the only task left is to determine the tree parameters (nodes $r_{i,j}$ and/or probabilities $q_{i,j}$) in order to match the prices of traded fixed-income securities, such as bonds, and/or options. The methodology is usually recursive, starting from the root of the tree and building it forward.

17.3.1.1 The Ho and Lee Model The **Ho and Lee model** is likely the simplest model and thus provides an excellent starting point. The model is as follows: let $r_{i,j}$ be the (annualized) interest rate in time/node (i, j), then

$$\begin{cases} \text{up:} & r_{i+1,j} = r_{i,j} + \eta(i)\Delta t + \sigma\sqrt{\Delta t} \text{ with } q = 1/2 \\ \text{down:} & r_{i+1,j+1} = r_{i,j} + \eta(i)\Delta t - \sigma\sqrt{\Delta t} \text{ with } 1 - q = 1/2 \end{cases} \tag{17.26}$$

where σ is the annualized volatility of the interest rate, $\eta(i)$ is a quantity that is chosen step-by-step to fit exactly the term structure of interest rate, as illustrated next, and Δt is the time step on the tree in annual units (e.g., $\Delta t = 0.5$ for semiannual steps). It is easy to verify that the Ho–Lee model above generates a recombining tree. We now illustrate the steps to calibrate the Ho–Lee model to zero-coupon bond data on a specific date.

17.3.1.2 Example: Calibration of the Ho–Lee Tree on January 28, 2014 On January 28, 2014, the zero-coupon bonds fitted to the Treasury bonds have values $Z(0.5) = 99.9327$, $Z(1) = 99.8600$, $Z(1.5) = 99.6468$, $Z(2) = 99.2242$, and $Z(2.5) = 98.5667$. We now sequentially choose the parameter $\eta(i)$ to ensure that the Ho and Lee binomial tree prices exactly these zero-coupon bonds. First, from $Z(0.5) = 1/(1 + r(0)\Delta t)$, we obtain the root of the tree as $r(0) = (100/Z(0.5) - 1)/\Delta t = 0.13\%$. Given a volatility value $\sigma = 0.0086\%$ (we will discuss later where we get this number), we compute sequentially the quantity $\eta(i)$, $i = 0, 1, 2, 3$ in order to exactly match the remaining four zero-coupon bonds. That is, we choose $\eta(0)$ to match $Z(1) = 99.8600$, we choose $\eta(1)$ to match $Z(1.5) = 99.6468$, and so on. The left-hand side panels of Table 17.6 report the resulting interest rate tree (Panel A) and the binomial trees of the four zero-coupon bonds (Panels B–E). The values of $\eta(i)$ are at the bottom of the interest rate tree, for reference. As it can be seen, the interest rate tree prices the zero-coupon bonds exactly.

17.3.1.3 The Simple Black, Derman, and Toy Model One drawback of the Ho and Lee model is that it may generate negative interest rates, as it is apparent from the left-hand side of Panel A of Table 17.6. Negative nominal rates imply that an investor is willing to pay more than \$100 today in order to receive \$100 in the future. This fact is apparent in the binomial trees for

TABLE 17.6 Ho–Lee and Simple Black–Derman–Toy Model on January 28, 2014

	Ho–Lee model						Simple Black–Derman–Toy model					
	Panel A: Interest Rate Tree											
$t \Rightarrow$	0	0.5	1	1.5	2	2.5	0	0.5	1	1.5	2	2.5
$i \Rightarrow$	0	1	2	3	4	5	0	1	2	3	4	5
j												
0	0.135%	0.756%	1.650%	2.687%	3.785%		0.135%	0.267%	1.446%	5.369%	16.209%	
1		−0.461%	0.433%	1.471%	2.569%			0.024%	0.131%	0.485%	1.464%	
2			−0.783%	0.255%	1.353%				0.012%	0.044%	0.132%	
3				−0.961%	0.136%					0.004%	0.012%	
4		$q = 0.5$			−1.080%			$q = 0.5$			0.001%	
$\eta(i)$	0.000255	0.00572	0.008588	0.009793		$\eta(i)$	−1.034019	0.973243	0.219291	−0.194529		
	Panel B: 1-Year Zero-Coupon Bond											
0	99.8600	99.6236	100				99.8600	99.8666	100			
1		100.2309	100					99.9879	100			
2			100						100			
	Panel C: 1.5-Year Zero-Coupon Bond											
0	99.6468	99.1084	99.1819	100			99.6468	99.4755	99.2820	100		
1		100.3194	99.7837	100				99.9523	99.9347	100		
2			100.3929	100					99.9941	100		
3				100						100		
	Panel D: 2-Year Zero-Coupon Bond											
0	99.2242	98.3875	98.1624	98.6742	100		99.2242	98.7016	97.8641	97.3855	100	
1		100.1946	99.3560	99.2699	100			99.8805	99.8029	99.7580	100	
2			100.5715	99.8728	100				99.9822	99.9781	100	
3				100.4831	100					99.9980	100	
4					100						100	
	Panel E: 2.5-Year Zero-Coupon Bond											
0	98.5667	97.4377	96.9202	97.1322	98.1427	100	98.5667	97.5033	95.6800	93.3812	92.5032	100
1		99.8285	98.6913	98.3071	98.7319	100		99.7628	99.5872	99.3625	99.2732	100
2			100.5058	99.5033	99.3283	100			99.9625	99.9421	99.9339	100
3				100.7216	99.9319	100				99.9948	99.9940	100
4					100.5429	100					99.9995	100
5						100						100

zero-coupon bonds, as their values become more than 100 at times. It is normally thought that negative nominal rates imply a simple arbitrage opportunity, as keeping the cash at home is better than investing it in Treasuries.[2]

A solution is to work with logarithms. Define $z_{i,j} = \log\ (r_{i,j})$ and then consider the Ho and Lee model in logarithms, namely,

$$\begin{cases} \text{up:} & z_{i+1,j} \quad = z_{i,j} + \eta(i)\Delta t + \sigma\sqrt{\Delta t} \text{ with } q = 1/2 \\ \text{down:} & z_{i+1,j+1} = z_{i,j} + \eta(i)\Delta t - \sigma\sqrt{\Delta t} \text{ with } 1 - q = 1/2 \end{cases} \tag{17.27}$$

Clearly, in this case, even if for some (i, j) we have $z_{i,j} < 0$, we still obtain positive interest rates, as $r_{i,j} = e^{z_{i,j}} > 0$. This model is a special case of a more elaborate model by Black, Derman, and Toy, and thus we call it the *simple* BDT *model.*

17.3.1.4 Example: Calibration of the Simple Black, Derman, and Toy Model on January 28, 2014 Going back to the example in Section 17.3.1.2, we again choose sequentially the parameters $\eta(i)$ to ensure that the zero-coupon bond prices from the simple BDT binomial tree exactly match the zero-coupon bonds in the data. We now choose a volatility $\sigma = 1.7$ (i.e., 170%), and again we discuss later how we choose this volatility level. The resulting binomial tree is on the right-hand side of Table 17.6.

[2]Still, in a world with frictions it is possible to see negative nominal rates. For instance, the 2-year German bond saw negative yields in June 2012 when there were speculations of a break of the Euro. Holding cash at home may actually be worse than investing at negative rates in this case, as a break of the Euro may imply that German bond would convert into Deutsche Marks, as opposed to a weaker currency.

As is apparent, all of the interest rates are positive in this case, although very small for down movements in the tree. Panels B–E show that the simple BDT model also fits the zero-coupon bonds exactly.

17.3.2 The Pricing of European Options

We can exploit binomial trees to calculate the price of European options on interest rates or bonds. We illustrate the methodology by considering real-world securities. In particular, we consider European callable bonds issued by Freddie Mac, a government-sponsored enterprise (GSE) that was taken over by the U.S. Treasury in 2008. Because Freddie Mac is essentially part of the U.S. Treasury, we can consider its bonds as risk-free. Therefore, we can apply the binomial trees that we fitted earlier to zero-coupon bonds in order to price a Freddie Mac security, since such security has comparable risk.[3]

In particular, we consider Freddie Mac callable bonds. A *callable* (or *redeemable*) *bond* is a fixed-rate bond that allows the issuer to retain the privilege of redeeming the bond at a preagreed value before the bond reaches its date of maturity. The callable bond is said to be *European* if there is a single redemption date, and *Bermudan* if it is redeemable on a periodic basis (e.g., quarterly) according to a preagreed time and price schedule. A *lockout condition* forces the issuer to delay redemption after bond issuance by a minimum period of time called *the lockout period*. For each redemption date, the issuer is required to declare its decision to the holder of the bond at *the announcement date* according to a schedule that is contractually specified.

The callable bond payoff can be decomposed into the payoff of a long position in an equivalent, noncallable bond and that of a short position on a call option. That is, it is as if the issuer sold a straight noncallable bond to its investors but purchased from them the option to buy it back at the preagreed price:

$$\text{Callable bond} = \text{Straight bond–Call option}$$

To obtain the price of callable bond, therefore we must first compute the value of the call option. Such call option has payoff

$$\text{Payoff call option} = \max(P_{nc}(T_O, T) - K, 0)$$

where $P_{nc}(T_O, T)$ is the value of the underlying noncallable bond at maturity of the call option T_O. We can then compute the value of the callable bond on a binomial tree in three simple steps:

1. **Compute the value of the underlying noncallable bond on the tree.** The valuation of noncallable, coupon-bearing securities on binomial trees can be achieved using the same recursive formula in Equation 17.25, with the only additional difficulty of adding the periodic coupon. We can easily modify the recursive formula to include such coupons as follows:

$$V_{i,j} = Z_{i,j}(i+1)\left[q_{i,j}V_{i+1,j} + (1-q_{i,j})V_{i+1,j+1} + c\Delta t\right] \tag{17.28}$$

   where c is the coupon rate and Δt is the frequency of payments. This formula provides "ex-coupon" prices, as it is the value of *future* coupons. The value of a coupon bond with maturity $i^* = T\Delta t$ starts with $V_{i^*,j} = 100$ for all nodes j and then applies Equation 17.28 recursively, assuming that coupons are paid every period in the tree (i.e., the binomial step tree coincide with the frequency of payments). It is simple to modify the recursive formula to take into account any periods in which coupons are not paid.
2. **Compute the value of the call option on the noncallable bond on the tree.** Let $\hat{i} = T_O\Delta t$ be the maturity of the call option on the binomial tree. The call option has final payoff given by

$$V^{Call}_{\hat{i},j} = \max(V_{\hat{i},j} - 100, 0)$$

   for every j. This payoff is justified by the fact that by exercising the option, the issuer pays \$100 to purchase back the underlying security whose value is $V_{\hat{i},j}$ in node j. Given the final payoff of the options, we can then move back on the binomial tree using the usual recursive formula:

$$V^{Call}_{i,j} = Z_{i,j}(i+1)\left[q_{i,j}V^{Call}_{i+1,j} + (1-q_{i,j})V^{Call}_{i+1,j+1}\right] \tag{17.29}$$

   where $Z_{i,j}(i+1) = 1/(1 + r_{i,j}\Delta t)$.
3. **Take the difference between the noncallable bond and the option.** That is, the value of the callable bond on the tree is

$$V^{Callable}_{i,j} = V_{i,j} - V^{Call}_{i,j}$$

We illustrate the methodology in the next example.

[3]The liquidity of U.S. Treasuries and Freddie Mac bonds is likely very different, and thus discrepancies in prices may occur. We do not investigate the issue of liquidity here.

17.3.2.1 Example: The Pricing of Freddie Mac 2-Year, 0.5% European Callable Bond on January 28, 2014 Consider the following debt security offered by Freddie Mac for an aggregate amount of $500,000,000 on January 2, 2013. The security pays a fixed (annual) coupon rate equal to 0.50% of the principal. Coupon payments take place on a semiannual basis with payment dates January 28 and July 28 starting from July 28, 2013. At maturity, which is fixed at January 28, 2016, the amount reimbursed will correspond to 100% of the principal. At the option of Freddie Mac, upon notice to holders, the security is redeemable on January 28, 2015, only (European feature) and the redemption price is set to 100% of the principal plus accrued interest until the redemption date.

Let today be January 28, 2014. From Bloomberg, this security is trading at $99.95. We now use the binomial tree in Table 17.6 to value this security. Table 17.7 contains the calculations, using both the Ho and Lee model (left-hand side panels) and the simple BDT model (right-hand side panels). We illustrate the methodology using the Ho and Lee model. In Panel A, we report the price of a noncallable, 2-year, 0.5% bond. This value starts at 100 at maturity and then uses the recursive formula 17.28. Panel B reports the value of the call option. Concentrating on time $i = 2$, it is apparent that the value of the noncallable bond is above 100 only in node $j = 2$. Therefore, the call option at time $i = 2$ gives a positive payoff only in node $j = 2$ equal to $V_{2,2}^{Call} = \$1.073955$. Using the usual recursive formula back on the binomial tree, we can compute the value of the option at time 0, which is $V_0^{Call} = \$0.268927$. Panel C reports the value of the callable bond, which is valued today at $V_0^{Callable} = \$99.95$ (rounded). Performing the same computations as above for the simple BDT model also recovers a value of the callable bond equal to $V_0^{Callable} = \$99.95$.

17.3.2.2 Fitting Interest Rate Volatility In the example illustrated in Table 17.7, both the Ho and Lee model and the simple BDT model give the same value to the 2-year, 0.5% European callable Freddie Mac security of $99.95. This is no coincidence. In fact, *we chose the volatility σ in both models to match exactly the value of this Freddie Mac bond.* Indeed, one can fit the term structure of interest rates with many choices of volatility σ by choosing appropriately the function $\eta(i)$. In order to pin down one value of the volatility σ, however, it is customary to use options – or securities with embedded options – to compute it. In this case, we call such volatility "implied volatility," which could in fact be different from the "realized volatility" of interest rates. Indeed, for the simple BDT model, we had to use a $\sigma = 170\%$ in order to match the value of the callable bond, which is very large.[4]

17.3.2.3 Using the Fitted Model to Price Other Securities In summary, we used Treasury bonds (viz., the zero-coupon $Z(i)$) and one Freddie Mac security to obtain two interest rate trees that fit exactly the input data used. An important question is then the following:

How do these models perform to price other securities?

TABLE 17.7 Freddie Mac, 2-Year, 0.5% European Callable Bond on January 28, 2014

	Ho–Lee model						Simple Black–Derman–Toy model					
$i \Rightarrow$	0	1	2	3	4	5	0	1	2	3	4	5
	Panel A: 2-Year, 0.5% Noncallable Bond											
0	100.2209	99.1303	98.6557	98.9209	100		100.2209	99.4467	98.3569	97.6289	100	
1		100.9464	99.8539	99.5181	100			100.6300	100.3022	100.0074	100	
2			101.0740	100.1225	100				100.4821	100.2280	100	
3				100.7343	100					100.2480	100	
4					100						100	
	Panel B: Call Option with Maturity $i = 2$											
0	0.2689	0.0000	0.0000				0.2713	0.1509	0.0000			
1		0.5382	0.0000					0.3921	0.3022			
2			1.0740						0.4821			
	Panel C: 2-Year, 0.5% European Callable Bond with 1-Year Time to Call											
0	99.9519	99.1303	98.6557	98.9209	100		99.9495	99.2958	98.3569	97.6289	100	
1		100.4082	99.8539	99.5181	100			100.2379	100.0000	100.0074	100	
2			100.0000	100.1225	100				100.0000	100.2280	100	
3				100.7343	100					100.2480	100	
4					100						100	

[4]Note that for BDT the interest rate volatility σ is defined on log changes of interest rates, and thus it is expressed in units of percentage variation of interest rates. When the interest rate is almost zero, few basis points of variation imply a very large percentage variation of interest rates. On the other hand, for the Ho and Lee model, the volatility is in first difference of the interest rate levels, and thus the volatility σ is in the same units as the interest rate itself.

We now use the calibrated model above to price one additional European security to see if we get a value that is close to the data. That is, given the parameters that fit exactly the term structure of interest rates and the 2-year, 0.5% European Freddie Mac callable bond, do we get a good pricing of other Freddie Mac securities?

17.3.2.4 Example: The Pricing of Freddie Mac 2.5-Year, 0.65% European Callable Bond on January 28, 2014 Consider the following security issued by Freddie Mac on January 29, 2014. The security features semiannual payments in July and in January of each year, it expires on July 29, 2016, and it is redeemable by Freddie Mac on July 29, 2015. From Bloomberg, we find that on January 28, 2014, this callable security was trading at \$99.92.[5]

Table 17.8 contains the same calculations we made earlier in Table 17.7 but for this security. As we can see from Panel A, the value of the noncallable bond is \$100.1827 for both Ho and Lee model and BDT model. This is not surprising, given that both models are chosen to fit exactly the term structure of zero-coupon bonds on January 28, 2014, and a fixed-rate coupon is just a portfolio of zero-coupon bonds. The traded price of the callable security, \$99.92, is below \$100.1827, which means that on January 28, 2014, the call option embedded in the callable bond had positive value. We now check whether the binomial trees in Table 17.6 produce the proper call value. Panel B reports the valuation of the call options, which equal \$0.2296 if we use the Ho and Lee model, and \$0.3057 if we use the BDT model. Subtracting these values from the noncallable bonds, we obtain (in Panel C) $V_0^{Callable}$ = \$99.9531 and $V_0^{Callable}$ = \$99.8770 when we use the Ho and Lee and the simple BDT models, respectively.

17.3.2.5 Models and Prices The example in Table 17.8 highlights two facts: First, the valuation of the callable security differs depending on which model we use. Note that both interest rate trees were calibrated to the *same* data, namely, zero-coupon bonds and the 2-year Freddie Mac callable bond. Even if we use the same data, the outcome of the pricing of *other* securities differs depending on which model we use. In other words, even with the same inputs, the choice of the model matters for pricing. The different results are due to the different statistical properties of the interest rates under the various models. For instance, the Ho and Lee model implies that the distribution of interest rates $r_{i,j}$ approaches a normal distribution as the time step Δt decreases to zero. In contrast, the simple BDT model, which is the Ho and Lee model in logarithms, implies that $z_{i,j}$ approaches a normal distribution as the time step Δt decreases to zero. It follows that for this second model, the distribution of the interest rate $r_{i,j} = e^{z_{i,j}}$ approaches a *lognormal* distribution as Δt decreases to zero. The differences in statistical distribution generate different prices for derivatives.

TABLE 17.8 Freddie Mac, 2.5-Year, 0.65% European Callable Bond on January 28, 2014

	Ho–Lee model						Simple Black–Derman–Toy model					
$i \Rightarrow$	0	1	2	3	4	5	0	1	2	3	4	5
				Panel A: 2.5-Year, 0.65% Noncallable Bond								
0	100.1827	98.7200	97.8766	97.7686	98.4616	100	100.1827	98.7889	96.6316	94.0012	92.8039	100
1		101.1304	99.6593	98.9492	99.0528	100		101.0615	100.5600	100.0097	99.5958	100
2			101.4856	100.1513	99.6511	100			100.9373	100.5918	100.2587	100
3				101.3755	100.2567	100				100.6447	100.3190	100
4					100.8697	100					100.3245	100
5						100						100
				Panel B: Call Option with Maturity $i = 3$ (= 1.5 Years)								
0	0.2296	0.0376	0.0000	0.0000			0.3057	0.1525	0.0048	0.0000		
1		0.4219	0.0755	0.0000				0.4593	0.3005	0.0097		
2			0.7664	0.1513					0.6182	0.5918		
3				1.3755						0.6447		
				Panel C: 2.5-Year, 0.65% European Callable Bond with 1.5 Year Time to Call								
0	99.9531	98.6824	97.8766	97.7686	98.4616	100	99.8770	98.6364	96.6268	94.0012	92.8039	100
1		100.7084	99.5838	98.9492	99.0528	100		100.6021	100.2595	100.0000	99.5958	100
2			100.7192	100.0000	99.6511	100			100.3191	100.0000	100.2587	100
3				100.0000	100.2567	100				100.0000	100.3190	100
4					100.8697	100					100.3245	100
5						100						100

[5] Although the security is issued on January 29, 2014, it was priced on January 16, 2014, and Bloomberg has available traded prices since the pricing date.

Second, the Ho and Lee model overprices the callable bonds ($99.9531 instead of $99.92), while the simple BDT model underprices the callable bond ($99.877 instead of $99.92). This indicates that the volatility level used for Ho and Lee model is too low and the volatility level used for the simple BDT model is too high. Thus, in order to match both the 2-year, 0.5% callable bond in Example 17.3.2.1 and the 2.5-year, 0.65% callable bond in Example 17.3.2.4, we need different volatility levels depending on maturity and time to call (1 year for the first bond and 1.5 years for the second one). We now present a model with such flexibility.

17.3.2.6 The Black, Derman, and Toy Model Differently from the simple BDT model, the **Black, Derman, and Toy model** assumes that the volatility σ is time dependent. We denote by σ_i the volatility in step i. This additional flexibility allows the BDT model to better fit options with various maturities. Unfortunately, the algorithm to build a BDT model cannot be just taken from 17.27 by adding σ_i, as the tree would no longer be recombining. Instead, step-by-step, we proceed as follows (see Benninga and Wiener (1998), Brigo and Mercurio (2006), and Veronesi (2010)):

1. For given $z_{i,0}$, we have

$$z_{i,j} = z_{i,j-1} + 2\sigma_{i+1}\sqrt{\Delta t} \tag{17.30}$$

2. Choose $z_{i,0}$ to match the value of the bond maturing at time $i+1$.

Example 17.3.2.7 shows an example of the procedure. To save space, we also consider a different algorithm to price European callable bonds. Instead of decomposing the value of the callable bond into a "straight bond" minus a "call option," we consider the perspective of the issuer. At the call date, the issuer can decide to pay back the bond and pay 100, or keep the bond alive and keep the liability $P_{nc}(T_O, T)$. Thus, the value of the callable bond at call time $\hat{i}$ is

$$V_{\hat{i},j}^{Callable} = \min\left\{100, \frac{\left(q_{\hat{i},j}V_{\hat{i}+1,j}^{Callable} + (1-q_{\hat{i},j})V_{\hat{i}+1,j+1}^{Callable} + c\Delta t\right)}{1 + r_{\hat{i},j}\Delta t}\right\}$$

This algorithm gives the same answer as the previous one.

17.3.2.7 Example: A Calibration of the Black, Derman, and Toy Model on January 28, 2014 We can now try to choose the volatility σ_i to match both the 2-year, 0.5% European callable bond with 1-year time to call (ttc), as in Example 17.3.2.1, as well as the 2.5-year, 0.65% European callable bond with 1.5-year ttc, in Example 17.3.2.4. Given that the simple BDT was overpricing the latter callable bond, it must be that the volatility for the last step was too high, generating too much value for the option to call in year 1.5. Table 17.9 calibrates the full BDT model using $\sigma_i = 170\%$ for the first few steps, so as to price first European callable bond exactly as before. However, we choose the last volatility $\sigma_4 = 110\%$ so as to decrease the value of the embedded option. The interest rate tree in Panel A of Table 17.9 shows the interest rate tree, which is identical to the simple BDT on the right-hand side of Panel A in Table 17.6, except for the interest rates at $i = 4$. Hence, the zero-coupon bonds maturing at $i = 2$, 3, and 4 are identical to those reported in Panels B–D in Table 17.6. In Panel B in Table 17.9 we report the 2.5-year zero-coupon bond, which differs from the simple BDT because of the rates at $i = 4$. Still, the price of the bond at 0 is exactly correct.

Panel C of Table 17.9 shows the value of the 2-year callable security. As can be seen, and not surprisingly, this is the same tree obtained in Panel C of Table 17.7 (on the right-hand side). As mentioned earlier, the algorithm to compute this callable bond is different from the one used in the previous table, but it provides the same answer.

Finally, Panel D of Table 17.9 shows the value of the 2.5-year callable security. Thanks to a lower volatility $\sigma(4) = 110\%$, we can match exactly the value of this security as well.

17.3.3 The Pricing of American Options

Binomial trees are extremely useful for pricing American or Bermudan options. Unlike European options, American options can be exercised any time before maturity of the option, while Bermudan options can be exercised at specific dates before maturity. American and Bermudan options are widespread, and they are often embedded in several securities. For instance, mortgage-backed securities contain implicit American options as homeowners can pay back their mortgages early. Similarly, many corporate bonds are issued with a "callable feature," which give the issuer the right to buy back the corporate bond at par before maturity (typically after a lockout period).

TABLE 17.9 A Calibration of Black, Derman, and Toy Model on January 28, 2014

$i \Rightarrow$	0	1	2	3	4	5
j						
0	0.135%	0.267%	1.446%	5.369%	10.282%	
1		0.024%	0.131%	0.485%	2.170%	
2			0.012%	0.044%	0.458%	
3				0.004%	0.097%	
4					0.020%	
$\sigma(i)$	1.7	1.7	1.7	1.1		
	Panel B: 2.5-Year Zero-Coupon Bond					
0	98.5667	97.6244	96.1004	94.4819	95.1104	100
1		99.6418	99.4093	99.1087	98.9266	100
2			99.8984	99.8397	99.7715	100
3				99.9688	99.9517	100
4					99.9898	100
5						100
	Panel C: 2-Year, 0.5%, 1-Year ttc, European Callable					
0	99.9500	99.2967	98.3587	97.6289	100	
1		100.2379	100.0000	100.0074	100	
2			100.0000	100.2280	100	
3				100.2480	100	
4					100	
	Panel D: 2.5-Year, 0.65%, 1.5-Year ttc, European Callable					
0	99.9237	98.7908	97.0580	95.1140	95.4195	100
1		100.5411	100.1375	99.7558	99.2481	100
2			100.3191	100.0000	100.0958	100
3				100.0000	100.2765	100
4					100.3148	100
5						100

The algorithm to price American options on trees is straightforward. Because we are pricing securities from the end of the tree backward to the root of the tree, the only difference from the case discussed in the previous section is that at any node (i, j) we have to decide whether to exercise or not the option. The decision rule will be to maximize the value of the option for the option's holder. More specifically, denote the value of the option in node (i, j) by $O_{i,j}$ and let $\text{Payoff}_{i,j}$ be the option's payoff at the same node if the option's holder decides to exercise at that node. For instance, if the option is a simple call option on an interest rate, we could have $\text{Payoff}_{i,j} = \max(r_{i,j} - r_K, 0)$ where r_K is the strike rate. In this case, the recursive formula in Equation 17.23 becomes

$$O_{i,j} = \max\left\{\text{Payoff}_{i,j}, Z_{i,j}(i+1)\left[q_{i,j}O_{i+1,j+up} + (1-q_{i,j})O_{i+1,j+down}\right]\right\} \quad (17.31)$$

The difference from the earlier recursive formula in Equation 17.23 is the addition of a "maximum" between the payoff in the node (the first term) and the "continuation value" (the second term). The continuation value is just the value of the option if we do not exercise in node (i, j), in which case we get back the formula in Equation 17.23.

We illustrate the logic of American options using Bermudan-style bonds issued by Freddie Mac. A callable, Bermudan-style bond is a debt security issued by a firm, which can be redeemed by the issuer at given dates before maturity, upon providing notice to investors. In particular, we will consider the decomposition of a Bermudan bond as a fixed-rate bond minus a Bermudan option to buy back the bond at given dates. The option in the recursive formula 17.31 thus represents the Bermudan option, with

$$\text{Payoff}_{i,j} = \max(V_{i,j} - 100, 0)$$

where $V_{i,j}$ represents the value of the noncallable bond in node (i, j).

17.3.3.1 Example: Pricing a 2-Year, 0.45%, Bermudan Freddie Mac Security on January 28, 2014 Consider the following debt security offered by Freddie Mac for an aggregate amount of \$250,000,000, issued on January 28, 2014, paying 0.45% per annum, and due on January 28, 2016. The security is redeemable periodically, beginning on July 28, 2014.

Coupon payments take place on a semiannual basis with payment dates January 28 and July 28 starting from July 28, 2014. At maturity, the amount reimbursed will correspond to 100% of the principal. At the option of Freddie Mac, the security is redeemable on a quarterly basis on the 28th of January, April, July, and October and the redemption price is set to 100% of the principal plus accrued interest until the redemption date upon notice to holders no less than 5 business days nor more than 60 calendar days prior to redemption. According to Bloomberg, this security was trading on January 28, 2014 at \$99.93.

In order to price this Bermudan-style callable bond, we would need to first fit the binomial tree to at least the quarterly frequency, so as to take into account the exact date in which redemption can occur. In fact, we should also consider that the decision to redeem must be notified at least 5 days prior to redemption date, making the calculations more complicated. However, to simplify, we will only consider the semiannually fitted binomial trees discussed earlier. That is, we assume that the security can only be redeemed at semiannual frequency. Note that this restriction can only reduce the value of the Bermudan option and thus bias the value of the security upward.

Table 17.10 shows the Ho–Lee and simple BDT binomial trees discussed in Table 17.6. Panel A reports the two interest rate trees for reference. Panel B reports the binomial tree of the noncallable 2-year, 0.45% bond. The value is the same whether one uses the Ho and Lee model or the simple BDT model, as both trees fit the current term structure of interest rates. Panel C reports the Bermudan option, and here we see that the Ho and Lee model yields a higher value of this option compared to the simple BDT model. The explanation is that the Ho and Lee model does not prevent interest rates from becoming negative, and thus in low-interest-rate nodes the value of the noncallable bond is especially high. Exercising the Bermudan option in those nodes yields a large payoff. Panel D reports the value of the Bermudan-style callable bond. The value of the bond is \$99.67 according to the Ho and Lee model and \$99.78 according to the simple BDT model. Both values are lower than the traded value on Bloomberg, which is \$99.93.

TABLE 17.10 Freddie Mac, 2-Year, 0.45% Bermudan-Style Callable Bond on January 28, 2014

	Ho–Lee model					Simple Black–Derman–Toy model				
$i \Rightarrow$	0	1	2	3	4	0	1	2	3	4
					Panel A: Interest Rate Trees					
0	0.135%	0.756%	1.650%	2.687%	3.785%	0.135%	0.267%	1.446%	5.369%	16.209%
1		−0.461%	0.433%	1.471%	2.569%		0.024%	0.131%	0.485%	1.464%
2			−0.783%	0.255%	1.353%			0.012%	0.044%	0.132%
3				−0.961%	0.136%				0.004%	0.012%
4					−1.080%					0.001%
					Panel B: 2−Year, 0.45% Noncallable Bond					
0	100.1212	99.0560	98.6064	98.8962	100	100.1212	99.3722	98.3076	97.6046	100
1		100.8712	99.8041	99.4932	100		100.5551	100.2523	99.9825	100
2			101.0237	100.0975	100			100.4321	100.2030	100
3				100.7091	100				100.2230	100
4					100					100
					Panel C: Call Option with Maturity $i = 1$					
0	0.4474	0.0242	0.0000	0.0000	0	0.3403	0.1260	0.0000	0.0000	0
1		0.8712	0.0486	0.0000	0		0.5551	0.2523	0.0000	0
2			1.0237	0.0975	0			0.4321	0.2030	0
3				0.7091	0				0.2230	0
4					0					0
					Panel D: 2−Year, 0.45% Bermudan Callable Bond with 6−Month Time to First Call					
0	99.6738	99.0318	98.6064	98.8962	100	99.7809	99.2462	98.3076	97.6046	100
1		100.0000	99.7554	99.4932	100		100.0000	100.0000	99.9825	100
2			100.0000	100.0000	100			100.0000	100.0000	100
3				100.0000	100				100.0000	100
4					100					100

17.4 FROM DIFFUSION MODELS TO BINOMIAL TREES

Numerous interest rate models have been developed in the continuous time framework, and it is important to establish the relation between continuous time and binomial tree approximations. The logic is relatively straightforward, as it recognizes that conditional on a given interest rate level at time t, the properties of interest rates in the next instant are mainly driven by the random realization of the Brownian shock that moves interest rates. The logic is to impose conditions to fit such properties to a tree. The most difficult part is to ensure that the tree is recombining, which can normally be accomplished by defining some equations that relate the tree to the properties of the interest rate model. Here, we consider the simple case in which the volatility of the interest rate model is constant (see Nelson and Ramaswamy (1990) for an early contribution).

More explicitly, consider a generic diffusion process for the interest rate such as

$$dr_t = \mu(r_t, t)dt + \sigma dW_t \tag{17.32}$$

where $\mu(r,t)$ is a function of r and time t, σ is a constant, and $dW_t \sim N(0, dt)$ is the increment of a Brownian motion. Because we are interested in pricing securities, we assume this is the *risk-neutral* process for interest rates. Over a small interval Δt, we have that conditional on the current r and t, we have

$$E[dr] = \mu(r,t)\Delta t \tag{17.33}$$

$$Var[dr] = \sigma^2 \Delta t \tag{17.34}$$

Consider now a binomial tree and a given node (i, j). Let $q_{i,j}$ be the (risk-neutral) probability of moving up the tree. As before, denote the current interest rate by $r_{i,j}$ and the two adjacent nodes by $r_{i+1,j}$ and $r_{i+1,j+1}$. If we want the binomial tree to have similar properties to the diffusion process at node (i, j), we must require the following condition:

$$\mu(r_{i,j}, i)\Delta t = q_{i,j}(r_{i+1,j} - r_{i,j}) + (1 - q_{i,j})(r_{i+1,j+1} - r_{i,j}) \tag{17.35}$$

$$\sigma^2 \Delta t = q_{i,j}(r_{i+1,j} - r_{i,j} - \mu(r_{i,j}, i)\Delta t)^2 + (1 - q_{i,j})(r_{i+1,j+1} - r_{i,j} - \mu(r_{i,j}, i)\Delta t)^2 \tag{17.36}$$

Given the current interest rate $r_{i,j}$, we have two equations and three unknowns $q_{i,j}$, $r_{i+1,j}$, and $r_{i+1,j+1}$, and therefore we have infinite solutions. However, one important restriction is not reflected in the above equations, and this is that the tree must be recombining. We can then choose the three quantities $q_{i,j}$, $r_{i+1,j}$, and $r_{i+1,j+1}$ to ensure the resulting tree is in fact recombining.

To build intuition, consider first the case in which the drift rate is zero $\mu(r_{i,j}, t) = 0$. In this case, the two equations are

$$0 = q_{i,j}(r_{i+1,j} - r_{i,j}) + (1 - q_{i,j})(r_{i+1,j+1} - r_{i,j}) \tag{17.37}$$

$$\sigma^2 \Delta t = q_{i,j}(r_{i+1,j} - r_{i,j})^2 + (1 - q_{i,j})(r_{i+1,j+1} - r_{i,j})^2 \tag{17.38}$$

If we set $q_{i,j} = 1/2$ and choose the remaining quantities $r_{i+1,j}$ and $r_{i+1,j+1}$ to satisfy these two equations, we obtain a recombining tree. In fact, in this case we obtain the solution

$$r_{i+1,j} = r_{i,j} + \sigma\sqrt{\Delta t} \tag{17.39}$$

$$r_{i+1,j+1} = r_{i,j} - \sigma\sqrt{\Delta t} \tag{17.40}$$

It is straightforward to verify that this binomial tree is recombining.[6] When $\mu(r_{ij}, t)$ is a function of the interest rate, however, the requirement $q_{i,j} = 1/2$ does not generate a recombining tree. Indeed, in this case, the solution is

$$r_{i+1,j} = r_{i,j} + \mu(r_{i,j}, t)\Delta t + \sigma\sqrt{\Delta t} \tag{17.41}$$

$$r_{i+1,j+1} = r_{i,j} + \mu(r_{i,j}, t)\Delta t - \sigma\sqrt{\Delta t} \tag{17.42}$$

[6] Indeed, the same remains true if we have $\mu(r_{i,j}, t) = \mu(t)$, that is, just a function of time, as we have seen with Ho and Lee model.

We see immediately by substitution that an "up-and-down" movement leads to a different interest rate than a "down-and-up" movement. Starting from $i = 0$ and using the simpler notation u and d to denote up-and-down movement, we see

$$r_{1,u} = r_0 + \mu(r_0, 0)\Delta t + \sigma\sqrt{\Delta t}$$
$$r_{1,d} = r_0 + \mu(r_0, 0)\Delta t - \sigma\sqrt{\Delta t}$$

and

$$\begin{aligned} r_{2,ud} &= r_{1,u} + \mu(r_{1,u}, 1)\Delta t - \sigma\sqrt{\Delta t} \\ &= r_0 + (\mu(r_0, 0) + \mu(r_{1,u}, 1))\Delta t \\ r_{2,du} &= r_{1,d} + \mu(r_{1,d}, 1)\Delta t + \sigma\sqrt{\Delta t} \\ &= r_0 + (\mu(r_0, 0) + \mu(r_{1,d}, 1))\Delta t \end{aligned}$$

Unless $\mu(r_{1,d}, 1) = \mu(r_{1,u}, 1)$, we have $r_{2,ud} \neq r_{2,du}$.[7]

How can we obtain a recombining tree from the two restrictions 17.35 and 17.36 ? We can suitably choose q_{ij} so that the "nodes" of the tree are still "driftless," that is, so that $\mu(r_{i,j}, i)$ disappear from the equation. This is accomplished by choosing

$$q_{i,j} = \frac{1}{2}\left[1 + \frac{\mu(r_{i,j}, i)}{\sigma}\sqrt{\Delta t}\right] \tag{17.43}$$

$$1 - q_{i,j} = \frac{1}{2}\left[1 - \frac{\mu(r_{i,j}, i)}{\sigma}\sqrt{\Delta t}\right] \tag{17.44}$$

With this choice of probabilities, we have that the nodes satisfy the driftless process

$$r_{i+1,j} = r_{i,j} + \sigma\sqrt{\Delta t} \tag{17.45}$$

$$r_{i+1,j+1} = r_{i,j} - \sigma\sqrt{\Delta t} \tag{17.46}$$

We can verify that the interest rate process 17.45–17.46 with up-and-down probabilities 17.43 and 17.44 still satisfies the two main restrictions 17.35 and 17.36. In fact,

$$\begin{aligned} E[dr] &= q_{i,j}(r_{i+1,j} - r_{i,j}) + (1 - q_{i,j})(r_{i+1,j+1} - r_{i,j}) \\ &= \frac{1}{2}\left[1 + \frac{\mu(r_{i,j}, i)}{\sigma}\sqrt{\Delta t}\right](\sigma\sqrt{\Delta t}) + \frac{1}{2}\left[1 - \frac{\mu(r_{i,j}, i)}{\sigma}\sqrt{\Delta t}\right]\left(-\sigma\sqrt{\Delta t}\right) \\ &= \mu(r_{i,j}, i)\Delta t \end{aligned}$$

and similarly

$$\begin{aligned} Var[dr] &= q_{i,j}(r_{i+1,j} - r_{ij})^2 + (1 - q_{i,j})(r_{i+1,j+1} - r_{ij})^2 \\ &= \frac{1}{2}\left[1 + \frac{\mu(r_{i,j}, i)}{\sigma}\sqrt{\Delta t}\right](\sigma\sqrt{\Delta t})^2 + \\ &+ \frac{1}{2}\left[1 - \frac{\mu(r_{i,j}, i)}{\sigma}\sqrt{\Delta t}\right](-\sigma\sqrt{\Delta t})^2 \\ &= \sigma^2\Delta t \end{aligned}$$

Essentially, this methodology generates both an interest rate tree (which is recombining) and a probability tree, whose probabilities mechanically depend on the interest rate $r_{i,j}$. One important drawback of this methodology, however, is that we must ensure that the probabilities are always between zero and one, that is, $0 < q_{i,j} < 1$. This can be ensured by choosing Δt sufficiently small for the problem at hand.

[7] Indeed, a similar problem arises when the volatility σ also depends on the interest rate r_t. In such cases, Nelson and Ramaswamy (1990) suggest to find a monotonic transformation that makes the volatility constant.

17.4.1 The Hull and White Model

We now use the popular **Hull and White** model to provide an example of the procedure above. The Hull–White model assumes that the interest rate follows the process

$$dr = (\eta_t - \gamma r)dt + \sigma dW$$

This is similar to the Ho and Lee model discussed earlier, except that a mean reversion component $(-\gamma r)$ is inserted in the drift rate. If $\gamma > 0$, then the model implies that when the interest rate is high, namely, $r > \eta_t/\gamma$, then future interest rates tend to decrease (because the drift rate $(\eta_t - \gamma r)$ is negative), while when the interest rate is low, namely, $r < \eta_t/\gamma$, then future interest rates tend to increase (because the drift rate $(\eta_t - \gamma r)$ is positive). Like the Ho and Lee model, the Hull and White model may generate negative interest rates. Hull and White model has closed-form formulas for bond prices (see Tebaldi and Veronesi (2016, Chapter 19 in this handbook)) and thus can be easily fitted to the term structure of interest rates. However, we use the model here as an example of "binomial tree building." In particular, according to the formulas in the previous section, we have

$$\mu(r_{i,j}, i) = \eta(i) - \gamma r_{i,j}$$

Like the Ho and Lee model, we can search $\eta(i)$ step-by-step to fit the current term structure of interest rates. We illustrate the methodology by using the same examples as above, with the important caveat that the interest rates $r_{i,j}$ are now continuously compounded rates. Accordingly, the formula for a zero-coupon bond is now $Z_{i,j}(i+1) = \exp\,(-r_{i,j}\Delta t)$.

17.4.1.1 Example: Using Hull and White Model to Price a 2-Year, 0.5%, European Freddie Mac Security on January 28, 2014 Recall the example discussed in Table 17.7. We now consider applying the Hull and White model. One important notion is that because of mean reversion $\gamma > 0$, the distribution of interest rates in the future has lower dispersion than in a model in which $\gamma = 0$. Thus, to ensure we price the implicit call option correctly, we must increase the volatility σ. In particular, for illustration purposes, we choose the following parameters $\sigma = 0.01$ and $\gamma = 0.13$ (we discuss below how we chose them). Given these parameters, we now search for $\eta(i)$ to fit the current term structure of interest rates. Panels A and B of Table 17.11 contain the results. In particular, Panel A contains the driftless interest rate tree from Equations 17.45 and 17.46. Note that this tree only depends on σ and not on $\eta(i)$. Panel B reports the risk-neutral probability of an up movement $q_{i,j+up}$, using the formulas 17.43 and 17.44. These probabilities are not 50% and grow as time passes and as interest rates increase. While in principle, for a given

TABLE 17.11 Calibration of Hull and White Model to a Binomial Tree

$i \Rightarrow$	0	1	2	3	4	$i \Rightarrow$	0	1	2	3	4
j		Panel A: Driftless Interest Rate Tree						Panel B: Probability $q_{i,j+up}$			
0	0.1346%	0.8418%	1.5489%	2.2560%			0.508595	0.669673	0.750531		
1		−0.5725%	0.1346%	0.8418%				0.734673	0.815531		
2			−1.2796%	−0.5725%					0.880531		
3				−1.9867%							
$\eta(i)$	0.000418	0.005893	0.0091								
		Panel C: 1−Year Zero−Coupon Bond						Panel D: Noncallable, 2−year 0.5% Bond			
0	99.86	99.58001	100				100.2209	99.0642	98.78305	99.12555	100
1		100.2866	100					101.0466	100.1422	99.82896	100
2			100						101.52	100.5374	100
3										101.2508	100
4											100
		Panel E: 1.5−Year Zero−Coupon Bond						Panel F: Value of Option to Call			
0	99.6468	99.04343	99.22856	100			0.273841	0.046774	0		
1		100.4078	99.9327	100				0.509227	0.142195		
2			100.6418	100					1.520026		
3				100							
		Panel G: 2−Year Zero−Coupon Bond						Panel H: European 2−Year, 0.5% Callable Bond			
0	99.2242	98.32184	98.28926	98.87836	100		99.94702	99.01743	98.78305	99.12555	100
1		100.2941	99.64326	99.58001	100			100.5374	100	99.82896	100
2			101.0159	100.2866	100				100	100.5374	100
3				100.9983	100					101.2508	100
4					100						

γ, higher interest rates should lead to a lower probability $q_{i,j}$, in this case to fit an increasing term structure of interest rates, $\eta(i)$ increases (see bottom of Panel A), which pushes up the probabilities of an up movement.

Panels C, E, and G on the left-hand side of the table show that the binomial tree in Panel A and the probabilities in Panel B correctly price the 1-year, 1.5-year, and the 2-year zero-coupon bond, whose traded values are $Z_0(1) = 99.86$, $Z_0(1.5) = 99.6468$, and $Z_0(2) = 99.2242$, respectively.

Panels D, F, and H on the right-hand side of the table illustrate the application of this Hull and White model to the pricing of the 2-year, European-style, 0.5% callable Freddie Mac bond, already discussed in Table 17.7. In particular, Panel D contains the value of the noncallable equivalent bond, Panel F contains the value of the option to call, and finally Panel H contains the value of the callable bond. The value of the callable bond is $V_0 = 99.95$ (rounded), which equals the traded value on that day from Bloomberg. In fact, we chose the two parameters σ and γ to ensure that this is the case.

17.4.1.2 ***Bounding Probabilities between Zero and One*** Table 17.11 shows that we can find parameters σ and γ and the sequence $\eta(i)$ to fit both the current term structure of interest rates as well as the 2-year, 0.5% European, callable bond issued by Freddie Mac. In fact, because we have two parameters (σ and γ) to choose before fitting exactly the term structure of interest rates by choosing $\eta(i)$, we can try to choose parameter values in order to price more than just one option. Indeed, there could be infinite combinations of σ and γ that would price the same option. However, while theoretically such observation is correct, we practically clash against an important constraint, namely, that the risk-neutral probabilities $q_{i,j}$ have to be positive and less than 1: $0 < q_{i,j} < 1$. It turns out that as we were searching for the parameters to fit the other Freddie Mac securities discussed in earlier examples, this constraint became binding, and we end up with some $q_{ij} = 1$, which hindered the proper fitting of the term structure to start with. In principle, we can solve the problem by choosing small step sizes Δt, but the issue remains that with a binomial tree, the constraint $0 < q_{ij} < 1$ is especially problematic. We now turn to trinomial trees that offer more flexibility and partly solve this problem.

17.5 TRINOMIAL TREES

Calibrating a model to zero-coupon bond prices ensures that the pricing of derivative securities is consistent with observed interest rates. Hull and White (1993) show that their trinomial tree building technique can in fact be applied to Ho and Lee (1986), Black, Derman, and Toy (1990), Hull and White (1990, 1994a,b, 1996), and Black and Karasinski (1991). Their technique produces a unified numerical technique for no-arbitrage bond pricing. To explore this, assume that the short-term interest rate dynamics is given by the diffusion process

$$dr_t = \mu(r_t, t)dt + \sigma(r_t, t)dW_t$$

Let $Q(r, t)$ be the price at time 0 of an (Arrow–Debreu) security with unit payoff at time t if the level of interest is r, and zero otherwise. Then, $Q(r, t)$ satisfies the forward Kolmogorov equation:

$$\begin{aligned}-rQ(r,t) = {} & \frac{\partial}{\partial t}Q(r,t) + \left(\mu(r,t) - \frac{1}{2}\frac{\partial \sigma(r,t)^2}{\partial r}\right)\frac{\partial Q(r,t)}{\partial r} \\ & - \left(\frac{\partial \mu(r,t)}{\partial r} - \frac{\partial^2 \sigma(r,t)^2}{\partial r^2}\right)Q(r,t) - \frac{1}{2}\sigma(r,t)^2\frac{\partial^2 Q(r,t)}{\partial r^2}\end{aligned}$$

This equation is approximated by Hull and White (1993) with a directed recombining trinomial tree, where an internal node r has three recombining branches, $r + \Delta r$, r, and $r - \Delta r$ for each time step Δt. The tree is represented by the forward recursive equation:

$$Q(r_0, 0) = 1 \tag{17.47}$$

$$\begin{aligned}Q(r, t + \Delta t) = {} & p_u(r,t)Q(r - \Delta r, t)e^{-(r-\Delta r)\Delta t} + p_m(r,t)Q(r,t)e^{-r\Delta t} \\ & + p_d(r,t)Q(r + \Delta r, t)e^{-(r+\Delta r)\Delta t}\end{aligned} \tag{17.48}$$

$$p_u(r,t) = \frac{\sigma^2 \Delta t}{2\Delta r^2} + \frac{\mu \Delta t^2}{2\Delta r^2} + \frac{\mu \Delta t}{2\Delta r} \tag{17.49}$$

$$p_m(r,t) = 1 - \frac{\sigma^2 \Delta t}{\Delta r^2} - \frac{\mu \Delta t^2}{2\Delta r^2} \tag{17.50}$$

$$p_d(r,t) = \frac{\sigma^2 \Delta t}{2\Delta r^2} + \frac{\mu \Delta t^2}{2\Delta r^2} - \frac{\mu \Delta t}{2\Delta r} \tag{17.51}$$

which reproduces the continuous time and state equation up to an approximation error of order $O(\Delta t, \Delta r^2)$.

An important point from the recursive formula above is that while the recursive formula defines $Q(r, t + \Delta t)$ on a trinomial tree, *outside* the trinomial tree $Q(r, t + \Delta t) = 0$. To illustrate, consider the Arrow–Debreu security price at time Δt for the same starting interest rate r_0. In this case, the above recursion is

$$\begin{aligned} Q(r_0, \Delta t) &= p_u(r_0, 0)Q(r_0 - \Delta r, 0)e^{-(r_0-\Delta r)\Delta t} + p_m(r_0, 0)Q(r_0, 0)e^{-r_0\Delta t} \\ &+ p_d(r_0, 0)Q(r_0 + \Delta r, 0)e^{-(r_0+\Delta r)\Delta t} \\ &= p_m(r_0, 0)e^{-r_0\Delta t} \end{aligned}$$

where we used the fact that $Q(r, 0) = 0$ for $r \neq r_0$ and $Q(r_0, 0) = 1$. The logic is that today we know what the interest rate is (it is r_0). Therefore, the value of a security that pays \$1 *today* when $r \neq r_0$ must be zero, as we know we are not getting any payment. Similarly, for other times, we know that the only interest rates that have positive probability are those on the trinomial tree. Therefore, the value today of a security that pays \$1 for an interest rate scenarios that is outside the tree must be zero, as such scenario has zero probability of occurring. We return on this point in the example below.

The second important property to recall is that given Arrow–Debreu securities $Q(r, t)$, we can obtain the price of a security with specified payments at time t as a portfolio of Arrow–Debreu securities. In particular, a zero-coupon bond that pays \$1 at $t + \Delta t$ is just given by

$$Z(t + \Delta t) = \sum_{r=r_{\min}}^{r_{\max}} Q(r, t + \Delta t)$$

where $r_{\min}$ and $r_{\max}$ denote the extremes of the range over which rates are defined at t. In order to understand the recursive formula that we use below to fit the term structure of interest rate, it is useful to note that if we get to a node (r, t) on the trinomial tree, the value of a zero-coupon bond maturing at $t + \Delta t$ computed in node (r, t) is $\exp(-r\Delta t)$. It follows that we can express the value of a zero-coupon bond at time 0 as

$$Z(t + \Delta t) = \sum_{r=r_{\min}}^{r_{\max}} Q(r, t)e^{-r\Delta t} \tag{17.52}$$

that is, as the sum of values of Arrow–Debreu securities that pay \$1 at (r, t) times the value of the one-period zero-coupon bond in that node. The convenience of this formula is that we can express the zero-coupon bond maturing at time $t + \Delta t$ using only quantities defined up to time t.

17.5.1 Calibration to the Yield Curve

In order to fit the observed yield curve information, Hull and White (1993) propose a two-step calibration procedure for a mean-reverting constant volatility interest rate process:

$$dr_t = (\eta(t) - \gamma r_t)dt + \sigma dW_t$$

where the function $\eta(t)$ is determined using the observed zero-coupon yield curve and γ and σ are constants.

The first step is to implement on a trinomial tree the evolution of an instrumental variable r_t^0, which follows

$$dr_t^0 = -\gamma r_t^0 dt + \sigma dW_t$$

On a short time interval $\Delta t = h$, the expected increment of r_t^0 and its variance are given by

$$\begin{aligned} E_t\left[r_{t+h}^0 - r_t^0\right] &= -\gamma r_t^0 h + o\left(h^{3/2}\right) \\ Var_t\left[r_{t+h}^0 - r_t^0\right] &= \sigma^2 h \end{aligned}$$

Hence in a node of the trinomial tree the (risk-neutral) probabilities to go up p_u, down p_d, or to stay at the medium level p_m have to satisfy the three equations:

$$\begin{aligned} p_u\left(\Delta r^0\right) + p_d\left(-\Delta r^0\right) &= -\gamma r_t^0 h \\ p_u\left(\Delta r^0 + \gamma r_t^0 h\right)^2 + p_m\left(\gamma r_t^0 h\right)^2 + p_d\left(-\Delta r^0 + \gamma r_t^0 h\right)^2 &= \sigma^2 h \\ p_u + p_m + p_d &= 1 \end{aligned}$$

Simplifying these equations yields

$$p_u\ \left(\Delta r^0\right) + p_d\ \left(-\Delta r^0\right) = -\gamma r_t^0 h$$
$$p_u\ \left(\Delta r^0\right)^2 + p_d\ \left(-\Delta r^0\right)^2 = \sigma^2 h - \left(\gamma r_t^0 h\right)^2$$
$$p_u + p_m + p_d = 1$$

We can then exploit these transition probabilities to determine, via standard forward iteration, the price of an Arrow–Debreu security $Q_0(r_j, t)$ for the *fictitious* market with $\eta(t) = 0$ and r_t^0 such that at each node of the tree will assume a value $j\Delta r^0$, $j = 0, \pm 1, \pm 2, \cdots, \pm n$.

Note that for sufficiently large levels of $|r_t^0|$ the value of these probabilities could be negative. Hull and White prove that this cannot happen for $j < j_* = 1.84/(\gamma h)$ and it is optimal to use the upward or the downward ramification for some $\bar{j}$ in the interval $\bar{j} \in [j_*, j^*]$, where $j^* = 8.16/(\gamma h)$. Figure 17.1 represents the three possible branches.

The optimal (error-minimizing) selection of the spacing in the interest rate tree is given by $\Delta = \sigma\sqrt{3h}$, which then determines the transition probabilities in Table 17.12:[8]

It is important to note the probabilities $p_u(j)$, $p_m(j)$, and $p_d(j)$ only depend on the node $j = 0, \pm 1, \pm 2$ but not on time. As mentioned, these transition probabilities pertain to a fictitious market with $\eta(t) = 0$ and r_t^0 such that at each node of the tree will assume a value $j\Delta$, $j = 0, \pm 1, \pm 2, \cdots, \pm n$. We denote the difference between the artificial r_t^0 and the original r_t interest rate evolution as $\alpha(t) = r_t - r_t^0$. We can determine $\alpha(t)$ by noticing that it follows a deterministic path:

$$d\alpha(t) = d(r_t - r_t^0) = \left[\eta\,(t) - \gamma(r_t - r_t^0)\right] dt = [\eta(t) - \gamma\alpha(t)]dt$$

Hence, $\alpha(t)$ is determined uniquely by the choice of $\eta(t)$, which, on the other hand, is usually selected by the no-arbitrage condition to match the initial zero-coupon bond yields.

This is the second stage of the trinomial tree construction. In its implementation it is efficient to set up a forward recursion that computes iteratively the artificial discount rate $\alpha(jh)$ using the sequence of the zero-coupon bond prices $Z^{data}(m)$ with maturity mh. It is efficient to determine jointly $\alpha(mh)$ and the prices $Q(j\Delta, mh)$ at time 0 of the Arrow–Debreu security, which pays a unit

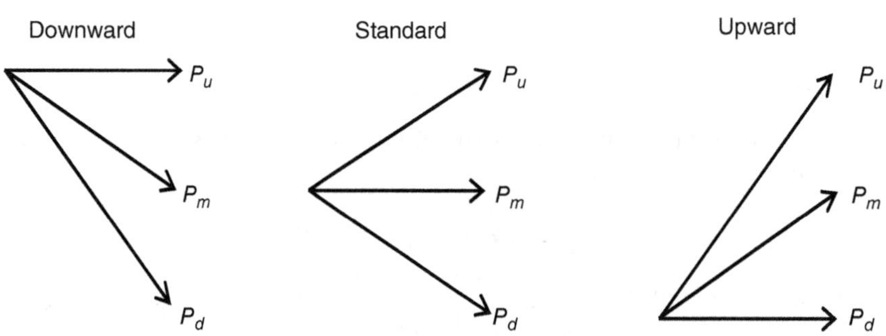

Figure 17.1 Potential branching in trinomial tree construction.

TABLE 17.12 Transition Probabilities in Trinomial Tree

	Downward (D)	Standard (S)	Upward (U)
$p_u(j)$	$\frac{1}{6} + \frac{(\gamma jh)^2 - \gamma jh}{2}$	$\frac{1}{6} + \frac{(\gamma jh)^2 - \gamma jh}{2}$	$\frac{7}{6} + \frac{(\gamma jh)^2 + 3jh}{2}$
$p_m(j)$	$-\frac{1}{3} - (\gamma jh)^2 + 2(\gamma jh)$	$\frac{2}{3} - (\gamma jh)^2$	$-\frac{1}{3} - (\gamma jh)^2 - 2(\gamma jh)$
$p_d(j)$	$\frac{7}{6} + \frac{(\gamma jh)^2 - 3jh}{2}$	$\frac{1}{6} + \frac{(\gamma jh)^2 + \gamma jh}{2}$	$\frac{1}{6} + \frac{(\gamma jh)^2 + \gamma jh}{2}$

[8]We indicate by Δ the optimal selection of the spacing in the interest rate tree instead of the more cumbersome Δr^0.

payoff in the tree node $j\Delta$ at time mh, consistent with the original interest rate r_t dynamics. The recursive procedure is initialized as follows:

- The Arrow–Debreu security at the root of the tree with initial interest rate r_0 is given by $Q(0,0) = 1$.
- Iteration Step 1. Computation of $\alpha(0)$: The price of the zero-coupon bond $Z(1)$ issued at time 0 with maturity h is given by

$$Z(1) = e^{-(\alpha(0))h}$$

Equating this to the observed zero-coupon bond $Z^{data}(1)$, we have

$$\alpha(0) = -\frac{\ln\,(Z^{data}(1))}{h} = r_0$$

In addition, the value today of the Arrow–Debreu securities that pay \$1 at time h in the nodes up ($j = 1$), medium ($j = 0$), and down ($j = -1$) are given by $Q(j\Delta, h)$ determined as follows:

$$Q(\Delta, h) = e^{-\alpha(0)h} \sum_{k=0}^{2} e^{-(k\Delta r)h} Q(k\Delta, 0)\,\Pr(k; 1) \tag{17.53}$$

$$= e^{-\alpha(0)h} p_u(0) \tag{17.54}$$

$$Q(0, h) = e^{-\alpha(0)h} \sum_{k=-1}^{1} e^{-(k\Delta r)h} Q(k\Delta, 0)\,\Pr(k; 0) \tag{17.55}$$

$$= e^{-\alpha(0)h} p_m(0) \tag{17.56}$$

$$Q(-\Delta, h) = e^{-\alpha(0)h} \sum_{k=-2}^{0} e^{-(k\Delta r)h} Q(k\Delta, 0)\,\Pr(k; -1) \tag{17.57}$$

$$= e^{-\alpha(0)h} p_d(0) \tag{17.58}$$

where $\Pr(k;j)$ denotes the probability of moving from time/node $(0, k)$ to time/node (h, j). For clarity, in the three cases above they are given by $\Pr(0; 1) = p_u(0)$, $\Pr(1; 1) = p_m(1)$, and $\Pr(1; 0) = p_d(1)$ for the top case; $\Pr(0; 0) = p_m(0)$, $\Pr(-1; 0) = p_u(-1)$, and $\Pr(0; 1) = p_u(0)$ for the middle case; and $\Pr(0; -1) = p_d(0)$, $\Pr(-1; -1) = p_m(-1)$, and $\Pr(-2; -1) = p_u(-2)$ for the bottom case. The probabilities in this case are for standard branching (see Figure 17.1) and are contained in Table 17.12.

- Iteration Step $m + 1$. Given the Arrow–Debreu security prices at time m, $Q(k\Delta, mh)$, $-k^m_{\max} \le k \le k^m_{\max}$, the pricing formula for the zero-coupon bond $Z(m + 1)$ is

$$Z(m+1) = e^{-(\alpha(mh))h} \sum_{k=-k^m_{\max}}^{k^m_{\max}} Q(k\Delta, mh) e^{-(k\Delta)h}$$

We can then compute $\alpha(m)$ by equating this bond to the observed $Z^{data}(m + 1)$, which implies

$$\alpha(mh) = \frac{1}{h}\left[\ln\left(\sum_{k=-k^m_{\max}}^{k^m_{\max}} Q\,(k\Delta, mh)\, e^{-(k\Delta)h}\right) - \ln\,\left(Z^{data}(m+1)\right)\right] \tag{17.59}$$

Arrow–Debreu security prices $Q(j\Delta, (m + 1)h)$ for $-j^{m+1}_{\max} \le j \le j^{m+1}_{\max}$ can be computed using the forward formula:

$$Q(0, 0) = 1 \tag{17.60}$$

$$Q(j\Delta, (m+1)h) = e^{-\alpha(mh)h} \sum_{k=-k^m_{\max}}^{k^m_{\max}} e^{-(k\Delta r)h} Q(k\Delta, mh)\,\Pr(k; j) \tag{17.61}$$

where $\Pr(k;j)$ is the probability of a transition from time/node $(mh, k\Delta)$ to time/node $((m + 1)h, j\Delta)$. These probabilities are determined by the $p_u(j)$, $p_m(j)$, and $p_d(j)$ in Table 17.12.

- Using the sequence $\alpha(mh)$ determined by the zero coupon bond prices $Z(m+1)$, it is immediate to derive the function $\eta(mh)$ using the difference equation:

$$\alpha((m+1)h) - \alpha(mh) = (\eta(mh) - \gamma\alpha(mh))h$$

and the construction of a short-term interest rate model consistent with the observed yields is complete.

17.5.1.1 Example: The Trinomial Hull–White Model on January 28, 2014 Table 17.13 reports the trinomial tree construction to match the data on January 28, 2014. We assume a mean reversion $\gamma = 0.1003927$and volatility $\sigma = 0.005927838$. Panel A reports the data, both in levels and yields. Panel B reports the results of the computations.

Panel C reports the demeaned interest rate tree $r^0_{i,j}$, whose dynamics is computed according to $j\Delta, j = 0, \pm 1, \pm 2, \cdots, \pm n$, and $\Delta = 0.00726009 = \sigma\sqrt{3h}$ with $h = 0.5$. The trinomial tree of $r^0_{i,j}$ is clearly symmetric. Panel D reports the final fitted interest rate tree, whose entries are given by $r_{i,j} = r^0_{i,j} + \alpha(i)$. The computation of $\alpha(i)$ is next.

Panel E reports the transition probabilities $p_u(j)$, $p_m(j)$, and $p_d(j)$ computed according to the formulas in Table 17.12. They do not depend on time but only the node j, that is, the level of the current (demeaned) interest rate $r^0_{i,j}$. Finally, Panel F reports the value of Arrow–Debreu securities, computed according to the recursion 17.61.

For each time step m, the values of the Arrow–Debreu securities is then used to compute $\alpha(m)$ through formula 17.59.

17.5.1.2 The Pricing of European-Style Securities The knowledge of all the prices $Q(j\Delta, (m+1)h)$ is sufficient to price any European-style security at time 0. In fact, by no-arbitrage the price of a security D paying $D_{j,m}$ in node j at time m will equal the price of the portfolio of Arrow–Debreu securities:

$$\pi_0(D) = \sum_{m=1}^{M} \sum_{-j_m^{\max} \le j_m \le j_m^{\max}} Q(j_m\Delta, mh) D_{j_m,m}$$

17.5.2 Pricing Bermudan Contracts Using the Trinomial Tree

Trinomial tree pricing of Bermudan exercise contracts is more involved than for the European contracts, as we also have to solve for the optimal exercise time. Optimal exercise (liquidation time) along a trinomial tree can be computed using a backward dynamic programming procedure. The algorithm is based on a backward iteration scheme starting at time T and ending at time 0. Each iteration is as follows:

- Initial iteration step: at time $M = T/h$ set the value of the security $V_{M,j}$ equal to the payoff at the terminal node $D_{M,j}$.
- Intermediate iteration step at time i, $0 < i < M$. The optimal exercise rule at time mh in each node is determined by selecting the maximum between:
  - — The immediate exercise payoff $D_{i,j}$
  - — The continuation value $V^C_{i,j}$, where $V^C_{i,j}$ is the expected risk-neutral value of the security, given by

$$V^C_{i,j} = e^{-r_{i,j}h}(p_u(j)V_{i+1,j+1} + p_m(j)V_{i+1,j} + p_d(j)V_{i+1,j-1}) \tag{17.62}$$

  Thus, we obtain

$$V_{i,j} = \max(D_{i,j}, V^C_{i,j})$$

In order to exemplify the trinomial tree approach to valuation of Bermudan securities, we reevaluate the Freddie Mac, Bermudan callable bond discussed in earlier examples.

17.5.2.1 The Pricing of Freddie Mac 2-Year, 0.45% Bermudan Callable Bond on January 28, 2014 Table 17.14 uses the trinomial tree fitted in Table 17.13 to compute the value of the Freddie Mac 2-year, 0.45% Bermudan callable bond. The methodology is very similar to the one illustrated for binomial trees. In Panel A, we report the ex-coupon prices of a straight (i.e., noncallable) bond with the same characteristics as Freddie Mac bond, that is, with coupon rate equal 0.45%, semiannual coupon payments, and 2-year maturity. Each value can be easily computed using a backward calculation

$$P^S_{i,j} = e^{-r_{i,j}h}(p_u(j)P^S_{i+1,j+1} + p_m(j)P^S_{i+1,j} + p_d(j)P^S_{i+1,j-1})$$

with final value $P^S_{M,j} = 100$.

TABLE 17.13 Hull–White Model on a Trinomial Tree on January 28, 2014

Panel A: Data

t	0	0.5	1	1.5	2	2.5
i	0	1	2	3	4	5
$Z^{Data}(t)$		99.9327	99.86	99.6468	99.2244	98.5667
Yields		0.001346	0.001401	0.002359	0.003893	0.005775
$\ln\left(Z^{data}(m)\right)$		−0.00067	−0.0014	−0.00354	−0.00779	−0.01444

Panel B: Recursive Computation of $\alpha(m)$

t	0	0.5	1	1.5	2	2.5
i	0	1	2	3	4	5
$\ln\left(\sum_j Q(j\Delta, mh)e^{-(k\Delta)h}\right)$	0	−0.00066	−0.00137	−0.00347	−0.00767	
$\alpha(m)$	0.001346	0.001473	0.004341	0.008639	0.013543	
$Z^{Model}(t)$	99.9327	99.86	99.6468	99.2244	98.5667	

Panel C: Demeaned Interest Rate Tree r_{ij}^0

5						0.0363
4					0.02904	0.02904
3				0.02178	0.02178	0.02178
2			0.01452	0.01452	0.01452	0.01452
1		0.00726	0.00726	0.00726	0.00726	0.00726
0	0	0	0	0	0	0
−1		−0.00726	−0.00726	−0.00726	−0.00726	−0.00726
−2			−0.01452	−0.01452	−0.01452	−0.01452
−3				−0.02178	−0.02178	−0.02178
−4					−0.02904	−0.02904
−5						−0.0363

Panel D: Fitted Interest Rate Tree r_{ij}

5					
4					0.042583
3				0.030419	0.035323
2			0.018862	0.023159	0.028063
1		0.008733	0.011601	0.015899	0.020803
0	0.001346	0.001473	0.004341	0.008639	0.013543
−1		−0.00579	−0.00292	0.001379	0.006283
−2			−0.01018	−0.00588	−0.00098
−3				−0.01314	−0.00824
−4					−0.0155
−5					

Panel E: Transition Probabilities

	p_u	p_m	p_d
5	0.82169	0.105638	0.072672
4	0.086431	0.626352	0.287217
3	0.102711	0.64399	0.2533
2	0.12151	0.656588	0.221902
1	0.142828	0.664147	0.193025
0	0.166667	0.666667	0.166667
−1	0.193025	0.664147	0.142828
−2	0.221902	0.656588	0.12151
−3	0.2533	0.64399	0.102711
−4	0.287217	0.626352	0.086431
−5	0.072672	0.105638	0.82169

Panel F: Arrow–Debreu Securities

5	0.0000	0.0000	0.0000	0.0000	0.0000	0.0000
4	0.0000	0.0000	0.0000	0.0000	0.0003	0.0009
3	0.0000	0.0000	0.0000	0.0028	0.0073	0.0122
2	0.0000	0.0000	0.0236	0.0465	0.0638	0.0758
1	0.0000	0.1666	0.2207	0.2348	0.2345	0.2290
0	1.0000	0.6662	0.5081	0.4233	0.3719	0.3372
−1	0.0000	0.1666	0.2223	0.2383	0.2397	0.2357
−2	0.0000	0.0000	0.0239	0.0478	0.0666	0.0803
−3	0.0000	0.0000	0.0000	0.0029	0.0078	0.0133
−4	0.0000	0.0000	0.0000	0.0000	0.0003	0.0010
−5	0.0000	0.0000	0.0000	0.0000	0.0000	0.0000

TABLE 17.14 Bermudan Freddie Mac Bond on a Trinomial Hull and White Model

$j \setminus m$	0	1	2	3	4
			Panel A: Straight Bond		
4					100
3				98.71216	100
2			98.32856	99.07114	100
1		98.81873	99.06222	99.43142	100
0	100.1134	99.95364	99.80137	99.79302	100
−1		101.1016	100.546	100.1559	100
−2			101.2963	100.5202	100
−3				100.8857	100
−4					100
			Panel B: Option Value		
4					0
3				0	0
2			0	0	0
1		0.003688	0	0	0
0	0.256184	0.108213	0.025932	0	0
−1		1.101597	0.546029	0.15593	0
−2			1.296251	0.520161	0
−3				0.885717	0
−4					0
			Panel C: Bermudan Bond Price		
4					100
3				98.71216	100
2			98.32856	99.07114	100
1		98.81505	99.06222	99.43142	100
0	99.85721	99.84543	99.77543	99.79302	100
−1		100	100	100	100
−2			100	100	100
−3					100
−4					

Panel B reports the value of the option to call. The payoff from exercising the option in node/time (j, m) is $P^S_{j,m} - 100$. Therefore, the value of the option along the tree is

$$V_{i,j} = \max\{e^{-r_{i,j}h}[p_u(j)V_{i+1,j+1} + p_m(j)V_{i+1,j} + p_d(j)V_{i+1,j-1}], P^S_{i,j} - 100\}$$

Panel C reports the final value of the Bermuda callable bond, given by

$$P^{Call}_{i,j} = P^S_{i,j} - V_{i,j}$$

17.5.3 Calibration to the Volatility Curve

Relative valuation of a callable security can be improved by making use of the information encoded in the implicit volatilities of cap and floors market quotes. Hull and White (1993) show that it is possible to fit a trinomial tree model consistent with volatility curves assuming a short-term interest rate model following:

$$dr_t = (\eta(t) - \phi(t)r_t) + \sigma r_t^\beta dW_t$$

which includes an additional time-dependent mean reversion speed $\phi(t)$ and a constant elasticity diffusion coefficient with elasticity parameter β.

As noted in Hull and White (1993), the trinomial tree construction technique illustrated in the previous section also generalizes to transformations of r, so that, for example, the Black–Karasinski model can be implemented in a similar fashion. In this case, the short rate evolution equation has to be modified to follow:

$$d\ln(r_t) = (\eta(t) - \gamma \ln(r_t)) + \sigma dW_t$$

Readers can refer to Hull and White (1993) for an extended treatment of this approach and to Hull and White (2015) for a novel generalized procedure for building trinomial trees.

REFERENCES

Benninga S, Wiener Z. Term structure of interest rates. Math Educ Res 1998;7(3):13–21.

Black F, Derman E, Toy W. A one-factor model of interest rates and its application to treasury bond options. Financ Anal J 1990;46(1):33–39.

Black F, Karasinski P. Bond and option pricing when short rates are lognormal. Financ Anal J 1991;47(4):52–59.

Brigo D, Mercurio F. *Interest Rate Models - Theory and Practice: With Smile, Inflation and Credit*. 2nd ed. Heidelberg: Springer-Verlag; 2006.

Ho TSY, Lee SB. Term structure movements and pricing interest rate contingent claims. J Finance 1986;41:1011–1029.

Hull J, White A. Pricing interest rate derivative securities. Rev. Financ. Stud. 1990;3(4):573–592.

Hull J, White A. One factor interest-rate models and the valuation of interest-rate derivative securities. J Financ Quant Anal 1993;28(2):235–254.

Hull J, White A. Numerical procedures for implementing term structure models I. J Derivat 1994a;2(1):7–16.

Hull J, White A. Numerical procedures for implementing term structure models II. J Derivat 1994b;2(2):37–48.

Hull J, White A. Using Hull-White interest rate trees. J Derivat 1996;3(3):26–36.

Hull J, White A. A generalized procedure for building trees for the short rate and its application to determining market implied volatility functions. Quant Finance 2015;15(3):443–454.

Nelson DB, Ramaswamy K. Simple binomial processes as diffusion approximations in financial models. Rev Financ Stud 1990;3(3):393–430.

Veronesi P. *Fixed Income Securities: Valuation, Risk, and Risk Management*. Hoboken, NJ: John Wiley and Sons; 2010.

18

Discounting and Derivative Pricing Before and After the Financial Crisis: An Introduction

Pietro Veronesi
Booth School of Business, University of Chicago, Chicago, IL, United States

18.1 INTRODUCTION

The size of the global fixed-income derivative market has been increasing steadily over the past two decades. Panel A of Figure 18.1 shows the increase in notional amount of over-the-counter (OTC) derivatives from June 1998 to June 2013, which moved from about \$50 trillion to over \$560 trillion over the 15-year period.[1] The figure also shows that the lion's share of the OTC fixed-income derivatives is made up by interest rate swaps.

While the 10-fold increase in the OTC market is impressive, we should remember that the global economy also expanded considerably over the same period. Panel B of Figure 18.1 renormalizes the notional amount of OTC derivatives in the previous figure by the world GDP. Even after normalization, the total notional of OTC fixed-income derivatives increased from being about 1.5 times the global GDP in 1998 to 7 times the global GDP at the end of 2012.

While the size of the OTC market appears large, we should remember that "notional value" does not correspond to the actual market value of a derivative. In fact, gross market values – defined as the cost of replacing all outstanding contracts at current market values – are several times smaller. This difference is illustrated in Panels A and B of Figure 18.2, which show the gross market value of OTC derivatives as reported by the Bank for International Settlements, both in U.S. dollars (Panel A) and scaled by global GDP (Panel B). We see that the historical maximum of reported gross market value is about 35% of global GDP in 2008, as opposed to the notional amount which was eight times bigger. Still, the size of the OTC derivatives market is relatively large. For instance, the total market capitalization of the G-20 countries in 2012 was about \$44 trillion,[2] that is, 61% of global GDP. The gross market value of OTC derivatives is thus about half of the G-20 market cap, a large value by any standard.

[1]Data are from the Bank for International Settlements and are available at *www.bis.org*. The biannual survey result of June 2013 is available at http://www.bis.org/publ/otc_hy1311.pdf, accessed on 1/17/2013.
[2]Data from *quandl.com*, accessed on January 20, 2014.

Handbook of Fixed-Income Securities, First Edition. Edited by Pietro Veronesi.

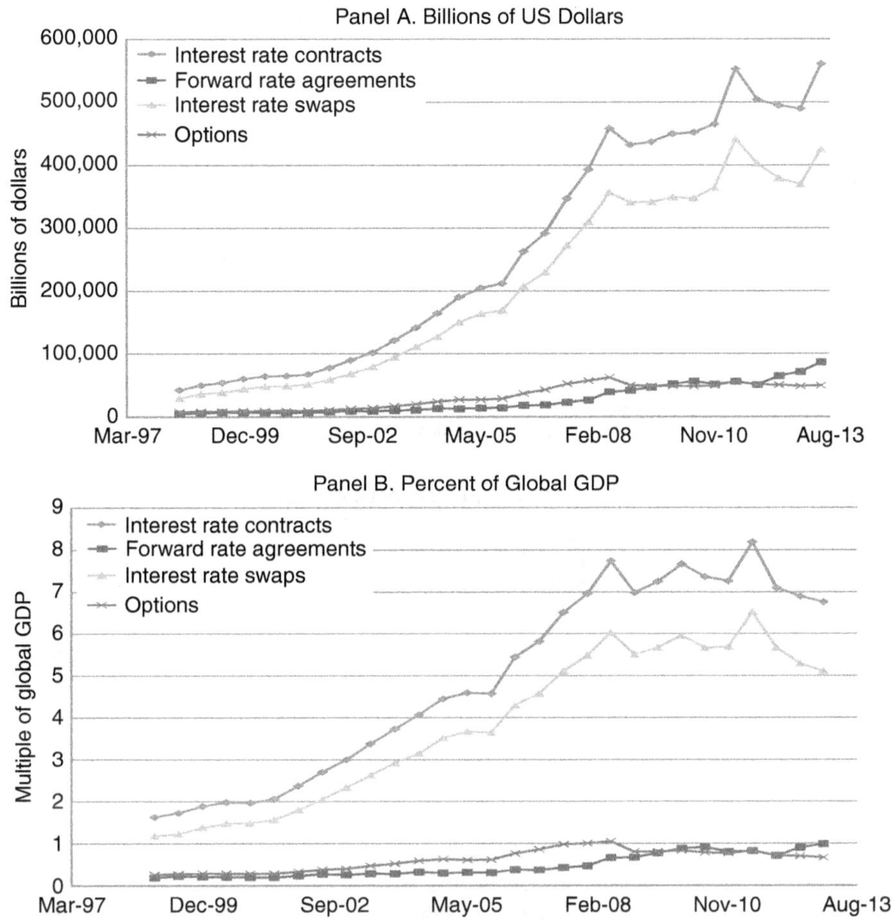

Figure 18.1 The notional amount of over-the-counter derivatives. Panel A shows the notional amount of OTC fixed-income derivatives from June 1998 to June 2013. Panel B reports the notional amount of OTC derivatives rescaled by the world global gross domestic product (GDP) from 1998 to 2012. OTC derivatives data are from the Bank for International Settlements, while global GDP data are from the World Bank.

Besides demonstrating the growth of OTC derivatives in the past 15 years, Figures 18.1 and 18.2 show that interest rate swaps are by far the largest component of the OTC derivatives. Indeed, interest rate swaps are a crucial component of the day-to-day hedging activities of corporations. As most firms, as well as governments, issue debt, they are subject to interest rate risk. Interest rate risk management can be efficiently implemented using plain vanilla interest rate swaps, which do not require any up-front payment – except for collateral – and can dramatically change the sensitivity of total liabilities to interest rates.

Swaps are part of the so-called "linear" derivative contracts, which are contracts whose payoffs depend linearly on a fluctuating interest rate index, such as the London Interbank Offer Rate (LIBOR), the Federal funds rate, the European OverNight Index Average (EONIA) rate, and so on. Forward Rate Agreements (FRAs) are the other "linear" contracts. The next few sections describe the contracts, their pricing, their implications for discounting, and especially the changes that took place after the 2007–2008 crisis hit. The last section contains some implications for "nonlinear" fixed-income contracts, such as LIBOR-based interest rate options.[3]

18.2 FORWARD RATE AGREEMENTS (FRAs)

FRAs are the simplest linear derivative contracts. Before discussing what they are for, let us define them. Consider three dates: today (time t), time T_1, and time T_2. Let $\Delta = T_2 - T_1$, and denote by $\ell(T_1)$ the LIBOR rate at time T_1 with maturity $T_2 = T_1 + \Delta$.[4]

[3]For more discussion on fixed-income derivative instruments, see Brigo and Mercurio (2006), Veronesi (2010), Tuckman and Serrat (2011), and Hull (2014).
[4]When there is no confusion about maturity, we denote the LIBOR rate at t as $\ell(t)$. Sometimes we have to differentiate LIBOR rates of different maturities, in which case we write $\ell(t, T)$ for a LIBOR rate at t with maturity T.

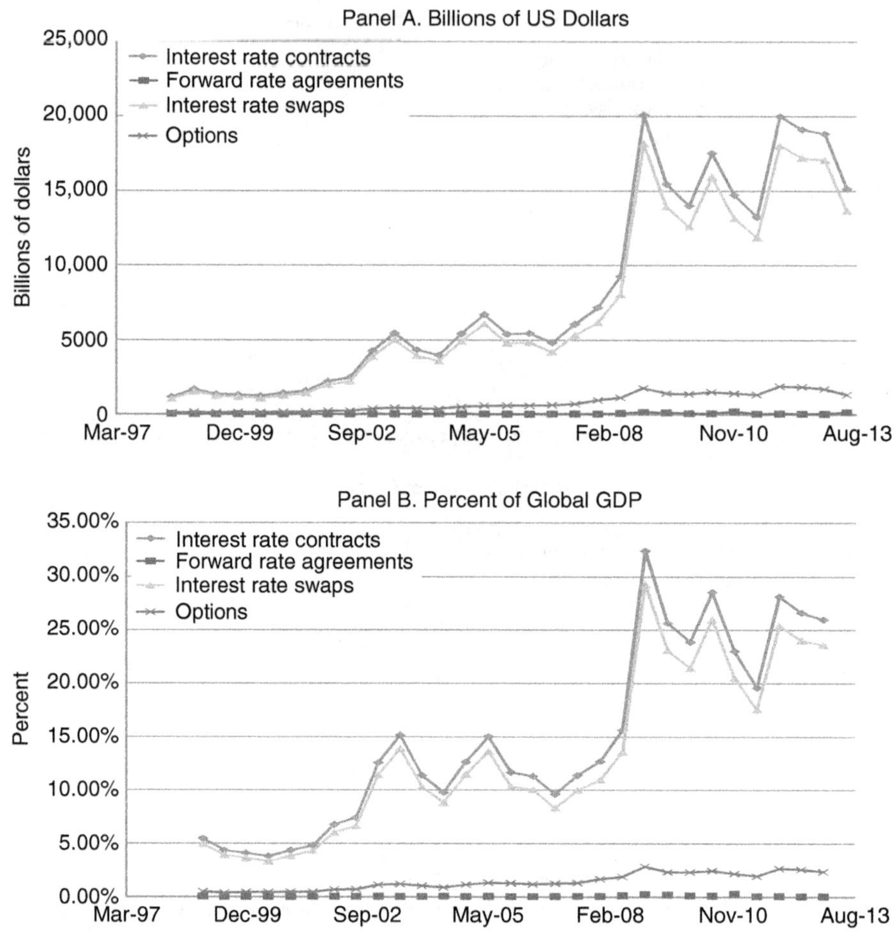

Figure 18.2 The market value of OTC derivatives. Panel A shows the market value of OTC fixed-income derivatives from June 1998 to June 2013. Panel B reports the market value of OTC derivatives rescaled by the world global GDP from 1998 to 2012. OTC derivatives data are from the Bank for International Settlements, while global GDP data are from the World Bank.

In an FRA, two counterparties agree today (time t) to exchange at T_2 the following net cash flow:[5]

$$\text{Net cash flow at } T_2 = N\Delta(\ell(T_1) - f) \tag{18.1}$$

where f is an interest rate decided today (time t), called the "forward rate," and N is called the notional of the FRA contract, which represents the size of the contract.

FRAs can effectively be used to "lock in" future borrowing or lending rates. Consider, for instance, a firm that is expecting a payment of \$$N$ in 6 months, and it desires to lock in a 3-month deposit rate for the period $T_1 = 0.5$ to $T_2 = 0.75$. In this case, the firm can enter into a FRA with $T_1 = 0.5$ and $T_2 = 0.75$ at the current forward rate f. In 6 months from now (T_1), the firm can deposit \$$N$ at the then 3-month LIBOR $\ell(T_1)$. The total payment at time T_2 from the FRA and LIBOR deposit is

$$\begin{aligned}\text{Total CF at } T_2 &= \underbrace{\$N(1 + \ell(T_1)\Delta)}_{\text{LIBOR deposit}} + \underbrace{\$N\Delta(f - \ell(T_1))}_{\text{FRA}} \\ &= \$N(1 + f\Delta)\end{aligned}$$

That is, the firm has "locked in" the FRA rate f.

[5] The market practice is to exchange the present value of 18.1 at T_1, which is equivalent given that at T_1 the LIBOR rate is $\ell(T_1)$ is known.

18.2.1 Forward Rates

How is the forward rate f determined? By no arbitrage. That is, by finding a portfolio of bonds that replicates the cash flow in expression 18.1.[6]

Consider $N = 1$ for simplicity. Let us decompose the cash flow 18.1 in its floating and fixed components as follows:

1. Replication of "$\ell(T_1)\Delta$":
   (a) Go long 1 zero-coupon bond maturing at T_1 and reinvest the principal received at T_1 at the LIBOR rate $\ell(T_1)$
   (b) Go short 1 zero-coupon bond maturing at T_2
   We obtain
$$\text{Total CF at } T_2 = \underbrace{1 + \ell(T_1)\Delta}_{\text{from } (a)} - \underbrace{1}_{\text{from } (b)} = \ell(T_1)\Delta$$
2. Replication of "$-f\Delta$"
   (a) Go short $f\Delta$ bonds maturing at T_2
$$\text{Total CF at } T_2 = -f\Delta$$

Clearly, 1 and 2 generate the exact cash flow from the FRA. Thus, to replicate the FRA cash flow, we need (i) go long 1 zero-coupon bond maturing at T_1 and reinvest the principal at T_1 at the then LIBOR rate $\ell(T_1)$, and (ii) go short $(1 + f\Delta)$ zero-coupon bonds maturing at T_2

What is the value of this portfolio at any time $t < T_1$? Denote $Z^\ell(t, T)$ as the value of a LIBOR-based zero-coupon bond at t with maturity T. Then

$$V_t^{FRA} = Z^\ell(t, T_1) - (1 + f\Delta)Z^\ell(t, T_2) \tag{18.2}$$

The forward rate f at time t is the value that makes $V_t^{FRA} = 0$. Because three dates are involved (today t, time T_1, and T_2), we denote $f(t, T_1, T_2)$ as the forward rate at time t for future borrowing (or lending) at T_1 with delivery at T_2. Thus, solving 18.2 for the forward rate gives

$$f^\ell(t, T_1, T_2) = \frac{1}{\Delta}\left(\frac{Z^\ell(t, T_1)}{Z^\ell(t, T_2)} - 1\right) \tag{18.3}$$

where the superscript ℓ denotes that this is the forward rate implied by the LIBOR-based zero-coupon bonds $Z^\ell(t, T_1)$ and $Z^\ell(t, T_2)$.

18.2.1.1 LIBOR Rates and Forward Rate Agreements on January 2, 2007 On January 2, 2007 ($t = 0$), the 3- and 6-month LIBOR rates were $\ell(0, 0.25) = 5.36\%$ and $\ell(0, 0.5) = 5.37\%$, respectively. Defining $T_1 = 0.25$ and $T_2 = 0.5$, this implies

$$Z^\ell(0, T_1) = \frac{1}{1 + .0536 \times 0.25} = 0.98677$$
$$Z^\ell(0, T_2) = \frac{1}{1 + 0.0537 \times 0.5} = 0.973852$$

Applying formula 18.3 we obtain

$$f^\ell(0, T_1, T_2) = 5.3089\%$$

Indeed, on the same day, the midquoted forward rate for a 3×6 FRA was

$$f^{FRA}(0, T_1, T_2) = 5.302\%,$$

which is quite close to the "theoretical value."

Figure 18.3 plots "theoretical" LIBOR-implied forward rates obtained from Equation 18.3 along with the quoted FRA from dealers from 2005 to mid-2007. As it can be seen, the series are very close to each other, demonstrating that formula 18.3 worked well, at least up to mid-2007.

[6] In this section, we often refer to bonds, even if we are talking about other forms of lending and borrowing. For instance, a deposit of \$$N$ at time T_1 with maturity $T_2 = T_1 + \Delta$ at the interest rate R can be equivalently expressed as buying a "bond" with unit price $Z(T_1, T_2) = \frac{1}{1+R\Delta}$ and principal \$$M$ = \$$N(1 + R\Delta)$. The value of this bond today is \$$N$, and at maturity it delivers the principal \$$M$ = \$$N(1 + R\Delta)$.

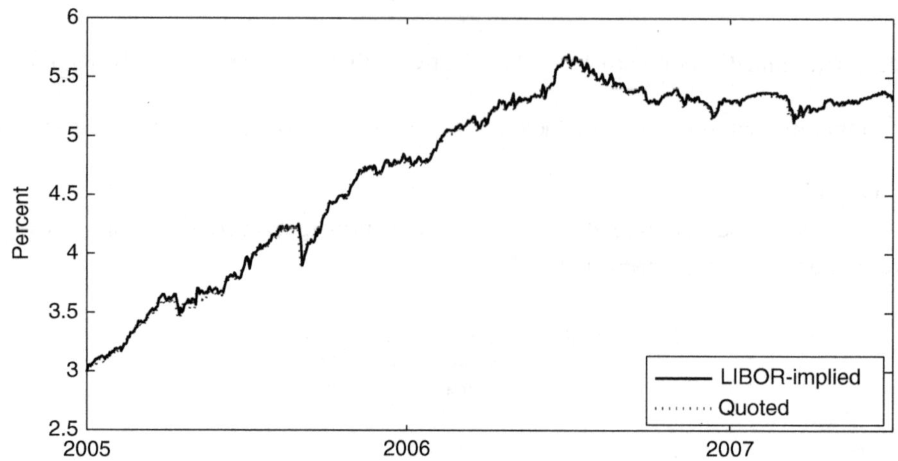

Figure 18.3 Quoted and LIBOR-based 3 × 6 forward rates. The figure shows the quoted and LIBOR-implied forward rate $f(t, T_1, T_2)$ with $T_1 = t+3$ months and $T_2 = T_1+3$ months. The LIBOR-implied forward rate is based on formula 18.3. Source: Data are from Bloomberg Inc.

18.2.2 Forward Rates after the Crisis

To motivate this section, let's do the same calculation as in the example in Section 18.2.1.1 but 2 years later. On January 2, 2009 ($t = 0$), the 3- and 6-month LIBOR rates were $\ell(0, 0.25) = 1.4125\%$ and $\ell(0, 0.5) = 1.7525\%$, respectively. Defining $T_1 = 0.25$ and $T_2 = 0.5$, this implies

$$Z^{\ell}(0, T_1) = \frac{1}{1 + .014125 \times 0.25} = 0.99648$$

$$Z^{\ell}(0, T_2) = \frac{1}{1 + 0.017525 \times 0.5} = 0.99131$$

Applying formula 18.3 we obtain

$$f^{\ell}(0, T_1, T_2) = 2.086\%$$

In contrast, on the same day, the midquoted forward rate for a 3 × 6 FRA was

$$f^{FRA}(0, T_1, T_2) = 1.174\%,$$

which is much lower than the "theoretical value."

This last numerical example is in stark contrast with the example in Section 18.2.1.1, as the theoretical LIBOR-implied forward rate (2.086%) is much higher than the quoted FRA rate (1.174%). Figure 18.4 shows that this was not an isolated episode but rather the norm after the crisis. Indeed, this figure plots again the "theoretical" forward rates obtained from Equation 18.3 from 2006 to mid-2013. As it can be seen, during the crisis the "theoretical forward rate" is much higher than the quoted forward rate. We denote the quoted forward rate in FRA as $f^{FRA}(t, T_1, T_2)$ while we keep the notation $f^{\ell}(t, T_1, T_2)$ for the theoretical forward rate in Equation 18.3. Figure 18.4 shows

$$f^{\ell}(t, T_1, T_2) > f^{FRA}(t, T_1, T_2) \tag{18.4}$$

for $T_1 = t+3$ months and $T_2 = T_1+3$ months. Similar plots can be obtained for other maturities.

What happened? Why are the quoted FRAs different from LIBOR-implied forward rates implied by no arbitrage? The 2007–2008 financial crisis happened and changed the perception of credit risk implicit in LIBOR borrowing/lending and in derivative transactions. In particular, while inequality 18.4 implies an arbitrage opportunity in a world without default or liquidity risk, such an "arbitrage" cannot be exploited when there is counterparty risk (see Mercurio (2009)).

What would be the arbitrage argument? Let $t = 0$. Given Equation 18.4, we want to borrow at T_1 at the quoted rate $f^{FRA}(0, T_1, T_2)$ and lend at the higher $f^{\ell}(0, T_1, T_2)$, which is only implicit in the LIBOR rates. We can do so as follows:

(a) Sell one bond $Z^{\ell}(0, T_1)$.

(b) Buy $M = \frac{Z^{\ell}(0,T_1)}{Z^{\ell}(0,T_2)}$ bonds maturing at T_2.

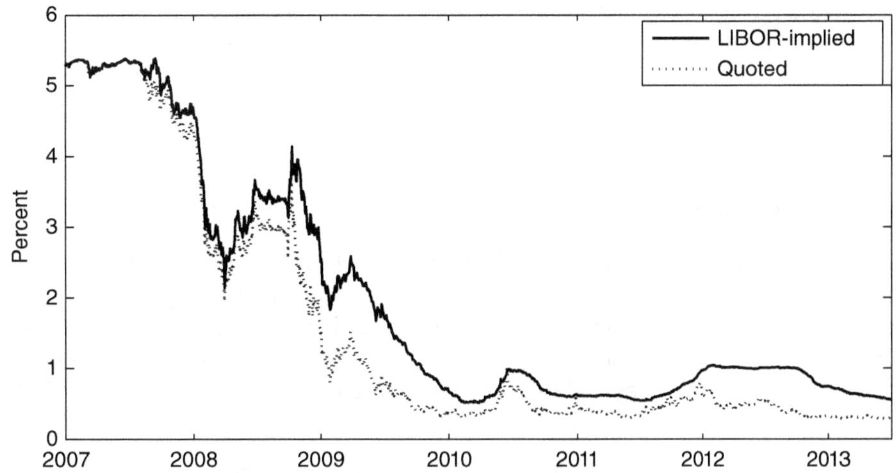

Figure 18.4 Quoted and LIBOR-based 3 × 6 forward rates. The figure shows the quoted and LIBOR-implied forward rate $f^{\ell}(t, T_1, T_2)$ with $T_1 = t$+3 months and $T_2 = T_1$+3 months. The LIBOR-implied forward rate is based on formula 18.3. Source: Data are from Bloomberg Inc.

(c) Enter into the quoted FRA to receive LIBOR and pay the quoted FRA rate, that is, $[\ell(T_1) - f^{FRA}(0, T_1, T_2)]\Delta$ at T_2.

At time $t = 0$ this strategy does not cost anything because the proceeds from (*a*) equal the cost of (*b*):

$$\underbrace{Z^{\ell}(0, T_1)}_{\text{Proceeds from (a)}} = \underbrace{M\, Z^{\ell}(0, T_2)}_{\text{Costs of (b)}}$$

(*d*) At time T_1, the arbitrageur must pay 1 from (*a*), which can be obtained by borrowing at the LIBOR $\ell(T_1)$.
(*e*) At time T_2 we then have the following cash flows:

$$\text{Pay LIBOR from } (d): \quad -[1 + \ell(T_1)\Delta]$$
$$\text{Receive } M \text{ from } (b): \quad M$$
$$\text{Receive net CF from FRA}: [\ell(T_1) - f^{FRA}(0, T_1, T_2)]\Delta$$

The total cash flow at T_2 is then

$$\text{Total cash flow at } T_2 = M - (1 + f^{FRA}(0, T_1, T_2)\Delta)$$

Recall that

$$M = \frac{Z^{\ell}(0, T_1)}{Z^{\ell}(0, T_2)} = 1 + f^{\ell}(0, T_1, T_2)\Delta$$

Therefore

$$\text{Total CF at } T_2 \text{is } [f^{\ell}(0, T_1, T_2) - f^{FRA}(0, T_1, T_2)]\Delta > 0$$

According to the textbook definition of arbitrage, there is an arbitrage opportunity if $f^{\ell}(0, T_1, T_2) > f^{FRA}(0, T_1, T_2)$ as an arbitrageur can make risk-free profits at T_2 without any investment of cash before T_2.

What goes wrong with this argument? Simply that the profit at T_2 is not actually free of risk or uncertainty, as there are risks implicit in the market structure that became in fact apparent during the 2007–2008 financial crisis. In particular:

1. Borrowing and liquidity: At 0 and T_1 the arbitrageur needs to borrow. What if he/she is prevented from doing so because of a liquidity crunch?
2. Counterparty risk 1: At 0 the arbitrageur needs to buy M LIBOR-based bonds (i.e., deposit cash in LIBOR-based deposits) maturing at time T_2. What if the counterparty fails and does not pay M at maturity?
3. Counterparty risk 2: At 0 the arbitrageur needs to enter into a FRA for delivery at T_2 of cash flow $[\ell(T_1) - f^{FRA}]\Delta$. What if the FRA counterparty fails before T_2?

The implication is that even OTC contracts, such as FRAs, require the collateralization of exposure from counterparties. Thus, the cash flow from FRA becomes inherently safer than what is implied from LIBOR rates, which instead imply uncollateralized borrowing. FRA quotes are lower as a different "discount" is applied to the FRA cash flows. The next section illustrates the effect of counterparty risk in a simple setting. For a discussion, see also Mercurio (2009), Ametrano and Bianchetti (2009, 2013), Brigo et al. (2015), and Hull and White (2015).

18.2.3 A Simple Explanation for the "Arbitrage"

As mentioned, the main reason why the LIBOR-implied forward rates differ from quoted FRA rates is that market participants now take into account that borrowing and lending at LIBOR entails some probability of default, while entering into FRA agreements may be "safer" due to collateralization. To see the effect of default in a simple way, consider a modification of the argument in Section 18.2.1 to take into account the possibility of counterparty default (see Mercurio (2009) for a similar example). Consider first the FRA's payoff discounted to time T_1. Because the rate $\ell(T_1)$ is known at T_1, the discounted value of the T_2 payoff is

$$\begin{aligned}\text{Net PV of FRA CF at } T_1 &= \frac{N\Delta[\ell(T_1) - f]}{1 + \ell(T_1)\Delta} \\ &= N - \frac{N(1 + f\Delta)}{1 + \ell(T_1)\Delta}\end{aligned}$$

Using the fact that $Z^\ell(T_1, T_2) = \frac{1}{1+\ell(T_1)\Delta}$, we can then write

$$\text{Net PV of FRA CF at } T_1 = N - N(1 + f\Delta)Z^\ell(T_1, T_2) \tag{18.5}$$

That is, the T_1 payoff of the FRA is notional, minus a LIBOR-based zero-coupon bond with notional $N(1 + f\Delta)$. If LIBOR zero-coupon bonds had no default, then V_t^{FRA} in 18.2 would converge to 18.5 at T_1. However, as mentioned, either or both of the two bonds $Z^\ell(t, T_i)$ may default before maturity.

If the FRA derivative is fully collateralized, we may assume that there is no default in the payoff 18.5. What is the default risk-free value at time t of the payoff 18.5 ? Denote by $Z(t, T)$ the value of a default-free zero-coupon bond at time t with maturity T. Clearly, in general, $Z(t, T) > Z^\ell(t, T)$ because market participants anticipate the probability of default of the LIBOR-based security.

How can we compute the default-free present value of the payoff 18.5 ? The default-free present value of the first term, "N," is just $NZ(t, T)$. The present value of the second term is more complex because its value depends on the LIBOR realization $\ell(T_1)$, which is not known before T_1.

Rather than modeling default explicitly,[7] we introduce here a credit derivative with maturity T_1 and price at t denoted by $C^\ell(t, T_1)$ with the following payoff at T_1:

$$C^\ell(T_1, T_1) = \begin{cases} 0 & \text{if no default before } T_1 \\ \frac{1}{1+\ell(T_1)\Delta} - Z^\ell_{Def}(T_1, T_2) & \text{if default before } T_1 \end{cases} \tag{18.6}$$

where $Z^\ell_{Def}(T_1, T_2)$ is the defaulted value at T_1 of the LIBOR-based bond $Z^\ell(t, T_1)$. That is, in case of default, the credit derivative pays what would have been the value of $Z^\ell(T_1, T_2)$ at T_1 if there was no default minus the recovery value $Z^\ell_{Def}(T_1, T_2)$ of the actually defaulted bond.[8]

Clearly, the portfolio $Z^\ell(t, T_2) + C^\ell(t, T_1)$ is the default-free present value of $Z^\ell(T_1, T_2)$ at time t; as whether the dealer defaults or not, the portfolio will be equal to $\frac{1}{1+\ell(T_1)\Delta}$ at T_1. It follows that the default-free value of the FRA payoff 18.5 at time t is

$$V_t^{FRA} = NZ(t, T_1) - N(1 + f\Delta)[Z^\ell(t, T_2) + C^\ell(t, T_1)] \tag{18.7}$$

Thus, the forward rate without default risk is the value of f that makes $V_0^{FRA} = 0$, that is,

$$f^{FRA}(0, T_1, T_2) = \frac{1}{\Delta}\left(\frac{Z(0, T_1)}{Z^\ell(0, T_2) + C^\ell(0, T_1)} - 1\right) \tag{18.8}$$

[7] See Mercurio (2009) for a similar example in which default is explicitly modeled.
[8] Recall that the LIBOR rate is an average of quotes across dealers. Even if a dealer defaults, the LIBOR rate exists nonetheless.

Note the following:

1. Because the credit derivative $C^{\ell}(t,T_1)$ only covers the credit risk of $Z^{\ell}(t,T_2)$ up to T_1 and not up to T_2, we have in general that
$$Z^{\ell}(t,T_2)+C^{\ell}(t,T_1)<Z(t,T_2)$$
The difference between left-hand side and right-hand side depends on the market assessment of the default risk the LIBOR loan between T_1 and T_2. Denote by $Q(t,T_1,T_2)$ the ratio
$$Q(t,T_1,T_2)=\frac{Z^{\ell}(t,T_2)+C^{\ell}(t,T_1)}{Z(t,T_2)}<1$$
The variable $Q(t,T_1,T_2)$ is closer to 1 when the assessment of default between T_1 and T_2 is small.
2. The forward rate $f^{FRA}(0,T_1,T_2)$ in 18.8 is less than the LIBOR-based FRA rate $f(0,T_1,T_2)$ in 18.3,
$$f^{\ell}(0,T_1,T_2)>f^{FRA}(0,T_1,T_2)$$
if and only if
$$\frac{Z^{\ell}(0,T_1)}{Z^{\ell}(0,T_2)}>\frac{Z(0,T_1)}{Z^{\ell}(0,T_2)+C^{\ell}(0,T_1)} \tag{18.9}$$
Denoting
$$sp(0,T_i)=y^{\ell}(0,T_i)-r(0,T_i) \tag{18.10}$$
the continuously compounded *credit spread* between the yield to maturity $y^{\ell}(0,T_i)$ of the LIBOR-bond $Z^{\ell}(0,T_0)=e^{-y^{\ell}(0,T_i)T_i}$ and the yield to maturity $r(0,T_i)$ of the risk-free bond $Z(0,T)=e^{-r(0,T_i)T_i}$, condition 18.9 translates into the following:[9]
$$\left(e^{sp(0,T_2)T_2-sp(0,T_1)T_1}\right)Q(0,T_1,T_2)>1 \tag{18.11}$$
The first term is larger than 1 if and only if
$$Slope(0,T_1)=\frac{sp(0,T_1+\Delta)-sp(0,T_1)}{\Delta}>-\frac{sp(0,T_1)}{T_2} \tag{18.12}$$
that is, if and only if the *slope* of the credit spread curve is not too negative. As mentioned, the second term in 18.11, $Q(0,T_1,T_2)$, is close to one whenever the expected default between T_1 and T_2 is not too high.

To summarize, it is likely to observe a quoted FRA $f^{FRA}(t,T_1,T_2)$ lower than the forward rate implied by LIBOR rates $f^{\ell}(t,T_1,T_2)$ whenever the credit spread curve is nondecreasing (too much) and the market assessment of a default between T_1 and T_2 is relatively small.

To illustrate the impact of credit spreads in condition 18.11 on the size of the "arbitrage" $f^{\ell}(t,T_1,T_2)-f^{FRA}(t,T_1,T_2)$, Figure 18.5 plots the credit spread 18.10 for T_1 =3 months (solid black line) and T_2 =6 months (dashed-dot gray line). More specifically, the plot uses the difference in (continuously compounded) yields of the LIBOR rate and the Overnight Index Swap (OIS) rate, which the market considers a risk-free rate. As explained in the next section, the OIS rate can be interpreted as the expected overnight Federal funds rate over the life of the swap maturity. The LIBOR–OIS spread is considered by market participants as an index of the credit worthiness of the banking sector. The LIBOR–OIS spread tends to be especially affected by potential funding liquidity problems in the banking sector. As it can be seen, the figure shows that before the 2007–2008 crisis hit, the LIBOR–OIS spreads were mostly close to zero. Instead, with the unfolding of the credit crisis, the LIBOR–OIS spread increased dramatically, with the 6-month LIBOR–OIS spread mostly higher than the 3-month spread. That is, the "slope" of the credit spread curve has been mostly positive.

[9]To see this, rewrite 18.9 as
$$\left(\frac{Z^{\ell}(0,T_1)}{Z(0,T_1)}\right)\left(\frac{Z(0,T_2)}{Z^{\ell}(0,T_2)}\right)\left(\frac{Z^{\ell}(t,T_2)+C^{\ell}(t,T_1)}{Z(t,T_2)}\right)>1$$
substitute the zero-coupon bond prices for their respective expressions with yields, and reorganize the expression.

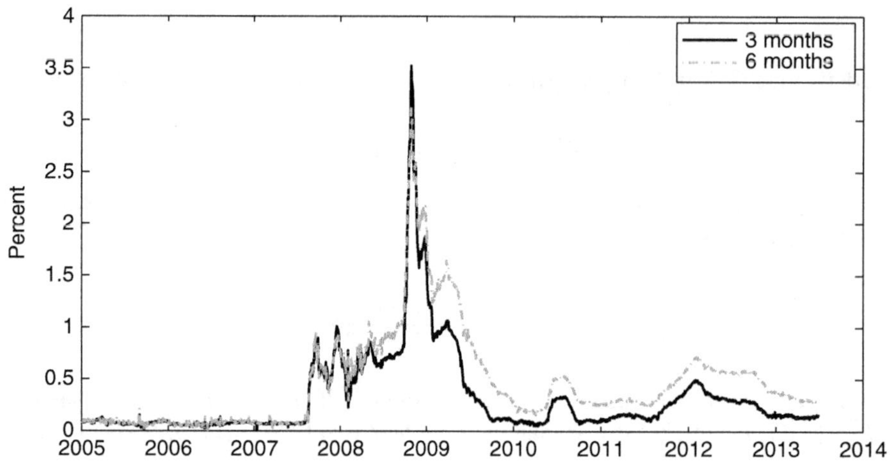

Figure 18.5 LIBOR–OIS credit spreads. The figure shows the credit spreads between LIBOR and OIS rate with maturities of 3 and 6 months. Source: Data are from Bloomberg Inc.

To show that indeed the slope of the credit spread plays an important role to explain the difference in $f^{\ell}(t, T_1, T_2)$ and $f^{FRA}(t, T_1, T_2)$, Figure 18.6 documents the time pattern of the FRA rates difference $f^{\ell}(t, T_1, T_2) - f^{FRA}(t, T_1, T_2)$ and the credit spread slope on the left-hand side of inequality 18.12. Both quantities were constant up to mid-2007, and then increased sharply. Indeed, except for a short episode in late 2008, when the credit spread slope was negative and the difference in LIBOR-implied and quoted FRA was positive, the time pattern of the slope and the FRA rate difference is remarkably similar. The correlation between the two series is over 75% over the full sample.[10]

18.3 OVERNIGHT INDEX SWAPS (OISs)

In an OIS, the two counterparties agree to exchange fixed-for-floating payments, where the floating payment is tied to the cumulative return from an overnight rate, such as the Federal funds effective rate in United States or the EONIA rate in Europe. More specifically, given a notional N, the floating rate payment at time T_i is given by the cumulative interest rate earned on N during $[T_{i-1}, T_i]$

$$CF(T_i) = N\left(\prod_{j=1}^{n_j}\left(1 + r_{t_j}\delta\right) - 1\right) \tag{18.13}$$

where δ is the daily interval; r_t is the reference (annualized) overnight rate, such as the Federal funds rate; and n_j is the number of days between reset periods. The day count convention is normally Actual/360. In the continuous time limit ($\delta \to 0$), we have that

$$CF(T_i) = N\left(e^{\int_{T_{i-1}}^{T_i} r(u)du} - 1\right) \tag{18.14}$$

OISs with maturity less than 1 year have only one payment at maturity. OISs with longer maturities have normally quarterly payments.

What is the value of an OIS at any time t? As in any swap, the value of an OIS is the difference between the value of the floating leg minus the value of the fixed leg:

$$V_t^{OIS} = V_t^{Floating} - V_t^{Fixed} \tag{18.15}$$

Let us start with the floating leg, $V_t^{Floating}$. At reset dates, and assuming the payment of the principal at maturity of the swap, the value of the floating leg is par. To see this, note that the simple strategy of investing the notional N in the overnight index daily gives at T_i:

$$N\prod_{j=1}^{n_j}(1 + r_{t_j}\Delta) = CF(T_i) + N$$

[10] A regression of the FRA difference on the slope generates a $R^2 = 56\%$ and a strongly significant regression coefficient. In first differences, a regression of changes of FRA difference on changes of credit spread slope gives a $R^2 = 20\%$ and also a strongly significant regression coefficient.

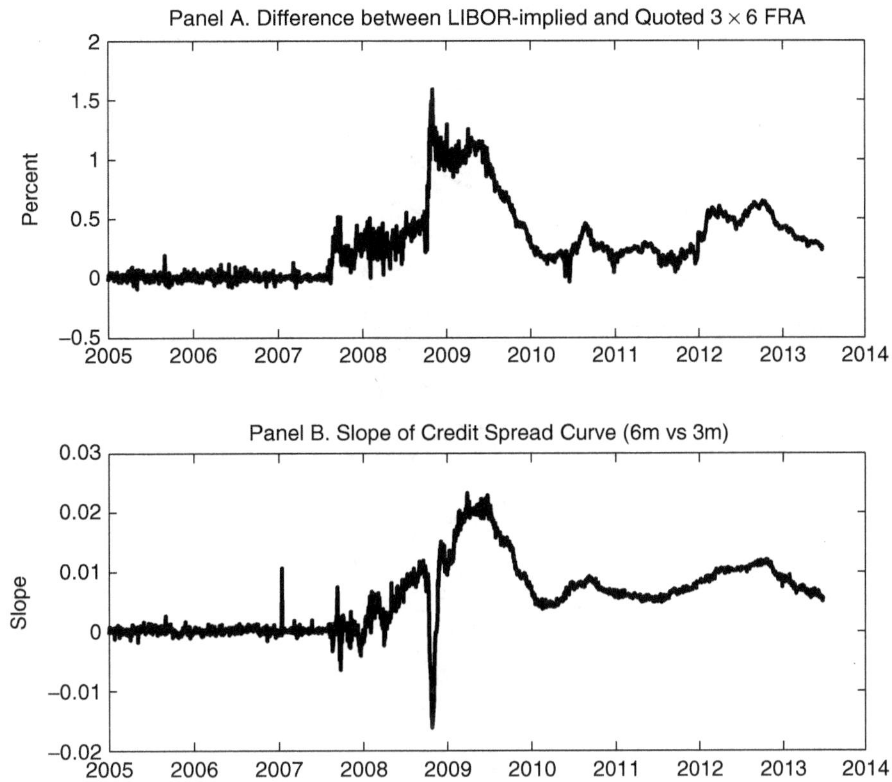

Figure 18.6 The difference between implied and quoted FRA and the slope of credit spread curve. Panel A plots the difference between LIBOR-implied and quoted 3 × 6 FRA rates. Panel B plots the slope of the OIS–LIBOR credit spread curve between 3 and 6 months. Source: Data are from Bloomberg Inc.

Therefore, we can replicate the floating payments, plus a residual of notional at maturity T_i, with an investment N at time 0. It follows

$$V_0^{Floating} = N$$

The value of the fixed leg is the value of a bond with the proper discount function $Z^{OIS}(0, T_i)$, where the superscript "OIS" indicates that this is the discount bond proper for this instrument, which may differ, say, from other derivatives such as LIBOR discounts. Given the zero-coupon curve $Z^{OIS}(0, T_i)$, we obtain

$$V_0^{Fixed} = N\, c\, \Delta \sum_{i=1}^{n} Z^{OIS}(0, T_i) + N\, Z^{OIS}(0, T_n) \tag{18.16}$$

As in any swap, the value of the contract at inception is zero, $V_0^{OIS} = 0$. It follows from 18.15 then that

$$V_0^{OIS} = V_0^{Floating} - V_0^{Fixed} = 0 \tag{18.17}$$

This equation implies that given the zero-coupon curve $Z^{OIS}(0, T_i)$, the swap rate c can be computed from

$$1 = c\, \Delta \sum_{i=1}^{n} Z^{OIS}(0, T_i) + Z^{OIS}(0, T_n) \tag{18.18}$$

which gives

$$c(T_n) = \frac{1}{\Delta} \frac{1 - Z^{OIS}(0, T_n)}{\sum_{i=1}^{n} Z^{OIS}(0, T_i)} \tag{18.19}$$

where we now emphasize that the coupon rate c is for a swap with maturity T_n and thus write $c(T_n)$.

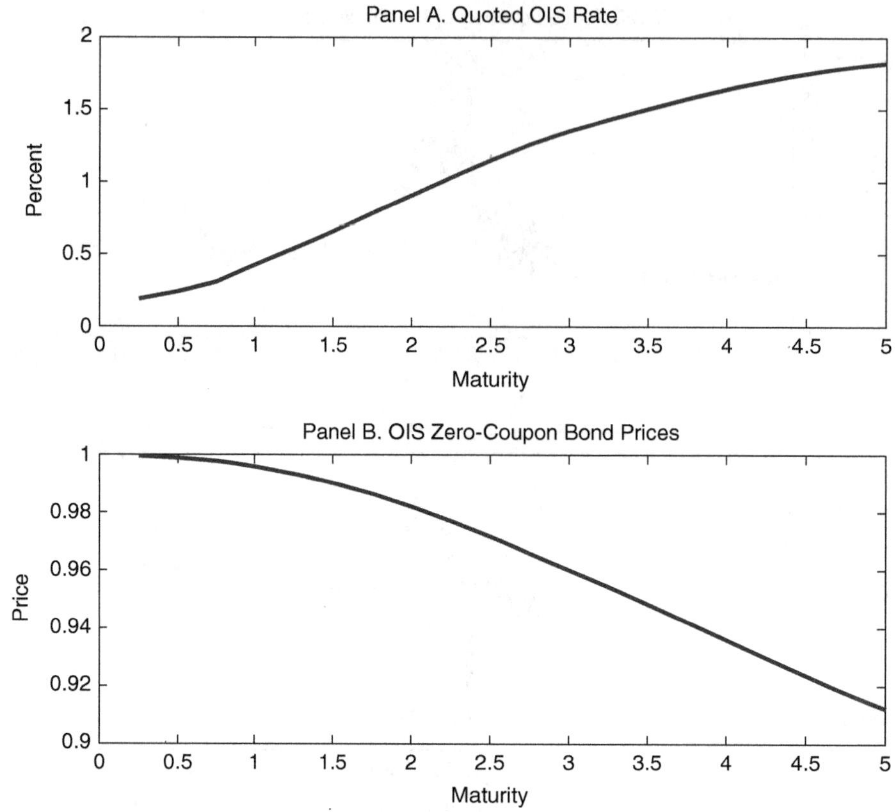

Figure 18.7 OIS discount curve on January 2, 2009. Panel A shows the OIS quotes on January 2, 2009. Panel B plots the implied zero-coupon curve $Z^{OIS}(0, T)$ from Equation 18.20. Source: Data are from Bloomberg Inc.

18.3.1 OIS Discount Curve

Given the OIS quotes $c(T_i)$ for every maturity T_i the OIS zero-coupon curve can be bootstrapped out from the same relation 18.17. That is, rather than solving for $c(T_n)$ given $Z^{OIS}(0, T_i)$ we can do the opposite and extract $Z^{OIS}(0, T_i)$ from the OIS quotes $c(T_n)$. In particular, we obtain the relation:

$$Z^{OIS}(0, T_i) = \frac{1 - c(T_i)\ \Delta\ \sum_{j=1}^{i-1} Z^{OIS}(0, T_j)}{1 + c(T_i)\Delta} \tag{18.20}$$

recalling, however, that OIS with maturity less than or equal to 1 year generally have only one payment. Figure 18.7 shows an example of bootstrapping from OIS quotes, on January 2, 2009. Panel A reports the original OIS quotes from Bloomberg. Panel B uses the quotes from Panel A along with bootstrap methodology 18.20 and defines the OIS discount function $Z^{OIS}(0, T)$.

18.4 LIBOR-BASED SWAPS

A LIBOR-based fixed-for-floating swap is an agreement between two counterparties to exchange net payments:[11]

$$\text{Swap CF at } T_i = N\Delta[\ell(T_{i-1}) - c] \tag{18.21}$$

for the periods $T_1, T_2, \ldots, T_n$ with $T_i = T_{i-1} + \Delta$, where c is called the swap rate. Such a contract is an extension of FRA to multiple dates, and it is typically used to manage interest rate risk or for debt management.

[11]Standard, plain vanilla swaps have floating payments at the quarterly frequency and fixed payments at the semiannual frequency. For simplicity, we consider here common payment times. In addition, we abstract from day count conventions and "counting days" issues. For instance, 3 months is $\Delta = 0.25$ and 6 months is $\Delta = 0.5$.

Consider, for instance, a corporation with a large amount of floating rate debt outstanding tied to LIBOR (e.g., LIBOR plus a spread). Suppose that the firm is worried about a hike in interest rates, which would generate large cash outflows. A simple way to "convert to fixed" its debt is simply to enter into a fixed-for-floating interest rate swap, in which the corporation receives floating (i.e., LIBOR) and pays fixed rate. In this case, the net payment of the corporation is

$$\begin{aligned}\text{Total payment} &= \underbrace{(\text{LIBOR} + \text{spread})}_{\text{Floating rate bond}} + \underbrace{(\text{swap rate} - \text{LIBOR})}_{\text{Swap}} \\ &= \text{swap rate} + \text{spread}\end{aligned}$$

which is fixed.

The swap rate c can then be obtained directly from the FRA quotes. Indeed, consider the net cash flow in 18.21. The random variation of LIBOR $\ell(T_i)$ can be hedged using an FRA with the payoff

$$\text{FRA CF at } T_i = N\Delta[f(0, T_{i-1}, T_i) - \ell(T_{i-1})] \tag{18.22}$$

Putting these two cash flows together, we obtain

$$\begin{aligned}\text{Swap CF} + \text{FRA CF at } T_i &= N\Delta[\ell(T_{i-1}) - c] + N\Delta[f(t, T_{i-1}, T_i) - \ell(T_{i-1})] \\ &= N\Delta[f(t, T_{i-1}, T_i) - c]\end{aligned}$$

This net cash flow at T_i is deterministic and known at time t. Therefore, the value at time t of the swap plus FRA is the discounted value of this future cash flow for an appropriate discount factor $Z(0, T_i)$

$$\text{PV of swap} + \text{FRA CF at } T_i = Z(0, T_i)N\Delta[f(0, T_{i-1}, T_i) - c] \tag{18.23}$$

Because at time $t = 0$ the value of the FRA is also zero, the expression in 18.23 is also the present value of the swap cash flow itself. Therefore, the value today of the swap is just given by the summation

$$V_0^{SWAP} = \sum_{i=1}^{n} Z(0, T_i)N\Delta[f(0, T_{i-1}, T_i) - c] \tag{18.24}$$

The value of a swap at inception of the contract is zero. Thus, from the condition

$$V_0^{SWAP} = 0 \tag{18.25}$$

we obtain

$$\sum_{i=1}^{n} Z(0, T_i)\, f(0, T_{i-1}, T_i) = c \sum_{i=1}^{n} Z(0, T_i) \tag{18.26}$$

This formula also provides another way to compute the swap rate from the quotes of FRA

$$c = \frac{\sum_{i=1}^{n} Z(0, T_i)\, f(0, T_{i-1}, T_i)}{\sum_{i=1}^{n} Z(0, T_i)} \tag{18.27}$$

Equivalently, we can reexpress this as a weighted average of forward rates

$$c(T_n) = \sum_{i=1}^{n} w_i f(0, T_{i-1}, T_i) \tag{18.28}$$

where we now also emphasize that the swap rate c is for a swap with maturity T_n, that is, $c(T_n)$. In this formula, the weights are

$$w_i = \frac{Z(0, T_i)}{\sum_{j=1}^{n} Z(0, T_j)} \tag{18.29}$$

The swap rate is a weighted average of forward rates, where the weights are given by the relative discount of each fixed payment over the total discounts. That is, forward rates of shorter maturities have a larger weight.

18.4.1 LIBOR Discount Curve with Single-Curve Pricing

In the previous section, we obtain the swap rate $c(T_n)$ from primitive discounts $Z(0, T_i)$ and forward rates $f(0, T_{i-1}, T_i)$, without specifying where they are coming from. In reality, the swap market grew so much over the years that we can think of swap rates $c(T_n)$ as being determined by standard supply and demand effects. That is, if a large number of corporations desire to enter into swaps and pay fixed, then the fixed rate $c(T_n)$ increases to clear the market (if there are more counterparties who desire to pay fixed than counterparties willing to take the risk of paying floating rate, the fixed rate needs to increase to induce some counterparty to accept to be a counterparty). That is, we can think of $c(T_n)$ as being determined from the interplay of corporation desires for debt management and speculators desires to take risk by being on the other side of the trades.

The question then becomes which discounts $Z(0, T_i)$ and forward rates $f(0, T_{i-1}, T_i)$ should we use in formula 18.28. So far, we have seen LIBOR discounts $Z^{\ell}(0, T_i)$ and OIS discounts $Z^{OIS}(0, T_i)$, and there could be many more. Similarly, we have seen LIBOR-implied forward rates $f^{\ell}(0, T_{i-1}, T_i)$ and FRA quotes $f^{FRA}(0, T_{i-1}, T_i)$. Like for FRA, there have been important changes in the swap market around the crisis, and the type of discounts and forward rates that market participants use in the formula 18.28 also changed.

Before the crisis, given the swap rates $c(T_n)$ for many maturities, it was customary to use LIBOR discounts $Z^{\ell}(0, T_i)$ and LIBOR-based forwards $f^{\ell}(0, T_{i-1}, T_i)$. This is called "single-curve pricing" as the discount function used to discount the payoff is the same as that used to determine the future cash flows. Under this assumption, we note that we can rewrite

$$c(T_n) = \sum_{i=1}^{n} w_i^{\ell} f^{\ell}(0, T_{i-1}, T_i) \quad \text{with} \quad w_i^{\ell} = \frac{Z^{\ell}(0, T_i)}{\sum_{j=1}^{n} Z^{\ell}(0, T_j)} \tag{18.30}$$

Substituting $f^{\ell}(0, T_{i-1}, T_i)$ from 18.3, we obtain the alternate, but equivalent, expression

$$c(T_n) = \frac{1}{\Delta} \frac{1 - Z^{\ell}(0, T_n)}{\sum_{j=1}^{n} Z^{\ell}(0, T_j)} \tag{18.31}$$

Because we can think of the swap rates $c(T_n)$ as being determined by market forces, we can actually compute the implicit zero-coupon curve $Z^{\ell}(0, T_i)$ by inverting 18.31.

More specifically, for maturities up to the maturity of LIBOR rates, we can consider the LIBOR curve as determined by

$$Z^{\ell}(0, T_i) = \frac{1}{1 + \ell(0, T_i)\, T_i}$$

where $\ell(0, T_i)$ is the LIBOR rate today (time 0) with maturity T_i. Such LIBOR fixes are available up to 1 year to maturity. For maturities larger than 1 year, traders use Eurodollar futures and swaps, as well as other LIBOR-based instruments.

Before the crisis, the LIBOR curve for longer maturities used to be computed using swap rates. In particular, inverting Equation 18.31 one can obtain the bootstrap algorithm

$$Z^{\ell}(0, T_n) = \frac{1 - c(T_n)\, \Delta \left(\sum_{j=1}^{n-1} Z^{\ell}(0, T_j) \right)}{1 + c(T_n)\Delta} \tag{18.32}$$

To illustrate, Figure 18.8 shows the LIBOR curve and OIS curve on January 2, 2007, where LIBOR curve uses LIBOR rates up to 1 year, and then swap rates. The two zero-coupon discounts (in Panel A) are very close to each other, and so are the implied continuously compounded yields in Panel B. That is, before the crisis, discounting from OIS curve or LIBOR curve would have had very little impact on valuation. Moreover, swap quotes were available up to 30 years to maturity, while OIS quotes only up to 5 years to maturity. Thus, the LIBOR curve was easier to implement using only LIBOR-based swaps.

18.5 THE CRISIS AND THE DOUBLE-CURVE PRICING OF LIBOR-BASED SWAPS

After the crisis, however, things changed quite dramatically. Indeed, if we blindly use the same formula 18.32 for the LIBOR curve 2 years later, on January 2, 2009, we obtain Figure 18.9. Clearly, the two curves are not close to each other, with the LIBOR curve substantially higher than the OIS curve, especially at the short horizon. The hump-shape difference between the LIBOR curve and the OIS curve points at something potentially "wrong" in the data. The source of the "hump" is that LIBOR rates are used up to 1 year, and the LIBOR-based swap rates are used for maturities longer than 1 year. Judging from the shape of the LIBOR curve – and also from the LIBOR discount curve in Panel A – it seems that there is a change in type of data as we

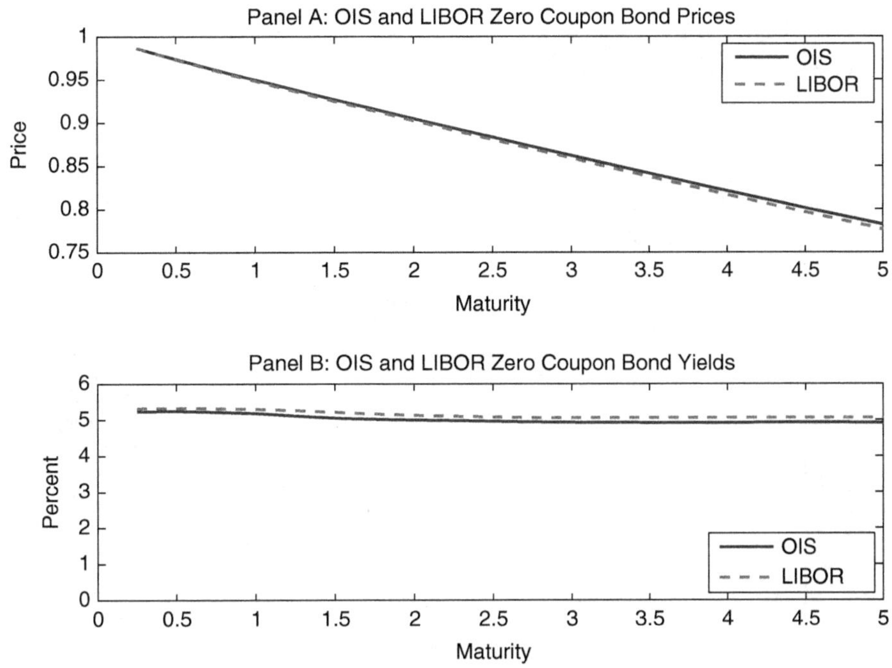

Figure 18.8 OIS and LIBOR discount curve on January 2, 2007. Panel A shows the implied zero-coupon discounts $Z^{OIS}(0,T)$ and $Z^{\ell}(0,T)$ from Equations 18.20 and 18.32, respectively. Panel B plots the continuously compounded rates from OIS and LIBOR discount curves. Source: Data are from Bloomberg Inc.

move from LIBOR rates and swap rates to back out $Z^{\ell}(0,T)$. Indeed, like FRA quotes discussed earlier, now swap rates are also affected by the perception of lower default risk compared to outright LIBOR borrowing. Like for FRAs, there is a difference between "LIBOR-implied" swap rates and actual swap rates.

The decoupling of the two curves is because of the increase in the perceived credit risk of security dealers – which affects LIBOR-based discounting – and the consequent increase in collateralization required for OTC derivative instruments (such as FRA or swaps). The pricing of derivative instruments now have to take into account the new costs and benefits that are implicit in the additional collateral and credit risk.

What is the swap pricing methodology in the aftermath of the crisis? As mentioned, in the after-crisis period, we witnessed a change in the collateralization required to discount derivatives payoffs. Consider again the LIBOR-based swap discussed in the previous section, which was hedged through a sequence of FRA. Because each FRA is zero at initiation, we obtained that the value of the swap had to satisfy 18.24, reported here again:

$$V_0^{SWAP} = \sum_{i=1}^{n} Z(0,T_i)N\Delta[f(0,T_{i-1},T_i) - c] \tag{18.33}$$

While this formula is general, the question again is what forward rates and discounts to use. As we saw in Section 18.2.1, quoted FRA rates are different from LIBOR-based forward rates after the crisis. Because we would be hedging the swap cash flows using a traded (and hence quoted) FRA, after the crisis we have $f^{FRA}(0,T_{i-1},T_i)$ that are used in formula 18.33. Similarly, because of the low default risk due to higher collateralization, it is customary to now discount the swap cash flows using the OIS discounts illustrated in Section 18.3.1.

We therefore obtain

$$V_0^{SWAP} = \sum_{i=1}^{n} Z^{OIS}(0,T_i)N\Delta\left[f^{FRA}(t,T_{i-1},T_i) - c\right] \tag{18.34}$$

The value of an FRA is zero. The swap rate c is the one that makes the swap also equal to zero. Thus, we obtain the condition

$$V_0^{SWAP} = 0$$

which leads to the swap rate formula

$$c(T_n) = \sum_{i=1}^{n} w_i^{OIS} f^{FRA}(0,T_{i-1},T_i) \tag{18.35}$$

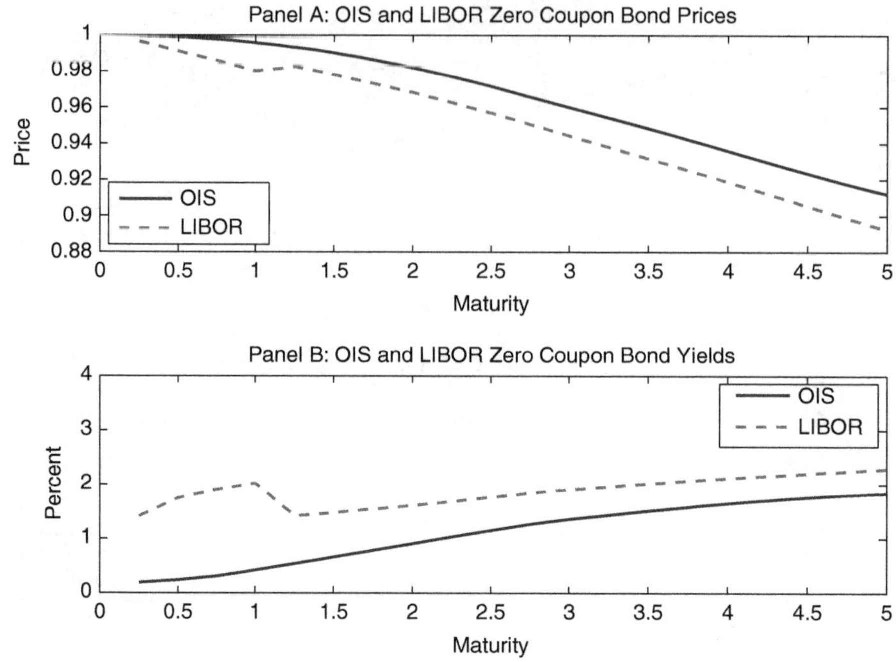

Figure 18.9 OIS and LIBOR discount curve on January 2, 2009. Panel A shows the implied zero-coupon discounts $Z^{OIS}(0,T)$ and $Z^{\ell}(0,T)$ from Equations 18.20 and 18.32, respectively. Panel B plots the continuously compounded rates from OIS and LIBOR discount curves. Source: Data are from Bloomberg Inc.

where now

$$w_i^{OIS} = \frac{Z^{OIS}(0,T_i)}{\sum_{j=1}^{n} Z^{OIS}(0,T_j)}$$

To reiterate, note two crucial differences between formula 18.35 developed in this section and formula 18.28 developed in Section 18.4:

1. The weights w_i use the OIS zero-coupon bond $Z^{OIS}(0,T_i)$ instead of the LIBOR-based (and risky) $Z^{\ell}(0,T_i)$.
2. The forward rates are given by market-based FRAs $f^{FRA}(0,T_{i-1},T_i)$ and not the LIBOR-based forward rates $f^{\ell}(0,T_{i-1},T_i)$. As shown in Section 18.2.2, after the crisis LIBOR-based forward rates are much higher than the market FRA rates.

18.5.1 Extracting FRA Rates from Swap Quotes

Given that in Equation 18.35 the risk-free discount $Z(0,T)$ is already given by the OIS discount, we can use the quoted swap rates to extract the market-implied forward rates $f^{FRA}(0,T_{i-1},T_i)$ for maturities for which FRA contracts are not observable. In particular, developing 18.35 we obtain

$$c(T_n) = \frac{\sum_{i=1}^{n} Z^{OIS}(0,T_i) f^{FRA}(0,T_{i-1},T_i)}{\sum_{j=1}^{n} Z^{OIS}(0,T_j)} \tag{18.36}$$

Therefore, multiplying both sides by $\sum_{j=1}^{n} Z^{OIS}(0,T_j)$ and isolating $f^{FRA}(0,T_{n-1},T_n)$ in the sum on the right, we obtain the recursive formula

$$f^{FRA}(0,T_{n-1},T_n) = c(T_n) + \frac{\sum_{i=1}^{n-1} Z^{OIS}(0,T_i)[c(T_n) - f^{FRA}(0,T_{i-1},T_i)]}{Z^{OIS}(0,T_n)} \tag{18.37}$$

For instance, the solid line in Figure 18.10 shows the FRA extracted from swap rates on January 2, 2009.

18.5.2 Extracting the Discount Curve from FRA Rates

Finally, we can use the FRA rates $f^{FRA}(0,T_{n-1},T_n)$ to compute a proper discount curve that "justifies them" from no-arbitrage principles. This can be accomplished by reversing formula 18.3. I will denote the discount curve $Z^{FRA}(0,T_i)$, as it is extracted

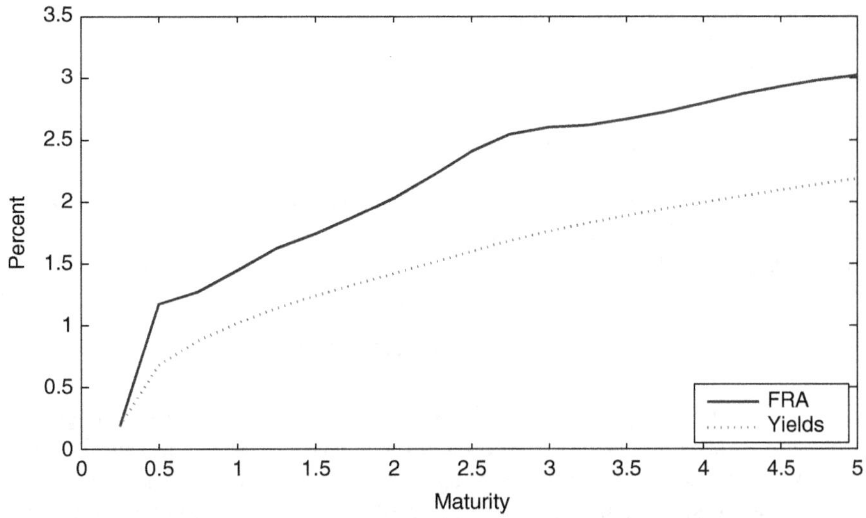

Figure 18.10 FRA rates and yields from swap quotes on January 2, 2009. The figure shows the FRA rates and the corresponding yields extracted from OIS-discounted LIBOR-based swap quotes. Data are from Bloomberg Inc.

by FRA rates $f^{FRA}(0, T_{n-1}, T_n)$. More explicitly, because for every T_{i-1} and T_i we must have

$$f^{FRA}(t, T_{i-1}, T_i) = \frac{1}{\Delta}\left(\frac{Z^{FRA}(0, T_{i-1})}{Z^{FRA}(0, T_i)} - 1\right) \tag{18.38}$$

We can solve this equation for $Z^{FRA}(0, T_i)$ and obtain the recursive formula

$$Z^{FRA}(0, T_i) = \frac{Z^{FRA}(0, T_{i-1})}{1 + f^{FRA}(t, T_{i-1}, T_i)\Delta} \tag{18.39}$$

Given a zero-coupon curve, we can extract the corresponding yield by using the usual formula

$$y^{FRA}(0, T_i) = \frac{1}{\Delta}\left(\frac{1}{Z^{FRA}(0, T_i)^{\Delta/T_i}} - 1\right)$$

For illustration, the dotted line in Figure 18.10 is the quarterly compounded yield from the FRA rates (solid line) on January 2, 2009.

18.5.3 Summing Up

The 2008–2009 financial crisis profoundly, and likely permanently, changed the way market participant discount the cash flows of derivative instruments. In a nutshell, before the crisis, discount rates were computed through the following sequence:

1. LIBOR curve extracted from LIBOR rates and LIBOR-based swaps (formula 18.32)[12]
   ↪ 2. FRA rates extracted from LIBOR curve (formula 18.3)
      ↪ 3. OIS curve not really used for derivative pricing (formula 18.20)

In contrast, after the crisis, the order of these computations has essentially been inverted:

1. OIS curve used to extract a "risk-free" discount curve (formula 18.20)
   ↪ 2. FRA rates obtained from OIS curve and LIBOR-based swap quotes (formula 18.37)
      ↪ 3. LIBOR curve extracted from FRA rates (formula 18.39)

[12]As mentioned, market participants also used Eurodollar futures.

Note that in both cases, before and after crisis, we have:

(a) A correspondence between FRA rates and LIBOR curve and the fact that they are related by the standard formula 18.3 or 18.38.
(b) The LIBOR curve is extracted from LIBOR-based swap rates.

The difference between before and after the crisis is just that after the crisis the discounting applied to LIBOR-based derivatives is different from the one implied by the LIBOR rates themselves due to the fact that collateralization reduces the risk of derivative transactions compared to uncollateralized borrowing/lending.

18.6 THE PRICING OF LIBOR-BASED INTEREST RATE OPTIONS

In the aftermath of the crisis, the pricing formulas for LIBOR-based interest rate options also changed. Like for linear securities, after the crisis two different curves are used: one for the projection of LIBOR rates (through the FRA rates) and another for discounting. In this section, I will look at the impact of these changes on some nonlinear derivatives. The formal analytical setup to justify the formulas in this section is significantly more complicated, and for this reason I will only mainly show the difference pricing formulas and refer the reader to the formal derivations in, for example, Mercurio (2009) and Bianchetti and Carlicchi (2012).

18.6.1 Black's Option Pricing Formula

In this section, we discuss the pricing formulas used by market participants to evaluate plain vanilla LIBOR-based options. Such plain vanilla contracts are the following:

1. **Interest Rate Caps**: A buyer of an interest rate cap is entitled to the sequence of payments at times $T_1, T_2, \ldots, T_n$, with $T_i = T_{i-1} + \Delta$:
$$\text{Cap CF at } T_i = N\Delta\max(\ell(T_{i-1}) - r_K, 0) \tag{18.40}$$
where $\ell(T_{i-1})$ denotes the LIBOR rate at time T_{i-1} with maturity T_i, and r_K is the strike rate. Each cash flow 18.40 is called a *caplet*. In exchange for receiving payments 18.40, the cap buyer makes an up-front payment to the cap seller at initiation of the contract. In a cap, the buyer receives payments only when interest rates increase.
2. **Interest Rate Floors**: An interest rate floor is the same as a cap but in which payments occur when interest rate declines. That is, the buyer receives the payments:
$$\text{Floor CF at } T_i = N\Delta\max(r_K - \ell(T_{i-1}), 0) \tag{18.41}$$
3. **Interest Rate Swaptions**: A buyer of an interest rate swaption has the right, but not the obligation, to enter into a swap at a given maturity T_O, for a given tenor τ_n, and at a predetermined swap rate r_K. In a *receiver* swaption, the buyer has the right to receive the fixed payment implied by the strike swap rate in the swaption contract in exchange of paying LIBOR rates, while in a *payer* swaption, the buyer has the right to pay the fixed payment implied by the strike rate. In particular, denote by $c(T_O, T_n)$ the market swap rate at time T_O for a swap with maturity T_n. The buyer of a receiver swaption with maturity T_O will receive the payoffs at the swap payments $T_i, T_{i+1}, \ldots, T_n$, with $T_i > T_O$, given by
$$\text{Receiver swaption payoff at } T_i = N\Delta\max(r_K - c(T_O, T_n), 0) \tag{18.42}$$
To understand this equation, note that if the market swap rate $c(T_O, T_n)$ at the expiration of the option was larger than the swaption strike rate r_K, then it is not optimal for the receiver swaption buyer to exercise the option: by entering in the swap at market value he/she will receive $c(T_O, T_n)$, while if she exercises she will only receive $r_K < c(T_O, T_n)$. So, it is optimal to exercise only when $r_K > c(T_O, T_n)$. The total additional payment the swaption buyer will receive compared to the alternative to enter into the swap at market rates is $r_K - c(T_O, T_n)$.
Symmetrically, in a payer swaption, the payoff at each $T_i > T_O$ is given by
$$\text{Payer swaption payoff at } T_i = N\Delta\max(c(T_O, T_n) - r_K, 0) \tag{18.43}$$
In this case, by exercising the option when $c(T_O, T_n) > r_K$, the buyer of the payer swaption makes lower payments every T_i from T_O to T_n compared to the alternative of entering into a swap at market rates. Therefore, the saving per period will be $c(T_O, T_n) - r_K$.

Market participants price these securities using the Black's formula for options pricing. In essence, the basic assumption is that the future reference interest rate – LIBOR for caps and floors and the swap rate for swaptions – has a log-normal risk-adjusted distribution. The proper "risk adjustment" allows us to discount such random payoff at maturity simply by the risk-free rate.

18.6.2 Caps and Floors before and after the Crisis

Consider the caplet and the floorlet discussed in points 1 and 2 previously. The Black's formula then assumes that

$$\log\,(\ell(T_{i-1})) \sim N(\mu(T_{i-1}), \sigma_i^2\, T_{i-1}) \tag{18.44}$$

where $N(a,b)$ denotes the normal distribution with mean a and variance b. Above, the mean of the distribution $\mu(T_{i-1})$ is such that

$$f(0, T_{i-1}, T_i) = \text{risk-adjusted } E[\ell(T_{i-1})] \tag{18.45}$$

Then, the Black option pricing formulas with notional N and time interval Δ are obtained from the pricing equation

$$V_0^{Caplet}(T_i) = \text{PV of risk-adjusted } NE[\max(\ell(T_{i-1}) - r_K, 0)\Delta]$$

$$V_0^{Floorlet}(T_i) = \text{PV of risk-adjusted } NE[\max(r_K - \ell(T_{i-1}), 0)\Delta]$$

and they are given explicitly by

$$V_0^{Caplet}(T_i) = Z(0, T_i)N\Delta\left[f(0, T_{i-1}, T_i)\mathcal{N}(d_1) - r_K\mathcal{N}(d_2)\right] \tag{18.46}$$

$$V_0^{Floorlet}(T_i) = Z(0, T_i)N\Delta[r_K\mathcal{N}(-d_2) - f(0, T_{i-1}, T_i)\mathcal{N}(-d_1)] \tag{18.47}$$

where $\mathcal{N}(.)$ is the cumulative standard normal distribution, and

$$d_1 = \frac{1}{\sigma_i\sqrt{T_{i-1}}}\log\left(\frac{f(0,T_{i-1},T_i)}{r_K}\right) + \frac{1}{2}\sigma_i\sqrt{T_{i-1}} \tag{18.48}$$

$$d_2 = \frac{1}{\sigma_i\sqrt{T_{i-1}}}\log\left(\frac{f(0,T_{i-1},T_i)}{r_K}\right) - \frac{1}{2}\sigma_i\sqrt{T_{i-1}} \tag{18.49}$$

The values of the cap and the floor are then given by the sum of the values of caplets

$$V_0^{Cap}(T_n) = \sum_{i=1}^{n} V_0^{Caplet}(T_i) \tag{18.50}$$

$$V_0^{Floor}(T_n) = \sum_{i=1}^{n} V_0^{Floorlet}(T_i) \tag{18.51}$$

What forward rates and discount rates should we use in these formulas? Like for FRAs and swaps, before the crisis, market participants used the LIBOR discount $Z^{\ell}(0, T_i)$ and the LIBOR-based forward rates $f^{\ell}(0, T_{i-1}, T_i)$ obtained from Equation 18.3. After the crisis, and for the same reason as discussed earlier, market participants have adopted the OIS discount $Z^{OIS}(0, T_i)$ as a discount rate and the FRA forward rate $f^{FRA}(0, T_{i-1}, T_i)$.

The effect on pricing is substantial, as illustrated in the next example.

18.6.2.1 Example: Floorlet Valuation Before and After Crisis On January 2, 2009 ($t = 0$), a 6-month floor with strike price $r_K = 1.174\%$ had volatility $\sigma = 85.22\%$. In a 6-month floor, there is only one floorlet because the 3-month floorlet depends on today's interest rate and it is not included in the pricing. What is the value of the floor? Denote $T_1 = 0.25 = 3$ months and $T_2 = 0.5 = 6$ months. We have the following data:

- 3×6 FRA rate $f^{FRA}(0, T_1, T_2) = 1.174\%$
- 3 months LIBOR $= \ell(0, T_1) = 1.4125\%$
- 6 months LIBOR $= \ell(0, T_2) = 1.7525\%$
- 6 months OIS rate $= 0.2405\%$

We can compute d_1 and d_2 from formulas 18.48 and 18.49:

$$d_1 = \frac{1}{0.8522\sqrt{0.25}} \log\left(\frac{1.174}{1.174}\right) + \frac{1}{2}0.8522\sqrt{0.25} = 0.21305$$

$$d_2 = \frac{1}{0.8522\sqrt{0.25}} \log\left(\frac{1.174}{1.174}\right) - \frac{1}{2}0.8522\sqrt{0.25} = -0.21305$$

From the 6-month OIS rate, we obtain $Z^{OIS}(0, T_2) = 0.998798$. Thus, from 18.47 and assuming a \$100 notional, the dollar value of the floor is

$$\begin{aligned} V_0^{Floor} &= 99.8798 \times 0.25 \times [.01174 \times N(0.21305) - 0.01174 \times N(-0.21305)] \\ &= 0.04946 \end{aligned}$$

If we were to use only the LIBOR-based quantities, instead, we would obtain a very different number. Indeed, in this case, we have $Z^{\ell}(0, T_1) = 0.996481$, $Z^{\ell}(0, T_2) = 0.991314$, and thus the LIBOR-based forward rate

$$f^{\ell}(0, T_1, T_2) = 2.0851\%$$

Using the same formulas as above, but with $f^{\ell}(0, T_1, T_2)$ instead of $f^{FRA}(0, T_1, T_2)$, we obtain

$$d_1 = \frac{1}{0.8522\sqrt{0.25}} \log\left(\frac{2.0851}{1.174}\right) + \frac{1}{2}0.8522\sqrt{0.25} = 1.5611$$

$$d_2 = \frac{1}{0.8522\sqrt{0.25}} \log\left(\frac{2.0851}{1.174}\right) - \frac{1}{2}0.8522\sqrt{0.25} = 1.1350$$

Using the 6-month LIBOR discount to discount the cash flows, moreover, yields

$$\begin{aligned} V_0^{Floor,\ell} &= 99.1314 \times 0.25 \times [.01174 \times N(-1.135) - 0.020851 \times N(-1.5611)] \\ &= 0.00667 \end{aligned}$$

This value is much smaller than the value obtained from FRA-based option pricing formula.

This example shows how the new discounting and the new FRA-based pricing affect the value of caps and floors. The option pricing formulas are the same, but it is change in the proper discounting as well as the impact in the valuation of FRA that affect the prices of options.

18.6.3 Swaptions before and after the Crisis

A similar effect occurs for swaptions, discussed in point 3 previously. In this case, the underlying stochastic variable is the market swap rate for a swap with tenor τ_n, $c(t, \tau_n)$. The assumption now is that the swap rate has a log-normal distribution under the proper risk adjustment of probabilities. That is, the assumption is now

$$\log\,(c(T_O, T_n)) \sim N(\mu_s(T_O), \sigma^2 T_O) \tag{18.52}$$

where $\mu_s(T_O)$ is such that the forward swap rate

$$f_{swap}(0, T_O, T_n) = \text{Risk-adjusted } E[c(T_O, T_n)] \tag{18.53}$$

The forward swap rate is nothing more than a forward rate for a swap that starts in the future, in this case at the option's expiration T_O. Using the same argument as in Section 18.4 (before the crisis) or Section 18.5 (after the crisis), we see that the swap rate of a swap that starts at some point in the future would have exactly the same formula as weighted average of forward rates but for longer maturities. More specifically, let i^* be the first time index when $T_{i^*} > T_O$, and then the forward swap rate is

$$f_{swap}(0, T_O, T_n) = \sum_{i=i^*}^{n} w_i\, f(0, T_{i-1}, T_i) \tag{18.54}$$

where

$$w_i = \frac{Z(0,T_i)}{\sum_{j=i^*}^{n} Z(0,T_j)} \tag{18.55}$$

Before the crisis, the forward rate used was the LIBOR-based forward rate $f^{\ell}(0, T_{i-1}, T_i)$, and the weights were computed using LIBOR discounts $Z^{\ell}(0, T_i)$. Instead, as in the case for plain vanilla swaps, the forward swap rate after the crisis is computed using the FRA-based forwards $f^{FRA}(0, T_{i-1}, T_i)$ and the weights use the OIS discount $Z^{OIS}(0, T_i)$.

The Black formula for the valuation of swaptions is given by

$$V_0^{Payer} = \text{PV of Risk-adjusted } E[\max(c(T_0, T_n) - r_K, 0)]$$

$$V_0^{Receiver} = \text{PV of Risk-adjusted } E[\max(r_K - c(T_0, T_n), 0)]$$

and they are given explicitly by

$$V_0^{Payer} = \sum_{i=i^*}^{n} Z(0,T_i)\Delta[f_{swap}(0, T_O, T_n)N(d_1) - r_K N(d_2)] \tag{18.56}$$

$$V_0^{Receiver} = \sum_{i=i^*}^{n} Z(0,T_i)\Delta[r_K N(-d_2) - f_{swap}(0, T_O, T_n)N(-d_1)] \tag{18.57}$$

where here

$$d_1 = \frac{1}{\sigma\sqrt{T_O}} \log\left(\frac{f_{swap}(0, T_O, T_n)}{r_K}\right) + \frac{1}{2}\sigma\sqrt{T_O} \tag{18.58}$$

$$d_2 = \frac{1}{\sigma\sqrt{T_O}} \log\left(\frac{f_{swap}(0, T_O, T_n)}{r_K}\right) - \frac{1}{2}\sigma\sqrt{T_O} \tag{18.59}$$

Note a few features of the swaption pricing formula:

1. The sums in Equations 18.56 and 18.57 run from the first time i after the option expiration to the maturity of the swap underlying the option T_n. If the swaption buyer exercises the option at T_O, she will receive a benefit not at T_O but at every time T_i in which a swap payment should be made, as it would pay less (if it was a payer) or receive more (if it was a receiver) than the alternative of entering in the swap at T_O at market values.
2. The term within parentheses in Equations 18.56 and 18.57 do not depend on the running index i. That is, this is the value today of the expected difference between the future market swap rate and the strike rate. As mentioned, the benefit of the option being in the money at T_O accrue over time (from T_{i^*} to T_n), but the amount of benefit is constant period by period.
3. As for other derivatives, before the crisis the market used the LIBOR discount $Z^{LIBOR}(0, T_i)$ to discount future payments, but after the crisis the OIS discount $Z^{OIS}(0, T_i)$ has been used more frequently. Similarly, as discussed earlier, the methodology to compute the forward swap rate $f_{swap}(0, T_O, T_n)$ has also changed after the crisis.

18.7 CONCLUSIONS

In this chapter, I overviewed the new challenges to derivative pricing that sprang out of the recent financial crisis. The decoupling of the curve used for discounting from the one used for computing the projection of future (LIBOR based) cash flows has generated numerous new formulas and procedures. There is also an ongoing debate on the proper way to account for the various costs from setting up a derivative trade and properly take into account for credit risk. Brigo et al. (2015) discuss the recent challenges and cover in detail the new pricing techniques.

REFERENCES

Ametrano FM, Bianchetti M. Bootstrapping the illiquidity: multiple curves construction for market coherent forward rates estimation. In: Mercurio F, editor. *Modeling Interest Rates: Latest Advances for Derivatives Pricing*. Risk Books; 2009.

Ametrano FM, Bianchetti M. Everything You Always Wanted to Know About Multiple Interest Rate Curve Bootstrapping But Were Afraid To Ask, Working Paper; 2013.

Bianchetti M, Carlicchi M. Interest Rates After The Credit Crunch: Multiple-Curve Vanilla Derivatives and SABR, Working Paper; 2012.

Brigo D, Liu Q, Pallavicini A, Sloth D. Nonlinear valuation under margining and funding costs with residual credit risk: a unified approach. In: Veronesi P, editor. *Handbook of Fixed Income*. John Wiley and Sons; 2015.

Brigo D, Mercurio F. *Interest Rate Models: Theory and Practice*. 2nd ed. Berlin Hedelberg: Springer Finance; 2006.

Hull J. *Options, Futures and Other Derivatives*. 9th ed. Upple Saddle River (NJ): Prentice Hall; 2014.

Hull J, White A. OIS discounting, interest rate derivatives, and the modeling of stochastic interest rate spreads. J Invest Manage 2015;13(1):64–83.

Mercurio F. Interest Rates and The Credit Crunch: New Formulas and Market Models, Working Paper. Bloomberg; 2009.

Tuckman B, Serrat A. *Fixed Income Securities*. Hoboken (NJ): John Wiley and Sons; 2011.

Veronesi P. *Fixed Income Securities: Valuation, Risk, and Risk Management*. Hoboken (NJ): John Wiley and Sons; 2010.

PART VII

Advanced Topics in Derivatives Pricing

19

Risk-Neutral Pricing: Monte Carlo Simulations

Claudio Tebaldi[a] and Pietro Veronesi[b]

[a]*Department of Finance and IGIER, Bocconi University, Milano, Italy*
[b]*Booth School of Business, University of Chicago, Chicago, IL, United States*

19.1 INTRODUCTION

This chapter covers the modern techniques of derivative security pricing using the risk-neutral pricing methodology. Ito calculus offers a powerful tool to analyze the impact of risk and uncertainty on prices and on their evolution. For this reason, stochastic differential equations (SDEs) are frequently used to define the temporal evolution of prices and the relevant state variables in stochastic market models. As a result, prices are typically represented as expectations of stochastic future payoffs conditioned on current information. Their analytical computation is unfeasible in many cases, and numerical simulation offers a reliable and efficient alternative approach. A vast and technically exhaustive description of Monte Carlo methods in finance can be found in Glasserman (2004). In the following discussion, we illustrate the basic steps that are to be followed to set up a simulation approach to valuation. As real-life examples, we implement the valuation procedure required to price a callable bond.

19.2 RISK-NEUTRAL PRICING

We start by considering single-factor models and showing later that the extension to multifactor models is as simple. Consider a continuous time process for the instantaneous interest rate r_t given by

$$dr_t = m(r_t, t)dt + s(r_t, t)dW_t \tag{19.1}$$

where $m(r, t)$ and $s(r, t)$ represent the functions of the interest rate r and time t and dW_t is a Brownian motion, that is, heuristically,

$$dW_t \sim N(0, dt)$$

The choice of $m(r, t)$ and $s(r, t)$ gives rise to different models, as we will see in the following. Some restrictions on $m(r_t, t)$ and $s(r_t, t)$ are usually imposed to ensure that the SDE in Equation 19.1 is well defined. See, for example, Duffie (2010) for discussion and details.

Handbook of Fixed-Income Securities, First Edition. Edited by Pietro Veronesi.

Consider two fixed-income securities that depend on the interest rate. Let the first one be an option, denoted by $V(r,t)$, and the second be a zero-coupon bond with maturity T, denoted by $Z(r,t)$. We want to establish a no-arbitrage relation between $V(r,t)$ and $Z(r,t)$.

As a matter of notation, we often suppress the arguments of the functions V and Z, for example, write V instead of $V(r,t)$, unless it is important to emphasize the dependence on r and t. Similarly, we sometimes indicate partial derivatives with subscripts with respect to the variable against which we differentiate. For instance,

$$V_t = \frac{\partial V}{\partial t}; \quad V_r = \frac{\partial V}{\partial r}; \quad V_{rr} = \frac{\partial^2 V}{\partial r^2} \tag{19.2}$$

We proceed as follows:

1. **Portfolio**: Set up a portfolio that is long one unit of the security $V(r,t)$ and N units of the zero-coupon bond $Z(r,t)$ with maturity T. The value of this portfolio at any time t is

$$\Pi(r,t) = V(r,t) + NZ(r,t). \tag{19.3}$$

2. **Hedging**: Choose N to make the portfolio riskless, that is, such that

$$\frac{\partial \Pi(r,t)}{\partial r} = 0 \tag{19.4}$$

This condition says that the sensitivity of the portfolio $\Pi(r,t)$ to changes of interest rates is null. This condition translates into the equation

$$\frac{\partial V(r,t)}{\partial r} + N\frac{\partial Z(r,t)}{\partial r} = 0 \tag{19.5}$$

We can solve for N as

$$N = -\frac{\partial V(r,t)/\partial r}{\partial Z(r,t)/\partial r} \tag{19.6}$$

The optimal hedge ratio N is given by the sensitivity of the security we want to hedge (V) to changes in interest rates divided by the sensitivity of the security we use to hedge (Z) to changes in interest rates.

3. **No-arbitrage**: The portfolio Π is risk-free between t and $t + dt$, because given N its value is independent of interest rate movements. Although intuitive, to show this formally we have to use Itô's lemma. **Itô's lemma** states that for any function $f(r,t)$, we have that its change between t and $t + dt$, namely, df, is given by[1]

$$df = \left\{ f_t + f_r m(r,t) + \frac{1}{2} f_{rr} s(r,t)^2 \right\} dt + f_r s(r,t) dW_t \tag{19.7}$$

Therefore, applying Itô's lemma to the portfolio (and thus function) $\Pi(r,t)$, we obtain

$$d\Pi = \left\{ \Pi_t + \Pi_r m(r,t) + \frac{1}{2}\Pi_{rr} s(r,t)^2 \right\} dt + \Pi_r s(r,t) dW_t \tag{19.8}$$

However, note that hedging gives $\Pi_r = \partial\Pi/\partial r = 0$, and thus two terms drop out, yielding

$$d\Pi = \left\{ \Pi_t + \frac{1}{2}\Pi_{rr} s(r,t)^2 \right\} dt \tag{19.9}$$

Because the interest rate risk dW_t does not affect the portfolio, this portfolio is riskless (today). It follows that its capital gain return must equal the risk-free rate

$$d\Pi = r\Pi dt \tag{19.10}$$

[1]Heuristically, this can be seen by using a second-order Taylor expansion:

$$f(t + dt, r + dr) \approx f(t,r) + f_t\, dt + f_r\, dr + \frac{1}{2} f_{rr}\, dr^2$$

Substituting dr in this equation, exploiting the fact that $dW_t^2 = dt$ (quadratic variation), and finally deleting "dt" terms of order higher than 1, we obtain Equation 19.7.

Otherwise an arbitrage would be available: for instance, if $d\Pi > r\Pi dt$, then we can borrow $\$\Pi$ at the risk-free rate r, invest it in one unit of $V(r,T)$ and N units of $Z(r,t)$, wait one period "dt," and unravel everything tomorrow, including paying the risk-free rdt on our loan $\$\Pi$. Such strategy yields $d\Pi - r\Pi dt > 0$ between today and tomorrow, which is a risk-free profit that required no initial investment, i.e., an arbitrage.

4. **Reshuffle**: The no-arbitrage relation 19.10 generates an equation that is obtained by substituting $d\Pi$ from 19.9 on the left-hand side:

$$\Pi_t + \frac{1}{2}\Pi_{rr}s(r,t)^2 = r\Pi$$

Substitute $\Pi(r,t) = V(r,t) + NZ(r,t)$ on the right-hand side and the analogous $\Pi_t = V_t + NZ_t$ and $\Pi_{rr} = V_{rr} + NZ_{rr}$ on the left-hand side and reorganize to obtain

$$V_t + \frac{1}{2}V_{rr}s(r,t)^2 - rV = N\left[Z_t + \frac{1}{2}Z_{rr}s(r,t)^2 - rZ\right]$$

Substituting also for N from Equation 19.6, we finally get

$$\frac{V_t + \frac{1}{2}V_{rr}s(r,t)^2 - rV}{V_r} = \frac{Z_t + \frac{1}{2}Z_{rr}s(r,t)^2 - rZ}{Z_r} \tag{19.11}$$

Note that the left-hand side is identical to the right-hand side. Because we have not specified the type of security we are considering – and in fact, even the right-hand side need not be a zero-coupon bond – it follows that restriction 19.11 must hold for every pair of securities. Therefore, we can give a generic "name" to this common ratio across fixed-income securities. We call it "$-m^*(r,t)$," where the negative sign is just for notational convenience in what follows. That is, every security V must satisfy

$$\frac{V_t + \frac{1}{2}V_{rr}s(r,t)^2 - rV}{V_r} = -m^*(r,t) \tag{19.12}$$

for some $m^*(r,t)$. Reorganizing, we obtain the following equation:

$$V_t + V_r m^*(r,t) + \frac{1}{2}V_{rr}s(r,t)^2 = rV \tag{19.13}$$

This is called the **fundamental pricing equation**. Any security must satisfy this pricing equation – a partial differential equation (PDE) – subject to the boundary condition that the security value converges to its payoff at maturity T, $g(r_T,T)$, that is, subject to

$$V(r,T) = g(r,T) \tag{19.14}$$

5. **Risk-neutral probabilities**: It turns out that the solution to Equation 19.13 can be achieved through the **Feynman–Kac Theorem.** It is useful to state it under a slightly different notation: consider the PDE

$$V_t + V_r p(r,t) + \frac{1}{2}V_{rr}s(r,t)^2 = c(r,t)V \tag{19.15}$$

where $p(r,t)$ and $c(r,t)$ are two functions of r and t. Then the solution to PDE 19.15 with boundary condition $g(r,T)$ at T is given by

$$V(r,T) = E^p\left[e^{-\int_t^T c(r_u,u)du}g(r_T,T)\right] \tag{19.16}$$

where the expectation $E^p[\cdot]$ is taken under the stochastic process

$$dr = p(r,t)dt + s(r,t)dX_t \tag{19.17}$$

and dX_t is a standard Brownian motion $dX_t \sim N(0,dt)$.

The Feynman–Kac theorem provides a methodology to solve the fundamental pricing equation 19.13: comparing 19.13 with the generic equation 19.15, we see that by setting $p(r,t) = m^*(r,t)$ and $c(r,t) = r$, the Feynman–Kac theorem implies the price of the derivative security $V(r,t)$ is given by

$$V(r,T) = E^*\left[e^{-\int_t^T r_u du}g(r_T,T)\right] \tag{19.18}$$

where the expectation is taken under the stochastic process

$$dr = m^*(r,t)dt + s(r,t)dX_t \tag{19.19}$$

The process 19.19 with $m^*(r,t)$ as its drift rate is called the **risk-neutral process**, or **risk-adjusted process**, for interest rates. It has this name because under this process, the valuation of derivative securities uses formula 19.18 in which the stochastic payoff $g(r_T, T)$ is discounted at the risk-free rate r. Such behavior would characterize a "risk-neutral investor." However, we have to remember that our investors are not risk neutral, as we changed the process for interest rates from 19.1 to 19.19 to price derivatives by no-arbitrage. As we will see, the change in drift from $m(r,t)$ to $m^*(r,t)$ exactly represents an adjustment for a risk premium.

19.2.1 Interest Rate Models

The choice of the functions $m^*(r,t)$ and $s(r,t)$ determines the type of the model we are considering and the price of securities. For instance, in the following four cases, we have that the value of a zero-coupon bond at t with maturity T is given by

$$Z(r,t;T) = e^{A(t,T)-B(t,T)r} \tag{19.20}$$

However, the choice of $m^*(r,t)$ and $s(r,t)$ determines the values of $A(t,T)$ and $B(t,T)$. Specifically,

1. **Vasicek:** $m^*(r,t) = \eta^* - \gamma^* r$ and $s(r,t) = \nu$ and

$$B(t,T) = \frac{1}{\gamma^*}\left(1 - e^{-\gamma^*(T-t)}\right) \tag{19.21}$$

$$A(t,T) = \frac{1}{(\gamma^*)^2}(B(t,T) - (T-t))\left(\eta^*\gamma^* - \frac{1}{2}\nu^2\right) - \frac{\nu^2 B(t;T)^2}{4\gamma^*} \tag{19.22}$$

2. **Cox, Ingersoll, and Ross (CIR):** $m^*(r,t) = \eta^* - \gamma^* r$ and $s(r,t) = \sqrt{\alpha r}$:

$$B(t;T) = \frac{2(e^{\psi_1(T-t)} - 1)}{(\gamma^* + \psi_1)(e^{\psi_1(T-t)} - 1) + 2\psi_1} \tag{19.23}$$

$$A(t;T) = 2\frac{\eta^*}{\alpha}\log\left(\frac{2\psi_1 e^{(\psi_1+\gamma^*)\frac{(T-t)}{2}}}{(\gamma^* + \psi_1)(e^{\psi_1(T-t)} - 1) + 2\psi_1}\right) \tag{19.24}$$

with

$$\psi_1 = \sqrt{(\gamma^*)^2 + 2\alpha}$$

3. **Ho and Lee:** $m^*(r,t) = \eta^*(t)$ and $s(r,t) = \nu$:

$$B(t,T) = T - t$$

$$A(t,T) = -\int_t^T \eta^*(\tau)(T-\tau)d\tau + \frac{1}{6}\nu^2(T-t)^3$$

4. **Hull and White:** $m^*(r,t) = \eta^*(t) - \gamma^* r$ and $s(r,t) = \nu$:

$$B(t,T) = \frac{1}{\gamma^*}\left(1 - e^{-\gamma^*(T-t)}\right)$$

$$A(t,T) = -\int_t^T B(\tau;T)\eta^*(\tau)d\tau + \frac{\nu^2}{2(\gamma^*)^2}\left(T - t + \frac{1 - e^{-2\gamma^*(T-t)}}{2\gamma} - 2B(t;T)\right)$$

19.2.2 The Market Price of Risk

To understand the notion of the market price of risk, consider the expected return from an investment in the security V. According to Itô's lemma, we have

$$\frac{dV}{V} = \mu_V dt + \sigma_V dW$$

where the diffusion component is

$$\sigma_V = \frac{V_r}{V} s(r,t) \tag{19.25}$$

and the expected return μ_V on investment over the period t to $t + dt$ is given by

$$E\left[\frac{dV}{V}\right] = \mu_V dt = \frac{1}{V}\left\{V_t + V_r m(r,t) + \frac{1}{2}V_{rr}s^2(r,t)\right\} dt$$

Note that the two terms, $V_t + \frac{1}{2}V_{rr}s^2(r,t)$, also appear in the pricing PDE 19.13. That is, from that equation, we have

$$V_t + \frac{1}{2}V_{rr}s^2(r,t) = rV - V_r m^*(r,t)$$

Substitute to obtain the expected return as

$$E\left[\frac{dV}{V}\right] = \left\{r + \frac{V_r}{V}(m(r,t) - m^*(r,t))\right\} dt$$

Using expression 19.25, we can rewrite this equation as follows:

$$\frac{E\left[\frac{dV}{V}\right] - r\,dt}{\sigma_V} = \frac{1}{s(r,t)}(m(r,t) - m^*(r,t))dt \tag{19.26}$$

On the left-hand side, the numerator is the expected return on the security V in excess of the risk-free rate r. That is, it is the risk premium for holding V. The denominator is the diffusion of dV/V, that is, the sensitivity of the security to the Brownian shocks dW that hit it. This is the risk. The ratio on the left-hand side is thus a **Sharpe ratio**, called the **market price of interest rate risk**. The right-hand side shows that such ratio does not depend on the particular security, because all of the quantities on the right-hand side are security independent. The terms $m(r,t)$ and $s(r,t)$ are just the drift and diffusion of the original process, and the $m^*(r,t)$, recall, is common across securities. For this reason, we can give a "name" to the right-hand side and define

$$\lambda(r,t) = \frac{1}{s(r,t)}(m(r,t) - m^*(r,t)) \tag{19.27}$$

The above derivation shows that for every security V, we must have

$$E\left[\frac{dV}{V}\right] = [r + \sigma_V\ \lambda(r,t)]dt \tag{19.28}$$

If agents require a large risk premium to hold interest rate securities (per unit of risk), then $\lambda(r,t)$ is large (in absolute value).

Given an estimate of $\lambda(r,t)$, we also see that the risk-neutral drift $m^*(r,t)$ is in fact equal to

$$m^*(r,t) = m(r,t) - \lambda(r,t)s(r,t) \tag{19.29}$$

that is, it is equal to the original drift adjusted for the market price of risk. The risk-neutral process is a "risk-adjusted" process.

19.2.3 Valuation under P and under Q

To obtain a bit more of intuition about the market price of risk, consider again the pricing equation

$$V_t + V_r m^*(r,t) + \frac{1}{2}V_{rr}s(r,t)^2 = rV \tag{19.30}$$

Add on both sides the term $V_r m(r,t)$ and rearrange to obtain

$$V_t + V_r m(r,t) + \frac{1}{2}V_{rr}s(r,t)^2 = \left(r + \frac{V_r}{V}(m(r,t) - m^*(r,t))\right)V \tag{19.31}$$

Using the definition of market price of risk 19.27, we obtain

$$V_t + V_r m(r,t) + \frac{1}{2}V_{rr}s(r,t)^2 = (r + \sigma_V\lambda(r,t))V \tag{19.32}$$

We can apply the Feynman–Kac theorem to this last PDE, with $p(r,t) = m(r,t)$ and $c(r,t) = (r + \sigma_V\lambda(r,t))$, with $\sigma_V = V_r/V\,s(r,t)$ (see Eq. 19.25). We obtain that the value of the security is given by

$$V(r,T) = E\left[e^{-\int_t^T r_u + \sigma_V\lambda(r_u,u)du}g(r_T,T)\right] \tag{19.33}$$

where now the expectation is taken under the original process

$$dr = m(r,t)dt + s(r,t)dW \tag{19.34}$$

Note that we can also express the value of a derivative security as the expectation of future payoff under the true probabilities but simply discounted at the (presumably) higher discount rate $r_u + \sigma_V\lambda(r_u,u)$. In contrast, under risk-neutral pricing, we change both the discount rate, that is, just r_u, and the probabilities underlying the expectation, from $m(r,t)$ to $m^*(r,t) = m(r,t) - \lambda(r,t)s(r,t)$ (see Eq. 19.29), that is, they now incorporate a risk adjustment. The two pricing methodologies, namely, the risk-neutral methodology (pricing under Q) in Equations 19.18 and 19.19 and the risk natural methodology (pricing under P) in Equations 19.33 and 19.34, have to give the same result, as they are solutions to the same PDE.[2]

Why do not we use this latter, more intuitive methodology under P then? For convenience: note that under the physical probability P (Eqs 19.33 and 19.34), the proper discount depends on $\sigma_V = s(r,t)V_r/V$. That is, in order to compute the proper discount required to value the future payoff $g(r_T,T)$, we need to know already the function $V(r,t)$. But this is exactly what we are trying to find out! In order to solve for V in this case, we would need to appeal to a fixed point within a functional space (given that $V(r,t)$ is a function). In contrast, the risk-neutral pricing methodology in Equations 19.18 and 19.19 is more convenient, as we just discount at the risk-free rate – which we know – and the probabilities are adjusted by considering a process that depend on $m^*(r,t)$. The key is that the latter is *not* specific to a given security and thus can be estimated from the data.

19.2.4 Multifactor Models

The methodology illustrated in the previous section readily extends to multifactor models. Assume that bond prices and derivatives depend only on n factors $\mathbf{X}_t = (X_t^1, X_t^2, \ldots, X_t^n)'$. We denote the price of a fixed-income security – derivative or bond – simply as $V(\mathbf{X}_t, t)$. Let the short-term riskless rate r_t also be some function

$$r = \phi(\mathbf{X}_t)$$

What are these factors $\mathbf{X}_t$? They could be macroeconomic factors (e.g., inflation, gross domestic product (GDP) growth, unemployment) or some unobservable factors that move bond prices (e.g., market participants' expectations about monetary policy). Assume that $\mathbf{X}$ follows the joint process

$$d\mathbf{X} = \mathbf{m}(\mathbf{X}_t,t)dt + \mathbf{s}(\mathbf{X}_t,t)d\mathbf{W}_t \tag{19.35}$$

where $\mathbf{W}_t$ is an n-dimensional vector of independent Brownian motions

$$d\mathbf{W}_t \sim \mathcal{N}(0, \mathbf{I}_n dt)$$

and $\mathbf{I}_n$ is the n-dimensional identity matrix. What is the price of a security $V(\mathbf{X}_t,t)$ with maturity T and payoff $g_T = G(\mathbf{X}_T,T)$? We proceed as before:

[2] This is of course true if the partial differential equation has a unique solution. In the case of potential multiple solutions, parameter restrictions may need to be imposed.

1. **Portfolio:** Consider the portfolio with $N_1 = 1$ units of the first bond, hedged using n additional bonds (as there are n sources of risk):

$$\Pi(\mathbf{X}_t, t) = N_1 V_1(\mathbf{X}_t, t) + \sum_{j=2}^{n+1} N_j V_j(\mathbf{X}_t, t) \tag{19.36}$$

2. **Dynamics:** To obtain the dynamics of Π, we need the multivariate version of **Itô's lemma**. In particular, Itô's lemma applied to each security i states

$$dV_i = \mu_{V,i} dt + \boldsymbol{\sigma}_{V,i} d\mathbf{W}_t$$

where

$$\mu_{V,i} = \frac{\partial V_i}{\partial t} + \frac{\partial V_i}{\partial \mathbf{X}} \mathbf{m}(\mathbf{X}_t, t) + \frac{1}{2} Tr\left(\frac{\partial^2 V_i}{\partial \mathbf{X} \partial \mathbf{X}'} \mathbf{s}(\mathbf{X}_t, t)\, \mathbf{s}(\mathbf{X}_t, t)' \right) \tag{19.37}$$

$$\boldsymbol{\sigma}_{V,i} = \frac{\partial V_i}{\partial \mathbf{X}} \mathbf{s}(\mathbf{X}_t, t) \tag{19.38}$$

Above, $Tr(.)$ is the "trace" of a matrix, that is, the sum of the elements on its principal diagonal.[3] We thus obtain

$$d\Pi = \sum_{j=1}^{n+1} N_j dV_j = \mathbf{N}'\, \boldsymbol{\mu}_V dt + \mathbf{N}'\, \boldsymbol{\sigma}_V\, d\mathbf{W}_t \tag{19.39}$$

3. **Hedge:** Choose $\mathbf{N}$ so that the last term drops out. That is, impose

$$\mathbf{N}'\, \boldsymbol{\sigma}_V = \mathbf{0} \tag{19.40}$$

These are n equations in n unknowns $N_2, \ldots, N_{n+1}$ (recall that $N_1 = 1$).

4. **No arbitrage:** Given Equation 19.40, the last term of 19.39 is zero, and thus

$$d\Pi = \mathbf{N}'\, \boldsymbol{\mu}_V dt \tag{19.41}$$

is risk-free between t and $t + dt$. Therefore, we can impose no-arbitrage

$$d\Pi = r\Pi dt \tag{19.42}$$

5. **Reshuffle:** Substitute expression 19.41 on the left-hand side of 19.42 and expression 19.36 on its right-hand side to obtain

$$\mathbf{N}'(\boldsymbol{\mu}_V - r\mathbf{V}) = 0 \tag{19.43}$$

We do not have any degrees of freedom left, because $\mathbf{N}$ was already determined in the system of Equations 19.40. So, given Equations 19.40, Equation 19.43 is satisfied if and only if it can be obtained as a linear combination of the system 19.40. That is, Equation 19.43 is satisfied if and only if there is an n−dimensional vector $\lambda(\mathbf{X}, t)$ such that

$$\underset{(n+1)\times 1}{\boldsymbol{\mu}_V - r\mathbf{V}_t} = \underset{((n+1)\times n)}{\boldsymbol{\sigma}_V}\ \underset{\times (n \times 1)}{\lambda(\mathbf{X}, t)}$$

That is, for each security, we have

$$\mu_{V,i} - rV_i = \sum_{j=1}^{n} \lambda_j(\mathbf{X}, t)\, \sigma_{V,i,j} \tag{19.44}$$

[3]Explicitly, we have

$$Tr\left(\frac{\partial^2 V_i}{\partial \mathbf{X} \partial \mathbf{X}'} \mathbf{s}(\mathbf{X}_t, t)\, \mathbf{s}(\mathbf{X}_t, t)' \right) = \sum_{i=1}^{n} \sum_{j=1}^{n} \frac{\partial^2 V_i}{\partial X_i \partial X_j} \mathbf{s}_i(\mathbf{X}_t, t) \mathbf{s}_j(\mathbf{X}_t, t)'$$

where $\mathbf{s}_i(\mathbf{X}_t, t)$ is the ith row of $\mathbf{s}(\mathbf{X}_t, t)$.

where recall $\sigma_{V,i,j} = \frac{\partial V_i}{\partial x_j} s_j(\mathbf{X}, t)$. The return premium (=LHS) depends on loadings λ_j on the n sources of risk. As discussed for the univariate case, we call

$$\lambda_j(\mathbf{X}, t) = \text{Market price of risk factor } j$$

Since this relation must hold for *any* bond (and in fact, any security that depends on $\mathbf{X}_t$), we can eliminate the subscript i from now on.

6. **Obtain PDE:** The fundamental pricing equation is finally obtained by substituting back μ_V and $\boldsymbol{\sigma}_V$ from 19.37 and 19.38 into Equation 19.44 :

$$rV = \frac{\partial V}{\partial t} + \frac{\partial V}{\partial \mathbf{X}}[\mathbf{m}(\mathbf{X}_t, t) - \mathbf{s}(\mathbf{X}_t, t)\lambda_t] + \frac{1}{2}Tr\left(\frac{\partial^2 V}{\partial \mathbf{X}\partial \mathbf{X}'}\mathbf{s}\left(\mathbf{X}_t, t\right)\mathbf{s}(\mathbf{X}_t, t)'\right) \tag{19.45}$$

To summarize, the price of *any* derivative security $V(\mathbf{X}, t)$ has to satisfy the PDE 19.45 subject to the final condition $V(\mathbf{X}, T) = g_T$, where g_T is the final payoff of the security. For instance, if the security is a zero-coupon bond, then $g_T = 1$.

7. **Risk-neutral pricing:** The solution to PDE 19.45 can be obtained by using the Feynman–Kac theorem, which establishes that the solution to the PDE 19.45 for a security V is given by

$$V(\mathbf{X}, t) = E_t^*\left[e^{-\int_0^T r_u du} g_T\right] \tag{19.46}$$

where the expectation is taken with respect to the risk-neutral process

$$d\mathbf{X} = \mathbf{m}^*(\mathbf{X}_t, t)dt + \mathbf{s}(\mathbf{X}_t, t)d\mathbf{W}_t^* \tag{19.47}$$

with

$$\mathbf{m}^*(\mathbf{X}_t, t) = \mathbf{m}(\mathbf{X}_t, t) - \mathbf{s}(\mathbf{X}_t, t)\lambda(\mathbf{X}_t, t) \tag{19.48}$$

As for the case of single-factor models (see Equation 19.29), Equation 19.48 shows that to move from the risk natural physical probability P to the risk-neutral pricing probability Q, we have to modify the drift rate of the state variable process by subtracting the product of the market prices of factor risk $\lambda(\mathbf{X}_t, t)$ times the factors "quantity of risk" $\mathbf{s}(\mathbf{X}_t, t)$.

As in the case of single-factor models, the choice of $r = \phi(\mathbf{X})$, $\mathbf{m}^*(\mathbf{X}_t, t)$, and $\mathbf{s}(\mathbf{X}_t, t)$ determines the valuation formulas for bonds and derivatives. Three relatively popular classes of models are the following:

1. **Affine models**. This class of models assumes:

$$\text{Risk-free rate:} \quad r_t = \delta_0 + \boldsymbol{\delta}_1'\mathbf{X}_t \tag{19.49}$$

$$\text{Risk-neutral drift:} \quad \mathbf{m}^*(\mathbf{X}_t, t) = \widetilde{\mathcal{K}}(\widetilde{\boldsymbol{\theta}} - \mathbf{X}_t) \tag{19.50}$$

$$\text{Diffusion term:} \quad \mathbf{s}(\mathbf{X}_t, t) = \boldsymbol{\Sigma}\sqrt{\mathbf{S}_t} \tag{19.51}$$

where $\widetilde{\mathcal{K}}$ is an $n \times n$ matrix, $\widetilde{\boldsymbol{\theta}}$ is an $n \times 1$ vector, and $\mathbf{S}_t$ is an $n \times n$ diagonal matrix, with diagonal element

$$[\mathbf{S}_t]_{ii} = \alpha_i + \boldsymbol{\beta}_i{}'\mathbf{X}_t \tag{19.52}$$

The price of the bond is given by the exponential-affine formula

$$Z(\mathbf{X}_t, t; T) = e^{A(t;T) - \mathbf{B}(t;T)'\mathbf{X}_t} \tag{19.53}$$

where $A(T; T) = 0$ and $\mathbf{B}(T; T) = \mathbf{0}$, and they satisfy the system of ordinary differential equations (ODEs)

$$0 = \frac{\partial \mathbf{B}'}{\partial t} + \boldsymbol{\delta}_1' - \mathbf{B}(t; T)'\widetilde{\mathcal{K}} - \frac{1}{2}\sum_{i=1}^{n}[\boldsymbol{\Sigma}'\mathbf{B}(t; T)]_{ii}\boldsymbol{\beta}_i'$$

$$0 = \frac{\partial A}{\partial t} - \delta_0 - \mathbf{B}(t; T)'\widetilde{\mathcal{K}}\widetilde{\boldsymbol{\theta}} + \frac{1}{2}\sum_{i=1}^{n}[\boldsymbol{\Sigma}'\mathbf{B}(t; T)]_{ii}\alpha_i$$

Solving a system of ODEs is far easier and faster than solving the PDE, and so it is common to refer to these solutions as analytical solutions.[4]

The affine class of term structure models has been widely investigated in the literature (see, e.g., Duffie and Kan (1996), Dai and Singleton (2000), Singleton (2009)), and conditions need to be imposed in order to ensure that the factor processes are well defined (see Dai and Singleton (2000)). There are three subclasses of this general class that are worth mentioning. They differ from each other depending on special assumptions on the parameters:

(a) **Completely affine models.** This subclass of affine models assumes that the market price of risk is given by

$$\lambda_t = \sqrt{\mathbf{S}_t}\lambda_1 \tag{19.54}$$

This choice is convenient, as it implies that the drift rate of factors $\mathbf{X}_t$ under the physical P probability is also affine. In fact, by inverting the transformation in Equation 19.48, we obtain

$$\begin{aligned}\mathbf{m}(\mathbf{X}_t) &= \mathbf{m}^*(\mathbf{X}_t) + \mathbf{s}(\mathbf{X}_t, t)\lambda(\mathbf{X}_t, t)\\ &= \widetilde{\mathcal{K}}\left(\widetilde{\theta} - \mathbf{X}_t\right) + \left(\mathbf{\Sigma}\sqrt{\mathbf{S}_t}\right)\left(\sqrt{\mathbf{S}_t}\lambda_1\right)\\ &= \mathcal{K}\theta - \mathcal{K}\mathbf{X}_t\end{aligned}$$

where

$$\begin{aligned}\mathcal{K} &= \widetilde{\mathcal{K}} - \mathbf{\Sigma} Diag(\lambda_1)\boldsymbol{\beta}\\ \mathcal{K}\theta &= \widetilde{\mathcal{K}}\widetilde{\theta} + \mathbf{\Sigma} Diag(\lambda_1)\boldsymbol{\alpha}\end{aligned}$$

(b) **Essentially affine models**. This subclass of affine models assumes that the market price of risk is given by

$$\lambda_t = \sqrt{\mathbf{S}_t}\lambda_1 + \widehat{\mathbf{S}}_t^{-1/2}\lambda_2\mathbf{X}_t$$

where λ_2 is an $n \times n$ matrix and $\widehat{\mathbf{S}}_t$ is a diagonal matrix such that

$$[\widehat{\mathbf{S}}_t]_{ii} = \begin{cases}\alpha_i + \beta_i\mathbf{X}_t & \text{if} \quad \min(\alpha_i + \beta_i\mathbf{X}_t) > 0\\ 0 & \text{otherwise}\end{cases}$$

Under the physical probabilities, the model is still affine. In fact, the drift rate under the physical probability is now given by

$$\begin{aligned}\mathbf{m}(\mathbf{X}_t) &= \widetilde{\mathcal{K}}(\widetilde{\theta} - \mathbf{X}_t) + \mathbf{\Sigma}\mathbf{S}_t^{\frac{1}{2}}\left(\mathbf{S}_t^{\frac{1}{2}}\lambda_1 + \widehat{\mathbf{S}}_t^{-\frac{1}{2}}\lambda_2\boldsymbol{\phi}_t\right)\\ &= \mathcal{K}\theta - \mathcal{K}\mathbf{X}_t\end{aligned}$$

where now

$$\begin{aligned}\mathcal{K} &= \widetilde{\mathcal{K}} - \mathbf{\Sigma} Diag(\lambda_1)\boldsymbol{\beta} + \mathbf{\Sigma}\widehat{\mathbf{I}}\lambda_2\\ \mathcal{K}\theta &= \widetilde{\mathcal{K}}\widetilde{\theta} + \mathbf{\Sigma} Diag(\lambda_1)\boldsymbol{\alpha}\end{aligned}$$

and $\widehat{\mathbf{I}}$ is the identity matrix but with zeros wherever $[\widehat{\mathbf{S}}_t]_{[ii]} = 0$.

[4] At $t = T$ we have $\mathbf{B}(T;T) = 0$ and $A(T;T) = 0$. And then we work backwards by discretizing time in dt intervals to get

$$\frac{\partial \mathbf{B}(t;T)}{\partial t} \approx \frac{\mathbf{B}(t;T) - \mathbf{B}(t-dt;T)}{dt}; \quad \frac{\partial A(t;T)}{\partial t} \approx \frac{A(t;T) - A(t-dt;T)}{dt}$$

To obtain the recursive backward equations,

$$\mathbf{B}'(t-dt;T) = \mathbf{B}'(t;T) + \left(\delta_1' - \mathbf{B}(t;T)'\widetilde{\mathcal{K}} - \frac{1}{2}\sum_{i=1}^{n}[\mathbf{\Sigma}'\mathbf{B}(t;T)]_{ii}\beta_i'\right)dt$$

$$A(t-dt;T) = A(t;T) + \left(-\delta_0 - \mathbf{B}(t;T)'\widetilde{\mathcal{K}}\widetilde{\theta} + \frac{1}{2}\sum_{i=1}^{n}[\mathbf{\Sigma}'\mathbf{B}(t;T)]_{ii}\alpha_i\right)dt$$

Duffie (2002) and Dai and Singleton (2002) show that essentially affine models do much better than the completely affine model to match not only the static properties of the term structure of interest rates but also its dynamic properties, such as the predictability of future bond excess returns from term spreads. See also Singleton (2009) for more discussion.

(c) **Gaussian models**. This is a special case of the affine class, but it merits its own discussion, given its popularity. We will use a special parameterization of these models in Section 19.5. This class of model assumes that the interest rate and $\mathbf{m}^*(\mathbf{X}, t)$ are still given by Equations 19.49 and 19.50, respectively, but that the diffusion term is instead the constant matrix

$$\text{Diffusion term } \mathbf{s}(\mathbf{X}_t, t) = \mathbf{\Sigma} \tag{19.55}$$

In this special case of affine models, $\boldsymbol{\beta} = 0$ and $\alpha_i = 1$ so that $\mathbf{S}_t = \mathbf{I}$ is the identity matrix. The value of a zero-coupon bond is still given by Equation 19.53, where $A(t, T)$ and $\mathbf{B}(t, T)$ still satisfy the same system of ODEs but with the stated restrictions.

Gaussian models are widely used in the literature, and they are normally paired with a market price of risk that is also linear in the factors

$$\lambda_t = \lambda_0 + \lambda_1 \mathbf{X}_t$$

It is simple to see that this specification implies that the drift rate under the physical probabilities P is still affine. Gaussian models are especially convenient as they can be easily studied also in discrete time. See, for example, Ang and Piazzesi (2003), Singleton (2009), Joslin, Singleton, and Zhu (2011), and Hamilton and Wu (2012).

2. **Linear quadratic models** . This class of models makes the following assumptions:

$$\text{Risk-free rate:} \quad r_t = \delta_0 + \delta_1' \mathbf{X}_t + \frac{1}{2}\mathbf{X}_t' \delta_2 \mathbf{X}_t \tag{19.56}$$

$$\text{Risk-neutral drift:} \quad \mathbf{m}^*(\mathbf{X}_t, t) = \widetilde{\mathcal{K}}(\widetilde{\theta} - \mathbf{X}_t) \tag{19.57}$$

$$\text{Diffusion term:} \quad \mathbf{s}(\mathbf{X}_t, t) = \mathbf{\Sigma} \tag{19.58}$$

where $\boldsymbol{\delta}_2$ is an $n \times n$ matrix. Note the dynamics of the state variables $\mathbf{X}_t$ are still Gaussian, as in the Gaussian models previously. However, the quadratic structure of the interest rates generates a different bond pricing formula. The price of the bond is given by the exponential–linear–quadratic formula

$$Z(\mathbf{X}_t, t; T) = e^{A(t;T) - \mathbf{B}(t;T)\mathbf{X}_t + \frac{1}{2}\mathbf{X}_t'\mathbf{C}(t;T)\mathbf{X}_t} \tag{19.59}$$

where $A(T; T) = 0$, $\mathbf{B}(T; T) = \mathbf{0}$, $\mathbf{C}(T; T) = \mathbf{0}$, and they satisfy another set of ODEs. This model was proposed by Ahn, Dittmar, and Gallant (2002) and further studies by Leippold and Wu (2002) and Brandt and Chapman (2003), among others.

19.3 RISK-NEUTRAL PRICING: MONTE CARLO SIMULATIONS

In general terms, consider the risk-neutral process of a state variable vector $\mathbf{X}_t$:

$$d\mathbf{X} = \mathbf{m}^*(\mathbf{X}, t)dt + \mathbf{s}(\mathbf{X}, t)d\mathbf{W} \tag{19.60}$$

Let the risk-free rate be $r_t = \phi(\mathbf{X}_t)$, and the risk-neutral pricing formula is then given by

$$V = E^* \left[e^{-\int_0^T \phi(\mathbf{X}_u)du} g_T \right] \tag{19.61}$$

The fact that a derivative security's value is given by an expectation suggests a simple way to compute it numerically: we can use Monte Carlo simulations to approximate the expectation on the right-hand side of Equation 19.61.

To elaborate, consider the case in which $\mathbf{X}$ is a scalar. The simplest, yet universal, way to produce a discrete representation of the stochastic evolution described by the process in Equation 19.60 is the construction of a matrix $\mathcal{X} = [\mathcal{X}_{n,k}]$ with row index $n = 1, \ldots, NoPaths$ and column index $k = 0, \ldots, K = \lfloor T/h \rfloor$, where h is the sampling interval and $K = \lfloor T/h \rfloor$ is the largest integer not exceeding T/h (see Table 19.1).

The element $\mathcal{X}_{n,k}$ represents the observation of the process at time kh along a sampled process path. While the initial ($t = 0$) value of the state variable is known, say, $X_0 = x_0$, the presence of a random forcing term in the process described in Equation

TABLE 19.1 Simulation Matrix $\mathcal{X}$

k	0	1	…	K
Sample 1	$\mathcal{X}_0$	$\mathcal{X}_{1,1}$	…	$\mathcal{X}_{1,K}$
Sample 2	$\mathcal{X}_0$	$\mathcal{X}_{2,1}$	…	$\mathcal{X}_{2,K}$
…	…	…	…	…
Sample *NoPaths*	$\mathcal{X}_0$	$\mathcal{X}_{NoPaths,1}$	…	$\mathcal{X}_{NoPaths,K}$

19.60 implies that the evolution is nonunique and depends on the realizations of that random term. Each column of the matrix thus represents a sample of observations at time t of the state variable X_t for different realizations of the random process. Notice that the reduction of the continuous time process X_t to the matrix $\mathcal{X}$ of size $NoPaths \times K$ involves two selection procedures: the sampling of a continuous time process on a discrete grid and the selection of a finite set of paths. Hence, to organize an efficient numerical scheme, the first critical step is the selection of an efficient discretization scheme for the continuous time process. The best choice of the sampling scheme is model specific and depends on the type of process we are considering. In order to illustrate the challenges involved in this choice, we discuss next the discretization of two benchmark one-dimensional processes widely used in financial applications: the Vasicek (1977) and the Cox, Ingersoll, and Ross (1985) interest rate processes.

19.3.1 Discretization of the Vasicek Model

The (Ornstein–Uhlenbeck) process

$$\begin{aligned} dX_t &= \kappa(\theta - X_t)dt + \sigma dW_t \\ X_0 &= x_0 \end{aligned}$$

describes the evolution of interest rates in the Vasicek (1977) model. This process has a well-defined solution on the real line $X_t \in \mathbb{R}$ for any choice of the parameters κ, θ, σ and for any initial condition x_0. Application of a standard Euler discretization scheme gives

$$\begin{aligned} X_{kh} - X_{(k-1)h} &\approx \kappa(\theta - X_{(k-1)h})h + \sigma\sqrt{h}\varepsilon_k, \quad \varepsilon_k \sim N(0,1) \\ X_0 &= x_0 \end{aligned}$$

which shows that the discrete-time version of the Vasicek model corresponds to an autoregressive process of order 1:

$$\mathcal{X}_{k,n} = \kappa\theta h + (1-\kappa h)\mathcal{X}_{(k-1),n} + \sigma\sqrt{h}\varepsilon_k$$

The conditional expectations for the continuous and discretized processes are, respectively

$$\begin{aligned} E[X_{kh} \mid X_{(k-1)h}] &= \theta(1-e^{-\kappa h}) + e^{-\kappa h}X_{(k-1)h} \\ E[\mathcal{X}_k \mid \mathcal{X}_{(k-1)}] &= \kappa\theta h + (1-\kappa h)\mathcal{X}_{(k-1)} \end{aligned}$$

while the conditional variance for the continuous and discretized processes are, respectively

$$\begin{aligned} Var[X_{kh} \mid X_{(k-1)h}] &= \sigma^2\frac{1-e^{-2\kappa h}}{2\kappa} \\ Var[\mathcal{X}_k \mid \mathcal{X}_{(k-1)}] &= \sigma^2 h \end{aligned}$$

It is immediate to verify that discretization is exact at order h in the drift (first moment), while it is of order $h^{1/2}$ in the diffusion term. In fact, the random forcing term is proportional to the conditional standard deviation, which is (for $h \to 0$) proportional to the square root of the variance. An alternative discretization scheme, the Milstein scheme, also includes the additional terms in the Taylor expansion required to reproduce also the diffusion component up to the order h in the discretization formula. For this scheme, the discretized equations become

$$\mathcal{X}_{k,n} = \kappa\theta h + (1-\kappa h)\mathcal{X}_{(k-1),n} + \frac{1}{2}h\sigma^2(\varepsilon_k^2 - 1) + \sigma\sqrt{h}\varepsilon_k$$

It is worth noticing a special feature of the Vasicek model, namely, that both the continuous time and the discretized processes have a Gaussian distribution. The discretization procedure does not affect the distributional properties of the process. This property turns out to be important to achieve good convergence properties of the estimators, by removing the small sample distortion of the statistical estimator distributions. The situation is strikingly different for the discretization of another popular model, which is discussed in the next section.

Figure 19.1 plots simulated paths from the Vasicek model. Table 19.2 contains the parameters used in simulations, which are based on the estimation of risk-neutral parameters from fixed-income securities traded in different markets for different periods of time.[5]

19.3.2 Discretization of the Cox–Ingersoll–Ross Model

Cox, Ingersoll, and Ross (1985) introduced a simple alternative single-factor interest rate model where the evolution of the short rate is described by a square root or Feller diffusion:

$$dX_t = \kappa(\theta - X_t)dt + \sigma\sqrt{X_t}dW_t$$
$$X_0 = x_0$$

This process is well defined on the nonnegative real line $X_t \in \mathbb{R}_+$. The volatility of the process is proportional to the square root of the process level. Given a positive initial condition $x_0 \in \mathbb{R}_{++}$, it is necessary to impose some parametric conditions in order to ensure that the process remains positive in any positive interval $[0, T]$, $T > 0$.

The Feller condition

$$\nu = \frac{2\kappa\theta}{\sigma^2} > 1$$

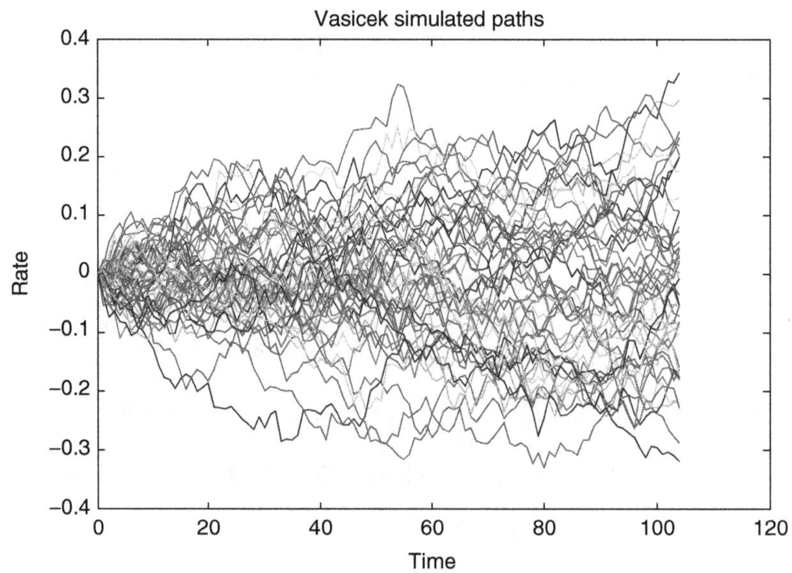

Figure 19.1 Simulated paths from the Vasicek model.

TABLE 19.2 Parameters Used in Sample Simulations

	κ	θ	σ
Vasicek	0.4417	0.0983	0.1326
CIR no Feller	0.08541	0.0255	0.4359
CIR Feller	0.1429	0.1339	0.3875

[5]The parameters for Vasicek and CIR satisfying the Feller condition are from Linetsky and Lim (2012). The κ and σ for CIR without Feller conditions are from Feng and Xie (2012), while its θ is chosen to best fit the term structure of interest rates on January 28, 2014. We use these parameters also for a later real-world exercise.

guarantees that the process, started at a positive initial level, never reaches zero. The weaker condition

$$\kappa\theta > 0$$

is sufficient to ensure that the process started at a positive level remains nonnegative.

The presence of the zero boundary creates a serious complication for the simulation procedure. In fact a simple Euler discretization scheme introduces a positive probability for the process to become negative. With positive probability the realization of a discretized random Gaussian noise can be sufficiently large to drive the discretized CIR process negative, which is out of the continuous time CIR (positive) state space. This possibility prevents convergence of the discretized process to the continuous one. The discretization is further complicated by the property of the continuous time CIR process when the Feller condition is verified: the probability to reach the zero boundary is zero.

This situation illustrates the typical problem in simulation procedures when the state space has boundaries and the behavior of the diffusion process close to the boundaries depends on the state variable itself. For such processes, a correct simulation scheme requires the selection of a discretization procedure consistent with the boundary behavior of the continuous time solution.

In the specific case of the square root diffusion process, a number of technical solutions have been proposed to overcome these difficulties: some of them involve nonlinear transformations of the state variable, while others suggest an adapted grid with variable step size.

19.3.2.1 Autoregressive Gamma Process of Order 1 An unconventional yet nearly optimal discretization scheme has been recently introduced by Gourieroux and Jasiak (2006). It is based on an autoregressive gamma process of order 1 and is as follows:

1. Define the discretization parameters:

$$\nu = \frac{2\kappa\theta}{\sigma^2}, \quad \Phi_h = 1 - \kappa h, \quad \Sigma_h = \frac{\sigma^2 h}{2}$$

2. Generate a Poisson distributed random variable with intensity $\Phi_h \frac{\mathcal{X}_{k-1,n}}{\Sigma_h}$:

$$\mathcal{P} \mid \mathcal{X}_{k-1,n} \sim Poisson\left(\Phi_h \frac{\mathcal{X}_{k-1,n}}{\Sigma_h}\right)$$

3. Generate a Gamma distributed random variable with shape parameter $\nu + \mathcal{P}$:

$$\frac{\mathcal{X}_{k,n}}{\Sigma_h} \mid (\mathcal{P}, \mathcal{X}_{k-1,n}) \sim Gamma(\nu + \mathcal{P})$$

This procedure generates a random variable $\mathcal{X}_{kh}$ whose first and second conditional cumulants are

$$E[\mathcal{X}_k \mid \mathcal{X}_{(k-1)}] = \nu\Sigma_h - \Phi_h \mathcal{X}_{k-1}$$
$$Var[\mathcal{X}_k \mid \mathcal{X}_{(k-1)}] = \nu\Sigma_h^2 + 2\Sigma_h \mathcal{X}_{k-1}$$

Introducing the following definition of the innovation shock

$$\widetilde{\varepsilon}_{k,n} := \frac{\mathcal{X}_{k,n} - E[\mathcal{X}_k \mid \mathcal{X}_{(k-1)}]}{\sqrt{Var[\mathcal{X}_k \mid \mathcal{X}_{(k-1)}]}}$$

the dynamic evolution of the autoregressive gamma process is

$$\mathcal{X}_{k,n} = \nu\Sigma_h - \Phi_h \mathcal{X}_{k-1,n} + \sqrt{\nu\Sigma_h^2 + 2\Sigma_h \mathcal{X}_{k-1,n}}\widetilde{\varepsilon}_{k,n}$$

which appears as a standard Euler discretization of the CIR process, with the difference that the innovation $\widetilde{\varepsilon}_k$ is Gamma rather than Gaussian distributed. The central limit theorem (and the infinite divisibility of the gamma process) guarantees that $\mathcal{X}_{k,n}$ converges to the continuous time CIR process as $h \to 0$.

This discretization procedure offers a number of advantages. First of all, the process $\mathcal{X}_{k,n}$ is positive by definition, and in fact the Gamma distribution has positive support. Notice also that the discretized process maintains the affine property of the CIR:

the conditional expectation and conditional variance of the process are affine functions of the state variable. Last but not least the (discretized) bond price is still an exponential-affine function of the initial state variable, and its exact expression can be computed in closed form using a simple recursion. Figures 19.2 and 19.3 offer graphical illustrations of typical realizations of sample paths of the CIR model, with and without enforcement of the Feller condition. The parameters used in the simulation are reported in Table 19.2.

19.3.2.2 CIR Model, Feller Condition, and No-Arbitrage An important issue in pricing securities under the risk-neutral CIR model arises from the fact that if the Feller condition is not satisfied, then the model admits arbitrage opportunities in continuous time (see, e.g., Cox, Ingersoll, and Ross (1985), Heston, Loewenstein, and Willard (2007).) In current markets with extremely low interest rates, the restriction imposed by the Feller condition is especially binding because it becomes hard to fit the term structure of interest rates. In contrast, it is possible to obtain a better fit of the term structure of interest rates when the Feller condition is not satisfied. Thus, we have a trade-off between a better match of the model to the data and ensuring the model does not admit an arbitrage opportunity. We note however that in discrete time, for any size of the time step "dt," it is possible

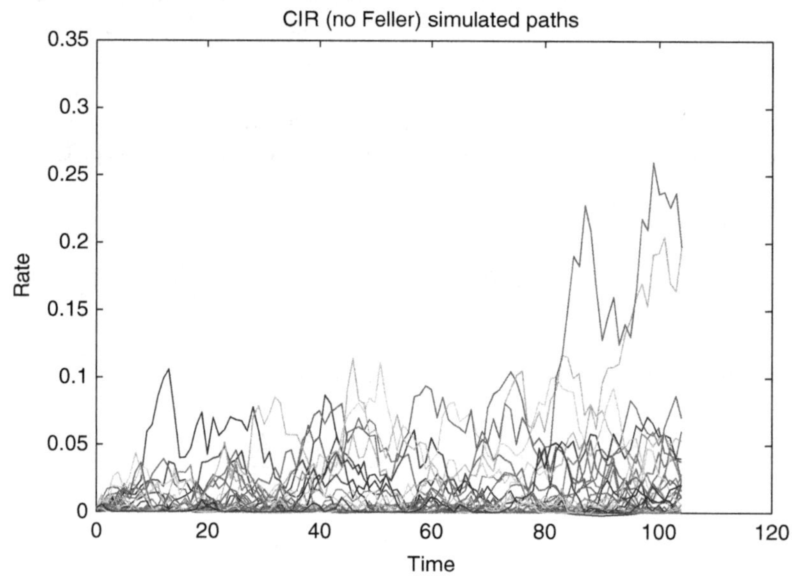

Figure 19.2 Simulated paths of CIR model without Feller condition.

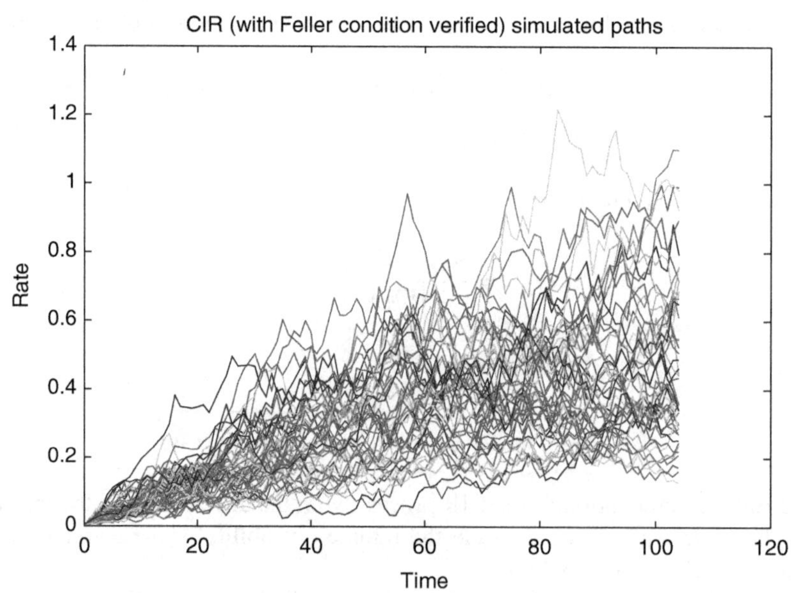

Figure 19.3 Simulated paths of CIR model with Feller condition.

to show that no-arbitrage is satisfied by the CIR model even when the Feller condition is not satisfied but only when the weaker condition $\kappa\theta > 0$ is satisfied (see Le, Singleton, and Dai (2010)). However, one can also show that the discrete-time formula for bond pricing converges to the continuous time formula as dt converges to zero. In what follows, we will keep using the convenient continuous time formulas for bond prices, but we will not impose the Feller condition so as to (slightly) improve the fit of the term structure of interest rates. We will therefore interpret the continuous time formulas as (very good) approximations of the discrete-time formulas. It should be noted that the Monte Carlo simulation methodology that we employ to price securities entails a discrete-time grid in the simulation of state variables, which further justifies our "approximation" interpretation of the continuous time analytical formulas.

19.3.3 Interest Rate Modeling at the Zero Lower Bound

In the aftermath of the 2008 financial crisis, the current environment with near-zero interest rates creates difficulties for many existing term structure models. Gaussian models predict negative rates with positive probability, while lognormal processes preserve positivity of nominal rates, but the "zero lower bound" (ZLB) is not reachable. Square root diffusion models preserve the ZLB by construction but introduce overly rigid restrictions on volatility levels. Hence, in practice, accurate pricing of interest rate derivatives when the short-term rates are close to zero requires elaboration of more sophisticated solutions. In the following, we illustrate two simple approaches that overcome these difficulties.

19.3.3.1 ***Black Shadow-Rate Models*** In the Black (1995) "shadow-rate model," the dynamics are generated by an unobserved state variable X_t, which can become negative, and the observed nominal rate is a nonlinear function of X_t:

$$r_t = \max(X_t, 0)$$

In this way the nominal rate is always greater than or equal to zero. While the nonlinearity of the "max" function introduces serious complications in the derivation of analytical pricing formulas, numerical simulation approaches that will be discussed in the next sections can easily handle this modification and produce reliable security valuations.

19.3.3.2 ***Autoregressive Gamma Process of Order Zero*** More recently, Monfort, Pegoraro, Renne, and Roussellet (2014) propose a mild modification of the CIR discretized process, namely, an autoregressive gamma process of order 0, to accommodate the possibility that the short-term rate stays at the ZLB for extended periods of time. This result is achieved by considering an autoregressive gamma process (see Section 19.3.2.1), setting $\nu = 0$, and then shifting the process by $\mu_h(1 - \Phi_h)$:

$$\begin{aligned} H_{k+1,n} &= \mu_h(1 - \Phi_h) + \Sigma_h w_{k+1,n} \\ w_{k+1,n} &\sim Gamma(z_{k+1}, 1) \\ z_{k+1,n} &\sim Poisson(e_i \Phi_h w_{k,n}) \end{aligned}$$

Thanks to the exponential-affine expression of the Laplace transform, it is possible to verify that this process hits the ZLB with finite probability. The probability to stay at 0 for a period of time kh is given by

$$\mathbb{P}(T^{Soujourn} = k) = p_h^{k-1}(1 - p_h)$$

where

$$p_h = e^{-\frac{\mu_h}{\Sigma_h}(1-\Phi_h)}$$

Hence, the average time spent at zero depends on μ_h and is given by

$$\langle T^{Soujourn} \rangle = \frac{1}{1 - p_h}$$

As an illustration, Figure 19.4 shows a sample of paths for this process, determined by $\mu_h = h$ and $r_0 = 0.25\%$.

19.4 VALUATION BY MONTE CARLO SIMULATION

The second critical step to define an efficient Monte Carlo simulation scheme is the definition of a statistical inference procedure in order to recover the probabilistic information encoded in the original process from the matrix representation of paths, in the stochastic limit of a vanishing grid spacing $h \to 0$ and for a diverging number of sampled paths $NoPaths \to +\infty$.

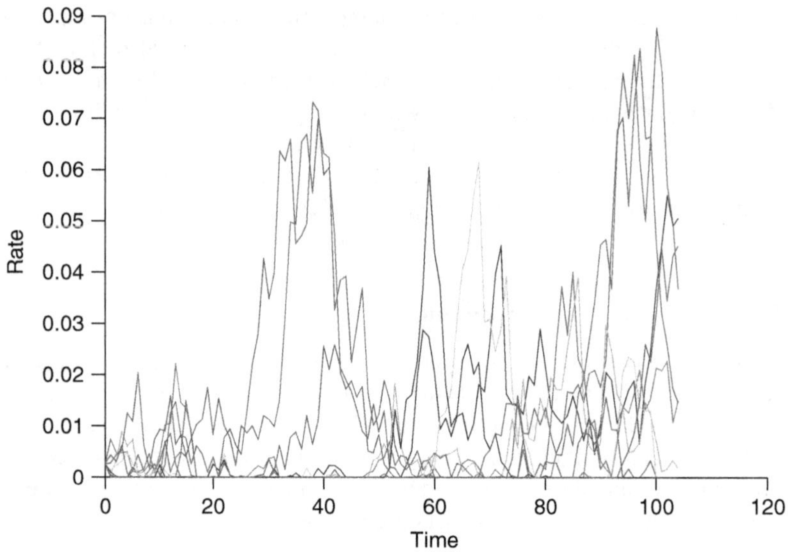

Figure 19.4 Simulated paths of autoregressive gamma process of order 0.

19.4.1 Valuation of Securities with Payoff at Fixed Date

We begin by considering the pricing of securities whose payoff is realized at a given future date T. These include simple securities, such as a zero-coupon bond with maturity T, as well as more complex securities, such as a European callable bond. In general, let $g_T = g(\mathbf{X}_T)$ denote the payoff at maturity T of the security, and then recall from Equation 19.61 that risk-neutral pricing implies that the arbitrage-free price of the security is

$$V = E^* \left[e^{-\int_0^T \phi(\mathbf{X}_u)du} g_T \right] \tag{19.62}$$

where the risk-free rate is given by the function

$$r_u = \phi(\mathbf{X}_u)$$

and $E^*[.]$ denotes that the expectation is taken with respect to the risk-neutral process for the state variables $\mathbf{X}_t$.

The simplest MC evaluation scheme is based on the law of large numbers, which guarantees that the sample average of a sequence of independent random variables converges to the (unconditional) expectation. In particular, for a given number *NoPath* of simulations with time step size h, define the average discounted payoff of the security by

$$G^{NoPaths}(h) := \frac{1}{NoPaths} \sum_{n=1}^{NoPaths} \exp \left(- \sum_{j=0}^{J-1} \phi\left(\mathcal{X}_{n,j}\right) h \right) g(\mathcal{X}_{n,J})$$

where $J = T/h$ is the time step corresponding to maturity T. Then, in the limit as $h \to 0$ and *NoPath* $\to \infty$, we have

$$G^{NoPaths}(h) \underset{NoPaths \to +\infty}{\overset{h \to 0, (T/h) \to +\infty}{\to}} = E^* \left[e^{-\int_0^T \phi(\mathbf{X}_u)du} g\left(X_T\right) \right]$$

where the sample mean is used to approximate the unconditional risk-neutral expectation. We provide a simple example next.

19.4.1.1 Example: Monte Carlo Valuation of Zero-Coupon Bonds on January 28, 2014 In this example, we illustrate the use of MC simulation to value a simple security: a zero-coupon bond. We perform this example on January 28, 2014, as we will use the same data for other valuation examples later.

Assume that the interest rate follows a CIR process so that the zero-coupon bond price is also known in closed analytic form (see Eqs 19.20, 19.23, 19.24). For the given discretization parameters h and *NoPath*, we can use the analytic formula to check on the accuracy of the MC valuation. In particular, for every maturity T the MC estimation of the zero-coupon bond price is

$$\widetilde{Z}(\mathcal{X}_0; T) = \frac{1}{NoPaths} \sum_{n=1}^{NoPaths} \exp \left(- \sum_{j=0}^{T/h-1} \mathcal{X}_{n,j} h \right)$$

where we recall that the short-term interest rate at time τ in simulation n is $r_{\tau,n} = \mathcal{X}_{\tau,n}$ (and we suppress the time index "0" from the argument of $\widehat{Z}(.)$ for simplicity).

We use the parameter estimates in Table 19.2, under the "no Feller condition" as they better fit the term structure of interest rates on January 28, 2014, and also because without the Feller condition, the interest rate r_0 can in fact hit zero, which is a reality of current market conditions (see discussion in Section 19.3.2.2.) The simulated paths of interest rates are shown in Figure 19.2.

Panel A of Figure 19.5 plots the zero-coupon bond prices from the CIR formula (solid line) and the one obtained from MC simulations, with $NoPath = 50,000$ and $h = 0.0052$ (dashed line). The two lines are very close to each other. The "circles" represent the data used and illustrate one of the drawbacks of using the CIR model compared to, for example, the Ho–Lee or Black, Derman, and Toy model, and this is that the model does not exactly fit the data but only approximates them.

Panel B of the figure plots the term structures of interest rates, which further highlights the very little difference between MC simulations and analytical formula and the difference between CIR model and the data. Indeed, the data display a mildly "inverted hump" term structure of interest rates, which is known to be difficult to fit using the one-factor CIR model.

We describe in the next sections two simple tools that can be used to improve the accuracy of the estimation through a refinement of the inference scheme.

19.4.1.2 Control Variates for Variance Reduction Iteration of the simulation procedure will produce a sequence of independent MC price estimates. If the estimator is unbiased, the sample mean of the sequence will represent the best price estimate, while the standard deviation will represent its statistical uncertainty. A popular variance reducing method, which is easy to implement, is the so called method of control variates.

For a concrete example, consider the pricing of a callable bond. Let its simulated value – discussed later – be given by $\widetilde{V}_0(\mathcal{X}_0)$. Assume that the interest rate follows a CIR or a Vasicek process, and then the zero-coupon bond price is known in closed analytic form (see Eq. 19.20). Hence on any maturity $\tau_i = 1, \ldots, K$, it is possible to compare the MC estimation of the zero-coupon bond price,

$$\widetilde{Z}(\mathcal{X}_0; \tau_i) = \frac{1}{NoPaths} \sum_{n=1}^{NoPaths} \exp\left(- \sum_{j=0}^{\tau_i/h-1} \mathcal{X}_{n,j} h \right)$$

with its exact price $Z(\mathcal{X}_0; \tau_i)$ (where we suppress here the current time "0" from the argument for notational simplicity).

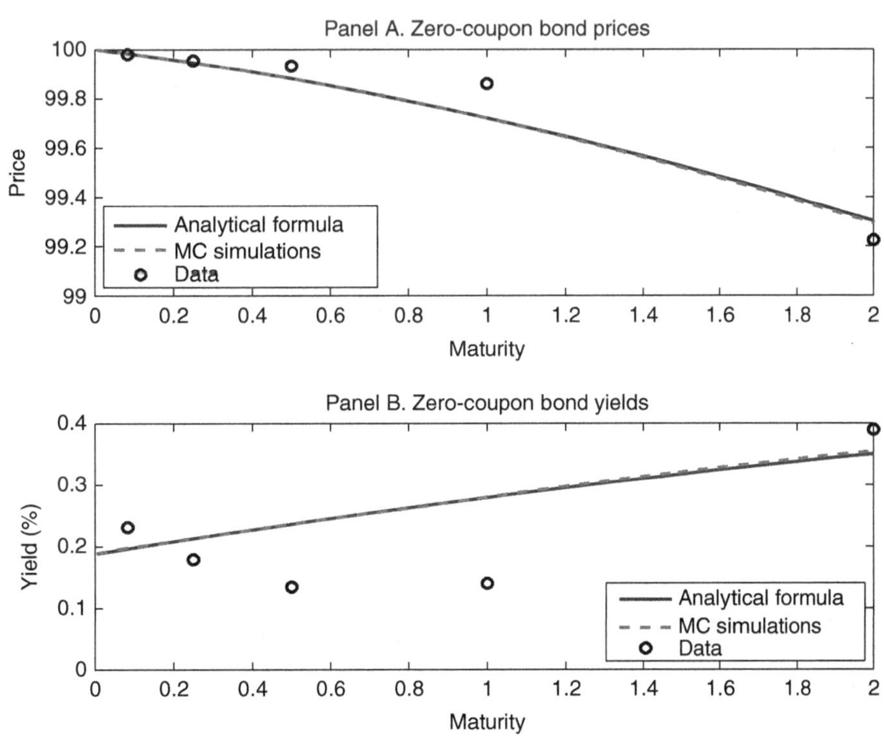

Figure 19.5 Simulated zero-coupon bond prices and yields under CIR model. Source: Data are from Gürkaynak, Sack, and Wright (2007), updated series.

The idea of control variate variance reduction is to exploit the information about the errors in estimates of known quantities (in this example the prices of zero-coupon bonds with expiration τ_i) to reduce the error of an estimate of an unknown quantity (in this example, the price of the callable bond) $\widetilde{V}_0(\mathcal{X}_0)$.

This can be done observing that the quantity

$$\widetilde{V}_0^{\eta}(\mathcal{X}_0) = \widetilde{V}_0(\mathcal{X}_0) + \sum_{i=1}^{I} \eta_i(\widetilde{Z}(\mathcal{X}_0;\tau_i) - Z(\mathcal{X}_0;\tau_i)),\ \eta_i \in \mathbb{R}$$

is an unbiased estimator of the true price of the callable bond for any value of the parameter η_i. The coefficients η_i are then selected by the condition that the variance of the estimation is minimized:

$$\eta^* = \arg \min_{\eta \in \mathbb{R}^I} Var(\widetilde{V}_0^{\eta}(\mathcal{X}_0))$$

It is easy to verify that the solution is

$$\eta_i^* = -\frac{Cov(\widetilde{Z}(\mathcal{X}_0;\tau_i), \widetilde{V}_0(\mathcal{X}_0))}{Var(\widetilde{Z}(\mathcal{X}_0;\tau_i))}$$

The minimum variance estimator controlling for the zero-coupon bond price is then given by $\widetilde{V}_0^{\eta^*}(\mathcal{X}_0)$. The variance of the estimated value of the security is expected to reduce by a factor $1 - \sum_{i=1}^{I} \rho_{i,C}^2$, where $\rho_{i,C}$ is the correlation between the ith zero-coupon bond price and the callable bond prices.

19.4.1.3 Richardson Extrapolation Recall that the computation of discrete-time sample estimators $G(h)$ are only an intermediate step with respect to the final goal, which is the identification of the true continuous time expectation value, the limit

$$G^* = \lim_{h\to 0, NoPaths\to +\infty} G^{NoPaths}(h)$$

Assume that the MC simulations produced a sequence of estimations $G(h_1), G(h_2), \ldots, G(h_N)$, with h_n a decreasing sequence of discretization step sizes. If the sequence of estimations converges to a value independent from h_n within the simulation error, then the limiting value is simply given by $G^* \approx G(h_N)$. On the contrary, if the dependence of $G(h_n)$ with respect to h_n does appear to be systematic, then a simple extrapolation scheme, called the Richardson extrapolation scheme, can be used to improve the estimate. The simplest version of this scheme is derived from the assumption that the leading correction to the exact value G^* is linear in the discretization step:

$$G(h) \approx G^* + Ch + O(h^2)$$

Then the value of the correction C can be estimated using a sequence of transformations. In particular, consider the case where $G(h_1), G(h_2)$ are known with $h_1 = h, h_2 = h/2$, then

$$G(h) = G^* + Ch + O(h^2)$$
$$G\left(\frac{h}{2}\right) = G^* + C\frac{h}{2} + O\left(\left(\frac{h}{2}\right)^2\right)$$

Then solving the linear system, one gets

$$C\frac{h}{2} = G(h) - G\left(\frac{h}{2}\right) + O\left(\left(\frac{h}{2}\right)^2\right)$$
$$G\left(\frac{h}{2}\right) = G^* + G(h) - G\left(\frac{h}{2}\right) + O\left(\left(\frac{h}{2}\right)^2\right)$$

and the best estimate of the limiting value is given by

$$G^* \approx 2G\left(\frac{h}{2}\right) - G(h) + O\left(\left(\frac{h}{2}\right)^2\right)$$

19.4.2 MC Valuation of Callable Bonds

The explicit valuation of a callable bond contract offers an illustration of the practical implementation issues involved in a valuation by MC simulation. As a first step let us recall the basic features of this contract. A *callable* (or *redeemable*) *bond* is a fixed rate bond that allows the issuer to retain the privilege of redeeming the bond at a preagreed value before the bond reaches its date of maturity.

The callable bond is said to have a *European* style if there is a single redemption date and a *Bermudan* one if the bond is redeemable on a periodic basis (e.g., quarterly) according to a preagreed time and price schedule. A *lockout condition* forces the issuer to delay redemption after bond issuance by a minimum period of time, called *the lockout period.* For each redemption date, the issuer is required to declare its decision to the holder of the bond at *the announcement date* according to a schedule, which is contractually specified.

The callable bond payoff can be decomposed as the payoff of a long position in a bond and that of a short position on a call:

$$\textit{Callable bond} = \textit{Straight bond} - \textit{Call option}$$

The option has the same exercise style as the one of the callable bonds. The payoff of the straight bond is the same as the callable bond one under the assumption that the option to redeem is never exercised. Hence the straight bond position will pay off a stream of coupons c_{T_i} according to a known time schedule T_i, $i = 1, \ldots, N$ (mostly, $c_{T_i} = c$ are constant over time) and the principal at maturity T.

In the one-dimensional factor models, the price of zero-coupon bonds is available in closed form. Zero-coupon bond prices can be computed as a function of the initial state variable (interest rate) for both the Vasicek and CIR models using the explicit solutions. Assuming that the level of the interest rate at time t is given by X_t, the value of a zero-coupon bond expiring at time T is given by

$$Z(t, X_t; T) = e^{A(t;T) - B(t;T)X_t}$$

where the expressions of $A(t; T)$ and $B(t; T)$ are specified in Equations 19.21 through 19.24.[6] Then, the unique arbitrage-free price of the straight coupon bond price with unit principal at time t and with N coupons to be paid at $T_1, T_2, \ldots, T_N$ is given by

$$P(t, X_t; T) = \sum_{i=1}^{N} Z(t, X_t; T_i) c_{T_i} + Z(t, X_t; T)$$

In case of a European-style contract, the call option has a maturity equal to the *redemption date* T_{RD} and a payoff equal to

$$\textit{Call option payoff} = g(X_{T_{RD}}) = \max[P(T_{RD}, X_{T_{RD}}; T) - K_{RD}, 0]$$

where the strike price of the option K_{RD} is set by the redemption price. For $t < T_{RD}$ we can compute the value of the call option by Monte Carlo simulations. In particular, note that for each simulation path $\mathcal{X}_{n,\cdot}$, the payoff $g(X_{T_{RD}})$ can be computed by using the CIR formula of zero-coupon bonds, $P(T_{RD}, \mathcal{X}_{n,J}; T)$, where $J = T_{RD}/h$ is the time step corresponding to the redemption date. Thus, we have that at time 0

$$\begin{aligned}
\widetilde{Call}_0 &= \frac{1}{NoPaths} \sum_{n=1}^{NoPaths} e^{-\sum_{j=0}^{J-1} \mathcal{X}_{n,j} h} \; g(\mathcal{X}_{n,J}) \\
&= \frac{1}{NoPaths} \sum_{n=1}^{NoPaths} e^{-\sum_{j=0}^{J-1} \mathcal{X}_{n,j} h} \; \max[P(T_{RD}, \mathcal{X}_{n,J}; T) - K_{RD}, 0]
\end{aligned}$$

In general, at any time t prior to redemption date T_{RD}, the price of the callable security is given by

$$P_t^{\textit{Callable Bond}} = P_t^{\textit{Straight Bond}} - Call_t \quad \text{for} \quad t \le T_{RD}$$

For $t > T_{RD}$, instead, if the bond is redeemed at T_{RD}, it ceases to exist; otherwise the redemption option remains unexercised, $P_t^{Call} = 0$, and hence

$$P_t^{\textit{Callable Bond}} = P_t^{\textit{Straight Bond}} \quad \text{for} \quad t > T_{RD}$$

[6]Similarly, the zero-coupon bond price solution for the discretized version of the model is determined by discrete-time difference equations whose explicit solution can be found in Le, Singleton, and Dai (2010).

Given a simulated value $\widetilde{Call}_0$ of the call option and the value $P(t, X_0; T)$ of the straight bond, the value of the callable bond at time 0 is thus

$$\widetilde{P}_0^{Callable\ Bond} = P(t, X_0; T) - \widetilde{Call}_0$$

We illustrate this procedure in the next example.

19.4.2.1 Example: Freddie Mac 0.5% Callable Bond Consider the following debt security offered by Freddie Mac for an aggregate amount of $500,000,000 on January 2, 2013. The security pays a fixed (annual) coupon rate equal to 0.50% of the principal. Coupon payments take place on a semiannual basis with payment dates January 28 and July 28 starting from July 28, 2013. At maturity, which is fixed at January 28, 2016, the amount reimbursed will correspond to 100% of the principal. At the option of Freddie Mac, upon notice to holders, the security is redeemable on January 28, 2015 only (European feature), and the redemption price is set to 100% of the principal plus accrued interest until the redemption date.

Let today be January 28, 2014. From Bloomberg, this security is trading at $99.95.

We use the parameter estimates in Table 19.2, under the "no Feller condition" as they better fit the term structure of interest rates on January 28, 2014, and also because without the Feller condition, the interest rate r_t can hit zero, which is a reality of current market conditions (see discussion in Section 19.3.2.2). The simulated paths of interest rates are shown in Figure 19.2.

The straight bond price is $100.33, which can be computed without MC simulations. The valuation of the option to call is quite small

$$\widetilde{Call}_0 = \$0.3721$$

The small value of the option to call is not surprising, given the environment with extremely low interest rates. Thus, the simulated value of the callable bond on January 28, 2014, is

$$\widetilde{P}_0^{Callable\ Bond} = \$100.33 - \$0.3721 = \$99.93$$

which is very close to the traded price.

19.4.3 MC Valuation of Securities with American or Bermudan Exercise Style

Many securities, such as callable bonds, are often issued with a Bermudan exercise style, that is, the issuer retains the right to redeem the bond at a sequence of possible redemption dates and of call prices.[7] Let us denote such sequence of redemption times and strike prices as

$$\begin{bmatrix} T_L & T_{L+1} & \cdots & T_I \\ K_L & K_{L+1} & \cdots & K_I \end{bmatrix}$$

where T_L denotes the end of the lockout period and T_I is the last redemption date. In this case the valuation of the Bermudan-style security is conditioned to the determination of the optimal time to exercise the option, which requires the construction of a backward dynamic programming procedure.

To be concrete, we illustrate the procedure using again the example of callable bonds, but the procedure can be applied to any security. To illustrate the logic of backward dynamic programming, note that at any available redemption date T_i, $i = L, \ldots, I$, the issuer must decide whether to redeem the callable bond or keep the option to call alive and redeem the security in the future. Assume for now that the notice period is zero and that the redemption strike price is par $K_{RD} = 100$, for simplicity. Because the issuer holds the call option to redeem, it is in the interest of the issuer to maximize the value of such call option. Thus, at any T_i, the issuer will compare the payoff from exercising the option, that is, $P(T_i, X_{T_i}; T) - 100$, and the value of keeping the option alive $Call(T_i, X_{T_i})$ and take the maximum of the two:

$$\max[P(T_i, X_{T_i}; T) - 100, Call(T_i, X_{T_i})]$$

The value to keep the option alive $Call(T_i, X_{T_i})$ is normally referred to as continuation value of the call option. It follows that the value of the option to call at time T_{i-1} is given by the risk-neutral present value of the payoff at time T_i, obtaining the rule

$$Call(T_{i-1}, X_{T_{i-1}}) = E^* \left\{ \exp\left(-\int_{T_{i-1}}^{T_i} r_u du \right) \max[P(T_i, X_{T_i}; T) - 100, Call(T_i, X_{T_i})] | X_{T_{i-1}} \right\} \tag{19.63}$$

where recall that the risk-free rate is $r_u = \phi(X_u)$.

[7] If the sequence of possible redemption dates is determined ex ante, the security has Bermudan exercise style. If redemption can occur any time before or at maturity, the security has American exercise style. We review the methodology for the case of Bermudan exercise style, but the same methodology can be applied to the American exercise style by choosing the sequence of redemption dates sufficiently close to each other. See Longstaff and Schwartz (2001).

This backward procedure requires us to start the computation of the valuation of the option to call at the last time available to call T_I and then move backward to T_{I-1}, T_{I-2}, and so on until T_L. Note that because Monte Carlo simulations move "forward," that is, we simulate the state variables $X_{n,j}$ from 0 to T, the procedure is not straightforward, as it is on, for example, binomial trees (see Tebaldi and Veronesi (2015, Chapter 17)). It is in fact incorrect to compute the earlier maximization path by path (i.e., for each path of interest rates, say, just compute the maximum along that path), as the call option in the maximization 19.63 $Call(T_i, X_{T_i})$ is itself an expectation of future values of the option to call and thus must be computed by taking into account all possible future realizations of paths of state variables $\{\mathcal{X}_{m,i}\}$. Next section discusses the procedure.

19.4.3.1 Backward Dynamic Programming In this section, we discuss concretely how to value a callable bond by dynamic programming. We also take into account the announcement date of the redemption, which we assume it occurs a short period δ before each redemption date T_i, that is, at $T_i - \delta$.

We first notice that we can rewrite the maximization of the option to call in Equation 19.63 as the minimum between the payment to investors, K_i, and the value of the callable bond if not exercised, referred to as a continuation value. More precisely, a rational issuer will decide to exercise the option to redeem the bond if at the announcement date, when the state variable is in state $X_{T_i-\delta}$, the ex coupon continuation price $C_{T_i-\delta}(X_{T_i-\delta})$ is larger than the redemption price K_i discounted from T_i to $T_i - \delta$. That is, the value of the callable bond at time $T_i - \delta$ is

$$V_{T_i-\delta}(X_{T_i-\delta}) = \min\{Z(\delta, X_{T_i-\delta})K_i, C_{T_i-\delta}(X_{T_i-\delta})\} + Z(\delta, X_{T_i-\delta})c_{T_i} \tag{19.64}$$

where with a slight abuse of notation, we denote here by $Z(\delta, X_{T_i-\delta})$ the "δ-period" risk-free discount at time $T_i - \delta$. To interpret this expression, the first term on the right-hand side is the minimum between the discounted value (to $T_i - \delta$) of the redemption price K_i and the current (continuation) value of the callable bond if not exercised $C_{T_i-\delta}(X_{T_i-\delta})$. The latter is ex coupon, because independent of the decision to exercise, the coupon c_{T_i} needs to be paid at T_i, as captured by the last term.

The value function $V_{T_i-\delta}(X_{T_i-\delta})$ can now be computed by backward induction as follows: first, at maturity T, set

$$V_T(X_T) = 1 + c_T$$

which is the final payoff *if* the bond is not redeemed before maturity T. Given this final condition, we now iterate backwards to compute the continuation value at time $T_{i-1} - \delta$ as the discounted conditional expectation of the future value of the callable bond at time $T_i - \delta$. That is, for every i with $L < i \leq I$, we have

$$C_{T_{i-1}-\delta}(X_{T_{i-1}-\delta}) = E^*\left[e^{-\int_{T_{i-1}-\delta}^{T_i-\delta} r_u du} V_{T_i-\delta}(X_{T_i-\delta}) \mid X_{T_{i-1}-\delta}\right] \tag{19.65}$$

where recall $r_u = \phi(X_u)$.

Because redemption can only start after the lockout period at time T_L, the initial price of a callable bond is then

$$V_0(X_0) = \sum_{i=1}^{L-1} Z(0, X_0; T_i)c_{T_i} + P^{CB}(X_0; T_L - \delta)$$

$$P^{CB}(X_0; T_L - \delta) = E^*\left[e^{-\int_0^{T_L-\delta} r_u du} V_{T_L-\delta}(X_{T_L-\delta}) \mid X_0\right]$$

That is, it is equal to the present value of future coupons c_{T_i} before redemption time T_L (and hence the sum runs only up to $L - 1$) plus the present value of the callable bond as of redemption time $T_L - \delta$, where again we take into account the announcement date must be δ before actual redemption. This latter term is given by $P^{CB}(X_0; T_L - \delta)$ in the expressions previously.

The important question is how we can compute the continuation value $C_{T_{i-1}-\delta}(X_{T_{i-1}-\delta})$ in Equation 19.65, as this involves the conditional expectation of future continuation values, conditional on the current value of state variables. We illustrate the methodology in the next section.

19.4.3.2 Computation of the Conditional Expectation by Least-Squares Regression The numerical approximation of the conditional expectation is a critical element for an efficient implementation of the backward dynamic programming procedure. Longstaff and Schwartz (2001) introduced a solution that is numerically efficient and well grounded on the probabilistic definition of conditional expectation .

Consider a simple framework in which the process is Markov and all the information is known at time t if the value of an underlying process X_t is known. Then the conditional expectation $E[F_{T_2}(X_{T_2}) \mid X_{T_1}]$ of a function $F_{T_2}(.)$ of the random variable

X_{T_2} is simply a function of the current value X_{T_1}. That is, different conditioning values X_{T_1} lead to different expectations. Denoting such function $f_{T_1}(X_{T_1})$, we can write

$$E[F_{T_2}(X_{T_2}) \mid X_{T_1}] = f_{T_1}(X_{T_1}) \tag{19.66}$$

Intuitively, if $F_{T_2}(X_{T_2})$ represents the payoff from the option to exercise a callable bond, where X_{T_1} is the level of the interest rate, Equation 19.66 indicates that the conditional expectation of the call option to redeem depends on the current level of the interest rate. If the interest rate is very high today, it is unlikely that the callable bond will be redeemed in the future, and thus the value of the option to redeem is close to zero. Vice versa, if the interest rate is very low today, it is likely that the callable bond will be redeemed at the next opportunity, and thus the conditional expectation of the payoff is high today. Thus, we would expect $f_{T_1}(X_{T_1})$ to be a decreasing function of X_{T_1}.

The conditional expectation in Equation 19.66 can be thought of as the forecast of $F_{T_2}(X_{T_2})$ given the information at time T_1. Define the forecast error as

$$\varepsilon_{T_2} = F_{T_2}(X_{T_2}) - E[F_{T_2}(X_{T_2}) \mid X_{T_1}] \tag{19.67}$$

$$= F_{T_2}(X_{T_2}) - f_{T_1}(X_{T_1}) \tag{19.68}$$

If we had a parametric functional form for $f_{T_1}(X_{T_1})$, then we could estimate the conditional expectation by estimating the parameters of the functional form. What data can we use for this estimation? Such data are provided by Monte Carlo simulations, as explained next.

In particular, Longstaff and Schwartz (2001) suggest to approximate the conditional expectation function $f_{T_1}(X_{T_1})$ using a linear combination of nonlinear functions $\{\mathcal{H}_1(X_{T_1}), \mathcal{H}_2(X_{T_1}), \ldots, \mathcal{H}_K(X_{T_1})\}$ of the underlying observed conditioning state variable X_{T_1}:[8]

$$E[F_{T_2}(X_{T_2}) \mid X_{T_1}] = f_{T_1}(X_{T_1}) \approx \sum_{k=1}^{K} \beta_k^* \mathcal{H}_k(X_{T_1}) + \varepsilon_{T_1}$$

The calculation of the conditional expectation is thus reduced to the determination of the coefficients $\{\beta_k\}_{k=1,\ldots,K}$, which minimizes the square forecast error in Equation 19.68, namely,

$$\{\beta^*_{T_1,k}\}_{k=1,\ldots,K} = \underset{\{\beta_{T_1,k}\}_{k=1,\ldots,K}}{\arg\min} E\left[\left(F_{T_2}(X_{T_2}) - \sum_{k=1}^{K} \beta_{T_1,k}\mathcal{H}_k\left(X_{T_1}\right)\right)^2\right]$$

In the numerical implementations, we use the first five Hermite polynomials. However, the valuation of conditional expectations is robust with respect to the choice of different basis functions.

19.4.3.3 Approximation of the Backward Induction Algorithm Longstaff and Schwartz (2001) propose an approximate determination of the value function $V_{T_i-\delta}(X_{T_i-\delta})$ based on a backward induction procedure. At each step the continuation value is computed using a least-squares regression approach. In the case of a callable bond, the approximate algorithm works as follows:

- Set a minimum discretization step h and convert all the redemption, coupon dates in grid units: $\tau_i = T_i/h$. Letting $d = \delta/h$ the announcement dates are $\tau_i - d = (T_i - d)/h$ and maturity is $J = T/h$.
- Simulate *NoPaths* paths of the discretized interest rate process with initial condition $\mathcal{X}_0$ (see Table 19.1).
- At maturity $J = T/h$, set the final value of the callable bond equal to the principal plus the last coupon c_T

$$\widetilde{V}_N(\mathcal{X}_{n,J}) = 1 + c_T, \quad \text{for} \quad n = 1, 2, \ldots, NoPath$$

- For each exercise time i with $L < i \leq I$, we compute the value function using the following procedure:
    1. Compute the least-squares approximation of continuation value at time $(\tau_{i-1} - d)$ for each realized simulated path n, that is, conditional on the realized value $\mathcal{X}_{(\tau_i-d),n}$. The continuation value is determined by the discounted conditional expectation:

$$\widetilde{C}_{(\tau_{i-1}-d)}(\mathcal{X}_{(\tau_{i-1}-d),n}) = \sum_{m=1}^{M} \psi^*_{(\tau_{i-1}-d),m}\mathcal{H}_m(\mathcal{X}_{(\tau_{i-1}-d),n}) \tag{19.69}$$

[8]The set of nonlinear functions is typically a family of orthogonal polynomials that form a basis in an Hilbert space of square integrable functions.

where $\psi^*_{\tau_i-1,m}$ for $m = 1, \ldots, M$ are obtained as the result of cross-sectional regression at time $\tau_{i-1} - d$ *across simulated paths*. Specifically, given the value of the callable bond already computed at time $\tau_i - d$ $\widetilde{V}_{\tau_i-d}(\mathcal{X}_{(\tau_i-d),n})$ for each possible realization of the simulated state variable $\mathcal{X}_{(\tau_i-d),n}$, we can move one step backward to time $\tau_{i-1} - d$, and for each simulation $n = 1, \ldots, NoPath$, we can define the discounted value of future payoff as

$$\mathcal{Y}_{(\tau_{i-1}-d),n} = \exp\left(-\sum_{j=\tau_{i-1}-d}^{\tau_i-d-1} r_{n,j}\, h\right)\widetilde{V}_{\tau_i-d}(\mathcal{X}_{(\tau_i-d),n})$$

In this expression, recall that the risk-free interest rate in simulation n and step j is given by $r_{n,j} = \phi(\mathcal{X}_{n,j})$. Because the quantity $\mathcal{Y}_{(\tau_{i-1}-d),n}$ can be computed for each simulation $n = 1, \ldots, NoPath$, we can then run the cross-sectional ordinary least square (OLS) regression to determine the coefficients $\psi^*_{(\tau_{i-1}-d),m}$, $m = 1, \ldots, M$ as a solution to the minimization of squared errors:

$$\min_{\psi_m\ m=1,\ldots,M} \sum_{n=1}^{NoPath}\left(\mathcal{Y}_{(\tau_{i-1}-d),n} - \sum_{m=1}^{M}\psi_m \mathcal{H}_m(\mathcal{X}_{(\tau_{i-1}-d,n)})\right)^2$$

2. Select the approximate value function $\widetilde{V}_{(\tau_{i-1}-d),n}$ at time $(\tau_{i-1} - d)$ in simulation n by applying the rational exercise, namely, solve the minimization in Equation 19.64 path by path. This translates in the following rule: for any $n = 1, \ldots, NoPath$

   (A) If $K_{i-1}Z(\delta, \mathcal{X}_{(\tau_{i-1}-d),n}) \leq \widetilde{C}_{(\tau_{i-1}-d)}(\mathcal{X}_{(\tau_{i-1}-d),n})$:

   $$\widetilde{V}_{(\tau_{i-1}-d)}(\mathcal{X}_{(\tau_{i-1}-d),n}) = K_{i-1}Z(\delta, \mathcal{X}_{(\tau_{i-1}-d),n}) + c_{\tau_{i-1}}Z(\delta, \mathcal{X}_{(\tau_{i-1}-d),n})$$

   (B) If $K_{i-1}Z(\delta, \mathcal{X}_{(\tau_{i-1}-d),n}) > \widetilde{C}_{(\tau_{i-1}-d)}(\mathcal{X}_{(\tau_{i-1}-d),n})$:

   $$\widetilde{V}_{(\tau_{i-1}-d)}(\mathcal{X}_{(\tau_{i-1}-d),n}) = \widetilde{C}_{(\tau_{i-1}-d)}(\mathcal{X}_{(\tau_{i-1}-d),n}) + c_{\tau_{i-1}}Z(\delta, \mathcal{X}_{(\tau_{i-1}-d),n})$$

   To interpret, case (A) says that if paying off the callable bond at τ_{i-1} is less expensive than keeping the callable bond alive, then the issuer should redeem the callable bond at τ_{i-1}. Thus, the value at announcement time $(\tau_{i-1} - d)$ of the callable bond is just the present value of the call price plus the next coupon, which are both paid at τ_{i-1}. Case (B) instead says that if paying off the callable bond at τ_{i-1} is more onerous than leaving it alive, the value at $\tau_{i-1} - d$ of the callable bond equals its continuation value plus the present value of the coupon that will be paid at τ_{i-1}.
3. At $i = L$ stop the iteration and compute the time zero discounted expectation of the residual value at the first announcement date $T_L - \delta = (\tau_L - d)h$:

   $$\widetilde{P}^{CB}(\mathcal{X}_0; T_L - \delta) = Z(0, \mathcal{X}_0; T_L - \delta)\frac{1}{NoPaths}\sum_{n=1}^{NoPaths}\widetilde{V}_{\tau_L-d}(\mathcal{X}_{\tau_L-d,n})$$

   and compute the initial prices of the callable bond as

   $$\widetilde{V}_0(\mathcal{X}_0) = \sum_{i=1}^{L-1} Z(0, \mathcal{X}_0; T_i)c_{T_i} + \widetilde{P}^{CB}(\mathcal{X}_0; T_L - \delta)$$

If the exact conditional expectation functional can be written as a linear combination of the selected set of nonlinear functions, then Clément, Lamberton, and Protter (2002) prove that in the limit of the number of paths going to infinity the numerical estimation of the price converges to the no-arbitrage one.

19.4.3.4 Estimation of Upper and Lower Bounds The approximate value iteration procedure used to determine the callable bond price could induce some bias on the numerical estimation. Glasserman and Yu (2004) and Haugh and Kogan (2004) have introduced some simple numerical procedures in order to quantify the systematic biases induced by the approximations. Their arguments can be easily adapted to the valuation of a callable bond.

19.4.3.5 Summary Summing up the previous discussion, the general scheme that has been applied to price a structured security by using a simulation approach is the following:

- Step 0: Generation of the underlying paths
- Step 1: Construction of the vector of structured security payoffs
  - Decomposition of the structured derivative as a sum of elementary products
  - Generation of the fundamental (underlying) securities payoffs (bond payoffs)
  - Generation of the derivative securities payoffs
- Step 2: Finite sample statistics estimation for decreasing discretization step and increasing sample size
- Step 3: Application of variance reduction techniques and extrapolation of the continuous time limit estimates
- Step 4: Quality check of the numerical solution
- Step 5: Estimation of upper and lower bounds and sensitivity analysis beyond price: a closer look to the statistical information hidden in the simulated sample paths
- Step 6: Calibration of the model to market data

19.4.3.6 Simulated versus Analytic Prices: A Comparison Evaluation for the Büttler and Waldvogel (1996) Benchmark Contract In order to quantify the accuracy achieved by a simulation procedure, it is useful to compare the performance of the simulation results with the value obtained with alternative valuation approaches and in particular with analytical solutions, whenever available. In the specific case of callable bond securities, Lim, Li, and Linetsky (2012) report analytical prices for a benchmark callable bond determined assuming the Vasicek and CIR interest rate models. The benchmark callable bond, which is used in the literature to assess the quality of a valuation model, is a 4.25% callable bond issued by the Swiss Confederation, over the period 1987–2012, originally priced in Büttler and Waldvogel (1996). At the pricing date $t_0 = 0$, December 23, 1991, the time to maturity was $T = 20.172$ years; the coupon $c = 0.0425$, paid once a year, had the next coupon coming at time $t_1 = 0.172$ years from now; and the protection period was $T_L = 10.172$ years from now. The bond could be redeemed at coupon times $T_L = T_{11} = 10.172, T_{12} = 11.172, \ldots, T_{21} = T = 20.172$ by giving a notice period of 2 months (i.e., $\delta = 0.1666$). The call prices are not constant but decreasing over time and equal to $K_{11} = 1.025$, $K_{12} = 1.020$, $K_{13} = 1.015$, $K_{14} = 1.010$, $K_{15} = 1.005$, and $K_{16} = \cdots = K_{21} = 1$. The parameter values used in the valuation are $\theta = 0.098397028$, $\kappa = 0.44178462$, $\sigma = 0.13264223$ for the Vasicek model and $\theta = 0.133976855$, $\kappa = 0.14294371$, $\sigma = 0.38757496$ for the CIR model. In the latter case, it is easy to see that the parameters satisfy the Feller condition.

In Table 19.3, we compare the numerical valuation obtained by MC simulation, its upper and lower bounds, and the exact valuation of the benchmark contract. As expected, the Longstaff and Schwartz (2001) procedure produces an estimated price that is very close to the exact values. Upper bounds are tight and within a standard error indistinguishable from the exact value, while the determination of the lower bound is very imprecise.

19.4.3.7 Pricing a 2-Year, 0.45% Bermudan Freddie Mac Security on January 28, 2014 In this section, we illustrate the methodology discussed in the previous sections by pricing a specific callable bond issued by Freddie Mac. Specifically, consider the following debt security offered by Freddie Mac for an aggregate amount of $250,000,000 issued January 28, 2014, paying 0.45% per annum and due January 28, 2016. The security is redeemable periodically beginning on July 28, 2014.

Coupon payments take place on a semiannual basis with payment dates January 28 and July 28 starting from July 28, 2014. At maturity, the amount reimbursed will correspond to 100% of the principal. At the option of Freddie Mac, the security is

TABLE 19.3 The Value of Callable Bonds for Benchmark Contract

	Upper	LS	Exact	Lower
Vas $r_0 = 0.04$	0.7964 (0.0031)	0.7953 (0.0028)	0.7942	0.7596 (0.0032)
Vas $r_0 = 0.05$	0.7800 (0.0024)	0.7787 (0.0023)	0.7795	0.7470 (0.0034)
CIR $r_0 = 0.04$	0.8719 (0.0011)	0.8717 (0.0007)	0.8712	0.8297 (0.0036)
CIR $r_0 = 0.05$	0.8504 (0.001)	0.8501 (0.0009)	0.8498	0.8054 (0.0028)

Results are based on *NoPaths* = 5000 simulations and with $h = 1/48$.
Standard deviations are reported with in parentheses.

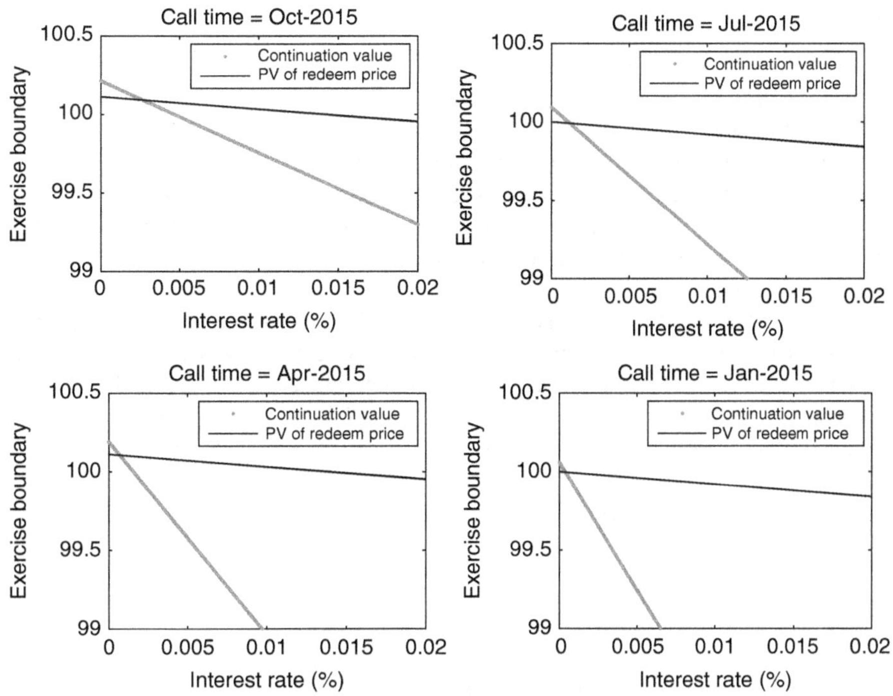

Figure 19.6 Call prices and simulated continuation values on four dates for the pricing of the 2-year, 0.45% Bermudan Freddie Mac.

redeemable on a quarterly basis on the 28th of January, April, July, and October, and the redemption price is set to 100% of the principal plus accrued interest until the redemption date upon notice to holders not less than 5 business days nor more than 60 calendar days prior to redemption. According to Bloomberg, this security was trading on January 28, 2014, at \$99.93.

The backward induction/Monte Carlo simulation methodology illustrated in previous sections produces an estimated "exercise threshold" at every exercise time $T_i - \delta$. For illustration, the four panels of Figure 19.6 plot such thresholds that trigger the decision to redeem the callable bond at four of the eight possible redemption dates. For each date, we plot the present value of the call price $100\, Z(\delta, \mathcal{X}_{(\tau_{i-1}-d),n})$ and the estimated continuation value

$$\widetilde{C}_{(\tau_{i-1}-d)}(\mathcal{X}_{(\tau_{i-1}-d),n}) = \sum_{m=1}^{M} \psi^*_{(\tau_{i-1}-d),m} \mathcal{H}_m(\mathcal{X}_{(\tau_{i-1}-d),n})$$

against the corresponding simulated interest rate scenarios on the x-axis. As we move further from maturity, the continuation value declines for each interest rate level, reflecting an increase in value of the option to call the bond in the future. As can be seen, the model predicts that for very low interest rates – which do happen with high frequency in the CIR model without the Feller condition being satisfied – the exercise of the Bermudan callable bond is optimal, as the continuation value is above the call price.

The backward calculation of the callable bond yields a price on January 28, 2014, equal to \$99.72, a bit smaller than the traded price on the same date.

19.5 MONTE CARLO SIMULATIONS IN MULTIFACTOR MODELS

It is well known at least since Litterman and Scheinkman (1991) that in order to match dynamic or cross-sectional properties of observed yields and returns, it is necessary to use models with three or more factors. Hence, it turns necessary to extend the simulation scheme introduced for single-factor models to multifactor stochastic interest rate models.

The typical challenges and advantages introduced by the multidimensional extension are best illustrated by analyzing the MC simulation approach on a specific class of multifactor processes, the class of affine term structure models introduced in Duffie and Kan (1996). This class of processes has the conditional mean and the conditional variance that are affine functions of the state variable levels and can be considered as the natural multidimensional extension of Vasicek and CIR processes.

19.5.1 Discretization Procedure of the Affine Factor Models

Affine factor models are said to be admissible in a domain $\mathcal{D}$ according to the terminology of Dai and Singleton (2000) if their evolution is well defined for any future time, and thus the term structure is well defined for any future maturity.

In the case of a single-factor model, the admissibility condition for a CIR process, which is defined on the positive line $\mathcal{D} = \mathbb{R}_+$, is precisely the condition that the process remains nonnegative for any positive initial condition. In the case of a multidimensional affine process, the admissibility conditions are those ensuring that the process does not exit from a domain $\mathcal{D} \subset \mathbb{R}^p$. The most common class of admissible affine models, which is used in the literature, is the class of models $\mathbb{A}_m(p)$ with domain $\mathcal{D} = \mathbb{R}^m_+ \times \mathbb{R}^{p-m}$, where the first m factors evolve in a positive state space (CIR-like factors), while the last $p - m$ evolve in an unrestricted (Gaussian) state space.

The discretization procedure preserving admissibility and extending the single-factor procedure proposed by Gourieroux and Jasiak (2006) to the class of multifactor affine models has been derived by Creal and Wu (2015). By convention, the discretization of the vector of positive factors at time kh for simulation n will be denoted by $H_{k,n} \in \mathbb{R}^m_+$, and the discretization of the vector of Gaussian factors at time kh for realization n will be denoted by $G_{k,n} \in \mathbb{R}^{p-m}_+$.

The discretized dynamics of the affine process is determined as follows:

- The discretized evolution of the CIR-like factors is

$$\underset{m\times 1}{H_{k+1,n}} = \underset{m\times m}{\Sigma_H} \cdot \underset{m\times 1}{w_{k+1,n}}$$

$$(w_{k+1,n})_i \sim Gamma(\nu_i^H + z_{i,k+1}, 1) \quad i = 1, \ldots, m$$

$$(z_{k+1,n})_i \sim Poisson(e_i(\Sigma^H)^{-1}\Phi^H\Sigma^H w_{k,n}) \quad i = 1, \ldots, m$$

  where $\nu^H = (\nu_1^H, \ldots, \nu_m^H)$ are the shape parameters, Φ^H is an $m \times m$ matrix controlling the autocorrelation, Σ_H is an $m \times m$ scale matrix, and e_i denotes the ith column of an $m \times m$ identity matrix. Admissibility conditions to guarantee that h_{t+1} remains positive require that all elements of Σ_H must be nonnegative, and to ensure that the mean of the Poisson distribution is nonnegative, $\Sigma_H^{-1}\Phi^H\Sigma_H$ must be nonnegative definite.
- The discretized evolution of the Gaussian factors is

$$\underset{m\times 1}{G_{k+1,n}} = \underset{m\times 1}{\mu^G} + \underset{m\times m}{\Phi^G} \cdot \underset{m\times 1}{G_{k,n}} + \underset{m\times m}{\Phi^{GH}} \cdot \underset{m\times 1}{H_{k,n}} + \underset{m\times m}{\Sigma^{GH}} \underset{m\times 1}{\varepsilon^H_{k+1,n}} + \underset{m\times 1}{\varepsilon^G_{k+1,n}}$$

$$\varepsilon^H_{k+1,\cdot} := H_{k+1,\cdot} - E[H_{k+1} \mid H_k]$$

$$\varepsilon^G_{k+1,\cdot} \sim Normal\left(\underline{0}, \Sigma_{G,0}\Sigma_{G,0}^T + \sum_{i=1}^m \Sigma_{G,i}\Sigma_{G,i}^T \left(H_{k,\cdot}\right)_i\right)$$

  where $\Sigma_{G,i}$ must be the lower triangular for $i = 1, \ldots, m$. The Gaussian factors are functions of the non-Gaussian state variables through both the autoregressive term Φ^{GH} and the covariance term Σ^{GH}. Notice that the complete representation of the process $\mathcal{X}_{k,n} = (H_{k,n}, G_{k,n})$ at a fixed time k requires an array (a pile of matrices) where each element is specified by three indices (i, k, n) where $i = 1, \ldots, p$ is the component index ($i = 1, \ldots, m$ are CIR-like components, while $i = p - m + 1, \ldots, p$ are Gaussian-like components), $k = 0, \ldots, K$ is the time index, and $n = 1, \ldots, NoPaths$ is the path index.

This class of processes, by far the most common class of processes used in financial valuation, has both conditional mean and conditional variance, which are affine in the state vector, both in discrete and continuous time. The conversion rules to pass from the continuous to the discrete-time parameters are the same as those discussed for the single-factor Vasicek and CIR models.

If $m = 0$ the discretized process reduces to a standard VAR(1) autoregressive process. The conditional variance of $G_{k+1,n}$ is also a function of the non-Gaussian factors, which introduces conditional heteroskedasticity into bond prices.

19.5.2 MC Simulations for Callable Securities in Multifactor Models

The price of a callable bond is determined by the shape of the yield curve. It is well known since Littermann and Scheinkman (1991) that the evolution of the yield curve can be decomposed according to principal components, corresponding to changes of level, slope, and curvature. It is interesting to analyze the variation on simulated prices of the callable securities previously computed when a more accurate description of the yield curve is adopted introducing additional factors.

19.5.2.1 Interest Rate Model Selection A model recently proposed by Christensen, Diebold, and Rudebusch (2011) (CDR hereafter) offers a good illustration of the potential accuracy improvements achievable by means of a simple affine multidimensional model, which offers a dynamic, arbitrage-free counterpart of the Littermann and Scheinkman (1991) decomposition.

This model belongs to the class of Gaussian models discussed in Section 19.2.4. The model features three factors L_t, S_t, and C_t (level, slope, and curvature) whose dynamics are specified to generate a modified extended Nelson and Siegel (1987) model as the resulting no-arbitrage bond price. More specifically, the short-rate evolution is determined by

$$r_t^S = L_t + S_t$$

while the continuous time (risk-neutral) evolution is given by

$$d\begin{pmatrix} L_t \\ S_t \\ C_t \end{pmatrix} = K^{\mathbb{Q}}\left[\begin{pmatrix} \theta^L \\ \theta^S \\ \theta^C \end{pmatrix} - \begin{pmatrix} L_t \\ S_t \\ C_t \end{pmatrix}\right] + \mathbf{\Sigma}\begin{pmatrix} dW_t^1 \\ dW_t^2 \\ dW_t^3 \end{pmatrix}$$

$$K^{\mathbb{Q}} = \begin{bmatrix} 0 & 0 & 0 \\ 0 & \lambda & -\lambda \\ 0 & 0 & \lambda \end{bmatrix}$$

This model is affine in the state variables, and its bond pricing formula is

$$Z(t,T) = e^{A(t,T)+B_1(t,T)L_t+B_2(t,T)S_t+B_3(t,T)C_t} \tag{19.70}$$

where

$$B_1(t,T) = -(T-t)$$

$$B_2(t,T) = -\frac{1-e^{-\lambda(T-t)}}{\lambda}$$

$$B_3(t,T) = (T-t)e^{-\lambda(T-t)} - \frac{1-e^{-\lambda(T-t)}}{\lambda}$$

and $A(t,T)$ solves the ODE

$$\frac{\partial A(t,T)}{\partial t} = -\mathbf{B}(t,T)K^{\mathbb{Q}}\theta^{\mathbb{Q}} - \frac{1}{2}\sum_{j=1}^{3}[\mathbf{\Sigma}\mathbf{B}(t,T)\mathbf{B}(t,T)'\mathbf{\Sigma}']_{i,j}$$

with $\theta^{\mathbb{Q}} = [\theta^L, \theta^S, \theta^C]'$ and final condition $A(T,T) = 0$. The zero-coupon yields are then given by

$$y_t(\tau) = L_t + S_t\left(\frac{1-e^{-\lambda\tau}}{\lambda\tau}\right) + C_t\left(\frac{1-e^{-\lambda\tau}}{\lambda\tau} - e^{-\lambda\tau}\right) + \frac{A(t,T)}{\tau} \tag{19.71}$$

The main property of this specification is that the first three components, those proportional to L_t, S_t, and C_t, are consistent with a Nelson–Siegel parameterization, which is commonly used by central banks and financial market practitioners to fit the cross section of yields. This model is usually termed **arbitrage-free Nelson–Siegel model**, since it generates an affine dynamics, which is consistent with the absence of arbitrage opportunities and simultaneously, at fixed time t, offers a parameterization of the yield curve consistent with the Nelson–Siegel model.

The interpretation of the three factors as the dynamic counterparts to level L_t, slope S_t, and curvature C_t is easily explained by looking at Figure 19.7, which reports the impact of a shock to each state variable (L_t, S_t, C_t) on yields of different maturities, that is, the coefficients of L_t, S_t, and C_t in Equation 19.71. The solid flat line, for instance, shows that an increase in factor L_t produces the same impact on yields independently of their maturity, that is, it changes the level of the yield curve. Similarly, the dashed line shows that an increase in factor S_t increases the yield with short maturity by much more than the yields with long maturity. That is, the impact of S_t is to change the slope of the yield curve. Finally, the dashed-dotted line shows that an increase in factor C_t increases medium-term yields by more than short-term and long-term yields. That is, the impact of C_t is to change the curvature of the yield curve.

The evolution of each factor in the CDR model is described by Gaussian Ornstein–Uhlenbeck processes with a constant volatility matrix Σ. The instantaneous interest rate is the sum of level and slope factors, while the curvature factor's sole role

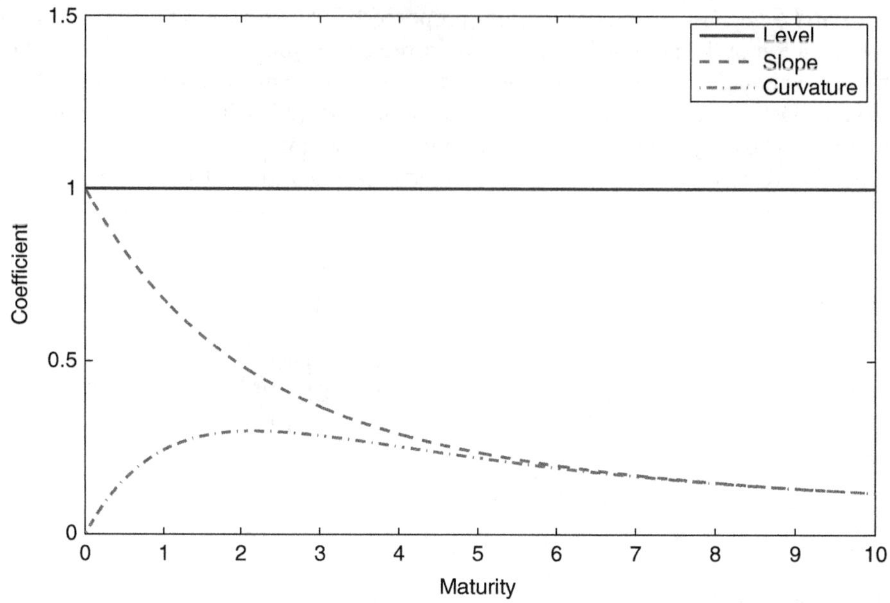

Figure 19.7 The coefficients of level L_t, slope S_t, and curvature C_t factors in the yield function $y_t(\tau)$.

is as a stochastic time-varying mean for the slope factor. λ is a constant in the CDR model and has the interpretation as the mean-reversion rate of the curvature and slope factors as well as the scale by which a deviation of the curvature factor from its mean affects the mean of the slope factor. The discretized processes with step size h evolve like the VAR(1):

$$G_{k+1,n} = \mu^G + \Phi^G \cdot G_{k,n} + \varepsilon^G_{k+1,n}$$
$$\varepsilon^G_{k+1,\cdot} \sim Normal(\underline{0}, \Sigma_{G,0}\Sigma^T_{G,0})$$

with the parameters and state variable identification:

$$G_{k,n} = \begin{pmatrix} \mathcal{L}_{k,n} \\ S_{k,n} \\ C_{k,n} \end{pmatrix}$$

$$\mu^G = [\mathbb{I} - \exp{(-K^{\mathbb{Q}}h)}] \begin{pmatrix} \theta^L \\ \theta^S \\ \theta^C \end{pmatrix}$$

$$\Phi^G = \exp{(-K^{\mathbb{Q}}h)} \quad \Sigma_{G,0} = \sqrt{h}\Sigma$$

The parameter choice that will be used in the valuation exercise has been estimated in Creal and Wu (2015) and are

$$\lambda = 0.4896,$$
$$\Sigma_0 = \begin{bmatrix} 0.0211 & 0 & 0 \\ -0.0192 & 0.004 & 0 \\ -0.0292 & -0.0009 & 0.0177 \end{bmatrix}$$

*19.5.2.2 **Multidimensional Regression Methods for the Computation of the Conditional Expectation Functional*** Longstaff and Schwartz (2001) show in a number of examples that the approximate backward regression procedure is efficient to price structured products with a payoff structure that involves multiple underlying factors. In particular it is shown that a mild number of polynomial regressors are sufficient to produce good estimates of the conditional expectation operator. In the multifactor model under discussion, we consider products of single-factor polynomial regressors. That is, our regressors take the form

$$\{\mathcal{H}_{n_L,n_S,n_C}(G_t)\}_{0\le n_L+n_S+n_C\le 3}$$

with

$$\mathcal{H}_{n_L,n_S,n_C}(G_t) := \mathcal{H}_{n_L}(\mathcal{L}_t)\mathcal{H}_{n_S}(\mathcal{S}_t)\mathcal{H}_{n_C}(\mathcal{C}_t)$$

where recall that $\mathcal{H}_m(X_t)$ denotes a (Hermite) polynomial, as discussed in Section 19.4.3.2. As an extension of formula 19.66 to the case with multiple factors, the expected value will now be approximated by the combination:

$$E[F_{T_2}(G_{T_2}) \mid G_{T_1}] \approx \sum_{0\le n_L+n_S+n_C\le 3} \beta_{n_L,n_S,n_C}\mathcal{H}_{n_L}(\mathcal{L}_t)\mathcal{H}_{n_S}(\mathcal{S}_t)\mathcal{H}_{n_C}(\mathcal{C}_t) + v_t$$

The backward dynamic programming computation is otherwise identical to the one described in Section 19.4.3.3.

19.5.2.3 Example: Multiple Factor Model Valuation by Simulation of Freddie Mac Callable Bonds In order to illustrate the accuracy gain when passing from single factors to multiple factor models, Figure 19.8 plots the fit of the CDR model to the zero-coupon yield curve. This figure should be compared with Figure 19.5 which reported the fit of the CIR model to the same data. In the case of the multifactor CDR model, the fit of the initial curve is closer to the data, which is a positive property of the model. However, on the negative size, the Gaussian dynamics implied by the CDR model is not realistic when the rates are near the zero boundary, as the likelihood of negative interest rates is very high.

The simplest way to overcome this problem is to apply the Black "shadow-rate model" and consider the real rate as the nonlinear function of the rate r_t^S:

$$r_t = \max(r_t^S, 0)$$

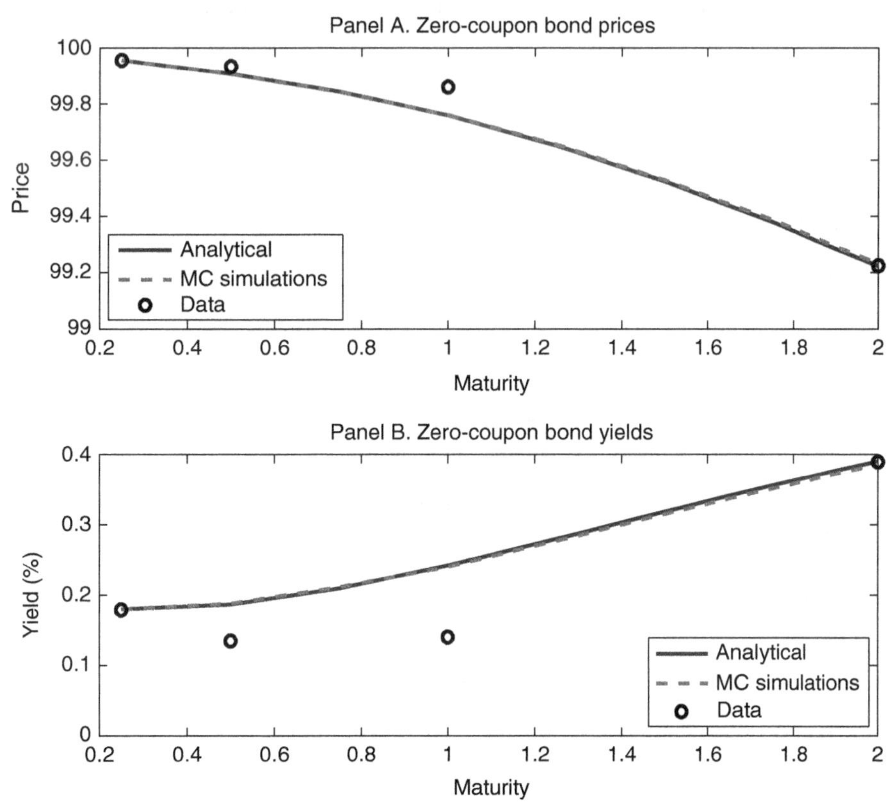

Figure 19.8 Fitted CDR model on January 28, 2014. Source: Data are from Gürkaynak, Sack, and Wright (2007), updated series.

Of course, in this case we need to recalibrate the CDR model to fit the current term structure of interest rates. The critical step of this procedure is the calibration for the yield curve. The presence of the zero lower bound implies that the price $P_{ZCB}(t, T)$ of the zero-coupon bond with maturity T is given by the price of a shadow bond minus the call option on values of the bond above par:

$$Z(t,T) = Z^{Shadow}(t,T) - C_{Am}^{Callable}(t,T;T;1)$$

where $Z^{Shadow}(t, T)$ is the price of the shadow zero-coupon bond (the one computed using negative rates) with the same maturity and $C_{Am}^{Callable}(t, T; T; 1)$ is the value of an American call option written on the shadow zero-coupon bond with strike 1 expiring at time T. The Longstaff and Schwartz regression method offers a natural approach to the estimation of the yield curve in the shadow-rate model: for each relevant maturity T, the American call is approximated by a Bermudan one, and the price of each zero-coupon bond is then determined as the prices of a Bermudan callable bond with the same maturity and strike at par. Initial conditions of the factors are then determined by the condition that the model reproduces the observe yield curve at time t.

Figure 19.9 reports the result of the new fit. In this case, the price of the security is only obtained through Monte Carlo simulations, and hence we only have one line in each plot. The additional restriction that the interest rate must be nonnegative still allows us to fit the model to the data well and much better than what we obtained with the CIR model (see Figure 19.5).

We finally return to the pricing of the 2-year, 0.45% Freddie Mac security already discussed earlier but now priced using both the CDR model and the CDR–shadow rate model. The former allows for interest rates to become negative, while the second truncates the interest rates to its positive domain. Table 19.4 reports the results, together with the CIR results obtained earlier, for comparison.

By comparing the CDR–shadow rate with the unconstrained CDR model, we first see that the shadow rate model produces a slightly higher price of the straight bond. This is due to difference in fit of the models with the data, as shown in Figures 19.9. In contrast, however, we see that the CDR model produces a much lower price of the callable bond than the CDR – Shadow rate model. The reason is that the CDR model allows for negative interest rates, which increase the value of the option to redeem early. Because investors are short for such option (which was implicitly sold to the issuer), the value of the callable bond is lower when such option is more valuable. This comparative exercise demonstrates that in an environment of very low interest rates, it is critical to use models that constrain interest rates to be nonnegative. Indeed, models such as CIR and CDR–shadow rate produce prices for the callable bond that are much closer to the traded price on January 28, 2014, which recall was \$99.93.

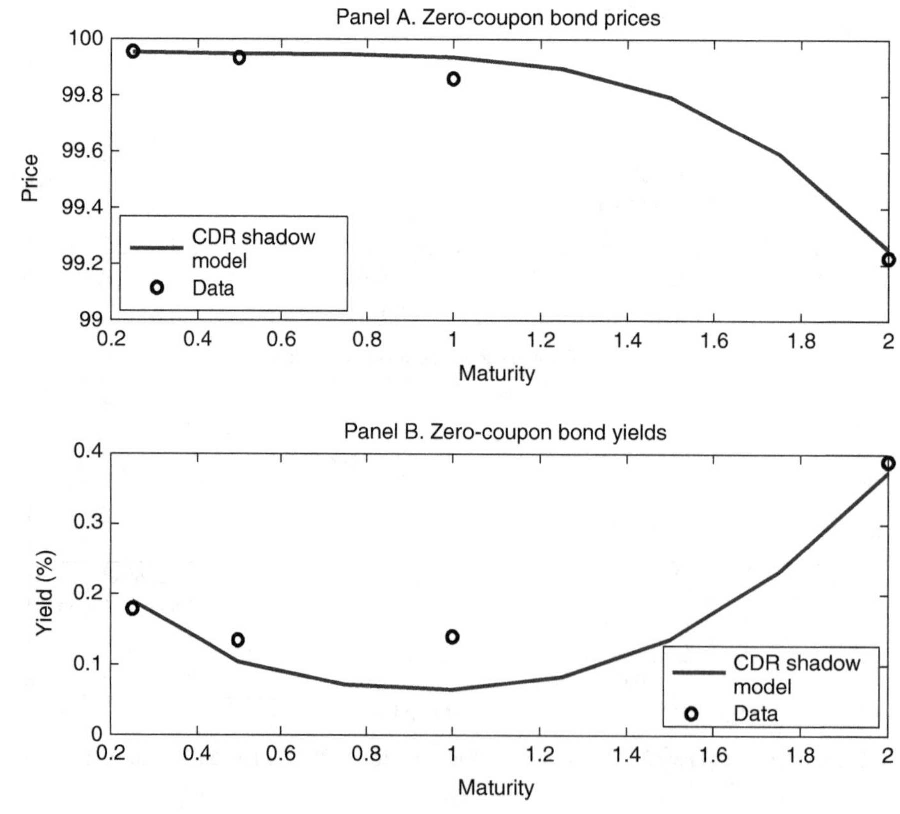

Figure 19.9 Fitted CDR model with shadow rate on January 28, 2014. Source: Data are from Gürkaynak, Sack, and Wright (2007), updated series.

TABLE 19.4 Price of Freddie Mac Security with Different Models

	Straight bond	Callable bond
CIR	100.18	99.73
CDR	100.01	98.77
CDR – Shadow rate	100.15	99.85

19.6 CONCLUSION

This chapter covered the foundations of risk-neutral pricing and its implementation using Monte Carlo simulations. The risk-neutral pricing formula we obtain from no-arbitrage principles shows that the value of a derivative security can be computed as the expected presented value of its cash flows – discounted at the risk-free rate – where the expectation is taken under a risk-adjusted (or risk-neutral) process for the underlying state variables. The fact that no-arbitrage pricing implies that a derivative's value can be computed as an expectation provides the foundation to the Monte Carlo simulation approach to valuing derivative securities. In fact, from the law of large numbers, the average of independent random variables converges to its population value, that is, its expectation. It is then possible to estimate the value of a derivative security by simulating a large number of scenarios under the proper risk-adjusted probabilities, compute the present value of each simulated payoff, and then take the average.

The biggest complication of the procedure, however, is to deal with derivatives whose exercise style is American. In this case, if we hold the option, we must decide not only whether to exercise or not, but also *when* it is the best time to exercise. That is, the decision rule must take into account that if we do not exercise today, we may always exercise the same option in the future, under potentially different market conditions. This implies we must know the value of the option conditional on no exercise, a "continuation" value that we can only know if we already solved the same decision problem at future times. The algorithm to implement an optimal decision rule thus must move backward from maturity to zero, and this is a problem because Monte Carlo simulations instead move forward from zero to maturity. The main technique we discussed in this chapter is to exploit the large number of simulated paths and estimate the continuation value of the derivative – its value if we do not exercise today – from the cross section of potential scenarios through a least-square regression. This methodology is very powerful and widely used in practice. Our examples in this chapter show also the flexibility of the approach and the possibility of valuing even relatively complicated securities in models with multiple factors.

REFERENCES

Ahn DH, Dittmar RF, Gallant AR. Quadratic term structure models: theory and evidence. Rev Financ Stud 2002;15(1):243–288.

Ang A, Piazzesi M. A no-arbitrage vector autoregression of term structure dynamics with macroeconomic and latent variables. J Monet Econ 2003;50(4):745–787.

Black F. Interest rates as options. J Finance 1995;50(5):1371–1376.

Brandt M, Chapman D. Comparing multifactor models of the term structure, working paper. Duke University; 2003.

Büttler HJ, Waldvogel J. Pricing callable bonds by means of green's functions. Math Finance 1996;6(1):53–88.

Christensen JH, Diebold FX, Rudebusch GD. The affine arbitrage-free class of Nelson–Siegel term structure models. J Econom 2011;164(1):4–20.

Christensen JH, Rudebusch GD. Estimating shadow-rate term structure models with near-zero yields. J Financ Econom 2014.

Clément E, Lamberton D, Protter P. An analysis of a least squares regression method for American option pricing. Finance Stochastics 2002;6(4):449–471.

Cox JC, Ingersoll JE, Ross SA. A theory of the term structure of interest rates. Econometrica 1985;53(2):385–407.

Creal DD, Wu JC. Estimation of affine term structure models with spanned or unspanned stochastic volatility. J Econom 2015;185(1):60–81.

Dai Q, Singleton KJ. Specification analysis of affine term structure models. J Finance 2000;55(5):1943–1978.

Dai Q, Singleton KJ, Expectation Puzzles, Time-varying Risk Premia, and Affine Models of the Term Structure, Journal of Financial Economics, 2002, 63: 415–441.

Duffie D. *Dynamic Asset Pricing Theory*. Princeton (NJ): Princeton University Press; 2010.

Duffie D, Kan R. A yield-factor model of interest rates. Math Finance 1996;6(4):379–406.

Feng X, Xie D. Bayesian estimation of CIR model. J Data Sci 2012;10(2):271–280.

Glasserman P. *Monte Carlo Methods in Financial Engineering*. Volume 53. New York: Springer Science & Business Media; 2004.

Glasserman P, Yu B. Simulation for American options: regression now or regression later? In: *Monte Carlo and Quasi-Monte Carlo Methods 2002*. Berlin Heidelberg: Springer-Verlag; 2004. p 213–226.

Gourieroux C, Jasiak J. Autoregressive gamma processes. J Forecast 2006;25(2):129–152.

Gürkaynak RS, Sack B, Wright J. The U.S. Treasury yield curve: 1961 to the present. J Monet Econ 2007;54:2291–2304.

Hamilton JD, Wu JC. The effectiveness of alternative monetary policy tools in a zero lower bound environment. J Money Credit Bank 2012;44(s1):3–46.

Haugh MB, Kogan L. Pricing American options: a duality approach. Oper Res 2004;52(2):258–270.

Heston SL, Loewenstein M, Willard GA. Options and bubbles. Rev Financ Stud 2007;20(2):359–390.

Joslin S, Singleton KJ, Zhu H. A new perspective on Gaussian dynamic term structure models. Rev Financ Stud 2011;24(3):926–970.

Le A, Singleton KJ, Dai Q. Discrete-time affine term structure models with generalized market prices of risk. Rev Financ Stud 2010;23(5):2184–2227.

Leippold M, Wu L. Asset pricing under the quadratic class. J Financ Quant Anal 2002;37(02):271–295.

Lim D, Li L, Linetsky V. Evaluating callable and putable bonds: an eigenfunction expansion approach. J Econ Dyn Control 2012;36(12):1888–1908.

Litterman RB, Scheinkman J. Common factors affecting bond returns. J Fixed Income 1991;1(1):54–61.

Longstaff FA, Schwartz ES. Valuing American options by simulation: a simple least-squares approach. Rev Financ Stud 2001;14(1):113–147.

Monfort A, Pegoraro F, Renne JP, Roussellet G. Staying at zero with affine processes: a new dynamic term structure model. Paris December 2014 Finance Meeting EUROFIDAI-AFFI Paper; 2014.

Nelson CR, Siegel AF. Parsimonious modeling of yield curves. J Bus 1987;60:473–489.

Singleton KJ. *Empirical Dynamic Asset Pricing: Model Specification and Econometric Assessment*. Princeton (NJ): Princeton University Press; 2009.

Vasicek O. An equilibrium characterization of the term structure. J Financ Econ 1977;5(2):177–188.

20

Interest Rate Derivatives and Volatility

Antonio Mele[a,b] **and Yoshiki Obayashi**[c]

[a]*Swiss Finance Institute, University of Lugano, Lugano, Switzerland*
[b]*CEPR, London, United Kingdom*
[c]*Applied Academics LLC, New York, NY, United States*

20.1 INTRODUCTION

Interest rate volatility (IRV) affects a wide base of individuals, investors, companies, and even governments. Individuals who have borrowed through adjustable-rate retail products, such as student loans and mortgages, are susceptible to greater uncertainty about the magnitude of their liabilities from one payment period to the next when short-term interest rates are volatile. For individual and institutional investors in fixed-income products like corporate bonds and mortgage-backed securities, IRV translates directly into undesirable, and sometimes devastating, portfolio volatility. Routine issuers of debt, such as financial institutions, corporations, and governmental agencies, are also forced to deal with the impact of IRV on their vital funding decisions.

As with other asset classes, IRV trading resides in the domain of interest rate derivative (IRD) markets. However, unlike volatility trading in spot instruments such as equity indexes, commodities, and currency cross rates, fixed-income assets and derivatives require significantly different mathematical treatments to address added complexities such as annuities and credit risk to name a few. This chapter aims to equip the reader with a foundational understanding of the vast IRD market and the quantitative tools for measuring and managing IRV.

Section 20.2 provides perspective on the immensity of over-the-counter (OTC) and listed IRD markets and gives context to how IRV affects market participants. Section 20.3 introduces notation and foundational concepts required to understand various IRD contracts and their risks. Section 20.4 surveys a portion of the large literature on IRD pricing methodologies to the extent relevant to the subject of IRV. Section 20.5 reviews existing volatility trading practices, introduces model-free option-based volatility measures for various interest rates, and covers recent developments in the standardization of IRV trading. Section 20.6 concludes. A technical appendix contains additional details aiming to make the chapter as self-contained as possible.

20.2 MARKETS AND THE INSTITUTIONAL CONTEXT

20.2.1 Market Size

IRDs constitute the largest segment of the OTC derivative market. At a notional amount outstanding of US $561.3 trillion as of June 2013 as reported by the Bank for International Settlements (BIS), the IRD market dwarfs all other OTC markets, with foreign exchange derivatives being a distant second at US $73.1 trillion (see Figure 20.1).

Handbook of Fixed-Income Securities, First Edition. Edited by Pietro Veronesi.

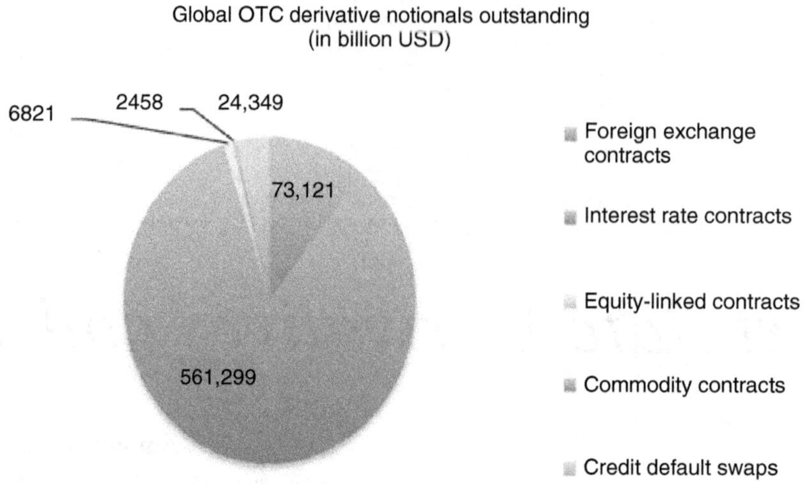

Figure 20.1 Global OTC derivative notional outstanding. Source: Bank of International Settlements.

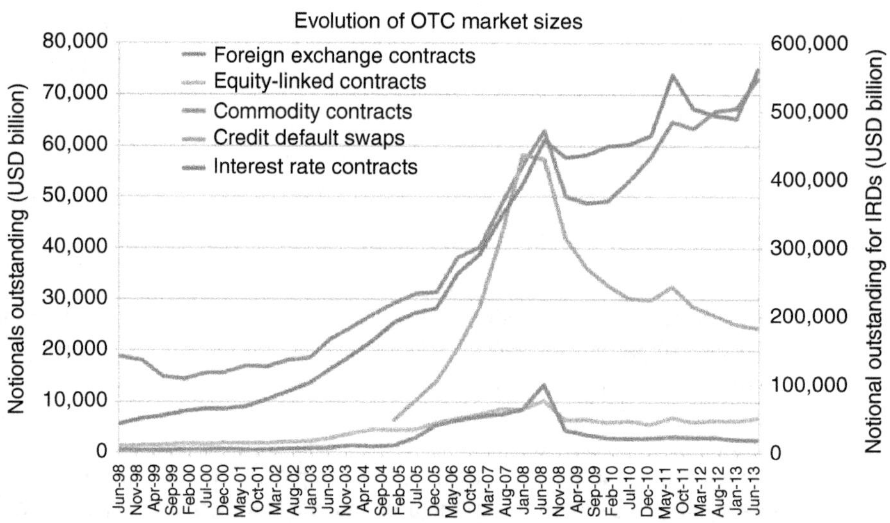

Figure 20.2 Evolution of OTC market sizes. Source: Bank of International Settlements.

Many factors come together to drive the activity and resulting size of the IRD market. The underlying fixed-income asset base has large notional amounts outstanding and a wide range of varied debt instruments such as interbank loans, mortgages, and corporate and government bonds to name just a few. Financial institutions are heavy users of IRDs for hedging against, or modifying the risk profile of, such assets on their books. IRDs such as fixed-for-floating swaps also serve as popular tools globally among large corporations, municipalities, and other nonfinancial and financial institutions alike for asset liability and cash flow management. IRDs moreover allow speculators to make leveraged bets to express their investment views on various interest rates and fixed-income asset prices.

Over the past 15 years, OTC derivativetrading activity has increased significantly across all asset classes as can be seen in Figure 20.2. The steady growth since the late 1990s hit a speed bump during the financial crisis of 2007–2008 as market makers and end users were forced to reduce risk. Notably, credit derivatives, commonly thought to have been at the epicenter of the global market collapse, has since had a sharp decline in market size to just about half its peak of US $58 trillion notional outstanding in 2007. In contracts, the IRD market has continued to grow in size postcrisis and stands at 13 times its size 15 years ago, which is more than double the growth rate of other OTC derivative markets.

While the bulk of IRD trading has traditionally taken place OTC, certain types of IRDs, such as futures and options on government bonds and time deposits, are actively traded on derivative exchanges such as Chicago Mercantile Exchange (CME) Group, Eurex, and NYSE LIFFE. Listed IRDs across exchanges have a total notional outstanding of US $24.2 trillion, which pales in comparison to their OTC counterparts, but are still an order of magnitude larger in notional outstanding compared to other listed derivatives such as those on currencies and equity indexes (see Figure 20.3).

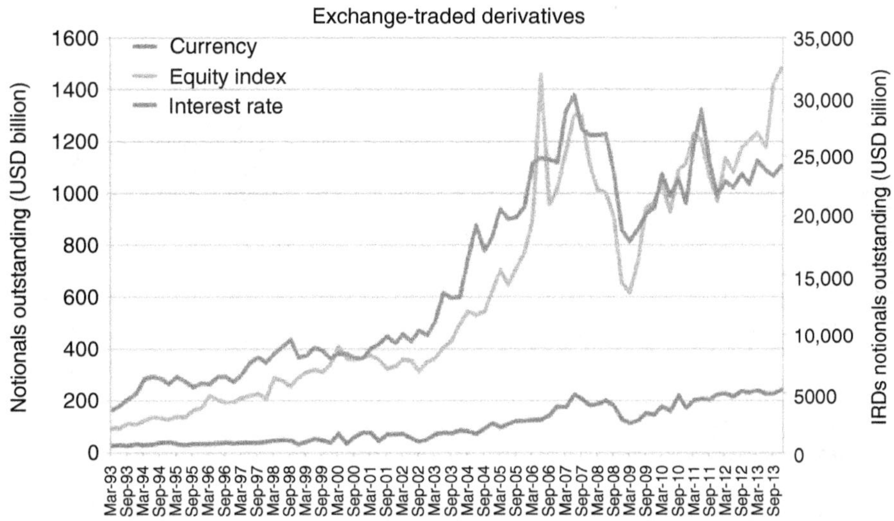

Figure 20.3 Exchange-traded derivatives. Source: Bank of International Settlements.

20.2.2 OTC IRD Trading and Volatility

The OTC fixed-for-floating interest rate swap (IRS) is by far the most liquid and actively traded IRD, with a notional amount outstanding of US $425.6 trillion as of June 2013. In a vanilla IRS, one party makes a stream of fixed-rate payments to its counterparty over a period of time, typically ranging from 1–30 years, in exchange for a stream of floating-rate payments. The floating leg of the IRS references a short-term interbank lending rate, most commonly the 3- and 6-month London Interbank Offered Rates (Libors). The British Bankers' Association had historically calculated Libor until its administration was recently transferred to ICE Benchmark Administration Limited in February 2014. Libor is designed to indicate the average rate at which a panel of banks is able to obtain unsecured funding in various currencies and terms and is calculated on a daily basis as the panel's interquartile average. Libor is frequently used as the reference rate for a wide range of debt instruments ranging from floating-rate notes issued by corporations, adjustable-rate mortgages, and student loans, which are quoted and traded at a spread to Libor.

The fixed leg of an IRS, known as the "swap rate," may be interpreted as the market's expectation of a break-even rate that provides the same net present value as the floating leg over the life of the IRS and thus closely relates to the term funding cost for highly rated financial institutions and corporations. In turn, the zero-coupon yield curve based on Libor/swaps, and variants thereof, are used to discount cash flows and drive the pricing of a large pool of fixed-income securities and derivatives.

At the most general level, volatility of swap rates affects individual and institutional investors in fixed-income assets by translating into volatility of their portfolios, which is a key risk driving investment decisions. Even with careful diversification, correlation across assets has the tendency to increase in times of heightened volatility to reduce the intended benefits of holding a mix of assets believed to smooth out returns. Figure 20.4 plots various historical realized basis point (BP) volatilities, the 1Y–10Y forward swap rate, and the Chicago Board Options Exchange (CBOE) SRVX Index, which is an implied volatility index based on 1Y–10Y swaptions. The "shrink fwd 1y10y BP vol" is the realized basis point volatility based on the 10-year swap rate 1 year forward, 1 year minus 1 day forward, 1 year minus 2 days forward, and so forth.

On the other side of the fence, issuers of Libor/swap-sensitive debt instruments are also affected by swap rate volatility. Greater volatility makes a corporate treasurer's job generally more difficult. For instance, in times of acute uncertainty about the future path of interest rates, corporate bond issuers have been known to delay or cancel the pricing of new issues in the primary market until volatility subsides. In other examples, companies with large fixed-income portfolios deliberately constructed to offset specific liabilities arising from their core businesses, such as insurance companies, or bond funds benchmarked to certain indexes face increased risk of tracking errors when interest rates experience large moves.

For both investors and issuers of fixed-income securities, spikes in volatility also have a secondary, but no less pernicious, effect of being accompanied by the evaporation of liquidityas dealers widen the width and reduce the depth of their markets or step to the sidelines altogether as seen during the crisis of 2007–2008. In extreme market panics, reduced liquidity leads to smaller trades having disproportionate price impact, and a vicious cycle between increased volatility and reduced liquidity can ensue.

Hedging and expressing views on swap rate volatility are traditionally done through trading swaptions, that is, option on IRS, which are part of the third largest OTC IRD category – interest rate options – with US $49.4 trillion outstanding as of June 2013. At maturity, a payer (receiver) swaption gives the buyer the right, but not obligation, to pay (receive) a predetermined fixed rate,

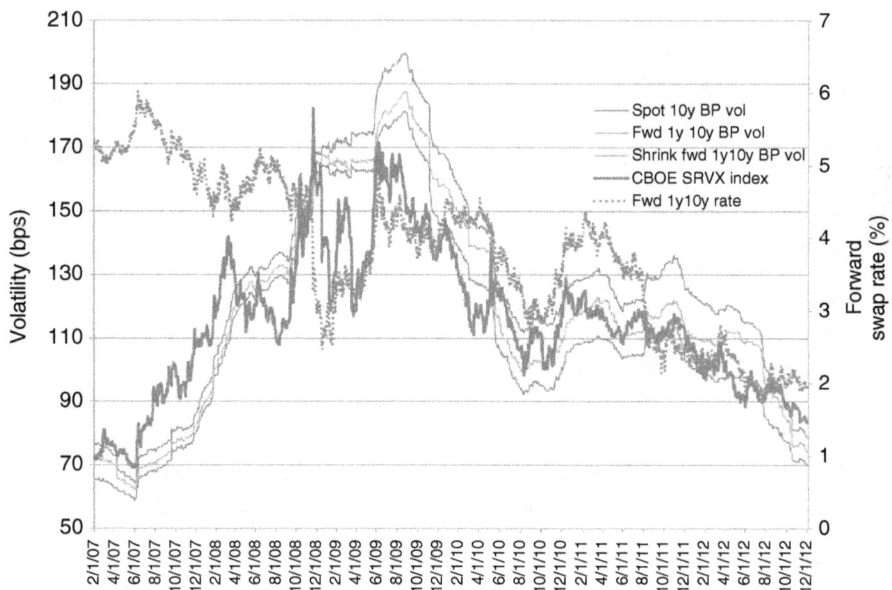

Figure 20.4 Realized and traded volatility indexes. Source: Chicago Board Options Exchange and Bloomberg.

that is, strike, on an IRS. Unlike equity options, which have only one temporal dimension, swaptions are defined by two time horizons – the maturity of the swaption and the tenor of the underlying swap – and therefore give rise to a volatility cube defined by (maturity, tenor, strike) coordinates, which offers a rich set of trading opportunities. Some maturity–tenor combinations, such as USD 1Y–10Y, are generally more active than others, but the distribution of liquidity morphs through time depending on the nature of events driving the market.

The most common directional volatility trades are at-the-money (ATM) swaptionstraddles in which one buys (sells) a payer and a receiver swaption, both struck ATM, to be long (short) volatility. According to a major global interdealer broker (IDB), such trades constitute the majority of swaption trades they broke between dealers on most days. To remain delta neutral throughout the trade, ATM straddles require dynamic hedging using, for example, forward swaps, which are part of the US \$88.3 trillion OTC forward rate agreement (FRA) market. Even with delta hedging, there can be significant P&L noise arising from the path-dependent nature of the strategy's payoffs, as explained in Section 20.5.1, which has been cited by some funds as a reason, among others, such as collateral requirements, for abstaining from OTC swap volatility trading.

Swap rate volatility trading is also done in the form of forward volatility Agreements (FVAs)whereby one party agrees to buy or sell on some future date an ATM swaption straddle at a predetermined strike. This is a form of forward volatility trading in which one takes a view on the change in implied volatility over time. The perception of the FVA market's activeness varies significantly depending on which dealer one speaks to, ranging from nearly nonexistent to a burgeoning business. More obscure forms of OTC IRV trading include variance swaps on bond exchange-traded funds (ETFs) in which one party agrees to pay another the realized variance of daily returns of the reference ETF.

A comprehensive survey of the entire OTC IRD landscape is outside the scope of this chapter, but the essential building blocks for OTC IRV trading have been introduced.

20.2.3 Exchange-Listed IRD Trading and Volatility

Some of the larger derivative exchanges have succeeded in capturing the market for certain types of IRDs, the most historically successful of which are futures and options on government bonds and time deposits.

Government bond futures and options include those listed on the U.S. Treasuries at the CME, on Euro Bund/Schatz/Bobl at Eurex, on Gilts at NYSE LIFFE, and on Japanese Government Bonds at the Osaka Securities Exchange. In a departure from the rate-based OTC IRDs described earlier, futures and options on government bonds are quoted and traded in terms of prices as opposed to yields. Moreover, unlike OTC FRA, listed bond futures involve additional contract specifications such as the cheapest-to-deliver option, which adds a layer of complexity to the pricing of futures but is a topic that is by now well understood. Liquidity in options on government bond futures is concentrated in the short term, such as the front 3 serial months, and does not go nearly as far out as in the swaption market. Such shorter-dated options are commonly thought to be useful for trading volatility around macro announcements and policy events and are also used by OTC IRD dealers as additional sources of liquidity to hedge against their OTC positions.

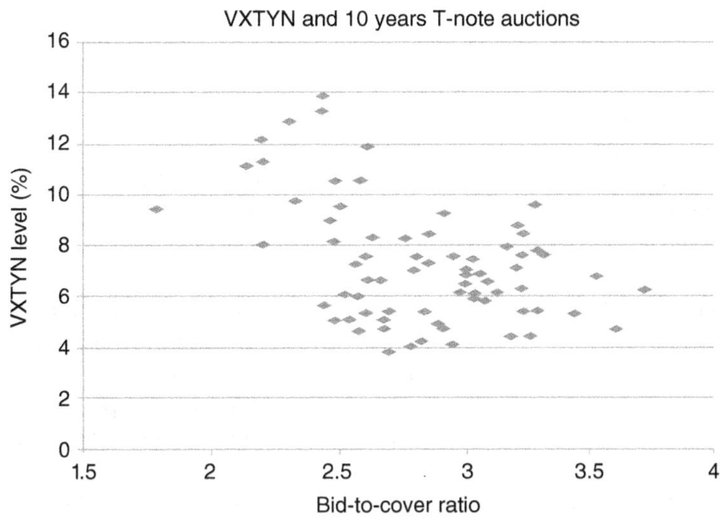

Figure 20.5 VXTYN and 10-year T-note auctions. Source: Chicago Board Options Exchange and Bloomberg.

In parallel with the discussion previously regarding the effect of swap rate volatility on corporate bond issuers, even the U.S. Treasury is not immune to IRV. Figure 20.5 illustrates how the bid-to-cover ratio in the 10-year Treasury Note auctions, a measure of demand for Treasury securities, is inversely related to IRV as measured by the CBOE/CBOT 10-year U.S. Treasury Note Volatility Index, VXTYN.[1]

The other successful category of exchange-listed IRDs includes futures and options on time deposits such as Eurodollar and Fed Funds at CME and Euribor and Sterling at NYSE LIFFE. A full listing of IRDs, their contract specifications, and volume statistics are maintained and publicly accessible on the various exchanges' websites.

20.2.4 Recent Developments in the IRD Market

The 2007–2008 financial crisis set in motion a tidal wave of reforms over the OTC derivative markets, and IRDs are one of the focal points of it given its sheer size and importance to the orderly functioning of global financial markets. Among the mind-numbing set of issues, regulators in various domiciles are focusing their efforts around implementing centralized clearing, settling, and reporting for a growing set of OTC IRDs. In response, various market utilities, from well-established exchanges and IDBs to a slew of new entrants, are adapting their businesses and positioning themselves the best they can for what the postreform landscape may look like.

While a detailed description of OTC reforms is not salient to this chapter, it is worth noting that the resulting shift in the longstanding dynamics between the listed and OTC worlds has already led to some previously unthinkable product innovations that are relevant to the subject at hand. For instance, in June 2012, CBOE announced that it had obtained swaption data licenses from multiple top IDBs in the IRD space to create a real-time index, named SRVX (in Figure 20.4), for tracking 1Y 10Y swap rate volatility. It is a safe bet to assume that a derivative exchange looking to enter the swaption volatility space would have had little chance of collaborations with IDBs before the crisis. What is more, many of the major IRD dealers have even expressed interest in the idea of an exchange-owned tradable swap rate volatility index, presumably in part because it overcomes the challenge dealers faced when trying to instill a sense of objectivity and credibility in their proprietary swap rate volatility indexes based on prices coming from their own trading desks. Other examples of such innovations include CME's deliverable IRS futures, which have garnered public support from multiple IRD dealers.

20.3 DISSECTING THE INSTRUMENTS

Evaluating IRDs poses new challenges compared to the equity derivative space. First, interest rate risk can take on different meanings: for example, it can relate to possibly imminent rate changes or to longer-term developments. Concerns about the former risk give rise to contracts such as time deposits (see Section 20.3.2), and concerns about the latter can be mitigated through IRS (see Section 20.3.3). The notion of risk adjustment differs in these two examples as it depends on varied risks affecting each market.

[1]Note that TYVIX has replaced VXTYN as the new ticker symbol while this article was in press.

A second issue is that the payoffs to IRDs are obviously interest rate dependent, and yet we need to discount them relying on the very same interest rates – or at least relying on other interest rates that presumably correlate with the payoffs (see Chapter 18 for discussions regarding "multiple yield curves"). Is there a way to express the value of IRDs in a compact manner that also incorporates the random character of the discounting factors?

Standard financial theory holds that absence of arbitrage in frictionless markets implies that there is indeed a unit of account such that the price of all securities denominated in this account is martingales under a given probability. We term such unit of account *numéraire* to honor Léon Walras (1874) that famously concluded that any market is in equilibrium, given the equilibrium in the remaining markets, such that we can take the price of any commodity as given and study the equilibrium price of any other commodity in terms of the chosen numéraire.

The evaluation of fixed-income derivatives is facilitated by the relevant notion of numéraire that applies to each fixed-income asset class. Evaluating equity derivatives assuming constant rates typically requires no more than making reference to the money market account and the associated and well-known risk-neutral probability – "discounted asset prices are martingales under Q" (Cox, Ross, and Rubinstein, 1979; Harrison and Kreps, 1979). In contrast, we have appropriate notions of numéraire applying to each of the fixed-income asset classes we consider. In terms of the previous introductory example, the numéraire applying to time deposits is not the same as that applying to IRS.

This section provides foundations regarding IRDs that hinge upon these appropriate notions of numéraire. It develops representations of IRD prices, which we shall use in later sections to pin down their value based on specific modeling assumptions and as benchmarks to deal with the fundamental scope of the chapter to explain how to set a standard for forward-looking measures of IRV. We cover three markets, one for bonds (Section 20.3.1), one for time deposits (Section 20.3.2), and one for forward rate agreements and IRS (Section 20.3.3), as well as the main derivatives based on the third market (Section 20.3.4).

20.3.1 Government Bonds

This section deals with derivatives written on bonds, referred to as "government bonds," that are not subject to default risk – credit risk is not taken into account in any juncture of this chapter. Our objective is to develop basic representations for the price of forwards, futures, and options written on these bonds expressed in terms of the numéraire for this market that facilitates their evaluation.

Throughout this and the following section, we shall make reference to the following basic notation. We denote the instantaneous rate process with r_t and the price of a zero-coupon bond at t and expiring at T with $P_t(T)$, assuming no default risk. Hereafter, we shall also refer to r_t as the *short-term rate* relying on a standard terminology. We let the risk-neutral probability be Q and $\mathbb{E}_t$ be the risk-neutral expectation taken conditional upon the information set at time t; Chapter 19 provides a survey on risk-neutral pricing. Let $B_t(\mathbb{T})$ be the price at t of a coupon-bearing bond expiring at $\mathbb{T} \geq t$.

We assume the bond pays off coupons $\frac{C_i}{n}$ over the sequence of dates T_i, $i = 1, \ldots, N$, where n is the frequency of coupon payments and $\mathbb{T} \equiv T_N$. For example, $n = 2$ denotes semiannual coupon payments, in which case $T_i - T_{i-1} = \frac{1}{2}$. In the absence of arbitrage,

$$B_t(\mathbb{T}) \equiv \sum_{i=i_t}^{N} \frac{C_i}{n} P_t(T_i) + P_t(\mathbb{T}) \tag{20.1}$$

where T_{i_t} is the first coupon payment date after t.

We now discuss two basic derivative instruments referencing nondefaultable coupon-bearing bonds, which help formulate views on developments in sovereign bond markets – futures and forwards on coupon-bearing bonds. While an important portion of trading activity is concentrated in exchanges such as CME and in regard to bond futures, OTC markets still host trading in bond forwards, and so both are interesting instruments to survey.

We have one additional source of motivation to deal with both instruments in this chapter. Markets for trading government bond volatility rely upon highly liquid American-style options on futures. Chicago Board Options Exchange publishes an index of Treasury volatility based on American options on the 10-year U.S. Treasury Note futures traded at Chicago Mercantile Exchange. At the same time, we shall explain that a "model-free" forward-looking volatility gauge should rely on European options on zero-coupon bond forwards (see Section 20.5). Understanding how American *futures* options are priced relative to European *forward* options is therefore an element of paramount interest in the context of this chapter.

We now proceed with technical details. Theoretically, futures and forwardsdiffer because futures are expectations taken under the risk-neutral probability, and forwards are expectations under a different probability measure called the forward probability. We explain in the following how the risk-neutral and the forward probability are the same when the short-term rate is constant or nonrandom. Therefore, futures and forwards differ in the context of this chapter for the obvious reason that interest rates are taken to be random.

20.3.1.1 Futures Denote with $\tilde{F}_t(S, \mathbb{T})$ the value at t of a future expiring at S on a coupon-bearing bond expiring at $\mathbb{T}$. Intuitively, a future position entails a continuous marking to market such that the expected instantaneous changes in the future position are zero under the risk-neutral probability, $\mathbb{E}_t(d\tilde{F}_t(S, \mathbb{T})) = 0$, and because of the boundary condition, $\tilde{F}_S(S, \mathbb{T}) = B_S(\mathbb{T})$, the future value satisfies,

$$\tilde{F}_t(S, \mathbb{T}) = \mathbb{E}_t(B_S(\mathbb{T})) \tag{20.2}$$

In Section 20.5, we shall rely on Equation 20.2 to explain how to gauge the error made by approximating a Treasury volatility index calculated through American options on bond futures, rather than European options on bond forwards.

20.3.1.2 Forwards Next, let$F_t(S, \mathbb{T})$ be the price at t of a forward expiring at $S \leq \mathbb{T}$. The payoff for going long the forward is $B_S(\mathbb{T}) - F_t(S, \mathbb{T})$, and the position is costless at inception such that, in the absence of arbitrage, the forward satisfies

$$F_t(S, \mathbb{T}) = \frac{1}{P_t(S)} \mathbb{E}_t \left(e^{-\int_t^S r_\tau d\tau} B_S(\mathbb{T}) \right) = \frac{B_t(\mathbb{T})}{P_t(S)}$$

where the second equality follows because the discounted coupon-bearing bond is a martingale under the risk-neutral probability. Alternatively, elaborating as follows on the first equality, heuristically,

$$F_t(S, \mathbb{T}) = \frac{1}{P_t(S)} \mathbb{E}_t \left(e^{-\int_t^S r_\tau d\tau} B_S(\mathbb{T}) \right) = \mathbb{E}_t(\xi_S^F B_S(\mathbb{T})) = \mathbb{E}_t^{Q_{FS}}(B_S(\mathbb{T})) \tag{20.3}$$

where Q_{FS} is a new probability, defined through the Radon–Nikodym derivative,

$$\xi_S^F \equiv \left. \frac{dQ_{FS}}{dQ} \right|_{\mathcal{F}_S} = \frac{e^{-\int_t^S r_\tau d\tau}}{P_t(S)} \tag{20.4}$$

and $\mathcal{F}_S$ denotes the information set at time S. The probability Q_{FS}, referred to as S-forward probability, was introduced by Geman (1989) and Jamshidian (1989) and further analyzed by Geman, El Karoui, and Rochet (1995).[2]

We assume $F_t(S, \mathbb{T})$ is a diffusion process. By Equation (20.3), it is a martingale under the S-forward probability, and it is also strictly positive, and the forward price satisfies

$$\frac{dF_\tau(S, \mathbb{T})}{F_\tau(S, \mathbb{T})} = v_\tau(S, \mathbb{T}) \cdot dW_\tau^{FS}, \quad \tau \in (t, S) \tag{20.5}$$

where $v_\tau(S, \mathbb{T})$ is an instantaneous volatility process adapted to W_τ^{FS}, which is a multidimensional Brownian motion under the S-forward probability. Note that $v_\tau(S, \mathbb{T}) = \sigma_\tau^B(\mathbb{T}) - \sigma_\tau(S)$ where $\sigma_\tau^B(\mathbb{T})$ denotes the instantaneous volatility of the log-changes in the coupon-bearing bond price in Equation 20.1 and $\sigma_\tau(S)$ is the instantaneous volatility of the log-changes of a zero-coupon bond expiring at S.

20.3.1.3 Options While OTC options commonly reference forwards or cash bonds, exchanges such as CME host trading of American options on futures. Section 20.5 explains that model-free volatility indexes should rely on European options on forwards, rather than American options on futures. We shall also deal with the latter in Section 20.5. In this section, we provide some details regarding the pricing of European options on forwards – with the option expiration being set equal to that of the forward.

Let $C_t^b(T, S)$ denote the price of a European option expiring at T and referencing a zero-coupon bond expiring at time S:

$$\begin{aligned} C_t^b(T, S) &= \mathbb{E}_t \left[e^{-\int_t^T r_\tau d\tau} \left(P_T(S) - K \right)^+ \right] \\ &= P_t(S) \cdot \mathbb{Q}_{FS}(P_T(S) \geq K) - K P_t(T) \cdot \mathbb{Q}_{FT}(P_T(S) \geq K) \end{aligned} \tag{20.6}$$

where $(x)^+ \equiv \max(x, 0)$ and $\mathbb{Q}_{Fj}(\cdot)$ denotes the cumulative distribution function under the j-forward probability.

[2] To explain heuristically how to arrive to the Radon–Nikodym derivative in Equation 20.4, consider a simple three-period market, with the current date being date-0, n states of nature occurring at date-2, and finally, the coupon-bearing bond (CBB) expiring at some date beyond date-2. Let B_i be the date-2 price of the CBB in state i and z_i be the discounting factor applying to payments contingent on the state of nature being i at date-2 – the counterpart to the numerator in Equation 20.4. Clearly, the arbitrage-free price of a zero-coupon bond expiring at date-2 is $P = \sum_{i=1}^n z_i q_i$, where q_i denotes the risk-neutral probability that state i will occur at date-2. Then, the price of the forward is, analogously to Equation 20.3, $F = \sum_{i=1}^n \frac{z_i B_i}{P} q_i = \sum_{i=1}^n B_i q_{F,i}$, where $q_{F,i}$ is defined through $\frac{q_{F,i}}{q_i} = \frac{z_i}{P}$. The meaning of this ratio parallels that of the Radon–Nikodym derivative in Equation 20.4, and it is immediate to verify that the "weights" $q_{F,i}$ sum to 1: $q_{F,i}$ is a probability, the counterpart to the forward probability in the continuous-time model.

Equation 20.6, derived in the appendix, is the bond option counterpart to the Black and Scholes (1973) formula in that (i) the underlying asset is a zero-coupon bond expiring at S, the current price of which, $P_t(S)$, multiplies the probability $\mathbb{Q}_{FS}$, and (ii) the present value of the strike price, $KP_t(T)$, multiplies the probability for the market numéraire in this problem, $\mathbb{Q}_{FT}$. Jamshidian (1989) first obtained Equation 20.6 in the context of a specific model for the short-term rate, reviewed in Section 20.4.2.

20.3.2 Time Deposits

A large portion of interest rate transactions involves interbank trading of time deposits as mentioned in Section 20.2, with the Libor being the best-known indicative cost of these transactions. The Libor serves as the basis of many IRDs surveyed in this chapter, such as interest rate futures and options, FRA, and IRS, caps, and floors, to mention the most important few. The focus of this section is on interest rate futures and options traded on exchanges, such as the CME's Eurodollar futures and options based on 3-month Libor.

Time deposit derivatives have in common with government bond derivatives the feature that their pricing is facilitated by making reference to the forward probability. Let $l_t(\Delta)$ be the simply compounded interest rate on a deposit for the time period from t to $t+\Delta$ (e.g., the 3-month Libor),

$$P_t(t+\Delta) \equiv \frac{1}{1+\Delta l_t(\Delta)}$$

where $P_t(t+\Delta)$ still denotes the time t price of a default-free zero-coupon bond expiring at $t+\Delta$, assuming that there is no counterparty risk. To simplify the exposition, we shall refer to $l_t(\Delta)$ as the Libor.

20.3.2.1 Forwards Consider a forward contract on the Libor, originated at time t, in which one party promises to pay the counterparty $100 \times (1 - l_S(\Delta)) - Z_t(S, S+\Delta)$ at time S. The forward Libor price, $Z_t(S, S+\Delta)$, is defined as the clearing price for this derivative, that is, such that its initial value is zero at inception,

$$Z_t(S, S+\Delta) = 100 \times (1 - \hat{f}_t(S, S+\Delta)) \tag{20.7}$$

where

$$\hat{f}_t(S, S+\Delta) \equiv \mathbb{E}_t^{Q_{FS}}(l_S(\Delta))$$

and $\mathbb{E}_t^{Q_{FS}}$ denotes the expectation under the S-forward probability introduced in Equation 20.4. We refer to $\hat{f}_t(S, S+\Delta)$ as the forward Libor. It is obviously a martingale under Q_{FS}, with $\hat{f}_S(S, S+\Delta) = l_S(\Delta)$. Therefore, assuming that information is driven by Brownian motions, the forward price in Equation 20.7 satisfies

$$\frac{dZ_\tau(S, S+\Delta)}{Z_\tau(S, S+\Delta)} = v_\tau^z(S, \Delta) dW_\tau^{FS}, \quad \tau \in (t, S) \tag{20.8}$$

where $W_{FS}(\tau)$ is a multidimensional Brownian motion under Q_{FS} and $v_\tau^z(S, \Delta)$ is a vector of instantaneous volatilities adapted to $W_{FS}(\tau)$.

Note the timing of the forward contract. The payoff takes place at S, that is, at the beginning of the debt servicing period, the Libor refers to $[S, S+\Delta]$. Section 20.3.3 reviews FRA and IRS, which are contracts for which the timing of payments occurs at the end of the debt servicing period.

20.3.2.2 Futures and Options Futures and options are determined exactly as in the government bond case and are not dealt with in this chapter to simplify the presentation. However, for reference, the appendix provides evaluation formulas and discussion regarding option evaluation in this context (see Eqs 20.115 and 20.116).

20.3.3 Forwards Rate Agreements and Interest Rate Swaps

20.3.3.1 Forward Agreements FRAs (in the sequel) are contracts that freeze the cost of capital for institutions such that at the end of a given debt servicing period, say, $[T, S]$, a counterparty (i) pays a fixed interest rate, K, and (ii) receives the variable interest rate that had prevailed over $[T, S]$. Assuming the variable interest rate to be the Libor $l_t(\Delta)$ introduced in the previous section, such a swap in interest rate payments has a time S payoff equal to

$$\Delta_S \times (l_T(\Delta_S) - K) \qquad \Delta_S \equiv S - T$$

such that its value for any K is

$$FRA_t(T,S;K) \equiv \mathbb{E}_t\left[e^{-\int_t^S r(\tau)d\tau}\Delta_S\left(l_T\left(\Delta_S\right)-K\right)\right]$$
$$= \Delta_S(f_t(T,S)-K)P_t(S) \tag{20.9}$$

where

$$f_t(T,S) \equiv \mathbb{E}_t^{Q_{FS}}(l_T(\Delta_S)) = \frac{1}{\Delta_S}\left(\frac{P_t(T)}{P_t(S)}-1\right) \tag{20.10}$$

and the last equality in Equation 20.9 follows by a change of probability. We shall return to the second equality in Equation 20.10 in a moment.

We refer to $f_t(T,S)$ as the forward swap rate: it is the value of K that makes the FRA worthless at origination, that is, $FRA_t(T,S;K)=0$. Note that $f_t(T,S)$ can actually be cast in a model-free fashion, that is, independent of any pricing model. Indeed, because $l_T(\Delta_S)$ is known at T, the value at T of $1+\Delta_S l_T(\Delta_S)$ dollars to be delivered at S is simply \$1 and, obviously, $P_t(T)$ dollars at t, such that the value of $\Delta_S l_T(\Delta_S)$ to be delivered at time S is simply $P_t(T)-P_t(S)$ at time t. Hinging upon this reasoning leads to the following simplification of Equation 20.9:

$$FRA_t(T,S;K) = P_t(T)-(1+\Delta_S K)P_t(S) \tag{20.11}$$

Solving for the value of K that renders $FRA_t(T,S;K)$ equal to zero yields the second equality in Equation 20.10.[3]

We now proceed with generalizing this basic contract with only one payment at S, to one in which periodic IRS take place.

20.3.3.2 Interest Rate Swaps Consider a basket of interest rate forwards, that is, one in which a party receives from another a payoff equal to $\pi_{T_i} \equiv \delta_{i-1}(l_{T_{i-1}}(\delta_{i-1})-K)$ at the reset date T_i, where K is the constant interest rate and $\delta_{i-1} \equiv T_i - T_{i-1}$, and n times. It is a forward-starting IRS, and the period over which the IRS payments will take place $T_n - T_1$ is known as the tenor of the contract.

A forward-starting IRS is valued as the present value of these single payoffs occurring over the reset dates,

$$v_{irs}^p(t) \equiv \sum_{i=1}^n FRA_t(T_{i-1},T_i;K)$$
$$= \sum_{i=1}^n [P_t(T_{i-1})-P_t(T_i)] - K\sum_{i=1}^n \delta_{i-1}P_t(T_i) \tag{20.12}$$

where $FRA_t(\cdot)$ is as in Equation 20.11. The superscript p in v_{irs}^p stands for payer – by convention, the party who pays the fixed interest rate enters a swap *payer*, and the counterparty enters a swap *receiver*.

The forward swap rate is defined as the value of K such that the value of the IRS is zero at inception, that is, $v_{irs}^p(t)=0$, and equals

$$R_t(T_1,\ldots,T_n) \equiv \frac{P_t(T_0)-P_t(T_n)}{PVBP_t(T_1,\ldots,T_n)} \tag{20.13}$$

$$PVBP_T(T_1,\ldots,T_n) \equiv \sum_{i=1}^n \delta_{i-1}P_t(T_i) \tag{20.14}$$

Note that $PVBP_T(T_1,\ldots,T_n)$ is the value of an annuity paying out \$1 at each reset date. It is also known as the "price value of the basis point," that is, the present value impact of 1 basis point moves in the forward swap rate at T. Replacing the expression for $R_t(T_1,\ldots,T_n)$ in Equations 20.13 and 20.14 into Equation 20.12 leaves the following intuitive expression for a forward swap payer:

$$v_{irs}^p(t) = PVBP_t(T_1,\ldots,T_n)(R_t(T_1,\ldots,T_n)-K) \tag{20.15}$$

[3]The standard assumption that allows for this reasoning is that settlement does indeed occur at S. Should settlement occur at $T<S$ (say), the value of $1+\Delta_S l_T(\Delta_S)$ at T would obviously be higher than 1, and the previous reasoning would not go through: a payoff of $1+\Delta_S l_T(\Delta_S)$ at T is the same as a payoff of $(1+\Delta_S l_T(\Delta_S))^2$ at S. Brigo and Mercurio (2006, Chapter 13) and Veronesi (2010, Chapter 21) explain standard market practice to deal with this "convexity" issue.

The forward swap rate displays a property to consider while pricing products referencing it, which we shall discuss in the next section. Consider the following equalities:

$$\begin{aligned}R_t(T_1, \dots, T_n) &= \frac{P_t(T_0) - P_t(T_n)}{PVBP_t(T_1, \dots, T_n)} \\ &= \mathbb{E}_t\left(\frac{e^{-\int_t^T r_\tau d\tau}}{PVBP_t(T_1, \dots, T_n)}(P_T(T_0) - P_T(T_n))\right) \\ &= \mathbb{E}_t(\xi_T^{sw,n} R_T(T_1, \dots, T_n)) \\ &= \mathbb{E}_t^{sw,n}(R_T(T_1, \dots, T_n))\end{aligned}$$

where the second equality holds by the martingale property of the discounted prices of the zero-coupon bonds expiring at T_0 and at T_n, the third by the definition of the forward swap rate in Equations 20.13 and 20.14 and the definition of $\xi_T^{sw,n}$ below:

$$\xi_T^{sw,n} \equiv \left.\frac{dQ_{sw,n}}{dQ}\right|_{\mathcal{F}_T} = e^{-\int_t^T r_\tau d\tau} \frac{PVBP_T(T_1, \dots, T_n)}{PVBP_t(T_1, \dots, T_n)} \tag{20.16}$$

and the fourth by a change of probability, with $\mathbb{E}_t^{sw,n}(\cdot)$ denoting the expectation under $Q_{sw,n}$. That is, the forward swap rate is a martingale under the new probability, $Q_{sw,n}$ and, in a diffusion setting, satisfies

$$dR_\tau(T_1, \dots, T_n) = R_\tau(T_1, \dots, T_n)\sigma_\tau(T_1, \dots, T_n) dW_\tau^{sw,n}, \quad \tau \in [t, T] \tag{20.17}$$

for some instantaneous volatility process $\sigma_\tau(\cdot)$ adapted to the Brownian motion $W_\tau^{sw,n}$ defined under $Q_{sw,n}$. The probability $Q_{sw,n}$ is known as *annuity probability* and was introduced by Jamshidian (1997).

20.3.4 Caps, Floors, and Swaptions

We review other major derivatives written on Libor besides those on time deposits considered in Section 20.3.2.

First consider a cap, which is the same as an IRS except that it gives the holder the option to proceed with the swap and reach reset date only if it is convenient to do so, that is, when interest rates turn out to be higher than a strike. Therefore, a cap protects the holder from an increase in interest rates. A cap is made up of caplets, each delivering a payoff at the reset date T_i equal to

$$\delta_{i-1}(l_{T_{i-1}}(T_i) - K)^+, \quad i = 1, \dots, n$$

where K is a strike.[4] Therefore, the price of a caplet at t equals

$$\begin{aligned}Cap_t &\equiv \sum_{i=1}^n \mathbb{E}_t\left[e^{-\int_t^{T_i} r_\tau d\tau}\delta_{i-1}\left(l_{T_{i-1}}(T_i) - K\right)^+\right] \\ &= \sum_{i=1}^n \delta_{i-1} P_t(T_i) \mathbb{E}_t^{Q_{F^{T_i}}}(l_{T_{i-1}}(T_i) - K)^+\end{aligned} \tag{20.18}$$

The benefit to be long a cap is to be protected period-by-period so to speak. It is the same as a basket of options with different maturities. A swaption works differently, in that the optionality kicks in "bundled." Suppose, for example, we anticipate that 1 year from now, we might want to enter a 5-year payer swap to hedge against variable interest rates. At the same time, we would like to be sure that we would only benefit from interest rates going up while fixing the downside. Swaptions allow for this optionality as they provide their holder the right to enter a swap contract on a future date and at a certain strike.

Consider a payer swaption expiring at time T_0 with tenor period T_n–T_1 and strike K. Its payoff is the maximum between zero and the value of a payer IRS at T_0, which by Equation 20.15 is

$$(v_{irs}(T_0))^+ = PVBP_{T_0}(T_1, \dots, T_n)(R_{T_0}(T_1, \dots, T_n) - K)^+ \tag{20.19}$$

[4]Floors are defined in a symmetrically opposite way. They protect against a downward movement in interest rates, in that they are baskets of single *floorlets* that pay off, $\delta_{i-1}(K - l_{T_{i-1}}(T_i))^+$, at time T_i, $i = 1, \dots, n$. Floors could be priced through the put–call parity for caps and floors.

such that the value at t is

$$Swpn_t^{\mathrm{p}} = \mathbb{E}_t\left[e^{-\int_t^{T_0} r(\tau)d\tau} PVBP_{T_0}\left(T_1, \dots, T_n\right)\left(R_{T_0}(T_1, \dots, T_n) - K\right)^+\right]$$
$$= PVBP_t(T_1, \dots, T_n)\mathbb{E}_t^{Q_{sw,n}}(R_{T_0}(T_1, \dots, T_n) - K)^+ \tag{20.20}$$

where $\mathbb{E}_t^{Q_{sw,n}}$ denotes the time t expectation taken under the annuity probability $Q_{sw,n}$ defined through Equation 20.16. Swaption receivers work in the exactly opposite way and can be evaluated through the swaption parity,

$$Swpn_t^P(K) = v_{irs}^P(t) + Swpn_t^{\mathrm{r}}(K)$$

where $v_{irs}(t)$ is the value of the forward IRS in Equation 20.12.

20.4 EVALUATION PARADIGMS

This section examines the main evaluation paradigms for the instruments reviewed in the previous section. The literature on IRD evaluation is vast, relying on dozens of models either addressing empirical regularities or providing a standard for a convenient analytical framework. We cannot even attempt to review this literature and refer the reader to classical textbooks such as Brigo and Mercurio (2006) or Veronesi (2010). Rather, our focus in this section is to provide a broad illustration of models that are commonly used in practice and related to our main theme in this chapter.

Section 20.4.1 provides an overview of one of the earliest approaches that emerged in the literature, which is based on models of the short-term rate that determine the entire yield curve, possibly in combination with additional factors. This approach suffers from a drawback: it cannot fit the entire yield curve without error. Suppose a financial institution is pricing a set of IRDs with a model built up through this approach. How can we rely on a model that is not even able to pin down the initial yield curve? A second class of "no-arbitrage models" aims to fix this issue and is succinctly reviewed in Section 20.4.2. Finally, Section 20.4.3 surveys models designed to fit the cross section of IRD relying on notions of "implied volatility."

20.4.1 Models of the Short-term Rate

20.4.1.1 The Seminal Work Vasicek (1977) derives a model of the yield curve assuming the short-term rate r_τ is a continuous-time mean-reverting process with constant basis point volatility,

$$dr_\tau = \kappa(\bar{r} - r_\tau)d\tau + \sigma d\tilde{W}_\tau, \quad \bar{r} \equiv \mu - \frac{\lambda\sigma}{\kappa} \tag{20.21}$$

where $\tilde{W}_\tau$ is a Brownian motion under the risk-neutral probability, μ is the unconditional expectation of r_τ, κ is the speed of mean reversion, and finally, $\bar{r}$ is the unconditional expectation of r_τ taken under the risk-neutral probability Q, with λ denoting a risk adjustment arising through Girsanov theorem: that is, μ is the unconditional expectation of r_τ under the physical probability.

The model's major drawback is that the transition density of r_τ in Equation 20.21 is normal, which can lead to negative values of r_τ. Cox, Ingersoll, and Ross (1985) propose an alternative model in which the short-term rate is the solution to the so-called "square-root" process

$$dr_\tau = \hat{\kappa}(\hat{r} - r_\tau)d\tau + \hat{\sigma}\sqrt{r_\tau}d\tilde{W}_\tau \tag{20.22}$$

where basis point volatility is now time varying (although locally deterministic) and notation is similar to that utilized for the Vasicek model. It is well known that under these dynamics, the transition density of r_τ is noncentral chi-square, and the short-term rate is always positive under regularity conditions.

Both models lead to a closed-form solution for the price of a zero-coupon bond, which has the form

$$P_t(r_t; T) \equiv e^{a(T-t)-b(T-t)r_t} \tag{20.23}$$

for two functions $a(\cdot)$ and $b(\cdot)$ given in the appendix (Eqs 20.106 and 20.107 for Vasicek and Eqs 20.108 and 20.109 for Cox, Ingersoll, and Ross). For example, in Vasicek's model, the bond price exposure to the short-term rate is

$$b(T-t) = \frac{1 - e^{-\kappa(T-t)}}{\kappa} \tag{20.24}$$

The higher the persistence of the short-term rate, the lower the κ, the higher the exposure of the bond price to the short-term rate, and in turn the higher the bond return volatility. In the limit where κ is very small, the volatility of the return on the bond maturing in n years is equal to $v(n) \equiv \sigma \cdot n$. Even if the basis point volatility of the short-term rate is as small as, say, 2 bps, the model predicts that for a 10-year zero-coupon bond, return volatility $v(n)$ reaches 20%. The high persistence of the short-term rate creates a "risk for the long run" so to speak. The bond exposure for the Cox, Ingersoll, and Ross model is obviously different from b in Equation 20.24, but one can reach a similar conclusion with this model.

The fact that both models predict the price of a zero-coupon bond with the form in Equation 20.23 is due to a precise mathematical property reviewed in the next section.

20.4.1.2 Stochastic Volatility and Multifactor Extensions The Cox, Ingersoll, and Ross (1985) model surveyed previously predicts the short-term rate to have random basis point volatility but driven by the level of the short-term rate. This is now understood to be somehow a counterfactual feature, which led to formulations of models in which short-term rate volatility is driven by other factors than the level of interest rates.

Fong and Vasicek (1991) consider the following model, generalizing the Vasicek (1977) model in 20.21:

$$\begin{cases} dr_\tau = \kappa_r(\bar{r} - r_\tau)d\tau + v_\tau d\tilde{W}_{1\tau} \\ dv_\tau^2 = \kappa_v(\omega - v_\tau^2)d\tau + \xi v_\tau d\tilde{W}_{2\tau} \end{cases} \tag{20.25}$$

where $\tilde{W}_{i\tau}$ are two standard Brownian motions under the risk-neutral probability. It is a natural extension of the Vasicek model. The short-term rate is still mean reverting, but its basis point variance is now random and also mean reverting.

Longstaff and Schwartz (1992) propose another model, grounded in general equilibrium, for which the short-term rate is a linear combination of two factors,

$$r_\tau = \beta_1 y_{1\tau} + \beta_2 y_{2\tau} \tag{20.26}$$

for two constants β_i and two uncorrelated processes $y_{1\tau}$ and $y_{2\tau}$ – leading to an "affine" model, as explained later (see, also, the appendix). The Longstaff and Schwartz model also exhibits stochastic volatility, and like Fong and Vasicek, it has a solution with the following form:

$$P_t(r_t, v_t^2; T) \equiv e^{a(T-t)-b(T-t)r_t+c(T-t)v_t^2} \tag{20.27}$$

for three functions $a(\cdot)$, $b(\cdot)$, and $c(\cdot)$ (see Appendix) and where v_t^2 denotes the instantaneous basis point variance of the changes in the short-term rate in Equation 20.26, just as in Fong and Vasicek.[5]

Note that there are now two factors driving the variation of the bond price. Persistence of either can inflate volatility of bond returns. Due to stochastic volatility, bond return volatility itself fluctuates. While very old, these two models are trailblazers for the new area of IRV pricing surveyed in this chapter and will also serve as an inspiration in Section 20.5 for the design of an evaluation model for derivatives on government bond volatility indexes.

An issue regarding both models is that there are only two factors driving the entire yield curve, which is counterfactual: it is well known since at least Litterman and Scheinkman (1991) (see also Knez, Litterman, and Scheinkman, 1994), that most of the variation of the yield curve is driven by at least three factors. Can we build up an analytically tractable multifactor model that predicts a bond price generalizing Equations 20.23 and 20.27?

Duffie and Kan (1996) prove the following result. Suppose that the short-term rate is the following generalization of the Longstaff and Schwartz equation 20.26:

$$r_\tau = \alpha + \beta \cdot y_\tau \tag{20.28}$$

where α is a constant, β is a vector, and y_τ is a diffusion in $\mathbb{R}^n$ solution to

$$dy_\tau = \kappa(\mu - y_\tau)d\tau + \Sigma V(y_\tau)d\tilde{W}_\tau \tag{20.29}$$

where $\tilde{W}_\tau$ is an n-dimensional Brownian motion under the risk-neutral probability, Σ is a full rank $n \times n$ matrix, and V is a full rank $n \times n$ diagonal matrix with elements

$$V(y)_{(ii)} = \sqrt{s_{1i} + s_{2i} \cdot y}, \quad i = 1, \ldots, n$$

[5] Mele (2003) studies the mapping from the instantaneous volatility of the short-term rate and the yield curve in more general models, identifying conditions leading to sign the relation between volatility and the yield curve – for example, the sign of $c(\cdot)$ in Equation 20.27.

for some scalars s_{1i} and vectors s_{2i}. Then, the price of a zero-coupon bond has the following form that generalizes both Equations 20.23 and 20.27:

$$P(y_t, T-t) = e^{a^o(T-t)+a^y(T-t)\cdot y_t} \tag{20.30}$$

for some functions $a^o(\cdot)$ and $a^y(\cdot)$ (see Appendix for further details on these two functions).

This class of *affine* models is thoroughly surveyed by Piazzesi (2010), and all of the models described in the current section fall within this class. Note that affine models do not constitute the only analytically tractable class of models; the so-called "quadratic" formulation of the term structure discussed by Ahn, Dittmar, and Gallant (2002) also leads to closed-form solutions for the price of zero-coupon bonds.

20.4.2 No-Arbitrage Models

The approach in the previous section is to take the short-term rate process as given and price the entire yield curve. Obviously, this approach cannot lead to a perfect fit of the current yield curve. We now succinctly review models that help achieve this goal. These models are known as "no-arbitrage" simply because it is as if they relied on (rather than determine) current prices to imply the dynamics of the future yield curve through no-arb restrictions – no arbitrage is essentially the only assumption made, on top of standard price dynamics such as prices driven by Brownian motions.

20.4.2.1 Early Formulations Ho and Lee (1986) consider the first no-arbitrage model of the yield curve. In continuous time, the model assumes that the short-term rate is the solution to

$$dr_\tau = \theta_\tau d\tau + \sigma d\tilde{W}_\tau, \quad \tau \geq t \tag{20.31}$$

where $\tilde{W}_\tau$ is a Brownian motion under Q, σ is a constant basis point volatility, and θ_τ is an "infinite-dimensional" parameter (i.e., a curve continuous in calendar time and known at time t), which allows fitting of the initial yield curve without error.

Note that the model is clearly affine, and the price at τ of a zero-coupon bond expiring at T can be expressed as

$$P_\tau(r_\tau, T) = e^{\int_\tau^T \theta_s(s-T)ds+\frac{1}{6}\sigma^2(T-\tau)^3-(T-\tau)\cdot r_\tau}$$

Matching the instantaneous forward rate for T predicted by the model, $\varphi_\tau(T) \equiv -\frac{\partial}{\partial T}\ln P_\tau(r_\tau, T)$, to its hypothetically observed market counterpart, $\varphi_\tau^\$(T)$, gives

$$\theta_\tau = \frac{\partial}{\partial \tau}\varphi_t^\$(\tau) + \sigma^2(\tau - t) \tag{20.32}$$

By construction, the model fits the entire yield curve without error because the price satisfies $P_t(T) = e^{-\int_t^T \varphi_t^\$(\tau)d\tau}$ and the parameter θ_τ in Equation 20.32 is indeed shown to guarantee that $\varphi_t(\tau) = \varphi_t^\$(\tau)$ for each τ.

Note that with this θ_τ, the model predicts that the short-term rate in Equation 20.31 satisfies

$$r_t = \varphi_0^\$(t) + \frac{1}{2}\sigma^2 t^2 + \sigma\tilde{W}_t$$

and the instantaneous forward rate

$$d\varphi_\tau(T) = \sigma^2(T-\tau)d\tau + \sigma d\tilde{W}_\tau$$

That is, the model does not impose any restrictions on the drift of the forward rates other than one arising from no-arbitrage, but it is still able to match any observed price. These are the reasons we refer to this model as "no-arbitrage."

Hull and White (1990) generalize the previous model to 1 in which the short-term rate has a mean-reverting component,

$$dr_\tau = (\theta_\tau - \kappa r_\tau)d\tau + \sigma d\tilde{W}_\tau \tag{20.33}$$

where $\tilde{W}_\tau$ is a Q-Brownian motion, θ_τ is the infinite-dimensional parameter, and κ, σ are constants.[6] They find that the price of a bond predicted by the model is

$$P_\tau(r_\tau, T) = e^{\frac{1}{2}\sigma^2\int_\tau^T b^2(T-s)ds-\int_\tau^T \theta_s b(T-s)ds-b(T-\tau)\cdot r_\tau}$$

[6]Hull and White do in fact consider a more complex model in which κ and σ are both time varying.

where the function $b(\cdot)$ is the same as in Equation 20.24 and

$$\theta_\tau = \frac{\partial}{\partial \tau}\varphi_t^{\$}(\tau) + \kappa f_{\$}\varphi_t^{\$}(\tau) + \frac{\sigma^2}{2\kappa}\left(1 - e^{-2\kappa(\tau-t)}\right) \tag{20.34}$$

The reason one may prefer the Hull and White model over the Ho and Lee model is that while the latter is capable of fitting the entire yield curve, a more complex model might be better to price derivatives. In fact, we may take this reasoning one step further and consider even more complex models than Hull and White. Brigo and Mercurio (2006) survey a rich variety of such models and examine their behavior vis-à-vis market data in detail.

*20.4.2.2 **Pricing Coupon-Bearing Bonds*** The Hull and White (1990) model does, of course, generalize Vasicek (1977). The latter is obtained from the former when θ_τ in Equation 20.33 is constant. In this section, we develop a pricing example to emphasize the importance of having θ_τ determined to fit the yield curve, as in Equation 20.34. The pricing problem concerns an option written on a coupon-bearing bond. In Section 20.5, we shall utilize this example to illustrate how to address a number of issues regarding the implementation of government bond volatility indexes.

First, recall the price of a call option expiring at T, written on a zero-coupon bond expiring at S, and struck at K, is given in Equation 20.6. Jamshidian (1989) shows that the two probabilities, $\mathbb{Q}_{Fj}$, can be calculated in closed form, such that

$$\overline{Call}_t^b(T; P_t(r_t, S), K, v) = P_t(r_t, S) \cdot \Phi(d_1) - KP_t(r_t, T) \cdot \Phi(d_1 - v_{[T,S]}) \tag{20.35}$$

where

$$d_1 = \frac{\ln \frac{P_t(r_t,S)}{KP_t(r_t,T)} + \frac{1}{2}v_{[T,S]}^2}{v_{[T,S]}}, \quad v_{[T,S]}^2 = \sigma^2\frac{1 - e^{-2\kappa(T-t)}}{2\kappa}b^2(S-T)$$

and $b(\cdot)$ is as in Equation 20.24 and $\Phi(\cdot)$ denotes the cumulative normal distribution.

Note that we have been silent regarding whether we are using Equation 20.34 to determine the "underlying" price $P_t(r_t, S)$ and the "discounting" price $P_t(r_t, T)$ in Equation (20.35). It does not really matter for the purpose of the current pricing exercise. It does matter, though, when it comes to pricing more complex instruments like options written on a coupon-bearing bond. Consider the payoff of such an option, given by

$$\left[\sum_{i=1}^{n} \frac{C_i}{n} P_{T_0}(T_i) + P_{T_0}(r_{T_0}, T_n) - K\right]^+ = \sum_{i=1}^{N} \bar{C}_i \cdot [P_{T_0}(r_{T_0}, T_i) - \mathcal{K}_i^*(K)]^+ \tag{20.36}$$

where $\bar{C}_i \equiv \frac{C_i}{n}$, for $i = 1, \ldots, N-1$, $\bar{C}_n \equiv \frac{C_n}{n} + 1$, $\mathcal{K}_i^*(K) \equiv P_{T_0}(r^*(K), T_i)$ and $r^*(K)$ is the solution to the following equation:

$$P_{T_0}(r^*, T_n) + \sum_{i=1}^{n} \frac{C_i}{n} P_{T_0}(r^*, T_i) = K \tag{20.37}$$

A unique solution to Equation 20.37 exists under mild regularity conditions because the bond price is inversely related to the short-term rate, in which case Equation 20.36 should also hold. Therefore, a call on a coupon-bearing bond is the same as a basket of call options with strike $\mathcal{K}_i^*(K)$, and its value is

$$Call_t^b(T_0; B_t(\mathbb{T}), K) \equiv \sum_{i=1}^{n} \bar{C}_i \cdot \overline{Call}_t^b(T_0; P_t(r_t, T_i), \mathcal{K}_i^*(K), v_{[T_0,T_i]}) \tag{20.38}$$

where $\overline{Call}_t^b$ is the call price in Equation 20.35. The price of a put can be determined through put–call parity. This formula is due to Jamshidian (1989).

A critical point to note is that the value of $r^*(K)$ and, hence, that of $\mathcal{K}_i^*(K)$ and ultimately that of $Call_t^b(\cdot)$ depends on the entire yield curve whenever θ_τ is calibrated to market data through Equation (20.37). In other words, different values of the yield curve lead to different values of $Call_t^b(\cdot)$ through the fictitious strike $\mathcal{K}_i^*(K)$.

*20.4.2.3 **Heath, Jarrow, and Morton*** Heath, Jarrow, and Morton (1992) (HJM, henceforth) generalize the early approach to no-arbitrage pricing in the fixed-income space. Their arguments can be understood as follows. Consider the following representation of a bond price in terms of the instantaneous forward rates:

$$P_\tau(T) = \frac{P_t^\$(T)}{P_t^\$(\tau)} \cdot e^{-\int_\tau^T (\varphi_\tau(\ell)-\varphi_t(\ell))d\ell} \tag{20.39}$$

Given the current prices, $P_t^\$(\tau)$ and $P_t^\$(T)$, the goal is to model the future forward rate movements,

$$\varphi_\tau(\ell) - \varphi_t(\ell)$$

Note that by construction, the current yield curve is fitted without error: set $\tau = t$ in Equation 20.39 and obtain $P_t(T) = P_t^\$(T)$ for each T.

HJM assume that under the risk-neutral probability, $\varphi_\tau(T)$ satisfies; for fixed T,

$$d\varphi_\tau(T) = \alpha_\tau(T)d\tau + \sigma_\tau^f(T)d\tilde{W}_\tau, \quad \tau \in (t, T] \tag{20.40}$$

where $\tilde{W}_\tau$ is a multidimensional process and α_τ and σ_τ^f are some adapted processes with $\varphi_t(T)$ given. A restriction can be found on the drift $\alpha_\tau(T)$ once we require the no-arbitrage condition that the expected returns of the zero-coupon bond must be equal to the short-term rate under the risk-neutral probability, Q. The restriction is

$$\alpha_\tau(T) = \sigma_\tau^f(T) \int_\tau^T \sigma_\tau^f(\ell)^\top d\ell \tag{20.41}$$

The appendix contains a derivation of Equation 20.41. Replacing the previous restriction in Equation 20.40 leads to the following expression for the short-term rate, $r_\tau \equiv \varphi_\tau(\tau)$:

$$r_\tau \equiv \varphi_\tau(\tau) = \varphi_t(\tau) + \int_t^\tau \alpha_s(\tau)ds + \int_t^\tau \sigma_s^f(\tau)d\tilde{W}_s, \quad \tau \in (t, T] \tag{20.42}$$

where $\alpha_.(\cdot)$ is as in Equation 20.41. In principle, we could use Equation 20.42 to price IRDs. We would be simply left with specifying the volatility of the forward rates. For example, it is straightforward to check that once $\sigma_s(\tau)$ is constant, one is back to the Ho and Lee model.

More generally, one could specify richer dynamics than Ho and Lee and price IRDs by simulations relying on Equation 20.42. Needless to mention, one can rely on models much richer than the single factor in Equation 20.40 and derive restrictions generalizing Equation 20.41 and price IRDs accordingly. We now describe a simple class of models used in practice.

20.4.2.4 Market Models The original HJM framework relies on the notion of continuously compounded forward rates; yet in practice one must deal with discretely compounded rates. Black's (1976)formula is often used in practice to price IRDs such as caps, floors, and swaptions. The question then arises as to how to make the HJM framework consistent with market practice. Brace, Gatarek, and Musiela (1997), Jamshidian (1997), and Miltersen, Sandmann, and Sondermann (1997) develop restrictions the HJM should satisfy to address these issues, which lead to the "market model."

Assume that the forward rate $f_{i\tau} \equiv f_\tau(T_i, T_{i+1})$ in Equation 20.10 under the risk-neutral probability Q is the solution to

$$\frac{df_{i\tau}}{f_{i\tau}} = m_{i\tau}d\tau + \gamma_{i\tau}d\tilde{W}_\tau, \quad \tau \in [t, T_i], \quad i = 0, \dots, n-1 \tag{20.43}$$

where $\tilde{W}_\tau$ is a vector of standard Brownian motions under Q, $m_{i\tau}$ is a function measurable with respect to $\tilde{W}_\tau$, and $\gamma_{i\tau}$ is a *deterministic* vector-valued function of time.

Note, also, that by Equation 20.10,

$$\ln\left(\frac{P_\tau(T_i)}{P_\tau(T_{i+1})}\right) = \ln(1 + \delta_i f_{i\tau})$$

The idea is to expand both sides of the previous equation and identify the diffusion terms. Relying on Itô's lemma,

$$\sigma_\tau^B(T_i) - \sigma_\tau^B(T_{i+1}) = \frac{\delta_i f_{i\tau}}{1 + \delta_i f_{i\tau}}\gamma_{i\tau}, \quad \tau \in [t, T_i] \tag{20.44}$$

where $\sigma_\tau^B(T_i)$ denotes the time τ instantaneous return volatility of a zero-coupon bond expiring at T_i, consistent with the notation after Equation 20.5.

Note that this restriction arises because a market model is being used to price IRDs. One could use any other no-arbitrage model (e.g., multifactor extensions of Hull and White, 1990) to price IRDs. The market model is, however, commonly used in practice. In the following, we shall see how Equation 20.44 is used to determine the price of a number of IRDs consistently (see Eq. 20.51).

20.4.2.5 *Applications to Derivative Pricing* Consider evaluating a cap through the market model. By Equation 20.18 and the relation $f_{i-1,T_{i-1}} \equiv f_{T_{i-1}}(T_{i-1}, T_i) = l_{T_{i-1}}(T_i)$,

$$Cap_t = \sum_{i=1}^{n} \delta_{i-1} P_t(T_i) \cdot \mathbb{E}_t^{Q_{FT_i}} (f_{i-1,T_{i-1}} - K)^+ \tag{20.45}$$

We know already from Equation 20.10 that the forward rate $f_{i-1,\tau}$ is a martingale under Q_{FT_i}. Assuming that it has deterministic volatility as in Equation 20.43

$$\frac{df_{i-1,\tau}}{f_{i-1,\tau}} = \gamma_{i-1,\tau} dW_\tau^{FT_i}, \quad \tau \in [t, T_{i-1}], \quad i = 1, \dots, n \tag{20.46}$$

under Q_{FT_i}. The expectation in Equation 20.45 can be determined through Black's (1976) formula,

$$\mathbb{E}_t^{Q_{FT_i}} (f_{i-1,T_{i-1}} - K)^+ = Bl76(f_{i-1,t}; T_{i-1} - t, K, s_{i-1}) \tag{20.47}$$

where

$$Bl76(f_{i-1,t}; T_{i-1} - t, K, s_{i-1}) \equiv f_{i-1,t}\Phi(d_{i-1,t}) - K\Phi(d_{i-1,t} - s_{i-1}),$$

$$d_{i-1,t} = \frac{\ln \frac{f_{i-1,t}}{K} + \frac{1}{2} s_{i-1}^2}{s_{i-1}}, \quad s_{i-1}^2 = \int_t^{T_{i-1}} \gamma_{i-1,\tau}^2 d\tau$$

and Φ denotes the cumulative normal distribution.

Swaptions are priced similarly. Consider Equation 20.17 and assume that $\sigma_\tau(\cdot) \equiv \gamma_{n,sw,\tau}$, for some deterministic $\gamma_{n,sw,\tau}$. Because the forward swap rate is a martingale under the annuity probability, Equation 20.20 tells us that we can use Black's formula and obtain the price of a swaption payer expiring at T_0 as

$$Swpn_t^{\mathrm{p}}(K, R_{n,t}) = PVBP_t(T_1, \dots, T_n) \cdot Bl76(R_{n,t}; T_0 - t, K, \sqrt{\bar{V}}) \tag{20.48}$$

where $R_{n,t} \equiv R_t(T_1, \dots, T_n)$ to simplify notation and

$$Bl76\left(R_{n,t}; T_0 - t, K, \sqrt{\bar{V}}\right) = R_{n,t}\Phi\left(d_t\right) - K\Phi\left(d_t - \sqrt{\bar{V}}\right)$$

$$d_t = \frac{\ln \frac{R_{n,t}}{K} + \frac{1}{2}\bar{V}}{\sqrt{\bar{V}}}, \quad \bar{V} = \int_t^{T_0} \gamma_{n,sw,\tau}^2 d\tau$$

In practice, the market convention is to price swaptions through an implied Black's volatility, defined as the value of $\sqrt{\bar{V}}$ in Equation 20.48 that makes the Black's pricer return the market price,

$$\sigma_{iv}(K, R_{n,t}, T_0 - t)$$

$$Bl76(R_{n,t}; T_0 - t, K, \sigma_{iv}(K, R_{n,t}, T_0)) = \frac{Swpn_t^{\mathrm{p}}(K)}{PVBP_t(T_1, \dots, T_n)} \tag{20.49}$$

where $Swpn_t^{\mathrm{p}}(K)$ denotes the market price of the swaption payer struck at K.

An issue that arises here is that we cannot assume that Equations 20.17 and 20.46 simultaneously hold through their deterministic instantaneous volatilities. According to the model, the forward swap rate cannot be lognormal if we assume the forward is lognormal, and vice versa. One approach would be to price caps and floors using the previous lognormal model and proceed to price the swaptions through simulation. For example, one could consider a slightly different representation of the swaption payoff than in Equation 20.19, obtained by using Equation 20.9 in the definition in 20.12,

$$(v_{irs}^p(t))^+ = \left[\sum_{i=1}^{n} FRA_t(T_{i-1}, T_i; K)\right]^+$$

and by taking expectation of the previous payoff and a change in probability:

$$Swpn_t^{\mathrm{P}} = P_t(T_0)\mathbb{E}_t^{Q_{F^{T_0}}}\left[\sum_{i=1}^{n} \delta_{i-1}\left(f_{i-1,T_0} - K\right) P_{T_0}(T_i)\right]^+ \tag{20.50}$$

Then, it can be shown that by Girsanov's theorem, the "fundamental restriction of the market model," Equation 20.44, implies

$$\frac{df_{i-1,\tau}}{f_{i-1,\tau}} = \gamma_{i-1,\tau}\sum_{j=0}^{i-1}\frac{\delta_j f_{j,\tau}}{1+\delta_j f_{j,\tau}}\gamma_{j,\tau}d\tau + \gamma_{i-1,\tau}dW_\tau^{F^{T_0}}, \quad i = 1, \ldots, n \tag{20.51}$$

The various forward rates in Equation 20.50 may be simulated through Equation 20.51, leading to Monte Carlo approximations to the price in Equation (20.50). There are more complex models and numerical procedures devised in the literature to deal with these issues (see, e.g., Brigo and Mercurio, 2006, for a survey), but the logic remains the same as that described in this section: to use the market model's restrictions to price IRDs consistently.

20.4.3 Volatility

20.4.3.1 Local Volatility The logic underlying the previous no-arbitrage models is to price IRDs while making sure that, at the same time, the initial yield curve is fitted without error. We now deal with a similar issue regarding the *volatility* of fixed-income securities. Consider the pricing of swaptions and assume that the forward swap rate has nonrandom volatility, such that the price of a swaption payer is just as in Equation 20.48.

There is ample empirical evidence suggesting that the assumption of a nonrandom volatility is counterfactual (see, e.g., Mele and Obayashi, 2014a). Moreover, it is well known that the implied volatilities in Equation 20.49 are decreasing over moneyness, $K/R_{n,t}$ (setting for simplicity $R_{n,t} \equiv R_t(T_1, \ldots, T_n)$) – a well-known empirical phenomenon known as the "skew." The presence of a skew poses quite a few challenges, both theoretical and practical. Theoretically, it implies an internally inconsistent conclusion that a model for the forward swap rate is needed for each swaption price corresponding to a specific strike. Practically, it does not allow for a consistent IRD risk management framework.

Naturally, these issues are very well known in the equity derivatives literature. In fact, research undertaken in the equity derivatives space suggests that stochastic volatility could be responsible for the skew (see, e.g., the early survey of Renault, 1997). Dupire (1994) provides a first fundamental step for dealing with these issues by introducing the so-called "local volatility" model. While this model was initially conceived to deal with equity derivatives, it may well be used to price IRDs such as swaptions.

Local volatility addresses an inverse problem. Let us continue with the forward swap example and consider Equation 20.17, assuming that $W_\tau^{n,sw}$ is scalar and that the volatility $\sigma_\tau(\cdot)$ is a function of both the forward swap rate and calendar time, $\sigma(R_{n,\tau}, \tau)$, say, such that

$$\frac{dR_{n,\tau}}{R_{n,\tau}} = \sigma(R_{n,\tau}, \tau)dW_\tau^{n,sw} \tag{20.52}$$

A standard approach in financial economics is to determine asset price restrictions given the dynamics of fundamentals and other assumptions. The local volatility model does, instead, reverse this protocol and, in the case of Equation 20.52, searches for the volatility function $\sigma(R_{n,\tau}, \tau)$ such that the price predicted by the model matches the market for each strike K. Mele and Obayashi (2014a; Appendix B) show that the resulting volatility function, say, $\sigma_{loc}(R_{n,\tau}, \tau)$, can be expressed in terms of the available swaption prices, similar to Dupire (1994) on the equity side,

$$\sigma_{loc}(K,\tau) = \sqrt{\mathbb{E}_t^{sw,n}(\sigma^2(R_{n,\tau},\tau)|R_{n,\tau} = K)} = \sqrt{2\frac{\frac{\partial Swpn_t^P(K;\tau)}{\partial \tau}}{K^2\frac{\partial^2 Swpn_t^P(K;\tau)}{\partial K^2}}} \tag{20.53}$$

where we have emphasized the maturity of the swaption in the second argument of the swaption payer, $Swpn_t^P(K;\tau)$.[7]

By construction, the model does "fit the skew" through a function $\sigma_{loc}(R_{n,\tau}, \tau)$ that allows the model to match every market swaption price.[8] This local volatility, $\sigma_{loc}(R_{n,\tau}, \tau)$, is nonparametric in nature, entirely relying on data, and could be used to price illiquid swaptions or any other products relying on Monte Carlo simulations, for example.

[7] In deriving Equation 20.53, we have neglected the impact of the change in $PVBP_t$ occurring after a change in T; see Mele and Obayashi (2014a; Appendix B) for additional details.

[8] As usual in this context, this fit is only theoretical as it relies on continuous dependence on the data.

Finally, note that we can use the previous expression to find an expression for the expectation of the integrated local variance from the time period $[T_1, T_2]$

$$\int_{T_1}^{T_2} \mathbb{E}_t^{sw,n}(\sigma^2(R_{n,\tau}, \tau))d\tau =$$

$$= \int_{T_1}^{T_2} \int_0^{\infty} (\mathbb{E}_t^{sw,n}(\sigma^2(R_{n,\tau}, \tau)|R_{n,\tau} = K)\phi_\tau(K)dK)d\tau$$

$$= \frac{2}{PVBP_t} \int_0^{\infty} \frac{Swpn_t^P(K;T_2) - Swpn_t^P(K;T_1)}{K^2} dK \tag{20.54}$$

where we have used the expression for the marginal density of $R_{n,\tau}$ under the annuity probability, $\phi_\tau(K) = \frac{1}{PVBP_t}\frac{\partial^2 Swpn_t^P(K;\tau)}{\partial K^2}$.

Equation 20.54 provides a model-free expression for expected percentage realized variance in swap markets, which is reminiscent of the model-free expression derived by Britten-Jones and Neuberger (2000) for equities. A remarkable difference is that this formula is rescaled by the $PVBP_t$, and the expectation is taken under the annuity probability, which are two themes we shall return to in great detail in Section 20.5.

20.4.3.2 SABR Local volatility models such as that in Equation 20.52 do, however, suffer from a drawback as pointed out by Hagan et al. (2002). Consider, for example, Equation 20.52 and for simplicity assume that the local volatility is a function of only the forward swap rate, $\sigma_{loc}(R_{n,\tau})$. Consider a generic "forward risk," denoted as X_τ, which is a martingale under a certain pricing probability, just as the forward swap rate under the annuity probability. Hagan and Woodward (1999) use perturbation methods and show that for any maturity, the implied Black's volatility of a European-style option with the forward risk X as the underlying is

$$\sigma_{iv}(K,X) = \sigma_{loc}\left(\frac{1}{2}(K+X)\right)\left(1 + \frac{1}{24}\frac{\sigma''_{loc}\left(\frac{1}{2}(K+X)\right)}{\sigma_{loc}(12(K+X))}(X-K)^2 + \cdots\right.$$

where the omitted terms are likely to be numerically negligible for practical purposes.

What are the dynamics of the market smile implied by this local volatility model? To illustrate, consider what happens to the first term in the previous expansion, say, $\hat{\sigma}_{iv}(K,X)$, when the forward increases from X to $X + \Delta X$,

$$\hat{\sigma}_{iv}(K, X + \Delta X) \equiv \sigma_{loc}\left(\frac{1}{2}(K + X + \Delta X)\right) = \hat{\sigma}_{iv}(K + \Delta X, X)$$

In other words, provided σ_{loc} is decreasing, the local volatility model predicts that as the forward X increases, the skew moves to the left, which might contradict market behavior. For example, let us assume the local volatility function is $\sigma_{loc}(x) = 0.04 \cdot x^{-1/2}$. Panel A of Figure 20.6 plots the implied volatility $\hat{\sigma}_{iv}(K,X)$ for $X = 3\%$ (solid line) and $X = 4\%$ (dashed line).

Hagan et al. (2002) consider a richer model, which they call SABR for "stochastic $\alpha\beta\rho$," in which the forward X_t satisfies

$$\begin{cases} dX_\tau = v_\tau X_\tau^\beta dW_{1\tau} \\ dv_\tau = \xi v_\tau \left(\rho dW_{1\tau} + \sqrt{1-\rho^2} dW_{2\tau}\right), \quad v_t \equiv \alpha_t \end{cases} \tag{20.55}$$

where $W_{i\tau}$ are two standard Brownian motions under the market probability; β, ρ, and ξ are constants; and α_t is interpreted as the initial condition for the unobserved stochastic volatility component of the forward. Note that the model allows the forward and its volatility to be conditionally correlated with instantaneous correlation equal to ρ.

HKLW show that the implied volatility predicted by this model is

$$\sigma_{iv}(K, X_t; \alpha_t) = \frac{\alpha_t}{(X_t K)^{(1-\beta)/2}} \frac{1 + \left(\frac{(1-\beta)^2}{24}\frac{\alpha_t^2}{(X_t K)^{1-\beta}} + \frac{1}{4}\frac{\rho\beta\xi}{(X_t K)^{(1-\beta)/2}}\alpha_t + \frac{2-3\rho^2}{24}\xi^2\right)T + \cdots}{\left(1 + \frac{(1-\beta)^2}{24}\ln^2\frac{X_t}{K} + \frac{(1-\beta)^4}{1920}\ln^4\frac{X_t}{K} + \cdots\right.} \frac{z_t}{u(z_t)} \tag{20.56}$$

where

$$z_t \equiv \frac{\xi}{\alpha_t}(X_t K)^{(1-\beta)/2} \ln\frac{X_t}{K}, \quad u(z_t) \equiv \ln\frac{\sqrt{1 - 2\rho z_t + z_t^2} + z_t - \rho}{1-\rho}$$

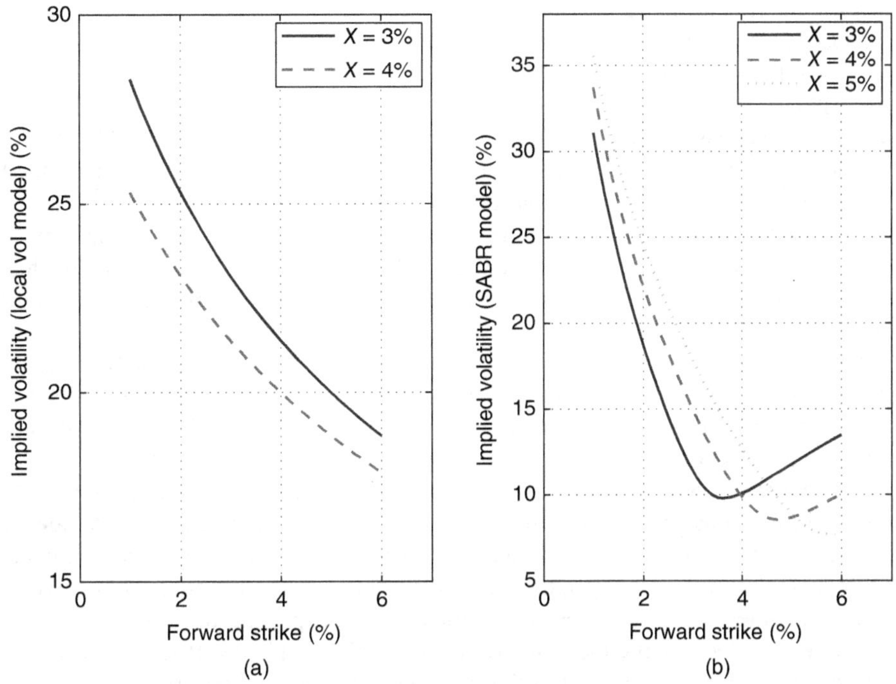

Figure 20.6 Panel A depicts the approximated implied volatility $\hat{\sigma}_{iv}(K, X)$ generated by a local volatility model with $\sigma_{loc}(x) = 0.04 \cdot x^{-1/2}$. Solid and dashed lines correspond to values of the forward X_t equal to 3% and 4%, respectively. Panel B depicts the approximated implied volatility $\sigma_{iv}(K, X_t; \alpha_t)$ in Equation 20.56 predicted by the stochastic alpha, beta, rho (SABR) model in Equation 20.55, with $\alpha_t = 0.02$, $\rho = -0.5$, $\beta = 0.5$, $\xi = 0.5$, and $T = 1$. Solid, dashed, and dotted lines correspond to values of the forward X_t equal to 3%, 4%, and 5%, respectively.

Panel B of Figure 20.6 depicts the behavior of the approximated implied volatility predicted by the SABR model obtained with hypothetical parameter values. The model can fix the counterfactual behavior of the skew predicted by a local volatility model: as the forward increases, the implied volatility shifts to the right while at the same time generating a downward-sloping "backbone," defined as the curve traced by the ATM volatility as the forward varies.[9]

The reason for a downward-sloping backbone is the coefficient $\beta < 1$ in Panel B of Figure 20.6. HKLW also show the origins of the asymmetric smile, that is, the skew, generated by their model, due to (i) a coefficient $\beta < 1$, which makes the instantaneous volatility in Equation 20.55, $\upsilon X^{\beta-1}$, decreasing in X, and (ii) a $\rho < 0$, which makes the transition density of the log-changes in X skewed toward the left, as in classical explanations of Heston (1993) given in related contexts. Finally, the volatility of volatility parameter ξ helps determine the curvature of the skew. The implied volatility shifts up as α_t increases – option prices increase with volatility in this model (e.g., Romano and Touzi, 1997) and so does implied volatility.

The SABR model is widely used in the market practice, especially while modeling the swaption skew. Note, however, that the model does not allow for a perfect matching of all available swaption prices, which by construction the local volatility can, at least theoretically. Finally, at the time of writing, it is not clear how this model could be incorporated in a market model of the kind surveyed in Section 20.4.2.4.

20.5 PRICING AND TRADING VOLATILITY

Volatility trading aims to produce P&L correlated with the volatility of a target asset class occurring over a given horizon. The portfolio design typically includes derivatives. Consider, for example, the swaption contract discussed in Section 20.3. Its value depends on the current forward swap rate and is mechanically determined through the Black's implied volatility as explained. The higher the Black's volatility, the higher the swaption value. One may attempt to create a certain portfolio of swaptions to bet on swap rate volatility.

[9]The comparative statics exercise in Figure 20.6 regards a change in the forward. Because the forward is correlated with volatility, an alternative comparative statics exercise is one in which both the forward changes and volatility change in accordance with their assumed correlation (see Bartlett, 2006). It is possible to show that in this case with negative correlation, an increase in the forward accompanied by a decrease in the volatility (consistent with the negative correlation) implies the skew shifts toward the left although the backbone is still downward sloping.

The question arises as to whether such swaption-based portfolio returns correlate "enough" with volatility. Consider the previous swaption contract as a potential case to trade swap rate volatility. The price of a swaption payer, say, can increase both because volatility increases and the forward swap rate increases. To insulate the volatility component, one needs to consider a portfolio with more than just a swaption payer, aiming to hedge against the forward swap rate. A straddle, for example, is a portfolio including a payer and a receiver swaption, with the payer's delta roughly compensated by the receiver's. A position in this straddle does indeed succeed in insulating volatility in the short term, although we shall explain that for longer horizons, it could well deliver returns quite poorly correlated with realized volatility of the forward rate.

By construction, a portfolio with returns perfectly correlated with realized variance is valued the same as a contract delivering this variance at expiration against a threshold – a *variance swap*. We shall explain that the value of this contract is actually a portfolio that should theoretically include *many* derivatives written on the risk we are pricing the volatility of, in contrast with the previous simple two-option straddle.

While the literature on equity variance swaps is well known (see, e.g., the early work of Neuberger, 1994; Dumas, 1995; Demeterfi et al. 1999a,b; Bakshi and Madan, 2000; Britten-Jones and Neuberger, 2000; and Carr and Madan, 2001), that on IRV is still in its infancy and presents many new aspects to deal with, which were unknown in the equity case. This section surveys recent developments aiming to fill this void.

Section 20.5.1 develops an introductory example, which illustrates pitfalls arising while trading rate volatility through standard portfolio designs. Section 20.5.2 explains how to overcome these pitfalls through dedicated interest rate variance swap. Sections 20.5.3 and 20.5.4 discuss the pricing of interest rate variance swaps for three asset classes (government bonds, time deposits, and IRS) and ensuing indexes of forward-looking gauges of volatility. In practice, indexes cannot be traded directly, but one may trade derivatives referencing the index, such as futures and options, to gain exposure to movements in the index. Section 20.5.5 explains the main challenges encountered while modeling derivatives relating to IRV. It also presents a simple pricing model, which illustrates how the insights gained while constructing a government bond volatility index helps determine the value of these new products.

20.5.1 Standard Volatility Trading Practice

A standard practice to trade IRV relies on straddles. It is well known that equity option straddles might fail to lead to profits consistent with directional volatility views, due to "price dependency," that is, the circumstance that the straddle returns are affected by the direction of price movements rather than their absolute movements – that is, volatility. It is probably fair to say that this issue played a key role in the emergence of variance swap contracts, which aligns volatility views and payoffs by construction and also the redesign of the VIX index maintained by the CBOE since 2003.

Mele and Obayashi (2012, 2014a, Chapter 3) study the P&L of straddles in the important IRS segment, both theoretically and empirically. Theoretically, they show that ATM straddles' P&L inherit the same price dependency problem arising in the equity case, in that their daily P&L at the swaption expiry (say N days after entering the straddle) is, approximately,

$$P\&L_N \approx \sum_{n=1}^{N} \Gamma_n^{\$} \cdot [(\sigma_n^2 - \sigma_{iv}^2) PVBP_N] + \sum_{n=1}^{N} Straddle_n \cdot Vol_n(PVBP) \cdot \widetilde{\frac{\Delta R_n}{R_n}} \tag{20.57}$$

where $\Gamma_n^{\$}$ is the Dollar Gamma on day n (i.e., the swaption's Gamma times the square of the forward swap rate), $Straddle_n$ is the straddle value at n, σ_n is the instantaneous vol of the forward swap rate at n, σ_{iv} is the swaption Black's implied volatility on the first day the strategy is implemented, $Vol_n(PVBP)$ is the volatility of the annuity factor growth at n, and finally, $\widetilde{\frac{\Delta R_n}{R_n}}$ denotes the series of shocks affecting the forward swap rate.

That is, the P&L in 20.57 has two components: the first is an average of the "volatility views," $\sigma_n^2 - \sigma_{iv}^2$, weighted with Dollar Gamma, $\Gamma_n^{\$}$ (and the *PVBP* at the swaption expiry). The presence of Dollar Gamma generates a *price dependency*: even if the difference $\sigma_n^2 - \sigma_{iv}^2$ were positive for most of the time, inconvenient realizations of σ_n^2 could occur precisely when the Dollar Gamma is high, such that the first term in 20.57 could be negative even if $\sigma_n^2 - \sigma_{iv}^2$ is positive for most of the time. This price dependency is a feature common to equity option straddles. In the swaption straddle case, the annuity factor $PVBP_t$ in Equation 20.20 introduces an additional source of noise in the P&L (the second term in 20.57), making it even more unlikely that straddle returns would align with realized variance.

Empirically, Mele and Obayashi conclude that in a sample covering more than 10 years including the 2007–2009 financial crisis, straddle returns are "dispersed," with a P&L preserving the same sign of the changes in the realized variance for approximately 62% of the time for 1-month trades, as illustrated in Figure 20.7, and for approximately 65% of the time for 3-month trades. These findings motivate their security design of variance swaps on IRS, surveyed in Sections 20.5.2 and 20.5.3. In fact, the P&L labeled "volatility contract" originates from trades that have the design in Equation 20.69 of Section 20.5.2.4.

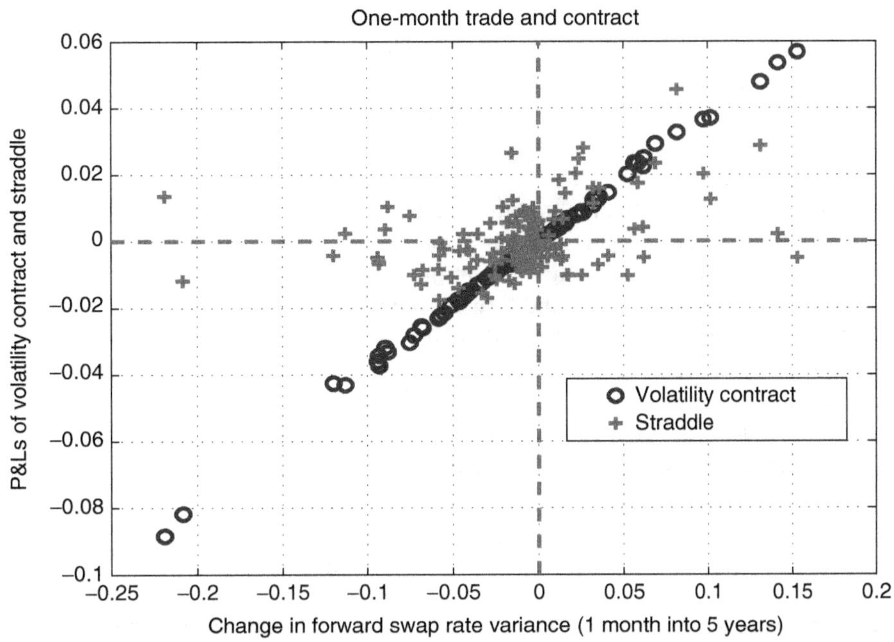

Figure 20.7 Empirical performance of directional volatility trades regarding interest rate swap markets. Source: Bloomberg.

20.5.2 An Introduction to Interest Rate Variance Swaps

One fundamental theme of this chapter relates to the evaluation of contracts referencing realized IRV. The idea underlying these contracts parallels that underlying equity variance swaps: the holder of the contract receives compensation from a counterparty, which is linked to the variance of a variable of interest realized in excess of a threshold determined in advance. This threshold is the "price of volatility," so to speak, and provides forward-looking information about volatility over the life of the variance swap. This section highlights general issues arising while pricing volatility in a model-free fashion and provides an evaluation framework leading to three concrete applications in Section 20.5.3.

20.5.2.1 From Equity to Rate Volatility Contracts The new definition of the CBOE VIX index in 2003 aims to incorporate advances made by financial theory over the previous decade on equity variance swaps. The new VIX index reflects the theoretically fair value of an equity variance swap cast in a "model-free" fashion – one that does not rely on any modeling assumptions beyond specification of standard price dynamics and absence of arbitrage. While variance swaps in the fixed-income space are still hypothetical at the time of writing, their importance as benchmarks for determining the fair value of volatility has already been actualized with the CBOE maintaining two indexes of IRV as discussed in Section 20.5.4.

A variance swap in the fixed-income space works similarly as in the equity case. Consider, for example, the instantaneous volatility of the forward bond price, $v_\tau(S, \mathbb{T})$ in Equation 20.5, and define the so-called realized integrated variance over the time interval $[t, T]$,

$$V(t, T, S, \mathbb{T}) \equiv \int_t^T \|v_\tau(S, \mathbb{T})\|^2 d\tau \tag{20.58}$$

Andersen, Bollerslev, and Diebold (2010) survey the literature of realized variance by highlighting estimation methods. Our emphasis in this chapter is different, motivated as we are to determine the economic value of this variance for a variety of fixed-income securities. Accordingly, assume that the risk we want to be protected against is that the realized variance of some fixed-income security is higher than a strike determined at the inception of the contract at time t. To illustrate, consider a swap linked to the realized variance of the forward bond price in Equation 20.58,

$$\pi(T, S, \mathbb{T}) \equiv V(t, T, S, \mathbb{T}) - \mathbb{P}_t(T, S, \mathbb{T}), \quad T \leq S \tag{20.59}$$

where T is the expiration of the variance swap and $\mathbb{P}_t(T, S, \mathbb{T})$ is the value of the strike, set such that the variance swap is worthless at origination,

$$\mathbb{P}_t(T, S, \mathbb{T}) = \frac{1}{P_t(T)} \mathbb{E}_t \left[e^{-\int_t^T r_\tau d\tau} V(t, T, S, \mathbb{T}) \right] = \mathbb{E}_t^{Q_{FT}} (V(t, T, S, \mathbb{T})) \tag{20.60}$$

The second equality follows by a change of probability similar to that leading to the forward price in Equations 20.3 and 20.4. Therefore, the strike of a government bond variance swap is the expectation of the future variance under the *forward* probability. In contrast, the strike of an equity variance swap reflects the *risk-neutral* expectation of future variance, assuming interest rates are constant. Naturally, we cannot assume that interest rates are constant when evaluating fixed-income variance swaps, for the value of the latter would then be identically zero.

20.5.2.2 Model-Free Pricing The previous example suggests that while pricing IRV, reference needs to be made to the notion of numéraire and risk-adjusted probability applying to each asset class of interest. In particular, while the pricing probability of *equity* variance swaps is the risk-neutral probability assuming constant interest rates, Equation 20.60 reveals the pricing probability of government bond variance swaps to be the forward probability.

A desirable property of a variance swap is that it could be priced in a *model-free* fashion. "Model-free" means absence of reliance on assumptions rather than absence of arbitrage or standard assumptions on price dynamics and no-arbitrage. An example would suffice to further illustrate the meaning of model-free pricing in our context. Consider the SABR model in Section 20.4.3.2 (Eq. 20.55), which is a model that yields predictions about future expected volatility. For example, if $\beta = 1$, the model predicts that the expected integrated variance of the percentage changes in X_τ over an investment horizon equal to $T - t$ is

$$\mathbb{E}_t\left(\int_t^T v_\tau^2 d\tau\right) = v_t^2 \cdot \frac{e^{\xi^2(T-t)} - 1}{\xi^2} \tag{20.61}$$

which is unknown because the parameter ξ is unknown, even assuming we could observe the current variance level, v_t^2. The parameter ξ could be estimated, but uncertainty surrounding statistical inference translates to uncertainty regarding the estimate of the market expectations about future volatility.

A model-free approach to the evaluation of future volatility aims to infer the market's expectations about volatility by looking into the entire spectrum of implied volatilities embedded in the price of out-of-the-money options. An implication of this approach is that the fair value of a variance swap should only link to the price of already tradable assets, such as (i) ATM interest rate options, (ii) the entire strip of out-of-the-money interest rate options, and (iii) zero-coupon bonds. It turns out this task is more involved than in the equity case due to the need to find the correct risk adjustment to be made while accounting for the numéraire in each market. For example, there is no guarantee that the appropriate probability to use while taking expectations is the risk-neutral probability, as in the hypothetical example of Equation 20.61.

To illustrate, consider the government bond variance swap in Equation 20.59. Does this payoff imply that the resulting variance swap could be priced in a model-free fashion? In the following, we shall see that in general, a model-free design of a variance contract is obtained by (i) rescaling the contract payoff by the market numéraire at the time of expiration of the variance swap and (ii) expressing the fair value of the contract as the expectation of future volatility under the market probability. In terms of the previous government bond example, the rescaling of item (i) is just $P_T(T) = 1$, such that we do not need to rescale by anything in the definition of the payoff $\pi(T, S, \mathbb{T})$ in Equation 20.59. Note, however, and importantly, that items (i) and (ii) are both required to price variance swaps in a model-free fashion.

For example, and consistently with item (ii), the expectation in Equation 20.60 is model-free whenever $T = S$. Intuitively, it is so because if $T = S$, the expectation in Equation 20.60 is proportional to the value of a portfolio of out-of-the-money options maturing at T and referencing a forward expiring at T. However, as soon as the expiration of the available options is shorter than that of the forward, $T < S$, the very same options cannot span risks generated by the volatility of the forwards. This situation is typical in Treasury markets, as we shall argue later, and a model-free expression for the variance swap is then typically only an approximation to its true value – a quite reasonable one in practice, as explained in the following.

We now proceed with a few technical details that formalize the previous conclusions. First, we provide a few additional albeit basic definitions regarding the notions of volatility we are interested in while modeling fixed-income securities.

20.5.2.3 Basis Point versus Percentage Volatility Unlike in equity markets, the appropriate gauge of IRV does not always rely on a "percentage notion," as in the government bond volatility example of Equation 20.58. An alternative market standard is to quote volatility in "basis points." While percentage volatility appears to be the right notion when reference is made to *price* movements, basis point volatility may be a more natural notion of uncertainty in *interest rate* movements. A rate increase from 10 bps to 15bps leads to the same percentage change as one from 100 bps to 150 bps, but, all else equal and accounting for convexity, the latter is a nearly 10-fold P&L and risk event. In this basic example, rate traders might find it more useful to speculate on whether a position might likely experience 5 bps moves or 50 bps moves over a given horizon.

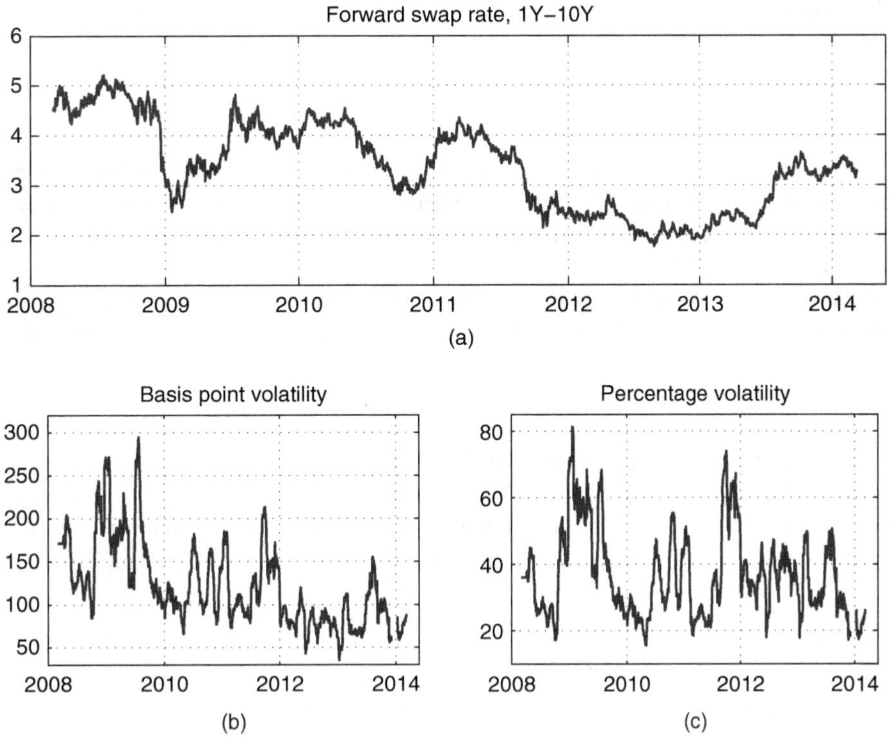

Figure 20.8 Panel A depicts the time series of the forward swap rate with 1-year maturity and 10-year tenor. Panels B and C depicts 1-month basis point realized volatility (Panel B) and 1-month percentage realized volatility (Panel C), both annualized. Source: Bloomberg.

To illustrate the notion of basis point volatility, consider the instantaneous volatility of the forward swap rate, $\sigma_\tau(\cdot)$, in Equation 20.17. The basis point and the percentage variance of the forward swap rate realized over the time interval $[t, T]$ are, respectively,

$$V_n^{\text{bp}}(t,T) \equiv \int_t^T R_\tau^2(T_1, \ldots, T_n)\, \|\sigma_\tau(T_1, \ldots, T_n)\|^2\, d\tau \qquad \text{and} \tag{20.62}$$

$$V_n(t,T) \equiv \int_t^T \|\sigma_\tau(T_1, \ldots, T_n)\|^2\, d\tau \tag{20.63}$$

While the concept of percentage variance is very well known and widely used in equity markets, our IRV contract design also needs to consider a basis point notion of volatility because absolute changes describe risk more effectively than relative changes in the context of yields and spreads.

Consider Figure 20.8, which depicts the 1Y–10Y forward swap rate, along with 1-month annualized realized volatilities, both basis point and percentage. During financial turmoil, basis point volatility appears to spike more when the forward swap rate is high. For example, basis point volatility over the second half of 2009 was more volatile than over the first half when interest rates were lower. The general downward trend in the forward swap rate over the sample period in Figure 20.8 is accompanied by a similar trend in basis point volatility. In contrast, percentage volatility seems to be less related to the general trend in the level of the forward swap rates.

Section 20.5.2.5 develops contract designs for variance swaps that are based on both basis point and percentage notions of realized variance. These contracts are cast in a context with random interest rates and numéraires and lead to technical issues unknown previously. For example, while in the standard equity case a percentage variance swap links to the so-called "log-contract," a basis point variance swap links to the "quadratic contract" under the numéraire probability. Furthermore, under standard conditions, the fair value can be decomposed as the product of a general fear factor and the level of interest rates consistently with the informal evidence in Figure 20.8 (see Eq. 20.81). We now explain these properties in detail.

20.5.2.4 Numéraire Matching To illustrate the main issues arising while pricing IRV, consider an interest rate variance swap that delivers the percentage variance $V_n(t, T)$ in Equation 20.63,

$$\hat{\pi}_{irs}(T, n) \equiv V_n(t, T) - \hat{\mathbb{P}}_t(T, n) \tag{20.64}$$

where $\hat{\mathbb{P}}_t(T, n)$ is the fair value of the variance swap, determined at t, such that the contract has zero value. We argued earlier that a more compelling IRS variance contract should use the basis point notion of volatility. However, we start by pricing Equation 20.64 because we wish to emphasize how variance swaps are priced in connection with the notion of numéraire in this market – the annuity factor in Equation 20.15.

By standard arguments, and in analogy with the fair value of a government bond variance swap, $\mathbb{P}_t(T, S, \mathbb{T})$ in Equation 20.60, the fair value of the interest rate variance swap is determined as the expectation taken under the forward probability,

$$\hat{\mathbb{P}}_t(T, n) = \mathbb{E}_t^{Q_{FT}}(V_n(t, T)) \tag{20.65}$$

Next, let us attempt to determine the expectation on the right-hand side of Equation 20.65, by relying on standard "spanning arguments" developed in the equity case (see, e.g., Bakshi and Madan, 2000; Carr and Madan, 2001). First, consider a log-contract (Neuberger, 1994) on the forward swap rate, that is, a contract that promises to pay a payoff equal to $\ln \frac{R_T}{R_t}$ at expiration T. We are interested in the log-contract because of its linkage to realized variance. Applying Itô's lemma to Equation 20.17 leaves

$$\mathbb{E}_t^{sw,n}\left(\ln \frac{R_T}{R_t}\right) = -\frac{1}{2}\mathbb{E}_t^{sw,n}(V_n(t, T)) \tag{20.66}$$

where we have set the forward swap rate $R_\tau \equiv R_\tau(T_1, \dots, T_n)$ to simplify notation.

Moreover, the appendix reviews the arguments leading to the following expression for the log-contract on the forward swap rate:

$$\ln \frac{R_T}{R_t} = \frac{R_T - R_t}{R_t} - \left(\int_0^{R_t} (K - R_T)^+ \frac{1}{K^2} dK + \int_{R_t}^{\infty} (R_T - K)^+ \frac{1}{K^2} dK\right) \tag{20.67}$$

The first term on the right-hand side of the previous equation, once rescaled by the annuity factor $PVBP_T$, is the value at T of $\frac{1}{R_t}$ positions in a forward-starting IRS; the second term, rescaled by $PVBP_T$, is the time T payoff of a portfolio of out-of-the-money swaptions, with weights inversely proportional to the square of the strike.

In other words, the payoff of a log-contract can be linked to a portfolio comprising a forward and out-of-the-money derivatives, whence the "spanning" term. In particular, by taking expectations under the annuity probability and relying on results surveyed in Section 20.3,

$$\mathbb{E}_t^{sw,n}\left(\ln \frac{R_T}{R_t}\right) = -\frac{1}{PVBP_t(T_1, \dots, T_n)}\left(\int_0^{R_t} Swpn_t^{\mathrm{r}}(K) \frac{1}{K^2} dK + \int_{R_t}^{\infty} Swpn_t^{\mathrm{p}}(K) \frac{1}{K^2} dK\right) \tag{20.68}$$

with the same notation as in Section 20.3.

Note that there is no way to match Equations 20.66 and 20.68 to Equation 20.65: the expectation in Equation 20.65 is under the forward probability, whereas the expectations in Equations 20.66 and 20.68 are taken under the annuity probability. In other words, the forward swap rate R_τ is a martingale under the annuity probability, such that a model-free expression for the expected volatility (i.e., in terms of available swaption quotes) is only available under the annuity probability, not under the forward probability as required by Equation 20.65.

Now consider the following payoff design as an alternative to that in Equation (20.64)

$$\pi_{irs}(T, n) \equiv PVBP_T(T_1, \dots, T_n) \times (V_n(t, T) - \mathbb{P}_t(T, n)) \tag{20.69}$$

where the fair value is now the expectation of realized variance under the annuity probability

$$\mathbb{P}_t(T, n) = \mathbb{E}_t^{Q_{sw,n}}(V_n(t, T)) \tag{20.70}$$

We can now match Equations 20.66–20.68 to Equation 20.70, obtaining

$$\mathbb{P}_t(T, n) = \frac{2}{PVBP_t(T_1, \dots, T_n)}\left(\int_0^{R_t} Swpn_t^{\mathrm{r}}(K) \frac{1}{K^2} dK + \int_{R_t}^{\infty} Swpn_t^{p}(K) \frac{1}{K^2} dK\right) \tag{20.71}$$

That is, we can price an interest rate variance swap in a model-free fashion once we rescale the payoff through the numéraire in this market, just as in Equation 20.69. In the next sections, we generalize to other markets and the notion of basis point volatility.

Before moving on to the theoretical generalization, we develop a numerical example to illustrate how Equation 20.71 can be implemented in practice, and an ensuing IRV index can be calculated.

20.5.2.5 A Numerical Example We provide an example regarding the implementation of the fair value of a variance swap on an IRS, $\mathbb{P}_t(T,n)$, in Equation 20.71, relying on hypothetical implied Black's volatilities for swaptions maturing in 1 month and tenor equal to 5 years (i.e., $\sigma_{iv}\left(K, R_{n,t}, T_0 - t\right)$ in Equation 20.49, with $T_0 - t = \frac{1}{12}$ and $T_n - T_0 = 5$) and regarding hypothetical market conditions on February 12, 2010. Panel A of Table 20.1 displays strike K (first column), implied vol (second), and basis point volatility (third), defined as

$$\sigma_{iv}^{bp}\left(K, R_{n,t}, T_0 - t\right) \equiv \sigma_{iv}(K, R_{n,t}, T_0 - t) \cdot R_{n,t} \tag{20.72}$$

TABLE 20.1 Calculation of the Fair Value of a Hypothetical Variance Swap on an IRS

Panel A

Strike rate (%)	Black's implied vol (%)	Basis point implied vol	Black's prices: Receiver swaption	Black's prices: Payer swaption
1.7352	36.1900	98.9869	≈ 0	$10.0000 \cdot 10^{-3}$
1.9852	36.1900	98.9869	$0.0007 \cdot 10^{-3}$	$7.5007 \cdot 10^{-3}$
2.2352	36.1200	98.7954	$0.0259 \cdot 10^{-3}$	$5.0259 \cdot 10^{-3}$
2.4352	35.9900	98.4398	$0.1773 \cdot 10^{-3}$	$3.1773 \cdot 10^{-3}$
2.5352	35.9300	98.2757	$0.3692 \cdot 10^{-3}$	$2.3692 \cdot 10^{-3}$
2.6352	35.8600	98.0843	$0.6793 \cdot 10^{-3}$	$1.6793 \cdot 10^{-3}$
2.6852	35.8300	98.0022	$0.8855 \cdot 10^{-3}$	$1.3855 \cdot 10^{-3}$
2.7352 (ATM)	35.8000	97.9202	$1.1272 \cdot 10^{-3}$	$1.1272 \cdot 10^{-3}$
2.7852	35.7600	97.8108	$1.4037 \cdot 10^{-3}$	$0.9037 \cdot 10^{-3}$
2.8352	35.7300	97.7287	$1.7142 \cdot 10^{-3}$	$0.7142 \cdot 10^{-3}$
2.9352	35.6700	97.5646	$2.4270 \cdot 10^{-3}$	$0.4270 \cdot 10^{-3}$
3.0352	35.6000	97.3731	$3.2406 \cdot 10^{-3}$	$0.2406 \cdot 10^{-3}$
3.2352	35.4700	97.0175	$5.0644 \cdot 10^{-3}$	$0.0644 \cdot 10^{-3}$
3.4852	35.3100	96.5799	$7.5092 \cdot 10^{-3}$	$0.0092 \cdot 10^{-3}$
3.7352	35.1400	96.1149	$10.0010 \cdot 10^{-3}$	$0.0010 \cdot 10^{-3}$

Panel B

Strike rate (%)	Swaption type	Price	Weights: Basis point ΔK_i	Weights: Percentage $\Delta K_i/K_i^2$	Contributions to strikes: Basis point contribution	Contributions to strikes: Percentage contribution
1.7352	Receiver	≈ 0	0.0025	8.3031	≈ 0	≈ 0
1.9852	Receiver	$0.0007 \cdot 10^{-3}$	0.0025	6.3435	$0.0018 \cdot 10^{-6}$	$0.0046 \cdot 10^{-3}$
2.2352	Receiver	$0.0259 \cdot 10^{-3}$	0.0022	4.5035	$0.0583 \cdot 10^{-6}$	$0.1167 \cdot 10^{-3}$
2.4352	Receiver	$0.1773 \cdot 10^{-3}$	0.0015	2.5294	$0.2660 \cdot 10^{-6}$	$0.4485 \cdot 10^{-3}$
2.5352	Receiver	$0.3692 \cdot 10^{-3}$	0.0010	1.5559	$0.3692 \cdot 10^{-6}$	$0.5744 \cdot 10^{-3}$
2.6352	Receiver	$0.6793 \cdot 10^{-3}$	0.0008	1.0800	$0.5095 \cdot 10^{-6}$	$0.7337 \cdot 10^{-3}$
2.6852	Receiver	$0.8855 \cdot 10^{-3}$	0.0005	0.6935	$0.4428 \cdot 10^{-6}$	$0.6141 \cdot 10^{-3}$
2.7352	ATM	$1.1272 \cdot 10^{-3}$	0.0005	0.6683	$0.5636 \cdot 10^{-6}$	$0.7533 \cdot 10^{-3}$
2.7852	Payer	$0.9037 \cdot 10^{-3}$	0.0005	0.6446	$0.4518 \cdot 10^{-6}$	$0.5825 \cdot 10^{-3}$
2.8352	Payer	$0.7142 \cdot 10^{-3}$	0.0007	0.9330	$0.5357 \cdot 10^{-6}$	$0.6664 \cdot 10^{-3}$
2.9352	Payer	$0.4270 \cdot 10^{-3}$	0.0010	1.1607	$0.4270 \cdot 10^{-6}$	$0.4956 \cdot 10^{-3}$
3.0352	Payer	$0.2406 \cdot 10^{-3}$	0.0015	1.6282	$0.3609 \cdot 10^{-6}$	$0.3917 \cdot 10^{-3}$
3.2352	Payer	$0.0644 \cdot 10^{-3}$	0.0023	2.1497	$0.1448 \cdot 10^{-6}$	$0.1384 \cdot 10^{-3}$
3.4852	Payer	$0.0092 \cdot 10^{-3}$	0.0025	2.0582	$0.0229 \cdot 10^{-6}$	$0.0188 \cdot 10^{-3}$
3.7352	Payer	$0.0010 \cdot 10^{-3}$	0.0025	1.7919	$0.0024 \cdot 10^{-6}$	$0.0017 \cdot 10^{-3}$
				SUMS	$4.1567 \cdot 10^{-6}$	$5.5405 \cdot 10^{-3}$

Source: Bloomberg.

The current forward swap rate is $R_{n,t} = 2.7352\%$ such that the ATM implied volatility is $\sigma_{iv}(K, R_{n,t}, T_0 - t)|_{K=R_{n,t}} = 35.80\%$ and $\sigma_{iv}^{bp}(K, R_{n,t}, T_0 - t)|_{K=R_{n,t}} = 2.7352\% \times 35.80\% = 0.979202\%$, that is, 97.9202 basis point volatility. Basis point volatilities are not needed to compute $\mathbb{P}_t(T, n)$ in 20.71 but are given for comparison purposes.

We plug the skew in the second column of Table 20.1 into the Black's formula, Equation 20.49, and calculate hypothetical swaption prices (normalized by the $PVBP_t$), reported in columns four and five of Table 20.1 (labeled "Black's prices"). We then approximate the integral in 20.71 using discretization steps equal to $\Delta K_i = \frac{1}{2}(K_{i+1} - K_{i-1})$ for $1 \le i < M$, $\Delta K_0 = (K_1 - K_0)$ and $\Delta K_M = (K_M - K_{M-1})$, where K_0 and K_M are the lowest and the highest available strikes and $M + 1$ is the total number of swaptions.

Panel B of Table 20.1 reports strikes (first column), swaption types used to estimate the fair value $\mathbb{P}_t(T, n)$ in 20.71 (second), and swaption prices (third). The fifth column reports the weight each price is given toward the estimation of $\mathbb{P}_t(T, n)$, before the final rescaling of 2; finally, the seventh column (labeled "percentage contribution") provides each swaption price multiplied by its weight (i.e., the third column multiplied by the fifth).

For later reference, the fourth column of Table 20.1 (Panel B) displays values for the weight ΔK_i, and the sixth column (labeled "basis point contribution") provides each swaption price rescaled by ΔK_i (i.e., the third column multiplied by the fourth). To anticipate, we shall utilize the values of column six while calculating the fair value of a basis point variance swap on an IRS (see Section 20.5.3.3, Eq. 20.95).

So we estimate the fair value of the variance swap $\mathbb{P}_t(T, n)$ to be $2 \times 5.5405 \cdot 10^{-3}$ in this example. We could, then, determine an index of percentage volatility based on this variance swap by annualizing this estimate of $\mathbb{P}_t(T, n)$ and expressing it in percentage terms, yielding the following forward-looking gauge of IRS volatility (1 month) on 5-year tenor forward swap rates:

$$\widehat{IRS\text{-}VI}_n(t, T) \equiv 100 \times \sqrt{\frac{2}{12^{-1}} \times 5.5405 \cdot 10^{-3}} = 36.4653$$

In comparison, the ATM implied volatility is $\sigma_{iv}(K, R_{n,t}, T_0 - t)|_{K=R_{n,t}} = 35.80\%$ as we mentioned earlier.

20.5.2.6 Contract Design Our goal is to design a contract that pays off an amount that depends on the realized variance of the risk of interest (say, the variance of the forward swap rate). However, a number of conceptual difficulties arise while attempting to price this contract in a model-free fashion, as interest rates for discounting are not independent of their volatility. How can we disentangle discounting from realized volatility of discounting, thereby pricing the pure volatility component? The answer is that we shall need to rescale the variance payoff with the market numéraire regarding the class of interest. This section provides introductory details.

Consider a forward-starting agreement originating at t, promising the following payoff at time T:

$$\Pi_T \equiv N_T \times (X_T - K) \tag{20.73}$$

where K is a constant; N_τ denotes the price of a tradable process, which is measurable with respect to the information at time τ

Concretely, N_τ is the value of the market numéraire and X_τ is a "forward risk." For example, X_τ can be the price of a forward expiring at T and written on a coupon-bearing bond, in which case $N_\tau \equiv P_\tau(T)$ and $N_T \equiv 1$. As another example, X_τ can be the forward swap rate, in which case $N_\tau \equiv PVBP_\tau$, such that the payoff Π_T in Equation 20.73 is that of an IRS payer. Even simpler, X_τ can be the price of a forward on a stock, and the numéraire is the price of a zero-coupon bond in a market with constant interest rates $\bar{r}$, say, $N_\tau \equiv e^{-\bar{r}(T-\tau)}$.

We are interested in pricing the realized volatility of X_τ to be formally defined later. We assume that X_τ is a diffusion process. Under standard regularity conditions, the clearing process X_τ is such that $X_t = K$ and is a martingale under the "market probability" Q_N, defined through the Radon–Nikodym derivative,

$$\xi_T^N \equiv \left.\frac{dQ_N}{dQ}\right|_{\mathcal{F}_T} = e^{-\int_t^T r_\tau d\tau} \frac{N_T}{N_t} \tag{20.74}$$

Therefore, X_τ satisfies

$$\frac{dX_\tau}{X_\tau} = \sigma_\tau \cdot dW_\tau \tag{20.75}$$

where W_τ is a vector Brownian motion under Q^N and σ_τ is the instantaneous volatility process adapted to W_τ.

As noted, market practice is to quote implied volatilities for fixed-income instruments both in percentage and basis point terms. Accordingly, we aim to price two notions of realized variance defined similarly as in the interest rate swap volatility case (see Eqs 20.62 and 20.63): one based on *arithmetic*, or *basis point*, changes of X_t in Equation 20.75 and another based on the *logarithmic*, or *percentage*, changes of X_t. Let $V^{bp}(t,T)$ and $V(t,T)$ denote the realized BP variance and percentage variance in the time interval $[t,T]$, namely,

$$V^{bp}(t,T) \equiv \int_t^T X_\tau^2 \|\sigma_\tau\|^2 d\tau \quad \text{and} \quad V(t,T) \equiv \int_t^T \|\sigma_\tau\|^2 d\tau \tag{20.76}$$

We are searching for variance contracts linked to $V^{bp}(t,T)$ and $V(t,T)$ that can be priced in a model-free fashion.

Mele and Obayashi (2014a, Chapter 2) consider the following forward contracts with "stochastic multiplier," ones that are zero at the time of inception, t, and that at maturity T, pay off

$$\Phi_T^{bp} \equiv Y_T \times (V^{bp}(t,T) - K_Y^{bp}), \quad \Phi_T \equiv Y_T \times (V(t,T) - K_Y) \tag{20.77}$$

where Y_τ is measurable with respect to the Brownian motion W_τ in Equation 20.75 and K_Y^{bp} and K_Y are the fair values of the contracts to be determined. Naturally, we have that

$$K_Y^{bp} = \mathbb{E}_t^{Q_Y}(V^{bp}(t,T)), \quad K_Y = \mathbb{E}_t^{Q_Y}(V(t,T)) \tag{20.78}$$

where $\mathbb{E}_t^{Q_Y}$ denotes expectation at t under Q_Y and Q_Y is a probability defined formally through ξ_T^N in Equation 20.74, with $N \equiv Y$, and referred hereafter as *forward multiplier probability*.

Mele and Obayashi (2014a, Proposition 2.II) prove the following result:

Proposition 1 ***(model-free contracts.)*** *The fair values of K_Y^{bp} and K_Y in Equation 20.77 are model-free if and only if the Radon–Nikodym derivative of the forward multiplier probability Q_Y against the market numéraire probability Q_N is uncorrelated with $V^{bp}(t,T)$ and $V(t,T)$. They are given by*

$$K_Y^{bp} = \frac{2}{N_t}\left(\int_0^{X_t} Put_t(K)\,dK + \int_{X_t}^{\infty} Call_t(K)dK\right) \text{ (basis point pricing)} \tag{20.79}$$

and

$$K_Y = \frac{2}{N_t}\left(\int_0^{X_t} \frac{Put_t(K)}{K^2}dK + \int_{X_t}^{\infty} \frac{Call_t(K)}{K^2}dK\right) \quad \text{(percentage pricing)} \tag{20.80}$$

where

$$\frac{Call_t(K)}{N_t} = \mathbb{E}_t^{Q_N}\left(\frac{\max\{\Pi_T, 0\}}{N_T}\right), \quad \frac{Put_t(K)}{N_t} = \mathbb{E}_t^{Q_N}\left(\frac{\max\{-\Pi_T, 0\}}{N_T}\right)$$

and Π_T is the payoff in Equation 20.73.

Note that the previous proposition is not merely restating the famous conclusion that in the absence of arbitrage, there exists a numéraire N and a probability Q_N, such that security prices rescaled by the numéraire are martingales under Q_N. It states a stronger result about security design, namely, that *model-free* pricing of variance swaps is possible once we rescale the payoff of these contracts with the appropriate numéraire.

Indeed, Mele and Obayashi identify a host of possible variance swap "tilters" that make the fair value of the resulting contracts model-free, with the "numé raire" tilter being a specific case. However, given the economic appeal of the numéraire, and the familiarity with it among academics and practitioners, we will build upon this notion to develop our model-free security designs of interest rate variance swaps. Consider, for example, the previous interest rate variance swap with payoff rescaled by the annuity numéraire $PVBP_t$ in Equation 20.69. The ensuing strike, $\mathbb{P}_t(T,n)$ in Equation 20.71, is just the same as K_Y in Equation 20.80, once we account for the definition of the various derivative payoffs and risks.

Mele and Obayashi (2014a, Chapter 2) also show that if implied volatilities are homogeneous of degree zero in X and K ("sticky delta"),[10] then, K_Y in Equation 20.80 is independent of X_t, and there exists a function independent of X, $Sk(t,T)$, say, such that K_Y^{bp} in Equation 20.79 can be written as

$$K_Y^{bp} = X_t^2 \times Sk(t,T) \tag{20.81}$$

[10] A well-known example of models leading to "sticky delta" is the SABR model (when $\beta = 1$) in Section 20.4.3.2.

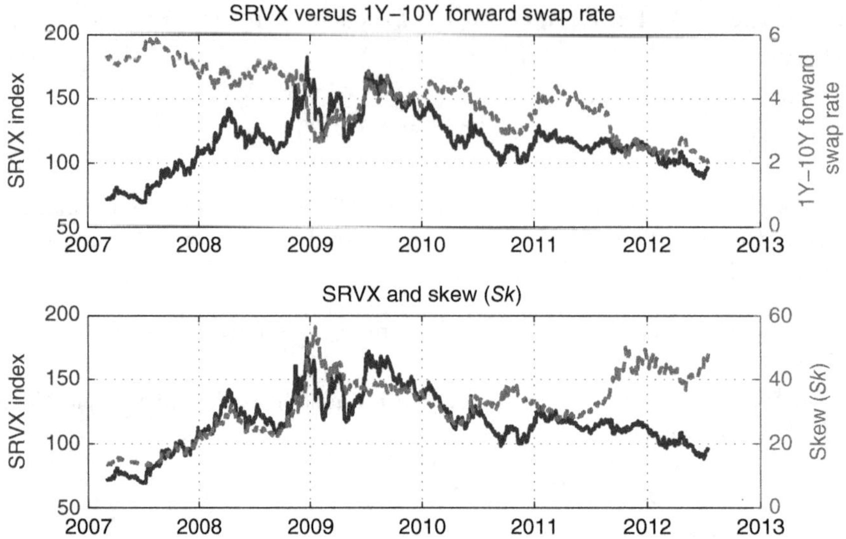

Figure 20.9 The CBOE SRVX interest rate swap volatility index (see Sections 20.5.4 and 20.5.5), along with the 1Y–10Y forward swap rate (Panel A) and the skew factor, $\sqrt{\frac{1}{T-t}Sk(t,T)}$, where $Sk(t,T)$ is as in Equation 20.81. Source: Chicago Board Options Exchange and Bloomberg.

The term $Sk(t,T)$ summarizes a pure "fear effect" or a "skew factor" and is shown to link to the entire skew of the options entering into the strike calculation.

Consider, for example, the SRVX index of swap rate volatility maintained by the CBOE (regarding volatility of 1Y–10Y forward swap rates), which is based on the strike K_Y in 20.79 (see Sections 20.5.4 and 20.5.5). Figure 20.9 depicts the behavior of the SRVX and both the forward swap rate and the annualized square root of the skew factor, $\sqrt{\frac{1}{T-t}Sk(t,T)}$. Mele, Obayashi, and Shalen (2015) analyze the empirical behavior of the CBOE SRVX and indeed show that this behavior can sometimes be determined by changes in the forward swap rate and at other times by the skew factor. For example, Figure 20.9 illustrates that the increase in the SRVX over the 2008 crisis is mostly driven by a fear factor; however, the SRVX decline in 2012 is explained by lower prevailing interest rates.

Section 20.5.3.3 explains that a basis point volatility index has additional properties, which could be utilized to assess uncertainty regarding developments in the *level* of interest rates and apply this property to swap markets (see Figure 20.11).

20.5.2.7 A Few Technical Details: Quadratic Contracts While the expression for the portfolio of out-of-the-money derivatives in Equation 20.80 may look familiar to those acquainted with the formula underlying the CBOE VIX index (see, e.g., Chicago Board Options Exchange, 2009), the expression in Equation 20.79 may be less familiar, and we therefore review the steps leading to it.

Suppose that the forward contract stochastic multiplier in Equation 20.77 is the same as the market numéraire, $Y_T = N_T$, and consider a "quadratic contract," one that delivers a payoff equal to X_T^2 at time T. The appendix shows that

$$X_T^2 - X_t^2 = 2X_t(X_T - X_t) + 2\left(\int_0^{X_t} (K - X_T)^+ dK + \int_{X_t}^{\infty} (X_T - K)^+ dK\right) \tag{20.82}$$

The first term on the right-hand side, once rescaled by the numéraire, N_T, is just the payoff Π_T in Equation 20.73 of $2X_t$ positions in a forward-starting agreement; the second term, rescaled by N_T, is the time T payoff of a portfolio of out-of-the-money options, with constant weights. By taking expectations under Q_N of both sides of the previous equation leaves

$$\mathbb{E}_t^{Q_N}(X_T^2) - X_t^2 = \frac{2}{N_t}\left(\int_0^{X_t} Put_t(K)\,dK + \int_{X_t}^{\infty} Call_t(K)dK\right) \tag{20.83}$$

Moreover, by applying Itô's lemma to Equation 20.75 leaves

$$\mathbb{E}_t^{Q_N}(X_T^2) - X_t^2 = \mathbb{E}_t^{Q_N}(V^{bp}(t,T)) \tag{20.84}$$

Matching Equations 20.83 and 20.84 to K_Y^{bp} in Equation 20.78 for $Y = N$ produces Equation 20.79. Note that in earlier work, Carr and Corso (2001) explain how to hedge the variance of price changes in markets with constant interest rates. In Mele and

Obayashi (2014a, Chapter 2), we explain that their elegant replication arguments fail to work if interest rates are random. In subsequent chapters, we also show that the numéraire inherent in each market of interest can be incorporated into replicating portfolios that contain fixed-income securities.

The next subsection applies the general framework underlying Proposition I to analyze a number of cases that are relevant to market practice.

20.5.3 Pricing Volatility in Three Markets

20.5.3.1 Government Bonds Webegin with a case regarding the pricing of a government bond variance swap, which does not exactly conform with the previous framework. Consider the strike $\mathbb{P}_t(T, S, \mathbb{T})$ in Equation 20.60 and recall the variables it depends upon (i) the maturity of the contract, $T - t$; (ii) the maturity of the underlying forward price, $S - T$; and (iii) the expiration time of the coupon-bearing bond underlying the forward, $\mathbb{T}$.

Guided by intuition gained over the previous sections, we would like to find a model-free expression for $\mathbb{P}_t(T, S, \mathbb{T})$ based on options expiring at T and written on the forwards expiring at S. It turns out that this is impossible: the short-dated option cannot span the risks generated by the bond forward volatility. Let us explain the main issue. The dynamics of $F_\tau(S, \mathbb{T})$ under the "variance swap" pricing measure are those under Q_{FT}, not under Q_{FS} as in Equation 20.5, and by Girsanov theorem,

$$\frac{dF_\tau(S,\mathbb{T})}{F_\tau(S,\mathbb{T})} = v_\tau(S,\mathbb{T})(v_\tau(S,\mathbb{T}) - v_\tau(T,\mathbb{T}))d\tau + v_\tau(S,\mathbb{T}) \cdot dW_\tau^{F^T}, \quad \tau \in (t,T) \tag{20.85}$$

where $W_\tau^{F^T}$ is a multidimensional Brownian motion under Q_{FT} and the nonzero drift reflects the adjustment made while moving from the probability Q_{FS} to Q_{FT}. Mele and Obayashi (2014a,b, Chapter 4) show that

$$\begin{aligned}\mathbb{P}_t(T,S,\mathbb{T}) &= 2(1 - \mathbb{E}_t^{Q_{FT}}(e^{\tilde{\ell}(t,T,S,\mathbb{T})} - \tilde{\ell}(t,T,S,\mathbb{T}))) \\ &\quad + \frac{2}{P_t(T)}\left(\int_0^{F_t(S,\mathbb{T})} Put_t^b(K)\frac{1}{K^2}dK + \int_{F_t(S,\mathbb{T})}^{\infty} Call_t^b(K)\frac{1}{K^2}dK\right)\end{aligned} \tag{20.86}$$

where $Put_t^b(K)$ and $Call_t^b(K)$ denote the price of European out-of-the-money options written on the bond forward and struck at K and

$$\tilde{\ell}(t,T,S,\mathbb{T}) \equiv \int_t^T v_\tau(S,\mathbb{T})(v_\tau(S,\mathbb{T}) - v_\tau(T,\mathbb{T}))d\tau \tag{20.87}$$

Therefore, an index of forward-looking government bond volatility can be based on the annualized value of $\mathbb{P}(t, T, S, \mathbb{T})$,

$$GB - VI(t,T,S,\mathbb{T}) \equiv \sqrt{\frac{1}{T-t}\mathbb{P}_t(T,S,\mathbb{T})} \tag{20.88}$$

This index is model dependent as the term $\tilde{\ell}(t, T, S, \mathbb{T})$ in Equation 20.87 cannot be spanned through available fixed-income securities. Mele and Obayashi (2014a, Chapter 4) report that the effects of this maturity mismatch are limited whenever $T - S$ (the difference between the futures and option maturity) is as small as 2 months. For example, the CBOE/CBOT 10-year Treasury Note Volatility Index maintained by the CBOE relies on 1-month options and an underlying expiring in 3 months, such that the maturity mismatch is small and, at least in this case, so is the bias of not accounting for a model-dependent adjustment, that is, the first term on the right-hand side of Equation 20.86.[11]

Table 20.2 contains details regarding the implementation of the government bond volatility index in Equation 20.88 using hypothetical quotes reflecting market conditions on April 27, 2012, for 1-month options written on a 1-month forward on 10-year U.S. Treasury Notes (therefore, the term $\tilde{\ell}(t, T, S, \mathbb{T})$ in 20.87 is zero) and assuming these hypothetical data relate to *European* options on *forwards*, rather than *American* options on *futures*. The first column of Panel A reports strike K, with the ATM being equal to $K = 132$; the second column is given for reference and provides Black's implied volatilities for each strike[12]; finally, the third and fourth columns provide the option premiums.

Panel B of Table 20.2 contains details leading to an estimate of the index in Equation 20.88: the strikes (first column); the type of option used to implement the index (second); the option premiums (third); the weights used while approximating the integral

[11] Another complication is that the underlying of the future is actually the "cheapest to deliver" from a set of deliverable bonds into a futures contract. Throughout this chapter, we assume that the coupon-bearing bond underlying the index is one with fixed and known maturity date.

[12] Black's volatilities are defined similarly as in Equation 20.49 but with the price of 1-month zeros replacing the $PVBP_t$ and obviously the option premiums replacing the swaptions.

TABLE 20.2 Calculation of the Fair Value of a Hypothetical Government Bond Variance Swap

Panel A

Strike price (%)	Black's implied vol (%)	Premiums	
		Put option	Call option
125.00	9.10	$0.2343 \cdot 10^{-3}$	$7.0234 \cdot 10^{-2}$
125.50	8.53	$0.2346 \cdot 10^{-3}$	$6.5234 \cdot 10^{-2}$
126.00	7.32	$0.1326 \cdot 10^{-3}$	$6.0132 \cdot 10^{-2}$
126.50	6.78	$0.1328 \cdot 10^{-3}$	$5.5132 \cdot 10^{-2}$
127.00	7.24	$0.3423 \cdot 10^{-3}$	$5.0342 \cdot 10^{-2}$
127.50	6.64	$0.3465 \cdot 10^{-3}$	$4.5346 \cdot 10^{-2}$
128.00	6.33	$0.4516 \cdot 10^{-3}$	$4.0451 \cdot 10^{-2}$
128.50	6.15	$0.6567 \cdot 10^{-3}$	$3.5656 \cdot 10^{-2}$
129.00	5.81	$0.8557 \cdot 10^{-3}$	$3.0855 \cdot 10^{-2}$
129.50	5.63	$1.2506 \cdot 10^{-3}$	$2.6250 \cdot 10^{-2}$
130.00	5.35	$1.7225 \cdot 10^{-3}$	$2.1722 \cdot 10^{-2}$
130.50	5.05	$2.3656 \cdot 10^{-3}$	$1.7365 \cdot 10^{-2}$
131.00	4.82	$3.3632 \cdot 10^{-3}$	$1.3363 \cdot 10^{-2}$
131.50	4.71	$4.9229 \cdot 10^{-3}$	$9.9229 \cdot 10^{-3}$
132.00 (ATM)	4.53	$6.8864 \cdot 10^{-3}$	$6.8864 \cdot 10^{-3}$
132.50	4.43	$9.5398 \cdot 10^{-3}$	$4.5398 \cdot 10^{-3}$
133.00	4.40	$1.2865 \cdot 10^{-2}$	$2.8655 \cdot 10^{-3}$
133.50	4.38	$1.6705 \cdot 10^{-2}$	$1.7053 \cdot 10^{-3}$
134.00	4.40	$2.0979 \cdot 10^{-2}$	$0.9793 \cdot 10^{-3}$
134.50	4.58	$2.5619 \cdot 10^{-2}$	$0.6192 \cdot 10^{-3}$
135.00	4.78	$3.0400 \cdot 10^{-2}$	$0.4000 \cdot 10^{-3}$
135.50	4.93	$3.5246 \cdot 10^{-2}$	$0.2462 \cdot 10^{-3}$
136.00	5.17	$4.0169 \cdot 10^{-2}$	$0.1696 \cdot 10^{-3}$
136.50	5.21	$4.5090 \cdot 10^{-2}$	$9.0837 \cdot 10^{-5}$

Panel B

Strike price (%)	Option type	Premiums	Weights	Contributions to strikes
			$\Delta K_i/K_i^2$	Premiums × weights
125.00	Put	$0.2343 \cdot 10^{-3}$	$3.2000 \cdot 10^{-3}$	$7.4976 \cdot 10^{-7}$
125.50	Put	$0.2346 \cdot 10^{-3}$	$3.1745 \cdot 10^{-3}$	$7.4494 \cdot 10^{-7}$
126.00	Put	$0.1326 \cdot 10^{-3}$	$3.1494 \cdot 10^{-3}$	$4.1762 \cdot 10^{-7}$
126.50	Put	$0.1328 \cdot 10^{-3}$	$3.1245 \cdot 10^{-3}$	$4.1512 \cdot 10^{-7}$
127.00	Put	$0.3423 \cdot 10^{-3}$	$3.1000 \cdot 10^{-3}$	$1.0613 \cdot 10^{-6}$
127.50	Put	$0.3465 \cdot 10^{-3}$	$3.0757 \cdot 10^{-3}$	$1.0658 \cdot 10^{-6}$
128.00	Put	$0.4516 \cdot 10^{-3}$	$3.0517 \cdot 10^{-3}$	$1.3781 \cdot 10^{-6}$
128.50	Put	$0.6567 \cdot 10^{-3}$	$3.0280 \cdot 10^{-3}$	$1.9887 \cdot 10^{-6}$
129.00	Put	$0.8557 \cdot 10^{-3}$	$3.0046 \cdot 10^{-3}$	$2.5710 \cdot 10^{-6}$
129.50	Put	$1.2506 \cdot 10^{-3}$	$2.9814 \cdot 10^{-3}$	$3.7289 \cdot 10^{-6}$
130.00	Put	$1.7225 \cdot 10^{-3}$	$2.9585 \cdot 10^{-3}$	$5.0963 \cdot 10^{-6}$
130.50	Put	$2.3656 \cdot 10^{-3}$	$2.9359 \cdot 10^{-3}$	$6.9454 \cdot 10^{-6}$
131.00	Put	$3.3632 \cdot 10^{-3}$	$2.9135 \cdot 10^{-3}$	$9.7990 \cdot 10^{-6}$
131.50	Put	$4.9229 \cdot 10^{-3}$	$2.8914 \cdot 10^{-3}$	$1.4234 \cdot 10^{-5}$
132.00	ATM	$6.8864 \cdot 10^{-3}$	$2.8696 \cdot 10^{-3}$	$1.9761 \cdot 10^{-5}$
132.50	Call	$4.5398 \cdot 10^{-3}$	$2.8479 \cdot 10^{-3}$	$1.2929 \cdot 10^{-5}$
133.00	Call	$2.8655 \cdot 10^{-3}$	$2.8266 \cdot 10^{-3}$	$8.0999 \cdot 10^{-6}$
133.50	Call	$1.7053 \cdot 10^{-3}$	$2.8054 \cdot 10^{-3}$	$4.7842 \cdot 10^{-6}$
134.00	Call	$0.9793 \cdot 10^{-3}$	$2.7845 \cdot 10^{-3}$	$2.7271 \cdot 10^{-6}$
134.50	Call	$0.6192 \cdot 10^{-3}$	$2.7632 \cdot 10^{-3}$	$1.7116 \cdot 10^{-6}$
135.00	Call	$0.4000 \cdot 10^{-3}$	$2.7434 \cdot 10^{-3}$	$1.0975 \cdot 10^{-6}$
135.50	Call	$0.2462 \cdot 10^{-3}$	$2.7232 \cdot 10^{-3}$	$6.7062 \cdot 10^{-7}$
136.00	Call	$0.1696 \cdot 10^{-3}$	$2.7032 \cdot 10^{-3}$	$4.5864 \cdot 10^{-7}$
136.50	Call	$9.0837 \cdot 10^{-5}$	$2.6835 \cdot 10^{-3}$	$2.4376 \cdot 10^{-7}$
			SUM	$1.0268 \cdot 10^{-4}$

Source: Bloomberg.

of premiums in 20.86 (fourth), determined just as we did for the weights in Section 20.5.2.5 regarding variance swaps on IRS; and the contributions to strike (fifth). The fair value of the variance swap $\mathbb{P}_t(T, S, \mathbb{T})$ is estimated to equal $2 \times 1.0268 \cdot 10^{-4}$, such that the government bond volatility index can be estimated as

$$\widehat{GB\text{-}VI} = 100 \times \sqrt{\frac{1}{0.9980} \frac{2}{(1/12)} \times 1.0268 \cdot 10^{-4}} = 4.9692 \tag{20.89}$$

where 0.9980 is the price of a hypothetical 1-month zero on April 27, 2012. In comparison, the ATM implied volatility in Table 20.2 is 4.53%. Our estimate in 20.89, 4.9692, is well in line with the official value taken by the CBOE/CBOT VXTYN index (see Section 20.5.4) on that day, which was 4.87% (closing value).

The previous calculations rely on the assumption that European-style options on forwards are available for trading, which unfortunately does not hold in practice, as the options available to calculate a government bond volatility index are typically American options written on futures. This issue potentially affects the accuracy of the index as an indicator of the fair value of volatility due to the likely presence of an early exercise premium, and an index relying on American options likely overstates the true fair value of volatility.

Mele and Obayashi (2014a, Chapter 4) undertake a simple experiment aimed at gauging this bias. They consider a model without stochastic volatility, that is, the Vasicek model in Equation 20.21. While this model obviously predicts that the fair of volatility is constant, the authors' main concern is to assess the impact of the early exercise premium unconditionally, that is, independent of any particular value taken by the volatility of the short-term rate.

In a nutshell, the algorithm they use is the following. First, they determine the theoretical value of futures on the coupon-bearing bond based on Equation 20.2. Second, they estimate the parameter values of the Vasicek model under the physical probability. Third, they calibrate the risk premium coefficient, λ in Equation 20.21, to minimize a certain criterion of distance between the price of American call options on futures and the model-based price of American options on the futures. This step requires utilizing methods combining time discretizations and Monte Carlo simulations based on an algorithm proposed by Longstaff and Schwartz (2001); see Chapter 19 for a survey of methods regarding these approaches.

This procedure amounts to extract a pricing kernel from the cross section of American options on futures and parallels similar work attempted in the literature (see, e.g., Broadie, Chernov, and Johannes, 2007; Bikbov and Chernov, 2011). One then uses this risk premium coefficient to calculate the value of European options on forwards based on the Jamshidian (1989) formula (see Eq. 20.38). Alternative to a minimization criterion, one could extract a "risk premium skew," that is, a λ for each strike, but numerical experiments in Mele and Obayashi (2014a, Chapter 4) are only available for the first algorithm based on a minimization criterion. The experiments reveal that under realistic market conditions, a government bond volatility index based on American options written on futures overstates the true index value (i.e., based on European options on forwards) by approximately one relative percentage point.

20.5.3.2 *Time Deposits* Government bonds and time deposits share the same numéraire (see Section 20.3), and we can price a time deposit variance swap using the forward probability. In contrast to the government bond case, however, we translate the results into *basis point volatility of rates* to match market convention.

We convert forward Libor *prices* into forward Libor *rates* through Equation 20.7, which by Equation 20.8 satisfy

$$\frac{d\hat{f}_\tau(S, S+\Delta)}{\hat{f}_\tau(S, S+\Delta)} = v_\tau^f(S, \Delta) dW_\tau^{F^S}, \quad \tau \in (t, S) \tag{20.90}$$

where $v_\tau^f(S, \Delta) \equiv (1 - \hat{f}_\tau^{-1}(S, S+\Delta)) v_\tau^z(S, \Delta)$ by It ô's lemma.

The basis point Libor integrated rate variance is

$$V_t^{f,bp}(T, S, \Delta) \equiv \int_t^T \hat{f}_\tau^2(S, S+\Delta) \, \|v_\tau^f(S, \Delta)\|^2 d\tau$$

such that, by arguments similar to those leading to Equation 20.60, the fair value of the time deposit rate variance swap starting at t and paying off at T

$$V_t^{f,bp}(T, S, \Delta) - \mathbb{P}_t^{f,bp}(T, S, \Delta), \quad T \le S,$$

is

$$\mathbb{P}_t^{f,bp}(T, S, \Delta) = \mathbb{E}_t^{Q_{FT}}(V_t^{f,bp}(T, S, \Delta))$$

As in the government bond case, we face the complication that the maturity of the variance swap is T, while the forward Libor is a martingale under the S-forward probability as Equation 20.90 indicates. Moreover, we are dealing with a notion of basis point variance. Mele and Obayashi (2014a,b, Chapter 4) show that the expression for $\mathbb{P}_f^{bp}(t,T,S,\Delta)$ includes a model-dependent term

$$\mathbb{P}_t^{f,bp}(T,S,\Delta) = 2\left(\hat{f}_t^2(S,S+\Delta)\left(\mathbb{E}_t^{Q_{FT}}\left(e^{\tilde{\ell}_f(t,T,S)}\right)-1\right)-\mathbb{E}_t^{Q_{FT}}\left(\tilde{\ell}^{bp}(t,T,S)\right)\right)$$
$$+\frac{2}{P_t(T)}\left(\int_0^{\hat{f}_t(S,S+\Delta)} Put_t^f(K_f,T,S,\Delta)\,dK_f+\int_{\hat{f}_t(S,S+\Delta)}^{\infty} Call_t^f(K_f,T,S,\Delta)\,dK_f\right) \tag{20.91}$$

where $\tilde{\ell}_f(t,T,S)$ and $\tilde{\ell}^{bp}(t,T,S)$ are given in the appendix (see Eqs 20.113 and 20.114) and

$$Put_t^f(K_f,T,\Delta) = \frac{Call_t^z(100(1-K_f),T,S,\Delta)}{100}$$
$$Call_t^f(K_f,T,\Delta) = \frac{Put_t^z(100(1-K_f),T,S,\Delta)}{100}$$

with $Put_t^z(K_z,T,S,\Delta)$ and $Call_t^z(K_z,T,S,\Delta)$ denoting the prices of out-of-the-money puts and calls written on the forward Libor price $Z_t(S,S+\Delta)$ with strike price K_z and maturity T, and $Put_t^f(K_f,T,S,\Delta)$ and $Call_t^f(K_f,T,S,\Delta)$ are hypothetical out-of-the-money puts European-style options on the forward Libor rate (see Eqs 20.115 and 20.116 in the appendix).

Accordingly, an index of basis point time deposit rate volatility is

$$TD-VI_f^{bp}(t,T,S,\Delta) \equiv \sqrt{\frac{\mathbb{P}_t^{f,bp}(T,S,\Delta)}{T-t}} \tag{20.92}$$

where $\mathbb{P}_t^{f,bp}(T,S,\Delta)$ is as in Equation 20.91.

We estimate the fair value of the time deposit variance swap, $\mathbb{P}_t^{f,bp}(T,S,\Delta)$, and the index in Equation 20.92, based on option quotes on hypothetical market conditions as of June 26, 2012. Options relate to 3-month Eurodollars and are taken to be 3-month European options on forwards so that there is no maturity mismatch between options and forwards, that is, $\tilde{\ell}_f(t,T,S)=\tilde{\ell}^{bp}(t,T,S)=0$ in Equation 20.91. Table 20.3 reports strike K, implied volatilities, and option premiums, defined similarly as in Tables 20.1 and 20.2. The only difference is the way the implied volatilities in basis points are defined; they rely on a model in which the forward Libor price follows a Gaussian process with constant volatility as explained in the appendix.

Figure 20.10 plots the option premiums used for estimating $\mathbb{P}_t^{f,bp}(T,S,\Delta)$ (italicized in Table 20.3).[13] The weighted average of these premiums (with weights ΔK_i determined as in Tables 20.1 and 20.2 and equal to $0.1250 * 10^{-2}$) is $1.9210 \cdot 10^{-6}$, yielding an estimate of the basis point variance swap fair value equal to $\frac{1}{0.9996}\times 2\times 1.9210\cdot 10^{-6}$, where 0.9996 is the price as of June 26, 2012, of a hypothetical 3-month zero. An estimate of Equation 20.92 is

$$\widehat{TD\text{-}VI}^{bp} = 100\times 100\times\sqrt{\frac{1}{0.9996}\frac{2}{(3/12)}\times 1.9210\cdot 10^{-6}} = 39.2101 \tag{20.93}$$

In comparison, the ATM basis point volatility in Table 20.3 is 27.22 basis points, with the average basis point skew equal to 48.24 basis points.

20.5.3.3 Swaps In Section 20.5.2, we derived an expression for the fair value of an interest rate variance swap expressed in percentage terms (see Eq. 20.71) and argued that a model-free solution could be implemented by tilting the payoff of the contract by the annuity factor, $PVBP_t(T_1,\ldots,T_n)$. Now, how is a *basis point* variance contract valued? Consider a variance swap with the following payoff:

$$\pi_{irs}^{bp}(T,n) \equiv PVBP_T(T_1,\ldots,T_n)\times\left(V_n^{bp}(t,T)-\mathbb{P}_t^{bp}(T,n)\right)$$

where $V_n^{bp}(t,T)$ is as in Equation 20.62 and $\mathbb{P}_t^{bp}(T,n)$ is its fair value. By an application of Proposition I, it equals

$$\mathbb{P}_t^{bp}(T,n) = \frac{2}{PVBP_t(T_1,\ldots,T_n)}\left(\int_0^{R_t} Swpn_t^r(K)\,dK+\int_{R_t}^{\infty} Swpn_t^p(K)\,dK\right)$$

[13] Note that the out-of-the-money puts (calls) on forward Libor prices in Table 20.3 correspond to the out-of-the-money calls (puts) on forward Libor rates in Equation 20.91.

TABLE 20.3 Determination of Usable Options to Calculate the Fair Value of a Hypothetical Basis Point Time Deposit Variance Swap

	Implied volatility		Premiums	
Strike price (%)	Black's implied vol (%)	Basis point implied vol	Put option	Call option
98.750	0.91	89.75	*9.0197* $\cdot 10^{-5}$	7.5871 $\cdot 10^{-3}$
98.875	0.79	78.18	*9.2048* $\cdot 10^{-5}$	6.3395 $\cdot 10^{-5}$
99.000	0.67	66.27	*9.6557* $\cdot 10^{-5}$	5.0945 $\cdot 10^{-3}$
99.125	0.59	58.79	*1.3910* $\cdot 10^{-4}$	3.8876 $\cdot 10^{-3}$
99.250	0.49	48.66	*1.9261* $\cdot 10^{-4}$	2.6916 $\cdot 10^{-3}$
99.375	0.38	38.20	*2.8781* $\cdot 10^{-4}$	1.5373 $\cdot 10^{-3}$
99.500 (ATM)	0.27	27.22	*5.3566* $\cdot 10^{-4}$	*5.3566* $\cdot 10^{-4}$
99.625	0.24	23.66	1.3405 $\cdot 10^{-3}$	*9.1043* $\cdot 10^{-5}$
99.750	0.24	24.25	2.5069 $\cdot 10^{-3}$	*7.9202* $\cdot 10^{-6}$
99.875	0.31	27.50	3.7628 $\cdot 10^{-3}$	*3.8729* $\cdot 10^{-6}$

Source: Bloomberg.

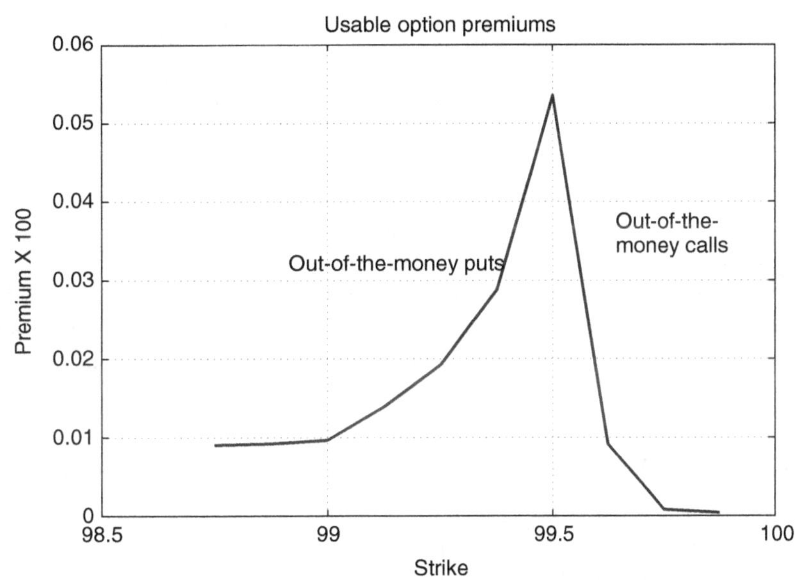

Figure 20.10 Option premiums used to determine the fair value of a time deposit basis point variance swap, $\mathbb{P}_t^{f,bp}(T,S,\Delta)$, in Equation 20.91, with $\tilde{\ell}_f(t,T,S) = \tilde{\ell}^{bp}(t,T,S) = 0$. The basis point time deposit volatility index based on these premiums is estimated to be $\widehat{TD\text{-}VI}^{bp} = 39.2101$ (see Eq. 20.93). Source: Bloomberg.

Then, an index of IRS basis point volatility can be formulated as the square root of the annualized value of this strike:

$$IRS - VI_n^{bp}(t,T) \equiv \sqrt{\frac{1}{T-t}\mathbb{P}_t^{bp}(T,n)} \tag{20.94}$$

Using the same hypothetical market conditions on February 12, 2010, underlying Table 20.1 (Panel B, column six), we estimate the fair value $\mathbb{P}_t^{bp}(T,n)$ of the basis point variance swap on a 1-month into 5-year IRS to be $2 \times 4.1567 \cdot 10^{-6}$ and calculate an estimate of IRS-$VI_n^{bp}(t,T)$ as

$$\widehat{IRS\text{-}VI}_n^{bp}(t,T) \equiv 100 \times 100 \times \sqrt{\frac{2}{12^{-1}} \times 4.1567 \cdot 10^{-6}} = 99.8803 \tag{20.95}$$

Note that this estimate is rescaled by 100^2 to make the index gauge be consistent with market practice to express basis point implied volatility as the product of rates times percentage volatility, where both rates and percentage volatilities are rescaled by 100.[14] In comparison, the ATM implied basis point volatility in Equation 20.72 is $\sigma_{iv}^{bp}(K, R_{n,t}, T_0 - t)|_{K=R_{n,t}} = 97.9202$ as determined in Section 20.5.2.5.

As anticipated, Mele and Obayashi (2012) first proposed this index of BP IRS volatility on the basis of the variance contract design in this section. Trolle and Schwartz (2013) arrive at the same expression in Equation 20.94 while solving for the conditional second moment of the swap rate distribution, which Mele, Obayashi, and Shalen (2015) label as "point-to-point" volatility, as opposed to the more familiar basis point "incremental" volatility $V_n^{bp}(t, T)$ in Equation 20.62,

$$V_{n,p-t-p}^{bp}(t, T) \equiv \sqrt{\frac{(R_T(T_1, \ldots, T_n) - R_t(T_1, \ldots, T_n))^2}{T - t}} \tag{20.96}$$

In contrast to $V_n^{bp}(t, T)$, point-to-point volatility tracks dispersion in changes of the forward swap rate over two distinct points in time. In other words, $V_{n,\text{p-t-p}}^{bp}(t, T)$ is a measure of distance between current and future forward swap rates and does not take into account movements that occur over the entire trading period, that is, $V_{n,\text{p-t-p}}^{bp}(t, T)$ could be small despite a period of market turbulence between t and T.

Incremental and point-to-point basis point volatilities can take on vastly different realizations, but they have the same expectation under the market probability. For simplicity, let $R_{n,\tau} \equiv R_\tau(T_1, \ldots, T_n)$ and $\sigma_{n,\tau} \equiv \sigma_\tau(T_1, \ldots, T_n)$, then

$$\begin{aligned}
\mathbb{E}_t^{sw,n}(R_{n,T} - R_{n,t})^2 &= \mathbb{E}_t^{sw,n}\left[\int_t^T R_{n,\tau}\sigma_{n,\tau} dW_\tau^{sw,n}\right]^2 \\
&= \mathbb{E}_t^{sw,n}\left[\int_t^T R_{n,\tau}^2 \|\sigma_{n,\tau}\|^2 d\tau\right] \\
&= \mathbb{E}_t^{sw,n}[V_n^{bp}(t, T)]
\end{aligned}$$

where the first equality follows by Equation 20.17, the second by the so-called isometry property of Itô's integrals (e.g., Øksendal, 1998; p. 26), and the third by the definition of $V_n^{bp}(t, T)$ in Equation 20.62.

The fair value of a variance swap on an incremental and on a point-to-point basis are the same. Mele, Obayashi, and Shalen (2015) rely on this property and calculate approximate confidence bands for the forward swap rate forecasts based on the CBOE SRVX, which are reproduced in Figure 20.11.[15] Naturally, the longer the forecast horizon, the higher the dispersion of the forward swap rate forecasts.

20.5.4 Current Forward-Looking Indexes of IRV

There are many practical considerations when implementing the volatility indexes surveyed in this section, including the microstructure of each asset class considered, across both time and geographies. The indexes are made more robust by greater price discovery, breadth of option strikes, and depth of liquidity in the options driving the index. These characteristics also increase the viability of derivatives to be written on the indexes, such as volatility futures and options. Successful IRV index derivatives may in turn create a positive feedback loop by increasing the liquidity of the options used to calculate the indexes.

CBOE currently maintains two indexes of IRV that have the potential to satisfy the previous properties: (i) the SRVX index of IRS volatility, launched in June 2012, which relies on 1-year/10-year USD swaptions (based on Eq. 20.94); and (ii) the VXTYN, launched in May 2013, which is based on near-month CBOT options on 10-year T-note futures (based on Eq. 20.88). This section reviews some of the empirical properties of these indexes and explores their potential as possible benchmarks of volatility products designed to provide access to standardized IRV.

20.5.4.1 Market Disconnects How do current IRV indexes compare with the equity VIX? Figures 20.12 and 20.13 depict the behavior of the CBOE VIX vis-à-vis the CBOE SRVX and the CBOE/CBOT VXTYN. The two samples cover daily data from February 2007 (SRVX) and January 2008 (VXTYN) through February 2014, for a total of 1818 (SRVX) and 1525 (VXTYN) observations.

While equity volatility and IRV seem to respond similarly to pronounced global events, the timing and nature of their responses do differ. For example, the correlation between the daily changes of the VXTYN and VIX is less than 30%, yet the daily changes

[14] That is, consider the basis point variance in Equation 20.62, $V_n^{bp}(t, T)$, and suppose that the forward swap rate, $R_\tau(T_1, \ldots, T_n)$, and its instantaneous vol, $\sqrt{\|\sigma_\tau(T_1, \ldots, T_n)\|^2}$, are both expressed in decimals, as in Table 20.1. Then, reexpressing $R_\tau(T_1, \ldots, T_n)$ and $\sqrt{\|\sigma_\tau(T_1, \ldots, T_n)\|^2}$ in percentage terms implies rescaling $V_n^{bp}(t, T)$ by $100^2 \times 100^2$, leading to the scaling factor 100×100 in Equation 20.95.

[15] The bands in Figure 20.11 are only approximate because the forward swap rate is a martingale under the annuity probability but not necessarily Gaussian.

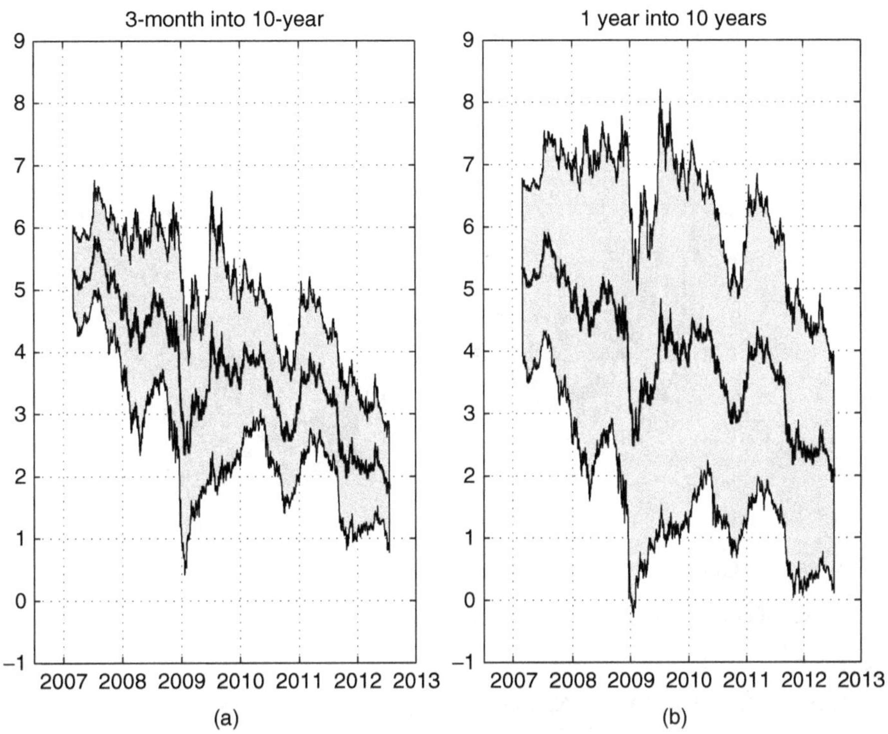

Figure 20.11 Panel A: Time series behavior of the 3-month into 10-year forward swap rate along with approximate confidence bands constructed by adding and subtracting 1.96 times the CBOE SRVX with maturity 3 months and tenor equal to 10 years. Panel B: Times series behavior of forward swap rates and approximate confidence bands regarding 1 year into 10 years forward rates. Source: Chicago Board Options Exchange and Bloomberg.

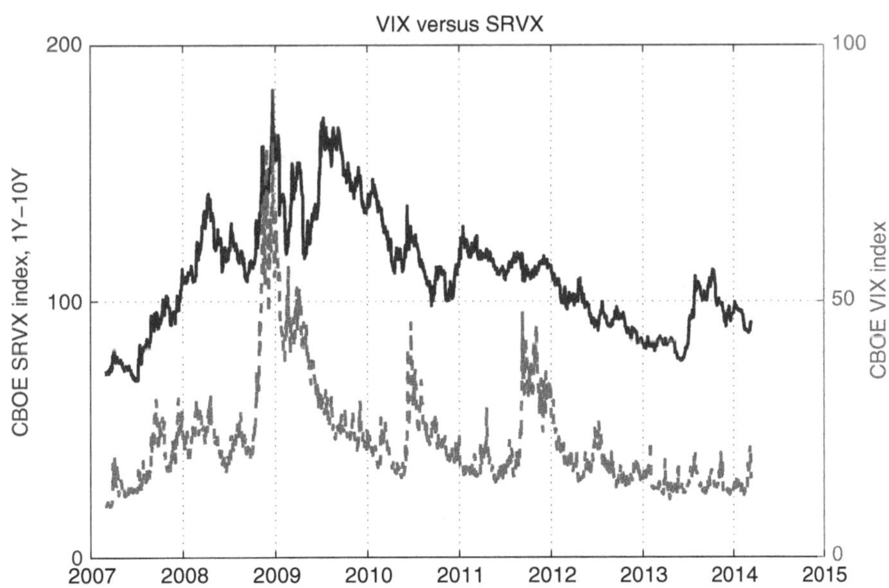

Figure 20.12 CBOE indexes of equity (VIX) and interest rate swap (SRVX) volatility. Source: Chicago Board Options Exchange.

of VXTYN and SRVX are correlated at more than 50%. There are at least five historical instances that vividly illustrate episodes of clear diversion between fixed-income and equity market volatilities.

First, right at the beginning of the crisis over summer 2007, the SRVX begins to trend upward for over 1 year, while over the same period, the VIX fluctuates without any apparent trend. Only in 2008 does the VIX experience a pronounced increase.

A second period of divergence occurs in 2009. Consider spring 2009 when positive economic news in the United States are accompanied by a bond sell-off and a stock market rally, with the VIX decreasing and both the SRVX and VXTYN increasing.

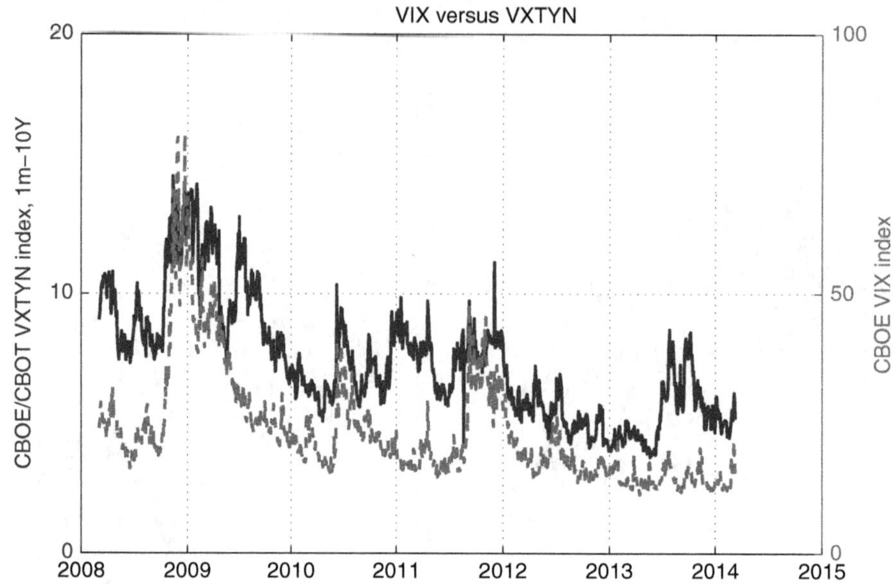

Figure 20.13 CBOE indexes of equity (VIX) and Treasury bond (VXTYN) volatility. Source: Chicago Board Options Exchange.

TABLE 20.4 Behavior of VXTYN, VIX, and S&P 500 over Days with Increasing Yields

10Y Yield up by:	No Obs.	VXTYN average Δ change (std error)	VIX average Δ change (std error)	S&P500 average change (std error)
>0	685	5.06 bps (1.70 bps)	−63.49 bps (7.23 bps)	0.51% (0.05)
>5 bps	297	14.17 bps (2.88 bps)	−90.07 bps (13.32 bps)	0.79% (0.10)
>10 bps	112	18.41 bps (6.09 bps)	−113.48 bps (28.77 bps)	1.06% (0.23)
>12 bps	73	29.01 bps (6.17 bps)	−101.95 bps (6.09 bps)	0.98% (0.27)
>15 bps	25	34.48 bps (12.40 bps)	−114.72 bps (32.70 bps)	0.68% (0.65)

Source: CBOE and Bloomberg.

A rate sell-off is indeed good news for the aggregate stock market but may still increase fixed-income portfolio risk and "rate fear," a theme we shall return to later.

Third, the sovereign debt problems over 2011–2012 lead IRV to be suppressed through the use of monetary policy, while the equity VIX starts a downward trend only after 2012.

Fourth, both SRVX and VXTYN enter another high regime during the "FED Watch" episode over May–September 2013 – when QE tapering comes into focus. In this period, the VXTYN doubles in a matter of a few weeks, with the fluctuations of the equity VIX over these months, which seem to be independent of this episode.

Fifth, Yellen's "regime" over the last months of our sample seems to have stabilized IRV with virtually no apparent effects on the dynamics of the VIX.

20.5.4.2 The Index Tail Behavior How does expected IRV behave in times of extreme rate movements? Tables 20.4 and 20.5 document a few summary statistics regarding the VXTYN, with similar results reported by Mele, Obayashi, and Shalen (2015) regarding the SRVX.

Table 20.4 reveals a clear pattern – the VXTYN significantly increases over rate sell-offs, while the VIX decreases. An interpretation is that this negative dependence is a "reverse flight-to-quality" effect, in which investors flock back to the equity market as in the 2009 episode described previously. This interpretation is corroborated by the last column of Table 20.4, which shows that during days with increasing yields, the S&P 500 index increases, albeit with a nonmonotonic pattern. In particular, on days with moderate increases in the 10-year yield, the S&P increases, possibly driven by a reverse flight-to-quality effect; on days in which the 10-year yield moves up more drastically, a possible fear effect seems to curb equity market rallies.

TABLE 20.5 Behavior of VXTYN, VIX, and S&P 500 over Days with Falling Yields

10Y yield down by:	No obs.	VXTYN average Δ change (std error)	VIX average Δ change (std error)	S&P500 average change (std error)
<0	723	−4.61 bps (1.45 bps)	63.39 bps (8.75 bps)	−0.48% (0.06)
>−2 bps	605	−4.52 bps (1.66 bps)	73.67 bps (10.21 bps)	−0.58% (0.07)
>−3 bps	468	−3.58 bps (2.04 bps)	91.93 bps (12.79 bps)	−0.76% (0.08)
>−5 bps	312	−0.19 bps (2.85 bps)	119.17 bps (17.38 bps)	−0.92% (0.11)
>−10 bps	100	13.71 bps (7.39 bps)	212.69 bps (42.41 bps)	−1.50% (0.29)
>−12 bps	55	23.63 bps (11.78 bps)	212.90 bps (64.60 bps)	−1.81% (0.40)
>−15 bps	28	44.03 bps (19.05 bps)	300.64 bps (113.99 bps)	−2.44% (0.69)

Source: CBOE and Bloomberg.

Table 20.5 reports the statistics regarding index behavior when the 10-year yield goes down. The VXTYN response is negative on days when yields are down by 5 bps, although this response is economically not important and not always statistically significant. When yields experience large falls, both the VXTYN and the VIX increase, possibly driven by a common fear that a fall in long-term yields might reflect bad times to come, which policy makers may have to handle in future rate cuts. This explanation seems to be corroborated by the fact that the S&P is indeed on average significantly negative during days on which the 10-year yield is down.

While forward-looking measures of volatility certainly bring valuable sources of information, they do not represent investable products. While a variety of investable products exist on the VIX, such as futures and options (see, e.g., Rhoads, 2011), only futures on VXTYN are available for trading since November 2014 at the time of writing. The next section provides an introduction to how to evaluate these products based on the variance swap pricing framework in the previous sections.

20.5.5 Products on IRV Indexes

The previous sections highlight that to price volatility in a model-free fashion, precise reference needs to be made to the appropriate market space – for example, the forward space for government bonds and time deposits and the annuity space for IRS.

We now illustrate how this explicit reference helps formulate models that jointly determine expected IRV and the price of derivatives thereon. For example, while pricing futures on an index of government bond volatility, we need to make sure that reference is made to risk-neutral expectations (needed to model future prices) of future expectations taken under the forward probability (needed to model government bond variance swaps). This added dimensionality defines a further difference of treatment between fixed-income and equity volatility – in the equity space, expected volatility and futures on it are both determined under the risk-neutral probability, Q, assuming as is standard that rates are constant.

Another key issue regards the very nature of IRV. A typical and pragmatic approach in the equity space is to model volatility in partial equilibrium, that is, separately from the stock price (see, e.g., Mencía and Sentana, 2013), by juxtaposing the dynamics of volatility to those of the asset returns as, for example, in the Heston (1993) model. This approach likely fails in the fixed-income space. Consider, for example, government bond volatility. Because the price of a zero-coupon bond converges to par, volatility cannot be taken to be exogenous, even ruling out stochastic volatility. Rather, it is determined endogenously, arising through no-arbitrage restrictions on bond price dynamics.

To illustrate, consider the following model with stochastic volatility,[16] which is an extension of the Ho and Lee (1986) model reviewed in Section 20.4, in which the short-term rate r_τ displays random and mean-reverting basis point volatility v_τ,

$$\begin{cases} dr_\tau = \theta_\tau d\tau + v_\tau dW_{1\tau} \\ dv_\tau^2 = k\left(m - v_\tau^2\right) d\tau + \xi v_\tau dW_{2\tau} \end{cases} \tag{20.97}$$

where $W_{i\tau}$ are Brownian motions under the risk-neutral probability; θ_τ is the infinite-dimensional parameter utilized to perfectly fit the initial yield curve at $\tau = t$ without error; k and m are the speed of mean reversion and the risk-neutral expectation of basis

[16]This model is introduced by Mele and Obayashi (2014a, Chapter 4, Appendix C) and is a special case of Mele and Obayashi (2014c).

point variance, v_τ^2; and ξ is a "volatility of variance" parameter. The model is similar to the random volatility models encountered in Section 20.4.1, except it allows for a perfect fit of the yield curve through θ_τ.

The ability to fit the initial yield curve is a desirable property, as it allows feeding the model with information concerning the entire *current* yield curve and not only the current short-term rate as explained in Section 20.4. A particularly interesting feature in our context would be that the entire *current* yield curve can feed expected future *developments* in IRV, an aspect we discuss in the following. Fitting the current yield curve is also important for market making purposes as explained in Section 20.4: in our context, it offers a consistent framework for the risk management of IRD books that contain both IRV derivatives as well as more traditional IRDs and fixed-income assets.

The model predicts that the price of a zero-coupon bond at time $\tau \geq t$ and expiring at time $\mathcal{T} \geq \tau$ when the state is (r_τ, v_τ) is

$$P_\tau(r_\tau, v_\tau^2, \mathcal{T}) \equiv e^{\int_\tau^{\mathcal{T}}(s-\mathcal{T})\theta_s ds + km\int_\tau^{\mathcal{T}} C_{\mathcal{T}}(s)ds - (\mathcal{T}-\tau)r_\tau + C_{\mathcal{T}}(\tau)v_\tau^2} \tag{20.98}$$

where $C_{\mathcal{T}}(\tau)$ is the solution to the following Riccati's equation:

$$\dot{C}_{\mathcal{T}}(\tau) = kC_{\mathcal{T}}(\tau) - \left(\frac{1}{2}(\mathcal{T}-\tau)^2 + \frac{1}{2}\xi^2 C_{\mathcal{T}}^2(\tau)\right), \quad C_{\mathcal{T}}(\mathcal{T}) = 0 \tag{20.99}$$

and the dot denotes differentiation with respect to τ. Moreover, set the parameter θ_τ to

$$\theta_\tau = \frac{\partial f_\$(t,\tau)}{\partial \tau} + km\int_t^\tau \frac{\partial^2 C_\tau(u)}{\partial \tau^2} du + \frac{\partial^2 C_\tau(t)}{\partial \tau^2} v_t^2$$

where $f_\$(t, \tau)$ is the forward rate at time t for maturity τ. Then, it can be shown that the model matches the yield curve initially observed (i.e., at t) without error, in that

$$P_t(r_t, v_t^2, \mathcal{T}) = e^{-\int_t^{\mathcal{T}} f_\$(t,\tau)d\tau} \equiv P_t(\mathcal{T}), \quad \text{for all } \mathcal{T}$$

The motivation leading to this model is to make predictions regarding the future yield curve and the price of government bond volatility products while feeding the model with all the bond prices observed at time t, not only the short-term rate. Methods and rationale underlying the model are then the same as those underlying the no-arbitrage approach reviewed in Section 20.4.

The attractive feature of this approach in our context is its potential to generate "price feedbacks," that is, the fact that a given shape of the yield curve today might convey information about the volatility to be expected within a given horizon. Mele and Obayashi (2014c) show this feature of the model does indeed arise once we consider the pricing of *coupon-bearing bonds*, although it does not, once we consider the volatility of *zero-coupon bonds*. However, in this introductory chapter, we illustrate the main features of government bond volatility pricing by making reference to the simplest zero-coupon bond case.

Consider, then, and again for simplicity, a forward expiring at S on a Zero-coupon bond expiring at $\mathbb{T}$, which by Equation 20.5 and a change in probability is shown to satisfy

$$\begin{cases} \frac{dF_\tau(S,\mathbb{T})}{F_\tau(S,\mathbb{T})} = v_\tau\left(-(\mathbb{T}-S)\,dW_{1,\tau}^{F^S} + \xi(C_{\mathbb{T}}(\tau) - C_S(\tau))dW_{2,\tau}^{F^S}\right) \\ dv_\tau^2 = (km - (k - \xi^2 C_S(\tau))v_\tau^2)d\tau + \xi v_\tau dW_{2,\tau}^{F^S} \end{cases} \tag{20.100}$$

where $W_{1,\tau}^{F^S}$ and $W_{2,\tau}^{F^S}$ are two independent Brownian motions under the forward probability Q_{F^S} and $C_S(\tau)$ is the bond price exposure to the basis point variance of the short-term rate in Equation 20.98, solution to Equation 20.99 for $\mathcal{T} \equiv S$. Therefore, the instantaneous percentage variance of the forward is

$$\|v_\tau(S,\mathbb{T})\|^2 \equiv \phi_\tau(S,\mathbb{T}) \cdot v_\tau^2 \tag{20.101}$$

where $\phi_\tau(S, \mathbb{T})$ is a time-varying, albeit nonrandom parameter, equal to

$$\phi_\tau(S,\mathbb{T}) \equiv (\mathbb{T}-S)^2 + \xi^2(C_{\mathbb{T}}(\tau) - C_S(\tau))^2$$

By taking the time t conditional expectation under Q_{F^S} of $\|v_\tau(S,\mathbb{T})\|^2$ in Equation 20.101, then annualizing and finally integrating the result over the time interval $[t, T]$, we have the following expression for the percentage volatility index predicted by the model for GB-VI$(t, T, S, \mathbb{T})$ in Equation 20.88:

$$GB\text{-}VI^z(v_t^2; t, T, S, \mathbb{T}) \equiv \sqrt{\Phi_1(t,T,S,\mathbb{T}) + \Phi_2(t,T,S,\mathbb{T}) \cdot v_t^2} \tag{20.102}$$

where

$$\Phi_j(t,T,S,\mathbb{T}) \equiv \frac{1}{T-t}\int_t^T \phi_\tau(S,\mathbb{T})\bar{\phi}_{j\tau}(t,T)d\tau, \quad j=1,2$$

$$\bar{\phi}_{1\tau}(t,T) \equiv km \cdot \int_t^\tau e^{-\int_u^\tau (k-\xi^2 C_T(x))dx}du, \quad \bar{\phi}_{2\tau}(t,T) \equiv e^{-\int_t^\tau (k-\xi^2 C_T(x))dx} \tag{20.103}$$

and the superscript z on GB-VI emphasizes it is a volatility index regarding zero-coupon bonds.

The square of the government bond volatility index predicted by the model is affine in the basis point variance of the short-term rate, v_t^2, reflecting mean reversion under the forward probability: it is higher than its realized counterpart when v_t^2 is sufficiently small, and vice versa.[17] Naturally, the intercept Φ_1 and the variance loading Φ_2 in Equation 20.102 inflate the basis point variance of the short-term rate through the exposure of the bond price to volatility arising through the time-varying parameter $\phi_\tau(S,\mathbb{T})$ in Equation 20.103, just as the instantaneous bond volatility is magnified against v_t^2 by this very same parameter in Equation 20.101.

This case does not give rise to price feedbacks: the entire yield curve at t is indeed informative about developments in the entire yield curve through the parameter θ_τ; yet it does not inform us about expected volatility because Φ_1 and Φ_2 are independent of the yield curve at t. The situation differs in the case of coupon-bearing bonds as already mentioned.

Given Equation 20.102 and the assumptions made on the dynamics of v_t^2 in Equation 20.97, we can solve for the price of products written on the index. Consider, for example, evaluating a future on the index level in Equation 20.102, for delivery at time $t+\Delta$,

$$\begin{aligned}\mathcal{F}_t(v_t^2;\Delta,T,S,\mathbb{T}) &\equiv \mathbb{E}_t(GB-VI^z(v_{t+\Delta}^2;t+\Delta,T+\Delta,S+\Delta,\mathbb{T}+\Delta))\\ &= \int_0^\infty \sqrt{\Phi_1(t,T,S,\mathbb{T})+\Phi_2(t,T,S,\mathbb{T})\cdot x}\cdot f_\Delta(x|v_t^2)dx\end{aligned} \tag{20.104}$$

where $f_\Delta(x|v_t^2)$ is the transition density of the basis point variance at time $t+\Delta$ in Equation 20.97. Because v_t^2 is a square-root process just as the short-term rate in Equation 20.22, this density is noncentral chi-square by results reviewed in Section 20.4.

The model predicts market cycles between contango and backwardation. The market is in contango when the current basis point variance v_t^2 is low, such that due to mean reversion, the index level in Equation 20.102 is lower than its risk-neutral expectation of its future value, $\mathcal{F}_t(v_t^2;\Delta,T,S,\mathbb{T})$ in Equation 20.104. It then switches to backwardation as soon as the realized basis point variance increases to a sufficiently high level to make futures valued less than the current index levels.

The model could be equally used to evaluate options on the index levels. For example, the price of a call option expiring at time $t+\delta$ and struck at K is given by

$$\begin{aligned}&\mathcal{C}_t(v_t^2;\delta,T,S,\mathbb{T})\\ &\equiv \frac{1}{P_t(t+\delta)}\mathbb{E}_t^{Q_{Ft+\delta}}(\text{GB-VI}^z(v_{t+\delta}^2;t+\delta,T+\delta,S+\delta,\mathbb{T}+\delta)-K)^+\\ &= \frac{1}{P_t(t+\delta)}\int_0^\infty (\sqrt{\Phi_1(t,T,S,\mathbb{T})+\Phi_2(t,T,S,\mathbb{T})\cdot x}-K)^+\cdot f_\delta^F(x|v_t^2)dx\end{aligned} \tag{20.105}$$

where $f_\delta^F(x|v_t^2)$ denotes the transition density of basis point variance at time $t+\delta$ given v_t^2 under the forward probability $Q_{Ft+\delta}$, which is the same as that implied by the variance equation in 20.100 with $S\equiv t+\delta$.

Mele and Obayashi (2014,c) show how to generalize Equation 20.105 to the coupon-bearing bond case and note that the current yield curve does indeed affect option evaluation in this context.

20.6 CONCLUSIONS

IRV is a topic that is receiving a great deal of attention at the time of writing. Institutional and retail investors alike have become increasingly aware of IRV's potentially significant effects on their portfolio performance, especially with respect to their fixed-income positions. While volatility benchmarking and trading is now well established in equity markets, analogous

[17] Formally, the expected realized variance under Q_{FT} is $\mathbb{E}_t^{Q_{FT}}(\|v_\tau(S,\mathbb{T})\|^2) = \phi_\tau(S,\mathbb{T})(\bar{\phi}_{1\tau}(t,T)+\bar{\phi}_{2\tau}(t,T)v_t^2)$, and it can be higher or lower than the realized variance, $\|v_\tau(S,\mathbb{T})\|^2$ as described for ξ sufficiently small. Indeed, it is possible to show that for a fixed T, $\infty > C_T(x) \geq 0$ for all $x \leq T$ and $\xi \geq 0$, such that $\exists \xi^o : k-\xi^2 C_T(x) > 0$ in Equation 20.100, for all $\xi < \xi^o$ and $x \leq T$.

initiatives are still in their infancy in the fixed-income space. This chapter surveys the main issues arising while dealing with this new topic and outlines solutions that have already been adopted. We describe both the institutional context and the pricing framework that is needed. This framework points to a new role IRDs might play while designing new tools to manage interest rate risks.

20.7 APPENDIX

Derivation of Equation 20.6. Let $\mathbb{I}_{.}$ be the indicator function. We have

$$
\begin{aligned}
& C_t^b(T,S) \\
&= \mathbb{E}_t\left[e^{-\int_t^T r_\tau d\tau} P_T(S)\cdot \mathbb{I}_{P_T(S)\geq K}\right] - K\cdot \mathbb{E}_t\left[e^{-\int_t^T r_\tau d\tau}\cdot \mathbb{I}_{P_T(S)\geq K}\right] \\
&= \mathbb{E}_t\left[e^{-\int_t^S r_\tau d\tau}\cdot \mathbb{I}_{P_T(S)\geq K}\right] - K\cdot \mathbb{E}_t\left[e^{-\int_t^T r_\tau d\tau}\cdot \mathbb{I}_{P_T(S)\geq K}\right] \\
&= P_t(S)\cdot \mathbb{E}_t^{Q_{FS}}(\mathbb{I}_{P_T(S)\geq K}) - KP_t(T)\cdot \mathbb{E}_t^{Q_{FT}}(\mathbb{I}_{P_T(S)\geq K}) \\
&= P_t(S)\cdot \mathbb{Q}_{FS}(P_T(S)\geq K) - KP_t(T)\cdot \mathbb{Q}_{FT}(P_T(S)\geq K)
\end{aligned}
$$

where the second equality follows by the law of iterated expectations,

$$
\begin{aligned}
\mathbb{E}_t\left[e^{-\int_t^T r_\tau d\tau} P_T(S)\cdot \mathbb{I}_{P_T(S)\geq K}\right] &= \mathbb{E}_t\left[\mathbb{E}_T\left(e^{-\int_t^T r_\tau d\tau} P_T(S)\cdot \mathbb{I}_{P_T(S)\geq K}\right)\right] \\
&= \mathbb{E}_t\left[e^{-\int_t^T r_\tau d\tau}\cdot \mathbb{I}_{P_T(S)\geq K}\mathbb{E}_T\left(e^{-\int_T^S r_\tau d\tau}\right)\right] \\
&= \mathbb{E}_t\left[\mathbb{E}_T\left(e^{-\int_t^S r_\tau d\tau}\cdot \mathbb{I}_{P_T(S)\geq K}\right)\right] \\
&= \mathbb{E}_t\left[e^{-\int_t^S r_\tau d\tau}\cdot \mathbb{I}_{P_T(S)\geq K}\right]
\end{aligned}
$$

and the third equality by a change in probability to the S-forward (the first term) and the T-forward (the second term). Q.E.D.

Bond prices in Vasicek (1977) and Cox, Ingersoll, and Ross (1985). The bond price predicted by Vasicek and Cox, Ingersoll, and Ross model are as in Equation 20.23. For the Vasicek model, the two functions $a(\cdot)$ and $b(\cdot)$ are given by

$$a(T-t) = \left(\frac{1-e^{-\kappa(T-t)}}{\kappa} - (T-t)\right)\left(\mu - \frac{1}{2}\left(\frac{\sigma}{\kappa}\right)^2\right) - \frac{\sigma^2}{4\kappa^3}(1-e^{-\kappa(T-t)})^2, \tag{20.106}$$

$$b(T-t) = \frac{1-e^{-\kappa(T-t)}}{\kappa} \tag{20.107}$$

and for Cox, Ingersoll, and Ross,

$$a(T-t) = \frac{2\hat{\kappa}\hat{r}}{\hat{\sigma}^2}\ln\left(\frac{2\gamma e^{\frac{1}{2}(\hat{\kappa}+\gamma)(T-t)}}{(\hat{\kappa}+\gamma)(e^{\gamma(T-t)}-1)+2\gamma}\right), \tag{20.108}$$

$$b(T-t) = \frac{2(e^{\gamma(T-t)}-1)}{(\hat{\kappa}+\gamma)(e^{\gamma(T-t)}-1)+2\gamma}, \quad \gamma = \sqrt{\hat{\kappa}^2+2\hat{\sigma}^2}. \tag{20.109}$$

Derivation of Equation 20.41. The price of a zero-coupon bond satisfies $P_t(T) = e^{Y_{t,T}}$, where $Y_{t,T} \equiv -\int_t^T \varphi_t(u)du$, such that by Itô's lemma,

$$\frac{dP_\tau(T)}{P_\tau(T)} = dY_{\tau,T} + \frac{1}{2}dY_{\tau,T}^2, \tag{20.110}$$

where

$$
\begin{aligned}
dY_{\tau,T} &= \varphi_\tau(\tau)d\tau - \int_\tau^T d\varphi_\tau(u)du \\
&= r_\tau d\tau - \int_\tau^T (\alpha_\tau(u)d\tau + \sigma_\tau^f(u)d\tilde{W}_\tau)du \\
&= (r_\tau - \alpha_\tau^I(T))d\tau - \sigma_\tau^{If}(T)d\tilde{W}_\tau
\end{aligned}
$$

where we have used the definition of the short-term rate, $r_\tau \equiv \varphi_\tau(\tau)$, and Equation 20.40 and defined

$$
\alpha_\tau^I(T) \equiv \int_\tau^T \alpha_\tau(u)du, \quad \sigma_\tau^{If}(T) \equiv \int_\tau^T \sigma_\tau^f(u)du
$$

Equation 20.110 implies that in the absence of arbitrage,

$$
\begin{aligned}
\mathbb{E}_\tau\left(\frac{dP_\tau(T)}{P_\tau(T)}\right) &= r_\tau d\tau \\
&= \mathbb{E}_\tau(dY_{\tau,T}) + \frac{1}{2}\mathbb{E}_\tau\left(dY_{\tau,T}^2\right) \\
&= (r_\tau - \alpha_\tau^I(T))d\tau + \frac{1}{2}\|\sigma_\tau^{If}(T)\|^2 d\tau
\end{aligned}
$$

leaving

$$
\alpha_\tau^I(T) = \frac{1}{2}\|\sigma_\tau^{If}(T)\|^2 \tag{20.111}
$$

Differentiating Equation 20.111 with respect to T yields Equation 20.41. Q.E.D.

Derivation of Equation 20.67. We rely on standard arguments (see, e.g., Bakshi and Madan, 2000; Carr and Madan, 2001). Consider a twice-differentiable function f. By a Taylor's expansion with remainder, we have that

$$
\begin{aligned}
f(x) &= f(x_0) + f'(x_0)(x - x_0) + \int_{x_0}^x (x-k)f''(k)dk \\
&= f(x_0) + f'(x_0)(x - x_0) + \int_0^{x_0} f''(k)(k-x)^+ dk \\
&+ \int_{x_0}^\infty f''(k)(x-k)^+ dk
\end{aligned} \tag{20.112}
$$

Equation 20.67 follows by taking $f \equiv \ln x$, $x \equiv R_T$, and $x_0 \equiv R_t$ in Equation 20.112. Q.E.D.

Derivation of Equation 20.82. This follows by Equation 20.112 after setting $f \equiv x^2$, $x \equiv X_T$, and $x_0 \equiv X_t$. Q.E.D.

The functions $\tilde{\ell}_f$ (t, T, S) and $\tilde{\ell}^{bp}$ (t, T, S) in Equation 20.91. The function summarizing the maturity mismatch $\tilde{\ell}_f(t, T, S)$ is the counterpart to that regarding the government volatility case in Equation 20.87, $\tilde{\ell}(t, T, S, \mathbb{T})$, and equals

$$
\tilde{\ell}_f(t, T, S) \equiv -\int_t^T v_\tau^f(S, \Delta)(v_\tau^f(T, \Delta) - v_\tau^f(S, \Delta))d\tau \tag{20.113}
$$

Regarding $\tilde{\ell}^{bp}(t, T, S)$, we have

$$
\tilde{\ell}^{bp}(t, T, S) \equiv -\int_t^T f_\tau^2(S, S+\Delta)v_\tau^f(S, \Delta)(v_\tau^f(T, \Delta) - v_\tau^f(S, \Delta))d\tau \tag{20.114}
$$

Gaussian model with constant volatility and basis point implied volatility. Consider the price of a European call option maturing at time T on a forward Libor price maturing at T,

$$\begin{aligned} Call_t^Z(K,T,\Delta) &= \mathbb{E}_t\left[e^{-\int_t^T r_\tau d\tau}\left(Z_T(T,T+\Delta)-K\right)^+\right] \\ &= P_t(T)\mathbb{E}_t^{Q_{FT}}(Z_T(T,T+\Delta)-K)^+ \end{aligned} \tag{20.115}$$

where the second equality follows by the usual change of probability. The price of a put option follows by the put–call parity,

$$Put_t^Z(K,T,\Delta) = Call_t^Z(K,T,\Delta) + P_t(T)(K - Z_t(T,T+\Delta)) \tag{20.116}$$

A standard benchmark to evaluate options relies on the assumption that the forward price in 20.8 is lognormal, with instantaneous volatility equal to a constant σ,

$$\frac{dZ_\tau(T,T+\Delta)}{Z_\tau(T,T+\Delta)} = \sigma dW_\tau^{F^T}, \quad \tau \in (t,T) \tag{20.117}$$

which leads to evaluate $Call_t^Z(K,T,\Delta)$ through Black's formula,

$$\begin{aligned} \frac{Call_t^Z(K,T,\Delta)}{P_t(T)} &= \mathbb{E}_t^{Q_{FT}}(Z_T(T,T+\Delta)-K)^+ \\ &= Bl76(Z_t(T,T+\Delta);T-t,K,\sigma) \end{aligned} \tag{20.118}$$

where

$$Bl76(Z_t;T-t,K,\sigma) \equiv Z_t\Phi(d_t) - K\Phi(d_t-\sigma), \quad d_t = \frac{\ln\frac{Z_t}{K}+\frac{1}{2}\sigma^2}{\sigma}$$

The Black's skew of implied volatilities in Table 20.3 is the mapping $K \mapsto \sigma(Z_t,K,T-t)$ where $\sigma(Z_t,K,T-t)$ denotes the value of σ such that Equation 20.118 holds when its left-hand side is replaced with market data.

An alternative model to 20.117 is one in which the instantaneous volatility $v_\tau^Z(T,\Delta)$ in Equation 20.8 is such that the forward Libor price follows a Gaussian process with constant volatility σ_N,

$$dZ_\tau(T,T+\Delta) = \sigma_N dW_\tau^{F^T} \tag{20.119}$$

Assuming Equation 20.119 holds true, the expectation in Equation 20.115 is

$$\mathbb{E}_t^{Q_{FT}}(Z_T(T,T+\Delta)-K)^+ = (Z_t(T,T+\Delta)-K)\Phi(\delta_t) + \frac{\sigma_N\sqrt{T-t}}{\sqrt{2\pi}}e^{-\frac{1}{2}\delta_t^2} \tag{20.120}$$

where

$$\delta_t \equiv \frac{Z_t(T,T+\Delta)-K}{\sigma_N\sqrt{T-t}}$$

The basis point implied volatility skew in Table 20.3 is defined as the mapping $K \mapsto \sigma^{bp}(Z_t,K,T-t)$, where $\sigma^{bp}(Z_t,K,T-t)$ is the value of σ_N such that the model-based option price implied by Equation 20.120 equals the market price.

Details regarding affine models. We collect a few well-known results regarding affine models. We derive the two functions $a(\cdot)$ and $b(\cdot)$ in Equation 20.27 in the Longstaff and Schwartz (1992) model and, later, characterize them as solutions to ordinary differential equations in a more general context (see Eqs 20.128 and 20.129).

The basic assumption underlying the Longstaff and Schwartz model is that the two state processes $y_{1\tau}$ and $y_{2\tau}$ are uncorrelated and that under the risk-neutral probability, they are solutions to

$$dy_{i\tau} = \hat{\kappa}_i(\bar{y}_i - y_{i\tau})d\tau + \sqrt{y_{i\tau}}d\tilde{W}_{i\tau} \tag{20.121}$$

with obvious notation.

The bond price predicted by the model is

$$P_t(y_{1t}, y_{2t}; T) = \mathbb{E}_t\left(e^{-\int_t^T r_\tau d\tau}\right) = \mathbb{E}_t\left(e^{-\int_t^T \beta_1 y_{1\tau} d\tau}\right)\mathbb{E}_t\left(e^{-\int_t^T \beta_2 y_{2\tau} d\tau}\right)$$
$$= F_t(y_{1t}; T)F_t(y_{2t}; T) \tag{20.122}$$

where the second equality follows by Equation 20.26 and the assumption that $y_{1\tau}$ and $y_{2\tau}$ are uncorrelated, the two processes $y_{i\tau} \equiv \beta_i y_{i\tau}$, and are therefore solutions to the following square-root processes:

$$dy_{i\tau} = \hat{\kappa}_i(\hat{y}_i - y_{i\tau})d\tau + \hat{\sigma}_i\sqrt{y_{i\tau}}d\tilde{W}_{i\tau}, \qquad \hat{y}_i \equiv \beta_i\bar{y}_i, \quad \hat{\sigma}_i \equiv \sqrt{\beta_i}$$

such that by Equation 20.22, the two functions $F_t(\cdot\,; T)$ are the same pricing functions as in the Cox, Ingersoll, and Ross (1985) model,

$$F_t(y_{it}; T) = e^{a(T-t)-b(T-t)y_{it}} \tag{20.123}$$

with the two functions $a(\cdot)$ and $b(\cdot)$ being defined by Equations 20.108) and 20.109 and replacing $\hat{r} \equiv \hat{y}_i$, $\hat{\kappa} \equiv \hat{\kappa}_i$, and $\hat{\sigma} \equiv \hat{\sigma}_i$.

Finally, note that by Equations 20.26 and 20.121, the instantaneous variance of the short-term rate is

$$v_\tau^2 d\tau \equiv var(dr_\tau) = (\beta_1^2 y_{1\tau} + \beta_2^2 y_{2\tau})d\tau \tag{20.124}$$

Equations 20.26 and 20.124 can be used to express $y_{i\tau}$ in terms of the short-term rate r_τ and its instantaneous variance, v_τ^2, namely,

$$y_{1\tau} = \frac{\beta_2 r_\tau - v_\tau^2}{\beta_1(\beta_2 - \beta_1)}, \quad y_{2\tau} = \frac{v_\tau^2 - \beta_1 r_\tau}{\beta_2(\beta_2 - \beta_1)} \tag{20.125}$$

By plugging 20.125 into 20.123 and, then, 20.122 leaves Equation 20.27 for suitable functions $a(\cdot)$, $b(\cdot)$, and $c(\cdot)$ and by abusing notation.

The model is a special case of the affine model in 20.29 introduced by Duffie and Kan (1996), yielding the pricing formula 20.30, where the two functions $a^o(\cdot)$ and $a^y(\cdot)$ are determined as follows. Note that in the absence of arbitrage, the expected return on a zero equals the short-term rate,

$$\mathbb{E}_\tau\left(\frac{dP_\tau}{P_\tau}\right) = r_\tau d\tau \tag{20.126}$$

By Itô's lemma, and the assumption that y_τ is as in Equation 20.29,

$$\mathbb{E}_\tau\left(\frac{dP}{P}\right) = \left(\frac{\partial P/\partial\tau}{P} + \frac{P_y}{P}\kappa(\mu - y) + \frac{1}{2}\mathrm{Tr}\left([\Sigma V(y)][\Sigma V(y)]^\top \frac{P_{yy}}{P}\right)\right)d\tau$$
$$= \left(-a^o + -a^y y + a^y\kappa(\mu - y) + \frac{1}{2}\sum_{i=1}^n (a^y\Sigma)_i^2 s_{1i} + \frac{1}{2}\sum_{i=1}^n (a^y\Sigma)_i^2 s_{2i} y\right)d\tau \tag{20.127}$$

where subscripts denote partial derivatives, dots denote differentiation with respect to time left to maturity, and the second equality follows by the assumption that the pricing function P_τ is as in Equation 20.30. Therefore, matching 20.127 and 20.28 through 20.126 produces that $a^o(\cdot)$ and $a^y(\cdot)$ are solutions to the following Riccati's equations:

$$\begin{cases} a^o(\tau) = -\alpha + a^y(\tau)\kappa\mu + \frac{1}{2}\sum_{i=1}^n (a^y(\tau)\Sigma)_i^2 s_{1i} \\ a^y(\tau) = -\beta - a^y(\tau)\kappa + \frac{1}{2}\sum_{i=1}^n (a^y(\tau)\Sigma)_i^2 s_{2i} \end{cases} \tag{20.128}$$

subject to the boundary conditions

$$a^o(0) = 0 \quad \text{and} \quad a^y(0) = 0$$

Consider, for example, the Fong and Vasicek (1991) model in 20.25. This model is still a special case of the general affine model 20.29, namely, after setting

$$r_\tau = y_{1\tau}, \quad v_\tau^2 = y_{2\tau}$$

and

$$\begin{cases} dy_{1\tau} = \kappa_r(\bar{r} - y_{1\tau})d\tau + \sqrt{y_{2\tau}}d\tilde{W}_{1\tau} \\ dy_{2\tau} = \kappa_v(\omega - y_{2\tau})d\tau + \xi\sqrt{y_{2\tau}}d\tilde{W}_{2\tau} \end{cases}$$

Therefore, the price is as in Equation 20.27 as claimed in the main text and by Equation 20.128, with the three functions $a(\cdot)$, $b(\cdot)$, and $c(\cdot)$ satisfying

$$\begin{cases} a(\tau) = -b(\tau)\kappa_r\bar{r} + c(\tau)\kappa_v\omega \\ b(\tau) = 1 - b(\tau)\kappa_r \\ \dot{c}(\tau) = -c(\tau)\kappa_v + \frac{1}{2}(b^2(\tau) + c^2(\tau)\xi^2) \end{cases} \quad (20.129)$$

subject to the boundary conditions $a(0) = b(0) = c(0) = 0$.

ACKNOWLEDGMENTS

We wish to thank Pietro Veronesi for his detailed and invaluable comments although we retain full responsibility for any remaining inaccuracies and mistakes.

REFERENCES

Ahn D-H, Dittmar RF, Gallant AR. Quadratic term structure models: theory and evidence. Rev Financ Stud 2002;15:243–288.

Andersen T, Bollerslev T, Diebold F. Parametric and nonparametric measurements of volatility. In: Yacine A-S, Hansen LP, editors. *Handbook of Financial Econometrics: Tools and Techniques*. Volume 1, Chapter 2. North Holland; 2010. p 67–137.

Bakshi G, Madan D. Spanning and derivative security evaluation. J Financ Econ 2000;55:205–238.

Bartlett B. Hedging Under SABR Model. Wilmott Magazine; July/August 2006.

Bikbov R, Chernov M. Yield curve and volatility: lessons from eurodollar futures and options. J Financ Econom 2011;9:66–105.

Black F. The pricing of commodity contracts. J Financ Econ 1976;3:167–179.

Black F, Scholes M. The pricing of options and corporate liabilities. J Polit Econ 1973;81:637–659.

Brace A, Gatarek D, Musiela M. The market model of interest rate dynamics. Math Finance 1997;7:127–155.

Brigo D, Mercurio F. *Interest Rate Models – Theory and Practice, with Smile, Inflation and Credit*. 2nd ed. Springer-Verlag; 2006.

Britten-Jones M, Neuberger A. Option prices, implied price processes and stochastic volatility. J Finance 2000;55:839–866.

Broadie M, Chernov M, Johannes M. Model specification and risk premia: evidence from futures options. J Finance 2007;62:1453–1490.

Carr P, Corso A. Commodity covariance contracting. Energy Power Risk Manage 2001;4:42–45.

Carr P, Madan D. Optimal positioning in derivative securities. Quant Finance 2001;1:19–37.

Chicago Board Options Exchange. The CBOE Volatility Index® – VIX®." White paper underlying the CBOE-VIX Volatility Index; 2009. Available from http://www.cboe.com/micro/VIX/vixintro.aspx.

Cox JC, Ingersoll JE, Ross SA. A theory of the term structure of interest rates. Econometrica 1985;53:385–407.

Cox JC, Ross SA, Rubinstein M. Option pricing: a simplified approach. J Financ Econ 1979;7:229–263.

Demeterfi K, Derman E, Kamal M, Zou J. A guide to variance swaps. Risk 1999a;12(6):54–59.

Demeterfi K, Derman E, Kamal M, Zou J. A guide to volatility and variance swaps. J Derivat 1999b;6(4):9–32.

Duffie D, Kan R. A yield-factor model of interest rates. Math Finance 1996;6:379–406.

Dumas B. The meaning of the implicit volatility function in case of stochastic volatility; 1995. Unpublished appendix of: Dumas B, Fleming J, Whaley RE. Implied volatility functions: empirical tests. J Finance 1998;53:2059–2106.

Dupire B. Pricing with a smile. Risk 1994;7:18–20.

Fong GH, Vasicek OA. Fixed income volatility management. J Portf Manage 1991;17:41–46.

Geman H. The Importance of the Forward Neutral Probability in a Stochastic Approach to Interest Rates. Unpublished working paper, ESSEC; 1989.

Geman H, El Karoui N, Rochet J-C. Changes of numéraire, changes of probability measures and pricing of options. J Appl Probab 1995;32:443–458.

Hagan PS, Kumar D, Lesniewski AS, Woodward DE. Managing Smile Risk. Wilmott Magazine; Sept 2002. p 84–108.

Hagan PS, Woodward DE. Equivalent black volatilities. Appl Math Finance 1999;6:147–157.

Harrison JM, Kreps DM. Martingales and arbitrage in multiperiod securities markets. J Econ Theory 1979;20:381–408.

Heath D, Jarrow R, Morton A. Bond pricing and the term-structure of interest rates: a new methodology for contingent claim valuation. Econometrica 1992;60:77–105.

Heston SL. A closed form solution for options with stochastic volatility with applications to bond and currency options. Rev Financ Stud 1993;6:327–344.

Ho TSY, Lee SB. Term structure movements and the pricing of interest rate contingent claims. J Finance 1986;41:1011–1029.

Hull J, White A. Pricing interest rate derivative securities. Rev Financ Stud 1990;3:573–592.

Jamshidian F. An exact bond option pricing formula. J Finance 1989;44:205–209.

Jamshidian F. Libor and swap market models and measures. Finance Stochastics 1997;1:293–330.

Knez PJ, Litterman R, Scheinkman J. Explorations into factors explaining money market returns. J Finance 1994;49:1861–1882.

Litterman R, Scheinkman J. Common factors affecting bond returns. J Fixed Income 1991;1:54–61.

Longstaff FA, Schwartz ES. Interest rate volatility and the term structure: a two-factor general equilibrium model. J Finance 1992;47:1259–1282.

Longstaff FA, Schwartz ES. Valuing American options by simulation: a simple least-squares approach. Rev Financ Stud 2001;14:113–147.

Mele A. Fundamental properties of bond prices in models of the short-term rate. Rev Financ Stud 2003;16:679–716.

Mele A, Obayashi Y. An Interest Rate Swap Volatility Index and Contract. Technical white paper underlying the CBOE Interest Rate Swap Volatility Index; 2012. Available from http://www.cboe.com/micro/srvx/default.aspx.

Mele A, Obayashi Y. *The Price of Fixed Income Market Volatility*. Book manuscript, Lugano: Swiss Finance Institute; 2014a.

Mele A, Obayashi Y. Interest Rate Variance Swaps and the Pricing of Fixed Income Volatility. GARP Risk Professional: Quant Perspectives; March 1-8 2014b.

Mele A, Obayashi Y. Pricing Options and Futures on a Government Bond Volatility Index. Working Paper, Swiss Finance Institute; 2014c.

Mele A, Obayashi Y, Shalen C. Rate fears gauges and the dynamics of interest rate swap and equity volatility. J Bank Finance 2015;52:256–265.

Mencía J, Sentana E. Valuation of VIX derivatives. J Financ Econ 2013;108:367–391.

Miltersen K, Sandmann K, Sondermann D. Closed form solutions for term structure derivatives with lognormal interest rate. J Finance 1997;52:409–430.

Neuberger Anthony. Hedging volatility: the case for a new contract. J Portf Manage 1994;20:74–80.

Øksendal B. *Stochastic Differential Equations – An Introduction with Applications*. Berlin: Springer-Verlag; 1998.

Piazzesi M. Affine term structure models. In: Yacine A-S, Hansen LP, editors. *Handbook of Financial Econometrics: Tools and Techniques*. Volume 1, Chapter 12. North Holland; 2010. p 691–766.

Renault E. Econometric models of option pricing errors. In: Kreps D, Wallis K, editors. *Advances in Economics and Econometrics*. Volume 3. Cambridge: Cambridge University Press; 1997. p 223–278.

Rhoads R. *Trading VIX Derivatives*. John Wiley and Sons; 2011.

Romano M, Touzi N. Contingent claims and market completeness in a stochastic volatility model. Math Finance 1997;7:399–412.

Trolle AB, Schwartz ES. The Swaption Cube. Working paper EPFL and Swiss Finance Institute; 2013.

Vasicek OA. An equilibrium characterization of the term structure. J Financ Econ 1977;5:177–188.

Veronesi P. *Fixed Income Securities*. John Wiley and Sons; 2010.

Walras L. *Éléments d'économie politique pure, ou théorie de la richesse sociale*. Lausanne: Corbaz & Cie; 1874; English translation:*Elements of Pure Economics*. Homewood (IL): R.D. Irwin; 1954.

21

Nonlinear Valuation under Margining and Funding Costs with Residual Credit Risk: A Unified Approach

Damiano Brigo[a], **Qing Liu**[a], **Andrea Pallavicini**[a,b] **and David Sloth**[c]

[a]*Department of Mathematics, Imperial College, London, United Kingdom*
[b]*Financial Engineering Department, Banca IMI, Milan, Italy*
[c]*Danske Bank, Copenhagen, Denmark*

21.1 INTRODUCTION

In the wake of the financial crisis in 2007–2008, dealers and financial institutions have been forced to rethink how they value and hedge contingent claims traded either in the over-the-counter (OTC) market or through Central Counterparty Clearing Houses (CCPs) . OTC derivatives are bilateral financial contracts negotiated between two default-risky entities. Yet, prior to the crisis, institutions tended to ignore the credit risk of high-quality rated counterparties, but as recent history has shown, this was a particularly dangerous assumption. Moreover, as banks became reluctant to lend to each other with the crisis rumbling through the Western economies, the spread between the rate on overnight indexed swaps (OISs) and the London Interbank Offered Rate (LIBOR) rate blew up.

To keep up with this sudden change of game, dealers today make a number of adjustments when they book OTC trades. The credit valuation adjustment (CVA) corrects the price for the expected costs to the dealer due to the possibility that the counterparty may default, while the so-called debt valuation adjustment (DVA) is a correction for the expected benefits to the dealer due to his own default risk. The latter adjustment has the controversial effect that the dealer can book a profit as his default risk increases and is very hard if not impossible to hedge. Finally, dealers often adjust the price for the costs of funding the trade. In the industry, this practice is known as a liquidity valuation adjustment and funding valuation adjustment (LVA, FVA). When a derivatives desk executes a deal with a client, it backs the trade by hedging it with other dealers in the market and by posting/receiving collateral and by receiving/paying interest on the collateral posted. This involves borrowing or lending money and other assets. Classical derivatives pricing theory rests on the assumption that one can borrow and lend at a unique risk-free rate of interest, a theoretical risk-free rate that is proxied by a number of market rates. The seminal work of Black–Scholes–Merton showed that in this case an option on equity can be replicated by a portfolio of equity and risk-free debt over any short period of time. Prior to the crisis, this assumption may have been reasonable with banks funding their hedging strategies at LIBOR. However, with drastically

Handbook of Fixed-Income Securities, First Edition. Edited by Pietro Veronesi.

increasing spreads emerging as the crisis took hold, it became apparent that LIBOR is contaminated by credit and liquidity risk and as such is an imperfect proxy of the risk-free rate. We should briefly mention that LIBOR has been undergoing reform due to the market manipulation problems that had been investigated since June 2012, with NYSE Euronext taking over LIBOR in January 2014. We will not be concerned with fraud risk here. Going back to our main focus, while overnight rates have replaced LIBOR as proxies for the risk-free rate, it would be preferable for a pricing framework not to feature theoretical rates in the final valuation equations.

In this paper, we develop an arbitrage-free framework for consistent valuation of collateralized as well as uncollateralized trades under counterparty credit risk, collateral margining, and funding costs . The need to consistently account for the changed trading conditions in the valuation of derivatives is stressed by the sheer size of the OTC market. Indeed, despite the crisis and the previously neglected risks, the size of derivatives markets remains staggering; the market value of outstanding OTC derivative contracts equaled \$24.7 trillion by the end of 2012 with a whopping \$632.6 trillion in notional value (Bank for International Settlements, 2013). Adopting the risk-neutral valuation principle, we derive a general pricing equation for a derivative deal where the new or previously neglected types of risks are included simply as modifications of the payout cash flows. We address the current market practices in accordance with the guidelines of the International Swaps and Derivatives Association (ISDA) without assuming restrictive constraints on the collateral margining procedures and closeout netting rules. In particular, we allow for asymmetric collateral and funding rates as well as exogenously given liquidity policies and hedging strategies. We also discuss rehypothecation of collateral guarantees.

When dealing with funding costs, one may take a single deal (micro) or homogeneous (macro) cost view. In the microview, funding costs are determined at deal level. This means that the trading desk may borrow funds at a different rate than at which it can invest funds, and the rates may vary across deals even in the same desk. In a slightly more aggregate cost view, average funding spreads are applied to all deals yet the spread on borrowing funds may still be different from that on lending. Finally, if we turn to the macro- and symmetric view, funding costs of borrowing and lending are assumed the same, and a common funding spread is applied across all deals. Clearly, the treasury department of a bank plays an active part in the microapproach and works as an operational center, while in the macroapproach, it takes more the role of a supporting function for the trading business. In this work we stay as general as possible and adopt a microcost view. Naturally, the macroview is just a special case of the microview. This will be implicit in making the otherwise exogenously assigned funding rates a function of the specific deal value. One should notice that the specific treasury model one adopts also impacts the presence of credit risk, and in particular of DVA, on the funding policy. This effect is occasionally referred to as DVA2, but we will not adopt such terminology here.

The introduction of funding risk makes the pricing problem recursive and nonlinear. The price of the deal depends on the trader's funding strategy in future paths, while to determine the future funding strategy, we need to know the deal price itself in future paths. This recursive structure was also discovered in the studies of Pallavicini, Perini, and Brigo (2011), Crépey (2011), and Burgard and Kjaer (2011a), yet the feature is neglected in the common approach of adding a funding spread to the discount curve.

Valuation under funding risk poses a significantly more complex and computationally demanding problem than standard CVA and DVA computations (except possibly CVA/DVA under replacement closeout), since it requires forward simulation and backward induction at the same time. In addition, FVA does not take the form of a simple additive term as appears to be commonly assumed by market participants. Funding and credit costs do not split up in a purely additive way. A consequence of this is that valuation becomes aggregation dependent as portfolio prices do not add up. It is therefore difficult for banks to create CVA and FVA desks with separate and clear-cut responsibilities. This can be done at the expense of tolerating some degree of double counting in the different adjustments (to which we refer simply as "double counting" in the following). In this respect, we introduce NVA, defined as a nonlinearity valuation adjustment, measuring the degree of valuation error one has when removing nonlinearities through symmetrization of borrowing and lending rates and through a risk-free closeout substituting a replacement closeout at default. More generally, nonlinearity implies organizational challenges, which we hint at in the conclusions.

To thoroughly explore valuation under funding costs, we show how the general pricing equation can be cast as a set of iterative equations that can be conveniently solved by means of least-squares Monte Carlo (see, e.g., Carriere (1996), Longstaff and Schwartz (2001), Tilley (1993), Tsitsiklis and Van Roy (2001)), and we propose an efficient simulation algorithm. Also, we derive a continuous-time approximation of the solution of the pricing equation as well as the associated partial differential equation (PDE), showing that the risk-free rate disappears.

Despite its general market acceptance, the practice of including an adjustment for funding costs has stirred quite some controversy among academics and practitioners (see the debate following Hull and White (2012)). At the center of this controversy is the issue that funding-contingent pricing becomes subjective due to asymmetric information. The particular funding policy chosen by the client is not (fully) known to the dealer and vice versa. As a result, the price of the deal may be different to either of the two parties. Theoretically, this should mean that the parties would never close the deal. However, in reality, the dealer may not be able to recoup his full funding costs from the client, yet traders say that funding risk was the key factor driving bid–ask spreads wider during the crisis.

The importance of the FVA in terms of impact has been stressed by J.P. Morgan's results in January 2014. The Wall Street Journal in Rapoport (2014) reports that the "FVA" cost J.P. Morgan Chase a $1.5 billion charge in its fourth-quarter earnings.

In terms of available literature in this area, several studies have analyzed the various valuation adjustments separately, but few have tried to build a valuation approach that consistently takes collateralization, counterparty credit risk, and funding costs into account. Under unilateral default risk, that is, when only one party is defaultable, Brigo and Masetti (2005), consider valuation of derivatives with CVA, while particular applications of their approach are given in Brigo and Pallavicini (2007), Brigo and Chourdakis (2009), and Brigo, Morini, and Tarenghi (2011b), see Brigo, Morini, and Pallavicini (2013) for a summary. Bilateral default risk appears in Bielecki and Rutkowski (2002), Brigo and Capponi (2008), Brigo, Pallavicini, and Papatheodorou (2011c), and Gregory (2009)who price both the CVA and DVA of a derivatives deal. The impact of collateralization on default risk has been investigated in Cherubini (2005) and more recently in Brigo, Capponi, and Pallavicini (2014) and Brigo et al. (2011a).

Assuming no default risk, Piterbarg (2010) provides an initial analysis of collateralization and funding risk in a stylized Black–Scholes economy. Yet, the introduction of collateral in a world without default risk is questionable since its main purpose is to mitigate such risk. Fujii, Shimada, and Takahashi (2010) analyze the consequences of multicurrency features in collateral proceedings. Morini and Prampolini (2011), Fries (2010), and Castagna (2011) consider basic implications of funding in the presence of default risk. However, these works focus only on simple financial products, such as zero-coupon bonds or loans, and do not offer the level of generality needed to include all the required features. Thus, a general framework for consistent valuation under the new risks is still missing. The most comprehensive attempts are those of Burgard and Kjaer (2011a,b), Crépey (2011, 2012a,b), and Pallavicini, Perini, and Brigo (2011, 2012). Nonetheless, as Burgard and Kjaer (2011a,b) resort to a PDE approach, their results are constrained to low dimensions. Also, they neglect the hidden complexities of collateralization and mark-to-market discontinuities at default. The approach of Crépey (2011, 2012a,b) is more general although it does not allow for credit instruments in the deal portfolio.

We follow the work of Pallavicini, Perini, and Brigo (2011, 2012) and Sloth (2013) and consider a general pricing framework for derivative deals that fully and consistently takes collateralization, counterparty credit risk, and funding risk into account. The framework is conceptually simple and intuitive in contrast to previous attempts. It is based on the celebrated risk-neutral valuation principle, and the new risks are included simply by adjusting the payout cash flows of the deal. We present a numerical case study that extends the benchmark theory of Black–Scholes for equity options to credit gap risk (CVA/DVA after collateralization), collateral, and funding costs. We find that the precise patterns of funding-inclusive values depend on a number of factors, including the asymmetry between borrowing and lending rates. We stress such inputs in order to analyze their impact on the funding-inclusive price. Our numerical results confirm that funding risk has a nontrivial impact on the deal price and that double counting can be relevant as well.

As we point out in the conclusions, the violation of the bilateral nature of valuation and the aggregation dependence lead to doubts about considering the funding-inclusive value as a price. Should this value be charged to a client? This prompts to the old distinction between price and value and whether funding costs should be considered as a profitability/cost analysis tool rather than as an adjustment to be charged to a client. This is often reinforced by the fact that a bank client has no direct control on the funding policy of a bank.

It is also worth pointing out that the theory we illustrate here on the Black–Scholes benchmark case has also been applied to pricing under multiple interest rate curves, see Pallavicini and Brigo (2013), and to pricing under CCPs in presence of default risk of clearing members, closeout delays, and initial and variation margins, see Brigo and Pallavicini (2014).

The paper is organized as follows. Section 21.2 describes the general pricing framework with collateralized credit, debit, liquidity, and FVAs. Section 21.3 derives an iterative solution of the pricing equation as well as a continuous-time approximation. Section 21.4 describes a least-square Monte Carlo algorithm and provides numerical results on deal positions in European call options on equity under the benchmark model of Black and Scholes. In addition, an NVA is introduced and computed. Section 21.5 extends the pricing framework to cases where the dealer hedges the trade using other derivatives. Finally, Section 21.6 concludes the paper.

21.2 COLLATERALIZED CREDIT AND FUNDING VALUATION ADJUSTMENTS

In this section, we develop a general risk-neutral valuation framework for OTC derivative deals. The section clarifies how the traditional precrisis derivative price is consistently adjusted to reflect the new market realities of collateralization, counterparty credit risk, and funding risk. We refer to the two parties of a credit-risky deal as the investor or dealer ("I") on one side and the counterparty or client ("C") on the other.

Fixing the time horizon $T \in \mathbb{R}_+$ of the deal, we define our risk-neutral pricing model on the probability space $(\Omega, \mathcal{G}, (\mathcal{G}_t)_{t\in[0,T]}, \mathbb{Q})$. $\mathbb{Q}$ is the risk-neutral probability measure. The filtration $(\mathcal{G}_t)_{t\in[0,T]}$ models the flow of information of the whole market, including credit, such that the default times of the investor τ_I and the counterparty τ_C are $\mathcal{G}$-stopping times. We adopt the notational convention that $\mathbb{E}_t$ is the risk-neutral expectation conditional on the information $\mathcal{G}_t$ while $\mathbb{E}_{\tau_i}$ denotes the conditional risk-neutral expectation given the stopped filtration $\mathcal{G}_{\tau_i}$. Moreover, we exclude the possibility of simultaneous defaults for simplicity and define the time of the first default event among the two parties as the stopping time:

$$\tau \triangleq (\tau_I \wedge \tau_C)$$

In the sequel, we adopt the view of the investor and consider the cash flows and consequences of the deal from his perspective. In other words, when we price the deal we obtain the value of the position to the investor. As we will see, with funding risk this price will often not just be the value of the deal to the counterparty with opposite sign.

The gist of the valuation framework is conceptually simple and rests neatly on the classical finance disciplines of risk-neutral pricing and discounting cash flows. When a dealer enters into a derivatives deal with a client, a number of cash flows are exchanged, and just like valuation of any other financial claim, discounting these cash in- or outflows gives us a price of the deal. Postcrisis market practice distinguishes four different types of cash flow streams occurring once a trading position has been entered: (i) cash flows coming directly from the derivatives contract such as payoffs, coupons, dividends, and so on. We denote by $\pi(t,T)$ the sum of the discounted payoff happening over the time period $(t,T]$. This is where classical derivatives pricing would usually stop and the price of a derivative contract with maturity T would be given by

$$V_t = \mathbb{E}_t[\ \pi(t,T)]$$

This price assumes no credit risk of the parties involved and no funding risk of the trade. However, present-day market practice requires the price to be adjusted by taking further cash flow transactions into account: (ii) cash flows required by collateral margining. If the deal is collateralized, cash flows happen in order to maintain a collateral account that in the case of default will be used to cover any losses. $\gamma(t,T;C)$ is the sum of the discounted margining costs over the period $(t,T]$ with C denoting the collateral account. (iii) Cash flows exchanged once a default event has occurred. We let $\theta_\tau(C,\epsilon)$ denote the on-default cash flow with ϵ being the residual value of the claim traded at default. Finally, (iv) cash flows required for funding the deal. We denote the sum of the discounted funding costs over the period $(t,T]$ by $\varphi(t,T;F)$ with F being the cash account needed for funding the deal. Collecting the terms we obtain a consistent price $\overline{V}$ of a derivative deal taking into account counterparty credit risk, margining costs, and funding costs:

$$\overline{V}_t(C,F) = \mathbb{E}_t[\ \pi(t,T\wedge\tau) + \gamma(t,T\wedge\tau;C) + \varphi(t,T\wedge\tau;F) + \mathbf{1}_{\{t<\tau<T\}} D(t,\tau)\theta_\tau(C,\epsilon)] \tag{21.1}$$

where $D(t,\tau)$ is the risk-free discount factor.

By using a risk-neutral valuation approach, we see that only the payout needs to be adjusted under counterparty credit and funding risk. In the following paragraphs, we expand the terms of 21.1 and carefully discuss how to compute them.

21.2.1 Trading under Collateralization and Closeout Netting

The ISDA master agreement is the most commonly used framework for full and flexible documentation of OTC derivative transactions and is published by the ISDA (2009). Once agreed between two parties, the master agreement sets out standard terms that apply to all deals entered into between those parties. The ISDA master agreement lists two tools to mitigate counterparty credit risk: *collateralization* and *closeout netting*. Collateralization of a deal means that the party which is out-of-the-money is required to postcollateral – usually cash, government securities, or highly rated bonds – corresponding to the amount payable by that party in the case of a default event. The credit support annex (CSA) to the ISDA master agreement defines the rules under which the collateral is posted or transferred between counterparties. Closeout netting means that in the case of default all transactions with the counterparty under the ISDA master agreement are consolidated into a single net obligation, which then forms the basis for any recovery settlements.

21.2.1.1 Collateralization Collateralization of a deal usually happens according to a margining procedure. Such a procedure involves that both parties postcollateral amounts to or withdraw amounts from the collateral account C according to their current exposure on pre-fixed dates $\{t_1,\cdots,t_n=T\}$ during the life of the deal, typically daily. Let α_i be the year fraction between t_i and t_{i+1}. The terms of the margining procedure may, furthermore, include independent amounts, minimum transfer amounts, thresholds, and so on, as described in Brigo et al. (2011a). However, here we adopt a general description of the margining procedure that does not rely on the particular terms chosen by the parties.

We consider a collateral account C held by the investor. Moreover, we assume that the investor is the collateral taker when $C_t>0$ and the collateral provider when $C_t<0$. The CSA ensures that the collateral taker remunerates the account C at an accrual rate. If the investor is collateral taker, he remunerates the collateral account by the accrual rate $c_t^+(T)$, while if he is the collateral provider, the counterparty remunerates the account at the rate $c_t^-(T)$.[1] The effective accrual collateral rate $\tilde{c}_t(T)$ is defined as

$$\tilde{c}_t(T) \triangleq c_t^-(T)\mathbf{1}_{\{C_t<0\}} + c_t^+(T)\mathbf{1}_{\{C_t>0\}} \tag{21.2}$$

To fix ideas, let us resort to a toy example.

Collateral Example. Suppose we are at time t_1 during the trade of an equity return swap, and that the swap value is negative now with a mark to market equal to \$2M (US \$2 million) in favor of our counterparty. In this case we have $C_{t_1} = -\$2M$ in the collateral account, posted by us in the past margining activity. Since $C_{t_1} = -\$2M < 0$, we receive collateral interest c^-, say 1% annually, on this. With simple compounding we will receive $1\% \times \$2M \times 1/250 = \$80$ on this day. Now time moves to the next day at $t_2 = t_1 + 1/250$, the market swings heavily, the mark to market turns around and goes to $+\$2M$ to us, or $-\$2M$ for the counterparty, so that we expect to receive \$2M in collateral while we take back the amount we had posted previously from the collateral account. As we receive collateral, $C_{t_2} = \$2M$, we now have to pay interest c^+ to the counterparty, say 1.2% annually, so that we pay $1.2\% \times \$2M \times 1/250 = \$96$ as interest over the next day. Clearly we see that the asymmetry of rates makes the interest on collateral posted or received on an opposite mark to market not symmetric. We will return to this example later on.

More generally, to understand the cash flows originating from collateralization of the deal, let us consider the consequences of the margining procedure to the investor. At the first margin date, say t_1, the investor opens the account and posts collateral if he is out-of-the-money, that is, if $C_{t_1} < 0$, which means that the counterparty is the collateral taker. On each of the following margin dates t_k, the investor posts collateral according to his exposure as long as $C_{t_k} < 0$. As collateral taker, the counterparty pays interest on the collateral at the accrual rate $c_{t_k}^-(t_{k+1})$ between the following margin dates t_k and t_{k+1}. We assume that interest accrued on the collateral is saved into the account and thereby directly included in the margining procedure and the closeout. Finally, if $C_{t_n} < 0$ on the last margin date t_n, the investor closes the collateral account given no default event has occurred in between. Similarly, for positive values of the collateral account, the investor is instead the collateral taker, and the counterparty faces corresponding cash flows at each margin date. If we sum up all the discounted margining cash flows of the investor and the counterparty, we obtain

$$\gamma(t, T \wedge \tau; C) \triangleq \sum_{k=1}^{n-1} \mathbf{1}_{\{t \le t_k < (T \wedge \tau)\}} D(t, t_k) C_{t_k} \left(1 - \frac{P_{t_k}(t_{k+1})}{P_{t_k}^{\tilde{c}}(t_{k+1})}\right) \tag{21.3}$$

with the zero-coupon bond $P_t^{\tilde{c}}(T) \triangleq [1 + (T-t)\tilde{c}_t(T)]^{-1}$ and the risk-free zero-coupon bond, related to the risk-free rate r, given by $P_t(T)$. If we adopt a first-order expansion (for small c and r), we can approximate

$$\gamma(t, T \wedge \tau; C) \approx \sum_{k=1}^{n-1} \mathbf{1}_{\{t \le t_k < (T \wedge \tau)\}} D(t, t_k) C_{t_k} \alpha_k (r_{t_k}(t_{k+1}) - \tilde{c}_{t_k}(t_{k+1})) \tag{21.4}$$

where with a slight abuse of notation we call $\tilde{c}_t(T)$ and $r_t(T)$ the continuously (as opposed to simple) compounded interest rates associated with the bonds $P^{\tilde{c}}$ and P. This last expression clearly shows a cost-of-carry structure for collateral costs. If C is positive to "I," then "I" is holding collateral and will have to pay (hence the minus sign) an interest c^+, while receiving the natural growth r for cash, since we are in a risk-neutral world. In the opposite case, if "I" posts collateral, C is negative to "I" and "I" receives interest c^- while paying the risk-free rate, as should happen when one shorts cash in a risk-neutral world.

A crucial role in collateral procedures is played by rehypothecation. We discuss rehypothecation and its inherent liquidity risk in the following.

21.2.1.2 Rehypothecation Often the CSA grants the collateral taker relatively unrestricted use of the collateral for his liquidity and trading needs until it is returned to the collateral provider. Effectively, the practice of rehypothecation lowers the costs of remuneration of the provided collateral. However, while without rehypothecation the collateral provider can expect to get any excess collateral returned after honoring the amount payable on the deal, if rehypothecation is allowed the collateral provider runs the risk of losing a fraction or all of the excess collateral in case of default on the collateral taker's part.

We denote the recovery fraction on the rehypothecated collateral by R_I' when the investor is the collateral taker and by R_C' when the counterparty is the collateral taker. The general recovery fraction on the market value of the deal that the investor receives in the case of default of the counterparty is denoted by R_C, while R_I is the recovery fraction received by the counterparty if the

[1] We stress the slight abuse of notation here: a plus and minus sign does not indicate that the rates are positive or negative parts of some other rate, but instead it tells which rate is used to accrue interest on the collateral according to the sign of the collateral account.

investor defaults. The collateral provider typically has precedence over other creditors of the defaulting party in getting back any excess capital, which means $R_I \leq R'_I \leq 1$ and $R_C \leq R'_C \leq 1$. If no rehypothecation is allowed and the collateral is kept safe in a segregated account, we have that $R'_I = R'_C = 1$.

Collateral Example (Continued). As in our previous case, suppose we have posted \$2*M* in the collateral account and we receive 1% annual interest from the counterparty. If the counterparty can rehypothecate collateral, they can use this collateral and post it in another trade and gain interest on that. This will offset the \$80 daily cost they pay us and ease their funding costs. Clearly we may also like to rehypothecate collateral when we receive it for the same reason. Suppose however that the mark to market moves in our favor at t_2 as in the previous example to +\$2*M*. We move to t_2 but before the counterparty may post \$2*M* collateral it defaults. This is the worst case. Not only we face a loss on our mark to market, since there is no collateral in the account to cover our loss, but also when we go to the account to take back at least the collateral we posted the previous day, we find that we can only get a recovery of that since the counterparty had rehypothecated our collateral and has now defaulted. We may only receive a recovery on that collateral. If the recovery rate R'_C is 20%, we will receive back only 20% × \$2*M*, namely, \$400, 000, losing \$2*M* on the mark to market of today and \$1.6*M* on the collateral posted yesterday.

21.2.1.3 Closeout Netting In case of default all terminated transactions under the ISDA master agreement with a given counterparty are netted and consolidated into a single claim. This also includes any posted collateral to back the transactions. In this context, the closeout amount plays a central role in calculating the on-default cash flows. The closeout amount is the costs or losses that the surviving party incurs when replacing the terminated deal with an economic equivalent. Clearly, the size of these costs will depend on which party survives so we define the closeout amount as

$$\epsilon_\tau \triangleq \mathbf{1}_{\{\tau=\tau_C<\tau_I\}}\epsilon_{I,\tau} + \mathbf{1}_{\{\tau=\tau_I<\tau_C\}}\epsilon_{C,\tau} \tag{21.5}$$

where $\epsilon_{I,\tau}$ is the closeout amount on the counterparty's default priced at time τ by the investor and $\epsilon_{C,\tau}$ is the closeout amount if the investor defaults. Recall that we always consider the deal from the investor's viewpoint in terms of the sign of the cash flows involved. This means that if the closeout amount $\epsilon_{I,\tau}$ as measured by the investor is positive, the investor is a creditor of the counterparty, while if it is negative, the investor is a debtor of the counterparty. Analogously, if the closeout amount $\epsilon_{C,\tau}$ to the counterparty but viewed from the investor is positive, the investor is a creditor of the counterparty, and if it is negative, the investor is a debtor to the counterparty.

We note that the ISDA documentation is, in fact, not very specific in terms of how to actually calculate the closeout amount. Since 2009 ISDA has allowed for the possibility to switch from a risk-free closeout rule to a replacement rule that includes the DVA of the surviving party in the recoverable amount. Parker and McGarry (2009) and Weeber and Robson (2009) show how a wide range of values of the closeout amount can be produced within the terms of ISDA. We refer to Brigo et al. (2011a) and the references therein for further discussions on these issues. Here, we adopt the approach of Brigo et al. (2011a) listing the cash flows of all the various scenarios that can occur if default happens. We will net the exposure against the predefault value of the collateral $C_{\tau-}$ and treat any remaining collateral as an unsecured claim.

If we aggregate all these cash flows and the predefault value of collateral account, we reach the following expression for the on-default cash flow:

$$\begin{aligned}\theta_\tau(C,\epsilon) \triangleq\ & \mathbf{1}_{\{\tau=\tau_C<\tau_I\}}(\epsilon_{I,\tau} - \text{L}_{\text{GD}_C}(\epsilon^+_{I,\tau} - C^+_{\tau-})^+ - \text{L}_{\text{GD}}'_C(\epsilon^-_{I,\tau} - C^-_{\tau-})^+) \\ & +\mathbf{1}_{\{\tau=\tau_I<\tau_C\}}(\epsilon_{C,\tau} - \text{L}_{\text{GD}_I}(\epsilon^-_{C,\tau} - C^-_{\tau-})^- - \text{L}_{\text{GD}}'_I(\epsilon^+_{C,\tau} - C^+_{\tau-})^-)\end{aligned} \tag{21.6}$$

We use the short-hand notation $\mathcal{X}^+ := \max(\mathcal{X}, 0)$ and $\mathcal{X}^- := \min(\mathcal{X}, 0)$, and define the loss given default as $\text{L}_{\text{GD}_C} \triangleq 1 - R_C$ and the collateral loss given default as $\text{L}_{\text{GD}}'_C \triangleq 1 - R'_C$. If both parties agree on the exposure, namely, $\epsilon_{I,\tau} = \epsilon_{C,\tau} = \epsilon_\tau$, when we take the risk-neutral expectation in 21.1, we see that the price of the discounted on-default cash flow,

$$\mathbb{E}_t[\mathbf{1}_{\{t<\tau<T\}}D(t,\tau)\theta_\tau(C,\epsilon)] = \mathbb{E}_t[\mathbf{1}_{\{t<\tau<T\}}D(t,\tau)\ \epsilon_\tau)] - \text{C}_{\text{VA}}(t,T;C) + \text{D}_{\text{VA}}(t,T;C), \tag{21.7}$$

is the present value of the closeout amount reduced by the positive collateralized CVA and DVA terms

$$\Pi_{CVAcoll}(s) = (\text{L}_{\text{GD}_C}(\epsilon^+_{I,s} - C^+_{s-})^+ + \text{L}_{\text{GD}}'_C(\epsilon^-_{I,s} - C^-_{s-})^+) \geq 0$$

$$\Pi_{DVAcoll}(s) = -(\text{L}_{\text{GD}_I}(\epsilon^-_{C,s} - C^-_{s-})^- + \text{L}_{\text{GD}}'_I(\epsilon^+_{C,s} - C^+_{s-})^-) \geq 0$$

and

$$\begin{aligned} \text{CVA}(t, T; C) &\triangleq \mathbb{E}_t[\mathbf{1}_{\{\tau=\tau_C<T\}} D(t, \tau)\Pi_{CVAcoll}(\tau)] \\ \text{DVA}(t, T; C) &\triangleq \mathbb{E}_t[\mathbf{1}_{\{\tau=\tau_I<T\}} D(t, \tau)\Pi_{DVAcoll}(\tau)] \end{aligned} \tag{21.8}$$

Also, observe that if rehypothecation of the collateral is not allowed, the terms multiplied by LGD'_C and LGD'_I drops out of the CVA and DVA calculations.

The above expressions contain a lot of positive and negative part operators, or more colloquially "option terms." This is because, depending on rehypothecation and on the recovery assumption, one may need to check the sign of the exposure and of the collateral account before netting them. Take, for example, the term $(\epsilon^+_{I,s} - C^+_{s-})^+$. This means that when the counterparty defaults first, at their default time we check the exposure sign and the collateral sign. If both are positive, and this is checked by the internal positive parts on ϵ and C, meaning that we were expecting a payment and that collateral was in the account as a guarantee for that, we then check the difference between exposure and collateral at default. If this is positive, and this is the external positive part outside round brackets, then collateral is smaller than exposure and is not enough to cover our loss. We then face a loss on the part of exposure not covered by collateral, namely, $(\epsilon^+_{I,s} - C^+_{s-})^+$, except for a recovery rate. Other terms derivations are similar and are given in full detail, for example, in Pallavicini, Perini, and Brigo (2011).

21.2.2 Trading under Funding Risk

The hedging strategy that perfectly replicates the no-arbitrage price of a derivative is formed by a position in cash and a position in a portfolio of hedging instruments. When we talk about a derivative deal's funding, we essentially mean the cash position that is required as part of the hedging strategy, and with funding costs we refer to the costs of maintaining this cash position. If we denote the cash account by F and the risky-asset account by H, we get

$$\overline{V}_t = F_t + H_t$$

In the classical Black–Scholes–Merton theory, the risky part H of the hedge would be a delta position in the underlying stock, whereas the riskless part F would be a position in the risk-free bank account. If the deal is collateralized, the margining procedure is included in the deal definition insuring that funding of the collateral is automatically taken into account. Moreover, if rehypothecation is allowed for the collateralized deal, the collateral taker can use the posted collateral as a funding source and thereby reduce or maybe even eliminate the costs of funding the deal. Thus, we have the following two definitions of the funding account: If rehypothecation of the posted collateral is allowed,

$$F_t \triangleq \overline{V}_t - C_t - H_t \tag{21.9}$$

and if such rehypothecation is forbidden, we have

$$F_t \triangleq \overline{V}_t - H_t. \tag{21.10}$$

By implication of 21.9 and 21.10, it is obvious that if the funding account $F_t > 0$, the dealer needs to borrow cash to establish the hedging strategy at time t. Correspondingly, if the funding account $F_t < 0$, the hedging strategy requires the dealer to invest surplus cash. Specifically, we assume the dealer enters a funding position on a discrete time-grid $\{t_1, \cdots, t_m\}$ during the life of the deal. Given two adjacent funding times t_j and t_{j+1}, for $1 \le j \le m-1$, the dealer enters a position in cash equal to F_{t_j} at time t_j. At time t_{j+1} the dealer redeems the position again and either returns the cash to the funder if it was a long cash position and pays funding costs on the borrowed cash, or he gets the cash back if it was a short cash position and receives funding benefits as interest on the invested cash. We assume that these funding costs and benefits are determined at the start date of each funding period and charged at the end of the period.

Without any loss of generality, the contracts used by the investor to fund the deal can be introduced as adapted price processes. Let $P^{f^+}_t(T)$ represent the price of a borrowing contract measurable at t where the dealer pays one unit of cash at maturity $T > t$, and let $P^{f^-}_t(T)$ be the price of a lending contract where the dealer receives one unit of cash at maturity. Moreover, the corresponding accrual rates are given by

$$f^{\pm}_t(T) \triangleq \frac{1}{T-t}\left(\frac{1}{P^{f^{\pm}}_t(T)} - 1\right)$$

In other words, if the hedging strategy of the deal requires borrowing cash, this can be done at the funding rate f^+ while surplus cash can be invested at the lending rate f^-. We define the effective funding rate $\tilde{f}_t$ faced by the dealer as

$$\tilde{f}_t(T) \triangleq f_t^-(T)\mathbf{1}_{\{F_t<0\}} + f_t^+(T)\mathbf{1}_{\{F_t>0\}} \tag{21.11}$$

Following this, the sum of discounted cash flows from funding the hedging strategy during the life of the deal is equal to

$$\varphi(t, T\wedge\tau; F) \triangleq \sum_{j=1}^{m-1} \mathbf{1}_{\{t\leq t_j<(T\wedge\tau)\}} D(t,t_j) F_{t_j}\left(1 - \frac{P_{t_j}(t_{j+1})}{P_{t_j}^{\tilde{f}}(t_{j+1})}\right) \tag{21.12}$$

where the zero-coupon bond corresponding to the effective funding rate is defined as $P_t^{\tilde{f}}(T) \triangleq [1 + (T-t)\tilde{f}_t(T)]^{-1}$. This is, strictly speaking, a discounted payout, and the funding cost or benefit at time t is obtained by taking the risk-neutral expectation of the above cash flows.

As before with collateral costs, we may rewrite the cash flows for funding as a first-order approximation in continuously compounded rates $\tilde{f}$ and r associated to the relevant bonds. We obtain

$$\varphi(t, T\wedge\tau; F) \approx \sum_{j=1}^{m-1} \mathbf{1}_{\{t\leq t_j<(T\wedge\tau)\}} D(t,t_j) F_{t_j}\alpha_j(r_{t_j}(t_{j+1}) - \tilde{f}_{t_j}(t_{j+1})) \tag{21.13}$$

We should also mention that, occasionally, we may include the effects of repo markets or stock lending in our framework. In general, we may borrow/lend the cash needed to establish H from/to our treasury, and we may then use the risky asset in H for repo or stock lending/borrowing in the market. This means that we could include the funding costs and benefits coming from this use of the risky asset. In this paper, we assume that the bank Treasury automatically recognizes this benefit/cost to us at the same rate $\tilde{f}$ used for cash, but for a more general analysis involving repo rate $\tilde{h}$, see, for example, Pallavicini, Perini, and Brigo (2012). See Section 21.5 for a quick summary.

The particular positions entered by the dealer to either borrow or invest cash according to the sign and size of the funding account depend on the bank's liquidity policy. In the following we discuss two possible cases: one where the dealer can fund at rates set by the bank's treasury department, and another where the dealer goes to the market directly and funds his trades at the prevailing market rates. As a result, the funding rates and therefore the funding effect on the price of a derivative deal depend intimately on the chosen liquidity policy.

21.2.2.1 Treasury Funding If the dealer funds the hedge through the bank's treasury department, the treasury determines the funding rates $f^\pm$ faced by the dealer, often assuming average funding costs and benefits across all deals. This leads to two curves as functions of maturity; one for borrowing funds f^+ and one for lending funds f^-. After entering a funding position F_{t_j} at time t_j, the dealer faces the following discounted cash flow:

$$\Phi_j(t_j, t_{j+1}; F) \triangleq -N_{t_j} D(t_j, t_{j+1})$$

with

$$N_{t_j} \triangleq \frac{F_{t_j}^-}{P_{t_j}^{f^-}(t_{j+1})} + \frac{F_{t_j}^+}{P_{t_j}^{f^+}(t_{j+1})}$$

Under this liquidity policy, the treasury – and not the dealer himself – is in charge of DVAs due to funding-related positions. Also, being entities of the same institution, both the dealer and the treasury disappear in case of default of the institution without any further cash flows being exchanged, and we can neglect the effects of funding in this case. So, when default risk is considered, this leads to following definition of the funding cash flows:

$$\overline{\Phi}_j(t_j, t_{j+1}; F) \triangleq \mathbf{1}_{\{\tau>t_j\}} \Phi_j(t_j, t_{j+1}; F)$$

Thus, the risk-neutral price of the cash flows due to the funding positions entered at time t_j is

$$\mathbb{E}_{t_j}\left[\overline{\Phi}_j(t_j, t_{j+1}; F)\right] = -\mathbf{1}_{\{\tau>t_j\}}\left(F_{t_j}^- \frac{P_{t_j}(t_{j+1})}{P_{t_j}^{f^-}(t_{j+1})} + F_{t_j}^+ \frac{P_{t_j}(t_{j+1})}{P_{t_j}^{f^+}(t_{j+1})}\right)$$

If we consider a sequence of such funding operations at each time t_j during the life of the deal, we can define the sum of cash flows coming from all the borrowing and lending positions opened by the dealer to hedge the trade up to the first default event:

$$\begin{aligned}\varphi(t, T \wedge \tau; F) &\triangleq \sum_{j=1}^{m-1} \mathbf{1}_{\{t \leq t_j < (T\wedge\tau)\}} D(t, t_j)(F_{t_j} + \mathbb{E}_{t_j}[\, \overline{\Phi}_j(t_j, t_{j+1}; F)\,]) \\ &= \sum_{j=1}^{m-1} \mathbf{1}_{\{t \leq t_j < (T\wedge\tau)\}} D(t, t_j) \left(F_{t_j} - F^-_{t_j} \frac{P_{t_j}(t_{j+1})}{P^{f^-}_{t_j}(t_{j+1})} - F^+_{t_j} \frac{P_{t_j}(t_{j+1})}{P^{f^+}_{t_j}(t_{j+1})} \right) \end{aligned} \quad (21.14)$$

In terms of the effective funding rate, this expression collapses to 21.12.

21.2.2.2 Market Funding If the dealer funds the hedging strategy in the market – and not through the bank's treasury – the funding rates are determined by prevailing market conditions and are often deal specific. This means that the rate f^+ the dealer can borrow funds at may be different from the rate f^- at which funds can be invested. Moreover, these rates may differ across deals depending on the deals' notional, maturity structures, dealer–client relationship, and so forth. Similar to the liquidity policy of treasury funding, we assume a deal's funding operations are closed down in the case of default. Furthermore, as the dealer now operates directly on the market, he needs to include a DVA due to his funding positions when he marks to market his trading books. For simplicity, we assume that the funder in the market is default free so no funding CVA needs to be accounted for. The discounted cash flow from the borrowing or lending position between two adjacent funding times t_j and t_{j+1} is given by

$$\begin{aligned}\overline{\Phi}_j(t_j, t_{j+1}; F) \triangleq\; & \mathbf{1}_{\{\tau > t_j\}} \mathbf{1}_{\{\tau_I > t_{j+1}\}} \Phi_j(t_j, t_{j+1}; F) \\ & - \mathbf{1}_{\{\tau > t_j\}} \mathbf{1}_{\{\tau_I < t_{j+1}\}} (\mathrm{L{\scriptstyle GD}}_I \epsilon^-_{F,\tau_I} - \epsilon_{F,\tau_I}) D(t_j, \tau_I)\end{aligned}$$

where $\epsilon_{F,t}$ is the closeout amount calculated by the funder on the dealer's default

$$\epsilon_{F,\tau_I} \triangleq -N_{t_j} P_{\tau_I}(t_{j+1})$$

To price this funding cash flow, we take the risk-neutral expectation

$$\mathbb{E}_{t_j}[\, \overline{\Phi}_j(t_j, t_{j+1}; F)\,] = -\mathbf{1}_{\{\tau > t_j\}} \left(F^-_{t_j} \frac{P_{t_j}(t_{j+1})}{P^{f^-}_{t_j}(t_{j+1})} + F^+_{t_j} \frac{P_{t_j}(t_{j+1})}{\overline{P}^{f^+}_{t_j}(t_{j+1})} \right)$$

Here, the zero-coupon funding bond $\overline{P}^{f^+}_t(T)$ for borrowing cash is adjusted for the dealer's credit risk

$$\overline{P}^{f^+}_t(T) \triangleq \frac{P^{f^+}_t(T)}{\mathbb{E}^T_t\left[\mathrm{L{\scriptstyle GD}}_I \mathbf{1}_{\{\tau_I > T\}} + R_I\right]}$$

where the expectation on the right-hand side is taken under the T-forward measure. Naturally, since the seniority could be different, one might assume a different recovery rate on the funding position than on the derivatives deal itself (see Crépey (2011)). Extensions to this case are straightforward.

Next, summing all discounted cash-flows from the sequence of funding operations through the life of the deal, we get a new expression for φ that is identical to (21.14), where the $\overline{P}^{f^+}_t(T)$ in the denominator is replaced by_ $P^{f^+}_t(T)$. To avoid cumbersome notation, we will not explicitly write $\overline{P}^{f^+}$ in the sequel, but just keep in mind that when the dealer funds directly in the market then P^{f^+} needs to be adjusted for funding DVA. Thus, in terms of the effective funding rate, we obtain 21.12.

21.3 GENERAL PRICING EQUATION UNDER CREDIT, COLLATERAL, AND FUNDING

In the previous section, we analyzed the discounted cash flows of a derivative deal, and we developed a framework for consistent valuation of such deals under collateralized counterparty credit and funding risk. The arbitrage-free pricing framework is captured in the following theorem.

Theorem 1 (General pricing equation) *The consistent arbitrage-free price $\overline{V}_t(C,F)$ of collateralized OTC derivative deals with counterparty credit risk, and funding costs takes the form*

$$\overline{V}_t(C,F) = \mathbb{E}_t[\ \pi(t,T\wedge\tau) + \gamma(t,T\wedge\tau;C) + \varphi(t,T\wedge\tau;F) + \mathbf{1}_{\{t<\tau<T\}}D(t,\tau)\theta_\tau(C,\epsilon)] \tag{21.15}$$

where

1. *$\pi(t,T\wedge\tau)$ is the discounted cash flows from the contract's payoff structure up to the first default event.*
2. *$\gamma(t,T\wedge\tau;C)$ is the discounted cash flows from the collateral margining procedure up to the first default event and is defined in 21.3.*
3. *$\varphi(t,T\wedge\tau;F)$ is the discounted cash flows from funding the hedging strategy up to the first default event and is defined in 21.12.*
4. *$\theta_\tau(C,\epsilon)$ is the on-default cash flow with closeout amount ϵ and is defined in 21.6.*

If funding and collateral margining costs are discarded, while collateral is retained for loss reduction at default, this pricing equation collapses to the formula derived in Brigo et al. (2011a) for the price of a derivative under bilateral counterparty credit risk. If further collateral guarantees are dropped, the formula reduces to the bilateral credit valuation formula in Brigo and Capponi (2008).

While the pricing equation is conceptually clear – we simply take the expectation of the sum of all discounted cash flows of the deal under the risk-neutral measure – solving the equation poses a recursive, nonlinear problem. The future paths of the effective funding rate $\tilde{f}$ depend on the future signs of the funding account F, that is, whether we need to borrow or lend cash on each future funding date. At the same time, through the relations 21.9 and 21.10, the future sign and size of the funding account F depend on the adjusted price $\overline{V}$ of the deal, which is the quantity we are trying to compute in the first place. One crucial implication of this recursive structure of the pricing problem is the fact that FVA is generally not just an additive adjustment term, in contrast to CVA and DVA. More importantly, the conjecture identifying the DVA of a deal with its funding is not appropriate in general. Only in the unrealistic setting where the dealer can fund an uncollateralized trade at equal borrowing and lending rates, that is, $f^+ = f^-$, do we achieve the additive structure often assumed by practitioners. If the trade is collateralized, we need to impose even further restrictions as to how the collateral is linked to price of the trade $\overline{V}$.

Remark 1 (The law of one price.) On the theoretical side, the pricing equation shakes the foundation of the celebrated Law of One Price prevailing in classical derivatives pricing. Clearly, if we assume no funding costs, the dealer and counterparty agree on the price of the deal as both parties can – at least theoretically – observe the credit risk of each other through CDS contracts traded in the market and the relevant market risks, thus agreeing on CVA and DVA. In contrast, introducing funding costs, they will not agree on the FVA for the deal due to asymmetric information. The parties cannot observe each others' liquidity policies nor their respective funding costs associated with a particular deal. As a result, the value of a deal position will not generally be the same to the counterparty as to the dealer just with opposite sign. In principle, this should mean that the dealer and the counterparty would never close the trade, but in practice trades are executed as a simple consequence of the fundamental forces of supply and demand. Nevertheless, among dealers it is the general belief that funding costs were one of the main factors driving the bid–ask spreads wider during the recent financial crisis.

Finally, as we adopt a risk-neutral valuation framework, we implicitly assume the existence of a risk-free interest rate. Indeed, since the valuation adjustments are included as additional cash flows and not as ad hoc spreads, all the cash flows are discounted by the risk-free discount factor $D(t,T)$ in 21.15. Nevertheless, the risk-free rate is merely an instrumental variable of the general pricing equation. We clearly distinguish market rates from the theoretical risk-free rate avoiding the false claim that the overnight rates (e.g., EONIA) are risk free. In fact, as we will show in continuous time, if the dealer funds the hedging strategy of the trade through cash accounts available to him – whether as rehypothecated collateral or funds from the treasury, repo market, and so on – the risk-free rate vanishes from the pricing equation.

21.3.1 Discrete-Time Solution

Our purpose here is to turn the recursive pricing equation 21.15 into a set of iterative equations that can be solved by least-squares Monte Carlo methods. These methods are already standard in CVA and DVA calculations (Brigo and Pallavicini, 2007). To this end, we introduce the auxiliary function

$$\overline{\pi}(t_j,t_{j+1};C) \triangleq \pi(t_j,t_{j+1}\wedge\tau) + \gamma(t_j,t_{j+1}\wedge\tau;C) + \mathbf{1}_{\{t_j<\tau<t_{j+1}\}}D(t_j,\tau)\theta_\tau(C,\epsilon) \tag{21.16}$$

which defines the cash flows of the deal occurring between time t_j and t_{j+1} adjusted for collateral margining costs and default risks. We stress the fact that the closeout amount used for calculating the on-default cash flow still refers to a deal with maturity T. If we then solve pricing equation 21.15 at each funding date t_j in the time-grid $\{t_1, \cdots, t_n = T\}$, we obtain the deal price $\overline{V}$ at time t_j as a function of the deal price on the next consecutive funding date t_{j+1}

$$\overline{V}_{t_j} = \mathbb{E}_{t_j}\left[\overline{V}_{t_{j+1}} D(t_j, t_{j+1})\right] + \overline{\pi}(t_j, t_{j+1}; C) + \mathbf{1}_{\{\tau > t_j\}}\left(F_{t_j} - F^-_{t_j}\frac{P_{t_j}(t_{j+1})}{P^{f^-}_{t_j}(t_{j+1})} - F^+_{t_j}\frac{P_{t_j}(t_{j+1})}{P^{f^+}_{t_j}(t_{j+1})}\right)$$

where, by definition, $\overline{V}_{t_n} \triangleq 0$ on the final date t_n. Recall the definitions of the funding account in 21.9 if no rehypothecation of collateral is allowed and in 21.10 if rehypothecation is permitted, we can then solve the above equation for the positive and negative parts of the funding account. The outcome of this exercise is a discrete-time iterative solution of the recursive pricing equation, provided in the following theorem.

Theorem 2 (Discrete-Time solution of the general pricing equation) *We may solve the full recursive pricing equation in Theorem 1 as a set of backward-iterative equations on the time-grid* $\{t_1, \cdots, t_n = T\}$ *with* $\overline{V}_{t_n} \triangleq 0$*. For* $\tau < t_j$*, we have*

$$\overline{V}_{t_j} = 0$$

while for $\tau > t_j$*, we have*

(i) If rehypothecation is forbidden:

$$(\overline{V}_{t_j} - H_{t_j})^{\pm} = P^{\tilde{f}}_{t_j}(t_{j+1})\left(\mathbb{E}^{t_{j+1}}_{t_j}\left[\overline{V}_{t_{j+1}} + \frac{\overline{\pi}(t_j, t_{j+1}; C) - H_{t_j}}{D(t_j, t_{j+1})}\right]\right)^{\pm}$$

(ii) If rehypothecation is allowed:

$$(\overline{V}_{t_j} - C_{t_j} - H_{t_j})^{\pm} = P^{\tilde{f}}_{t_j}(t_{j+1})\left(\mathbb{E}^{t_{j+1}}_{t_j}\left[\overline{V}_{t_{j+1}} + \frac{\overline{\pi}(t_j, t_{j+1}; C) - C_{t_j} - H_{t_j}}{D(t_j, t_{j+1})}\right]\right)^{\pm}$$

where the expectations are taken under the $\mathbb{Q}^{t_{j+1}}$ *forward measure.*

The $\pm$ sign in the theorem is supposed to stress the fact that the sign of the funding account, which determines the effective funding rate, depends on the sign of the conditional expectation. Further intuition may be gained by going to continuous time, which is the case we will now turn to.

21.3.2 Continuous-Time Solution

Let us consider a continuous-time approximation of the general pricing equation. This implies that collateral margining, funding, and hedging strategies are executed in continuous time. Moreover, we assume that rehypothecation is allowed, but similar results hold if this is not the case. By taking the time limit, we have the following expressions for the discounted cash flow streams of the deal:

$$\pi(t, T \wedge \tau) = \int_t^{T\wedge\tau} \pi(s, s + ds) D(t, s)$$

$$\gamma(t, T \wedge \tau; C) = \int_t^{T\wedge\tau} (r_s - \tilde{c}_s) C_s D(t, s) ds$$

$$\varphi(t, T \wedge \tau; F) = \int_t^{T\wedge\tau} (r_s - \tilde{f}_s) F_s D(t, s) ds$$

whereas before $\pi(t, t + dt)$ is the payoff coupon process of the derivative contract and r_t is the risk-free rate. These equations can also be immediately derived by looking at the approximations given in Equations 21.4 and 21.13.

Then, putting all the above terms together with the on-default cash flow as in Theorem 1, the recursive pricing equation yields

$$\begin{aligned}\overline{V}_t = & \int_t^T \mathbb{E}_t\,[(\mathbf{1}_{\{s<\tau\}}\pi(s,s+ds) + \mathbf{1}_{\{\tau\in ds\}}\theta_s(C,\epsilon))D(t,s)] \\ & + \int_t^T \mathbb{E}_t\,[\mathbf{1}_{\{s<\tau\}}(r_s - \tilde{c}_s)C_s D(t,s)]ds \\ & + \int_t^T \mathbb{E}_t\,[\mathbf{1}_{\{s<\tau\}}(r_s - \tilde{f}_s)F_s]D(t,s)ds \end{aligned} \tag{21.17}$$

By recalling Equation 21.7, we can write the following.

Proposition 3 *The value $\overline{V}_t$ of the claim under credit gap risk, collateral, and funding costs can be written as*

$$\overline{V}_t = V_t - CVA_t + DVA_t + LVA_t + FVA_t \tag{21.18}$$

where V_t is the price of the deal when there is no credit risk, no collateral, and no funding costs; LVA is a liquidity valuation adjustment accounting for the costs/benefits of collateral margining; FVA is the funding cost/benefit of the deal hedging strategy, and CVA/DVA are the familiar credit and debit valuation adjustments after collateralization. These different adjustments can be written by rewriting Formula 21.17. One obtains

$$V_t = \int_t^T \mathbb{E}_t\{D(t,s)1_{\{\tau>s\}}[\pi(s,s+ds) + 1_{\{\tau\in ds\}}\epsilon_s]\} \tag{21.19}$$

and the valuation adjustments

$$\begin{aligned} CVA_t &= -\int_t^T \mathbb{E}\Big\{D(t,s)1_{\{\tau>s\}}[-\mathbf{1}_{\{s=\tau_C<\tau_I\}}\Pi_{CVAcoll}(s)]\Big\}du \\ DVA_t &= \int_t^T \mathbb{E}\Big\{D(t,s)1_{\{\tau>s\}}[\mathbf{1}_{\{s=\tau_I<\tau_C\}}\Pi_{DVAcoll}(s)]\Big\}du \\ LVA_t &= \int_t^T \mathbb{E}_t\{D(t,s)1_{\{\tau>s\}}(r_s - \tilde{c}_s)C_s\,ds \\ FVA_t &= \int_t^T \mathbb{E}\{D(t,s)1_{\{\tau>s\}}[(r_s - \tilde{f}_s)F_s]\}ds \end{aligned}$$

As usual, CVA and DVA are both positive, while LVA and FVA can be either positive or negative. Notice that if $\tilde{c}$ equals the risk-free rate LVA vanishes. Similarly, FVA vanishes if the funding rate $\tilde{f}$ is equal to the risk free rate.

The proof is immediate. Notice that 21.19 simplifies further under a risk-free closeout:

$$\epsilon_\tau = V_\tau$$

Indeed, in such a case the presence of τ does not alter the present value. In fact, one can show that since the unwinding at τ happens at the fair price V_τ and with recovery one, this is equivalent, in terms of valuation at time t, to valuing the whole deal:

$$V_t = \int_t^T \mathbb{E}_t\{D(t,s)\pi(s,s+ds)\}$$

Remark 2 (Separability?) As pointed out earlier and in Pallavicini, Perini, and Brigo (2011), valuation Formula 21.18 is not really splitting risk components in different terms. For example, $\tilde{f}$ needs to know future signs of F and hence future $\overline{V}$'s. Such future $\overline{V}$'s depend on all risks together and so does $\tilde{f}$. Hence interpreting the $\tilde{f}$-dependent term FVA as a pure funding adjustment is misleading. Similarly, if we adopt a replacement closeout at default where $\epsilon_\tau = \overline{V}_{\tau-}$, then the CVA and DVA terms will depend on future $\overline{V}$ and hence on all other risks as well. Therefore, CVA is no longer a pure CVA. If enforcing the above separation a posteriori after solving the total equation for $\overline{V}$, then one has to be careful in interpreting this as a real split of risks. A further point concerns the presence of the short rate r_t in the terms above. Since r is a theoretical rate with no direct market counterpart, this decomposition is not ideal. To implement the pseudodecomposition, one would have to proxy r with a real market rate, such as an overnight rate.

By recalling that $\overline{V}_t = F_t + H_t + C_t$, we may rewrite Equation 21.17 as

$$\begin{aligned}\overline{V}_t = & \int_t^T \mathbb{E}_t\left[(\mathbf{1}_{\{s<\tau\}}\pi(s,s+ds) + \mathbf{1}_{\{\tau\in ds\}}\theta_s(C,\epsilon))D(t,s)\right] \\ & + \int_t^T \mathbb{E}_t\left[\mathbf{1}_{\{s<\tau\}}(\tilde{f}_s - \tilde{c}_s)C_s D(t,s)\right]ds \\ & + \int_t^T \mathbb{E}_t\left[\mathbf{1}_{\{s<\tau\}}(r_s - \tilde{f}_s)(\overline{V}_s - H_s)D(t,s)\right]ds\end{aligned}$$

For simplicity, we now switch to the default-free market filtration $(\mathcal{F}_t)_{t\geq 0}$. This step implicitly assumes a separable structure of our complete filtration $(\mathcal{G}_t)_{t\geq 0}$. In other words, $\mathcal{G}_t$ is generated by the pure default-free market filtration $\mathcal{F}_t$ and by the filtration generated by all the relevant default times monitored up to t. We are also assuming that the basic portfolio cash flows $\pi(0,t)$ are $\mathcal{F}_t$ measurable and that default times of all parties are conditionally independent given filtration $\mathcal{F}$ (see, for example, Bielecki and Rutkowski (2002) or Brigo and Pallavicini (2014) for the full details in the present setup). We assume all needed technical conditions to be satisfied. This allows us to rewrite the previous price equation as

$$\begin{aligned}\overline{V}_t = & \mathbf{1}_{\{\tau>t\}}\int_t^T \mathbb{E}_t\left[(\pi(s,s+ds) + \lambda_s\theta_s(C,\epsilon)ds)D(t,s;r+\lambda)|\mathcal{F}\right] \\ & + \mathbf{1}_{\{\tau>t\}}\int_t^T \mathbb{E}_t\left[(\tilde{f}_s - \tilde{c}_s)C_s D(t,s;r+\lambda)|\mathcal{F}\right]ds \\ & + \mathbf{1}_{\{\tau>t\}}\int_t^T \mathbb{E}_t\left[(r_s - \tilde{f}_s)(\overline{V}_s - H_s)D(t,s;r+\lambda)|\mathcal{F}\right]ds\end{aligned}$$

where λ_t is the first-to-default intensity and the discount factor is defined as $D(t,s;\xi) \triangleq e^{-\int_t^s \xi_u du}$. We further denote $\mathbb{E}_t\,[\,\cdot|\mathcal{F}\,]$ the conditional expectation with respect to $\mathcal{F}_t$. Assuming the relevant technical conditions are satisfied, the Feynman–Kac theorem now allows us to formally write down the corresponding predefault PDE of the pricing problem. The formal proof is the same as that of Feynman–Kac for the linear case and relies on the stochastic integral term being a martingale and applying Itô's formula twice. So the first step is applying Feynman–Kac and writing the above expectation as a PDE. Once this has been done, assume that the underlying market risk factors are Markov processes with infinitesimal generator $\mathcal{L}_t$ (see, for example, Friedman (2007)), that the risk-free rate r_t is bounded, and that we have sufficient smoothness of the price function $\overline{V}$. Hence, for $\tau > t$, we get the PDE

$$(\partial_t - \tilde{f}_t - \lambda_t + \mathcal{L}_t)\overline{V}_t - (r_t - \tilde{f}_t)H_t + (\tilde{f}_t - \tilde{c}_t)C_t + \lambda_t\theta_t + \pi_t = 0 \tag{21.20}$$

with boundary condition

$$\overline{V}_T = 0 \tag{21.21}$$

where

$$\pi_t dt = \pi(t, t+dt)$$

for small dt, where the single argument in π avoids confusion on which π we are referring to, and where π_t is assumed $\mathcal{F}_t$ adapted. In Brigo and Pallavicini (2014), a BSDE derivation of the PDE is provided, avoiding the Feynman–Kac argument.

If we, furthermore, assume that the underlying risk factors are diffusions and consider delta hedging of the deal value $\overline{V}$ in continuous time, the generator $\mathcal{L}$ can be expanded in terms of first- and second-order operators:

$$\mathcal{L}_t\overline{V}_t \triangleq (\mathcal{L}_t^1 + \mathcal{L}_t^2)\overline{V}_t \triangleq r_t H_t + \mathcal{L}_t^2\overline{V}_t$$

As a result, for $\tau > t$, the pricing PDE reduces to

$$(\partial_t - \tilde{f}_t - \lambda_t + \mathcal{L}_t^{\tilde{f}})\overline{V}_t + (\tilde{f}_t - \tilde{c}_t)C_t + \lambda_t\theta_t + \pi_t = 0 \tag{21.22}$$

where $\mathcal{L}_t^{\tilde{f}}\overline{V}_t \triangleq \tilde{f}_t H_t + \mathcal{L}_t^2\overline{V}_t$. Observe that the predefault PDE no longer depends on the risk-free rate r_t. This equation may be solved numerically as in Crépey (2012a). On the other hand, if we apply the Feynman–Kac theorem again – this time going from the predefault PDE to the pricing expectation – and integrate by parts, we arrive at the following result.

Theorem 4 (Continuous-time solution of the general pricing equation) *If we assume collateral rehypothecation and delta hedging, we can solve the iterative equations of Theorem 2 in continuous time. We obtain*

$$\overline{V}_t = \int_t^T \mathbb{E}^{\tilde{f}}\{D(t,u;\tilde{f}+\lambda)[\pi_u + \lambda_u\theta_u + (\tilde{f}_u - \tilde{c}_u)C_u]|\mathcal{F}_t\}du \tag{21.23}$$

where expectations are taken under the pricing measure $\mathbb{Q}^{\tilde{f}}$ for which the underlying risk factors grow at the rate $\tilde{f}$ if no dividend is paid.

Theorem 4 decomposes the deal price $\overline{V}$ into three intuitive terms. The first term is the value of the deal cash flows discounted at funding plus credit. The second term is the price of the on-default cash flow in excess of the collateral, which includes the CVA and DVA of the deal after collateralization. The last term collects the cost of collateralization. In addition, we see that any dependence on the hedging strategy H can be dropped by taking all expectations under the pricing measure $\mathbb{Q}^{\tilde{f}}$. At this point it is very important to appreciate once again that $\tilde{f}$ depends on F and hence on V.

Remark 3 (Deal-dependent pricing measure, local risk-neutral measures). Since the pricing measure depends on $\tilde{f}$ which in turn depends on the very value $\overline{V}$ we are trying to compute, we have that the pricing measure becomes deal dependent. Every deal or portfolio has a different pricing measure.

Finally, we stress once again a very important invariance result that first appeared in Pallavicini, Perini, and Brigo (2012) and Brigo, Morini, and Pallavicini (2013).

Theorem 5 (Invariance of the Valuation Equation with Respect to the Short Rate r_t) *Equations 21.22 or 21.23 for valuation under credit, collateral, and funding costs are completely governed by market rates; there is no dependence on a risk-free rate r_t. Whichever initial process is postulated for r, the final price is invariant to it. This confirms our earlier conjecture that the risk-free rate is merely an instrumental variable of our valuation framework and we do not, in fact, need to know the value of such a rate.*

The proof is immediate by inspection.

21.4 NUMERICAL RESULTS: EXTENDING THE BLACK–SCHOLES ANALYSIS

This section provides a numerical study of the valuation framework outlined in the previous sections. We investigate the impact of funding risk on the price of a derivatives deal under default risk and collateralization. To this end, we propose a least-squares Monte Carlo algorithm inspired by the simulation methods of Carriere (1996), Longstaff and Schwartz (2001), Tilley (1993), and Tsitsiklis and Van Roy (2001) for pricing American-style options. As the purpose is to understand the fundamental implications of funding risk, we focus on relatively simple deal positions in European call options. However, the Monte Carlo method we propose below can be applied to more complex derivative contracts, including derivatives with bilateral payments.

21.4.1 Monte Carlo Algorithm

Recall the recursive structure of the general pricing equation: the deal price depends on the funding decisions, while the funding strategy depends on the future price itself. The intimate relationship among the key quantities makes the pricing problem computationally challenging.

We consider K default scenarios during the life of the deal – either obtained by simulation, bootstrapped from empirical data, or assumed in advance. For each first-to-default time τ corresponding to a default scenario, we compute the price of the deal $\overline{V}$ under collateralization, closeout netting, and funding costs. The first step of our simulation method entails simulating a large number of sample paths N of the underlying risk factors X. We simulate these paths on the time-grid $\{t_1, \cdots, t_m = T^*\}$ with step size $\Delta t = t_{j+1} - t_j$ from the assumed dynamics of the risk factors. T^* is equal to the final maturity T of the deal or the consecutive time-grid point following the first default time τ, whichever occurs first. For simplicity, we assume the time periods for funding decisions, and collateral margin payments coincide with the simulation time grid.

Given the set of simulated paths, we solve the funding strategy recursively in a dynamic programming fashion. Starting one period before T^*, we compute for each simulated path the funding decision F and the deal price $\overline{V}$ according to the set of backward-inductive equations of Theorem 2. The algorithm then proceeds recursively until time zero. Ultimately, the total price of the deal is computed as the probability-weighted average of the individual prices obtained in each of the K default scenarios.

The conditional expectations in the backward-inductive funding equations are approximated by across-path regressions based on least-squares estimation similar to Longstaff and Schwartz (2001). We regress the present value of the deal price at time t_{j+1}, the adjusted payout cash flow between t_j and t_{j+1}, the collateral account, and funding account at time t_j on basis functions ψ of realizations of the underlying risk factors at time t_j across the simulated paths. To keep the notation simple, let us assume that we are exposed to only one underlying risk factor, for example, a stock price. Extensions to higher dimensions are straightforward. Specifically, the conditional expectations in the iterative equations of Theorem 2, taken under the risk-neutral measure, are equal to

$$\mathbb{E}_{t_j}\left[\Xi_{t_j}(\overline{V}_{t_{j+1}})\right] = \theta'_{t_j}\,\psi(X_{t_j}) \tag{21.24}$$

where we have defined $\Xi_{t_j}(\overline{V}_{t_{j+1}}) \triangleq D(t_j, t_{j+1})\overline{V}_{t_{j+1}} + \overline{\pi}(t_j, t_{j+1}; C) - C_{t_j} - H_{t_j}$. Note the C_{t_j} term drops out if rehypothecation is not allowed. The usual least-squares estimator of θ is then given by

$$\hat{\theta}_{t_j} \triangleq \left[\psi(X_{t_j})\psi(X_{t_j})'\right]^{-1} \psi(X_{t_j})\, \Xi_{t_j}(\overline{V}_{t_{j+1}}) \tag{21.25}$$

Orthogonal polynomials such as Chebyshev, Hermite, Laguerre, and Legendre may all be used as basis functions for evaluating the conditional expectations. We find, however, that simple power series are quite effective and that the order of the polynomials can be kept relatively small. In fact, linear or quadratic polynomials, that is, $\psi(X_{t_j}) = (\mathbf{1}, X_{t_j}, X_{t_j}^2)'$, are often enough.

Further complexities are added, as the dealer may – realistically – decide to hedge the full deal price $\overline{V}$. Now, the hedge H itself depends on the funding strategy through $\overline{V}$, while the funding decision depends on the hedging strategy. This added recursion requires that we solve the funding and hedging strategies simultaneously. For example, if the dealer applies a delta-hedging strategy

$$H_{t_j} = \frac{\partial \overline{V}}{\partial X}_{t_j} X_{t_j} \approx \frac{\overline{V}_{t_{j+1}} - (1 + \Delta t_j \tilde{f}_{t_j})\overline{V}_{t_j}}{X_{t_{j+1}} - (1 + \Delta t_j \tilde{f}_{t_j})X_{t_j}} X_{t_j} \tag{21.26}$$

we obtain, in the case of rehypothecation, the following system of nonlinear equations

$$\begin{cases} F_{t_j} - \dfrac{P^{\tilde{f}}_{t_j}(t_{j+1})}{P_{t_j}(t_{j+1})}\, \mathbb{E}_{t_j}\left[\Xi_{t_j}(\overline{V}_{t_{j+1}})\right] = 0 \\ H_{t_j} - \dfrac{\overline{V}_{t_{j+1}} - (1 + \Delta t_j \tilde{f}_{t_j})\overline{V}_{t_j}}{X_{t_{j+1}} - (1 + \Delta t_j \tilde{f}_{t_j})X_{t_j}} X_{t_j} = 0 \\ \overline{V}_{t_j} = F_{t_j} + C_{t_j} + H_{t_j} \end{cases} \tag{21.27}$$

where all matrix operations are on an element-by-element basis. An analogous result holds when rehypothecation of the posted collateral is forbidden.

Each period and for each simulated path, we find the funding and hedging decisions by solving this system of equations, given the funding and hedging strategies for all future periods until the end of the deal. We apply a simple Newton–Raphson method to solve the system of nonlinear equations numerically, but instead of using the exact Jacobian, we approximate it by finite differences. As initial guess, we use the Black–Scholes delta position:

$$H^0_{t_j} = \Delta^{BS}_{t_j} X_{t_j}$$

The convergence is quite fast, and only a small number of iterations are needed in practice. Finally, if the dealer decides to hedge only the risk-free price of the deal, that is, the classic derivative price V, the pricing problem collapses to a much simpler one. The hedge H no longer depends on the funding decision and can be computed separately, and the numerical solution of the nonlinear equation system can be avoided altogether.

Now we move on to analyzing numerical results on the impact of funding for both a long and a short position in a European call option. Before doing so, we fully specify our modeling setup.

21.4.2 Market, Credit, and Funding Risk Specification

We assume that the underlying stock S_t evolves according to a geometric Brownian motion $dS_t = rS_t dt + \sigma S_t dW_t$ where W is a standard Brownian motion under the risk-neutral measure. The risk-free interest rate r is 100 bps, the volatility σ is 25%, and the current price of the underlying is $S_0 = 100$. The European call option is in the money and has strike $K = 80$. The maturity T of the deal is 3 years, and, in the full case, we assume that the investor delta hedges the deal according to 21.26. The usual default-free, funding-free, and collateral-free Black–Scholes price V_0 of the call option deal is given by

$$V_t = S_t\Phi(d_1(t)) - Ke^{-r(T-t)}\Phi(d_2(t)), \quad d_{1,2} = \frac{\ln\,(S_t/K) + (r \pm \sigma^2/2)(T-t)}{\sigma\sqrt{T-t}}$$

for $t = 0$ and is

$$V_0 = 28.9$$

with our choice of inputs. As usual, Φ is the cumulative distribution function of the standard normal random variable. In the usual setting the hedge would not be 21.26 but a classical delta-hedging strategy based on $\Phi(d_1(t))$.

We consider two simple discrete probability distributions of default. Both parties of the deal are considered default risky but can only default at year 1 or at year 2. The localized joint default probabilities are provided in the matrices below. The rows denote the default time of the investor, while the columns denote the default times of the counterparty. For example, in matrix D_{low} the event $(\tau_I = 2yr, \tau_C = 1yr)$ has a 3% probability and the first-to-default time is 1 year. Simultaneous defaults are introduced, and we determine the closeout amount by a random draw from a uniform distribution. If the random number is above 0.5, we compute the closeout as if the counterparty defaulted first and vice versa.

For the first default distribution, we have a low dependence between the default risk of the counterparty and the default risk of the investor

$$D_{low} = \begin{array}{r} \\ 1yr \\ 2yr \\ n.d. \end{array}\!\!\begin{array}{c} \begin{array}{ccc} 1yr & 2yr & n.d. \end{array} \\ \begin{pmatrix} 0.01 & 0.01 & 0.03 \\ 0.03 & 0.01 & 0.05 \\ 0.07 & 0.09 & 0.70 \end{pmatrix} \end{array}, \quad \tau_K(D_{low}) = 0.21 \tag{21.28}$$

where $n.d.$ means no default and τ_K denotes the rank correlation as measured by Kendall's tau. In the second case, we have a high dependence between the two parties' default risk:

$$D_{high} = \begin{array}{r} \\ 1yr \\ 2yr \\ n.d. \end{array}\!\!\begin{array}{c} \begin{array}{ccc} 1yr & 2yr & n.d. \end{array} \\ \begin{pmatrix} 0.09 & 0.01 & 0.01 \\ 0.03 & 0.11 & 0.01 \\ 0.01 & 0.03 & 0.70 \end{pmatrix} \end{array}, \quad \tau_K(D_{high}) = 0.83 \tag{21.29}$$

Note also that the distributions are skewed in the sense that the counterparty has a higher default probability than the investor. The loss given default is 50% for both the investor and the counterparty, and the loss on any posted collateral is considered the same. The collateral rates are chosen to be equal to the risk-free rate. We assume that the collateral account is equal to the risk-free price of the deal at each margin date, that is, $C_t = V_t$. This is reasonable as the dealer and client will be able to agree on this price in contrast to $\overline{V}_t$ due to asymmetric information. Also, choosing the collateral this way has the added advantage that the collateral account C works as a control variate, reducing the variance of the least-squares Monte Carlo estimator of the deal price.

21.4.3 Preliminary Analysis without Credit Risk and with Symmetric Funding Rates

To provide some ballpark figures on the effect of funding risk, we first look at the case without default risk and without collateralization of the deal. We compare our Monte Carlo approach to four alternative (simplified) approaches:

(i) Simple discounting of the risk-free Black–Scholes price with a symmetric funding rate $\hat{f} = f^+ = f^-$. We obtain

$$V_t^{(i)} = e^{-\hat{f}T}(S_t\Phi(d_1(t)) - Ke^{-r(T-t)}\Phi(d_2(t)))$$

assuming a continuously compounded funding rate.

(ii) The Black–Scholes price where both discounting and the growth of the underlying happens at the symmetric funding rate

$$V_t^{(ii)} = (S_t\Phi(g_1(t)) - Ke^{-\hat{f}(T-t)}\Phi(g_2(t)))$$
$$g_{1,2} = \frac{\ln\ (S_t/K) + (\hat{f} \pm \sigma^2/2)(T-t)}{\sigma\sqrt{T-t}}$$

(iii) Simple discounting of the forward price with the symmetric funding rate. This approach can be justified by the fact that the price of a deep out-of-the-money call will approximately equal that of a forward contract:

$$V_t^{(iii)} = S_t - Ke^{-\hat{f}(T-t)}$$

(iv) We use the above FVA formula in Proposition 3 with some approximations. Since in a standard Black–Scholes setting $F_t = -Ke^{-r(T-t)}\Phi(d_2(t))$, we compute

$$\begin{aligned}\text{FVA}^{(iv)} =& (r-\hat{f})\int_0^T \mathbb{E}_0\{e^{-rs}[F_s]\}ds \\ =& (\hat{f}-r)Ke^{-rT}\int_0^T \mathbb{E}_0\{\Phi(d_2(s))\}ds\end{aligned}$$

We illustrate the four approaches in the case of an equity call option (long position). Moreover, let the FVA in each case be defined by $\text{FVA}^{(i,ii,iii,iv)} = V^{(i,ii,iii,iv)} - V$. Figure 21.4 plots the resulting FVA with credit and collateral switched off under the four different approaches and under the full-valuation approach. Recall that if the funding rate is equal to the risk-free rate, the value of the call option collapses to the Black–Scholes price and the FVA is zero.

Remark 4 (Current market practice for FVA). Looking at Figure 21.1, it is important to realize that at the time of writing this paper, most market players would adopt a methodology like (ii) or (iv) for a simple call option. Even if borrowing or lending rates were different, most market players would average them and apply a common rate to borrowing and lending in order to avoid nonlinearities. We will discuss the approximation error entailed in this symmetrization later when introducing the NVA. For the time being, we notice that method (iv) produces the same results as the quicker method (ii) that simply replaces the risk-free rate by the funding rate. In the simple case of a long position in a call option without credit and collateral, and with symmetric borrowing and lending rates, we can show that this method is sound since it stems directly from our rigorous Formula 21.23. We also see that both methods (ii) and (iv) are quite close to the full numerical method we adopt. Occasionally, the

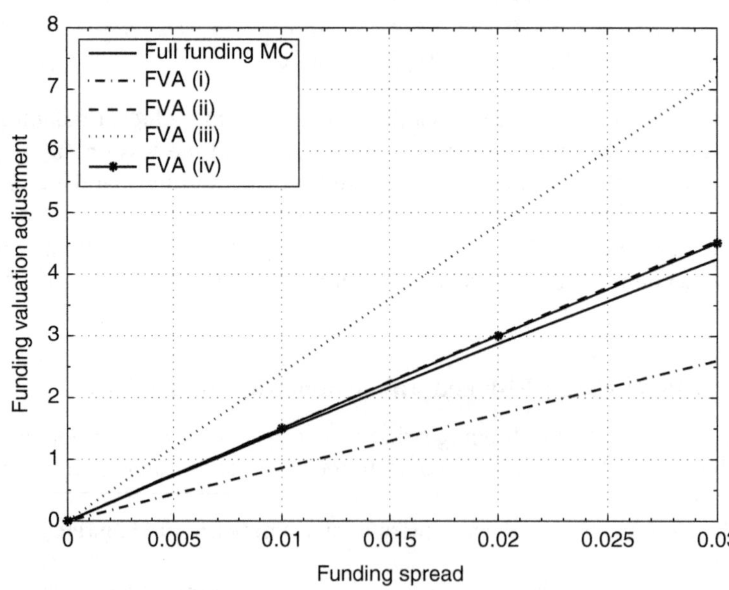

Figure 21.1 Funding valuation adjustment of a long call position as a function of symmetric funding spreads $s_f := \hat{f} - r$ with $\hat{f} := f^+ = f^-$. The adjustments are computed under the assumption of no default risk nor collateralization.

industry may adopt methods such as (i), but this is not recommended, as we can see from the results. Method (iii) is not accurate either, since it ignores optionality, and would not be used by the industry in a case like this. Overall industry-like methods such as (ii) or (iv) work well here, and there would be no need to implement the full machinery. However, once collateral and credit risk are in the picture, and once nonlinearities due to replacement closeout at default and asymmetry in borrowing and lending are present, there is no way we can keep using something like (ii) or (iv), and we need to implement the full methodology.

21.4.4 Full Analysis with Credit Risk, Collateral, and Funding Costs

Let us now switch on credit risk and consider collateralized deals. The recursive structure of our simulation method makes the pricing problem particularly demanding in terms of computational time, so we are forced to choose a relatively small number of sample paths. We use 1000 sample paths but, fortunately, the presence of collateral as a control variate mitigates too large errors. In Tables 21.1 and 21.2 we conduct a ceteris paribus analysis of funding risk under counterparty credit risk and collateralization. Specifically, we investigate how the value of a deal changes for different values of the borrowing (lending) rate f^+ (f^-) while

TABLE 21.1 Price Impact of Funding with Default Risk and Collateralization

	Default risk, low[b]		Default risk, high[c]	
Funding[a]	Long	Short	Long	Short
Borrowing rate f^+				
0 bps	29.36 (0.12)	−26.20 (0.17)	29.67 (0.22)	−26.60 (0.36)
100 bps	28.70 (0.15)	−28.72 (0.15)	29.06 (0.21)	−29.07 (0.21)
200 bps	28.05 (0.21)	−31.37 (0.32)	28.45 (0.22)	−31.66 (0.25)
300 bps	27.38 (0.29)	−34.26 (0.55)	27.83 (0.23)	−34.48 (0.46)
400 bps	26.67 (0.38)	−37.24 (0.86)	27.17 (0.26)	−37.38 (0.80)
Lending rate f^-				
0 bps	26.17 (0.18)	−29.38 (0.11)	26.59 (0.36)	−29.68 (0.22)
100 bps	28.70 (0.15)	−28.72 (0.15)	29.06 (0.21)	−29.07 (0.21)
200 bps	31.37 (0.32)	−28.07 (0.22)	31.67 (0.25)	−28.46 (0.22)
300 bps	34.28 (0.55)	−27.41 (0.30)	34.51 (0.47)	−27.85 (0.23)
400 bps	37.28 (0.88)	−26.69 (0.39)	37.45 (0.82)	−27.17 (0.26)

Standard errors of the price estimates are given in parentheses:
[a]Ceteris paribus changes in one funding rate while keeping the other fixed to 100 bps.
[b]Based on the joint default distribution D_{low} with low dependence.
[c]Based on the joint default distribution D_{high} with high dependence.

TABLE 21.2 Price Impact of Funding with Default Risk, Collateralization, and Rehypothecation

	Default risk, low[b]		Default risk, high[c]	
Funding[a]	Long	Short	Long	Short
Borrowing rate f^+				
0 bps	29.33 (0.12)	−25.56 (0.22)	29.65 (0.22)	−25.96 (0.41)
100 bps	28.70 (0.15)	−28.73 (0.15)	29.07 (0.22)	−29.08 (0.22)
200 bps	28.07 (0.22)	−32.14 (0.36)	28.47 (0.22)	−32.43 (0.29)
300 bps	27.42 (0.30)	−35.93 (0.68)	27.88 (0.24)	−36.16 (0.61)
400 bps	26.75 (0.41)	−39.95 (1.14)	27.26 (0.27)	−40.10 (1.09)
Lending rate f^-				
0 bps	25.53 (0.22)	−29.36 (0.11)	25.95 (0.41)	−29.66 (0.22)
100 bps	28.70 (0.15)	−28.73 (0.15)	29.07 (0.22)	−29.08 (0.22)
200 bps	32.14 (0.37)	−28.10 (0.22)	32.44 (0.29)	−28.49 (0.22)
300 bps	35.94 (0.69)	−27.45 (0.31)	36.19 (0.61)	−27.89 (0.24)
400 bps	39.99 (1.17)	−26.77 (0.42)	40.17 (1.12)	−27.27 (0.27)

Standard errors of the price estimates are given within parentheses:
[a]Ceteris paribus changes in one funding rate while keeping the other fixed to 100 bps.
[b]Based on the joint default distribution D_{low} with low dependence.
[c]Based on the joint default distribution D_{high} with high dependence.

keeping the lending (borrowing) rate fixed to 100 bps. When both funding rates are equal to 100 bps, the deal is funded at the risk-free rate and we are in the classical derivatives pricing setting.

Remark 5 (Potential arbitrage). Note that if $f^+ < f^-$ arbitrage opportunities might be present, unless certain constraints are imposed on the funding policy of the treasury. Such constraints may look unrealistic and may be debated themselves from the point of view of arbitrageability, but since our point here is strictly to explore the impact of asymmetries in the funding equations, we will still apply our framework to a few examples where $f^+ < f^-$.

Table 21.1 reports the impact of changing funding rates for a call position when the posted collateral may not be used for funding the deal, that is, rehypothecation is not allowed. First, for the long position, increasing the lending rate f^- while keeping the borrowing rate f^+ fixed causes an increase in the deal value. On the other hand, an increase in the borrowing rate while fixing the lending rate decreases the value of the short position, that is, the negative exposure of the investor increases. As a call option is just a one-sided contract, increasing the borrowing rate for a long position only has a minor impact. Recall that F is defined as the cash account needed as part of the derivative replication strategy or, analogously, the cash account required to fund the hedged derivative position. To hedge a long call, the investor goes short in a delta position of the underlying asset and invests excess cash in the treasury at f^-. Correspondingly, to hedge the short position, the investor enters a long delta position in the stock and finances it by borrowing cash from the treasury at f^+, so changing the lending rate only has a small effect on the deal value. Finally, due to the presence of collateral, we observe an almost similar price impact of funding under the two different default distributions D_{low} and D_{high}.

Finally, assuming cash collateral, we consider the case of rehypothecation and allow the investor and counterparty to use any posted collateral as a funding source. If the collateral is posted to the investor, this means it effectively reduces his costs of funding the delta-hedging strategy. As the payoff of the call is one sided, the investor only receives collateral when he holds a long position in the call option. But as he hedges this position by short selling the underlying stock and lending the excess cash proceeds, the collateral adds to his cash lending position and increases the funding benefit of the deal. Analogously, if the investor has a short position, he posts collateral to the counterparty, and a higher borrowing rate would increase his costs of funding the collateral he has to post as well as his delta hedge position. Table 21.2 reports the results for the short and long positions in the call option when rehypothecation is allowed. Figures 21.2 and 21.3 plot the values of collateralized long and short positions in the call option as a function of asymmetric funding spreads. In addition, Figure 21.4 reports the corresponding FVA defined as the difference between the full funding-inclusive deal price and the full deal price but symmetric funding rates equal to the risk-free rate. Recall that the collateral rates are equal to the risk-free rate, so the LVA collapses to zero in these examples.

This shows that funding asymmetry matters even under full collateralization when there is no repo market for the underlying stock. In practice, however, the dealer cannot hedge a long call by shorting a stock he does not own. Instead, he would first borrow

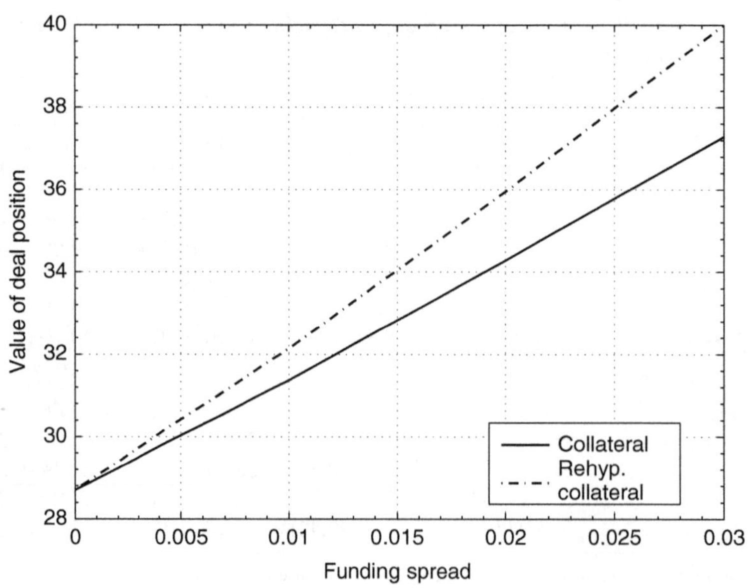

Figure 21.2 The value of a long call position for asymmetric funding spreads $s_f^- = f^- - r$, that is, fixing $f^+ = r = 0.01$ and varying $f^- \in (0.01, 0.02, 0.03, 0.04)$.

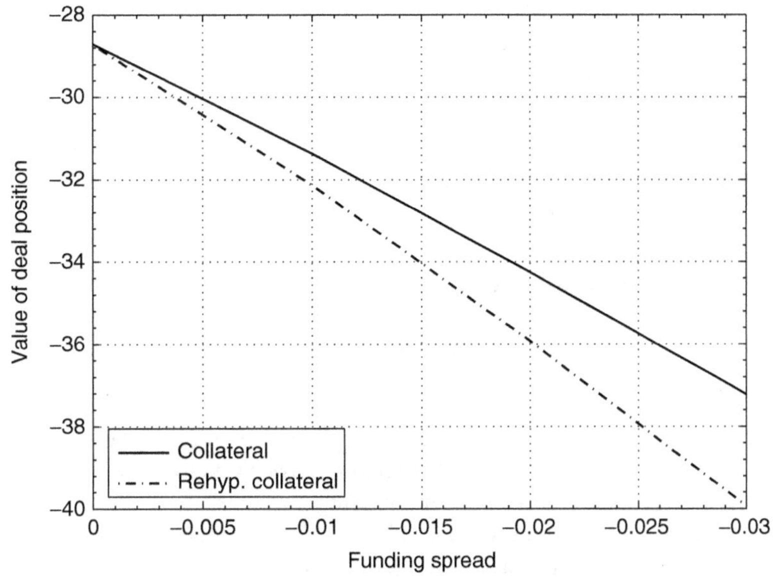

Figure 21.3 The value of a short call position for asymmetric funding spreads $s_f^+ = f^+ - r$, that is, fixing $f^- = r = 0.01$ and varying $f^+ \in (0.01, 0.02, 0.03, 0.04)$.

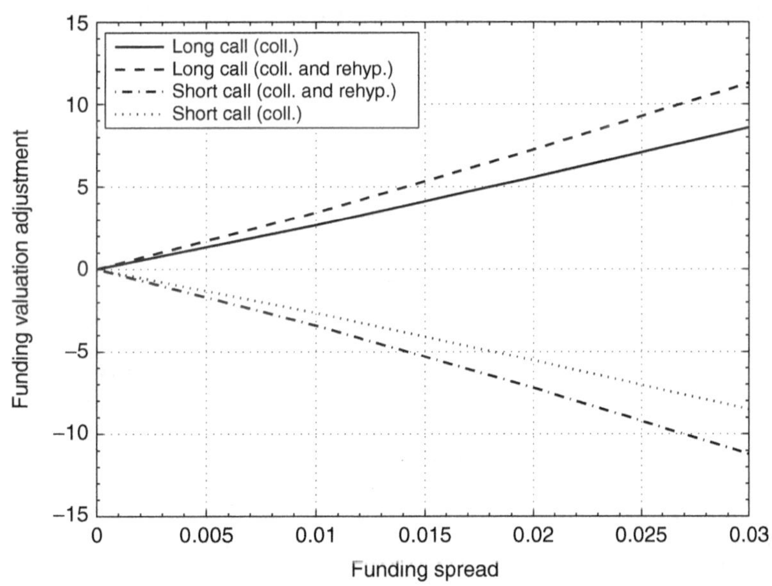

Figure 21.4 Funding valuation adjustment as a function of asymmetric funding spreads. The adjustments are computed under the presence of default risk and collateralization.

the stock in a repo transaction and then sell it in the spot market. Similarly, to enter the long delta position needed to hedge a short call, the dealer could finance the purchase by lending the stock in a reverse repo transaction. Effectively, the delta position in the underlying stock would be funded at the prevailing repo rate. Thus, once the delta hedge has to be executed through the repo market, there is no FVA (meaning any dependence on the funding rate $\tilde{f}$ drops out) given the deal is fully collateralized, but the underlying asset still grows at the repo rate. If there is no credit risk, this would leave us with the result of Piterbarg (2010). However, if the deal is not fully collateralized or the collateral cannot be rehypothecated, funding costs enter the picture even when there is a repo market for the underlying stock.

21.4.5 Nonlinearity Valuation Adjustment

In this last section, we introduce NVA. The NVA is – to the best of our knowledge – proposed here for the first time and is defined by the difference between the correct price $\overline{V}$ and a version of $\overline{V}$ where nonlinearities have been approximated away through blunt symmetrization of rates and possibly a change in the closeout convention from replacement closeout to risk-free closeout.

This entails a degree of double counting (both positive and negative interest). In some situations, the positive and negative double counting will offset each other, but in other cases this may not happen. Moreover, as pointed out by Brigo, Buescu, and Morini (2012), a further source of double counting might be neglecting the first-to-default time in bilateral CVA/DVA pricing. This is done in a number of industry approximations.

Let $\hat{V}$ be the resulting price of our full pricing algorithm when we replace both f^+ and f^- by $\hat{f}$, and we adopt a risk-free closeout at default. A further approximation in $\hat{V}$ could be to neglect the first-to-default check in the closeout, along with the previous point. We have the following.

Definition 1 (Nonlinearity Valuation Adjustment, NVA)

$$NVA_t \triangleq \overline{V}_t - \hat{V}_t$$

As an illustration, we revisit the previous example of an equity call option and analyze the NVA in a number of cases. The results are reported in Tables 21.3 and 21.4. Since we also here adopt a risk-free closeout, the examples highlight primarily the double counting error due to symmetrization of borrowing and lending rates.

We can see that, depending on the direction of the symmetrization, NVA may be either positive or negative, and the order of magnitude is about 10–15% of the full funding-inclusive deal price $\overline{V}$. This is definitely a relevant figure, especially in a valuation context.

Our examples previously take a large asymmetry in the funding rates to stress the nonlinear effect. However, even for more modest differences, NVA can be sizeable. For example, with a credit and funding risk-free option price at 29, $f^+ - f^- = 25$bps may result in NVA $= -0.5$ circa, while with $f^+ - f^- = 50$bps we have NVA $= -1$, which are of 1.7% and 3.4%, respectively, on the risk-free price.

Finally, we point out that the previous framework can be applied to fixed income instruments such as interest rate swaps. This has been done for example in Pallavicini and Brigo (2013), and Brigo and Pallavicini (2014), to which we refer for the details.

TABLE 21.3 NVA with Default Risk and Collateralization

Funding rates			Default risk, low[a]		Default risk, high[b]	
			Long	Short	Long	Short
f^+	f^-	$\hat{f}$				
200 bps	100 bps	150 bps	−1.61 (5.7%)	−1.68 (5.4%)	−1.57 (5.5%)	−1.64 (5.2%)
100 bps	200 bps	150 bps	1.71 (5.5%)	1.62 (5.8%)	1.65 (5.2%)	1.56 (5.5%)
300 bps	100 bps	200 bps	−3.27 (11.9%)	−3.60 (10.5%)	−3.16 (11.4%)	−3.50 (10.1%)
100 bps	300 bps	200 bps	3.63 (10.6%)	3.25 (11.8%)	3.52 (10.2%)	3.13 (11.3%)

The percentage of the total call price corresponding to the NVA is reported in parentheses:
[a]Based on the joint default distribution D_{low} with low dependence.
[b]Based on the joint default distribution D_{high} with high dependence.

TABLE 21.4 NVA with Default Risk, Collateralization, and Rehypothecation

Funding rates			Default risk, low[a]		Default risk, high[b]	
			Long	Short	Long	Short
f^+	f^-	$\hat{f}$				
200 bps	100 bps	150 bps	−1.98 (7.1%)	−2.06 (6.4%)	−1.93 (6.8%)	−2.01 (6.2%)
100 bps	200 bps	150 bps	2.09 (6.5%)	1.98 (7.0%)	2.04 (6.3%)	1.93 (6.8%)
300 bps	100 bps	200 bps	−4.02 (14.7%)	−4.45 (12.4%)	−3.91 (14.0%)	−4.35 (12.0%)
100 bps	300 bps	200 bps	4.50 (12.5%)	4.03 (14.7%)	4.40 (12.2%)	3.92 (14.0%)

The percentage of the total call price corresponding to the NVA is reported within parentheses:
[a]Based on the joint default distribution D_{low} with low dependence.
[b]Based on the joint default distribution D_{high} with high dependence.

21.5 EXTENSIONS

So far, we have more or less tacitly assumed that the dealer hedges the derivatives position by trading in the spot market of the underlying asset(s). Nonetheless, to be in business, the dealer might decide or even be forced to implement a hedging strategy that involves trading the underlying assets through stock lending or repo markets or by entering other derivatives positions, for example, (synthetic) forward contracts on the underlying risk factors. As a result, the dealer may incur additional costs or revenues, which we obviously need to include when pricing the deal. To address this issue, we introduce two general adapted processes: $h_t^-(T)$ is the rate of hedging revenue for lending risky assets from time t to T, while $h_t^+(T)$ is the hedging cost rate for asset borrowing. The corresponding effective hedging rate is defined as

$$\tilde{h}_t(T) \triangleq h_t^-(T)\mathbf{1}_{\{H_t<0\}} + h_t^+(T)\mathbf{1}_{\{H_t>0\}}$$

For example, if the dealer hedges in the stock lending or repo market, we can apply the quoted repo rate as the hedging rate. Another example is hedging by trading in collateralized markets, that is, markets where only collateralized financial contracts are quoted. The money market falls in this category and contracts traded in this market are collateralized on a daily basis at the overnight rate. So, if the hedging strategy implies trading directly in the money market, the effective hedging cost is simply given by the collateral rate itself.

If we assume the hedging strategy is implemented on the same time grid as the funding procedure of the deal, we can sum both the funding and hedging costs in a single term. This leads us to redefine φ in 21.12 so it explicitly takes the dependence on the hedging strategy into account:

$$\begin{aligned}\varphi(t, T\wedge\tau) \triangleq & \sum_{j=1}^{m-1} \mathbf{1}_{\{t\le t_j<(T\wedge\tau)\}} D(t,t_j) F_{t_j}\left(1-\frac{P_{t_j}(t_{j+1})}{P_{t_j}^{\tilde{f}}(t_{j+1})}\right)\\ & - \sum_{j=1}^{m-1} \mathbf{1}_{\{t\le t_j<(T\wedge\tau)\}} D(t,t_j) H_{t_j}\left(\frac{P_{t_j}(t_{j+1})}{P_{t_j}^{\tilde{f}}(t_{j+1})} - \frac{P_{t_j}(t_{j+1})}{P_{t_j}^{\tilde{h}}(t_{j+1})}\right)\end{aligned} \tag{21.30}$$

where the zero-coupon hedging bond is defined as $P_t^{\tilde{h}}(T) \triangleq [1+(T-t)\tilde{h}_t(T)]^{-1}$. As done previously, we can approximate this expression with a more direct cost-of-carry-like expression:

$$\begin{aligned}\varphi(t, T\wedge\tau) \approx & \sum_{j=1}^{m-1} \mathbf{1}_{\{t\le t_j<T\wedge\tau\}} D(t,t_j)(F_{t_j}+H_{t_j})\alpha_k(r_{t_j}(t_{j+1}) - \tilde{f}_{t_j}(t_{j+1}))\\ & - \sum_{j=1}^{m-1} \mathbf{1}_{\{t\le t_j<T\wedge\tau\}} D(t,t_j) H_{t_j}\alpha_k(r_{t_j}(t_{j+1}) - \tilde{h}_{t_j}(t_{j+1}))\end{aligned}$$

Moreover, if we take the continuous-time limit, assuming that rehypothecation is allowed, we obtain

$$\begin{aligned}\varphi(t, T\wedge\tau) = & \int_t^{T\wedge\tau} (r_s - \tilde{f}_s)[\bar{F}_s + H_s]D(t,s)ds\\ & - \int_t^{T\wedge\tau} (r_s - \tilde{h}_s)H_s D(t,s)ds\end{aligned} \tag{21.31}$$

which assumes funding and hedging of the deal takes place in continuous time. For the case when rehypothecation is forbidden, the result can be obtained analogously. We can now repeat the calculations of Section 21.3.2 to obtain the predefault PDE for the continuous-time pricing problem in the case of hedging costs, which is given by

$$(\partial_t - \tilde{f}_t - \lambda_t + \mathcal{L}_t)\bar{V}_t - (r_t - \tilde{h}_t)H_t + (\tilde{f}_t - \tilde{c}_t)C_t + \lambda_t\theta_t + \pi_t = 0, \quad \tau > t \tag{21.32}$$

with boundary condition 21.21. Assuming diffusive underlying risk factors and delta hedging, this collapses to the PDE:

$$(\partial_t - \tilde{f}_t - \lambda_t + \mathcal{L}_t^{\tilde{h}})\bar{V}_t + (\tilde{f}_t - \tilde{c}_t)C_t + \lambda_t\theta_t + \pi_t = 0, \quad \tau > t$$

where the generator is defined as $\mathcal{L}_t^{\tilde{h}}\overline{V}_t \triangleq \tilde{h}_t H_t + \mathcal{L}_t^2 \overline{V}_t$. Importantly, this equation does not depend on theoretical unobservable quantities such as the risk-free rate r_t. Again, we could solve this equation numerically, but we choose to apply the reasoning of Section 21.3.2 to reach a similar result of Theorem 4 when the dealer needs to implement the hedging strategy by trading in the derivatives market and not just the spot market.

Corollary 6 [Continuous-time solution with hedging costs] *If we assume collateral rehypothecation and delta hedging, we can solve the iterative equations of Theorem 2 in continuous time when the hedging strategy is implemented by trading on a derivative market where the effective hedging rate is $\tilde{h}$. We obtain*

$$\overline{V}_t = \mathbb{E}^{\tilde{h}}\left\{\int_t^T D(t,u;\tilde{f})1_{\{\tau>u\}}[\pi_u \quad du + 1_{\{\tau\in du\}}\theta_u + (\tilde{f}_u - \tilde{c}_u)C_u \quad du]|\mathcal{G}_t\right\} \tag{21.33}$$

where the expectations are taken under a pricing measure $\mathbb{Q}^{\tilde{h}}$ for which the underlying risk factors grow at the rate $\tilde{h}$.

Analogous to the case of hedging in the spot market, we incorporate the additional hedging costs by altering the drift of the price processes of the underlying risk factors. Moreover, by handling hedging costs via a change of measure, we observe that the explicit dependence on H_t disappears from the pricing equation. See Pallavicini, Perini, and Brigo (2012) and Brigo and Pallavicini (2014) for full details.

21.6 CONCLUSIONS: BILATERAL PRICES OR NONLINEAR VALUES?

We have developed an arbitrage-free framework for consistent valuation of derivative trades with collateralization, counterparty credit risk, and funding costs. Based on the risk-neutral pricing principle, we derived a general pricing equation where CVA, DVA, LVA, and FVA are introduced by simply modifying the payout cash flows of the deal. The pricing problem is nonlinear and recursive. The price of the deal depends on the trader's funding strategy, while to determine the funding strategy we need to know the deal price itself. This means that FVA is not generally an additive adjustment, let alone a discounting spread, as commonly assumed by most market participants in simplified approaches.

Despite starting from a risk-neutral formulation, the continuous-time limit of our equations does not depend on unobservable rates, such as the risk-free rate, but only on directly observable rates such as credit spreads, CSA rates, and bank treasury funding rates. Our valuation framework addresses common market practices of ISDA and CSA governed deals without restrictive assumptions on collateral margin payments and closeout netting rules and can be also tailored to pricing trades under CCPs with initial and variation margins, as shown in Brigo and Pallavicini (2014). In particular, we allow for asymmetric collateral and funding rates.

The introduction of funding risk breaks the bilateral nature of the deal price. The particular funding policy chosen by the client is not known to the dealer and vice versa. As a result, the price of the deal would be different to the two parties. Theoretically, this should mean that the parties would never close the deal, but in reality dealers say this was the key factor driving bid–ask spreads wider during the crisis.

A further consequence of the nonlinearity of the valuation equation is that portfolio asset values do not add up. Valuation is not additive for portfolios in the presence of funding costs and/or default risk with replacement closeout. This makes valuation aggregation dependent and has organizational consequences. Given the impossibility to split valuation adjustments into purely additive credit and funding ones, it is difficult for banks to create CVA and FVA desks with separate and clear-cut responsibilities. This can be done only at the cost of double counting. To initiate an analysis of this problem, we introduced NVA measuring the degree of valuation error one has when removing nonlinearities through symmetrization of borrowing and lending rate and through a risk-free closeout substituting a replacement closeout at default.

We show that the general nonlinear pricing equation under credit, collateral, and funding can be cast as a set of backward-iterative equations. These equations can be solved recursively by means of least-squares Monte Carlo, and we propose such a simulation algorithm. We apply our numerical framework to the benchmark case of the Black–Scholes model for options on equity. The precise patterns of funding adjustments depend on a number of factors, including the asymmetry between borrowing and lending rates. We stress such parameters to analyze their impact on the funding-inclusive price. Our numerical results confirm that funding risk does have a nontrivial impact on the deal price and that double counting can be relevant as well.

As a concluding remark, we point out that the violation of the bilateral nature of valuation and aggregation dependence, among other issues, leads to doubts about the funding-inclusive value being a price. This prompts to the old distinction between price and value, and funding costs could be considered as a profitability/cost analysis tool rather than as a quantity used to charge an adjustment to a client. This is often reinforced by the fact that a bank client has no direct control on the funding policy of a bank and would therefore have no way to influence or remedy potential inefficiencies for which she would have to pay if charged.

REFERENCES

Bank for International Settlements. Statistical release: OTC derivatives statistics at end-December 2012. Technical report; May 2013. Available at http://www.bis.org/publ/otc_hy1305.pdf. Accessed 2015 Nov 4.

Bielecki T, Rutkowski M. *Credit Risk: Modeling, Valuation and Hedging*. Berlin: Springer Finance; 2002.

Brigo D, Buescu C, Morini M. Counterparty risk pricing: impact of closeout and first-to-default times. Int J Theor Appl Finance 2012;15:1250039.

Brigo D, Capponi A. Bilateral counterparty risk with application to CDSs. Working Paper; 2008. p 241–268.

Brigo D, Capponi A, Pallavicini A. Arbitrage-free bilateral counterparty risk valuation under collateralization and re-hypothecation with application to CDS. Math Finance 2014;24(1):125–146.

Brigo D, Chourdakis K. Counterparty risk for credit default swaps: impact of spread volatility and default correlation. Int J Theor Appl Finance 2009;12(07):1007–1026.

Brigo D, Capponi A, Pallavicini A, Papatheodorou V. Collateral margining in arbitrage-free counterparty valuation adjustment including rehypotecation and netting, Working Paper; 2011a.

Brigo D, Morini M, Tarenghi M. Equity return swap valuation under counterparty risk. In: Bielecki T, Brigo D, Patras F, editors. *Credit Risk Frontiers: Sub- prime crisis, Pricing and Hedging, CVA, MBS, Ratings and Liquidity*. Hoboken (NJ): John Wiley and Sons; 2011b. p 457–484.

Brigo D, Pallavicini A, Papatheodorou V. Arbitrage-free valuation of bilateral counterparty risk for interest-rate products: impact of volatilities and correlations. Int J Theor Appl Finance 2011c;14(6):773–802.

Brigo D, Masetti M. Risk neutral pricing of counterparty risk. In: Pykhtin M, editor. *Counterparty Credit Risk Modeling: Risk Management, Pricing and Regulation*. London: Risk Books; 2005.

Brigo D, Morini M, Pallavicini A. *Counterparty Credit Risk, Collateral and Funding with Pricing Cases for All Asset Classes*. Chichester: John Wiley and Sons; 2013.

Brigo D, Pallavicini A. Counterparty risk under correlation between default and interest rates. In: Miller J, Edelman D, Appleby J, editors. *Numerical Methods for Finance*. London: Chapman and Hall; 2007.

Brigo D, Pallavicini A. Nonlinear consistent valuation of CCP cleared or CSA bilateral trades with initial margins under credit, funding and wrongway risks. J Financ Eng 2014;1(1):1–60.

Burgard C, Kjaer M. Partial differential equation representations of derivatives with counterparty risk and funding costs. J Credit Risk 2011a;7(3):1–19. Available at http://ssrn.com/abstract=1605307.

Burgard C, Kjaer M. The Balance. Risk Magazine; Oct 2011b.

Carriere JF. Valuation of the early-exercise price for options using simulations and nonparametric regression. Insur Math Econ 1996;19(1):19–30.

Castagna A. Funding, liquidity, credit and counterparty risk: links and implications, Working Paper; 2011. Available at ssrn.com.

Cherubini U. Counterparty risk in derivatives and collateral policies: the replicating portfolio approach. In: Tilman L, editor. *ALM of Financial Institutions*. London: Institutional Investor Books; 2005.

Crépey S. A BSDE approach to counterparty risk under funding constraints, Working Paper; 2011. Available at http://grozny.maths.univ-evry.fr/pages_perso/crepey/. Accessed 2015 Nov 4.

Crépey S. Bilateral counterparty risk under funding constraints - Part I: Pricing. Math Finance 2012a. Forthcoming.

Crépey S. Bilateral counterparty risk under funding constraints - Part II: CVA. Math Finance 2012b. Forthcoming.

Friedman A. *Stochastic Differential Equations and Applications*. New York: Dover Publications Inc.; 2007.

Fries C. Discounting revisited: valuation under funding, counterparty risk and collateralization, Working Paper; 2010. Available at ssrn.com.

Fujii M, Shimada Y, Takahashi A. Collateral posting and choice of collateral currency, Working Paper; 2010. Available at ssrn.com.

Gregory JK. Being two faced over counterparty credit risk. Risk Mag 2009;22:86–90.

Hull J, White A. The FVA debate. Risk Magazine; 2012. p 83–85.

ISDA. ISDA close-out amount protocol, Working Paper; 2009. Available at www.isda.com.

Longstaff FA, Schwartz ES. Valuing American options by simulation: a simple least-squares approach. Rev Financ Stud 2001;14(1):113–147.

Morini M, Prampolini A. Risky funding with counterparty and liquidity charges. Risk Mag 2011:70–75.

Pallavicini A, Brigo D. Interest-rate modelling in collateralized markets: multiple curves, credit-liquidity effects, CCPs; 2013. arxiv.org, ssrn.com.

Pallavicini A, Perini D, Brigo D. Funding valuation adjustment: a consistent framework including CVA, DVA, collateral, netting rules and rehypothecation; 2011. arXiv preprint.

Pallavicini A, Perini D, Brigo D. Funding, collateral and hedging: uncovering the mechanics and the subtleties of funding valuation adjustments; 2012. arXiv preprint arXiv:1210.3811.

Parker E, McGarry A. The ISDA master agreement and CSA: closeout weaknesses exposed in the banking crisis and suggestions for change. Butterworths Journal of International Banking Law, Volume 1; 2009.

Piterbarg V. Funding beyond discounting: collateral agreements and derivatives pricing. Risk Mag 2010;2:97–102.
Rapoport M. Funding value adjustment proves costly to J.P. Morgan's 4Q results. Wall St J 2014.
Sloth D. A journey into the dark arts of quantitative finance [PhD thesis]. Department of Economics and Business, Aarhus University; 2013.
Tilley JA. Valuing American options in a path simulation model. Trans Soc Actuar 1993;45(83):104.
Tsitsiklis JN, Van Roy B. Regression methods for pricing complex American-style options. IEEE Trans Neural Netw 2001;12(4):694–703.
Weeber P, Robson ES. Market practices for settling derivatives in bankruptcy. ABI J 2009;34-35(9):76–78.

PART VIII

Corporate and Sovereign Bonds

22

Corporate Bonds

Jens Dick-Nielsen and David Lando

Center for Financial Frictions (FRIC), Department of Finance, Copenhagen Business School, Copenhagen, Denmark

22.1 INTRODUCTION

A corporate bond is a debt obligation issued by a corporation. For large corporations, corporate bonds are an important source of debt financing supplementing bank loans. The Securities Industry and Financial Markets Association (SIFMA) estimates the nominal outstanding amount of the U.S. corporate bond market[1] to be US $9617 billion at the end of 2013. The market is thus of the same order of magnitude as that of the U.S. Treasury market (US $11,854 billion). A considerable amount of research has therefore gone into developing pricing models for corporate bonds and testing their performance empirically. Early pricing models have used option pricing techniques to price corporate bonds establishing a close link between the pricing of the equity and the bonds issued by a firm. This link has been essential – especially back in time when corporate bond markets were far less liquid – for using the more liquid stock markets to extract information about firm fundamentals and use this to price and assess the default risk of corporate bonds. Later, intensity models have established a closer link to fixed-income modeling, and this has greatly facilitated the modeling of credit derivatives. Intensity models have also been heavily used to try and understand the role of credit risk in money market instruments such as interbank lending rates and interest rate swaps. Both modeling approaches have been used to attack the fundamental problem of whether corporate bond investors are compensated excessively for their risk.

Instead of giving a comprehensive overview, this chapter will try to help a reader get a quick introduction to working with corporate bonds. This requires both data and pricing models. We therefore begin by describing the most important data sources for U.S. corporate bond data. We then provide two workhorse models that can be used to get started on working with the pricing of bonds. These models are useful for understanding how credit spreads and expected returns on corporate bonds depend on the bonds' risk characteristics and their time to maturity. We end up giving some further references to readers interested in understanding the role of illiquidity in credit spreads and also give a few references that may serve as a starting point to the extensive literature on the credit spread puzzle.

[1] See http://www.sifma.org/research/statistics.aspx

Handbook of Fixed-Income Securities, First Edition. Edited by Pietro Veronesi.

22.2 MARKET AND DATA

Most empirical studies analyzing corporate bonds focus on the U.S. market. According to debt market statistics[2] from the Bank for International Settlements (BIS), the U.S. corporate bond market is by far the largest in the world. According to the BIS statistics for total debt outstanding (all maturities) for nonfinancial corporations, U.S. issuers have a total amount outstanding of US $7097 billion. Other countries with large issuer volume are China (US $819 billion), Japan (US $733 billion), the United Kingdom (US $704 billion), Germany (US $174 billion), and Canada (US $385 billion). The size of the U.S. corporate bond market and the availability of data are the key reasons why empirical studies focus on this specific market. In the following, we will therefore describe the available data sources for U.S. corporate bonds and their scope.

22.2.1 Data on Bond Characteristics

The main legal document describing a corporate bond is the prospectus. The prospectus contains all financial terms (static information) of the corporate bond and the offering of that bond. In the United States, all bonds issued by a company for sale to the public are required to have a prospectus filed with the Securities and Exchange Commission (SEC). These prospectuses can be viewed via the SEC's EDGAR website[3]. Not all corporate debt is in the form of corporate bonds, but there is no exact definition of what constitutes a corporate bond. One way to define the universe of corporate bonds is to follow the broad classification used by SIFMA in their statistics. They include all nonconvertible corporate debt, medium-term notes (MTNs), and Yankee bonds (i.e., USD-denominated corporate bonds publicly issued in the United States by foreign corporations that have to be registered with SEC before issuance). SIFMA excludes certificates of deposits (CDs) and federal agency debt. Hybrid securities such as convertible bonds are excluded from their definition and so are money market instruments, which in this connection can be defined as any security with remaining time to maturity of less than 1 year.

Instead of extracting all bond characteristics directly from their respective prospectuses, one can use the Mergent Fixed Income Securities Database (Mergent FISD). This database contains all static information about bond issues in addition to some semistatic information. Static information includes all terms of the bond issue such as offering date, maturity date, coupon type and coupon size, covenants, and derivative features, all of which can be found in FISD. Semistatic information includes the following: *amount outstanding table* and the *historical ratings table*. The *amount outstanding table* tracks the historical amount outstanding for each bond issue and any change to this due to factors such as callability, sinking fund provisions, or redemption. This table is particularly useful since the amount outstanding during the lifetime of the bond may be a lot different from the offering amount and scaling by amount outstanding is a common procedure in empirical bond research. The *historical ratings table* is also very useful since it contains historical ratings information for each bond issue from the three major rating agencies and also from some minor agencies. Bloomberg, for example, only contains the current rating and not the series of historical ratings. One reason that it may still be interesting to look at the actual prospectus is that the prospectus contains information on the company's intended use of the proceeds of the debt issue –information that cannot be found in FISD.

22.2.2 Data on Market Prices

Besides knowing the terms of the corporate bonds, we also need information on their market prices. Primary market prices and information, for example, underwriter names, can be found in FISD, but secondary market trading information cannot. The secondary corporate bond market is a decentralized, dealer–broker-based, over-the-counter (OTC) market. Corporate bonds may be listed on an exchange, but the vast majority of trading takes place OTC. Therefore, earlier bond market studies relied on transaction information from a trading desk when analyzing transaction prices (see, e.g., Warga (1991), Hong and Warga (2000)), from insurance companies' transaction reporting (see, e.g., Chakravarty and Sarkar (2003), Schultz (2001), Campbell and Taksler (2003)), or prices from a data vendor, for example, Datastream or Bloomberg, when analyzing daily or monthly returns (see, e.g., Chen, Lesmond, and Wei (2007)).

Today there are two main sources for secondary market transaction prices for corporate bonds: Trade Reporting and Compliance Engine (TRACE) and the National Association of Insurance Commissioners (NAIC). Both these databases contain transaction reports for corporate bonds and therefore provide more accurate information on prices than daily prices based on quotes such as those provided by Datastream. These daily prices are often based on matrix pricing that can be misleading (Sarig and Warga, 1989), and to the extent that they are based on actual transactions, these are also available in TRACE and NAIC. The NAIC Financial Data Repository Database for Corporate Bonds collects all holdings and transactions for insurance companies based on their mandatory quarterly Schedule D filings. The transaction data include price, date, quantity, Counterparties, and other relevant

[2]See http://www.bis.org/statistics/secstats.htm. The numbers reported below are from the table "Total debt securities by residence of issuer." BIS has a different definition than that of SIFMA for what constitutes corporate debt so the BIS and SIFMA figures are not directly comparable.

[3]See www.sec.gov/edgar.shtml

information. Hence, the data are very detailed, but they only cover a specific group of investors, namely, insurance companies. Fortunately, insurance companies make up a very large fraction of the market participants, at least based on their holdings.

The alternative to using the NAIC data is the TRACE data. TRACE is maintained by FINRA (formerly NASD) and is a system that facilitates mandatory reporting of all OTC secondary market transactions. All FINRA members are required to report transactions in corporate bonds to TRACE, and most trade reports are disseminated shortly after being reported. TRACE therefore has the advantage over NAIC in that it essentially covers the entire universe of transactions in U.S. corporate bonds, but it has the disadvantage in that all counterparties are anonymous in TRACE.

TRACE was initiated in July 2002, but in the beginning, not all transactions were disseminated. The dissemination has taken place in three main phases and several minor phases with transactions in more bonds being included in each phase. Due to the uncertainty surrounding the effects of the dissemination of the data on the market, the transaction data were released in stages and not all at once. The first studies to use TRACE data, however, showed that the dissemination lowered transaction costs (see Edwards, Harris, and Piwowar (2007); Bessembinder, Maxwell, and Venkataraman (2006); and Goldstein, Hotchkiss, and Sirri (2007)).

Since October 2004, almost all transactions have been released within 15 minutes of execution. The most recent addition to the dissemination is that all transactions in bonds trading under rule 144A will be available starting June 2014. Corporate bonds trading under rule 144A are not required to be registered with the SEC. These unregistered bonds can only be traded by qualified institutional investors. Corporate bonds initially offered under rule 144A are often later on registered with the SEC and sold in an IPO.

The TRACE database comes in two versions: the standard TRACE dataset and the historic TRACE dataset. The standard TRACE dataset is updated every quarter and contains all transaction reports (according to the phases mentioned earlier). Each report consists of date, time, volume, price, (calculated) yield, and reporting party side, that is, buy- or sell-side transaction or interdealer transactions (this variable was added starting in November 2008). In the standard TRACE, volumes are capped at US $5 million for investment grade bonds and US $1 million for speculative grade bonds. The historic TRACE data is updated with an 18-month lag. However, it then contains transaction reports from bonds that were not originally disseminated. For example, in Phase 1 of TRACE, only transactions in large investment grade bonds and selected speculative grade bonds were disseminated, but the historic TRACE data also include all transactions for all other non-144A corporate bonds in Phase 1. Furthermore, the historic data has no cap on the volume and includes an indicator of reporting party (buy–sell-side indicator) as far back as July 2002. The historic data thus dominates the standard data in every way, the only downside of the historic data being the time lag of 18 months. Any study using corporate bond transactions more than 18 months prior should therefore be using the historic TRACE data at least for the available time period.

22.2.3 Understanding Market Data from TRACE

Before using TRACE data, one needs to clean up the data. Around 8% of all transaction reports in TRACE are erroneous and are for most parts marked as such[4]. Dick-Nielsen (2009) outlines a procedure for deleting these errors (the filters are implemented in SAS programs, which can be downloaded from the author's website). There are several issues in addition to the erroneous reports that need to be dealt with when using TRACE data. We will discuss three of them in the following: agency transactions, retail traders versus institutional traders, and data outliers.

When looking at transactions from TRACE, one will discover that a large number of transactions seem to be repeated. The same bond appears to be traded at the same price and volume twice within a short period of time or even within the same second. These reports are not the result of double counting of interdealer reports where both counterparties report the same transaction. Instead, they are the result of agency transactions where an introducing broker facilitates a transaction on behalf of a customer. The broker then buys or sells the corporate bond through a third party and conducts the opposite transaction with the customer. The broker will not always charge a trade-specific commission but could instead charge the customer an annual wrap fee. In an analysis that depends on the price sequence, one should consider deleting agency transactions since the unchanged price between adjacent transactions is not evidence that the bond could be traded without any price impact. Agency transactions account for approximately 10% of all reported transactions.

Another very important issue to consider is the relationship between investor sophistication and bond price. The same bond may trade at different prices depending on the bargaining power of the counterparties (Feldhütter, 2012). In general, retail traders will face a larger bid–ask spread than sophisticated institutional investors. This is illustrated in Figure 22.1 for a bond issued by Ford[5].

[4]In the historic TRACE data, the percentage of errors is much higher. The errors are by-products of the database design, and they need to the cleaned up or results will be biased.

[5]The bond has maturity date January 12, 2009, and CUSIP 345397SG9.

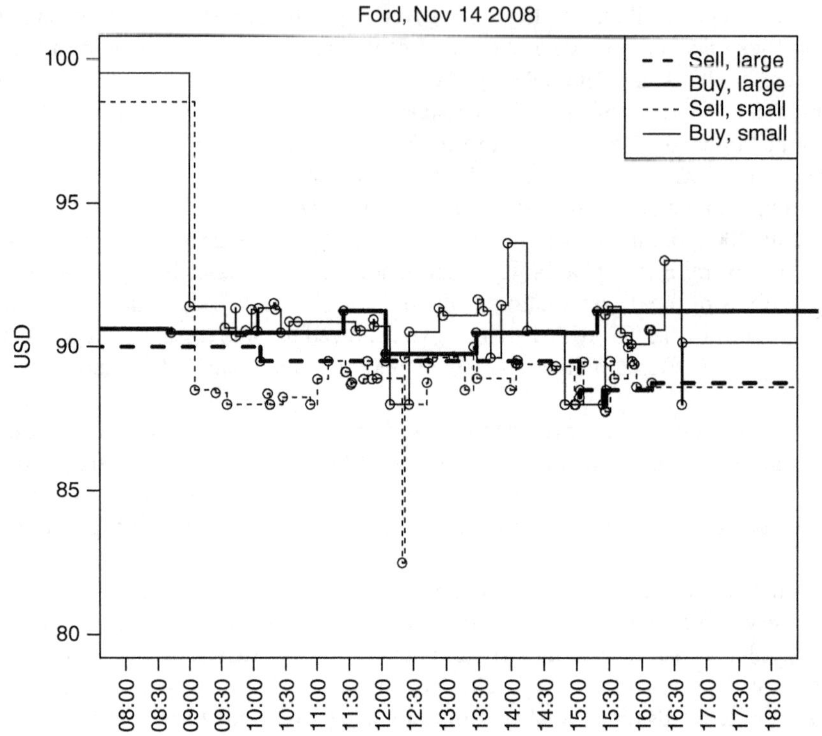

Figure 22.1 The figure shows all transactions on November 14, 2008, in the Ford bond with CUSIP 345397SG9 and maturity date January 12, 2009. Transactions are collected from TRACE, and we define small transactions to be those below US \$100,000 and large transactions US \$100,000 or above. The *x*-axis shows the time stamp for each transaction and the *y*-axis the price reported for each transaction.

The figure shows that prices for large transactions (US \$100,000 or above) form a more narrow price band than that for small transactions (below US \$100,000). Since we do not actually know the identity of the investors in TRACE, the usual procedure is to delete all small transactions below US \$100,000 in nominal value (Bessembinder et al., 2009) or even all transactions below US \$1 million in nominal value (Feldhütter, 2012). Institutional investors also execute small transactions, but retail investors rarely execute large transactions so when deleting small transactions, we should get a data sample with only institutional investors. Around 75% of all transactions are small transactions below US \$100,000 but they only account for 5–10% of the total aggregated transaction value. Small transactions are therefore not very representative of the majority of the traded volume.

Finally, it is usually desirable to delete both data errors and outliers before using TRACE. Data errors and outliers are not necessarily the same subset of observations. As already mentioned, Dick-Nielsen (2009) contains a procedure to detect data errors. The majority of these data errors, for example a wrong date or time stamp, will not stand out compared to the rest of the data and as such will not look like outliers. On the other hand, there will still be some very unusual observations that have not been marked as data errors that nevertheless are likely errors. We call the latter group of observations outliers. Typically, outliers have a price or a volume that is far from the level of the surrounding transactions. Outliers are most commonly the result of a wrongly placed decimal point in the price or of entering the traded dollar volume as opposed to the number of bonds traded. Both Friewald, Jankowitsch, and Subrahmanyam (2012) and Rossi (2014) address how to detect outliers in TRACE.

22.3 A VERY SIMPLE MODEL

There are several risk characteristics that separate the analysis of corporate bonds from that of Treasury bonds. Most importantly, there is the risk that the bond issuer may default in which case the owner of the bond typically receives only a partial compensation. The risk of default and recovery in default are going to be the key focus areas of this chapter. Market liquidity risk and risk related to derivative features of the corporate bond, primarily call risk, are also important factors, but we will not model these here. The sovereign crisis that emerged in the latter part of the great financial crisis has shed light on the fact that even Treasury bonds may be viewed as default risky. However, in this chapter, we will assume that there is a riskless benchmark so that we can quantify the price discount of a corporate bond compared to a similar bond with no default risk.

22.3.1 The Credit Spread Arising from Expected Loss

We begin with the simplest possible illustration of the main theme of this chapter, namely, the compensation for risk in corporate bonds. To readers familiar with asset pricing models, this example can be skipped. Assume that we have two periods, $t = 0$ and $t = 1$, and two possible states. The true state is revealed at time 1. The probability of states 1 and 2 are $p_1 = 0.98$ and $p_2 = 0.02$, respectively. Everybody agrees that the probabilities represent the "true" probabilities that the states will occur. A riskless bond and a bond with default risk are traded at time 0. The riskless bond pays 1 in both states at $t = 1$. The price of this bond at time 0 will determine the riskless interest rate, and we set the price such that it corresponds to a riskless rate of 2%, that is, set the price at $p(0, 1) = \frac{1}{1.02} = 0.98039$. The credit risky bond pays 1 in state 1, but in state 2, the bond has defaulted and pays only a recovery of 0.5. In a risk-neutral world, the price of this bond would be obtained by computing the expected, discounted payoff of the bond, that is,

$$p_c(0, 1) = \frac{1}{1.02}(0.98 \cdot 1 + 0.02 \cdot 0.5) = 0.9706$$

This price is of course smaller than the price of the riskless bond, and we can compute the yield on the bond as follows:

$$y_c(0, 1) = \frac{1}{0.9706} - 1 = 3.03\%$$

where we think of the time period as being 1 year and the yield as being an annual yield. Note that this yield is a promised yield – contrary to that of the riskless bond, it only represents the yield of the investment in one of the states, namely, the state where the bond does not default. The yield spread of the bond is the difference between the promised yield and the yield on the riskless bond, that is, the yield spread in this case is 1.03%. Note that the yield spread exists even if the bond is priced with no compensation for bearing risk. What does it mean that there is no compensation for bearing risk? If we compute the expected return on the corporate bond, it is 2% – just as for the riskless bond. In other words, the bond has a credit spread but no excess expected return. We say that the credit spread here is a compensation for expected loss – it is roughly the product of the default probability of 2% and loss in default that is 50%.

22.3.2 Adding a Risk Premium

A more realistic model assumes that agents are not risk-neutral and that they require compensation for bearing risk. In asset pricing, we can represent the compensation for risk by using risk-adjusted probabilities for the different states.[6] Assume that when agents in the economy price the bonds, they use probabilities $q_1 = 0.03$ and $q_2 = 0.97$. The intuition is that in the state where the corporate bond pays back its full principal, the economy is in good shape and the value of extra income is smaller than that obtained by using the real-world probabilities. In the state where the bond defaults, agents are willing to pay more for extra income than that implied by the real-world probabilities. If prices are computed using the q-probabilities, we get

$$p_c(0, 1) = \frac{1}{1.02}(0.97 \cdot 1 + 0.03 \cdot 0.5) = 0.9657$$

which corresponds to a yield on the bond of

$$y_c(0, 1) = \frac{1}{0.9657} - 1 = 3.55\%$$

This is a credit spread of 1.55%. We know from the above that the credit spread that follows just from the expected loss is 1.03%, and we see that the compensation for risk has added an extra 0.52%. Note that the bond now also has an excess expected return (over the riskless rate). The expected return of the corporate bond is

$$r_c(0, 1) = \frac{0.98 \cdot 1 + 0.02 \cdot 0.5}{0.9657} - 1 = 2.52\%$$

that is, it has an excess expected return (over the riskless rate) of 0.52%.

The credit spread of the bond depends only on the probabilities that the market uses for calculating the price (i.e., the q-probabilities in the example) and the recovery rate. The real-world probabilities are important if we want to understand which part of the credit spread comes from the expected loss on the bond. We also rely on the real-world probabilities if we want

[6]See Chapter 17 of this handbook by Tebaldi and Veronesi for the derivation of the risk-adjusted probabilities in binomial trees in the case where the two states correspond to different interest rates.

to compute the expected return on the bond and hence to understand the excess expected return. The more the q-probabilities deviate from the p-probabilities, the larger is the deviation between the expected return and the riskless rate.

One could easily explain observed credit spreads on corporate bonds by just assuming a high enough q-probability of default. However, we need some sort of reality check on the realism of the q-probabilities, and the reality check is to compute the excess expected returns that the q-probabilities imply for other types of assets, such as equities. Think of these markets as imposing a restriction on how much the q-probabilities can deviate from the physical probabilities. With such a restriction, the challenge of explaining observed credit spreads is to learn whether the actual default probabilities are high enough (and recovery low enough) to justify the size of the spreads.

In summary, there are three ways we can affect the spreads: through the recovery rate, through the physical default probabilities (when the risk premium is fixed), and through the risk premium (i.e., for given physical default probabilities, increase the compensation for bearing risk through the q-probabilities). We need more elaborate model structures to analyze these questions thoroughly. Such structure is offered by the structural models of corporate bonds.

22.4 STRUCTURAL MODELS

Structural models for corporate bonds are models that take as starting point a model of the firm's asset value or the firm's earnings. Equity and bonds are priced as derivative securities whose cash flows depend on either the firms' asset values or the firms' earnings. The power of structural models is that, in principle, they allow for a coherent model of all liabilities of a firm, that is, equity, bonds with different seniority, and hybrid instruments such as convertible bonds or warrants. A key challenge is that the fundamental variable in the model – the market value of the firm's assets – is not directly observable.

22.4.1 Merton's Model with Beta

We follow the original approach of Merton (1974) and start by considering a model for the firm's asset value V assumed to follow a geometric Brownian motion. We add to the original setup a decomposition of firm asset volatility into a systematic and a nonsystematic part so that we may discuss the beta of firm asset value, equity, and corporate bonds. We will assume that assets earn an expected excess return given by a capital asset pricing model (CAPM) relation. Assume that there is a market portfolio whose value V_m is given as

$$dV_m(t) = \mu_m V_m(t)dt + \sigma_m V_m(t)dW_0(t) \tag{22.1}$$

This portfolio represents purely systematic risk and its instantaneous Sharpe ratio is

$$\lambda = \frac{\mu_m - r_f}{\sigma_m}$$

In the single factor model we consider here, this Sharpe ratio determines the instantaneous excess return of all risky securities in the sense that only exposure to the systematic factor is rewarded with expected excess return.

The asset value of firm i evolves (under P) according to

$$dV_i(t) = \mu_i V_i(t)dt + V_i(t)(\beta_{im}\sigma_m dW_0(t) + v_i dW_i(t))$$

The total volatility of the firm is equal to

$$\sigma_i = \sqrt{(\beta_{im}\sigma_m)^2 + v_i^2} \tag{22.2}$$

If the CAPM holds, we have

$$\mu_i - r_f = \beta_{im}(\mu_m - r_f) \tag{22.3}$$

In the standard Merton model, we assume that the firm is financed by equity and a single zero-coupon debt issue with principal D and maturity date T. The payoffs at maturity to equity S_T and to debt B_T at maturity are given as

$$S_T = \max(V_T - D, 0)$$
$$B_T = \min(V_T, D) = D - \min(D - V_T, 0)$$

where we have now suppressed the superscript i. In the model above, the asset value is a geometric Brownian motion with volatility σ (again suppressing i), and hence, the prices at time t of the claims follow directly by applying the Black–Scholes model:

$$S_t = V_t\Phi\left(\frac{\log \frac{V_t}{D} + (r + \frac{1}{2}\sigma^2)(T-t)}{\sigma\sqrt{T-t}}\right) \tag{22.4}$$

$$- D\exp\left(-r(T-t)\right)\Phi\left(\frac{\log \frac{V_t}{D} + (r - \frac{1}{2}\sigma^2)(T-t)}{\sigma\sqrt{T-t}}\right) \tag{22.5}$$

where $\Phi(\cdot)$ is the cumulative distribution function of a standard normal distribution. We will use the conventional notation

$$d_1 = \frac{\log \frac{V_t}{D} + (r + \frac{1}{2}\sigma^2)(T-t)}{\sigma\sqrt{T-t}} \tag{22.6}$$

$$d_2 = \frac{\log \frac{V_t}{D} + (r - \frac{1}{2}\sigma^2)(T-t)}{\sigma\sqrt{T-t}} \tag{22.7}$$

Since the sum of debt and equity pays off the entire firm value, the value of the debt at time t can be computed simply as $B_t = V_t - S_t$, but we could of course also use the representation of debt as the difference between riskless debt and a put option to obtain the expression

$$B_t = D\exp\left(-r(T-t)\right) - P^{BS}(V_t, D, r, \sigma, T-t)$$

where P^{BS} is the expression for the price of a put option in the Black–Scholes model.

Since prices are difficult to compare across maturities and across different choices of leverage, it is common to discuss the prices of corporate bonds in terms of their promised yield or the quantity by which this quantity exceeds the yield of a comparative riskless benchmark, the credit spreads. Using continuous compounding, we define the promised yield and the yield spread as

$$y(T) = \frac{1}{T}\log\frac{D}{B_0}$$

and

$$s(T) = y(T) - r(T)$$

where $r(T)$ is the yield to maturity on a riskless bond with the same maturity. In the Merton model, we have assumed a riskless rate r that is independent of the time to maturity, but it is easy to incorporate a term structure of interest rates derived using a deterministic evolution of the short rate. A full modeling of the term structure that incorporates a stochastic model for interest rates becomes more involved. Even if the discount factor may have a simple closed-form expression, the drift of firm asset value under the risk-neutral measure must be equal to the stochastic short rate, and this complicates the calculation of the option value. For more on this, see Lando (2004). As in our simple one-period, binomial example, remember that the promised yield is the yield to maturity obtained if you buy the bond at time 0 at the price B_0 and hold it to maturity and you receive the full principal.

It is a consequence of the option pricing theory behind these price expressions that they are independent of the drift (i.e., the expected return) of the underlying assets. This is also true then for the risk-neutral probability of default (which is the price of a derivative paying off 1 if V_T is below D and 0 otherwise), but the real-world probability of default of course depends on the actual drift of the underlying process:

$$\begin{aligned} P(V_T < D) &= P(V_0\exp\left((\mu - \frac{1}{2}\sigma^2)T + \sigma W_T\right) < D) \\ &= \Phi\left(-\frac{\log(V_0/D) + (\mu - \frac{1}{2}\sigma^2)T}{\sigma\sqrt{T}}\right) \end{aligned}$$

where with CAPM holding, we would have $\mu = \mu_i = r_f + \beta_{im}(\mu_m - r_f)$ Note that in the expression for total volatility 22.2, we can keep volatility constant but let a larger fraction of the volatility be due to systematic risk. This is done by increasing β_{im} and simultaneously decreasing the contribution from the nonsystematic part v_i. Because the drift increases in 22.3 when β_{im} increases, this decreases the actual probability of default. Since volatility is kept constant, the credit spread is unchanged. Stated differently, we can have the same credit spreads and very different actual default probabilities. Similarly, we can have the same actual default probabilities for two firms but have different credit spreads. This can be obtained by letting the firm with the higher volatility have a higher beta. The higher beta gives a higher drift under the physical measure, and this tends to offset the increase in default probability that comes from the higher volatility. Having the same actual default probabilities means having the same ratings in a rating system that assigns ratings based on the probability of default, and therefore it is no surprise that bonds with the same ratings can have different credit spreads. Furthermore, since there is an interval of physical default probabilities, which corresponds to a certain rating, this leaves even more room for yield spread variations within a given rating class. Below, we have combined different values of beta and total volatility that produce the same physical default probability both over a 1-year horizon (Table 22.1) and over a 5-year horizon (Table 22.2). As we see, the different combinations of volatility and systematic risk can lead to considerable variations in credit spreads. We have included both the credit spreads that apply in the Merton model presented above and a modified version in which the bond holders receive a fixed fraction (equal to 0.5) of debt principal in the event of default, regardless of firm asset value. We will provide more details in the section below on bankruptcy costs.

Note that even though the firm's assets have a constant volatility, the volatility of equity is stochastic and increases with leverage:

$$\sigma_S(t) = \Phi(d_1)\frac{V_t}{S_t}\sigma_V$$

In empirical work, this relation is often used to argue that except for highly levered firms, the volatility of equity is roughly the leverage (measured as total assets over equity) multiplied by the asset value. For example, if the face value of debt is 60, and the value of the firm is 100, and we use an asset volatility of 0.3, a riskless rate equal to 0.02, and time to maturity of 1 year, we have $\Phi(d_1) = 0.973$. For a face value of 50, it is 0.994.

We can also derive an instantaneous beta for stocks, which is

$$\beta_S(t) = \Phi(d_1)\frac{V_t}{S_t}\beta_V$$

confirming that with higher leverage equity, gets higher beta. This is what is referred to as the leverage effect: in the Merton model (ignoring the effect of shortening maturity of the option), a loss in equity value is due to a fall in the firm's asset value. With debt fixed, this implies higher leverage, hence higher equity beta and therefore a higher expected return on the equity.

TABLE 22.1 Yield Spreads in Basis Points When Holding the Physical Default Probability Constant at 5% Over a 1-Year Horizon

Volatility	Beta	Credit spread in Merton model	Spread with recovery 0.5 of face value
0.332	0.6	80	316
0.344	1.0	95	360
0.356	1.4	112	405

Market volatility is assumed to be 0.25, and the expected excess return on the market portfolio is assumed to be 0.06. Firm value at time 0 is 100, debt maturity is 1 year, face value is 58, and the riskless rate is 0.02.

TABLE 22.2 Yield Spreads in Basis Points When Holding the Physical Default Probability Constant at 25% over a 5-year horizon

Volatility	Beta	Credit spread in Merton model	Spread with recovery 0.5 of face value
0.286	0.6	231	381
0.326	1.0	308	442
0.363	1.4	385	493

Market volatility is assumed to be 0.25, and the expected excess return on the market portfolio is assumed to be 0.06. Firm value at time 0 is 100, debt maturity is 1 year, the face value is assumed to be 70, and the riskless rate is 0.02.

For an unlevered firm, equity volatility equals asset volatility, of course. The expressions for bond volatility and bond beta are similar:

$$\sigma_B(t) = (1 - \Phi(d_1))\frac{V_t}{B_t}\sigma_V$$

$$\beta_B(t) = (1 - \Phi(d_1))\frac{V_t}{B_t}\beta_V$$

Here lower leverage means lower volatility, and as leverage goes to zero, debt volatility also goes to zero because debt becomes risk-free. In this limit, the beta is also zero.

22.4.2 Bankruptcy Costs

The option pricing approach in its cleanest form immediately produces one empirical problem. Because of the shape of the lognormal distribution, we should see that except for highly distressed bonds, the more likely recovery rates on defaulted bonds would be close to 1. That is, the conditional distribution of $\frac{B_T}{D}$ should have an increasing mass near 1. This is not observed in practice as seen from recovery studies such as Acharya, Bharath, and Srinivasan (2007) and those published annually by rating agencies, such as Moody's.

As a consequence, empirical implementations of the Merton model often impose a bankruptcy cost, which reduces the payoff to bond holders with some exogenously given fraction. This can be done by assuming either that a fixed fraction of the asset value is lost in default or that a fixed fraction of the bond principal is lost. The assumption that a fixed fraction of the asset value is lost is perhaps closer to the spirit of the structural model's emphasis on firm asset value as the key variable. If we assume that only a fraction δ of asset value remains after default, that is, that a fraction $1 - \delta$ of asset value is lost due to financial distress, we obtain the following payoff to bond holders:

$$\begin{aligned} B_T &= \delta V_T 1_{\{V_T<D\}} + D1_{\{V_T\geq D\}} \\ &= \delta \min(V_T; D) + (1-\delta)D1_{\{V_T\geq D\}} \end{aligned}$$

where we use the notation $1_{\{V_T\geq D\}}$ for the indicator function that is 1 whenever $V_T \geq D$ and 0 otherwise. Recall that the risk-neutral probability of the event $V_T \geq D$ is equal to $\Phi(d_2)$ and therefore the price at time 0 becomes

$$B_0 = \delta(D\exp(-rT) - P^{BS}(V_0, D, r, \sigma, T)) + (1-\delta)D\exp(-rT)\Phi(d_2)$$

If we let the payoff to bond holders in default be a fixed fraction δ of the principal, that is,

$$B_T = \delta D1_{\{V_T<D\}} + D1_{\{V_T\geq D\}} \tag{22.8}$$

then the value at time 0 becomes simply

$$B_0 = \delta D\exp(-rT) + (1-\delta)D\exp(-rT)\Phi(d_2)$$

representing the fact that debt holders then have a riskless payoff of δD and get the remaining part of the principal when the firm survives. Note that in this representation, only the default probability under the risk-neutral measure is used as an input to the bond price. It is thus much closer in spirit to the reduced-form models presented below in that there is really no option pricing involved.

The effect of choosing exogenous recovery is significant. We have computed in Table 22.3 the effect on yield spreads that follows from applying an exogenous recovery rate instead of using the recovery that follows endogenously from the evolution of V. Tables 22.1 and 22.2 contain additional examples for the case of recovery of face value.

It is also worth noticing that empirical applications of the model very often make the simplifying assumption that one can reduce the firm's debt to being equivalent to a zero-coupon bond issue of a fixed maturity (typically 1 year). Exactly how the firm's coupon bearing debt of several maturities is reduced varies, but the so-called KMV approach proposes using the sum of short-term debt (i.e., debt of maturity 1 year or less) and one half the notional of all long-term debt (i.e., debt of maturity more than 1 year), and this choice has been influential. One reason for this simplification is that it is not easy to deal rigorously with coupons. Modeling becomes a lot more complicated in the structural setting when we have to take into account the lump-sum nature of the payments and the fact that default boundaries and valuation depend critically on how debt repayments are financed. Are the owners of the firm allowed to sell assets to repay debt, or does debt have to be repaid using new equity, new debt, or a mixture of the two? For more on the role of whether asset sales are permitted, see Lando (2004).

TABLE 22.3 Yield Spreads in Basis Points When Using Exogenously Specified Recovery Rates on Credit Spreads

Face value of debt	Merton model	Recovery 0.5 of assets	Recovery 0.5 of face
30	0.03	0.23	0.21
40	1.2	8.0	7.4
50	12	71	65
60	60	298	267
70	181	793	696
80	405	1591	1361

We compare the pure Merton model, a model in which debt receives 50% of asset value, and a model with 50% recovery of face value in default regardless of asset value. Firm value at time 0 is 100, debt maturity is 1 year, the riskless rate is 0.02, and asset volatility is 0.3.

22.4.3 Early Default

The model presented here has viewed default as happening at a fixed point in time coinciding with a maturity date of a debt issue. An important extension of this framework is due to Black and Cox (1976). They model default as occurring not only when a firm's assets fall short of face value at maturity but also when the asset value crosses some exogenously specified barrier, which is modeled as a continuous function of time. This barrier could represent, for example, a covenant related to asset value that – if breached – allows the debt holders to take over the assets of the firm. In terms of getting more realistic credit spreads out of structural models, this model does not help a lot in that the presence of the default barrier actually increases the value of debt and hence decreases the yield spreads. This is because there are states of the world in which bond holders take over all the firm's assets where in a model with default only at maturity, there would still be a strictly positive part of the firm value belonging to the equity owners. For more details, see Lando (2004).

An important strand of literature, starting with Leland (1994), extends this framework into a model where the default boundary is chosen optimally by equity owners who seek to maximize equity value after the firm has issued debt and who choose to default if the value of retaining the option value of equity does not match the expense of the debt service. In this model, there is a trade-off when issuing debt between a tax advantage that increases with the debt level, and bankruptcy costs suffered by the debt holders when the firm defaults. The optimal debt level is the level of debt that maximizes total cash flow to debt and equity holders taking into account that equity owners will behave in their own interest when the firm has issued its debt. Davydenko (2012) finds empirical evidence consistent with the predictions of this trade-off theory, but they are far from explaining the default barrier exactly. A weakness of Leland (1994) is that the firm does not change its debt issuance when firm value increases. A model that takes into account that a firm will seek to maintain a stationary leverage ratio, that is, issue more debt in good times and retire debt in bad times, is presented in Collin-Dufresne and Goldstein (2001), but here we are back to an exogenously specified capital structure that does not involve any kind of optimization. Goldstein, Ju, and Leland (2001) present a model more in the spirit of Leland (1994) in which there is a possibility of recapitalization. Chen (2010) is a recent reference that is state of the art in terms of generalizing the framework.

22.5 REDUCED-FORM MODELS

The risk structure of interest rates that we obtain from a structural model graphs the credit spread of a zero-coupon bond as a function of time to maturity. It cannot be used in the same way as a term structure of default-free interest rates for pricing a coupon bond by pricing each coupon separately and adding up the components. The reduced-form models or intensity models build a framework similar to the framework we know from pricing default-free bonds. Of course, this framework should be used with caution. It cannot be used to infer the price of a new corporate bond issue if this drastically increases a company's debt unless one is able to find another firm whose leverage and characteristics are similar to the firm after its new bond issue. The intensity framework is extremely useful for studying credit default swaps (CDSs). CDS contracts, as they are commonly named, are contracts that insure the buyer against default of bonds issued by a default-risky firm (the reference firm) or a sovereign. The buyer of a CDS pays a premium proportional to the notional amount insured until whichever comes first: default of the firm or maturity of the CDS contract. In the event of default before maturity of the CDS contract, the seller of the CDS compensates the buyer with an amount equal to the loss suffered by a bond investor who holds the insured notional of bonds issued by the defaulting firm. The intensity model works well because CDS contracts do not affect the capital structure of the reference firm.

The reduced-form setting is also extremely useful when studying money market rates and fixed income securities such as swaps whose underlying floating rate often depends on a rate with a credit risk element in it. It is extremely useful to model the credit risk component of interbank rates, such as LIBOR rates, without having to propose a structural model for the banks that are used as panel banks for setting the LIBOR rates.

The starting point of an intensity model is a model for the instantaneous default probability of the issuing firm. The mathematical theory of intensity modeling is quite involved, and we focus here on a class of intensity models that allow you to do calculations using only properties of conditional expectations. This class of models builds on the following link between the stochastic intensity process λ and the default time τ of a firm: intuitively, given survival up to time t and the information set $\mathcal{F}_t$, the intensity satisfies that

$$\lambda(t) = \lim_{\Delta t \to 0} \frac{1}{\Delta t} P(\tau < t + \Delta t | \mathcal{F}_t)$$

that is, the probability of a default in the next small time interval Δt is $\lambda(t)\Delta t + o(\Delta t)$, where λ_t is allowed to depend on the information $\mathcal{F}_t$ at time t. Note that the definition is different from the hazard function of the default time, which would be a deterministic function giving conditional probabilities of default given survival up to time t with no other information added since time 0.

To mathematically construct a default time with the desired property of having default intensity λ, let the default time τ be given as

$$\tau = \inf\{t \geq 0 : \int_0^t \lambda(s)ds > \epsilon_1\} \tag{22.9}$$

where ϵ_1 is an exponential random variable with mean 1, which is independent of the process λ. This will ensure that we get the "local default probability" interpretation; see Lando (2004) for more details. Here we focus on the computational implications of this formulation. We obtain the key relationships:

$$P(\tau > t | (\lambda(s))_{0 \leq s \leq t}) = \exp\left(-\int_0^t \lambda(s)ds\right)$$

$$P(\tau > t) = E\left[\exp\left(-\int_0^t \lambda(s)ds\right)\right]$$

The last expression is of the exact same form as the expression for the price of a default-free bond obtained in continuous-time term structure theory. To be specific, assume that we have a short rate process r and that we have a money market account accumulating at the short rate, that is,

$$B(t) = \exp\left(\int_0^t r(s)ds\right)$$

In an arbitrage-free system, we know that there is a risk-neutral measure Q, such that all zero-coupon prices of riskless bonds are given at time t as

$$\begin{aligned} p(t,T) &= E_t^Q\left[\frac{B(t)}{B(T)}\right] \\ &= E_t^Q\left[\exp\left(-\int_t^T r(s)ds\right)\right] \end{aligned}$$

where E_t denotes the expectation conditional on information at time t. The similarity between the survival probability of a firm with default intensity λ and the price of a zero-coupon bond will help us obtain analytical expressions for corporate bond prices. Assume for maximum simplicity that the risky issuer has issued a defaultable zero-coupon bond that matures at date T and that has zero recovery in the event of default. We assume that the intensity of the default process is λ under the risk-neutral measure Q. The price (given no default at t) is then given as

$$\begin{aligned} v(t,T) &= E_t^Q\left[\exp\left(-\int_t^T r(s)ds\right) 1_{\{\tau > T\}}\right] \\ &= E_t^Q\left[\exp\left(-\int_t^T (r+\lambda)(s)ds\right)\right] \end{aligned}$$

We often assume independence between the short rate process and the intensity process, because there are no convincing arguments in favor of a strong dependence (in fact, the sign is not even clear) and the pricing effects for realistic levels of correlation are small. The price at time 0 is then given as

$$v(0,T) = p(0,T)S(0,T) \tag{22.10}$$

where

$$S(0,T) = E^Q\left[\exp\left(-\int_0^T \lambda(s)ds\right)\right] \tag{22.11}$$

If we assume a recovery of δ paid at the maturity date in the event of default, then we obtain

$$v(0,T) = \delta p(0,T) + (1-\delta)p(0,T)S(0,T) \tag{22.12}$$

which is exactly of the same form as the formula obtained in the structural model with exogenously specified recovery, except that the survival probability is now modeled from an intensity process instead of using the distribution of the market value of a firm's assets. This loses the link to the capital structure of the firm, but it on the other hand opens up an approach for linking empirically data on defaults with pricing using hazard rate regressions; see Duffie, Saita, and Wang (2007) for an example.

The intensity framework can handle more general types of defaultable claims. For example, we may want to model a claim paying a constant cash flow of c continuously until default at τ or maturity T – whichever comes first. For this we find (maintaining the assumption of independence between the short rate and the default intensity) the following expression for the value:

$$E^Q\left[\int_0^T c1_{\{\tau>s\}} \exp\left(-\int_t^s r(u)du\right) ds\right]$$
$$= c\int_0^T P(0,u)S(0,u)du$$

We may also want to consider a time-dependent recovery of $\delta(s)$ paid at the default date τ if this event happens before a maturity date T. The time dependence can handle, for example, recovery rates that depend on the remaining time to maturity of a bond:

$$E^Q\left[\exp\left(-\int_0^\tau r(u)du\right)\delta(\tau)\right]$$
$$= \int_0^T \delta(u)p(0,u)h(u)\exp\left(-\int_0^u h(s)ds\right)du$$
$$= \int_0^T \delta(u)h(u)p(0,u)S(0,u)du \tag{22.13}$$

where $h(s)$ is the deterministic hazard function (not the intensity) of the default time τ defined by

$$h(t) = -\frac{d}{dt}\log S(0,t)$$

22.5.1 A Useful Approximation

Even if we have the integral representation 22.13, it is common, especially when looking at CDS and cash flows from structured products, to make an approximation that removes this integral and leads us back to a pricing formula that depends only on the expression for the survival probability 22.11. Imagine that we want to price the so-called protection leg of a CDS contract. Assume that the reference bond underlying the CDS has a recovery of face value of δ at the time of default. We think here of δ as a function of time, but it will often be assumed to be a constant. In the event of a default of the reference bond before the CDS expires, the protection seller will have to pay $1-\delta$ to the protection buyer at the default time. The approximation now works as follows: divide the time interval between 0 and T into intervals with the division points $0 = t_0 < t_1 < \cdots < t_{n-1} < t_n = T$. Assume that if the default of the bond happens in the time interval $[t_{i-1}, t_i]$, then the repayment of the loss (i.e., the difference between the insured principal and the recovery in default) takes place in the middle $\frac{t_{i-1}+t_i}{2}$ of the time interval and is given from the recovery function δ evaluated at the midpoint of the interval $\delta\left(\frac{t_{i-1}+t_i}{2}\right)$. Then (again assuming independence between the short rate and the default event) we obtain the following approximation for the value $\Pi^s(T)$ of the protection leg:

$$\Pi^s(T) = \sum_{i=1}^{n} \left[1 - \delta\left(\frac{t_{i-1}+t_i}{2}\right)\right] p\left(0, \frac{t_{i-1}+t_i}{2}\right)(S(0,t_{i-1}) - S(0,t_i))$$

Note that this only requires computation of the survival probability $S(0, t)$ as a function of t. The length of the time interval (t_i, t_{i+1}) would be chosen (ignoring day-count conventions) to equal $\frac{1}{4}$ corresponding to 3 months.

The value of a running premium on a CDS, that is, the quarterly payment made by the buyer of the CDS contract until default or maturity (whichever comes first), also needs to make use of this approximation. This is because that in the event of default, a partial payment is made that represents the fraction of a quarter that has elapsed since the last coupon date. To see how this is done, we denote the quoted annual CDS premium $C(T)$. It is constant throughout the life of the contract but depends on the maturity T. The quarterly payment is $\frac{C(T)}{4}$, and the payment is "in arrears," that is, at the end of the quarter. If a default happens at date $\tau \in (t_{i-1}, t_i]$, then in practice the final premium payment that covers the period in which the default occurred is proportional to the length of time in which the company survived in the interval, that is, the payment would be $\frac{\tau - t_{i-1}}{t_i - t_{i-1}} \frac{C(T)}{4}$. Due to our simplifying midpoint assumption, we will just set this payment equal to $\frac{1}{2}\frac{C(T)}{4}$. Still assuming independence between interest rates and the loss process – an assumption almost always made in practice when pricing CDS contracts – we get the following value of the premium payment (if paid as a running premium, i.e., there is no initial payment between the parties to the CDS at initiation):

$$\begin{aligned}
\Pi^b(T) &= \sum_{i=1}^{n} P(0,t_i)\frac{C(T)}{4} E^Q 1_{\{\tau > t_i\}} \\
&+ \sum_{i=1}^{n} P\left(0, \frac{t_i + t_{i-1}}{2}\right) \frac{C(T)}{8} E^Q 1_{\{\tau \in (t_{i-1}, t_i]\}} \\
&= \frac{C(T)}{4} \sum_{i=1}^{n} P(0,t_i) Q(\tau > t_i) \\
&+ \frac{C(T)}{8} \sum_{i=1}^{n} P\left(0, \frac{t_i + t_{i-1}}{2}\right)(Q(\tau > t_{i-1}) - Q(\tau > t_i))
\end{aligned}$$

The fair running premium $C(T)$ on a CDS contract with notional 1 and maturity T is found by choosing $C(T)$ such that the expressions for $\Pi^s(T)$ and $\Pi^b(T)$ are equal.

22.5.2 Closed-Form Solutions

It is clear from the applications above that we can go far with models that deliver closed-form solutions for expression of the form

$$S(0,t) = E \exp\left(-\int_0^t \lambda_s ds\right)$$

Fortunately, this machinery is developed in great detail in the theory of so-called affine term structure models, and this can be directly translated into our models here. A rich model to work with assumes that the intensity process follows the so-called *affine jump-diffusion process*:

$$d\lambda_t = \kappa(\theta - \lambda_t)dt + \sigma\sqrt{\lambda_t}dW_t + dJ_t \tag{22.14}$$

where $J_t = \sum_{i=1}^{N_t} \epsilon_i$ and N_t is a Poisson process with constant intensity π and $(\epsilon_i)_{i=1}^{\infty}$ is a sequence of iid, exponentially distributed random variables with mean η. Following Duffie and Garleanu (2001), we use the notation

$$\lambda \sim AJD(\lambda(0), \kappa, \theta, \sigma, \pi, \eta)$$

We are interested in $S(0, t)$, the probability of survival up to time t, that is,

$$S(0,t) = E\left[e^{-\int_0^t \lambda_s ds}\right] \tag{22.15}$$

But as a convenience when working with a factor model (see below), we will also consider the expression

$$S^{\rho}(0,t) = E\left[e^{-\rho\int_0^t \lambda(s)ds}\right]$$

It is shown in Duffie and Garleanu (2001) using the theory of exponentially affine processes that $S^{\rho}(0,t)$ has a closed-form solution of the form

$$S^{\rho}(0,t) = \exp\ (\alpha(t) + \beta(t)\lambda(0))$$

where

$$\beta(t) = \frac{1 - e^{b_1 t}}{c_1 + d_1 e^{b_1 t}}$$

$$\alpha(t) = -\frac{\kappa\theta(c_1 + d_1)}{b_1 c_1 d_1}\log\frac{c_1 + d_1 e^{b_1 t}}{c_1 + d_1} + \frac{\kappa\theta}{c_1}t + \pi\frac{a_2 c_2 - d_2}{b_2 c_2 d_2}\log\frac{c_2 + d_2 e^{b_2 t}}{c_2 + d_2} + \left(\frac{\pi}{c_2} - \pi\right)t$$

and

$$c_1 = \frac{-\kappa - \sqrt{\kappa^2 + 2\sigma^2\rho}}{2\rho}$$

$$d_1 = \frac{\kappa - \sqrt{\kappa^2 + 2\sigma^2\rho}}{2\rho}$$

$$b_1 = \frac{d_1(\kappa + 2\rho c_1) - (\kappa c_1 - \sigma^2)}{c_1 + d_1}$$

$$a_2 = \frac{d_1}{c_1}$$

$$b_2 = b_1$$

$$c_2 = 1 - \frac{\eta}{c_1}$$

$$d_2 = \frac{d_1 + \eta}{c_1}$$

Note that when computing

$$S^{\rho}(0,t) = E\left[e^{-\rho\int_0^t \lambda(s)ds}\right]$$

one may also use the formula above with $\rho = 1$ and use the fact that

$$\rho\lambda \sim AJD(\rho\lambda(0), \kappa, \rho\theta, \sqrt{\rho}\sigma, \pi, \rho\eta)$$

If we want to study excess returns of bonds, we need to understand how the evolution of the intensity can be modeled under P and Q and to model portfolios we need to learn how we can model correlated default intensities. We will cover these topics in the next few sections.

22.6 RISK PREMIA IN INTENSITY MODELS

The mathematics of risk-premia in continuous-time models is closely linked to martingale theory and especially to a type of theorems that are referred to as "Girsanov theorems" that stipulate under what conditions probability measures are equivalent, that is, they agree on which sets have probability zero and which have positive probability. Rather than giving a mathematically rigorous restatement of this theory for jump diffusions and affine processes, we will give a more intuitive guide to the structure of risk premia in intensity models. It gives rise to the important distinction of whether variation in default risk or jump-to-default risk or both is priced for corporate bonds.

Consider once more the model for the stochastic intensity

$$d\lambda_t = \kappa(\theta - \lambda_t)dt + \sigma\sqrt{\lambda_t}dW_t + dJ_t \tag{22.16}$$

and assume that these dynamics are given under the real-world probability measure P. Remember that if we want there to be expected excess returns on corporate bonds (and not just a compensation for expected loss in the credit spread), we need the dynamics of the intensity process to behave differently under the risk-neutral pricing measure Q than under the real-world probability measure P. If we just look at the intensity process itself, there are essentially three different things we can do, which all serve to increase the level of the intensity and hence make default more likely under the risk-neutral measure:

1. Increase the jump intensity π of the process J. Since the jumps are all positive, this will increase the level of the intensity.
2. Increase the mean jump size η of the exponentially distributed jumps in the intensity.
3. Change the drift of the process by changing the drift in the Brownian motion. With the chosen square-root process dynamics, it is common to change the drift in such a way that the mean reversion level θ of the process is higher. The mean reversion force κ is left unchanged here, but it need not be.

This will produce positive expected returns for the corporate bond, but as we see, the effects on the credit spreads are qualitatively similar. In Table 22.4, we have listed a base case set of parameters, which we think of as the P-parameters. The associated yield spreads shown in Figure 22.2 are then compensation for expected loss only, that is, they are credit spreads that would apply if all agents used expectations under the real-world measure P to compute prices of securities. We have assumed independence between the riskless rate and the default intensity and zero recovery, so that the spreads are a function of the default intensity process only.

Table 22.4 also lists parameter choices for the three cases listed above, and Figure 22.2 shows the associated spreads.

The changes above are all changes that we could also make to a short rate process in interest rate modeling under an equivalent change of measure. But it is important to realize that there is an additional degree of freedom in changing the dynamics of the default process, which we would not be able to perform for the short rate process. Recall that in the construction of the default time 22.9, there is an independent exponential distribution that adds randomness to the default time even if we know the path of the stochastic default intensity. It is possible to change the mean of this random variable under an equivalent change of measure, and this results in a different intensity process under the pricing measure whose dynamics are a multiple of the intensity process under P. Again, not going for maximum generality, it is possible to have an intensity process of λ under P and to have market prices computed under a measure Q under which $\mu\lambda$ with $\mu > 0$ is the intensity of default. If we want a contribution to positive excess expected returns, we need to choose $\mu > 1$. In this case, the starting value of the intensity under Q is $\mu\lambda_0$, and we see that this has strong effects in the short end of the spread curve as well, as seen from the top curve labeled "event risk premium" in Figure 22.2.

This presentation is simplified. In the mathematical theory, one can change drift to make it time-varying and random, and the same applies for mean reversion level, jump intensity – and we do not need to even preserve the exponential distribution (but we must have the same support). But in real-world applications, we worry about computation, and we want the behavior under

TABLE 22.4 Parameter Choices Used for Comparing Different Specifications of Risk Premia in an Intensity Model Where the Default Intensity Follows an Affine Jump Diffusion of the Form 22.16

Parameter	Base case	Case 1	Case 2	Case 3	Event risk premium
λ_0	0.03	0.03	0.03	0.03	0.03
κ	0.3	0.3	0.3	0.3	0.3
θ	0.02	0.02	0.02	0.04	0.02
σ	0.05	0.05	0.05	0.05	0.05
π	0.1	0.3	0.1	0.1	0.1
η	0.05	0.05	0.15	0.05	0.05
μ	1	1	1	1	2

The base case should be thought of as corresponding to the evolution under the physical measure P. The other cases correspond to different ways of modeling the intensity under the risk-neutral measure Q. Three cases modify the parameters of the diffusion process. Case 1 increases the intensity of jumps. Case 2 increases the mean jump size, and case 3 increases the mean reversion level of the process. The case labeled event risk premium corresponds to applying an intensity process under Q that is the intensity process under P multiplied by a factor 2. All types of adjustment may be applied simultaneously.

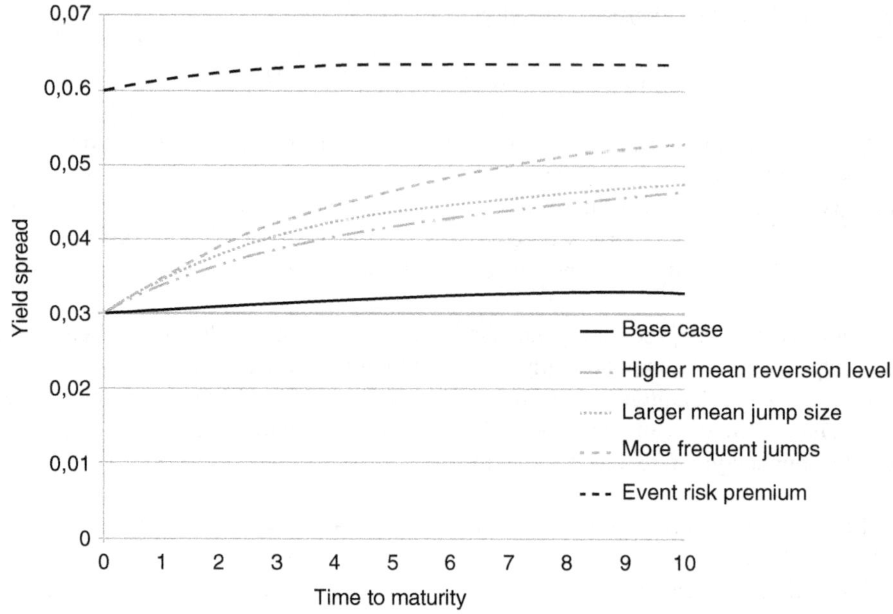

Figure 22.2 The figure shows how different Q-dynamics of the default intensity 22.16 change the yield spreads. The base case is to be thought of as the case where there is only compensation for expected loss. Cases 1 through 3 correspond to modifying a parameter of the process, as outlined in Table 22.2. The top graph corresponds to having an event risk premium in which case the intensity under Q is a multiple of the intensity under P.

the P-measure to be tractable, so that we can compute moments and at least approximate likelihood-functions. We also want it to be tractable under the Q-dynamics, so that we can compute prices in closed form. Therefore, even if the possibilities listed above are by no means exhaustive from a mathematical point of view, they are very close to how we would proceed in practice.

Jarrow, Lando, and Yu (2005) discuss the economic meaning of the different risk premium specifications. Simply put, a condition under which there is no event risk compensation is when default risk is conditionally diversifiable in the sense that the default event itself can be diversified away in a large portfolio even if the portfolio is sensitive to variations in default risk. Driessen (2005) tests for the presence of event risk. A natural setting for having common factors that carry systematic variations in default risk is to have a factor intensity model. We will present an example of such a model in the next section.

22.7 DEALING WITH PORTFOLIOS

Having the default intensity specified for a single firm is useful in many applications, but if we want to consider portfolios of bonds, we need a correlation structure between the different intensities. The natural way to obtain this is to specify a factor intensity model. We present here an outline of how calculations of distributions of portfolios of bonds can be performed in such a model. The model we will present is similar to Duffie and Garleanu (2001) but with a modification due to Mortensen (2006), and the exposition here builds on the latter.

In this model, the default intensity of the i'th issuer in the underlying index is given as

$$\lambda_i(t) = a_i Y(t) + X_i(t)$$

where, as above, the dynamics are assumed to be of the affine jump diffusion type

$$dY(t) = \kappa_Y(\theta_Y - Y(t))dt + \sigma_Y\sqrt{Y(t)}dW_Y(t) + dJ_Y(t)$$
$$dX_i(t) = \kappa_i(\theta_i - X_i(t))dt + \sigma_i\sqrt{X_i(t)}dW_i(t) + dJ_i(t)$$

where Y is thought of as the economy-wide factor, X_i is the firm-specific factor, Y and all X_i's are independent processes, and a_i is a firm-specific loading on the economy-wide factor. The economy-wide factor would naturally have Q-dynamics that differ from P-dynamics using one or all of the three cases listed in the previous section but have no multiplicative risk premium.

In a heterogeneous pool, it is important to allow for the different values of a_i across firms. Without the a_i we would force the common factor to be smaller than the smallest default intensity (assuming that work with positive X_i's). This in turn would imply that the idiosyncratic component would be large for low-grade issuers, which then would imply high correlation for high-grade issuers and low correlation for low-grade issuers, which is not what we find empirically. We do need a restriction on the a_i's to get statistical identification also of the Y process parameters, for example, by having $\sum_i a_i = 1$.

In the notation given earlier, we have

$$Y \sim AJD(Y(0), \kappa_Y, \theta_Y, \sigma_Y, l_Y, \mu_Y)$$
$$X_i \sim AJD(X_i(0), \kappa_i, \theta_i, \sigma_i, l_i, \mu_i)$$

To ensure that Y stays strictly positive, we assume $2\kappa_Y\theta_Y > \sigma_Y^2$ and similarly for the X_i's. The default probabilities of individual firms are now expressible in closed form because the AJDs for X_i and Y are independent, so the survival probability becomes

$$S(0,t) = E\left[e^{-a_i \int_0^t Y(s)ds}\right] E\left[e^{-\int_0^t X_i(s)ds}\right]$$

A numerical integration is required when computing the distribution of payouts on a portfolio of bonds. Introduce $Z(t) = \int_0^t Y(s)ds$ and note that conditional on $Z(t) = z$ defaults of firms are independent. It is too restrictive to assume that all default probabilities are the same, but to simplify the notation here, we assume that principal values and recovery in default are the same for each bond, and therefore it is sufficient for the payoff on a portfolio to know the number of firms that default. We cannot use the binomial distribution since default probabilities are different, but there is an easy recursion that allows us to compute the probability of j defaults in a portfolio of N bonds. Imagine labeling the individual bonds $k = 1, \cdots, N$, and define $P(D^k(t) = j|Z(t) = z)$ to be the probability given $Z(t) = z$ that there are j defaults among the first k firms. Then we have the following recursion for $P(D^k(t) = j|Z(t) = z)$

$$\begin{aligned} &P(D^k(t) = j|Z(t) = z) \\ &= P(D^{k-1}(t) = j|Z(t) = z) \times (1 - p_k(t|z)) \\ &= P(D^{k-1}(t) = j - 1|Z(t) = z) \times p_k(t|z) \end{aligned}$$

where $p_k(t|z)$ is the probability that firm k defaults before t given $Z(t) = z$. Note that the recursion starts by setting $k = 1$ and use information on bond 1 to obtain $P(D^1(t) = j)$ for $j = 0, 1$. It then sets $k = 2$ and computes $P(D^2(t) = j|Z(t) = z)$ for $j = 0, 1, 2$, and so forth. This recursion can easily be extended to allow for more nonhomogeneity in the portfolio having, for example, some variation in recovery rate or principal. Having different principals or recovery rates for every bond in the sample will quickly take up to much space as the sum of every payoff combination has to be stored. When the recursion is finished for a given z, then all that is left is to integrate over the density of $Z(t)$. The characteristic function for $Z(t)$ can be found in closed form and the density then is found by Fourier inversion. Note that we only need to perform this inversion once. This is essentially the only nonanalytical part. This model has mainly been used in connection with CDO modeling, but it clearly can be applied to analyze portfolios of corporate bonds in a reduced-form setting.

22.8 ILLIQUIDITY AS A SOURCE OF SPREADS

Even if we get our model of the credit risk and recovery dynamics in place, the credit spread is difficult to measure because other factors may influence spreads and expected returns. The factor that has received the most attention in recent years is the price of illiquidity. If investors worry that it is or may become difficult or expensive to sell corporate bonds, then the price of corporate bonds reflects this worry. Some models of illiquidity emphasize the role of search costs, that is, that it takes time and is costly for dealers to find customers or other dealers willing to trade; see, for example, Duffie, Garleanu, and Pedersen (2007). From an investor's perspective, the bid–ask spread is a cost of trading, and the larger this is, the larger the discount that should be applied to the bond's price is. Remember that there is not only the direct cost of trading the bond "next time." The bond's price will also reflect the costs incurred by future investors of getting rid of the bond before maturity should this need arise; see, for example, Acharya and Pedersen (2005).

An early attempt to show that corporate bond spreads are affected by illiquidity is the paper by Longstaff, Mithal, and Neis (2005). In this paper, CDS premia are used to quantify the credit risk component of corporate bond spreads. The difference between the corporate bond spread and the CDS premium measured at the same maturity (5 years) is defined as a nondefault component, that is, a component that is not due to credit risk. If at least part of this spread is due to illiquidity, then it should be the case that proxies for illiquidity help explain both cross-sectional and time-series variations in the nondefault component. The authors do find evidence – most convincingly in the cross section – that illiquidity helps explain corporate bond spreads.

Note that the definition of a corporate bond spread must use a benchmark riskless rate. The choice of this benchmark rate may significantly influence the size of the estimated liquidity component. Longstaff, Mithal, and Neis (2005) use three different riskless benchmarks: the first is the yield on Treasury securities; the second is the yield on so-called refcorp bonds, which are bonds that have an explicit government guarantee without enjoying the special status enjoyed by Treasury securities; and the third is the swap curve. Swap rates do contain an element of credit risk because the LIBOR rate that defines the floating rate payments itself contains an element of interbank credit risk, and therefore the fixed leg that balances the stream of floating rate payments contains an element of credit risk; see Collin-Dufresne and Solnick (2001) and Lando (2004) for more details. Whether Treasury bonds are trading at prices that are in a sense higher than what would be justified by their extremely low default risk is addressed, for example, in Vissing-Jorgensen and Krishnamurthy (2012) and in Feldhütter and Lando (2008), who estimate a latent riskless rate based on swap, corporate bond, and Treasury data.

Later papers have attempted to assess the size of the credit spread using the TRACE database, which we discussed in the first section. These data have greatly changed our ability to define proxies for illiquidity, since it is possible to define measures based on trading frequency, volume, price impact, and costs. Since CDS data are not available for most of the bonds available in TRACE, several papers have attempted to instead control for credit risk using both market prices of traded securities and accounting information. Examples include Bao, Pan, and Wang (2011) and Dick-Nielsen, Feldhütter, and Lando (2012), both of which include much more comprehensive overviews of the literature.

It is interesting to what extent CDS premia are pure measures of credit risk. Bongaerts, Driessen, and de Jong (2011) study this question and find some evidence of liquidity in CDS contracts. During the financial crisis, the difference between CDS premia and corporate bond spreads has been surprisingly large, especially for speculative grade bonds; see, for example, Bai and Collin-Dufresne (2013). And perhaps more surprisingly, the CDS premia have been smaller than the bond spreads, which suggests that the "easy" arbitrage of buying corporate bonds and buying CDS protection would be at play here. If the yield on this position is larger than the funding rate of the arbitrageurs, one should think that the negative basis would be traded away or at least narrowed considerably. An explanation that seems capable of capturing at least the magnitudes of these spreads is in Garleanu and Pedersen (2011), who stress the role of capital constraints and differences in how much capital is needed to finance different trading strategies.

22.9 SOME ADDITIONAL READINGS

Pricing models for corporate bonds depend on simplifying assumptions, and the problem is striking a balance between analytical tractability and realism. The fact that there still is no consensus on which model to use to price corporate bonds is perhaps consistent with an outsider's view of economics as a discipline that has a tough time drawing firm conclusions. Since structural models are the most explicit in terms of characterizing the connection between the default triggering event and the pricing of bonds, most of the testing has gone into these models. Part of the difficulty in testing structural models is that within this class of models, there is a wide range of exogenous specifications of the default boundary and the recovery in the event of default; these factors give a lot of flexibility in terms of empirical specification. One could argue that they in fact bring these models a lot closer to reduced-form models. An early benchmark for the debate on structural models is[7] Huang and Huang (2012), and many papers have followed up. A recent paper that emphasizes the role of potential estimation biases is the paper by Feldhütter and Schaefer (2014), which contains a survey of many of the important earlier papers on testing structural models.

An interesting study of where the default boundary lies empirically is carried out by Davydenko (2012). Davydenko finds that a default boundary at a level of 66% of total debt is the best approximation, but he finds considerable dispersion in this level and he concludes that it may be beneficial to avoid using a boundary of default, which is a deterministic function of observed variables. Whether the problem is that we have not found the "right" variables or whether there is a more fundamental problem of incomplete information that makes it impossible for investors to replicate the firm's decision to default is not clear. Duffie and Lando (2001) present a structural model with an endogenously determined default boundary in which investors have incomplete information on the firm's assets. This has significant implications for bond spreads, especially in the short end, and it actually leads to a setting in which investors view the default event as a Poisson-type event driven by an intensity process. In this sense, it gives us an underpinning for using reduced-form models in the spirit of Duffie, Saita, and Wang (2007) and also for pricing, although the focus of applying these models has been default prediction thus far.

[7]The working paper predates the published version by more than a decade.

22.10 CONCLUSION

This chapter gives a basic toolkit for someone wishing to work quantitatively with the pricing of corporate bonds and CDS contracts. The toolkit should allow the reader to get started both with structural models and intensity models. We have emphasized the structure of the risk premia in the models since the risk premia are important for understanding how much of the credit spread represents compensation in addition to the compensation for the expected loss. It is this part of the credit spread that generates excess expected returns. Hopefully, the intuition gained from the models presented here will make it easy to venture into more elaborate models.

REFERENCES

Acharya V, Bharath S, Srinivasan A. Does industry-wide distress affect defaulted firms? Evidence from creditor recoveries. J Financ Econ 2007;85(3):787–821.

Acharya VV, Pedersen LH. Asset pricing with liquidity risk. J Financ Econ 2005;77(2):375–410.

Bai J, Collin-Dufresne P. The CDS-Bond Basis. Working Paper. NY Fed and EPFL Lausanne; 2013.

Bao J, Pan J, Wang J. The illiquidity of corporate bonds. J Finance 2011;66(3):911–946.

Bessembinder H, Kahle K, Maxwell W, Xu D. Measuring abnormal bond performance. Rev Financ Stud 2009;22(10):4219–4258.

Bessembinder H, Maxwell W, Venkataraman K. Market transparency, liquidity externalities, and institutional trading costs in corporate bonds. J Financ Econ 2006;82(2):251–288.

Black F, Cox J. Valuing corporate securities: some effects of bond indenture provisions. J Finance 1976;31:351–367.

Bongaerts D, Driessen J, de Jong F. Derivative pricing with liquidity risk: theory and evidence from the credit default swap market. J Finance 2011;66(1):203–240.

Campbell J, Taksler G. Equity volatility and corporate bond yields. J Finance 2003;58:2321–2350.

Chakravarty S, Sarkar A. Trading costs in three U.S. bond markets. J Fixed Income 2003;13:39–48.

Chen H. Macroeconomic conditions and the puzzles of credit spreads and capital structure. J Finance 2010;65:2171–2212.

Chen L, Lesmond D, Wei J. Corporate yield spreads and bond liquidity. J Finance 2007;62(1):119–149.

Collin-Dufresne P, Goldstein RS. Do credit spreads reflect stationary leverage ratios? J Finance 2001;56:1929–1957.

Collin-Dufresne P, Solnik B. On the terms structure of default premia in the swap and LIBOR markets. J Finance 2001;56(3):1095–1115.

Davydenko SA. When do firms default? A study of the default boundary. Working paper, University of Toronto; 2012.

Dick-Nielsen J. Liquidity biases in TRACE. J Fixed Income 2009;19(2):43–55.

Dick-Nielsen J, Feldhütter P, Lando D. Corporate bond liquidity before and after the onset of the subprime crisis. J Financ Econ 2012;103:471–492.

Driessen J. Is default event risk priced in corporate bonds? Rev Financ Stud 2005;18(1):165–195.

Duffie D, Gârleanu N. Risk and valuation of collateralized debt obligations. Financ Anal J 2001;57(1):41–59.

Duffie D, Gârleanu N, Pedersen LH. Valuation in over-the-counter markets. Rev Financ Stud 2007;20(6):1865–1900.

Duffie D, Lando D. Term structures of credit spreads with incomplete accounting information. Econometrica 2001;69(3):633–664.

Duffie D, Saita L, Wang K. Multi-period corporate default prediction with stochastic covariates. J Financ Econ 2007;83:635–665.

Edwards AK, Harris LE, Piwowar MS. Corporate bond market transaction cost and transparency. J Finance 2007;62(3):1421–1451.

Feldhütter P. The same bond at different prices: identifying search frictions and selling pressures. Rev Financ Stud 2012;25(4):1155–1206.

Feldhütter P, Lando D. Decomposing swap spreads. J Financ Econ 2008;88:375–405.

Feldhütter P, Schaefer SM. The credit spread puzzle -myth or reality. Working Paper, London Business School; 2014.

Friewald N, Jankowitsch R, Subrahmanyam MG. Illiquidity or credit deterioration: a study of liquidity in the US corporate bond market during financial crises. J Financ Econ 2012;105:18–36.

Gârleanu N, Pedersen LH. Margin-based asset pricing and deviations from the law of one price. Rev Financ Stud 2011;24(6):1980–2022.

Goldstein MA, Hotchkiss ES, Sirri ER. Transparency and liquidity: a controlled experiment on corporate bonds. Rev Financ Stud 2007;20(2):235–273.

Goldstein R, Ju N, Leland H. An EBIT-based model of dynamic capital structure. J Bus 2001;74(4):483–512.

Hong G, Warga A. An empirical study of corporate bond market transactions. Financ Anal J 2000;56:32–46.

Huang J-Z, Huang M. How much of the corporate-treasury yield spread is due to credit risk? Rev Asset Pricing Stud 2012;2(2):153–202.

Jarrow R, Lando D, Yu F. Default risk and diversification: theory and empirical implications. Math Finance 2005;15:1–26. 34 David Lando. Credit Risk Modeling: Theory and Applications. Princeton (NJ); 2004.

Lando L. *Credit Risk Modeling: Theory and Applications.* Princeton (NJ): Princeton University Press; 2004.

Leland HE. Corporate debt value, bond covenants, and optimal capital structure. J Finance 1994;49:157–196.

Longstaff F, Mithal S, Neis E. Corporate yield spreads: default risk or liquidity? New evidence from the credit-default swap market. J Finance 2005;60(5):2213–2253.

Merton RC. On the pricing of corporate debt: the risk structure of interest rates. J Finance 1974;29:449–470.
Mortensen A. Semi-analytical valuation of basket credit derivatives in intensity-based models. J Derivat 2006;13(4):8–26.
Rossi M. Realized volatility, liquidity, and corporate yield spreads. Q J Finance 2014;4(1):1–42.
Sarig O, Warga A. Bond price data and bond market liquidity. J Financ Quant Anal 1989;24(3):367–378.
Schultz P. Corporate bond trading costs: a peek behind the curtain. J Finance 2001;56:677–698.
Vissing-Jorgensen A, Krishnamurthy A. The aggregate demand for treasury debt. J Polit Econ 2012;120(2):233–267.
Warga A. Corporate bond price discrepancies in the dealer and exchange markets. J Fixed Income 1991;1:7–16.

23

Sovereign Credit Risk

Gerardo Manzo and Pietro Veronesi

University of Chicago, Booth School of Business, Chicago, IL, United States

23.1 INTRODUCTION

The outbreak of the Financial Crisis in the Summer of 2007 has resulted in the collapse of banks worldwide, forcing local governments to ramp up debt issuance to bail out the financial sector. This intervention has caused a rapid widening of sovereign credit spreads, making borrowing more costly for these countries. The higher cost of financing has led to difficulties in rolling over the debt, increasing the risk that governments may be unable to meet their obligations, thus making sovereign default risk a real concern.

Credit-sensitive instruments, such as sovereign credit default swaps (CDSs), reflect the market expectation about sovereign defaults as well as its degree of risk aversion toward such potentially devastating events. A CDS is a derivative contract that insures the buyer against a counterparty default. In the aftermath of the 2007–2008 Financial Crisis, the net notional of sovereign CDS contracts has followed a positive trend with respect to other categories of credit derivatives. Figure 23.1 plots the CDS notional outstanding amount in trillions of dollars over the period 2006–2012.

The growing sovereign CDS market is a signal that investors have been seeking protection from countries' defaults since 2006, with a steeper increase from 2009 when the growing indebtedness of European countries threatened the stability of the European Union. Figure 23.2 corroborates such a hypothesis, as it shows how the outstanding amount of sovereign CDS has grown more than the outstanding public debt. In particular, the former has experienced a growth of 225.9% over the sample period, as opposed to a growth of 56.6% in the world's outstanding public debt.

The sovereign CDS market emerged in 2001 and saw rapid growth thanks to the relative simplicity of the contracts, whose price embeds market expectations of default probability and recovery. A CDS is a financial derivative contract agreed between two parties: the buyer and the seller. The buyer makes semiannual or quarterly payments to the seller and is compensated upon the occurrence of a specific credit event related to an underlying debt obligation such as a bond or a loan. In other words, upon the realization of the credit event, the buyer will receive the difference between the face value of a bond and its market value.

While for a company a credit event may be the bankruptcy or default, for a country it is not accurate to talk about a pure default. The most appropriate definition for a sovereign credit event is provided by the International Swaps and Derivatives Association (ISDA), which references four types of credit events: acceleration, failure to pay, restructuring, and repudiation. This classification is due to the fact that countries rarely default outright. Instead, governments may restructure or renegotiate their debt. As pointed out by Duffie, Pedersen, and Singleton (2003), a sovereign default is mostly the result of political decisions, namely, when the government considers it is optimal to default. Indeed, the government faces a trade-off between the cost of

Handbook of Fixed-Income Securities, First Edition. Edited by Pietro Veronesi.

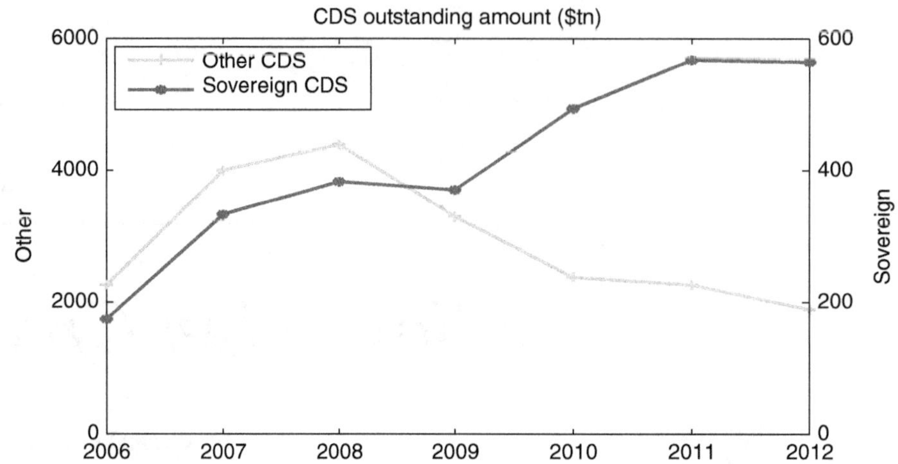

Figure 23.1 This figure compares the trend of the single-name sovereign CDS notional outstanding amount versus the rest of the CDS market over the period 2006–2012. The latter includes financial and nonfinancial firms, securities products, asset-backed securities, and mortgage-backed securities. Source: Bank for International Settlements (BIS).

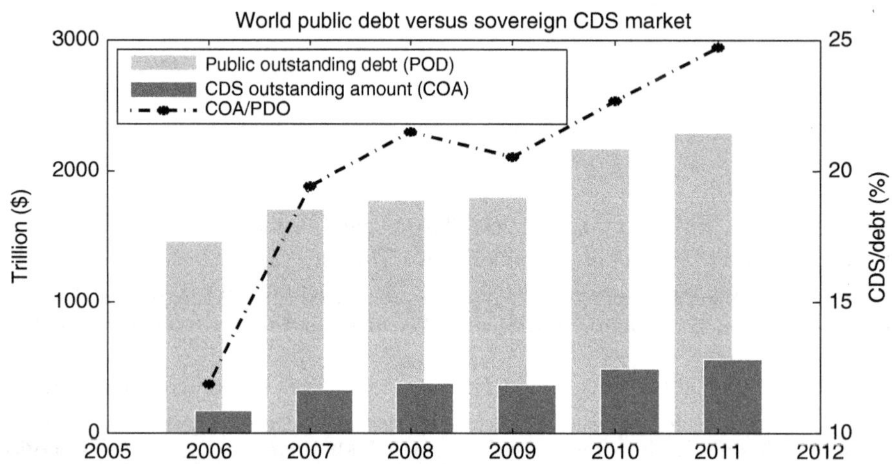

Figure 23.2 This figure plots the outstanding public debt, the outstanding amount of CDS contracts, and the ratio between the two (right y-axis), over the yearly period from 2006 to 2011. Source: BIS and FRED.

making debt payments against reputation costs (Eaton and Gersovitz, 1981) and the cost of losing access to international financial markets. In a study on the duration of capital market exclusion, Richmond and Dias (2008) report that, over the period from 1980 to 2005, countries regain full (partial) market access after 8.4 (5.7) years on average.

The absence of an international bankruptcy court that applies to sovereign issuers leaves open room for serious debates as to whether certain credit events count as CDS triggers. Indeed, at the beginning of 2012, a dispute erupted after several bondholders agreed on a Greek debt swap,[1] a decision that followed several failed attempts by third parties to bail out the Hellenic Republic. The agreement staved off a disorderly default but raised doubts about the definition of such an event. While Standard & Poor's defined it as a *selective default*, the ISDA declared that the restructuring credit event did not occur because neither debt subordination nor a collective action clause (CAC) were in place at that time.[2] Only after Greece used the CAC, forcing holders of bonds governed by domestic law to take the debt swap, the ISDA declared that Greece's restructuring represented a credit event and the CDS was executed following the ISDA declaration. This event provides an example of a particular risk embedded in sovereign CDSs, namely, the risk of disagreement about the occurrence of the event. Such risk is rarely taken into account when a CDS contract is evaluated.

[1]The agreed bond swap required private holders to incur a nominal loss of 53.5% on their Greek debt, in addition to a 20% loss in future interest payments, for a total loss of about 74%.

[2]As reported in Section 4.7(a) of the 2003 Credit Event Definition, a restructuring is considered a credit event when, among others, it requires that all the bondholders participate in a debt swap with the approval of a quorum of bondholders.

In the next sections, we introduce theoretical approaches to model credit risk and to decompose the credit spread into risk premium and default risk. We then show how to calibrate such models to market data. The last two sections are empirical applications of the framework to Emerging Economies and the European Debt Crisis.

23.2 LITERATURE REVIEW

Research on sovereign credit risk has grown since the late 1990s when turbulence in the currency markets of East Asia caused the default of a number of Emerging Economies. Recent studies that have focused on the determinants of sovereign credit risk have found arguments in favor of both local and global factors. One common empirical and theoretical approach is to decompose credit spreads into a risk premium and a default risk component, as global factors and country characteristics can have separate impacts. Zhang (2003) measures the risk premia of Argentina as the difference between the risk neutral and the historical default probabilities, and finds that it is associated with changes in business cycles and credit spillover from the U.S. economy. Pan and Singleton (2008) introduce a new pricing model to measure the risk premium associated with unpredictable variations in default probabilities, and estimate it for three Emerging Economies: Turkey, Mexico, and Korea. Their findings mainly show that the principal component of the risk premia of these three dissimilar economies is highly correlated with proxies of global financial uncertainty (VIX), global default risk (U.S. credit spread), and macroeconomic policies (currency-implied volatility). A wider view on how sovereign risk is driven by global factors is given by Longstaff, Pan, Pedersen, and Singleton (2011), who analyze a larger set of emerging markets and find that global market factors, risk premiums, and investment flows matter more for sovereign risk than country-specific characteristics. Ang and Longstaff (2013) build a pricing model to measure the dependence of a system of countries upon a common factor that they call systemic risk. Their findings indicate that this common component is mostly related to financial markets rather than macroeconomic fundamentals.

In related work, Remolona, Scatigna, and Wu (2008) decompose credit spreads of some emerging markets into a market-based measure of expected loss, or simply default risk, and a risk premium in order to study how these two components are related to global factors and country characteristics. They find evidence that characteristics such as inflation, industrial production, GDP growth consensus forecasts, and foreign exchange reserves are the main determinants of the sovereign default risk, whereas global factors such as the VIX and the JP Morgan Risk Tolerance Index are the main drivers of the sovereign risk premia. In line with Remolona, Scatigna, and Wu (2008), Caceres, Guzzo, and Segoviano Basurto (2010) employ a similar analysis to show that much of the Eurozone credit spread variation is explained by shifts in global risk aversion, country characteristics, and spillover from other countries. They show that at the very beginning of the Financial Crisis, credit spreads were mostly driven by global factors, whereas in the last stage of the crisis, they were mainly affected by country fundamentals such as public debt and budget deficit over GDP. Hilscher and Nosbusch (2010) analyze the effect of macroeconomic fundamentals on emerging markets, such as terms of trade and its volatility, and find that they have a significant impact on credit spreads. Additionally, they also show that global factors such as the VIX, the U.S. spread, the 10-year Treasury yield, and the TED spread all have a significant effect on credit spreads. In support of the "local" view, they argue that, even in controlling for global factors, macroeconomic fundamentals still explain a significant portion of spread variation. Carr and Wu (2007) conjecture that economic and political instability in a country leads to a deterioration in sovereign credit quality and currency depreciation, thus increasing currency volatility. Their paper empirically documents the comovement between credit spreads and option-implied currency volatilities, and proposes a theoretical model in which credit spread and currency volatility are jointly priced.

The widening credit spreads in the Eurozone in the aftermath of the 2007–2009 Financial Crisis has shifted attention away from emerging markets to developed European economies whose debt increased dramatically as a result of bank bailouts. Sgherri and Zoli (2009) find that changes in sovereign risk premia of 10 European countries mirror global risk factors such as expected inflation, the Euribor spread, and the implied volatility of the DAX stock market index. Dieckmann and Plank (2012) study 18 developed European countries and show that size, precrisis health, and country-specific financial markets strongly explain the variation in credit spreads. Additionally, they stress the potential role of the private-to-public risk transfer channel, that is, the impact of more government financial sector guarantees, significant extension of loans to the banking system, and the like, on investors' expectations about future banks' bailouts. Acharya et al. (2011) present a theoretical model to test the two-way feedback effect between sovereign systems and financial markets. When a country rescues an insolvent financial system with debt expansion financed by taxes, it induces a positive signal in the market that subsequently deteriorates into a negative one due to an increase in the sovereign's marginal cost of raising tax revenue and more limited debt capacity. Hence, a distressed sovereign may exacerbate the solvency of the financial sector, as it would be unable to make further transfers to the banking system. They find empirical evidence of such a two-way feedback effect reflected in credit spreads.

In summary, there is evidence that sovereign credit spreads are highly correlated across countries due to a common set of global market factors, risk premia, and liquidity patterns. However, further research is needed to reach a general conclusion about the source of sovereign credit spreads, as existing research utilizes relatively short sample periods of credit default spreads that include irregular economic periods driven by the 2007–2009 Financial Crisis and subsequent European Debt Crisis.

23.3 MODELING SOVEREIGN DEFAULT

Modeling credit risk means making assumptions on the default event. Structural models *à la* Merton (1974) assume that the default occurs when the value of a firm's assets falls below the promised debt repayment at maturity.[3] But a sovereign default embeds more complex dynamics. For instance, the government may release fictitious budget statistics, so a serious measurement issue could give wrong estimates of the probability of default. Moreover, a default is mostly a political decision that might be driven also by personal incentives of politicians (Duffie, Pedersen, and Singleton, 2003).

Given such practical issues, reduced-form models have been employed to overcome the nonobservability and nontradability of firms', or countries', fundamentals values. The default time is then modeled as an exogenous process that arrives as a "surprise" (see Jarrow and Turnbull (1992)).

23.3.1 Risk-Neutral Pricing

The key concept in pricing credit-sensitive securities is the *risk-neutral valuation* approach, according to which the price of a security is the discounted expected value of future cash flows, discounted at the risk-free rate, where the expectation is computed using "risk-adjusted," or "risk-neutral," probabilities. The theoretical pricing method is preference free, as it does not assume that investors are risk neutral but rather states that the price of a security can be computed *as if* they were risk neutral (Björk, 2004). Investors' risk aversion is instead reflected in the risk-neutral probabilities that are used to compute expectations of future cash flows. Thus, a credit risk premium is priced in the market as long as the risk-neutral default probability differs from the actual or *physical* one. Therefore, modeling credit risk allows for the decomposition of the credit spread into its two main components: the credit risk premium and the default risk. The former is the reward for the investor to bear the risk of default or of unexpected variations in the arrival rate of the default event, whereas the default risk captures the probability and size of a sudden negative jump in the price upon default.

23.3.1.1 A Simple Example To understand the logic of risk-neutral pricing and the distinction between risk-neutral and physical probabilities, consider the following simple example.

A country issues a zero-coupon bond at time t with maturity T. On every small time interval Δt, there is constant probability $\lambda \times \Delta t$ that the country defaults, and in case of default, the investor gets nothing. λ is usually called "default intensity." The probability of surviving until T is then[4]

$$\Pr(\text{no default between } t \text{ and } T) = P(t, T; \lambda) = e^{-\lambda(T-t)} \tag{23.1}$$

Therefore, while the *promised* payoff at T is \$1, in fact the actual payoff is stochastic, and it depends on whether the country defaults before T or not. Let g_T be a random variable with $g_T = 1$ if the country does not default before T and $g_T = 0$ if the country defaults. Then, the expected payoff at T is

$$\mathbb{E}_t^{\mathbb{P}}[g_T|\lambda] = P(t, T; \lambda) \times \$1$$

where the notation $\mathbb{E}_t^{\mathbb{P}}[.|\lambda]$ denotes that the expectation is taken under the physical (i.e. true) probability, conditional on the intensity λ, that is, $P(t, T; \lambda)$.

Assume now that λ is itself a random variable. That is, investors do not know the default intensity λ, but they know it has probability distribution $F(\lambda)$. In this case, the probability of no default is given by

$$\Pr(\text{no default between } t \text{ and } T) = \mathbb{E}_t^{\mathbb{P}}[P(t, T; \lambda)] = \mathbb{E}_t^{\mathbb{P}}[e^{-\lambda(T-t)}]$$

where the notation $\mathbb{E}_t^{\mathbb{P}}[.]$ denotes the expectation is taken with respect to the physical probability distribution, that is, $F(\lambda)$.

Because of the uncertainty about λ and the possibility of losses, investors discount the future promised payment at the risk-free rate r plus a risk premium μ. What is the value of the defaultable bond at t? We have to compute the discounted value of the expected cash flow, that is,

$$V(t, T) = \mathbb{E}_t^{\mathbb{P}}[e^{-(r+\mu)(T-t)} g_T] \tag{23.2}$$

[3]Several extensions of the Merton model have been proposed, such as Black and Cox (1976); Fischer, Heinkel, and Zechner (1989), Longstaff and Schwartz (1995), and Leland and Toft (1996), among others.

[4]To see this, note that the probability of surviving n periods is $P(n\Delta t) = (1 - \lambda\Delta t)^n$. Thus, with time to maturity $T - t = n\Delta t$, we can take the limit as $n \to \infty$ and thus $\Delta t = (T - t)/n \to 0$. We have $P(t, T) = (1 - \lambda\Delta t)^n \to e^{-\lambda(T-t)}$.

We can write

$$V(t,T) = \mathbb{E}_t^{\mathbb{P}}[e^{-(r+\mu)(T-t)} g_T] \tag{23.3}$$
$$= \mathbb{E}_t^{\mathbb{P}}[e^{-(r+\mu)(T-t)} \mathbb{E}_t^{\mathbb{P}}[g_T|\lambda]] \tag{23.4}$$
$$= \mathbb{E}_t^{\mathbb{P}}[e^{-(r+\mu)(T-t)} P(t,T;\lambda)\$1] \tag{23.5}$$
$$= \mathbb{E}_t^{\mathbb{P}}[e^{-(r+\mu+\lambda)(T-t)}] \tag{23.6}$$

where in the last equation we dropped the unit cash flow for simplicity. We can now define a new variable $\lambda^{\mathbb{Q}} = \lambda + \mu$, which has the same distribution as λ except for a higher mean, which is shifted by μ. We denote the distribution of $\lambda^{\mathbb{Q}}$ as $F^{\mathbb{Q}}(\lambda^{\mathbb{Q}})$ and the expectation with respect to this distribution as $\mathbb{E}^{\mathbb{Q}}[.]$. We then obtain

$$V(t,T) = \mathbb{E}_t^{\mathbb{P}}[e^{-(r+\mu+\lambda)(T-t)}] \tag{23.7}$$
$$= \mathbb{E}_t^{\mathbb{Q}}[e^{-(r+\lambda^{\mathbb{Q}})(T-t)}] \tag{23.8}$$

That is, in order to price the defaultable security, we only need information about the risk-neutral intensity $\lambda^{\mathbb{Q}}$ and not about the true intensity λ and the risk premium μ. The risk-neutral intensity λ^{Q} can be high either because the true intensity λ is high or because the risk premium μ is high (or both). Either case will give the same value to the defaultable security.

To better understand the terminology "risk-neutral pricing," we can proceed one step further and define $Q(t,T;\lambda^{\mathbb{Q}}) = e^{-\lambda^{\mathbb{Q}}(T-t)}$ the surviving probability for given *known* $\lambda^{\mathbb{Q}}$. Given the distribution $F^{\mathbb{Q}}(\lambda^{\mathbb{Q}})$, we have that the risk-neutral survival probability is $\mathbb{E}^{\mathbb{Q}}[Q(t,T;\lambda^{\mathbb{Q}})] = \mathbb{E}^{\mathbb{Q}}[e^{-\lambda^{\mathbb{Q}}(T-t)}]$. We thus obtain

$$V(t,T) = \mathbb{E}_t^{\mathbb{Q}}[e^{-(r+\lambda^{\mathbb{Q}})(T-t)}] \tag{23.9}$$
$$= \mathbb{E}_t^{\mathbb{Q}}[e^{-r(T-t)} Q(t,T;\lambda^{\mathbb{Q}})\$1] \tag{23.10}$$
$$= \mathbb{E}_t^{\mathbb{Q}}[e^{-r(T-t)} g_T] \tag{23.11}$$

Under the risk-neutral (or risk-adjusted) probabilities, then, it is *as if* we are pricing the security under the assumption of risk neutrality, as we are discounting the future cash flow g_T using the risk-free rate r. In reality, the risk premium is embedded in the probability used for the expectation. The next section generalizes this approach to the more realistic case of time-varying default intensities.

23.3.1.2 Time-Varying Default Intensities The common approach in credit risk modeling is to first model the default times under the physical probability measure, $\mathbb{P}$, and then include the risk premium, or the market price of risk, to calculate the value of the security under the risk-neutral probability measure, $\mathbb{Q}$.

Assume a complete probability space $(\Omega, \mathcal{F}, \mathbb{P})$ and a filtration $\mathcal{G}_t \geq 0$ of sub-σ-algebras of $\mathcal{F}$ that satisfies the *usual conditions*.[5] Additionally, assume there exists a nonexplosive counting process $\{K_t\}$ with intensity $\{\lambda_t\}$ that records the number of events occurring up to time t (excluded), K_t.[6]

Credit risk is mostly modeled in a *doubly stochastic* framework, in which a stopping time process, and so its underlying counting process, has a stochastic intensity. Technically, we say that a $\mathcal{F}_t$-measurable nonexplosive counting process $\{K_t\}$ is doubly stochastic if its intensity $\{\lambda_t\}$ is $\mathcal{F}_t$-measurable and if, for all t and $T > t$, conditional on the σ-algebra $\mathcal{G}_t \vee \mathcal{F}_t$, $K_T - K_t$ is Poisson distributed with parameter $\int_t^T \lambda_u du$.[7] Intuitively, the filtration $\mathcal{F}_t$ collects information about the intensity but does not embed enough information to reveal the event times of the counting process $\{K_t\}$. Hence, the physical probability of no event between time t and T, namely, the probability of the realization of the event $A = K_T - K_t = 0$, can be obtained by the law of iterated expectation. Let τ denote the realization of the first event, we have

$$\Pr(\tau > T|\mathcal{G}_t) = \mathbb{E}^{\mathbb{P}}[1_A|\mathcal{G}_t] \tag{23.12}$$
$$= \mathbb{E}^{\mathbb{P}}[\mathbb{E}^{\mathbb{P}}(1_A|\mathcal{G}_t \vee \mathcal{F}_s)|\mathcal{G}_t] \tag{23.13}$$
$$= \mathbb{E}^{\mathbb{P}}[\Pr(K_T - K_t = 0|\mathcal{G}_t \vee \mathcal{F}_s)|\mathcal{G}_t] \tag{23.14}$$
$$= \mathbb{E}^{\mathbb{P}}\left[e^{-\int_t^T \lambda_s ds}|\mathcal{G}_t\right] \tag{23.15}$$

[5]See Appendix B in Duffie (2005).

[6]The counting process has an intensity $\{\lambda_t\}$ if λ_t is a nonnegative predictable process that satisfies $\int_0^t \lambda_s ds < \infty$ a.s. for all t.

[7]A random variable x is Poisson distributed with parameter λ if for integers $k = 0, 1, \ldots$ we have $\Pr(x = k) = \lambda^k e^{-\lambda}/k!$. We also have $E[x] = Var[x] = \lambda$.

where the expectation is taken under the physical or actual probability measure $\mathbb{P}$. Equation 23.15 embeds an important interpretation: the surviving probability $P(\tau > T|\mathcal{G}_t)$ can be seen as the value of a zero-coupon bond discounted at the stochastic interest rate λ_t. Indeed, the case with constant λ leads back to the surviving probability in Equation 23.1 in the simple example.

For later reference, note that for every Δt, the probability of default between T and $T + \Delta t$ is

$$\begin{aligned}\Pr(T < \tau < T + \Delta t|\mathcal{G}_t) &= \Pr(\tau > T|\mathcal{G}_t) - \Pr(\tau > T + \Delta t|\mathcal{G}_t)\\ &= \mathbb{E}^{\mathbb{P}}\left[e^{-\int_t^T \lambda_s ds} - e^{-\int_t^{T+\Delta t} \lambda_s ds}|\mathcal{G}_t\right]\end{aligned}$$

Multiplying and dividing by Δt, and taking the limit as $\Delta t \to dT$, we obtain that the probability density function of default at T is

$$\Pr(T < \tau < T + dT|\mathcal{G}_t) = -\mathbb{E}^{\mathbb{P}}\left[\frac{\partial e^{-\int_t^T \lambda_s ds}}{\partial T}|\mathcal{G}_t\right] dT \tag{23.16}$$

$$= \mathbb{E}^{\mathbb{P}}\left[\lambda_T e^{-\int_t^T \lambda_s ds}|\mathcal{G}_t\right] dT \tag{23.17}$$

From a practical point of view, one can assume that the intensity is a function of some state variables, $\mathbf{X}_t$, that is, $\lambda_t = \Lambda(\mathbf{X}_t)$ for some measurable $\Lambda : \mathbb{R}^d \to [0, \infty)$, where $\mathbf{X}_t$ in $\mathbb{R}^d$ solves a stochastic differential equation (SDE) of the form

$$d\mathbf{X}_t = \boldsymbol{\mu}(\mathbf{X}_t)dt + \boldsymbol{\sigma}(\mathbf{X}_t)d\mathbf{B}_t^{\mathbb{P}} \tag{23.18}$$

for some $\mathcal{G}_t$-standard Brownian motion $\{\mathbf{B}_t^{\mathbb{P}}\}$ in $\mathbb{R}^d$, and with $\boldsymbol{\mu}(\cdot)$ and $\boldsymbol{\sigma}(\cdot)$ subject to *regularity conditions* for the solution to be unique. Under this framework, the probability in Equation 23.15 can be written as

$$\Pr(\tau > T|\mathcal{G}_t) = \mathbb{E}_t^{\mathbb{P}}[e^{-\int_t^T \Lambda(\mathbf{X}(s))ds}|\mathbf{X}(t)] \tag{23.19}$$

$$= f(t, \mathbf{X}(t)) \tag{23.20}$$

Applying the Feynman–Kac formula, $f(\cdot)$ solves the following partial differential equation (PDE):

$$\mathcal{D}f(t, \mathbf{X}(t)) - \Lambda(\mathbf{X}(t))f(t, \mathbf{X}(t)) = 0 \tag{23.21}$$

where $\mathcal{D}f(t, \mathbf{x})$ is given by

$$\mathcal{D}f(t, \mathbf{x}) = \frac{\partial f(t, \mathbf{x})}{\partial t} + \sum_i \frac{\partial f(t, \mathbf{x})}{\partial x_i}\mu_i(\mathbf{x}) + \frac{1}{2}\sum_{i,j} \frac{\partial f(t, \mathbf{x})}{\partial x_i \partial x_j}\sigma_i(\mathbf{x})\sigma_j(\mathbf{x}) \tag{23.22}$$

with the boundary condition $f(\mathbf{x}, T) = 1$.

Similarly to the simple example in Section 23.3.1.1, the appendix shows that a defaultable security with promised payoff g_T at T and zero recovery can be evaluated using the risk-neutral pricing formula:

$$V_t = \mathbb{E}_t^{\mathbb{Q}}\left[e^{-\int_t^T r_s + \lambda_s^{\mathbb{Q}} ds} g_T\right] \tag{23.23}$$

where $\lambda_t^{\mathbb{Q}}$ is the risk-neutral default intensity. Like in the simple example, the risk-neutral default intensity depends on the true intensity of default λ plus a risk premium that investors require to hold the security.

In addition, the appendix shows that the risk-neutral intensity $\lambda_t^{\mathbb{Q}}$ has both a dynamics under the physical $\mathbb{P}$ and risk-neutral $\mathbb{Q}$ probabilities. The dynamics of $\lambda_t^{\mathbb{Q}}$ under the physical probabilities $\mathbb{P}$ capture the variation in the discount rate that is due to default risk. Such variation may stem from the variation in the true default probabilities (λ_t) or from the variation in the default risk premium itself (μ in the simple example in Section 23.3.1.1). The dynamics of $\lambda_t^{\mathbb{Q}}$ under the risk-neutral probabilities $\mathbb{Q}$ adds another source of risk premium, namely, the risk premium that investors require to hold a security whose value may change because of default risk changes. That is, a defaultable security may decrease in price not only because it defaults but also because the *risk of default* increases (i.e., $\lambda_t^{\mathbb{Q}}$ increases). The variation in the risk of default is a source of risk itself and requires an additional risk premium. The appendix contains further details.

23.3.2 Pricing Sovereign Credit Default Swaps

Even if a CDS contract written on a company's bond differs from that written on a sovereign bond in its credit event definition, the theoretical pricing framework is still valid.

A CDS contract with maturity M consists of two components: the buyer's premium, defined as $CDS_t(M)$ and paid quarterly or semiannually, and the amount the buyer gets from the seller upon the occurrence of a credit event. Assuming a semiannual payment and a notional equal to one, the premium leg, that is, the present value of the premium flows, is then equivalent to a portfolio of defaultable zero-coupon bonds with zero recovery (because if default occurs, the buyer of the CDS stops making payments to the seller). Using formula 23.23, we obtain

$$\frac{1}{2}CDS_t(M)\sum_{j=1}^{2M}\mathbb{E}_t^{\mathbb{Q}}[e^{-\int_t^{t+.5j}(r_s+\lambda_s^{\mathbb{Q}})ds}] \tag{23.24}$$

where the expectation is taken under the risk-neutral measure $\mathbb{Q}$, and the term in brackets catches the risk-neutral survival-dependent nature of the payments.

Instead, the present value of the contingent amount the seller will pay upon a credit event is

$$L^{\mathbb{Q}}\int_t^{t+M}\mathbb{E}_t^{\mathbb{Q}}[\lambda_u^{\mathbb{Q}}e^{-\int_t^u(r_s+\lambda_s^{\mathbb{Q}})ds}]du \tag{23.25}$$

where $L^{\mathbb{Q}} = 1 - R^{\mathbb{Q}}$ is the loss given default (LGD), expressed as the face value minus the recovery rate, $R^{\mathbb{Q}}$.[8] This last equation can be easily understood by recalling that the probability density function of default occurring at time s is $\mathbb{E}_t^{\mathbb{Q}}[\lambda_s^{\mathbb{Q}}e^{-\int_t^s\lambda_u^{\mathbb{Q}}du}]$, as shown in Equation 23.17.

Like many other "swap" contracts, a CDS is worth zero at inception. Therefore, we can infer the contract-implied spread by setting the premium leg equal to the contingent leg and then inverting for the spread:

$$\frac{1}{2}CDS_t(M)\sum_{j=1}^{2M}\mathbb{E}_t^{\mathbb{Q}}[e^{-\int_t^{t+.5j}(r_s+\lambda_s^{\mathbb{Q}})ds}] = L^{\mathbb{Q}}\int_t^{t+M}\mathbb{E}_t^{\mathbb{Q}}[\lambda_u^{\mathbb{Q}}e^{-\int_t^u(r_s+\lambda_s^{\mathbb{Q}})ds}]du \tag{23.26}$$

such that

$$CDS_t(M) = \frac{2L^{\mathbb{Q}}\int_t^{t+M}\mathbb{E}_t^{\mathbb{Q}}[\lambda_u^{\mathbb{Q}}e^{-\int_t^u(r_s+\lambda_s^{\mathbb{Q}})ds}]du}{\sum_{j=1}^{2M}\mathbb{E}_t^{\mathbb{Q}}[e^{-\int_t^{t+.5j}(r_s+\lambda_s^{\mathbb{Q}})ds}]} \tag{23.27}$$

The pricing of a CDS requires a solution to the expectations in Equations 23.24 and 23.25. A common simplifying assumption is to assume independence between the risk-free rate and the default intensity. In this case the expectation in Equation 23.25 can be split accordingly as follows:

$$\int_t^{t_M}\mathbb{E}_t^{\mathbb{Q}}[\lambda_u^{\mathbb{Q}}e^{-\int_t^u(r_s+\lambda_s^{\mathbb{Q}})ds}]du = \int_t^{t_M}D(t,u)\mathbb{E}_t^{\mathbb{Q}}[\lambda_u^{\mathbb{Q}}e^{-\int_t^u\lambda_s^{\mathbb{Q}}ds}]du \tag{23.28}$$

where $D(t,u)$ represents the price of a default-free zero-coupon bond issued at time t and maturing at time u, whereas the term in the expectation is nothing more than the risk-neutral probability density of default at u. The default-free discount function can be obtained in several ways: it can be bootstrapped either from constant maturity Treasury (CMTs) bonds or from swap-LIBOR curves[9].

[8] We put a superscript $\mathbb{Q}$ to the LGD to emphasize that the recovery rate may be stochastic as well, and thus one more risk premium may apply to this additional random variable. As pointed out by Pan and Singleton (2008), the risk-neutral default intensity has a clear interpretation in a reduced-form model. Assume that each of the four ISDA credit events has its own default intensity $\lambda_t^{\mathbb{Q}}$ and LGD $L^{\mathbb{Q}}$. Then the default intensity is simply the sum of the four intensities, whereas the LGD is a weighted sum of event-specific LGDs, that is,

$$\lambda_t^{\mathbb{Q}} = \lambda_{t,acc}^{\mathbb{Q}} + \lambda_{t,fail}^{\mathbb{Q}} + \lambda_{t,rest}^{\mathbb{Q}} + \lambda_{t,repud}^{\mathbb{Q}}$$

$$L_t^{\mathbb{Q}} = \frac{\lambda_{t,acc}^{\mathbb{Q}}}{\lambda_t^{\mathbb{Q}}}L_t^{\mathbb{Q}} + \frac{\lambda_{t,fail}^{\mathbb{Q}}}{\lambda_t^{\mathbb{Q}}}L_t^{\mathbb{Q}} + \frac{\lambda_{t,rest}^{\mathbb{Q}}}{\lambda_t^{\mathbb{Q}}}L_t^{\mathbb{Q}} + \frac{\lambda_{t,repud}^{\mathbb{Q}}}{\lambda_t^{\mathbb{Q}}}L_t^{\mathbb{Q}}$$

In fact, since in a doubly stochastic framework the conditional probability of two events occurring at the same time is zero, conditional on the intensity path, $\lambda_t^{\mathbb{Q}}$ catches the sudden nature of the arrival of the credit event of any type. Once the event i has occurred, the LGD is realized with probability $\lambda_{t,i}^{\mathbb{Q}}/\lambda_t^{\mathbb{Q}}$.

[9] As pointed out in Duffie (1999), under some assumptions, a credit spread on a defaultable security can be replicated in an arbitrage-free setting, where the risk-free discount function plays a negligible role.

23.3.3 Pricing in a Lognormal Model

One of the most commonly used approaches to solve the expectation in Equation 23.28 is to assume an *affine* structure for the state process in Equation 23.18. We instead follow Pan and Singleton (2008) to price sovereign CDSs and assume that the dynamics of the default intensity is described by a mean-reverting lognormal process. The lognormal assumption has its own advantages. Indeed, a lognormal distribution presents fatter tails than the classical noncentral chi-square distribution of the frequently used Cox, Ingersoll, and Ross (1985) process. Additionally, it insures the strict positivity of the intensity whose distribution is skewed to the right. However, Sandmann and Sondermann (1997) show the main drawback of such an assumption is that the model is *double exponential*, that is, the exponential function is itself an argument of an exponential function, giving rise to infinite expectations under the risk-neutral probability measure. Moreover, since the seminal work of Black and Karasinski (1991), it is known that the implied default probability is not available in closed form, since the distribution of sums of lognormals is never lognormal, and there is no explicit formula for the convolution of lognormal distributions. This shortcoming can be overcome by numerical approximations of the corresponding PDE, such as, the fully implicit and the Crank–Nicolson methods.

As explained in Section 23.3.1, we need to specify the dynamics of the process under both the risk-neutral ($\mathbb{Q}$) and physical ($\mathbb{P}$) probability measure. Such a specification is important to define the two components of credit risk: the credit risk premium and the default risk. The former is the premium an investor demands to bear more risk; therefore, it captures the degree of risk aversion of the market. This is quantified by the difference of the price of the security under both probability measures. Default risk, instead, reflects the physical probability of a sudden negative jump in the price of the underlying security upon the realization of the credit event.

Measuring the physical default probability requires knowledge of the true intensity process (or dynamics) that generates it. But a sovereign default is a rare event, thus, it is hard to infer it from traded prices alone (Pan and Singleton (2008) and Longstaff et al. (2011)). Indeed, market prices can convey information only on the risk-neutral intensity $\lambda_t^{\mathbb{Q}}$ under the objective probability measure. Such an intensity will give rise to *pseudo*-credit spreads, whose default intensity is risk neutral but driven by parameters under the physical probability measure.

To make the point clearer, let the risk-neutral intensity $\lambda_t^{\mathbb{Q}}$ have the following representation under the physical probability measure:

$$d \ln \lambda_t^{\mathbb{Q}} = k^{\mathbb{P}}(\theta^{\mathbb{P}} - \ln \lambda_t^{\mathbb{Q}})dt + \sigma_{\lambda_t^{\mathbb{Q}}} dB_t^{\mathbb{P}} \tag{23.29}$$

where $k^{\mathbb{P}}$ is the mean-reversion speed, $\theta^{\mathbb{P}}$ the long-term mean level, and $\sigma_{\lambda_t^{\mathbb{Q}}}$ the local volatility for local changes in $\ln \lambda_t^{\mathbb{Q}}$. Assuming an affine market price of risk η_t of the form

$$\eta_t = \delta_0 + \delta_1 \ln \lambda_t^{\mathbb{Q}} \tag{23.30}$$

and applying the Girsanov theorem, we obtain the following risk-neutral dynamics:

$$d \ln \lambda_t^{\mathbb{Q}} = k^{\mathbb{Q}}(\theta^{\mathbb{Q}} - \ln \lambda_t^{\mathbb{Q}})dt + \sigma_{\lambda_t^{\mathbb{Q}}} dB_t^{\mathbb{Q}} \tag{23.31}$$

where $k^{\mathbb{Q}} = k^{\mathbb{P}} + \delta_1 \sigma_{\lambda_t^{\mathbb{Q}}}$ and $k^{\mathbb{Q}}\theta^{\mathbb{Q}} = k^{\mathbb{P}}\theta^{\mathbb{P}} - \delta_0 \sigma_{\lambda_t^{\mathbb{Q}}}$. Thus, the characteristics of the process are preserved under the equivalent probability measure.

23.4 CREDIT RISK PREMIA

Reduced-form models applied to defaultable securities present an important limit. Yu (2002) shows how these models can only be applicable prior to default, since they suffer a survival bias, which is related to the true process under the objective probability that can never be revealed from quotes alone.

Credit risk premium or *distress risk* is priced in the market as long as the risk-neutral default probability differs from the physical one. Such a premium is a compensation investors demand for bearing the risk due to unexpected variations in the arrival of default events, that is, the default intensity. Therefore, following Pan and Singleton (2008), we measure the distress risk as the difference between the credit spread and the *pseudo*-credit spread. The *pseudo*-credit spread is the credit spread that would hold under agents' risk neutrality, and it is computed using the expectation under the physical probability measure:

$$CDS_t^{\mathbb{P}}(M) = \frac{2L^{\mathbb{Q}} \int_t^{t+M} \mathbb{E}_t^{\mathbb{P}}[\lambda_u^{\mathbb{Q}} e^{-\int_t^u (r_s + \lambda_s^{\mathbb{Q}})ds}]du}{\sum_{j=1}^{2M} \mathbb{E}_t^{\mathbb{P}}[e^{-\int_t^{t+.5j}(r_s+\lambda_s^{\mathbb{Q}})ds}]} \tag{23.32}$$

where $\lambda_t^{\mathbb{Q}}$ follows the dynamics in Equation 23.29. Therefore, the credit risk premium at time t and for the maturity M, $CRP_t(M)$, is

$$CRP_t(M) = CDS_t(M) - CDS_t^{\mathbb{P}}(M) \tag{23.33}$$

If agents were risk neutral, then $CDS_t(M) = CDS_t^{\mathbb{P}}(M)$. However, agents are risk averse, and they require a higher (insurance) premium to insure against default. Therefore, in general, $CDS_t(M) > CDS_t^{\mathbb{P}}(M)$ implying the existence of a risk premium in the credit market.

Longstaff et al. (2011) argue that the default risk can be estimated as the residual from the quoted CDS spread after subtracting the CRP. In other words, according to the interpretation of the expected return in Yu (2002), the risk premium derived from the difference between a defaultable and a default-free bond consists of the sum of two components. The first component is due to the risk of price jump upon default, while the second is due to the risk of unexpected variation in default intensity. The methodology in this section only allows for the identification of the latter component.[10]

23.5 ESTIMATING INTENSITY MODELS

The calibration of a reduced-form model to market data can be performed according to several procedures. One of the most commonly used estimation strategies is the maximum likelihood estimator (MLE) that allows for the estimation of the parameters under both probability measures.[11] This estimation method is employed in the dated works of Longstaff and Schwartz (1992) and Chen and Scott (1993), and in the recent works of Duffee (2002), Pan and Singleton (2008), and Longstaff et al. (2011).

Essentially, the MLE method looks for those values of the parameters that maximize the likelihood function, that is, it maximizes the probability of the observed data under the resulting distribution. Therefore, it is a very suitable approach when the assumption about the probability distribution of the underlying data is reliable. Additionally, it might be the case that the probability distribution of the data is not known, so that a different or simplified form of the actual likelihood function is used instead. In this case we talk about *Quasi*-MLE. As we shall show, instead of using the actual probability of CDS spreads, we estimate the parameters with respect to the distribution of the CDS-implied default intensity, which is lognormal.

In order to implement the MLE approach, it is common to assume that a CDS contract over a specified maturity is priced without error. Under this assumption, the model for that maturity can be inverted to get the latent variable, that is, the unobservable default intensity $\lambda_t^{\mathbb{Q}}$. This is possible thanks to the availability of a term structure of CDS spreads. A widely used empirical approach is to choose the most liquid maturity, which usually corresponds to the 5-year one (Longstaff et al., 2011). In the following empirical application, we estimate the model assuming that the 5-year maturity for each country is priced without error.

The stochastic intensity in Equation 23.31 has a lognormal density with the following time-varying mean $m_{\Delta t}$ and variance $v_{\Delta t}$:

$$m_{\Delta t} = \ln(\lambda_{t-1}^{\mathbb{Q}})e^{-k^{\mathbb{P}}\Delta t} + \frac{\theta^{\mathbb{P}}}{k^{\mathbb{P}}}(1 - e^{-k^{\mathbb{P}}\Delta t}) \tag{23.34}$$

$$v_{\Delta t} = \frac{\sigma^2_{\lambda_t^{\mathbb{Q}}}}{2k^{\mathbb{P}}}(1 - e^{-2k^{\mathbb{P}}\Delta t}) \tag{23.35}$$

Let $CDS_t(M)$ be the vector of CDS spreads for some maturities $M = 1, 3, 7$, and 10. We assume that for these maturities the pricing errors are normally distributed with mean zero and constant variance. Therefore, we estimate the following model:

$$CDS_t(M) = h(\lambda_t^{\mathbb{Q}}) + \epsilon_t \tag{23.36}$$

where $h(\cdot)$ is the pricing function in Equation 23.29 and the pricing error, ϵ_t, is jointly estimated according to the following joint density:

$$f^{\mathbb{P}}(\lambda_t^{\mathbb{Q}}, \epsilon_t) = f^{\mathbb{P}}(\lambda_t^{\mathbb{Q}} | \mathcal{F}_{t-1}) \times f^{\mathbb{P}}(\epsilon_t | \lambda_t^{\mathbb{Q}}, \mathcal{F}_{t-1}) \tag{23.37}$$

$$= f^{\mathbb{P}}(\lambda_t^{\mathbb{Q}} | \lambda_{t-1}^{\mathbb{Q}}) \times f^{\mathbb{P}}(\epsilon_t | \lambda_t^{\mathbb{Q}}, \mathcal{F}_{t-1}) \tag{23.38}$$

[10]In the literature, there exists two main approaches to decompose a credit spread. One consists in building a pricing model, such as the one we are presenting, whose market calibration gives a direct estimate of the credit risk premium. The second approach requires the estimation of the real probability of default of a sovereign. Using Moody's default probabilities as a proxy for the underlying objective process that drives the spreads, one can get a direct estimate of the default risk and so the credit risk premium emerges as a residual component from the quoted spreads (see Amato and Remolona (2003), Driessen (2005), Berndt et al. (2005) and Remolona, Scatigna, and Wu (2007)).

[11]Other used approaches are the nonlinear least square (NLS) and the Kalman Filter. While the former can only estimate the risk-neutral parameters by minimizing the squared errors between the actual and the fitted quotes (see Cornuejols and Tutuncu (2006) and Ang and Longstaff (2013)), the Kalman Filter and its extensions use the MLE as a second step in the estimation, thus capturing the process dynamics under both probability measures (see Carr and Wu (2007 and 2010)).

where the first RHS term is derived from the Markov assumption[12] and where $f^{\mathbb{P}}(\epsilon_t|\lambda_t^{\mathbb{Q}}, \mathcal{F}_{t-1}) \sim N(0, \Omega)$, with $\Omega = diag\{\sigma(1), \sigma(3), \sigma(7), \sigma(10)\}$. Hence, the final set of parameters, Θ, is comprised of $k^{\mathbb{P}}$, $k^{\mathbb{P}}\theta^{\mathbb{P}}$, $k^{\mathbb{Q}}$, $k^{\mathbb{Q}}\theta^{\mathbb{Q}}$, $\sigma_{\lambda_t^{\mathbb{Q}}}$, $\sigma(1)$, $\sigma(3)$, $\sigma(7)$, and $\sigma(10)$. The likelihood function to be maximized is obtained by summing up the log transformation of Equation 23.38 across time.

We can compute the likelihood function once we know the default intensity $\lambda_t^{\mathbb{Q}}$. As mentioned, this is computed from the inversion of the CDS pricing formula for the maturity $M = 5$ years. We now describe the procedure in detail:

Step 1. (*Model inversion*) Choose a set of initial risk-neutral parameters to compute fitted 5-year CDS spreads (the function $h(\cdot)$ in Eq. 23.36). For that set of parameters, compute the intensity that gives the smallest pricing error with respect to the quoted spread.

Step 2. (*Joint distribution*) The *known* value of the intensity $\lambda_t^{\mathbb{Q}}$ at time t is then used to get both the pricing errors and the probability density by plugging it into the Equation 23.38.

Step 3. (*Log-likelihood*) Compute the log-likelihood by summing up the logarithm of the probability distribution over time as follows:

$$\mathcal{L}(\Theta|\lambda_1^{\mathbb{Q}}, \cdots, \lambda_N^{\mathbb{Q}}) = \sum_{t=1}^{N} \ln f^{\mathbb{P}}(\lambda_t^{\mathbb{Q}}, \epsilon_t) \tag{23.39}$$

Step 4. (*ML estimator*) The final set of parameters will give the maximum log-likelihood, that is,

$$\{\hat{\Theta}^{mle}\} \subseteq \{\arg\max \mathcal{L}(\Theta|\lambda_1^{\mathbb{Q}}, \cdots, \lambda_N^{\mathbb{Q}})\} \tag{23.40}$$

To complete the estimation, we also need the risk-free discount functions. Several methods can be used for this purpose, but their effect in pricing CDSs is negligible, since it enters the pricing equation symmetrically. Indeed, Duffie (1999) shows that the sensitivity of CDSs to interest rate variations is very small, as under some specific conditions a CDS contract can be replicated by an arbitrage-free portfolio that is long a default-free floater and short a defaultable floater. For our empirical analysis, we bootstrap the risk-free discount functions from constant maturity bonds (CMT) collected from the H.15 release of the Federal Reserve system.

23.6 APPLICATION TO EMERGING MARKETS

Emerging markets have been examined for years due to their worldwide economic and financial implications. Even if there exists no proper definition for emerging markets, they are typically referred to as less-developed economies with a high potential in terms of economic growth but with high risk and market volatility. The view of a sustainable future growth path is typically supported by demographic reasons (large and young populations), growing domestic consumption, relatively low debt, high private saving rates, and high potential for productivity growth boosted by infrastructural and technological improvements. However, a serious downside risk exists: these are often countries with insufficient monetary moderation that causes a significant potential inflation risk. Moreover, their capital markets do not require the stringent accounting standards and disclosures expected in the developed economies, leading to limited protection of investors in terms of fraud and information disclosure. Currency and liquidity risk also contribute to high volatility in the short run (Domowitz et al., 1998). Last but not least, political risk plays a significant role as it may adversely affect the return on investments (see Diamonte et al. (1996), Cuadra and Sapriza (2008), and Pastor and Veronesi (2012 and 2013)).

Nowadays, an important debate is taking place about the potential for an emerging market crisis similar to the *Asian Contagion* of 1997.[13] Shin (2013) argues that a *Second Phase of Global Liquidity* is at stake due to an increased vulnerability of emerging economies to a reversal of permissive financial conditions. Indeed, emerging markets have shown bond yields that increasingly tend to "move in sync with those of advanced economy bonds," as well as a widespread propensity of local corporations to hold cash in local currencies financed with U.S. dollar liabilities. An improvement in the economic conditions in both Europe and the United States that leads to a monetary tightening may trigger significant shocks in the emerging markets, such as a rise in the borrowing cost for emerging market corporations, currency depreciation, runs of corporate deposits from the domestic banking sector, declines in corporate expenditures leading to a slowdown in growth, and asset managers on the run from those markets due to the weakening economic conditions.

[12]A process is said to be Markovian if the conditional probability distribution of future states of the process, conditional on past information, depends only on the present state, not on the entire filtration that has generated it, that is, $\mathcal{F}_{t-1}$.

[13]*Asian Contagion* refers to the Asian Financial Crisis burst in the Summer of 1997 after the collapse of the Thai baht that brought about declines in Asian stock markets and import revenues and government upheavals.

TABLE 23.1 Emerging Economies (2012 IMF Classification)

Emerging country	Code	Region	Per capita GDP ($)	Debt to GDP (%)	Unem (%)	Growth rate (%)
Argentina	ARG	South America	6813	75.7	11.4	4.6
Brazil	BRA	South America	6850	68.5	8.9	3.3
Bulgaria	BGR	East Europe	4750	32.4	11.2	3.5
Chile	CHL	S. America	9251	9.6	8.5	4.4
China	CHN	Central Asia	2877	20.1	4.1	10.0
Colombia	COL	South America	4432	37.3	12.3	4.3
Estonia	EST	East Europe	12102	6.0	9.9	4.3
Hungary	HUN	East Europe	11063	68.0	8.3	1.6
India	IND	South Asia	953	75.2	3.8	7.0
Indonesia	IDN	South Asia	1923	45.8	8.4	5.5
Latvia	LVA	East Europe	9292	21.7	12.0	4.2
Lithuania	LTU	East Europe	9339	25.9	11.6	4.5
Malaysia	MYS	South Asia	6774	46.4	3.4	4.7
Mexico	MEX	Central America	8253	42.4	4.1	2.1
Peru	PER	South America	3854	32.6	8.5	5.9
Philippines	PHL	South Asia	1598	51.8	8.9	4.9
Poland	POL	East Europe	9509	47.9	13.4	3.6
Romania	ROM	East Europe	5915	24.9	7.1	3.6
Russia	RUS	North Asia	7611	21.1	7.3	4.6
South Africa	ZAF	South Africa	5344	36.6	25.2	3.4
Turkey	TUR	Asia Minor	7640	50.7	10.4	4.2
Ukraine	UKR	E. Europe	2344	30.5	8.1	4.2
Venezuela	VEN	South America	8035	39.4	10.8	3.4
Mean	–	–	6370	39.6	9.5	4.4

The table reports the list of Emerging Economies as of the 2012 IMF classification, together with average values, over the period 2001–2013, of *per capita GDP*, *debt-to-GDP* ratio, unemployment rate as a percentage of total labor force (*Unem*), and the *Growth rate*.
Source: World Bank, International Monetary Fund and Eurostat.

As of July 2012, the International Monetary Fund (IMF) labels 25 countries as emerging markets according to their *per capita* GDP, which is, assumed to range between $2,000 and $12,000. Table 23.1 reports a list of these economies together with their main statistics averaged over the period 2001–2013. The per capita GDP ranges from a minimum of $953 in India to a maximum of $12,102 in Estonia, which has been recently included among the developed economies. The debt-to-GDP ratio depicts a very safe scenario if compared to that of the most developed countries. Such a ratio is mostly used to proxy for the ability of a government to commit to its debt. But, as already mentioned, in the case of emerging markets, geopolitical and economic risks might negatively influence the ability to pay back debts. Additionally, such economies have, on average, an unemployment rate of 9.5% and a growth rate of 4.4%.

23.6.1 Credit Markets of Emerging Economies

The heterogeneity in the economic fundamentals of these economies is reflected in their credit markets as shown in Table 23.2. Panel A reports summary statistics of 5-year CDS spreads across three subsamples: the pre-crisis period from 2001 to 2007, the crisis period 2008–2009, and the post-crisis period 2010–2013. The relevance of such a period classification lies in the fact that the 2000's began with a significant slowdown in growth of Latin American economies (Barajas and Steiner, 2002). In fact, the slowdown period of Latin America, namely, the years between 1980 and 2000, was also characterized and followed by unprecedented political changes over the period 1998–2011. Gonzalez (2008) labels the period 2000–2007 as a "nontraditional crisis" for seven countries including Argentina, Venezuela, and Peru. As reported in Table 23.2, the first two countries have the highest credit spreads, together with Brazil that had just recovered from a currency crisis at the end of 1999. In the second subsample period, the highest mean spreads are those of Argentina, Venezuela, and some European countries such as Ukraine, Latvia, and Lithuania. The latter countries experienced very high spreads during the Financial Crisis because their underdeveloped banking system led them to rely mostly on foreign borrowing, thus leading them to suffer negative spillovers. The third period is mostly characterized by the European Debt Crisis, and indeed, the highest spreads are those of Eastern European economies. Interestingly, both Argentina and Venezuela have always been perceived among the riskiest by the market across the three periods, possibly due to their persistent political crises.

TABLE 23.2 Credit Markets of Emerging Economies

Panel A: Credit Default Spread Summary Stats

	Precrisis		Crisis		Postcrisis	
	Mean	Std dev	Mean	Std dev	Mean	Std dev
India	58.6	24.6	219.8	146.6	–	–
Argentina	2174.0	2922.2	1470.5	1262.3	1342.8	871.0
Venezuela	702.7	512.5	1091.0	761.2	952.1	184.5
Ukraine	247.8	113.6	1201.7	1202.3	680.6	174.6
Hungary	29.5	8.9	214.5	160.3	358.5	117.8
Romania	162.8	165.2	266.9	199.1	290.0	83.8
Latvia	8.3	3.5	417.4	309.3	245.3	102.5
Bulgaria	169.0	160.7	235.6	173.5	227.8	90.3
Lithuania	28.9	31.8	281.5	227.9	217.5	74.6
Turkey	517.0	327.9	271.4	109.2	187.7	48.6
Russia	232.9	189.8	262.5	234.1	172.5	39.3
Indonesia	280.4	118.1	314.3	201.6	169.8	36.9
South Africa	116.3	63.8	196.5	128.5	159.3	30.0
Poland	33.5	19.0	113.6	96.2	147.6	59.7
Philippines	383.9	140.5	243.5	105.3	141.5	32.4
Brazil	744.3	759.2	174.8	99.2	133.8	26.5
Peru	349.1	239.0	181.6	103.3	127.9	24.2
Colombia	448.7	279.3	206.5	99.9	124.4	24.3
Mexico	152.8	94.1	168.7	114.4	119.9	21.8
Malaysia	66.7	49.3	116.2	82.0	100.4	24.8
Estonia	7.4	2.2	238.8	196.0	98.9	29.9
China	35.1	16.9	84.6	61.0	90.5	27.1
Chile	71.1	74.1	94.9	74.4	87.5	19.6

Panel A: Principal Component Analysis

	Expl var	Total	Expl var	Total	Expl var	Total
PC1	0.2527	0.2527	0.7292	0.7292	0.6972	0.6972
PC2	0.0839	0.3366	0.0825	0.8117	0.0764	0.7736
PC3	0.063	0.3996	0.0518	0.8635	0.0428	0.8164

The table reports summary statistics of 5-year CDS spreads in bps (*Panel A*) and the principal component analysis (*Panel B*) across three subsamples: *precrisis* (2001–2007), *crisis* (2008–2009 Financial Crisis) and *postcrisis* (2010–2013).
Source: Markit.

The principal component analysis in Panel B of Table 23.2 highlights the degree of heterogeneity of the credit markets of these Emerging Economies. It is performed on the correlation matrix of changes in the 5-year CDS spreads. To gauge the global nature of the 2008–2009 Financial Crisis and European Debt Crisis 2010/2013, the explanatory power of the first principal component increases from 25% during the first part of the sample to 73 and to 70% during the subsequent periods, respectively.

Figure 23.3 plots the loadings on the first three principal components over the period 2008–2013. The loadings on the first PC, which explains 70% of the variability in the credit market, are all positive, reflecting "parallel shifts" in the cross section of the CDS spreads (Longstaff et al., 2011). Interestingly, the second PC loads positively and heavily only on Eastern Europe economies. Therefore, this component may reflect the spread between European and non-European countries. Finally, the third PC weighs positively on those countries that have been experiencing serious political crisis such as Argentina, Venezuela, and Ukraine.

23.6.2 Credit Risk Premia in Emerging Credit Markets

In order to measure the credit risk premia of emerging markets, we estimate the model using the CDS term structure at maturities 1, 3, 5, 7, and 10 years and according to the procedure in Section 23.5. To analyze the degree of correlation of credit risk premia across different macroregions, we select a country for each region and estimate the model separately. We select Turkey for Asia

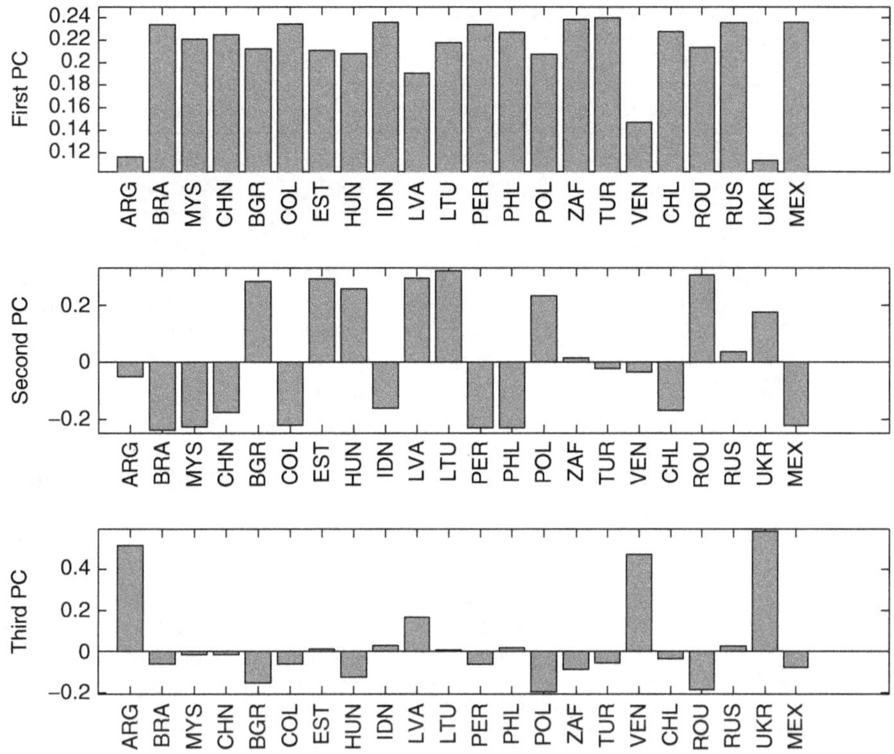

Figure 23.3 The figure plots the loading of the first three principal components of the PCA performed on the correlation matrix of weekly 5-year CDS spread changes over the period 2008–2013. Source: Markit.

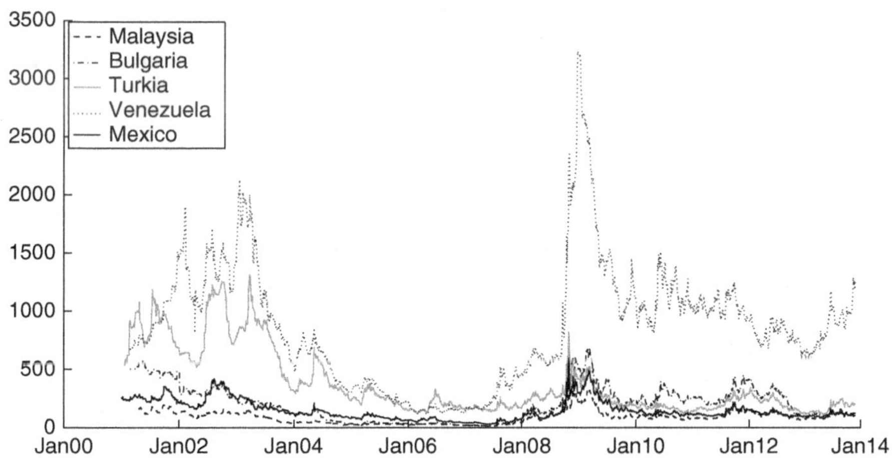

Figure 23.4 The figure plots the 5-year credit default swap spreads in basis points of Malaysia, Bulgaria, Turkey, Venezuela, and Mexico over the weekly period from January 2001 to November 2013. Source: Markit.

Minor, Mexico for Central America, Venezuela for South America, Malaysia for South Asia, and Bulgaria for Eastern Europe. The idea behind the selection is to choose countries that are geographically dispersed so as to assess how these markets are driven by common factors.

Figure 23.4 plots the CDS spreads of these five economies.

The beginning of 2000s was characterized by high credit spreads, in particular for Venezuela. We may find several reasons for these high spreads. As explained previously, emerging markets have been concerned with local economic and political shocks. As an example, Longstaff et al. (2011, fn. 9) find that for some Latin American countries such as Venezuela, percentage changes

TABLE 23.3 Maximum Likelihood Estimated Parameters and CRP Statistics

Panel A: Maximum Likelihood Estimation					
	Bulgaria	Malaysia	Turkia	Mexico	Venezuela
$\sigma_{\lambda_t^{\mathbb{Q}}}$	1.524	0.530	1.244	0.632	0.497
	(0.004)	(0.0171)	(0.0023)	(0.0059)	(0.0053)
$k^{\mathbb{Q}}\theta^{\mathbb{Q}}$	1.398	6.681	5.716	3.776	1.682
	(0.0081)	(0.0122)	(0.0052)	−0.0133	(0.0119)
$k^{\mathbb{Q}}$	−0.523	−0.687	−1.067	0.233	−1.788
	(0.0004)	(0.0024)	(0.0002)	(0.0023)	(0.0015)
$\theta^{\mathbb{P}}$	−2.107	−1.055	−2.989	−2.463	−0.733
	(0.0044)	(0.0072)	(0.0055)	(0.0055)	(0.0054)
$k^{\mathbb{P}}$	0.013	0.070	0.151	0.156	0.050
	(0.0004)	(0.0013)	(0.0005)	(0.0007)	(0.0007)
$\sigma(1)$	0.306	0.076	0.037	0.265	0.002
	(0.0002)	(0.0001)	(0.00004)	(0.00001)	(0.00001)
$\sigma(3)$	0.002	0.000	0.006	0.007	0.001
	(0.00000)	(0.00000)	(0.00052)	(0.00000)	(0.00000)
$\sigma(7)$	0.005	0.000	0.023	0.008	0.000
	(0.00000)	(0.00001)	(0.00000)	(0.00000)	(0.00000)
$\sigma(10)$	0.003	0.000	0.029	0.001	0.000
	(0.00000)	(0.00000)	(0.00001)	(0.00026)	(0.00000)
Panel B: Credit Risk Premia Summary Statistics					
CRP mean (bps)	112.64	50.81	145.31	72.65	466.98
CRP std dev (bps)	87.68	44.87	96.33	48.17	296.20
%-CRP mean	0.55	0.51	0.46	0.48	0.54
%-CRP std dev	0.03	0.11	0.21	0.03	0.01

The table reports the maximum likelihood estimated parameters (Panel A) and summary statistics of the credit risk premia (Panel B) for Bulgaria, Malaysia, Turkey, Mexico, and Venezuela. Numerical standard errors in parenthesis. The estimation is performed on the term structure of 1-, 3-, 5-, 7-, and 10-year credit default swap spreads over the weekly period January 2001–November 2013.
Source: Markit.

in oil price have a significant explanatory power for sovereign credit spreads. Pan and Singleton (2008) report that in the early 2000s, Turkey was affected by financial and political crises such as the devaluation of the Turkish lira and political elections. After a period of lower spreads, the credit risk of these economies increased again during the Financial Crisis (2007–2009), with Venezuela reaching the highest spread of about 3200 basis points.

Turning to the estimation, Table 23.3 reports the estimated parameters with standard errors within parentheses (Panel A) and summary statistics of the credit risk premia (Panel B).

The standard deviations are small enough to claim that the model fits the term structure well, with the exception of the 1-year contract. The calibration confirms some empirical characteristics found in Pan and Singleton (2008): the credit environment is worse under the risk-neutral probabilities than the objective ones, $k^{\mathbb{Q}}\theta^{\mathbb{Q}} > k^{\mathbb{P}}\theta^{\mathbb{P}}$, allowing for large and more persistent ($k^{\mathbb{Q}} > k^{\mathbb{P}}$) default intensities under $\mathbb{Q}$ than under $\mathbb{P}$; finally, $k^{\mathbb{P}} > 0$ for each country, meaning that the process $\lambda_t^{\mathbb{Q}}$ is $\mathbb{P}$-stationary.

Panel B reports summary statistics for the credit risk premia both in absolute value and as a percentage of the actual CDS spread. The mean credit risk premia is on average 169.68 basis points, with that of Venezuela being the highest and the most volatile. On an average, the credit risk premia accounts for 51% of the quoted CDS spread.

To further explore the dynamics of the credit risk premia across macroregions, we employ a principal component analysis on the correlation matrix of 5-year CRPs and plot the first PC against two global variables: the VIX index and the U.S. spread. While the former is used as a proxy for the global financial uncertainty, the U.S. spread, computed as the difference between the 10-year BBB corporate yield and the 3-month T-Bill rate, captures two important risks: the slope of the term structure of interest rates and the credit risk. The former is an indicator of the U.S. monetary policy and, therefore, of the condition of the U.S. economy, whereas the BBB corporate yield resembles the two components of a credit spread: the credit risk premium and the expected default loss rate. Figure 23.5 plots these (standardized) time series. The first PC, which accounts for about 77% of the variability in the credit risk premia across macroregions, is highly correlated with both global measures. In line with Pan and Singleton (2008) and Berndt et al. (2005), the U.S. spread is highly correlated (84%) with our measure of risk premia, implying

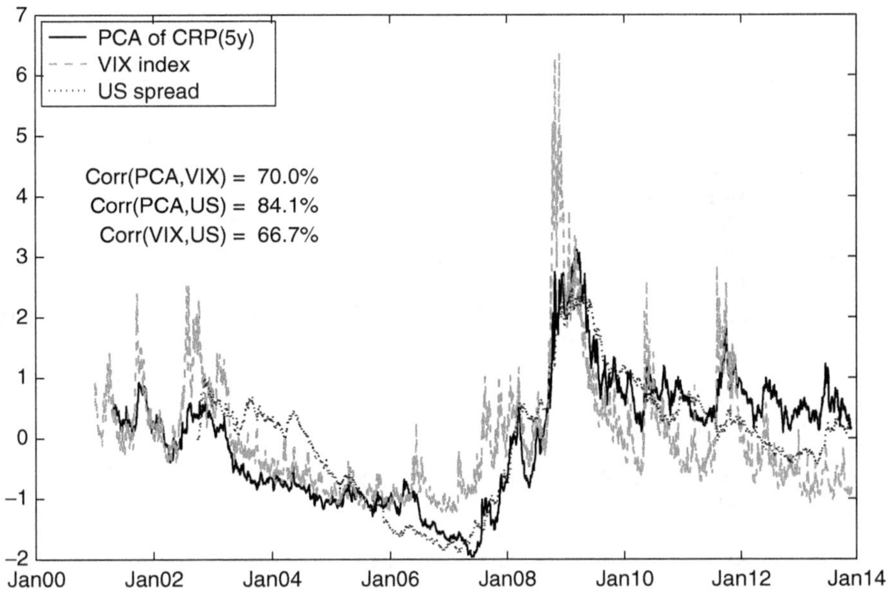

Figure 23.5 This figure plots the first Principal Component (PCA) of 5-year Credit Risk Premia of Bulgaria, Malaysia, Turkey, Mexico, and Venezuela (CRP), the VIX index and the U.S. spread (difference between the 10-year BBB U.S. Corp and the 3-month T-Bill rate). All the series are standardized to have the same mean and standard deviation. Source: Markit, CBOE, and Federal Reserve Board.

that the U.S. spread is mostly related to changes in the credit risk premium component rather than the default *event* risk premium component. This finding supports the view that an increase in risk aversion of international investors make them dump all of the risky securities, including risky BBB corporate bonds and sovereign bonds.

23.7 APPLICATION TO THE EUROPEAN DEBT CRISIS

As a result of the 2008–2009 Financial Crisis, a wave of sovereign debt increases aimed at rescuing local banking systems has swept through European economies. The growing amount of debt has resulted in a rapid widening of credit spreads that has brought about serious difficulties in repaying or refinancing the debt in the short term. Fears about a potential outbreak of a European Debt Crisis appeared at the beginning of 2010 when serious concerns on the ability of countries such as Greece, Ireland, and Portugal to commit to their debt payments emerged as a possible factor of contagion to other countries.

The first bailout agreement in the European Union history was reached in May 2010 for Greece when the Troika, a committee formed by the European Commission; the European Central Bank; and the IMF approved a bailout package worth $147 billion. Such intervention was followed by the bailouts of Ireland ($67.5 billion) in November 2010, Portugal ($78 billion) in the first half of 2011, Greece for the second time ($130 billion) in October 2011, Spain ($100 billion) in June 2012, and Cyprus ($10 billion) in December 2013.[14] Even if these economies are small compared to the rest of the Eurozone (with the exception of Spain)[15], they highlight two different but related risks: the financial risk and political risk, which raise doubts about the stability of the whole European Union. The former is mostly related to the high degree of interconnectedness of the financial markets, given that a large portion of the debt of these economies was held by foreign creditors.

Instead, political risk has become apparent in different ways. The debate about the first Greek bailout took 4 months before an agreement was reached in May 2010. Indeed, Greece was rescued after a long period of hesitation that saw a drop in Athens Stock Exchange (ASE) index of 13% and a significant increase in the 1-year and 10-year Greek bond yield to 276% and 116%, respectively. Interestingly, the bond and CDS markets embedded two different expectations about a possible Greek default. Over the period January-May 2010, the slope, computed as the difference between the 10-year and the 1-year contract, was +2.19%, on average, in the bond market, whereas negative (−1.47%) in CDS market. Therefore, the latter was showing an expectation by market participants of a Greek default in the short run. Then, after the second bailout and before the first default in March 2012, the Greek spreads in both markets increased exponentially, embedding a risk-neutral default probability close to one. Other episodes of political instability shocked the European Union in the last months of 2011, when the Italian and Greek Prime Ministers resigned, and when strikes and protests arose throughout Europe, threatening the stability of the European Union.

[14]Source: European Stability Mechanism (ESM) website, ESM/EFSF press release.

[15]Those countries account for the 12% of the GDP of the Eurozone.

TABLE 23.4 European Sovereign Credit Markets

Panel A: Summary Statistics

Region	Country	Code	DEBT/GDP	Precrisis Mean	Precrisis StdDev	Financial Crisis Mean	Financial Crisis StdDev	Euro crisis Mean	Euro crisis StdDev
	Belgium	BEL	99.8	4.2	1.6	38.6	33.8	145.5	80.6
	France	FRA	90.2	3.9	2.1	23.7	21.3	105.3	50.9
	United Kingdom	GRB	88.7	1.6	0.2	44.5	42.7	61.9	18.2
	Germany	DEU	81	4.2	2.6	20.4	19.7	52.0	24.1
Core	Austria	AUT	74	3.7	1.7	54.3	59.1	88.6	51.4
	Nether	NLD	71.3	2.5	1.2	30.1	31.9	62.2	27.3
	Finland	FIN	56.9	3.3	1.3	21.9	20.8	40.5	19.3
	Denmark	DNK	45.4	3.1	0.9	34.3	38.1	57.3	37.5
	Sweden	SWE	38.2	3.4	1.6	38.9	40.4	36.4	16.4
	Hungary	HUN	79.8	29.5	8.9	214.5	160.3	358.5	117.8
	Poland	POL	55.6	33.5	19.0	113.6	96.2	147.6	59.7
	Croatia	HRV	55.5	99.7	68.2	189.3	144.9	329.9	99.3
	Slovenia	SVN	54.4	14.4	10.5	56.9	52.5	225.5	133.1
	Slovak	SVK	52.4	43.5	50.1	67.2	57.2	130.6	72.3
East	Czech	CZE	46.2	17.1	11.4	79.8	74.3	93.7	30.5
	Latvia	LVA	40.7	8.3	3.5	417.4	309.3	245.3	102.5
	Lithuania	LTU	40.5	28.9	31.8	281.5	227.9	217.5	74.6
	Romania	ROM	37.9	162.8	165.2	266.9	199.1	290.0	83.8
	Ukraine	UKR	35.8	247.8	113.6	1201.7	1202.3	680.6	174.6
	Bulgaria	BGR	18.5	169.0	160.7	235.6	173.5	227.8	90.3
	Estonia	EST	9.8	7.4	2.2	238.8	196.0	98.9	29.9
	Greece	GRC	156.9	12.7	4.0	98.6	81.1	2275.8	3089.2
	Italy	ITA	132.6	9.1	2.1	67.0	52.0	277.3	123.9
	Portugal	PRT	124.1	7.1	2.1	51.1	34.6	612.9	355.3
Periph	Ireland	IRL	117.4	3.5	1.3	98.7	95.3	423.0	252.8
	Cyprus	CYP	86.6	16.1	10.4	59.8	49.9	744.7	464.4
	Spain	ESP	86	4.5	1.9	56.2	39.6	296.8	111.6
	Malta	MLT	71.3	10.4	5.4	57.4	45.1	245.0	91.5

Panel B: Principal Component Analysis

	ExpVar	Tot	ExpVar	Tot	ExpVar	Tot
PC1	0.11	0.11	0.65	0.65	0.60	0.60
PC2	0.09	0.20	0.11	0.76	0.07	0.67
PC3	0.18	0.26	0.70	0.81	0.64	0.72

The table reports the summary statistics of the European sovereign Credit Default Swap markets (*Panel A*. The 5-year CDS spreads are in basis points and cover three periods: *precrisis* (2001–2007), *Financial Crisis* (2008–2009), and *European crisis* (2010–2013). The *debt/GDP* ratio is for 2013 and is shown as a percentage. *Panel B* reports the PCA on the correlation matrix of 5-year CDS spread changes across subsamples. Source: Markit and Eurostat.

In this section, we analyze the European Debt Crisis through the lens of the sovereign CDS market. Table 23.4 reports the credits spreads and debt-to-GDP ratios of 28 European countries inside and outside the European Union and the European Monetary Union.

Panel A reports summary statistics for the 5-year CDS spread of those countries across three subsamples: the *precrisis* period from 2001 to 2007, the 2008–2009 *Financial Crisis*, and the *European Debt Crisis* from 2010 to 2013. Countries are classified into three regions: the *core*, the *Eastern*, and the *peripheral* economies and are sorted on their debt over GDP ratio at the end of 2013.

The precrisis is a quiet period in terms of credit risk for both core and peripheral economies. The situation is different for Eastern countries. As shown in Section 23.6, some of them are also classified as Emerging Economies, thus, sharing additional sources of risk. The 2008–2009 Financial Crisis has particularly affected the credit markets of Eastern economies. The high mean spreads and volatilities in their credit markets are in line with the view that these economies have suffered negative spillovers from the U.S. economy as their underdeveloped banking systems have made them rely heavily on foreign borrowing, especially from the biggest U.S. banks. The postcrisis period, that is, the European Debt Crisis, resembles the fragile stability of the Eurozone. The peripheral economies are the most affected by credit risk concerns. Indeed, over the period 2008–2013, their debt-to-GDP ratio increase by 72% on average, reaching very high levels in 2013.[16] Indeed, this period has been particularly significant in term of debt increase for Cyprus, Ireland, Portugal, and Spain as their ratio has grown by 77%, 166%, 73%, and 114%, respectively. The Eastern economies have also experienced large increases in their debt-to-GDP ratio but without reaching levels as high as those of the peripheral economies. Indeed, this region has an average ratio of 43%, significantly lower than that of the core (72%) and of the peripherals (111%). Moreover, the Eastern economies have shown good performances in terms of real GDP growth and unemployment rates over the sample period.

Panel B in Table 23.4 reports the results of a principal component analysis performed on the correlation matrix of changes in the 5-year CDS spread across the three subperiods. Interestingly, the first PCs increase from 11 percent in the precrisis period to 65% and 60% during the 2008–2009 Financial Crisis and the European Debt Crisis, respectively. Figure 23.6 plots the loading on the first three PCs.

As for the credit markets of Emerging Economies, the first PC resembles parallel shifts in the spreads as it loads positively on all of the sovereign CDS spreads. The second one weighs positively on Eastern economies, while it gives negative loadings to the rest of Europe. Thus, this second PC can be seen as a spread between the Eastern and the rest of Europe as it reflects the structural differences in terms of fundamentals between the two macroregions. The third PC displays an interesting pattern in the European credit market. It weighs largely and positively on the most indebted countries.[17] Conversely, it has large and negative weights on the healthiest countries, with that of Sweden being the largest, as its debt-to-GDP ratio has decreased by 1.5% over the period 2008–2013.

To show differences in sovereign credit spreads in the Eurozone during the European Debt Crisis, we plot in Figure 23.7 the CDS spreads of five economies: Germany, Sweden, Greece, Ireland, and Italy.

Since 2010, credit spreads of the most indebted economies such as Italy, Ireland, and Greece have diverged from those of efficient economies such as Germany and Sweden. The Greek spread reached a peak of 22,065 basis points in March 2012 when an agreement about a selective default was reached. Instead, the spreads of both Germany and Sweden are comparable in magnitude across the financial and European debt crises.

To further explore the heterogeneity in the economic fundamentals of European economies, we plot in Figure 23.8 the GDP growth rates averaged across three macroregions: the core, the PIIGS, and the Eastern economies.

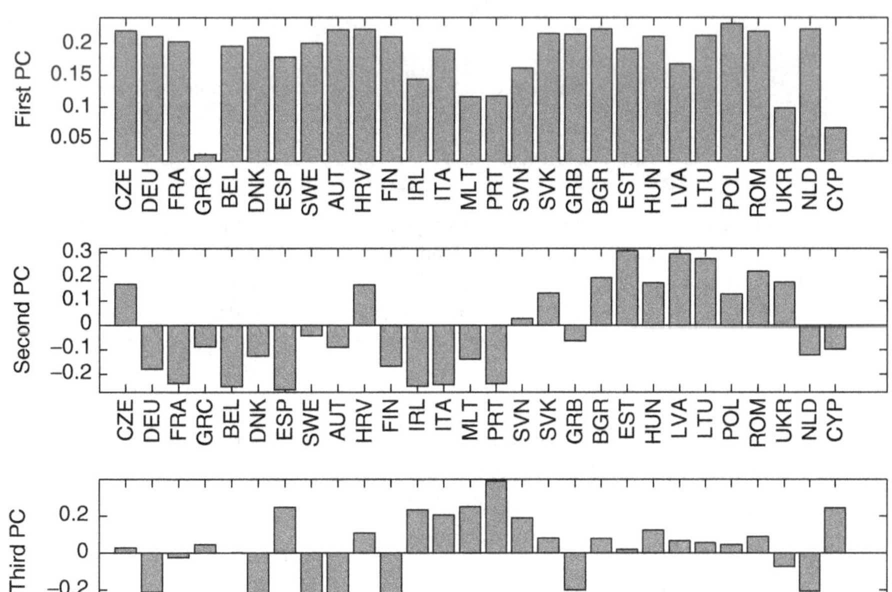

Figure 23.6 This figure plots the loading of the first three principal components of the PCA performed on the correlation matrix of weekly 5-year CDS spread changes over the period 2008–2013. Source: Markit.

[16]We compute the percentage variation of the debt/GDP ratio over the period 2008–2013 and then take the within-region average.

[17]The low loading on Greece is driven by data availability as its sample ends in March 2012 when the country declared the selective default.

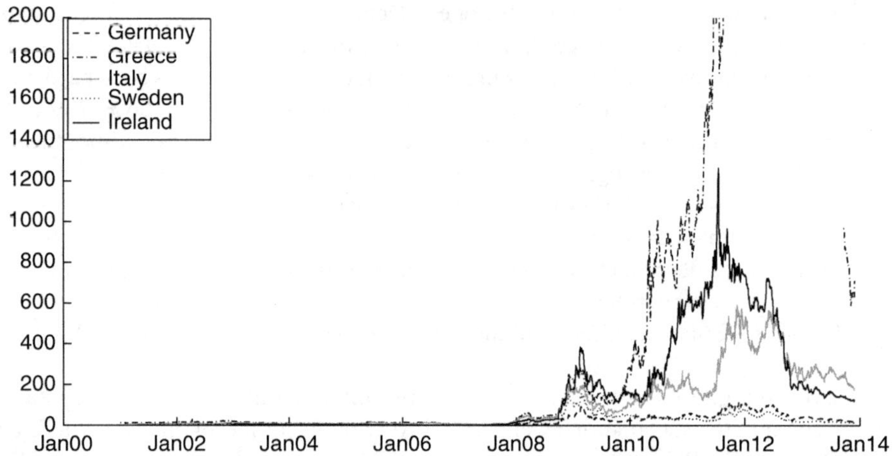

Figure 23.7 The figure plots the 5-year credit spreads of five European economies where debt-to-GDP ratios ranged from 38.2% (Sweden) to 156.9% (Greece) in 2013. Although the Greek spread reached a maximum of 22,065 bps in March 2012, the graph is trimmed to 2000 bps for graphical reasons. Source: Markit.

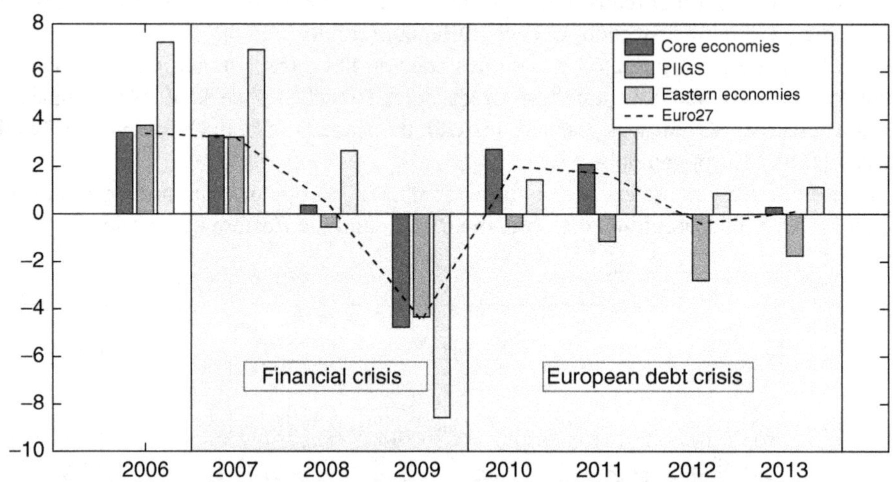

Figure 23.8 The figure plots the average percent GDP growth for each year across three macroregions: core Economies are shown in dark gray bars (Germany, France, Belgium, Denmark, Sweden, Austria, Finland, Netherlands, and United Kingdom), the most indebted countries or PIIGS in medium gray (Portugal, Italy, Ireland, Greece, and Spain), and Eastern Economies in light gray (Czech Republic, Croatia, Slovenia, Slovakia, Bulgaria, Estonia, Hungary, Latvia, Lithuania, Poland, Romania, and Ukraine). The dashed line is the GDP growth rate of the Euro27. Vertical lines split the sample between the 2007–2009 Financial Crisis and the 2010/2013 European Debt Crisis. Source: Eurostat.

The interesting scenario shows how the PIIGS countries have recorded negative growth rates since the Financial Crisis in 2008, as opposed to positive mean growth rates for the rest of Europe. Divergences in credit market may be the result of a combination of negative growth rates and high indebtedness that give rise to doubts about the creditworthiness of such countries.

23.7.1 Credit Risk Premia in the Eurozone

We calibrate the sovereign CDS pricing model for the 28 European countries. Estimated parameters are not reported here but they have the same features found for the Emerging Economies. Table 23.5 reports summary statistics of the absolute and percentage 5-year credit risk premia. Interestingly, the premium accounts for about 45% of the variation in the European credit market on average. Among the peripheral economies, Greece, Cyprus, and Portugal have the highest risk premia and negative slopes, which indicates that the market not only required a higher premium but also that it expected a default for these countries in the short run. While the percentage risk premium is almost the same across regions, significant differences arise when considering the average of the absolute value, which is only 23 bps for the core economies, compared to 120 bps for the Eastern economies, and 133 bps for the peripheral economies.

TABLE 23.5 Credit Risk Premia in the Eurozone

		CRP			%-CRP	
Region	Country	Mean	Std dev	Slope	Mean	Std dev
	Belgium	36.0	53.8	35.78	39.3	18.9
	France	29.5	40.3	38.85	43.2	18.5
	United Kingdom	33.6	20.0	52.43	39.2	14.6
	Germany	16.9	19.3	24.7	47.9	10.6
Core	Austria	25.2	33.8	14.21	43.0	6.4
	Nether	26.1	23.7	31.02	47.4	14.8
	Finland	12.2	13.3	9.27	48.7	0.3
	Denmark	19.3	25.4	24.17	45.5	12.3
	Sweden	13.4	18.2	15.66	42.2	14.7
	Hungary	88.0	91.2	37.03	36.2	0.7
	Poland	50.2	47.0	36.92	46.2	3.9
	Croatia	112.6	86.4	62.17	48.4	2.5
	Slovenia	57.0	75.2	28.95	51.2	1.1
	Slovak	43.3	42.4	31.38	46.7	2.8
East	Czech	30.9	32.7	38.17	36.5	13.1
	Latvia	136.0	150.4	38.19	38.8	17.0
	Lithuania	92.0	102.8	24.34	39.7	14.1
	Romania	135.8	101.3	75.25	46.7	4.8
	Ukraine	403.5	461.2	41.35	49.8	3.1
	Bulgaria	119.4	91.6	77.84	47.1	4.5
	Estonia	66.4	87.1	22.96	43.7	9.6
	Greece	363.7	1213.4	−349.95	48.4	4.9
	Italy	62.9	86.4	41.97	45.1	5.6
	Portugal	138.7	227.6	−3.8	35.8	15.4
Periph	Ireland	122.6	174.1	4.26	47.3	15.7
	Cyprus	176.3	280.3	−34.09	48.1	5.8
	Spain	73.2	101.1	31.07	47.7	12.7
	Malta	76.2	77.2	1.05	49.8	2.1
Mean	.	91.5	134.9	16.11	44.6	8.9

The table reports the summary statistics of the absolute and percentage 5-year credit risk premia (*CRP*) in the Eurozone. The slope is computed as the difference between the 10-year and 1-year CRP. Countries are classified in macroregions, *core*, *East*, and *periphery*, and are sorted according to their debt over GDP ratio as of 2013.
Source: Markit.

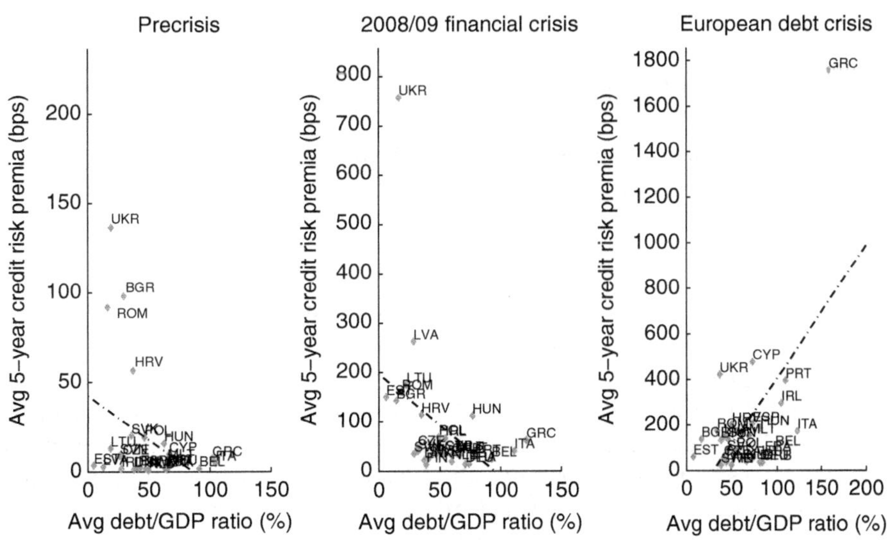

Figure 23.9 The figure plots the relation between average CDS spreads and debt over GDP ratios across three subsamples: *precrisis* (2001–2007), *Financial Crisis* (2008–2009), and *European Crisis* (2010–2013). Each point is an average value over that specific period. Source: Markit, Eurostat, and authors computation.

Dieckmann and Plank (2012) find that the country indebtedness, measured by the debt-to-GDP ratio, accounts for 27 basis points of European sovereign CDS spreads. Acharya et al. (2011) analyze the correlation between sovereign CDS and debt-to-GDP ratio of European countries before and after the bank bailout and find evidence of a strong relationship between the two in the aftermath of the financial rescue. In light of this finding, we employ a naive regression analysis and plot in Figure 23.9 the relation between 5-year CRPs and debt-to-GDP ratios averaged over the three periods: the *precrisis*, the 2008–2009 *Financial Crisis*, and the *European Debt Crisis*. While acknowledging that this naive OLS regressions are just suggestive results and should be taken with a grain of salt, the negative relation in the period preceding the debt crisis may be seen as a signal that increasing indebtedness was welcome by the market as it was needed to rescue a distressed banking systems. But then the situation reversed and investors have been requiring a higher premium to hold government debt as doubts arose about the sustainability of many countries' government debts.

23.8 CONCLUSION

In this chapter, we review recent techniques to model sovereign credit risk and apply them to the credit markets of both emerging and European economies.

We show how to model the sovereign credit risk in a reduced-form setting and how to price CDS contracts written on sovereign debt. The modeling framework enables us to decompose the credit spread into two components: the credit risk premium and the default risk. The former captures the compensation investors demand for bearing the risk due to unexpected variations in the default intensity, whereas the default risk captures the real probability of default of a country or of an institution. We then describe how to estimate the pricing model with market data using the Quasi-MLE that exploits the features of the probability distribution of the default intensity to match actual CDS spreads.

In the last two sections, we empirically analyze the credit markets of Emerging Economies and the European economies in light of the European Debt Crisis. Using the 2012 classification from the IMF, we collect CDS data on 23 emerging countries over the period from 2001 to 2013. Interestingly, the first principal components of CDS explain 73% and 70% of the market variability across the crisis and postcrisis period, respectively. We then pick up a country for each macroregion, representing Europe, Asia, Asia Minor, and Central and South America, and calibrate each country separately to extract the credit risk premium component. We find that these risk premia are highly correlated and that their first principal component correlates positively with both the VIX index (about 70%) and the U.S. spread (about 84.1%), as proxies for the global financial uncertainty and the default risk in the U.S. economy, respectively.

The last section shows how the European crisis is a debt crisis. Indeed, sovereign credit risk has always been deemed as a unique concern for Emerging Economies till the outbreak of the 2008–2009 Financial Crisis that has brought about serious implications for the stability of developed economies, such as that of the Eurozone. Relying on a sample of 28 European countries inside and outside the European Union and the European Monetary Union, we show how the European crisis in the post 2008–2009 Financial Crisis period is mostly driven by debt dynamics. Indeed, in this period, higher credit risk premia are associated with higher levels of indebtedness.

23.9 APPENDIX: NO ARBITRAGE PRICING

In this appendix, we derive the no arbitrage pricing formula 23.23 in the simple case in which the state variables $\mathbf{X}_t$ in Equation 23.18 are $\mathbf{X}_t = (r_t, \lambda_t)$. Assume in addition that they follow the pair of processes

$$dr_t = \mu_r(r_t, t)dt + \sigma_r(r_t, t)dB^{\mathbb{P}}_{r,t} \tag{23.41}$$

$$d\lambda_t = \mu_\lambda(\lambda_t, t)dt + \sigma_\lambda(\lambda_t, t)dB^{\mathbb{P}}_{\lambda,t} \tag{23.42}$$

where $\{B^{\mathbb{P}}_{r,t}\}$ and $\{B^{\mathbb{P}}_{r,t}\}$ are Brownian motions with correlation $\rho(r, \lambda, t)$.

In this setting, a defaultable bond $V_1(t, r_t, \lambda_t)$ with maturity T is subject to three sources of risk, namely, the shocks to interest rate r_t (if rates increases, the bond price decreases), the shock to intensity of default λ_t (if the intensity increases and default is more likely, the bond price decreases), and the outright default of the issuer, that is, the event realization $dK^{\mathbb{P}}_t = 1$ (where we now emphasize that the counting process $\{K_t\}$ is defined under the physical probability measure $\mathbb{P}$).

In order to hedge three sources of risk, we have to construct a hedge portfolio with three securities that span the same risks. Consider the portfolio composed by other three securities $V_i(t, r_t, \lambda_t)$, $i = 2, 3, 4$ that also depend on default of the same issuers (e.g., other bonds issued by the same issuers but with different maturity or credit derivatives) and the interest rate. For instance, one of these securities could be a Treasury zero-coupon risk-free bond $D(t, r_t)$ in order to hedge the interest rate risk of the portfolio of securities. The total portfolio is then

$$\Pi(t, r_t, \lambda_t) = V_1(t, r_t, \lambda_t) + \sum_{i=2}^{4} N_{i,t} V_i(t, r_t, \lambda_t) \tag{23.43}$$

We choose $N_{2,t}, \ldots, N_{4,t}$ to hedge the exposure to shocks of defaultable bond $V_1(t, r_t, \lambda_t)$. For notational simplicity, we use the shorter notation $V_{i,t} = V_i(t, r_t, \lambda_t)$ to indicate functions of time and state variables.

To proceed forward, we need an assumption about the losses incurred by investors in case of default. We follow Duffie and Singleton (1999) and assume that in case of default at τ, each defaultable security i can recover R_i of its *market value* before default, that is, the recovery value after default is $R_i V_{i,\tau-}$, where R_i is the recovery rate. The percentage LGD is then $L_i = 1 - R_i$.

Ito's lemma implies that the process for each defaultable security $V_{i,t}$ can be described by the jump-diffusion process:

$$dV_{i,t} = V_{i,t}\mu_{i,t}dt + V_{i,t}\sigma_{i,r,t}dB^{\mathbb{P}}_{r,t} + V_{i,t}\sigma_{i,\lambda,t}dB^{\mathbb{P}}_{\lambda,t} - V_{i,t}L_i dK^{\mathbb{P}}_t \tag{23.44}$$

where

$$\mu_{i,t} = \frac{1}{V_{i,t}} DV_i(t, r_t, \lambda_t) \tag{23.45}$$

$$\sigma_{i,r,t} = \frac{1}{V_{i,t}} \frac{\partial V_{i,t}}{\partial r} \sigma_r(r_t, t) \tag{23.46}$$

$$\sigma_{i,\lambda,t} = \frac{1}{V_{i,t}} \frac{\partial V_{i,t}}{\partial \lambda} \sigma_\lambda(\lambda_t, t) \tag{23.47}$$

are the expected (percentage) return of $V_{i,t}$ and its sensitivity to the diffusive shocks $dB^{\mathbb{P}}_{r,t}$ and $dB^{\mathbb{P}}_{\lambda,t}$, respectively. The last term in Equation 23.44 is the loss to the security $V_{i,t}$ due to default.

We can describe the dynamics of the portfolio explicitly as follows:

$$\begin{aligned} d\Pi_t &= \left(\sum_{i=1}^{4} N_{i,t}\mu_{i,t}\right) dt + \left(\sum_{i=1}^{4} N_{i,t} V_{i,t}\sigma_{i,r,t}\right) dB^{\mathbb{P}}_{r,t} \\ &+ \left(\sum_{i=1}^{4} N_{i,t} V_{i,t}\sigma_{i,\lambda,t}\right) dB^{\mathbb{P}}_{\lambda,t} - \left(\sum_{i=1}^{4} N_{i,t} V_{i,t} L_i\right) dK^{\mathbb{P}}_t \end{aligned}$$

where recall that $N_{1,t} = 1$ for all t. We now choose $N_{2,t}, N_{3,t}, N_{4,t}$ to eliminate the three sources of risk. That is, we impose

$$0 = \sum_{i=1}^{4} N_{i,t} V_{i,t}\sigma_{i,r,t} \tag{23.48}$$

$$0 = \sum_{i=1}^{4} N_{i,t} V_{i,t}\sigma_{i,\lambda,t} \tag{23.49}$$

$$0 = \sum_{i=1}^{4} N_{i,t} V_{i,t} L_i \tag{23.50}$$

These are three equations in three unknowns ($N_{2,t}, N_{3,t}, N_{4,t}$, as recall $N_{1,t} = 1$) that can be easily solved.

Given the choice of $N_{i,t}$, $i = 2, 3, 4$, the portfolio Π_t is hedged at t against variation in interest rates, default intensity, and default itself. That is, because the three coefficients of $dB^{\mathbb{P}}_{r,t}$, $dB^{\mathbb{P}}_{\lambda,t}$, and dK_t are all zero, we are left with

$$d\Pi_t = \left(\sum_{i=1}^{4} N_{i,t}\mu_{i,t}\right) dt \tag{23.51}$$

It follows that the portfolio is riskless, and therefore it must yield the risk-free rate as a rate of return between t and $t+dt$. That is, no arbitrage implies that we must have

$$d\Pi_t = r_t\Pi_t dt$$

Substitute Equation 23.51 on the left-hand side, and Equation 23.43 on the right-hand side, to obtain yet one more equation:

$$0 = \sum_{i=1}^{4} N_{i,t}(\mu_{i,t} - r_t)V_{i,t} \tag{23.52}$$

We do not have any more degrees of freedom because $N_{i,t}$, $i = 2, 3, 4$ are already fixed to solve the previous system of Equations 23.48 –23.50. It follows that this last equation – and hence no arbitrage – can be satisfied if and only if it is a linear combination of the previous three equations. That is, if and only if there are three quantities $\eta_{r,t}$, $\eta_{\lambda,t}$, and $\eta_{K,t}$ such that:

$$\mu_{i,t} - r_t = \eta_{r,t}\sigma_{i,r,t} + \eta_{\lambda,t}\sigma_{i,\lambda,t} + \eta_{K,t}L_i \tag{23.53}$$

for $i = 1, 2, 3$. Each $\eta_{j,t}$, for $j = r, \lambda, K$, is called **market price of risk** j, where $j = r$ is the interest rate risk, $j = \lambda$ is default intensity risk, and $j = K$ is the default risk itself. To understand the terminology, Equation 23.53 shows that the risk premium of a defaultable security $\mu_{i,t} - r_t$ depends on three risk factors: the interest rate risk, the default intensity risk, and default risk itself. Each factor j's impact on the risk premium is given by its market price of risk $\eta_{j,t}$ times the sensitivity of the security to that risk. Note that the sensitivity of the security to default itself is L_i, as that's what the investor stands to lose in case of default. Equation 23.53 also applies to nondefaultable securities, such as risk-free Treasury bonds. In this case, the sensitivity of such bond to intensity risk or default is just zero, that is, $\sigma_{i,\lambda,t} = 0$ and $L_i = 0$.

Finally, note that the market prices of risk are *security independent*, that is, they are the same independently of what security we are considering. Therefore, we can safely eliminate the subscript i from Equation 23.53.

Before proceeding to our main pricing equation, we note that the market price of default risk should be zero when the default intensity hits zero. If $\lambda_t = 0$, the defaultable security is locally riskless, and therefore for the next instant, $\eta_{K,t} = 0$, as investors should not require a risk premium for default risk, when default risk is zero. Thus, it is natural to assume $\eta_{K,t} = \eta_K(\lambda)$ for some function $\eta_K(.)$ such that $\eta_K(0) = 0$.

Substituting also Equations 23.45 –23.47 into Equation 23.53, we obtain the **fundamental pricing equation**:

$$\begin{aligned}(r + \eta_K(\lambda)L)V = {} & \frac{\partial V}{\partial t} + \frac{\partial V}{\partial r}(\mu_r(r,t) - \eta_{r,t}\sigma_r(r,t)) + \frac{1}{2}\frac{\partial^2 V}{\partial r^2}\sigma_r(r,t)^2 \\ & + \frac{\partial V}{\partial \lambda}(\mu_\lambda(\lambda,t) - \eta_{\lambda,t}\sigma_\lambda(\lambda,t)) + \frac{1}{2}\frac{\partial^2 V}{\partial \lambda^2}\sigma_\lambda(\lambda,t)^2 \\ & + \frac{\partial^2 V}{\partial \lambda \partial r}\sigma_\lambda(\lambda,t)\sigma_r(r,t)\rho(r,\lambda,t)\end{aligned} \tag{23.54}$$

with final condition $V_i(T, r_T, \lambda_T) = g_T$, where g_T is the promised payoff of the defaultable security at maturity.

Applying Feynman–Kac formula, we obtain that the solution to this equation can be expressed as

$$V_t = \mathbb{E}_t^{\mathbb{Q}}\left[e^{-\int_t^T r_s + \eta_K(\lambda_s)L ds} g_T\right] \tag{23.55}$$

where $\mathbb{E}_t^{\mathbb{Q}}[.]$ indicates that the expectation is not taken with respect to the original processes 23.41 and 23.41 but the *risk-neutral* (or risk-adjusted) processes:

$$dr_t = \mu_r^{\mathbb{Q}}(r_t,t)dt + \sigma_r(r_t,t)dB_{r,t}^{\mathbb{Q}} \tag{23.56}$$

$$d\lambda_t = \mu_\lambda^{\mathbb{Q}}(\lambda_t,t)dt + \sigma_\lambda(\lambda_t,t)dB_{\lambda,t}^{\mathbb{Q}} \tag{23.57}$$

where

$$\mu_r^{\mathbb{Q}}(r_t,t) = \mu_r(r_t,t) - \eta_{r,t}\sigma_r(r_t,t); \quad \mu_\lambda^{\mathbb{Q}}(\lambda_t,t) = \mu_\lambda(\lambda_t,t) - \eta_{\lambda,t}\sigma_\lambda(\lambda_t,t)$$

and $\{B_{r,t}^{\mathbb{Q}}\}$ and $\{B_{r,t}^{\mathbb{Q}}\}$ are two new Brownian motions with correlation $\rho(r,\lambda,t)$.[18]

[18]Because dr_t and $d\lambda_t$ have to be the same under the probability measures $\mathbb{Q}$ and $\mathbb{P}$, equating 23.41 with 23.56, and 23.42 with 23.57, we obtain the relation

$$dB_{r,t}^{\mathbb{Q}} = \eta_{r,t}dt + dB_{r,t}^{\mathbb{P}}; \quad dB_{r,t}^{\mathbb{P}} = \eta_{r,t}dt + dB_{r,t}^{\mathbb{P}}$$

23.9.1 The Risk-Neutral Default Intensity

Consider again the security $V(t, r, \lambda)$, and let it follow the jump-diffusion *risk-neutral* process:

$$dV_t = V_t\mu^{\mathbb{Q}}_{V,t}dt + V_t\sigma_{V,r,t}dB^{\mathbb{Q}}_{r,t} + V_t\sigma_{V,\lambda,t}dB^{\mathbb{Q}}_{\lambda,t} - V_tLdK^{\mathbb{Q}}_t \tag{23.58}$$

where $\{K^{\mathbb{Q}}_t\}$ denotes a counting process under the risk-neutral measure $\mathbb{Q}$ with a risk-neutral intensity $\lambda^{\mathbb{Q}}_t$, and the underlying state variables follow the risk-neutral processes 23.56 and 23.57. Because $V_t = V(t, r_t, \lambda_t)$, from Ito's lemma we must have

$$\begin{aligned}\mu^{\mathbb{Q}}_{V,t}V_t =& \frac{\partial V}{\partial t} + \frac{\partial V}{\partial r}\mu^{\mathbb{Q}}_r(r,t) + \frac{1}{2}\frac{\partial^2 V}{\partial r^2}\sigma_r(r,t)^2\\ &+\frac{\partial V}{\partial \lambda}\mu^{\mathbb{Q}}_\lambda(\lambda,t) + \frac{1}{2}\frac{\partial^2 V}{\partial \lambda^2}\sigma_\lambda(\lambda,t)^2 + \frac{\partial^2 V}{\partial\lambda\partial r}\sigma_\lambda(\lambda,t)\sigma_r(r,t)\rho(r,\lambda,t)\end{aligned}$$

The total risk-neutral expected return over the next instant dt, however, must take into account the jump component as well. Because $\mathbb{E}^{\mathbb{Q}}_t[dK^{\mathbb{Q}}] = \lambda^{\mathbb{Q}}dt$, we have

$$\mathbb{E}^{\mathbb{Q}}_t[dV_t] = \mu^{\mathbb{Q}}_{V,t}V_tdt - V_tL\lambda^{\mathbb{Q}}_tdt$$

Because we are under risk-neutral probabilities, we must also have that the expected total return on the defaultable security equals the risk-free rate:

$$\mathbb{E}^{\mathbb{Q}}_t[dV_t] = r_tV_tdt$$

Equating the two expected returns, we obtain the equation

$$r_tV_t = \mu^{\mathbb{Q}}_{V,t}V_tdt - V_tL\lambda^{\mathbb{Q}}dt$$

Substituting on the right-hand side for $\mu^{\mathbb{Q}}_{V,t}$, we obtain

$$\begin{aligned}rV =& \frac{\partial V}{\partial t} + \frac{\partial V}{\partial r}(\mu_r(r,t) - \eta_{r,t}\sigma_r(r,t)) + \frac{1}{2}\frac{\partial^2 V}{\partial r^2}\sigma_r(r,t)^2\\ &+\frac{\partial V}{\partial \lambda}(\mu_\lambda(\lambda,t) - \eta_{\lambda,t}\sigma_\lambda(\lambda,t)) + \frac{1}{2}\frac{\partial^2 V}{\partial \lambda^2}\sigma_\lambda(\lambda,t)^2\\ &+\frac{\partial^2 V}{\partial\lambda\partial r}\sigma_\lambda(\lambda,t)\sigma_r(r,t)\rho(r,\lambda,t) - \lambda^{\mathbb{Q}}LV\end{aligned}$$

This PDE is identical to the fundamental pricing equation 23.54 if the risk-neutral default intensity equals the market price of default risk itself:

$$\lambda^{\mathbb{Q}}_t = \eta_K(\lambda_t) \tag{23.59}$$

Thus, the risk-neutral default intensity is related to the true default intensity through its market price of risk. If, for instance, the function $\eta_K(\lambda_t)$ is linear, $\lambda^{\mathbb{Q}}_t = \eta_K(\lambda_t) = \lambda_t\eta_K$, it is clear that a high risk-neutral default intensity may occur either because the true default intensity λ_t is high or because the market price of default risk η_K is high. In what follows, we then normally write the risk-neutral price of a defaultable security as

$$V_t = \mathbb{E}^{\mathbb{Q}}_t\left[e^{-\int_t^T r_s + \lambda^{\mathbb{Q}}_s Lds}g_T\right] \tag{23.60}$$

in which we use $\lambda^{\mathbb{Q}}_s$ instead of $\eta_K(\lambda_s)$.

Note that because $\lambda^{\mathbb{Q}}_t = \eta_K(\lambda_t)$ and λ_t has both dynamics under the physical $\mathbb{P}$ and risk-neutral $\mathbb{Q}$ probabilities, so does $\lambda^{\mathbb{Q}}_t$. That is, using Ito's lemma and assuming the function $\eta_K(\lambda_t)$ is invertible, we can write the process for the risk-neutral intensity $\lambda^{\mathbb{Q}}$ under both the physical and risk-neutral probabilities as

$$d\lambda^{\mathbb{Q}}_t = \mu_{\lambda^{\mathbb{Q}}}(\lambda^{\mathbb{Q}}, t)dt + \sigma_{\lambda^{\mathbb{Q}}}(\lambda^{\mathbb{Q}}, t)dB^{\mathbb{P}}_t \tag{23.61}$$

$$d\lambda^{\mathbb{Q}}_t = \mu^{\mathbb{Q}}_{\lambda^{\mathbb{Q}}}(\lambda^{\mathbb{Q}}, t)dt + \sigma_{\lambda^{\mathbb{Q}}}(\lambda^{\mathbb{Q}}, t)dB^{\mathbb{Q}}_t \tag{23.62}$$

That is, by Girsanov theorem, the new probability measure $\mathbb{Q}$ is generated by the two new Brownian motions that are adjusted by their respective market prices of risk.

for some functions $\mu_{\lambda^{\mathbb{Q}}}(\lambda^{\mathbb{Q}}, t)$ and $\sigma_{\lambda^{\mathbb{Q}}}(\lambda^{\mathbb{Q}}, t)$ and where

$$\mu^{\mathbb{Q}}_{\lambda^{\mathbb{Q}}}(\lambda^{\mathbb{Q}}, t) = \mu_{\lambda^{\mathbb{Q}}}(\lambda^{\mathbb{Q}}, t) - \eta_{\lambda,t}\sigma_{\lambda^{\mathbb{Q}}}(\lambda^{\mathbb{Q}}, t)$$

The above derivations can be greatly generalized to have many correlated factors that affect interest rates, default intensities, stochastic recovery rates, and the like.

REFERENCES

Acharya VV, Drechsler I, Schnabl P. A pyrrhic victory? Bank bailouts and sovereign credit risk. No. w17136. National Bureau of Economic Research; 2011.

Amato J, Remolona E. The credit spread puzzle. BIS Quarterly Review; Dec 2003.

Ang A, Longstaff FA. Systemic sovereign credit risk: Lessons from the US and Europe. J Monet Econ 2013;60(5):493–510.

Barajas A, Steiner R. Credit Stagnation in Latin America. International Monetary Fund; 2002.

Berndt A, Douglas R, Duffie D, Ferguson M, Schranz D. Measuring default risk premia from default swap rates and EDFs. Working Paper; 2005.

Black F, Cox JC. Valuing corporate securities: some effects of bond indenture provisions. J Finance 1976;31(2):351–367.

Black F, Karasinski P. Bond and option pricing when short rates are lognormal. Financ Anal J 1991;47(4):52–59.

Björk T. *Arbitrage Theory in Continuous Time.* Oxford: Oxford University Press; 2004.

Caceres C, Guzzo V, Segoviano Basurto M. Sovereign spreads: global risk aversion, contagion or fundamentals?. IMF working papers; 2010. p 1–29.

Carr P, Wu L. Theory and evidence on the dynamic interactions between sovereign credit default swaps and currency options. J Bank Finance 2007;31(8):2383–2403.

Carr P, Wu L. Stock options and credit default swaps: a joint framework for valuation and estimation. J Financ Econom 2010;8(4):409–449.

Chen R-R, Scott L. Maximum likelihood estimation for a multifactor equilibrium model of the term structure of interest rates. J Fixed Income 1993;3(3):14–31.

Cornuejols G, Tutuncu R. *Optimization Methods in Finance.* Volume 5. The Edinburgh Building, Cambridge, CB2 2RU, UK: Cambridge University Press; 2006.

Cox JC, Ingersoll JE Jr., Ross SA. A theory of the term structure of interest rates. Econometrica 1985;53(2):385–407.

Cuadra G, Sapriza H. Sovereign default, interest rates and political uncertainty in emerging markets. J Int Econ 2008;76(1):78–88.

Diamonte RL, Liew JM, Stevens RL. Political risk in emerging and developed markets. Financ Anal J 1996;52(3):71–76.

Dieckmann S, Plank T. Default risk of advanced economies: an empirical analysis of credit default swaps during the financial crisis. Rev Finance 2012;16(4):903–934.

Domowitz I, Glen J, Madhavan A. International cross-listing and order flow migration: evidence from an emerging market. J Finance 1998;53(6):2001–2027.

Driessen J. Is default event risk priced in corporate bonds? Rev Financ Stud 2005;18(1):165–195.

Duffee GR. Term premia and interest rate forecasts in affine models. J Finance 2002;57(1):405–443.

Duffie D. Credit swap valuation. Financ Anal J 1999;55(1):73–87.

Duffie D. Credit risk modeling with affine processes. J Bank Finance 2005;29(11):2751–2802.

Duffie D, Pedersen LH, Singleton KJ. Modeling sovereign yield spreads: a case study of Russian debt. J Finance 2003;58(1):119–159.

Duffie D, Singleton KJ. Modeling term structures of defaultable bonds. Rev Financ Stud 1999;12(4):687–720.

Eaton J, Gersovitz M. Debt with potential repudiation: theoretical and empirical analysis. Rev Econ Stud 1981;48(2):289–309.

Fischer EO, Heinkel R, Zechner J. Dynamic capital structure choice: theory and tests. J Finance 1989;44(1):19–40.

González LE. Political Crises and Democracy in Latin America Since the End of the Cold War, Helen Kellogg Institute for International Studies; 2008.

Hilscher J, Nosbusch Y. Determinants of sovereign risk: macroeconomic fundamentals and the pricing of sovereign debt. Rev Finance 2010;14:235–262.

Jarrow R, Turnbull S. Credit risk: drawing the analogy. Risk Mag 1992;5(9):63–70.

Leland HE, Toft KB. Optimal capital structure, endogenous bankruptcy, and the term structure of credit spreads. J Finance 1996;51(3):987–1019.

Longstaff FA. The subprime credit crisis and contagion in financial markets. J Financ Econ 2010;97(3):436–450.

Longstaff FA, Pan J, Pedersen LH, Singleton KJ. How sovereign is sovereign credit risk? Am Econ J Macroecon 2011;3(2):75–103.

Longstaff FA, Schwartz ES. A simple approach to valuing risky fixed and floating rate debt. J Finance 1995;50(3):789–819.

Longstaff FA, Schwartz ES. A two-factor interest rate model and contingent claims valuation. J Fixed Income 1992;2(3):16–23.

Merton RC. On the pricing of corporate debt: the risk structure of interest rates*. J Finance 1974;29(2):449–470.

Pan J, Singleton KJ. Default and recovery implicit in the term structure of sovereign CDS spreads. J Finance 2008;63(5):2345–2384.

Pastor L, Veronesi P. Uncertainty about government policy and stock prices. J Finance 2012;67(4):1219–1264.

Pastor L, Veronesi P. Political uncertainty and risk premia. J Financ Econ 2013;110(3):520–545.

Remolona EM, Scatigna M, Wu E. The dynamic pricing of sovereign risk in emerging markets: fundamentals and risk aversion. 20th Australasian Finance & Banking Conference; 2007.

Remolona EM, Scatigna M, Wu E. A ratings?based approach to measuring sovereign risk. Int J Finance Econ 2008;13(1):26–39.

Richmond C, Dias DA. *Duration of Capital Market Exclusion: Stylized Facts and Determining Factors*. Los Angeles (CA): Department of Economics, University of California; 2008.

Sandmann K, Sondermann D. A note on the stability of lognormal interest rate models and the pricing of Eurodollar futures. Math Finance 1997;7(2):119–125.

Sgherri MS, Zoli ME. Euro area sovereign risk during the crisis. IMF Working Papers; 2009. p 1–23.

Shin HS. The Second Phase of Global Liquidity and its Impact on Emerging Economies. working paper; 2013.

Veronesi P. *Fixed Income Securities: Valuation, Risk, and Risk Management*. Hoboken (NJ): John Wiley and Sons; 2010.

Yu F. Modeling expected return on defaultable bonds. J Fixed Income 2002;12(2):69–81.

Zhang FX. What Did the Credit Market Expect of Argentina Default?: Evidence from Default Swap Data. Volume 3. Division of Research & Statistics and Monetary Affairs, Federal Reserve Board; 2003.

Index

Handbook of Fixed-Income Securities, First Edition. Edited by Pietro Veronesi.

and inflation expectations, 9
and the spanning of macroeconomic expectations, 296
nominal, 9
real, 9, 19, 42
survey forecasts, 292